The Two-Ocean War

A Short History of the United States Navy
in the Second World War

For
Captain S. E. Morison –
with all good wishes –
Ernest J. King
January 20, 1947

Admiral Ernest J. King USN

The Two-Ocean War

A Short History of the United States Navy in the Second World War

BY SAMUEL ELIOT MORISON

WITH ILLUSTRATIONS

An Atlantic Monthly Press Book

LITTLE, BROWN AND COMPANY · BOSTON · TORONTO

Published simultaneously in Canada
by Little, Brown & Company (Canada) Limited

PRINTED IN THE UNITED STATES OF AMERICA

To my Wartime Shipmates in

U.S.S. *Baltimore*

U.S.S. *Brooklyn*

U.S.S. *Buck*

U.S.C.G.C. *Campbell*

U.S.S. *Honolulu*

U.S.S. *Montpelier*

U.S.S. *Tennessee*

U.S.S. *Washington*

Preface

THIS BOOK has been written in the hope of bringing the exploits of the United States Navy in World War II to the attention of new readers. For I have already written, and Little, Brown and Company have published, a fifteen-volume *History of the United States Naval Operations in World War II*, as follows:

I *The Battle of the Atlantic*, September 1939–May 1943
II *Operations in North African Waters*, October 1942–June 1943
III *The Rising Sun in the Pacific*, 1931–April 1942
IV *Coral Sea, Midway and Submarine Actions*, May 1942–August 1942
V *The Struggle for Guadalcanal*, August 1942–February 1943
VI *Breaking the Bismarcks Barrier*, 22 July 1942–1 May 1944
VII *Aleutians, Gilberts and Marshalls*, June 1942–April 1944
VIII *New Guinea and the Marianas*, March 1944–August 1944
IX *Sicily — Salerno — Anzio*, January 1943–June 1944
X *The Atlantic Battle Won*, May 1943–May 1945
XI *The Invasion of France and Germany*, 1944–1945
XII *Leyte*, June 1944–January 1945
XIII *The Liberation of the Philippines: Luzon, Mindanao, the Visayas*, 1944–1945
XIV *Victory in the Pacific*, 1945
XV *Supplement and General Index*

In this book I have not attempted a uniform condensation of the fifteen volumes, but rather to select the most important battles and campaigns. Consequently, many minor actions, convoy struggles, fights of naval armed guards against U-boats, individual submarine exploits, air clashes in the "central blue," in which sailors fought and died, have had to be omitted. For these, and for illustrations and more charts, the reader is referred to the appropriate volume of my larger History. On the other hand, Chapter I on the Navy between wars is more detailed than the coverage of that period in *The Battle of the Atlantic.*

Whilst research for the larger History has generally served for this, I have consulted all printed works covering the naval war in both oceans which have appeared since my own volumes, and profited by many. Among these, especially valuable were the following:

† E. B. Potter and Chester W. Nimitz *The Great Sea War* (1960)

† M. Fuchida and M. Okumiya *Midway, the Battle that Doomed Japan* (1955)

* Kent R. Greenfield (ed.) *Command Decisions* (1960)

Ernest R. May (ed.) *The Ultimate Decision* (1960)

* Julius A. Furer *Administration of the Navy Department in World War II* (1959)

† Arnold S. Lott *Most Dangerous Sea. A History of Mine Warfare* (1959)

Roberta Wohlstetter *Pearl Harbor Warning and Decision* (Stanford, 1962)

In the * *U. S. Army in World War II* series, Louis Morton *The Fall of the Philippines* (1953); George F. Howe *Northwest Africa* (1957); Maurice Matloff *Strategic Planning for Coalition Warfare 1943-1944* (1959); Philip A. Crowl *Campaign in the Marianas* (1960); Crowl and Edmund G. Love *Seizure of the Gilberts and Marshalls* (1955); Samuel Milner *Victory in Papua* (1957)

* *History of U. S. Marine Corps Operations in World War II,* of which only Volume I by F. O. Hough et al., *Pearl Harbor to Guadalcanal* (1958), has yet appeared

† S. W. Roskill *White Ensign, the British Navy at War 1939-1945* (1960)

† Paul Auphan and Jacques Mordal *The French Navy in World War II* (1959)

† Marc' A. Bragadin *The Italian Navy in World War II* (1957)

† These books are published by the U. S. Naval Institute, Annapolis, Md.

* These books are published by the Superintendent of Documents, U. S. Government Printing Office, Washington, D. C.

S. L. A. Marshall *Night Drop, the American Airborne Invasion of Normandy* (Atlantic-Little, Brown, 1962)

In J. R. M. Butler (ed.) *History of the Second World War. United Kingdom Military Series*, S. W. Roskill *The War at Sea 1939-45* (4 vols., 1954-61); S. Woodburn Kirby *The War Against Japan* (3 vols. 1957-61); John Ehrman et al. *Grand Strategy* (6 vols., not all yet out). These are published by H. M. Stationery Office, London.

In the *Australia in the War of 1939-1945* series, G. H. Gill's Vol. I of *Royal Australian Navy* (Canberra, 1957), and Dudley McCarthy *South-West Pacific Area — First Year* (Canberra, 1959)

K. W. L. Bezemer *Zij Vochten op de Zeven Zeeën* (1960) — the best history of the Royal Netherlands Navy

Jacques Mordal *La Bataille de Casablanca* (Paris, 1952)

Emilio Faldella *Lo Sbarco e la Difesa della Sicilia* (Rome, 1957)

Admiral Karl Doenitz *Memoirs. Ten Years and Twenty Days.* R. H. Stevens trans. (London: Weidenfeld & Nicholson 1959)

Masanori Ito and Roger Pineau *The End of the Japanese Navy* (New York, 1962)

Herbert Feis *Japan Subdued: The Atomic Bomb and the End of the War* (Princeton, 1961)

Tameichi Hara *Japanese Destroyer Captain* trans. by F. Saito and R. Pineau (New York, 1961)

My deepest feeling of gratitude is towards my beloved wife, Priscilla Barton Morison, for her support and encouragement which enabled me to complete this volume, and for many perceptive suggestions when I read it aloud to her in proof.

My obligations to naval officers and historians of the United States and other navies are so many and great that I cannot begin to name them. Special thanks are due to Rear Admiral Ernest M. Eller USN (Ret.), Director of Naval History, for permitting me to use charts and material from my 15-volume History; to two members of his staff, Mr. Jesse D. Thomas and Mr. Donald R. Martin, for doing research on sundry points; and to Captain Ralph C. Parker USN (Ret.) and Vice Admiral Morton L. Deyo USN (Ret.), for helpful advice on the opening and closing chapters.

SAMUEL ELIOT MORISON

44 BRIMMER STREET
BOSTON
February, 1963

Contents

Illustrations

(*All photographs not otherwise described are Official United States Navy*)

List of Charts

Abbreviations

Service designations:

(jg) Junior Grade
RAN — Royal Australian Navy
RN — Royal Navy
RNN — Royal Netherlands Navy
USA — United States Army
USCG — United States Coast Guard; USCGR, Reserve of same
USMC—United States Marine Corps; USMCR, Reserve of same
USN — United States Navy; USNR, Reserve of same
(All officers and men not otherwise designated may be assumed to be USN)

Terms most frequently used in text:

AGC — Amphibious Force Command Ship
AKA — Attack cargo vessel
A.A.F. — Army Air Force or Forces
ABDA — American, British, Dutch, Australian Command
APA — Attack Transport
APD — High-speed Destroyer Transport
C.A.P. — Combat Air Patrol
C.C.S. — Combined Chiefs of Staff
C. in C. — Commander in Chief
C.N.O. — Chief of Naval Operations
C.O. — Commanding Officer
C.T.F. — Commander Task Force; C.T.G. — Commander Task Group
Cinclant — Commander in Chief, Atlantic Fleet
Cincmed — Commander in Chief, Mediterranean
Cincpac, Cincpoa — Commander in Chief Pacific Fleet, Pacific Ocean Areas
Cominch — Commander in Chief, United States Fleet; Comsopac, Commander in Chief, South Pacific; Comairspac, Commander Air, South Pacific
CVE — Escort Carrier
DD — Destroyer
DE — Destroyer escort

DMS — Fast Minesweeper
dukw — 2½ ton amphibian truck
Dumbo — patrol seaplane equipped for rescue

exec. — Executive officer on board a ship

HF/DF (Huff-Duff) — High-frequency Direction-Finder
H.M.A.S. — His Majesty's Australian Ship
H.M.C.S. — His Majesty's Canadian Ship
H.M.N.Z.S. — His Majesty's New Zealand Ship
H.M.S. — His Majesty's Ship (Royal Navy)
H.N.M.S. — Her Netherlands Majesty's Ship

J.C.S. — Joint Chiefs of Staff

Maru (lit. "chubby") is added to the names of Japanese merchant ships and many naval auxiliaries
MTB or PT — Motor Torpedo Boat

O.N.I. — Office of Naval Intelligence
op plan — Operation plan
O.T.C. — Officer in Tactical Command

PC — Patrol craft
P.M. — Prime Minister (Churchill)

R.A.F. — Royal Air Force
RCT — Regimental Combat Team
RN — Royal Navy

SC — Submarine chaser
SOPA — Senior Officer Present Afloat

TBS — Talk Between Ships (voice radio)
TF — Task Force; TG — Task Group

UDT — Underwater Demolition Team

YMS — Motor Minesweeper

Landing Craft and Ships [(A), (G), (L), (M), (R) after these mean armored, gunboat, large, mortar, rocket]:
LCI — Landing Craft, Infantry
LCP — Landing Craft, Personnel
LCT — Landing Craft, Tank
LCM — Landing Craft, Mechanized
LCVP — Landing Craft, Vehicles and Personnel
LSD — Landing Ship, Dock
LSM — Landing Ship, Medium
LST — Landing Ship, Tank
LVT — Landing Vehicle, Tracked (Amphtrac)

Principal United States Planes (engine number in parentheses):

ARMY

A–20 — Hudson light bomber (2)
B–17 — Flying Fortress heavy bomber (4); B–24 — Liberator heavy bomber (4); B–25 — Mitchell medium bomber (2); B–26 — Marauder medium bomber (2); B–29 — Superfortress heavy bomber (4); P–35, –36, –39, –40 — fighters (1); P–38 — Lightning fighter (2)

NAVY

F4F — Wildcat, fighter (1)
F4U — Corsair, fighter (1)
F6F — Hellcat, fighter (1)
OS2U — Kingfisher float plane (1)
PBM — Mariner, patrol bomber (2)
PBY — Catalina (2) patrol seaplane
PB4Y — Liberator bomber (4)
PV–1 — Ventura medium bomber (2)
SBD–5 — Dauntless dive-bomber (1)
SB2C — Helldiver dive-bomber (1)
TBD — Devastator torpedo-bomber (1)
TBF, TBM — Avenger torpedo-bomber (1)

Japanese Planes

"Betty" — Mitsubishi Zero–1 (2)
"Jill" — Nakajima, Navy (2) medium torpedo-bomber
"Judy" — Aichi, Navy (1) dive-bomber
"Kate" — Nakajima, Navy (2) torpedo-bomber
"Val" — Aichi 99, Navy (1) dive-bomber
"Zeke" — Mitsubishi Zero–3, Navy (1) fighter (also called "Zero")

The Two-Ocean War

A Short History of the United States Navy in the Second World War

CHAPTER I

The Twenty Years' Peace

1919–1939

1. *Naval Limitation, 1922–1937*

ALTHOUGH THE UNITED STATES participated heavily in World War I, the nature of that participation was fundamentally different from what it became in World War II. The earlier conflict was a one-ocean war for the Navy and a one-theater war for the Army; the latter was a two-ocean war for the Navy and one of five major theaters for the Army. In both wars a vital responsibility of the Navy was escort-of-convoy and anti-submarine work, but in the 1917-1918 conflict it never clashed with the enemy on the surface; whilst between 1941 and 1945 it fought some twenty major, and countless minor engagements with the Japanese Navy. American soldiers who engaged in World War I were taken overseas in transports and landed on docks or in protected harbors; in World War II the art of amphibious warfare had to be revived and developed, since assault troops were forced to fight their way ashore. Air power, in the earlier conflict, was still inchoate and almost negligible; in the latter it was a determining factor. In World War I the battleship still reigned queen of the sea, as she had, in changing forms, since the age of Drake, and Battle Line fought with tactics inherited from the age of sail; but in World War II the capital naval force was the aircraft carrier task group, for which completely new tactics had to be devised.

America entered World War I late, almost three years after it began; owing to unpreparedness for battle she had to borrow everybody else's weapons, and in Europe left the reputation of a brave, almost foolhardy, amateur. In World War II, America became not only the "arsenal of democracy" for her Allies (who before had daintily been called "Associates"), but participated with greater man power, weapon power, sea power and air power than any other belligerent except, as respects ground forces, Russia. And American strategists showed themselves at least the equals of those of the Old World in the art of war.

After the earlier conflict ended with defeat of Imperial Germany, America turned her back on Europe, indulged in futile dreams of everlasting peace, and to all intents and purposes disarmed; but World War II was no sooner over than the "cold war" with Communism opened, and we rearmed with new and deadlier instruments of destruction which threaten, whenever and by whomsoever employed, to snuff out civilization itself. Thus, World War I was a hit-and-run war; we struck late but hard, and quickly withdrew into our shell, like a hermit crab; but World War II was a hit-and-stay war; we struck even harder, and stayed in Europe, Asia and Africa. In 1963, American air and ground forces are in Great Britain, Germany, North Africa, Japan, Korea, Formosa, South Vietnam, and a score of Pacific islands formerly in enemy possession; and the United States Navy not only patrols every verge of Asia, and dives under the polar ice, but protects the lifeline between America and all other bastions of freedom.

The important point in "turning our back on Europe" was rejection by the United States Senate in 1920 of the Treaty of Versailles and the League of Nations. Although this action was taken mainly for political and personal reasons — revenge against President Wilson, and Wilson's own stubbornness — the rejection was undoubtedly popular. There was a feeling of national frustration over the unsatisfactory outcome of the Paris Peace Conference, a belief that we had been "sold down the river" by Lloyd

George and Clemenceau, and that adherence to the League would involve us in conflicts contrary to our permanent interests. President Wilson prophesied on 4 September 1919 that the League "is the only conceivable arrangement which will prevent us sending our men abroad again very soon. . . . The only thing that can prevent the recurrence of this dreadful catastrophe." This warning the people heeded not.

Americans nevertheless were devoted to the idea of world peace, and the Harding administration, elected in the fall of 1920, felt obliged to do something spectacular to satisfy that aspiration. This took the form of the Naval Arms Limitation Conference at Washington. In 1916, on the eve of war, Congress had passed an act authorizing the building of a navy which, had it been carried out, would have made it the equal to any other two navies of the world. The British government and people, after the war was over, foolishly regarded this as a challenge to the Royal Navy, which had borne the brunt of blue-water fighting. The war had thrown such financial burdens on the British that they could not match us ship for ship; and, so far as anyone could see, America would always be on their side. Yet British pride and sense of history were too powerful to brook a superior rival; for history seemed to prove that Britain's allies in one war would be her enemies in the next.

The suggestion from London of a naval limitation agreement between the five leading naval powers (Great Britain, the United States, Japan, France and Italy) was eagerly taken up at Washington. There the conference opened spectacularly on 12 November 1921 with an American offer to scrap a large part of the naval tonnage then building, if other powers would forgo building warships themselves; and as the United States had the capability to build the world's most powerful navy, the delegates of those nations hailed Secretary Hughes's offer with almost indecent joy. The results of this conference, after weeks of deliberation, were the famous treaties signed 6 February 1922 setting up the 5:5:3 ratio in battleship and aircraft carrier tonnage between England, America and Japan; France and Italy each receiving a 1¾ ratio; a ten-year "holiday" on building capital ships, and a restriction on the burthen of all battleships to 35,000 tons.[1] Although this ratio allowed Japan to become the strongest naval power in the Western Pacific (since America had two, and Britain three, oceans to defend), Japanese consent had to be purchased by a supplementary agreement on military bases. The United States renounced strengthening, in a military sense, any of her bases, such as Guam and Manila, that lay west of Pearl Harbor; and England renounced strengthening any of hers east of Singapore or north of Australia. This provision actually reversed the ratio to 5:3:2 in favor of Japan, as the United States and Great Britain learned to their sorrow twenty years later.

The American government and people confidently expected that this agreement would prove the entering wedge for limitation of other types of combatant ships, and to general disarmament on land and sea; but three later conferences, called to effect these objects, ended in nothing of importance except an agreement to limit cruisers to 10,000 tons, which we respected and Japan flouted.

Having, as they fondly thought, started the ball rolling toward universal peace, the British and American people allowed their armed forces to drift into obsolescence. For about ten years this hardly mattered, but in the 1930's the German, Italian and Japanese governments began planning war as a short cut to wealth and power, and building up their armed forces. If "England slept," America not only slept but snored. The Army was neglected as much or more than the Navy, which Congress did not allow to be built up even to what the treaties permitted. Congress would probably have done even less but for the Navy League, a civilian organization founded in 1902, dedicated to keeping the Navy in

[1] See NOTE at end of this chapter for details.

proper shape. Ironically, the League celebrated its first Navy Day on 27 October 1922, immediately after the administration had consigned some of our best ships to the wreckers' yards.

Several factors, besides a general revulsion against war and aversion from Europe, conspired to bring about this lamentable state of affairs. The recession of 1921-1922 and the depression of 1929-1933 made Congress unwilling to vote money for armaments that might never be used. Pacifist propaganda in this era was very powerful; one remembers with shame the sneers and jeers at Congressional hearings, directed toward conscientious officers who were trying to obtain a few million dollars for Army buildup, fleet maintenance and new construction.

President Coolidge, although he hated the sea and even disliked reviewing a naval regatta from the presidential yacht, did more for the Navy than any President between Wilson and Roosevelt. Disappointed and irritated that the second Naval Limitation Conference at Geneva in 1927 could not agree to cut down the world's navies further, he urged the then chairman of the House of Representatives' committee on naval affairs to introduce legislation which would bring the United States Navy to full parity with the British. Chairman Butler did so, submitting a program that called for the building of 71 new ships (including 5 aircraft carriers and 25 cruisers) in nine years. The peace societies then got into action, congressmen were overwhelmed with protests, and the program was pared to 15 heavy cruisers and one carrier. Even this bill was rejected in the Senate. President Coolidge returned to the subject in his Armistice Day address of 1928, the "cruiser bill" was re-introduced, and this time became law. That was the origin of the *Astoria*, *Indianapolis* and *Brooklyn* classes; but no keels were laid before 1930 (no *Brooklyn* keels until 1935), and only two of these ships were in commission before 1934.

President Hoover, a Quaker and a congenital pacifist, trusted to a sort of incantation — the Kellogg-Briand treaty "outlawing war"

— to keep the peace. He found the British premier, Ramsay MacDonald, very congenial. After MacDonald on 24 July 1929 had announced that the Royal Navy would stop work on two heavy cruisers, four destroyers and two submarines, Hoover, when proclaiming the Kellogg-Briand treaty in force, announced that the keels of three cruisers authorized as far back as 1924 would not be laid, pending another effort to limit navies. The Hoover administration has the sad distinction of being the only one since the eighteenth century in which not a single naval combatant ship was laid down.

Another influence that kept the Navy weak was the propaganda by Brigadier General William Mitchell USA to the effect that armies and navies — even aircraft carriers — were obsolete; that land-based air bombers could overcome all the ships and armies in the world. When a prophet habitually prophesies around the clock, he is sure to score some bull's-eyes as well as numerous misses; but "Billy" Mitchell, although now canonized by airmen for his few hits, made a very high percentage of bloopers — such as:

> The surface ship as an element of war is disappearing.
>
> Airplane carriers are useless instruments of war against first-class powers.
>
> Effectiveness [of antiaircraft guns] is constantly diminishing [and] never can improve much.
>
> A superior air power will dominate all sea areas when they act from land bases, and no seacraft, whether carrying aircraft or not, is able to contest their aërial supremacy.
>
> An attempt to transport large bodies of troops, munitions and supplies across a great stretch of ocean, by seacraft, as was done during the World War from the United States to Europe, would be an impossibility.

This line of argument appealed to the people and to Congress, since aircraft were not only the newest weapons but relatively cheap. And some practice sinkings of moored, unarmed and defenseless naval hulks by air bombing in 1921 were cited as proof that no ship could ever threaten our shores if we had a powerful air force. Yet, when the Army's planners first asked for appropriations for B–17s, the Flying Fortresses that played so great a rôle in World War II, the Deputy Chief of Staff (General Stanley D. Embick) told them to forget it, since Congress deemed long-range bombers "aggressive."

As a result of this public attitude, which Congress represented, and of presidential indifference, the Navy from 1920 to 1933 remained static, with an average complement of 7900 officers and 100,000 enlisted men, manning about a million tons of warships. The Royal Navy was almost identical in strength. "Except for cruisers," wrote Fleet Admiral King, "hardly any combatant ships (no battleships or destroyers) were added to our own fleet during that period and few were under construction. . . . Moreover, advances in the science of naval construction were hampered by the lack of opportunity to prove new design." Although the naval limitation treaty helped the American taxpayer by suspending battleship construction for ten years, almost all other naval construction stopped too. Battleships were not only the most expensive warships (until the super-carrier came on the scene), but took the longest to build. Before Pearl Harbor, construction of a battleship required an average of 39 months; after that, 32; fleet carriers before Pearl Harbor required 32 months; after it, 15. Submarines and destroyers before Pearl Harbor required 13 to 14 months; after it, five to seven months.

Many senior officers of the Navy envisaged the battles of the next war as long-range gunfire duels between battle lines, as at Jutland, an action so intensively studied at the Naval War College in Newport that one witty officer called Jutland "a major defeat of the United States Navy."

Actually, only one major battle in which our Navy engaged during the war, the night action off Guadalcanal on 14-15 November 1942, was decided by gunfire. All the others were won by ships' torpedoes, and by bombs and torpedoes delivered to the target by aircraft. Accurate gunfire, nevertheless, proved to be indispensable in World War II, both to repel air attack and for shore bombardment to cover an amphibious assault.

Although air bombing of an objective supplemented rather than superseded naval bombardment, it was largely the development of air power that doomed the "battlewagon" to a secondary rôle. In the face of unwelcome attention from bomber planes, she could no longer hold a battle line. Very few ranking officers of any navy appreciated this. Germany put mighty efforts into producing *Bismarck* and *Tirpitz;* and although Admiral Ozawa reached the same conclusion as the progressive American naval leaders, Japan built 18.1-inch-gunned *Musashi* and *Yamato,* and concentrated on battleships in its attack on Pearl Harbor, assuming that their elimination would leave the Japanese Navy supreme.

Battleships were very useful in World War II. All those present at Pearl Harbor on 7 December 1941 were "old enough to vote," but five of the seven sunk or badly damaged, after being raised, repaired and modernized, proved indispensable in covering amphibious operations and for shore bombardment; even *Arkansas, New York* and *Texas* were still "dishing it out" in the European theater at the age of thirty or more in 1944. That is not what they were designed to do; but no matter, many classes of naval vessels have proved useful in unintended directions. The submarine was originally conceived by us as a coast defense vessel, to torpedo enemy ships approaching our shores; it proved incapable of doing that at Luzon in December 1941, but in the Pacific war the submarine proved to be especially potent in sinking the enemy merchant fleet. Destroyers — originally "torpedo boat destroyers" — superseded the torpedo boats to become, first, the "cavalry of the sea" for scouting, and finally, a protective screen for convoys and carriers. Motor torpedo boats were supposed to sneak up on capital ships after dark and torpedo them, a feat seldom performed in

World War II; but they became very effective as small, fast gunboats.

Nevertheless, a much too big slice of the thin appropriation pie was spent on battleships between wars. This was due, fundamentally, to Captain Alfred Thayer Mahan's teachings to the effect that all other classes of warships would be so outranged and outgunned by them in fleet actions as to be useless. And it was fed by a belief that lighter men of war — cruisers, destroyers, auxiliaries and patrol craft — could be constructed quickly in an emergency.

Not only in harping on battleships, but in other matters too, the Navy itself must share the blame with Congress and the public for unpreparedness. One cause was overemphasis on ship-to-ship competition. Gunnery competition, instituted by President Roosevelt in 1902 as a result of the Navy's bad shooting in the Spanish-American War, was extended to torpedo firing, propulsive engineering and communications, the whole comprising the "battle-efficiency competition." For several years this helped the Navy, and probably the net result was beneficial — certainly it was better than no competition at all. But the rivalry thus engendered became almost an end in itself. In order to ensure fairness, rules were standardized and contests held under optimum conditions of fair weather and smooth seas, off the New England coast in summer and in the Caribbean in winter, such as are seldom encountered in battle. A somewhat complacent attitude, to the effect that the United States Navy could outshoot every other Navy, developed. But competition and battle practice were useful in discovering defects in ordnance and matériel, and in improving the design of warships.

To quote a recent letter from Vice Admiral Deyo to the writer:

> The surface Navy, despite lack of funds from Congress or interest by its civilian heads, produced a reasonable semblance of a balanced fleet and operated effectively as one in its training. The spur of officer selec-

tion and ship competition was most noticeable. But gradually the means became the end. Thus, while everyone worked hard, we began going in circles. The Fleet became more and more tied to bases, operating out of Long Beach–San Diego on a tight fuel budget, chained to the increasingly artificial, detailed mandates of the Office of Fleet Training whose word was law. The pencil became sharper than the sword, everyone tried to beat the target practice rules and too many forgot there was a war getting closer. There was a waiting line for top commands, and tenure of office was so short — often only a year or less — that high commanders came and went, leaving little impression. Paper work wrapped its deadly tentacles around cabin and wardroom. Smart ship handling, smart crews, eager initiative received little attention, as did the reverse. Glaring defects in guns, ammunition, torpedoes, battle tactics, went unnoticed so long as the competition rules made due allowances and gave everyone similar conditions.

Fortunately the "battle-efficiency competition" was abolished in 1935 by the then C.N.O., Admiral Standley, and our ships began to train under conditions that more nearly approximated what they were to face in war. Even so, there was little if any practice in night fighting, on which the Japanese Navy specialized. That they were so doing in the East China Sea was apparent in 1937-1939 to the United States Asiatic Fleet, whose C. in C., Admiral Yarnell, repeatedly called it to the attention of the C.N.O. in Washington; but nothing was done. And, although our development in central-directed gunfire subsequent to 1934 was outstanding, no improvements were made in our torpedoes.

Poor design and performance of our torpedoes was due partly to obsolescence (leftover stock from World War I), partly to economy (it was a major offense to lose a live torpedo), partly to between-wars inefficiency of the Bureau of Ordnance, and partly to politics in the torpedo factory at Newport. Rhode Island politicians regarded civilian labor there as part of their patronage, and supported the local union in resisting efficiency. As one United States naval officer remarked ruefully, "If I fired an incompetent or insubordinate workman, the Secretary of the Navy was visited next day by both Rhode Island senators and a congressman insisting that he be reinstated." After war broke with Japan we discovered the hard way that not only our torpedo exploders and depth-regulation mechanisms were fatally defective, but that the enemy had an oxygen-propelled torpedo which carried half a ton of TNT (compared with our 780-pound charge), and could travel eleven miles at 49 knots, compared with our range of 7.5 miles at 26.5 knots. And, while the United States Navy, expecting to fight daylight Jutlands at long range with high-caliber guns, took the torpedo tubes off its cruisers, the Japanese kept theirs, and prepared for the close-range nocturnal "hugger-mugger" clinch, making abundant use of torpedoes. With these tactics they reaped rich rewards during the battles around Guadalcanal in 1942-1943. The United States Navy, in contrast, was like a city police force equipped only with high-powered rifles, but with no weapons to meet thugs jumping patrolmen at night with automatic pistols and blackjacks.

2. *Naval Aviation and Amphibious Training*

Nevertheless, the Navy strove to attain excellence within the required framework. After 1930, under the lead of wise and aggressive Chiefs of Naval Operations such as Admirals William V. Pratt and William H. Standley, the Fleet made substantial progress in several directions, especially naval aviation. The Navy's first aircraft, a bamboo-and-canvas single-engined biplane, the Curtiss A–1, dates from 1910. Pilot Eugene Ely landed it successfully on an inprovised flight deck of cruiser *Pennsylvania* on 18 January 1911. The Navy's small air arm did so well in World War I that in May 1919 the General Board declared for an immediate development of fleet aviation: "a naval air service must be established capable of accompanying and operating with the Fleet in all waters of the globe." That year the catapult was invented to enable spotting planes to take off from the decks of battleships and cruisers. The use of planes on board ship incorporated the new weapon and the newly trained aviators with the existing naval organization, instead of keeping it at arm's length, as the Army did with the A.A.F. These young aviators, unhampered by obsolete equipment or doctrine, injected new life into ships' wardrooms, and there was enough time before war again broke for many to become senior officers and some to reach flag rank. This early integration of air power with the United States Navy, and our Navy's successful resistance to every effort to deprive it of the air arm, was the basis for the remarkable performances of American aircraft carriers and their planes in World War II.

It was also in May 1919 that Lieutenant Commander Albert C. Read USN, pilot of *NC-4*, with a crew of four, flew the first airplane to cross the Atlantic.[2] The first seaplane tender, *Wright*, and the first aircraft carrier, appropriately named *Langley* after another American poineer in aviation, were commissioned in 1921. The Bureau of Aeronautics (Buaer) was added to the Navy bureaus that same year. The creation of an Assistant Secretary of the Navy for Aviation followed. Aircraft and carriers participated, from 1923 on, in the annual fleet "problems," which were maneuvers aimed at some definite objective, such as attacking the Panama Canal. *Langley's* performance in the 1925 problem so impressed the C. in C. that he pressed the speedy completion of *Lexington* and *Saratoga*. Both carriers participated in fleet maneuvers and problems from 1929 on; and in 1938 *Saratoga* launched a successful "surprise attack" on Pearl Harbor, a hint probably not lost on Admiral Yamamoto of the Imperial Japanese Navy. Commen-

[2] Commander Read called at the Azores; the first nonstop flight was made from Newfoundland to Ireland by two Royal Air Force officers, J. W. Alcock and A. W. Brown, 14-15 June 1919. Charles Lindbergh's, the first nonstop solo flight, was in 1927.

surate improvement went on in carrier aircraft types (fighters, torpedo-bombers, dive-bombers), but the Japanese Navy improved the first two types faster than we did. U.S.S. *Ranger*, first of our aircraft carriers to be built as such from the keel up, was completed in 1934.

The performance of these vessels and their planes brought about a new conception of the aircraft carrier's place in naval warfare. Formerly their functions were to scout for and provide an "air umbrella" over the Battle Line. Now rôles were reversed; the carrier became the nucleus of a striking force capable of projecting fire power deep into enemy-held waters, and the proud battlewagon, when not employed in shore bombardment, joined the protective screen to the carrier.

Other important developments came in connection with amphibious training. A military expedition the object of which is to land troops on enemy-held territory and establish a beachhead there, is called an amphibious operation. This, the most ancient form of naval warfare, in which the Greeks, Phoenicians and Norsemen distinguished themselves, became discredited in World War I and for years thereafter was neglected by all naval powers except Japan. This neglect arose from the misleading claims made by air-power fanatics, and from the costly failure of the Dardanelles operation in 1915. Both combined to create the impression that land-based aircraft and modern coast defense guns would slaughter any landing force before it reached the beach.

Credit for the revival of amphibious training, and for adapting amphibious tactics to an age of air power and increased gunfire potential, is due to the United States Marine Corps; primarily to Major Earl H. Ellis USMC, who disappeared mysteriously when reconnoitering the Palau Islands in 1923. He was probably murdered by the Japanese because he knew too much; but he had already planted the seed. He pointed out that Japan's insular spiderweb would have to be swept up in case of war, and that the

Marines would have to wield the broom — provided the Navy could get them there and cover their landings with gunfire. He even anticipated that we would have to take Okinawa before defeating Japan. Major Ellis's plans were approved by General Lejeune, Commandant of the Marine Corps, in 1921, a Marine expeditionary force was organized, and in 1923 it performed the first amphibious attack "problem" on Culebra Island east of Puerto Rico. Next year a bigger problem, with 1700 troops engaged, resulted in a complete foul-up. This convinced the Navy that far more study and training were required before an amphibious assault could dislodge a determined enemy. New landing craft types, even the precursor of the LVT amphibian tractor, were tried out, and in 1933 the Fleet Marine Force was established. Next year it issued a *Tentative Manual for Landing Operations* which Marine Corps historians regard as "the Pentateuch and the Four Gospels" of amphibious warfare. As Bob Sherrod writes, the establishment of Fleet Marine Force marks the evolution of the Marine Corps "from a simple, rough-and-ready gang, which could fight banana wars . . . to a specialized organization with a primary mission" — the seizure of beachheads as bases for military operations.[3] General John H. Russell, acting Commandant of the Corps, was largely responsible.

Gradually the Marines drew more of the Navy and Coast Guard into their maneuvers. After France fell, and the Army realized that no future American Expeditionary Force could land at Brest on stone jetties and proceed to the battle area in *40 hommes, 8 chevaux* boxcars, it too consented to learn from the Marines, and began to take part in their amphibious exercises.

[3] *History of Marine Corps Aviation in World War II* (1952) p. 30.

3. *Pacific Ocean Strategy*

Until September 1939, when World War II broke in Europe, the Navy hardly knew what it would be called upon to do in the Atlantic; but for over forty years it had known what would be expected of it in the Pacific. Responsibility for the Philippines, which (together with a formidable insurrection) we bought from Spain in 1898, involved us in Far Eastern power politics and made war with Japan difficult to escape, if not inevitable. And, as an example of the haphazard, nonstrategic nature of the decision to buy the Philippines, we failed to acquire island approaches to the archipelago on which Spain had put a "For Sale" sign — excepting Guam, which was of slight value without nearby Saipan and Tinian.

Out of the welter of events in the Pacific between 1900 and 1941 there emerged two major factors — the growing disorganization of China and the increasing power of Japan. We tried to arrest the one by the "Open Door" policy of John Hay, which meant dissuading European powers and Japan from annexing parts of China or acquiring special privileges in her ports. Then came the Russo-Japanese War of 1904-1905 in which Japan acquired Korea and a new area of influence in Manchuria. It was generally expected that this would not long satisfy Japan, and that the Philippines would be her next objective.

As early as 1903 our great authority on naval strategy, Captain Mahan, urged that the United States Navy concentrate in the Pacific. The joint Army-Navy Board, precursor of the Joint Chiefs of Staff, so recommended in 1905; it proposed that the Battle Fleet be based on Subic Bay, Luzon. President Theodore Roosevelt declined to support this. Had he done so, and if Congress had built up shore installations there as a "deterrent," it is possible that Japan would never have attacked us. But one can never tell when something intended as a deterrent may instead become a mere irritant. Basing the Battle Fleet in the Philippines might have provoked Japan to a sneak attack on Subic Bay, before the opening of the Panama Canal in June 1914 permitted warships to be shifted rapidly from one ocean to another.

Japan again increased her power by joining World War I as the ally of Britain, and, with very little exertion and minimum loss, acquiring Germany's insular empire — the Marshall and Caroline Islands, and all the Marianas except Guam. President Wilson, more farseeing about Japan than Theodore Roosevelt had been, protested against these acquisitions at the Paris Peace Conference, and the 1916 naval program, which he strongly supported, had the deterrence of Japan principally in view. Wilson was overruled on the first point, and the planned big navy, as we have seen, was scrapped after the war. Japan kept her insular spiderwebs, on which dozens of airfields and numerous naval bases could be built and were built after 1936. In the event of war with Japan, the United States Navy's "Orange" plan looked to the Army to defend Manila and hold out for an estimated three to four months until the Battle Fleet could cross the Pacific and raise the siege. Japanese possession of the mandated islands made this task impossible unless key positions in the Marshalls and Carolines were first secured, and the spiders cleaned out; that increased the estimated time for the Army to hold out in Luzon to nine months. And, as we have seen, a part of the 1922 Washington agreement was our renouncing the right to strengthen our bases in Guam and the Philippines.

An impossible situation in grand strategy had been created for us, largely by our own folly. We were promising to defend the integrity of China and of the Philippines, without anything near the military means to implement such a policy.

In the meantime the liberal, Western-oriented groups in Japanese politics, which had been participating in the collective security measures of the League of Nations, were being harassed and terrified by a movement roughly parallel to Hitler's Nazis. *Kodo-Ha,* as it was called, aimed to place Japan under Army control, "liberate" China, India, the Philippines and all East Asia from "foreign imperialists," and place all Asiatic countries under Japanese hegemony. Liberal politicians were assassinated, and in 1931 the Japanese Kwantung Army moved into Manchuria. Secretary Stimson was unable to persuade President Hoover to do more than protest against the Japanese invasion of Manchuria, and of Shanghai later in the same year. A commission of the League of Nations condemned the Japanese action and demanded that she retire from Manchuria; Japan's reply was to withdraw from the League of Nations and to announce that on her part the naval limitation treaties would end in 1936.

Harbinger of fairer weather for the Navy was the appointment of the Honorable Carl Vinson of Georgia, in 1931, to be Chairman of the Naval Affairs Committee of the House of Representatives; a position that he still held, as chairman of an enlarged House Armed Services Committee, in 1962. Mr. Vinson was not only well disposed toward the Navy; he made himself an expert on its technique and supported its aspirations to help defend the country. "No Member of Congress," writes Rear Admiral Furer, "has ever shown a greater understanding of naval needs . . . nor a greater mastery of the practical politics necessary to get the legislative branch of the government to recognize these needs, than Carl Vinson." Among the promoters of a powerful Navy Carl Vinson deserves a high place. But the No. 1 architect of victory was the former Assistant Secretary of the Navy in World War I, who became President of the United States on 4 March 1933. Franklin D. Roosevelt brought a New Deal for the armed forces as well as for the nation. Yet he was not yet ready to end appeasement of Japan.

4. *Naval Buildup under Roosevelt, 1933–1939*

Even though Japan had bowed out of naval limitation, both Britain and America regarded themselves bound by the treaties. But the United States Navy had been allowed to fall so low that there was a vast gap to be filled before even treaty strength could be attained. Congress finally began responding to frequent prods from President Roosevelt, Mr. Vinson and the leading admirals. The first new construction authorized in years — of the *Brooklyn* class light cruisers, *Craven* class destroyers, carriers *Enterprise* and *Yorktown* and four submarines — came as a corollary to the National Industrial Recovery Act of 16 June 1933, the avowed purpose being to relieve unemployment.

This buildup taxed the ingenuity of the Navy bureaus (especially Ships and Yards and Docks) because during the lean decade many shipbuilding and other firms that depended on naval orders had been liquidated, and their designers, draftsmen and skilled workers had obtained other jobs or gone on relief. Thus the rearmament program started almost from scratch and could not be greatly accelerated until wartime. For example, the Vinson-Trammel Act of 1934 provided an eight-year replacement program which would require ten years to attain "treaty strength."

The first five "treaty 10,000-ton" heavy cruisers of the *New Orleans* class, which had been authorized five years earlier, joined the Fleet in 1934. Despite nation-wide unemployment, Congress for several years refused to increase the authorized personnel of the Navy, which in 1935, with only 8063 officers and 82,500 men, had to operate ships with about 80 per cent of their proper complement. Two years later a new ceiling of 100,000 bluejackets was established. Between 1935 and 1940 the *Atlanta* class of antiaircraft cruisers was designed and several types of fleet auxiliaries, including minesweepers, were transferred from the drafting boards to the building ways. All battleships of the *North Carolina*, *South Dakota* and *Iowa* classes were designed in these years; but only *North Carolina* and *Washington* were completed before we entered the war — our first battleships in eighteen years. These ships were characterized by 16-inch main batteries, thick armored decks for protection from air bombing, heavy fragment protection around important control stations, modern 5-inch antiaircraft guns in twin mounts, and the forerunners (found by battle experience to be inadequate) of the present types and numbers of close-range antiaircraft weapons.

In August 1939, when Admiral William D. Leahy was relieved as C.N.O. by Admiral Harold R. Stark, he could look back with some satisfaction at the increase of naval strength during the two and a half years of his incumbency. But, as he wrote in his last report, "The Navy must be sufficiently strong in every essential element, and it must be adequately trained," in order to take the offensive in the event of war and "defeat the enemy fleet wherever it can be brought to action." In several respects the Navy was not well rounded. Very few fast, modern auxiliaries had been finished. On 1 July 1939 the Navy had only two transports, three cargo ships, three oilers and one ammunition ship in commission; and on 1 December 1941 Cincpac had only one transport and one oiler ready to accompany the fleet's trans-Pacific trek, if and when war broke out. But the chief worry that Leahy bequeathed to his successor was the subject of bases.

It was probably a good thing in the long run that the United States Navy was ill-provided with bases in the Pacific, in comparison with the Imperial Japanese Navy and the Royal British. Want of them made American officers more self-reliant, and their ships more self-sufficient. Nevertheless, failure to develop adequately what bases we had meant a rapid withdrawal of American sea power from the western Pacific when the Japanese struck. After Japan denounced the naval limitation treaty in

1936, the United States was free to strengthen all bases, anywhere. But all that could be got out of Congress was a few million dollars for seaplane bases at Wake and Midway islands, and at Kodiak (Alaska) and Dutch Harbor in the Aleutians. These were indeed useful; only the first-named was lost to the enemy. In 1938 a special board headed by Admiral Hepburn recommended the building of a fully equipped fleet and air base at Guam, to help defend the Philippines. Congress, after a heated debate, turned this down, largely for fear of provoking Japan. And the little that was done to strengthen the defenses of Manila Bay proved to be wholly inadequate.

Immediately upon the outbreak of war in Europe, in September 1939, the appropriate bureaus of the Navy drew up comprehensive estimates of warship requirements. The problem was no longer one of designing the best ship of a limited size, but of selecting the most desirable combination of basic characteristics. With the aid of previous experience, designs were completed for new types of destroyers, cruisers, and aircraft carriers. By 7 December 1941, plans had been completed for the *Fletcher* class destroyers, the 6-inch *Cleveland* class cruisers, the 8-inch *Baltimore* class heavy cruisers, the *Essex* class aircraft carriers, the first destroyer escorts, and a dozen different classes of auxiliaries. In order to meet the demands of modern warfare, more ammunition was required for an increased number of guns, more crews to man the gunmounts, more fuel capacity for a wider cruising radius, more powerful machinery to deliver greater shaft horse power and develop more speed. Increased tonnage was inescapably necessary to carry the added weight, with sufficient reserve buoyancy and stability for the ship to survive serious damage. New main propulsion plants, using high-pressure, high-temperature steam, were introduced during the prewar period. These reached such a state of development that United States ships were able to travel enormous distances without shipyard upkeep and overhaul — in many cases over 100,000 miles within a single year. Vast improvements in the diesel engine industry provided another source of propulsive power which would be utilized to the staggering total of 35 million out of a total of some 90 million shaft horse power during the war.

A number of experimental laboratories and testing stations, maintained by various bureaus of the Navy, were staffed with technicians and scientists. Among such establishments were the Taylor ship-model basin, wind tunnels, powder, gun, torpedo, mine and aircraft factories, ordnance proving grounds, as well as testing and experimental stations. A Naval Research Laboratory was established in 1928 for high-level work. Owing to meager appropriations, it lost primacy in radar to the Royal Air Force laboratory in England; but that eventually benefited us too, and our research laboratory helped the Royal Navy in other fields. The National Research Council collaborated with the Naval Research Laboratory and also with the research activities of private industry. This laid foundations for the phenomenal success of the Navy in mobilizing American scientists and scientific resources for wartime purposes.

During Franklin D. Roosevelt's first administration and the first two years of his second (1937-1939), progress in national defense was substantial but slow. A five-day week law, designed to spread employment, made construction lag. Nor did our foreign policy substantially change. What the Japanese called the "China Incident" of 7 July 1937 inaugurated their invasion of China proper, in the course of which they sank United States River Gunboat *Panay* without producing a noticeable dent on the American people's determination to avoid war.

The widely publicized report of a committee headed by Senator Gerald Nye, in 1934, "proved" by innuendo that bankers and munitions makers ("merchants of death") had got America into World War I, and Congress responded to the public opinion thereby created by passing a series of neutrality acts. These renounced most of the neutral rights for which we had fought England in 1812 and Germany in 1917. Sale or transport of munitions to a belligerent was forbidden (1935), loans to belligerents were prohibited (1936); these were applied to the civil war in Spain, but sale of munitions was permitted on a "cash and carry" basis (1937). And the President was authorized to prohibit American ships from entering "danger zones" so as to prevent "incidents" (1939). Thus, to peace by naval limitation and peace by incantation (the Kellogg-Briand pact) we added peace by an ostrich-like isolation.

When war broke in Europe in September 1939, the vast majority of the American people wished to stay out of it. American sympathies were strongly pro-Ally, but it was assumed that Hitler's Third Reich was a big bluff, and that the French Army and Royal Navy could defeat him in short order.

Note on "Scrapping" under the 1922 Treaties

There were a few exceptions allowed to the 5:5:3 ratio: the most fortunate for us being permission to convert two 43,500-ton battle cruiser hulls, still on the ways, into carriers *Lexington* and *Saratoga*, of 33,000 tons each — despite a treaty limitation of 25,000 tons on aircraft carrier construction. Japan by way of compensation converted battle cruiser *Akagi* and battleship *Kaga* (substituted for *Amagi*, destroyed in the great earthquake) to carriers. In accordance with the 1922 treaties, the United States Navy scrapped the 76 per cent completed battleship *Washington*, six 43,200-tonners of *South Dakota* class 11 to 38 per cent complete, and four battle cruisers building, sisters to *Lexington* and *Saratoga*. On these ships three hundred million dollars had already been spent. In addition, "Dreadnoughts" *Delaware*, *North Dakota*, *Michigan* and *South Carolina* (twelve years old), were scrapped and 15 pre-Dreadnoughts, some as old as the Spanish-American War, were broken up, used as targets, or made museum pieces. Originally the United States Navy was also to have scrapped *Colorado* and *West Virginia*, retaining only *Maryland* as a postwar 16-inch-gunned battleship; England to have kept *Hood*, and Japan *Nagato*, to balance *Maryland*. Japan, however, presented a plea to keep new battleship *Mutsu*, since Japanese schoolchildren had contributed their pennies to pay for her; so there was another compromise, whereby the United States Navy kept *Colorado* and *West Virginia* and England built two new equalizers, *Nelson* and *Rodney*. The Royal Navy in accordance with the treaty scrapped 14 "Dreadnought" battleships and 6 "Dreadnought" battle cruisers, 7 to 15 years old, totaling 415,000 tons, and renounced building four "super-*Hood*" class battle cruisers. Japan used as a target and sank the completed 40,000-ton battleship *Tosa*, gave up constructing two more battle cruisers, and scrapped 8 pre-Dreadnought battleships, 11 to 16 years old. A re-examination after World War II makes the balance fairer than it seemed at the time; 8 of the 18 battleships retained by the United States Navy were completed in 1917 or later, but only 3 of the 16 battleships retained by the Royal Navy, and 5 of the 6 battleships retained by Japan, were that new. Both Britain and Japan had in the blueprint stage eight 18-inch-gunned battleships, which they gave up building. I am indebted to Mr. Samuel A. Smiley of Falls Church, Virginia, for information on this subject.

CHAPTER II

Short of War

1939–1941

1. *Impact of the European War*

THE SIXTH YEAR of the appeasement of Hitler by England and France ended on 3 September 1939, when he invaded Poland. For another year American policy toward the European war was dictated by the public's overwhelming desire to keep out of it, at almost any price. At the same time that President Roosevelt announced American neutrality, he declared a "limited emergency" (8 September). The immediate effects of this on Congress, as respects the Navy, were to increase authorized enlisted strength to 191,000, and to allow the President to recall reserve officers and men to active duty as needed.

Our first positive action toward the war, typically if paradoxically negative, was to organize the Neutrality Patrol. This was decided at the Congress of American Republics at Panama, on 2 October. Hitler had been nourishing "fifth columns" of Nazis in many Latin American republics, and the gravest danger to the Americas at that time appeared to be German subversion. The idea behind the Neutrality Patrol was to create and protect a neutral zone extending an average of 300 miles off the American coastline, except off Canada; for Canada loyally declared war when her mother country did. West of this line, belligerents were forbidden by the Congress of American Republics to conduct military operations. Eight groups of the United States Navy, mostly destroyers and cruisers, covered the North American sector from Newfoundland to Trinidad. This, writes Captain Roskill RN, "was unquestionably an unfavorable move from the Allies' point of view." On the other hand, Admiral Doenitz, commander of the German U-boat fleet, regarded the Neutrality Patrol as an outrageous limitation on the operations of his submarines.

Although naval and military men are often accused of trying to fight a new war with the tactics of the last one, the reverse was true here; neither Germany nor England realized that World War II in the Atlantic would closely resemble World War I. In both wars, Germany tried to disrupt England's communications and sink Allied tonnage with U-boats, whilst England counterattacked the submarines and imposed a surface blockade of Germany. But neither side thought it would be like this in 1939. Germany had fewer than fifty submarines ready for offensive operations when war broke, and a very low production schedule. The Royal Navy was not provided with mines to protect British harbors or with nearly enough ships for escort-of-convoy and antisubmarine work. The reasons given for this lack, by Admiral Sir William James, are equally applicable to the United States Navy when it entered the war more than two years later: it was thought better to spend limited budgets on battleships, carriers, and other big ships that took a long time to build, rather than on a multitude of escorts and other small craft which, it was believed, could be improvised when war broke out.

Another lesson of the last war was the necessity of convoying merchant shipping, and the folly of trying to cope with submarines by hunting them all over the place — "looking for a needle in a haystack," as Captain Mahan described such tactics. The Royal Navy did organize merchant convoys to the extent of its supply of escorts; but, spurred by Winston Churchill and other civilians, it also wasted time and effort on hunter groups. After a big fleet carrier, H.M.S. *Courageous*, had fallen victim to a U-boat while engaged in one of these hunts, the British stopped them; and after the United States entered the war, Admiral King set his face sternly against anything of the sort.

To anticipate: The entire experience of the war demonstrated that the heavily escorted merchant convoy, supplemented by an escort carrier group on its flank, was by far the best way to get U-boats, because the merchantmen acted as bait. The convoy was not a defensive weapon, as so often charged by ignorant or prejudiced people, but the best sort of offensive, besides being the only way to insure safe transportation of men and matériel.

With the aid of the land-based Coastal Command of the R.A.F., now under Admiralty control, the Royal Navy did well against U-boats in 1939-1940, the winter of the "phony war" on the European Continent. German moored magnetic mines and surface raiders proved more destructive than submarines at this period. The Royal Navy quickly learned to cope with these, and passed on its findings to us, which enabled the United States Navy to repair its former neglect of mine warfare.

2. *The Fall of France and "Short of War" Strategy*

Up to mid-1940 it was the general opinion in the United States that the French Army and British Navy between them could defeat Hitler. The blitzes that Hitler exploded in the spring of 1940, culminating in the fall of France in June, administered a rude jolt to this attitude. It took time for the implications to sink into the public mind; but we now know that the fall of France was the greatest upset to world balance of power between 1871 and 1949, when China went Red.

With Germany in control of such French outposts as Brest, Lorient, Saint-Nazaire and La Pallice, her U-boats' cruising radius was doubled; and the air blitz laid on England at the same time carried the grave threat of Hitler's acquiring bases in the British Isles. If North Africa too were brought under German control, there was a fair prospect that Nazi governments would be set up in South America and the French and Dutch West Indies be taken over.

Naturally there were repercussions in the Far East. The Tokyo press reacted violently to the United States holding its annual fleet exercise in the Pacific. At the conclusion of this 1940 Fleet Problem, and at the request of the State Department, the Fleet was ordered to remain based on Pearl Harbor, in the hope of its exercising a "deterrent effect" on Japanese aggression. The Imperial government had already proclaimed the "Greater East Asia Co-Prosperity Sphere," aiming at Japanese political, economic and military hegemony over Indochina, Thailand, Netherlands East Indies and the Philippines. On 27 September 1940, Japan formally joined the European Axis in the Tripartite Pact, which stipulated that if one of the three got into war with the United States the other two would pitch in. For the United States Navy this posed the problem of fighting a two-ocean war with a much less than one-ocean Fleet.

President Franklin D. Roosevelt had a political calculating machine in his head, an intricate instrument in which Gallup polls, the strength of armed forces and the probability of England's survival; the personalities of governors, senators and congressmen, and of Mussolini, Hitler, Churchill, Chiang, and Tojo; the Irish, German, Italian, and Jewish votes in the approaching presidential election; the "Help the Allies" people and the "American Firsters," were combined with fine points of political maneuvering. The fall of France, fed into the F.D.R. calculating machine, caused wheels to whir and gears to click with dynamic intensity. Out came a solution: the "short of war" policy (1) to help keep England fighting in Europe, (2) to gain time for American rearmament, and (3) to restrain Japan by diplomacy and the Fleet's "deterrence." Whether Roosevelt really believed that this policy would "keep us out of war" is debatable. But he had to assume that it would, until after the presidential election of 1940, in which he flouted tradition by running for a third term, and until events abroad convinced the American people that war was their only alternative to a shameful and ultimately disastrous appeasement.

In any case, an essential and most beneficial part of the "short of war" policy was to build up the Navy. On 14 June 1940, the day that Hitler took Paris, President Roosevelt signed a naval expansion bill that had been under discussion for months. Three days later, Admiral Stark asked Congress for four billion dollars more to begin building a "two-ocean navy," and got it. The Navy then had about 1,250,000 tons of combatant shipping; this bill authorized a more than double increase. But, as Admiral Stark said, "Dollars cannot buy yesterday." For two years at least, the Americas would be vulnerable in the event of a German victory in Europe.

To meet this emergency, President Roosevelt adopted the political strategy of helping England and (after June 1941) Russia in their war with Germany. This meant violating all the old international laws of neutrality. Hitler had completely flouted neutral rights by his invasion of Denmark, Norway, Belgium and Holland; hence Germany forfeited the right to demand neutrality of others. Most Americans were loath to discard a concept so deeply rooted in the national tradition — they had just been trying to embalm neutrality in acts of Congress! But they were willing to build a two-ocean Navy, hoping that a wall of ships in the blueprint stage or on the building ways would deter Hitler from setting up satellite states in America.

On 15 June 1940, the day after approving the first of these new navy bills, President Roosevelt appointed a group of eminent civilian scientists members of a new National Defense Research Committee. These included Vannevar Bush, President of the Carnegie Institution of Washington; James Bryant Conant, President of Harvard University; Karl T. Compton, President of the Massachusetts Institute of Technology; Frank B. Jewett, President of the National Academy of Sciences; and Rear Admiral J. A. Furer. Since late 1939 Dr. Bush had been working on the mobilization of American scientists for war, but it took the fall of France to bring matters to a head. From this N.D.R.C. stemmed most of the essential civilian research done for the armed forces during the "short of war" period, and during the war itself.

At the same time, in order to emphasize the nation's danger and obtain nation-wide support, President Roosevelt appointed two leading Republicans Secretary of the Navy and Secretary of War. Frank Knox, who had been Republican candidate for Vice President in the last election, quickly acquired a grasp of naval business and became one of the best secretaries the Navy ever had. The office of Under Secretary of the Navy was created and first filled by Knox's future successor, James V. Forrestal, on 22 August 1940. Henry L. Stimson, who had been Secretary of War under President Taft and Secretary of State under President Hoover, became Secretary of War again in July 1940. Upon his urgent recommendation, Congress passed the Selective Training and Service Act on 16 September. This was the first time that the United States had adopted compulsory military training in time of peace.

During the summer and fall of that year, President Roosevelt initiated several important steps in high-level strategy in the Atlantic. He held a conference with Mackenzie King, Prime Minister of Canada, in August. A United States–Canada Mutual Defense Pact included complete reciprocity in the use of the naval shipyards of both countries. Now that the British Commonwealth was the one power fighting Germany, it became urgent to keep her strong and pugnacious while the American "two-ocean navy" was being built. President Roosevelt and Winston Churchill concluded on 2 September the naval bases–destroyers deal. Britain ceded to the United States sovereign rights for ninety-nine years over sites for naval, military and air bases in the West Indies in exchange for fifty four-stack destroyers built during or shortly after the last war. The Argentia (Newfoundland) and Bermuda bases were also granted to the United States as free gifts.

Information from United States naval attachés in the Axis countries furthered the "short of war" policy. For instance, Commander A. E. Schrader reported from Berlin on 18 December 1940 that Hitler already had seven to nine million men available to be called to the colors, that there was no possibility of an internal revolt against him, that all six of the occupied countries were being systematically plundered for Germany's benefit, and that the British "heart of oak" was admirably taking the German air blitz on a "chin of armorplate." He even predicted that Germany would next attack Russia to annex the Ukraine and the Caucasus, and warned that the whole world would be "an empty shell" if Germany won. One of our military attachés in Berlin obtained a copy of Hitler's plan for an attack on Russia six months in advance; the important news went to Stalin via Roosevelt and Churchill, but Stalin refused to believe it.

Postwar revelations of discussion in the German high command prove that President Roosevelt's estimate that Hitler would overlook direct American aid to England, rather than declare war, was absolutely right. The arrogant Nazi government chose to accept the destroyer deal and plenty more, because it knew very well that the United States at war would be far more formidable than the United States "short of war." And the time gained by us for preparation was of inestimable value.

The next unneutral measure was Lend-Lease. By existing neutrality legislation it was still illegal for American merchant ships to trade with, or for private investors to lend their money to, belligerent countries. Whatever war supplies Britain or Canada procured in the United States had to be paid for with cash, and carried in their own ships; and they were "scraping the bottom of the barrel." The Lend-Lease plan was briefly this: The United States would embark on an all-out military and naval defense program, both by giving orders to private firms and by building new government plants; but would lend or lease as much production as could be spared to Great Britain. Congress passed the first Lend-Lease Act on 11 March 1941. "This decision," said the President on 15 March, "is the end of any attempt at appeasement in our land; the end of urging us to get along with the dictators; the end of compromise with tyranny and the forces of oppression."

It was not quite that; certainly not, respecting Japan; but the Nazis had to "take it." Hitler, who attacked Russia in June 1941, informed his navy chief in July that it was "vitally important to put off America's entering into the war for another one or two months." He wanted no "incidents" calculated to provoke America. But he got plenty, as we shall see.

Even more important in early 1941 was the ABC–1 Staff Agreement which constituted the basic agreement for Anglo-American coöperation if and when we entered the war, and the basic strategic decision of the war: to "beat Hitler first." In July 1940, Admiral Harold R. Stark, Chief of Naval Operations, sent Rear Admiral R. L. Ghormley to London for "exploratory conversations" with the Admiralty. These were so fruitful in acquiring information about antisubmarine and other aspects of the war that, on the advice of C.N.O., a secret staff conversation with the British was convened at Washington at the end of January 1941. Rear Admirals Ghormley and Richmond Kelly Turner and Captains Alan G. Kirk and DeWitt C. Ramsey represented the United States Navy; Major General Embick, Brigadier General Sherman Miles and Colonel L. T. Gerow, the Army; Air Vice Marshal John C. Slessor was there for the Royal Air Force; Rear Admirals Roger Bellairs and Victor Danckwerts for the Royal Navy. After long deliberations, this conference concluded the "ABC–1 Staff Agreement" of 27 March 1941. This provided that, if and when the United States entered the war, it would exert "the principal U.S. military effort" in the European theater. America would try to avoid war with Japan, but, even if that proved impossible, operations in the Pacific would be conducted in such a manner as "to facilitate" the effort against the European Axis. Naturally this decision pleased the British, but the Americans initiated it. The reasons behind so sound a decision — which, as Slessor wrote, continued to govern our combined action throughout the war, although "at times a bit frayed at the edges" — were (1) Germany had a far greater military potentiality than Japan; (2) Germany already controlled almost the entire Atlantic coast of Europe and threatened the Americas; (3) England was already fighting Germany and could be assisted immediately, whilst Japan at that time was fighting only China, which foreign aid could not reach — Japan having already seized the Chinese coast, part of Indochina, and the Burma Road.

The two staffs also agreed that, if and when the United States entered the war, the American Joint Chiefs of Staff and the British Chiefs of Staff would meet as the Combined Chiefs of Staff to make strategic plans and decisions for the Allied nations. And other decisions about command structures, areas of responsibility, and exchange of information were loyally carried out on both sides. Thus, even before America entered the war, the basic strategic decision had been made, and machinery had been set up for close coöperation. This forehandedness prevented an infinite amount of friction, misunderstanding and fruitless effort, such as had taken place in World War I.

One Washington agreement went into effect immediately — that the United States Navy share responsibility for escorting transatlantic convoys as soon as the Atlantic Fleet could do so.

The Atlantic Fleet was reactivated 1 February 1941 under Admiral Ernest J. King as Commander in Chief — "Cinclant" for short. "Ernie" King, born in Ohio in 1878, a graduate of the Naval Academy in 1901, was not only a great naval officer but a military strategist. He had shown outstanding ability in almost every branch of the Navy — ordnance, engineering, assistant chief of staff to the C. in C. in World War I, logistics, submarines, naval aviation, General Board, C.O. of a reefer, of destroyers, of a naval air station, and of *Lexington*. A hard man with little sense of humor, he was more respected than liked in the Navy; his eagerness to get things done quickly with no unnecessary palaver, coupled with an abrupt and often rude manner, infuriated many Americans and dismayed his British opposite numbers. No officer on either side or in any armed service had so complete a strategic view of the war as King's. Neither General Marshall nor any of the British had time or energy to concentrate on the war in the Pacific; but King not only grasped that and the Atlantic war; he had a better strategic savvy of the land phases of the European war than most of the generals. Secretary Stimson hated him, Winston Churchill and Sir Alan Brooke hated him, Admiral Sir Andrew B. Cunningham hated him, many even in the United States Army and Navy hated him. But Tojo, Hitler, and Doenitz had even greater reason to hate King, because, with Churchill, Roosevelt and Eisenhower, he was a principal architect of Allied victory.

By the time the "short of war" measures were being organized, German U-boats were coming in increasing numbers off the assembly line, enabling Admiral Doenitz to set up new "wolf-pack" tactics. His submarines, in groups of eight to twenty, were sent out fanwise into the North and South Atlantic, and, daily controlled by radio from the command post in Lorient, would shadow a convoy by day and attack by night. On the night of 3-4 April 1941 one of these wolf-packs sank 10 out of 22 ships in a slow transatlantic convoy. Admiral Stark at once saw that the United States Navy would have to pitch in to help escort-of-convoy, or the lend-lease aid would never reach its destination.

On 4 April he transferred the new carrier *Yorktown*, three battleships, four light cruisers and two destroyer squadrons from the Pacific to the Atlantic Fleet. On 9 April the minister of Denmark (now occupied by the Germans) at Washington invited the United States to become the protector of Greenland, which she promptly did; and Greenland became a base for weather stations and for airfields, both important in the antisubmarine campaign. On 18 April Admiral King issued his Operation Plan 3-41 in which he ordered that any belligerent warship or aircraft — other than those of powers which had West Indian colonies — which approached within 25 miles of the Western Hemisphere (Greenland included) to be "viewed as actuated by an intention immediately to attack such territory." The Fleet was ordered to be in constant readiness for combat, but to make no attack without orders from C.N.O. In May came the break-out of German battleship *Bismarck*, sunk after a long chase by torpedo bombers and gunfire of the Royal Navy on the 27th. That day President Roosevelt declared an "Unlimited National Emergency." The decimation of transatlantic convoys by U-boats continued. Hitler invaded Russia on 22 June. After a tardy invitation from a sulky Icelandic government, United States Marines occupied Iceland on 8 July. The United States Navy formally began escort duties by protecting merchant ships, of whatever flag, in convoys from East Coast ports to Iceland. On 16 September the Navy began helping the Canadians to escort transatlantic convoys to a mid-ocean meeting point ("Momp") south of Iceland, where the Royal Navy took over.

First blood for Germany was narrowly averted on 20 June 1941 when *U-203* sighted battleship *Texas* between Newfoundland and Greenland and, assuming that she had been lend-leased to England, tried to attack but could not catch her. On 4 September United States destroyer *Greer* and *U-652* played a cat-and-mouse game with depth charges and torpedoes. Both missed, but the President took this occasion to have orders issued to shoot on sight any ship interfering with American shipping. It worked both ways; on the black night of 17 October U.S.S. *Kearny*, one of Captain Hewlett Thébaud's destroyer division escorting a slow convoy, was torpedoed. She lost eleven men, but reached port. On 30 October a naval oiler, *Salinas*, was torpedoed in mid-ocean, but survived. The first sinking of a combatant ship came next day when U. S. S. *Reuben James* (Lieutenant Commander H. L. Edwards) was sunk by *U-562* while helping to escort a fast convoy from Halifax, with a loss of 115 officers and men.

Thus, "short of war" was not so very short for the Atlantic Fleet. Autumn and winter escort work in the North Atlantic was arduous and exhausting for men and ships. That section of it covered by United States destroyers, between Newfoundland, Greenland and Iceland, is the roughest part of the western ocean in winter. Winds of gale force, mountainous seas, biting cold, body-piercing fog and blinding snow squalls were the rule rather than the exception. The continual rolling and pitching, coupled with the necessity for constant vigilance night and day — not only for enemy attack, but to guard against collisions with other escort vessels and the convoy — wore men down. The so-called "rest periods" at Hvalfjordur and Argentia were rests merely from enemy attack, not from the weather; for in both ports the holding ground was bad and the weather terrible. Destroyers dragged all over these harbors in winter gales, and vigorous effort was required to avoid fouling other vessels and running aground.

The strain was not only physical but psychological. These officers and men were enduring all the danger and hardship of war; yet it was not called war. They were forbidden to talk of their experiences ashore, or even to tell where they had been and what they were doing, and so had none of the satisfaction derived from public recognition. After going through cold hell at sea, they would reach port to find other young men making money in safe industries, and college football stars featured as heroes of the day.

Barroom isolationists and (it is suspected) enemy agents worked on the men in Boston, taunting them with "fighting England's battles" and tempting them to desert. But our bluejackets had seen for themselves the new terror that the Nazi had added to the perils and dangers of the deep. Few realized better than they the threat to America in this German strike for sea supremacy. And the fact that morale in the destroyers remained high, throughout this period of bitter warfare that yet was not war, attests the intelligence, the discipline, and the fortitude of the United States Navy.

3. *Japan Moves Toward War*

As we have seen, the United States Fleet, commanded by Admiral James O. Richardson, had been based at Pearl Harbor, as a "deterrent" to Japanese aggression, since April 1940. Admiral Richardson, after expressing to the President in no uncertain terms his dislike of Pearl Harbor as a fleet base, was relieved by Admiral Husband E. Kimmel on 1 February 1941; and on the same day the United States Fleet was renamed the Pacific Fleet.[1] It was still an unbalanced fleet, incapable of promptly performing its assigned mission in the revised Orange (now called Rainbow 5) plan of capturing key points in the Marshall and Caroline Islands with the help of the Marine Corps, and then relieving the Philippines. There, it was assumed, the Army under General Douglas MacArthur, who was also Field Marshal of the armed forces of the Philippine Commonwealth, would be holding out against the Japanese. Kimmel, an energetic, devoted naval officer, applied himself to fleet training, both of ships and planes, so as to provide a core of

[1] The Pacific Fleet, as then constituted, included all ships in the Navy except (1) the Atlantic Fleet which was set up on 1 Feb. 1941; and (2) the Asiatic Fleet under Admiral Thomas C. Hart, a very small fleet with no ship larger than a cruiser, based at Manila Bay.

experienced officers and petty officers for the flood of new construction that the two-ocean navy and other recent acts provided. He frequently sent out task groups to exercise the men and the guns but he made a practice of mooring most of the Fleet in Pearl Harbor over weekends, to keep officers and men happy. It must be remembered that the average young American of that era, conditioned by twenty-one years of antimilitarist indoctrination by movies, books, preachers and teachers, could be induced to enlist in the armed forces, or reënlist if his term had expired, only by making things pleasant for him — not too much work and plenty of recreation. That situation, besides the two-thousand-mile haul for supplies, was why Admiral Richardson objected to the fleet's being based away from California.

The situation in Oahu of the United States Army, responsible for the defense of the Territory, was similar. Lieutenant General Walter Short had two divisions under his command. He too was deeply concerned with training and replacement. Flying Fortresses (B–17s) as fast as built were flown to Oahu for their final arming and equipment, after which most of them flew on to Manila via Wake Island and Guam. There seems to have been no expectation that they might be needed in Hawaii.

In contrast to the United States Pacific Fleet, the Japanese Combined Fleet was well balanced, thoroughly trained and spoiling for a fight. Owing to the operation of the 5:5:3 ratio, and to Japan's kicking over even that in 1936 and embarking on an intensive building program, the Japanese Navy was more powerful in combatant ships than the United States Navy in the Pacific; more powerful even if one added the British and Dutch warships in that ocean.[2] It had plenty of freighters convertible to transports, fleet oilers, or other auxiliaries; it was rugged from annual ma-

2 On 1 Dec. 1941: Pacific Fleet, 9 battleships, Japan, 10; Pacific Fleet, 3 carriers, Japan, 10; United States Pacific and Asiatic Fleets, 13 heavy and 11 light cruisers, Japan, 18 and 17; Pacific and Asiatic Fleets, 80 destroyers, Japan, 111; Pacific and Asiatic Fleets, 55 submarines, Japan, 64.

neuvers in rough northern waters. Japanese gunnery and navigation were excellent; their torpedoes were far more speedy, accurate and destructive than those of any other navy, and their carrier planes were superior in the fighter and torpedo-bomber categories.

Admiral Yamamoto, Commander in Chief Combined Fleet, had been attached to the Japanese embassy in Washington, where he was respected for his naval knowledge, and also for his excellent game of poker. Knowing America's military potential very well, he begged Prince Konoye, the prime minister who preceded General Tojo, to endeavor to avoid war; but when war was decided upon, Yamamoto set his ingenious brain to work on the best method of neutralizing the United States Navy at the start. He had, in fact, been working on that problem since January 1941, when he decided that a surprise air attack on the Pacific Fleet at Pearl Harbor was the answer.

The decision, for a man of Yamamoto's intelligence, was strange; for as strategy it was not only wrong but disastrous. The Pacific Fleet, as we have seen, had been sent to Pearl Harbor as a "deterrent," and as such it was fatally effective. The Japanese war lords had made up their minds in 1940 to take advantage of the European situation and conquer all European or American colonies or dependencies in eastern Asia. The only deterrents that they feared were the B–17s at Manila and the Pacific Fleet at Pearl Harbor. In view of the weakness of that Fleet (of which they were well apprised), and the length of time that it would take to reach Philippine waters, it is unaccountable that Yamamoto thought its destruction necessary before war fairly began. Apparently he felt that Japan could not suffer a "fleet in being" (one of Mahan's concepts) on her flank, even though thousands of miles distant. Actually the Fleet would have been as much of a deterrent in California harbors as at Pearl, but harder to get at. And if we had based it at Singapore, as the British urged us to do, it would have been even more vulnerable, besides being in an impossible position logistically.

The Japanese war plan, brought together at a Supreme War Council on 6 September 1941, was as follows: First, prior to a declaration of war, destruction of the United States Pacific Fleet and the British and American air forces on the Malay Peninsula and Luzon. Second, while the British and American Navies were decimated and disorganized, a quick conquest of the Philippines, Guam, Wake, Hong Kong, Borneo, British Malaya (including Singapore), and Sumatra. Third, when these were secure, the converging of Japanese amphibious forces on the richest prize, Java, and a mop-up of the rest of the Dutch islands. Fourth, an intensive development of Malayan and Indonesian resources in oil, rubber, etc.; and, to secure these, establishment of a defensive perimeter running from the Kurile Islands through Wake, the Marshalls, and around the southern and western edges of the Malay Barrier to the Burmese-Indian border. With these bases the Japanese Navy and air forces could cut all lines of communication between Australia, New Zealand and the Anglo-American powers, which would then be forced to sue for peace. Fifth and finally, Japan would proceed completely to subjugate China. Over half the world's population would then be under the economic, political and military control of the Emperor.

This scheme of conquest was the most enticing, ambitious and far-reaching in modern history, not excepting Hitler's. It almost worked, and might well have succeeded but for the United States Navy.

This being Japan's plan, it is astonishing to find her American apologists claiming that she was goaded, provoked and coerced into making war on us by the Roosevelt administration. What F.D.R. did (with the support of Congress and popular approval, as judged by acts of Congress, Gallup polls and the newspapers) was to impose embargoes on iron, steel, oil, and other strategic materials going to Japan, and to "freeze" Japanese financial assets in America. This process, applied gradually, began in mid-1940 and finally reached effectiveness at the end of July 1941, after Japan had announced her determination to occupy southern Indochina.

Now, in the second half of 1941, the British and the Dutch co-operated in both freeze and embargoes; and as Japanese oil stocks dwindled, the government found itself in a dilemma. It must either renounce an imposing plan of conquest, on which the army insisted, to get oil from the United States and the Netherlands East Indies; or it must fight the United States, the Dutch and the British, to conquer oil for more conquests. It chose the second alternative deliberately, as the more honorable and potentially profitable. Better to defeat America in a quick blitz, as Hitler had France, and then, impregnable, get on with the conquest of China.

It is now perfectly clear that nothing short of force could have stopped Japan from embarking on her Southeast Asia plan, or have persuaded her to withdraw from China. But war might have been at least postponed, allowing the United States to catch up somewhat in the arms race, if Prince Konoye's proposal in August 1941 of a summit conference between himself and President Roosevelt had been accepted. Joseph Grew, our sapient and sensitive ambassador at Tokyo, was for it; F.D.R. was for it; but Secretary of State Cordell Hull opposed it on the grounds that Konoye was a slippery character, and that a summit conference should take place only to cap a prior agreement on principles, such as Japan's abandoning the Tripartite Pact. Hull did not understand that for Japan that treaty with Germany and Italy was part "face," part minatory gesture, and that she did not intend to honor it if it did not suit her. Prince Konoye sincerely wished to start liquidating Japan's dreams of conquest; but he was on a spot, with a ministry of jingo militarists, and Hull gave him no help to get off. As prince of the royal house he had the Emperor's ear, and Hirohito himself was anxious for peace. So there was a chance that if Konoye brought a promise from Roosevelt to lift the oil embargo and unfreeze the assets, in return for Japan's promising to start a military evacuation of Indochina and eventually of China itself, the prince might have persuaded the Emperor to expel the militarists from the cabinet. Of course it is even more likely that Konoye would have been assassinated; but he was willing to take the chance, and he should have been given the opportunity. In any event, a summit conference would have gained time; it could not have met until late October, and Japan could hardly have dispatched the Pearl Harbor striking force while it was sitting.

After toying with the summit idea for almost two months, Hull persuaded F.D.R. to reject it definitely on 2 October. Konoye then resigned, and General Tojo became prime minister. And as the Japanese Supreme War Council had in the meantime set up the grandiose war plan already described, any complete change of Japanese policy would have been difficult to carry out, even by the Emperor.

The negotiations at Washington dragged along fruitlessly. On 10 November Winston Churchill declared in a speech that he did not know whether "the effort of the United States to preserve peace in the Pacific will be successful"; and he promised that "if the United States should become involved in war with Japan, a British declaration would follow within the hour." That threat did not deter the Japanese government for a moment.

You can always keep the peace if you are willing to pay the asking price; and it is a matter of high strategic decision whether the price demanded is worse than refusal with its risk of war. Tojo's price for peace, his ultimatum as he called it, was presented by his ambassador at Washington on 20 November 1941. America must concede Japan a free hand in Indochina and China, and render Chiang no more assistance. She must restore trading relations with Japan and send no more military forces to the South Pacific or the Far East, even to the Philippines. In return for these extraordinary concessions, which could only have been accepted by a nation defeated in war, all Japan offered was to send no more armed forces into Southeast Asia, and to evacuate French Indochina after peace had been imposed on China.

Tojo had already twice postponed the deadline at which war would begin if the United States did not knuckle under. Time was running out, and time was what the leaders of the American armed forces, especially General Marshall, Admiral Stark, and General MacArthur in the Philippines, most wanted. Largely to please them, the Department of State drafted a three months' *modus vivendi*, according to which Japan would start a token withdrawal from Indochina and America would partially resume trade with Japan, as a preliminary to a fresh approach to the China problem. Of the friendly governments to which this was submitted on 25 November, Chiang Kai-shek "violently opposed" it, and the British, Dutch and Australian governments were lukewarm or unfavorable; many people high in the United States government, too, thought that this proposal smelt of Munich. The President decided, on Hull's advice, that the slight prospect of Japan's agreeing to this *modus vivendi* did not warrant the risks to Chinese and American morale that backtracking at this time would involve. Actually, Tojo had already rejected the essential idea of the *modus vivendi* — halting conquest in return for oil — in a dispatch of 20 November, so the whole thing was bad diplomacy.

Hull's next move was even less fortunate. On 26 November he presented to the Japanese ambassadors at Washington an outline of a "proposed basis for agreement" which went absolutely counter to Tojo's plans; for it required an eventual Japanese evacuation of China and recognition of Chiang in return for restoration of trading relations with the United States. While such stipulations made no sense at that crisis, it must be emphasized that this note was not an ultimatum, an alternative to war. There was no threat, express or implied, that the President would ask for a declaration of war on Japan if Tojo rejected it. The cold war could have gone on indefinitely, so far as Washington was concerned (and we now know how long a cold war can go on), provided Japan made no fresh aggressive move. And it is doubtful whether Congress would have considered as *casus belli* a Japanese move into Thailand, British Malaya or the Netherlands East Indies.

On 26 November, the very day that Hull's outline was presented, the Japanese striking force for Pearl Harbor sortied from Tankan Bay in the Kuriles. The "day of infamy" was already set for 7 December, and several other Japanese task forces were set in motion to strike or invade Hong Kong, Malaya, Thailand and the Philippines. If Washington had knuckled under completely before 5 December, the Pearl Harbor force would have been recalled; but the conquest of the Philippines, Malaya and the Netherlands East Indies would have gone on according to schedule. Those were Japanese objectives from which they could not have been dissuaded, no matter how abject the appeasement.

History is studded with ironies, but never were there greater ironies that these: The fundamental reason for America's going to war with Japan was our insistence on the integrity of China; yet all our efforts and sacrifices, instead of strengthening friendly relations with China, have resulted in making her our greatest potential enemy. America in 1939-1941 wanted neither world power nor world responsibility, only to be let alone; but world power and responsibility were forced upon her by the two nations, Germany and Japan, that badly wanted both. And those nations are now numbered among America's firmest allies. In terms of the ancient Greek drama, the gods of Olympus must be roaring with laughter over the state of the world twenty years and more after the Pearl Harbor attack, which one might think had been especially arranged by them to destroy American complacency.

CHAPTER III

Disaster at Pearl Harbor

7 December 1941

1. *Last Days of "Peace" in the Pacific*

THE PEARL HARBOR STRIKING FORCE, under Vice Admiral Chuichi Nagumo, was strong, well organized, and intensively trained for the double purpose of wiping out the major part of the Pacific Fleet at Pearl Harbor, and destroying all military aircraft on Oahu. It included the six newest and largest carriers of the Imperial Navy[1]; a screen of nine destroyers and a light cruiser; a support force of two battleships and two heavy cruisers; three fleet submarines to patrol the flanks, and a supply train of seven or eight tankers. These ships departed the Inland Sea in deuces and treys so as not to arouse suspicion, rendezvoused at desolate Tankan Bay in the Kuriles, and sailed for Pearl Harbor 26 November. Course was shaped over a part of the North Pacific generally avoided by merchant shipping, and the advance screen of destroyers was ordered to sink at sight any American, British or Dutch vessel encountered. The weather was foul, many men were washed overboard, fueling at sea was accomplished with difficulty; but Striking Force pounded along according to schedule.

Admiral Nagumo did not relish his assignment and rather hoped that his force would be detected by 5 December, in which case Yamamoto had instructed him to abandon mission and return. But

[1] *Akagi, Kaga, Shokaku, Zuikaku, Horyu, Soryu,* carrying 423 combat planes.

only one ship, a Japanese freighter, was encountered; and not one aircraft. By listening to the Honolulu commercial broadcasts, the Admiral was assured that nobody ashore anticipated the lethal strike that he was about to deliver. His sailors had been hopped up by anti-American propaganda to a black, bitter hatred of Americans; and it apparently never occurred to anyone that to attack an unsuspecting people, when your government was still negotiating, and in defiance of the Hague Convention of 1907 which Japan had ratified, was dirty ball. Treaties, for the Japanese government of that time, were to be honored or broken according to the Emperor's presumed interest. Early on 6 December the latest report from the Japanese consulate in Honolulu on American ships present in Pearl Harbor was received via Tokyo. The Battle Fleet was there all right, but no carriers — a great disappointment.

At 2100 that evening Striking Force reached the meridian of Oahu at a point about 490 miles north of the island. All hands on the carriers who could be spared from duties below were summoned to the flight decks, officers made speeches, and the actual flag which had been displayed from Admiral Togo's flagship before the Battle of Tsushima in 1905 was raised to the masthead of *Akagi*. It was a high moment of frenzied patriotic emotion. Course now was shaped due south, the oilers and supply ships were left behind, and during a night of thick overcast through which the moon (three days after full) showed a faint light, Striking Force charged forward at 26 knots. Heavy cruisers *Tone* and *Chikuma* thrust ahead to catapult two float planes for reconnaissance. They reported everything calm in Pearl Harbor; not one ship under way. Nagumo reached his launching point, lat. 26° N, long. 158° W, about 275 miles north of Pearl Harbor, at 0600. It was still dark, and the carriers pitched badly in the swell, but the launching of the first attack was effected without mishap, and the 183 planes orbited waiting for their strike commander, Captain Fuchida, to give the word to go. Again emotion welled high in Japa-

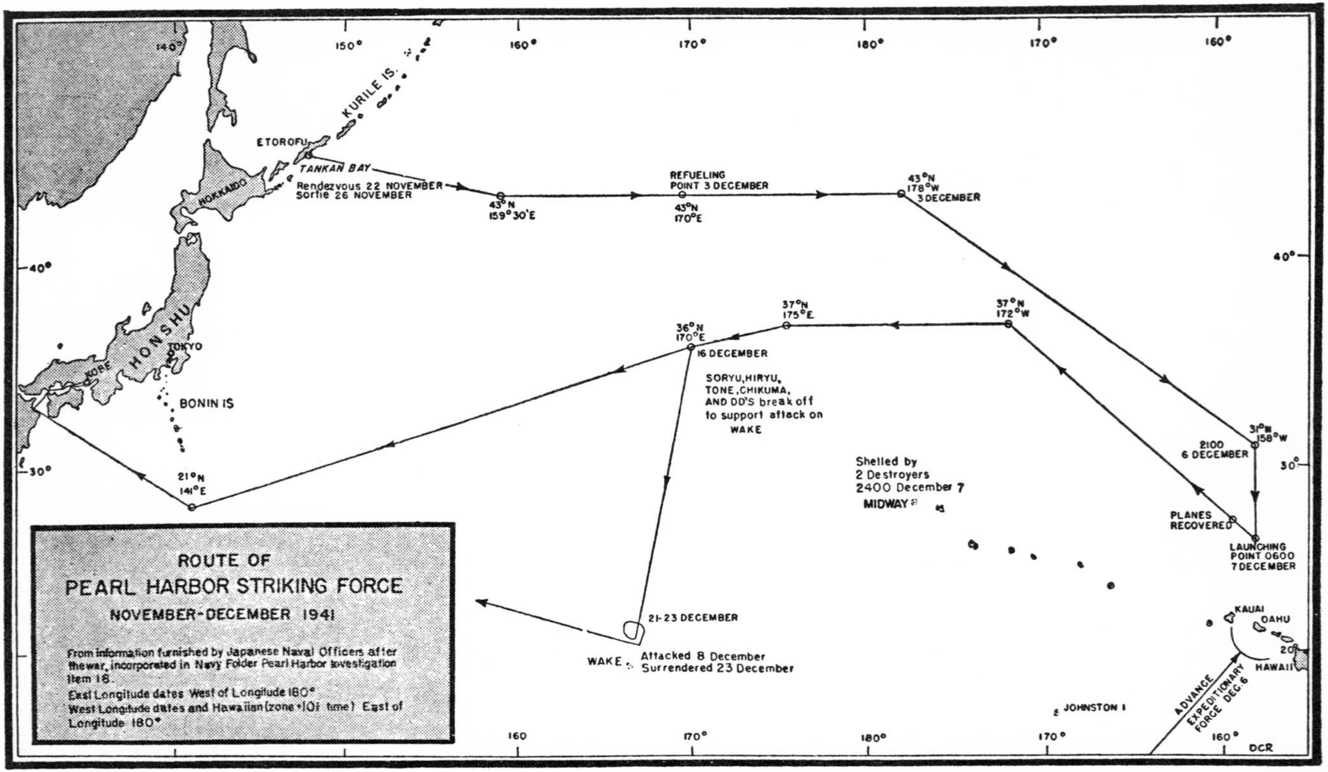
ROUTE OF
PEARL HARBOR STRIKING FORCE
NOVEMBER-DECEMBER 1941
From information furnished by Japanese Naval Officers after the war, incorporated in Navy Folder Pearl Harbor Investigation Item 18.
East Longitude dates West of Longitude 180°
West Longitude dates and Hawaiian (zone +10½ time) East of Longitude 180°
KURILE IS.
ETOROFU
TANKAN BAY
Rendezvous 22 NOVEMBER
Sortie 26 NOVEMBER
HOKKAIDO
HONSHU
TOKYO
KURE
BONIN IS
43°N 159°30'E
REFUELING POINT 3 DECEMBER
43°N 170°E
43°N 178°W 3 DECEMBER
37°N 175°E
37°N 172°W
36°N 170°E
16 DECEMBER
SORYU, HIRYU, TONE, CHIKUMA, AND DD'S break off to support attack on WAKE
21°N 141°E
21-23 DECEMBER
WAKE
Attacked 8 December
Surrendered 23 December
Shelled by 2 Destroyers 2400 December 7
MIDWAY
31°N 158°W
2100 6 DECEMBER
PLANES RECOVERED
LAUNCHING POINT 0600 7 DECEMBER
KAUAI
OAHU
HAWAII
JOHNSTON I
ADVANCE EXPEDITIONARY FORCE DEC. 6
DCR

nese breasts; all who could came topside and shrilled "Banzai!" into the gray dawn.

2. *The Unsuspecting Victim*

First blow of Japan against the United States was scheduled not for the Emperor's "eagles" but for his Advance Expeditionary Force of submarines. These, 27 in number, left Kure and Yokosuka around 19 November and fueled at Kwajalein in the Marshalls. Five of the I-boats carried midget two-man submarines. These had the mission of penetrating Pearl Harbor, while the big ones took stations on 6 December about Oahu, to torpedo any American ship that escaped the air strike. The midgets were cast off at midnight 6-7 December, a few miles outside the harbor's mouth.[2]

Before taking up the story of what happened on that "day of infamy," let us see what the high commands at Hawaii and Washington were doing to prevent surprise. The answer is, Almost nothing.

Admiral Stark in Washington sent Admiral Kimmel in Pearl Harbor a "war warning" on 27 November, to expect "an aggressive move by Japan within the next few days . . . against either the Philippines, Thai, Kra Peninsula or possibly Borneo." He ordered Kimmel to prepare to execute "defensive deployment preparatory to carrying out" the existing war plan.[3] The Chief of Naval Operations did not mention Hawaii as a possible target, and neither Ad-

[2] One of these was sighted by Lieutenant James O. Cobb about 3 miles off Diamond Head, by daylight on the 6th. Since it was near one of our "submarine sanctuaries," he felt obliged to radio ashore for permission to attack, but by the time permission arrived the I-boat had submerged. After the war he met the submarine's skipper, who remembered the occasion.

[3] In addition, Kimmel received a dispatch from C.N.O. on 28 Nov.: "Hostile action is possible at any moment," but ordered him to "undertake no offensive action until Japan has committed an overt act."

miral Kimmel nor Lieutenant General Walter Short, commanding the Army in Hawaii, believed it to be menaced. They did not even notify the commanders of their respective air arms, Rear Admiral Bellinger and Brigadier General Martin, of the "war warning" dispatch. There had been no Army-Navy air raid drill since 12 November. On 2, 3, 4 and 5 December air patrols were sent out as much as 400 miles to the northwestward, not with any idea of discovering an enemy but to train pilots and break in new PBY Catalinas; but on the 6th the air reconnaissance was again reduced to little more than harbor-mouth patrol. General Short took the war warning as indicating danger only from local sabotage, and ordered all Army planes to be parked wing-to-wing; he so informed Washington, but, owing to a recent renumbering of the three degrees of alert, Washington assumed that his alert was complete instead of local. In general, routine patrol and training schedules were maintained after 27 November, and the usual leaves and liberties were granted for that weekend and the next. Pearl Harbor and Oahu were unprepared, mentally and physically, for what happened on the 7th. As one officer expressed it, "there was a state of mind of being fed up with the unproductive vigilance of the several months preceding."

One very important new measure Admiral Kimmel did take in good time. On 28 November he sent carrier *Enterprise* from Pearl Harbor, under Rear Admiral Halsey, to deliver Marine Corps fighter planes to Wake Island; and Halsey, to his credit, ordered his men to shoot down any suspicious ships or planes encountered. On 4 December Halsey delivered the planes, and on the 7th was on his way back to Oahu. Also, on 5 December, Admiral Kimmel sent a task force built around carrier *Lexington*, under Rear Admiral Newton, to deliver 25 scout bombers to Midway Island. *Saratoga*, the third Pacific Fleet carrier, had left Pearl Harbor for upkeep and repairs on the West Coast. Thus the three carriers, whose destruction would have been far more disastrous than that of the entire Battle Fleet, were absent on 7 December — a slight concession that the god of battles made to us on that fateful day.

Now let us turn to Washington. There, Army and Navy Intelligence had been "reading the Japanese mail" — intercepting, decrypting and translating dispatches between Tokyo and its representatives in Washington and elsewhere. These told them that war was likely to break out in the Far East on the weekend of 29 November; but whereabouts, or on what date, the Japanese government was too cagey to admit even in the top-secret diplomatic code. Every bit of intelligence received from this and many other sources was ambiguous; neither date nor target was mentioned. And when Sunday, 30 November, passed and nothing happened, a sort of numbness seemed to creep over official Washington. Commander Arthur H. McCollum of the Office of Naval Intelligence felt that the situation was serious enough to send another war warning to Hawaii on 4 December, but Admiral Stark declined to do so; felt there had been too much crying "Wolf!"

The two Japanese dispatches decrypted and translated before 7 December which might have suggested an attack on Pearl Harbor, were orders from Tokyo to an agent in Honolulu, to report not only all ship movements in and out of Pearl Harbor, but where each ship was berthed within the harbor. Admiral Kimmel might have perceived the significance of these now famous "berthing orders," but he never had the chance. Naval Intelligence discounted them because similar orders were being sent to Japanese agents in all principal world ports, and in that context these particular demands on Honolulu no more indicated an attack on Pearl Harbor than an attack on San Diego, the Panama Canal, New York, London, Rio or Sydney. Nevertheless, the failure to transmit this material to Pearl Harbor is a black mark against Washington. One may argue, as Admiral Turner did at the hearings, that the 27 November war warning should have been enough to put Kimmel on his toes. But, as Roberta Wohlstetter well says, "There seems little doubt that if the sender had been more alarmed, the warning itself would have been more alarming." [4]

On Saturday, 6 December, Tokyo began transmitting to its Washington embassy in diplomatic code a long note for the State Department, breaking diplomatic relations. Army Intelligence had the first thirteen parts decrypted, translated, and in the hands of Brigadier General Sherman Miles, head of Army Intelligence, and Captain Theodore S. Wilkinson, head of Naval Intelligence, by 2230. These thirteen parts were a long rehash of Japanese-American relations, accusing us of warmongering in East Asia. President Roosevelt received and read them that evening and exclaimed, "This means war!" But the note gave no hint of a projected attack on Hawaii, or anywhere in particular. General George C. Marshall, Army Chief of Staff, and Admiral Stark, Chief of Naval Operations, were not informed that evening by the officers whose duty it was to do so.

Admiral Stark and Rear Admiral Turner, the Navy War Plans chief, were in Stark's office at 0915 Sunday, 7 December, when Captain Wilkinson, chief of Naval Intelligence, and Commander McCollum, head of his Far East Section, brought in the translation of Tokyo's Part 14, the "snapper" which broke off diplomatic relations. But even Part 14 did not declare war or threaten immediate attack. About an hour later, Commander McCollum brought in the "time of delivery" message, an order from Tokyo to its ambassadors to destroy all coding machines after presenting the fourteen-part note to Secretary Hull at 1300. Sunday was an

[4] *Pearl Harbor: Warning and Decision* (1962), p. 336. And, as Mrs. Wohlstetter says on p. 383, "If our intelligence system . . . failed to produce an accurate image of Japanese intentions . . . it was not for want of the relevant materials. Never before have we had so complete an intelligence picture of the enemy." And on p. 392: "What these examples illustrate is . . . the very human tendency to pay attention to the signals that support current expectations about enemy behavior."

odd day, and one P.M. a strange hour, for presenting a diplomatic note. What could it mean?

McCollum and his assistant, Lieutenant Commander A. D. Kramer, and Colonel Rufus S. Bratton of Army Intelligence, guessed the answer by consulting a time chart on the wall. One P.M. in Washington was 0730 at Pearl Harbor. That might be only a coincidence, but it might also mean an attack there, and there only — for one P.M. in Washington is nighttime at Manila and Guam. Wilkinson suggested that Admiral Stark at once call Admiral Kimmel on the telephone. Stark demurred, feeling that since the Army was responsible for the defense of Hawaii, General Marshall should do it. Marshall, contacted on returning from his Sunday morning horseback ride, came into Stark's office at about 1115. In tense silence he read all fourteen parts, agreed that they meant immediate war, and that Pearl Harbor and Manila should be alerted at once. Marshall's communicator said he could get the word to Pearl in twenty minutes. Rear Admiral Leigh Noyes, Director of Naval Communications, offered to send it through Navy channels. Stark declined (again Navy-Army punctilio), and the message — JUST WHAT SIGNIFICANCE THE HOUR SET MAY HAVE WE DO NOT KNOW, BUT BE ON THE ALERT ACCORDINGLY — was filed at noon, 0630 in Hawaii. General Marshall called the Army communication center thrice to make sure that the message had been filed and sent, and was assured that it had been sent, which it had — but by Western Union! There was a foul-up that morning in Army radio, and the officer in charge entrusted the message to commercial channels. A boy on a bicycle delivered it to General Short some hours after the attack was over.

The night of 6-7 December was not uneventful in and around Oahu. While officers and men on leave enjoyed themselves in Honolulu, as sailors do on a Saturday night, a routine patrol was maintained off Pearl Harbor entrance. At 0355 U.S.S. *Condor* sighted a periscope less than two miles off shore and passed the word by blinker to destroyer *Ward*, also on patrol. The two captains discussed the contact by radio. Their talk was overheard at Bishop's Point radio station ashore, but nobody there thought it worth while to relay this to naval headquarters; nor did the captains.

Almost three hours passed, and Pearl Harbor slept. At 0633 a patrolling Catalina sighted the same or another midget submarine, dropped smoke pots on the spot, and informed *Ward*. The destroyer closed, shot at, depth-charged and sank the midget at 0645. *Ward's* commanding officer, Captain Outerbridge, sent the word at 0651 to naval district headquarters where, owing to an unexplained delay, Lieutenant Commander Harold Kaminsky, the duty officer, never got it until 0712. Kaminsky, one of the few communicators really on the ball that morning, made frantic efforts to pass this word to fleet headquarters, but he had only one telephone operator, a Hawaiian who spoke little English, and found it difficult to raise anyone at that hour of a Sunday morning.

In the meantime, at 0700, another PBY had sunk a second midget a mile off Pearl Harbor entrance; but, contrary to instructions, reported the incident in code. So this message was not ready for circulation until 0730, when the Pacific Fleet staff duty officer telephoned it to Rear Admiral Bellinger's operations officer at Ford Island. They discussed these reports over the telephone with Admiral Bloch, the naval district commandant. All three, who suspected these contacts to be false, were still talking about them when the bombs began to drop.

Thus, the Navy, largely through faulty or lax communications, lost an opportunity to alert the Fleet that midget submarines were lurking about Pearl Harbor in the early morning. Admiral Kimmel himself, on 14 October, had warned the Fleet that "a single submarine attack may indicate the presence of a considerable surface force probably composed of fast ships accompanied by a carrier." But this was imbedded in a very prolix and involved fleet letter, which nobody except Kaminsky appears to have digested.[5]

And the Army lost an even better chance to give advance warning of the main air attack. It was responsible for five or six mobile search radar stations, spotted around the coast of Oahu. Search radar had saved England from destruction during the German air blitz of 1940, and it might have done so here; but these Army radars were being operated on Sunday only from 0400 to 0700, and at all times on a training basis, to train radar operators, not with any serious idea of watching for enemy aircraft.

The radar set at Opana on the northern point of Oahu was manned on the morning of 7 December by Privates Lockard and Elliott. Between 0645 and 0700 they tracked what we now know to have been a Japanese cruiser plane reconnoitering ahead of the bombers to make sure that the Battle Fleet was really in harbor. One of the lads reported this to radio information center at Fort Shafter near Honolulu, where the duty officer was an inexperienced second lieutenant, also under training. He ordered them to secure for the day. Instead of so doing, the two privates, eager to improve their technique, continued to work the radar. Elliott, at the controls at 0702, saw on the screen "something completely out of the ordinary" — blips indicating an enormous flight of planes, bigger than anything he had ever observed. The flight was then 132 miles north of Oahu, approaching at 182 m.p.h. He telephoned the switchboard operator at the information center, who insisted on calling the duty officer to hear what the privates had to say. The green lieutenant listened in a bored manner and told them to "forget it." For he had heard that a flight of our B–17s was ex-

[5] One midget actually penetrated Pearl Harbor, the gate to which had carelessly been left open, and was sunk therein by a destroyer. One ran aground and was captured, and the rest disappeared without leaving a trace. Nor did the big I-boats accomplish anything, owing to our aggressive patrolling after the air attack. *I-70* was sunk by planes from *Enterprise* 10 December. Two proceeded to the West Coast and sank a few merchant ships, giving the West Coast a big scare.

pected to arrive from the mainland that morning. But these could only have been a dozen planes at most, and the Opana radar screen showed a flight numbering over a hundred.

Note that if even one of the people responsible, either in Washington or on Oahu, had been really brisk, the Fleet and Army could have had at least an hour's warning, and hundreds of lives would have been saved. It seems that the Fates were determined to humble American pride.

3. *The Assault*

Shortly after 0700 the sun, rising over the Tantalus Mountains, cast its first rays on Pearl Harbor, heightening the green of the canefields that stretch up the slopes above Aiea and deepening the blue of the lochs, as the arms of this harbor are called. Even for Oahu, favored by nature, this was an uncommonly bright and peaceful Sabbath morning. On board ships the forenoon watch was piped to breakfast while the men it would relieve at 0800 concluded their various duties, such as cleaning brass and wiping dew off the machine guns and the 5-inch dual purpose guns. Of these, only about one in four was fully manned. The main batteries were not manned, nor were the plotting rooms, directors, and ammunition supply; ready ammunition was in locked boxes whose keys were in the hands of the Officer of the Deck. All ships had at least one boiler lighted, but few had enough steam up to get under way in a hurry. Among the 70 combatant ships and 24 auxiliaries in the harbor, only one, a destroyer, was under way.

At about 0740 the first Japanese attack wave, 40 torpedo-bombers, 49 high-level bombers, 51 dive-bombers and 51 fighters, sighted the Oahu coastline. They then deployed — the fighters to destroy parked planes at Wheeler Field and Kaneohe, the high-

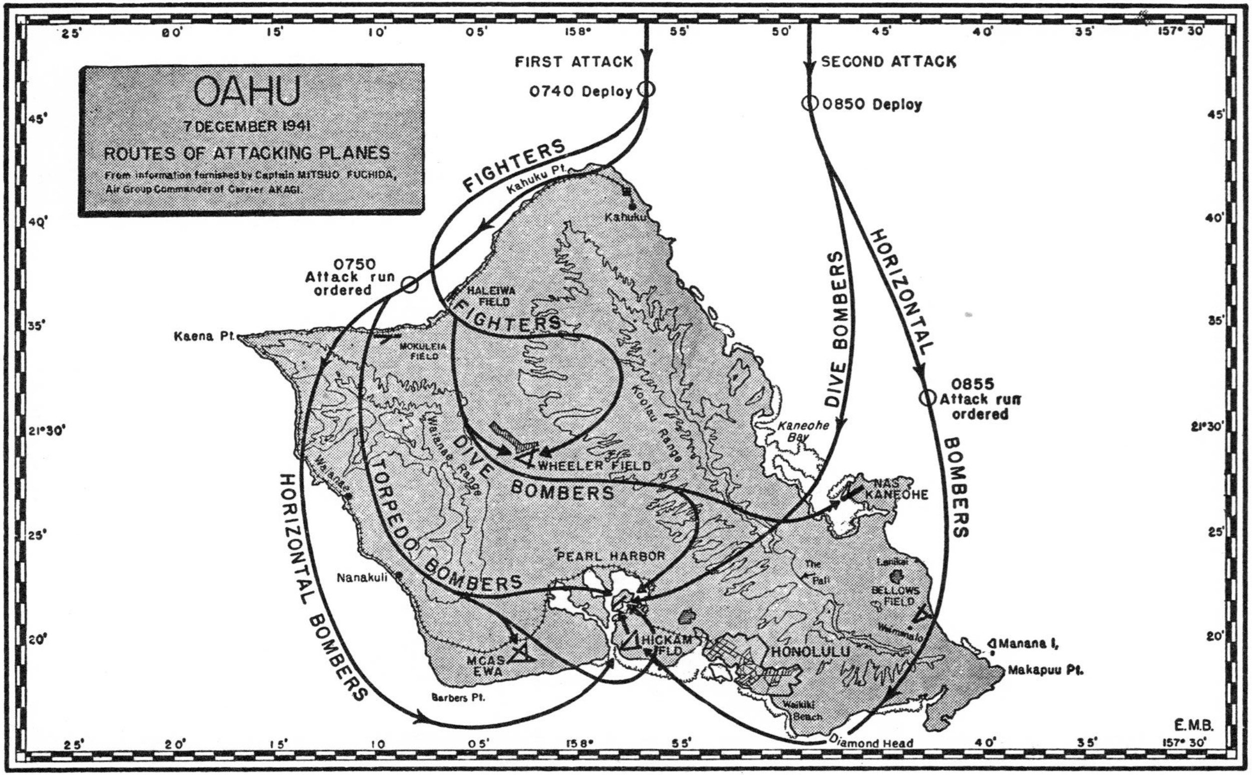
OAHU
7 DECEMBER 1941
ROUTES OF ATTACKING PLANES
From information furnished by Captain MITSUO FUCHIDA, Air Group Commander of Carrier AKAGI.
FIRST ATTACK
0740 Deploy
SECOND ATTACK
0850 Deploy
FIGHTERS
0750 Attack run ordered
0855 Attack run ordered
DIVE BOMBERS
HORIZONTAL BOMBERS
TORPEDO BOMBERS
Kahuku Pt.
Kahuku
Kaena Pt.
HALEIWA FIELD
MOKULEIA FIELD
WHEELER FIELD
Waianae Range
Koolau Range
Kaneohe Bay
NAS KANEOHE
Waianae
Nanakuli
PEARL HARBOR
MCAS EWA
Barbers Pt.
HICKAM FLD
HONOLULU
The Pali
Lanikai
BELLOWS FIELD
Waimanalo
Manana I.
Makapuu Pt.
Waikiki Beach
Diamond Head
E.M.B.
158°
157° 30'
21°30'

level bombers for Hickam Field, the torpedo planes and dive-bombers for "Battleship Row." By 0750 they were ready to strike and Captain Fuchida, the strike commander, gave the word.

The sound of church bells at Honolulu, ringing for eight o'clock mass, came over the harbor, whose calm surface was only lightly rippled by the breeze. Many officers were at breakfast, others were just rising; seamen were lounging on deck talking, reading, or writing letters home. As the hour for morning colors approached, sailors in white uniforms removed the jack and ensign from their lockers, a bluejacket on the signal bridge hoisted the Blue Peter, and boatswains were set to pipe the preparatory signal at 0755.

A few seconds before or after that hour — nobody could remember which — the air suddenly seemed filled with strange planes, hovering, darting, diving. A brisk dive-bomber got in the first lick, on Ford Island naval air headquarters, where Commander Ramsey, the operations officer, who had been discussing the midget submarine sinkings over the telephone, thought it was accidental, from an overzealous Army plane. Hardly anyone, for seconds or even minutes, even after seeing the red "meat ball" on the fuselages, recognized the planes as Japanese. Some thought they were United States Army planes camouflaged as Japanese to give the Navy a scare. Others assumed that this was an air drill and thought it too realistic. Across the harbor, Rear Admiral William R. Furlong, in minelayer *Oglala*, who had studied Japanese plane types, recognized the torpedo-bombers when they zoomed up the main channel between him and Ford Island; and as he happened to be senior officer present afloat, he ordered the signal hoisted, "All Ships in Harbor Sortie." Almost simultaneously, someone in the signal tower ashore made the same observation and telephoned to Cincpac headquarters, "Enemy air raid — not drill." The Navy air arm on Ford Island took a little longer to realize the truth, so it was not until 0758 that Admiral Bellinger broadcast a message which shook the United States as nothing had since the firing on Fort Sumter: —

AIR RAID, PEARL HARBOR — THIS IS NO DRILL.

Now, to quote John Milton, "All hell broke loose." The Sabbath calm was shattered by bomb explosions, internal explosions, and machine-gun fire, with the hoarse signal of General Quarters as obbligato. At least two battleships were already doomed and hundreds of American seamen dead by 0758.

Let us now concentrate on the first phase of the attack, from 0755 to 0825, during which about 90 per cent of the damage was done.

Battleship Row was located along the southeast shore of Ford Island, a few hundred yards across the main channel from the Navy Yard. The battlewagons were moored, some singly and others in pairs, to massive quays a short distance off the island shore. *Nevada* occupied the northeasterly berth, with an ammunition lighter outboard. Next came *Arizona*, with tender *Vestal* outboard. Southwest of them were *Tennessee* and *West Virginia* side by side, and the next pair was *Maryland* and *Oklahoma*. *California* alone had the southernmost berth. *Pennsylvania* was in drydock across the harbor, where five cruisers were also berthed. Twenty-six destroyers and minecraft were moored in groups in various parts of the harbor.

The Japanese aviators knew exactly where to find the battleships, completely unprotected from torpedo attack, and made first for *Arizona* and the two pairs. The major attack was made by twelve "Kate" torpedo-bombers launching torpedoes from low altitudes — 40 to 100 feet above the water. Four more Kates followed. Almost simultaneously, "Val" dive-bombers began combing battleship row fore and aft, dropping not only conventional bombs but converted 16-inch armor-piercing shells which penetrated the decks and exploded below. Then five more planes attacked cruiser *Raleigh* and three other ships moored on the northwest side of Ford Island. Most of these planes, after they had dropped bombs or topedoes, flew back over their targets, strafing viciously in order to kill as many sailors as possible.

Imagine the consternation that this sudden onslaught created among the officers and men on board! A surprise attack in war is bad enough to cope with, but this was a surprise attack in time of peace when, so far as anyone in Hawaii knew, diplomatic negotiations at Washington were continuing. What made defense even more difficult was the absence on weekend leave of many senior officers and chief petty officers to whom juniors were accustomed to look for orders and guidance. Yet the junior officers and bluejackets' reaction, against fearful odds, was superb. Between explosions one could hear sailors knocking off the padlocks from ready ammunition chests with axes and mauls. Dive-bombers swooped so near that sailors could see the Japanese pilots' toothy grins, and in exasperation hurled monkey wrenches at them. At what moment return gunfire was opened is still uncertain. Some said within a minute, others within five; but photos taken by the Japanese as late as 0805, when *California* was torpedoed, show not a single black burst of ack-ack in the sky, and all but one or two of the first wave of torpedo-bombers got away unscathed. The Navy's machine guns at that time were not very effective — the 3-inch was not rapid-fire enough, and the 1.1-inch was liable to heat and jam after a few rounds; it was not until next year that the 20-mm Oerlikon and 40-mm Bofors were installed.

Oklahoma, outboard of the southernmost pair of battlewagons, one of our 1916 "Dreadnoughts," never had a chance to fight back. While the crew were running to battle stations, a few moments after the first bomb exploded on Ford Island, three torpedoes blasted huge holes in her and she promptly listed 30 degrees. There was no time to set Condition Zed (complete watertight integrity), or to counterflood, or to bring machine guns to bear. Before 0800 the senior officer on board ordered Abandon Ship. Men crawled over the starboard side as she rolled over, and two more torpedo hits completed her doom. Fifteen minutes later, parts of her bottom were facing the sky. Many survivors climbed on board *Maryland* alongside, to help her fight. She, protected by *Oklahoma* from the torpedoes, got off with only two bomb hits, and became the first of the stricken Battle Fleet to return to active service. *Oklahoma* lost 415 officers and men killed out of 1354 on board.

Tennessee and *West Virginia* made the next couple on Battleship Row. The latter, outboard, took six or seven torpedoes, the first before 0756, and two bombs. An exceptionally well-trained crew, who loved their "Wee Vee," as they called the ship, saved her from the fate of *Oklahoma*. Ensign Brooks, officer of the deck, saw the first bomb hit Ford Island and immediately ordered "Away Fire and Rescue Party!" This brought everyone topside on the double, and saved hundreds of lives. She listed so rapidly that the guns on the starboard side, which opened fire promptly, could be served only by organizing a double row of ammunition handlers — one to pass and the other to hold the passer upright. Lieutenant Ricketts ordered counterflooding on his own initiative, and, ably assisted by Boatswain's Mate Billingsley, corrected a 28-degree list to 15 degrees; this allowed her to settle on the bottom almost upright. Captain Bennion, disemboweled by fragments from a bomb that exploded on *Tennessee* alongside, was *in extremis;* his only thoughts were for his ship and crew until his life flickered out a few minutes later; but his fighting spirit lived on. All hands fought fires, although frequently dive-bombed and strafed. "Their spirit was marvelous," reported the surviving executive officer. "Words fail in attempting to describe the magnificent display of courage, discipline and devotion to duty of all." *West Virginia* lost 105 killed out of about 1500 on board.

Tennessee, moored inboard, naturally suffered less. She received two bombs early in the action, but most of her damage came from fires started by flaming debris from *Arizona*, exploding 75 feet astern. Fire-fighting continued all the rest of that day and the following night, and she did not sink. Her losses were only 5 killed; and within three weeks she, in company with *Maryland* and *Pennsylvania*, sailed to the West Coast for a complete overhaul.

Arizona was moored inboard of a short repair ship which afforded her slight protection. Within one minute of the opening attack the battleship was literally torn apart by torpedo and bomb explosions. A bomb exploded in the forward magazine before it could be flooded, wrecking half the ship, killing Captain Van Valkenburgh and Rear Admiral Kidd who were on the bridge, and causing the ship to settle so fast that hundreds of sailors were trapped below. Even so, the machine guns topside opened fire on the enemy planes, and she was not abandoned until 1032. Owing to lack of warning and to the magazine explosion, *Arizona*'s casualties were over half those suffered by the entire Fleet at Pearl Harbor — 1103 officers and men killed out of some 1400 on board. Her remains, and most of theirs, are still there today; she has never been formally decommissioned, and every day a color guard faithfully raises and lowers the ensign on a mast built on a platform over the wreck.

Battleship Row tapered off to a lone battlewagon at each end. Southernmost was *California*, flagship of Admiral Pye and, at the age of twenty, youngest of the Battle Fleet. At 0805 she was the last to be hit, but in the worst condition to take it — completely "unbuttoned" in preparation for an admiral's inspection — so that the two torpedoes that hit her, together with one bomb that exploded below and set off a magazine, were enough to cause her to settle into the mud. Prompt counterflooding, directed by Reserve Ensign Fair, prevented her from capsizing, which would have meant a far greater loss of life than the 98 officers and men actually killed. *California* was also restored to the Fleet and performed excellent service in the latter half of the war.

Nevada, at the northern end, oldest battleship present — well past her 25th birthday — had a little more grace than her immediate neighbors; Color guard began making morning colors and the band struck up "The Star-spangled Banner" before anything lethal came her way. A Kate that had torpedoed *Arizona* skimmed across her stern during the ceremony and the rear gunner tried to strafe the sailors at attention, but managed only to rip the ensign. A second strafer came in, but the band finished the national anthem without a pause; nobody broke ranks. Ensign Taussig, officer of the deck, then ordered Battle Stations, set Condition Zed, and *Nevada* went into action with her machine guns and port 5-inch battery. One and possibly two torpedo-bombers were hit, and the rest gave *Nevada* a wide berth; but one torpedo tore a hole in her side, 45 by 30 feet. Prompt counterflooding corrected the list, and as her power plant was intact, Lieutenant Commander Francis J. Thomas, senior officer present, eighth in the chain of command — made the wise decision to get under way. In the meantime she had taken two bomb hits amidships, causing many casualties and great damage. Ordinarily, four tugs were required to get a battleship under way from the mooring quays, but *Nevada* did it unaided; Chief Boatswain E. J. Hill jumped onto the quay, cast off the lines under strafing fire, and swam back to the ship. Down the ship channel she stood, fighting off dive-bombers of the second Japanese attack wave who concentrated on her, and at one time surrounded by a curtain of smoke and spray so dense that spectators thought her gone; but most of the bombs were near-misses. A proud and gallant sight she made, with her tattered ensign streaming from the fantail. She could easily have gone to sea, but in the confusion Admiral Bloch or Kimmel, fearing lest she sink and block the channel, sent her an urgent signal not to leave the harbor. Commander Thomas then decided to anchor off Hospital

Point. Just as she was about to drop the hook, dive-bombers attacked and made three hits, one of which "opened the forecastle like a sardine can" and killed the entire anchoring detail, including Boatswain Hill. *Nevada* then slid gently aground. The Captain now came on board and ordered her towed across the harbor to Waipio Point where, despite strenuous effort at damage control, she flooded and settled. Fifty officers and men had been killed, and the old battlewagon was thoroughly wrecked topside. Floated in February, she steamed to Puget Sound under her own power and, after modernization, rejoined the Fleet in 1943.

Pennsylvania, flagship of the Pacific Fleet, was happily in dry dock at the Navy Yard and so could not be reached by torpedo-bombers. She threw up powerful antiaircraft fire, took but one severe bomb hit, and lost only 18 men. But several bombs meant for her hit destroyers *Cassin* and *Downes* in the same dry dock, and pretty well demolished them.

Thus, in half an hour the Japanese bombers accomplished their most important objective, wrecking the Battle Line of the Pacific Fleet beyond any possibility of offensive action within a year.

Too much praise cannot be given to the officers and bluejackets in these and other ships. Once they had recovered from the initial surprise they served their vessels nobly, and the damage control parties were especially effective. There was no flinching, no attempt to escape. On the contrary, from the moment of the first alarm, officers and men on leave in Honolulu and elsewhere began hastening to their stations. Dozens of barges, gigs, launches and small yard craft took men out to their own ships, evacuated the wounded from the stricken vessels, and helped fight fires, with complete disregard for their own safety. Chief Jansen, commanding *YG–17*, one of the yard's garbage lighters, received high praise for closing *West Virginia* to fight her fires until they were quenched, when he moved over to another post of danger, alongside *Arizona*. Ensign Sears of *West Virginia* was taken to the wrong ship but jumped overboard and swam to his own to bear a hand. Chief Boatswain Hill of *Nevada*, and every one of his detail, and the exposed gunners of the 5-inchers, fought like one man, and that man a hero; and almost every one of them lost his life. So, while we deplore the surprise, let us never forget the heroic reaction. "That strife was not inglorious, though the event was dire."

During the initial phase of the attack, between 0755 and 0825, the enemy inflicted severe punishment on military aircraft in Oahu. A flight of dive-bombers worked over Ford Island and in a few minutes Patrol Wing Two lost 33 planes, almost half its number. At Ewa, the Marine Corps air base, halfway between West Loch and the ocean, some 50 planes were based. Captain Ashwell, officer of the day, was having breakfast when he heard aircraft, stepped out, sighted the first flight of torpedo-bombers making for Battleship Row, immediately recognized them; and, as he ran to the guardhouse to sound an alarm, saw 21 "Zeke" fighter planes roaring in over the Waianae mountains. They struck Ewa before sprinting Ashwell reached his goal. Swooping low, they attacked with short bursts of gunfire the planes parked wing to wing, and destroyed over thirty in a couple of minutes. By the time a second attack came in the Marines had organized defense, dragging one undamaged plane to a good position to use as a machine-gun mount, breaking out spare machine guns from ordnance rooms and wrenching them off damaged planes to set up elsewhere. These were able to keep the would-be strafers at a healthy distance, and threw back a third attack by 15 Zekes. Only four men were killed in these attacks, but the Marine air arm on Oahu was almost completely destroyed.

Yamamoto had also placed the Indian sign on Kaneohe, a Navy patrol wing station on the windward side of Oahu. A squadron of Vals made for the Catalinas parked there at 0755. Almost everyone was asleep; the duty officer thought they were Army planes gone berserk, and telephoned to Pearl Harbor for help. Another strike came in at 0820, blasted a hangar and destroyed three Catalinas inside; an hour later, a third strike mopped up. As a result, 27 of the 36 PBYs at Kaneohe were destroyed, and six more damaged; the three saved were out on patrol when the attack came in.

Three principal Army airfields on Oahu caught it badly. At Hickam, adjoining Pearl Harbor Navy Yard, a dozen A–20s, 33 B–18s and 6 B–17s were lined up in the open, wing to wing. A few seconds after 0755, bombers earmarked to destroy them barreled in. One bomb crashed through the roof of the mess hall and exploded in the midst of the breakfast tables, killing 35 men. Others destroyed the parked planes. It was even more difficult to fight back ashore than on board ship, since many antiaircraft guns spotted around Hickam and in the Navy Yard, all operated by the Army, were not manned, and none had ready ammunition. Soldiers had to run to the depots and break down doors to get bullets; others wrenched machine guns off planes and blazed away. At Wheeler Field, in the central valley of Oahu, 62 P–40s and other planes too were parked as close as possible, in lines only 20 feet apart. Most of these were destroyed by 25 dive-bombers which attacked at 0802. Two small squadrons of P–40s at Bellows Field near Lanikai were also pretty much wiped out. Army Air Force had 231 aircraft on Oahu when the attack came in, but at close of day had only 166 units left, half of them damaged. Navy and Marine Corps had only 54 left out of about 250.

From 0825 to 0840 there was a lull, broken only by a few laggards from the first wave. Then the second wave struck. It consisted of 50 Kates equipped for high-level bombing, 80 Val dive-bombers, and 40 fighter planes. These came in around Diamond Head, concentrating largely on Hickam, on *Nevada*, and on other ships already hit. But this second wave of Japanese attackers was met by a lethal barrage of antiaircraft fire and did comparatively little damage. The destroyers which were moored in groups of three to five in East Loch, the cruisers tied up at docks in Southeast Loch, and the minecraft moored off the Naval Hospital in Middle Loch were under way by this time, and escaped serious damage.

At 0945 all Japanese planes over Oahu returned to their carriers. All but 29 got back, though some 70 were shot full of holes. One plane crash-landed on the island of Niihau, where the pilot, with the aid of a local Japanese, managed to terrorize the unarmed native populace for a week. At the end of that time a burly Hawaiian grappled with the pilot and, although shot by him in divers places, managed to kill him with bare hands and a stone.

By the end of two morning hours on 7 December, the Navy had lost over 2000 officers and men killed and 710 wounded, about thrice as many as in the two wars of 1898 and 1917-1918. The Army and Marine Corps together lost 327 killed and 433 wounded. In addition, some 70 civilians were killed — mostly men who happened to be on one of the airfields, but some in Honolulu where a few naval antiaircraft shells, whose fuses in the confusion had not been cut, exploded on city streets.

The rest of this terrible day was passed in expectation of worse to come. Japanese ships were reported to be on every side of Oahu, preparing to land troops. In the Hawaiian Islands were 160,000 people of Japanese blood; surely from among them Black Dragon bands had been recruited, to assassinate Americans? Japanese maids and butlers, it was said, told their employers to "scram," as their house had been assigned to a Japanese general. Every one of these rumors was later found to be false, and not one disloyal act was committed by the local Nipponese. General Short, for whom that day marked the end of a distinguished Army career, promptly executed his plans for deployment in the event of enemy attack. At about 1000, Army contingents in trucks or afoot began to move toward the supposed danger spots, now that the danger had passed.

Sunset over the Pacific inaugurated a hideous night for all hands. Fire-fighting continued on many of the stricken ships. Surgeons and nurses in the overcrowded hospitals were up all night attending the wounded and dying; hundreds of women and children whose husbands' quarters had been bombed huddled miserably in the university auditorium, or in a storage tunnel at Red Hill. Trigger-happy sentries and machine-gunners fired at everything that moved, supposing it to be a Japanese invader. Saddest of all accidents was the shooting down at night of four dive-bombers from carrier *Enterprise.* These had landed at Ford Island during the morning lull and were then sent out to search for the enemy. When they returned after nightfall with running lights on, an anti-aircraft gunner, who failed to get the word because the airbase communications had been ruptured, opened fire and started a panic of shooting all around the harbor.

Daybreak 8 December revealed a "dismal situation waste and wild" — half the aircraft on the island destroyed, seven battleships sunk or badly damaged, three destroyers reduced to junk. And the atmosphere was one of tormenting uncertainty. Nobody knew where the Japanese task force was; the one radar fix on it was interpreted 180 degrees wrong, so many a ship and most of the flyable planes were sent scurrying southward.

But, as the days elapsed, one saw that the situation might well have been worse. Our three aircraft carriers were safe; the repair shops, which did an amazingly quick job on damaged ships, were almost untouched, as was the fuel-oil tank farm, filled to capacity, whose loss would have tied up the Fleet for months.

Nevertheless, the armed forces and the nation had been struck a treacherous, devastating and humiliating blow. When someone in Washington proposed that a medal be issued to Pearl Harbor combatants, one of the survivors replied, "Better make the ribbon of black crepe."

4. *Who Was Responsible?*

The Pearl Harbor disaster made a tremendous emotional impact on the American people. The Japanese high command, by their idiotic act, had made a strategic present of the first order to the United States; they had united the country in grim determination to win victory in the Pacific. Isolationism and pacifism now ceased to be valid forces in American politics; but some of their exponents, and many well-meaning people too, became violent propagandists for the bizarre theory that the Roosevelt administration, with the connivance of leading generals and admirals in Washington, knew perfectly well that the attack was coming and deliberately withheld knowledge of it from Kimmel and Short in order, for their own foul purposes, to get us into the war.

Even if one can believe that the late President of the United States was capable of so horrible a gambit, a little reflection would indicate that he could not possibly have carried it off. He would have needed the connivance of Secretaries Hull, Stimson and Knox, Generals Marshall, Gerow and Miles, Admirals Stark, Turner and Wilkinson, and many of their subordinates, too — all loyal and honorable men who would never have lent themselves to such monstrous deception. More reflection might suggest that if Roosevelt and his cabinet ministers and armed service chiefs had schemed to get us into the war, their purpose would have been better served by warning the Hawaiian commanders in time to get the Fleet to sea and the planes airborne. Even a frustrated attempt to strike Pearl Harbor would have been sufficient *casus belli* to satisfy the most isolationist congressman. Actually, the administration and the heads of the armed forces, as we have seen, were doing their best to prevent or postpone a war with Japan. Roosevelt even sent a personal appeal to Hirohito on the evening of 6 December.

After any overwhelming disaster there is a search for the culprit; and this search is still being pursued, for partisan purposes, after two Navy and two Army investigations and a lengthy congressional one have combed every phase of omission and commission. No military event in our or any other country's history, not even the Battles of Gettysburg and Jutland, has been the subject of such exhaustive research as the air assault on Pearl Harbor.

A principal reason why Washington and Pearl Harbor were caught unawares was their inability to imagine that Japan would do anything so stupid and suicidal. But Joseph Grew in Tokyo — one of the most alert and perceptive ambassadors in United States history — warned Washington on 3 November 1941 against any possible misconception "of the capacity of Japan to rush headlong into a suicidal conflict with the United States. National sanity would dictate against such an event, but Japanese sanity cannot be measured by our own standards of logic. . . . Japan's resort to [war] measures . . . may come with dramatic and dangerous suddenness." Grew's warning fell on deaf ears.

Three weeks later, almost everyone in a responsible position in Washington expected Japan to make an aggressive move on the weekend of 29 November; but not on Pearl Harbor. And the curious lethargy into which official Washington seemed to fall after the "war warning" is partly explained by the decrypting of a whole series of dispatches from Tokyo to its ambassadors, to the effect that the deadline was approaching, time was running out, etc. There were no fewer than 19 such messages between 2 and 26 November, yet nothing had happened.

The Army and Navy cryptographers in Washington were experts, but grossly overworked. The stuff was coming in faster than they could deal with it, and one could not tell which dispatch was important and which was not until all were decrypted.[6] A message from the Japanese consulate at Honolulu dated 6 December, which ended, "There is a considerable opportunity . . . to take advantage for a surprise attack against these places" (Pearl Harbor and vicinity), was not decrypted until after the attack. The "berthing plan" message and Honolulu's replies were not assigned their proper significance at Washington, because they were mixed in with hundreds of messages, which had to be decrypted and translated, from all parts of the world. Observers in China, for instance, were sending as many as fifty messages a week, warning of forthcoming Japanese attacks on Siberia, Peru, and other unlikely places.

Army and Navy Intelligence officers in Washington were somewhat in the position of a woman with a sick child trying to take instructions from a doctor over the telephone while the neighbors are shouting contrary advice in her ear, dogs are barking, children screaming, and trucks roaring by the house. The noise overwhelmed the message. Personalities also entered into it. Rear Admiral Turner, Navy War Plans officer, was highly opinionated and difficult to work with. He actually forbade the Japanese language officers who did the decrypting and translating, or even the Chief of Naval Intelligence, to make estimates from the dispatches, insisting on doing that himself. And Turner, until late November, was obsessed by the idea that Japan was going to attack Russia, not American or British possessions.

Intelligence data received in Washington was handled in a manner that dissipated its impact. Copies of all decrypted messages that the translators thought significant, sometimes running to 130 a day,

[6] In the subsequent "conspiracy" theory of the surprise, much is made of one of the decoding machines being given to the British instead of to Kimmel. It was actually exchanged for machines that the British invented, and Washington wanted, for decrypting certain German ciphers; and since Britain had interests in the Far East at least equal to ours, the exchange was natural and proper. Another machine destined for Pearl Harbor was being constructed when war began. Admiral Hart already had one at Cavite.

were placed in locked briefcases and carried by special messengers to the President, the Secretaries of State, War, and Navy, and about six top-ranking members of the armed forces. The recipient, without taking notes, had to read these signals in the presence of the messenger, who returned them to Army or Navy Intelligence office, where all copies but one were burned. This system, devised for security, denied to all these important people the opportunity to digest data and draw conclusions. It was nobody's particular and exclusive business to study all intelligence material and come up with an estimate. Nobody got anything but excerpts and driblets.

It must also be remembered that in the late months of 1941 all high Army, Navy and State Department officials in Washington were deeply concerned with the "short of war" conflict in the Atlantic, and with Europe, where it then seemed probable that Hitler would gobble up Russia as he had France, order American merchantmen to be sunk, and step up his subversive activities in Central and South America.

Every one of the Japanese messages decrypted and translated before 7 December was ambiguous. None mentioned Pearl Harbor. None even pointed clearly at Japanese intent to attack the United States anywhere. Thus, no clear warnings were sent to Hawaii because Washington saw no reason to anticipate an attack on Hawaii. Washington, moreover, was determined not to begin a war with Japan. That was the meaning of the passage in the diary of War Secretary Stimson, recording the cabinet meeting of 25 November, after one of Tojo's deadline messages had been decrypted and translated. "The President predicted that we were likely to be attacked perhaps next Monday. . . . The question was how we should maneuver them into the position of firing the first shot." This quotation has been made much of by those trying to prove conspiracy between F.D.R. and his cabinet to get us into war. Mr. Stimson's use of the verb "maneuver" was unfortunate, but his intent is clear — we were not going to provoke the Japanese by an overt act; peace would continue until and unless they chose to strike. This was exactly the same attitude as President Lincoln's about Fort Sumter; or, to go further back, Colonel Parker's classic speech to the Minutemen at Lexington on 19 April 1775: "Don't fire unless fired upon, but if they mean to have a war, let it begin here."

Pearl Harbor, besides lacking the complete Intelligence picture, had the additional handicap of divided responsibility. General Short was charged with the defense of Oahu, including Pearl Harbor and antiaircraft batteries ashore; Admiral Bloch, commandant Fourteenth Naval District, was responsible for the defense of the Navy Yard, and Admiral Kimmel for that of the Fleet. Relations between them were friendly but inadequate; each one, as we have seen, assumed that the others were doing something that they didn't do.

A series of false assumptions, both at Washington and Oahu, added up to something as serious as the sins of omission. In Hawaii, the Navy assumed that the Army had gone on full alert, and that the radar warning net was completely operational. The Army assumed that the Navy was conducting an effective air reconnaissance around the island. Admiral Kimmel assumed that aërial torpedoes could not operate in the shoal waters of Pearl Harbor. Both Army and Navy Intelligence officers assumed that Japan was sending all her naval forces south, and that in any event Japan would not be so stupid as to attack Pearl Harbor. In Washington, Colonel Bratton of Army Intelligence assumed that the Pacific Fleet would go to sea after the 27 November "war warning," so to him the intercepted reports of ships' positions by the Japanese consulate registered waste effort; and Captain Wilkinson of Naval Intelligence assumed that these reports were simply evidence of the Japanese inordinate love for detail. Rear Admiral Turner of War Plans assumed that this and all other relevant intelligence was going to Admiral Kimmel, and General Gerow of Army War Plans assumed that Kimmel and Short were exchanging every scrap of what they did get, which was considerable. Washington was as vague and uncertain about what was going to happen on the first or second weekend after 27 November as Pearl Harbor itself. It was a case of the blind *not* leading the blind; false assumptions at both ends of the line.

The gravest charge against Admiral Kimmel and General Short is that they virtually ignored the "war warning" dispatch of 27 November from Washington. Admiral Kimmel, as we have seen, did send air reinforcement promptly to Wake and Midway Islands. He had already (with Admiral Bloch's coöperation) set up the surface and air patrol off the mouth of Pearl Harbor which encountered the midget submarines. He had, on 14 October, warned the Fleet against a submarine attack as a herald of something worse. Thus, the charge whittles down to this: that he did not repeat this warning and beef-up air patrol after 27 November. He thought that he had done everything that could reasonably be expected, in view of the intelligence received. Nevertheless, an "unwarranted feeling of immunity from attack" prevailed in Oahu at the crucial moment, as Admiral King observed; and it is not unfair to hold Kimmel and Short responsible.

Finally, we have to consider the "East Wind, Rain" dispatch which, by people bent on proving dastardly deception by Washington, has been blown up to a definite word from Tokyo that Pearl Harbor was about to be attacked. Actually, it was nothing of the sort. On 19 November, Tokyo notified the principal Japanese representatives abroad, in a dispatch that Washington decrypted, that if all other means of communication failed, they would be ordered to destroy codes in a plain-language weather broadcast. In this broadcast, "East Wind, Rain" would mean, "Japanese-United States relations in danger"; "North Wind, Cloudy" would mean the same as to Russia; "West Wind, Clear" would mean the same as to England. There was no mention of Pearl Harbor, or any other target; not even a clear forecast of war. This "Winds" message, however, was taken seriously in Washington where a number of officers were alerted to watch Japanese broadcasts for the false weather forecast. Whether or not that was ever sent is disputed; but in no case would it have told Washington or Hawaii anything more than what they already knew, viz., that Japanese embassies had been ordered to destroy their codes.

Fundamentally, however, it was the system, the setup both at Washington and at Pearl, rather than individual stupidity or apathy, which muffled and confused what was going on. No one person knew the whole picture that the intelligence data disclosed; no one person was responsible for the defense of Pearl Harbor; too many people assumed that others were taking precautions that they did not take.

There is an old saying, "Give every dog two bites"; but Kimmel and Short were not even allowed one; they were relieved from active duty forthwith. Admiral Turner, however, was conceded two bites — Pearl Harbor and the Battle of Savo Island, after which he became a highly successful practitioner of amphibious warfare. General Marshall functioned brilliantly as Chief of Staff; and Admiral Stark, as Commander United States Naval Forces Europe in London, acquitted himself very well. Admiral Kimmel and General Short were so shaken by the attack that they had to be relieved anyway; but they might, with justice, have been given honorable commands elsewhere.

Since World War II the methods and systems of obtaining military intelligence and, what is more important, evaluating it and seeing that the proper people get it, have been vastly improved. But let us not forget that we were surprised by the North Koreans in June 1950; surprised when China entered the war later that year; surprised in 1961 by discovery of the attempt to overthrow Castro in Cuba; surprised by the building of the East Berlin wall.

In a tense international situation, such as we have been in ever since the end of World War II, it is important not only to gather intelligence but to see that the right people get it, and to have it evaluated intelligently. It is vital to ascertain not only the capabilities of a potential enemy but his intentions.

So, I conclude this sad story of disaster with the warning which Sophocles, over twenty-three centuries ago in his tragedy of the Siege of Troy, placed in the mouth of Ajax: —

> Far-stretching, endless Time
> Brings forth all hidden things,
> And buries that which once did shine.
> The firm resolve falters, the sacred oath is shattered;
> And let none say, "It cannot happen here."

CHAPTER IV

Disaster in the Far East

July 1941–May 1942

1. *Loss of the Philippines, December 1941–May 1942*

ONE OF THE STRANGE THINGS in popular psychology is the different reaction of the American people to disaster at Pearl Harbor, and to disaster at Manila. The one completely overshadowed the other; it seemed so overwhelming that people could take in no bad news elsewhere. Yet the attack on Pearl Harbor was the lesser of the two evils. It was a hit-and-run raid, and the hit was not decisive. By 1000 December 7 the Japanese planes had retired, and they never returned; nor was there any attempt by the enemy to land troops on Oahu and take over. All we had to do was to count the losses, begin salvage and bury the dead. In the Philippines, the events of 7 December here (8 December there) were not so devastating as at Oahu, but they proved to be but the first of a series of body blows — and what blows! General MacArthur's Army forced to evacuate Manila and Admiral Hart's Fleet to evacuate Cavite; after a rear-guard campaign the entire Philippine archipelago surrendered to Japan; General MacArthur retired to Australia. Nor were these all. Defeat at Pearl Harbor brought no immediate consequences except the capture of Wake Island; but the Japanese blitz in the Philippines was followed by the seizure of Guam, Hong Kong, Thailand, North Borneo, Singapore; and, after a last-ditch campaign in the Java Sea, the entire Netherlands East Indies. Our inability to defend the Philippines in 1941-1942 cost us tens of thousands of lives, and uncounted billions of dollars, before the archipelago could be liberated in 1944-1945.

If surprise at Pearl Harbor is hard to understand, surprise at Manila is completely incomprehensible. Some eight or nine hours after General MacArthur was informed of the attack on Pearl Harbor, his planes were caught grounded, and his air force was as badly destroyed as that of the Army at Pearl Harbor. Yet General MacArthur was given a "second bite"; his mistakes on 8 December were overlooked — fortunately.

Again and again, since the turn of the century, American military commanders in the Philippines had warned that, with the meager forces assigned, they could not possibly defend the archipelago against Japan. Their plan, in case of war, was to abandon Manila, retire the army to Bataan, but to defend Manila Bay from Corregidor and other small island fortresses until the Pacific Fleet managed to arrive on the scene.

This plan and attitude changed after General MacArthur became Commander United States Army Forces Far East in July 1941. The General convinced Army authorities in Washington that, if properly reinforced before war broke out, and if the clash could be postponed until the spring of 1942, his army and the United States Asiatic Fleet could keep the Japanese out of Luzon until the Pacific Fleet arrived. His opinion was based on the hope, and expectation, that his command would receive at least one hundred B–17s. The performance of these Flying Fortresses was so outstanding that in October 1941 General MacArthur advised the War Department that the "citadel type of defense" of the Philippines, as envisaged by the "Rainbow 5" war plan, be changed to a dynamic and offensive plan. MacArthur's enthusiasm was infectious; General Marshall told him to go ahead with new plans, which provided for an offensive strike by B–17s on the Formosa airfields when and if war came with Japan. The Chief of Staff at a press conference in Washington on 15 November 1941 told selected correspondents that we were on the brink of war with Japan, that our position was "highly favorable" in the Philippines, where we had 35 B–17s — "greatest concentration of heavy bomber strength anywhere in the world" — which could counterattack, set the "paper cities" of Japan afire, and make the Philippines garrison independent of sea power.

General MacArthur's opposite number on the naval side was Admiral Thomas C. Hart, Commander in Chief of the Asiatic Fleet. Small, taut, wiry and irascible, Admiral Hart was a year older than Admiral King and had served 44 years in the Navy. In the autumn of 1940 he transferred most of his small fleet from China to Manila Bay. The Asiatic Fleet in the existing war plan was responsible for the naval defense of the Philippines. It must support the Army there "so long as that defense continues." Its total strength, when war broke, was a heavy cruiser *Houston,* two light cruisers, 13 World War I destroyers, 28 submarines, and a number of auxiliaries. Obviously, all that this fleet could do in the event of a Japanese invasion of the Philippines was to retire, or fight a delaying action. "Tommy" Hart, a real fighter, preferred the second alternative, but on 20 November the Navy Department ordered him to fall back. The Admiral then began deployment southward of all except his submarines, which were wanted to repel invasion, and Seaplane Wing 10 of PBYs, which were wanted for reconnaissance. On 8 December, four destroyers, six river gunboats, five "bird" class minesweepers, two fleet oilers, floating dry dock *Dewey* and a couple of tugs were still in Manila Bay. The 4th Marine Regiment was also in barracks at Cavite. Admiral Hart tried his best to remove Marines of the China embassy guard in time, and did get most of them out in river gunboat *Wake;* but merchant ship *President Harrison,* sent for the rest, was captured by the Japanese on 8 December.

Both commanders in the Philippines took the 27 November war warning very seriously and expected the blow to come soon. Ocean search by the PBYs was stepped up, and General MacArthur ordered all Flying Fortresses around Manila to be flown to Davao Field, Mindanao, for safety from a surprise air attack. But by 7 December only about half of them had gone, because room had to be left at the small Mindanao base for more B–17s expected presently from Hawaii. Nevertheless, the new war plan called for a counter-attack on the Formosan airfields as soon as Japan made war, or declared war.

News of the Pearl Harbor attack reached Admiral Hart's headquarters in Manila at 0230 December 8 (East Longitude date), which was 0800 December 7, Hawaiian time. There was nothing he could do but alert the Asiatic Fleet to prepare for air attack. General MacArthur got the word about an hour later, and official confirmation arrived from Washington at 0530. At dawn a flight of 22 planes from Japanese carrier *Ryujo* attacked U.S. seaplane tender *William B. Preston* in Davao Gulf, Mindanao. That overt act inaugurated war in the Philippines. At 0930 two flights of bombers from Formosa struck Baguio and the Tugugarao airfield in northern Luzon. So there was no possible doubt that we were at war with Japan, or that the Philippines were on her list for conquest. Yet, in the face of this, there was hesitation at Manila about unleashing the B–17s against Formosa, or the fighter planes to intercept a bomber strike from Formosa that might reasonably be expected at any moment. General Sutherland, General MacArthur's chief of staff, and General Brereton, commanding MacArthur's army air forces, have given each other the lie as to why the planned attack on Formosa was not promptly executed. Each claims that he wanted to do it but that the other dragged his feet, or his wings, insisting that first there be a photographic reconnaissance of the Formosa airfields. And why had that not been done earlier? The surprise at Manila has never been thoroughly investigated, and Dr. Louis Morton, the official Army historian, failed to get to the bottom of it. This naval historian can only venture a guess — that the real trouble was bad blood between Sutherland and Brereton, of which, unfortunately, General MacArthur seems to have been ignorant.

Whatever the cause, by 1130 almost all B–17s and fighter planes were grounded on Clark, Nichols, Iba and other fields of the airdrome complex around Manila. The ground crews then began arming the bombers for a raid on Formosa, which had finally been ordered to take place that afternoon, and the pilots went to lunch. A force of 108 twin-engined Japanese bombers, escorted by 34 fighters, was then well on its way from Formosa to Manila.

At about 1130, warnings of this approaching strike, from observers in northern Luzon, began to reach the Air Force plotting board at Nielson Field. Thence, about a quarter of an hour later, a warning message was ordered sent to Clark and other fields by teletype. Some claim that it never did go out; that the radio operator was at lunch. Nevertheless, one pursuit squadron of American fighter planes took off promptly from Iba Field, and another was just about to take off from Clark, at 1215, when the first group of 27 Japanese bombers appeared. Their delighted pilots found the B–17s all lined up like "sitting ducks," dropped their bombs from about 22,000 feet altitude, and were off and away. Then came a similar formation which bombed for fifteen minutes, completely unmolested by American antiaircraft, whose ancient ammunition (vintage 1932) and corroded bomb fuses could not reach so high. Finally came a full hour's strafing attack by 34 fighter planes. The scene was one of horror and destruction, relieved by many acts of individual heroism similar to those of the victims at

Pearl Harbor. Iba Field was struck by 54 Japanese planes, just as the pursuit squadron, which had gone forth a little before noon, was about to land. That squadron gave a good account of itself but lost all but two of its planes. Total losses to our side were 18 of the 35 B–17s present destroyed, 56 fighter planes, 25 miscellaneous aircraft, and many installations destroyed, 80 men killed and 150 wounded at a cost to the enemy of only seven fighters. After one day of war, and despite ample warning, the Far Eastern Air Force as an effective combat unit had been eliminated.

After this debacle there was no possibility of a counterattack, and Japan retained the initiative she had so easily won. December 9 was comparatively quiet, but the 10th was Navy Day for the enemy, who sent part of an 80-bomber and 52-fighter group to rub out the Cavite Navy Yard. While a substantial segment of this attack group neutralized airfields, some 54 bombers flew back and forth over Cavite at 20,000 feet elevation, beyond the range of our 3-inch antiaircraft guns, bombing at will. The Navy Yard and a large part of the city of Cavite were completely destroyed, as were a dockside submarine, a minesweeper, and the entire reserve stock of submarines' torpedoes.

On 12 December, all the PBYs of Patwing 10, returning from a fruitless search for an enemy carrier force that wasn't there, were destroyed by Japanese Zero fighters at their Olongapo moorings. The surviving aviators were sent south. The United States Navy had completely lost control of the waters and air surrounding Luzon; no supplies or reinforcements could reach MacArthur's army, ever. Let us humbly remember this humiliating fact and not bury it under the memory of MacArthur's gallantry, or the Navy's part in spearheading his return to the Philippines.

Across the South China Sea the Royal Netherlands Navy and the Royal British were faring no better.

Japan actually began hostilities in that quarter two days before her strike on Pearl Harbor. Minelayer *Tatsumiya Maru,* beginning on the evening of 6 December (East Longitude date), laid 456 mines in British territorial waters between Tiuman Island and the Malay Peninsula, not far from Singapore. This was done to protect the forthcoming Japanese landings on that peninsula from interference by British ships in Singapore. Netherlands submarine *O–16,* and probably *K–XVII* too, were sunk in this minefield in mid-December.

Worse things had already happened. Japanese bombers based on Indochina sank H.M. battleship *Prince of Wales* and battle cruiser *Repulse* on 10 December. By that time Japanese forces had already landed on the Malay Peninsula, taken Hong Kong from the British, and Guam from us. Nor is this all that happened on the 10th, which should be regarded as an even greater "day of infamy" than the 7th at Pearl Harbor. On that day the Japanese executed the first of their five amphibious landings on Luzon, at Aparri. The others coming up were at Vigan and Legaspi (11th and 12th), Lingayen (21st) and Lamon Bay (24th). The pitifully few ships and aircraft of Admiral Hart's fleet were unable to prevent the enemy from landing whenever and wherever he chose, or even to delay his timetable of conquest. Not that Asiatic Fleet failed to try. Its submarines were deployed to intercept the landings, and sank a couple of transports or freighters; but that did not stop the Japanese. Our efforts only served to prove that a properly equipped amphibious force cannot be stopped by submarines alone. And a Japanese amphibious group led by Rear Admiral Tanaka in light cruiser *Jintsu,* of whom (and of which) we shall hear much more, landed at Davao, Mindanao, on 20 December and then proceeded to take Jolo.

Japanese air forces so completely controlled the air over Manila Bay that reinforcements could not be brought in by sea, and the B–17s fleeted up from Mindanao were soon expended. On 21 De-

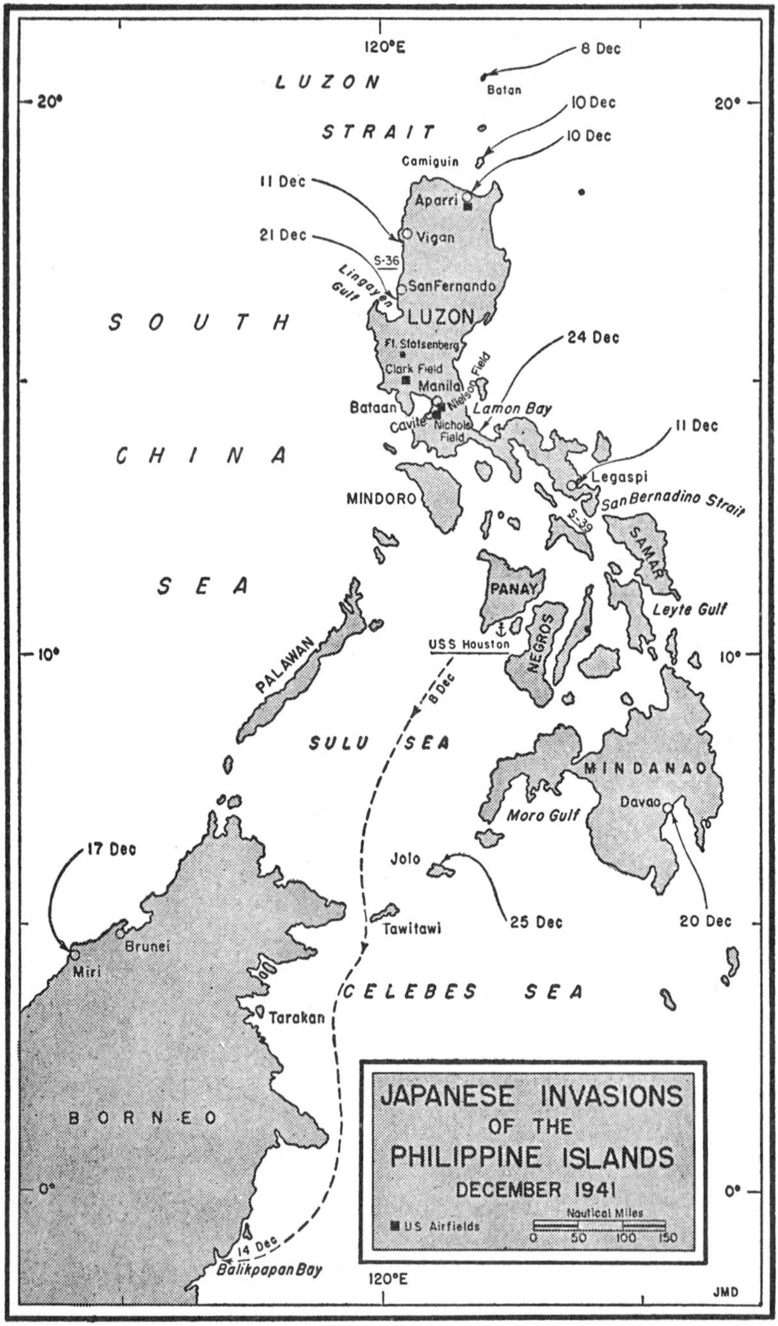
JAPANESE INVASIONS
OF THE
PHILIPPINE ISLANDS
DECEMBER 1941
U.S. Airfields
Nautical Miles
0 50 100 150
120°E
20°
10°
0°
LUZON STRAIT
SOUTH CHINA SEA
SULU SEA
CELEBES SEA
8 Dec
Batan
10 Dec
10 Dec
Camiguin
11 Dec
Aparri
21 Dec
Vigan
S-36
Lingayen Gulf
San Fernando
LUZON
Ft. Stotsenberg
Clark Field
Manila
Nielson Field
24 Dec
Bataan
Cavite
Nichols Field
Lamon Bay
11 Dec
Legaspi
San Bernadino Strait
S-39
MINDORO
SAMAR
PANAY
Leyte Gulf
NEGROS
USS Houston
PALAWAN
MINDANAO
Davao
Moro Gulf
Jolo
25 Dec
20 Dec
Tawitawi
17 Dec
Brunei
Miri
Tarakan
BORNEO
14 Dec
Balikpapan Bay
JMD

cember Rear Admiral Francis W. Rockwell, Commandant Sixteenth Naval District, established new headquarters in a tunnel on "The Rock," Corregidor. On Christmas Eve General MacArthur decided to evacuate Manila (daily being bombed) and to deploy his army in the ultimate defense area, the Bataan Peninsula. Admiral Hart at the same time ordered the only two destroyers left in Manila Bay to Java, where Rear Admiral William A. Glassford, in cruiser *Marblehead*, was rallying the Asiatic Fleet. Hart himself departed for Java in submarine *Shark* the day after Christmas, leaving tender *Canopus* and a handful of minecraft, gunboats and motor torpedo boats, under Admiral Rockwell, to be expended. That they were, covering the flanks of the Army in its stubborn defense of Bataan.

There was no lack of individual bravery. A colorful character, Commander Francis J. Bridget of an already expended PBY squadron, organized a weird Naval Battalion of about 200 men from grounded aviators, Marines, Filipinos or anyone who would join. Wearing white Navy uniforms dyed bright yellow, these tough hombres not only protected General MacArthur's headquarters at Mariveles from capture by one Japanese landing force several times their strength, but forced a second Japanese group to hole up in caves on the coastal cliff, whence they were "disinfected" by Lieutenant John D. Bulkeley's PT boats. It was no use. On 21 February 1942 submarine *Swordfish* took President Quezon of the Philippine Commonwealth out of danger, and on 11 March, on orders from Washington, Lieutenant Bulkeley's PT carried General MacArthur and Admiral Rockwell to Mindanao, whence B-17s flew them to Australia.

General Jonathan M. Wainwright, left in command of the Army, evacuated Bataan on 8 April, to Corregidor. "The Rock," gallantly defended by Colonel S. L. Howard's 4th Marines and the remnants of the Army, held out for another month. Finally on 6 May came the bitterest event of all, when General Wainwright, hoping to prevent further effusion of blood, surrendered Corregidor and all armed forces in the Philippines to the enemy.

This was the greatest surrender in American history, not excepting Appomattox. But unlike that one, in which the Southern dream of empire faded, Corregidor inspired a grim determination on the part of General MacArthur to return, and of the country to see that he did return, in sufficient force to reverse the verdict. A new bond of brotherhood between Americans and Filipinos was forged, and it has never since been sundered.

2. *The ABDA Command*

By the new year Japan could afford to neglect the Philippines, since both United States and Commonwealth forces there were completely neutralized, and to the southward Japan was fast realizing her bold scheme of conquest.

England, the Netherlands and America had to fight for the Malay Barrier, a name then applied to the string of big islands from the Malay Peninsula to New Guinea, most of them belonging to the Netherlands East Indies. If Japan got possession of these rich territories, teeming with oil, rubber and other strategic materials, she would be well-nigh self-sufficient; and, once in control of the Molucca, Sunda, Lombok and other straits between the islands, the warriors of Nippon might pour into the Indian Ocean and threaten British India and Australia.

In April 1941 an attempt was made to arrive at an international staff agreement about the conduct of war in the Far East, similar to the Anglo-American one at Washington. Representatives of the United States, Great Britain, the Netherlands, Australia and New Zealand met at Singapore. This conference came to no useful result, largely because of divergent views about Singapore itself. The British had spent vast sums on creating the military and naval base there, and regarded it as a symbol of empire, a pledge to the Antipodes that England in her time of greatest peril had not forgotten them. Rear Admiral Turner and other Americans took a dim view of Singapore as a strategic base. Owing to its lack of defenses on the land side, they predicted that Singapore could not long hold out in the event of war with Japan, nor did it. Even after H.M.S. *Prince of Wales* and *Repulse* had been sunk, the British continued to insist that Singapore must and could be defended. Divergent aims bedeviled the new ABDA (American-British-Dutch-Australia) combined command, set up on 15 January 1942, throughout the six stormy weeks of its existence. The British wanted more troops to be poured into Singapore, and to use the combined naval forces to escort them; the Dutch wished to protect their East Indies; the Australians to prevent an invasion of their country; and the Americans to prepare a comeback.

Thus ABDA as a combined command was very creaky at the joints. Communication and language difficulties were never solved. No combined system of signaling was worked out. The native Indonesians, unlike the Filipinos, were apathetic or hostile. The supreme ABDA commander, Field Marshal Sir Archibald Wavell, had proved himself in Africa to be one of England's most distinguished soldiers, but here he failed, as anyone under like conditions would have failed. Under Wavell, Admiral Hart commanded the combined naval forces, a Dutch lieutenant general the ground forces, and a British air chief marshal the air forces. The Asiatic Fleet was now based at Surabaya on the north coast of Java, and its principal units were organized into the ABDA striking force under Vice Admiral Helfrich of the Royal Netherlands Navy. Port Darwin, Australia, 1200 miles distant, was the nearest service and supply base for the United States Asiatic Fleet.

Two powerful Japanese attack groups, the Eastern under Vice Admiral Takahashi, and the Western under Vice Admiral Ozawa, composed of heavy cruisers and destroyers escorting army transports, and with Admiral Nagumo's still intact carriers of the Pearl Harbor Striking Force in wide-ranging support, slithered into the Netherlands East Indies like the arms of two giant octopi. The Western octopus worked down the South China Sea to North Borneo and Sumatra; the Eastern to East Borneo, the Celebes, Ambon, Timor and Bali. Aircraft would pound down a beachhead, amphibious forces would then move in and activate another airfield and soften up the next objective for invasion. Nothing possessed by the three Allied powers could stop this grim process. Dutch and United States submarines inflicted considerable damage, but the enemy forces were overwhelming. The Allies, owing to their diverse interests, dissipated their forces in various directions and on gallant but futile missions.

Commander Paul Talbot in *John D. Ford*, with three other World War I destroyers, broke into the Japanese force landing at Balikpapan, Borneo, on the night of 23-24 January 1942, and sank four *Marus* and a patrol craft; but this did not delay the Japanese timetable by even a day. By 3 February Japanese airplanes, now established at Kondari in the Celebes, began raiding Surabaya, forcing Admiral Hart to send his tenders south to Tjilatjap; none too soon, for light cruiser *Marblehead* was so badly mauled off Banka next day that she had to be sent home. Another air-surface battle between planes from carrier *Ryujo*, and an ABDA striking force under Admiral Doorman RNN on 15 February, forced the ships to retire through Gaspar Strait to the Java Sea. And on that very day, Singapore surrendered — as bitter a draught for Britain as Pearl Harbor had been for America.

3. *The Battle of the Java Sea, 27 February 1942*

Now, in quick succession, the Japanese occupied Timor and Nagumo's carrier planes bombed Port Darwin, heavily damaging the

Allied supply ships, and forcing the abandonment of that port as a supply base. The octopi would soon put the final squeeze on Java.

By the time they were ready for that, ABDA command had been "reorganized upon the floor," like the person described in T. S. Eliot's "Sweeney among the Nightingales." Admiral Hart had been a good skipper in a bad storm, using the little that he had to fight to best advantage, but on 12 February, owing to the Netherlands government's desire that in their East Indies a Dutch admiral should be in command, "Tommy" Hart was relieved by Admiral Helfrich RNN. This change did not help the desperately bad situation. All fighting ships and sailors had been worked beyond their capacity. Facilities for repairs were inadequate at Surabaya, and almost nonexistent at Tjilatjap on the south coast of Java, which most of the Asiatic Fleet now had to use as base, owing to frequent air attacks on the north-coast ports.

Field Marshal Wavell was ordered home, and on 25 February departed. General Brereton of the United States Army Air Force had already gone, together with most of the planes that he had managed to evacuate from the Philippines. Units of the British, of United States and of the Netherlands Navy remained. ABDA no longer existed in fact, only in theory. Dutch officers were now in full control of all armed forces left in the area.

Rear Admiral Karel Doorman RNN now commanded the Striking Force of the three Allied navies, based at Surabaya. It was far from negligible as a fighting array: heavy crusiers *Houston* and H.M.S. *Exeter*, light cruisers H.M.A.S. *Perth*, H.M.N.S. *De Ruyter* and *Java;* four American, three British and three Dutch destroyers. Collectively, these ships were not strong enough to stop the major Japanese thrust, and they had never worked together as a team. Two massive amphibious forces were approaching — 56 transport types under Rear Admiral Ozawa to the westward, and 41 under Rear Admiral Nishimura to the eastward. And the eastern one, which Doorman hoped to intercept since it seemed headed for Surabaya, was covered by a formidable support force under Rear Admiral Takeo Takagi, which included heavy cruisers *Nachi* and *Haguro*, and two destroyer squadrons with light cruiser flagships (*Naka* and *Jintsu*) under Rear Admirals Nishimura and Tanaka. Vice Admiral Nagumo's Pearl Harbor Striking Force was hovering in the Indian Ocean to prevent reinforcement from that quarter and took no part in the battle. The air component was supplied by the Japanese cruisers' float planes. Their spotting and (after dark) illuminating may well have tipped the scales, for Doorman had no aircraft whatsoever. He had left his float planes ashore on the 26th, expecting a night battle, and when he called for air support from Java, the air commander there stupidly sent his few light bombers and fighters to make a fruitless attack on the Japanese transports.

Admiral Doorman, a fine type of fighting sailor, was about to enter Surabaya for rest and replenishment when he received reports of two Japanese convoys, the nearer but 80 miles distant. At 1525 February 27 Striking Force reversed course to give battle in waters between the north coast of Java and Bawean Island, which the Japanese had already taken. Doorman had no time to issue a battle plan, much less to distribute it; and there was confusion and delay from the necessity of translating every signal. About the only command that Doorman could get across during the battle was "Follow me!" and every ship that could, did. His object was simple enough, to beat off or get around Takagi's fighting ships and raise havoc among the transports waiting just over the northern horizon. Takagi's object, naturally, was to prevent this and clear the way for the invasion of Java.

The battle was such a series of thrusts and parries, bursts of gunfire and shoals of torpedoes, over a period of five or six hours, that it is difficult to follow. If you care to go with me, keep one eye on our chart. If you do not, skip to read only the result.

At the lower right of the chart, note the Allied order of battle:

three British destroyers (*Encounter*, *Electra*, *Jupiter*) in the van; H.N.M.S. *De Ruyter* (Doorman's ship) followed by H.M.S. *Exeter*, U.S.S. *Houston*, H.M.A.S. *Perth*, H.N.M.S. *Java* in column; two Dutch destroyers (*Witte de With* and *Kortenaer*) on the left flank, and four Americans (*John D. Edwards*, *Alden*, *John D. Ford*, *Paul Jones*) in the rear.

It was a calm, clear day with high visibility and a slight swell. At 1612 the enemy was sighted, in three columns — Tanaka's *Jintsu* and seven destroyers on the right flank; Takagi's two heavy cruisers *Nachi* and *Haguro* in the center, Nishimura's *Naka* and six destroyers on the left flank. At 1616 firing commenced between the two heavy groups at the extreme range of 28,000 yards, almost 14 miles. Tanaka's destroyer squadron closed *Electra* and *Jupiter* to 18,000 yards and straddled them, but they could not reach him with their 4.7-inch guns. As Doorman's course, if continued, would enable the Japanese to emulate Admiral Togo's famous Tsushima "crossing of the T," the Netherlands admiral changed course from northwest to west to parallel the enemy, and endeavored to close range so that his three light cruisers could use their 6-inch guns. In the gunfire duel that ensued, the Japanese, with planes spotting for them, had the advantage, and at 1631 made the first hit, fortunately a dud, on *De Ruyter*. Takagi now ordered the first torpedo attack; and he had 17 ships to launch from, as all Japanese cruisers carried torpedoes. Over a period of 19 minutes, 1633-1652, the Japanese launched 43 of their fast, powerful "long lances," but made not one hit; the range was too great. Both forces sped westward at about 25 knots or more, firing furiously but not hitting. This battle showed something that became increasingly evident during World War II: the ineffectiveness of naval gunfire at high speed and great range.

Again the Japanese took the initiative. At 1700, bold Tanaka peeled off to cross Doorman's bows and make a second torpedo attack. He would have had little chance to score against the thin

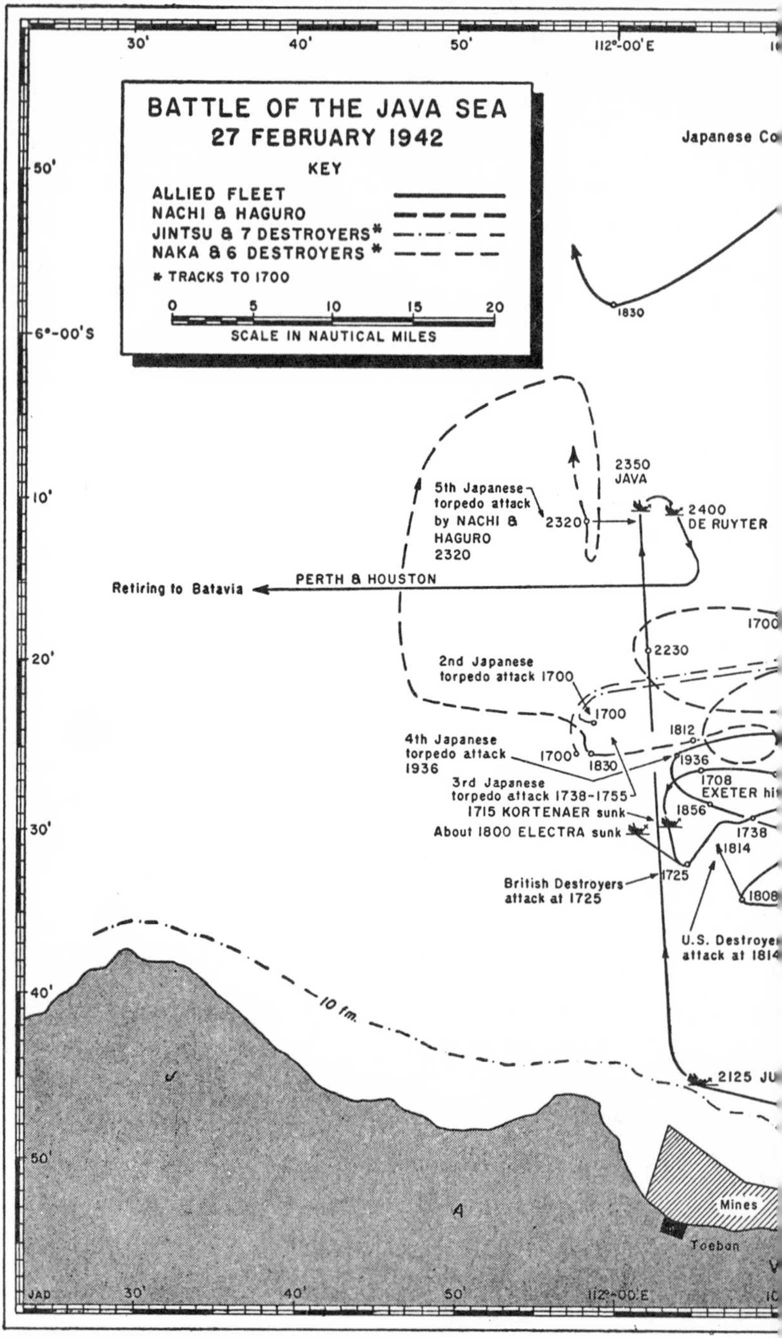

BATTLE OF THE JAVA SEA
27 FEBRUARY 1942
KEY
ALLIED FLEET
NACHI & HAGURO
JINTSU & 7 DESTROYERS*
NAKA & 6 DESTROYERS *
* TRACKS TO 1700
0 5 10 15 20
SCALE IN NAUTICAL MILES
30'
40'
50'
112°-00'E
50'
6°-00'S
10'
20'
30'
40'
50'
1830
2350
JAVA
5th Japanese torpedo attack by NACHI & HAGURO 2320
2320
2400
DE RUYTER
Retiring to Batavia
PERTH & HOUSTON
1700
2230
2nd Japanese torpedo attack 1700
1700
1812
4th Japanese torpedo attack 1936
1700
1830
1936
3rd Japanese torpedo attack 1738-1755
1708
1715 KORTENAER sunk
1856
About 1800 ELECTRA sunk
1738
1814
British Destroyers attack at 1725
1725
1808
10 fm.
2125
Mines
Toeban
JAD
30'
40'
50'
112°-00'E

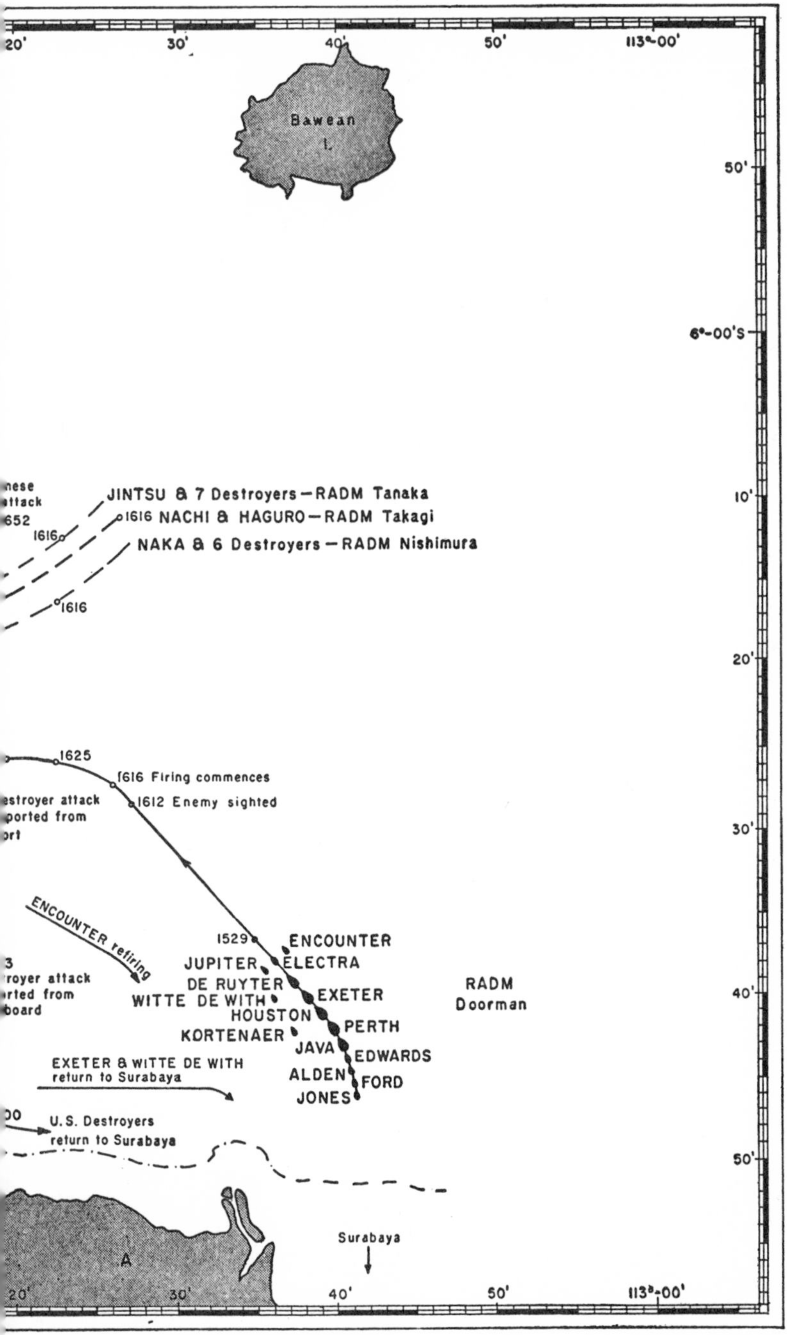

20'
30'
40'
50'
113°-00'
Bawean I.
50'
6°-00'S
10'
20'
30'
40'
50'
nese
attack
652
1616
JINTSU & 7 Destroyers — RADM Tanaka
1616 NACHI & HAGURO — RADM Takagi
NAKA & 6 Destroyers — RADM Nishimura
1616
1625
1616 Firing commences
1612 Enemy sighted
estroyer attack
ported from
ort
ENCOUNTER refiring
1529
ENCOUNTER
JUPITER
ELECTRA
DE RUYTER
WITTE DE WITH
EXETER
HOUSTON
PERTH
KORTENAER
JAVA
EDWARDS
ALDEN
FORD
JONES
RADM
Doorman
3
royer attack
rted from
board
EXETER & WITTE DE WITH
return to Surabaya
00
U.S. Destroyers
return to Surabaya
Surabaya
A

frontal silhouette of Doorman's column, but for a cruiser's 8-inch hit, at 1708, on H.M.S. *Exeter,* which put six of her eight boilers out, slowed her down and caused her to sheer out of line, about 90 degrees to port. *Houston, Perth* and *Java,* assuming that Doorman (whom they could not see in the smoke) must have ordered a 90-degree left turn, followed suit; and so flagship *De Ruyter,* after continuing west for a minute or two, had to do the same. As a result, the Allied force became scattered in a confused pattern right slap into Tanaka's torpedo water. He could hardly fail to score, and he did. At 1715 H.N.M.S. *Kortenaer* exploded, jackknifed, and sank.

Takagi, seeing his chance with the Allied force in confusion and slowed down to 15 knots by *Exeter*'s mishap, ordered his entire force in for the kill. Doorman sent the three British destroyers to counterattack through smoke to the northwestward, where Tanaka's squadron was milling about and trying pot shots. By this time, in the gathering dusk, the entire battle area was shrouded in smoke, through which only an occasional blinker signal from Admiral Doorman reached his ships.

Electra, which received this latest order at 1725, scored a hit on *Jintsu,* but in return was stopped dead by a shell exploding in a boiler room. Tanaka now drove in to try and finish off limping *Exeter,* but was frustrated by the nimble footwork of destroyers *Jupiter, Witte de With* and *Encounter.* The enemy then doubled back to gang up on *Electra.* She fulfilled the tragic implication of her name at 1800.

Doorman in the meantime had ordered *Exeter,* escorted by *Witte de With,* to Surabaya, and reformed his column in this order: *De Ruyter, Perth, Houston, Java,* with the four United States destroyers flank and rear. The cruisers now engaged in another long-range gunfire duel, in which *Houston* took two duds. As Doorman was steering south, Takagi assumed that he was retreating, advised the convoy (which had turned north) to resume course for the landing beaches, and sent Nishimura's squadron to finish off the Allies. Nishimura scored not one hit with the 24 torpedoes his squadron launched.

Doorman now ordered the United States destroyers to cover his retirement. Their squadron commander, T. H. Binford, regarding attack as the best means to cover, turned north to torpedo *Nachi* and *Haguro*. Unfortunately the American torpedoes had been set so that they could only be fired broadside, and under these circumstances to close to a proper range would mean almost certain destruction by the cruisers' gunfire before launching. Binford therefore took a chance shot at 10,000 yards, and all torpedoes missed. After a short gunfire duel with destroyer *Asagumo*, possibly holing her, the "four-pipers" hastened to catch up with Admiral Doorman.

That great sea-dog never acknowledged defeat. At 1830 he had radioed to Admiral Helfrich ashore: "Enemy retreating west, where's the convoy?" At that very moment Takagi ordered the convoy to reverse course and stand northward — it was then only 30 miles away. The Japanese did not underestimate the ability of Doorman, now steering northwesterly, to get at the convoy; and if the Allies had had any air reconnaissance they might have evaded Takagi's ships and struck a fatal blow. But the dice were loaded against them.

At about 1927 the converging cruisers sighted each other again in the gathering darkness. *Nachi* led *Haguro*, *Jintsu* and several destroyers; 13,000 yards to the southeastward was *De Ruyter* followed by *Perth*, *Houston*, *Java* and four American destroyers; H.M.S. *Jupiter* was stationed about a mile on *De Ruyter's* port bow. *Perth* and *Houston* opened fire at 1933, but their shells fell short. The enemy fired star shells to illuminate, and at 1936, when Captain Waller RAN of *Perth* saw a row of flashes in the enemy column, he rightly suspected that they meant torpedo launchings and swung hard right to course 60°. The other ships followed suit and this, the fourth, Japanese torpedo attack was successfully evaded.

Doorman now planned to escape these troublesome ships and get at the convoy by following the coast of Java west. So, at 1955, he swung his column south and at flank speed steamed toward the Java coast, which soon loomed up in the moonlight. There could be no escape, since he was continually illuminated by Japanese float planes dropping flares. When his column reached shoal water, at 2100, Admiral Doorman turned right to parallel the coast. The United States destroyers at this point left the formation and turned east for Surabaya; Doorman had instructed them to do that when their torpedoes were expended, as now they were. As Doorman's force continued westward along the coast, it skirted a newly laid Dutch minefield whose exact position had been broadcast at frequent intervals. At high speed the cruisers, followed by two destroyers, cleared the mined area safely; but at 2125 an explosion racked H.M.S. *Jupiter*, and she dropped out, victim either of a floating mine that had broken loose, or of an internal explosion. She sank four hours later.

Shortly after *Jupiter* exploded, Admiral Doorman turned his four cruisers north again. Although he now had but one destroyer with him and no air support, this brave officer determined to make one last desperate thrust to thwart the invasion of Java. It was a suicidal move. Zigzagging slightly, the column steamed northward, hoping to avoid further attention from the enemy. Over an hour passed and nothing happened, except that destroyer *Encounter* dropped out to pick up survivors from *Kortenaer* on life rafts. Then *Nachi*, *Haguro* and several destroyers were sighted in bright moonlight on the port beam, steering south. Takagi reversed course to parallel Doorman, and the two columns exchanged long-range gunfire for twenty minutes, hoping for a lucky hit. Salvos came slowly now, since both sides were low on ammunition and their crews were near exhaustion. At 2320, when the two columns were almost parallel, 8000 yards apart, the Japanese cruisers launched 12 torpedoes. *De Ruyter* and *Java,* caught in the wide spread, burst into flames, exploded and stopped dead. *Java* lived for only fifteen minutes; *De Ruyter* defiantly floated for about three hours. Their captains and Admiral Doorman followed the hard ritual of the sea and went down with them.

Before he lost contact with *Perth* and *Houston,* Doorman had ordered them not to stand by him but to retire to Batavia. They headed for Tanjong Priok, where they signaled to Admiral Helfrich the tragic results of the Battle of the Java Sea.

In one afternoon and evening, half the ships of Admiral Doorman's Striking Force had been destroyed; the Japanese had not lost a single ship, and only one destroyer was damaged. The convoy was never touched.

The main factors in this battle, any one of which would have doomed the Allies to defeat, were complete lack of air power, bad communications, and the enemy's superiority in torpedoes. The most surprising thing about the battle was its duration. Before World War II, most strategists thought that gun and torpedo fire had been developed to such a degree that naval battles would be decided in a few minutes, at the end of which one side would either be annihilated or so crippled that it could fight no more. Several battles in this war — notably, Savo Island — were of that description. But in the Battle of the Java Sea the two opponents slugged each other intermittently over a period of some seven hours before one had to break off and admit defeat. That it lasted so long was due to Admiral Doorman's stubborn determination and the admirable manner in which men of the three navies under his command fought and fought until they could fight no more.

Java Sea was indeed a decisive battle. There was nothing now to stop the Japanese invasion. And when brave Doorman went down, his country's colonial empire was doomed; even the eventual Allied victory could not eradicate the effects of this Japanese triumph. Never again would the Netherlanders rule over these beautiful islands and their volatile people.

4. *Bloody Sequel, March–April 1942*

One Allied disaster after another followed the Java Sea battle. Seaplane tender *Langley*, pioneer carrier of the United States Navy, was sunk by air bombing south of Tjilatjap on 27 February while trying to bring in plane reinforcements. On the last night of February, U.S.S. *Houston* and H.M.A.S. *Perth*, survivors of the Java Sea, gallantly charged into Banten Bay, adjoining Sunda Strait, to break up one of the major Japanese amphibious forces that was being landed. If only Doorman and his other ships had been with them, they could have realized the ABDA dream of breaking up a Japanese invasion force at its most vulnerable moment. But, alas, it was so late, they were so few, and Admiral Kurita's Western Covering Group, built around four heavy cruisers, was too strong.

Destroyer *Fubuki* almost caught *Houston* and *Perth* as they entered Banten Bay. She fired torpedoes at them at a range of about 2700 yards, missed them but hit and sank a couple of Japanese transports on their port hand. The cruisers swung around the bay, shooting up transports as they passed; one was sunk outright and three others had to be beached.[1]

As they roared through the narrow channel between Panjang Island and Saint Nicholas Point, the two cruisers ran into a fatal trap. On the port hand a Japanese destroyer squadron blocked

[1] John Toland *But Not in Shame* (1961) states that from Japanese sources all four transports were sunk by Japanese torpedoes from the heavy cruisers. This cannot be correct; the cruisers were too far away to score with torpedoes, and Panjang Island lay between them and the transports.

Sunda Strait, their escape hatch; on the starboard hand, freshly replenished, oversize heavy cruisers *Mogami* and *Mikuma* opened up on the two depleted, exhausted "treaty" cruisers. The Japanese shooting, from almost point-blank range, was inaccurate but so overwhelming that only a miracle could have changed the result. H.M.A.S. *Perth* came under fire at 2326. At 0005 March 1 she took a torpedo in her forward engine room that almost lifted her out of the water, then another, and in a few moments she went down, taking Captain Waller and hundreds more.

Now every Japanese ship concentrated on putting *Houston* away. She was already listing dangerously to starboard. Around 0010 she took a salvo in her after engine room which burst all the steam lines and scalded to death the entire engine room force. A torpedo hit forward smashed up main battery plot, whose crew was wiped out by a shellburst as they ran topside. Turrets went to local control, and for a few moments the gunners profited by a mistake that the enemy made, illuminating his own ships; they hit three different destroyers and sank a minesweeper. A shell hit No. 2 turret just as powder bags were being loaded, starting a fire which forced Captain Rooks to have both magazines flooded. Now the two 8-inch turrets had no ammunition except what was already in the hoists. Three torpedoes hit the ship on her starboard side and shrapnel from small-caliber fire ricocheted about her superstructure. Around 0025, standing near a machine-gun mount, Rooks and the gun crew were killed by a bursting shell. Men stood by the other guns and fired every bit of ammunition until all was expended. Then, as the ship lost headway, Japanese destroyers swarmed about her, machine-gunning the quarterdeck and the port hangar where many of the survivors from below had congregated. Commander David Roberts, the exec., ordered Abandon Ship, and Seaman Stafford, standing on the careening fantail, sounded the call on his bugle, at 0033. Within ten or twelve minutes *Houston* rolled over and sank. Swimming survivors could see her ensign defiantly flying until it dipped below the waters of Sunda Strait.

On this same bloody first of March, H.M.S. *Exeter* tried to lead U.S. destroyer *Pope* and H.M.S. *Encounter* through the Surabaya minefields to safety. All three were sunk by enemy naval gunfire and carrier bombing planes.

Japanese troops swarmed over Java, and on the 9th the Dutch commanding general surrendered the Netherlands East Indies.

Admiral Nagumo's carrier force was now free to raid the Indian Ocean, where Admiral Sir James Somerville RN, one of England's senior and most versatile flag officers, awaited him with the British Far Eastern Force — five old battleships, three small carriers, eight cruisers and 15 destroyers. The Japanese had it pretty much their own way from 25 March to 8 April, striking Colombo and Trincomalee, sinking carrier *Hermes* and two heavy cruisers, and about 136,000 tons of merchant shipping. In four months' time Nagumo had operated one third of the way around the world. He had conducted strikes against ships and shore installations at Pearl Harbor, Rabaul, Ambon, Darwin, Java, and Ceylon. He had sunk five battleships, an aircraft carrier, two cruisers and seven destroyers; had damaged several more capital ships, disposed of some 200,000 tons of fleet auxiliaries and merchant men, and hundreds of Allied aircraft. Yet not one ship of his Striking Force had been even damaged by enemy action. There was no longer any doubt as to what type would be the capital ship of the future.

The Malay Barrier was now shattered. Except for isolated pockets of resistance, such as Corregidor, the colonial empires of the United States, the Netherlands, and Great Britain, as far west as India and as far south as Australia, had joined that of the French, already liquidated. Within four months of the Pearl Harbor strike, Japan had achieved her Greater East Asia Co-Prosperity Sphere. She was poised to lash backward into China; or, if America and

Britain did not throw in the sponge, forward by the right flank into India and by the left flank into the Aleutians and Hawaii.

Were our efforts, then, to defend the Malay Barrier a waste of men and matériel? Admiral King is reported to have characterized the whole Southwest Pacific campaign as "a magnificent display of very bad strategy." He never said what he thought good strategy would have been; probably he meant abandoning Singapore and concentrating on defending Java, which might possibly have worked. Be that as it may, the Allies did well to fight for the Malay Barrier, although fighting alone could not save it. Recent experience of the French showed the moral cost of too easy and complacent a capitulation. Another such in Southeast Asia might have been too much for the Allies to bear.

So, while we mourn *Houston* and the other gallant ships of three navies that went down with most of their officers and men after fighting so bravely and well, we should not regard their efforts as vain; their desperate exploits should forever be held in proud and affectionate remembrance by the ABDA nations — America, Britain, the Netherlands and Australia.

CHAPTER V

Destruction in the Atlantic

1942

1. *Transatlantic Convoys, January–April 1942*

THE JAPANESE ATTACK on Pearl Harbor was as much of a surprise to Hitler as to the United States; he had been trying to persuade Japan to attack Russia. The *Chicago Tribune* on 4 December printed a purloined document in which the ABC Conference decision of March to beat Germany first was embodied, and the German chargé at Washington promptly transmitted this to Berlin. But the revelation, instead of encouraging Hitler to continue his policy of avoiding war with the United States as long as possible, caused him to declare war on the United States (11 December 1941). Mussolini obediently followed, and that afternoon Congress declared war on Germany and Italy.

Admiral King, appointed Commander in Chief United States Fleet (Cominch) on 20 December 1941 at the age of sixty-three, was relieved ten days later as Commander in Chief Atlantic Fleet (Cinclant) by Admiral Royal E. Ingersoll. As the functions of the Chief of Naval Operations overlapped those of a shore-based Cominch, President Roosevelt gave King the C.N.O. job too, on 12 March 1942.

King was a "man of adamant," as Mahan described Sir John Jervis. Tall, spare and taut, with piercing brown eyes, a powerful Roman nose and deeply cleft chin, he looked the part and filled the part of Commander in Chief of the Fleet. King was a sailor's sailor. He believed that what was good for the Navy was good for the United States, and indeed the world. In that sense and that alone he was narrow. But he had a firm grasp of naval strategy and tactics, an encyclopedic knowledge of naval detail, an immense capacity for work, and complete integrity. Endowed with a superior intellect himself, he had no toleration for fools or weaklings. He hated publicity, did not lend himself to popular buildup, and was the despair of interviewers. Unlike Admiral Stark's decisions, King's were made quickly and without much consultation; when anyone tried to argue with him beyond a certain point, a characteristic bleak look came over his countenance as a signal that his mind was made up and further discussion was useless. Although he had nothing of the courtier in his make-up, King acquired and retained the confidence and esteem of President Roosevelt. The two men were in a sense complementary. Each had what the other lacked, and in concert with General Marshall, who shared the qualities of both, they formed a perfect winning team. The Republic has never had more efficient, intelligent and upright servants than these three men.

Admiral King made Rear Admiral Russell Willson his chief of staff, and brought with him to Washington from the Atlantic Fleet Rear Admiral Richard S. Edwards as deputy chief of staff, Captain Francis S. Low as operations officer, and Commander George L. Russell as flag secretary. As assistant chiefs of staff he appointed Rear Admirals Richmond K. Turner and Willis Augustus Lee. When Turner went to Guadalcanal he was relieved as assistant chief of staff for plans by Rear Admiral Charles M. ("Savvy") Cooke. Apart from Edwards, Willson, Russell and Cooke, and Vice Admiral Frederick J. Horne, who became Vice Chief of Naval Operations in March 1942, Admiral King kept a continual turnover on his staff. Senior officers were constantly being brought in from different theaters of war, retained on duty with Cominch-

CNO for a few months, then sent back to sea. Thus the fighting Navy point of view was maintained at Washington.

Since escort-of-convoy was every day becoming more important, and required heavy communications facilities, Admiral King took the direction of it with him from Newport to Washington. Shortly after becoming Cominch, he exchanged views on the subject with the Admiralty. This resulted in transatlantic convoy routes being shifted southward, and the Canadian Navy being given a greater share in escorting slow convoys to a "momp"[1] at long. 22° W (about five hundred miles from Northern Ireland), where Royal Navy escorts could take over, and the Canadians proceed to Londonderry to fuel. The fast Halifax–U.K. convoys were escorted by United States destroyers to Momp, where they, too, were relieved by the Royal Navy, refueled at Londonderry, and escorted a fast convoy home. This change of the turnaround point from Iceland to Ireland was most welcome to bluejackets; Londonderry, a dour Presbyterian city, seemed like Coney Island after Reykjavik, and the green Irish countryside looked like heaven after the barren wastes of Iceland. Repair facilities also were superior, since Londonderry was already an important base of the Royal Navy, and the main British center for antisubmarine training. The British "dome teacher," in which sailors were trained to the use of antiaircraft guns in a sort of planetarium, was of immense value to American gunners, as were the British "tame submarines" on which escort vessels practised both day and night attacks.

Admiral Ingersoll as Cinclant exercised complete responsibility for troop convoys, the first of which sailed from Halifax 10 January 1942 and arrived Londonderry about two weeks later. It was desirable to build up United States Army forces in the United Kingdom immediately, so that there would be no shortage of troop-lift, as in 1918, when the Army was ready to strike. In

[1] Abbreviation for Mid-ocean Meeting Point.

February the Navy organized a series of troop convoys, partly with British transports, and a heavy American escort, including battleships and cruisers as well as destroyers. These convoys also enjoyed all the blimp and airplane escort that was available at each end of the route. Heavy weather was often encountered, and an occasional sound contact on a submarine was made, but a speed of 12.5 to 14.5 knots was maintained and not a ship or a soldier was lost.

Fueling at sea was another problem. The old "short-legged" 1200-ton destroyers had been designed in the light of World War I experience, when all that was expected of an escort was a 48-hour run outbound or inbound. But the necessities of escort duty in 1941-1942 were such that every United States destroyer had to cover the route Argentia–Momp–Iceland, or the reverse, which required at least ten days' steaming. It was impossible for such ships, in winter weather, to conduct the active, aggressive patrolling enjoined on all by the fate of U.S.S. *Kearny* and *Reuben James*. Before the war, fueling at sea had been practised largely in calm weather, and only from battleships; now it had to be done from merchant tankers. On one transatlantic convoy four tankers, rigged for ocean fueling abreast or astern, made twenty fuelings of escorts, four or five times on some of them.

The scarcity of suitable escorts was the greatest handicap during this period. Coast Guard Cutter *Campbell*, employed as escort in November 1941, proved so effective that most of her sister ships of the "Treasury" class were diverted to this duty. These big seagoing cutters had everything that a destroyer had except speed and torpedoes; and seldom does an opportunity arise to use torpedoes in escort-of-convoy. U.S.C.G.C. *Alexander Hamilton* was torpedoed and sunk ten miles off Iceland 29 January 1942, when towing a disabled storeship.

Air cover at this period could only be provided at each end of the transatlantic route, and from Iceland. In antisubmarine warfare, air search proved so valuable for locating and destroying U-boats that every effort was made to extend and enlarge the coverage. By the end of 1942, a squadron of four-engined Liberators operating out of Greenland proved a great help in mid-ocean, but even they left a big "dark pocket" around the Azores, where U-boats operated with impunity and even refueled from special submarine "milch cows" sent out for that purpose. The Navy was eager to light up this pocket by occupying the Azores and installing airfields there, but Dr. Salazar, premier of Portugal, would not allow this until late 1943, when he had decided that the Allies were going to win; and the Allies could not violate their own principles by seizing part of a neutral country.

A convoy is beautiful, whether seen from a deck or from the sky. The inner core of stolid ships in several columns is never equally spaced, for each has her individuality; one is always straggling or ranging ahead until the commodore becomes vexed and signals angrily, "Number So-and-so, take station and keep station!" Around the merchant ships is thrown the screen like a loose-jointed necklace, the beads lunging to port or starboard and then snapping back as though pulled by a mighty submarine elastic; each destroyer nervous and questing, all eyes topside looking for the enemy, sound gear below listening for him, radar antennae like cats' whiskers feeling for him. On dark nights only a few shapes of ships a little darker that the black water can be discerned; one consults the radar screen to ascertain that the flock is all there. To one coming topside for the dawn watch, it is a recurring wonder to see the same ships day after day, each in her appointed station, each with her characteristic top-hamper, bow-wave, lift and dip; the inevitable straggler, the inveterate smoker, the vessel with an old shellback master who "knew more about shipping forty years ago than any goddam gold-braid in a tin can," and whose sullen fury at being convoyed translates itself into belated turns, unanswered signals and insolent comebacks. When air cover is furnished there are darting, swooping planes about the convoy; upon approaching port, the stately silver bubble of a blimp comes out, swaying in the breeze and blinking a cheery welcome.

There is nothing beautiful, however, about a night attack on a convoy, unless you see it from a submarine's periscope. A torpedo hit is signaled by a flash and a great orange flare, followed by a muffled roar. Guns crack at imaginary targets, star shell breaks out, a rescue ship hurries to the scene of the sinking, and sailors in other ships experience a helpless fury and dread. If the convoy has a weak escort it can only execute an emergency turn and trust that the rest of the wolf-pack will be thrown off or driven down; if the escort is sufficient a "killer group" peels off, searching relentlessly with radar and sonar, while everyone stands by hoping to feel underfoot the push of distant depth charges that tells of a fight with a submerged enemy.

The only American-escorted convoy that lost heavily during the first four months of 1942 was ON–67 of 35 ships in eight columns which crossed westward during the full moon of February. The ocean escort, consisting of the United States destroyers *Edison*, *Nicholson*, *Lea* and *Bernadou*, under Commander A. C. Murdaugh USN, steamed south to join from Iceland. Shortly after they took over, at 1305 February 22 two ships were torpedoed and sunk. In the early hours of 24 February, four more were torpedoed and two sank. All day the screen made wide sweeps and aggressive patrols, which continued throughout the night. Two U-boats were sighted in the moonlight and depth-charged, but both escaped. Commander Murdaugh's officers were alert and zealous, but deficient in attack technique.

Escort units, composed usually of two United States destroyers and four Canadian corvettes, directed by such seasoned commanders as W. K. ("Sol") Phillips in *Mayo*, P. R. Heineman in *Benson,* H. C. Fitz in *Niblack,* John B. Heffernan in *Gleaves* and R. W. Hungerford in *Bristol,* were getting the ships across safely — but they were not sinking any U-boats. When March came in like a lion, weather became more deadly than the submarine. A convoy cannot heave-to like a single steamship, because vessels act so differently hove-to that collisions and wide scattering would result. It has to keep going somewhere, somehow. Except for two ships sunk out of Convoy ON–68, the casualties in March were caused by the weather.

2. *The Assault on Coastal and Caribbean Shipping, January–July 1942*

A prompt attack by U-boats on American coastal shipping should have been anticipated, since they had done just that during World War I. No U-boats happened to be in position to raid American coasts when Germany declared war on the United States in December 1941, but Admiral Doenitz chose five of his best "aces" (and followed them by six more) to devastate the American East Coast shipping lanes. These originate in the Saint Lawrence River, cross the Gulf of Maine, pass New York (where at least fifty ships arrived and departed daily), and extend past the Capes of Delaware, the Chesapeake, and Hatteras, into the Caribbean, the Gulf of Mexico, and down past the bulge of Brazil.

Operation PAUKENSCHLAG ("Roll of the Drums"), as the Germans called it, opened on 12 January 1942, when a British steamer was torpedoed and sunk about 300 miles east of Cape Cod by *U–123.* Two days later, enemy submarines moved into the shipping bottleneck off Cape Hatteras. Three tankers in succession were sunk on 14 and 15 January. Next day the U-boats sank a Canadian "Lady boat" and two freighters, then three tankers in succession and three more before the end of the month. Thirteen vessels in all, measuring 95,000 gross tons (and 70 per cent of this tanker tonnage), were lost in a little over two weeks.

No more perfect setup for rapid and ruthless destruction could have been offered the Nazi sea lords. The massacre enjoyed by the U-boats along our Atlantic Coast in 1942 was as much a national disaster as if saboteurs had destroyed half a dozen of our biggest war plants. The damage in the Eastern Sea Frontier was wrought by no more than 12 U-boats operating at any one time, and every month the Germans were building 20 or more new 740- and 500-tonners. Each U-boat carried fourteen torpedoes, including some of the new electrically propelled type that showed no air bubbles in the wake, so could not be sighted or dodged. In addition they carried guns of sufficient caliber to sink most merchant vessels by shellfire alone. The 500-tonners carried enough fuel for a cruise of at least 42 days. Allowing two weeks for the outward passage and the same for homeward to a French port, they could spend two weeks in the Atlantic coastal lanes. Their usual tactics, in the early months of 1942, were to approach a trade route at periscope depth, lie in wait on the surface at night, and launch torpedoes from seaward against a vessel whose silhouette might be seen against shore lights.

One of the most reprehensible failures on our part was the neglect of local communities to dim their waterfront lights, or of military authorities to require them to do so, until three months after the submarine offensive started. When this obvious defense measure was first proposed, squawks went all the way from Atlantic City to southern Florida that the "tourist season would be ruined." Miami and its luxurious suburbs threw up six miles of neon-light glow, against which was silhouetted southbound shipping that hugged the shore to avoid the Gulf Stream. Ships were sunk and seamen drowned in order that the citizenry might enjoy pleasure as usual. Finally, on 18 April 1942, the Eastern Sea Frontier ordered waterfront lights and sky signs doused, and the

Eastern Defense Command of the Army ordered a stringent dim-out on 18 May.

If one or two torpedoes did not fatally hole the attacked ship, the submarine finished her off by shellfire. In the spring, when the nights became shorter and the ineffectiveness of our anti-submarine warfare had been demonstrated, the U-boats became bolder and attacked in broad daylight, even surfaced. Although they invariably attacked without warning, they commonly gave the crew a chance to get away before opening gunfire, and refrained from machine-gunning survivors in lifeboats, as had been done freely in the early part of the war. Survivors were often questioned as to the identity of the ship and the nature of her cargo, were sometimes offered water, provisions or cigarettes and dismissed with a standardized joke about sending the bill to Roosevelt or Churchill. The healthy and sunburned German submariners appeared to be having a glorious field day. They later referred to this period as "the happy time."

This assault temporarily stunned the defense forces of the United States and Canada. Such protection as the Navy furnished to shipping was pitifully inadequate. Destroyers could not be spared from the transatlantic route. The entire antisubmarine fleet when the U-boats struck along the East Coast consisted of three 110-foot wooden subchasers (SC) and two 173-foot patrol craft (PC), together with a score of Eagle boats left over from World War I and a few converted yachts. Orders for sixty PCs and SCs had already been placed, but they were not due for completion until the summer and fall of 1942. Consequently there were no escorts to organize coastal convoys; and Admiral King judged, rightly, that a convoy without escort was worse than no convoy at all. The question has often been asked why the Navy was so unprovided with these indispensable small craft for antisubmarine warfare. The reason was its desperate concentration on building destroyers and larger ships to fight an impending two-ocean war.

Small craft were neglected in the belief that they could be improvised and rapidly reproduced in quantities at small shipbuilding yards. It was the same with antisubmarine aircraft. Vice Admiral Adolphus Andrews, Commander Eastern Sea Frontier — which extended from the Canadian border to Jacksonville, Florida — had no naval planes at his disposal in December capable of searching far out to sea. Offshore air patrol was therefore undertaken by the nine available planes of the Army Air Force. But by 1 April 1942 the antisubmarine patrol had been built up to 84 Army and 86 Navy planes at 19 bases between Bangor, Maine, and Jacksonville.

The total number of Allied, American and neutral merchant vessels sunk in the North Atlantic in January 1942, between our coast and the Western Approaches to the British Isles, was 58; only three of these were in transatlantic convoys. The tonnage lost was 307,059 gross, of which 132,348 tons consisted of tankers of 5,000 to 12,000 tons each; the rest were mostly freighters up to 10,000 tons each. In February, the score was almost identical for the same area; but the sinkings in the Eastern Sea Frontier alone passed the 100,000-ton mark, and new zones were raided: east coast of Florida, and, in the latter half of the month, the Caribbean. Admiral Andrews's attempt to hunt U-boats with two or three destroyers taken out of transatlantic duty was a costly failure. *U-578* sank destroyer *Jacob Jones* off the Delaware Capes on the last day of February.

The aggregate loss increased in March 1942: 28 vessels of 159,340 tons sunk by U-boats in the Eastern Sea Frontier alone; 15 more of 92,321 tons (over half of it tanker tonnage) in the Gulf and Caribbean; 86 vessels and almost half a million gross tons for the entire Atlantic. The coastline from Norfolk to Wilmington was the scene of numerous sinkings. Submarines lay off Diamond Shoals buoy "pickin' 'em off"; at least three U-boats maintained patrol off Cape Hatteras, lying on the bottom by day and hunting at night. Some of the details of these sinkings,

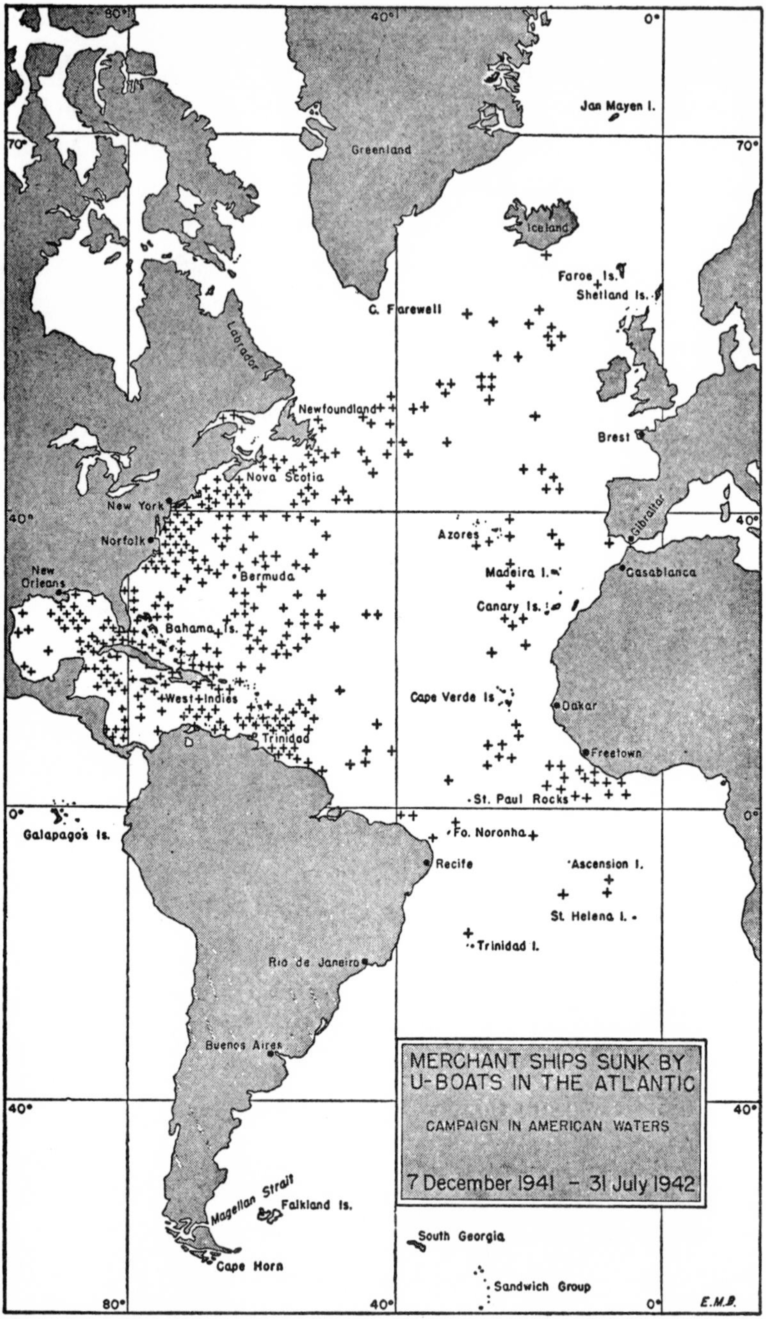
MERCHANT SHIPS SUNK BY U-BOATS IN THE ATLANTIC
CAMPAIGN IN AMERICAN WATERS
7 December 1941 – 31 July 1942
Greenland
Jan Mayen I.
Iceland
Faroe Is.
Shetland Is.
C. Farewell
Labrador
Newfoundland
Nova Scotia
Brest
New York
Norfolk
New Orleans
Bermuda
Bahama Is.
West Indies
Trinidad
Azores
Gibraltar
Madeira I.
Casablanca
Canary Is.
Cape Verde Is.
Dakar
Freetown
St. Paul Rocks
Fo. Noronha
Recife
Ascension I.
St. Helena I.
Trinidad I.
Galapagos Is.
Rio de Janeiro
Buenos Aires
Magellan Strait
Falkland Is.
Cape Horn
South Georgia
Sandwich Group
80°
70°
40°
0°
E.M.B.

especially of the tankers, are pitiful to relate: oil scum ignited by signal flares on life preservers, men attempting to swim in a heavy viscous layer of fuel oil, men trying to swim underwater to avoid flames. A Chilean freighter was torpedoed and sunk 30 miles off Ambrose Channel, New York, and only one man survived. A tugboat and three barges, shelled by *U-574*, sank on the last night of March off Cape Charles and there were only two survivors. The same night, a tanker was sunk off Cape Henry when maneuvering to pick up a pilot; on the following night, between Cape Charles and Cape Henlopen, an unarmed collier was sunk by a submarine's gunfire at a range of about 600 yards. Her crew of 27, denied any opportunity to abandon ship, were slaughtered by machine-gun fire and only three men survived.

A poor substitute for coastal convoys, nicknamed the "bucket brigade," was set up on 1 April 1942. Net-protected anchorages were established at places where there were no harbors, such as Cape Hatteras and Cape Fear, so that ships could be escorted by daylight from one harbor to another by such small craft as were available in the naval districts. By mid-May enough proper escorts were available to organize convoys between New York and Halifax, N.S., and between Hampton Roads and Key West. By August a completely interlocking convoy system had been organized: two main lines (New York–Guantanamo and New York–Key West) with local branch lines from all important points on the East Coast, Gulf, Caribbean, Brazil and West Africa feeding in.

As soon as Admiral Doenitz learned that coastal convoys were being organized along the Eastern Sea Frontier, he diverted U-boats southward, into the Gulf Sea Frontier. Organized 6 February 1942, with headquarters at Key West,[2] this naval frontier covered the Straits of Florida, most of the Bahamas, the entire Gulf of Mexico, the Yucatan Channel and most of Cuba. Available defense

[2] Removed to Miami 17 June 1942.

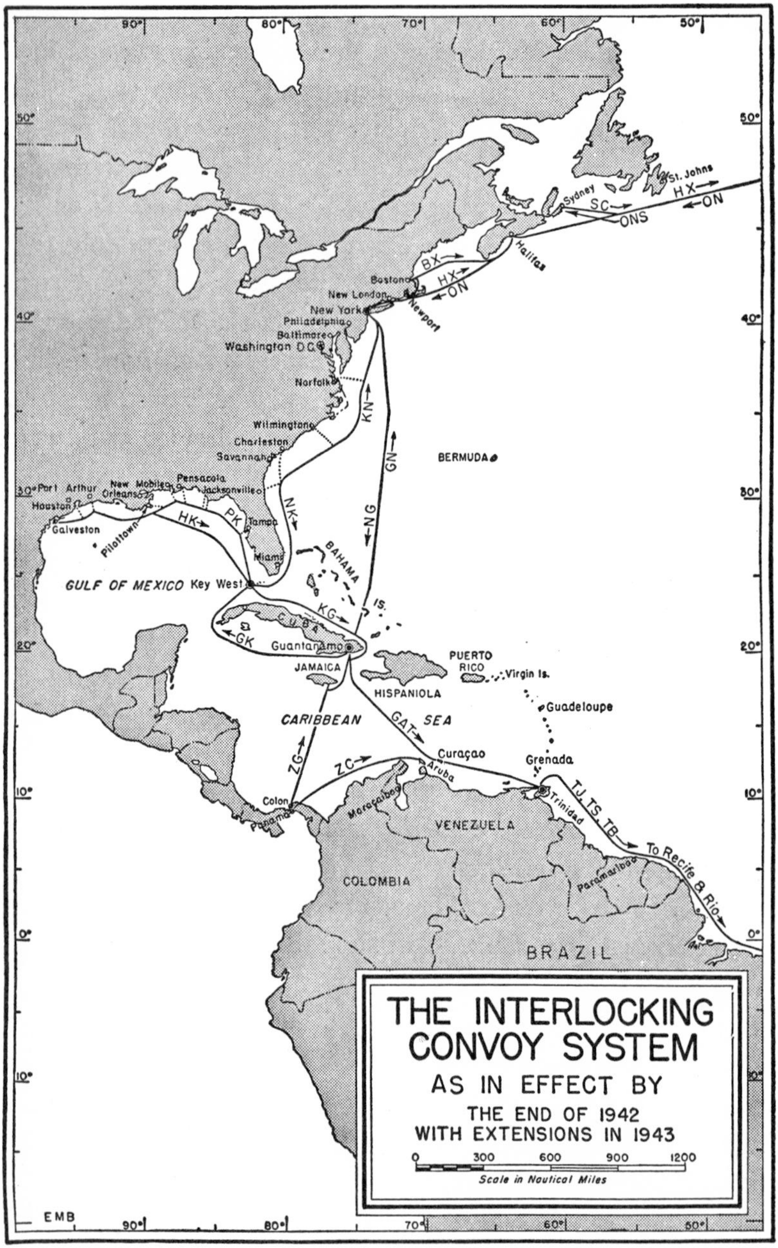

THE INTERLOCKING CONVOY SYSTEM
AS IN EFFECT BY
THE END OF 1942
WITH EXTENSIONS IN 1943
0 300 600 900 1200
Scale in Nautical Miles
GULF OF MEXICO
CARIBBEAN SEA
BERMUDA
BAHAMA IS.
CUBA
JAMAICA
HISPANIOLA
PUERTO RICO
Virgin Is.
Guadeloupe
Grenada
Curaçao
Aruba
Trinidad
VENEZUELA
COLOMBIA
BRAZIL
Paramaribo
Maracaibo
Colon
Panama
Guantanamo
Key West
Miami
Tampa
Pilottown
Galveston
Houston
Port Arthur
New Orleans
Mobile
Pensacola
Jacksonville
Savannah
Charleston
Wilmington
Norfolk
Washington D.C.
Baltimore
Philadelphia
New York
New London
Newport
Boston
Halifax
Sydney
St. Johns
HX
ON
SC
ONS
BX
KN
GN
NG
NK
HK
PK
KG
GK
GAT
ZG
ZC
TJ, TS, TB
To Recife & Rio
EMB

forces were a small converted yacht, three Coast Guard cutters, and, in emergency, the craft used for instruction at the Key West Sound School. Air protection was almost nil. The first U-boat known to enter this frontier, *U-128*, signaled her presence on 19 February 1942 by sinking tanker *Pan Massachusetts* about forty miles SE of Cape Canaveral. Two more ships were sunk on the 21st by *U-504*, and one on the 22nd. This was merely a foretaste of woe. By traveling at night surfaced and submerging during daylight hours, the U-boats bucked the Stream through the Straits of Florida into the Gulf or else chose the Windward Passage—Yucatan Channel route. One of their most fruitful hunting grounds in May and June 1942 lay off the Passes of the Mississippi. This U-boat blitz gave the Gulf Sea Frontier the melancholy distinction of having the most sinkings in May (41 ships, 219,867 gross tons) of any one area in any month during the war, and 55 per cent of this was tanker tonnage, which made it all the worse. And it was wrought by not more than six submarines operating at one time.

The Navy was not idle while these things went on. Every submarine spotted was hunted; but the hunters, few in number, had not yet acquired the necessary technique to kill. Between 8 and 10 May, the following measures were taken: night patrol by a radar-equipped Catalina between Cape Canaveral and Fowey Rocks, a squadron of Hudson bombers based on Jacksonville, and six B-25s staged in to Miami; merchantmen routed from the Canal to New Orleans through the Old Bahama Channel and past Key West. Several of those sunk in the Yucatan Channel, or in the Gulf between there and the Passes, had disregarded routing orders. A detachment of B-25s was sent to Havana, to patrol the Yucatan Channel, and preparations were made to take over the San Julian airfield near Cape San Antonio and to build an airfield on Grand Cayman. A Yucatan Channel patrol began on 21 May.

Rear Admiral James L. Kauffman, appointed Commander Gulf Sea Frontier on 3 June 1942, did much to make this a less profitable hunting ground for U-boats. "Reggie" Kauffman, who had had plenty of experience with submarines in his Iceland command, believed that the best way to sink them was by organized killer groups of properly equipped ships and planes that would go out on any favorable contact and stick to it until they scored. He lost no time in organizing such a group from the frontier craft at his disposal, and between 10 and 13 June they enjoyed a memorable and successful hunt, which in the end sank *U-157*. Everybody enjoyed the hunt and it paid dividends in training and morale; but the experiment was not repeated. For the diversion of large numbers of aircraft and armed vessels for several days left shipping unprotected, and it was proved that better results could be obtained by using the same number of craft to beef-up escort units.

U-boats showed the utmost insolence in the Caribbean, their happiest hunting ground, which they began working over in February. With devilish economy, Admiral Doenitz concentrated on two particularly soft spots — the Dutch islands of Curaçao and Aruba, where over half a million barrels of gasoline and oil derivatives were produced daily; and Trinidad, through or by which most of our shipping to and from South America, and all the bauxite trade, had to pass. Rear Admiral John H. Hoover, Commander Caribbean Sea Frontier at San Juan, had to do the best he could with even less than most sea frontier commanders.

At Aruba, where one Dutch motor whaleboat, three 7.5-inch coast defense guns and a few Army Air Force medium bombers defended this valuable oil industry, a submarine shelled a shore refinery on 16 February 1942. On the same day a successful attack was made on the light-draft tankers that carried oil from Lake Maracaibo to the islands, and on seagoing tankers just departing; six were sunk. *U-161* sneaked into the Gulf of Paria on 18 February, and torpedoed two big ships anchored at Port of Spain. Kapitänleutnant Albrecht Achilles ("Ajax," as this bold bantumweight skipper was called) steamed boldly out through the Bocas, surfaced and showing running lights. He then entered Castries Harbor, Saint Lucia, where *U–161* torpedoed a Canadian passenger steamer and a freighter lying alongside the dock.

A glance at the map will show the peculiar strategic importance of Trinidad. It blocks off the Gulf of Paria, an inland sea which, if properly protected, is an ideal center for handling traffic between the Atlantic and Gulf ports of the United States and the Guianas, Brazil, the River Plate and Africa. Tanker traffic between the Dutch West Indies and Europe or Africa passes the same way. Trinidad itself has an oil industry, and nearby there are oilfields in Venezuela. Port of Spain was the clearinghouse for bauxite, an ore essential for the manufacture of aluminum. The bauxite mines in British and Dutch Guiana were situated up the Demerara, Berbica, Cottica and Surinam Rivers, at the mouths of which were bars that admitted a maximum draft of 17 feet. In order to economize shipping, a small fleet of British and Dutch bauxite ships maintained a shuttle service between the Guianas and Trinidad, where they transferred their cargoes to big ore carriers, diverted from the Great Lakes. Already important at the opening of the war in Europe, Trinidad gradually built up until in 1943 it was one of the world's greatest centers of sea traffic.

The right to establish ground facilities for naval, army and air bases in Trinidad had been ceded to the United States as part of the original destroyer-naval base deal of 2 September 1940. N.O.B. Trinidad was commissioned 1 August 1941, with Captain A. W. Radford USN, our future C.N.O., as commanding officer. During the first few months of the war the chief concern of his command was to push construction, which was delayed by enemy activities, such as the sinking of a freighter that was bringing two million dollars' worth of equipment to Port of Spain. The arrival of *SC–453*, a 110-foot subchaser, first vessel of the "Hummingbird Navy" to be equipped with sound gear, was an event comparable to the addition of an *Essex* class carrier to the Pacific Fleet. But the deadly count went up and up — 31 ships of 154,779 gross tons sunk in the Caribbean Sea Frontier (west) in February and March 1942; 41 ships of 198,034 tons in April and May; 42 ships of 218,623 tons in June and July. During June, German submarines disposed of more shipping in the Gulf, the Caribbean and approaches thereto than they had sunk the world over during any month of 1940-41.

ADMIRAL LOW'S GRAPH OF THE ANTISUBMARINE WAR

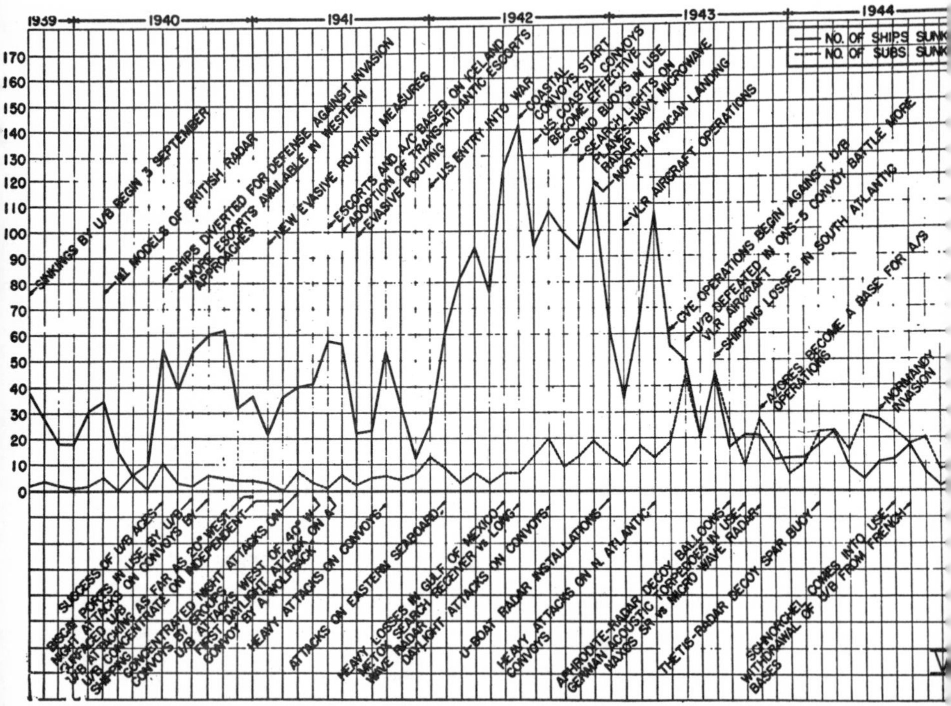

Panama, the only sea frontier with a foot in each ocean, had a baffling task. Relative to its responsibilities and extent, it was the most poorly provided with means of defense. On the Atlantic side alone, this frontier included the entire coast from the Yucatan Peninsula to Punta de Gallinas, Colombia. But its prime, overriding charge was defense of sea approaches to the Panama

Canal and of shipping in transit — the Army protected the Canal from sabotage, land attack or air attack. They also had to cope with a difficult political situation. Only the ten-mile wide Canal Zone was under United States' control; the rest of the frontier was divided among several independent republics, officially at war with Japan and Germany but somewhat dubious as to who would win. In any case, these republics had no naval vessels capable even of inshore patrol; thus, the entire burden of their defense fell on the United States Navy. The same was true of the two republics in Hispaniola. Authorities in the British and Dutch West Indies were most coöperative. Venezuela, Colombia and Mexico were rather "sticky" and the French islands remained stiffly neutral until a commissioner from De Gaulle took over in 1943. Mexico finally declared war on the Axis after one of her fully lighted tankers had been sunk by a U-boat off Miami; Colombia, too, became a loyal ally after some of her small freighters had been sunk. Cuba was our most useful ally in North America, excepting Canada; her fleet of small gunboats took care of her coastal traffic and helped to escort the Florida-Havana seatrains. *CS–13*, an 83-foot Cuban Navy subchaser which sank *U–176* in the Old Bahama Channel in May 1943, was the only small craft of any navy to kill a submarine in American waters.

Enemy submarines entered Panama Sea Frontier in June, 1942, a very favorable moment for attack. Reinforcements for the Pacific Fleet were constantly passing through the Canal. Rear Admiral Clifford E. Van Hook had at his disposal only four old destroyers, *Borie*, *Barry*, *Tattnall* and *Goff;* gunboat *Erie*, two PCs, two small converted motor yachts, and 24 Catalinas. In view of the Japanese attacks on the Aleutians and Midway during the first week of June, the Frontier had to prepare for a possible carrier or submarine raid on the Pacific side, and its most watchful care was extended in that direction. It was a rude shock when *U–159* sank eight ships in four days, two of them right off the Canal entrance. On 17 June, a British tanker bringing diesel oil to Cristobal was shelled by two U-boats and sunk within 75 miles of her destination. Shortly after, two ships were sunk off Santa Marta, and on 2 July the redoubtable "Ajax" Achilles in *U-161* put into Puerto Limon, Costa Rica, and torpedoed a steamer loading at a dock. That concluded this blitz on the Panama Canal approaches. No more than five submarines had disposed of an average of a ship a day for two weeks, and retired without damage — without even being attacked, except from the air.

Many new precautionary and defense measures were now adopted. Puerto Limon was closed by a net. The first Canal Zone–Guantanamo convoy sailed 10 July. Air patrol out of Coco Solo was reinforced with radar-equipped PBYs and so extended that any submarine contact could be followed night and day for 36 hours. Four Catalinas were stationed at Grand Cayman, two at Port Royal Bay, Jamaica, and a few short-range patrol planes operated from Almirante, Panama. VI Army Air Force covered the Colombian Coast and Venezuela up to Curaçao. A seaplane base with tender was set up at Puerto Castillo, Honduras.

Before these measures were completed, a well-coördinated attack resulted in Panama Sea Frontier's first kill. On 11 July net tender *Mimosa*, about 60 miles off Almirante, was attacked by *U-153* with five torpedoes, some of which passed right under her keel. All available ships and planes were then ordered to that position. Destroyer *Lansdowne* (Lieutenant Commander William R. Smedberg III) on the 13th sank *U-153* with four depth charges, fifteen minutes after relieving one of the patrol craft; an exploit that started "Smeddy" on his career to flag rank.

This was only the eighth kill of a German submarine by United States naval forces since we entered the war. The first, of *U-656*, had been made on 1 March 1942 off Cape Race, Newfoundland, by Ensign William Tepuni USNR, when piloting a Lockheed-Hudson of Squadron VP-82 based on Argentia. Donald Francis Mason, Chief Aviation Machinist's Mate of the same squadron, has the credit of the second, *U–503*, on 15 March, near the southeast corner of the Grand Bank of Newfoundland. One month later destroyer *Roper* (Lieutenant Commander H. W. Howe) became the first United States naval vessel to make a kill, of *U–85*, off Wimble Shoal near Hatteras. *U–352* on her first war patrol was caught in shoal water off Cape Lookout by Coast Guard Cutter *Icarus* (Lieutenant Commander Maurice Jester USCG) on 9 May 1942. The other two kills in the first half of 1942 were that of *U–157*, victim of Kauffman's killer hunt, and *U–158*, sunk off Bermuda 30 June. The first two weeks of July brought a couple more, Smedberg's *U–153*, and *U–701*. The latter was caught flatfooted off Diamond Shoal Lightship by an A.A.F. bomber and killed with three depth charges. Eight kills in six and a half months — about as many U-boats as were being produced every ten days!

Admiral Doenitz was naturally delighted with the performance of his boys. On 15 June he reported to Hitler the gratifying number of sinkings compared with the small number of submarines employed, and predicted "vast possibilities through the rapid increase in number of U-boats and the use of supply submarines." He dwelt on the poor quality of American defenses, the heavy destruction of tankers and the failure of new construction to replace shipping losses. In a press interview that summer Doenitz declared: "Our submarines are operating close inshore along the coast of the United States of America, so that bathers and sometimes entire coastal cities are witnesses to that drama of war, whose visual climaxes are constituted by the red glorioles of blazing tankers."

No frantic boast, this; burning tankers were not infrequently sighted from fashionable Florida resorts, and on 15 June two large American freighters were torpedoed by a U-boat within full view of thousands of pleasure-seekers at Virginia Beach.

3. *The Organization of Antisubmarine Warfare*

Having described the havoc wrought by the U-boats during the first six months of the war, we may now relate some of the principle countermeasures adopted, which bore fruit in the latter half of the year and in 1943. Of these, by far the most important were the building of more escort vessels (although the best of these, the DE or destroyer escort, did not come out until 1943), and the interlocking coastal convoys which we have already mentioned.

The amount of study, energy and expense necessary to combat a few hundred U-boats is appalling. The major naval effort of the Allied navies in the Atlantic was so employed for two years. In money terms alone, counting the sunken ships and cargoes, time lost at sea, and expense of operating naval vessels and planes to protect the seaways, the efforts of the American republics and the British Empire amounted to some hundreds of billions of dollars; whilst the lives lost by submarine action reached tens of thousands. Beaten Nazis may take comfort in reflecting that no army, fleet or other unit in World War II, with the exception of their own people who murdered defenseless civilians, wrought such destruction and misery as the U-boats.

There was no administrative center of the Navy's efforts against the U-boats until March 1942, when Admiral King designated Captain Wilder D. Baker to set up an antisubmarine section of his staff in Washington. This section was responsible for matériel, supply, development and training.

An important step toward unified control of merchant shipping was taken on 15 May 1942, when the Convoy and Routing Section of C.N.O., headed by Rear Admiral M. K. Metcalf, became a section of Cominch headquarters. About 1 July "C. and R." assumed full responsibility for the routing and reporting of all merchant shipping in the United States strategic area, and for troop convoys. Cinclant, Admiral Ingersoll, provided the escorts and many of the transports; C. and R. organized the convoy, and, in conjunction with the British Admiralty, laid down its route.

Until Tenth Fleet was organized in May 1943, Admiral Ingersoll directed antisubmarine warfare. Living on board his flagship U.S.S. *Vixen*, steaming from one Atlantic port to another as occasion required, he kept his finger on the U-boat pulse. The public knew nothing of him; even to most of the Atlantic Fleet he remained a shadowy, almost a legendary figure. But to Admiral Ingersoll's sagacity and seasoned "sea-cunning," to use an Elizabethan phrase, the Allied nations owed in large measure their progress against the submarine in 1942-1943.

Besides improved depth charges, which were tossed off a vessel's stern, two ahead-thrown weapons were adopted by the United States Navy in 1942: "hedgehog" and "mousetrap." Hedgehog, adapted from a British design which Captain Paul Hammond USNR called to the attention of the Royal Navy, consisted of a steel cradle from which projected six rows of spigots firing 24 projectiles. As the ship fired these ahead before breaking her sound contact with a submarine, it gave her a better chance of inflicting damage. Depth charges went off at the determined depth, whether they hit anything or not, but hedgehog shells exploded only on contact. The smaller mousetrap, which fired a pattern of four to eight small rocket projectiles, was developed for PCs and SCs. Antisubmarine ships also mounted the usual types of naval ordnance suitable for their burthen. Machine guns proved to be useful in clearing a surfaced submarine's deck, but there is no record of any U-boat being sunk with a gun smaller than 3-inch.

Both the British and ourselves, between the two wars, invented supersonic echo-ranging sound which they called "asdic" and we named "sonar." Housed in a streamlined retractable dome which projected beneath the ship's bottom but was operative only at moderate speeds owing to water noises, sonar could be employed in two ways: listening for the U-boat's propeller noises, and echo-ranging with a sharp "ping" which the U-boat's hull returned, the time giving the range and the direction indicating the bearing. The echo reached the operator with varying degrees of pitch, depending on the nature and movements of the target. This variation in the pitch, known as the "doppler effect," told a trained operator with a sensitive ear whether the target was a ship or a whale, whether it was stationary or moving, and its direction and speed.

In order to thwart sonar, German submarines were equipped with *Pillenwerfer*. This device shot out from a special tube a multitude of small, stationary gas bubbles, which returned an echo similar to that of a submarine. Trained sound operators, however, could detect a submarine's echo from that returned by *Pillenwerfer*. There were many other pitfalls for inexperienced operators. Schools of blackfish, whales, wrecks, coral reefs, and even a layer of water of different temperature echoed in a way which only an expert could distinguish from echoes on a steel hull. Snapping shrimps on the ocean bottom made a curious crackling noise that disturbed sound-listeners. The Navy's monthly *Anti-Submarine Warfare Bulletin* had to print special articles about the habits of cetaceans and crustaceans in order to diminish false alarms.

Intensive training was necessary for a bluejacket to operate sonar, or an officer use it intelligently. Atlantic Fleet Sound School, originally established in 1939, at the submarine base in New London, was shifted to Key West. During the first three months of 1943, 250 officers passed through the eight-weeks course, 1033 enlisted men began basic sound training, and 969 were graduated. In addition, the Key West Sound School trained 1016 officers and men of seven different foreign Navies during the war. And the West Coast Sound School at San Diego kept up a steady enrollment of about 1200 students.

In order to study details of fights with submarines and ascertain the causes of success or failure, an Atlantic Fleet Anti-Submarine Warfare Unit was commissioned 2 March 1942 at Boston. Collection and correlation of data, analysis and deduction, were its primary functions; but it also trained instructors for the Key West Sound School, the Subchaser School at Miami, and for the various "attack teachers," British mechanical devices set up at naval bases from Iceland to Brazil. Thus the Boston Unit became a sort of teachers' college for antisubmarine warfare.

In every aspect of this planetary struggle, men of science worked in laboratories, inventing, developing and testing new weapons, devices and military equipment for the armed forces. One group of civilian scientists worked side by side with naval officers, even on board ships and in planes. This was the Anti-Submarine Warfare Operations Research Group (Asworg), an offshoot of the National Defense Research Committee. James B. Conant, then President of Harvard University, and other scientists, visited England during the Battle for Britain and returned convinced that one of the main factors which saved England from destruction under the long sustained assaults of the Luftwaffe was a group of "operational" scientists, working closely with R.A.F. fighter command to coördinate coast warning radar with fighter plane defense. As Professor P. M. S. Blackett pointed out, "Relatively too much scientific effort has been expended hitherto in the *production* of new devices and too little in the *proper use* of what we have got." When assigned to antisubmarine warfare, scientists were called upon to answer such questions as "What pattern of depth charges at what settings has the best mathematical chance of killing a submarine? What sort of track should a ship steer to have best chance of regaining a lost underwater contact? How large an expanse of ocean, under varying atmospheric conditions, can a ship or a plane profitably patrol in one hour? What disposition of escorts around a convoy gives optimum protection?" Answers to these and a thousand other questions on antisubmarine warfare could not be left to mere trial and error, or the Battle of the Atlantic might be lost before the right answer was found. And it was not sufficient for scientists to invent a new device; they must observe its use in action, in order to make improvements.

At Captain Baker's suggestion, Asworg was organized 1 April 1942, with Professor Philip M. Morse, sound physicist of M.I.T., as director. Asworg was centered at Washington, but individual members were sent to Norfolk, Argentia, sea frontier headquarters, Trinidad and Brazil. And very important work was done at these outlying bases. It sounds odd today, when all armed services are scientifically indoctrinated; but in 1942 "practical seamen" had a deep suspicion of "long-haired scientists" that had to be overcome. Dr. Morse, however, "sold" Asworg by laying down the principle that no scientist was to claim credit for anything, since he took no responsibility for the ultimate decision; that his duty was simply to help the fighting Navy improve its antisubmarine technique.

The Asworg mathematicians and analysts worked out a whole complex of search problems, including patterns of "box search" by ships, on Greek key patterns, for regaining underwater contact with a submarine; they worked up data on effective search speed, altitude, and airborne time for patrol planes; they proved that three destroyers searching abreast were more than three times as effective as a single destroyer, that an "air umbrella" over a convoy gave far less protection than a wide-ranging air search on front and flanks; they drafted blueprints for the Atlantic Narrows air patrol that caught several German blockade runners, and for the Straits of Gibraltar patrol; they worked up countermeasures which stymied the German acoustic torpedo as soon as it appeared.

Radar was invented by Sir Robert Watson-Watt, but some of its developments and refinements were produced in the United States from sheer necessity. By the summer of 1942 almost every combatant ship in the Atlantic Fleet had been equipped with some form of radar, and an improved model, the SG — in which the scope gives a picture of what lay ahead — had passed the test of experiment and was ready to be installed in October. For aircraft, the value of radar was even greater than for ships, because it enabled planes to pick up a surfaced submarine far beyond visible distance, to deliver a surprise attack, and to home in other planes and ships. The first sets installed in planes were on meter-wave. The Germans invented a search receiver for it which ended its usefulness as a detecting device, and inventing a microwave plane radar to take its place became urgent. That was done, and a variety of 10-cm sets did the trick; the Germans never could figure out a way to detect or jam these. Microwave radar made possible the large number of kills by aircraft in the spring and early summer of 1943. Hitler referred to it peevishly, in his New Year's 1944 address, as "one invention of our enemy" which had thwarted his submarine fleet.

A convoy is no stronger than its ears and eyes. Radar furnished our convoys with cat's eyes, sonar with ears, while the high-frequency direction-finders (HF/DF, pronounced "Huff-Duff"), by picking up and plotting radio transmissions of U-boats at sea, acted as highly sensitive, elongated cat's whiskers. The Royal Navy was the first to adopt this method of locating submarines. Estimated positions of U-boats, plotted at Washington and London, were sent out to sea on "Fox" schedule, which was a secret radio bulletin transmitted several times a day on a fixed schedule. While HF/DF fixes were seldom accurate within 50 or 100 miles, they enabled an escort commander to order an evasive change of course which, by Admiral Doenitz's admission, frequently frustrated his wolf-packs.

There is no better example of the effectiveness of the land-based HF/DF than that of the following submarine kill. About noon 30 June 1942, HF/DF ranges were obtained by the stations at Bermuda, Hartlant Point, Kingston and Georgetown. Operations officers at N.O.B. Bermuda plotted the bearings, which made a perfect fix. Lieutenant Richard E. Schreder USNR in a Mariner of Squadron VP–74, patrolling out of Bermuda, was then about fifty miles away. Immediately notified, he laid his course accordingly and found *U–158* idling on the surface with the crew sunning themselves on deck. He dropped a depth charge which stuck to the superstructure and detonated as the submarine went down, for keeps.

The next step was the shipborne HF/DF, which began to be installed in key escort vessels in October 1942. The Germans long ignored the danger of this to them; their U-boats continued to chatter among themselves and to Doenitz when closing a convoy, thus revealing their position.

As the number of escort craft increased it was necessary to provide special training for the young reservists who were to man them. A Submarine Chaser Training Center was commissioned at Miami in March 1942, with Lieutenant Commander E. F. McDaniel as commandant. His school opened with about 50 pupils, but by 1 January 1944 10,396 officers and 37,574 enlisted men had been trained there for the United States Navy alone. These included the crews of 285 DEs, 256 PCs, 397 SCs, and 150 other craft. McDaniel was a lean, thin-lipped officer whose eyes burned with hatred of the enemy and all his works, and whose heart glowed with devotion to the Navy, especially the antisubmarine part of it. He had a sense of organization and a natural teaching ability. His "faculty," like his "student body," was constantly changing; for McDaniel would have for instructors none but officers who had actually hunted submarines, and back to sea they went after a few months.

Before this Miami institution was many months old, the United States began to deliver subchasers under lend-lease to Allied European and American nations, and the task of training their crews too was thrown on McDaniel. In 1942-1943, 360 officers and 1374 men were trained there for fourteen different foreign navies.

4. *Air Power, Auxiliaries and Amateurs*

The Army Air Force, which controlled almost the entire supply of United States military land-based planes in 1941, did not expect to include antisubmarine warfare among its duties. Army pilots were not trained to fly over water or protect shipping or bomb small moving targets like submarines. And the Navy did not have the planes to fill the rôle so successfully assumed by the British Coastal Command. This was due not to lack of foresight, but to a principle decided on in 1920, that the Army should control land-based and the Navy sea-based aviation. Consequently the Army received the entire American production of military land planes; while the Navy received the entire production of seaplanes and carrier types, and the numbers were inadequate for both kinds. When British experience showed the value of large land-based bombers in antisubmarine warfare, the Army modified this agreement. On 7 July 1942, General Marshall consented to a reallocation of production that promised the Navy a fair share of Liberators and other long-range bomber types. But by that time the submarines had done their worst off the Atlantic Coast.

The Navy badly wanted four-engined land-based bombers for antisubmarine work, and the Army responded to the best of its ability. By the end of July 1942, the Army had 141 planes available for antisubmarine work in Eastern Sea Frontier, and the naval air arm had grown to 178 planes and 7 blimps. These were spread among 26 fields along the coast from Argentia to Jacksonville.

This coverage was far from effective, partly because the Army and Navy had different communications system, partly because of a deficient command organization. At General Marshall's suggestion, Antisubmarine Army Air Command was formed in October 1942, with Brigadier General Westside T. Larson as commander. Admiral King, however, had no intention of permanently sharing with the Army what he considered to be a naval responsibility, the protection of shipping. He conceived of Army participation in antisubmarine air warfare as a temporary expedient. So, as fast as the Navy obtained land-based planes and trained pilots, they were moved into sea frontiers and Iceland and Greenland, to relieve the Army Air Force of this special duty. But it should be remembered that the Army Air Force came to the Navy's assistance at a critical moment, stood by as long as it was needed, contributed to the technique of antisubmarine warfare, and killed several submarines.

The naval air squadrons based at Argentia, under the successive command of Rear Admirals Bristol and Brainard, were particularly useful in covering convoys during the critical moment of changing escort groups, and also in killing submarines. Amphibious Catalinas found a new sphere of usefulness in air-sea rescue work, and by the time the war ended many were trained and equipped for that purpose alone. Throughout the war, the PBY was the Navy's workhorse of the air. It did everything — search, reconnaissance, transport, bombing, rescue. It was slow, ungainly, a big target for the enemy — but what a plane!

Air search and attack, because of the delicate instruments and the mathematical factors involved, were peculiarly subject to improvement through the efforts of the operational scientists. The Navy set up early in 1943 the Anti-Submarine Development Detachment (Asdevlant) at Quonset Point, Rhode Island, to which many scientists were attached. This opened a new and brilliant chapter for naval air in antisubmarine warfare.

In addition to the efforts, methods and procedures to master the U-boats that we have already described, there were several auxiliary operations which accomplished little good, yet must be mentioned for their brave efforts. Probably the most useful was the Northern Ship Lane Patrol, consisting of big converted yachts such as *Migrant* and *Guinevere*, which patrolled the main convoy routes to a considerable distance off shore, and reported some useful information on submarines that enabled convoys to elude them. Second was the Coastal Picket Patrol, nicknamed the "Hooligan Navy." Organized by the Coast Guard in May 1942, this consisted of auxiliary yachts and motor boats under 100 feet in length. These were taken over by the Coast Guard, often with their civilian owners as skippers, manned mostly by yachtsmen who could not pass qualifications for the Navy, armed with small guns and depth charges, and sent forth to hunt U-boats. This was too late to help repel Doenitz's first blitz along the East Coast, but they patrolled faithfully during the hard winter of 1942-1943. The "Hooligans" were too small, slow and feebly armed to make any kills. At top strength, in February 1943, there were no fewer than 550 of these boats patrolling between Eastport, Maine, and Galveston, Texas. From that time the numbers were progressively reduced, and their duties assumed by 83-foot Coast Guard cutters.

The Civil Air Patrol, organized in March 1942, was much the same thing in the air. Civilian pilots ineligible for the armed forces — some even veterans of World War I with wooden legs — contributed their planes and their services, and many of the ground crews were women. All served without pay. At the height of its strength the C.A.P. had several hundred planes operating from bases between Bar Harbor, Maine and Corpus Christi, Texas. They never killed a submarine, but they spotted survivors from sinkings in rafts and lifeboats, and performed many auxiliary services for the armed forces. Down to September 1943, when it was disbanded, C.A.P. had reported the positions of 173 enemy submarines, 91 vessels in distress, and rafts or lifeboats containing 363 survivors.

In addition to their direct services, the C.A.P. and the "Hooligans" trained hundreds of young boys to be pilots, sailors and coastguardsmen. Both organizations are outstanding examples of fusing civilian with military effort. At least 90 per cent of their personnel consisted of men and women who had to earn their livings, and who could have made big money in war industries or the merchant marine. But they were people who wanted to serve, not to gain; they proved that the call to work and sacrifice is stronger, and produces better service, than the lure of money.

There was also a "Mystery" or "Q" ship project which consumed an inordinate amount of effort and lost the lives of about one quarter of the sailors who volunteered, without accomplishing anything. These were heavily armed vessels disguised as peaceful merchantmen which, on the approach of a U-boat, were supposed to unmask powerful batteries and sink the submarine. The Q ships had done some good in World War I, but not nearly so much as the thriller books written about them claimed; and the U-boats of World War II were too fast and smart to be taken in by such a ruse. Nevertheless, in early 1942, the situation was so serious that Admiral King very reluctantly, in response to pressure from President Roosevelt, organized a Mystery Ship program. The first three sailed from New England ports in March. U.S.S. *Atik* was sunk with all hands by a U-boat off the Capes of the Chesapeake when only four days out. *Foam* met a similar fate in May off Nova Scotia. Two others which never made a contact and a third which made three unsuccessful attacks were finally converted to weather-reporting ships; and a fourth, a three-masted schooner, almost sank in a hurricane and was decommissioned.

The building of new merchant ships to replace and surpass those lost by enemy action, under the Maritime Commission and the War Shipping Administration Board headed by Rear Admiral Emory S. Land, was highly successful, and got under way before formal war began. The first Liberty ship of 10,800 deadweight tonnage, *Patrick Henry*, was launched in September 1941; the first Victory ship, of about the same size but 50 per cent faster, two years later. In 1942, 727 ships of 55.5 million tons were constructed. By April 1943 the Maritime Commission was building 140 ships of a million tons per month; and by the end of the year these figures were doubled and the time of construction had been lowered from 244 days to an average of 42 days for a Liberty. These ships were manned by merchant mariners, for whom training schools had to be organized.

Although the best protection of merchant ships from the enemy was to travel in convoy, many had to ply routes for which no escort could be spared, and sailed alone. For their protection, the Navy began in early 1942 to provide merchantmen with one or more guns and a naval armed guard of bluejackets. This led to a great deal of friction between the merchant mariners and the naval ratings who were not under union control or interested in pay, bonuses or overtime.[3] Of course the merchant marine might have been absorbed by the Navy or made an auxiliary service like the famous Seabees. This was not done, mainly for two reasons. It would have antagonized the National Maritime Union, headed by the truculent Joe Curran; and it would have required far more man power; naval regulations would have about doubled the number of each crew. And many "ancient mariners" with decayed teeth or ruptures, who made good seamen for a merchant ship, could never have passed the Navy's physical requirements.

As the war continued, naval armed guards and ships' crews, facing a common danger, learned to coöperate; and there were several instances of armed merchant vessels driving off and even sinking submarines.

By June of 1942 the United States Navy and the Army Air Force were coming to grips with the U-boat problem, but were far

[3] The Navy bluejackets' pay started at $50 per month; the merchant seaman's at $100 for a 44-hour week (85 cents for every hour over that), plus $100 war bonus in the Atlantic, plus various sums around $100 for each different combat area entered. On 15 Mar. 1943 this last bonus, greatly to the indignation of the National Maritime Union, was commuted to a flat rate of $125 per man for every air raid occurring when the ship was in port, whether or not the ship was hit. Although the merchant seaman was not paid when on the beach, continuous employment was guaranteed during the war. He did not, however, receive the family allowances and retirement pay of the naval seaman.

from attaining mastery. The shortage of escorts was still critical; no DE had yet joined the Fleet. No killer groups of escort carriers had yet been organized. On the other side, Admiral Doenitz had not exhausted his repertoire, and tough days were to come for the convoys. The Admiral, who relieved Raeder as commander in chief of the German Navy in January 1943, later regarded the next two months as the peak of U-boat achievement.

A fair example of a transatlantic convoy crossing in June 1942 and of the comparatively slight improvement in antisubmarine warfare to that time, is furnished by the story of Convoy ONS–102, from Londonderry to Halifax. There were 63 ships in eleven columns, protected by nine escorts — U.S.S. *Leary*, three big Coast Guard cutters, one Canadian destroyer, and four Canadian corvettes. Commander P. R. Heineman was escort commander in U.S.C.G.C. *Campbell*. Speed of advance was 8 knots. At 0725 June 16, two contacts were made through HF/DF, and two escorts were detached to run them down. Both made unsuccessful depth-charge attacks, but the convoy was left at peace that night. The following night two U-boats managed to worm in between the convoy columns, and at 0125 torpedoed a ship. A few minutes later *Campbell*, patrolling two and a half miles ahead, sighted a submarine headed for the convoy, distant 500 yards. This U-boat submerged and was depth-charged, unsuccessfully. Admiral Brainard, at Argentia, Newfoundland, now sent four Canadian corvettes to help Heineman. One of them, H.M.C.S. *Agassiz*, sighted a U-boat a mile ahead at 2242 June 20. It dove, and *Agassiz* attacked with depth charges, one of which made such a terrific explosion that several merchantmen thought themselves torpedoed and fired star shell. The resulting illumination revealed a second submarine in the middle of the convoy. The nearest merchant ship, which had a naval armed guard, attacked with gunfire and forced it to submerge. Escorts dashed about the now brightly illuminated convoy throwing depth charges to no purpose. Radar broke down, and the U-boat escaped. Convoy ONS–102 was lucky to get through with the loss of but one ship.

Commander Heineman, one of the best of our escort commanders, was red-faced about the whole thing, and reported seven different classes of errors that prevented him from getting a U-boat. The most important was the lack of uniform antisubmarine doctrine. Escort vessels needed a definite set of principles concerning how to hunt a submerged U-boat in order to make best use of available detection gear and weapons. A good beginning was made by the issuance on 9 July 1942 of a Cominch information bulletin on antisubmarine warfare, the result of intensive study by officers of the Boston Anti-Submarine Warfare Unit and its attached scientists. In clear, precise language it described the German submarine and its capabilities, and laid down rules and methods for escort-of-convoy and patrol operations, for sound, sight and radar searching, and for surface, air and joint attacks.

Looking backward, the increasing number of escorts, uniform doctrine, the training and analysis systems set up, and plain hard experience seem to be the most important contributions toward controlling the U-boat menace during the first half of that woeful year 1942. Convoys were increasingly successful in protecting trade routes, but escorts were not killing enough U-boats. Only 21 of these, together with seven Italian submarines, were sunk by both Allied navies during the first six months of 1942; and only five of these kills were by United States forces. During the same period Germany built 123 new U-boats, and in June 1942 there were 60 of them, on an average, patrolling the Atlantic.

This period of antisubmarine warfare closed with a stern warning, delivered by General Marshall to Admiral King on 19 June 1942:

The losses by submarines off our Atlantic seaboard and in the Caribbean now threaten our entire war effort. The following statistics bearing on the subject have been brought to my attention.

> Of the 74 ships allocated to the Army for July by the War Shipping Administration, 17 have already been sunk. Twenty-two per cent of the Bauxite fleet has already been destroyed. Twenty per cent of the Puerto Rican fleet has been lost. Tanker sinkings have been 3.5 per cent per month of tonnage in use.
>
> We are all aware of the limited number of escort craft available, but has every conceivable improvised means been brought to bear on this situation? I am fearful that another month or two of this will so cripple our means of transport that we will be unable to bring sufficient men and planes to bear against the enemy in critical theatres, to exercise a determining influence on the war.

Admiral King's and the Navy's response to this challenge will be related in a later chapter. For we must now turn to the Pacific, where the tide of war had already turned in the great Battle of Midway.

CHAPTER VI

Carrier Strikes, Coral Sea and Midway

December 1941–June 1942

1. *Wake Island and the Tokyo Raid, December 1941–April 1942*

"THE PACIFIC SITUATION is very grave," signaled President Roosevelt to Winston Churchill on 9 March 1942. The first four months of 1942 were the grimmest period of the war for the Allies, everywhere. It looked as if America's entry would mean only one more victim for the Axis and Japan to strike down and tear apart. In Eastern Europe, after a winter's stalemate, the German armies had resumed their victorious advance toward the Caucasus. Crippling attacks by U-boats and Italian midget subs in Alexandria Harbor had reduced the British Mediterranean Fleet to a squadron of cruisers and destroyers. In the broad Atlantic and the Caribbean, merchant shipping was being sunk by submarines much faster than it could be replaced. In the Middle East, Hitler had turned Rommel loose on the British, with devastating effects. In the Far East, the Japanese were about to throw the Americans, British and Dutch out of their last strongholds. Then came a ray of light for the Allies out of the Coral Sea, dawn broke over Midway, Russia successfully defended Moscow and Stalingrad, Auchinleck won the First Battle of El Alamein in the Libyan desert, and hope returned to the forces of freedom.

In the Central Pacific, the first few months after Pearl Harbor were dark indeed. Wake Island, the most important outpost between Oahu and Guam, was garrisoned by a little over 500 officers and men, mostly Marines, under Commander W. Scott Cunningham USN and Major James Devereux USMC. With the help of a squadron of fighter planes and a few coast defense guns, none larger than 5-inch, they beat off a Japanese invasion on 11 December — the only occasion in the entire war when an amphibious assault was thrown back with loss. But the Japanese came back with greater force on 23 December, and captured Wake, after a strong Naval relief force under Rear Admiral Frank Jack Fletcher, built around carrier *Saratoga,* had been recalled by Cincpac.[1] The American combatant prisoners were sent to Shanghai, the Japanese commander beheading a couple of them en route to amuse his men. About one hundred civilian workers were detained on Wake, to work for the enemy. These were later executed.

On the last day of 1941, when Admiral King became Cominch at Washington, Admiral Chester W. Nimitz became Cincpac. At his first meeting with Admiral Kimmel's former staff at Pearl Harbor, he assured them of his confidence and announced that they would serve him too. That act alone raised morale at Pearl Harbor from an all-time low. Nimitz, calm in demeanor and courteous in speech, with blue eyes, a pink complexion, and tow-colored hair turning white, was a fortunate appointment. He restored confidence to the decimated Pacific Fleet. He had the prudence to wait through a lean period; to do nothing rash for the sake of doing something. He had the capacity to organize both a fleet and a vast war theater, the tact to deal with sister services and Allied commands, the leadership to weld his own subordinates into a great fighting team, the courage to take necessary risks, and the

[1] Admiral William S. Pye, who had relieved Admiral Kimmel. This fiasco, however, was more the fault of Admiral Fletcher, who wasted time on unnecessary fueling, when he should have pressed on to relieve Wake.

wisdom to select, from a variety of intelligence and opinions, the correct strategy to defeat Japan.

For the time being nothing was practicable but hit-and-run raids, such as the British were making in Europe. In the Pacific, aircraft carriers served this strategy of weakness. Admiral Halsey's *Enterprise* group raided Kwajalein in the Marshall Islands on 1 February 1942, sank a transport, badly damaged nine other ships and killed the Japanese atoll commander. Next, Admiral Wilson Brown's *Lexington* group raided Rabaul. The Japanese air force based there hit back, and on 20 February an air battle between Japanese and American planes was joined. Our airmen won this round, John S. Thach and "Butch" O'Hare particularly distinguishing themselves. On 10 March Wilson Brown, his force augmented by *Yorktown,* launched planes from a point off Port Moresby, and flew them over the Owen Stanley Range to pound the Japanese at Lae and Salamaua on the north coast of Papua.

That raid, however, paled in comparison with the Halsey-Doolittle one on Tokyo, in April. As the Fleet then had no carrier bombers with enough range to operate from outside the limit of the Japanese offshore air patrol, the Army Air Force lent sixteen B–25 Mitchells, which made a deckload for carrier *Hornet* (Captain Marc A. Mitscher). *Enterprise* (Captain George D. Murray) went along to provide combat air patrol; Rear Admiral Raymond A. Spruance commanded the cruisers and Captain Richard Conolly the destroyers of the screen. Although B–25 pilots could be trained to take off from a carrier, the deck was too short for recovery; so the planes had to fly 668 miles from *Hornet*'s launching point to Tokyo, bomb the city, and thence fly another 1100 miles to friendly Chinese airfields. The strike group, led by Lieutenant Colonel James H. Doolittle USA, were airborne by 0824 April 18, and over the city by noon. They completely surprised the Japanese, as we had been surprised by them at Pearl Harbor, and not one B–25 was lost over Japan; but some made crash landings in China or splashed off the coast, and two pilots picked up by the Japanese were executed — an unpleasant practice which persisted through the Pacific war, and led to some of the officers responsible being hanged when it was over.

This "answer to Pearl Harbor" did not inflict one thousandth part of the damage it was supposed to revenge; but it gave the American public, which had had nothing but bad news for nineteen weeks, a great lift. The Japanese authorities, who never guessed where the bombers came from (President Roosevelt's announcement that they flew from "Shangri-la" didn't help much) pinned down hundreds of planes to defend Tokyo. And, what is more important, the event expedited plans for an overextension that led to the Japanese defeat at Midway.

2. *The Battle of the Coral Sea, 3–8 May 1942*

"Strategic Over-stretch" Captain Liddell Hart calls it; "Victory Disease" a Japanese admiral named it after the war. Imperial General Headquarters, not content with the most rapid, stupendous conquest made in modern times, now embarked on a plan for still further aggression. First, Tulagi in the Solomons and Port Moresby in Papua would be seized to secure air mastery of the Coral Sea. The Combined Fleet would cross the Pacific to "annihilate" the United States Pacific Fleet, and at the same time capture Midway Island and the Western Aleutians; then set up a "ribbon defense" anchored at Attu, Midway, Wake, and the Marshalls and Gilberts. This effort, had it not been thwarted by the Battle of Midway, would have been followed by invasion of New Caledonia, the Fijis and Samoa, to isolate Australia.

The one really sound part of this grandiose plan, even though it failed, was Admiral Yamamoto's challenge to the Pacific Fleet. He knew that the destruction of the Fleet must be completed before 1943, when American war production would make it too late. With Pacific Fleet wiped out, Japan could make her ribbon defense impregnable and organize her conquests; Americans would tire of a futile war and negotiate a peace which would leave Japan master of the Pacific. Such was the plan and the confident expectation of the war lords in Tokyo.

The Coral Sea is one of the world's most beautiful bodies of water. Typhoons pass it by; the southeast trades blow fresh across its surface almost the entire year, raising whitecaps which build up to long surges that crash on Australia's Great Barrier Reef in a 1500-mile line of white foam. Lying between the Equator and the Tropic of Capricorn, it knows no winter, and the summer is never uncomfortably hot. The islands on the eastern and northern verges — New Caledonia, the New Hebrides, the Louisiades — are lofty, jungle-clad and ringed with coral beaches and reefs. Here the interplay of bright sunlight, pure air and transparent water may be seen at its best; peacock-hued shoals over the coral gardens break off abruptly from an emerald-hued fringe into deeps of brilliant amethyst. Under occasional overcasts the Coral Sea becomes a warm dove-gray instead of assuming the bleak dress of the ocean in high latitudes. Only in its northern bight — the Solomon Sea — does the Coral Sea wash somber shores of lava and volcanic ash. That bight had been dominated by Japan since January 1942, from her easily won base at Rabaul. It was now time, in the view of her war planners, that she swing around the New Guinea bird's tail, and move into the dancing waters of the broad Coral Sea.

Cincpac Intelligence smoked out the gist of this plan by 17 April, and Admiral Nimitz saw to it that Task Force 17, a two-carrier group (*Lexington* and *Yorktown*) under Rear Admiral Fletcher, was there to spoil it. That is why the Coral Sea, where no more serious fights had taken place in days gone by than those between trading schooners and Melanesian war canoes, became the scene of the first great naval action between aircraft carriers — the first naval battle in which no ship on either side sighted the other.

The Japanese operation plan was not simple; her naval strategists believed in dividing forces. There were three main divisions: (1) a left prong (Rear Admiral Shima) to occupy Tulagi in the lower Solomons and establish a seaplane base whence Nouméa could be neutralized; (2) a right prong (Rear Admiral Kajioka's Port Moresby invasion group, floating a sizeable army in a dozen transports, covered by heavy cruisers and light carrier *Shoho*) to start from Rabaul, whip through Jomard Passage in the Louisiades, and capture Port Moresby; (3) Vice Admiral Takagi's big carrier striking force, including *Shokaku* and *Zuikaku*, veterans of Pearl Harbor, to enter the Coral Sea from the East, and destroy anything the Allies might offer to interfere with this plan. The whole was to be directed from Rabaul by Commander in Chief Fourth Fleet, Vice Admiral Inouye.

Admiral Nimitz did not have even half this force at his disposal; but he put together under Admiral Fletcher's command all he had and gave him no more specific orders than to stop the enemy. Fletcher in *Lexington*, familiar with the Coral Sea, came steaming west from Pearl Harbor. *Yorktown*, already known as the "Waltzing Matilda of the Pacific Fleet," was ordered to cut short a period of upkeep at Tongatabu, waltz over to the Coral Sea, and rendezvous with "Lady Lex." Most of the ships of "MacArthur's Navy," not yet named Seventh Fleet, also joined. These were three cruisers — H.M.A.S. *Australia* and *Hobart*, U.S.S. *Chicago* — and a few destroyers, under the command of Rear Admiral J. G. Crace RN.

The ensuing action was full of mistakes, both humorous and tragic, wrong estimates and assumptions, bombing the wrong ships, missing great opportunities and cashing in accidentally on minor ones.

The Japanese won the first trick. Admiral Shima's group occupied Tulagi unopposed, on 3 May. They took the second, too, on 4 May, when *Yorktown*'s planes bombed Tulagi and did only minor damage. At the same time, however, Japan missed her best chance to win this game, through false economy. To save an extra ferrying mission, *Shokaku* and *Zuikaku* were ordered to deliver nine fighter planes to Rabaul; this delayed the two big carriers two days, so that on the 4th they were too far away to counterattack Fletcher.

Nothing much happened on the 5th and 6th, when each big carrier force was searching for its enemy without success. At one time they were only 70 miles apart. That 6th day of May, when General Wainwright surrendered Corregidor in the Philippines, marked the low point of the entire war for American arms. But the next day opened with a bright dawn. This transition from Corregidor to the Coral Sea is startling and dramatic.

At dawn on the 7th *Shokaku* and *Zuikaku* sent out a search mission for an enemy force they suspected to be in the Coral Sea. The search planes sighted Fletcher's retiring fueling group, fleet oiler *Neosho* and destroyer *Sims*, and made the second big mistake of this error-crowded battle by reporting them to be a carrier and a cruiser. Admiral Takagi promptly ordered an all-out bombing attack on this hapless couple and sank them both. This caused Rear Admiral Hara, the carrier division commander under Takagi, "much chagrin," cost him six planes, and saved the American carriers from attack.

The American planes, however, were off on a similar wild-goose chase. That particular "boo-boo" had resulted from the report of a *Yorktown* search plane, at 0815 May 7, of "two carriers and four heavy cruisers" about 175 miles northwest of the American force. Fletcher, naturally assuming that this meant Takagi's Striking Force, launched full deckloads to go after it. When these aircraft were already airborne it was discovered that the "two carriers and four heavy cruisers," owing to a disarrangement of the pilot's code contact pad, should have been reported as "two heavy cruisers and two destroyers." [2] Nevertheless, by good luck the *Lexington* and *Yorktown* fliers encountered light carrier *Shoho*, piled in on her, and put her under in a matter of ten minutes — a record for the entire war. "Scratch one flattop!" signaled *Lexington*'s dive-bomber commander.

It was not the right flattop, but the loss of *Shoho* so discouraged Admiral Inouye that he ordered the Port Moresby invasion group, instead of pressing on through Jomard Passage, to jill around at a safe distance north of the Louisiades. Thus, our attack on the wrong carrier thwarted the enemy's main object.

More grim humor on the 7th was furnished by "Crace's Chase." Fletcher gallantly weakened his carriers' screen by detaching Rear Admiral Crace RN with his two Australian cruisers, U.S.S. *Chicago* and a few destroyers, to find and attack the Port Moresby invasion force. Crace handled this mixed group so efficiently as to beat off 31 land-based bombers from Rabaul without receiving a scratch; and he also fought off three United States Army Air Force B–17s from the Townsville (Queensland) base, which thought his ships were Japanese. To cap this comedy, the thwarted Japanese planes claimed to have sunk two battleships and a heavy cruiser.

Toward evening of the same day, 7 May, Takagi sent a search-attack mission to find and bomb Fletcher's carriers. They missed the flattops, but had a rough experience. First they were intercepted by Fletcher's fighter planes and lost nine of their number; then, after dark, six tried to land on *Yorktown*, mistaking her for Japanese; and eleven more were lost trying to make night landings on their own carriers.

[2] Post-battle information downgraded this contact still more, to two old light cruisers and three converted gunboats, which were escorting a seaplane tender to one of the Louisiades.

On 8 May came the payoff. The two major carrier groups under Fletcher and Takagi (or, to use the actual O.T.C.'s of the carriers, Fitch and Hara),[3] which had been fumbling for one another for the better part of three days and nights, finally came to grips. Each located the other and attacked. Never were forces more even. The Japanese admiral with the Irish name had 121 planes; "Jakey" Fitch had 122. Hara had a screen of four heavy cruisers and six destroyers; Fitch, now Crace was away, had but one more of each type. Nature, however, gave the Japanese carriers one great advantage. They were in a belt of heavy overcast which had moved into the Coral Sea from the Solomons, whilst the Americans were out in the clear under brilliant sunshine. Thus, the *Yorktown* attack group, 41 planes strong, missed *Zuikaku* under a rain squall, concentrated on *Shokaku* and obtained only two bomb hits; but one of these bent the flight deck so that she could no longer launch planes. Half *Lexington*'s attack group failed to find the fog-enshrouded enemy; the other half gave *Shokaku* another bomb hit. Takagi, who by this time (noon 8 May) believed that both American carriers were sinking, decided he could dispense with the damaged carrier and sent her back to Truk.

His assumption was about half correct. The Japanese attack group, amounting to about 70 planes, gave both American carriers a severe working-over. *Yorktown* took one bomb hit which killed 66 men; *Lexington* took two torpedoes and two bomb hits. The end of the battle found "Lady Lex" listing, with three fires burning but her power plant intact. There was every prospect of damage control quenching the fires, when suddenly she was racked by two internal explosions which forced Captain Frederick Sherman to abandon ship. This was done skillfully, some 150 wounded being lowered in basket stretchers into motor whale-

[3] Before the battle opened on the 8th Fletcher wisely made Rear Admiral Fitch, in *Lexington*, the O.T.C.; for Fitch had the more carrier experience. Similarly, Takagi made Hara in *Zuikaku* his O.T.C. Takagi wore his flag in *Myoko*; Fletcher's flagship was *Minneapolis*.

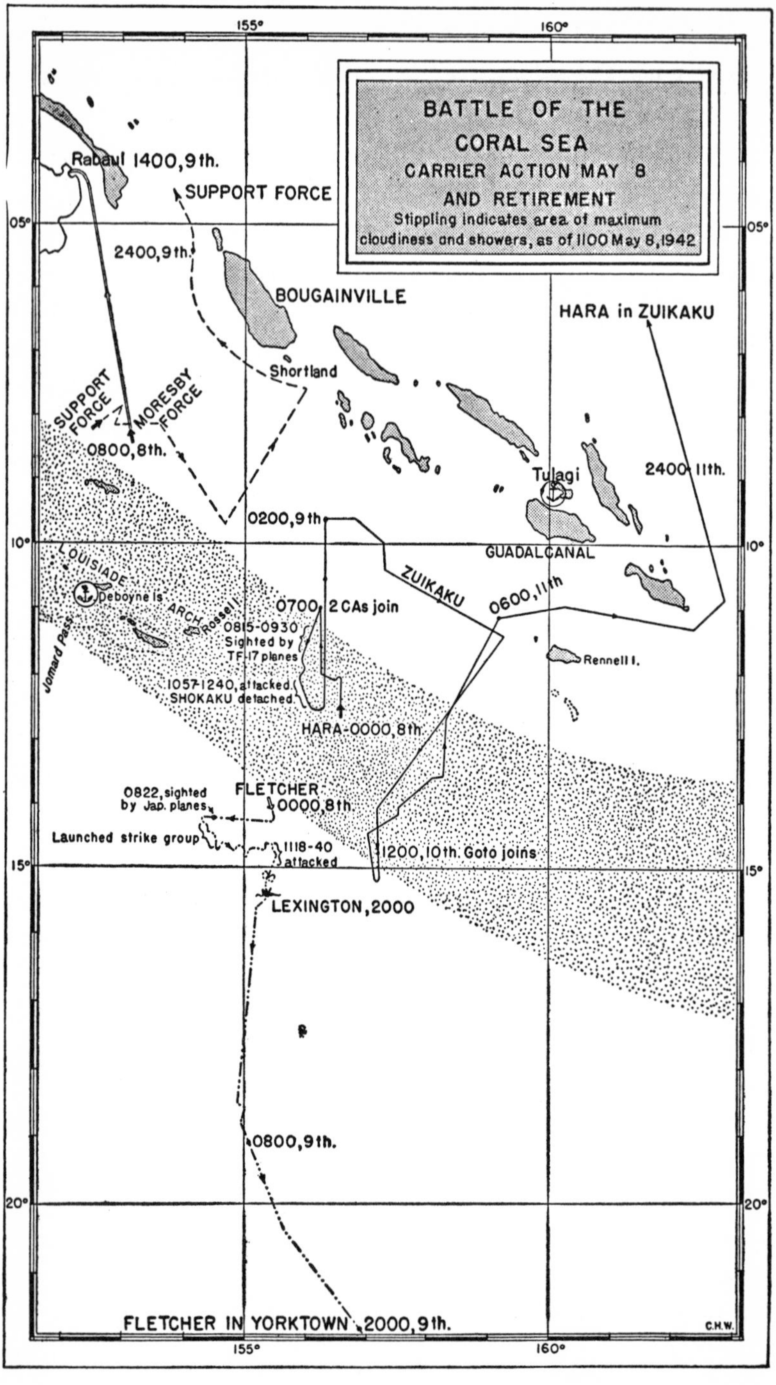

BATTLE OF THE
CORAL SEA
CARRIER ACTION MAY 8
AND RETIREMENT
Stippling indicates area of maximum cloudiness and showers, as of 1100 May 8, 1942
155°
160°
05°
10°
15°
20°
Rabaul 1400, 9th.
SUPPORT FORCE
2400, 9th.
BOUGAINVILLE
HARA in ZUIKAKU
Shortland
SUPPORT FORCE
MORESBY FORCE
0800, 8th.
Tulagi
2400 11th.
0200, 9th
GUADALCANAL
ZUIKAKU
LOUISIADE ARCH
Deboyne Is
Rossel I.
0700, 2 CAs join
0600, 11th
0815-0930 Sighted by TF-17 planes
Rennell I.
Jomard Pass
1057-1240, attacked. SHOKAKU detached.
HARA-0000, 8th.
0822, sighted by Jap. planes
FLETCHER
0000, 8th.
Launched strike group
1118-40 attacked
1200, 10th. Goto joins
LEXINGTON, 2000
0800, 9th.
FLETCHER IN YORKTOWN
2000, 9th.
C.H.W.

boats, while the able-bodied slid down lines into the water, where they were picked up by destroyers. Rear Admiral Tom Kinkaid, who handled these rescue operations, showed the qualities that helped him to emerge as one of our great flag officers.

Lady Lex, beloved as few warships have been by her crew, some of whom had been on board since she was commissioned in 1927, finally had to be sunk by a friendly destroyer's torpedoes. Her loss gave the Japanese the winning score in tonnage sunk; but that does not register the effect of the battle. Admiral Inouye, fearful of risking the Port Moresby Invasion Force south of Papua without air cover, ordered it to retire to Rabaul; and never again in this war did the keel of a Japanese warship vex the Coral Sea south of the Louisiades. Thus the battle was really won by the Americans owing to their biggest mistake, the sighting and bombing of *Shoho;* her loss led Inouye to throw in the sponge. Even the big carriers' battle turned out ill for the Japanese, because *Shokaku* took two months to repair, and *Zuikaku* took over one month to replace her plane losses. Thus, neither big flattop could take part in the great battle coming up. But *Yorktown* could and did.

3. *The Battle of Midway — First Blood, 3 June*

Even before the sea warriors of Japan began roaring into the Coral Sea, word had reached Admiral Nimitz at Pearl Harbor of a second offensive that threatened to be much the more powerful and dangerous. Imperial General Headquarters issued the order that put the wheels in motion on 5 May 1942: "Commander in Chief Combined Fleet will, in coöperation with the Army, invade and occupy strategic points in the Western Aleutians and Midway Island." The objectives were three-fold. The named islands were wanted as anchors in the new "ribbon defense," and Midway too as a base for air raids on Pearl Harbor. But most of all, Admiral Yamamoto intended this operation to draw out and "annihilate" the United States Pacific Fleet, in its hour of greatest weakness, before new construction could replace the losses of Pearl Harbor. The success of this battle was central to the entire Japanese strategic concept of the war. Had Japan won, Port Moresby, Fijis, anything else she wanted, would have fallen into her lap. But the yet small Pacific Fleet declined to accept the sacrificial role.

Midway, situated 1136 miles WNW of Pearl Harbor, is the outermost link of the Hawaiian chain. The entire atoll, smaller even than Wake, is but six miles in diameter. Only two islets, Sand and Eastern, the first less than two miles long and the other a little more than one, are dry land. It had been a Pan American Airways base since 1935, and a Naval Air Station since August 1941.

A comparison of the Combined Fleet thrown into this operation with what Admiral Nimitz could collect to withstand it indicates that Yamamoto's expectations of "annihilation" were justified. He commanded (1) an Advance Force of 16 submarines, (2) Nagumo's Pearl Harbor Striking Force, with four big carriers, (3) a Midway Occupation Force, some 5000 men in 12 transports, protected by two battleships, six heavy cruisers, and numerous destroyers, (4) a Main Body under Yamamoto's immediate command, comprising Japan's three most modern battleships and four older ones, with a light carrier; and (5) the Northern Area Force, with two light carriers, two heavy cruisers and four big transports, for the bombing of Dutch Harbor and occupation of Adak, Attu and Kiska. This added up to 162 warships and auxiliaries, not counting small patrol craft and the like — practically the entire fighting Japanese Navy. The total number that Admiral Nimitz could scrape together was 76, of which one-third belonged to the North Pacific Force and never got into the battle.

Nevertheless, Nimitz had certain assets which helped tip the scale. The senior commander of the Carrier Striking Force which did most of the fighting was Rear Admiral Fletcher in *Yorktown* (repaired at Pearl Harbor in two days, when by peacetime methods it would have taken ninety), and Fletcher had learned a thing or two at the Coral Sea. Junior to him, and in temporary command of Halsey's Task Force 16,[4] which had pulled off the Tokyo strike, was Rear Admiral Raymond A. Spruance. He, though not an aviator, showed in the forthcoming battle the very highest quality of tactical wisdom, the power to seize opportunities. *Enterprise* and *Hornet*, the carriers under him, had two superlative commanding officers, Captains George D. Murray and Marc A. Mitscher. In Midway itself, where 32 Navy Catalinas and six of the new torpedo-bombing Avengers, 54 Marine Corps planes, and 23 Army Air Force planes (19 of them B–17s) were based, we had an "unsinkable aircraft carrier." Finally, Nimitz had the inestimable advantage of knowing when and where the enemy intended to attack. But for early and abundant decrypted intelligence, and, what was more important, the prompt piecing together of these bits and scraps to make a pattern, "David" United States Navy could never have coped with the Japanese "Goliath."

Admiral Nimitz's orders to Fletcher and Spruance were to "inflict maximum damage on enemy by employing strong attrition tactics," which meant air strikes on enemy ships. He cannily ordered them to take initial positions to the northeastward of Midway, beyond search range of the approaching enemy, anticipating that the 700-mile searches by Midway-based planes would locate the Japanese carriers first. To this he added a special Letter of Instruction: "In carrying out the task assigned . . . you will be governed by the principle of calculated risk . . . the avoidance of exposure of your force to attack by superior enemy forces

[4] Admiral Halsey had been hospitalized after the Tokyo strike.

without good prospect of inflicting . . . greater damage on the enemy." No commander in chief's instructions were ever more faithfully and intelligently carried out.

Yamamoto really threw away his chance of a smashing victory by dividing his mammoth forces several ways, and by fitting his operation plan to what he assumed the Americans would do. Dividing forces was a fixed strategic idea with the Japanese. They loved diversionary tactics — fleets popping up at odd places to confuse the enemy and pull him off base. Their pattern for decisive battle was the same at sea as on land — lure the enemy into an unfavorable tactical situation, cut off his retreat, drive in his flanks and then concentrate for the kill. Their manual for carrier force commanders even invoked the examples of Hannibal at Cannae and Ludendorff at Tannenberg (probably studied in Schlieffen's works) to justify such naval strategy as Yamamoto tried at Midway. Thus, the preliminary air strike on Dutch Harbor, set for 3 June, was a gambit to pull the Pacific Fleet up north where it could not interfere with the occupation of Midway Island, due to take place at dawn 6 June. When the Pacific Fleet hastened south after a fruitless run up north, which could not be earlier than 7 June, Japanese carrier planes and Midway-based aircraft would intensively bomb the American ships. These, if they did not promptly sink, would be dispatched by gunfire from Yamamoto's battleships and heavy cruisers.

So very, very neat! But Nimitz, insteaded of falling for this trap, had three carriers already covering Midway as Nagumo approached. It was the "Nips" who were nipped.

The Japanese Aleutian prong struck first, on 3 June, with the triple object of deceiving Admiral Nimitz into the belief that this was the main show, destroying American installations at Dutch Harbor, and covering an occupation of the Western Aleutians. Besides separate occupation forces, Vice Admiral Hosogaya had light carriers *Ryujo* and *Junyo*, three heavy cruisers and a suitable number of destroyers and oilers. On our side, we had the North Pacific Force commanded by Rear Admiral Robert A. Theobald in light cruiser *Nashville*, with sister ships *St. Louis* and *Honolulu*, two heavy cruisers, a destroyer division, a nine-destroyer striking group, six S-class submarines and a flock of Coast Guard cutters and other small craft. Cincpac Intelligence smoked out Japanese intentions in this quarter, and informed the Admiral of them on 28 May, but "Fuzzy" Theobald, as usual, thought he knew better — that the enemy was going to seize Dutch Harbor. Consequently he deployed the main body of his force about 400 miles south of Kodiak, instead of trying to break up the Western Aleutians invasion force. This bad guess lost him all opportunity to fight; for Hosogaya's two light carriers, under the tactical command of Rear Admiral Kakuji Kakuta, slipped in between Theobald's force and the land, began bombing Dutch Harbor at 0800 June 3, and returned through a fog-mull for another whack at this Eastern Aleutians base next day, completely unmolested from the sea. The Japanese could have landed at Dutch Harbor, for all the protection it had from Theobald. Considerable damage was inflicted on this base, but it was far from being knocked out.

On 7 June undefended Attu and Kiska in the Western Aleutians were occupied by the Japanese according to plan, but Adak was not taken, because it seemed to be too near Unmak. Army P–40s based on the new A.A.F. field at Unmak had given Kakuta's carrier planes quite a run for their money.

Turning now to the main show, Old Man Weather seemed determined to help the Japanese here, as in the Coral Sea. Admiral Nagumo's Striking Force, built around carriers *Akagi*, *Kaga*, *Hiryu* and *Soryu*, veterans of Pearl Harbor, advanced toward Midway under heavy cloud cover; they could even hear the island-based search planes buzzing overhead, but themselves were not seen. The force allotted to occupy Midway was, however, sighted by a Catalina on 3 June. Captain Simard's island-based air force reacted quickly, though ineffectively. It made but one hit, on an oiler, at 0143 June 4. That was the first blow in this battle south of the Aleutians.

4. *The Battle of Midway — the Fourth of June*

All night 3-4 June the two opposing carrier forces were approaching each other on courses which, if maintained, would have crossed a few miles north of Midway Island. Day began to break around 0400. It was still overcast over the Japanese, clear over the Americans. A light wind blew from the southeast; another break for the Japanese, since wind is almost as important for aircraft carriers as for the old frigates. Contrary to what was desirable in the sailing navy — to get the weather gauge of your enemy — the lee gauge was now wanted, because a carrier has to steam into the wind to launch or recover planes. Thus, Fletcher and Spruance, having the weather gauge, had to lose mileage during flight operations. *Yorktown*, having to recover a search mission, had to lag behind when the big news arrived, shortly after 0600 June 4.

This news was a Midway-based PBY's contact report of two Japanese carriers, headed southeast. For four hours this was all the information that Fletcher and Spruance had of Nagumo's location and course; but it was enough. Fletcher promptly ordered Spruance, with *Enterprise* and *Hornet*, to "proceed southwesterly and attack enemy carriers when definitely located," promising to follow as soon as his search planes were recovered. Both admirals knew very well that Nagumo's Striking Force was Yamamoto's jugular vein, and that their only hope was to cut it.

Ten minutes after Fletcher issued that pregnant order, the next phase of the Battle of Midway opened, over the island itself. One hundred and eight Japanese planes, divided evenly between fighters, dive-bombers and torpedo-bombers, took off from the four carriers before sunrise. Midway search radar picked them up 93 miles away, and every fighter on the island was scrambled to intercept; but they were too few, and the Marine Corps "Buffaloes" too weak and slow, to stop the Japanese. The bombing of Midway began at 0630 and continued for twenty minutes. It did considerable ground damage, without breaking up the runways; and Midway antiaircraft fire was very good. Between that and the Marine fighters, 15 of which were lost, about one third of the Japanese attack group was shot down or badly damaged. In the meantime, four waves of American Midway-based bombers had flown off to counterattack Nagumo's carriers. They, too, lost heavily; but, as we shall see, their sacrifice was not in vain.

Now came the most decisive moment in a battle filled with drama. Admiral Nagumo, when sending off that 108-plane strike on Midway, reserved 93 aircraft armed with bombs and torpedoes to deal with enemy ships, if he could find any. Usually the Japanese were smarter than we in air search, but this time they failed, largely because, according to the Japanese plan, no American carriers should have been around for a couple of days. So Nagumo sent only a few cruiser float planes on routine search, and by 0700 they had found nothing. At that moment Lieutenant Tomonoga, commander of what was left of the 108-plane strike then returning to their carriers, signaled to Nagumo that Midway needed another pounding. Immediately after, there came in on the Japanese carriers the first Midway-based bombing attack, which seemed to second Tomonoga's motion — obviously Midway had plenty of bite left. So the Admiral "broke the spot," and ordered the 93 planes struck below to be rearmed with incendiary and fragmentation bombs for use against the island. Fifteen minutes elapsed, and the Admiral was dumfounded to receive a search plane's report of "ten enemy ships" to the northeast, where no American ships were supposed to be. What to do? Nagumo mulled it over for another quarter-hour, canceled the former change-bomb plan, and ordered the 93 planes again rearmed and readied to attack ships. That took time, and it was already too late to fly those planes off to attack enemy ships, because flight decks had to be kept clear to receive the rest of the Japanese aircraft which had been bombing Midway.

At 0835, when the returning bombers began landing on the Japanese carriers, American birds carrying death and destruction were already winging their way from *Enterprise* and *Hornet*. Spruance had taken over from Halsey, as chief of staff, Captain Miles Browning, one of the most irascible and unstable officers ever to earn a fourth stripe, but a man with a slide-rule brain. Browning figured out that Nagumo would order a second strike on Midway, that he would continue steaming toward the island, and that the golden opportunity to hit his carriers would arrive when they were refueling planes for this second strike. Spruance accepted these estimates and made the tough decision to launch at 0700, when about 175 miles from the enemy's calculated position, instead of continuing for another two hours in order to diminish the distance. Spruance also decided to make this an all-out attack — a full deckload of 20 Wildcat fighters, 67 Dauntless dive-bombers and 29 Devastator torpedo-bombers — and it took an hour to get all these airborne. Fletcher properly decided to delay launching from *Yorktown*, in case more targets were discovered; but by 0906 his six fighters, 17 SBDs and 12 TBDs were also in the air.

Imagine, if you will, the tense, crisp briefing in the ready-room, the warming-up of planes which the devoted ground crews have been checking, arming, fueling and servicing; the ritual of the take-off, as precise and ordered as a ballet; planes swooping in graceful curves over the ships while the group assembles. This Fourth of June was a cool, beautiful day; pilots at 19,000 feet could see all around a circle of 50 miles' radius. Only a few fluffy cumulus clouds were between them and an ocean that looked like a dish of wrinkled blue Persian porcelain. It was a long flight (and, alas, for so many brave young men, a last flight) over the superb ocean. Try to imagine how they felt at first sight of enemy flattops and their wriggling screen, with wakes like the tails of white horses; the sudden catch at their hearts when the black puffs of antiaircraft bursts came nearer and nearer, then the dreaded Zekes of Japanese combat air patrol swooping down out of the central blue; and finally, the tight, incredibly swift attack, when a pilot forgets everything but the target so rapidly enlarging, and the desperate necessity of choosing the exact tenth of a second to release and pull out.

While these bright ministers of death were on their way, Nagumo's Striking Force continued for over an hour, as Miles Browning had calculated, to steam toward Midway. The four carriers were grouped in a boxlike formation in the center of a screen of two battleships, three cruisers and eleven destroyers. Every few minutes messages arrived from reconnaissance planes that the enemy was approaching. At 0905, just before the last of the planes returning from Midway were recovered, Nagumo ordered Striking Force to turn 90 degrees left, to course ENE, "to contact and destroy the enemy Task Force." His carriers were in exactly the condition that Spruance and Browning hoped to find them — planes being refueled and rearmed in feverish haste.

Now came a break for Nagumo. His change of course caused the dive-bombers and fighters from *Hornet* to miss him altogether. *Hornet*'s torpedo-bombers, under Lieutenant Commander John C. Waldron, sighted his smoke and attacked without fighter cover. The result was a massacre of all fifteen TBDs. Every single one was shot down by Zekes or antiaircraft fire; only one pilot survived. The torpedo squadron from *Enterprise* came in next and lost ten out of fourteen; then *Yorktown*'s which lost all but four; and not a single hit for all this sacrifice. No wonder that these torpedo-bombers, misnamed Devastators, were struck off the Navy's list of combat planes.

The third torpedo attack was over by 1024, and for about one hundred seconds the Japanese were certain they had won the Battle of Midway, and the war. This was their high tide of victory. Then, a few seconds before 1026, with dramatic suddenness, there came a complete reversal of fortune, wrought by the Dauntless dive-bombers, the SBDs, the most successful and beloved by aviators of all our carrier types during the war. Lieutenant Commander Clarence W. McClusky, air group commander of *Enterprise*, had two squadrons of SBDs under him: 37 units. He ordered one to follow him in attacking carrier *Kaga*, while the other, under Lieutenant W. E. Gallaher, pounced on *Akagi*, Nagumo's flagship. Their coming in so soon after the last torpedo-bombing attack meant that the Zekes were still close to the water after shooting down TBDs, and had no time to climb. At 14,000 feet the American dive-bombers tipped over and swooped screaming down for the kill. *Akagi* took a bomb which exploded in the hangar, detonating torpedo storage, then another which exploded amid planes changing their armament on the flight deck — just as Browning had calculated. Fires swept the flagship, Admiral Nagumo and staff transferred to cruiser *Nagara*, and the carrier was abandoned and sunk by a destroyer's torpedo. Four bomb hits on *Kaga* killed everyone on the bridge and set her burning from stem to stern. Abandoned by all but a small damage-control crew, she was racked by an internal explosion that evening, and sank hissing into a 2600-fathom deep.

The third carrier was the victim of *Yorktown*'s dive-bombers, under Lieutenant Commander Maxwell F. Leslie, who by cutting corners managed to make up for a late start. His 17 SBDs jumped

Soryu just as she was turning into the wind to launch planes, and planted three half-ton bombs in the midst of the spot. Within twenty minutes she had to be abandoned. U.S. submarine *Nautilus*, prowling about looking for targets, pumped three torpedoes into her, the gasoline storage exploded, whipsawing the carrier, and down she went in two sections.

At 1024 Japan had been on top; six minutes later, on that bright June morning, three of her big carriers were on their flaming way to death. But Nagumo did not give up. He ordered *Hiryu*, the one undamaged carrier, to strike *Yorktown*. Her two attack groups comprised 18 dive-bombers, 10 torpedo-bombers and 12 fighters. Most of them were shot down by C.A.P. and antiaircraft fire, but three Vals of the first strike made as many bomb hits, and four Kates, breaking low through a heavy curtain of fire, got two torpedoes into *Yorktown* at 1445. These severed all power connections and caused her to list 26 degrees. Fifteen minutes later Captain Buckmaster ordered Abandon Ship. *Yorktown*'s watertight integrity had been impaired in the Coral Sea battle, and her repairs were so hasty that he feared she would turn turtle.

Admiral Fletcher, who shifted his flag to cruiser *Astoria* after the first attack, had already sent out a search mission to find the fourth Japanese carrier. Almost at the same moment that *Yorktown* was torpedoed, these planes found *Hiryu*. As a result of their contact, "Waltzing Matilda" was revenged just as her dancing career ended. *Enterprise*, at Spruance's command, turned into the wind at 1530 and launched an attack group of 24 SBDs, including ten refugees from *Yorktown*, and veterans of the morning's battle. Led by the redoubtable Gallaher, they jumped *Hiryu* and her screen at 1700. The carrier received four hits which did her in, and she took down with her Rear Admiral Yamaguchi, an outstanding flag officer who, it is said, would have been Yamamoto's successor had he lived.

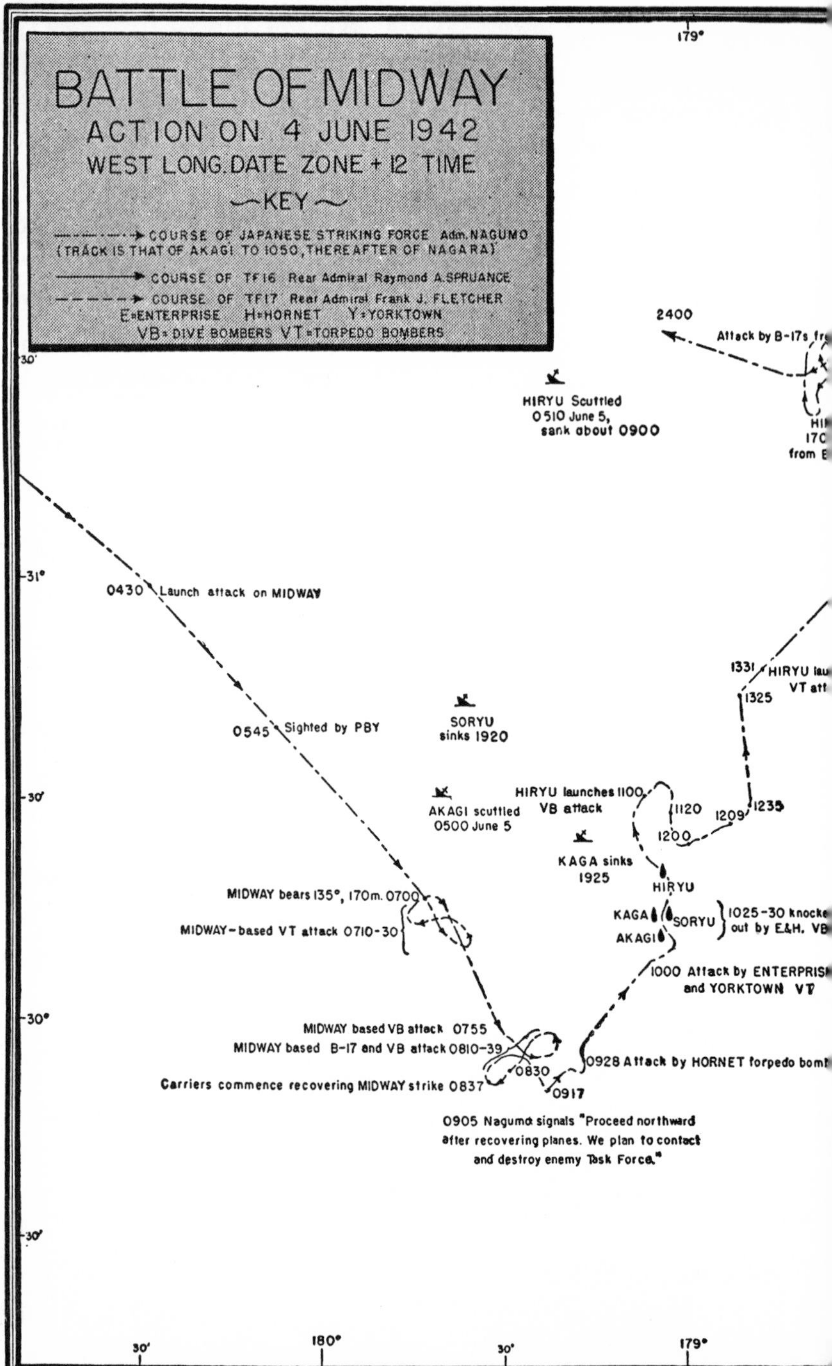
BATTLE OF MIDWAY
ACTION ON 4 JUNE 1942
WEST LONG. DATE ZONE + 12 TIME
KEY
COURSE OF JAPANESE STRIKING FORCE Adm. NAGUMO
(TRACK IS THAT OF AKAGI TO 1050, THEREAFTER OF NAGARA)
COURSE OF TF16 Rear Admiral Raymond A. SPRUANCE
COURSE OF TF17 Rear Admiral Frank J. FLETCHER
E=ENTERPRISE H=HORNET Y=YORKTOWN
VB=DIVE BOMBERS VT=TORPEDO BOMBERS
179°
2400
HIRYU Scuttled
0510 June 5,
sank about 0900
31°
0430 Launch attack on MIDWAY
0545 Sighted by PBY
SORYU
sinks 1920
AKAGI scuttled
0500 June 5
HIRYU launches 1100
VB attack
KAGA sinks
1925
1331
1325
1120
1200
1209
1235
HIRYU
KAGA
SORYU
AKAGI
MIDWAY bears 135°, 170m. 0700
MIDWAY-based VT attack 0710-30
1000 Attack by ENTERPRISE
and YORKTOWN VT
30°
MIDWAY based VB attack 0755
MIDWAY based B-17 and VB attack 0810-39
0830
Carriers commence recovering MIDWAY strike 0837
0917
0905 Nagumo signals "Proceed northward
after recovering planes. We plan to contact
and destroy enemy Task Force."
30'
180°
30'
179°

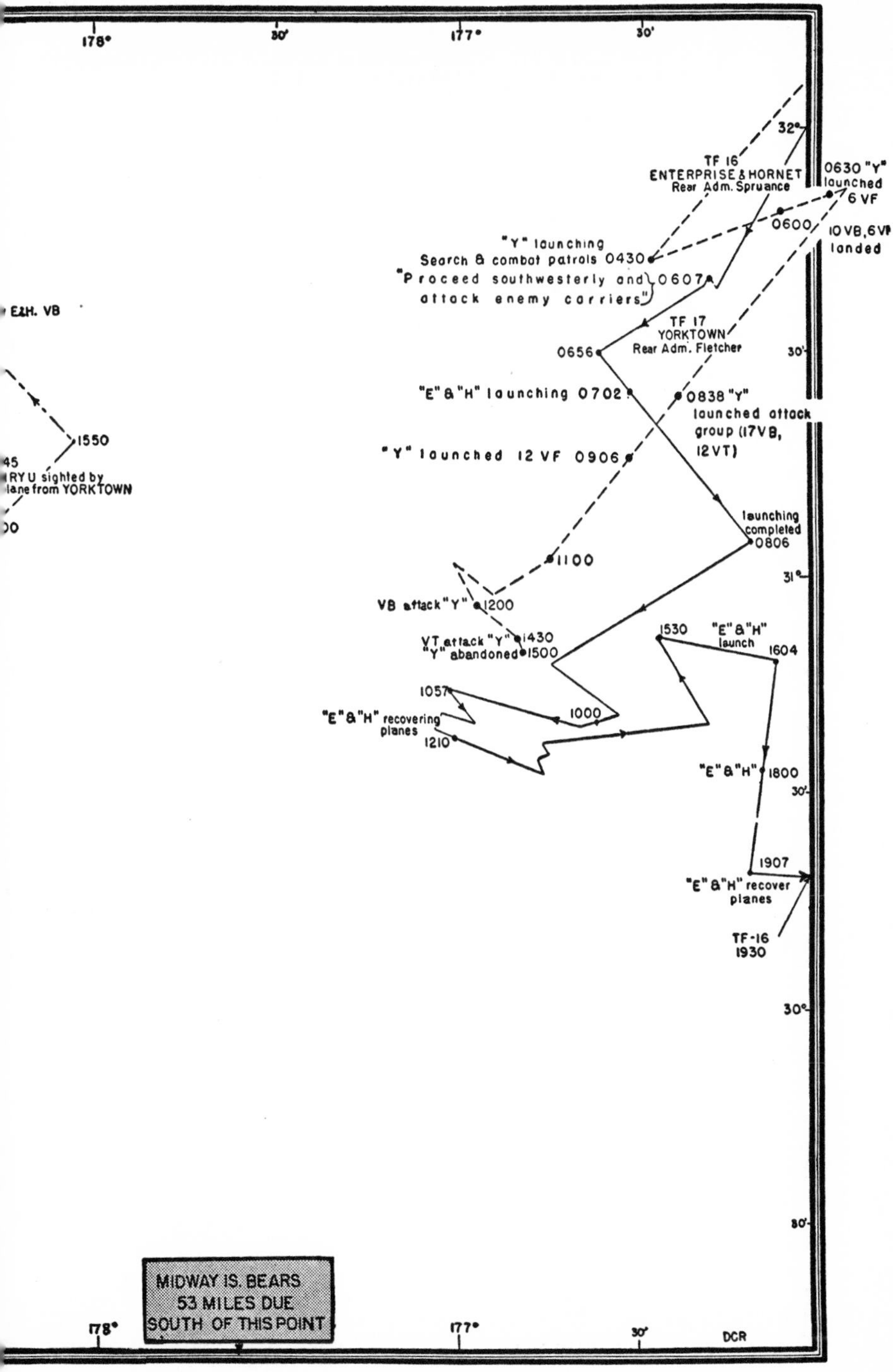

178°
30'
177°
30'
32°
TF 16
ENTERPRISE & HORNET
Rear Adm. Spruance
0630 "Y"
launched
6 VF
0600
10 VB, 6 VF
landed
"Y" launching
Search & combat patrols 0430
"Proceed southwesterly and attack enemy carriers"
0607
E&H. VB
TF 17
YORKTOWN
Rear Adm. Fletcher
0656
30'
"E" & "H" launching 0702
0838 "Y"
launched attack
group (17 VB,
12 VT)
1550
"Y" launched 12 VF 0906
45
RYU sighted by
lane from YORKTOWN
launching
completed
0806
1100
31°
VB attack "Y" 1200
1530
"E" & "H"
launch
1604
VT attack "Y" 1430
"Y" abandoned 1500
1057
1000
"E" & "H" recovering
planes
1210
"E" & "H" 1800
30'
1907
"E" & "H" recover
planes
TF-16
1930
30°
30'
MIDWAY IS. BEARS
53 MILES DUE
SOUTH OF THIS POINT
178°
177°
30'
DCR

Yamamoto, who according to plan was keeping well to the rear his Main Body, built around the mastodonic battleship *Yamato*, first reacted to these events aggressively. He ordered Kakuta's three light carriers down from the Aleutians, and Kondo's heavy cruiser Covering Group to join Main Body next day, to renew the battle. He still had overwhelming gunfire and torpedo superiority over anything that Spruance and Fletcher could offer. But, after news arrived that his four splendid carriers were either sunk or burning derelicts, he bowed to the logic of events and at 0255 June 5 ordered a general retirement. He had lost his entire fast carrier group, with their complement of some 250 planes, most of their pilots, and about 2200 officers and men. In all its long history, the Japanese Navy had never known defeat; no wonder that Yamamoto fell ill and kept close to his cabin during the homeward passage. Never has there been a sharper turn in the fortunes of war than on that June day when McClusky's and Leslie's dive-bombers snatched the palm of victory from Nagumo's masthead, where he had nailed it on 7 December.

5. *The Battle of Midway — Epilogue*

The Fourth of June — day that should live forever glorious in our history — decided the Battle of Midway. By destroying the four Japanese carriers and their air groups, the American aviators had extracted the sting from Combined Fleet. Everything that followed now appears to be anticlimax; but the situation during the night of 4-5 June was far from clear to the people at Midway, to Fletcher and Spruance, or, for that matter, to Nimitz and Yamamoto. Spruance knew that the Japanese supporting naval forces, which nobody had yet located, included carriers. With *Yorktown* disabled, the air groups of his own carriers decimated, and no support in sight, he had to balance the possible damage he could inflict by pressing westward that night against the risks involved. Consequently he retired *Enterprise* and *Hornet* to the eastward, and did not reverse course until midnight. It was fortunate that he refused to tempt fate further; for, had he steered westward that evening, he would have run smack into a heavy concentration of Yamamoto's battleships and cruisers around midnight, and have been forced to fight a night gunfire battle — just what the Japanese wanted.

Prior to ordering a general retirement at 0255 June 5, Yamamoto canceled a scheduled bombardment of Midway by Admiral Kurita's four heavy cruisers. Two of these, *Mikuma* and *Mogami*, which had sunk *Houston* and *Perth* in the Java Sea, were attacked by the bombers Captain Simard had left on Midway — six SBDs and six old Marine Corps Vindicators. Both cruisers were damaged, and *Mikuma* next day was sunk by dive-bombers from *Hornet*.

By 1000 June 5 Spruance's carriers were about 50 miles north of Midway. Five hours later they launched 58 SBDs to search for targets, but found only one destroyer. After continuing to a point some 400 miles west of Midway, and increasing his score only by the sinking of *Mikuma*, Spruance turned east on the evening of the 6th to keep a fueling rendezvous.

After the battle was over Yamamoto blamed his defeat on the failure of his advance screen of 16 submarines to accomplish anything. The fault, however, was the Admiral's. He had deployed them to catch the Pacific Fleet where he counted on its being, instead of where it was. Nevertheless, a Parthian shot by one of these boats scored for Japan in the last play of this big game. Her victim was *Yorktown*, abandoned after her hits on 4 June — unnecessarily, as proved by the fact that she floated for 24 hours with no human hand to help. She was taken in tow on the 5th by minesweeper *Vireo*, too small to cope with the carrier's 19,800-ton bulk. As *Yorktown* inched along toward home on 6 June, submarine *I-168* penetrated her destroyer screen and got two torpedoes home. A third torpedo sank destroyer *Hammann*, which was then alongside the carrier to furnish power and pumps for her salvage crew; she went down in four minutes, taking 81 officers and men with her. The two other torpedo hits finished old "Waltzing Matilda." During the night her list suddenly increased, and at dawn it was evident she was doomed. The escorting destroyers half-masted their colors, all hands came to attention, and at 0600, with her loose gear making a horrible death rattle, *Yorktown* rolled over and sank in a two-thousand-fathom deep.

Midway was a victory not only of courage, determination and excellent bombing technique, but of intelligence, bravely and wisely applied. "Had we lacked early information of the Japanese movements, and had we been caught with carrier forces dispersed . . . the Battle of Midway would have ended differently," commented Admiral Nimitz. So, too, it might have ended differently but for the chance which gave Spruance command over two of the three flattops. Fletcher did well, but Spruance's performance was superb. Calm, collected, decisive, yet receptive to advice; keeping in his mind the picture of widely disparate forces, yet boldly seizing every opening, Raymond A. Spruance emerged from this battle one of the greatest admirals in American naval history.

The Japanese knew very well that they were beaten. Midway thrust the war lords back on their heels, caused their ambitious plans for the conquest of Port Moresby, Fiji, New Caledonia and Samoa to be canceled, and forced on them an unexpected and unwelcome defensive role. The word went out from Imperial Headquarters that the name Midway was not to be mentioned.

Admirals Nimitz, Fletcher and Spruance are, as I write, very much alive; Captain Mitscher of *Hornet*, Captain Murray of *Enterprise* and Captain Miles Browning of the slide-rule mind have joined the threescore young aviators who met flaming death that day in reversing the verdict of battle.[5] Think of them, reader, every Fourth of June. They and their comrades who survived changed the whole course of the Pacific War.

[5] The squadron commanders killed were Lieutenant Commanders Lance E. Massey of *Yorktown*, Eugene E. Lindsey of *Enterprise*, John C. Waldron of *Hornet*, and Marine Corps Majors Floyd B. Parks, Loften R. Henderson and Benjamin W. Norris of the Midway-based Marine Aircraft Group.

CHAPTER VII

Guadalcanal

August 1942–February 1943

1. *The Landings, 7–8 August 1942*

THE GUADALCANAL CAMPAIGN, the most bitterly contested in American history since the Campaign of Northern Virginia in the Civil War, comprised seven major naval engagements, at least ten pitched land battles, and innumerable forays, bombardments and skirmishes. It began as a gleam in Admiral King's eye, in early February 1942. He saw clearly that the Japanese must not be permitted to consolidate the formidable prizes that they were then in the course of gathering. To the basic prewar strategic decision to beat Germany first, King always remained faithful; but he insisted that it would be fatal to adopt a purely defensive attitude in the Pacific, as General Sir Alan Brooke (Chief of the Imperial General Staff) and other British strategists demanded. Limited offensives against the Japanese must be begun, and bases secured by us for future advances. Otherwise, the Japanese would certainly advance from Rabaul in the Bismarck Archipelago into Papua and New Guinea, then into Australia, Samoa, and even New Caledonia.

The Joint Chiefs of Staff did not take kindly to the Admiral's "defensive-offensive" strategy, as he called it; they regarded it as a diversion. They were trying to block Churchill's diversion of our buildup for the main attack on Germany into North Africa; wasn't this the same sort of thing in the Pacific? King vigorously denied it. The Bismarck Archipelago, he pointed out, blocks a main road (General MacArthur would say the only road) to Tokyo, and Guadalcanal is the tollgate. If we don't pay the toll, the Japanese will — and sail through in the contrary direction to Nouméa, Fiji and Queensland.

On 3 May, as we have seen, the Japanese seized Tulagi, opposite Guadalcanal. Washington countered by allowing Vice Admiral Robert L. Ghormley, recently appointed Commander South Pacific Force, to move into Espiritu Santo and start a base there (28 May). The Free French had already allowed us to use Nouméa.

Japan's defeat at Midway caused General Tojo to shift his attention once more to the Southwest Pacific. A new Eighth Fleet under Vice Admiral Mikawa was created to spearhead a fresh advance from Rabaul, new airfields were built at Rabaul to accommodate an air flotilla, and troops were alerted to march on Port Moresby, Papua, across the Owen Stanley Mountains. In order to enable land-based bombers to cover this advance, more airfields would have to be constructed in the Solomons. Tulagi was fit only for a seaplane base.

Admiral King, with this intelligence in hand, overcame General Marshall's objections, and obtained a Joint Chiefs of Staff directive on 2 July 1942 for Operation WATCHTOWER. The South Pacific Force would first seize Tulagi and Guadalcanal. General MacArthur (in command of Southwest Pacific Forces and Area at Brisbane) would then assume responsibility for taking the rest of the Solomons and finally Rabaul. That would remove one major barrier, the Bismarck Archipelago, to the recovery of the Philippines and the defeat of Japan.

On 5 July South Pacific reconnaissance planes gathered a bit of news that sparked off Operation WATCHTOWER: the Japanese were beginning work on an airfield — the future Henderson Field — on Guadalcanal. Admiral King put his foot down, ordered WATCHTOWER to start within a month; and how right he was! The

Japanese expected to have the new Guadalcanal field ready for 60 bombers by 1 August, and by the end of the month to base a whole air flotilla there. That would menace our entire position in the South Pacific. Had we not attacked when we did, a new seaborne invasion of Port Moresby would have started in mid-August.

Preparations were so hasty and the forces available so lean that the officers concerned nicknamed this Operation SHOESTRING. And won on a shoestring it was, since the main Allied effort at the time was directed to Operation TORCH in North Africa.

Vice Admiral Ghormley, who remained in Nouméa, had over-all command. Under him, Rear Admiral Frank Jack Fletcher commanded the Expeditionary Force, as well as a carrier supporting force built around *Enterprise, Saratoga* and *Wasp.* Rear Admiral Richmond Kelly Turner, the rough, tough but highly intelligent flag officer who helped make the prewar strategic decision of March 1941, now became Commander South Pacific Amphibious Force. This comprised, on the naval side, two Australian heavy cruisers and one light cruiser, four United States heavy cruisers and 19 destroyers; and for ground forces, about 19,000 Marines under Major General Alexander A. Vandegrift USMC, embarked in 19 transports. Almost the entire Pacific Fleet at that time was involved. The operation was quickly mounted at Wellington, Sydney, San Diego and Nouméa; the Marines rehearsed in the Fijis at the end of July. This meant too short a period for training.

WATCHTOWER was the first amphibious operation undertaken by United States forces since 1898; and the feeling among the participants was anything but confident. The Japanese in Malaya, the Philippines and Java had acquired a reputation of invincibility, especially in jungle fighting. Despite their defeat at Midway, they still had plenty of ships and planes to throw into the Solomons. Furthermore, there is something sinister and depressing about that Sound, soon to be renamed Ironbottom, between Guadalcanal and Florida Islands. Men who rounded Cape Esperance in the darkness before dawn of 7 August remember that "it gave you the creeps." Even the land smell failed to cheer sailors who had been long at sea; Guadalcanal gave out a rank, heavy stench of mud, slime and jungle. And the serrated cone of Savo Island looked sinister as the crest of a giant dinosaur emerging from the ocean depths.

Everything went well, for a time. Surprise, one of the most essential conditions of a successful landing in enemy territory, was complete. The landings on Guadalcanal were effected in full daylight against slight and scattered opposition, and the incomplete airstrip was occupied at 1600. Tulagi, where the bulk of the defense force was located, took more time and effort, but was practically secured by the morning of 8 August.

On D-day, 7 August, there developed the first serious counterattack, a raid of some 43 Japanese bombers, with fighter cover, from Rabaul — in three groups. Intercepted successfully by Wildcats from Fletcher's three carriers, then operating southwest of Guadalcanal, they did no damage this time. But on the 8th, nine Japanese torpedo-bombers bored into the transport area, and one burning plane crashed transport *George F. Elliott*, which had to be abandoned.

By midnight 8-9 August, the beachheads and airstrip on Guadalcanal, and the three wanted islands on the Tulagi side of the Sound, were secured. Prospects looked bright indeed. Then, shortly after midnight, there opened the Battle of Savo Island, probably the worst defeat ever inflicted on the United States Navy in a fair fight.

2. *The Battle of Savo Island, 9 August 1942*

Early in the morning of 7 August news of the American landings reached Vice Admiral Mikawa at Rabaul. His decision was prompt and intelligent — to send reinforcements to the Tulagi-

Guadalcanal garrison, and to assemble a task group to attack the American ships unloading there. A few hundred troops were hastily assembled at Rabaul and embarked in transport *Meiyo Maru*, which was sent off to the endangered island with a light escort. When this transport was steaming about 14 miles off Cape St. George shortly before midnight 8 August, she encountered United States submarine *S–38* (Lieutenant Commander H. G. Munson), a veteran of the Java campaign, and was torpedoed and sunk. So much for that.

Mikawa's naval reaction is a very different story. One hour after receiving the bad news from Tulagi, he began collecting from Kavieng and Rabaul a task group to attack the American Expeditionary Force. It was a "scratch team," the ships had never trained together before, but it proved to be good enough for the task in hand. Heavy cruisers *Chokai* (flagship), *Aoba*, *Kako*, *Kinugasa* and *Furutaka*, light cruisers *Tenryu* and *Yubari*, and one destroyer, *Yunagi*, made rendezvous in St. George Channel around 1900 August 7 and started hell-bent for Guadalcanal. Mikawa's battle plan, sent by blinker to each ship, was to enter Ironbottom Sound in the small hours of the 9th, strike the warships guarding the expeditionary force, shoot up the unloading transports, and retire. An excellent plan; but the chances of detection were great, as the striking force had to steam in full daylight down the "Slot" between the central Solomon Islands before entering the cover of darkness.

Owing to a series of blunders on our side, the Slot was not properly covered by air search on 8 August, and the one sighting of Mikawa's force that day, by an Australian Hudson pilot at 1026, was so mishandled by him, as well as by the authorities who passed it along, that Admiral Turner did not receive it until over eight hours had passed. This contact report, moreover, was misleading, in that the pilot mistook two Japanese cruisers for seaplane tenders.[1] On that basis Turner made the bad guess that the Japanese were not coming through that night, but intended to set up a seaplane base at Santa Isabel Island, some 150 miles from Savo, and attack later.

Dogmatically deciding what the enemy would do, instead of considering what he could or might do, was not Turner's only mistake on that fatal night. He allowed his fighting ships to be divided into three separate forces to guard three possible sea approaches by the enemy. Rear Admiral Norman Scott with two light cruisers and two destroyers patrolled the transport area between Tulagi and Guadalcanal, and never got into the battle. The two western approaches, on each side of Savo Island, were guarded by six heavy cruisers and four destroyers (besides two more destroyers thrust out as pickets) under Rear Admiral Victor Crutchley RN. This British flag officer in the Australian Navy was a gallant and jovial figure, sporting a full red beard to hide a wound scar. He had taken part in the Battle of Jutland and won the Victoria Cross. For reasons unknown, Crutchley neither conferred with his cruiser captains before the battle, nor issued a battle plan; and his disposition was faulty. The cruisers were divided into two groups: the southern, under himself in H.M.A.S. *Australia*, with her sister ship *Canberra*, U.S.S. *Chicago* and two destroyers, guarded the southern entrance to the Sound; U.S.S. *Vincennes*, *Astoria*, and *Quincy*, with two destroyers, under the tactical command of Captain Riefkohl in *Vincennes*, guarded the northern entrance.

Turner was so certain that the enemy would not attack that night that he made the further mistake of summoning Crutchley, in *Australia*, to a conference on board his flagship *McCawley*, some 20 miles away, in Lunga Roads, Guadalcanal. This action of Turner's stemmed from the worst of all blunders that night: Admiral

[1] Seaplane tender *Akitsushinia* was coming down the Slot on 8 August to establish a seaplane base at Gizo Island; possibly the Hudson sighted her.

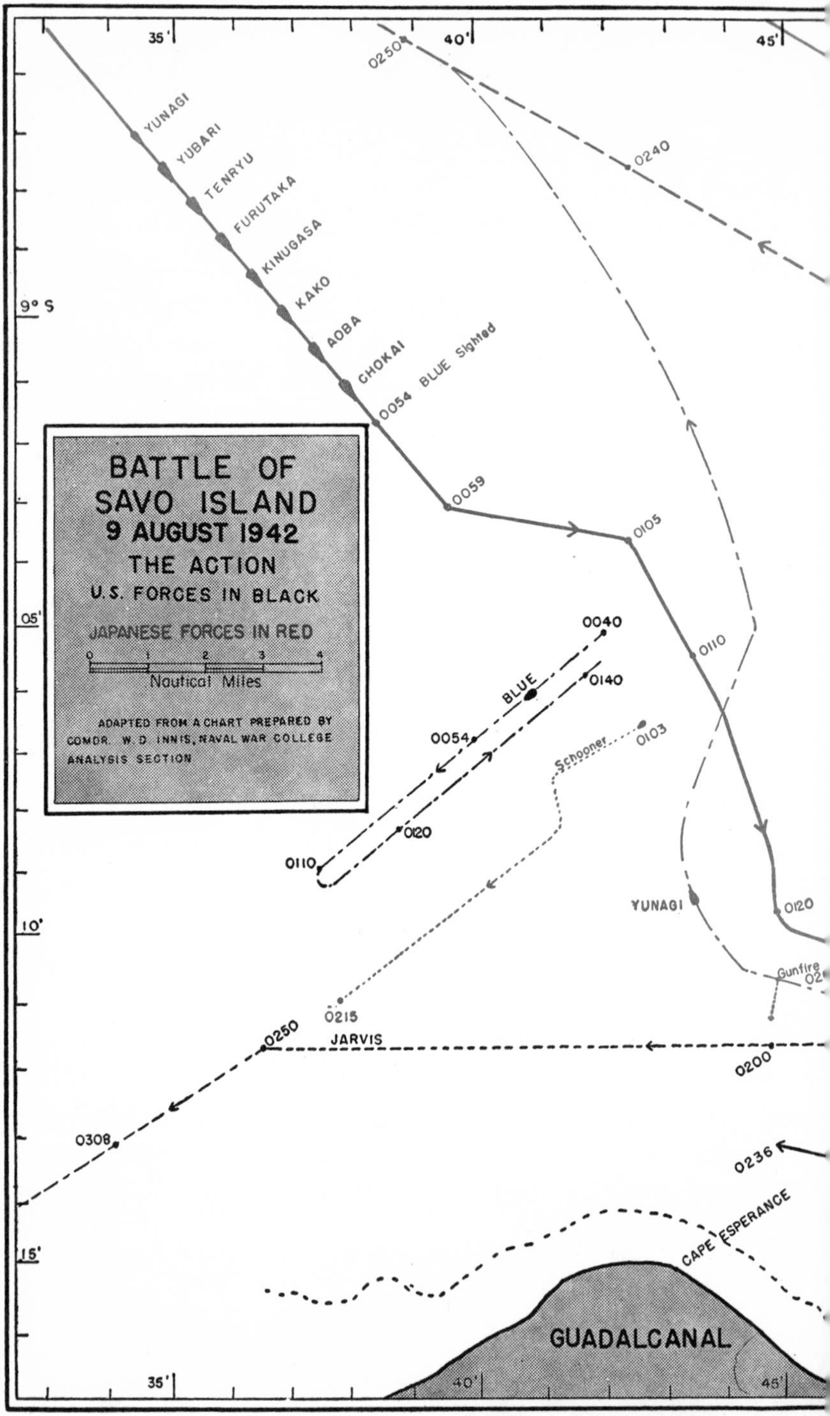

BATTLE OF SAVO ISLAND
9 AUGUST 1942
THE ACTION
U.S. FORCES IN BLACK
JAPANESE FORCES IN RED
Nautical Miles
ADAPTED FROM A CHART PREPARED BY COMDR. W. D. INNIS, NAVAL WAR COLLEGE ANALYSIS SECTION
YUNAGI
YUBARI
TENRYU
FURUTAKA
KINUGASA
KAKO
AOBA
CHOKAI
0054 BLUE Sighted
0059
0105
0110
0120
0240
0250
BLUE
0040
0140
0054
0120
0110
Schooner
0103
0215
JARVIS
0250
0200
0308
0236
Gunfire
CAPE ESPERANCE
GUADALCANAL
9° S
05'
10'
15'
35'
40'
45'

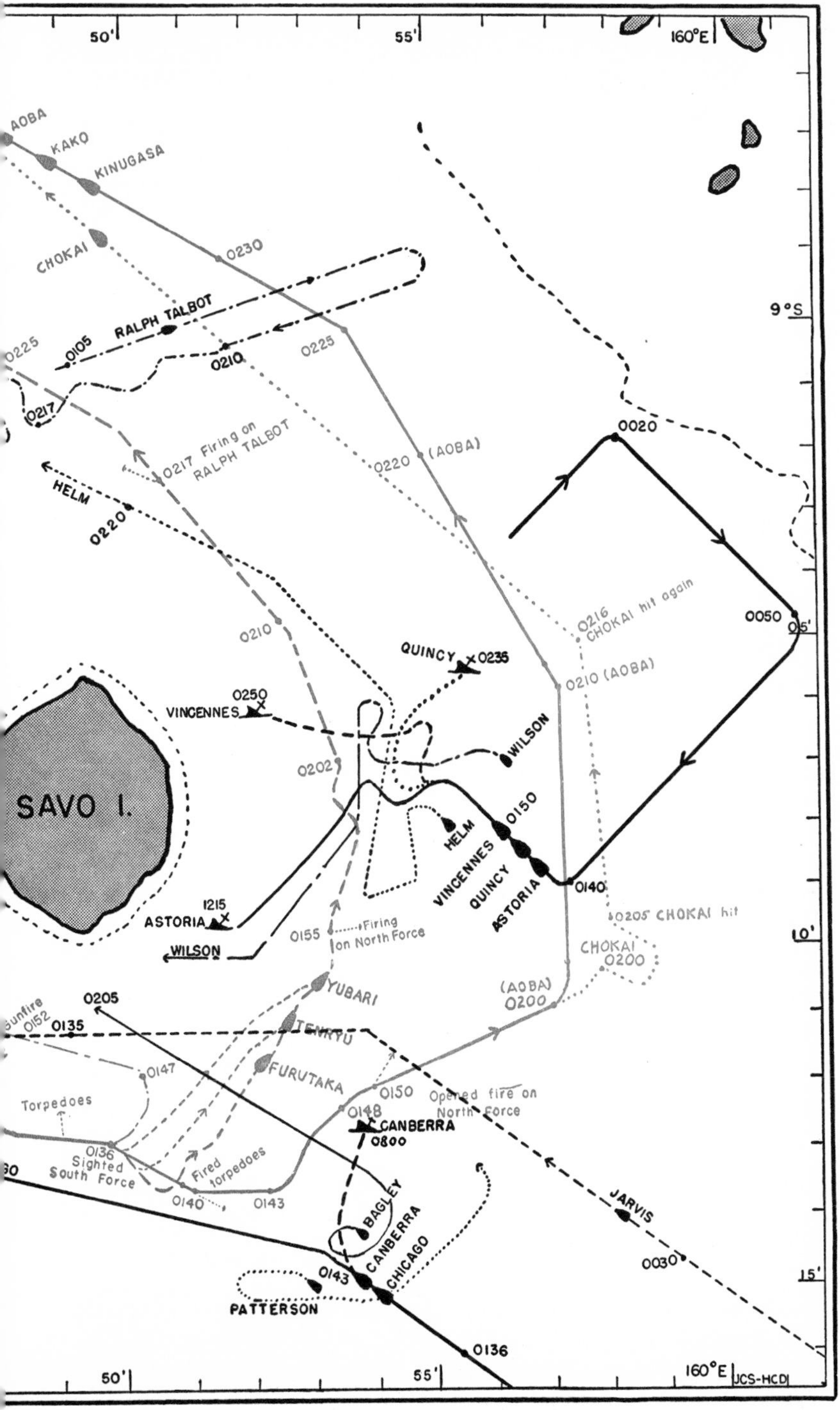

50'
55'
160°E
9°S
05'
10'
15'
SAVO I.
AOBA
KAKO
KINUGASA
CHOKAI
0230
RALPH TALBOT
0105
0210
0225
0217
0217 Firing on RALPH TALBOT
HELM
0220
0220 (AOBA)
0020
0050
0216 CHOKAI hit again
QUINCY
0235
0250
VINCENNES
0210 (AOBA)
WILSON
0202
0150
HELM
VINCENNES
QUINCY
ASTORIA
0140
1215
ASTORIA
0205 CHOKAI hit
0155
Firing on North Force
WILSON
CHOKAI
0200
YUBARI
(AOBA)
0200
0205
Gunfire
0152
0135
TENRYU
0147
FURUTAKA
0150
Opened fire on North Force
Torpedoes
0148
CANBERRA
0800
0136
Sighted South Force
Fired torpedoes
0140
0143
BAGLEY
CANBERRA
JARVIS
CHICAGO
0030
0143
PATTERSON
0136
JCS-HCD

Fletcher's decision to retire his three-carrier task force from its covering position, depriving the landing force of air cover next day. He did so on the flimsy ground that his fighter-plane strength had been reduced 21 per cent in two days' operations, and that his ships needed fuel — of which they were far from dangerously short. Probably the real reason was that "Frank Jack" had already lost *Lexington* and *Yorktown*, and did not intend to lose another carrier. He commenced this withdrawal at about 1810 August 8 without consulting Turner, who was below him in the chain of command. That was why Turner felt he had to confer with Crutchley and Vandegrift, to decide whether the partly unloaded transports should depart that night, or risk more Japanese air attack without air protection. Consequently, cruiser *Australia* and the O.T.C. were not on hand when badly needed, and the depleted cruiser group south of Savo Island was commanded by Captain Bode of *Chicago*, who acted as if dazed.

This was a hot, overcast and oppressive night, "heavy with impending doom," as a novelist would say. At 2315, when Turner's flag conference opened, the two cruiser groups off Savo Island were steaming at low speed on their monotonous patrol courses. Officers and men were dog-tired after two full days of incessant action. They had been at General Quarters for forty-eight hours.

At 2345 came the first disturbance: three unidentified planes reported by picket destroyer *Ralph Talbot*. Turner did not get this report; but the cruiser captains who did, and who even saw the planes overhead, assumed with incredible optimism that they were friendly. These planes had been catapulted by Mikawa's cruisers at 2310 to tell him what to expect, and to illuminate targets for his gunners. They droned unmolested over the sleepy American ships for an hour and a half, sending exact information of their movements that was very helpful to the Japanese admiral.

At 0040 August 9, Admiral Mikawa, having sighted Savo Island in the darkness, summoned his men to battle stations. He was using hooded blinkers, invisible outside his column, to signal his ships. Three minutes later, lookouts in flagship *Chokai* sighted a ship, obviously enemy, on their starboard bow. This was picket destroyer *Blue*. Mikawa wisely decided that this was no moment to alert the enemy by shooting. He ordered a slow-down to 22 knots, and the Japanese column padded silently by, every gun trained on *Blue*, just in case she opened up. Nobody in the destroyer suspected a thing. Her SC radar did not register, and her lookouts were looking the wrong way.

After another tense half-hour, the Japanese sighted ahead two American cruisers and two destroyers. At 0136 Mikawa ordered Commence Firing. Two minutes later a flock of torpedoes leaped out of their tubes, aimed at *Chicago*, *Canberra* and *Bagley*. For five minutes more the Japanese force approached undetected. Not until 0143 did Commander Frank Walker of destroyer *Patterson*, the only American ship properly awake that night, sight them. Immediately she broadcast the tocsin: —

WARNING, WARNING, STRANGE SHIPS ENTERING HARBOR!

Too late, too late! Three Japanese float planes, alerted by Mikawa, now dropped brilliant flares which silhouetted the American southern group; and at that moment the Japanese heavy cruisers opened gunfire. A few seconds later H.M.A.S. *Canberra*, with General Alarm sounding and her guns still trained in, was hit by two of the torpedoes launched at 0138. Next (range less than one mile) she was literally taken apart by 24 shell hits in less than one minute. Her captain and gunnery officer were killed, unquenchable fires spread, and this fine Australian cruiser had to be abandoned and eventually scuttled. *Chicago* was similarly surprised. Captain Bode, who in Crutchley's absence was O.T.C. of this group, was awakened out of sound sleep by gunfire, and, with a column of five heavy cruisers to shoot at, steamed off in pursuit of

Mikawa's lone destroyer,[2] little the worse for one shell hit and one torpedo explosion well forward. *Chicago* was out of the battle.

Having dealt with these two cruisers and their destroyers, Mikawa divided his yet untouched column to put the pincers on the northern group of American cruisers. They had heard *Patterson*'s warning at 0143, but no other word; shut off from the southern group by a heavy rain squall, they could not see what was going on and Captain Bode in the confusion forgot to signal their O.T.C. *Vincennes* was followed in column by *Quincy* and *Astoria*, with destroyers *Helm* and *Wilson* on their flanks. All were on the northwesterly leg of their box patrol when, at 0148, *Chokai* launched torpedoes at *Astoria*, the nearest. Captain Greenman was catching a little sleep after some 40 hours spent on the bridge. His gunnery officer, Lieutenant Commander Truesdell, commenced firing the main battery on his own initiative, at 0152½. *Chokai*'s torpedoes missed; but she poured salvo after salvo of 8-inch shell into hapless *Astoria*, which became a blazing shambles. She went dead in the water and, defying all efforts of her damage control crews, sank next day.

Quincy, next astern of *Astoria*, was the least prepared for action and took the worst beating; but, in the opinion of the Japanese, she put up the best fight of any Allied ship that night. A searchlight from *Aoba* which brilliantly illuminated her at about 0150 found her guns still trained in, fore and aft. Promptly she trained them on the target and got off two 9-gun salvos, from which two shells hit *Chokai*, one of them demolishing the Japanese admiral's staff chartroom. In avoiding collision with *Vincennes* ahead, she appeared to the enemy to be bearing down on them to ram. Although enveloped in flames from midships aft, a shellburst having

[2] This was *Yunagi*, which Mikawa had detached to deal with the picket destroyers. U. S. destroyer *Jarvis*, badly hit in the air attack of 8 August and ordered to Sydney, was limping through the battle area at the time. She received additional damage from *Yunagi* and was sunk with all hands at noon 9 August by torpedo planes from Rabaul.

lighted a plane on her fantail, her forward guns continued to fire. Now the doomed cruiser was caught by crossfire between the two Japanese columns. Turret No. 2 exploded after a shell hit, No. 4 fire room took a torpedo, engine rooms became sealed deathtraps, the sick bay was wiped out, a shell ignited the ammunition for a 5-inch gun, fires raged throughout. The only question now was whether she would burn to death or sink. Captain Moore, mortally wounded by a shell hit that killed almost everyone on the bridge, ordered the helmsman to try to beach her on Savo Island; then he gave up the ghost. The senior surviving officer — seventh in the chain of command — ordered Abandon Ship. At 0235 *Quincy* rolled over and sank, first piece of the steel carpet that now underlies Ironbottom Sound.

Leading the northern cruiser column and last to be engaged was *Vincennes*. At 0150 Captain Riefkohl and his executive officer were still speculating about *Patterson*'s warning, and what the sound of distant gunfire and airplane flares meant, when Japanese searchlights fastened on their ship. Riefkohl assumed that they were from the southern group, having strayed off its patrol course, and even signaled *Chicago* by radio to shut off the searchlights! An 8-inch salvo from *Kako* ended that line of thought. *Vincennes* replied in kind at 0153, and her second salvo made a hit on *Kinugasa;* enemy gunfire simultaneously exploded the planes on the American cruiser's fantail and their flames provided a brilliant illumination which helped the enemy, as he swept by, to destroy *Vincennes* methodically by gunfire and torpedoes. She took three of these in two fire rooms, floundered to a halt, and, pounded by repeated gunfire, with direct hits on every gun turret, went down into the depths a few minutes after *Quincy* took the plunge.

By this time the Japanese force was in disorder, owing to each ship's maneuvering to fire at best advantage, and Admiral Mikawa was not certain where they all were. So at 0220 he ordered all ships to re-form northwest of Savo Island, intending apparently to execute the second part of his battle plan and fall on the almost undefended transports. But Mikawa was uneasy in his mind, as he confessed after the war. At 0240 he thought better of returning to the fray, and ordered all ships to make for Rabaul at top speed. His reason, strangely enough, was a fear of being bombed in the approaching daylight by planes from Admiral Fletcher's carriers, which by that time were hightailing to safety.[3]

Even though Mikawa lacked the strategic savvy to gather more fruits of victory, a resounding victory it was. In a battle lasting exactly 32 minutes he had sunk or put in a sinking condition four heavy cruisers and chased away a fifth, with negligible damage to his own force, and at a cost of only 35 men killed and 57 wounded.

An investigation by the United States Navy so evenly distributed the blame that nobody was punished. Military commanders, wrote Churchill, "should not be judged by results, but by the quality of their effort"; and it was well that Admiral Turner was retained, since he became the leading practitioner of amphibious warfare in the Pacific. Admiral Crutchley, exonerated because not present, retained his position in the Australian Navy, and was even knighted. Captain Riefkohl of *Vincennes*, who had made about as many mistakes as a commanding officer could make, was broken in spirit by the loss of his ship. He used to go about, like Kipling's "Matun the Old Blind Beggar," telling "over and over the story" to anyone who would listen, of how his ship had prevented Mikawa from attacking the transports by wrecking the flag chartroom (*Quincy* did that) and that the battle should be called an American victory. Captain Bode of *Chicago*, whose stupidity was largely responsible for that cruiser's inglorious part in the battle, committed suicide.

[3] Captain Forrest Sherman of *Wasp*, on hearing a flash report of the action, begged permission to turn back and launch planes at daylight to pursue the Japanese ships, but was denied. However, the 17-year-old submarine *S-44* (Captain John R. Moore) encountered cruiser *Kako* off Kavieng on 10 August and sank her with four torpedoes — first retribution for Savo Island.

Many lessons were learned from this disastrous battle. *Canberra* and *Astoria* might have been saved but for their heavily upholstered wardroom furniture, and the layers of paint and linoleum on their bulkheads and decks. All inflammable furniture and bedding was now ordered ashore, and every ship in the Navy was ordered to scrape down her interior to bare steel; day and night for the rest of 1942, sounds of chipping hammers were never still. Improved fire-fighting technique and the "fog nozzle," far superior to a solid stream of water, were developed; communications were improved; and officers adopted a more reasonable battle-readiness condition which relieved them and their men from continual tension.

Thus, Savo Island was neither a decisive battle nor an unprofitable defeat, although the cost was heavy — four heavy cruisers and one destroyer sunk, 1270 officers and men killed and 709 wounded. It opened a bloody and desperate campaign for control of an island that neither side really wanted, but which neither could afford to abandon to the enemy.

3. *The Battle of the Eastern Solomons, 24 August 1942*

Guadalcanal is mountainous, covered with dark-green rain-forest jungle, interspersed with patches of light-green kunai grass, whose tall, saw-toothed blades can inflict a nasty wound on walkers. Along the north coast, where the Japanese had built their landing strip, there is a narrow plain where the Australians had planted coconut groves. The fuzzy-haired Melanesians, whose labor converted the ripe nuts into copra, were uniformly hostile to the Japanese, who had pushed them around too violently, and friendly to the Allies. They, as well as the Australian "coast watchers" who concealed themselves in the Japanese-held central and upper Solomons, were an important factor in the eventual Allied victory.

The main factor, however, was the Marines. When the transports and surviving naval vessels departed on 9 August, they had landed over 16,000 Marines, but less than half their supplies and weapons had been unloaded. The Leathernecks pulled in their belts and lived on two meals a day, using the large stores of rice which the Japanese had obligingly left; but they could not continue to fight without naval support — witness what had happened at Wake. For the present, they concentrated on setting up a five-mile long defense perimeter from the Tenaru (Ilu) River to the native village of Kukum, and, by using abandoned Japanese equipment, turning the airstrip, then no more than a piece of level ground, into Henderson Field. It was ready for the first flight of Marine Corps planes on 15 August. On the same day the Marines received their first reinforcements — aviation gas, ammunition, and a "Cub" unit to service planes — in three fast destroyer-transports; and these returned on the 20th with rations.

During the twelve days following the Battle of Savo Island, the Japanese lost their best opportunity to reinforce their small garrison and run us off the island. They had full sea-and-air command; there was nothing to stop them but submarines — and Marines. But the high command was more interested in its Papuan operation; and General Hyakutake at Rabaul, estimating that only 3000 Marines were on the island, thought that a thousand more Japanese could do the trick. Accordingly, the Ichiki Detachment, originally slated to occupy Midway, was loaded in the six destroyers of Rear Admiral Raizo Tanaka's squadron and landed east of the Marines' perimeter, in the night of 18-19 August. Two days later Colonel Ichiki and his 815 men were completely wiped out by a part of the 1st Marines under Lieutenant Colonel E. A. Pollock, who lost only 34 men killed. This Battle of the Tenaru River, a model of perfectly coördinated effort, freed the Marines' eastern flank and had far-reaching effects. The Corps' first stand-up fight with the much-touted jungle-fighting Jap, it proved that the American was the better fighting man, even on his enemy's chosen terrain. From that time on, United States Marines were invincible.

It also proved what a mistake it is to commit forces piecemeal, but the Japanese war lords did not heed this lesson; not even Yamamoto did. An old Chinese proverb says, "A lion uses all its might in attacking a rabbit." Yamamoto had acted on that principle at Midway, but the rabbit won; and he reverted to the piecemeal doctrine, saving his best capital ships for a future all-out offensive. His biggest commitment came now, in the third week of August: 3 carriers, 3 battleships, 9 cruisers, 13 destroyers, 36 submarines and several auxiliaries to cover a reinforcement of only 1500 men to the garrison in western Guadalcanal. The reinforcement unit, under Rear Admiral Tanaka, was to run down the Slot and land the troops at night. In the meantime, a fleet carrier force under Vice Admiral Kondo, spearheaded by *Shokaku* and *Zuikaku*, with two battleships and three heavy cruisers, advanced into waters northeast of the Solomons to engage whatever ships Admiral Ghormley ventured to deploy. Admiral Hara's light carrier *Ryujo*, thrusting ahead, would play the dual role of flying off bombers to pound Henderson Field, and baiting the American carrier planes into attacking her, while formidable air groups from the two big carriers punished Frank Jack Fletcher's flattops. Six submarines steamed ahead to scout, six others were deployed southwest of the Santa Cruz Islands, and four groups of three each thrust down to the south and west. It looked like a sure thing.

Warned by Australian coastwatchers and American reconnaissance planes, Admiral Ghormley now ordered Fletcher's strong carrier force (*Enterprise*, *Saratoga*, *Wasp*) north to cover sea lanes into the Solomons. By daybreak 23 August they were east of Malaita, and about 150 miles from Henderson Field. Admiral Kondo did not yet know their exact position, and Fletcher, misinformed by Pacific Fleet Intelligence that the Japanese force still lay north of Truk, decided at the close of the 23rd that there would be no battle for several days. So he sent the *Wasp* group to a fueling rendezvous. This was a bad move; for Yamamoto had already ordered Kondo to press ahead and engage him.

At 0905 August 24 an American PBY spotted carrier *Ryujo* about 280 miles northwest of Fletcher's now two-carrier force. At 1345 Fletcher took the offensive, launching 38 bombers and torpedo planes to snap at the bait. Within one hour, his search planes discovered *Shokaku* and *Zuikaku* some 60 miles farther north than *Ryujo*. Fletcher attempted to divert his strike to the big carriers; but communications that afternoon were abominable and he could not reach the pilots. Commander N. D. Felt's air group attacked *Ryujo* successfully, and at 2000 she was swallowed up by the sea.

Admiral Nagumo decided that the hour had come to avenge Midway. At 1507 and 1600, two attack groups rolled off the decks of *Zuikaku* and *Shokaku*.

Poseidon and Aeolus had arranged a striking setting for this battle. Towering cumulus clouds, constantly rearranged by the 16-knot southeast tradewind in a series of snowy castles and ramparts, blocked off nearly half the depthless dome. The ocean, two miles deep at this point, was topped with merry whitecaps dancing to a clear horizon, such as navigators love. The scene — dark shadows turning some ships purple and sun illuminating others in sharp detail, a graceful curl of foam at the bow of each flattop, the long bow of *North Carolina* (a recent arrival from the Atlantic), *Atlanta* bristling like a porcupine with antiaircraft guns, heavy cruisers stolid and businesslike and the destroyers thrusting, lunging and throwing spray — was one for a great marine artist to depict. To practical carrier seamen, however, the setup was far from perfect. Those handsome clouds could hide a hundred vengeful aircraft; that high equatorial sun could provide a concealed path for pouncing dive-bombers; that reflected glare of blue, white and gold bothered and even blinded the lookouts, and made aircraft identification doubtful. Altogether it was the kind of weather a flattop sailor wants the gods to spread over the enemy's task force, not his own.

As at Midway and Coral Sea, each carrier group, in a tight circle about two miles in diameter, was independent of the other. *Enterprise* operated ten miles northwest of *Saratoga*. Later they combined.

Fletcher was ready for Japanese bombers with 51 Wildcats, mostly from *Enterprise*, stacked in three layers as Combat Air Patrol. At 1629 August 24 the attack group was only ten miles away. Dive-bombers and torpedo planes helped C.A.P. to intercept it. About 24 dive-bombers got through, one diving about every seven seconds. *Enterprise* took three bombs — which killed 74 men, ruptured her decks and wrecked the 5-inch guns; but good damage control saved the ship. *North Carolina* also attracted enemy attention, but she drove off or shot down 14 bombers that got through C.A.P. By 1647 this main attack was finished, and *Enterprise* at 1749 headed into the wind to recover planes. But "Big E's" troubles were not over; delayed effects of two bombs stifled the steering engine and jammed her rudder. By amazingly quick and courageous work this was brought under control at 1859, just when the second Japanese attack wave should have come in; but it missed the carriers altogether.

None of the attackers got through to *Saratoga*, but she hit back at the enemy. Five TBF and two SBD under Lieutenant Harold H. Larsen were scrambled to counterattack. At 1745 they attacked Kondo's Advance Force, badly damaging seaplane carrier *Chitose*, and were back on board "Sara" by 1930. They had no fighter cover, and they were only seven, on a mission for which tenfold the number of planes would have been assigned later in the war. Gallant lads these; none braver.

Admiral Fletcher now decided to call it a day, and turned southward toward a fueling rendezvous. His two carriers, amazingly, had lost only 17 planes. Kondo sent his van of battleships and cruisers in pursuit, but gave it up and retired before midnight.

Neither commander regarded the battle as finished, but to all intents and purposes it was, except for Admiral Tanaka's reinforcement unit. His destroyers pranced up and down off Lunga Point that night, bombarding the Marines' perimeter. Next morning, 25 August, the Marines' own air group, from Henderson Field, badly damaged Tanaka's flagship *Jintsu* and a transport; while a B–17 actually sank a destroyer, which caused amazement on both sides. The Battle of the Eastern Solomons was over.

It is generally accounted an American victory, though far from clean-cut, since two big Japanese carriers remained afloat and undamaged. But the study of this engagement by American airmen and technicians led to great improvements in aircraft tactics and carrier construction in the immense pilot-training and shipbuilding programs under way. An unfortunate epilogue was the torpedoing of *Saratoga*, about 260 miles southeast of Guadalcanal, by submarine *I–26* on 31 August. She was saved, but her repairs took three months to complete. Admiral Fletcher, flying his flag in her at the time, was now relieved, and during the rest of the war received commands more commensurate with his abilities.

4. *The Battle of Cape Esperance, 11–12 October 1942*

This Guadalcanal campaign ran from one crisis to another. After the Battle of the Eastern Solomons each side concentrated on reinforcing its island garrison. Admiral Ghormley initiated an almost continuous reinforcement by freighters, covered by combatant ships and by planes. The Japanese kept thrusting reinforcements into the island after dark in fast destroyers, covered by naval bombardments which made night life hideous for the Marines. Ashore there was fighting every day in the week, and two big offensives. The one laid on by the island commander, General Kawaguchi, 12-14 September, was known as the Battle of the Bloody Ridge, in which the Japanese lost a cool thousand men, against 40 dead Marines. This was followed by a westward thrust by the Marines themselves, along and around the Matanikau river on their west flank, which lasted for two weeks from 23 September.

Apart from these battles, a curious tactical situation developed: a virtual exchange of sea mastery every twelve hours. The Americans ruled the waves from sunup to sundown. Big ships discharged cargoes, little ships dashed through the Sound, landing craft ran errands between Lunga Point and Tulagi. But as the tropical twilight performed a quick fadeout and the pall of night fell on Ironbottom Sound, big ships cleared out like frightened children running home from a graveyard and small craft holed up in Tulagi Harbor. Then the Japanese took over. The "Tokyo Express" of troop-laden destroyers and light cruisers dashed in to discharge soldiers or freight where their troops controlled the beach, and, departing, tossed shells in the Marines' direction. But the Rising Sun flag never stayed to greet its namesake; by dawn the Japanese were well away and the Stars and Stripes reappeared. Such was the pattern cut to fit the requirements of this strange campaign; any attempt to reshape it meant a bloody battle. The Japanese rarely, and then only disastrously, attempted daytime raids with ships; the Americans more frequently interfered with the Tokyo Express, but any such attempt was apt to be fatal — as was that of destroyer-transports *Little* and *Gregory* on 5 September. Both were sunk.

It was not easy to get American reinforcements to Guadalcanal. To protect a convoy of six transports carrying the 7th Marine Regiment, which departed Espiritu Santo on 14 September, Admiral Ghormley committed two carriers, *Wasp* and *Hornet*. Japanese submarines *I–19* and *I–15*, which had missed their opportunities in the Battle of the Eastern Solomons, now hit the jackpot.

The one penetrated *Wasp*'s destroyer screen on 15 September, got three torpedoes into her, and sank that big carrier. The other took a crack at *Hornet*, missed her, but got one torpedo each into destroyer *O'Brien* and the *North Carolina*. Both survived, though *O'Brien* sank on her way to the West Coast. Admiral Turner, in command of the transport echelon, decided to push on; and never was the old naval adage "Stout hearts make safe ships" better tested. The Marines, 4000 in number, were safely landed at Guadalcanal on 18 September.

Some effort had to be made to break this deadlock. Could not more help be obtained from the Southwest Pacific? A conference to discuss this subject was held at Nouméa on 28 September. Admirals Nimitz, Ghormley and Turner, General MacArthur's chief of staff General Sutherland, and General "Hap" Arnold, head of the Army Air Force, attended.

MacArthur had 55,000 troops, American and Australian, in Port Moresby. The Japanese attempt to take Port Moresby by marching troops across the Owen Stanley Range had been halted on 17 August, and Nimitz thought that MacArthur might now spare troops for Guadalcanal. Sutherland rejected this idea flat; he expected the Japanese to start another Coral Sea operation. Nobody on our side knew that on 31 August the Japanese high command had decided to throw everything it had into Guadalcanal, and until that island was secured, to leave their Papuan army out on a limb. The two Admirals at the Nouméa conference, even without that knowledge, warned that unless Guadalcanal were reinforced the enemy could push us off the island whenever he really tried.

Try he did, and thrice; but not quite hard enough, as we were trying a little harder. The next naval battle, that of Cape Esperance, was sparked off by the dispatch of a reinforced regiment of the Americal Division to Guadalcanal, in two big transports and eight destroyer types, on 9 October. Admiral Turner commanded this echelon, and Ghormley sent up a cruiser group to run interference. The cruisers were commanded, in *San Francisco*, by Rear Admiral Norman Scott, a young and brilliant flag officer. He had had three weeks to give his task force intensive training in night action, and it paid off well.

For a week or more, the Japanese had been running nightly Tokyo Expresses to northwestern Guadalcanal, and a particularly strong one was due on the night of 11-12 October: two seaplane carriers and six destroyers carrying troops and a vast amount of ammunition and matériel, commanded by Rear Admiral Joshima. In addition, Rear Admiral Goto brought down the Slot a bombardment group of three heavy cruisers and two destroyers. These were reported by a B–17 to Admiral Scott in the early afternoon of the 11th. He built up speed to intercept them west of Savo Island, launched his cruisers' float planes to track them, and Goto was completely surprised when Scott's cruisers opened gunfire at 2346. The American task force (five destroyers, heavy cruisers *San Francisco* and *Salt Lake City*, and light cruisers *Boise* and *Helena*) was just executing a countermarch, southwest of Savo Island and north of Cape Esperance, Guadalcanal, from which this battle is named. The range of *Aoba* at the head of the Japanese column, to *Helena*, was only 4800 yards.

So far, so good; but this might have been called the Battle of Mutual Errors. Scott, fearing that his cruisers were firing on van destroyer *Duncan*, ordered Cease Fire only one minute after firing began. Fortunately the American cruiser commanders, emulating Nelson at Copenhagen, turned deaf ears to this order and their gunners continued to pump shells into the enemy ships. Admiral Goto, thinking that Scott's column was Joshima's Reinforcement Group (then safely within the Sound), did the same, and ordered his column to turn right. A few seconds later the Admiral was mortally wounded by a shell explosion near his flag bridge. By

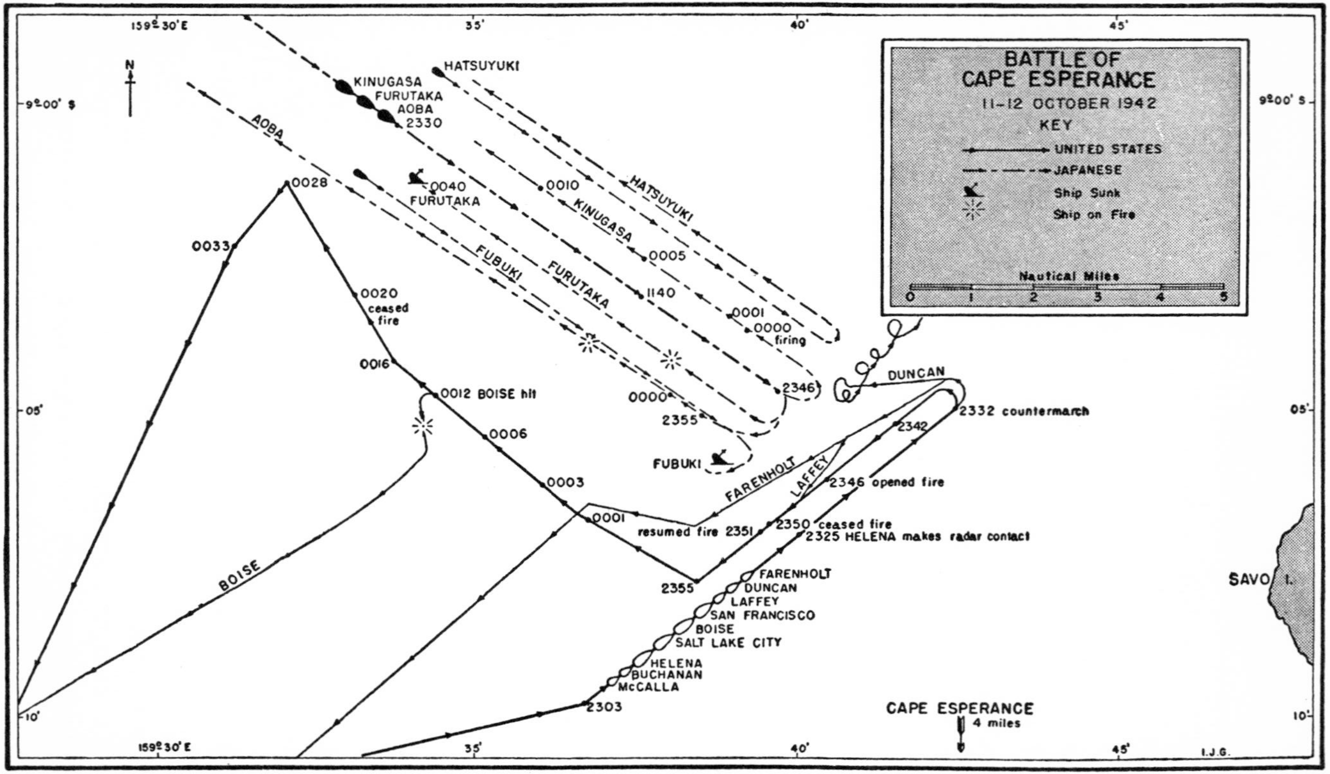
BATTLE OF
CAPE ESPERANCE
11-12 OCTOBER 1942
KEY
UNITED STATES
JAPANESE
Ship Sunk
Ship on Fire
Nautical Miles
0 1 2 3 4 5
159° 30' E
35'
40'
45'
9°00' S
05'
10'
N
HATSUYUKI
KINUGASA
FURUTAKA
AOBA
2330
AOBA
0040
FURUTAKA
0010
KINUGASA
HATSUYUKI
0005
FUBUKI
FURUTAKA
1140
0001
0000
firing
2346
0000
2355
FUBUKI
0028
0033
0020
ceased
fire
0016
0012 BOISE hit
0006
0003
0001
BOISE
DUNCAN
2332 countermarch
2342
FARENHOLT
LAFFEY
2346 opened fire
resumed fire 2351
2350 ceased fire
2325 HELENA makes radar contact
2355
FARENHOLT
DUNCAN
LAFFEY
SAN FRANCISCO
BOISE
SALT LAKE CITY
HELENA
BUCHANAN
McCALLA
2303
SAVO I.
CAPE ESPERANCE
4 miles
I.J.G.

that time, both *Aoba* and *Furutaka* were burning brightly. At 2351 Scott discovered his error and ordered Resume Firing. Four minutes later he swung his column northwest to parallel the Japanese. Partly as a result of Goto's bad guess and sudden death, the enemy never returned an effective fire, and lost cruiser *Furutaka* and destroyer *Fubuki* to gunfire and torpedo hits. On our side, *Duncan* was mortally wounded and *Farenholt* badly so; *Boise* was badly pounded by two enemy cruisers, her No. 1 turret breached and a magazine exploded. But the luck of the Irish and good damage control saved the "Galloping Ghost," as the men called Captain "Mike" Moran's cruiser, to fight another day. The main action was over at 0020 October 12.

In the meantime Admiral Joshima was setting ashore the contents of his Reinforcement Group. At 0250 a float plane from *Boise* sighted his formation steaming out of the Sound. Bomber planes summoned from Henderson Field sank two of his destroyers, which were combing the scene of the action for survivors.

Norman Scott fought the Battle of Cape Esperance with cool, determined courage, and, despite an intricate countermarch, never let the situation deteriorate into a mêlée. He became the hero of the South Pacific during the short month that remained of his valiant life. Unfortunately, because it is human to conclude that the result justifies the means, some fallacious conclusions were drawn from the Battle of Cape Esperance: that the single-column formation was all right, and that American gunfire could master any night battle situation. Actually, Scott's disposition was dangerously unwieldly and prevented the destroyers from exploiting their proper weapon, the torpedo. And because the surprised enemy did not get off his usual torpedo attack, that was assumed to be no longer a serious threat. One learns more from defeat than from victory.

The Japanese did accomplish their main mission, landing not only troops but heavy artillery while Goto and Scott were fighting. On the other hand, the 164th Infantry Regiment, Americal Division, whose journey to Guadalcanal was the reason for Scott's being where he was, landed safely on 13 October, bringing relief to the weary Marines in the perimeter.

Tokyo Express for the night of 13-14 October was a bombardment mission built around battleships *Kongo* and *Haruna*, under command of Admiral Kurita. They delivered a 90-minute shoot, which killed many Marines, blooded the newly arrived GIs, holed the airfield with yawning chasms, destroyed almost the entire supply of aviation gasoline and 48 aircraft.

The bombardment might have lasted even longer but for the PTs, the first motor torpedo boats to arrive at Tulagi. These piled in against the battleships, shooting and firing torpedoes briskly; and although no hits are recorded, they made Admiral Kurita so nervous (a quality he later showed in greater degree at the Battle off Samar), that he retired at 0230 October 14.

The following night, of 14-15 October, was another bad one for Americans ashore. Admiral Mikawa personally entered "Sleepless Lagoon" (as the Marines were beginning to call it) in cruiser *Chokai*, followed by lucky *Kinugasa*, to churn up the Henderson Field community with 752 eight-inch shell and cover the landing of another echelon of troops.

Dawn of the 15th revealed a humiliating spectacle. In full view were enemy transports lying-to off Tassafaronga, unloading troops and supplies with as much ease as if they had been in Tokyo Bay; and, hovering around and over them, destroyers and planes.

General Geiger, Marine air commander, was told there was no gas at Henderson Field. "Then, by God, find some!" he roared. Men scoured the dispersal areas, collected some 400 drums of aviation gas from swamps and thickets where they had been cached, and trundled them to the field. Even two disabled B–17s had their tanks siphoned dry. By these pint-pot methods enough fuel was procured to enable planes to make the ten-mile hop to the targets off Tassafaronga and back. Army, Navy and Marine pilots bombed and strafed the transports all day long 15 October, fighting off Zekes and dodging the darting tongues of antiaircraft tracers. Flying Fortresses flew up from Espiritu Santo and lent a hand. High over the revitalized airfield, Wildcat bullets and antiaircraft shells brought down twelve bombers and five fighters. Everybody who flew claimed damage that day, and for once they were right. Three large Japanese transports not yet completely unloaded had to be beached and became a total loss. By 1550 things had become so hot that the Japanese task force commander decided to retire. Not one transport escaped damage; not one troop unit landed without casualties and loss of equipment. This field day cost the Americans only three dive-bombers and four fighter planes.

That night, all hands ashore breathed easier. Even a downpour of 800 eight-inch shells from cruisers *Myoko* and *Maya* and 300 five-inch from Tanaka's destroyers failed to quench the spark of hope kindled by the feeling that the enemy had done his worst. But, alas, he had not.

On 15 October Admiral Nimitz expressed his estimate of the situation in three sober sentences: "It now appears that we are unable to control the sea in the Guadalcanal area. Thus our supply of the positions will only be done at great expense to us. The situation is not hopeless, but it is certainly critical."

The extremity of the American situation in mid-October is illustrated by gallant if pitiful efforts to keep the lifeline intact. Twin-engined Douglas Skytroopers became flying workhorses; each brought up from Espiritu Santo about enough gas to keep twelve Wildcats aloft for an hour. Submarine *Amberjack*, fitted to carry 9000 gallons of gasoline and ten tons of bombs, did her part. A barge-towing Allied expedition was made up of two cargo ships, motor torpedo boat tender *Jamestown*, fleet tug *Vireo* and two destroyers, each towing a barge carrying 2000 barrels of gasoline and 500 quarter-ton bombs. On 15 October, 75 miles from Guadalcanal, these lucrative targets were sighted and reported by a Japanese search plane. The bigger ships hastily returned to Espiritu Santo, but around noon *Meredith* was sunk by a 27-plane raid from carrier *Zuikaku.*

Mid-October marked the nadir of misery for the American at Guadalcanal.

5. *The Battle of the Santa Cruz Islands, 26–27 October 1942*

Admiral Nimitz was also confronted with the pressing problem of leadership in the South Pacific. Admiral Ghormley, a meticulous, conscientious officer with a long record of achievement, lacked the personal qualities needed to inspire American fighting men in a tough spot. Admiral Nimitz on 15 October decided that "the critical situation requires a more aggressive commander," and named Vice Admiral William F. Halsey.

Since May, "Bill" [4] Halsey had been on the binnacle list with dermatitis, but mid-October found him back to battery. On 18 October, with feelings of "astonishment, apprehension and regret," he relieved his old friend Ghormley. He brought his own staff, headed by Captain Miles Browning who had fought under Spruance at Midway. Halsey had already won a reputation for leadership, confidence and agressiveness. The announcement that he was now Comsopac was received on board ships of that force with cheers and rejoicing.

Other positive measures were taken. Admiral King released from Atlantic Fleet a task group powered by new battleship *Indiana*, which came through the Panama Canal to the South Pacific. A flock of 50 Army fighter planes migrated from the Central to the

[4] "Bill" was corrupted by news reports to "Bull"; but nobody who knew Halsey personally ever called him that.

South Pacific. Twenty-four submarines were ordered thither. Two squadrons of Army B–17s droned across the Equator to join the brood under Rear Admiral Aubrey W. Fitch, now Comairsopac at Espiritu Santo.

In Washington, Admiral King had his hands full. Our predicament in the Solomons was more than matched by that of the Atlantic Fleet. German submarines during October sank 88 merchant ships of 585,510 tons in the Atlantic, and the North African invasion was already at sea. British forces in Egypt and India were still being supplied by ships sailing around the Cape of Good Hope. Guadalcanal had to be fitted by the Joint Chiefs of Staff into a worldwide strategic pattern. The island could not be secured without drawing on forces committed to the buildup in the United Kingdom for a cross-channel operation in 1943, a date the British wished to postpone. Admiral King and General MacArthur argued against risking disaster in the Solomons and New Guinea in order to provide for a vague future operation in Europe. President Roosevelt broke this deadlock on 24 October by sending a strong message to each member of the Joint Chiefs of Staff, insisting that Guadalcanal must be reinforced, and quickly.

It could not be done too quickly, for the Japanese high command had now given the capture of Henderson Field top billing. Their plan was to devote the third week of October to softening up the Marines in preparation for "Y-day," the 22nd, when the Rising Sun was to be planted on Henderson Field by General Maruyama. The Combined Fleet, impatiently circling north of the Solomons, would then "apprehend and annihilate any powerful forces in the Solomons area, as well as any reinforcements." This reversed the classic strategy of first securing sea control which the Japanese had tried, unsuccessfully, in the Eastern Solomons battle. Admiral Yamamoto would better have stuck to Mahan. For the Marines and the GIs refused to be softened, and the stout fight they put up for a week (19-26 October) to defend Henderson Field, and the consequent postponement of Y-day, gave Admiral Kinkaid time to bring up carrier *Enterprise* and take a decisive part in the sea action.

The Japanese Guadalcanal garrison, now augmented by the 4500 troops landed by recent Tokyo Expresses, opened attack 20 October against the Marines' western flank on the Matanikau river. This was followed by an enveloping movement against the central and eastern flanks of the American perimeter. Each was beaten off with heavy loss, over a period of six days. And in this Battle for Henderson Field the GIs proved that they too could defeat jungle-fighting Japanese, if properly trained and led, as indeed they were. Lieutenant Colonel Timboe of the 164th belongs to the Hall of Fame with Lieutenant Colonels McKelvy, "Chesty" Puller, Sam Griffith and General Vandegrift of the Marine Corps.

During these ground actions there were several minor actions in Ironbottom Sound, and at least one Tokyo Express failed to deliver the goods; but these were overshadowed by the carrier-fought Battle of the Santa Cruz Islands, now making up.

Northeast and east of the lower Solomons are two small groups of islands, the Stewarts and the Santa Cruz. The center of the United States Navy's position in this forthcoming battle was about 280 miles east of the one and 125 miles north of the other; roughly 160 miles east of the spot where *Enterprise* was hit in the Battle of the Eastern Solomons two months earlier. The Santa Cruz Islands, glorified as the site of "Bali-hai" in the musical comedy *South Pacific*, were so infested with malignant malaria, and so rugged in terrain, that the Army Engineers sent there early in August to build an airfield had to give up and leave.

Admiral Yamamoto, who directed the show from Truk, really expected to clean up this time. He had four carriers, five battleships, 14 cruisers and 44 destroyers to throw in; he knew that *Wasp* had been sunk and that *Saratoga* was under repair, but did not know that "Big E" was back, under fighting Tom Kinkaid, with *South Dakota* in her screen. This new battleship, freshly provided with dozens of the new 40-mm antiaircraft guns, was commanded by one of the Navy's most remarkable characters, Captain Thomas L. Gatch. No ship more eager to fight ever entered the Pacific; for the skipper, by constant target practice on towed planes, ignoring lapses in spit-and-polish, and exercising a natural gift for leadership, had welded his green crew into a splendid fighting team. They "looked like a lot of wild men," said one of his officers, and they all adored Tom Gatch.

Combined Fleet was losing its edge, and the ships were running out of fuel, waiting for the Japanese ground forces to take Henderson Field. A premature paean of victory — later retracted — from the liaison officer on Guadalcanal, at 0126 October 25, sparked off the naval battle. Yamamoto did not know where the American carriers were; but a far-ranging Catalina from Espiritu Santo sighted Nagumo's spoiled children of victory, carriers *Shokaku* and *Zuikaku*, at noon. Kinkaid acted on this contact by launching a combined search-strike from *Enterprise* that afternoon. But they located nothing, as the Japanese had cagily reversed course, again waiting for certain news of victory ashore.

In the small hours of 26 October Admiral Kinkaid, who had been steering northwesterly at 20 knots, began to receive plane contacts on enemy carriers 200 miles away. In the gray hours before dawn Admiral Halsey on Nouméa riffled through the dispatches, glanced at his operations chart, and sent out these words:

ATTACK — REPEAT — ATTACK!

The sun rose at 0523 on a fair day — low broken cumulus clouds scattered over half the sky, the ocean rising and falling in a gentle swell, a languid 8-knot breeze from the southeast scarcely raising ripples on the sea's smooth surface. It was weather to the taste of dive-bomber pilots who could lurk in the clouds, but to the distaste of antiaircraft gunners — no cloud has a silver lining for them. Already *Enterprise* had launched a search mission, each SBD armed with a 500-pound bomb "just in case." At 0740, two bomber pilots sighted light carrier *Zuiho*, used their bombs, and knocked her out so far as this battle was concerned.

One hour earlier a Japanese search plane had sighted *Hornet*. Admiral Kondo, again Japanese O.T.C., ordered strikes to be launched at her immediately from his three viable carriers. Twenty minutes later *Hornet* followed suit. The two hostile groups passed one another in the air, each eying the enemy and wondering which would find a flight deck on its return. Half *Enterprise*'s group was shot down 100 miles short of its target by a dozen Zekes which had peeled off especially to get them.

Now came the most tense moment for the opposing commanders, Kinkaid and Kondo. Each had found the other, each was lashing out at the other.

Flagship *Enterprise* was the hub of a tight little circle rimmed by battleship *South Dakota*, heavy cruiser *Portland*, antiaircraft cruiser *San Juan* and eight destroyers. Ten miles to the southeast cruised Rear Admiral George D. Murray's flagship *Hornet*, similarly surrounded by floating gun platforms. Stacked in layers overhead were 38 fighters of Combat Air Patrol, all under *Enterprise* fighter-direction.

The Japanese strike, first to depart, was also the first to arrive at its target. At 0859 the American C.A.P. sighted Val dive-bombers at 17,000 feet. At about the same moment *Enterprise* entered a local rain squall which concealed her from the approaching enemy; but *Hornet* was in the clear and the enemy concentrated on her, commencing at 0910. Vals dove down, loosing a series of explosive bombs. *Hornet* and her protectors blackened the sky with shell-bursts. One bomb hit the starboard side of the flight deck aft. The Japanese squadron commander, crippled by a shellburst, made a spectacular suicide crash. His plane hit the stack, glanced off and burst through the flight deck, where two of its bomb detonated. Even more deadly were the torpedo-carrying Kates, which bored in low from astern, slugging nastily at *Hornet*'s tender groin. Two torpedoes exploded in the engineering spaces. The carrier, in a thick cloud of smoke and steam, lurched to starboard, slowed to a stop, lost all power and communications. She was now immobile — deaf, dumb and impotent. Three more quarter-ton bombs hit the flight deck. She was still writhing from this onslaught when a flaming Kate with a doomed pilot made a suicide run from dead ahead, piled into the port forward gun gallery, and blew up near the forward elevator shaft. In all, some 27 Japanese planes jumped this carrier, and only two got home; but that was a cheap price to pay for depriving the Pacific Fleet of one third of its carrier strength.

At 0925, when *Hornet* looked like a bad risk, 52 planes of her air group led by Lieutenant Commander "Gus" Widhelm were approaching the Japanese force. Eleven bombers under Lieutenant James E. Vose fought their way through to the pushover point, drew a bead on *Shokaku*, and roared down through flak with Zekes still on their tails. It was worth the risk. Three to six 100-pound bombs ripped the Japanese carrier's flight deck to shreds, destroyed the hangar and ignited severe fires. *Shokaku* was out of the war for nine months. *Hornet*'s second wave missed the Japanese carriers, but exploded two bombs on cruiser *Chikuma* and knocked her out — for a time.

Thus, by 1030 October 26, one large and one small Japanese flattop had been scratched, and *Hornet* almost finished; but *Zuikaku* and *Junyo* were still intact, and Admiral Kondo had already ordered their planes to go get Big E. His earlier strike would have done so, but for superb ship handling by Captain Hardison, and magnificent shooting by the "wild men" of *South Dakota*. She in this action secured for battlewagons the place of honor that they occupied during the rest of the war — defending carriers from attack. *Enterprise* took three bombs which killed 44 men but inflicted no lethal damage on the ship.

Forty minutes later, at 1101, *Junyo*'s dive-bombers tumbled out of the low overcast. One of them planted a bomb on *South Dakota*'s No. 1 turret; an armor-piercing bomb went right through the thin skin of antiaircraft cruiser *San Juan*, exploding below her keel and jamming her rudder.

Enemy planes kept dogging *Hornet*, when under tow by cruiser *Northampton;* she took three more hits, and had to be abandoned. Two Japanese destroyers then sank her. Had the later expedient of attaching powerful fleet tugs to each carrier group been in effect, she would have been towed out of enemy range and salvaged.

Kondo now shaped a retiring course northward, hoping to renew battle on the 28th; but Kinkaid by that time was too far away for him to make contact. The Battle of the Santa Cruz Islands was over. Measured in terms of sinking, the Japanese could claim victory. The loss of the new, powerful *Hornet* was serious, and left the United States Navy with only two carriers in the Pacific, "Sara" and "Big E," both under repair. But Japanese air strength had been reduced by about 100 planes, and some of the best pilots. The land battle, which the naval battle was supposed to cover, had failed. Moreover, this Santa Cruz set-to gained precious time for the Americans to prepare for the next expected onslaught.

6. *The Naval Battle of Guadalcanal, 12–15 November 1942*

As usual, that was not long a-coming. Admiral Yamamoto, contemptuous of earlier air and ground efforts to capture Henderson Field, now issued a new op plan to secure sea supremacy in the

Solomons. Admiral Halsey, exasperated over the loss of *Hornet*, drafted a plan to thwart him. Between 2 and 10 November the enemy brought in 65 destroyer loads and two cruiser loads of troops to western Guadalcanal. One of these detachments, landed at Koli Point east of the American perimeter, was exterminated by the Marines; Henderson Field flyers inflicted major damage on three destroyers, helped by the Tulagi PT squadron; minesweeper *Southard* sank one submarine. But by 12 November the Japanese garrison on Guadalcanal outnumbered the Americans for the first time.

The big American reinforcements, due to arrive on 11-12 November, were (1) three combat-loaded freighters escorted by Rear Admiral Scott in antiaircraft cruiser *Atlanta*, with four destroyers; and (2) four more transport types (including Admiral Turner's flagship *McCawley*), escorted by Rear Admiral Daniel J. Callaghan in *San Francisco*, with three more cruisers and five destroyers. Since intelligence reports indicated that the Japanese were about to dispatch an exceptionally strong and noxious Tokyo Express, Admiral Halsey deployed 24 submarines in and around Solomons waters and sent Tom Kinkaid's carrier task force (*Enterprise*, battleships *Washington* and *South Dakota*, two cruisers and eight destroyers) to cover Turner and counter Yamamoto. If Big E, still under repair at Nouméa, could not get there in time, the battleships and four destroyers would be detached for independent action, under the command of Rear Admiral Willis A. Lee in *Washington*. That is exactly what happened — and mighty fortunate that it did. Halsey inadvertently afforded "Ching" Lee his one big moment in the war, even though he later deprived him of an even greater opportunity in the Battle for Leyte Gulf.

Scott's reinforcement contingent unloaded successfully on 11 November, and Turner's was about half empty at 1317 on the 12th when word came from a coastwatcher at Buin that a formidable flock of fighter-escorted bombers was flying down the Slot. Their attack on the transports in Lunga Roads an hour later opened the Naval Battle of Guadalcanal. This first round resulted very ill for enemy aircraft. Admiral Turner, a past master at handling ships in such manner as to thwart air attack and bring all his own antiaircraft fire to bear, suffered only slight damage, and, helped by Wildcats from Henderson Field, allowed very few of the two-engined Bettys to return.

Tense calm followed the afternoon's elimination shoot. As Turner steamed back to the unloading area through floating remains of downed planes, he realized that the enemy had just begun to show his hand. Abundant intelligence from search planes and coastwatchers indicated that the Tokyo Express that night would include two battleships and at least four cruisers and ten destroyers — too much for Callaghan's two heavy and three light cruisers and eight destroyers to take on with much prospect of success. Yet, with Kinkaid's carrier-battleship force too far away to help, there was nothing else to do but for Callaghan to block, and block hard.

At dusk 12 November Turner pulled out his transports, Callaghan escorting them for a few hours only before he had to return to face the Japanese onslaught. "Uncle Dan" Callaghan, austere, deeply religious, a hard-working and conscientious officer who possessed the high personal regard of his fellows and the love of his men, had reached the acme of his career. There was something a little detached about this man, since his thoughts were often not of this world; something, too, that recalled the chivalrous warriors of other days. One could see him as Ossian's dark-haired Duth-maruno, with beetling-browed Turner in the role of Fingal, exhorting him, when they parted that night: "Near us are the foes, Duth-maruno. They come forward like waves in mist, when their foamy tops are seen above the low-sailing vapor. . . . Sons of heroes, call forth the steel!"

Callaghan passed through Lunga Channel into Ironbottom Sound, his ships in single column. Four destroyers were in the van, then cruisers *Atlanta* (with Rear Admiral Scott embarked), *San Francisco*, *Portland*, *Helena* and *Juneau*. Four destroyers brought up the rear. This disposition was supposed to be best for navigating restricted waters and for ship-to-ship communication. But it prevented the rear destroyers from making an initial torpedo attack; and, for reasons unknown, Callaghan did not place in the van two destroyers which had the latest SG radar — the kind that showed a picture on the screen.

Fast approaching was a beefed-up Tokyo Express — two battleships, screened by a light cruiser and 14 destroyers, under Vice Admiral Hiroaki Abe. Their mission was to knock out Henderson Field and slaughter the Marines with high explosive shells. Abe was not looking for a naval battle. He assumed that the Americans as usual would be gone with the sun, allowing him to prowl the Sound and bombard at will.

It was now Friday the thirteenth, last day of life for eight ships and many hundred sailors, including two rear admirals. The Americans' first radar contact, at 0124, showed Abe's battlewagons almost surrounded by his destroyer screen, approaching from the direction of Savo Island. Callaghan did not alter course to cross the enemy's "T"; that was his big mistake. At 0141 destroyer *Cushing*, leading the American column, sighted two Japanese destroyers about to cross her bows. She turned hard-a-port to unmask her torpedo batteries and avoid a collision. This maneuver threw the American column into partial disorder, which in a few minutes' time became almost complete. Now surprise was lost. Callaghan delayed eight minutes before opening gunfire, owing to the confusion engendered by *Cushing*'s turn and his fear of hitting friends. This gave Abe precious time to change his high-caliber bombardment shells for armor-piercing. If one American shell had exploded on his battleships while their decks were heaped with shells, they would have been destroyed.

At 0150, just as a Japanese destroyer's searchlight picked up the bridge of *Atlanta*, she began shooting. Other Japanese destroyers and the two battlewagons then deluged the helpless cruiser with shellfire. One snuffed out the lives of Admiral Scott and his staff on the bridge. *Atlanta* was out of the battle, which now became an unplanned, wild and desperate mêlée in black darkness, fitfully lighted by gunfire flashes, torpedo explosions and star shell.

So far as there was any order in this action, it was Callaghan's cruiser column, minus *Atlanta*, thrusting between two battleships, *Hiei* to port and *Kirishima* to starboard, while destroyers of both sides milled about, shooting at targets of opportunity. Although neither Japanese battleship was hit early in the action, Admiral Abe didn't like it and countermarched. *Hiei* sank *Cushing*, which had launched six torpedoes fruitlessly at her, and then had a brush with destroyer *Laffey*, so close that her 14-inch guns could not depress sufficiently to hit the destroyer, whose torpedoes were too close to arm; but *Laffey*'s machine-gun fire riddled the battleship's bridge and killed her C.O. A Japanese destroyer got a torpedo into *Laffey*, and sank her. *Sterett*, next destroyer astern, torpedoed Japanese destroyer *Yudichi* and then herself received three hits that put her out of the battle. *Hiei* at one time was burning from stem to stern, and she went dead in the water, but *Kirishima* took only one hit.

Admiral Callaghan, informed that his flagship *San Francisco* was shooting at disabled *Atlanta*, ordered "Cease Firing Own Ships!" When that order took effect, his ship was the first to suffer. *Kirishima* and two other Japanese ships hurled an avalanche of gunfire at her. Admiral Callaghan and almost every member of his staff, and Captain Cassin Young, were killed. Cruiser *Portland* (Captain Laurance DuBose), next astern, took a torpedo hit which bent her stern plates so that they acted as a giant fixed rudder; she could only steam in circles. As she sheered out of the column she let fly at *Hiei*, range 4000 yards, with both forward

After her magazine exploded

(Stern of *Tennessee* at left)

Blown in half

Death of Arizona, *7 December 1941*

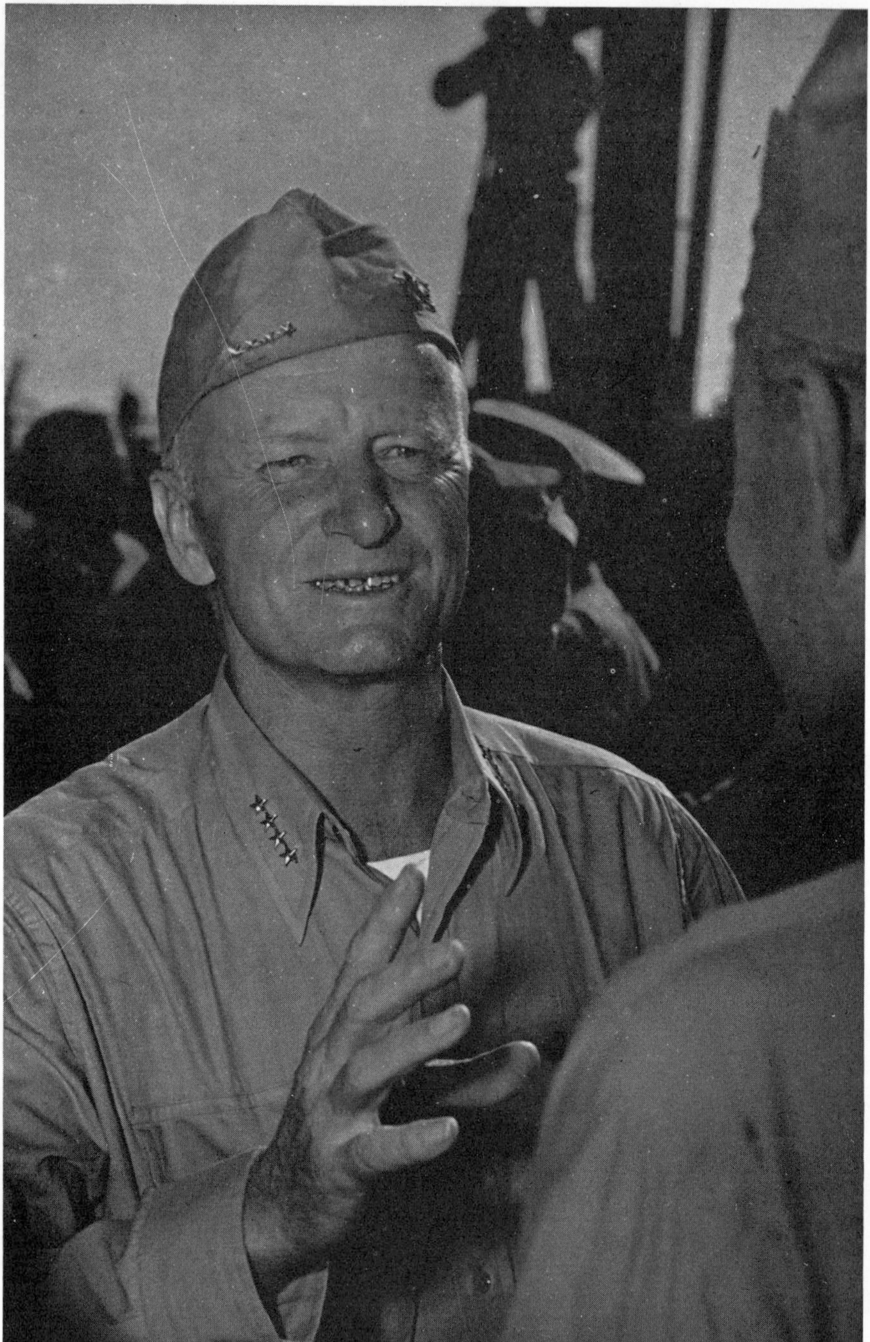

Admiral Chester W. Nimitz USN

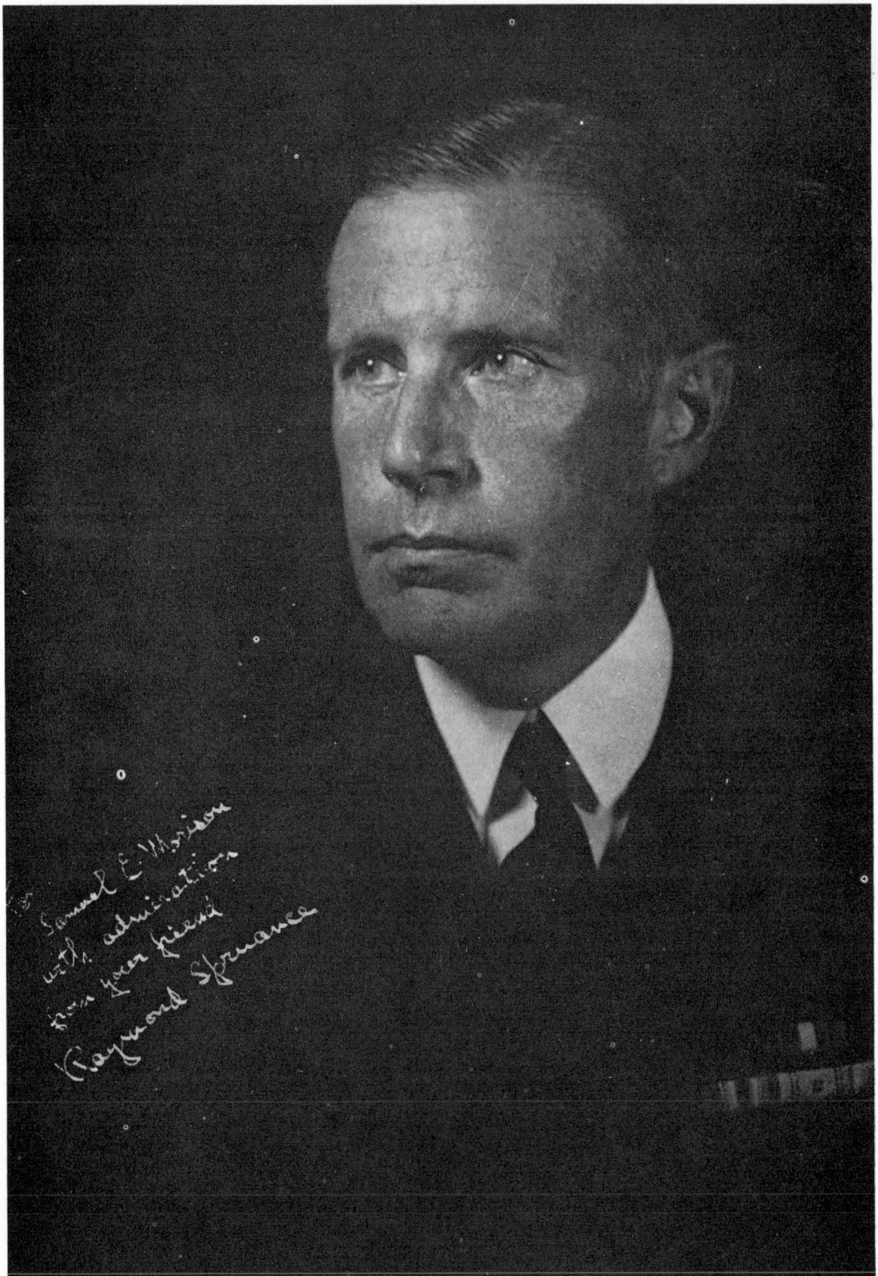

Admiral Raymond A. Spruance USN

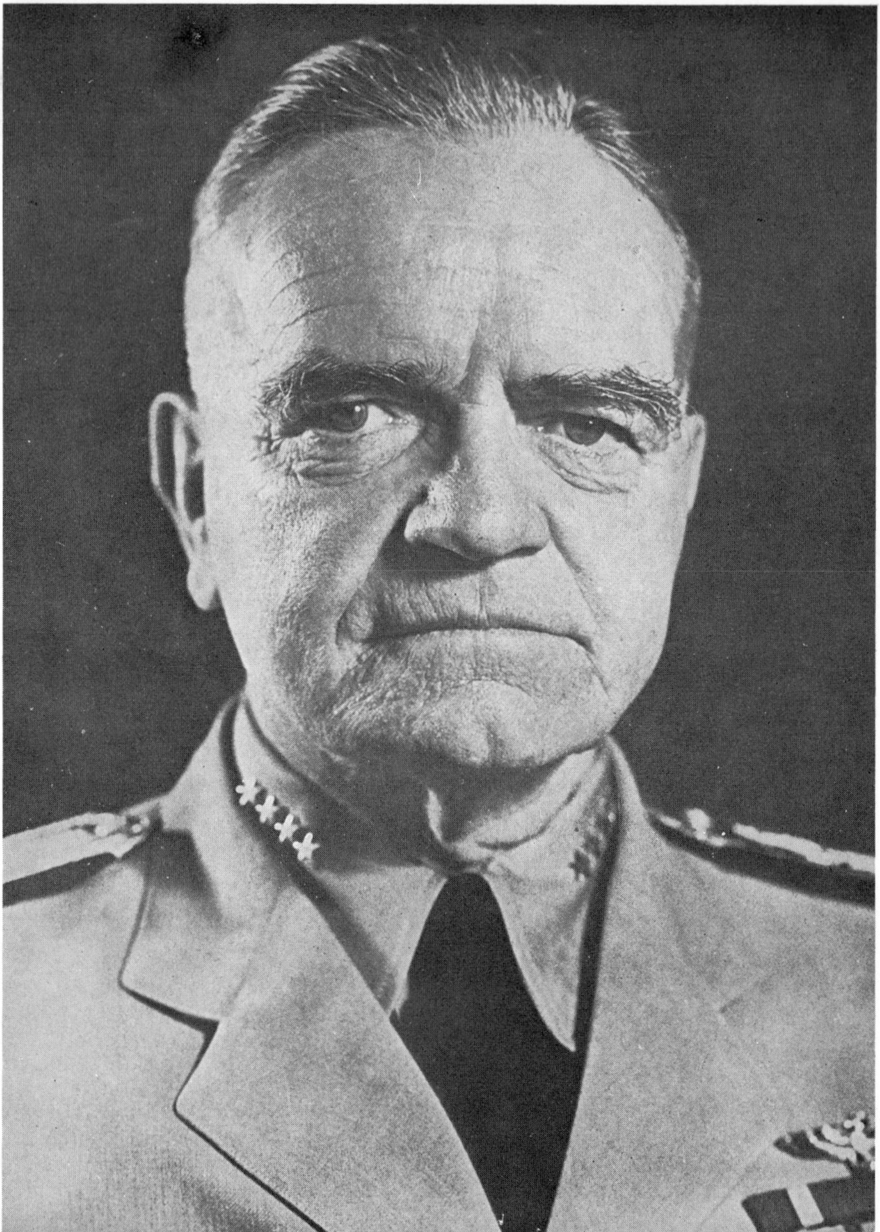

Admiral William F. Halsey USN

U.S.S. South Dakota *and* Enterprise *during the Battle of the Santa Cruz Islands*

Japanese transports burning on beach, Guadalcanal

U.S.S. *Washington*

15 November 1942

Vice Admiral Henry Kent Hewitt USN

Commander Task Force 34, 1942; Commander Eighth Fleet, 1943

From a painting by Albert K. Murray

Rear Admiral Richmond Kelly Turner USN *and Staff*

In the background: Colonel N. D. Harris USMC, Commander J. S. Lowis, Captain J. H. Doyle

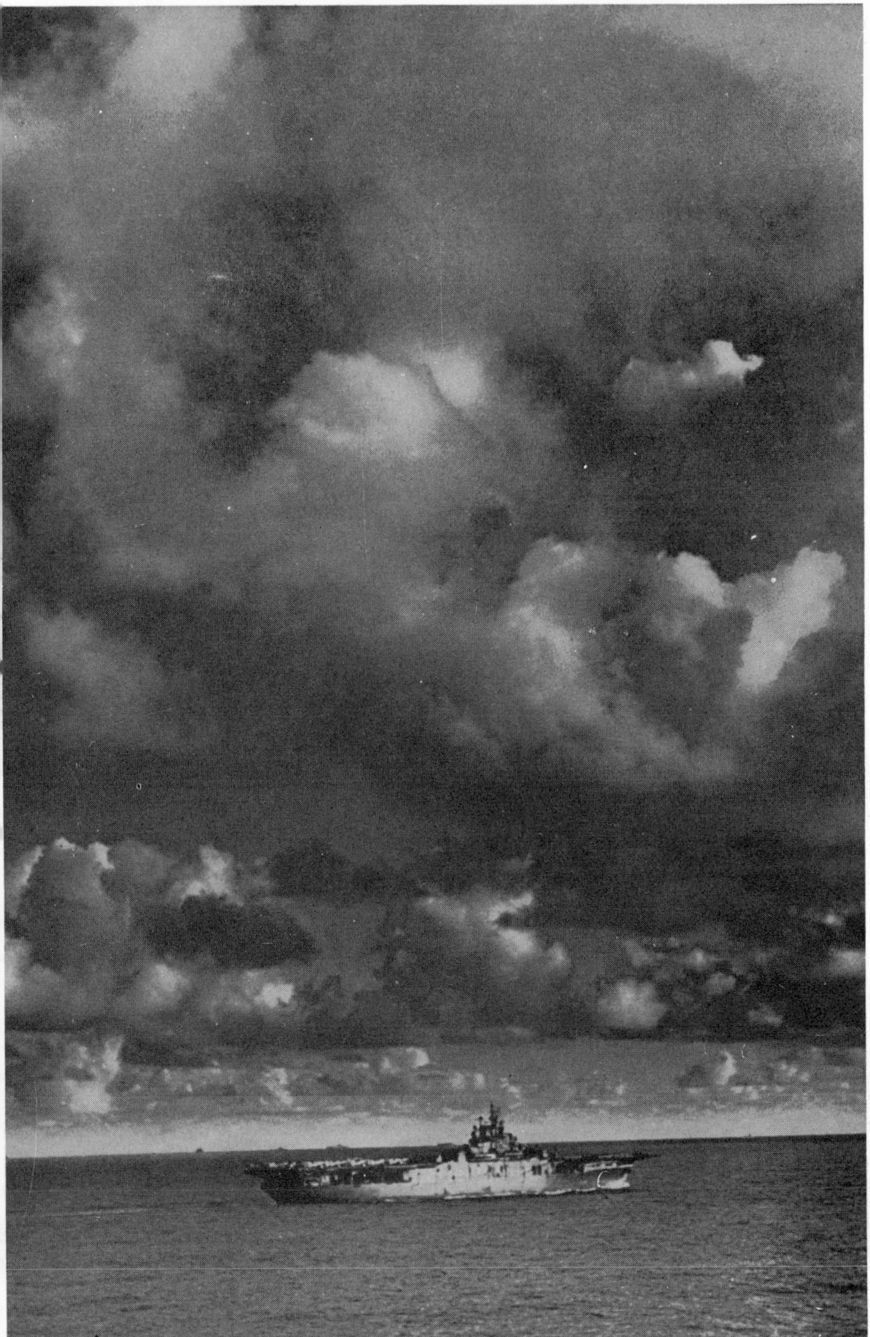

U.S.S. Essex *during Operation* GALVANIC

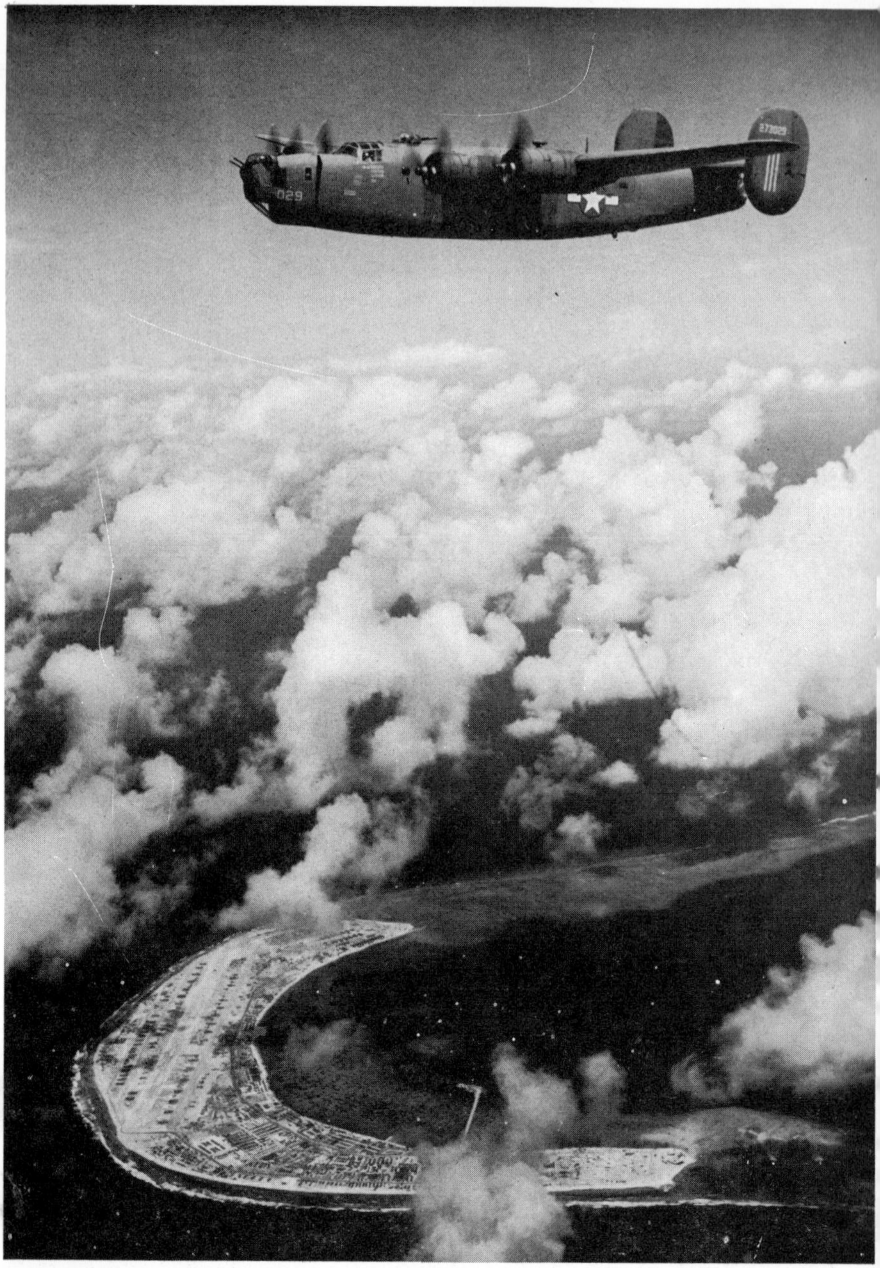

Photo by Army Air Force

Wings over Kwajalein

VII Army Air Force Liberator over Kwajalein Island, October 1944

Vice Admiral John S. McCain USN

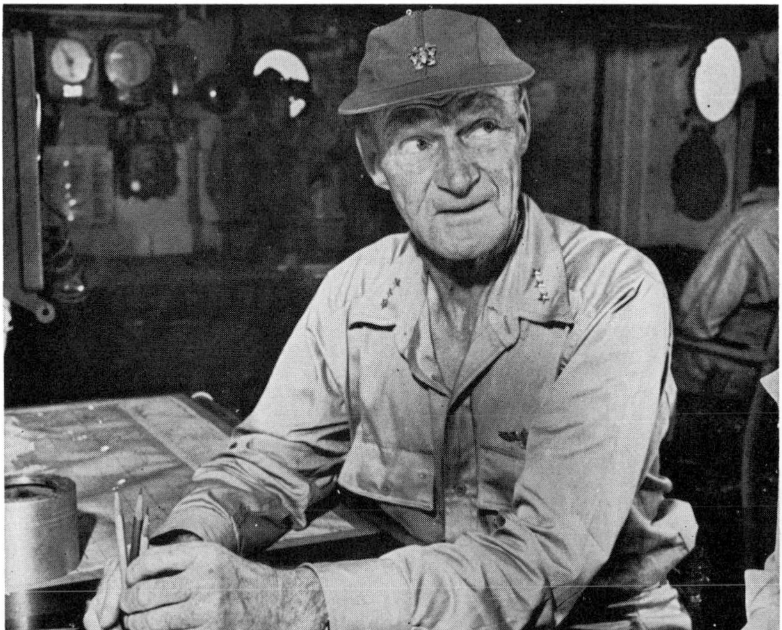

Vice Admiral Marc A. Mitscher USN in U.S.S. *Randolph*

CTF 38 and CTF 58

U.S. motor torpedo boat laying smoke

U.S.S. *Savannah* hit by radio-guided bomb

Salerno

turrets. Still churning loopwise, she found crippled destroyer *Yudichi* at first light, and finished her off. That concluded the night's performance for "Sweet Pea," as her sailors called this great fighting ship. *Helena,* next astern, did some useful shooting that helped speed the enemy on his way; but *Juneau,* the rear cruiser, was put out of action by a torpedo that exploded in her forward fire room.

Of the four rear destroyers, brand-new *Barton* had exactly seven minutes of life in combat. Two torpedo hits broke her in two, and down she went with most of her crew. *Monssen* was reduced to a burning hulk by some 37 shell hits. *Fletcher,* the tail-end Charlie with SG radar, useless in that position, threaded her way through the maelstrom, shooting, and emerged without even her paint being scratched.

Four bells of this sinister midwatch struck at the height of the battle. An infernal spectacle presented itself to the survivors. Greenish light from flares and star shell dimmed that of the silent stars. Red and white trails of tracer shell arched and crisscrossed overhead, magazines exploded in blinding bouquets of white flame, oil-fed fires sent up twisted columns of yellow flame and black smoke. Around the horizon smoldering hulks of abandoned ships now glowed dull red, now blazed up when fires reached fresh combustibles. Geysers from shells that missed their targets rose from the surface of the sea, now fouled with oil and flotsam.

At 0226 November 13, Captain Hoover of *Helena,* the senior undamaged cruiser, ordered all ships that could move to retire via Sealark Channel. Only *San Francisco, Juneau* and three destroyers were able to comply, and at 1100 submarine *I–26* sank *Juneau,* taking down almost 700 men, including the five Sullivan brothers.

A bloody postscript, this, to the most desperate sea fight since Flamborough Head; recalling Anglo-Dutch battles of the seventeenth century, when each side slugged the other until all but one went down. Ship losses were fairly well balanced; two American light cruisers and four destroyers as against two Japanese destroyers and a battleship so badly damaged that airmen could sink her next day. But the Japanese bombardment mission was completely frustrated; Yamamoto admitted as much by relieving Admiral Abe and depriving him of any further sea command. Callaghan, on the other hand, completed his mission; he had saved Henderson Field from a bombardment which would have been more serious than those of mid-October, and would certainly have stopped the American air operations, which next day disposed of eleven troop-laden transports.

Thus, in the end, mistakes were canceled out by valor. Let none deny praise to those who fell that bloody night, with two great seamen and gallant gentlemen, Daniel J. Callaghan and Norman Scott.

Dawn rose on a glassy, metallic sea, stippled by the floating litter of death and destruction. The mountains of Guadalcanal turned to purple and then to lush green. Sailors on crippled warships of both nations stood or slept by their remaining guns, grimly aware that between ship and ship no quarter would be given. Eight damaged ships, five of them American, were visible between Savo Island and Guadalcanal; *Atlanta* had edged painfully over to Kukum and landed her survivors, but she was past saving and had to be scuttled.

Each side now prepared for another night action. Admiral Kondo, who had been cruising off Ontong Java, pushed south with his yet uncommitted heavy cruisers and destroyers to gather up battleship *Kirishima* and cover a super-Tokyo Express commanded by Rear Admiral Tanaka, composed of eleven destroyers escorting eleven troop-laden transports. Admiral Kinkaid's carrier *Enterprise* and two new battleships were boiling up from the south, Big E ringing day and night with hammer blows and the sputter of welders' arcs to repair the forward elevator. Kinkaid decided that the best thing he could do for the cause was to fly off nine Avengers and six Wildcats to beef up General Geiger's air forces on Guadalcanal, and to do what good they could en route. They found *Hiei* limping along north of Savo Island, and got two torpedoes into her, proceeded to Henderson Field, refueled, picked up some Marine SBDs, and this time made the battleship go dead in the water. B–17s from Espiritu Santo added an "egg" or two to the collection, and at about 1800 she plunged, stern-first. *Hiei* was the first enemy battleship to be sunk by American forces.

That night the Americans on Guadalcanal were subjected to heavy bombardment by two heavy cruisers which Admiral Mikawa had sent down from Rabaul.

As 14 November dawned, airmen, ground crews and stranded sailors rolled out of their foxholes, and Henderson Field warmed up to one of the busiest days in its hectic history. The first strike holed a retiring light cruiser and heavy cruiser *Kinugasa*, which bombers from the deck of *Enterprise* then sank.

American airmen, both land- and carrier-based, now concentrated on Tanaka's transports that were barreling down the Slot In a series of bold attacks they succeeded in sinking six transports with all their supplies. But Tanaka the Tenacious refused to retire. He pressed on to Guadalcanal with four destroyers and four big transports. These landed their troops before dawn by running onto the beach, whence the ships never got off; but Tanaka and his destroyer escort scampered safely back to Shortlands. Seven more destroyers, which he had detailed to rescue survivors from the sunk transports, picked up almost 5000 men and carried them to safety.

As the third day of this almost continuous naval battle came to an end, orders were given which led to another night action. Kinkaid, as Halsey had planned, detached battleships *Washington* and *South Dakota* and four destroyers from *Enterprise*'s screen to thrust into Ironbottom Sound and clean up. Rear Admiral Willis Augustus Lee, O.T.C. of this group, knew exactly how to handle battleships, and had studied how to make the best use of radar. Coming south to meet him was Admiral Kondo in *Atago*, with the yet undamaged *Kirishima*, another heavy and two light cruisers, and more destroyers under Tanaka, bent on delivering the heavy bombardment on Henderson Field that Abe had been ordered to perform but Callaghan had prevented. Kondo, whom Commander Hara describes as "the British gentleman sort of man," had missed chances in the previous battle, but had been kept in as a favorite of Yamamoto. After this battle he was out.

At 2215 November 14 Admiral Lee entered Ironbottom Sound by the northern passage. A first-quarter moon was shining. Lookouts could pick up looming heights on every side and shore outlines appeared on radar screens, but neither eyes nor radar discerned any trace of enemy. A rich odor like honeysuckle floated out from the land over the calm waters, a pleasant change from the fecal smells usually exuded by the Guadalcanal jungle. This seemed a good omen to the sailors.

Lee badly wanted exact intelligence of the enemy. Light cruiser *Sendai* of Rear Admiral Hashimoto's advance screen had sighted him at 2210 — the Japanese, with their excellent night binoculars, usually picked us up first. Kondo now adopted a typically Japanese battle plan, splitting his 14-ship task force four ways, moving up big units at flank speed while *Sendai* shadowed Lee. The battle opened at 2317 when Lee, steering westerly from Ironbottom Sound toward its southern entrance, opened fire on *Sendai*. The Americans missed, and *Sendai* doubled back to the northward. Next, the destroyers in Lee's van encountered two Japanese destroyers, steaming so close to Savo Island that American radar was useless. The ensuing destroyer duel was disastrous to the Americans. Both *Preston* and *Walke* were sunk, and the other two went out of action.

Lee pressed on with two battleships only — his men tossing out life rafts to the destroyer sailors as they passed over their ships' graves. Captain Gatch was back on the bridge of *South Dakota,* but his luck and hers had run out. At the worst possible moment she suffered an electrical power failure, so that she was little help to Lee, except that she absorbed numerous hits which might have crippled his other battleship. *Washington,* superbly handled by Captain Glenn Davis, picked up *Kirishima* on her radar, and at midnight opened up on her at 8400 yards' range. Nine of her 75 sixteen-inch shells and 40 five-inch shells scored; and within seven minutes the Japanese battleship, steering gear wrecked and topsides aflame, was out of the battle. Admiral Lee now directed lone *Washington* to the northwestward to draw off the enemy cruisers and destroyers that were punishing *South Dakota,* and succeeded in so doing. At 0025 Kondo decided he had had enough, and retired. *Washington* and *South Dakota* rejoined south of Guadalcanal at 0900; helpless *Kirishima* had already been scuttled. The Naval Battle of Guadalcanal, which opened on the afternoon of November 12, was over by 0100 on the 15th.

This night battleship action was vastly better fought by the United States Navy than the unorganized brawl of two nights earlier. Admiral Lee had a positive doctrine that he maintained, despite the loss of his entire destroyer screen. He made quick, accurate analyses from the information on his radar screen. *Washington,* conned by Captain Glenn Davis and directed by Admiral Lee with a skill and imperturbability worthy of her eponym, saved the day for the United States.

The conclusion of this great battle marked a definite shift for America from defensive to offensive, and for Japan one in the opposite direction. Fortune now for the first time smiled on the Allies everywhere: not only here but in North Africa, at Stalingrad, and in Papua. President Roosevelt, while mourning the loss

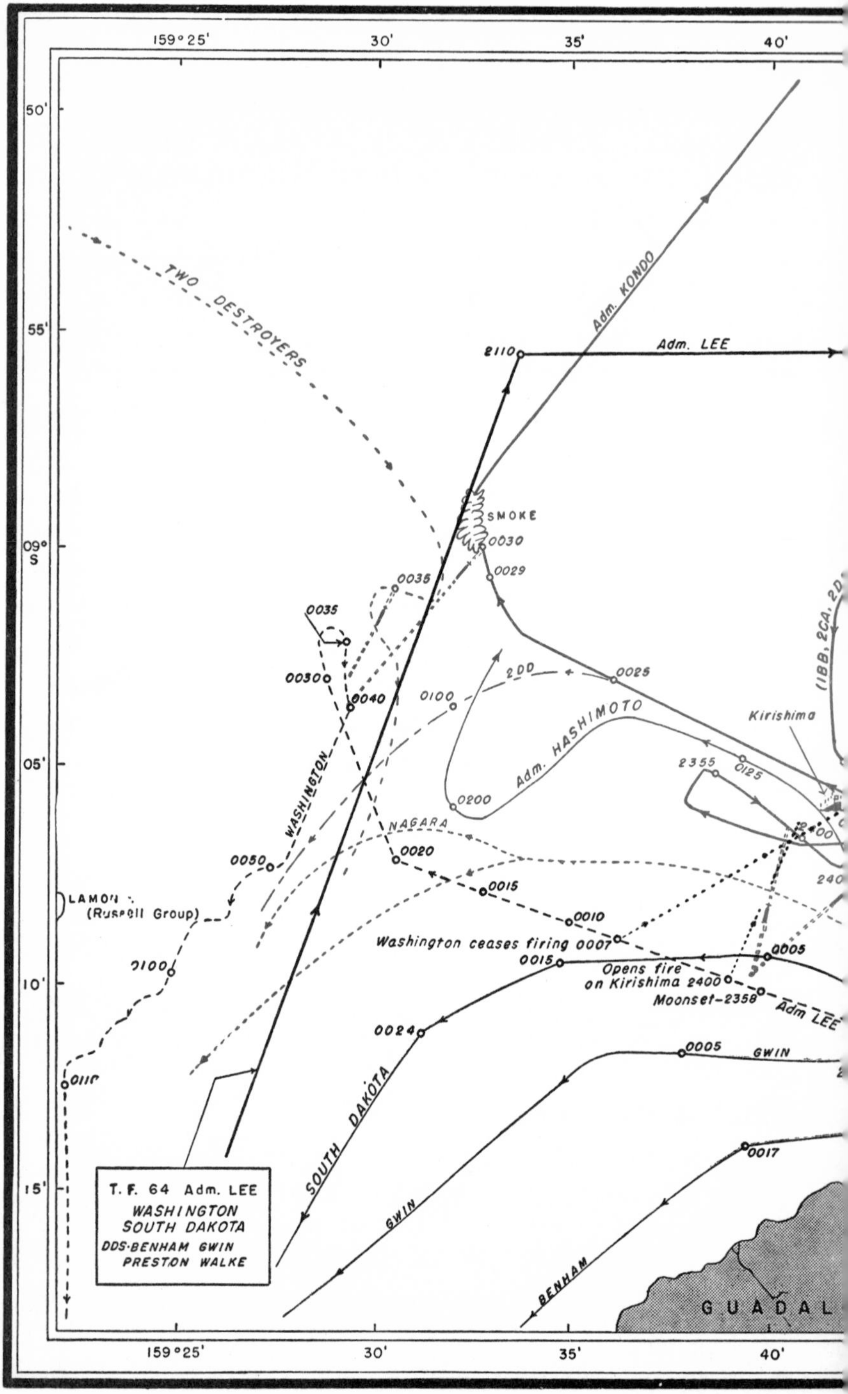

159°25'
30'
35'
40'
50'
55'
09° S
05'
10'
15'
TWO DESTROYERS
Adm. KONDO
Adm. LEE
2110
SMOKE
0030
0029
0035
0035
0030
0040
0025
200
0100
Adm. HASHIMOTO
Kirishima
2355
0125
0200
WASHINGTON
NAGARA
0020
0050
0015
0010
LAMON
(Russell Group)
Washington ceases firing 0007
0015
0005
Opens fire on Kirishima 2400
Moonset-2358
Adm LEE
0100
0024
0005
GWIN
0110
SOUTH DAKOTA
GWIN
0017
BENHAM
T. F. 64 Adm. LEE
WASHINGTON
SOUTH DAKOTA
DDS-BENHAM GWIN
PRESTON WALKE
G U A D A L
(IBB, 2CA, 2D

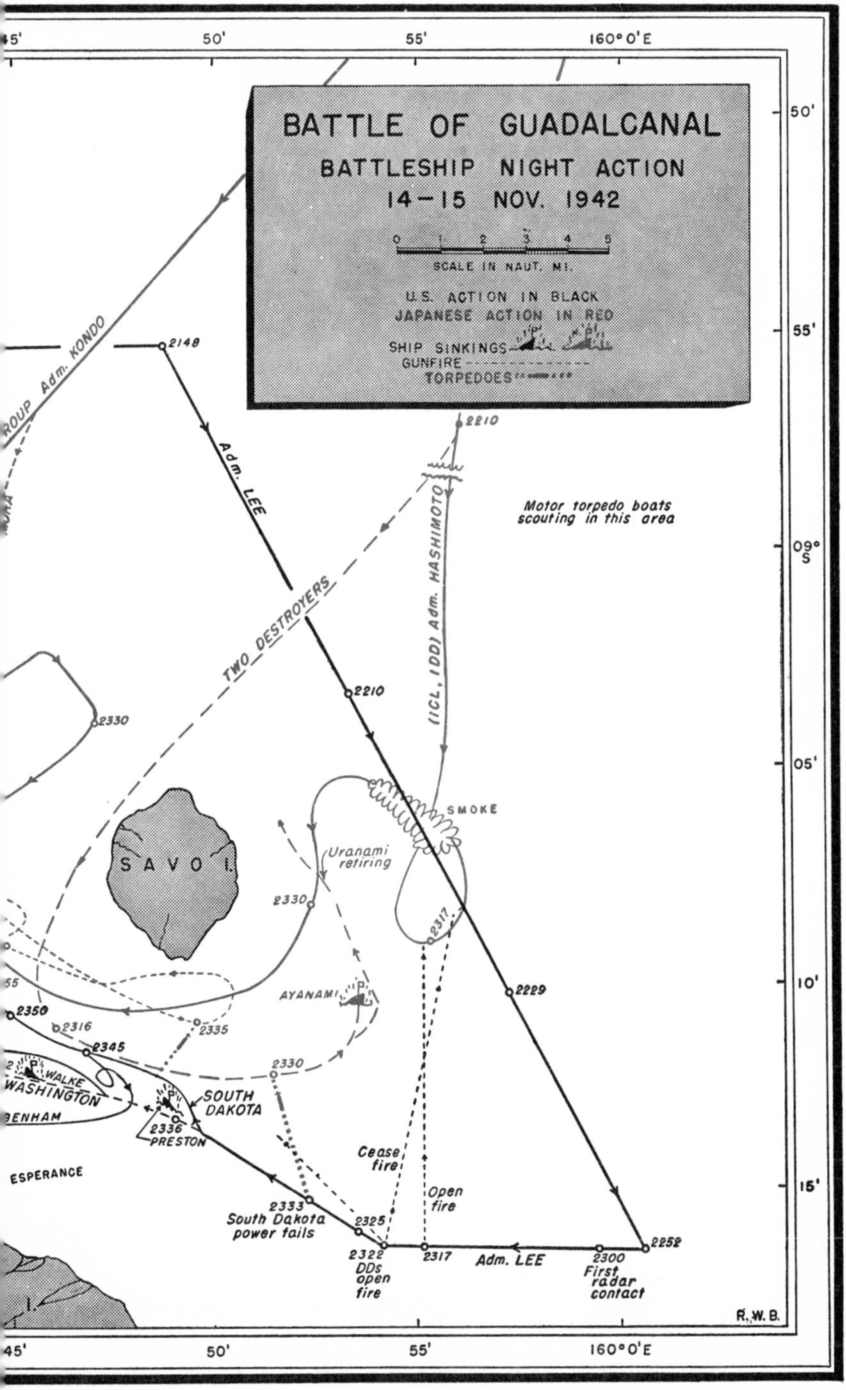
BATTLE OF GUADALCANAL
BATTLESHIP NIGHT ACTION
14-15 NOV. 1942
SCALE IN NAUT. MI.
U.S. ACTION IN BLACK
JAPANESE ACTION IN RED
SHIP SINKINGS
GUNFIRE
TORPEDOES
45'
50'
55'
160° 0'E
09° S
05'
10'
15'
Adm. KONDO
Adm. LEE
2148
2210
2229
2252
2300
First radar contact
2317
2322
DDs open fire
2325
2333
South Dakota power fails
2336
PRESTON
SOUTH DAKOTA
WASHINGTON
WALKE
BENHAM
2345
2350
2316
2335
2330
(1CL, 1DD) Adm. HASHIMOTO
TWO DESTROYERS
Motor torpedo boats scouting in this area
SMOKE
Uranami retiring
AYANAMI
SAVO I.
2317
Cease fire
Open fire
ESPERANCE
R. W. B.

of his friend Dan Callaghan, announced, "It would seem that the turning-point in this war has at last been reached." Churchill chose this moment to proclaim "the end of the beginning." And a captured Japanese document admitted: "It must be said that the success or failure in recapturing Guadalcanal Island, and the vital naval battle related to it, is the fork in the road which leads to victory for them or for us."

From 15 November 1942 until 15 August 1945 the war followed the right fork. It was rough, tough and uncharted, but it led to Tokyo.

7. *The Battles of Tassafaronga and Rennell Island, 30 November 1942–30 January 1943*

After losing the Naval Battle of Guadalcanal in November, the Japanese Navy proposed to abandon the island. Tojo, having switched his major South Pacific objective from New Guinea to the Solomons, refused to change back. So the struggle continued.

Captain Morton L. Deyo of Cincpac staff wrote a trenchant memorandum to Admiral Nimitz on 10 October. Commenting on the defeat at Savo Island and the far from satisfactory events that followed, he declared that unrealistic training of our destroyers and cruisers and the almost exclusive employment of them in escort of convoy had prevented the development of a tough, offensive spirit. He suggested the formation of a cruiser-destroyer group in the South Pacific, to be given a solid month of training, especially night fighting, and then thrown up the Slot to break up the Tokyo Expresses.

Belatedly, Admiral Halsey did just that, about a week after the Naval Battle of Guadalcanal. He appointed Rear Admiral Kinkaid commander of a new striking force, composed of heavy cruisers *Minneapolis*, *Pensacola*, *New Orleans* and *Northampton*, light cruiser *Honolulu* and four to six destroyers, based at Segond Channel, Espiritu Santo. Kinkaid took command 24 November, before the task force had all been collected, worked up an operation plan, conferred with the officers — and then was detached by Admiral Nimitz! Cincpac wanted Kinkaid to command the North Pacific Force based on Dutch Harbor, where "Fuzzy" Theobald was making a mess of things. As commander of the striking force, Kinkaid was relieved by Rear Admiral Carleton H. Wright, to whose unhappy lot it fell, on the second day of his command, to lead his yet untrained task force against a Tokyo Express led by the redoubtable Tanaka.

This Japanese reinforcement plan was comparatively modest. Tanaka's force, consisting of destroyers only, would dash into Ironbottom Sound and off Tassafaronga would jettison rubber-wrapped drums of provisions, shove troops overboard to be recovered by small craft operating from the shore, and quickly retire. On this particular night Tanaka had six destroyers crammed with troops and supplies, and two more not so encumbered. At 2225 November 30, before arriving off Tassafaronga, he encountered Admiral Wright's much stronger task force. The ensuing battle reflected slight credit on the United States Navy, but great luster on the Imperial Navy of Japan.

The surface of Ironbottom Sound that calm night was like a black mirror, and the American float planes detailed to illuminate Tokyo Express were unable to rise from the water. But Wright had the advantage of radar, and destroyer *Fletcher* in his van had the latest kind. At 2316 she picked up Tanaka's force, broad on the port bow, steaming slowly along the Guadalcanal shore toward the dumping-off place. The squadron commander in *Fletcher* asked permission for his four van destroyers to fire torpedoes; Wright hesitated for four minutes before granting it, and so lost the battle. For, by the time the torpedoes were launched, about 2321, the Japanese column had passed the Americans on a contrary course and the range was too great for American torpedoes to overtake them. Immediately after his last torpedo smacked the water, Wright ordered cruisers to open gunfire, and the flashes of his guns sparked off Tanaka's reaction. Despite initial handicaps of surprise, cluttered decks and enemy gunfire, Tanaka's disciplined crews in the first moments of battle managed to launch more than twenty fast-running torpedoes. And a large share of the American gunfire concentrated on one Japanese destroyer, *Takanami*, the only enemy ship sunk in this battle.

Not one American torpedo found its target, but at 2327 the Japanese "long lances" began to rip the bowels of Wright's cruisers. *Minneapolis* took two violent explosions and was out of the fight. *New Orleans*, maneuvering to avoid her, ran smack into another torpedo that sliced off her bow and everything up to No. 2 turret. *Pensacola*, turning to port to avoid her two burning sisters, became silhouetted by them for the enemy's benefit and took a torpedo hit directly below her mainmast, which became a torch blazing with oil from a ruptured fuel tank. *Honolulu* escaped by smart seamanship on the part of the officer of the deck, Lieutenant Commander George F. Davis.[5] *Northampton*, after firing 18 salvos from her 8-inch battery, took two torpedo hits, and sank, after more than three hours' frantic efforts by Damage Control to save her. By 0130 December 1, all Japanese ships except sinking *Takanami* were hightailing out of Ironbottom Sound, undamaged.

The three stricken heavy cruisers, saved by remarkable energy and ingenuity of their crews, were sent to major bases for repairs, and joined the Fleet again by next fall. But it is painfully true that the Battle of Tassafaronga was a sharp defeat, inflicted on an alerted and superior cruiser force by a surprised and inferior destroyer force whose decks were cluttered with freight. Tanaka

[5] Her C.O., Captain Robert W. Hayler, had a lot to do with this, but generously gave Commander Davis all the credit.

was prevented from delivering the goods, and that was held against him by the higher command.

By 3 December this remarkable flag officer was ready for another reinforcement dash into the Sound. General Imamura, who had succeeded to the top army command at Rabaul, now had some 60,000 troops, and planned to get two divisions of them into Guadalcanal. Successful runs were made on the nights of 3-4, 7-8, and 11-12 December, hampered but not defeated by PT boats based at Tulagi. *PT-59*, Lieutenant (jg) John M. Searles, sank a 2000-ton blockade-running submarine, *I-3*, on the 9th; and three PTs, commanded by Lieutenant (jg) Lester H. Gamble USNR, sank Tanaka's newest flagship, destroyer *Teruzuki*, on the 12th.

Japan had good reason to be proud of her destroyers; and their success was well earned. For forty years the Imperial Navy had put much thought and great effort into improved torpedoes, night fighting, and torpedo tactics. The 2300 ton *Fubuki* class destroyer, such as those of Tanaka's squadron, were equipped with nine torpedo tubes fitted for the deadly "long lances," the crews were trained to reload them in a matter of minutes, and the C.O.'s were all torpedo experts. American and British destroyers enjoyed no comparable matériel, technique, or training. Nevertheless, faulty tactics and stupid strategy doomed to failure Japan's effort to hold Guadalcanal.[6]

During the last weeks of November and the first of December, Allied forces on the island were both relieved and increased. The 1st Marine Division, which had fought almost incessantly for 17 seven-day weeks, was relieved by two regiments of the Second

[6] Rear Adm. Tanaka "Japan's Losing Struggle for Guadalcanal" U.S. Naval Inst. *Proceedings* LXXXII (1956) 698. On pp. 830-831 he discusses Japan's defeat at Guadalcanal, which may be summarized as lack of an over-all operation plan, committing forces piecemeal, "terrible" communications, "unendurable" relations with the Army, belittling the enemy, and inferiority in the air. "We stumbled along from one error to another," he concludes, "while the enemy grew wise."

Marine division. The balance of the Americal Division came up, and its commander, Major General Alexander M. Patch, relieved General Vandegrift on 9 December.

During the rest of December the Japanese refrained from sending anything but submarines to relieve their now starving Guadalcanal garrison. But they were building a new launching platform at Munda in the central Solomons for more and shorter air thrusts against Guadalcanal. It was constructed, very cannily, in a large coconut plantation, the trees being kept standing until the last minute. By 5 December a 2000-foot runway was ready. Since air bombing did not seem to stop the Japanese beavers, Halsey ordered bombardment missions on Munda by light cruisers and destroyers, beginning on the night of 4 January, 1943.

On that very day Tojo decided to evacuate Guadalcanal, but this decision was imparted only to the top Japanese commanders, and remained unknown to Allied forces until the operation was completed. A Tokyo Express run on the night of 10-11 January, 1943, cost us two PT boats and the Japanese a destroyer. On the night of 14-15 January, Rear Admiral Koyanagi, Tanaka's relief, led down the Slot nine destroyers, with a rear guard to cover the Japanese evacuation, and delivered it.

By 23 January, aërial reconnaissance had reported a large number of transports, freighters and destroyers at Rabaul and Buin, and carriers and battleships milling around Ontong Java, north of Guadalcanal. These were preparations for the final evacuation; but Admiral Halsey, assuming that they meant another major attempt at reinforcement, sent up four loaded transports powerfully covered and escorted, in the hope to tempting Yamamoto to another naval battle. C. in C. Combined Fleet declined the gambit; but, with the new Munda airfield as base, he laid on two successful bombing attacks which cost us the only heavy cruiser which had survived the Battle of Savo Island.

Rear Admiral Robert C. Giffen's covering group for the reinforcement echelon comprised heavy cruisers *Wichita*, *Chicago* and *Louisville*, three light cruisers, eight destroyers and two of the *Sangamon* class escort carriers, which had demonstrated their worth off Casablanca. "Ike" Giffen, a tough, colorful officer, had had slight experience in dealing with enemy aircraft. Thus, when Japanese torpedo-bombers jumped his task force in the twilight of 29 January, he was in a bad formation to meet air attack, his ships had no orders what to do, and (worst of all) he had left his escort carriers behind in order to meet an unimportant rendezvous, so had no air cover. He plugged doggedly ahead, trusting to antiaircraft fire alone, while the Japanese aviators pressed their attacks repeatedly. At 1945 *Chicago* was hit and went dead in the water. Giffen then countermarched, *Louisville* (Captain C. Turner Joy), took the stricken cruiser in tow, and, escorted by six destroyers, headed south at slow speed. At 1600 January 30, the Japanese caught up with them. Crippled *Chicago* now had air cover from *Enterprise*, which Admiral Halsey had ordered up; but the Combat Air Patrol provided by Big E was not strong enough to protect an almost stationary target. At a point a few miles east of Rennell Island, nine torpedo-toting Bettys ganged up on *Chicago* and put four "fish" into her already damaged starboard side. She sank in twenty minutes. This Battle of Rennell Island was the last of seven naval battles of the Guadalcanal campaign.

The American transports unloaded troops and matériel at Lunga Point without molestation, as did a second convoy of five transports which arrived 4 February 1943.

By that time, the Japanese were almost out of Guadalcanal. They had chosen the night of 1-2 February to begin the final evacuation, which had been going on in driblets for two or three weeks. American aircraft and destroyers and PTs were dispatched and a minefield was laid to stop these ships, which Admiral Halsey and General Patch still believed to be bringing troops in, not taking them out. Two more echelons, on the nights of 4-5 and 5-6 February, completed the job of removing over 11,000 men. American ground forces never realized what had happened until 9 February, when they covered the entire western end of the island without finding one living Japanese. That afternoon, General Patch radioed to Admiral Halsey:

> TOTAL AND COMPLETE DEFEAT OF JAPANESE FORCES ON GUADALCANAL EFFECTED TODAY . . . TOKYO EXPRESS NO LONGER HAS TERMINUS ON GUADALCANAL.

So now 2500 square miles of miasmic plain and savage jungle-covered mountains were in American hands, after six months of toil and suffering. The American ground force losses were not great; the Japanese lost far more heavily. The number of sailors lost on each side in the sea battles, the aviators lost over the Slot, the Sound and Henderson Field, have never been computed. Exactly 24 combatant ships, exclusive of PTs, patrol craft, auxiliaries and transports, were lost by each side. Tactically, Guadalcanal was a profitable lesson book for the United States Navy, Army and Marine Corps. Strategically, it stopped the enemy in his many-taloned reach for the Antipodes, and concluded task No. 1 of Operation WATCHTOWER — an arduous climb to Rabaul.

Guadalcanal should ever remain a proud name in American military history, recalling desperate fights in the air, furious night naval battles, frantic work at supply or construction, savage fighting in a sodden jungle, nights broken by screaming bombs and the explosion of naval shells. Hail to all who fell! The jagged cone of Savo Island, forever brooding over the once blood-thickened waters of Ironbottom Sound, stands as a perpetual monument to the men and ships who here rolled back the enemy tide.

CHAPTER VIII

North Africa and Sicily

(Operations TORCH and HUSKY)

January 1942–August 1943

1. *Strategic Discussions, January–June 1942*

IN THE PACIFIC the British too were at war with Japan, but they could contribute only to land operations in Burma and India, leaving the naval warfare to the United States. In the European theater, however, England was the senior partner. She had been fighting Germany and Italy since 1939-1940, most of the time alone; she had taken a terrific beating without flinching, and knew the weight of German might. This naturally gave her a great advantage in strategic discussions.

Whilst China remained the great enigma in the Pacific, in the European theater it was Soviet Russia. She had been fighting Germany from the summer of 1941, when Hitler decided to strike her down before resuming his blitz on England. When America entered the war, only the British in North Africa and the Russians were actually engaging the German Army. It was therefore a prime necessity for the Western Allies to keep Russia fighting until they were ready to establish a second front in the west. To get help to Russia, Britain and the United States at great sacrifice maintained convoys to Murmansk and Archangel. These were a Royal Navy responsibility, but about half the merchant ships and an even greater proportion of the cargoes were American. Convoy PQ–17, the worst damaged, lost 22 out of 33 ships to U-boats and

Norway-based German dive-bombers in July 1942. Freighters charged with lend-lease goods for Russia were also being sent around the Cape of Good Hope to ports on the Persian Gulf; and other cargoes in Soviet-flag ships (cautiously let alone by the Japanese) were crossing the Pacific to Vladivostok. But Russia, demanding more, had mobilized left-wing opinions in England and the United States behind the cry, "A Second Front — Now!"

The British Chiefs of Staff and Winston Churchill set their faces firmly against any premature invasion of the Continent, and with good reason. Thrice in this war — from Norway, Greece and Dunkirk — they had been thrown out of the Continent; next time they went in, they wished to be certain to stay. England by early 1942 had mobilized almost her entire man power, which added up to a small army but a first-rate Navy; so why not use the Navy to carry commandos on distant, peripheral operations until such time as the Allies had the requisite men and weapons for a massive invasion of the Continent? Churchill called this strategy "tightening the ring"; England's tradition was behind it. She had got at Napoleon by the back door of Spain, and Churchill always believed that his Gallipoli strategy, if implemented by proper amphibious tactics, could have defeated Germany in World War I. That was the only major war since Marlborough's time when England had gone into the Continent in a big way, and it had led to useless losses which all responsible Englishmen were determined not to repeat. Finally, the Royal Air Force was a convert to the Douhet-Billy Mitchell theory that the quick way to win a modern war was to bomb the hell out of your enemy's civilian population — destroy their homes and their morale. While Churchill and the British Chiefs of Staff were not entirely convinced that this could be done against Germany, they were determined to give it a good try.

The British, accordingly, concluded that it would make no sense to invade the Continent in 1942, perhaps to revive the agony of trench warfare, as long as there was any chance of persuading the Germans by other means into rising against Hitler and demanding peace.

With the policy of bombing Germany into submission, General H. H. ("Hap") Arnold, head of the Army Air Force, was thoroughly in accord. But the other American service heads favored a direct approach by ground forces, and began pressing for a massive cross-Channel operation to establish an army in France, thence to strike into the heart of Germany. The British admitted that this would have to be done eventually, but hoped to make it as painless as possible after a long stretch of "bleeding Germany to death" by air-bombing and jabs around the periphery. This basic difference in British and American strategic thinking was never really resolved until victory crowned the necessary compromise. The J.C.S., especially Marshall and King, continued to work for long-range commitments and a war of massed power aimed at the enemy's heart. The British Chiefs of Staff, always hoping that "something would turn up" to render a major continental campaign unnecessary, argued for a strategy of opportunism, attrition and peripheral attacks.

It had been agreed, in March 1941, that Germany was to be Number One enemy, even if Japan came in; but nothing had been decided as to how Enemy Number One was to be beaten That was debated at the three-weeks "Arcadia" Conference of the Combined Chiefs of Staff with President Roosevelt and Winston Churchill in Washington, in December 1941 and January 1942. Churchill came over with a plan in his pocket, of which the essence was: —

1. Continue all possible material aid to Russia.
2. Clear Axis forces out of Libya.
3. Invade Morocco and Algeria, to clear Axis forces out of the rest of North Africa.

This last, he argued, was essential. And Mr. Churchill finally had his wish — though not without a great deal of argument by the Joint Chiefs of Staff for the direct approach.

His three-weeks stay at the White House — interrupted only by short trips to Canada and Florida — was beneficial for Anglo-American coöperation. The two leaders had met but once before, briefly, at Argentia. They now had an opportunity to thrash things out and take each other's measure. In many ways Roosevelt and Churchill were extraordinarily alike; it has been well said that each had more in common with the other than with his military advisers. But there was one essential difference. F.D.R. did not pretend to be an authority on military strategy; the P.M. did. Just as Jefferson Davis felt he knew more about strategy than Johnston or Lee because he had been an officer in the Mexican War; so Churchill felt that his service in Queen Victoria's army, and subsequently as First Lord of His Majesty's Admiralty, made him an authority on strategy. It was often difficult for the British Chiefs of Staff to dissuade him from carrying out some of his peripheral plans for landing in Norway, Dakar, Rhodes, and so on. Roosevelt, too, would have enjoyed romantic military adventures, but he had a natural common sense on strategy and his military advisers kept him on the "straight and narrow." Both men were political maestros, adept at creating and using public opinion, and both had to deal with the opposition inevitable under democratic governments. Both — but Roosevelt to the greater extent — were regarded as "traitors to their class" and hated by the sort of people with whom they had grown up; but both had the enthusiastic support of the masses. Never has there been such a team in coalition warfare as "Winnie" and "F.D.R." Compared with the relations between these two, the principal protagonists in World War I — Lloyd George, Wilson and Clemenceau — were mutually suspicious strangers, and Hitler and Mussolini were a pair of gangsters, each fearing the other would win the most loot.

Before the Arcadia Conference met at Washington, the United States Army planners, led by General Embick, a member of the Supreme War Council during the First World War, had been doing some intensive thinking on ways and means of defeating Germany. After considering every possible method of getting at the heart of the Reich, they reached the conviction that the only way was to mount a large-scale Anglo-American assault in the British Isles and throw it across the Channel, the sooner the better. They were willing to contemplate small peripheral operations to "blood" American troops and "do something" [1] while preparing for the great push; but they opposed, as long as they could, a large-scale invasion of North Africa, as a diversion which would draw off forces needed for the invasion of Hitler's heartland.

The Arcadia Conference disbanded 14 January 1942 without deciding on any campaign for that year; but the British and American joint staffs continued planning as if the North African invasion would come off in May or June. The series of disasters in the Far East, the U-boat blitz, and the victories of Rommel over Auchinleck in Libya, made this timetable impossible to keep, and on 3 March the Combined Chiefs of Staff agreed to scrap it. In view of the beatings the Allies had already taken in Europe and in Asia, any invasion of North Africa must be done in sufficient force to ensure success. But where was the force to come from? The British agreed that we must place garrisons in Nouméa, Fiji, Johnston and Palmyra Islands to guard the lifeline to Australia, and shipping was in short supply — shortly to become shorter, thanks to the U-boats.

On the C.C.S. agenda, North Africa was now replaced by what was known as the "Marshall Memorandum." This was a plan for (1) a cross-Channel beachhead to be established in Normandy in

[1] General Marshall told the writer after the war that the one great lesson he learned in 1942 was that the political leaders must "do something"; they could not afford the imputation of fighting another "phony war" that year.

1942 (Operation SLEDGEHAMMER), to be followed by (2) an all-out cross-Channel offensive in 1943 (Operation ROUNDUP), and a push across the Rhine. This plan was accepted in principle by the British Chiefs of Staff on 14 April, after General Marshall and Harry Hopkins had gone to England especially to "sell" it. But, as Marshall realized, this was not, from the British point of view, a firm commitment. The more they looked at it, the less they liked it, especially the 1942 curtain-raiser. In any cross-Channel movement that early, the major part of the troops would have to be British; so the United States could not insist. Large numbers of landing craft would be required; and although, in the United States, Amphibious Force Atlantic Fleet was established with a training center at Little Creek, Virginia, and a construction program for 2500 craft for SLEDGEHAMMER and 8200 for ROUNDUP was set up on 4 April, these had to compete with so many other urgent shipbuilding demands that the target date could not possibly be met.

In May and June events came thick and fast. Molotov visited both Churchill and Roosevelt to plead for a "second front"; Rommel captured Tobruk, which rendered action in North Africa urgent, and the War and Navy Departments made frantic efforts to get more tanks and planes to the British in Egypt, and to the Russians by the dangerous Murmansk route. Churchill visited Washington again, in June, to tell Roosevelt flatly that England could not and would not undertake a cross-Channel operation in 1942.

2. *The "Torch" Is Lighted, July*

That opened a crisis in Anglo-American relations. The Joint Chiefs of Staff, especially Admiral King and General Marshall, felt that if the British would not set a firm date for a major invasion of

Europe, we were entitled to renege on the "Beat Germany First" decision of 1941, to stop preparing for an invasion that might never take place, and concentrate on the Pacific war. This proposed right-about-face in strategy would greatly have pleased General MacArthur, who in a long message to General Marshall of 8 May 1942 argued seriously that the "second front" should be established under his own command in the Pacific, where it would take the heat off Russia by seriously engaging the armies of Japan. But Japan was not then at war with Russia, nor would be until August 1945. Not only MacArthur, but King, Marshall, and Secretary Stimson strongly opposed the launching of a North African invasion in 1942, as certain to divert and absorb men, ships, aircraft and matériel that would postpone the direct cross-Channel assault indefinitely.

The President himself decided that to turn our backs on Europe was too drastic. Before Churchill left Washington they had convinced each other that something formidable must be laid on in the Atlantic theater for 1942. Since the British would not accept SLEDGEHAMMER, an invasion of North Africa was the only practical alternative. On 24 July 1942 the Combined Chiefs of Staff in London voted timidly and tentatively for Operation TORCH, a simultaneous occupation of Morocco and Algeria, but to postpone a definite decision until mid-September. President Roosevelt, sick of this wrangling and procrastination, used his authority as C. in C. Army and Navy to make it definite next day. Churchill, naturally, accepted what he had wanted all along. On the 26th, General Marshall informed General Eisenhower that he was to be Commander in Chief Allied Expeditionary Force in North Africa. The torch was lit.

This TORCH decision was one of the most momentous in the war. It set up what was supposed to be only a secondary front; but the force of logic, the natural desire to build on foundations that have already cost one dear, pulled more and more Allied forces into the Mediterranean theater — over a million Americans alone. In consequence, the cross-Channel operation was impossible before 1944; and we came measurably close to having it postponed another year.

At this time the Vichy government of France was in control of French Morocco, Algeria and Tunisia; no De Gaullist movement had developed there and no German armed forces were in occupation. Spanish Morocco opposite Gibraltar was under Franco's control, and so neutral. Libya or Tripolitania, the Italian colony between Tunisia and Egypt, was the battleground between Rommel and Auchinleck, who checked the Germans at the First Battle of El Alamein on 2 July, and was then relieved by the colorful Montgomery, because Churchill felt that Auchinleck had not done well enough. Egypt, nominally independent, was still under strong British occupation and control. On the north side of the Mediterranean, Gibraltar was British, Spain neutral, Southern France neutral under Vichy; Italy, the Balkans and Greece were under Axis control. Malta, after a heroic defense, held firm, and continued an indispensable strategic base for the Allies, and a thorn in the Axis.

The declared objectives of Operation TORCH were to gain control over French Morocco (where the one modern port Casablanca offered an excellent base for antisubmarine warfare), and of Algeria and Tunisia, as bases for further operations against the Axis. Planning began immediately at Combined Headquarters in Norfolk House, London. General Eisenhower arrived there in early August; Admiral Sir Andrew B. ("A.B.C.") Cunningham RN was appointed Allied Naval Commander. D-day was set for 8 November, the very latest date in the fall when amphibious landings on the ironbound outer coast of Morocco were considered possible. The entire operation was broken down as follows:

1. *Western Naval Task Force* — Rear Admiral H. Kent Hewitt USN; lifting and covering Western Task Force U. S. Army,

Major General George F. Patton USA: consisting initially of about 35,000 troops. This all-American section of TORCH was mounted at Norfolk, Virginia. Owing to its geographical separation from the rest of the operation, Western Naval Task Force was given a free hand by Eisenhower and Cunningham. It was divided in three groups for as many separate landings: (*a*) NORTHERN, Rear Admiral Monroe Kelly, to land at Mehedia and thrust up the Wadi Sebou to Port Lyautey; (*b*) CENTER, Captain Robert R. M. Emmet, to land at Fedhala near Casablanca; and (*c*) SOUTHERN, Rear Admiral Lyal A. Davidson, to land at Safi.

2. *Center Naval Task Force* — escorted and covered by the Royal Navy: about 39,000 American ground forces, mounted in the United Kingdom; to capture Oran in Algeria.

3. *Eastern Naval Task Force* — about 23,000 British and 10,000 American troops, mounted in the United Kingdom, escorted and covered by the Royal Navy; to capture Algiers.

We shall have most to say about the Western Naval Task Force, as it was all American, and many of its doings were original, almost fantastic. Except for the landings at Guadalcanal in August, this was the first amphibious operation conducted by the United States in forty-five years; and it is no exaggeration to say that it was one of the boldest ever undertaken.

Amphibious operations are divided into two main categories, of which the most common is the shore-to-shore. In this the troops are lifted a short distance in landing or beaching craft, which take them directly to the beaches; as, for instance, in Operation NEPTUNE-OVERLORD, the great cross-Channel movement of June 1944. In the other kind, ship-to-shore, of which TORCH is a good example, the troops are lifted over long distances in transports, and put ashore in small landing craft that the big ships carry on deck. This was the first time in history that a ship-to-shore operation had been projected across an ocean. It was extremely risky. There was danger of attack by the yet unmastered U-boats during the ocean passage, and while unloading. There was danger from high surf at the target — all landing places faced the Atlantic surges. The beaches selected were commanded by coast defense guns; the French had plenty of ground, air and naval forces to defend their positions in Morocco, and nobody knew what their attitude would be. Secret diplomacy had been at work for months to persuade the French there to welcome us as liberators; but they were all under command of Marshal Pétain at Vichy, and nobody knew whether he would respond to German pressure or to Allied persuasion.

One of the most amazing things about this bold operation was the secrecy with which so great an expeditionary force — 107 sail in the Western Task Force alone, and even more in the two others — was assembled and transported. The Germans knew that something was in the wind, but never guessed what. Hewitt's Western Naval Task Force they knew nothing of; and by careful work with HF/DF, the Navy was able to spot all U-boats then in the Atlantic and route this great force so that it avoided them all. Nevertheless, after it arrived, some U-boats slipped silently in to make easy kills.

All troops of the Western Task Force embarked at Norfolk, and with a strong naval escort sortied 23 October. The Air Group (carrier *Ranger* and converted escort carriers *Suwannee*, *Sangamon*, *Santee* and *Chenango*, commanded by Rear Admiral Ernest D. McWhorter) sortied from Bermuda and joined at long. 50° W on the 28th. There were two fuelings at sea, and every ship was a floating school of amphibious warfare. Nobody on board had ever participated in such an operation, and very few had even been in combat.

3. *The Assault on Fedhala and Casablanca, 7–11 November*

On 7 November the sun set at 1745, and enough stars appeared for a fix. At 2300 Commander James M. ("Shady") Lane, navigator of *Brooklyn* (in which your historian sailed) announced that we were closing "High Barbaree." Africa was never so dark and mysterious to ancient sea-rovers as she seemed that night, veiled in clouds and hushed in slumber. Not a light gleamed, not a dog barked, but the wind came off shore, blowing out to the ships the smell of charcoal smoke and of parched dry grass. What countless strategems of this sort have been practised on this very coast, since remotest antiquity! We might have been Portuguese caravels, with sails furled and yards on deck, waiting for the Pole Star clock to register two hours before dawn to move in and slaughter infidels. It has always been thus. You want a couple of hours' darkness to land and surprise the enemy, and then daybreak, so you can tell friend from foe, gold from brass, and wench from wife.

At a quarter-hour before midnight, flagship *Augusta* signaled "Stop," and the transports coasted into their planned unloading positions off Cape Fedhala, eight minutes in advance of schedule. Before eight bells ushered in 8 November, one could hear the clank and clash which told one that the transports were already lowering landing craft. . . . An hour passed. Assault troops were now leaping ashore, rifles in hand, running up the beach and striking for their first objectives. . . . A searchlight shot up from ashore, and then another — the French had heard the humming of landing craft engines and thought they were planes. At morning twilight *Brooklyn* moved toward her fire support position, to knock out a powerful coast defense battery known to Americans as "the Sherki." It and other shore batteries opened fire on us.

A few moments later, there came over the air from the flagship

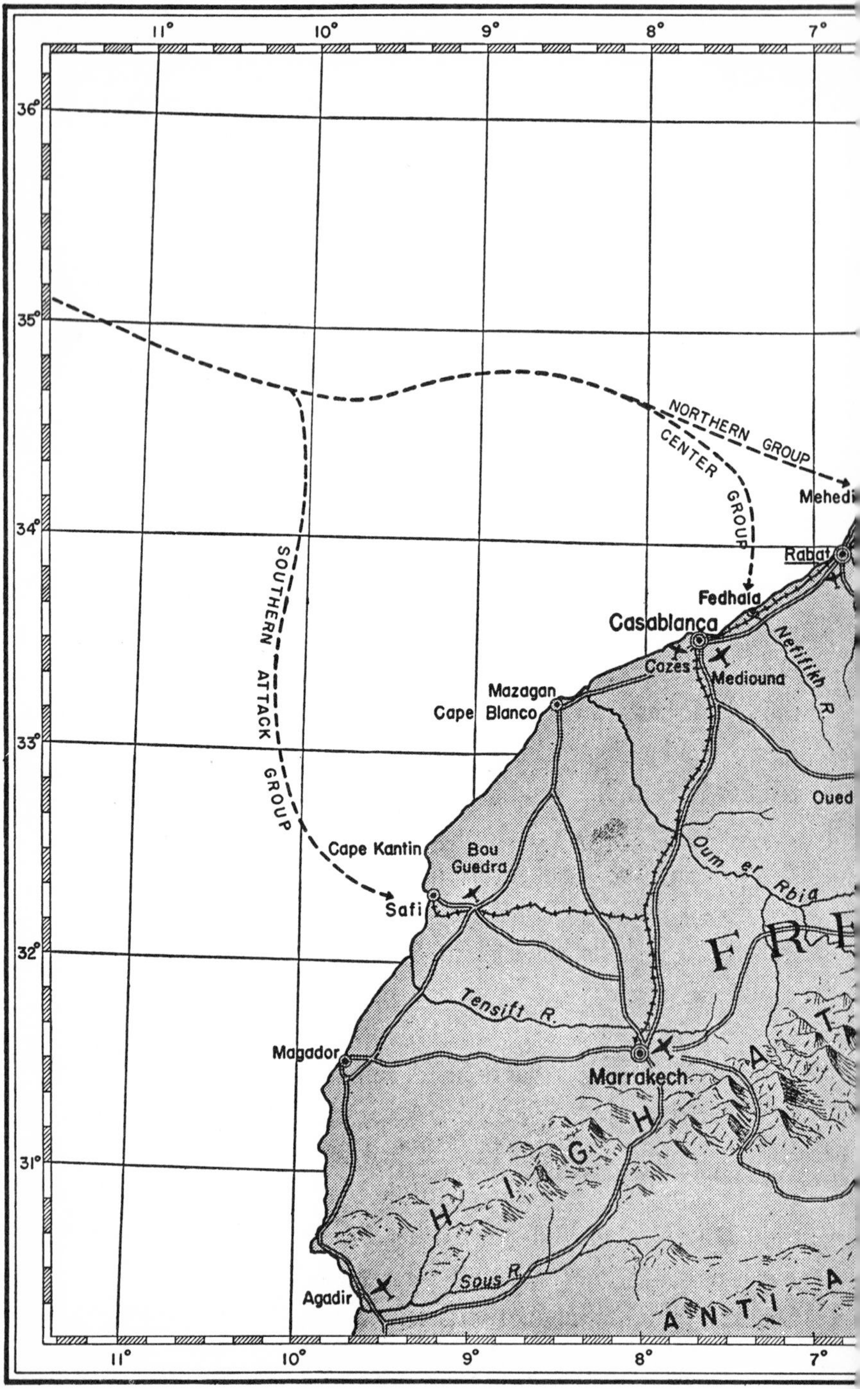

NORTHERN GROUP
CENTER GROUP
SOUTHERN ATTACK GROUP
Mehedi
Rabat
Fedhala
Casablanca
Cazes
Mediouna
Nefifikh R.
Mazagan
Cape Blanco
Oued
Cape Kantin
Bou Guedra
Safi
Oum er Rbia
FR
Tensift R.
Magador
Marrakech
HIGH AT
Sous R.
Agadir
ANTI A

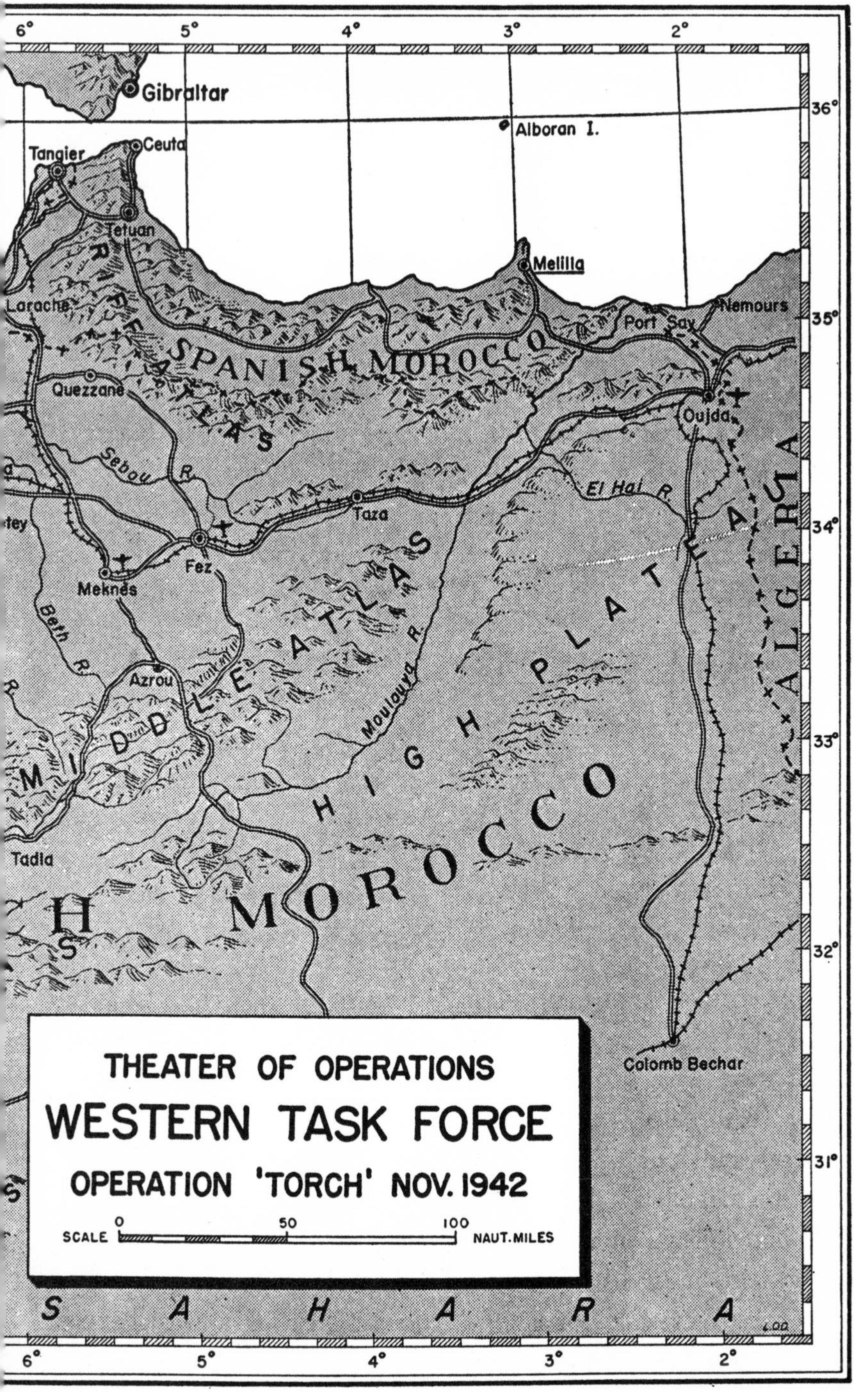

THEATER OF OPERATIONS
WESTERN TASK FORCE
OPERATION 'TORCH' NOV. 1942
SCALE 0 50 100 NAUT. MILES
Gibraltar
Alboran I.
Tangier
Ceuta
Tetuan
Melilla
Larache
Nemours
Port Say
SPANISH MOROCCO
RIF ATLAS
Quezzane
Oujda
Sebou R.
El Hai R.
Taza
Fez
Meknes
Beth R.
MIDDLE ATLAS
Moulouya R.
Azrou
HIGH PLATEAU
ALGERIA
MOROCCO
Tadla
Colomb Bechar
SAHARA
6° 5° 4° 3° 2°
36° 35° 34° 33° 32° 31°

Admiral Hewitt's long-anticipated signal for a general engagement: "Play Ball!" This little corner of the world, so dark and silent for five long hours, was now split with blinding gun flashes, shattered by machine-gun fire, shaken by the crash of heavy ordnance.

It was essential to silence batteries at each end of Fedhala, as they enfiladed the beaches and their approaches. *Brooklyn* scored a direct hit on one of the four guns at Sherki, and another on the fire control station. Ground troops then moved in. The batteries on Cape Fedhala were harder to find and still more difficult to knock out; they opened up intermittently on the landing craft and killed several men. But the landings went on, wave after wave of small craft, until by 1700 on D-day, 8 November, 7750 officers and men were ashore. French resistance here was almost nil, but surf, a falling tide and inexperienced crews brought heavy damage to landing craft; some 150 out of a total of 350 were expended.

From 0615, when it was barely light enough to launch planes, the Navy's carrier-based aircraft began to fight. *Ranger*'s Wildcats destroyed grounded planes at the three principal French airdromes in Morocco, while her dive-bombers hit the submarine basin in Casablanca Harbor, and both took part in the naval actions we are about to relate. *Suwannee*, commanded by Captain "Jocko" Clark, handled combat air and antisubmarine patrol for the Center Group.

Shortly after 0700 opened the first phase of the Naval Battle of Casablanca. This was a fight between Admiral Giffen's covering group (battleship *Massachusetts*, heavy cruisers *Wichita* and *Tuscaloosa*) and four 8-inch coast defense guns of El Hank battery near the Casablanca lighthouse, aided by French battleship *Jean Bart* immobilized in the harbor. The shore battery was only silenced temporarily; but *Jean Bart*, whose four 15-inch guns might have raised havoc in the transport area off Fedhala, was silenced for the day. The next phase began at 0815, when Contre-Amiral

Michelier, commanding French naval forces at Casablanca, took advantage of a moment when Giffen's big ships were 16 miles off shore to hurl his seven destroyers at the American transports.

Even at this late hour the French did not know whether the ships landing troops on their soil were German, British or American; and they didn't much care; the French Navy's honor was at stake, it was determined to fight. The sortieing destroyers made a few hits on landing craft and destroyer *Ludlow*, but before they could reach the vulnerable transports they were engaged by *Augusta*, *Brooklyn* and two destroyers. The French ships, led by Contre-Amiral Gervais de Lafond in destroyer-leader *Milan*, put up a stout and clever fight, laying a thick smoke screen in and out of which they dodged to shoot; but they were too few and feebly armed, even when assisted by light cruiser *Primauguet* and by eight submarines which had escaped the earlier bombardment of their mooring basin. American gunfire was faster, heavier and more accurate, and carrier-based aircraft had command of the air. Destroyers *Fougueux* and *Boulonnais* blew up and sank; *Primauguet* took a bad beating from the cruisers' gunfire, and was later finished off by air bombing; *Brestois* and *Frondeur* met the same fate. A hit by El Hank battery on *Wichita*, which wounded 14 men, was the only lethal one received by the American ships before action broke off at 1145.

The final score for this day of battle was very onesided. But by the day's end the French Navy had plenty of fight left. El Hank was still intact, and the 15-inch guns of *Jean Bart* were again ready for action.

4. *Mehedia and Safi Assaulted, and Cease-Fire, 7–15 November*

The objective of the Northern Attack Group, commanded by Rear Admiral Kelly in battleship *Texas* and carrying about 9000 men, mostly of the 9th Infantry Division under General Truscott, was to capture the important airdrome of Port Lyautey, several miles up the shoal and winding Wadi Sebou. Escort carrier *Sangamon* carried the fighter and bomber components, and her sister ship *Chenango* stood by waiting for a chance to fly army planes to the airdromes.

It was assumed that the town of Mehedia, with an ancient but well-fortified Kasba citadel at the mouth of the Sebou, must be taken before the river could be used. The Kasba took the initiative at 0700, shelling boat waves and transports, forcing transports to pull out to a point some 15 miles off shore. The result, as General Truscott reported, was that the landings were turned "into a hit-or-miss affair" which "would have spelled disaster" against a determined enemy. The French here were too strong (some 3500 Moroccan *tirailleurs* and Foreign Legionnaires and 14 tanks) and were alerted too early, and our troops got ashore too late, to have a walk-over as at Fedhala. The Kasba, despite efforts of cruiser *Savannah*, did not fall until 10 November — and then to the Army.

The leading naval exploit of this attack was the gallant passage of destroyer *Dallas* (Lieutenant Commander Robert Brodie), a twenty-two-year-old four-piper, up the Sebou. After her net-cutting party had severed the stout wire of the boom at the river-mouth, *Dallas*, carrying a raider detachment of 75 men and guided by a local French pilot, crashed through the rest of the boom at first light 10 November, under fire from the Kasba, threaded her way between sunken hulks, dragged her keel through the soft mud of the river bottom, silenced French guns that fired at her, and landed her raiders without a casualty. Coöperating with a battalion of the 2nd Armored Division United States Army, which marched overland, the raiders captured the airdrome in short order, and by 1030 it was being used by P–40s from *Chenango.*

Everything clicked in the southern attack, on Safi, a little town at a gap in the cliffs 150 miles south of Casablanca, where the French had constructed a small artificial harbor. It was selected as objective partly to box off French forces in Southern Morocco, but mainly as the one place to land tanks. One quay in the harbor was long enough and the water alongside deep enough to berth tank carrier *Lakehurst*, a converted seatrain. She had to be used, as no LST had been completed in time to take part in this operation. There was no other harbor in Morocco that she could enter, except Casablanca — and it was for the capture of Casablanca that these tanks were wanted.

The harbor and all possible beaches were well covered by French artillery. To permit *Lakehurst* to enter and discharge her tanks two 1919-vintage destroyers, *Bernadou* (Lieutenant Commander R. E. Braddy) and *Cole* (Lieutenant Commander G. G. Palmer) were shorn of most of their superstructures and loaded with 350 assault troops to rush into the harbor and take it over before daylight. It worked. *Bernadou*, guided by Ensign J. J. Bell in a rubber scout boat, was just entering the harbor at 0428 November 8 when the French shore artillery started giving her "the works." Cruiser *Philadelphia* and battleship *New York* then started throwing 6-inch and 14-inch shells at the Batterie Railleuse, four 130-mm coast defense guns north of the town, which was making most of the trouble. *Bernadou* miraculously came through unhurt, sweeping the jetties and piers with machine-gun fire, and grounded near the harbor head. Her assault troops clambered down landing nets onto the rocks, and a few minutes later were chasing

Foreign Legionnaires away from the water's edge. *Cole* followed with landing craft trailing, and tied up at a quay. The town of Safi was captured by the raiders, Marrakech airdrome was neutralized by flyers from escort carrier *Santee*, and in the afternoon seatrain *Lakehurst* made a dignified entry and began discharging tanks. They started rumbling along the road to Casablanca on 10 November; but before they had got very far word came through from Admiral Darlan that this little Franco-American war was over.

General Patton's staff on 10 November had drawn plans for an all-out assault on Casablanca next day, and Contre-Amiral Michelier had prepared for desperate resistance. But at 0700 November 11, fifteen minutes before this attack was to start, the French army commander sent Patton a flag of truce. He had received a cease-fire order from Admiral Darlan at Algiers. This was the result of protracted negotiations between that French admiral (Marshal Pétain's second in command in the Vichy government), Robert Murphy of the American Foreign Service, and General Mark Clark USA. Darlan's order, issued at 1120 November 10, brought peace between French and Allied forces in North Africa, but plenty of trouble for metropolitan France.

There was no surrender, no transfer of sovereignty; merely a cease-fire which developed into full coöperation between Allied and French authorities, military and civil. The French naval administration at Casablanca immediately placed port facilities, installations, tugs, pilots and divers at our disposal. Thus, after three days' sharp fighting, the traditional friendship was renewed under the happiest circumstance of making common cause against the Axis powers.

But we had not yet heard from the Axis.

On the evening of 11 November 15 transports and cargo ships of Admiral Hewitt's Western Naval Task Force were still at anchor in Fedhala roadstead. *U–173* worked in between them and the shore, evading their screen and a protective mine field; it torpedoed and sank transport *Joseph Hewes,* then torpedoed but failed to sink oiler *Winooski* and destroyer *Hambleton.* The following evening *U–130,* by using the same tactics, made three victims — transports *Edward Rutledge, Tasker H. Bliss* and *Hugh L. Scott.* Their cargoes were mostly lost, and over a hundred men were killed or died of wounds. On the 15th U.S.S. *Electra* was torpedoed about 17 miles off Fedhala by *U–173,* but, more fortunate than her British namesake in the Java Sea, she did not sink. That U-boat hung around Casablanca too long for its health. Through good teamwork between destroyers *Woolsey, Swanson* and *Quick,* it was sunk off the harbor entrance on 16 November. By that time almost every ship of Admiral Hewitt's group which had not departed was safely inside Casablanca Harbor.

As a definite seal to Darlan's cease-fire order of 10 November, the French admiral, secretly assured by Marshal Pétain of his approval, drew up a formal accord with General Eisenhower and Admiral Cunningham, which was ratified by Churchill and Roosevelt on the 15th. By virtue of this pact, Admiral Darlan became head of the civil government in North Africa and General Giraud, who had escaped from a German prison and been brought to Gibraltar in a submarine commanded by Captain Jerauld Wright, became head of the French armed forces in North Africa. This "Darlan deal" — denounced as a base truckling to Vichy by General de Gaulle and by British and American left-wingers — ensured French coöperation with the Allies, saved very many lives, and prevented an inestimable amount of sabotage and obstruction to Allied military operations.

5. *The Capture of Oran and Algiers, 8–11 November*

Simultaneously with Admiral Hewitt's landings in Morocco, and equally powerful and important, were those of American and British troops, escorted by the Royal Navy, near Oran and Algiers. Both forces were mounted in the United Kingdom, drawing on the United States Army contingents which General Marshall had hoped to use in a cross-Channel operation.

In the small hours of the morning of D-day, 8 November, H.M.S. *Hartland* and *Walney* (former United States Coast Guard cutters transferred to the Royal Navy in 1941) dashed into Oran Harbor carrying a small United States Naval and Marine guard and 400 picked American troops. Unlike *Bernadou*'s assault on Safi, this enterprise was a dismal failure. The local French, alerted, raked both vessels with point-blank fire, sank them, and killed about half their crews and passengers.

The main landings of troops lifted by Center Task Force (Commodore Thomas Troubridge RN), the 1st Infantry Division and part of the 1st Armored Division, United States Army, took place on two sets of beaches, each side of Oran. Those in the Gulf of Arzeu were noteworthy for the use of two British "Maracaibos" — shoal-draft oilers from Venezuela, fitted with a big bow ramp for landing tanks; these were prototypes of the famous LST. The two columns of troops converged on Oran, where all resistance ceased 9 November.

Algiers was taken by the Eastern Naval Task Force, Rear Admiral Sir Harold M. Burrough RN, lifting the Eastern Assault Force, comprising regimental combat teams of the 9th and 34th Infantry Divisions United States Army, and two brigade groups of the British Army, which here outnumbered the American contingent two to one. This force, too, was mounted in the United Kingdom and escorted by the Royal Navy. Five of the transports were American, one of which, *Thomas Stone*, was crippled by a U-boat's torpedo on 7 November, off the Spanish coast. The ships, boat crews and troops of this Force had had only a few days' amphibious training, with the result that the landing, though unopposed, was a complete foul-up. The same state of affairs characterized the unopposed landings from British transports west of Algiers. No fewer than 98 of the 104 landing craft used in all sectors of the Eastern Naval Task Force were expended; a loss so scandalous that the Army put in a bid for taking charge of all future landing operations.

French resistance ceased in and around Algiers on D-day, 8 November, but the Axis picked up the ball, and over a period of a week the big transports unloading were subjected to severe bombing and torpedo attacks by land-based Junkers and Heinkels. U.S.S. *Leedstown* was the principal casualty; she had to be abandoned, and sank.

As a result of this massive three-pronged amphibious operation, North Africa west of Tunisia was denied to the Axis, valuable airdromes, military, naval and antisubmarine bases were secured, and foundations laid for driving the Germans out of North Africa. The Royal and United States Navies had learned far more about amphibious operations than they ever could have done from the most prolonged training and rehearsal; later assaults in the European theater would have failed but for the lessons learned in TORCH. Those lessons were: —

(1) The need of better seamanship and design in small landing craft: the original plywood and rampless "Higgins Boat" proved inadequate, and the Navy henceforth concentrated on building

steel, diesel-powered and ramped types, such as the LCP(R), LCVP and LCM.

(2) The pressing need of big beaching craft — the Landing Ship Tank (LST), Landing Craft Tank (LCT) and Landing Craft Infantry (LCI), to bring in tanks, vehicles and large units of troops quickly.

(3) From the Navy's point of view, the advisability of renouncing tactical surprise in order to deliver gunfire support and land by daylight — a point of view the Army was not yet ready to accept. Owing to the half-hearted, sporadic resistance offered by the French, we had yet to experience a stoutly contested amphibious operation. The Germans would provide that at Salerno, and the Japanese at Tarawa, before the end of 1943.

Bold as Operation TORCH was, and successful within its sphere, it could well have been a little bolder and secured Tunisia too, as Admiral Cunningham wanted. There the Germans beat us at the draw. Admiral Esteva, head of the French government in Tunisia, was well disposed to the Allies but overpowered by German troops arriving by ferry plane. Frenzied efforts were made by the Germans to convert this country into an African bastion, since the British army led by General Montgomery, after winning the Second Battle of El Alamein on 3 November, was slowly and deliberately pursuing Rommel westward. This year 1942 closed on a static situation in Tunisia. The Anglo-American First Army was bogged down in Algerian mud; Montgomery's forces were dusted down by sandstorms; the Germans had occupied the ports of Bizerta, Sousse, Sfax and Gabes.

The Royal Navy, respecting the powerful air forces that the enemy had deployed, was not yet ready to challenge Axis control of the Straits of Sicily. Malta stood firm. But the Axis had won the race for Tunisia.

6. *The Casablanca Conference*

The military campaign for Tunisia, which lies outside the scope of this volume, did not end until 13 May 1943. Axis forces 275,000 strong, which had been pushed into Cape Bon, then completed their surrender to American II Corps (Major General Omar N. Bradley) and British Eighth Army (General Sir Harold Alexander). On 17 May the first Allied trans-Mediterranean convoy since 1941 left Gibraltar, and on the 26th it reached Alexandria without loss. The Suez lifeline now reopened; no longer did ships bound for the Indian Ocean and Australia have to round the Cape of Good Hope.

If TORCH put the Navy on its toes, the Tunisian experience was equally valuable for the Army. There it learned how to fight seasoned German troops, and developed the competence of corps and divisional commanders for a much bigger show. There Generals Bradley and Patton first had a chance to prove their exceptional, though diverse, military qualities. In all three elements — ground, sea and air — British and Americans had learned how to win battles together. Thus, whilst one can argue that TORCH was a mistake, and that the Marshall plan of cross-Channel operations in 1942-1943 should never have been allowed to lapse, almost everyone who studies the Tunisian campaign must conclude that the postponement was correct. We were simply not ready to launch, and still less to follow up, a massive assault on *Festung Europa* in 1942-1943.

Since that had to be postponed, a question arose as before: What could the Allies do in 1943 to engage the Axis and take pressure off Russia? A plenary Combined Chiefs of Staff conference, with President Roosevelt and Premier Churchill, met at Casablanca between 14 and 23 January 1943 to consider that and other questions. This conference ended in a strategic compromise. The

British removed their objection to America's exploiting the initiative she had won in the Pacific; America consented to take part in another Mediterranean operation, and to postpone the cross-Channel invasion until 1944. Both agreed that "the defeat of the U-boat must remain a first charge on the resources of the United Nations," since if that failed, everything would fail. In consequence of that decision, the United States gave "Triple-A" priority to the construction of destroyer escorts, escort carriers and antisubmarine aircraft, placing landing and beaching craft in a lower category. That is why a worldwide shortage of such craft occurred in 1944.

Admirals King and Pound now persuaded the Conference to make Sicily the next objective in order to secure the Mediterranean line of communications, increase pressure on Italy, and divert German forces from the Russian front. The Conference also adopted a rough plan for Operation HUSKY, an Anglo-American invasion of Sicily for July 1943, with General Eisenhower as supreme commander, Admiral Cunningham naval commander and Air Chief Marshal Tedder air commander. American strategists hoped that Sicily would put a stopper on Mediterranean campaigns, so that we could get on with the big cross-Channel invasion. The British, on the contrary, looked on Sicily as another rung of the ladder to what Churchill called the "soft underbelly" of the Axis. Thus, as Admiral King predicted, once we started in the Mediterranean, we would have to go on and on. And the "underbelly" turned out to be boned with the Apennines, plated with the hard scales of Kesselring's armor, and shadowed by the wings of the Luftwaffe.

The other important decision at Casablanca, and the only one made public, was a resolution to accept nothing less than "unconditional surrender" of Germany, Italy and, by implication, Japan. The P.M. and F.D.R. were jointly responsible for the principle, and Roosevelt for the publicity and the phrase, which he remembered vaguely from the history of the Civil War.[2] It was received with joy and acclamation in the Allied countries, where it dispelled the fear of a "Darlan deal" with Hitler, Mussolini and Hirohito, or the adoption of something like a Wilsonian "Fourteen Points," the meaning of which could be argued indefinitely. The decision to utter this rallying slogan was not lightly made. The American, Russian and British people, especially the last two, had suffered so severely that they had to be promised complete victory; no Peace of Amiens, no mere truce which would leave Germany strong enough to start up again. And the Americans felt the same about Japan. But did not "unconditional surrender" help the Axis leaders to persuade their people to fight *à l'outrance*, as the only alternative to virtual "slavery"? Possibly so; probably not. Italy's surrender in 1943 was highly conditional, and both the Nazis and the Japanese war lords, right up to the moment of their complete defeat, imagined that they could make a "deal." In my opinion "unconditional surrender" did not prolong the war a day, and can in no way be considered responsible for our postwar troubles.

7. *The Shipping and Submarine Situation, August 1942–May 1943*

The Casablanca conferees, meeting in an atmosphere of euphoria following the success of TORCH, had eyes bigger than their stomachs, and laid out a strategic menu that they could not digest. Although HUSKY did come off at the target date, it was at the expense of other things — a quick follow-up in the Pacific after the

[2] F.D.R. apparently thought that General Grant's initials were expanded to "Unconditional Surrender" owing to the Appomattox affair; he was, however, given the nickname owing to his successful demand for the unconditional surrender of Fort Donelson in February 1862.

securing of Guadalcanal and Papua, a drive from India toward Akyab in Burma; and the build-up of American forces in Britain for the now postponed cross-Channel operation. Shipping was the bottleneck for everything, and Admiral Doenitz was doing very well in his efforts to squeeze that neck.

In Chapter V, above, we left the antisubmarine situation in June 1942 considerably improved, but it did not long stay improved. Doenitz started a new U-boat blitz in August, which reached its acme in March 1943. He now had echelons of wolf-packs strung across all transatlantic convoy routes between Iceland and the Azores, especially in what we called the "Black Pit" outside the range of land-based aircraft. These tactics were exceedingly difficult to beat; and beaten they were not for eight months. In August 1942, the Allies lost 102 merchant ships of over half a million gross tons to submarine attack, in Atlantic and Arctic waters. Not one transatlantic merchant convoy escaped attack. During the next four months an average of almost a ship a day was lost on the North Atlantic convoy routes, and sinkings in the Caribbean and among unconvoyed merchants ships trying to round the Cape of Good Hope (access to Suez still being closed) were also heavy.

Although the convoy system had been extended, much transatlantic traffic was still carried in unescorted merchant ships with naval armed guards. Their fine fighting spirit is illustrated by the battle of Liberty ship *Stephen Hopkins* (Paul Buck, master) with two armed German ships, Raider "J" armed with six 5.9-inch guns, and blockade-runner *Tannenfels.* These two attacked *Hopkins* at lat. 28° S, long. 20° W, on 27 September 1942. Ensign K. M. Willett USNR and his naval armed guard, operating the freighter's one 4-inch gun, scored 35 hits on Raider "J" and forced her abandonment. After a German shell had exploded the magazine for Willett's gun, the ship's second mate and crew operated two 37-mm guns forward, firing at *Tannenfels,* which was raking their decks with machine-gun fire — Captain Buck maneuvering his ship so as to bring all possible gunfire to bear. This unequal battle continued for almost three hours, when *Stephen Hopkins*, aflame from stem to stern and holed below her waterline, plunged with colors flying; but Raider "J" had preceded her to the bottom. The one undamaged American lifeboat, without charts or navigation instruments, made the coast of Brazil after a voyage of 31 days, with only 15 men of the Liberty ship's crew still alive.

In January, while the C.C.S. and their guests were basking in the sunshine at Casablanca and planning great doings for 1943, one of the worst winters on record was lashing the Western Ocean. Hardly a day passed without snow squalls or bone-chilling rain. Heavy seas broke continuously over vessels' bows, icing their superstructures in the high latitudes. These conditions were even worse for merchant ships than for U-boats, which could get under. During most of the winter the weather was so foul that long-range land-based planes could not fly, and several of those that did never returned. Merchant ship losses by marine casualty alone, for the five months November 1942-March 1943, reached the unprecedented figure of 92 vessels in the Atlantic; 166 for all parts of the world. Sinkings from U-boat attack reached an all-time high in November 1942: 106 ships of 637,907 gross tons. In January 1943, a convoy escorted by four British corvettes from Trinidad to Gibraltar lost seven out of nine tankers.

As a sample, here is what happened to a couple of transatlantic convoys early in 1943. Westbound Convoy ON–166, 63 ships, escorted by Captain P. R. Heineman's unit, comprising U.S.C.G.C. *Spencer* and *Campbell*, five British and Canadian corvettes, and Polish destroyer *Burza*, between 12 and 25 February lost seven merchant ships, but sank two U-boats, one by *Spencer* with depth-charges, one by *Campbell* through ramming and gunfire, after *Burza* had depth-charged it. The escort unit had barely entered the uneasy shelter of Argentia, Newfoundland, when it was ordered out, augmented by U.S.S. *Greer*, to take charge of eastbound

Convoy SC–121, of 56 ships. Thrice in four days (6-9 March) this unfortunate convoy was set upon by wolf-packs. At least seven ships were torpedoed and all but one sunk, with unusually heavy loss of life, including that of the British convoy commodore. The sea was so rough that even *Greer*'s veteran sailors on one occasion could not pick up survivors from lifeboats and rafts, and had to let them go. Both in this and the next slow convoy (122), which lost nine ships, and in HX–229 which lost 11 ships on 8-10 March, there were numerous acts of heroism and self-sacrifice on the part of merchant seamen as well as coastguardsmen and bluejackets.

Few outside the two Navies and merchant marines realized how serious the situation had become in March 1943. The U-boats, in this and other areas, sank 108 ships that month, totaling 627,000 tons, and lost only 15 of their number. So many Allied escort vessels were under repair that the group organization was disintegrating. So many U-boats were at sea (an average of 116 operating daily in the North Atlantic) that evasive routing was futile; a convoy avoided one concentration of wolf-packs only to fall into the fangs of another. No enemy ever came so near to disrupting Atlantic communications as Doentiz did that month.

All this had a very damaging effect on Britain's imports. These, the Joint Chiefs of Staff had agreed, early in 1942, must be kept above a certain norm in order to keep her people fighting, producing, and even eating. British imports, owing largely to the work of the U-boats, had declined from a prewar average of over 50 million tons[3] to 23 million in 1942; and by the end of that year Britain was "eating her own tail." In November F.D.R. promised the P.M. to allot England enough newly built merchant ships to raise her imports to a marginal 27 million tons next year. But it was some months before this relief came forth. And as most of the

[3] Deadweight tonnage, in tons of 2,240 lbs. each. Apply factor of 1.5 for equivalent in gross tonnage.

follow-up TORCH convoys from the United Kingdom to North Africa had to be under the Red Ensign, food stocks in Britain fell off to a three-months supply in January 1943. In order that England might not "live from hand to mouth," Churchill reduced by half sailings to the Indian Ocean around the Cape, a drastic measure which brought Bengal to the verge of famine.

It was, unfortunately, typical of the hit-or-miss methods of wartime administration that the J.C.S. first heard of the President's promise from Sir John Dill, the C.C.S. representative in Washington. Thus Lieutenant General Brehon Somervell of the U. S. Army Service of Supply, attended the Casablanca Conference both uninstructed and confused. He neither knew what the President had promised, or what his country was able to do about it; and he made a fuzzy sort of agreement with his British opposite number which might be interpreted that we were to give the British 300,000 tons of shipping, or 7 million tons. In March 1943, with the situation clouded by protracted German resistance in Tunisia and U-boat achievements in the North Atlantic, this misunderstanding blew up in everybody's face. To implement the President's promise would require, in April-June, not only 9 million tons of cargo ships to Britain for the rest of 1943, but 14 sailings per month to the Mediterranean to support HUSKY, and 25 sailings per month to the Indian Ocean for the planned drive on Akyab. Churchill wrote severely to Roosevelt "We cannot live from hand to mouth on promises limited by provisos." Admiral King and the other members of the J.C.S. felt, on the contrary, that the important thing was to get on with the war; Britain must tighten her belt. A nasty situation was developing between the military heads of both countries when President Roosevelt took it out of their hands and gave it to a special board of civilians, presided over by Harry Hopkins. On 29 March, Hopkins, Lewis Douglas (then deputy chief of War Shipping Administration), and Sir Anthony Eden, the British Foreign Minister, met with the President at the White House. Douglas presented the case for maintaining the level of British imports if we wished to avoid weakening the entire war effort; he further declared that American armed services' estimates of necessary shipping were generally inflated, and that they wasted tonnage scandalously.[4] Roosevelt decided in Britain's favor, and gave strict orders that his November promise be implemented, as it was. The British import program rapidly revived, and in May the President directed the War Shipping Administration to transfer 15 to 20 new freighters a month to the Red Ensign.

But this presidential promise could never have been kept, and the British people would have approached famine in 1943 but for a dramatic reverse of fortune in the antisubmarine war in April and May.

First came success in antisubmarine operations. The glorious battle of a British escort group under Commander P. W. Gretton RN, to westbound Convoy ONS–5, is regarded both by the Allies and the Germans as a turning-point in the North Atlantic struggle. Doenitz deployed no fewer than 51 U-boats to destroy this 42-ship convoy. The battle raged almost continuously in foul weather from 28 April to 6 May. Thirteen merchantmen (including three Americans) were sunk; but an escort that never numbered more than nine ships sank five U-boats; and two Catalinas — one Canadian and one American — disposed of two more.

This victory was followed by another in the Bay of Biscay offensive which Air Vice Marshal Sir John Slessor of Coastal Command had been conducting since March. His plan was to train bomber planes based on southern England, operating in con-

[4] For instance, freighters at places like Nouméa swung around the hook for weeks and even months for lack of unloading facilities. Not until the Okinawa operation in 1945 did the Navy set up a proper administration for controlling shipping, seeing that the turnaround was expedited, and that cargo space was not wasted.

nection with Royal Navy corvettes, to catch U-boats going and coming near their French outports on the Bay. Aircraft-mounted microwave radar, which the Germans could not detect, picked up surfaced U-boats at night, then the new Leigh searchlight illuminated them; and if they were not sunk, a surface unit was homed in to do the job. In May 1943, the results of this Bay offensive, added to others, meant 38 U-boats sunk — 12 more than were built; and three less than the number of merchant ships lost in the Atlantic and Arctic Oceans. The Bay offensive, continuing to the end of the year with American Liberators pitching in to help, broke the back of Doenitz's submarine campaign.

There was also a vast improvement in organization and method. On 1 May 1943, Admiral King organized Tenth Fleet, with himself as commander and Rear Admiral Francis S. Low as chief of staff, to combine "all existing antisubmarine activities." Low — tough, intelligent and hard-working — was a perfect *alter ego* to King, who did not have the time to give this branch of warfare the detailed attention it required. He ruled with an iron hand, but had the respect of his subordinates, who were never allowed to doubt what he wanted, and were never let down.

The destroyer escort (DE) program finally bore fruit. Some 250 of these new escort vessels had been authorized in January 1942, but the shifting of priority work in American shipyards to beaching and landing craft for the cross-Channel operation that never came off so delayed the program that by 2 June only 42 had been launched. They were now produced in such abundance that by December 260 DEs were in commission.

There was a similar delay in building escort carriers. These CVEs, capable of carrying about 24 operating planes, were badly wanted as additional protection to convoys. The first, U.S.S. *Bogue*, got into action in March 1943.[5] At the same time the production of land-based aircraft types suitable for antisubmarine

[5] See Chap. XII for some of their exploits.

work so increased that in the second half of 1943 the Navy was able to relieve the Army Air Force of antisubmarine duties which it had assumed at a time of desperate need. Liberators (PB4Ys, same as the Army B–24s) had a radius of 900 miles from Newfoundland or the British Isles, and smaller bombers had a radius of 500 miles from Greenland or Iceland; but there was still a mid-ocean "black pit" where no air protection could reach a convoy unless brought to it by a CVE. This was not lighted up until late 1943 when Portugal gave the Allies permission to base antisubmarine planes on the Azores.

8. *Operation* HUSKY, *July 1943*

Not even Mr. Churchill expected Operation HUSKY to be soft. As an historian he knew that Greeks, Carthaginians, Romans, Byzantines, Saracens, Normans, Angevins and Spaniards in succession had had their will of this great and fair island, but each conquest had taken years to complete. Sicily had never been so defensible, at least in theory, as in 1943. It contained about a dozen airfields, and its garrison was formidable, at least on paper. The greater part of the island is mountainous, difficult to traverse except by main roads. The Strait of Messina is so narrow that reinforcements can easily be poured in from Italy.

The command setup for Operation HUSKY may best be presented in a diagram: —

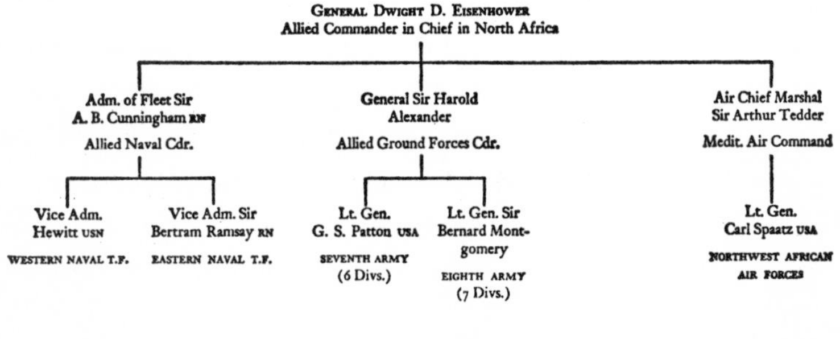

General Eisenhower, preoccupied with the Tunisian campaign and bedeviled by the rivalries of De Gaulle, Giraud and other French leaders in Africa, was unable to give much attention to planning HUSKY. Most of the essential work was done at Hewitt's and Cunningham's headquarters in Algiers, and General Patton's at Mostaganem, 165 miles distant — much too distant for proper planning. For D-day, the night of 9-10 July was chosen because the moon set around 0230; the Air Forces wanted moonlight for their paratroop drop, and the Army wanted darkness to commence landing at 0245. Nine Allied divisions (four American, four British and one Canadian) were available for the initial assault, and about the same number of German and Italian divisions were expected to be on hand to oppose. The plan finally selected in mid-May, after much wrangling, provided for Hewitt's Western Naval Task Force to land on three sets of beaches near Licata, Gela and Scoglitti on the southwest coast of Sicily, and the British to land on beaches around the southeastern cape of the island. Patton would drive across the island to secure Palermo, and then swing east to Messina, while Montgomery drove north to Syracuse, Augusta, Catania and Messina.

This was a poor strategic plan, better calculated to push the Axis forces out of Sicily than to trap them in Sicily. But its chief weakness lay in the refusal of the United States Army Air Forces to coöperate, largely because General "Tooey" Spaatz was wedded to the concept of "strategic" air operations — which meant the A.A.F. fighting its own war. He planned to devote practically his entire strength to fighting the Luftwaffe and the Royal Italian Air Force; and not until two weeks before D-day did Spaatz even let Hewitt and Patton know that this was his intention. The A.A.F. and R.A.F. opened this Sicilian campaign on 2 July with an implacable, day-and-night hammering of enemy headquarters and of ten or twelve Sicilian airfields, which were rendered temporarily unusable. But the amphibious expedition sailed and landed with no promise of tactical support from the air, and almost none did it obtain.

An important air unit, which came under Seventh Army, not the A.A.F., and which greatly helped, was the 82nd Airborne Division (Major General Matthew B. Ridgway USA). This, the first paratroop division in the United States Army, made its combat debut in HUSKY. Its mission was to seize high ground and the Ponte Olivo airfield behind the landing beaches, confuse the defense and prevent a prompt counterattack on the beachhead. This division no more than the Navy could obtain night fighter protection from the Army Air Force. The A.A.F. did have night-flying fighter planes and pilots, but had other uses for them.

"The capture of Sicily was an undertaking of the first magnitude," as Churchill wrote. Measured by the strength of the initial assault, it breaks all records for amphibious operations; even the Normandy landings next year exceeded it only if follow-up echelons are counted. Admiral Hewitt had 580 ships, and Admiral Ramsay had 795 ships under their respective commands. In addition Vice Admiral Sir Algernon Willis RN commanded a Royal Navy covering force of six battleships, six cruisers and 24 destroyers. The nature of the operation was part ship-to-shore, part shore-to-shore, this last being made possible by the arrival in North Africa of the first big beaching craft,[6] the 1500-ton, 328-foot Landing Ship Tank (LST), the 550-ton, 112-foot Landing Craft Tank (LCT), and the 200-ton, 158-foot Landing Craft Infantry Large — LCI(L). The biggest of these, the LST, modified from a British design, were built at Newport News, trained in Chesapeake Bay, and early in 1943 began crossing the Atlantic on their own bottoms, as the LCI did too. LCTs came over on the decks of LSTs or on freighters. Admirals Conolly and Hall,

[6] These three types, and the Landing Ship Medium (LSM), are designated "beaching craft" to distinguish them from the landing craft proper that are small enough to be carried on the decks or davits of transports. Dimensions here given are those of the three types used in HUSKY; later ones varied somewhat.

who had specially interested themselves in these types, experimented with them to ascertain their capabilities, and used them extensively in HUSKY.

According to Thucydides, the Greeks who invaded Syracuse in 413 B.C. had most to fear from the Sicilian cavalry, against which, for want of a Landing Ship Horse, their only defense was archery. Enemy tanks, the modern cavalry, are now the bane of amphibious landings. In order to prevent their working havoc on the GIs it was necessary to land our own tanks and antitank guns with or immediately after the assault troops. That was the main function of the LST and LCT. These craft were supposed to be able to ground on a beach and lower their ramps, over which tanks, guns and vehicles could roll ashore. The LCI beached and then lowered bow gangways, not unlike the "brows" of a Greek bireme, for infantry to land without boating or swimming. Unfortunately, most of the Sicilian beaches were protected by sand bars with enough water to float landing craft but not an LST. The dukw, an amphibious truck which could carry 25 troops or 2½ tons of cargo, swim in the water and roll over the land, and required only one driver, also made its European debut in HUSKY. The great advantage of the dukw was its ability to carry supplies from a ship to an inland dump without handling at the water's edge.

The Axis was partly, but not completely, surprised by the Sicilian assault. Hitler, swallowing a clever British "plant" to the effect that the real objectives were Sardinia and Greece, dispatched reinforcements to both places; but Marshal Kesselring, the German commander in Italy, was not fooled and sent a panzer division to Sicily as reinforcement. That added up to two German and four Italian combat divisions, in addition to six Italian coastal divisions which were composed mostly of over-age Sicilian reservists.

There were over 300,000 men under arms in Sicily when the Anglo-American expeditionary force landed on 10 July 1943,

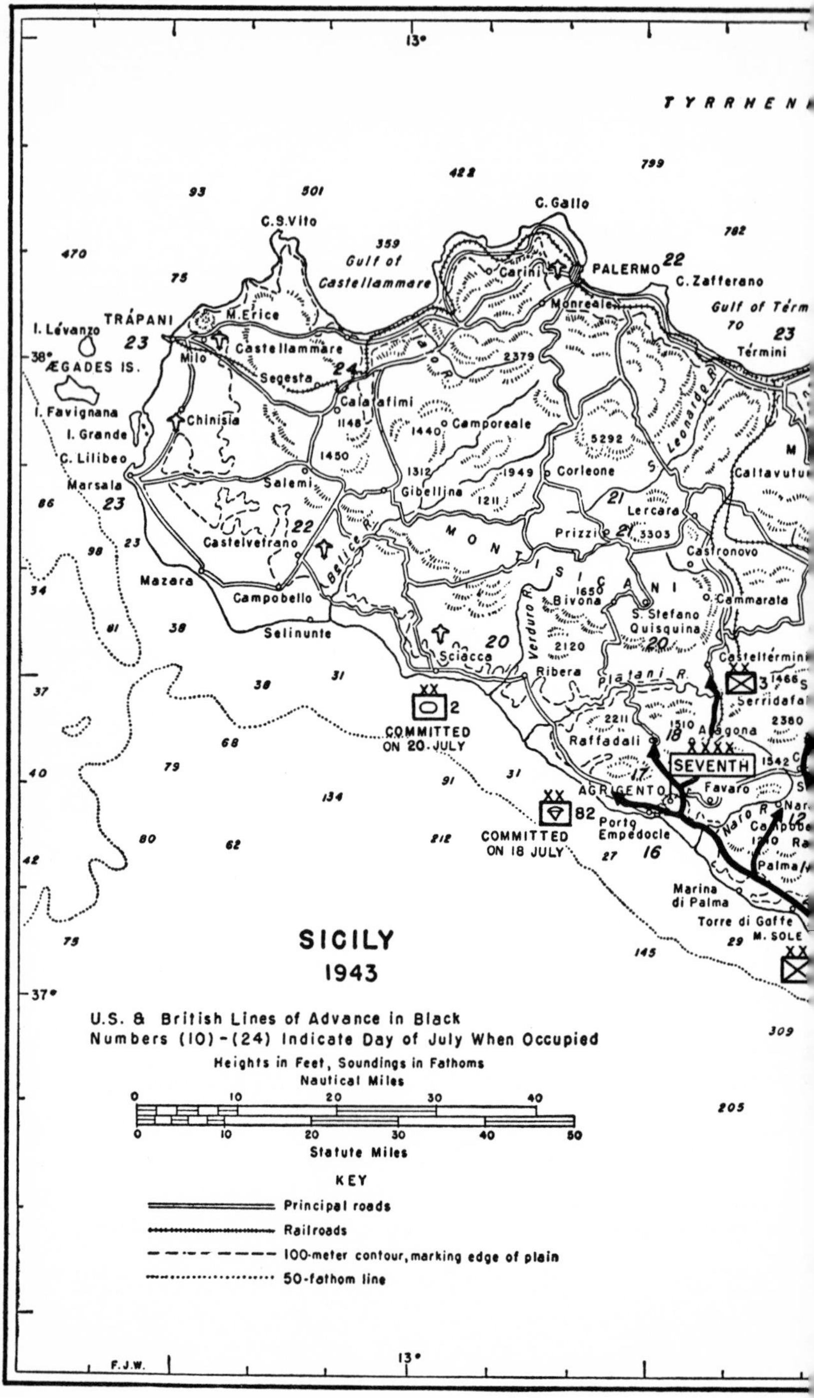

TYRRHENI
SICILY
1943
U.S. & British Lines of Advance in Black
Numbers (10)-(24) Indicate Day of July When Occupied
Heights in Feet, Soundings in Fathoms
Nautical Miles
Statute Miles
KEY
Principal roads
Railroads
100-meter contour, marking edge of plain
50-fathom line
TRÁPANI
PALERMO
C. Gallo
C. S. Vito
Gulf of Castellammare
C. Zafferano
Gulf of Térm
Términi
Carini
Monreale
M. Erice
Castellammare
Segesta
Calatafimi
Camporeale
Corleone
Lercara
Prizzi
Castronovo
Cammarata
Caltavutu
I. Lévanzo
ÆGADES IS.
I. Favignana
I. Grande
C. Lilibeo
Marsala
Milo
Chinisia
Salemi
Gibellina
Castelvetrano
Mazara
Campobello
Selinunte
Sciacca
Ribera
Bivona
S. Stefano Quisquina
Casteltérmini
Serridafa
Aragona
Raffadali
SEVENTH
AGRIGENTO
Favaro
Porto Empédocle
Marina di Palma
Torre di Gaffe
M. SOLE
Belice R.
Verduro R.
Platani R.
Naro R.
Leonardo R.
MONTI SICANI
COMMITTED ON 20 JULY
COMMITTED ON 18 JULY
F.J.W.

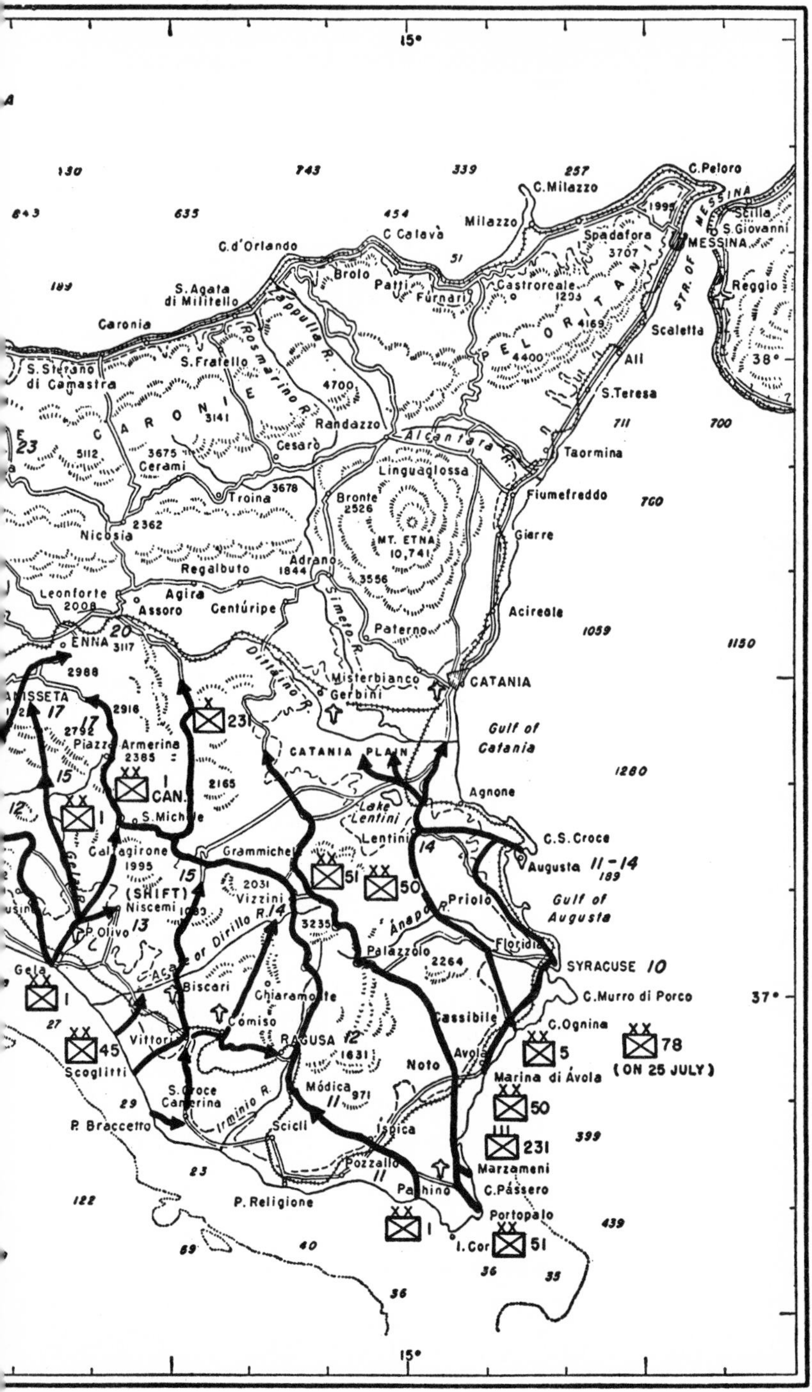
15°
C.Peloro
C.Milazzo
Milazzo
C Calavà
C.d'Orlando
Brolo
Patti
Furnari
Spadafora
3707
MESSINA
STR. OF MESSINA
Scilla
S.Giovanni
Reggio
Castroreale
1293
PELORITANI
4169
4400
Scaletta
Ali
S.Teresa
38°
S.Agata di Militello
Caronia
Zappulla R.
Rosmarino R.
S.Stefano di Camastra
S.Fratello
CARONIE
3141
4700
Randazzo
Alcantara R.
Cesarò
5112
3675
Cerami
Troina
3678
Linguaglossa
Taormina
Fiumefreddo
Bronte
2526
MT. ETNA
10,741
Gierre
2362
Nicosia
Adrano
1844
Regalbuto
3556
Leonforte
2008
Agira
Assoro
Centúripe
Simeto R.
Acireale
Paterno
ENNA
3117
Dittaino R.
2988
Misterbianco
Gerbini
CATANIA
Gulf of Catania
2916
2792
Piazza Armerina
2385
CATANIA PLAIN
1 CAN.
2165
231
Agnone
S.Michele
Lake Lentini
Lentini
C.S.Croce
Augusta
Caltagirone
1995
Grammichele
2031
Vizzini
51
50
Priolo
Gulf of Augusta
(SHIFT)
Niscemi
Dirillo R.
Anapo R.
3235
Floridia
P.Olivo
Palazzolo
2264
SYRACUSE
Gela
Acate or Dirillo R.
Biscari
Chiaramonte
C.Murro di Porco
37°
Comiso
Cassibile
C.Ognina
Vittoria
RAGUSA
1631
Noto
Avola
5
78
(ON 25 JULY)
45
Scoglitti
Marina di Ávola
S.Croce Camerina
Irminio R.
Módica
971
50
P. Braccetto
Scicli
Ispica
231
Pozzallo
Marzameni
Pachino
C.Pássero
P. Religione
Portopalo
I.Cor
51
17
15
12
13
14
11-14
10
11
20
23

and the Luftwaffe, the German Air Force, had about 1000 serviceable planes within flying distance of the landings. On the other hand, Mussolini prudently kept his Navy in protected harbors such as Spezia, the German Navy was represented by only a few U-boats and motor torpedo boats, and the Italian air force consisted largely of obsolete planes. Another asset to the invaders was the friendly attitude of the Sicilians, and of the Mafia or "Black Hand." Gangsters and peasants alike hated Germans, were fed up with the Duce, and looked on their invaders as liberators.

Admiral Hewitt's Western Naval Task Force, mounted at or staged through six different harbors along the Algerian and Tunisian littoral, ran into a sharp and sudden *mistral* north of Malta that blew up a high breaking sea. This tested the endurance of the new beaching craft and the seamanship of their crews; both met it magnificently.

Carrying to a lower level the diagram at the head of the last section, Hewitt's Western Naval Task Force was divided three ways from west to east: Rear Admiral Conolly's Joss Force, to land Major General Truscott's 3rd Infantry Division[7] on beaches near Licata; Rear Admiral John L. Hall's Dime Force, to land Major General Terry Allen's 1st Infantry Division on beaches near Gela; and Rear Admiral Alan G. Kirk's Cent Force, to land Lieutenant General Omar N. Bradley and II Corps staff, and Major General Troy Middleton's 45th Infantry Division, on beaches near Scoglitti. Conolly, Hall and Kirk, as well as Admiral Hewitt, were experienced practitioners of amphibious warfare. Kirk had relieved Hewitt as Comphiblant, and as such trained his Cent Force in Chesapeake Bay. Hall, who came to Africa as Hewitt's chief of staff, had been Comphibforce Northwest African Waters since early in the year.

[7] All these divisions were "reinforced" and had so many "attached" units that the average number of officers and men in each of these three landings was 24,000.

Up to a certain point the story of these three landings is similar. Although their targets were miles apart, the military objective was the same: to establish a beachhead as a base from which to begin the march on Palermo and Messina. It had to be deep enough so that boats, ships and beaches would be outside enemy artillery range.

On the evening of 9 July the Western Naval Task Force, still undetected, was fast approaching the Sicilian shore. Beacon submarines, to help the vessels find their targets with infra-red blinkers, were stationed about five miles off each set of beaches. In addition, Joss Force had destroyer *Bristol* five miles south of the submarines, and a PC south of her; three lampposts to help the new beaching craft find their way.

There is nothing in warfare to be compared with the hushed tension of the final approach in a night landing. Everything ahead is uncertain. There is no sound but the rush of waters, the throbbing of your ship's engines and of your own heart. You can see nothing but the ship ahead and the ship astern. The shore, if dimly visible, is shrouded in darkness. A few mistakes on our part, or clever thrusts by the enemy, may utterly wreck a vast, long-planned effort. There can be no drawn battle, no half-success, in an amphibious landing; it is win all splendidly or lose all miserably.

The enemy was not entirely surprised, but unready. Many officers of Italian coastal divisions, in view of the foul weather, turned in; and German search-radar crews could not believe the enormous "blips" they saw on their screens. Small groups of beach defenders commonly deserted their pillboxes in panic when they saw the imposing and terrifying spectacle revealed by the first light of dawn. There had been nothing like it in Sicilian history since the Athenian expedition against Syracuse, "no less famous for its wonderful audacity, and for the splendor of its appearance, than for its overwhelming strength," as Thucydides wrote. As

Sicilians later described the scene to me, "There were thousands of vessels in the roadstead; one couldn't see the horizon for the ships." The Allies had ringed a good third of Sicily with a wall of ships, no power on earth could prevent them from establishing beachheads, and it would take more power than the Axis had to keep them from taking the island.

Conolly's Joss landings around Licata were noteworthy for the skill with which the LCIs and LCTs beached in rough surf to land troops and tanks, and for naval gunfire support. Every large troop unit carried a shore fire control party which communicated by "walkie-talkie" radio with a destroyer or cruiser of Rear Admiral Laurance DuBose's Support Group (cruisers *Brooklyn* and *Birminghan*, destroyers *Buck* and *Ludlow*) and frequently asked them to put a few shells on a spot where the enemy showed resistance. By noon General Truscott was setting up his command post in the city of Licata. Already 3000 Italian troops had been taken prisoner. The Joss Force landings were smooth and successful, securing the left flank of the Allied assault, and a port for follow-up.

Rear Admiral Hall's Dime Force, which landed around Gela, encountered the toughest opposition, and had the satisfaction of repelling two enemy tank assaults with naval gunfire. Here most of the troops came in big transports and were taken ashore in landing craft. The first boats hit the beach exactly at H-hour, 0245. Everything went smoothly until dawn brought enemy air attacks. At 0458, just as daylight began to spread over the sea, destroyer *Maddox*, on antisubmarine patrol several miles off shore, was attacked by a Stuka. A bomb exploded under her propeller guard, demolishing the stern and exploding the after magazine. Within two minutes *Maddox* rolled over and sank, taking down her C.O., Lieutenant Commander Sarsfield, and most of her crew.

Cruisers of the Dime Force Support Group, without waiting for fire-support parties to issue invitations, catapulted their float planes to look for targets. One of these cruisers was *Boise*, repaired better than new after her battering in the Battle of Cape Esperance, and with Captain L. Hewlett Thébaud as C.O.; the other was *Savannah*, Captain R. W. Cary. Since their float planes had no fighter protection, most of them were shot down by Messerschmitts; but one at 0830 reported two columns of about 25 Italian tanks each approaching the beachhead. *Boise*'s 6-inch fire stopped one column and destroyer *Shubrick* deprived the other of several units. *Boise* also silenced a shore battery that was enfilading the beach, and Admiral Ramsay kindly lent Admiral Hall H.M. monitor *Abercrombie*, to plant a few 15-inch shells on Niscemi, eight miles inland. Thus naval gunfire played the role of the Athenian archers against Sicilian cavalry in the famous invasion of 413 B.C.

One of the bottlenecks in amphibious operations has always been the congestion of supplies on the beaches. Army shore parties are supposed to carry the bales, boxes and other stuff to supply dumps; but they hate the job, and never do it fast enough. By nightfall D-day the Gela beaches were so congested that some landing craft had to return to their ships fully loaded; others, which had managed to find a spot to beach, swamped through their open ramps because nobody would help their exhausted crews to unload. The enemy had almost complete control of the air over the beachhead, while A.A.F. and R.A.F. flew "strategic." A renewal of tank counterattacks at daylight was certain, but how could they be met? *LST–313*, carrying all antitank guns of Dime Force, had been destroyed at sunset on D-day by a Messerschmitt. Other LSTs carrying tanks could not get into the beach over the bars. Thus the main burden of supporting the 1st Infantry Division in a really tough assault by a German tank column on 11 July fell on the Navy. Intermittently, over a period of ten hours, two cruisers and eight different destroyers fired on enemy tanks and infantry, advancing or retreating, destroyed half the tanks and demoralized

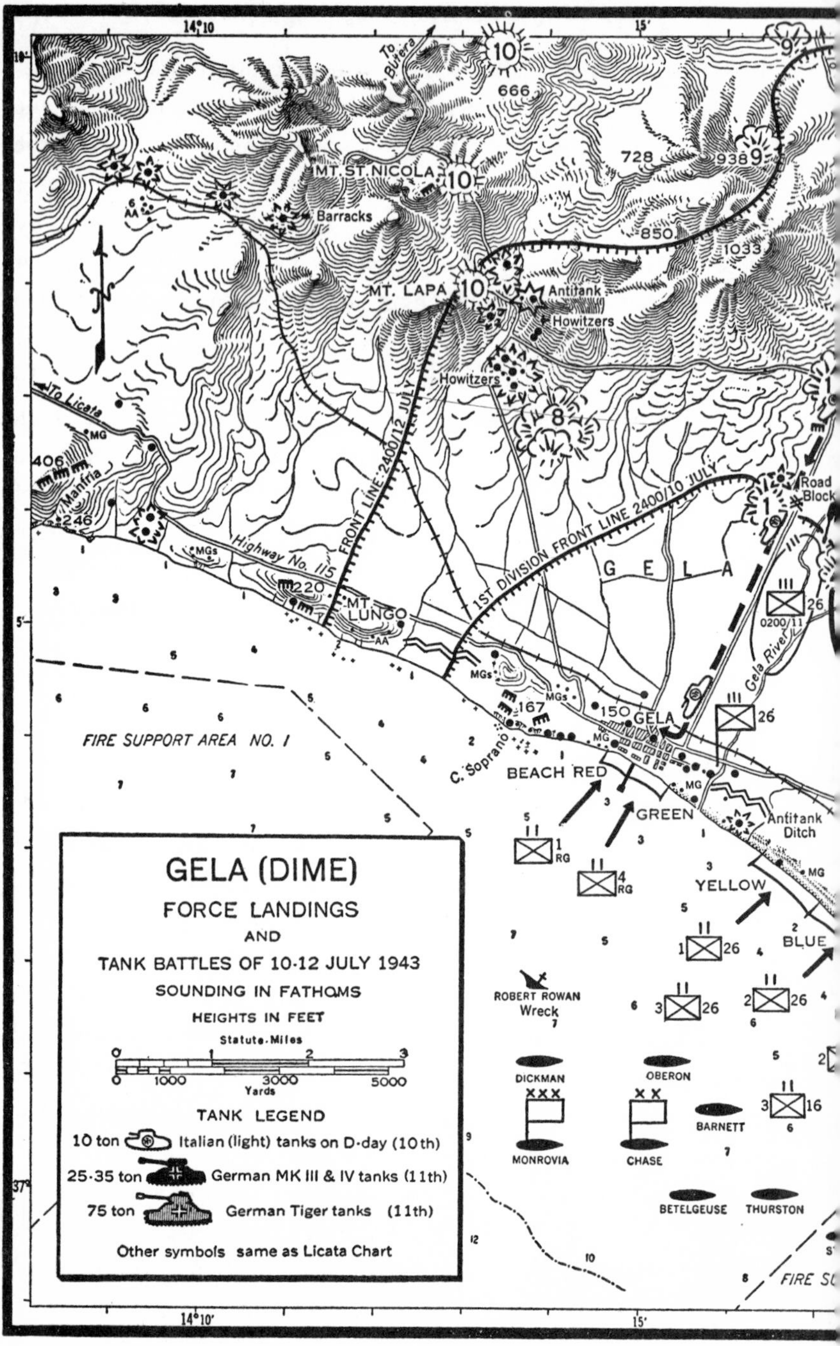

GELA (DIME)
FORCE LANDINGS
AND
TANK BATTLES OF 10-12 JULY 1943
SOUNDING IN FATHOMS
HEIGHTS IN FEET
Statute Miles
Yards
TANK LEGEND
10 ton Italian (light) tanks on D-day (10th)
25-35 ton German MK III & IV tanks (11th)
75 ton German Tiger tanks (11th)
Other symbols same as Licata Chart
To Butera
MT. ST. NICOLA
Barracks
MT. LAPA
Antitank
Howitzers
Howitzers
To Licata
MG
Manfria
Highway No. 115
FRONT LINE 2400/12 JULY
1ST DIVISION FRONT LINE 2400/10 JULY
GELA
MT. LUNGO
AA
MGs
Road Block
Gela River
0200/11
C. Soprano
GELA
BEACH RED
GREEN
YELLOW
BLUE
Antitank Ditch
FIRE SUPPORT AREA NO. 1
ROBERT ROWAN Wreck
DICKMAN
OBERON
MONROVIA
CHASE
BARNETT
BETELGEUSE
THURSTON

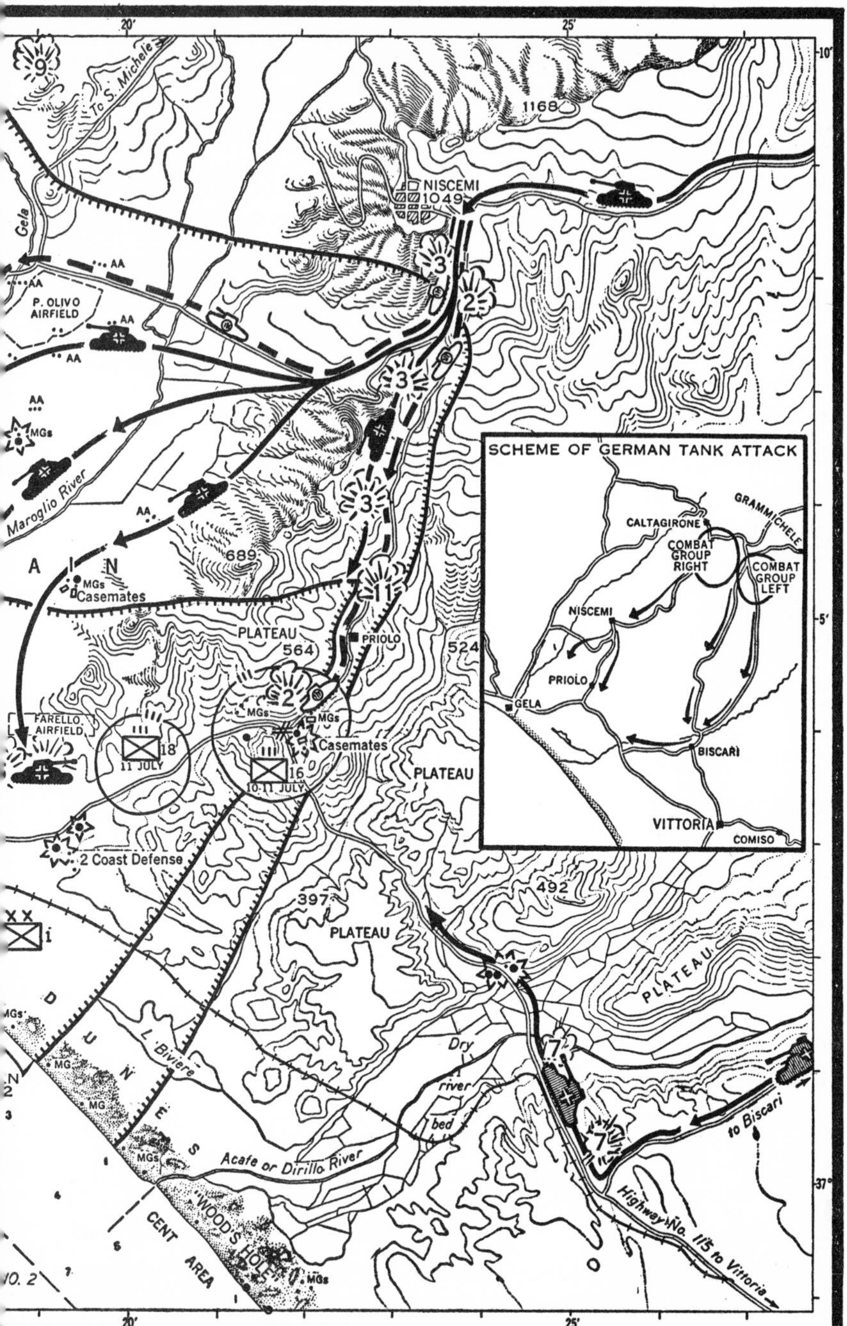

SCHEME OF GERMAN TANK ATTACK
CALTAGIRONE
GRAMMICHELE
COMBAT GROUP RIGHT
COMBAT GROUP LEFT
NISCEMI
PRIOLO
GELA
BISCARI
VITTORIA
COMISO
NISCEMI 1049
1168
To S. Michele
Gela
P. OLIVO AIRFIELD
AA
MGs
Maroglio River
689
Casemates
PLATEAU
564
PRIOLO
524
FARELLO AIRFIELD
18
11 JULY
16
10-11 JULY
Casemates
PLATEAU
2 Coast Defense
397
PLATEAU
492
PLATEAU
Dry river bed
L. Biviere
Acate or Dirillo River
"WOOD'S HOLE"
CENT AREA
to Biscari
Highway No. 115 to Vittoria
DUNES

the foot soldiers. Next day naval gunfire supported our own advancing troops, up to eight miles inland. "So devastating in its effectiveness," wrote General Eisenhower, was this shooting, "as to dispose finally of any doubts that naval guns are suitable for shore bombardment."

On the other hand, the paratroops won naval converts owing to the magnificent job done by Colonel James M. Gavin's RCT of the 82nd Airborne Division. This was the first troop airdrop ever attempted at night, so it is not surprising that the 3400 paratroops were dispersed along 60 miles of coast. But a part of one battalion which dropped behind Gela held up a German tank column on D-day, harassed the retreating tanks on the 11th, and greatly contributed to the confusion between the Italian and the German defenders. We shall later see Airborne playing a vital role in the Normandy operation.

In Admiral Kirk's Cent Force area, centered on the fishing village of Scoglitti, high surf and outlying rocks were very troublesome to landing craft. Here is a sample incident. A boat from transport *Thomas Jefferson*, commanded by Ensign G. P. Limberis USNR, seeking a small beach in pitchy darkness, hit instead a rocky point. The troops, understandably, flinched from debarking in heavy surf on a rockbound coast; but "after much persuasion," reported the ensign, "every man in my boat was on the beach, and crew and myself salvaged the two .30-caliber machine guns and a few rounds of ammunition." Four Italians who manned a nearby machine gun were so astounded at this exploit that they promptly surrendered. Presently Limberis and his men heard shouts and screams in the water. Two boats in the second wave, following the same erroneous course, had collided and swamped when their coxswains sighted the rocks and tried to sheer off. The first-comers scrambled down the steep and slippery rocks and managed to pull four GIs out of the water, but some 38 others were drowned. The third boat wave, at 0415, barely escaped crashing and put its troops ashore safely on the rocky point, but lost five boats out of seven. The combination of heavy surf, want of definite landmarks, and inexperienced boat crews made landing craft casualties in Cent area almost as great as in the Moroccan landings of Operation TORCH.

The saddest event in the American sector was the shooting down of transport aircraft towing gliders carrying American paratroops. General Ridgway decided on the morning of 11 July to lay a big airdrop on Farello, which, as he did not know, was already occupied by American troops. His opposite number ordered a similar one in the British sector. There was not enough time to inform ships and army units ashore what was coming. The route for the transport planes and gliders lay right along the battle front, and over the ships, whose antiaircraft gunners were trigger-happy after two days of frequent air attack. Between 2150 and 2300 the Germans sent in a heavy air raid — 24th of that busy day — wherein the Axis committed 381 planes against ships off the assault beaches. Right on top of that came our own transport planes. Recognition signals were of no avail in the tracer-filled night sky; antiaircraft gunners ashore and on shipboard fired at friend and foe alike. Twenty-three of the 144 planes which took off from Tunisia failed to return and 37 were badly damaged; almost one hundred officers and men were killed or missing. A special board was convened by General Eisenhower to study this airdrop, and a similarly shot-up one over the British sector. It concluded that these tragic fiascos were caused by not allowing sufficient time to notify friendly ground and naval forces, flying over them during an enemy bombing attack, and at such low altitudes as to make I.F.F. inoperative.[8] These errors were not repeated.

In justice to the Air Forces, we must remember that their

[8] I.F.F. ("Identification Friend or Foe") was a radio device by which friendly planes flashed a coded signal so that they would not be mistaken for enemy.

main efforts against enemy airfields and lines of communication were so successful that air attacks on the amphibious forces were kept to a minimum, and none were delivered in the American sector after 13 July. The British sector, lying nearer mainland airdromes, continued to catch it nightly under the waxing moon, and as soon as the United States naval forces came around to Palermo, the Luftwaffe found them again.

9. *Sicily Secured, July–August 1943*

For reasons of space, I shall have to pass rapidly over the British landings of Vice Admiral Sir Bertram Ramsay's Eastern Task Force, between Formiche, on the west side of Cape Passero, and Cassibile, not far south of Syracuse. The Royal Navy's part was conducted with the same verve and efficiency as that of the United States Navy. The British had the easier meteorological conditions for landing, as their beaches were sheltered from the wind on D-day, but they suffered more from enemy air attack. The American troops met stouter initial opposition, but after 15 July it was the other way round. Although the British and Americans landed on different sections of the coast, a close coördination was maintained between upper levels of command, and the two navies got along so well that a more intimate intermingling could be attempted in the next operation.

Before that could start, Sicily had to be conquered.

On the night of 12-13 July, after the beachheads were secure and enemy dispositions had been felt out, General Alexander's staff drew up a plan and issued directives. Montgomery was to thrust one army corps due north to Catania, while a second corps took the road to Enna and continued to the north coast at San Stéfano, "to split the island in half." Patton's Seventh Army would pivot on its left and overrun the central and western parts of the island. In other words, "Monty" was to wield the sword and "George" hold the shield. This unfortunate reversal of the rôles proper and congenial to their respective characters was the result of Alexander's belief that American troops were not much good.

Marshal Kesselring flew to General Guzzoni's headquarters at Enna on 12 July to find out what was going on. What he saw and heard deflated his optimism. The Allied landings everywhere had been successful. In two days' time, 80,000 men and 8200 vehicles, tanks and guns had been landed. The German tank attack had failed ignominiously. Syracuse and Augusta had fallen to the British. Several airfields were already in Allied possession. Kesselring realized that there was nothing left but to fight a delaying action. He flew back to Rome and informed Mussolini that, owing to the failure of his troops to stop the landings, it would be impossible to defend Sicily. Il Duce beat his breast and bellowed, "It must not be!" but it was; and two weeks later the King of Italy straightened his short back and fired Mussolini. His successor, Marshal Badoglio, issued a brash statement about prosecuting the war "with renewed vigor," but nobody believed that; and he told the little king that the war was absolutely and completely lost.

Seventh Army overran the western half of the island in record time. General Patton made a triumphal entry to Palermo on 22 July, riding between cheering throngs, and appropriately set up Seventh Army headquarters in the palace of *Il Re Ruggiero*, the twelfth-century Norman king. Only a few hours later, the United States Navy arrived at Palermo, in the shape of Motor Torpedo Boat Squadron 15, Lieutenant Commander Stanley M. Barnes. Next came Captain Charles Wellborn's Destroyer Squadron 8 (*Wainwright*, flag), and several minesweepers. On 27 July, when Palermo Harbor was first opened to Allied shipping, Admiral Hewitt organized these and the few other United States warships left in Sicilian waters into "General Patton's Navy" to support Seventh Army. As such, it had plenty to do: defending Palermo from an Italian Navy raid, giving gunfire support to Patton as he advanced along the coast, providing amphibious craft for "leap-frog" landings, and ferry duty for heavy artillery, supplies and vehicles to relieve congestion on the coastal road.

Rear Admiral Davidson commanded the support force. This tall, lanky flag officer, firm in decision and quiet of speech, never lost his temper. He inspired confidence. His flagship *Philadelphia*, with cruiser *Savannah* and six destroyers, steamed into Palermo during the forenoon watch 30 July. There was no chance of their collecting barnacles on their bottoms. General Patton asked for gunfire support next day and was obliged with a vigorous bombardment of shore batteries near San Stéfano. From Palermo, Patton pushed east along the coastal road to Messina, using the Navy to make short hops from place to place along the shore; but the Germans always kept one jump ahead of him.

In the British sector, Montgomery was held up for a week by stout German defense of the plain south of Catania. In contrast to Patton, "Monty" (as Admiral Cunningham has written) made no use of amphibious opportunities, and very little of naval gunfire support. Consequently General Patton, approaching Messina by two legs of the triangle, reached it first, on 17 August. But that was slight satisfaction, as Montgomery's slow and cautious advance along the coast gave the Axis sufficient time to evacuate three good German divisions with all their weapons and most of their armor across the Strait of Messina. The Italian Army, too, got out.

In the land campaign by Seventh Army it has been well said that the ordinary, run-of-the-mine GI now proved himself to be a first-class fighting man. The dash to Palermo, the battle of Troina, and other actions in Sicily deserve to be among the proudest in American military annals. One only regrets that, owing to General Alexander's bad judgment, General Patton was not allowed to wield the sword instead of the slow-moving, methodical Montgomery.

Leadership in the Western Naval Task Force was superb. Admirals Hewitt, Kirk, Hall and Conolly, to mention only the force commanders, showed intelligence in planning and skill in execution that marked them for honors and promotion. Yet the heroes of the western landings were the crews of the landing and beaching craft, mostly very young reservists, many of whom had never even smelled salt water before 1943. These were the last link in a chain that started in American shipyards and factories, which included military bases painstakingly developed in North Africa, warships and transports and three reinforced Army divisions, with their supplies, vehicles, armor and equipment. All these troops and the bulk of their matériel depended, to get ashore safely, on beaching or small landing craft. Boats under reserve ensigns or enlisted coxswains had to negotiate five miles or more of strange waters, often with nothing but a wobbly compass to guide them through the night, to locate targets in the dark, beach their craft, and provide their own support against enemy gunfire while discharging troops and equipment. Surprisingly few mistakes were made. The beaching craft, with slightly more experienced leadership, had even more complicated and difficult tasks. If these crews had failed, the entire American part of Operation HUSKY would have failed, and the British would have been left to carry the war into Sicily unsupported. All honor, then, to these lads of the last link, since they proved themselves to be brave, strong and resourceful. Although their names are not recorded on bronze tablets, let their deeds be kept in fresh memory by the nation and the cause that they served.

CHAPTER IX

Forward in the Pacific

March 1943–April 1944

1. *Alternate Plans for Defeating Japan*

WE LEFT the Pacific on 9 February 1943, with Guadalcanal secured. Three weeks earlier the Papuan campaign had been concluded. General Eichelberger, whom MacArthur had ordered "to take Buna or not come back alive," led his Australian and American troops through a stinking malarial jungle, and captured Gona (9 December), Buna (2 January), and Sanananda (18 January 1943). The naval aspect of this campaign was limited to bringing supplies from Australia via Milne Bay to an Allied base on the north coast of Papua, mostly by small armed Australian and Dutch merchant vessels, covered by American PTs. Rear Admiral Barbey's VII Amphibious Force was training in Australia, but as yet it had no LSTs or other beaching craft.

All this was part of Operation WATCHTOWER which started with Guadalcanal, and whose object was to breach the Bismarck barrier, the route to Japan favored by General MacArthur. He wished the entire weight of the Pacific Fleet to be placed under his command, to cover troop movements along this "New Guinea-Mindanao Axis" to the Philippines. Admirals King and Nimitz did not deny the value of that route, but wished to use an alternate one as well; to project a series of amphibious operations across the Central Pacific, via the Gilbert, Marshall, Caroline and Mariana Islands. Their chief argument against the MacArthur plan was very cogent.

As long as the Micronesian "spider webs" which Japan had spread over the Central Pacific were in her possession, enemy air forces could attack everything that moved along the New Guinea–Mindanao Axis. These webs must be swept up with the Pacific Fleet broom, and a second and shorter route opened to Tokyo.

A third plan which might have been incorporated with MacArthur's never came off. This was for a British comeback through the Indian Ocean and the Straits of Malacca to recover Burma and Singapore and control the South China Sea. Admiral King was eager to have this done by Admiral Lord Mountbatten, the British commander in Southeast Asia whom both he and General Marshall admired. Unfortunately it was postponed again and again, because whenever Lord Louis managed to build up landing craft and naval forces, they were taken away from him to feed the hungry maw of the Mediterranean.

The main thing, in early 1943, was to get on with Operation WATCHTOWER. But nothing substantial was done for five months. The Joint Chiefs of Staff could promise no reinforcement to the Pacific Fleet while U-boats remained a major threat, Tunisia was still being fought over, and the invasion of Sicily was coming up. But the principal reason for this delay was the same shipping shortage that bedeviled the Allies in Europe, and lack of aircraft carriers. When the *Essex*-class carriers began to come out, in answer to the prayers of Pacific sailors, we were ready to go.

2. *In Aleutian Waters, March–August 1943*

During this pause there were fleet and troop movements as far north as the Bering Sea. No operations in this region of almost perpetual mist and snow accomplished anything of importance or had any appreciable effect on the outcome of the war. It was a theater of military frustration. Both sides would have done well to leave the Aleutians to the few Aleuts unfortunate enough to live there. But the Japanese, as part of the Midway offensive, had occupied Attu and Kiska, the two westernmost islands, as northern anchors to their "ribbon defense"; and as such, American strategists felt obliged to set them adrift.

For over nine months after Midway, events in this sector were a sequence of naval bombardment by us which did no damage, reinforcement missions by the enemy which accomplished nothing, and operations by United States submarines which usefully diminished the Japanese merchant marine. Finally, on 26 March 1943, a really interesting event broke: the Battle of the Komandorski Islands. A small task group under Rear Admiral Charles H. McMorris fought a retiring action against a Japanese force of twice its size and fire power; the battle lasted without a break for three and a half hours of daylight; the contestants slugged it out with gunfire at ranges of eight to over twelve miles, without intrusion by air power or submarines. It was a miniature version of the sort of fleet action that the Navy, after World War I, expected to fight in the next war, with the important difference that neither side did the other any great damage.

Admiral McMorris's task group had been cruising on a north-south line west of Attu for several days in order to intercept Japanese reinforcement of that island. He flew his flag in twenty-year-old light cruiser *Richmond* (Captain T. W. Waldschmidt); with him were heavy cruiser *Salt Lake City* (Captain Bertram J. Rodgers), repaired and freshly overhauled since the Cape Esperance battle, and four destroyers under Captain Ralph S. Riggs.[1]

At 0800 March 26, a clear calm day with temperature just above freezing, this task group ran slap into Vice Admiral Hosogaya's Northern Area Force of two heavy cruisers (*Nachi*, flag), two light cruisers and four destroyers, about halfway between Attu

[1] *Bailey*, Lt. Cdr. J. C. Atkeson; *Coghlan*, Cdr. R. E. Tompkins; *Dale*, Cdr. A. L. Rorschach; *Monaghan*, Lt. Cdr. P. H. Horn.

and Kamchatka. The ensuing action, fought south of the Komandorski Islands, resembled the Battle of the Java Sea a year earlier. Hosogaya here, like Takagi there, was escorting and covering a reinforcement group of transports and freighters; and McMorris here, like Doorman there, first tried to get at the transports, but soon had to fight for his life. The outcome was very different.

At 0840, before the American ships had had time to change from scouting line to battle order, the enemy opened fire on *Richmond* at 20,000 yards, made a close straddle on the second salvo, then shifted gunfire to *Salt Lake City*. Throughout the action this heavy cruiser received almost all the enemy's attention. She commenced return fire with her forward turrets at 0842, and at a range of over ten miles made hits on *Nachi* with her third and fourth salvos, starting fires that were quickly brought under control.

Nachi now launched a salvo of eight torpedoes which failed to score because of the extreme range; and the same thing happened to all other Japanese torpedoes launched in this fight. *Salt Lake* was now doing some fancy shooting at long range, and all that time nimbly darting and pirouetting like a ballet dancer to throw off the enemy aim. Captain Rodgers "chased salvos" [2] with notable success. Flagship *Richmond* and the destroyers conformed their movements to hers; old "Swayback Maru," as the sailors called *Salt Lake City*, was Queen of the North Pacific that day.

The second Japanese heavy cruiser, *Maya*, at 0910 made her first hit on *Salt Lake*. It failed to stop or even slow her down. Ten minutes later, she and *Nachi* were swapping punches at a range of almost twelve miles. McMorris now turned his force north, hoping to make an end run around the Japanese warships and get at the transports; but Hosogaya was too fast for him. At 1002 *Salt Lake* briefly had steering trouble, and a few minutes later she took another hit. There was a big laugh on *Richmond*'s

[2] This means, changing your course quickly to cover the spot where the enemy's last salvo exploded in the water, so that when he corrects his aim he will miss again.

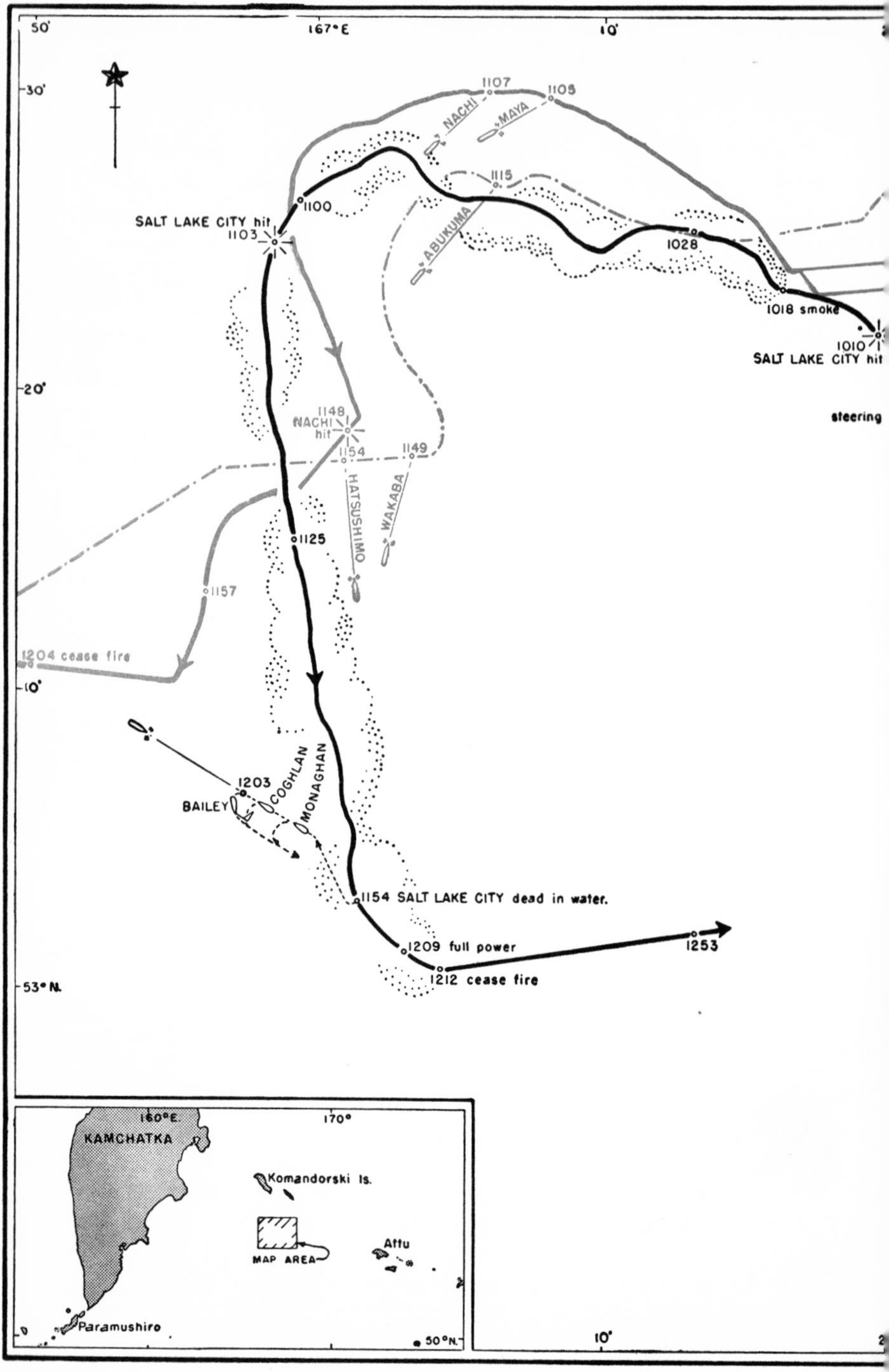

50'
167° E
10'
30'
20'
10'
53° N.
1107
1105
NACHI
MAYA
1115
ABUKUMA
1100
SALT LAKE CITY hit
1103
1028
1018 smoke
1010
SALT LAKE CITY hit
steering
1148
NACHI
hit
1154
1149
HATSUSHIMO
WAKABA
1125
1157
1204 cease fire
1203
BAILEY
COGHLAN
MONAGHAN
1154 SALT LAKE CITY dead in water.
1209 full power
1253
1212 cease fire
160° E.
170°
KAMCHATKA
Komandorski Is.
MAP AREA
Attu
Paramushiro
50° N.
10'

ASAKA MARU
SAKITO MARU

NACHI

MAYA

TAMA

WAKABA

HATSUSHIMO

ABUKUMA

IKAZUCHI

ASAKA MARU

SAKITO MARU

INAZUMA

ABUKUMA 1007

1022

0957

0840 open fire
0846
0850 NACHI hit
NACHI

MAYA 0907
0845
0842 SALT LAKE CITY opens fire.

SALT LAKE CITY hit 0910

0926
0920
SALT LAKE CITY hit.

BAILEY
COGHLAN
RICHMOND
SALT LAKE CITY
DALE
MONAGHAN

COGHLAN

0752 RICHMOND

BAILEY

DALE

0800

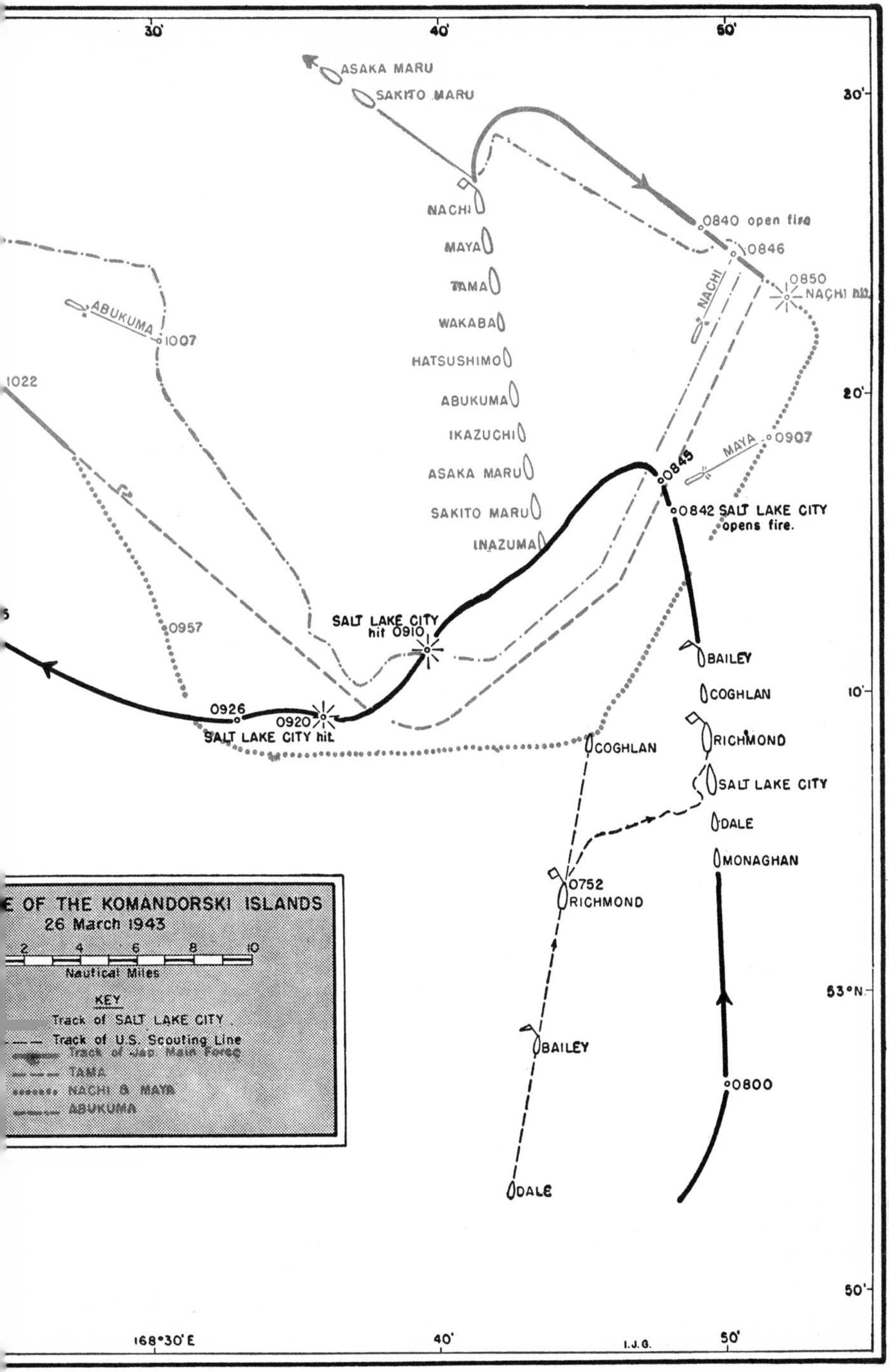

E OF THE KOMANDORSKI ISLANDS
26 March 1943

2 4 6 8 10
Nautical Miles

KEY
———— Track of SALT LAKE CITY
– – – Track of U.S. Scouting Line
━━━━ Track of Jap. Main Force
— — TAMA
•••••• NACHI & MAYA
-·-·- ABUKUMA

53°N

50'

30' 40' 50' 30'

20'

10'

168°30'E 40' I.J.G. 50'

bridge when the O.T.C. received a message from Admiral Kinkaid, at Adak, promising to get Army bombers out to help him "within five hours," and "suggesting that a retiring action be considered."

Retirement, indeed, was now the only thing to do. McMorris first steered west under good smoke cover which the Japanese rangefinders, having no radar, were unable to penetrate. But this course carried the Americans nearer and nearer to the Japanese base at Paramushiro. So at 1100 McMorris turned his force south to disengage. No sooner done than *Salt Lake* suffered a serious 8-inch hit which flooded the after engine room. She continued firing, at declining speed, for twenty miles and almost one hour longer; then she went dead in the water. McMorris reacted by closing in *Richmond* to make smoke and help defend Old Swayback, and (in a magnificent but desperate gesture), ordering three of his four destroyers to deliver a torpedo attack on the fast-approaching enemy. Everyone who could help damage control on board *Salt Lake* did, and everyone else prayed. Before the destroyers had been gone five minutes, what looked like a miracle occurred. Admiral Hosogaya broke off action and turned his entire force west, hotly pursued by *Bailey*, *Coghlan* and *Monaghan.*

Hosogaya really funked out. He was anxious to get home; smoke concealed from him *Salt Lake*'s desperate plight, and he feared that American air bombers from Dutch Harbor would arrive shortly. Destroyer *Bailey* gave *Nachi*'s superstructure a good dusting with close-in 5-inch fire to firm up his decision to depart. It is no wonder that this Japanese admiral was shortly put on the beach.

Salt Lake recovered propulsion as eight bells struck, then shaped a course for Dutch Harbor, and a repair base. *Nachi,* too, needed several jobs done on her; and as the Japanese transports also returned to Paramushiro, there was no doubt as to who won this battle. During the action *Salt Lake* fired 832 rounds, *Nachi* 707 and *Maya* 904 rounds of 8-inch shell. *Bailey*, the only American destroyer to get close enough to the retiring enemy to use torpedoes, fired five, which missed; the Japanese ships fired 43, and all missed. So this battle deserves a place in the history of naval warfare as the last heavy gunfire daylight action, with no interference by air power, submarines or torpedoes. The demonstration of superior gunnery was tremendously heartening to the United States Navy.

Before leaving Alaska's dreary shores for warmer climes, we must briefly mention the recovery of Attu. Amphibious Force North Pacific was set up to accomplish this, under Rear Admiral Francis W. Rockwell; the 7th Infantry Division United States Army had the unhappy ground assignment. Battleships *Pennsylvania* and *Nevada* emerged from naval shipyards in time to act as support group with *Idaho*, and "Soc" McMorris was back again, in light cruiser *Raleigh*, commanding a covering group. The landings, on 11 May 1943, were successful, but the Japanese garrison fought desperately, culminating in a thousand-man screaming suicide charge on 29 May. A big operation to take Kiska was laid on for late July, but the Japanese fooled us by evacuating their 5000-man garrison under fog cover, leaving only three yellow dogs to contest the American landing.

It was bad strategy to throw such heavy forces into capturing a few square miles of muskeg, at a time when troops and ships were desperately needed in the South and Southwest Pacific. Ironically, one of the main reasons for these efforts in the Aleutians was the desire of the Joint Chiefs of Staff to expedite aid to Russia, in the expected event of her going to war with Japan.

During the rest of the war the Aleutians offer little of interest. Harassing air raids on Paramushiro were varied by occasional shore bombardments and feeble Japanese retaliatory raids on Attu, Kiska and Adak. But there was a constant improvement both of bases and of flying efficiency in these difficult northern areas; and that was all to the good. For it may well be that in the future the

Bering, not the Caribbean, will be America's "Sea of Destiny." In any case, it was wonderful practice ground for armed forces; after a tour of duty in the Aleutians, every other field of action seemed good.

3. *Minor Operations in the South and Southwest Pacific, February–May 1943*

About 9000 infantrymen and Marines, lifted from New Caledonia, landed unopposed on the Russell Islands, 30 miles west of Cape Esperance, on 21 February 1943. This overstuffed affair might well have been omitted.

After the Japanese were thrown out of Buna and Gona, they began to strengthen their garrisons at Lae and Salamaua on Huon Gulf, General MacArthur's next objective. On 1 March 1943 a strong reinforcement convoy for Lae, about 7000 troops in eight transports and as many destroyers, departed Rabaul. By this time Major General George C. Kenney, air commander under MacArthur, had beefed-up his own and the Royal Australian Air Force in Papua to 207 bombers and 129 fighters. He had equipped one squadron of B–25s with 500-pound bombs having a five-second delay fuse that permitted a plane to come in on a ship almost at sea level, like a torpedo-bomber, drop its bomb and escape. The Lae-bound convoy was kept under observation and at 1000 March 3 the land-based Allied planes flew in to bomb it from over Papua. The ensuing battle was the most devastating air attack on ships of the entire war, excepting only that on Pearl Harbor. Out of 37 bombs dropped by the first wave of planes, 28 scored; and by noon, over 200 bombs had fallen upon and around the writhing ships. High above sea level, Army Air Force fighters tangled with the Japanese C.A.P.; others flew to Lae to prevent air reinforcement reaching the enemy. All afternoon the slaughter continued. Seven out of eight transports and two of the eight destroyers were sunk; four undamaged destroyers picked up survivors and fled; the sea was spotted with life rafts, rubber boats and swimmers. At daybreak 4 March the Army Air Force returned and sank two damaged destroyers.

Now the motor torpedo boats took a hand. *PT–143* and *PT–150,* after sinking the one transport still afloat, encountered a Japanese submarine taking on survivors from three big landing craft. The I-boat dived, the PTs sank the craft and machine-gunned the survivors. This may sound horrible, but it had to be done, as Japanese soldiers and sailors were trained to resist capture, or, if captured willy-nilly, to seek revenge on their saviors. There were innumerable incidents such as a wounded Japanese soldier at Guadalcanal seizing a scalpel and burying it in the back of a surgeon who was about to save his life by an operation; and a survivor of the Battle of Vella Lavella, rescued by *PT–163,* pulling a gun and killing a bluejacket in the act of giving the Japanese sailor a cup of coffee.

The total score of this Battle of the Bismarck Sea was eight Japanese transports and four destroyers sunk, and three to four thousand men killed — at a cost of two bombers and three fighters out of over 300 aircraft engaged. Unfortunately this smashing victory could never be repeated, because the Japanese never again risked a transport bigger than a barge in waters shadowed by American planes.

During this long lull in major operations, Japan was improving her defensive positions at Huon Gulf and westward in New Guinea, and in the central and upper Solomons. Munda airfield, on New Georgia, was greatly extended; a supporting field was established at Vila on Kolombangara; seaplane bases were set up at Shortlands and Santa Isabel; new airfields were built on Ballale near Shortlands and Kahiki on southern Bougainville. South Pacific cruiser task groups under Rear Admirals A. Stanton Merrill and

Walden L. Ainsworth raided these places frequently ("Tip" Merrill sank two enemy destroyers incidental to bombarding Vila on the night of 5-6 March); Airsols bombed them even more often, but the Japanese kept right on working. And Fleet Admiral Yamamoto was preparing a big campaign, which proved to be his last.

This "I" Operation, as he called it, was meant to be a crushing, annihilating air offensive, from Rabaul, against American ships and bases in Papua and the Solomons. To double the already strong air fleet at Rabaul, Admiral Ozawa contributed some 170 naval planes from four carriers. No fewer than 187 planes pulled off the first strike of "I" Operation, against Tulagi, on 7 April. There was a wild scene in Tulagi Harbor when the bombers roared in. They sank a tanker, a New Zealand corvette and destroyer *Aaron Ward*, losing only 21 of their own planes. On 11-12 April Yamamoto threw the "I" switch to Papua, burned two merchant vessels at Oro Bay, and sent 174 aircraft over the Owen Stanley Range to attack Port Moresby. MacArthur's antiaircraft guns prevented them from doing much damage. Small result for all this effort; but Yamamoto never learned the truth.

By decrypting Japanese communications, Halsey obtained the complete timetable of a forthcoming inspection tour by the Japanese C. in C., and both Nimitz and King encouraged him to profit thereby. Sixteen United States Army Lightnings flew up from Henderson Field to intercept Yamamoto's air cortege, and neatly shot down the two bombers carrying the Fleet Admiral and staff, killing him and five or six others. All Japanese writers admit that this was equivalent to a major defeat, since there was "only one Yamamoto."

4. *The Central Solomons Campaign, June–July 1943*

Everyone in the now crowded American bases at Nouméa, Espiritu Santo, Guadalcanal, Tulagi and Purvis Bay was asking, "When do we go?" Halsey was ready to start the South Pacific ball rolling in mid-April, but General MacArthur was not. He knew very well that military power is like a three-legged stool; if it lacks one of the three legs, land power, air power and sea power, it will be toppled. In 1942, MacArthur was sitting on one leg — land power. A second leg, air power, proved its strength in the Battle of the Bismarck Sea, and on 15 March a third leg, Seventh Fleet under Vice Admiral Arthur S. Carpender, was set up. But, being "at the end of the line," this was the last fleet to get beaching and landing craft and other instruments to enable Rear Admiral Daniel E. Barbey and his new VII Amphibious Force to go places. Everything in the South Pacific was held up until General MacArthur's third "leg," the amphibious force, was ready.

A Joint Chief of Staff directive of 29 March set Southwest Pacific two tasks: (1) to establish airfields on the Trobriand Islands; (2) to seize Japanese positions on Huon Gulf and along Vitiaz Strait, and Cape Gloucester on New Britain, in order to breach the Bismarck barrier at vital points. MacArthur chose the last day of June to start. It was a walkover, since Kiriwina and Woodlark (the two Trobriands) were occupied only by natives. But this was the first time in the Southwest Pacific that air, land and sea power had operated as a balanced team, and Barbey's plan for the Trobriands became the template for all later shore-to-shore leaps along the New Guinea coast. Before the war ended, VII 'Phib would have over fifty amphibious landings to its credit, and its commander would be known as "Uncle Dan the Amphibious Man."

Nassau Bay was occupied the same day, 30 June, by a shore-to-shore operation. General Eichelberger's troops were lifted 40 miles from Morobe in motor torpedo boats and in landing craft manned by the 2nd Engineer Special Brigade, all riding the crest of a southeast gale.

There was jubilation in the South Pacific when the word "Go!" was finally pronounced in the picturesque Melanesian pidgin: "Musket-he-fire-up." Munda on New Georgia, the annoying air base whence the Japanese raided Guadalcanal and Tulagi for months after they had been secured, was the objective. The amphibious forces, under Rear Admiral R. Kelly Turner in *McCawley*, comprised 10 large transports, 12 destroyer transports, 9 LST and 11 LCI, screened by 8 destroyers and supported by battleships, cruisers and escort carriers under Rear Admirals Ainsworth, Merrill and Glenn B. Davis. The major landing took place on Rendova Island across Blanche Channel from Munda. Troops had to be ferried thence to the New Georgia shore, and then fight Japanese step by step through the jungle to get at the coveted airdrome.

The naval part of this campaign for Munda was sparked off by hot clashes up the Slot between Japanese "Tokyo Expresses" to Vila (whence troops were transferred to Munda), and Rear Admiral Walden L. Ainsworth's light cruiser task force. On the night of 4-5 July it bombarded Vila and Bairoko, but lost destroyer *Strong* (Commander J. H. Wellings) to a mine. The following night, ordered back up the Slot by Halsey, Ainsworth fought the Battle of Kula Gulf, against a ten-destroyer force under Rear Admiral Akiyama. American gunfire sank one destroyer and drove another ashore, but cruiser *Helena* was sunk by three explosions of the Japanese "long lance" torpedoes.

On the night of 12-13 July Ainsworth performed his fifteenth combat mission up the Slot, and enjoyed another fight, the Battle of Kolombangara, in almost the same water as that of Kula Gulf. He had light cruisers *Honolulu* (Captain Robert W. Hayler) and *St. Louis* (Captain Colin Campbell), with H.M.N.Z.S. *Leander*

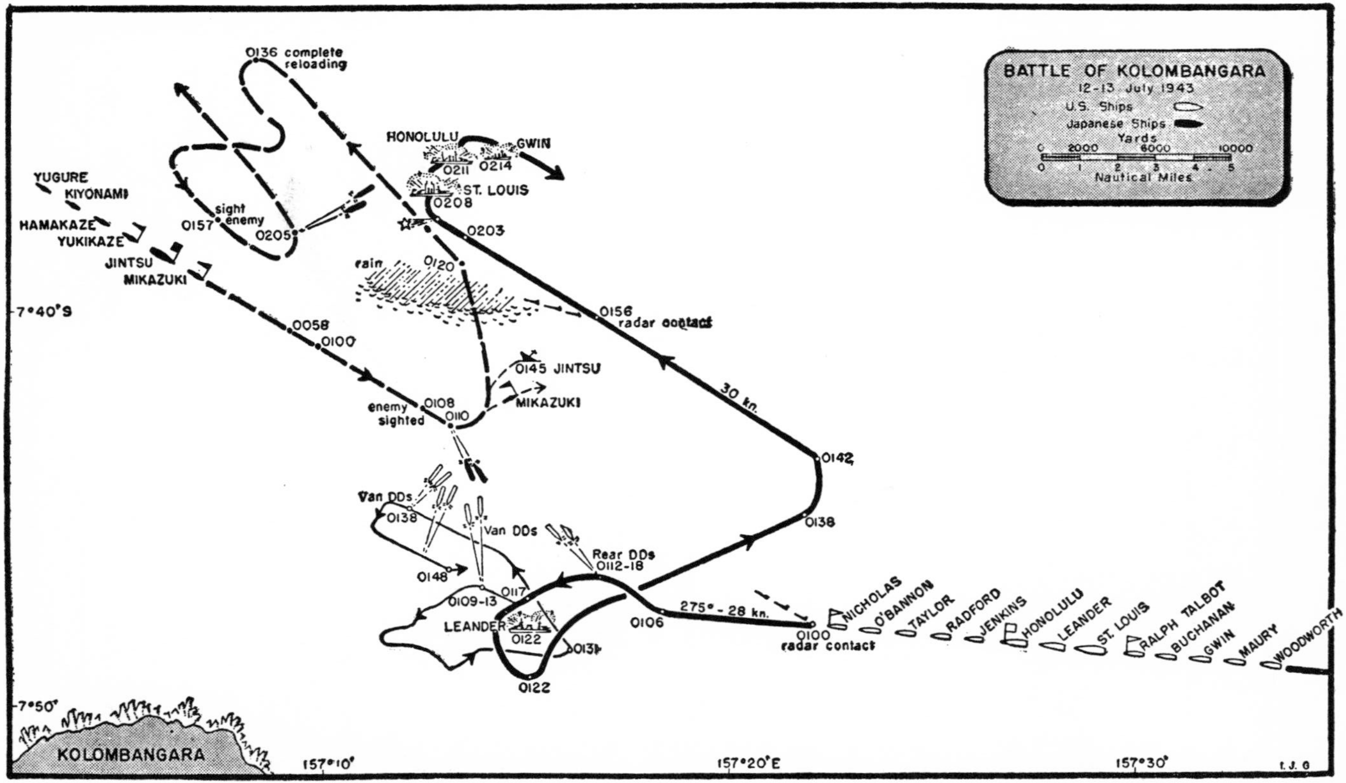
BATTLE OF KOLOMBANGARA
12-13 July 1943
U.S. Ships
Japanese Ships
Yards
0 2000 6000 10000
0 1 2 3 4 5
Nautical Miles
0136 complete reloading
HONOLULU
GWIN
0211
0214
ST. LOUIS
0208
0203
YUGURE
KIYONAMI
HAMAKAZE
YUKIKAZE
JINTSU
MIKAZUKI
sight enemy
0157
0205
rain
0120
0156 radar contact
-7°40'S
0058
0100
0145 JINTSU
MIKAZUKI
enemy sighted
0108
0110
30 kn.
0142
0138
Van DDs
0138
Van DDs
Rear DDs
0112-18
0148
0117
0109-13
LEANDER
0122
0131
0122
0106
275° - 28 kn.
0100 radar contact
NICHOLAS
O'BANNON
TAYLOR
RADFORD
JENKINS
HONOLULU
LEANDER
ST. LOUIS
RALPH TALBOT
BUCHANAN
GWIN
MAURY
WOODWORTH
-7°50'
KOLOMBANGARA
157°10'
157°20'E
157°30'
t. J. G

(Captain C. A. L. Mansergh RN) sister ship to the famous H.M.S. *Achilles* (to replace lost *Helena*), and two destroyer squadrons of five ships each. This time he tangled with Rear Admiral Izaki's support group, comprising Tanaka's old flagship *Jintsu*, five destroyers and four destroyer-transports. Although we had radar and the enemy none, he had a radar-detecting device which enabled him to track Ainsworth's progress up the Slot for an hour before American radar bounced off a Japanese ship. Izaki launched torpedoes at 0108 July 13, one minute before Captain McInerney's van destroyer squadron got off theirs. Ainsworth then waited until range closed to 10,000 yards before ordering his cruisers to commence firing. As usual in early days of radar fire control, the cruisers concentrated on the biggest blip, *Jintsu*, and so smothered her with 6-inch shell that she exploded and went down with all hands. A few minutes earlier a Japanese torpedo crashed into *Leander*, putting her out of the battle and almost out of the war.

While two destroyers stood by *Leander*, Ainsworth sent McInerney's destroyer squadron scampering up the Slot in the hope of catching the retiring Japanese destroyers, and followed with his remaining two cruisers and three destroyers. This bold bid for complete victory was thrown back in his face. The five Japanese destroyers, reloading torpedo tubes under cover of a rain squall in the remarkably fast time of eighteen minutes, countermarched and at 0156 appeared on the American cruisers' radar scopes. Ainsworth hesitated to open gunfire, fearing lest the blips represented McInerney's destroyers returning (I was in flag plot with him, seeing and feeling the agony of decision in such a case); and when at 0205 the Admiral ordered right turn to unmask his main batteries and commence firing, it was too late. The Japanese destroyers had already launched their 31-torpedo reload, and were speeding away. One "long lance" sank destroyer *Gwin*, one caught *Honolulu* and one exploded on *St. Louis*, each so far forward as to kill nobody and do but slight damage. A third, which hit the flagship square in her fantail without exploding, hung there a moment and then dropped out.

Although we who participated in these battles up the Slot felt pretty cocky at the time, thinking we had sunk at least twelve ships in the two actions, sober reassessment indicates that we were not so hot. The Japanese were still tops in torpedo work and night fighting. Incredible as it now seems, the speed, size and range of the Japanese "long lance" torpedo, invented ten years earlier and lavishly employed in every naval action of the war, was still unknown to the Pacific Fleet. One had been salvaged early in 1943 and analyzed by the Bureau of Ordnance, but these findings had not even reached Admiral Halsey. Had Ainsworth been apprised of its capacity, he would never have closed to 10,000 yards before opening gunfire, or maneuvered his cruisers in enemy torpedo water. As it was, he enjoyed good luck in bringing all three cruisers back to Tulagi on their own bottoms.

The Japanese continued to lose planes and ships which they could not replace, to save Munda and Vila; then they continued to lose more planes, ships and men, to get men out of Munda and Vila. Reinforcement and evacuation were very well done; but a string of such victories adds up to defeat.

The land campaign for Munda went very slowly. It was the worst kind of jungle fighting, too many of our troops were raw, and their top commander, until relieved by Major General Oscar W. Griswold, was unequal to the task. It took nearly 34,000 American troops six weeks to wrest this corner of New Georgia from about 8000 Japanese.

Subsequent to the two cruiser actions, the principal naval aid to the New Georgia campaign was contributed by PT boats. They successfully broke up reinforcements by Japanese *daihatsu* armed barges on the nights of 23-24 and 26-27 July. Another action, unsuccessful in a military sense, but important to a future President of the United States, took place on the night of 1-2 August 1943. Fifteen PTs, divided four ways, tried to block Blackett Strait south of Kolombangara to a Japanese destroyer express. They used torpedoes lavishly, but made not one hit on enemy ships going or coming. On the contrary, Commander Hanami of destroyer *Amagiri* had the distinction of running down and knifing in two *PT–109*, commanded by Lieutenant John F. Kennedy USNR. Eleven of the crew of 13 survived, and, with Kennedy swimming and towing a wounded sailor, and the rest on an improvised raft, they managed to reach a small island in five hours. Kennedy refused to give up; he spent most of the next night swimming in the Strait, hoping in vain to intercept a PT. In the morning he sent a message on a coconut shell via a friendly native to an Australian coastwatcher, who dispatched other natives to the rescue. Kennedy and his surviving shipmates were paddled to safety in a well-camouflaged canoe.

The capture of Munda on 5 August did not end the naval campaign up the Slot. For a full year, destroyer officers had been banging fists on wardroom tables and bellowing, "When are they going to cut us loose from the cruisers' apron strings?" In one battle after another the O.T.C. had kept destroyers in van and rear, instead of sending them to make independent torpedo attacks. And the performance of American torpedoes so far had been miserable. But "Just give us a chance!" was the destroyer sailors' reply to every criticism. Now, Rear Admiral Theodore S. Wilkinson, who had relieved Kelly Turner as Com III 'Phib, accepted this challenge from Commander Frederick Moosbrugger, who met it admirably.

The chance occurred because Wilkinson suspected on 5 August that the Japanese would run a Tokyo Express to Kolombangara the following night; and Wilkinson told Moosbrugger to fight the battle his own way. With six destroyers (*Dunlap*, *Craven*, *Maury*, *Lang*, *Sterett*, *Stack*, the last two under Commander Rodger Simp-

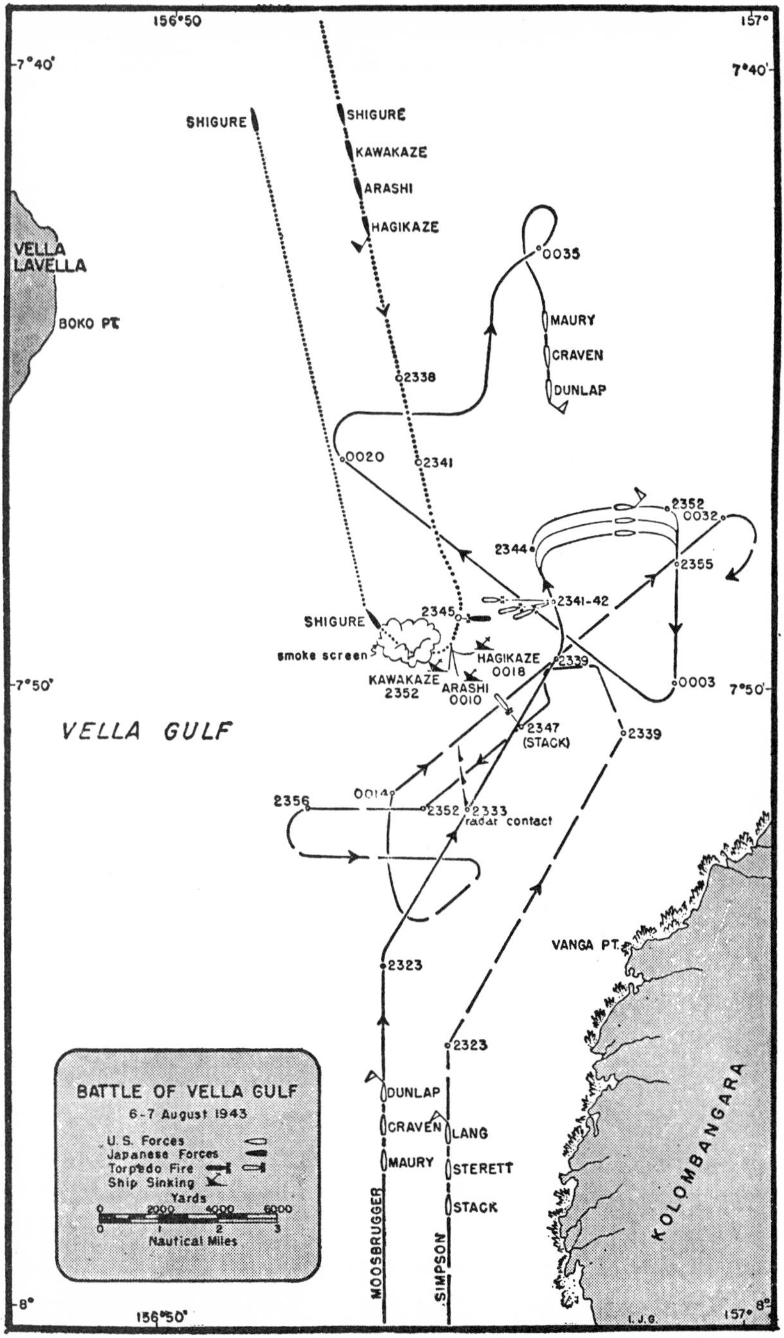

BATTLE OF VELLA GULF
6-7 August 1943
U. S. Forces
Japanese Forces
Torpedo Fire
Ship Sinking
Yards
2000 4000 6000
0 1 2 3
Nautical Miles
156°50
157°
7°40'
7°50'
8°
VELLA LAVELLA
BOKO PT.
VELLA GULF
VANGA PT.
KOLOMBANGARA
SHIGURE
KAWAKAZE
ARASHI
HAGIKAZE
MAURY
CRAVEN
DUNLAP
LANG
STERETT
STACK
MOOSBRUGGER
SIMPSON
smoke screen
KAWAKAZE 2352
ARASHI 0010
HAGIKAZE 0018
2347 (STACK)
2333 radar contact
0035
2338
2341
0020
2352
0032
2344
2355
2341-42
2345
2339
0003
2339
0014
2356
2352
2323
2323
I. J. G.

son) Moosbrugger gave battle in Vella Gulf, on the night of 6-7 August, to four Japanese destroyers under Captain Sugiura. He surprised them with a flock of torpedoes at a range of 4000 yards, and three of the enemy destroyers exploded with such a flash and roar that sailors on PT boats almost thirty miles away thought that the volcano on Kolombangara had blown its top. There was a brief exchange of gunfire after this initial hit, and lucky *Shigure*, the one that escaped, fired torpedoes; but no Japanese ship laid a finger on Moosbrugger. His Battle of Vella Gulf was one of the neatest victories of the war.

3. *Leapfrogging Begins, August–October 1943*

July of 1943 was a month of Allied victory in Sicily, on the Russian front, and in the Atlantic sea lanes. Japanese resistance at Munda, threatening to slow up the Pacific war, led to a notable acceleration in tactics. So far, MacArthur's strategy in New Guinea, like Halsey's in the Solomons, could not unfairly be described as "island hopping." If we had continued at that pace, it would have taken at least ten years to reach Japan, and the enemy's strategy of tiring us out by sheer stubbornness might have worked. But about this time, "leapfrogging" was substituted for "island hopping."

General Tojo, shortly before his death, told General MacArthur that leapfrogging was one of the three principal factors that defeated Japan; the other two being the depredations of United States submarines and the ability of fast carrier forces to operate for long periods away from their bases. There was nothing new about leapfrogging or bypassing enemy strong points or, as General MacArthur and Admiral Wilkinson called it in baseball phraseology, "Hitting 'em where they ain't." Wilkinson, a student of naval strategy, had long been eager to take advantage of Pacific topography, bypass the strongest Japanese garrisons, seal them off by air and sea, and leave them to "wither on the vine." So were General MacArthur's staff. Captain Harry R. Thurber of Halsey's staff advocated the bypassing of Munda early in 1943, but we had to take it instead, because there was then no place to leapfrog into.

The first demonstration of leapfrogging came about inadvertently, in the Aleutians. Admiral Nimitz skipped over Kiska to take the more important Attu, and the enemy then secretly evacuated Kiska. Nimitz on 11 July 1943 suggested to Halsey that Kolombangara be given the Kiska treatment — land troops on Vella Lavella to the northwest and skip the island with the long name. A plan was promptly drafted to place Vila airfield under the fire of American artillery, to sever the enemy's supply lines to Kolombangara, and seize lightly held Vella Lavella for a fighter-plane base.

The Vella Lavella landings, on 15 August at Barakoma Bay on the eastern foot of the island, were uncontested except from the air. During two weeks after the landings, Wilkinson's III 'Phib delivered 6305 men and 8626 tons cargo on the island, fought off Japanese planes in scores of air attacks, and turned back one enemy reinforcement echelon. Land operations continued slowly but systematically. On 18 September the American troops were relieved by the 3rd Division New Zealand Army, Major General Barrowclough. The New Zealanders pushed a pincer movement up both coasts, and by 1 October had cornered about 600 of the enemy on the northwest shore. There they stayed for another week, when the effort to evacuate them brought about the Naval Battle of Vella Lavella.

This battle occurred because the Japanese endeavored to evacuate the 600 waifs and strays left on that island. Rear Admiral Ijuin marshaled nine destroyers and a dozen small craft to rescue them, on the night of 6-7 October. Admiral Wilkinson sent Captain Frank R. Walker in command of six destroyers to intercept. Each side had a destroyer with a charmed life — *Shigure*, which had escaped Moosbrugger's slaughter at Vella Gulf and which would be the sole survivor of the Battle of Surigao Strait; and *O'Bannon*, which probably acquired more "hash marks" than any destroyer of the U. S. Navy.

In the ensuing Battle of Vella Lavella on the night of 6-7 October Walker won both the tactical maneuvering and the draw, launching torpedoes at 2255, range 7000 yards, one of which disembowled *Yugumo;* but a torpedo from that very destroyer had already exploded in *Chevalier*'s forward magazine, tearing off her bow as far aft as the bridge, and dooming her, besides causing a collision with *O'Bannon* which put that destroyer out of the battle. In the meantime the other two Japanese destroyers had registered on Captain Walker's radar screen. After them he galloped full cry in his now lone *Selfridge*. The range, over 10,000 yards, was too great for the sluggish products of the Newport Torpedo Station, but not for the Japanese long lances, sixteen of which at 2306 were boiling viciously around *Selfridge*. One caught her forward, exploded, and she shuddered to a stop. Eventually she had to be scuttled.

A Japanese plane sighted in the moonlight three destroyers dashing up to help Walker, and passed the word to Admiral Ijuin. That cautious commander then ordered retirement, and the three destroyers arrived a quarter-hour too late to engage. In the meantime the subchasers which Ijuin sent to rescue the Vella Lavella garrison quietly embarked them and got out.

Thus Ijuin performed his mission and inflicted the greater damage; but Captain Walker showed skill and guts in accepting the short end of three-to-one odds, and depriving the Japanese Navy of one more destroyer. It had now lost more than 40 by enemy action since the beginning of the war.

This battle concluded the Central Solomons campaign, second phase of Operation WATCHTOWER. It had cost the United States Navy six warships, and the Imperial Japanese Navy seventeen. It had brought us 250 miles nearer Rabaul — but three months was too much time to spend on getting less than one tenth of the way to Tokyo. Nevertheless, the Allies now had the strategic initiative: they would call the tunes, selecting where and when to fight.

6. *The Bougainville Battles, October–November 1943*

The next hop toward Rabaul from the South Pacific was to Bougainville. This operation was planned by the staffs of Rear Admiral Theodore S. Wilkinson and Lieutenant General Vandegrift, the last two at Guadalcanal. "Ping" Wilkinson, a scholarly officer with an excellent combat record, went into Bougainville as if he had been preparing for it all his life. He had, in fact, won a school prize some forty years earlier with an account of an amphibious operation by Alexander the Great.

Empress Augusta Bay, near the center of the long southwest coast of Bougainville, was chosen as target for this big leap. It was near enough Rabaul to be a good base for fighters to join bomber strikes from Munda, and separated from the Japanese garrisons on Bougainville by many miles of dense tropical rain forest. Thus our troops would have time to dig in and build airstrips before sustaining any serious counterattack by land.

Admiral Koga, Yamamoto's successor, guessing that something was coming up, sliced off 173 aircraft from his three biggest carriers to help defend Rabaul. Between 12 October and 2 November the Southwest Pacific air forces under General Kenney attempted to knock out Rabaul with eight massive raids of 54 to 349 planes each. Rabaul survived this treatment, but Kenney's raids were useful in diverting Japanese attention from Bougainville.

Although the Gilbert Islands operation was being mounted simultaneously in the Central Pacific, Admiral Wilkinson had enough transports and supporting warships for the task at hand. For ground forces he had a superb outfit, the I Marine Amphibious Corps commanded by General Roy S. Geiger USMC, comprising the 3rd Marine Division, the 37th Infantry Division U. S. Army, and a brigade group of New Zealand troops. Equally diverse was Airsols, comprising aircraft of the United States Army, Navy, Marine Corps and the Royal New Zealanders, the command rotating monthly between officers of the first three.

The landing at Cape Torokina, Empress Augusta Bay, of 14,000 Marines and 6200 tons of supplies from 12 transports, was pulled off successfully 1 November 1943. Wilkinson was not bothered by the local defense force, which consisted of 270 Japanese troops and one ancient *soixante-quinze*. But, remembering what happened when enemy planes from Rabaul attacked transports at Guadalcanal on 7-8 August 1942, he insisted on combat-loading his transports so that first things came out first, making for a quick landing and an even quicker getaway. How right he was! The first boat wave hit the beach at 0726; the first counterattack from Rabaul came in at 0735. Air cover from Vella Lavella and Munda took care of that, but about 100 more Japanese aircraft attacked at 1300. They were frustrated by 34 savagely aggressive Airsols fighters which were beautifully handled by a fighter-director team in destroyer *Conway*. In spite of these two interruptions, which forced the big transports to get under way, all but four were completely unloaded by 1730 and departed — a record performance.

Successful as the landings were, everyone expected the Japanese Navy to attempt another Savo Island, and they had not long to wait. Rear Admiral Omori, who hoped to repeat Mikawa's ex-

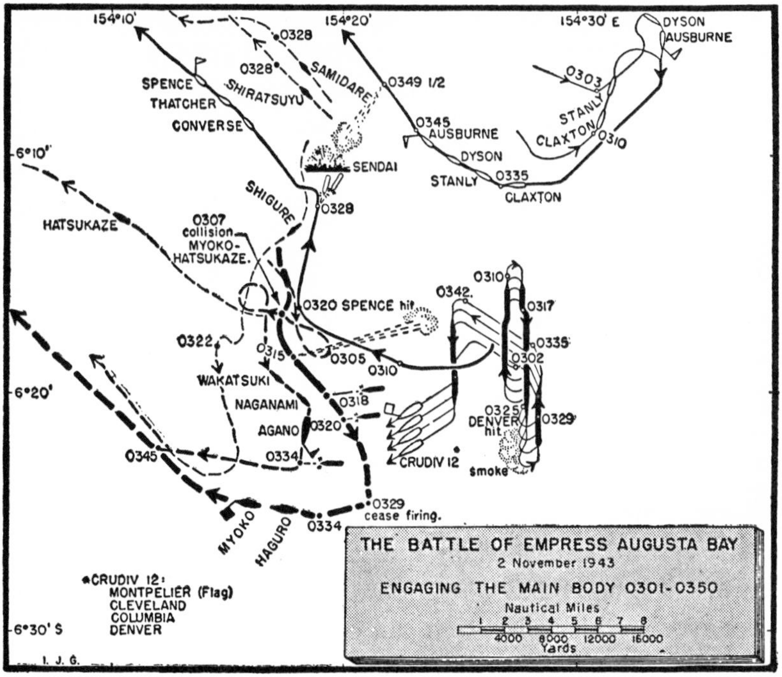

ploit, was given like him a pick-up task group to break up the landings. He had his own heavy cruiser division (*Myoko* and *Haguro*), two destroyer divisions (one commanded by Rear Admiral Ijuin, the victor at Vella Lavella), two light cruisers and six destroyers, including indestructible *Shigure*. Omori was steaming hell-bent to get the American transports in Empress Augusta Bay when he was intercepted by Rear Admiral Merrill's Task Force 39 — four light cruisers (*Montpelier*, *Cleveland*, *Columbia*, *Denver*) and two destroyer divisions of four ships each, one under Commander B. L. Austin and the other commanded by Captain Arleigh A. Burke, who had just won the nickname "31-knot Burke" for fast stepping on a recent bombardment mission. "Tip" Merrill certainly had plenty of talent under him.

The situation was now similar to that before the Battle of Savo

Island, with one important difference: from scout planes the Americans had accurate knowledge of Japanese movements. Merrill's battle plan was "to maintain the cruisers in a position across the entrance to Empress Augusta Bay and to prevent the entry therein of a single enemy ship." He proposed to push the enemy westward in order to gain sea room and to fight at ranges close to the maximum effective range of Japanese torpedoes, say 16,000 to 20,000 yards, in order to protect his cruisers from the fate of *Helena* and *Leander*. He planned to detach his destroyer divisions for an initial torpedo attack, to hold cruisers' gunfire until the "fish" struck home, and to give his destroyer commanders complete freedom of action once they were detached. Omori was in cruising disposition, in three columns 5000 yards apart; Ijuin's destroyers on the left, the two heavies in the center, other destroyers on the right. Some of the Japanese ships had radar, but the operators were green and Omori relied wholly on visual sighting. This time, Japanese eyes and binoculars were not equal to American radar.

The maneuvering in this Battle of Empress Augusta Bay was complicated. Actually there were three battles — one waged by Merrill's cruisers against the enemy cruisers, one by Burke's destroyers, and one by Austin's.

Initial torpedo salvos from both sides failed to score. The American cruisers' radar-controlled gunfire converged on the nearest ship, light cruiser *Sendai*, at 0250 November 2, and made five or more hits which jammed her rudder. At 0301 Merrill led his cruisers on a colossal figure eight, to hold an advantageous range, and spoil the enemy's aim. His cruisers dished out 6-inch gunfire as they zigzagged violently at 30 knots, but did little damage; and by 0315 Omori's 8-inch fire began to improve, straddling repeatedly. *Denver* alone was hit, but only by duds.

Japanese planes now approached Merrill's force and dropped both white and colored flares. At that point in the battle a cloud ceiling hung high over the cruisers, acting as a silver reflector to the flares and star shell. These brilliantly lighted up the four graceful vessels as their prows hissed through the black waters, in which their salvos were reflected as broken splashes of orange light. Geysers from the enemy's 8-inch misses rose deliberately from the sea like fountains in a princely garden. They flashed red, green and gold as they reflected the flares and the cruisers' gunfire, poised immobile for a split second, then tumbled in a shower of phosphorescent spume. It was one of those rare moments of awful beauty sometimes vouchsafed to those who do business in great waters.

Optimistic Omori, thinking that he had sunk two cruisers and completed a good night's work, ordered retirement at 0337.

The two destroyer divisions, although given the freedom of action that destroyer men craved, did not do well; they were like lusty children stumbling when just released from leading strings. Desdiv 45 became separated and it took Burke a full hour to get his ships back in formation. By that time there was not much left for them to do except pump a couple of torpedoes into disabled *Sendai.* Desdiv 46 finished off destroyer *Hatsukaze,* which had been damaged in a collision with Omori's flagship; but *Foote,* on the other hand, took a torpedo intended for the cruisers and lost her fantail. Both division commanders wanted to "chase the Japs back to Rabaul." But Merrill, expecting an air attack from that hornets' nest at dawn, called all units to him and started to retire at 0500. Three hours later his disposition was attacked by over 100 of the Japanese carrier planes now based at Rabaul. Merrill maneuvered his ships so nimbly that they received only two hits, neither lethal.

He thoroughly deserved victory over a force greatly his superior in torpedo power and gunfire. In a constantly changing tactical situation, he kept his poise and power of quick decision. His cruisers functioned as a well-drilled team. The Battle of Empress Augusta Bay is a refreshing contrast to earlier cruiser night actions.

Admiral Halsey now seized the initiative by ordering carrier strikes on Rabaul to eliminate the great number of aircraft still based there, and to bomb seven heavy cruisers which Koga had sent south from Truk, in the fatuous expectation of "cleaning up" on Merrill's "remnants." Rear Admiral Frederick Sherman's task force, built around *Saratoga* and the new light carrier *Princeton*, so damaged these ships on 5 November that the Japanese never again committed heavy cruisers to those waters. This performance was more than bettered on 11 November by Rear Admiral Alfred E. Montgomery's task group, built around *Essex*, *Bunker Hill* and *Independence*, which here made their debut. The Japanese counterattacked with Rabaul-based planes, but lost heavily, and Koga withdrew his crippled ships and the few remaining carrier planes, from Rabaul to Truk. He had expended another naval air group for nothing, and the Pacific Fleet had proved that carriers could profitably be pitted against a powerful land air base.

In the meantime, fresh echelons were pouring into the Bougainville beachhead. By 14 November 33,861 men and 23,137 tons of supplies had been landed at Empress Augusta Bay. But could the defensive perimeter set up around the beachhead be defended while the Seabees built airstrips and a full-fledged airdrome? The Marines were equal to it. A Japanese infantry regiment, first to press through the jungle and try Guadalcanal tactics on them, got "the treatment" on Thanksgiving Day.

On that same day, the 25th, there was even greater cause for thanksgiving, when Arleigh Burke's Desron 23, now reduced to five destroyers (two of them "Count" Austin's)[3] intercepted a Japanese five-destroyer team running reinforcements into Buka. Off Cape St. George, New Ireland, they clashed at 0156. The surprised Japanese lost two new 2000-ton destroyers from torpedo explosions, and a third by gunfire, without making a single hit. It was as good a cleanup as Moosbrugger's at Vella Gulf.

[3] *Charles F. Ausburne, Claxton, Dyson, Converse, Spence.*

The Allies were not long permitted to enjoy their Bougainville toehold in peace. General Hyakutake, the island commander, had some 40,000 soldiers and 20,000 sailors under him. All through January and February 1944 he was moving them along jungle trails, and in barges that hid out by day and crawled along shore by night, in the hope of rubbing out the Allied perimeter. General Griswold, to defend it, had about 27,000 combatant troops, the "Bougainville Navy" of small craft and PTs, commanded by the redoubtable Captain O. O. ("Scrappy") Kessing, and about one hundred Airsols planes. Halsey sent him six destroyers for naval gunfire support, and these were credited with defeating one of several enemy attacks on what was intended to be the fatal day — 9 March 1944. Two more attempts, both failures, were made by the Japanese within a week. Their losses were in the proportion of twenty to our one.

7. *Ringing Around Rabaul, September 1943–April 1944*

During July and August 1943, while Halsey and Wilkinson slowly masticated the Central Solomons, MacArthur and Barbey had to be content with digesting their easily won gains in the Trobriand Islands and Nassau Bay. To that minor landing the Japanese reacted by setting up a barge line to carry troops from New Britain to the threatened New Guinea bases. General MacArthur wisely decided to take both places and Finschhafen too. His prerequisite for success was local air superiority. MacArthur, at 64 somewhat elderly for active duty, was air-minded as the youngest pilot in the A.A.F. He had learned a great lesson of the air age — never needlessly to expose troops or ships to an enemy supreme in the air. A contingent of the Southwest Pacific air forces raided Wewak, the principal Japanese base in New Guinea, 17-18 August, and destroyed over 100 planes; General Kenney seized the Japanese airstrip at Nadzab on 5 September by a surprise paratroop drop of 1700 men. Next day, Australian troops, lifted by Dan Barbey's VII 'Phib from Milne Bay, landed on beaches near Lae, and seized that place on the 16th; Salamaua had already fallen to another group of Aussies; Finschhafen succumbed to a repeat performance by 2 October, 1943.

Seventh Fleet was now in reasonably full control of Vitiaz Strait, but General MacArthur wanted Dampier Strait too, in order to dominate all passages between New Britain and New Guinea. That was his reason for landing the 1st Marine Division (Major General Rupertus) on Cape Gloucester. It was a big shore-to-shore operation, mounted in beaching craft by VII 'Phib in Papua and covered by a mixed United States Navy and Royal Australian Navy cruiser group commanded by Admiral Crutchley RN. After passing a hot and stuffy Christmas at sea, the Marines were landed at Cape Gloucester on the 26th. They found that place to be even worse than Guadalcanal, because the rain never stopped. After suffering heavy losses they secured a beachhead and a perimeter, by 16 January 1944.

Since Rabaul had always been the main objective of Operation WATCHTOWER, it was a shock to General MacArthur when General Marshall on 21 July 1943 suggested that he leapfrog Rabaul instead of assaulting it. The Combined Chiefs of Staff at their Quebec meeting in August directed Halsey and MacArthur to do just that, and as Rabaul's substitute occupy Kavieng in New Ireland and Manus in the Admiralties. This major leap, coupled with a later decision to bypass Kavieng as well, proved to be fortunate. Rabaul still had close to 100,000 defenders under a tough and resourceful general. Since it had been a stockpiling base for various invasions which never came off, the Japanese garrison had plenty of provisions, munitions, weapons and

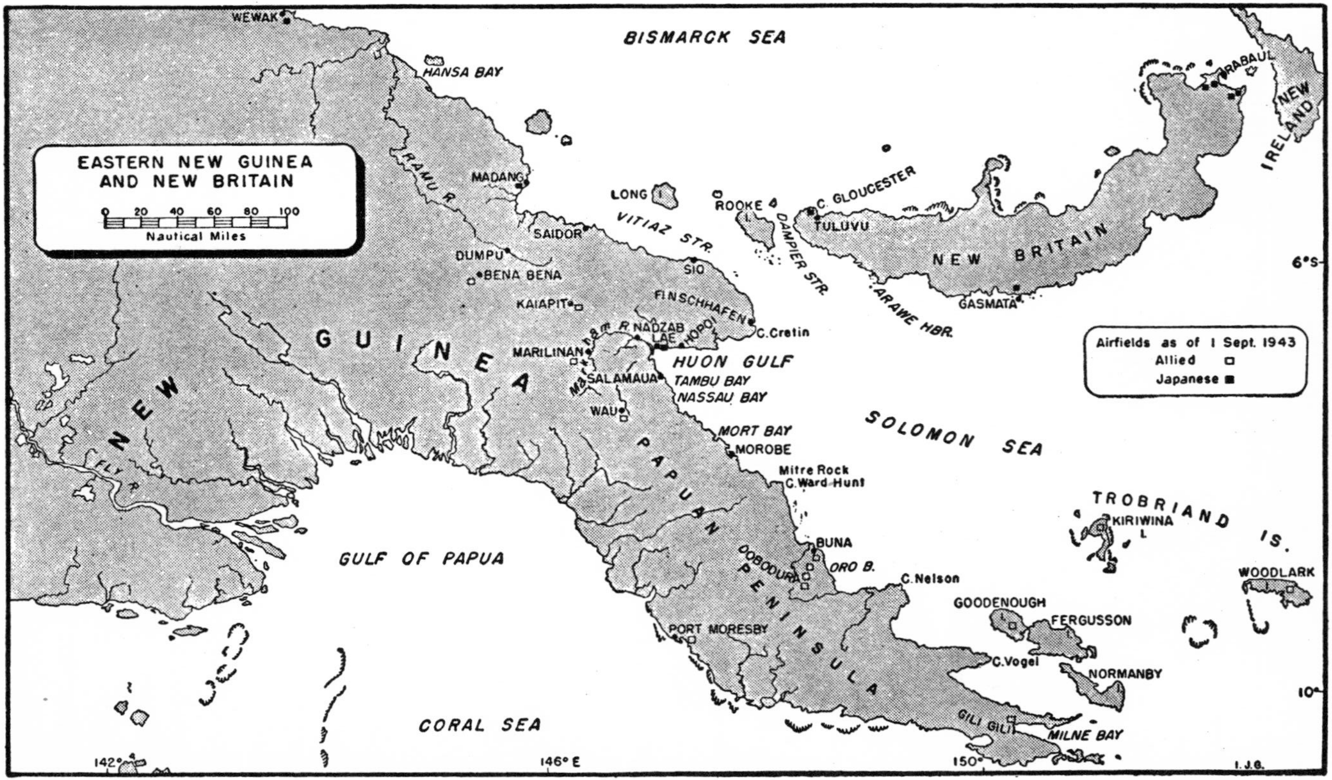
EASTERN NEW GUINEA
AND NEW BRITAIN
0 20 40 60 80 100
Nautical Miles
Airfields as of 1 Sept. 1943
Allied
Japanese
BISMARCK SEA
SOLOMON SEA
CORAL SEA
GULF OF PAPUA
NEW GUINEA
PAPUAN PENINSULA
NEW BRITAIN
NEW IRELAND
TROBRIAND IS.
WEWAK
HANSA BAY
RAMU R.
MADANG
SAIDOR
DUMPU
BENA BENA
KAIAPIT
MARILINAN
R. NADZAB
LAE
HOPOI
FINSCHHAFEN
SIO
C. Cretin
HUON GULF
SALAMAUA
TAMBU BAY
NASSAU BAY
WAU
MORT BAY
MOROBE
Mitre Rock
C. Ward Hunt
BUNA
DOBODURA
ORO B.
C. Nelson
PORT MORESBY
GOODENOUGH
FERGUSSON
NORMANBY
C. Vogel
GILI GILI
MILNE BAY
KIRIWINA
WOODLARK
LONG I.
VITIAZ STR.
ROOKE I.
DAMPIER STR.
C. GLOUCESTER
TULUVU
ARAWE HBR.
GASMATA
RABAUL
FLY R.
142°
146° E
150°
6° S
10°
I. J. G.

supplies. They kept busy, digging caves and concealed gun positions and constructing fields of fire and booby traps that should have enabled them to repulse any amphibious operation that the Allies could have laid on.

The last important leap that isolated Rabaul was made by MacArthur into the Admiralty Islands. This was not supposed to come off until 1 April 1944, but on the basis of a B–25 pilot's report that the islands were empty of Japanese, General MacArthur decided to pull off a reconnaissance in force, and to accompany it himself. This kind of reconnaissance means that you send enough men to stay if the target is weakly defended, but not too many to make a brisk retreat if the enemy is there in strength. The 1st Cavalry Division United States Army supplied over a thousand troopers (minus boots, saddles and sabers); Barbey's VII 'Phib lifted them as usual. The troopers were landed on Los Negros Island without opposition, on 29 February. It turned out that the B–25 pilot was wrong. About 4000 of the Japanese were present, and started making trouble that very night. But MacArthur decided to let the troopers stay and to reinforce them quickly, because from his knowledge of Japanese ground tactics he rightly predicted that the enemy would commit his army piecemeal, and that each small package could be defeated.

With the aid of almost the entire Seventh Fleet, abundant air power, and sundry ground troops, the Americans moved from Los Negroes into Manus, the biggest island of the group. By 3 April they were in control of the magnificent, deep, landlocked Seeadler Harbor, fifteen miles long and four wide. Far better as a base than Rabaul, and nearer Japan, the Admiralties became one of the most important staging points in the last fifteen months of the Pacific War.

In the meantime, there had been big doings along the other road to Tokyo — through the Central Pacific.

CHAPTER X

Gilberts and Marshalls

November 1943–July 1944

1. *The Gilberts — Operation* GALVANIC

IN ALLIED CIRCLES, very little was known of enemy activities in the Gilbert Islands, which the Japanese Navy captured in September 1942, and even less of the Marshalls, for which Japan obtained the mandate after World War I. Photographic reconnaissance could not stretch up to the Marshalls, even from Funafuti, which the United States occupied on 2 October 1942. Submarines *Pompano*, *Stingray* and *Plunger* reconnoitered Rongerik, Bikini, Eniwetok and several minor atolls in February–March; but a fish-eye view does not reveal what is going on ashore. Combined Fleet might have rendezvoused in Kwajalein Lagoon and half a dozen new airfields might have been constructed without the news reaching Pearl Harbor.

Admiral King, always alert to seize opportunities, on 9 February 1943 invited Admiral Nimitz's comment on an operation to secure the Gilbert Islands. Cincpac thought the suggestion premature. No ground troops were yet available, and no naval forces could be spared from the Central Solomons operation, coming up in June.

Modern warfare has to be planned far ahead; improvisation may lead to disaster. Why then did the Marshalls become a priority target in the Joint Chiefs' 20 May plan for the defeat of Japan? Their object was to attain positions in the Western Pacific from which Japan's unconditional surrender could be forced, possibly by air action alone, probably by invasion after repeated air strikes on her industrial cities. The key target to this plan, short of Japan itself, was a base at or near Hong Kong; and although that key fell — owing to Japan's sealing off the entire coast of China — a good part of the plan endured. In brief, it amounted to this: —

Parallel, simultaneous carrier and amphibious operations through (*a*) Gilberts and Marshalls, (*b*) the Bismarck Archipelago, and (*c*) from the Indian Ocean into Burma. The first (*a*) we are about to relate. Operation WATCHTOWER, which (as we have already told) was concluded with the neutralization of Rabaul, is (*b*); Burma (*c*) was postponed again and again. The basic idea was this: an offensive through Micronesia (Gilberts, Marshalls, Carolines) must be pushed at the same time as MacArthur's New Guinea–Mindanao approach to Japan. The one would support the other, and the fast carrier forces, now being augmented by the *Essex* class, could free-wheel between the two. It was a very bold plan. Nothing in past warfare told how amphibious forces could advance in great leaps across an ocean where the enemy had dozens of island bases. The series of operations we are about to relate were one of the finest achievements in World War II.

Cincpac, after a good photo reconnaissance of the Gilberts, convinced the J.C.S. that we had better take Tarawa and Makin for air bases before trying the Marshalls, and the J.C.S. issued the directive on 20 July 1943. Operation GALVANIC was now definitely on the timetable for November.

Fifth Fleet, organized 15 March 1943 from what had been the Central Pacific component of the Pacific Fleet, was at last formidable. It had the new *Lexington*, the new *Yorktown*, three light carriers, twenty new 2100-ton destroyers, and the new fast battleship *Alabama*. The J.C.S. informed Admiral Nimitz that by October he might count on double or triple these numbers, besides 27 transport types and a flock of new Kaiser-built escort carriers.

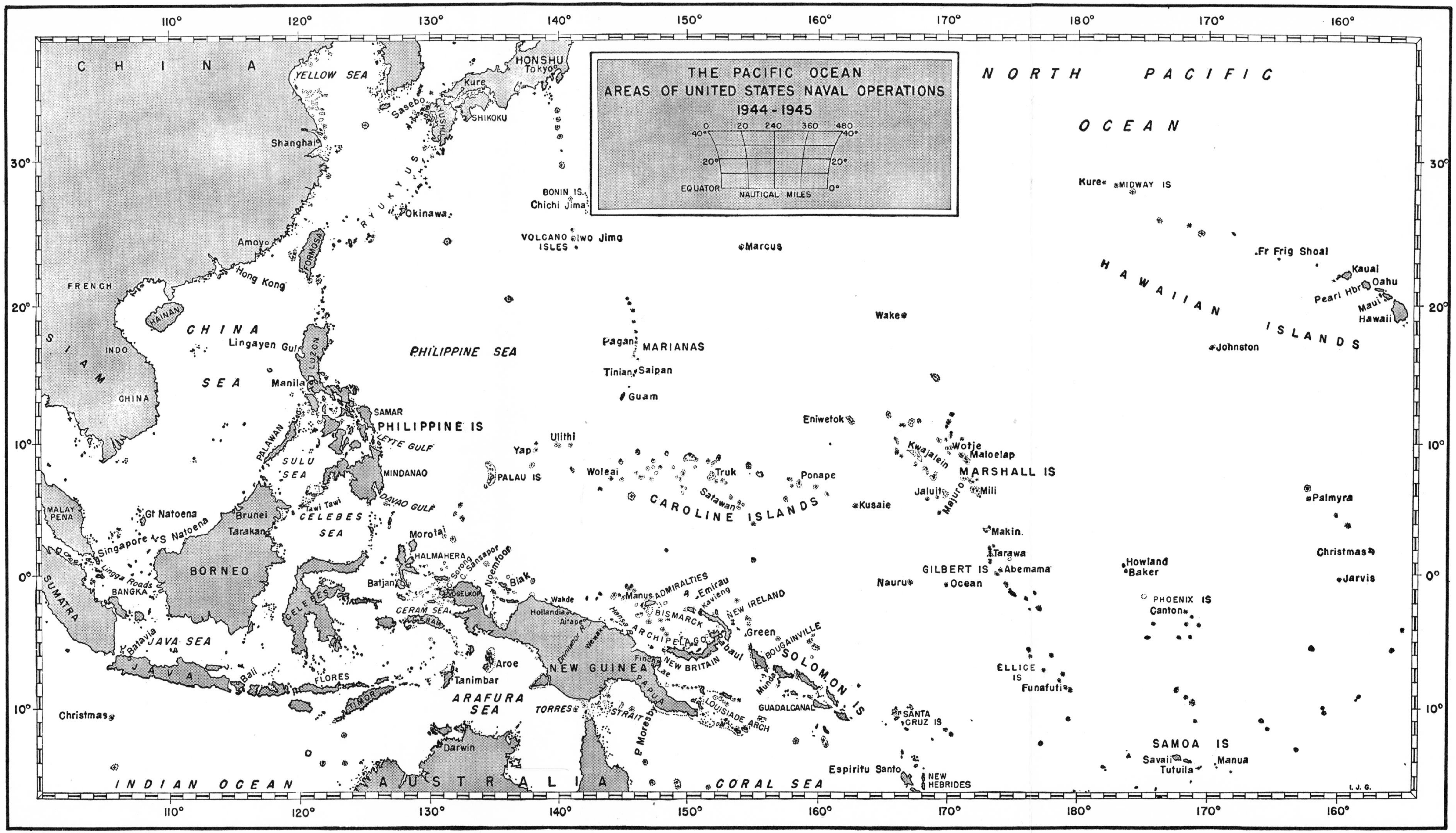
THE PACIFIC OCEAN
AREAS OF UNITED STATES NAVAL OPERATIONS
1944 - 1945
0 120 240 360 480
NAUTICAL MILES
EQUATOR
NORTH PACIFIC OCEAN
CHINA
YELLOW SEA
HONSHU
Tokyo
Kure
Sasebo
KYUSHU
SHIKOKU
Shanghai
RYUKYUS
Okinawa
BONIN IS.
Chichi Jima
VOLCANO ISLES
Iwo Jima
Marcus
Amoy
FORMOSA
Hong Kong
FRENCH INDO CHINA
HAINAN
SIAM
CHINA SEA
Lingayen Gulf
LUZON
Manila
PHILIPPINE SEA
Pagan
MARIANAS
Tinian
Saipan
Guam
Wake
Kure
MIDWAY IS
Fr Frig Shoal
HAWAIIAN ISLANDS
Kauai
Oahu
Pearl Hbr
Maui
Hawaii
Johnston
SAMAR
PHILIPPINE IS
LEYTE GULF
PALAWAN
SULU SEA
MINDANAO
DAVAO GULF
Ulithi
Yap
PALAU IS
Woleai
Truk
Satawan
Ponape
CAROLINE ISLANDS
Kusaie
Eniwetok
Kwajalein
Wotje
Maloelap
MARSHALL IS
Jaluit
Majuro
Mili
Palmyra
MALAY PENA
Gt Natoena
S Natoena
Singapore
Brunei
Tarakan
Tawi Tawi
CELEBES SEA
Morotai
HALMAHERA
Sorong
Sansapor
Noemfoor
Biak
VOGELKOP
Batjan
BORNEO
Lingga Roads
BANGKA
SUMATRA
CELEBES
CERAM SEA
CERAM
Wakde
Hollandia
Aitape
Manus
ADMIRALTIES
Emirau
Kavieng
NEW IRELAND
BISMARCK ARCHIPELAGO
Rabaul
Green
BOUGAINVILLE
SOLOMON IS
Makin
Tarawa
Abemama
GILBERT IS
Nauru
Ocean
Howland
Baker
PHOENIX IS
Canton
Christmas
Jarvis
Batavia
JAVA SEA
JAVA
Bali
FLORES
TIMOR
Aroe
Tanimbar
ARAFURA SEA
Digul R.
Sepik R.
Hansa
Wewak
NEW GUINEA
Finsch
Lae
NEW BRITAIN
PAPUA
Munda
GUADALCANAL
LOUISIADE ARCH
ELLICE IS
Funafuti
Christmas
TORRES STRAIT
P Moresby
Darwin
SANTA CRUZ IS
Espiritu Santo
NEW HEBRIDES
SAMOA IS
Savaii
Tutuila
Manua
INDIAN OCEAN
AUSTRALIA
CORAL SEA
I. J. G.

(Yamamoto was right: the Pacific Fleet had to be "annihilated" in 1942, or not at all.) Vice Admiral Raymond A. Spruance left Nimitz's staff to become Commander Fifth Fleet, and Rear Admiral R. Kelly Turner commanded the V Amphibious Force set up in August — leaving Rear Admiral Wilkinson to carry on, as we have seen, in the Solomons. The ground troops, the V Amphibious Corps, although not all Marines, were commanded by Major General Holland M. Smith USMC.

Planning and training for a big amphibious operation is probably the most difficult branch of military preparation. It never even approaches perfection because the units employed cannot be trained as a team; no one base is big enough to hold them all. In an operation requiring the most detailed planning and the nicest timing, Admiral Turner commanded men of the Army, Navy and Marine Corps attached to ships, planes and ground forces in points as far apart as New Zealand, Hawaii, San Diego and Alaska, organized in units very few of which he could even see before D-day.

There were preliminary carrier-plane strikes on Tarawa and Makin, submarine and photographic reconnaissance, and diversionary strikes on other islands such as Wake and Marcus, to confuse the Japanese. Every day for the week 13–20 November, Army and Navy Liberators bombed Tarawa and Makin. The sortie of surface forces from Pearl Harbor began as early as 21 October. Never before had there been such intensive activity in Pearl Harbor, in the Fijis and in the New Hebrides as during the last days of October and the first of November 1943. Then, suddenly, every harbor and roadstead was deserted. Over two hundred sail — the Fifth Fleet carrying 108,000 American soldiers, sailors, Marines and aviators under the command of taut Raymond Spruance, gallant Harry Hill, and bristling Kelly Turner — were on the high seas. By various and devious routes, they converged on two coral atolls whose names will be remembered as long as men prize valor: Makin and Tarawa.

We may dispose of the easier task first. This was Butaritari Island, Makin Atoll, defended by only 300 Japanese combat troops, with no higher officer than a lieutenant, and 500 labor troops. The landing was easy, but the ground troops made "infuriatingly slow" progress, as General "Howling Mad" Smith put it, despite a 23 to 1 superiority. These were two regiments from the 27th Infantry Division, a New York National Guard outfit that had gone stale from too long training. Thus, it was not until the fourth day of the assault, 24 November, that their commander could signal "Makin taken." The taking cost the Army 64 killed and 150 wounded; it was the Navy that paid dear. Admiral Koga, C. in C. Combined Fleet, committed nine submarines to break up the massive forces supporting the Gilbert Islands landings, and, owing to the slow work of our ground troops, which required naval forces to stay near the island, submarine *I–175* scored heavily. She torpedoed and sank escort carrier *Liscome Bay* on 24 November, taking the lives of Captain I. D. Wiltsie, Rear Admiral Henry M. Mullinnix, and 642 others.

All Japanese air counterattacks were thwarted by planes from aircraft carriers that Admiral Spruance brought up for that very purpose; their presence was a major factor in persuading Admiral Koga to keep Combined Fleet snug in Truk. But he fleeted up a few dozen land-based planes from Truk to Kwajalein; and these, after sunset Thanksgiving Day, 25 November, put on a beautiful show, a night attack on Admiral Turner's force of battleships, cruisers and escort carriers, operating about 60 miles east of Makin. The technique of Japanese night air attacks at this period of the war was spectacular. First, snoopers dropped strings of colored float lights to guide bombers to the enemy ships. When the bombers approached, the snoopers flew high over the ships and dropped parachute flares, of a brilliance that none of our pyrotechnicians could match. Then the dive- and torpedo-bombers bore in. Turner, an old hand at evading air attack, won this contest of wits. His ships had been intensively drilled in radical simultaneous turns on the voyage from Pearl Harbor, and they performed so many that night as to afford the enemy no opportunity to score.

On the same Thanksgiving Day night, when Arleigh Burke was sinking Japanese destroyers off Cape St. George, a group of Japanese planes attacked Rear Admiral Radford's Northern Carrier Group (*Enterprise*, *Belleau Wood*, *Monterey*), which had been furnishing air support for the Gilbert Islands operation. "Raddy" had trained a radar-equipped night combat air patrol, and a group of night fighters as well; they saw to it that not one hit was made on the carriers. But Commander E. H. ("Butch") O'Hare, one of the best pilots in the Navy, was shot down.

Thus, Makin was taken at slight cost by the Army, but at considerable cost to the Navy. It provided vivid proof of the necessity of speed in conquering an island, so as to release the covering naval forces promptly. But, in marked contrast to Guadalcanal, the main Japanese fleet was never committed, because it had been temporarily paralyzed by the air attacks on Rabaul.

2. *Tarawa, 19–23 November 1943*

Betio Island, at the southwest corner of Tarawa Atoll, in shape resembles an old-fashioned muzzle-loading musket, complete with stock, lock and barrel, pointing a little south of east. The total length is only 3800 yards; the width, 500 yards at the stock, 600 at the lock, tapering off to a point on the barrel; the area is less than 300 acres. An airfield occupied the wide center part; and the rest of the island was covered with a stand of coconut palms under

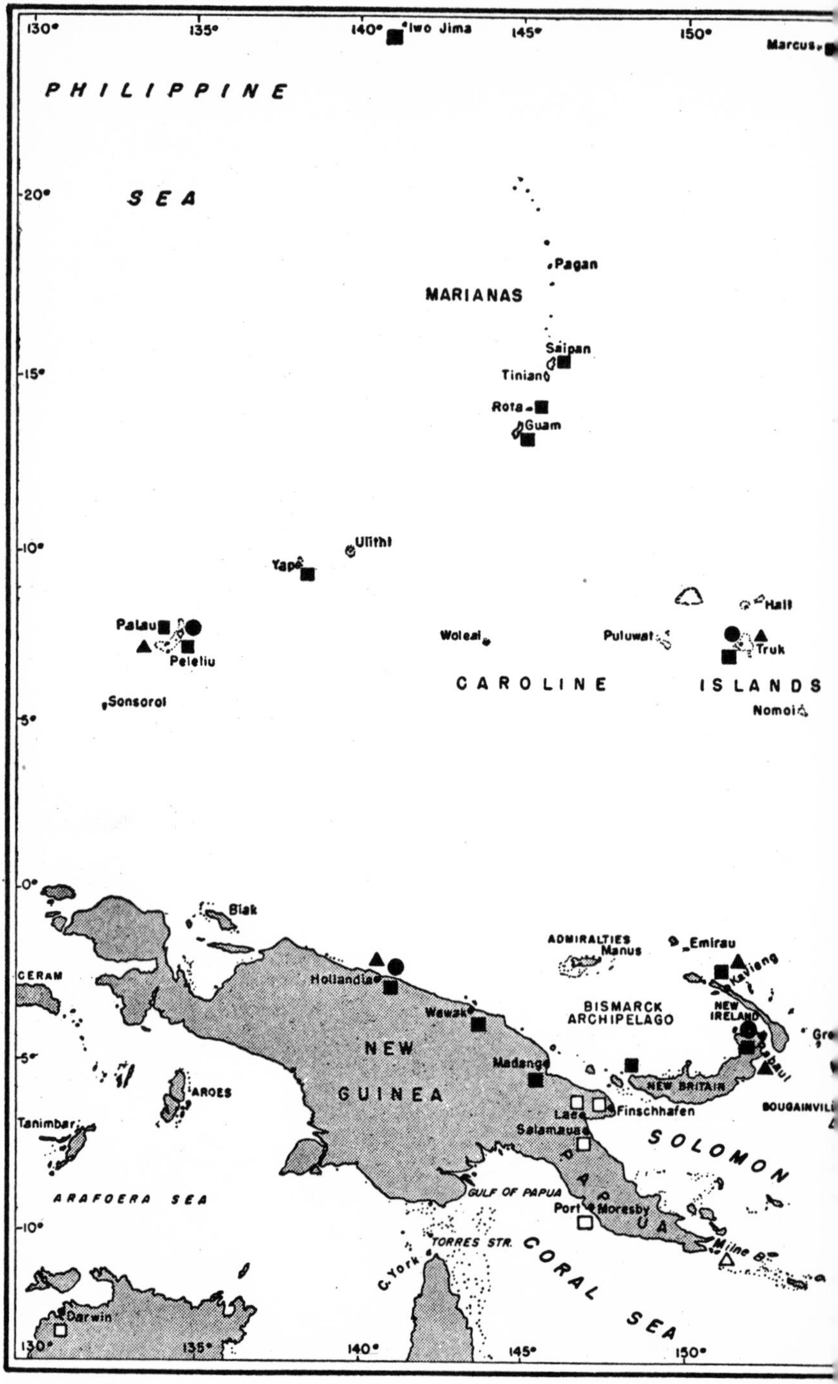

130°
135°
140°
Iwo Jima
145°
150°
Marcus
PHILIPPINE
SEA
20°
Pagan
MARIANAS
Saipan
Tinian
15°
Rota
Guam
Ulithi
10°
Yap
Palau
Peleliu
Woleai
Puluwat
Hall
Truk
CAROLINE
ISLANDS
Sonsorol
Nomoi
5°
0°
Biak
ADMIRALTIES
Manus
Emirau
CERAM
Hollandia
Kavieng
Wewak
BISMARCK
ARCHIPELAGO
NEW IRELAND
NEW
GUINEA
Madang
5°
AROES
NEW BRITAIN
Lae
Finschhafen
Salamaua
BOUGAINVILLE
Tanimbar
SOLOMON
PAPUA
GULF OF PAPUA
ARAFOERA SEA
Port Moresby
10°
TORRES STR.
CORAL SEA
C. York
Milne B.
Darwin
130°
135°
140°
145°
150°

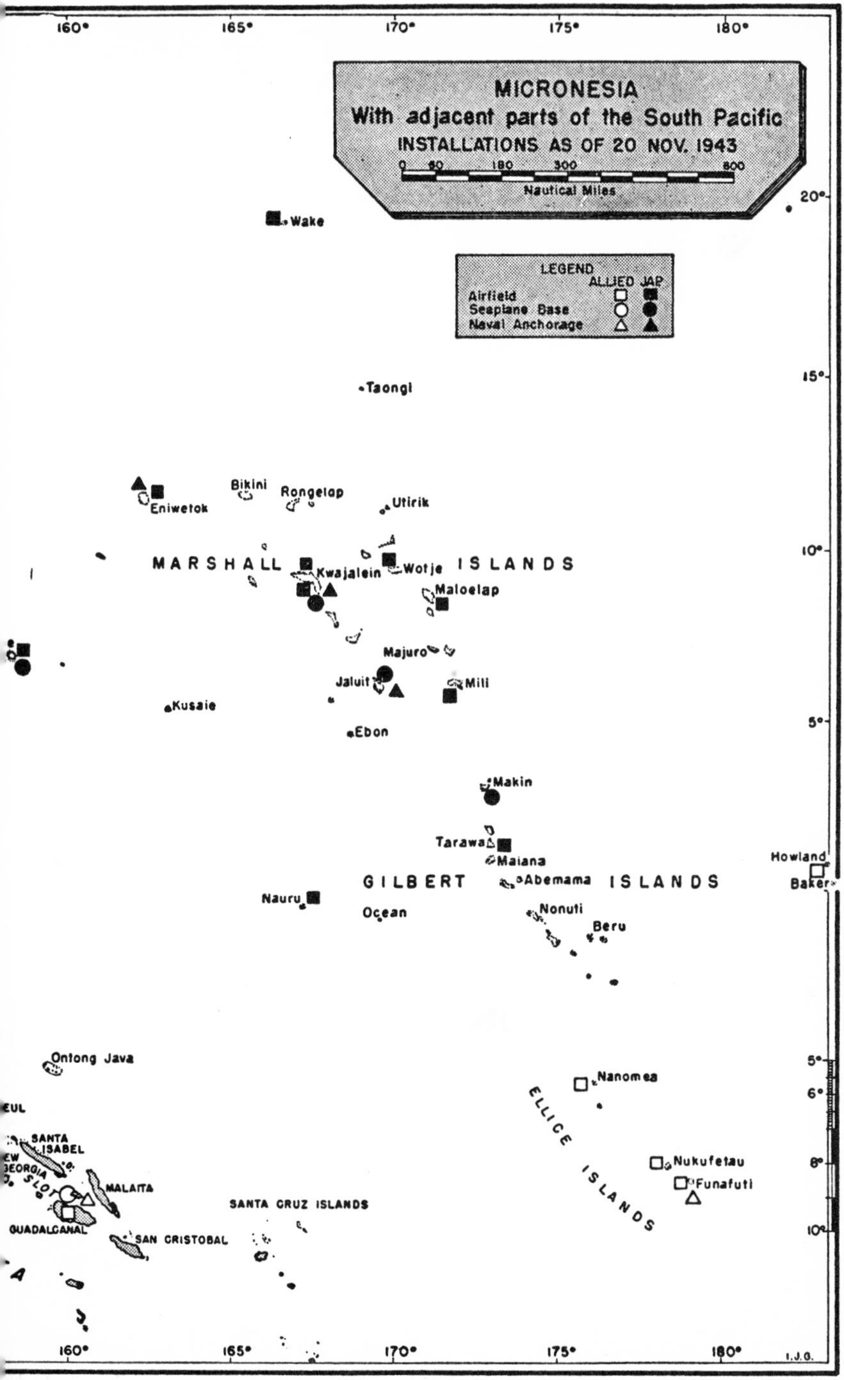

MICRONESIA
With adjacent parts of the South Pacific
INSTALLATIONS AS OF 20 NOV. 1943

0 50 100 300 500
Nautical Miles

• Wake

LEGEND
 ALLIED JAP.
Airfield □ ■
Seaplane Base ○ ●
Naval Anchorage △ ▲

• Taongi

▲■
Eniwetok Bikini Rongelap • Utirik

MARSHALL ■ Kwajalein ■ Wotje ISLANDS
 ● ▲ ■ Maloelap
 Majuro
 Jaluit ▲ ■ Mili

• Kusaie
 • Ebon

 • Makin
 ●

 Tarawa △■
 ⌀ Maiana
GILBERT ⌀ Abemama ISLANDS Howland □
 Baker □
Nauru ■ Ocean Nonuti
 Beru

Ontong Java

EUL □ Nanomea
 SANTA
 ISABEL
NEW
GEORGIA
 MALAITA □ Nukufetau
 SANTA CRUZ ISLANDS □ Funafuti
 △
GUADALCANAL SAN CRISTOBAL

 I.J.G.

which a complete defensive system had been installed. The atoll commander, Rear Admiral Shibasaki, had 4500 picked troops under him, tough as mountain goats, and indoctrinated to fight to the last man, as they did — only 17 were taken prisoner. These troops had been there over a year with nothing to do but pepper the island with strongpoints. They had plenty of weapons, even 8-inch British naval guns captured at Singapore, and enough bombproof shelters to hold the entire garrison. No small island was ever so well protected or stubbornly defended as Betio.

Rear Admiral Hill commanded the Southern Attack Force that took Tarawa. In contrast to the dour and saturnine Turner, Harry Hill was a sanguine, genial officer who thought and talked like a young man and preferred to lead rather than drive. The landing force, the 2nd Marine Division, reinforced to about 18,600 men, was commanded by Major General Julian C. Smith, a student of the art of war and of human nature, who had the complete confidence of his officers and men. Admiral Hill and General Smith came up in battleship *Maryland*, a rehabilitated victim of Pearl Harbor. Pacific Fleet as yet had no specially equipped amphibious command ship, such as Hewitt enjoyed in Sicily, and *Maryland's* communications system, inadequate at best, had an annoying habit of conking out with each main battery salvo.

Beaches on the lagoon side of Betio were chosen as the least difficult of three tough places. The planners hoped that by landing on a three-battalion front the Marines could sweep across the island and capture the airfield in short order. The trouble with this lagoon-side landing was that transports had to unload outside, so that a ten-mile trip with a turn was required for landing craft. And, if the boats could not float over a wide shelving coral reef, the troops would have to wade. Tarawa tides at this season were unpredictable, and we drew the worst.

The Navy badly miscalculated the amount of softening-up that could be done in two and a half daylight hours' bombardment on the morning of D-day, 20 November, preceded and followed by air bombing from the attendant carriers. All coast defense guns were silenced and some destruction was done — but not nearly enough; nobody yet realized how much punishment the Japanese could take when protected by heavy concrete or several layers of coconut logs and coral sand.

This was the first operation to use a large number of amphtracs, LVTs. These, developed from "alligators" used in the Florida Everglades before the war, were 25-foot amphibious tractors that could carry 25 men and two machine guns, make 4 knots in the water, climb over coral reefs if necessary, and operate as tanks on land. Ninety-three LVTs — of which 90 were expended — made up the first three assault waves commanded by Colonel David M. Shoup. Delayed by a heavy chop and westerly set of current, they began hitting the beach at 0913. That was already 28 minutes after an already once-postponed H-hour.

This delay wrecked the landing timetable, to which an amphibious operation has to stick rigidly for success. Admiral Hill did not dare deliver gunfire support after 0855, because both island and lagoon were under a pall of smoke, and he feared hitting the landing craft. The cease-fire afforded the Japanese twenty minutes' grace, which they employed to transfer troops from the south shore to rifle pits and machine-gun nests on the lagoon side. Many Japanese guns had the LVTs under crossfire before landing. After the amphtracs came a wave of tank-loaded LCMs from LSD *Ashland*. These, stranded on the coral apron by an unexpectedly low tide, had to discharge Sherman tanks in three to four feet of water, which drowned out some of the engines. And as no landing craft could float over the reef, troops had to wade for 400 to 500 yards under heavy fire, in water waist-deep, which meant death by drowning for a wound or a stumble.

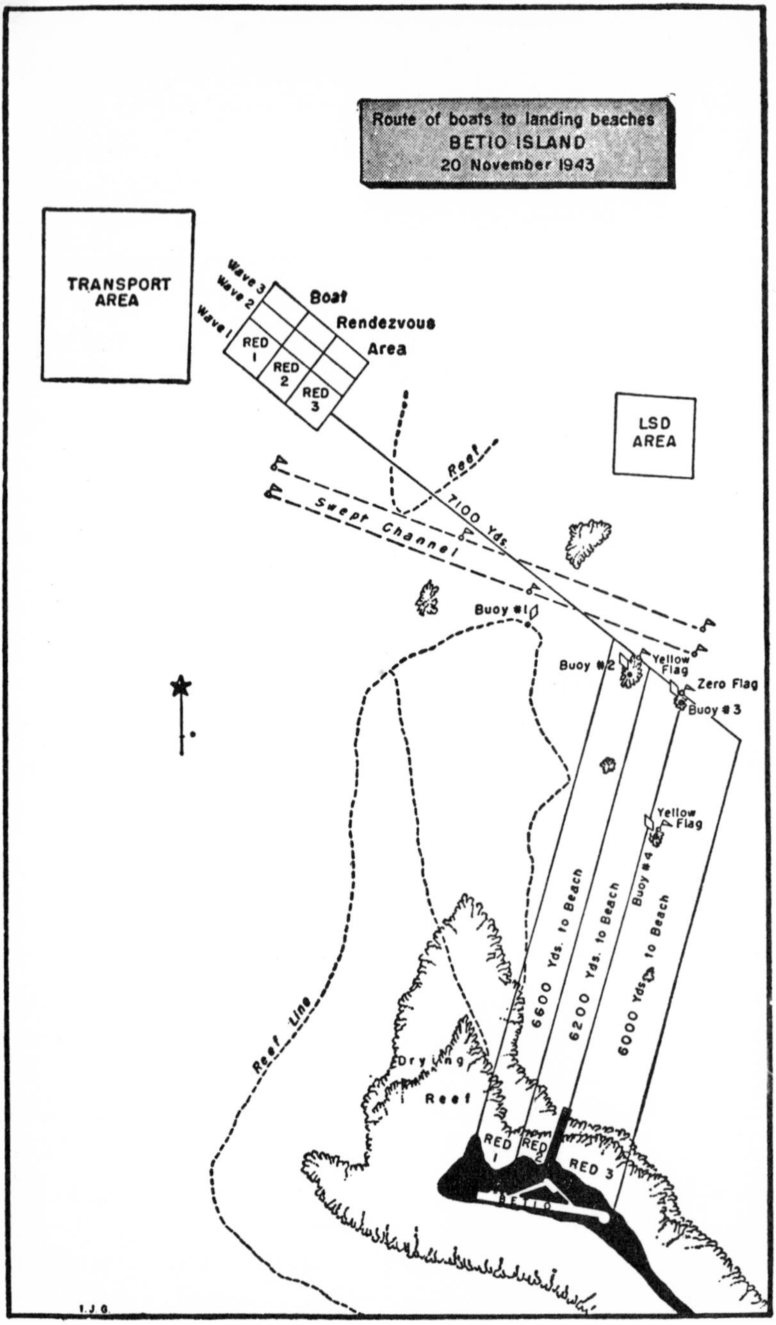

Route of boats to landing beaches
BETIO ISLAND
20 November 1943
TRANSPORT AREA
Wave 3
Wave 2
Wave 1
Boat
Rendezvous
Area
RED 1
RED 2
RED 3
LSD AREA
Reef
7100 Yds.
Swept Channel
Buoy #1
Buoy #2
Yellow Flag
Zero Flag
Buoy #3
Yellow Flag
Buoy #4
6600 Yds. to Beach
6200 Yds. to Beach
6000 Yds. to Beach
Reef Line
Drying
Reef
RED 1
RED 2
RED 3
BETIO
I.J.G.

Between noon and 1400, the situation ashore was very critical. Some 1500 Marines were pinned down on a narrow beach under a wall of coconut logs and coral blocks, behind which the enemy was shooting everything he had at men wading ashore. General Julian Smith at 1330 radioed General H. M. Smith, who was in battleship *Pennsylvania* off Makin, requesting release of the reserve, and ending with the ominous words: ISSUE IN DOUBT.

By the end of D-day, about 5000 Marines had landed, but at least 1500 had been killed or wounded. Intrepid officers led small squads inland, rooting out defenders as they advanced, and established a 300-yard-wide beachhead by evening.

Next day, 21 November, Major L. C. Hays's battalion of the divisional reserve fought its way ashore, losing 13 officers and 331 men in so doing. Around noon that day, when the laggard tide finally rose and landing craft could steam right up to the beach, the tide of battle turned. Next day the Japanese were thrust into two or three pockets, and by the end of the 23rd these had been eliminated. The first American plane landed on the airstrip at noon. It only remained to send a squad of Marines up the atoll to rescue the Catholic mission station in the northern part, and to exterminate the last of the Japanese garrison.

Tarawa was ours, at heavy cost — the lives of over 1000 Marines and sailors, with more than double that number of wounded. They were not wasted. As a result of intensive study of reports by everyone, from admirals and generals down to boat wave ensigns, many valuable lessons were learned, and these rendered most later amphibious operations in the Pacific, in comparison, pushovers. The relatively easy conquest of Kwajalein in January 1944 is owed to lessons learned at Tarawa; to a perfect take-off position, the triangle Tarawa–Makin–Abemama,[1] captured in November; and to

[1] Abemama, 75 miles southeast of Tarawa, was occupied 21 November by 78 Marines, lifted in submarine *Nautilus*. In three weeks Seabees built O'Hare Field, which became very useful in the Marshalls operation.

using this position, as well as carrier planes, for photographic reconnaissance and for neutralizing enemy air power in the Marshalls before D-day.

All honor, then, to the fighting heart of the United States Marine. Let the battle for that small stretch of coral sand called Betio of Tarawa be remembered as terrible indeed, but glorious, and the seedbed for victory in 1945.

3. *Kwajalein (Operation* FLINTLOCK*), January–February 1944*

Although it had long since been decided that the Marshalls would come next after the Gilberts, it was not determined until December what would happen after that. Should the now vastly stronger Pacific Fleet combine with Kinkaid's Seventh Fleet to help General MacArthur roll up the back of the New Guinea bird into the Celebes Sea, and on to Mindanao? Or should the General be left to do that with his own Navy, and Admiral Nimitz continue to hew out a second road to Tokyo across the Central Pacific? Admiral King won the approval of the C.C.S. in its "Sextant" Conference at Cairo, on 3 December 1943, for the Nimitz plan of dual approach. Their principal directive was as follows: —

"The advance along the New Guinea–N.E.I.–Philippine axis will proceed concurrently with operations for the capture of the Mandated Islands. A strategic bombing force will be established in Guam, Tinian and Saipan for strategic bombing of Japan proper."

This bombing force meant the Superfortresses, the B–29s. The need of a base for them in the Marianas was a principal reason why the King-Nimitz idea prevailed over the all-under-MacArthur plan. Other reasons were (1) the planned all-British amphibious operation to retake Burma as a "second front" against Japan had been scrapped; (2) fast carrier forces of the Pacific Fleet were not suitable for employment in the narrow seas south of the Philippines, with Japanese air bases on all sides; (3) Saipan would make an ideal advanced base for United States submarines, which with new and more effective torpedoes had finally got into their stride and were rapidly reducing Japanese merchant tonnage.

Momentum, a word that continually recurs in strategic discussions, was a great consideration. For, the closer that one offensive steps on the heels of the other, the greater will be one's gain and the enemy's loss and confusion. Japan had proved that in early 1942; we now intended to turn the same principle against her. Momentum settled the question of which Marshall atolls should be taken, and which leapfrogged. Nimitz's bold plan provided that undefended Majuro be taken first, for the sake of its anchorage; that both ends of Kwajalein, the hub of the enemy's defense system, be assaulted simultaneously the second day; and that Eniwetok be taken as soon as possible thereafter. All the rest of the atolls, even those with airfields, would be skipped. Admirals Spruance and Turner and General H. M. Smith argued against the plan as too bold, but Nimitz correctly estimated that his fast carrier forces, together with aircraft based on the Makin-Tarawa-Abemama triangle, could neutralize Japanese air power in the Marshalls before operation began. And he now had enough battleships and heavy cruisers to take on the Combined Fleet in case it sortied from Truk.

Fast Carrier Force Pacific Fleet had become really formidable by the first of the new year. Besides old "Big E" and "Sara," Rear Admiral Mitscher had *Essex* and three more of her class, six light carriers of the *Independence* class, with new *Iowa* class battleships and plenty of cruisers and destroyers to screen them. Divided into four task groups, they raided one or more atolls in the Marshalls every day from 29 January to 6 February, virtually destroying enemy air and sea power in the archipelago before the amphibious operation began. And they covered it thereafter. Escort carriers were also present, to furnish close air support.

Rear Admiral Turner (at last in an amphibious command ship, *Rocky Mount*) commanded the entire expeditionary force. Rear Admiral Conolly, fresh from participation in the Salerno operation, took charge of the northern half, lifting the new 4th Marine Division to occupy Roi and Namur Islands on Kwajalein Atoll. Turner himself commanded the southern half, lifting the 7th Infantry Division to take Kwajalein Island.

Japan made almost no attempt to counter this massive onslaught. The Halsey-MacArthur campaign against the Bismarcks Barrier had thrown her forces off balance. Admiral Koga dared not commit Combined Fleet, because his carrier air groups had been expended to defend Rabaul. The Marshalls were only a "holding" front for the Japanese; Imperial Headquarters decided to expend the garrisons and strengthen the next defensive perimeter, Timor–Western New Guinea–Truk–Marianas. A force of submarines was sent up from Truk to do what it could; but not one got a lethal hit, and four, including *I–175* which had torpedoed *Liscome Bay* off Makin, were sunk by our destroyers or destroyer escorts.

Majuro, the undefended atoll, was occupied 31 January 1944, by the attack group under Rear Admiral Hill which later went on to take Eniwetok. Compared with other atolls where the garrison had to camp among the debris of battle, Majuro proved a paradise for American soldiers and sailors. Its spacious lagoon, well served the new mobile supply force of auxiliaries, under Captain Worrall R. Carter, who became SOPA Majuro.

Kwajalein is the world's largest coral atoll, composed of a string of one hundred islands and islets, enclosing an irregularly shaped lagoon 66 miles long and at places 20 miles wide. At the southeast corner is Kwajalein Island, where the Japanese were constructing a bomber strip; at the northern tip were two small connected is-

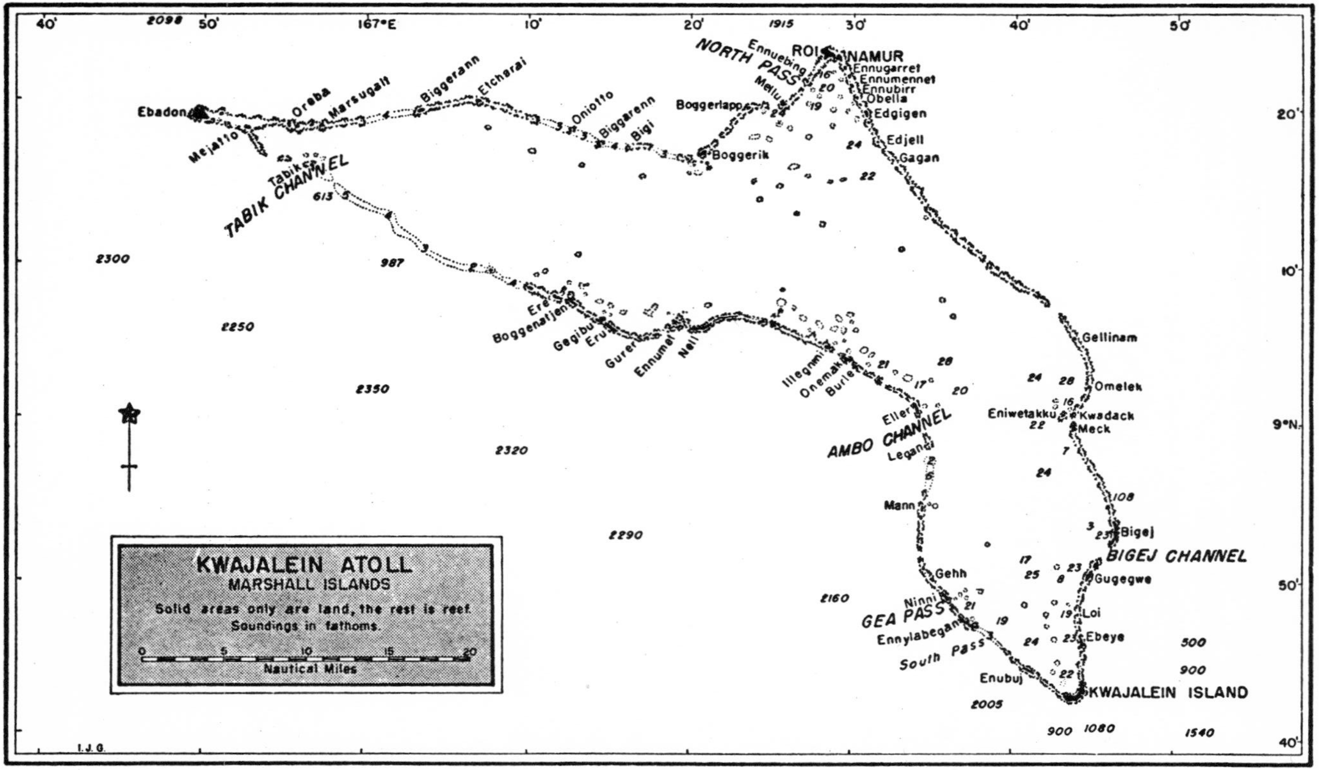
KWAJALEIN ATOLL
MARSHALL ISLANDS
Solid areas only are land, the rest is reef.
Soundings in fathoms.
0 5 10 15 20
Nautical Miles
ROI
NAMUR
NORTH PASS
TABIK CHANNEL
AMBO CHANNEL
GEA PASS
South Pass
BIGEJ CHANNEL
KWAJALEIN ISLAND
Ebadon
Mejatto
Oreba
Marsugalt
Biggerann
Etcharai
Oniotto
Biggarenn
Bigi
Boggerlapp
Boggerik
Mellu
Ennuebing
Ennugarret
Ennumennet
Ennubirr
Obella
Edgigen
Edjell
Gagan
Tabikes
Eres
Boggenatjen
Gegibu
Eru
Gurer
Ennumel
Nell
Illegmi
Onemak
Burle
Eller
Legan
Mann
Gehh
Ninni
Ennylabegan
Enubuj
Gellinam
Omelek
Eniwetakku
Kwadack
Meck
Bigej
Gugegwe
Loi
Ebeye
167°E
9°N.
I. J. G.

lands, Roi and Namur, within whose small area, a mile and a quarter long and three quarters wide, the Japanese had 3500 troops and an airfield. This pair was the objective of Admiral Conolly's Northern Force. Since it was impractical to make a surf landing on the outer coast, it was necessary to boat the assault troops outside, where the atoll made some sort of lee, and bring them into the lagoon through narrow passes which fortunately the enemy had neglected to fortify. But the landing plan had to be so fussy and complicated that plenty of things went wrong. Every foul-up was finally straightened out and every D-day (31 January) objective attained shortly before nightfall. Casualties amounted to 24 dead and missing and 40 wounded.

Then the real agony began. Three days' preliminary air bombing and naval bombardment (this at such close range that the admiral got the nickname "Close-in Conolly") were not enough to pulverize the Roi-Namur rectangle, although a vast amount of damage was done and possibly half the Japanese defenders killed. The rest had to be rooted out, man by man. Roi was secured by the evening of 1 February; Namur next day. It was a stinking mess of debris and dead Japanese. Hardly a tree was left alive in what had been a pretty wooded island, and of the hundred or more buildings not one was usable.

A dismal prospect met the garrison group when it steamed into the lagoon a few days later to relieve the 4th Division. All air protection was removed when the carriers retired, and the particular Seabee outfit sent in with the garrison was so lazy and inefficient that by 12 February the runways were not yet ready to receive planes. That day, these islands received a stinging backlash from the Japanese. A flight of several 4-engined bombers from Saipan, staged through Ponape, hit Roi-Namur and with its bombs touched off an ammunition dump whose explosion killed many Marines and destroyed immense quantities of food and equipment.

The southern attack, on boomerang-shaped Kwajalein Island,

was characterized by a large contingent of LVTs and dukws, and by perfect coöperation between Army and Navy. Here, too, D-day (31 January) was devoted to securing islets adjacent to the objective and basing artillery thereon for the main assault. Admiral Turner, first to admit that Tarawa had not been bombarded long enough or well enough, was determined that this island should be properly pulverized. To execute this worthy object, he started it with four battleships, three heavy cruisers, eleven destroyers and three escort carriers, on 30 January. He continued it all next day and on D-day, 1 February, from 0618 to 0840 and from 0905 to H-hour 0930. And a drop of 2000-pound bombs, flown up from Tarawa, was thrown in.

A well-executed amphibious assault is as beautiful a military spectacle as one can find in warfare, and this one was superbly done in a setting of deep blue white-capped sea, fluffy tradewind clouds, flashing gunfire and billowing smoke over the target, gaily colored flag hoists at the yardarms of the ships and on the signal halyards of the control craft. At 0928 all four LVT waves were approaching the beach in line, not one of the 84 amphtracs falling behind more than a couple of lengths, their cupped tracks churning the blue water into curling sheepskins of white foam, their square bows throwing spray until everyone on board was drenched, but nobody cared. This was what the 7th Division had come for, to kill more of those you-know-what who had cost them so many buddies on Attu. LCI gunboats were flashing and crackling; battleships off shore were booming and belching huge gobs of orange-tinted smoke, and on the island palm trees and parts of buildings were rising in the air.

First wave hit the beaches right at H-hour — 0930. Within twelve minutes, 1200 officers and men had landed without a single casualty. But the Japanese were not wiped out; Rear Admiral Akiyama, the island commander, had prepared his defenses well, and at least half of his more than 5000 troops were still alive.

In the center was a complex of trenches, antitank traps, pillboxes, blockhouses and air-raid shelters, and here the invading infantrymen ran into trouble. The island had to be taken inch by inch, and was not secured until the morning of 5 February. Except for about 35 men, who surrendered, the garrison was annihilated. It only remained, in this southern sector of the bit atoll, to take Ebeye, where there was a garrison of 400, and a few lesser islets.

By 7 February Kwajalein Atoll was entirely American. One of the most complicated amphibious campaigns in history, involving landings on 30 different islets, fights on at least ten, and bloody battles on three, had come to a successful conclusion within a week. The price was far less than had been paid for the Gilberts. The Navy suffered negligible casualties. Out of 41,000 troops committed, 372 soldiers and Marines died on this atoll; on the Japanese side, 7870 men out of 8675 were wiped out.

4. *Truk Bombed, Eniwetok Taken, February 1944*

With Kwajalein in the bag, flag officers and generals turned their attention to Eniwetok Atoll. Admiral Spruance asked Nimitz to let him push right on to this western outpost to the Marshalls, 326 miles WNW of Roi, and only 1000 miles from the Marianas. The very name Eniwetok, meaning "Land between West and East," suggests strategic importance. For the primitive Micronesians it had been a place of call and refreshment in their long canoe voyages from west to east; now it would become an important staging point for the United States Army, Navy and Marine Corps in their spectacular progress from east to west.

Spruance had his wish, and detailed planning began on board Turner's command ship *Rocky Mount* on 14 February. Captain D. W. Loomis's Reserve Force, waiting at Majuro Lagoon, was already tagged for CATCHPOLE — code name for the Eniwetok operation — and Admiral Hill eagerly assumed the top command. But the destructive attack of 12 February on Roi-Namur by Japanese long-range bombers from Saipan, staged through Ponape, proved that this island, and Truk, needed attention before Eniwetok could be captured. Liberators of General Willis Hale's VII Army Air Force, based at Tarawa, pounded Ponape between 15 and 26 February, to such good purpose that there could be no interference thence. And on Eniwetok D-day (17 February) the fast carrier forces began a two-day visit to Truk which rendered this "Gibraltar of the Pacific" little more use to Japan, and unnecessary for us to capture.

An Airsols reconnaissance plane on 4 February found a good part of Combined Fleet in Truk Lagoon, but Admiral Koga got most of his ships out in time. Light cruiser *Agano*, however, was sunk by U.S. submarine *Skate* (Lieutenant Commander W. F. Gruner) as she sortied. Mitscher's fliers found some 50 merchant ships in the lagoon and 365 aircraft on the airfields when they jumped the atoll at dawn 17 February. Their first strike of 72 fighters, followed by 18 Avengers dropping incendiaries, left fewer than 100 Japanese planes operational. In the meantime Mitscher's dive-bombers were merrily knocking off ships in the lagoon. That evening the enemy got off his one and only counterattack, and managed to make a hit on carrier *Intrepid*, whose propensity to collect Japanese bombs and torpedoes earned her a nickname, "The Evil I."

In the meantime, Admiral Spruance in battleship *New Jersey* was conducting a round-the-atoll cruise with *Iowa*, two heavy cruisers and four destroyers, to catch escaping ships. They sank light cruiser *Katori* and destroyer *Maikaze;* but destroyer *Nowaki*, straddled by the battlewagons' 16-inch salvos at ranges between 17 and 20 miles, managed to escape unhurt, and even launched a spread of torpedoes. That night Mitscher started bombing with specially equipped Avengers. Flight operations were resumed by *Enterprise*, *Yorktown*, *Essex* and *Bunker Hill* at dawn 18 February; and by noon, when Mitscher decided to pick up and retire, his aviators had destroyed 200,000 tons of merchant shipping, two destroyers and some 275 planes.

This two-days-and-one-night raid on Truk was one of the most successful of the war. For the first time a major enemy base was beaten down without the aid of land-based air power or an amphibious invasion. Truk was still usable for planes, and the buildings were not too badly damaged, but it had become as vulnerable to the Japanese as Pearl Harbor had been to the Pacific Fleet on 7 December 1941. Never again would the eight-rayed flag of C. in C. Combined Fleet meet the rising sun in Truk Lagoon.

The capture of Eniwetok could now proceed without interference from a single enemy plane. The landings at Engebi Island in the north on 17 February by the 22nd Marine Regiment (Brigadier General T. E. Watson USMC) were similar in character to those at Roi-Namur, and even more complicated. The thousand or more Japanese defenders were rendered punch-drunk by the preliminary bombardment and offered comparatively light resistance. Engebi was ours by 1640 February 18, at the cost of 85 Marines killed. But the southern operations against Parry and Eniwetok Islands turned up a number of surprises. The Japanese neatly fooled the invaders into believing that these islands were unoccupied. They had concealed themselves and their weapons from photo interpreters of the Pacific Fleet, and from the eyes of Admiral Hill's lookouts when his ships passed only a biscuit-toss from Parry to enter the lagoon. An Intelligence team, combing through the debris on Engebi, found papers indicating that Eniwetok and Parry Islands were actually defended by 2155 men of Major General Nishida's 1st Amphibious Brigade, a veteran unit of the toughest fighters bred in Japan. Faced with this situation, General Wat-

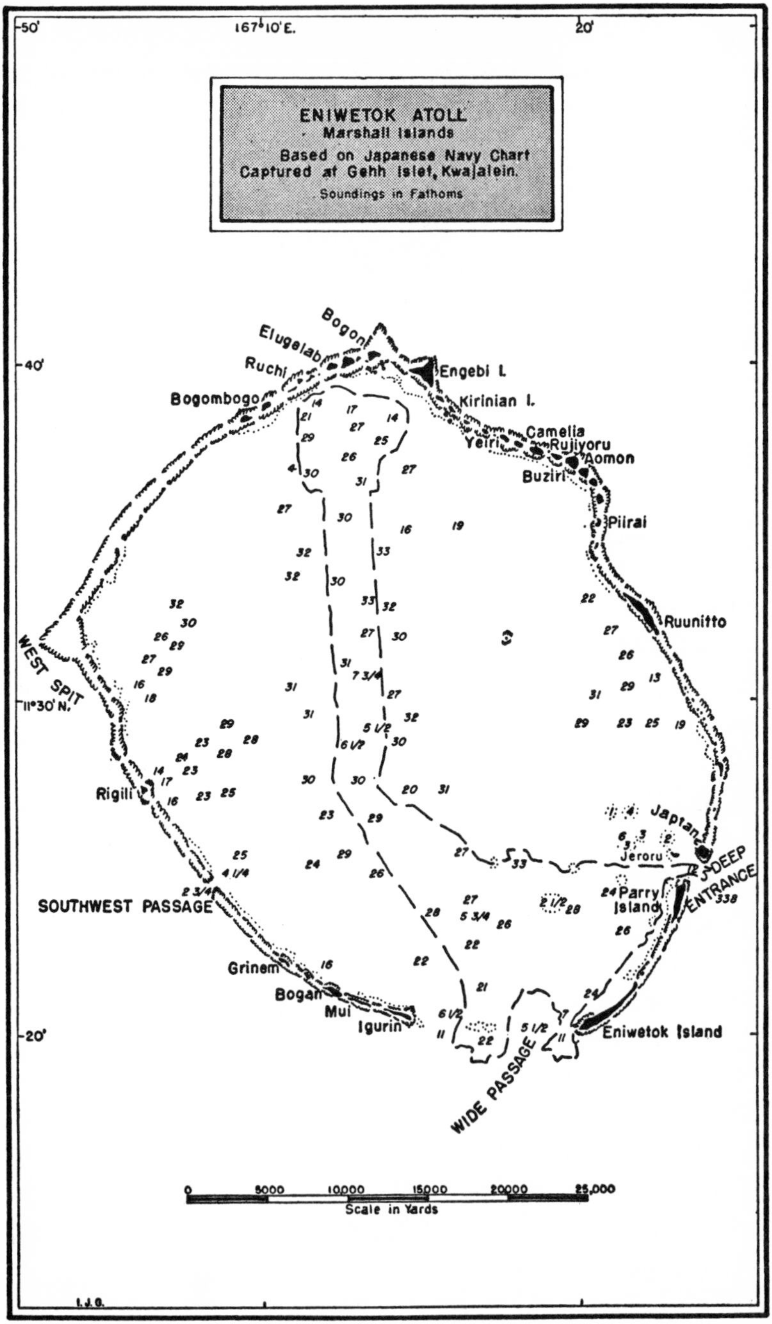
ENIWETOK ATOLL
Marshall Islands
Based on Japanese Navy Chart
Captured at Gehh Islet, Kwajalein.
Soundings in Fathoms
50'
167° 10' E.
20'
40'
11° 30' N.
20'
Bogon
Elugelab
Ruchi
Bogombogo
Engebi I.
Kirinian I.
Camelia
Yeiri
Rujiyoru
Aomon
Buziri
Piirai
Ruunitto
WEST SPIT
Rigili
Japtan
Jeroru
DEEP ENTRANCE
Parry Island
SOUTHWEST PASSAGE
Grinem
Bogan
Mui
Igurin
Eniwetok Island
WIDE PASSAGE
0
5000
10,000
15000
20000
25,000
Scale in Yards
I. J. G.

son brought all possible strength to bear upon each island in succession. He decided to throw both battalions of the 106th Infantry Regiment into Eniwetok Island, southernmost of the atoll, together with a Marine reserve battalion brought down from Engebi. Eniwetok Island was not secured until 1630 February 21. It cost only 37 American lives and 94 wounded; the Japanese garrison of about 800 men, except for 23 taken prisoner, was annihilated.

Gunfire support ships had plenty of time to pound Parry Island north of Eniwetok, fortunately, since 1350 hidey-hole Japanese were there. When the Marine Corps landings began at 0900 February 22 the enemy was still full of fight, and his emplacements were so well concealed as to be difficult to spot even a few feet away. Assault troops pushed rapidly forward behind tanks, with demolition and flame-thrower parties directly behind to burn out each enemy nest. But the terrain was studded with mines which detonated on 35 pounds' pressure and tore men apart horribly, blowing their bodies to bits. In the afternoon, in skirmish line, the Marines pushed on to their final goal, the southern end where the enemy was in the open. "Finally we killed them all," wrote Lieutenant Cord Meyer. "There was not much jubilation. We just sat and stared at the sand, and most of us thought of those who were gone — those whom I shall remember as always young, smiling and graceful, and I shall try to forget how they looked at the end, beyond all recognition."

It was one of those many, many times in the war when you had time to stop and think about it, and wonder why mankind is not wise enough to end this senseless suffering and slaughter.

Eniwetok Atoll was secured, at a cost of 339 Americans killed and missing, and 2677 Japanese. Four atolls of the Marshalls group where the enemy had air bases — Jaluit, Mili, Maloelap, Wotje — and Nauru, too, had been bypassed; but it was easy to keep them isolated until the war's end. In addition there were some fifty atolls where only a handful of Japanese, or none, were living; the now famous Bikini, for instance, was occupied by a detachment of Marines in one landing craft after the garrison of five Japanese had committed suicide.

Looking back, Admiral Dick Conolly said: "The Marshalls really cracked the Japanese shell. It broke the crust of their defenses on a scale that could be exploited at once. It gave them no time adequately to fortify their inner defense line that ran through the Marianas." Operations CATCHPOLE and FLINTLOCK and the strikes on Truk enhanced the reputation of the United States Navy. Courage and determination it had shown from the first; but in the Marshalls it demonstrated mastery of the art of amphibious warfare; of combining air, surface, submarine and ground forces to project fighting power irresistibly across the ocean.

CHAPTER XI

New Guinea and the Marianas

April–August 1944

1. *The Conquest of New Guinea*

WHILE SPRUANCE'S FIFTH FLEET and Turner's V 'Phib Force were crashing through the Central Pacific to Eniwetok, Kinkaid's Seventh Fleet and Barbey's VII 'Phib were making equally spectacular leaps along New Guinea. These were shore-to-shore operations, performed largely in the three leading types of beaching craft — LST, LCT and LCI, of which MacArthur never had enough. The last two types, the 114-foot Landing Craft Tank and the 173-foot Landing Craft Infantry, had to perform long hauls and house crews for months on end in compartments designed for a night run across the English Channel. Fast converted destroyer-transports were also used. The covering forces were meager compared with the array of powerful gunfire ships disposed of by Spruance. Rear Admiral Crutchley RN had two heavy cruisers (H.M.A.S. *Australia*, flag) and a few destroyers; Rear Admiral Berkey had three light cruisers (*Phoenix*, flag) and a few more destroyers. Seventh Fleet had four squadrons of amphibious Catalinas, each with its tender; but for air support it depended mainly on General Kenney's Southwest Pacific Air Force, with its many bases and ample strength on New Guinea. Under MacArthur, Generals Eichelberger and Krueger were in command of the ground operations.

We left the Southwest Pacific forces at Manus in the Admiralties in March 1944, after finally breaching the Bismarck Barrier and sealing off Rabaul. General MacArthur's next plan was to leapfrog the strong Japanese garrison at Wewak into Hollandia, and set up new advance headquarters there. Some 215 vessels, mostly beaching craft, were divided into three attack groups, commanded by Rear Admiral Barbey, Rear Admiral Fechteler, and Captain A. G. Noble, each in a destroyer — no luxurious amphibious command ships here. But each attack group had an LSD to bring preboated tanks to the targets.

By this time, it had become clear that the success of an amphibious operation depended in great measure on preliminary pounding of enemy air power at the target. By the end of March the Japanese had assembled 351 aircraft on the airfields about Hollandia. On the 30th and on 3, 5, and 12 April, General Kenney made massive air attacks, which almost completely knocked out Hollandia as an enemy air base; carrier aircraft added frosting to the cake on 21 April. For General MacArthur had obtained an order that Mitscher's flattops must support him at Hollandia. It turned out the help was not needed. Not one enemy plane rose from the five target fields to intercept the carrier-borne bombers.

The Hollandia operation was perfectly planned and smoothly executed. D-day was 22 April, and by 3 May the Japanese airfields at Lake Sentani in the hills above the town were in our possession.

Supreme Allied Commander Southwest Pacific needed no urging to push his westward advance rapidly along the New Guinea coast. General MacArthur had already outlined to his planning staff a series of assaults, all pointing toward Mindanao, target date 15 November. Four operations — Wakde, Biak, Noemfoor and Sansapor — carried him and his forces to the northwest point of New Guinea's Vogelkop, 550 miles west of Hollandia, in a little more than three months. Seventh Fleet handled the highly important seaborne aspects of this advance, since the ocean was the only possible road. Motor torpedo boat squadrons, as eager as the Army Air Force to secure forward bases, also took part in this breathless race.

Before the next operation came off — an invasion of the Wakde-Sarmi area on 17 May — the disquieting discovery had been made that heavy bombers could not use the Lake Sentani airfields, and that no site suitable for them existed in Dutch New Guinea, short of Biak Island. Hence, until Biak could be taken, the heavies would have to continue operating from Nadzab, 440 miles east of Hollandia, or from the Admiralties. The need for full speed ahead being evident, General MacArthur decided to simplify the Wakde-Sarmi operation and move on into Biak as soon as possible. Rear Admiral Fechteler, who commanded VII 'Phib in Admiral Barbey's absence, promised to assault Biak ten days after Wakde, which was taken by Captain Noble's group of VII 'Phib and the 163rd RCT, Brigadier General Jens Doe, after two days' fighting, on 19 May. Army engineers had made the airstrip operational even for Liberators. But it was a long, tough job for the Army to capture the adjacent mainland.

Biak is one of the Schouten Islands that close in Geelvink Bay, at the neck of the New Guinea bird. The occupation of this big, reef-fringed island started on 27 May. The landing force under Major General Horace F. Fuller USA and VII 'Phib under Admiral Fechteler were fortunate to get away with it, since the 10,000 Japanese defenders were amost as numerous as the attacking force and were not surprised. Colonel Kuzume, their commander, denied to us for a month the two Biak airfields within ten miles of the landing beaches by a skillful defense in depth — tactics later developed at Peleliu and Iwo Jima.

The Japanese Navy here tried to interfere with an amphibious operation for the first time since Bougainville. Admiral Toyoda[1]

[1] Admiral Koga, Yamamoto's successor as Commander in Chief Combined Fleet, was killed in an airplane accident around 1 April, and was succeeded by Admiral Soemu Toyoda, a much more aggressive character.

realized that heavy bombers based at Biak would be a handicap to his plan for a big naval battle in mid-1944—a plan of which we shall hear more shortly. He therefore decided to transport 2500 amphibious troops from Mindanao to Biak. Three attempts were made by a reinforcement echelon of destroyers under Rear Admiral Sakonju, who was no Tanaka. Once he was turned back by a false report of an aircraft carrier, and on 8 June he was chased off by Crutchley's cruiser-destroyer force. Toyoda now assembled a really powerful striking force, built around superbattleships *Yamato* and *Musashi*, which should have been able to sink anything in Seventh Fleet. Three days before it was to head for Biak, C. in C. Combined Fleet decided, correctly, that Spruance's Fifth Fleet was about to land in the Marianas, and pulled all naval forces north into the Philippine Sea.

Colonel Kuzume's stubborn but hopeless defense of Biak continued until 22 June. The capture of this island cost Allied ground forces 438 killed, 2300 battle wounded, and 3500 cases of typhus. It became an important air base in subsequent operations for the liberation of the Philippines.

When Biak was proving difficult, General MacArthur's planners began looking for airfield sites on the Vogelkop, the head of the New Guinea bird. They first pitched upon the almost circular island of Noemfoor, about eleven miles in diameter, midway between Biak and Manokwari. A task force was hurriedly assembled, a naval bombardment delivered on the morning of 2 July, and the landing made that afternoon. An important component of the assault force was boated in LCMs, the 50-foot open Landing Craft Mechanized, manned by amphibious Army engineers; it took them 12 days to make the 700-mile passage from Finschhafen.

To complete his control of New Guinea and prepare for the invasion of Mindanao, MacArthur wanted one more air base on the Vogelkop. This was obtained at Sansapor on 30 July by Admiral Fechteler, commanding 16 destroyer types and numerous beaching craft, mounted at Wakde. There was no opposition. Sansapor was MacArthur's last stop in New Guinea on his long return journey to the Philippines.

This advance of 550 miles from Hollandia to Cape Sansapor required little more than three months, with three big Japanese air bases —Hollandia, Wakde, Biak — picked up en route, and a fourth, Wewak, leapfrogged. Expert planning and a high order of teamwork between Army, Navy and Air Forces of the United States and Australia produced these results; but it is questionable whether they could have been attained under any other commander but Douglas MacArthur. Everyone who served under him, in whatever arm of the service or from whatever country, acquired a great respect for his military judgment and leadership. We have seen how smartly his operations were executed, on or very close to the target dates set, with few of the snarls usual in military affairs. We shall now leave him consolidating his positions and preparing for his heart's desire — his return to the Phillippines — while we shift our attention to great doings around the Marianas and in the broad reaches of the Philippine Sea.

2. *The Marianas (Operation* FORAGER*), February–June 1944*

The fifteen Mariana or Ladrone Islands stretch for some 425 miles in an arc, of which the 145th meridian east longitude is the chord. Starting with Farallon de Pájaros, 335 miles southeast of Iwo Jima, and ending with Guam, 250 miles north of the Carolines, this chain forms with the Bonins the upright bar of the big Micronesian "L," the foot of which is the Carolines and Marshalls. The four biggest Marianas — Saipan, Tinian, Rota and Guam, all at the southernmost end — are those with which we are concerned; only they had any military or economic value.

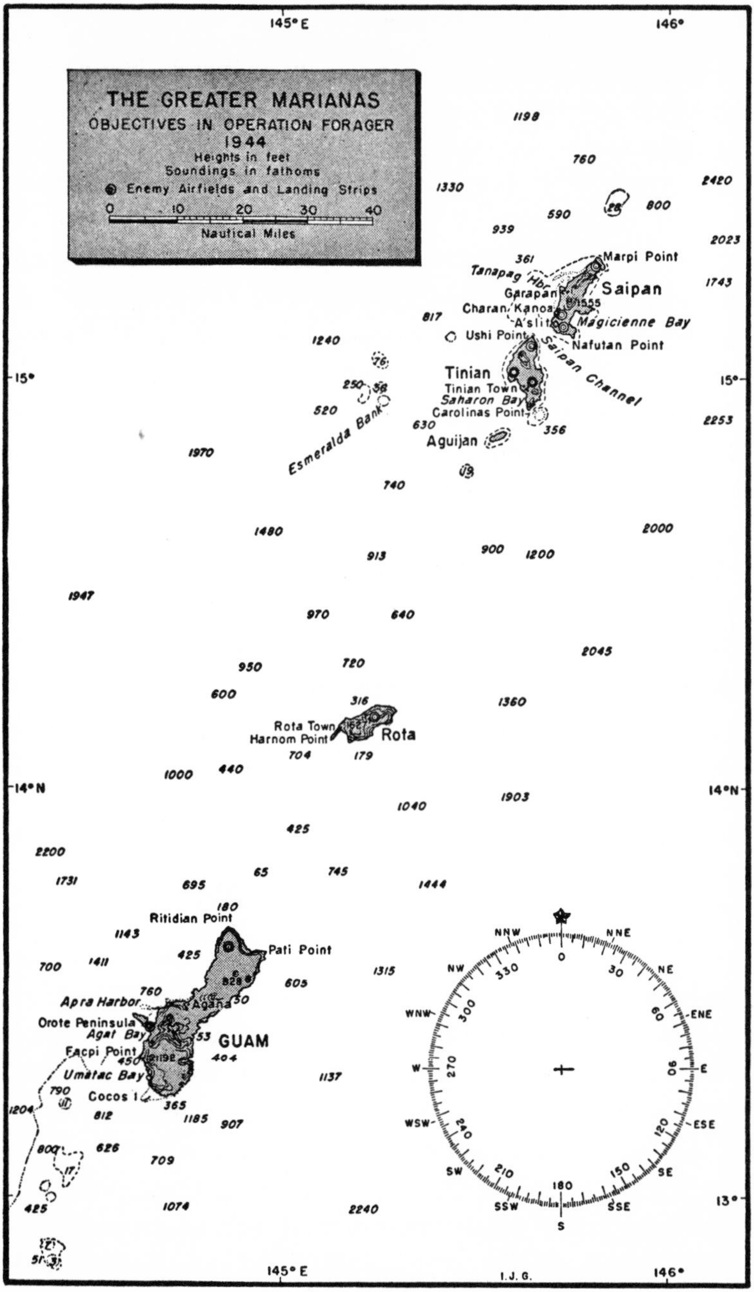
THE GREATER MARIANAS
OBJECTIVES IN OPERATION FORAGER
1944
Heights in feet
Soundings in fathoms
Enemy Airfields and Landing Strips
0 10 20 30 40
Nautical Miles
145° E
146°
15°
14° N
13°
Saipan
Marpi Point
Tanapag Hbr
Garapan
Charan Kanoa
A'slito
Magicienne Bay
Nafutan Point
Ushi Point
Saipan Channel
Tinian
Tinian Town
Saharon Bay
Carolinas Point
Aguijan
Esmeralda Bank
Rota
Rota Town
Harnom Point
GUAM
Ritidian Point
Pati Point
Apra Harbor
Agana
Orote Peninsula
Agat Bay
Facpi Point
Umatac Bay
Cocos I
I. J. G.

On 23 February 1944, five days after the big strike on Truk, planes from Admiral Mitscher's carriers dropped the first American bombs on the Marianas. Cincpac ordered this raid mainly to obtain photographic intelligence, no Allied plane having flown over these islands since the fall of Guam in December 1941. Pacific Fleet submarines were stationed around them to shoot surface game flushed by aircraft. Several ships sailed right into the periscope sights of *Sunfish* (Lieutenant Commander E. E. Shelby), which sank two *Marus* before and after daybreak on the 23rd. *Tang* (Lieutenant Commander R. H. O'Kane) sank four, in as many days; and the total bag of shipping, including those sunk by carrier planes, came to about 45,000 tons.

The decision to place Saipan, Tinian, and Guam next on the program of conquest after the Marshalls, with target date 15 June, was not made by the Joint Chiefs of Staff until 12 March 1944. It was high time for a decision. The Pacific Fleet had become immensely powerful in every type of combatant ship and auxiliary, and was ready to deal another hard blow to the Japanese Empire. Most American ground forces had been allotted to the great invasion of Europe, but three Marine and two Army divisions in the Pacific were ready to take part in a major amphibious operation that summer.

This was to be Vice Admiral R. Kelly Turner's fifth major amphibious operation. Schooled by adversity at Guadalcanal and Tarawa, he was not spoiled by success in the Marshalls. He had learned more about this specialized branch of warfare than anyone else ever had, or probably ever would. He supervised every detail himself; and there were plenty, because in an amphibious operation nothing can be left to chance, and perfect timing is the essence of success. Energetic, quick and nervous, Turner was apt to be abrupt to junior officers who came to him with new suggestions, then to think them over carefully and incorporate them in his next draft plan. For all his rugged personality and rough tongue, "Kelly" had a keen intellect and complete intellectual honesty. He drafted the concept, dated 4 April, on which Operation FORAGER was based: "The objective is the capture of Saipan, Tinian and Guam, in order to secure control of sea communications through the Central Pacific for the support of further attacks on the Japanese."

No amphibious operation on so vast a scale, with a final thousand-mile "hop," had before been planned, although Operation TORCH was a close approximation. Inherent difficulties peculiar to amphibious warfare were enhanced by the distance of the Marianas from any Allied continental base, and by the operation's size. Some 535 combatant ships and auxiliaries carried 127,571 troops, of which over two thirds were Marines. The destination lay 1000 miles' steaming from Eniwetok, the nearest advanced base, which was little more than an anchorage, and 3500 miles from Pearl Harbor. Logistics problems alone would have condemned this operation as impossible in 1941, for the distance meant that the entire expeditionary force had to be afloat at the same time, and that the ships allotted could do nothing else for at least three months.

It is difficult to change logistic plans for a series of naval offensives after the procession of shipborne supplies has started. The flow may be slowed down or diverted to alternate harbors and warehouses if available, but it cannot be reversed without immense confusion and waste. Operations of the magnitude and complexity of FORAGER and its successors were so new to American (or to any) logistics planners that few were capable of planning beyond the assault phase.[2] Fortunately, Admiral Spruance, Commander Fifth Fleet, was one of these few. He understood that

[2] The planning for OVERLORD (Normandy) may be cited to the contrary. But a cross-Channel operation, under various names, had been in the planning stage since early 1942, whilst Nimitz received his directive for FORAGER only three months before its D-day.

FORAGER was but a means to a further end; and he saw to it that his and Turner's plans for the assault were coördinated with those for base development in the Marianas. In this he had the intelligent coöperation of Vice Admiral William L. Calhoun, Commander Service Force Pacific Fleet, and his subordinates, Commodores W. R. Carter of the floating service force and Augustine Gray, "the oil king of the Pacific."

While the Joint Expeditionary Force was at sea, the Pacific Fleet was being reorganized, to accelerate the tempo of the Pacific war. The old South Pacific command was maintained at Nouméa, now a rear base, but Admiral Halsey was placed under Nimitz, with the title Commander Third Fleet, in the same echelon as Admiral Spruance. Thus, the Pacific Fleet command was divided into two teams, the first Spruance's and the second Halsey's. One would plan and train while the other fought, reducing time between operations. Vice Admiral Mitscher's Fast Carrier Force, designated TF 58 when under Spruance's command, and TF 38 when under Halsey's, operated almost continuously, together with most of the gunfire support ships. As Admiral Nimitz put it, "The team remains about the same, but the drivers change."

To invade Saipan was the greatest challenge that the Allies had yet thrown at Japan. She regarded that island as part of her home land, as well as a link in her inner defense perimeter. Yet, owing to the newly won command of the sea by the Pacific Fleet, Japan was unable to reinforce Saipan after April 1944. General Saito, the Army commander, had only 22,700 troops under him when the Americans landed. Admiral Nagumo, who had lost his carriers at Midway, was also on Saipan in command of a small-craft fleet and about 6700 sailors. We have Pacific Fleet submarines to thank for Saito's lack of reinforcement; one Japanese regiment lost all its weapons and ammunition and most of its men when several ships of the convoy lifting it to Saipan were sunk by *Shark*, *Pintado* and *Pilotfish*.

From 11 June Admiral Mitscher's four fast carrier groups carried the ball with heavy bombing attacks on the Marianas airfields. Seven new battleships under Admiral Lee's command were detached from Mitscher's TF 58 on 13 June to bombard Saipan. But this shore bombardment was a failure; the new battlewagons simply did not know how to do it. Next day, the old "Pearl Harbor survivors" did much better, and under their cover the Underwater Demolition Teams of "frogmen" charted channels through the lagoon that bordered the beaches on the leeward coast of Saipan. There were no boat mines or other obstacles such as those that did so much damage on the Omaha beaches in Normandy — the reason being that the Japanese never expected to defend anything, only to conquer, so they were not prepared with defensive matériel other than coast defense guns.

3. *Saipan Invaded, June 1944*

We have now reached Saipan D-day, 15 June. At 0542 Admiral Turner made the signal: "Land the Landing Force." Chaplains offered a last prayer and a blessing — over loud-speakers. Amphtracs laden with troops, taken on board at Eniwetok, poured from the maws of the LSTs. From the big transports other Marines crawled down landing nets into boats. Those who gazed at the shoreline through binoculars could see a narrow beach backed by sandy soil and low scrubby trees, with an occasional palm grove or flame tree blooming with vermillion flowers. The land rose in a series of low escarpments like steps, and Mount Tapotchau dominated the scene. It was not in the least like anything the Marines had assaulted before.

The landings took place on a two-division front on eight beaches, almost four miles long. The line of departure was established 4000 yards off shore, and fifteen hundred yards to seaward were stationed 64 LSTs with the assault troops. Twenty-four gunboats preceded the initial wave to deliver close 40-mm fire support. As the long waves of amphtracs, each trailing a plume of white spray, raced with their supporters toward the beaches, the fire support battleships, cruisers and destroyers, anchored only 1250 yards off shore, delivered frontal and enfilading fire on beach defenses. And as the amphtracs began crawling over the barrier reef, 72 planes from escort carriers, including 12 Avengers armed with rockets, came down in vicious, hawklike swoops to strafe the beaches and the area just behind, the rockets making a sound like the crack of a gigantic whiplash.

At 0844 the initial wave touched down and at once came under intense fire, but pressed resolutely on. Within eight minutes there were troops on every beach, and some were fighting their way across the Charan Kanoa airstrip. As the second wave came in, around 0857, amphtracs of the first were beginning to retract, passing through the second, third and fourth waves with expert helmsmanship. Among these 600 and more LVTs and landing craft, tearing to and fro for the space of two hours, there was not a single serious collision, so well had the training center done its work, and so expertly did Commodore Theiss and his 50 control craft direct the movement. Despite all hazards, 8000 Marines got ashore in the first 20 minutes; and all day long, and after dark, landing craft were plying furiously between the transports and the beaches.

Little, however, went according to plan after the troops were ashore. The reason for landing on so broad a front was to seize a big enough beachhead to allow deployment. Subsequent waves were to mop up behind the first, dig in for the night, next day capture the airfield and strike cross-island to Magicienne Bay. Saipan would be "in the bag," and the assault on Guam could start. But it did not work out that way. The No. 1 objective line was not reached for three days, nor Saipan secured for three weeks, and the assault on Guam had to be delayed until 21 July.

The main reason for this miscarriage was the skill of Japanese artillery and mortar fire, which prevented amphtracs from fulfilling their assignment to carry troops well inland, and forced most of them to disgorge their passengers near the water's edge. By nightfall, although 20,000 assault troops had been landed, one tenth of them were casualties, and only half of the planned beachhead had been occupied.

Unhappy hours lay ahead for the Marines. There is something particularly terrifying about the first night on a hostile beach, when you are the underdog. The Japanese saw to it that nobody slept for more than a few minutes. After a series of probes, their big effort was announced at 0300 June 16 by a bugler; and with much screaming, brandishing of swords and flapping of flags the enemy launched an attack that was supposed to drive the Marines into the sea. As the Japanese fell others replaced them, and the fighting on this flank did not reach its climax until sunrise, at 0545. Five Marine Corps tanks then stopped the last attack, and the Japanese withdrew under a blanket of gunfire from cruiser *Louisville* and destroyers *Phelps* and *Monssen*, leaving about 700 dead on the battlefield. Dawn came none too soon for the Marines — but it found them still there.

This was General Saito's last chance to "destroy the enemy at the beachhead." But he was far from downhearted, since he had been assured that an irresistible fleet was about to bring him succor. Unfortunately for him, Fifth Fleet had the same warning.

On D-day Admiral Spruance received word from submarine *Flying Fish* that a Japanese carrier force was heading in his direction from San Bernardino Strait; and at 0400 June 16 he received submarine *Seahorse*'s contact report on a second Japanese force, steaming north off Surigao Strait. Rightly assuming that these ships meant business, Spruance promptly canceled the 18 June date for landing on Guam and went on board Turner's flagship to confer with him and General Holland Smith. There, the decision was made to commit at once the reserve (the 27th Infantry Division) to Saipan, to detach certain cruisers and destroyers from the fire support ships to augment the fast carriers' screen, to continue unloading until dark 17 June, and then to send the transports safely eastward until the anticipated naval battle was over.

4. *Preparations for a Decisive Naval Battle*

While the forces under Nimitz, Halsey and MacArthur were advancing in the Central, South and Southwest Pacific, the Japanese Combined Fleet was swinging around the hook — either in Truk Lagoon, or at Lingga Roads off Singapore, or in the Inland Sea of Japan.

The explanation of this inactivity lay in America's vastly increased air power, while Japan was in the sad position of having a carrier fleet with no planes, having sacrificed them in the fruitless defense of Rabaul. But by the spring of 1944 new air groups were at least partially trained, and Admiral Toyoda felt strong enough to resume Yamamoto's strategy of annihilating the United States Pacific Fleet in one decisive battle. The right person was chosen to do that, if it could be done — Vice Admiral Jisaburo Ozawa. After relieving Admiral Nagumo in command of the carrier striking force in November 1943, Ozawa also became C. in C. First Mobile Fleet, which comprised at least 90 per cent of the surface part of the Japanese Navy. He was an officer with a scientific brain as well as a seaman's innate sense of what can be accomplished with ships; a worthy antagonist to Mitscher and Spruance.

On 3 May his immediate superior, Admiral Toyoda, issued preliminary orders for Operation A-GO, to annihilate Spruance. The intended victim was to be "lured" into waters between the Palaus,

Yap and Woleai, where both land-based and carrier-based planes could slaughter him. But in any event Fifth Fleet must be attacked.

Ozawa's six carriers, five battleships, seven heavy cruisers, 34 destroyers and six oilers rendezvoused at Tawi Tawi, westernmost island of the Sulu Archipelago, on 16 May. In that open roadstead they were snooped by submarines *Bonefish* and *Puffer*, and the latter sank two of Japan's dwindling tanker fleet. Submarine *Harder* (Commander S. D. Dealey) did even better, sinking three destroyers between 3 and 8 June. This was the first installment of the contribution by United States submarines to the forthcoming battle. The second was their two above-mentioned contact reports on Ozawa, which caused Admiral Spruance to postpone the invasion of Guam and prepare to give battle. These sightings were indeed vital, because even our Liberators' 1100-mile air searches from Manus failed to pick up Ozawa's approach; he was too cagey to pass within their range.

In preparation for the "decisive battle," Japan deployed several hundred land-based naval aircraft in the Marianas and Carolines with orders to sink at least one third of the American carriers before they clashed wth Ozawa's. The achievements of this First Air Fleet were miserably disappointing, and equally so were some 25 Japanese submarines deployed during the Marianas campaign. They gathered no valuable information; they hit not one ship. According to Japanese submarine doctrine, these boats were positioned in May in the "NA" line to bar waters into which the high command expected — and wanted — the American fleet to be "lured." Spruance, as at Midway, did not accommodate his movements to the enemy's wishes. On the contrary, Pacific Fleet found out where the enemy RO-boats were deployed, sent a flock of destroyer escorts to get them, and sank no fewer than 17. Of these, six were sunk in the last twelve days of May by destroyer escort *England* (Lieutenant Commander W. B. Pendleton), one of a hunter-killer group under Commander Hamilton Hains. This ex-

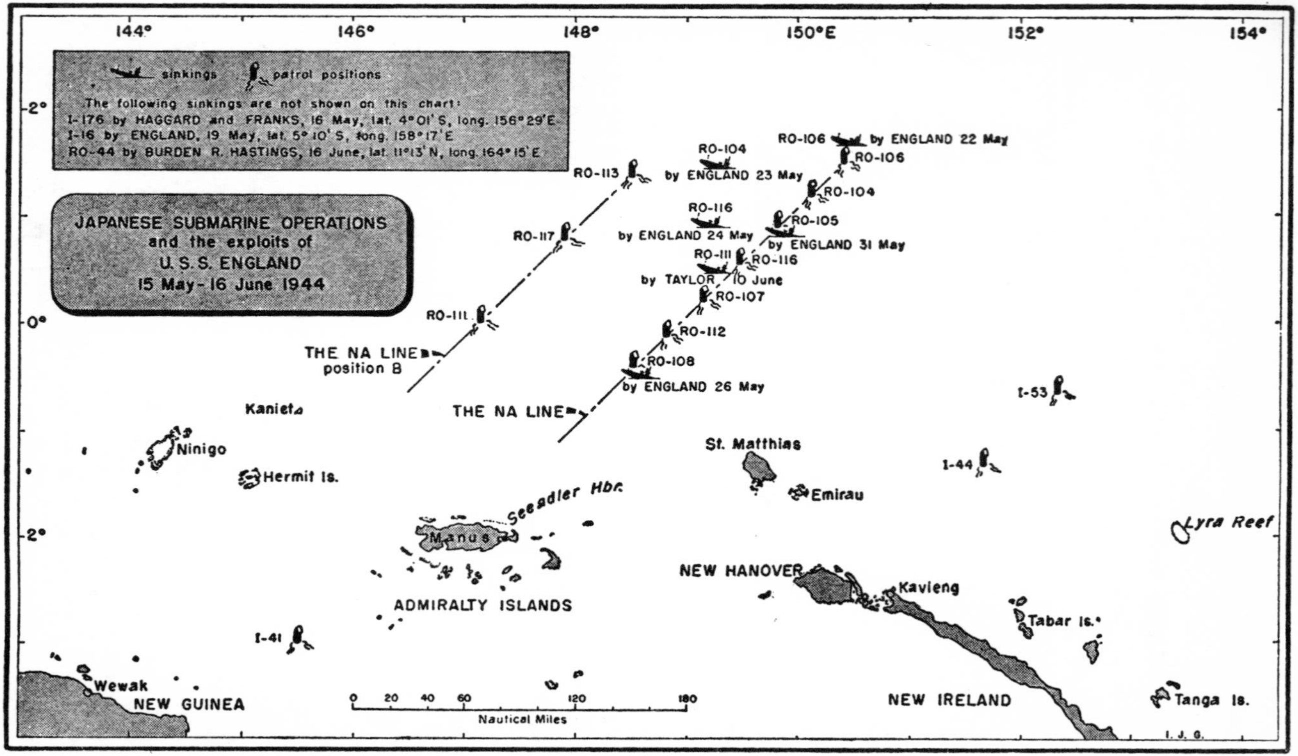
JAPANESE SUBMARINE OPERATIONS
and the exploits of
U. S. S. ENGLAND
15 May - 16 June 1944
sinkings
patrol positions
The following sinkings are not shown on this chart:
I-176 by HAGGARD and FRANKS, 16 May, lat. 4°01'S, long. 156°29'E
I-16 by ENGLAND, 19 May, lat. 5°10'S, long. 158°17'E
RO-44 by BURDEN R. HASTINGS, 16 June, lat. 11°13'N, long. 164°15'E
144°
146°
148°
150°E
152°
154°
2°
0°
2°
RO-106 by ENGLAND 22 May
RO-106
RO-104
by ENGLAND 23 May
RO-113
RO-104
RO-116
by ENGLAND 24 May
RO-105
by ENGLAND 31 May
RO-117
RO-111
RO-116
by TAYLOR, 10 June
RO-107
RO-111
RO-112
RO-108
by ENGLAND 26 May
THE NA LINE
position B
THE NA LINE
Kaniet
Ninigo
Hermit Is.
Manus
Seeadler Hbr.
ADMIRALTY ISLANDS
St. Matthias
Emirau
I-53
I-44
I-41
Lyra Reef
NEW HANOVER
Kavieng
Tabar Is.
NEW IRELAND
Tanga Is.
Wewak
NEW GUINEA
0
20
40
60
120
180
Nautical Miles
I. J. G.

ploit exceeded any of those in the Atlantic that we are about to record in the next chapter.

On 15 June, when Admiral Toyoda got news of the landings on Saipan, he activated Operation A-GO for the decisive battle. No more talk of "luring" the enemy south.

Between 15 and 18 June the two carrier forces were warily feeling for each other. Here is a tabular comparison of them: —

SHIPS

	Fleet Carriers	*Light Carriers*	*Battle-ships*	*Heavy Cruisers*	*Light Cruisers*	*Destroyers*
Japanese	5	4	5	11	2	28
United States	7	8	7	8	13	69

AIRCRAFT STRENGTH

	Fighters	*Dive-bombers*	*Torpedo-bombers*	*Total CVs*	*Float Planes*	*Grand Total*
Japanese	222	113	95	430	43	473
United States	475	232	184	891	65	956

Thus, Ozawa was inferior to Spruance in every naval category except heavy cruisers. But he possessed three tactical advantages that made him confident of victory. First, he intended to give battle within range of his 90 to 100 land-based planes at Guam, Rota and Yap, whilst Spruance could look to no such assistance. Second, Japanese carrier planes, owing to lack of armor and self-sealing fuel tanks, had greater range than the Americans. Ozawa's aircraft could search out to 560 miles, Mitscher's only to 325 or 350; Japanese planes could profitably attack at 300 miles, ours not much beyond 200, although they had to fly 300 on 20 June. And, third, the easterly tradewind gave Ozawa the lee gauge, enabling him to approach his enemy while launching and recovering planes. A further tactical advantage for Japan, of which Ozawa was ignorant, lay in the fact that he had but one objective, to destroy the enemy fleet; whilst Spruance's primary duty was to cover and protect the American invasion of Saipan. That tied him fairly closely to the vicinity of the Marianas.

These tactical advantages for the Japanese were more than offset by the poor training of their aviators. In the United States Navy at that time every naval aviator had two years' training and over 300 hours' flying time before he was considered fit to fly from a carrier, and most of Mitscher's air groups were already veterans. But the air groups of Ozawa's best carrier division had had only six months' training when they left Tawi Tawi; those of Cardiv 3, only three months; and those of Cardiv 2, only two months. Moreover, the month spent at Tawi Tawi before the sortie was wasted, because the fleet lay at anchor to save fuel, and, without an airfield or a moving flattop to practise from, aviators went stale.

Admiral Spruance, victor at Midway, Commander Fifth Fleet since mid-1943, was tried by experience and unspoiled by victory. Modest by nature, he had a prejudice against publicity in any form, and closed up like a clam in the presence of news correspondents. Spruance's leading characteristics were attention to detail, poise, and power of intelligent decision. He envied no man, regarded no one as rival, won the respect of all with whom he came in contact, and went ahead in his quiet way winning victories for his country. Typically, he chose for flagship no big new battleship but twelve-year-old heavy cruiser *Indianapolis*, because she was expendable.

Vice Admiral Mitscher, too, was a simple, unassuming gentleman with a soft voice and quiet manners. He, too, would have avoided publicity if he could; but his slight, wiry figure and leathery, wizened face, usually seen under a long-visored lobsterman's cap, "made copy" in spite of him. A pioneer of naval aviation, Mitscher had, as it were, grown up with the flattop. Since March 1944 he had commanded Fast Carrier Forces Pacific Fleet. He gained devotion and admiration, partly by exceptionally good performance, partly by unusual consideration for his officers and men. Rescue operations for him were as important as battle operations; preservation of aviators' lives as important as risking their lives to attain victory. Admiral Mitscher, in carrier *Lexington*, was in tactical command throughout the Battle of the Philippine Sea; but the major decisions were made, or concurred in, by Admiral Spruance.

Of the four task group commanders under Mitscher, Rear Admiral John W. Reeves, CTG 58.3 (*Enterprise*, flag) was senior. A stern, steady, dependable officer, he could always be counted on to get the most out of his men. Slightly junior to him but of longer aviation experience was Rear Admiral Alfred E. Montgomery, CTG 58.2 (*Bunker Hill*, flag), who had already commanded *Ranger* and an escort carrier division. Next, in *Hornet*, was Rear Admiral Joseph J. ("Jocko") Clark, part Cherokee Indian and part Southern Methodist, but all fighter. A picturesque character who looked more like a western desperado than a naval officer, he knew his business thoroughly and had more than his share of energy and dogged determination. A specialist in naval air, promoted to flag rank at the age of 50, he had just relieved Rear Admiral Frederick C. Sherman as CTG 58.1. Rear Admiral W. K. Harrill, an aviator since 1921, had recently relieved Rear Admiral Ginder as CTG 58.4, in *Essex* (Captain R. A. Ofstie).

As a good instance of Spruance's coolness, when he knew from submarine reports that the enemy was in the Philippine Sea, he calculated how long it would take him to cross, and let "Jocko" Clark perform a scheduled strike on Iwo Jima and Chichi Jima away up north. It was fortunate that he did, for Clark's planes destroyed dozens of Japanese aircraft waiting to attack the landing forces at Saipan.

Kelly Turner, agreeing with Spruance on the 16th that all signs pointed to a big sea battle for the supremacy of the Philippine Sea, lent him five of his heavy cruisers, three light cruisers and 21 destroyers, to augment his screen. Since "Jocko" was then engaged in pounding Iwo, Spruance set a rendezvous for the entire fleet at a point about 160 miles west of Tinian for 1800 June 18. At 1415 on the 17th, he issued this simple battle plan to Mitscher:

> Our air will first knock out enemy carriers, then will attack enemy battleships and cruisers to slow or disable them. Battle Line will destroy enemy fleet either by fleet action if the enemy elects to fight or by sinking slowed or crippled ships if enemy retreats. Action against the enemy must be pushed vigorously by all hands to ensure complete destruction of his fleet. Destroyers running short of fuel may be returned to Saipan if necessary for refueling.
>
> Desire you proceed at your discretion selecting dispositions and movements best calculated to meet the enemy under most advantageous conditions. I shall issue general directives when necessary and leave details to you and Admiral Lee.[3]

Spruance also cautioned Mitscher and Lee that "TF 58 must cover Saipan." Its movements were tied to that major objective.

All day 18 June the two forces continued to feel for each other, and the Japanese, owing to their greater search range, obtained much more information about Spruance than he did of them. Ozawa changed to a southerly course at 1540, intending to keep Vice Admiral Kurita's van (light carriers *Chitose*, *Chiyoda* and *Zuiho*) at a distance of about 300 miles, and his Main Body (including the five big carriers), about 400 miles, from Fifth Fleet. This would enable the Japanese to benefit by the longer range of their planes and choose their own time to fight. By 0415 June 19 Ozawa's battle disposition was complete, and all was set to hurl

[3] In every carrier campaign, starting with the Gilberts, a Battle Line of battleships, heavy cruisers and destroyers was set up under Vice Admiral Willis A. Lee, to be pulled out from the carrier groups' screens to engage Combined Fleet in a gunfire action, if need be. In this action, Mitscher formed Lee's Battle Line on 18 June and stationed it about 15 miles west or south of the carriers, to help them by its antiaircraft fire.

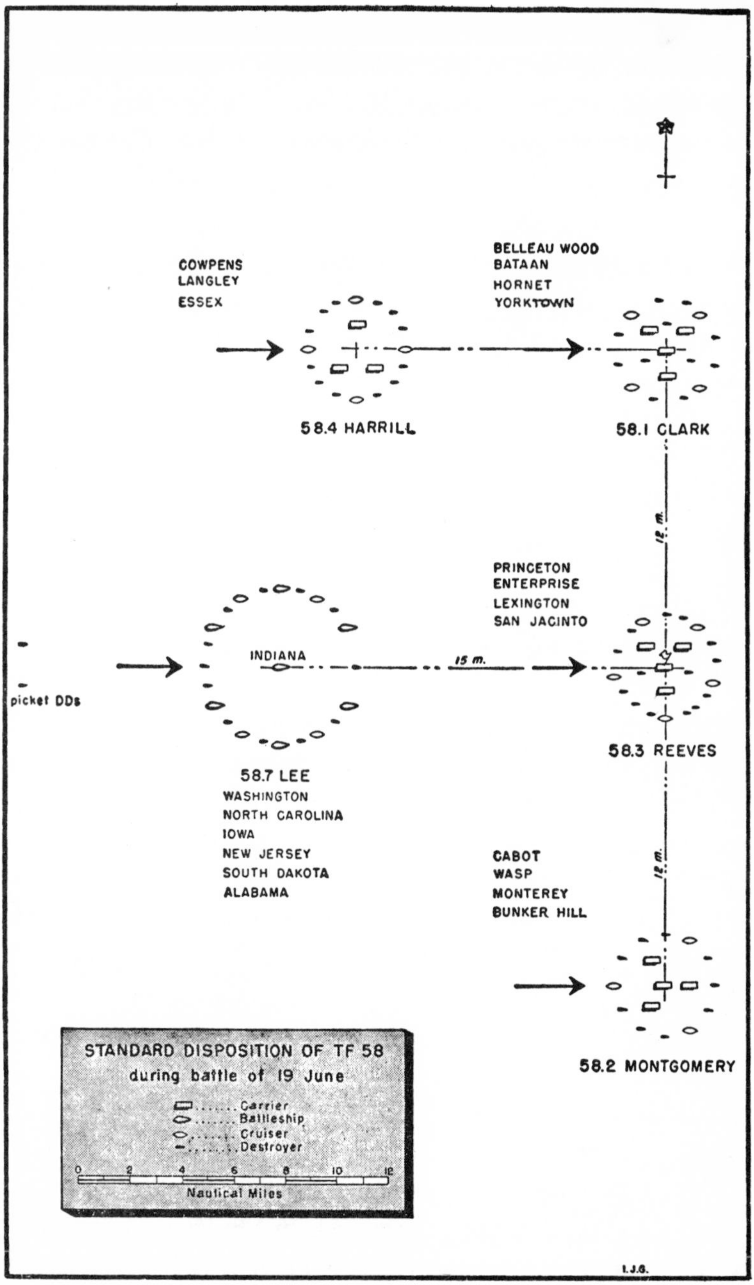

COWPENS
LANGLEY
ESSEX
BELLEAU WOOD
BATAAN
HORNET
YORKTOWN
58.4 HARRILL
58.1 CLARK
12 m.
PRINCETON
ENTERPRISE
LEXINGTON
SAN JACINTO
INDIANA
15 m.
picket DDs
58.3 REEVES
58.7 LEE
WASHINGTON
NORTH CAROLINA
IOWA
NEW JERSEY
SOUTH DAKOTA
ALABAMA
12 m.
CABOT
WASP
MONTEREY
BUNKER HILL
58.2 MONTGOMERY
STANDARD DISPOSITION OF TF 58
during battle of 19 June
Carrier
Battleship
Cruiser
Destroyer
0 2 4 6 8 10 12
Nautical Miles
I.J.G.

300 planes at Spruance. He, still ignorant of Ozawa's position, was steering east, apprehensive that the Japanese might try an "end run" around him to get at the amphibious forces off Saipan.

5. *The Battle of the Philippine Sea, 19–21 June*

June the 19th, to be as memorable as the 4th in naval annals, broke warm and fair around 0430, with a last-quarter moon in the sky. At a little before six the sun rose over a blue ocean, kindling the carriers' topsides to pure gold for a brief moment. Night clouds soon dissolved, and by the forenoon watch the sea had become all azure with argent high lights, and clouds so few as to afford no cover for pouncing aviators. Wind remained in the eastern quadrant, varying from ENE to ESE, with a strength of 9 to 12 knots. Ceiling and visibility were unlimited; from *Lexington*'s high superstructure one could see forty miles all around.

Fifth Fleet was on a north-south line of bearing, each task group in a circle four miles in diameter, their centers 12 miles apart, Lee's Battle Line lay 15 miles to the westward, so that the entire disposition covered an ocean area about 25 by 35 miles.

Flagship *Lexington* at sunrise was about 90 miles NW of Guam, and 110 miles SW of Saipan. As no enemy had yet been spotted, Spruance suggested to Mitscher a morning neutralization strike on Guam. Ozawa (as he rightly guessed) was counting on help from the land-based air forces there, and on using Guam fields to refuel his planes; it was an excellent idea to deprive him in advance of this backlog. First phase of the Battle of the Philippine Sea was a series of dogfights, starting about 0830, over and near Guam. Some 33 Hellcats accounted for more than their number of Japanese planes, but many more were taking off from Orote Field when the Hellcats found something better to do.

"The Great Marianas Turkey Shoot," as an aviator named the

principal phase of this battle, opened at 0959 June 19, when American radar picked up an attack group 150 miles to the westward. This was the first of four massive raids from Ozawa's carriers. At 1023 Mitscher's carrier groups sounded General Quarters, swung east into the wind, launched full teams of fighters to intercept and, to keep flight decks clear, sliced off bombers to orbit on call. This first Japanese raid was 69 planes strong. Hellcats from *Essex*, *Cowpens*, *Bunker Hill* and *Princeton* intercepted it well west of the Fleet, and shot down at least 25. As about 40 of them continued toward their targets, more Hellcats came out and destroyed 16 more. One that got through to Lee's Battle Line scored a direct hit on *South Dakota*. None reached the carriers, and of the 69 only 24 survived.

Ozawa's second raid, of 130 planes, was launched by his own carrier division around 0900. Immediately after it took off, submarine *Albacore* (Commander J. W. Blanchard) torpedoed fleet flagship *Taiho*, the newest and biggest flattop (33,000 tons) in the Japanese Navy, exceeded only by our *Saratoga*. *Taiho* was sunk by this single torpedo, plunging so suddenly as to take down three-quarters of her crew. And *Shokaku*, one of the two survivors of the Pearl Harbor strike, had preceded her to the bottom. She was victim of submarine *Cavalla* (Lieutenant Commander H. J. Kossler).

Ozawa's second raid did even worse than the first — 98 of the 130 planes never returned. About 20 closed Admiral Lee's Battle Line, gave his picket destroyer *Stockham* a terrific tussle, and near-missed three battleships. About six planes got through to the carriers, to be knocked down by C.A.P. and antiaircraft fire.

Of Ozawa's third raid of 47 planes, launched from *Junyo* and *Ryuho* at 1000, the greater part, luckily for themselves, made for a false contact point,[4] failed to find their enemy and returned safely.

[4] The point called "3 Ri" on the chart.

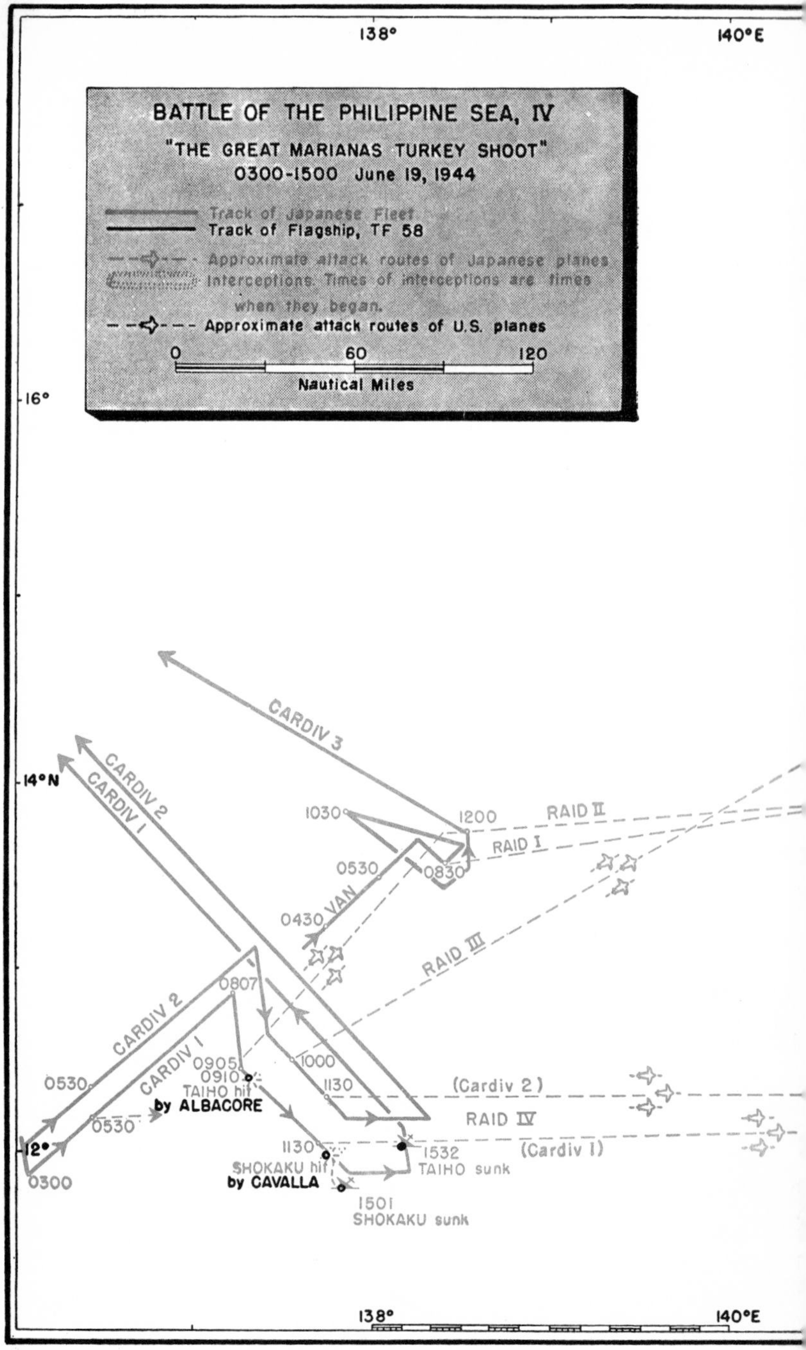

BATTLE OF THE PHILIPPINE SEA, IV
"THE GREAT MARIANAS TURKEY SHOOT"
0300-1500 June 19, 1944
Track of Japanese Fleet
Track of Flagship, TF 58
Approximate attack routes of Japanese planes
Interceptions. Times of interceptions are times when they began.
Approximate attack routes of U.S. planes
0
60
120
Nautical Miles
138°
140°E
16°
14°N
12°
CARDIV 3
CARDIV 2
CARDIV 1
RAID II
RAID I
RAID III
RAID IV
VAN
1030
1200
0530
0830
0430
0807
0905
0910
TAIHO hit
by ALBACORE
1000
1130
(Cardiv 2)
(Cardiv 1)
0530
0300
1130
SHOKAKU hit
by CAVALLA
1532
TAIHO sunk
1501
SHOKAKU sunk

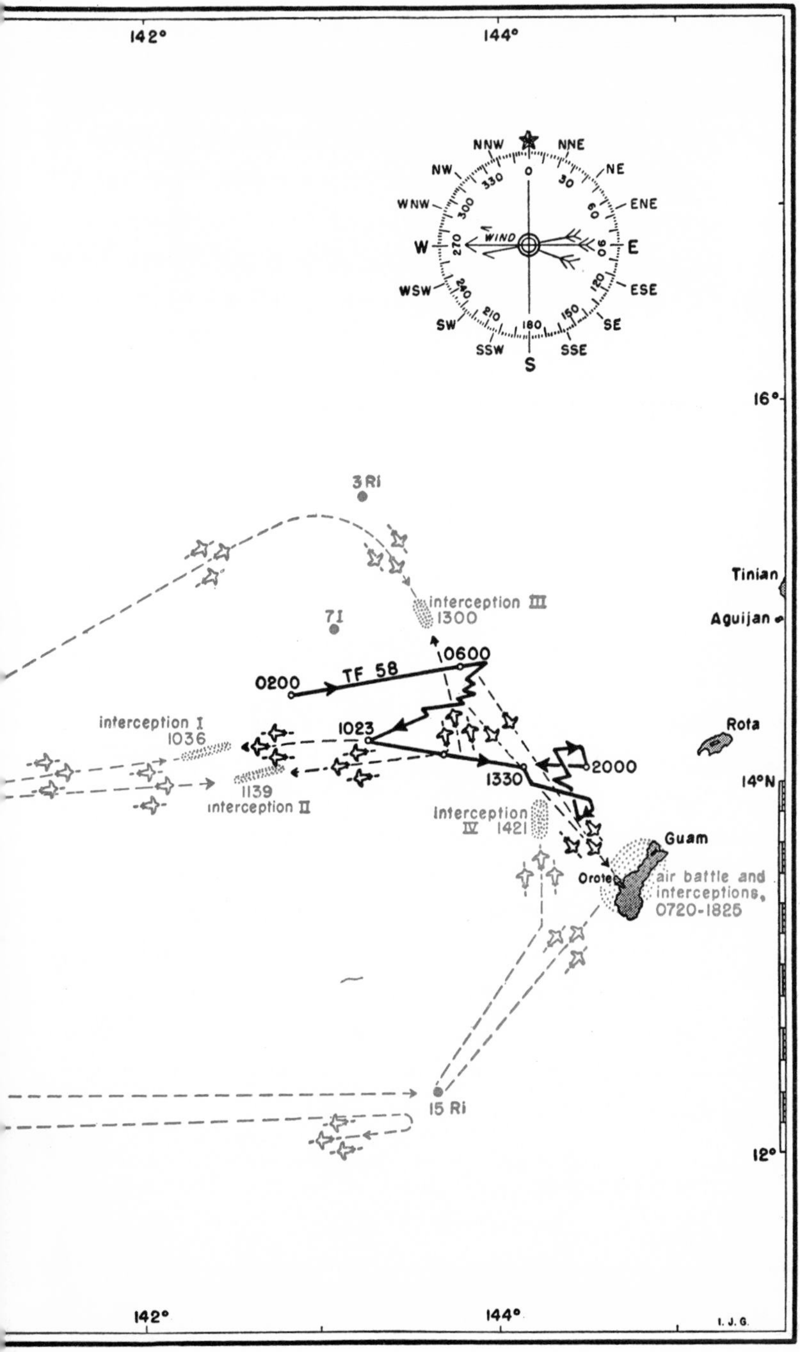

142°
144°
NNW
NNE
NW
NE
WNW
ENE
W
E
WSW
ESE
SW
SE
SSW
SSE
S
0
30
60
90
120
150
180
210
240
270
300
330
WIND
16°
3 Ri
Tinian
Aguijan
interception III
1300
71
0600
0200
TF 58
interception I
1036
1023
Rota
2000
1330
14°N
1139
interception II
Interception IV 1421
Guam
Orote
air battle and interceptions, 0720-1825
15 Ri
12°
142°
144°
I. J. G.

Only ten or twelve engaged, and seven of them were shot down by Hellcats from *Hornet*, *Yorktown* and other carriers.

Zuikaku, *Junyo* and *Ryuho* at 1100 began launching the fourth big raid, of 82 planes. These were sent to a phantom contact SW of Guam, which had been reported by a Japanese search plane with a bad compass.[5] Finding nothing there, they turned north. Six attacked Montgomery's carrier group, did no damage, and only one got back; 18 tangled with Hellcats and lost half their number; 49 when trying to land on Guam were attacked by 27 Hellcats from *Cowpens*, *Essex* and *Hornet*, which shot down 30; the other 19 crash-landed and were knocked useless. Thus only nine out of this raid of 82 planes returned to their carriers.

Guam and Rota were not neglected during the four big raids. Mitscher's bombers, which had been sloughed off in order to keep flight decks clear, were used to destroy grounded planes and to put the airfields out of business. A fighter sweep from *Yorktown* patrolled Guam until sundown, when it was relieved by planes from *Hornet* and *Essex*. On these fell the honor of fighting the last battle of this eventful day. Four Hellcats, led by Lieutenant Commander Brewer, who had distinguished himself in the morning's interception of the first Japanese raid, were patrolling over Orote Field when they saw a "Jill" coming in low. As the F6Fs flew down to pounce on her, they were jumped by an estimated four times their number of land-based Zekes. The American pilots managed to cut down the odds, but not before Brewer and his wingman had been killed. When darkness ended this fight at 1845 the air was completely clear of Japanese planes, except for those limping back to their own carriers.

This was the greatest carrier battle of the war. Forces engaged were three to four times those in Midway, and victory was so complete that Japanese naval air could never again engage on any

[5] The point called "15 Ri" on the chart.

other terms than suicidal. In the "Great Marianas Turkey Shoot" of 19 June Ozawa lost 346 planes and two carriers; the United States Navy lost 30 planes and sustained one bomb hit on a battleship, which did not even stop her. For over eight hours there was fierce, continuous action in the air, directed and supported by action on board ship. The brainwork of the carriers' combat information centers in tracking Japanese raids, and of the fighter-director units (in destroyers) arranging interceptions; the skilled energy of deck crews in rapid launching, recovering and servicing planes; the accuracy of antiaircraft gunners in Lee's Battle Line — all contributed. But, above all, the skill, initiative and intrepid courage of the young Hellcat pilots made this day one of the high points in the history of the American spirit.

Now the hunter became the hunted. At 2000 June 19, having recovered all planes, three out of four American carrier groups started west in search of the enemy, at the low speed of 23 knots to economize fuel. Harrill's TG 58.4, which was due to refuel next day, stayed behind to interdict remnants of the land-based aircraft on Rota and Guam.

Again, American air search failed. Not until 1540 June 20 did an Avenger pilot from *Enterprise* report Ozawa's position, 275 miles away. Mitscher then made the quick decision to launch an all-out strike, even though he knew that recovery must take place after dark. At 1620 TG 58 turned into the wind and completed launching full deckloads — 216 planes from ten carriers in the amazingly short time of ten minutes. At 1840 these aircraft sighted the enemy. Nature had provided a perfect setting from an artistic point of view, but from no other. The lower limb of the setting sun was just touching the horizon, and about half the sky was covered with brilliantly colored clouds. The thinnest golden sliver of a new moon was setting, promising a dark night for aviators' homing. American planes — after flying 300 miles — were so near the end of their tether that there was no time to organize coördinated attacks. Fortunately for them, Ozawa had not yet re-formed his battle disposition to receive air attack.

Six oilers, protected by as many destroyers, were the first group of enemy ships encountered; these had been left astern when Ozawa turned up speed. Some American dive-bombers concentrated on the oilers and disabled two, which had to be scuttled. Four Avengers from *Belleau Wood*, led by Lieutenant (jg) George B. Brown USNR, got two torpedoes into carrier *Hiyo* and sank her; but Brown lost his life. Hits were made on *Zuikaku* and other ships — none lethal. This action cost Ozawa 65 of the 100 carrier planes which had survived the "Turkey Shoot"; only 20 of the 216 American attackers were lost in action.

Many more were lost landing in a pitch-black night, between 2045 and 2300 — although Admiral Mitscher, disregarding carrier doctrine and defying submarines, ordered every ship to light up to make recovery easier. Almost half the aircraft landed on the wrong carriers, fourscore planes crashed, or ditched because they ran out of gas. Fortunately rescue work by destroyers was very efficient.

At midnight Spruance again turned his force westerly, not so much in hope of catching Ozawa as of recovering more splashed aviators and encountering crippled enemy ships. Ozawa, with the engineering plants of his ships still intact, opened distance during the night. Spruance called off the chase at 1920 June 21 and ordered course shaped for Saipan. On the return passage his ships, aided by tender-based planes from Saipan, rescued 59 floating aviators who otherwise would have perished in the Philippine Sea. Thus, all but 16 pilots and 33 crewmen who had taken part on 20 June were eventually recovered. Total losses of American aircraft on the two days of battle, from all causes, were 130; of airmen, 76.

A dispirited and defeated Japanese Mobile Fleet anchored at

Okinawa 22 June, with only 35 serviceable carrier planes out of the 430 which it had possessed on the morning of the 19th. In addition, 31 out of the 43 cruiser and battleship float planes were destroyed in action or crashed on landing, besides about 50 of those based on Guam. The three largest carriers had been sunk, some 480 planes destroyed, and almost that number of aviators. This was the third time that the Japanese carriers' air groups had been virtually wiped out, and there was no time to replace them by October, when the Battle for Leyte Gulf came up.

Although Admiral Spruance was criticized — bitterly so, by self-styled air strategists — for not taking the offensive on 18 June or pursuing more vigorously on the 20th, there can no longer be any doubt that his strategy was correct. If he had thrust aggressively westward instead of awaiting attack off Guam, as his pervading sense of a mission to cover Saipan compelled him to do, he could have accomplished no greater destruction of the enemy air groups, and might have lost some of his own ships. The one thing in this great battle on the American side which can be criticized is Mitscher's failure to send out searches for Ozawa after sundown 19 June. If he had, the air battle of the 20th could have been delivered in the morning, with better results. But Mitscher's refusal to fly night searches is a tribute to his humanity; he felt that his aviators, after fighting all day, were entitled to a little rest. All honor, then, to him for his tactical brilliance and his consideration for human lives; and to Spruance for his strategical savvy. He made the best dispositions to inflict maximum damage on the enemy, and lost not one of his own ships. Nor may we forget the submarines, who coöperated so vigorously and intelligently to make this Battle of the Philippine Sea one of the most decisive of the entire war.

6. *The Marianas Secured, June–August 1944*

After this battle, the fate of the Marianas was sealed, but the Japanese refused to admit it. Two weeks of tough fighting lay ahead on Saipan; Tinian and Guam remained to be taken. The main work at Saipan was done by the foot soldiers of one U. S. Army division and two Marine divisions; but the Navy was in there helping every day with gunfire support. As General Saito, the island commander, recorded, "If there just were no naval gunfire, we feel that we could fight it out with the enemy in a decisive battle."

Equally impressive was the quantity and quality of naval air support. At the beginning of the campaign the escort carriers of the expeditionary force, under the command of Rear Admirals Bogan, Sallada and Stump, maintained from dawn to dusk about 16 fighters and 20 bombers orbiting two air stations some eight miles off shore, to deliver call strikes promptly; a new wrinkle in amphibious warfare. From the 22nd, escort carrier planes of both groups of carriers and Army P-47s based on Isely (ex-Aslito) Field, Saipan, supplied this highly important component. Captain R. F. Whitehead, Commander Support Aircraft, directed the show from Admiral Turner's flagship *Rocky Mount*, receiving calls from shore fire-control parties with the advanced troops and relaying them to orbiting aircraft.

A battalion of Marines led by Colonel R. M. Tompkins captured the top of Mount Tapotchau on 27 June, but the Japanese continued to contest every yard of the island. By the time the last desperate banzai charge flickered out, both Saito and Nagumo, the admiral who in 1941 and 1942 had ranged victoriously with his carriers from Pearl Harbor to Trincomalee, had committed suicide.

The capture of Saipan cost the United States Army and Marine Corps 3426 killed and missing in action. About 24,000 Japanese were killed, by burial count, and 1780 (more than half Koreans) taken prisoner. Hundreds of Japanese civilians committed suicide by jumping off the cliffs of northern Saipan, and for days our patrolling warships sighted their floating bodies — grim reminders of Japanese no-surrender mentality.

The landing on Tinian, 24 July, was perfectly planned and almost faultlessly executed by the same Marine and naval units that had won Saipan. The Marines, unhampered here by slower-moving Army units, drove ahead with their customary *élan*, and in seven days secured the island, incurring casualties of 389 killed and 1816 wounded.

Guam, most important of the Marianas, an American possession for over forty years before the war, was the last to be secured. The unexpected toughness of the Saipan fight showed that the recovery of Guam would require three divisions instead of the two on hand. That meant lifting from Oahu the 77th Infantry Division, but it also meant no respite for the Japanese on Guam, as it gave Admiral Conolly time to plan and carry out the most meticulous prelanding bombardment of the war.

Amphibious operations are difficult and dangerous for people unfamiliar with the technique, but easy and formidable when both naval officers and troops are at home with the work, by constant and well-ordered practice. Rear Admiral Richard L. Conolly, robust, genial, thorough and methodical, loved planning as well as fighting, and he did a great deal of the planning for Guam himself at the Guadalcanal headquarters of Major General Roy Geiger, who was to command the landing force. Daily naval bombardment and air bombing began on 8 July and continued until D-day, the 21st. The UDTs cleared the way for almost faultless landings over difficult reefs. Marines and GIs alike fought with skill and courage against a tenacious enemy, where terrain was all on his side. Casualties, though heavy (1435 killed or missing in action, 5646 wounded) were less than half those on Saipan. Guam was a fitting climax to Operation FORAGER, completed in exactly two months from the first shot. On 12 August 1944, the Eastern Philippine Sea and the air over it, and the major Marianas, were under American control. These islands were as formidable and well defended as Guadalcanal and New Georgia had been — but what a difference in the time it took to take them!

General Tojo and cabinet resigned on 18 July, the day that the loss of Saipan was announced. This was the first move on the Japanese side toward peace; but so reluctant were the Japanese to face defeat that there was no peace for thirteen months.

We can now take a breather from the Pacific war and return to operations on the other side of the world. Throughout the Atlantic Ocean, in Italy and France, the Atlantic Fleet of the United States Navy had been doing its utmost to implement the great strategic decision of 1941: to beat the European Axis first.

CHAPTER XII

Mediterranean and Atlantic

August 1943–June 1944

1. *The Navy at Salerno (Operation* AVALANCHE*), September 1943*

ON 26 JULY 1943, when Sicily was almost overrun and Mussolini had fallen, the Combined Chiefs of Staff ordered General Eisenhower to plan an invasion of Italy — "landings in the Bay of Salerno, to be mounted at the earliest possible date, using the resources already available to you." This last clause registered American reluctance to become more deeply involved in Mediterranean operations. But the futility of resisting that involvement, once we had consented to TORCH, was soon evident. At the C.C.S. conference at Quebec in August, the 26 July directive was confirmed with the significant exception that the General need not be restricted to "resources already available" if he needed more — as of course he did.

Marshal Badoglio began negotiating for the surrender of Italy immediately after relieving Mussolini. If this dicker could have been quickly concluded, Italy might have been ours before August; but it was so protracted by the Italian propensity for bargaining that when a secret armistice was finally signed, on 3 September, it was no secret to the Germans. Even so, the greater part of Italy might have fallen into the Allied lap if an airdrop on Rome by the 82nd Airborne Division, simultaneous with the Salerno landings, had come off. It was canceled because the Italian general in command at Rome, a pro-German Fascist, convinced General Maxwell Taylor that there were too many German troops near Rome to make it a probable success. Rome underwent enemy occupation for eight months, and the Allies had to "crawl up the boot" of Italy, fighting Germans all the way.

The effects of the Italian surrender, upon which Churchill had set his heart, were not too favorable to the Allies. It enabled the Germans to take over most of Italy together with Rhodes and Leros in the Aegean. The Italian Navy did indeed surrender, but added little to Allied naval strength because the ships lacked radar and other modern improvements.

The Gulf of Salerno was chosen for the first important landing on the Italian mainland because it lies about 30 miles south of Naples, and at the then extreme limit of Allied fighter-plane support. Owing to the poor tactical air support provided by the A.A.F. and R.A.F. in Sicily, the Royal Navy added four escort carriers and their planes, as a support carrier force. The over-all commanders — Eisenhower, Cunningham, Alexander and Tedder — were the same as in Sicily. Vice Admiral H. Kent Hewitt commanded the entire amphibious force, which was divided into a Northern Attack Force, mainly British, under Commodore G. N. Oliver RN and Rear Admiral Richard L. Conolly; and a Southern Attack Force, mainly American, commanded by Rear Admiral John L. Hall. These landed, on two sets of beaches about eight miles apart, X Corps British Army and VI Corps U. S. Army. The two together made Fifth Army, General Mark W. Clark USA. The Royal Navy provided the covering force of four battleships and two fleet carriers. Assault convoys were mounted at four ports in North Africa, and Palermo and Términi in Sicily.

Of all decisions about Operation AVALANCHE, the most unfortunate — except giving up the airdrop — was the Army's insistence on no preliminary bombardment, in order to obtain tactical surprise. Admiral Hewitt argued against this in vain, as he had before HUSKY. He pointed out that the Germans were "on"; that it was fantastic to assume that we could surprise them. Implicit in the Army's denial was a fear that preliminary bombardment would attract German forces to Salerno. But on 6 September Marshal Kesselring had already sent there the 16th Panzer Division, which had several days to site artillery, cut down trees, build strongpoints, sight machine guns and fieldpieces on the beaches and their exits, bring up tanks, and cram nearby airfields with German planes. A good selective shoot on strongpoints on the edge of the Salerno plain, for a day or two before D-day, would have rendered the landings much less arduous.

At 1830 September 8, as both attack forces were approaching the Gulf of Salerno, they heard a broadcast in the familiar voice of General Eisenhower, announcing the armistice with Italy. This was singularly ill-timed with reference to the Allied troops. They proceeded to relax, mentally and otherwise; and instead of the tenseness that one usually feels before an amphibious assault, the approach continued under a sort of spell. It was a beautiful, calm, bright night. Capri was visible, swimming in a silver sea; the jagged outline of the Sorrento peninsula made a dark cutout against the star-studded heavens. Lookouts could even see the twinkling lights of Positano, and the flares of the Amalfi fishermen. The illusion of a pleasure cruise, to be followed by a peaceful landing and joyous reception by the Italians, lasted until the transports began easing into their release points at one minute past midnight. Then orders rang out, boatswains' whistles shrilled, and the clang and clatter of lowering landing craft broke the spell.

Admiral Hall's landings of the Southern Attack Force were directed to beaches overlooked by the famous temples of Paestum, all that was left of the Greek colony of Poseidonia destroyed by Saracens over a thousand years ago. As first light broke at 0330 on D-day, 9 September, the initial waves of landing craft were

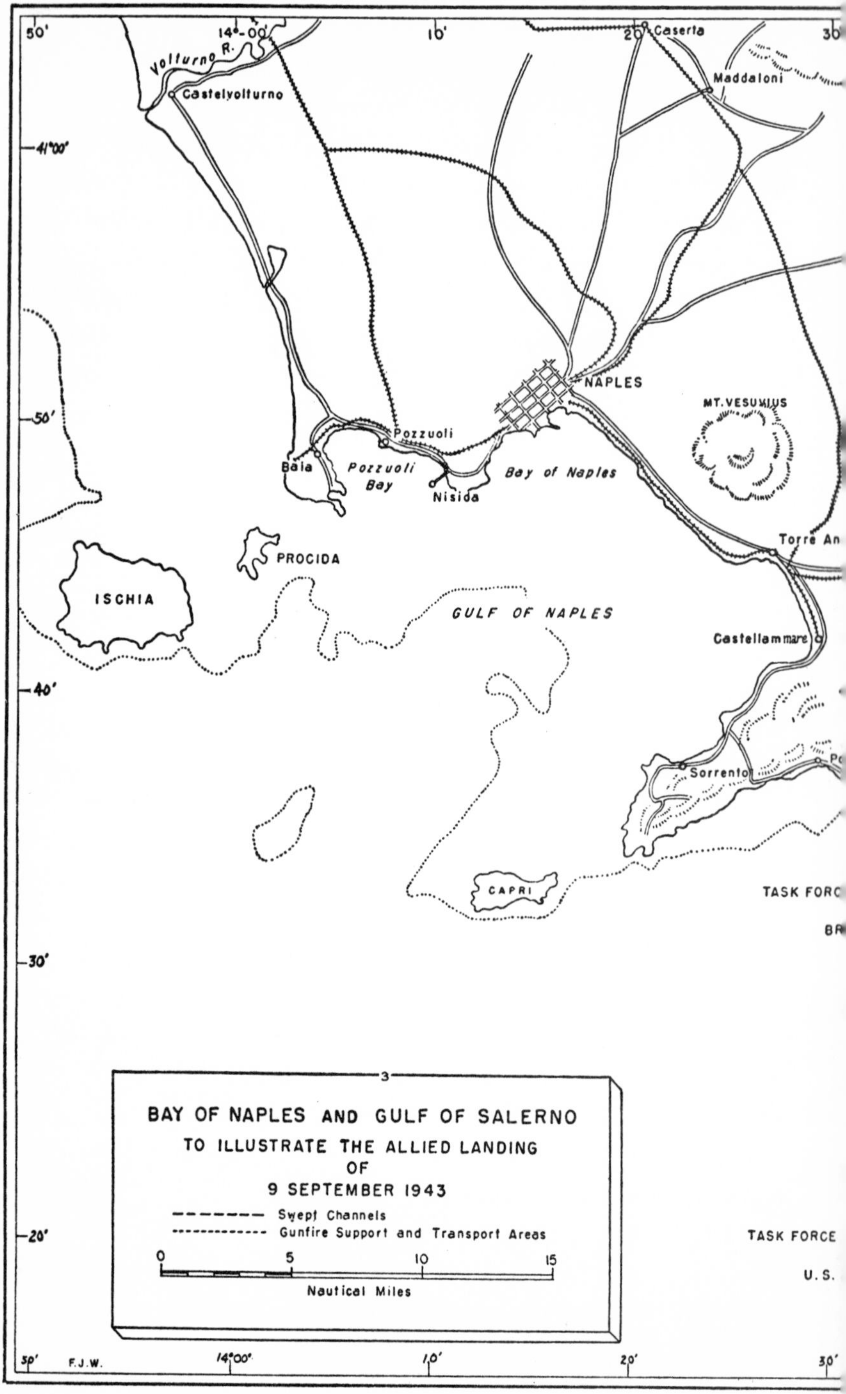
50'
14°-00'
10'
20
Caserta
30
Volturno R.
Castelvolturno
Maddaloni
41°00'
NAPLES
MT. VESUVIUS
50'
Pozzuoli
Baia
Pozzuoli Bay
Nisida
Bay of Naples
Torre An
PROCIDA
ISCHIA
GULF OF NAPLES
Castellammare
40'
Sorrento
CAPRI
TASK FORC
BR
30'
3
BAY OF NAPLES AND GULF OF SALERNO
TO ILLUSTRATE THE ALLIED LANDING
OF
9 SEPTEMBER 1943
Swept Channels
Gunfire Support and Transport Areas
0
5
10
15
Nautical Miles
20'
TASK FORCE
U.S.
50'
F.J.W.
14°00'
10'
20'
30'

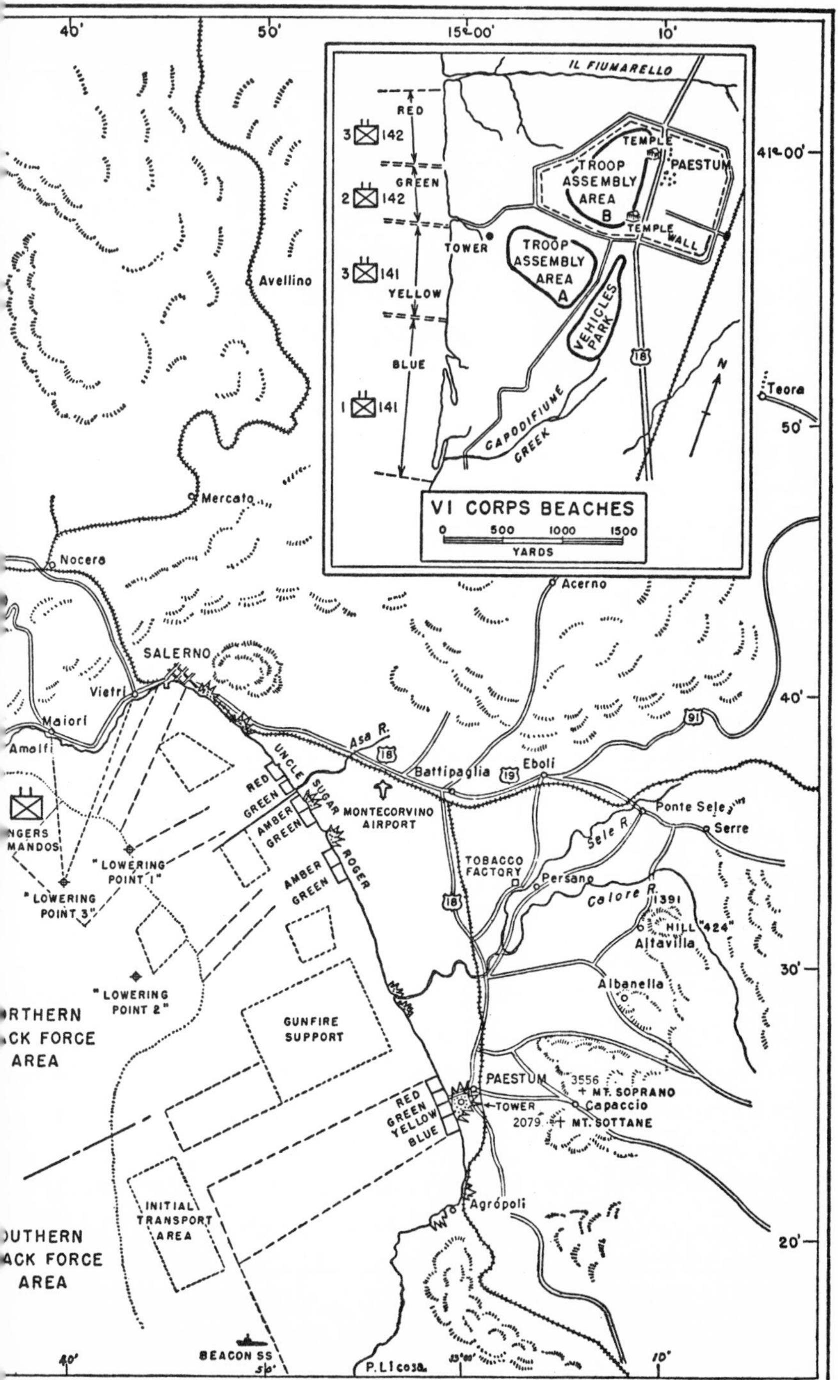

VI CORPS BEACHES
IL FIUMARELLO
RED
GREEN
YELLOW
BLUE
3 142
2 142
3 141
1 141
TEMPLE
PAESTUM
TROOP ASSEMBLY AREA B
TEMPLE
WALL
TOWER
TROOP ASSEMBLY AREA A
VEHICLES PARK
CAPODIFIUME CREEK
18
N
0 500 1000 1500
YARDS
40'
50'
15°00'
10'
41°00'
Avellino
Teora
Mercato
Nocera
Acerno
SALERNO
Vietri
Maiori
Amalfi
Asa R.
18
Battipaglia
19
Eboli
91
UNCLE
SUGAR
ROGER
RED
GREEN
AMBER
GREEN
AMBER
GREEN
MONTECORVINO AIRPORT
Ponte Sele
Serre
Sele R.
TOBACCO FACTORY
Persano
Calore R.
1391
HILL "424"
Altavilla
Albanella
NGERS
MANDOS
"LOWERING POINT 1"
"LOWERING POINT 3"
"LOWERING POINT 2"
RTHERN
CK FORCE
AREA
GUNFIRE SUPPORT
PAESTUM
3556
MT. SOPRANO
Capaccio
TOWER
2079
MT. SOTTANE
RED
GREEN
YELLOW
BLUE
INITIAL TRANSPORT AREA
Agropoli
UTHERN
ACK FORCE
AREA
BEACON SS
P. Licosa
30'
20'

nearing the end of their eight- to ten-mile run over a calm sea. All hit their respective beaches on time; second and third waves followed at the proper intervals. These craft had no close fire support or rocket craft or gunboats, as all landings had in the Pacific, because the United States Army would have none of it; imagining that they could obtain tactical surprise if they landed in the dark silently, and ignoring the fact that landing craft engines are the noisiest things afloat. Thus, for want of close fire support, many soldiers in the boats were killed by German gunners ready and waiting.

Fortunately, the assault troops, an RCT of the 36th Infantry Division, were not easily discouraged. Working under fire to their prearranged assembly area, they made it by sunrise, 0436. Dukws carrying 105-mm howitzers arrived from three British LSTs at 0530. No fewer than 123 dukw landings were made on the American beaches in the first two hours — a remarkable achievement. LSTs carrying tanks were no more fortunate than they had been in Sicily; heavy gunfire kept them off, and the 36th Division got very little armor ashore on D-day. German tanks, on the contrary, were active from 0700. The GIs, with the aid of bazookas, howitzers, and naval gunfire, prevented them from reaching the beaches.

Rear Admiral Lyal A. Davidson in *Philadelphia* commanded naval gunfire support in the American sector. He had cruiser *Savannah* and four destroyers at his disposal, while H.M.S. *Abercrombie*, screened by Royal Netherlands gunboat *Flores*, stood by to serve when 15-inch shell was wanted. (It is curious that the Royal Navy went right on building monitors, a type invented by the United States Navy in 1862, long after we gave them up; the type proved to be valuable in World War II for shore bombardment.) Unfortunately, *Abercrombie* struck a mine that afternoon, and had to retire to Palermo. *Savannah* and *Philadelphia*, shortly after 0900, established communication with their shore fire-control parties, and spent D-day pleasantly and profitably silencing or destroying enemy batteries, tanks, and even bridges. For spotting, the cruisers used their own SOC float planes, as well as Army Mustangs, which flew over from Sicily. These P–51s, flying in pairs, turned in an excellent performance; one would spot while the other covered against enemy air attack. When two SOCs discovered a covey of German tanks hiding in a thicket, *Philadelphia's* 6-inch guns flushed 35 of them, followed them with salvos as they rumbled to the rear, and destroyed about seven. Outstanding support was also given by destroyers *Bristol, Edison, Ludlow* and *Woolsey*, driving in through minefields to deliver accurate shoots. Their performance inspired a message from the 36th Division artillery commander, "Thank God for the fire of the blue-belly Navy ships. . . . Brave fellows these; tell them so."

Landing craft crews functioned even better here than in Sicily, although enemy fire on the boats was far more severe. Training counted — the men stuck by their craft, and worked around the clock to unload transports. When the operation was over, the incredibly small number of eleven boats had to be abandoned, and all but one of these had been knocked out by enemy action.

In the British Northern sector, the pattern of assault was similar and amphibious technique almost identical; the troops were aggressive and gunfire support ships assiduous. By the evening of D-day the British right flank joined the coast four miles northwest of the Sele River's mouth, leaving a gap of seven miles between their X Corps and the United States VI Corps. That gap proved to be serious; for if anyone imagined that the Germans had shot their bolt, he was destined for a great disappointment. They had at least partial control of the air, and full control over the roads and railways of southern Italy. Reinforcements were rolling in from the mountains, and an armored division was coming south from Naples; leading elements of another panzer division reached the Salerno beachhead at 1900, less than twenty-four hours after they had been ordered to break off contact with Montgomery's Eighth Army, which was marching along the coastal road from Calabria not much faster than Belisarius had done in A.D. 536.

Salerno beachhead ranks with those of Anzio, Tarawa and Normandy as the most fiercely contested in World War II. Few soldiers came under such severe fire on landing as did those of the American VI and the British X Corps, or came through it so well. Yet even these "valiant men of might" could not have carried on without naval gunfire. For three days, 10-12 September, as the tide of battle swept to and fro over the Salerno plain, both navies delivered gunfire support to the troops ashore. During this period the Luftwaffe attacked ships in the roadstead with a new glide bomb, radio-directed to its target from a high-flying plane. One put *Savannah* out of action and almost sank her, but she managed to make Malta under her own power. *Philadelphia* sidestepped two; H.M.S. *Uganda* was struck by one that penetrated seven decks and exploded below her hull, but she too was saved.

By 12 September General Vietinghoff, the local German commander, had built up his forces on the Salerno plain to three divisions with 600 tanks and mobile guns, with which he proposed to throw Mark Clark's Fifth Army into the sea before slow-motion "Monty" arrived to relieve him.[1] The Germans recaptured much of their lost ground that day, and on 13-14 September delivered repeated tank attacks on several parts of the beachhead. These were defeated by the combined efforts of infantry, field artillery and naval gunfire. Vietinghoff reported to Marshal Kesselring on the 14th: "The attack this morning . . . had to endure naval gunfire from at least 16 to 18 battleships, cruisers and large destroy-

[1] General Alexander on the 10th ordered Montgomery to hurry, and on the 12th sent his chief of staff to explain the urgent situation; but Monty's advance patrols did not make contact with VI Corps until 1400 September 16, after the crisis had passed. General Clark went so far as to request Admiral Hewitt to make plans for reëmbarking VI Corps and landing it in the British sector; but it is not true, as stated in Bernard Fergusson *The Watery Maze* (1961), that the General's headquarters actually did reëmbark.

ers. . . . With astonishing precision and freedom of maneuver, these ships shot at every recognized target with overwhelming effect." *Philadelphia* was to the fore. *Boise* relieved her, at 0844 September 14, firing almost continuously at tanks and troops. She and *Philadelphia* and the destroyers continued to spell one another until 0530 next morning. In the British sector gunfire support by four light cruisers and four destroyers was equally brisk and enterprising.

On 15 September German armored units made their last attempt to dislodge the Allies from the Salerno beachhead. Next day Marshal Kesselring ordered a general retirement, "in order to evade the effective shelling from warships," as he says in his memoirs.

2. *Naples and Anzio (Operation* SHINGLE*), October 1943–June 1944*

Fifth Army on 1 October entered Naples, which the Germans had done their best to destroy. Commodore William A. Sullivan, with a mixed Anglo-American salvage team, did a remarkable job clearing the bay and the waterfront, so that by the end of the year more tonnage was being discharged in Naples than in time of peace.

At the Volturno line north of Naples, with the great harbor secured, and the Foggia airdrome on the other side of Italy in Allied hands, the Italian campaign should have been halted. But Winston Churchill and Field Marshal Sir Alan Brooke, whose idea it was to fight all the way up the "boot," justified continuing on the ground that the battle of Italy pinned down and used up German divisions which might resist the Normandy landing in 1944. Actually the Italian campaign failed to draw German reserves from France, and by June 1944 the Allies were employing in Italy double the number of Germans in that area. It developed, as General Sir Henry Wilson ("Ike's" relief) said, into a "slow, painful advance through difficult terrain against a determined and resourceful enemy, skilled in the exploitation of natural obstacles by mines and demolition." Marshal Kesselring, fighting a series of rear guard actions along prepared mountain entrenchments, used every natural advantage to the full; and no Allied general except Guillaume, who commanded a French army corps, showed much ability to cope with him. From Naples to Rome is but a hundred miles; yet the Allies, with numerical superiority on land and in the air, and with control of adjacent waters, took eight months to cover that ground.

Churchill persuaded the C.C.S. to order an attempt to break the stalemate by an amphibious landing in the rear of the Germans at Anzio, 37 miles from Rome. This Operation SHINGLE was planned as an end run around the German Winter or Gustav Line, which ran through Monte Cassino, where the Allied advance had stalled. The original concept of SHINGLE was to land a division or two in the enemy's rear to coöperate with the Allied armies when they reached Frosinone on the road from Naples to Rome, by seizing the Alban Hills. Eisenhower accepted it reluctantly and with this assumption.

Fifth Army started its drive toward Frosinone on 1 December 1943, but bogged down at the base of Monte Cassino. The Anzio operation, accordingly, was canceled; but Churchill promptly revived it, on Christmas Day, as one of his favorite peripheral jobs. Eisenhower would have done well at that point to have uttered an emphatic "No!" — as Marshall did when Churchill demanded an attack on Rhodes; for the Anzio operation made no sense except to support Fifth Army, which was still too far away to profit by it.

The landings between Anzio and Nettuno on 22 January 1944 of one British and one American division, under Rear Admiral Frank J. Lowry USN and Major General John P. Lucas USA, were completely successful. The troops were lifted from the Bay of Naples, largely in beaching craft, and had ample gunfire support.

Since the concept of this operation was British, but the execution largely American, and most of the troops in the end were Americans too, it has been very tempting to British writers to pin the failure of Operation SHINGLE on their allies. General Lucas should, it is argued, on D-day itself, have ordered one column into the Alban Hills and another into Rome itself, which would have fallen like a ripe plum; Patton would have done just that.[2] Overextension, however, is one of the worst military blunders and the initial assault forces allotted to Anzio were much too weak to be stretched that far; reinforcements came too late to do anything but save the beachhead. Kesselring, though tactically surprised, had a plan ready both to contain Lucas's VI Corps on a narrow beachhead, and hold Clark's Fifth and Montgomery's Eighth Army as well. That is just what he did. Failure to appreciate the Germans' capability in rapid troop movement was a major lapse in Allied Intelligence. The air forces reported that their preliminary bombings had disrupted all rail and road communications in central Italy, but they had not done so. R.A.F. and A.A.F. firmly believed in the concept of "isolating the battlefield" by bombing bridges and the like; but it was not until the Normandy operation that such tactics, implemented by airdrops, seriously deterred enemy movements.

Even more quickly than Kesselring, the German Air Force reacted to the landings. On 23 January H.M.S. *Janus* was exploded and sunk by one of their new glide-bombs. Two days later over 100 bombers attacked the transport area repeatedly, making several hits and sinking a brightly illuminated British hospital ship.

There is no need here to dwell on the distressing details of the

[2] Actually Patton regarded the operation as suicidal. He flew to Naples to say good-by to Lucas, blurting out: "John, there is no one in the Army I hate to see killed as much as you, but you can't get out of this alive. Of course, you might be badly wounded. No one ever blames a *wounded* general!"

Anzio operation. The Germans turned an amphibious assault into a siege; even the Okinawa campaign in the Pacific was shorter. Four more American divisions and one more British division were sent in to beef up VI Corps. All through February, March, April and most of May there was trench warfare of World War I type on the beachhead. Off shore the two Navies stood by, bringing up supplies and reinforcements, rendering gunfire support, and beating off attacks by the Luftwaffe. Deadlock on the beachhead was a severe trial to the soldiers, and to sailors in ships standing by. Cold, drenching rains and gusty winds made any movement ashore difficult. Beaching craft in the roadstead rolled and tossed in the steep Mediterranean winter seas. Evening brought no rest to the weary sailor, who, like as not, had been at General Quarters since dawn, for twilight air attacks were the rule rather than the exception. The Germans had an air observation post high in the Alban Hills, from which they could identify and follow any ship and dispatch a guided missile attack from the Roman airfields at a few minutes' notice.

Special praise is due to the 450 American dukws employed. These "proved an invaluable asset in unloading Liberty ships moored at a distance off shore," recorded General Wilson; and British naval officers praised the Negroes who drove these dukws "for their cheerfulness, cleanliness and courage. Shelling or no shelling . . . those American Negroes and their white comrades kept the unending chain of 'ducks' running to and from the anchorage."

It was Mark Clark's Fifth Army which finally broke the deadlock on 11 May by an all-out attack on the Gustav Line.

Cisterna, which the Germans had turned into a miniature Monte Cassino, was captured by the Anzio forces on 25 May after two days' bitter fighting. *Brooklyn* fired her last shot in this campaign on the 26th, evoking complimentary comments from her spotters. French cruiser *Émile Bertin*, relieving *Philadelphia*, acquitted her-

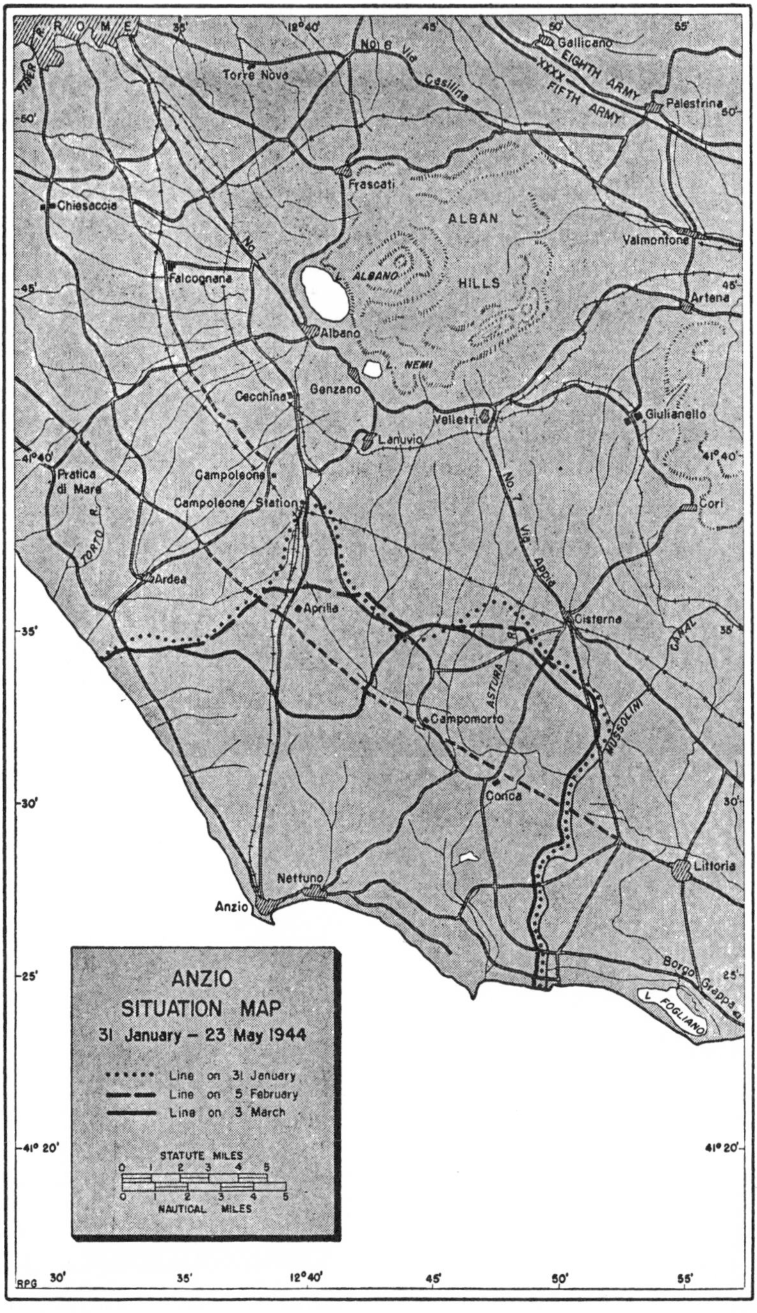
ANZIO
SITUATION MAP
31 January – 23 May 1944
Line on 31 January
Line on 5 February
Line on 3 March
STATUTE MILES
0 1 2 3 4 5
0 1 2 3 4 5
NAUTICAL MILES
ROME
TIBER R.
Torre Nova
No. 6 Via Casilina
Gallicano
EIGHTH ARMY
XXXX
FIFTH ARMY
Palestrina
Frascati
ALBAN
HILLS
Chiesaccia
No. 7
Valmontone
Falcognana
L. ALBANO
Artena
Albano
L. NEMI
Genzano
Cecchina
Velletri
Giulianello
Lanuvio
Pratica di Mare
Campoleone
Campoleone Station
No. 7 Via Appia
Cori
TORTO R.
Ardea
Aprilia
Cisterna
ASTURA R.
MUSSOLINI CANAL
Campomorto
Conca
Littoria
Nettuno
Anzio
Borgo Grappa
L. FOGLIANO
12°40'
35'
45'
50'
55'
30'
41°40'
41° 20'
25'
RPG

self with equal skill. With two United States destroyers screening, she silenced three enemy gun emplacements on the 27th. For the next two days these ships supported the Allied left flank at extreme ranges.

No more cruiser fire was wanted, but destroyers took over fire support as the Germans withdrew. From 31 May to 3 June, *Kendrick*, *Parker*, *Mackenzie*, *Champlin* and *Kearny* took turns pouring hundreds of rounds upon guns, vehicles and troops of the retreating enemy around Ardea and Practica di Mare. H.M.S. *Dido* and French *Émile Bertin* came up on 4 June, just in time to hear that it was all over. That night, 19 weeks after Admiral Lowry had landed VI Corps at Anzio, the Germans marched out of Rome and the Americans and British rolled in.

Operation SHINGLE was expensive to both Allies. The United States lost 526 sailors and about 3400 soldiers, the United Kingdom lost 366 sailors and about 1600 soldiers. German mines and bombs sank two cruisers, three destroyers, three LST, one LCI and a hospital ship of the Royal Navy, and two minecraft and six beaching craft of the United States Navy, besides two Liberty ships. Thus Churchill's baby turned out to be a costly and unrewarding brat. But Anzio beachhead should endure in our memories as a symbol of heroic tenacity on the part of British and American soldiers and sailors. Moreover, the two Navies performed an almost faultless landing, and then played the parts of ferry, feeder and gunfire support. The dogged valor of the foot soldiers and gunners repelled formidable counterattacks and eventually broke out to Rome. This was their battle, this their victory; of which the United States Navy is proud to say, "We helped you; and we too suffered, at Anzio beachhead."

3. *Sardinia, Corsica and Elba, September 1943–June 1944*

When the surrender of Italy was announced in September 1943, it became a matter of immediate concern to the Germans to withdraw their garrisons from Sardinia and Corsica, and to the Allies to get theirs in. Marshal Kesselring managed the former with his usual dexterity. By moving to Sardinia the ferries and other small craft used in the evacuation of Sicily, he transferred 25,800 men, hundreds of cannon, and 62 tanks to Corsica by 18 September. And on the same day the evacuation of Corsica to Leghorn began.

The responsibility for occupying Corsica was gladly accepted by the Fighting French. Using their own warships, cruisers *Jeanne d'Arc* and *Montcalm*, destroyers *Le Fantasque* and *Le Terrible*, they poured 6600 French and North African troops into one end of that island, while the Germans streamed out at the other. Over 30,000 enemy troops with their weapons and armor were transferred to the mainland, in one of the notable evacuations of the war. The oversight of the United States and Royal Navies in not attempting to attack this Bastia-Leghorn ferry route, covering 60 miles of deep water, is even more astonishing than their failure to halt the Sicilian evacuation; for here were no deterrents such as narrow seas and powerful coastal batteries.

American Army engineers were soon working on bomber bases in Sardinia and Corsica, which became useful to cover the invasion of Southern France the following year. And both islands were put to good use by Allied small craft. The Royal Navy established an advanced base for coastal forces at Maddalena before the end of September, and Lieutenant Commander Stanley M. Barnes reported there with his veteran MTBron 15 in early October. A second base was established at Bastia, Corsica. United States PTs operated thence with their British partners, under Royal Navy command, to the end of the war in the Mediterranean.

They conducted almost continuous hostilities with the heavily armed German F-lighters — 163-foot beaching craft similar to the LST — and R-boats — 85- to 115-foot escort vessels. These the enemy used to supply his forces in central Italy from Genoa and ports on the French Riviera. The Navies also contended with 30-knot Italian torpedo boats which the Germans had taken over.

The PTs here showed exemplary energy, courage and cunning. Operating with the British boats in mixed patrols, alternately under Commander Barnes and Commander R. A. Allan RNVR (known as "the Corsican Brothers"), they left a gallant record. Penetrating where larger vessels could not venture because of mines, they proved that properly designed and armed small naval craft have an important and useful function in modern warfare.

The most consistently unsung naval heroes of World War II, however, were the minecraft. U. S. Mine Squadron 11 (*Improve*, flag),[3] based since 27 August at Saint-Tropez and from 25 November at Cagliari and Bastia, was very active. In conjunction with British and French minesweepers and destroyers, they quietly pursued their dull, dangerous, but necessary work of clearing the coasts and sea lanes of the Mediterranean from anchored and floater mines which were constantly being planted or released by the retreating Germans.

Elba, least important of the three larger islands of the Tyrrhenian Sea, was not voluntarily evacuated by the Germans. Hitler insisted, probably because of its association with his hero Napoleon, on holding it "to the last man and the last cartridge." And the French Army of Liberation in Corsica insisted on taking Elba, because they wanted something to do before helping to liberate

[3] Successive C.O.'s were Capt. H. G. Williams and Cdr. Allan M. Robinson USNR.

their own country. So Operation BRASSARD, to capture Elba, was set up for a D-day of 17 June 1944.

The troops under General Henry-Martin, 12,000 in number, were French, North African and Senegalese. Since this was a shore-to-shore operation mounted in Corsica, the men were lifted in beaching craft and LCPRs towed by motor launches. The naval commander, the portly, genial and vigorous Rear Admiral Thomas Troubridge RN, had for flagship a converted LCI. His invasion flotilla included the ubiquitous Barnes with three PT squadrons, 40 or more Navy-manned LCI, and a few LST of the United States Navy. Gunfire support, in small supply, was rendered by three antique British river gunboats and three other small craft.

This rugged little island, about 30 miles long, was garrisoned by about 3000 Germans — many times the Intelligence estimate — and they were so well provided with coastal and mobile batteries that the convoy, steering into Golfo di Campo on the south shore, was met by murderous fire. Several LCI were sunk and for a time it looked as if nobody would get out alive; but the British SNOL (Senior Naval Officer Landing), Captain Errol Turner, gamely ordered troop-loaded craft to land on other beaches, the six small gunfire support craft did wonders, and by noon all beachheads were joined and only one battery was still giving trouble. The Germans, as soon as they saw the black faces of the *Sénégalais* and heard the wild whoops of the *goumiers* and *tabors*, surrendered in droves; and by 19 June the entire island was in French hands.

4. *The Escort Carriers and the U-Boats, May–December 1943*

Some people regarded the war against the U-boats as won because of the Bay Offensive and the spirited defense of northern transatlantic convoys. That was far from the truth. On 24 May 1943 Doenitz signaled to all U-boat captains, "The situation in the North Atlantic now forces a temporary shift of operations to areas less endangered by aircraft." He chose two areas of American responsibility, the central transatlantic convoy route and the South Atlantic; and one British theater, the Indian Ocean. If the Navies had now failed the merchantmen, there would have been a tonnage slaughter comparable to that of 1942. As it was, the Central Atlantic became the scene of a major tactical triumph over the U-boats, wrought by the American escort carriers.

On 26 May the Grossadmiral, having selected the horse latitudes as the best waters for filling his empty bag with merchant tonnage, ordered Group "Trutz" of 17 U-boats to form north-south line along the 43rd meridian between latitudes 32° and 39° N. Here the United States Navy was convoying hundreds of troop transports, fast tankers and slow freighters crammed with military supplies, in preparation for the invasion of Sicily. But we were well prepared to protect these convoys; and as soon as Group "Trutz" was on station it became the victim of an antisubmarine offensive unique for the rapidity with which tactical innovations were introduced.

The principal innovation was a roving U-boat killer outfit — a group composed of an escort carrier (CVE) equipped with Wildcat fighters and Avengers which could use bombs, depth charges or torpedoes, screened by old destroyers or destroyer escorts. In May 1943, Admiral Ingersoll, C. in C. Atlantic Fleet, gave the commanders of CVE groups discretion to hunt down submarines wherever HF/DF fixes indicated their presence. These orders were a joy to the young escort carrier commanders, making them feel as free off soundings as John Paul Jones or Lord Nelson.

First to profit was Captain Giles E. Short of *Bogue*, which, with four destroyers, departed Argentia 30 May under orders to conduct offensive operations in wide support of North African convoys. On 5 June a Wildcat and an Avenger executed a well-coordinated attack on *U-217* of Group "Trutz," then some 63 miles from *Bogue*. At 1507 June 8, a clear, calm day with glassy sea, a *Bogue* Avenger sighted *U-758* moving "at extremely high speed." She happened to be the first of the German submarine fleet to be equipped with a quadruple mount of 20-mm antiaircraft guns, and to have orders from Doenitz to fight planes on the surface instead of diving. This U-boat drove off two Avengers, then circled slowly on the surface, tempting one Wildcat pilot after another to try his luck. All were forced out of range except Lieutenant (jg) Phil Perabo USNR. He piled in, jammed the German 20-mm Oerlikons with strafing bullets, and mowed down most of the gunners. The C.O. then decided it was time to dive; and as he did so, at 1528, an Avenger dropped a load of bombs which should have been fatal, but were not. Heavy antiaircraft fire and smart tactics saved *U-758*; and incidentally encouraged all her teammates in the fatal belief that "fight back" doctrine was the answer to a German submariner's prayer.

Not until 1147 June 12 did one of *Bogue*'s patrol teams make a fresh contact: *U-118*, a 1600-ton fueling "milch cow" cruising 20 miles astern of the carrier. She did not fight back with anything like the vigor of *U-758*, but it took seven planes to sink her. Grossadmiral Doenitz, exasperated by the failure of Group "Trutz" to intercept convoys, ordered his boats to set up a new barrier south of Flores. After this had been successfully evaded by two convoys, he dissolved the group. No organized patrol line replaced frustrated "Trutz," but by 12 July there were 16 U-boats, including several milch cows, in waters east and south of the Azores.

Escort carrier *Core*, commanded by Captain Marshall R. Greer, stood out from the Capes of the Chesapeake 27 June on her first war cruise. Screened by destroyers *Bulmer*, *George E. Badger* and *Barker*, she remained within hailing distance of Convoy UGS-11 until 11 July when it was about 700 miles south of São Miguel.

Captain Greer than received a signal from Cinclant to join westbound Convoy GUS–9. On the afternoon of 13 July one of *Core*'s Wildcat-Avenger patrol teams, about 720 miles SSW of Fayal, sighted the 1600-ton tanker *U–487*, and sank it, losing one plane and pilot in the fight. Three days later, the *Core* group made a second kill, of *U–67*.

Santee (Captain Harold F. Fick), with destroyers *Bainbridge*, *Overton* and *MacLeish*, was equally successful. An Avenger-Wildcat team, patrolling about 150 miles north of the carrier at 0803 July 14, sighted *U–160*. *Santee*'s air squadron was now equipped with the homing torpedo "Fido," for which a new form of attack had been worked out. The Wildcat forced the sub to dive; the Avenger dropped a Fido which quickly smelt its target and sent *U–160* to the bottom with all hands. Next day, the same tactics disposed of another 740-tonner, *U–509*, about 180 miles south of Santa Maria. Fick joined a Gibraltar-Norfolk convoy, recognized as still the best bait for U-boats. Upon reaching mid-ocean on 30 July, a Wildcat pilot sighted two submarines: *U–43* playing milch cow to *U–403*. The fighter plane's strafing runs forced both boats to submerge; and while the larger still had decks awash an Avenger dropped two depth bombs and a Fido near enough to do the trick.

All these kills had been made by the escort carriers' aircraft; but on 23 July a member of *Bogue*'s screen, the 1920-vintage destroyer *George E. Badger* (Lieutenant Thomas H. Byrd USNR), scored. *U–613*, Florida-bound with a load of mines to close off the mouth of St. John's river, was the victim. After three depth-charge attacks there were heard on board *Badger* sounds that are music to a submarine hunter's ears — the horrible roarings, rumblings, cracklings, belchings and bubblings that mark the breaking up of a U-boat. Debris appeared on the surface: shattered woodwork, mattresses and clothing, dismembered and mutilated human bodies. Finally and appropriately the sea spewed up a German translation

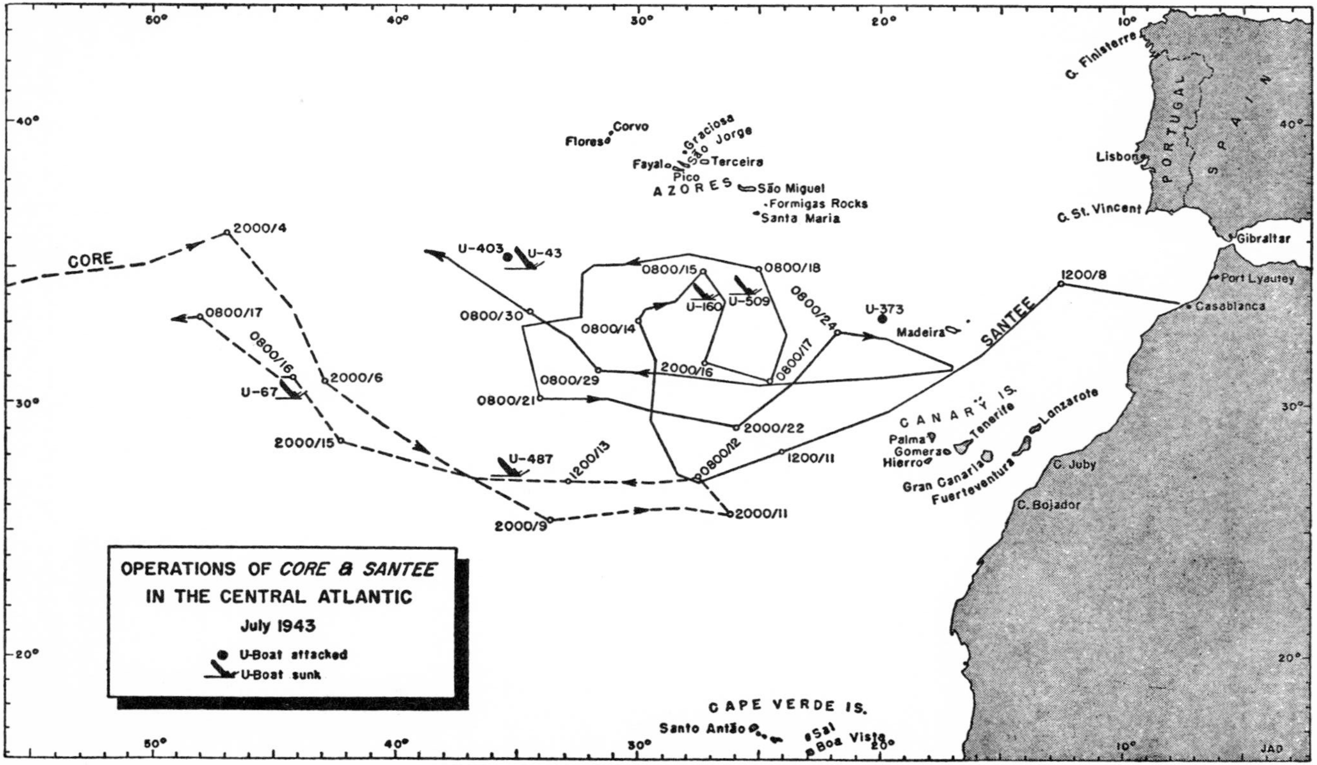
OPERATIONS OF CORE & SANTEE
IN THE CENTRAL ATLANTIC
July 1943
U-Boat attacked
U-Boat sunk
CORE
SANTEE
2000/4
2000/6
0800/16
0800/17
2000/15
2000/9
1200/13
2000/11
0800/12
1200/11
2000/22
0800/21
0800/29
0800/30
0800/14
0800/15
2000/16
0800/17
0800/18
0800/24
1200/8
U-403
U-43
U-67
U-487
U-160
U-509
U-373
Flores
Corvo
Graciosa
São Jorge
Fayal
Pico
Terceira
AZORES
São Miguel
Formigas Rocks
Santa Maria
Madeira
CANARY IS.
Palma
Gomera
Hierro
Tenerife
Gran Canaria
Fuerteventura
Lanzarote
C. Juby
C. Bojador
CAPE VERDE IS.
Santo Antão
Sal
Boa Vista
C. Finisterre
PORTUGAL
SPAIN
Lisbon
C. St. Vincent
Gibraltar
Port Lyautey
Casablanca
JAD

of Poe's *Murders in the Rue Morgue*. On the same day, one of *Bogue*'s Avengers sank *U-527*.

Escort carrier *Card* (Captain Arnold J. Isbell) and her screen of old four-pipers, *Barry*, *Goff* and *Borie*, now began a five-day battle with U-boats. On 7 August an Avenger, piloted by Lieutenant (jg) A. H. Sallenger USNR, spotted *U-66* about to fuel from *U-117*. With the help of two other planes the milch cow was sunk, but the other got away — to be sunk by *Buckley* nine months later. Next morning, Sallenger and a Wildcat piloted by Ensign John F. Sprague USNR spotted another brace, *U-664* and *U-262*, which had just battled their way past Jack Slessor's boys in the Bay of Biscay and were full of prunes and vinegar. They shot down both planes and killed Sprague; Sallenger and his gunner were picked up on a rubber raft by *Barry*. At noon 9 August, another patrol team spotted *U-664* charging batteries. Captain Isbell had been up all night working out new attack techniques to smother U-boats that tried to fight it out, and to such good purpose that *U-664* was bombed helpless and the crew abandoned ship, leaving 44 floating survivors for *Borie* to pick up. On the 11th, another Wildcat-Avenger team put down *U-525* for keeps with a Fido. The *Card* group returned to the Azorean hunting grounds on 27 August. At noon a three-team patrol sank *U-847*, which had been supplying other U-boats for over a week. She was the sixteenth submarine and eighth milch cow that Admiral Ingersoll's escort carrier groups had sunk in 98 days. In the same period the U-boats had sunk only one ship out of a convoy that the CVEs supported.

Doenitz now called off further operations in the Central Atlantic.

Lacking space to follow the fortunes of every escort carrier group, we shall continue wih Captain Isbell's *Card*. She had two weeks' overhaul at Norfolk in September 1943, then sortied in wide support of a Gibraltar-bound convoy. On 4 October this group hit the jackpot, four U-boats fueling within a radius of 500 yards, sank two of them then and a third on the 13th. After putting in at Casablanca, *Card* sortied and on 31 October sank one of a pair some 660 miles north of Flores. The other, *U-91*, escaped, and Captain Isbell sent destroyer *Borie* (Lieutenant Charles H. Hutchins USNR) to get it.

At 0200 November 1, *Borie* blew a different submarine, *U-405*, to the surface by a shower of depth charges. Hutchins opened fire with main 4-inch battery and machine guns at 1400 yards, closed range, tried to ram, and actually rode his destroyer right up over the U-boat's forecastle. The two ships remained locked in deadly embrace, one under the other, for ten minutes. Two of *Borie*'s 4-inch and three machine guns kept up continuous fire on the sub's conning tower and that part of her deck still above water. Negro mess attendants who manned a 20-mm battery fired right through the metal weather screen; bluejackets not otherwise occupied fired tommy guns, pistols, shotguns, rifles, or whatever they could lay hands on, at the Germans. A sheath knife hurled by a fireman buried itself in the belly of a submariner running to man a gun. In a heavy sea the two vessels pounded and rolled against each other, adding the noise of grinding steel to the roar of gunfire, the clatter of machine guns, and human shouts and screams. All this time *Borie*'s "black gang" was making a gallant fight to keep up steam. The destroyer's plates, light enough at her birth in 1920, had by now been chipped and rusted almost paper-thin, and the whole port side became crushed and holed as it ground against the U-boat's hard pressure hull. All hands, working in water chest-high, stuck to their stations and engineer officer M. R. Brown USNR managed to keep up full power even when salt water was lapping the boilers.

After ten minutes of this mêlée, the submarine managed to back out from under and opened the range to 400 yards; then went into a tight turn. *Borie* circled the submarine, trying to get into position to ram, firing furiously and launching a torpedo which missed. *U-405* straightened out and tried to escape. Now, ordering depth charges set shallow, Hutchins bent on 27 knots, turned on the searchlight and closed to ram. The U-boat skipper, Korvettenkapitän Hopman, had the same thought. Hutchins, with great presence of mind, ordered hard left rudder and, with port engine backing full and starboard engine stopped, slewed *Borie*'s fantail with its depth-charge projectors right across the path of the approaching submarine. Three charges made a perfect straddle around the conning tower, lifting *U-405* bodily and stopping it dead when its stem was only six feet from *Borie*'s stern. The submarine backed full and attempted to pull out. *Borie* swung rapidly to port and pursued, firing. One 4-inch shell blew the German bridge crew overboard; another shell hit the U-boat's exhaust tube, and the boat glided to a halt. Submariners were now coming on deck with hands raised, crying, "*Kamerad!*"

At 0257 November 1, one hour and twelve minutes after the first contact, *U-405* plunged stem-first and exploded under water. A yell of triumph went up from the deck of battered *Borie*.

The victor was in a bad way. When fuel for the radio's auxiliary generator was on the point of exhaustion, it was spliced with lighter fluid, kerosene, and rubbing alcohol so that a message could be put through to the escort carrier at 1100: "Commenced sinking." Captain Isbell got a bearing on this far-from-cheery message and immediately launched two Avengers. One sighted the destroyer at 1129, dead in the water, wallowing heavily and down by the stern. Next he sent *Goff* with hose and handy-billies to pump fresh water for *Borie*'s boilers, but it was now so rough, with swells up to 40 feet, that she could not close. Shortly before sunset 1 November, Lieutenant Hutchins reluctantly gave the word to abandon ship. Captain Isbell sent *Barry*, his one remaining escort, to assist this difficult process, leaving his carrier stripped of her screen. All night *Goff* and *Barry* searched for survivors in heavy seas, until 7 officers and 120 men were rescued. Throughout those hours of heroism and misery, *Card* circled nearby at 10 knots, a fair target for a roving submarine. Finally, an Avenger's depth bombs sent the gallant old destroyer to the bottom, at 0954 November 2.

This memorable battle took place in one of the loneliest stretches of the Atlantic, about halfway between Cape Race, Newfoundland, and Cape Clear, Ireland.

Captain Joseph B. Dunn's task group, composed of escort carrier *Bogue* and destroyers *George E. Badger, Osmond Ingram, Clemson* and *DuPont,* had the honor of delivering the final blows to German supply submarine activity in mid-Atlantic. On her eastward passage, *Bogue*'s aircraft ended the career of *U–86*. On 9 December she sortied from Casablanca with orders from Admiral Ingersoll to support a convoy until it had cleared a concentration of U-boats near the Azores. The object of Cinclant's present interest and of *Bogue*'s hunting was a 1600-ton milch cow, *U–219*, about to fuel *U–172*, outward bound to the Indian Ocean.

U–172 did not get any nearer the Indian Ocean than that, but she made a good try, sinking only after a fight which lasted intermittently from 0723 December 12 to 1021 next day. She received 14 depth-charge attacks by one destroyer, and gunfire attacks by all three. *U–219*, the milch cow, did escape, and ended the war under Japanese colors. *U–850* was sunk by *Bogue*'s planes 170 miles distant from her, on the 20th.

Captain Dunn now turned west to keep Christmas in Bermuda, while *Card*, with a new screen, destroyers *Schenck, Decatur* and *Leary*, again picked up the ball. This time, briefly, the hunters became the hunted, as Doenitz had directed one of his wolf-packs especially to get the escort carrier that had caused him so much grief. At 2200 December 23 *Card* ran afoul of this pack. In the early hours of the day before Christmas, *Schenck* sank *U–645* with depth charges, but *U-245* exploded two torpedoes on *Leary*, and sank her. The skipper, Commander James E. Kyes, gave his life-jacket to a mess attendant who had none, and was drowned — as were 41 others of the 100 who lived to abandon ship. The rest of the wolf-pack let *Card* alone to go after another convoy. But it was a sad Christmas at sea for the group, although they had sunk 11 U-boats as against 8 for *Bogue*, 5 for *Core*, 3 for *Santee*, and 2 each for H.M.S. *Tracker* and *Biter*.

In accordance with Admiral Doenitz's doctrine that it was the duty of his submarine fleet to score off merchant tonnage, no matter where, he began in February 1943 to send U-boats to operate off the Cape of Good Hope and in the Indian Ocean. They did very well, since the Royal Navy had not yet enough escorts to establish convoys in the Indian Ocean. Five U-boats sank 21 vessels of 125,000 tons, including two Liberty ships, in that ocean during the last four months of 1943. Doenitz set up a Far-Eastern submarine base on Penang, off the Malay Peninsula, for future operations. At the same time a number of Japanese I-boats conducted a blitz against Allied shipping in the Indian Ocean, and the Germans took over three Italian submarines. These, the I-boats, and U-boats returning to Germany, sank over 184,000 tons of neutral and Allied shipping in the first three months of 1944.

In order to service and fuel these high-scoring submarines out and home, Doenitz established two filling stations. He sent two supply ships to hang around Mauritius, and milch cows to operate among the Cape Verde Islands. Both supply ships were discovered and sunk by the Royal Navy in February–March 1944; and Admiral Ingersoll sent an escort carrier group built around *Block Island* (Captain Francis M. Hughes) to take care of the others. Her screen was composed of four new destroyer escorts, two of which, *Bronstein* (Lieutenant Sheldon H. Kinney) and *Thomas* (Lieutenant Commander D. M. Kellogg USNR), between them sank three U-boats en route, on 1 and 17 March 1944. On the 19th, having arrived in the Cape Verdes, two of the escort carrier's planes caught an 1100-ton milch cow, *U-1059*, surfaced with the crew in swimming. Lieutenant (jg) N. T. Dowty dropped a bomb right into the boat's ammunition locker and the explosion sank it, but Dowty's plane splashed and he was lost.

Block Island's next cruise, in May 1944, was to be her last. One of her night-flying pilots stalked *U-66*, and homed in DE *Buckley* (Lieutenant Commander Brent M. Abel USNR) of the screen. She opened gunfire on the U-boat in moonlight, at 0320 May 6, closed and rammed. There then ensued a hand-to-hand battle like *Borie*'s. Several of the German submariners attempted, 1812 fashion, to board the destroyer. Abel's merry men repelled them with small arms, shell cases, coffee cups and bare fists in a brawl lasting several minutes. The two vessels parted; *U-66* rammed *Buckley*, scraped clear and made off at high speed, burning furiously with open hatches. Shortly she went down sizzling, and *Buckley* recovered 36 survivors.

U-66 was amply revenged before the month was out. *Block Island* at 2013 May 29 was blasted by three torpedoes from *U-549*, which had slipped inside her screen, and went down quickly. Destroyer escorts recovered 951 survivors, and *Eugene E. Elmore* sank the U-boat. This action took place about 320 miles WSW of Funchal.

Four weeks later, at a point about halfway between the Canaries and the Cape Verdes, Captain Dan Gallery, commanding the *Guadalcanal* escort carrier group, performed the unusual feat of boarding and salvaging a U-boat. At 1110 June 4 a DE of his screen, *Chatelain* (Lieutenant Commander Dudley W. Knox Jr.) made a sound contact on *U-505*. Brisk action followed. Two other DEs bore in to assist, Wildcats circled overhead like hawks, and *Guadalcanal* swung clear at top speed since, as Captain Gallery wrote, "A carrier right smack at the scene of a sound contact is like an old lady in a barroom brawl. She has no business there, and can do nothing but get out of the way." *Chatelain* delivered a full depth-charge pattern which caught the Germans just as lunch was being served, holed the outer hull and rolled the boat on its beam ends, dumping crockery, food and sailors into the bilges. Some of the men, panic-stricken, rushed up to the conning tower shouting that the boat was sinking; the skipper, taking their word for it, blew his tanks and surfaced. A boarding party from DE *Pillsbury*, specially trained to profit by such circumstances, swarmed on board, closed sea cocks, disconnected demolition charges, and took over. *Guadalcanal* passed a towline and, until relieved in mid-ocean by a fleet tug, towed the captured boat toward Bermuda. *U-505*, after serving as a "tame submarine" during the remainder of the war, found a final resting place in the Chicago Museum of Science and Industry.

5. *Fighting U-Boats in Other Waters, May 1943–August 1944*

Between 18 May and 18 September 1943, 62 convoys comprising 3546 merchant ships crossed between America and Britain by the northern transatlantic route, and not one ship was lost. Winston Churchill reported this to the House of Commons with unusual gusto, even for him. He also declared that the excess of new merchant tonnage construction over all losses, since 1 January, was 6 million tons, and that the crisis in food and other imports for the United Kingdom was past. But he rightly predicted that the struggle was not yet over, and that Doenitz was about to spring another surprise.

This was the *Zaunkönig* (wren) homing torpedo, attracted to an escort vessel's propellers as our Fido was to a submerged hull. Doenitz first tried this new device on two northern transatlantic convoys which combined on their westward passage in September. He sank three Canadian and British destroyers and six merchant ships; but the other escorts, assisted by land-based Liberators, sank three of the 21 U-boats deployed against them.

After this convoy attack, Doenitz decided to call off surface warfare for his U-boats and kill time until he could get new and deadlier submarine types into production. One of his time-killing operations was an unsuccessful attempt of 13 U-boats, between June and October 1943, to mine harbor channels from St. John's, Newfoundland to the St. Johns River, Florida. Two of the boats were lost, and their total bag (including that of the mines) was four merchant ships and gunboat *Plymouth*. But they certainly gave a much-needed scare to Eastern Sea Frontier, which was getting careless after nine months' enemy inactivity in its teeming waters.

Doenitz also tried a summer blitz in the Caribbean and off Brazil. *U-615* spent the second half of July prowling about Curaçao in search of tankers. In a space of nine days she beat off attacks by a dozen aircraft and a PC, and sustained such serious damage that when destroyer *Walker*, dispatched from Port of Spain, sighted her on August 7, the skipper, knowing that his time was up, ordered all hands into life rafts, and grimly took his boat down for the last time. *Walker* rescued 43 of the crew. For the Germans, this Caribbean blitz was a disaster. Ten U-boats in six weeks sank only 16,231 tons of shipping, a bag that would have been considered small for one boat in 1942. Five U-boats were sunk in the Caribbean and two more never got home.

After withdrawing the battered remnants of this group in August, Doenitz left the Caribbean undisturbed until late October, when he tried a series of mine-planting missions that accomplished nothing; and, in November, tried a three-boat attack on Caribbean shipping. *U-516* (Kapitänleutnant Hans Tillessen) made the most sensational raid on the Isthmus of Panama since the days of Drake;

and, although he carried off no pieces of eight, he made a bigger bag of merchantmen than had all ten boats of the summer blitz. In the Pacific the Bougainville campaign was now on, Tarawa was coming up, and every day warships, tankers, LSTs and all manner of ships were passing through the Canal to reinforce Pacific Fleet, while troop transports were returning empty from San Diego. Plenty of targets for an enterprising U-boat, which *U–516* was. And, at the very moment when she paid her unexpected call on the Caribbean side, all Panama Sea Frontier forces were engaged in a tactical exercise on the Pacific side.

On 5 November 1943 the boat was sighted north of Curaçao and bombed unsuccessfully by a Ventura. Sea frontier officers sent out three submarine chasers to look for her, but Tillessen eluded them by hugging the coast. On 12 November he sank a small Panamanian freighter, and on the 17th a Colombian schooner; on the 23rd he torpedoed and sank a loaded tanker shortly after it had departed Cristobal, and the following night downed a Liberty ship seventy-five miles off the Canal entrance. Every available plane, including Avengers from an escort carrier transiting the Canal, was ordered out to look for *U–516;* but Tillessen eluded them all and sank another freighter off the Gulf of San Blas, on 8 December. The Aruba and Trinidad sectors now got into the act with minecraft, minesweepers, coast guard cutters and aircraft; Tillessen replied by sinking another tanker off Aruba on 16 December. Sonobuoys, which register propeller noises like a ship's sonar, were dropped around spots where *U–516* was sighted, but she escaped every attack and celebrated Christmas submerged off Saint Eustatius. She then steamed into the open sea by a narrow passage which sea frontier commanders had not troubled to patrol. Tillessen even brought *U–516* back next year and sank two more tankers.

Off Brazil and in the South Atlantic, Vice Admiral Ingram's Fourth Fleet waged relentless war against raiders, blockade run-

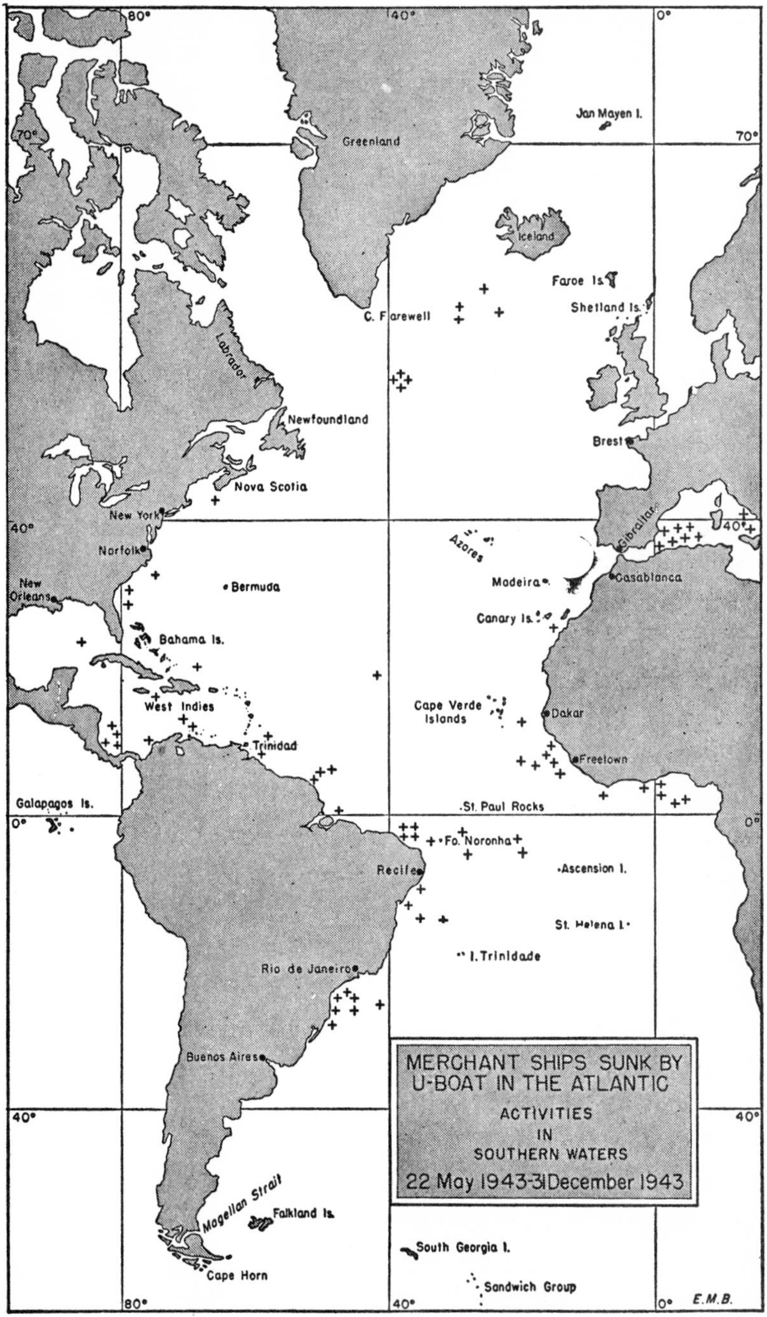

MERCHANT SHIPS SUNK BY U-BOAT IN THE ATLANTIC
ACTIVITIES
IN
SOUTHERN WATERS
22 May 1943-31 December 1943
80°
40°
0°
70°
Greenland
Jan Mayen I.
Iceland
Faroe Is.
Shetland Is.
C. Farewell
Labrador
Newfoundland
Nova Scotia
New York
Brest
40°
Norfolk
Gibraltar
Azores
New Orleans
Bermuda
Madeira
Casablanca
Canary Is.
Bahama Is.
West Indies
Cape Verde Islands
Dakar
Trinidad
Freetown
Galapagos Is.
St. Paul Rocks
Fo. Noronha
Recife
Ascension I.
St. Helena I.
I. Trinidade
Rio de Janeiro
Buenos Aires
Magellan Strait
Falkland Is.
Cape Horn
South Georgia I.
Sandwich Group
E.M.B.

ners and submarines, with the coöperation of the Brazilian government and armed forces. Jonas Ingram and President Vargas were thick as thieves, and everything that he wanted the Brazilian armed forces to do was done. The small, closely knit Fourth Fleet, less diluted by replacements than almost any other part of the Navy, ranked high in morale and aggressiveness. It included only five light cruisers of the twenty-year-old *Omaha* class, eight destroyers, and several small craft, but its air arm by the end of 1943 comprised ten squadrons of amphibious Catalinas, Venturas, Liberators and Mariners, located at five different bases on the Brazilian coast. There was also a squadron of Army bombers and some Navy Liberators on the lonely island of Ascension. Air forces were so much stronger and more mobile than surface forces, which were largely employed in escort duty, that all the antisubmarine fights in this theater were aircraft vs. U-boat. From Ascension Island, *U-848* was sunk on 5 November, her sister *U-849* on the 25th, the same Thanksgiving Day which Arleigh Burke was celebrating off Cape St. George in the Bismarcks. Fourth Fleet paid special attention to blockade runners which were trying to bring rubber, tin and wolfram from the Far East to Germany. *Weserland* was sunk by destroyer *Somers; Rio Grande* and *Burgenland* by *Omaha* and *Jouett*. This virtually ended blockade-running for the war.

The Mediterranean was an even more critical sea than the South Atlantic. Between December 1942 and March 1945, twenty-four troop convoys, escorted by the United States Navy, transported 536,134 troops from the United States to the Mediterranean; thirty "Oil-Torch" fast-tanker convoys, with an average of seven tankers each, sailed from the Caribbean to the Mediterranean at 32-day intervals between February 1943 and June 1944. And no loss or damage to any of them. Between November 1942 and VE day,

11,119 merchant ships were convoyed in 189 U.S.-Gibraltar and Gibraltar-U.S. slow convoys, with the loss of only nine ships sunk while under United States naval escort.

Although the largest number of U-boats present in the Mediterranean at any one time was eighteen, in February 1944, this was eighteen too many for the Allies. Staff officers of Cincmed (now Admiral Sir John Cunningham RN), Commander Eighth Fleet (Vice Admiral Hewitt) and Northwest Africa Coastal Command R.A.F. (Air Vice Marshal Hugh Lloyd) devised what they called "the SWAMP Operation," to keep submarines down to the point of exhaustion and attack them when forced up to breathe. On 13 December 1943 SWAMP scored an initial success on *U–593*, after a stubborn, persistent search lasting 72 hours by British and American destroyers and Wellington bombers. *U–73* succumbed a few days later to the efforts of four United States destroyers and SOC planes from *Brooklyn*, which happened to be lying at Oran. In May 1944 *U–371*, which had sunk H.M.S. *Penelope* in the Anzio operation, was downed after a 24-hour hunt. Next day the hunted became the hunter when *U–967* attacked a 107-ship convoy east of Gibraltar and sank destroyer escort *Fechteler*. But, during the same month, *U–616* succumbed to a 90-hour chase in which several British and American destroyers and numerous planes participated.

In April 1944, the German air offensive grew more intense. It was aimed at the big U.S.–Gibraltar–Suez convoys, principal means of supplying Allied armies in the Italian campaign, of building up for the invasion of Southern France, and of carrying matériel to India and Russia. Marshal Goering used all resources that he could spare from the Italian and Russian fronts and all the tactical ingenuity he could muster. His aircraft attacked only at night or in twilight. Elaborate tactics were worked out, with lines of acetylene float lights as long as sixty miles, and intensely bright flares, and coördinated bombing attacks similar to those that we have described the Japanese using off Makin. They were frustrated by a sufficient number of escorts well trained in antiaircraft fire, proximity-fused shells, smoke; and, perhaps even more by Coastal Command Beaufighters vectored out from Algerian fields to intercept the bombers. The only convoy roughly handled was an eastbound one on 20 April, in which destroyer *Lansdale* was sunk and S.S. *Paul Hamilton*, carrying 500 men of the Army Air Force and a crew of eighty, blew up with the loss of all hands. The escort commanders of the other convoys, Commander Jesse C. Sowell in U.S.C.G.C. *Campbell*, Commander W. R. Headden in DE *Stanton*, Captain H. S. Berdine USCG in *Decatur*, Captain Adelbert F. Converse in *Ellyson*, and Captain Charles C. Hartman in *Mervine*, rank high among our antisubmarine fighters. By 1 August, with operation DRAGOON coming up, German airfields in Southern France were interdicted, and the Mediterranean became so peaceful that, beginning with a convoy which passed Gibraltar 27 November 1944, all dispersed at Point Europa and the ships proceeded independently to their terminal ports.

The few U-boats that managed to slip past the Cape Verdes in 1944 did so by grace of the snorkel, which enabled them to cruise continuously submerged and escape the attentions of escort carrier groups and land-based planes. But the chief theater of activity for snorkel-equipped submarines was the North Atlantic. This device, which the Germans stole from the Royal Netherlands Navy, was a combined air-intake and gas-outlet that allowed submarines to run their diesels submerged, charging batteries if needed. It took the shape of a streamlined steel cylinder which was provided with an automatic float-valve to keep out sea water, and a small radar grid. When the snorkel was in use, it made a "feather" on the water scarcely bigger than that of a periscope head — almost impossible to pick up by the radar sets in use in 1944.

Doenitz regarded the snorkel as a mere stopgap until he had Type XXI, with diesel-electric propulsion and new, much more powerful batteries, in operation. In the spring of 1944 he began to send snorkel-equipped boats on nuisance raids to the East Coast of America in hope of sinking strategic cargoes destined for the invasion of Normandy. They accomplished nothing and, in spite of the snorkel spurt, total losses of merchant ships to U-boats fell, in May 1944, to an all-time low of four ships. The most dramatic evidence of Allied mastery of the U-boat came in the Normandy operation of June 1944. Doenitz alerted 58 U-boats to break it up, but not one got near the invasion area. Liberators of R.A.F. Coastal Command, including United States Fairwing Seven, in which Joseph P. Kennedy Jr., brother of the future President, was a pilot, operated a 24-hour patrol across the chops of the Channel, in conjunction with small warships, so close that every part of the surface was inspected by a plane every 35 minutes. All had microwave radar, and sonobuoys to drop if they spotted a U-boat after dark — and there isn't much dark in those northern waters in June. Thirteen U-boats were sunk by planes or surface craft in the Channel approaches in June; and their only successes were two British frigates, one corvette and one empty transport. In early August, after General Patton's breakthrough isolated the Brittany peninsula, the U-boats had to evacuate their Breton ports to operate from Norway.

But whenever the Allies thought they had the U-boats licked, Doenitz uncorked something new; and he was to give us many anxious hours in 1945.

CHAPTER XIII

The Navy in the Invasion of France

1944

1. *Preliminaries, January–June 1944*

IT WAS NO EASY MATTER to get the cross-Channel operation firmed-up for 1944. At the Casablanca Conference in January 1943, the Americans succeeded only in getting a vote to set up a Combined Planning Staff. That was done in March, when the able and enthusiastic Lieutenant General Sir Frederick E. Morgan became "Cossac" — Chief of Staff to Supreme Allied Commander (Designate). In May, at the "Trident" Conference in Washington, a tentative date was set for a twelvemonth thence, and in August at the Quebec "Quadrant" Conference, the J.C.S. persuaded the C.C.S. to accept Cossac's plan for OVERLORD, as the cross-Channel operation had been named, and to declare that it should be first charge on Allied resources in 1944.

The British chiefs of staff, especially General Marshall's opposite number, Field Marshal Sir Alan Brooke, never seemed to understand why Americans had to have commitments well in advance. Their own logistics problems being relatively simple, they thought we were unnecessarily inflexible. They did not appreciate the enormous difficulties of procurement, shipbuilding, troop training and supply necessary to place a million and a half troops in England, with armor, tanks and troop-lift ready to invade the Continent. The general idea in Britain seems to have been that America had an inexhaustible pool of man power, weapons, landing craft, aircraft and other lethal weapons which could be deployed at short notice. American production schedules had been upset in April 1942, to give top priority to landing and beaching craft for the cross-Channel operation that was canceled, and again in January 1943 schedules were upset to give top priority to ships for anti-submarine warfare. That is why there was a landing and beaching craft shortage in 1944. Admiral King was always loyal to the major strategic decision to "Beat Germany first," but he saw no sense in piling up men, landing craft and matériel in England while Mr. Churchill and the British chiefs of staff were making up their minds what, if anything, should be done with them. Too many high strategists in England regarded American and Canadian troops in Britain as a mere army of opportunity, to be thrown across the Channel if and when Germany showed signs of weakening.

Even after December 1943, when OVERLORD was refirmed at the Teheran conference between Roosevelt, Churchill and Stalin, the P.M. tried to have it postponed in order to get in a few more thrusts "around the ring," such as a landing on the island of Rhodes. Churchill told an American general in April 1944 that, had *he* been planning OVERLORD, he would first have recovered Norway, taken some Aegean islands and ensured Turkey's support. General Morgan had difficulty in inducing his planning staff to take OVERLORD seriously, because so many of his countrymen believed it would never be necessary, hoping that something would turn up, such as a crack in German morale, or bombing them into subjection, or the death of Hitler, to make it unnecessary. Planning for OVERLORD was also hampered by Roosevelt's procrastination. From August through December 1943 he was balancing the respective merits of Generals Marshall and Eisenhower as Supreme Commander. He selected "Ike" only at Christmastide, having been persuaded that Marshall was a key member of the Joint Chiefs of Staff who could not be spared from Washington.

After this appointment, which gave the hitherto headless Cossac an energetic director, the planners were absorbed into Shaef (Supreme Headquarters Allied Expeditionary Force). By New Year's 1944 Shaef's staff, at Norfolk House, St. James's Square, London, comprised 489 officers, about half American and half British, and 614 men, two thirds of them British.

The chain of command of naval and ground forces decided on to execute the final plan for NEPTUNE-OVERLORD, as the great cross-Channel operation came to be called,[1] may best be represented by a diagram, in which I have shown the assault elements only of the troops that landed on D-day.

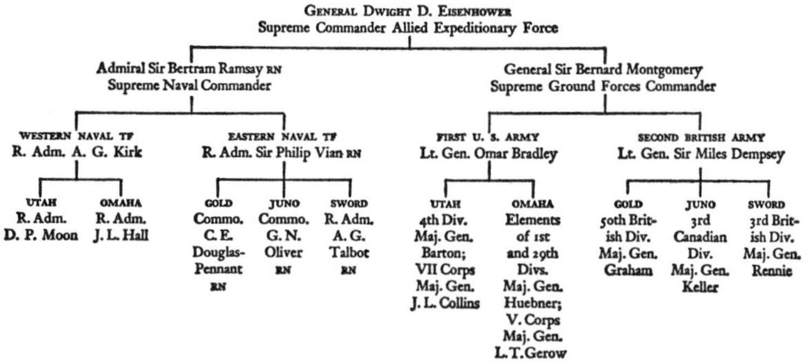

Before describing the vital air plan for the invasion, we must touch on Operation POINTBLANK, the R.A.F. and A.A.F. strategic air offensive against Germany. Its original purpose, in accordance with the Douhet-Mitchell theory of air warfare, was to render an invasion of Germany unnecessary by bombing her into submission. Judged by the results, this was a failure. Even the attacks on Hamburg, in July-August 1943, which wiped out over half the city, killed 42,000 and injured 37,000 people, did not seriously diminish Germany's well-dispersed war production, and failed to break civilian morale.

[1] The code NEPTUNE was generally used for the amphibious phase of the operation.

During 1944, with General Carl Spaatz commanding the U. S. Strategic Air Force in Europe, POINTBLANK was better directed. In the "Big Week" of 19-25 February 1944, 3300 heavy bombers of the England-based VIII, and over 500 of the Italy-based XV Army Air Forces, escorted by about the same number of fighter planes, pounded factories of the German aircraft industry, as far south as Ratisbon and Augsburg. Our losses were 226 bombers, 28 fighters and about 2600 men; but some 600 German planes were shot down, denying their use to the enemy when he needed them most. By 14 April, when Operation POINTBLANK ended and air operations with immediate reference to OVERLORD began, the Allied air forces had established a thirty-to-one superiority over the Luftwaffe. On D-day "Ike" told his troops, "If you see fighting aircraft over you, they will be ours," and they were.

Besides taking a terrific toll of the Luftwaffe, the air forces gave vital prior support to the invasion by their "transportation plan" to cripple the enemy's communications system. This was a sustained bombing of roads, railroads and marshaling yards in France, Belgium and western Germany. Results were spectacular. Some 600 trains carrying German army supplies were back-tracked, and by the end of May all rail traffic between Paris and the Channel was stalled. The Air Forces contributed heavily to blockading the Channel to U-boats. And they destroyed stockpiles of the newly invented German V–1 guided missiles (the so-called "buzz-bombs"), and some of their launching sites. These were too small — many of them mobile — and too well protected by antiaircraft guns to be eliminated by air bombing alone. But the result of this air operation CROSSBOW which cost the A.A.F. and R.A.F. hundreds of lives, was to destroy so many missiles that the Germans were unable to start them off until 12 June, when most of the invasion forces were already in France.

Finally, an essential part of the assault plan was two night air-drops of unprecedented size, two divisions in each sector. In the

American, behind Utah Beach, the 82nd and 101st Airborne, commanded by Major Generals Matthew B. Ridgway and Maxwell D. Taylor made the drop. The object was to confuse the Germans and seal off the land approaches to the Utah beachhead, which they did admirably. Thus, the air power leg to the Allied military tripod was more than sufficiently stout; it was unbreakable.

So, too, was the naval leg. Admiral Ramsay, the top Allied naval commander, after notable service in World War I, had been recalled to active duty at the age of fifty-six, to be Flag Officer, Dover. As such he had been the main instrument in the evacuation of the British Army from Dunkirk in 1940. After serving as Cunningham's chief naval planner for Operation TORCH, he took an important part in later Mediterranean amphibious operations. Rear Admiral Hall, who served under Ramsay, described him as "quiet, brilliant, intelligent, determined and easy to get on with."

Rear Admiral Alan G. Kirk as Commander Western Naval Task Force was the key American naval figure in NEPTUNE-OVERLORD, from the time of his reporting in mid-November 1943. At the age of fifty-six he was rounding out his thirty-ninth year of service in the United States Navy. While chief of staff to Admiral Stark in 1942, he had become thoroughly conversant with English ways, problems and personalities. As Commander Amphibious Forces Atlantic Fleet he had made himself master of that branch of naval warfare, and in the Sicilian operation he led the difficult assault on the eastern flank.

The essence of the over-all plan was to land two American and three British divisions simultaneously on a sixty-mile stretch of the coast of Normandy, on 5 June; with quick, strong reinforcements to keep up momentum and expand the beachhead. Although this was a shore-to-shore operation which required only one night spent in the English Channel, big transports with landing craft on davits were employed in addition to beaching craft. The shortage of what Churchill referred to as "some goddam things called LSTs" provoked the only sharp unpleasantness between Allies over this operation. The British accused the Americans of starving Europe of beaching craft in order to feed the Pacific; Admiral King denied this and accused the British of dragging their feet in producing or repairing their own beaching and landing craft.

A memorandum of the C.C.S. Planning Staff gives the only reliable figures on the deployment of beaching and landing craft. It tells how many of each nation was both operational and serviceable on 1 June 1944, eliminating those building, having shakedown, crossing the ocean, under repair, and so on. Here it is, for the six principal types used in the two operations for the invasion of France: —

1 June 1944	LST	LCI(L)	LCT	LCM	LCVP	LCA[2]
U.S.N. in United Kingdom	168	124	247	216	1089	0
R.N. in United Kingdom	61	121	664	265	0	646
U.S.N. in Mediterranean	23	59	44	185	395	0
R.N. in Mediterranean	2	32	64	95	0	138
U.S.N. on East Coast, U.S.	95[3]	89	58	57	341	0
U.S.N. on West Coast, U.S.	0	41	1	60	181	0
U.S.N. in all Pacific Areas	102	128	140	1198	2298	0
R.N. on E. Indies Station	0	4	2	67	0	46

The first two lines represent what went into Operation NEPTUNE-OVERLORD. Comparing these with the last three lines, it will be seen that the J.C.S. were far from niggardly in allotting beaching craft to the European theater, and that the only types of which the Pacific may be said to have had a superfluity were the LCM and LCVP, together with the LSM (Landing Ship, Medium, not in this table), which was not wanted for OVERLORD. It is also relevant to point out that 115 LST, 220 LCI(L), 171 LCT, 671 LCM, and 1333 of the smaller landing craft, were built in the United States for the Royal Navy during the war.

[2] A British landing craft similar to our LCVP.
[3] Of these, 93 were just completed and not yet allocated.

A legitimate complaint of both British and American officers in Shaef was Admiral King's tardiness in allocating battleships, cruisers and destroyers for gunfire support. This was crucial, since nothing was more certain than that very heavy naval gunfire would be necessary to break down Germany's Atlantic Wall; air bombs couldn't get at it. After Admiral Hall had sounded off on the subject to King's planning officer, C.N.O. allocated three old battleships, three cruisers and 31 destroyers. Yet even with these in hand, the Royal Navy supplied the lion's share of gunfire support, a majority of the minecraft, many specialized types of small craft, and all the Fairmile motor launches and dan-buoy layers.[4]

Rear Admiral John L. Hall had the most varied duties of any attack force commander. He not only commanded XI 'Phib Force, but supervised the training of ships in Force "U" as well as his own assault force. All United States fire support ships reported to him and conducted shore bombardment exercises under his command. "Jimmie" Hall was not only able; his calm, assured temperament spread confidence. Two nights before D-day, when the foul weather and the postponement were giving almost everyone the jitters, the Admiral said to a friend of mine, "I do not expect to be repulsed on *any* beach."

Training centers, supply depots and repair bases for the American troops and landing craft crews were established at Rosneath on the Clyde, at Plymouth, Dartmouth, Salcombe, Exeter and Tiverton in Devonshire, at Falmouth, Fowey, St. Mawes, Launceston, Calstock and Saltash in Cornwall, at Deptford on the Thames below London, and in a base hospital at Netley near Southhampton. Rear Admiral John Wilkes, with headquarters at Devonport, was responsible for the training and readiness of all landing and beaching craft and for amphibious training exercises. These started as early as December 1943 at Slapton Sands and Torquay, Devon-

[4] The French and Netherlands Navies between them contributed three cruisers, five destroyers and two gunboats.

shire. Admiral Kirk reported on 1 June that, owing to Wilkes's "splendid efforts," 99.3 per cent of all types of United States beaching and landing craft were ready to go. The corresponding British figure was 97.6 per cent. Both indicated an unusually high order of readiness.

On 26 April 1944 Admiral Ramsay and staff took up headquarters at Southwick House, an old country mansion seven miles from Portsmouth. Here Ramsay was frequently visited by Admiral Kirk, and by Generals Eisenhower and Montgomery. Southwick House now became the nerve center for NEPTUNE-OVERLORD, where the great decisions were made.

The culmination of the joint training program was a couple of full-scale rehearsals in late April and early May. Troops and equipment were embarked in the same ships, and for the most part in the same ports, whence they would leave for the Far Shore, as everyone now called the coast of Normandy. One rehearsal was ruined by German E-boats bursting into it in Lyme Bay and sinking two LSTs, with a loss of almost 200 sailors and over 400 soldiers.

Rehearsals completed, the troops returned to their embarkation ports and marshaling camps, where they were held until it was time for the assault. English harbors have never been so full of ships and sailors, or the English land so heavy with troops, as on the eve of NEPTUNE. Some 1,627,000 "Yanks" were bedded down on British soil before the invasion began, and the Admiralty estimate for sailors then afloat in the harbors or at sea was 52,889 Americans, 112,824 British. The latter assembled at Portsmouth, Southampton, Poole, the Solent and Spithead. American forces were assigned to harbors on the south coast between Portland and Falmouth, with the center of gravity at Plymouth. But these West Country ports were too small to hold all American forces afloat. The naval gunfire support ships and many destroyers were based on Belfast Lough in Northern Ireland, where they had plenty of room for maneuvering and training.

On 28 May Admiral Ramsay from Southwick House sent out the signal that started this vast operation in motion: "Carry out Operation NEPTUNE!" All crews were now "sealed" in their ships and craft. The troops had already been placed behind barbed wire in their long marshaling camps, with Counterintelligence Corps keeping a tight watch to prevent leaks and to stifle loose talk.

2. *The Start and the Crossing, 1–6 June*

"For now sits Expectation in the air." By 1 June 1944 southern England began to swarm with British, Canadian and American soldiers in battle uniform, with their weapons and field equipment, marching along country roads by day, rolling in trucks and tanks by night through blacked-out villages and towns, whose citizens had been cautioned to reveal nothing.

All night long, no sound was heard but the clatter of army boots on paved streets, the "*Hup*, two, three, four; *hup*, two, three, four" of sergeants, the rattle of vehicles and the roar and putter of engines, as men marched and machines rolled to the water's edge, there to board beaching craft on the "hards," and transports at the docks. Gunfire support ships converged from northern ports in England and Ireland, and at a score of airfields paratroops climbed on board transport planes and gliders. No music, no flags, no crowds; only women and old men offering a last cup of tea and a hearty "God bless you!" Thus, efficiently and in silence, supported by the prayers of the free world, began the great invasion to crush Germany and liberate France.

Vast, unprecedented, was the press of shipping. From Felixstowe on the North Sea, around the South Coast to Milford Haven in Wales, English harbors were crowded with ships. By 3 June almost

U-1229, with snorkel raised, under attack by aircraft of VC-42

U.S.S. *Bogue*

U.S.S. Bogue *and One of Her Victims*

"Ike," "Alan," and "Mort"

General Dwight D. Eisenhower, Rear Admiral Alan G. Kirk, and Rear Admiral Morton L. Deyo

On board U.S.S. *Tuscaloosa* at Belfast Lough, May 1944

From water color by Lieutenant Dwight Shepler USNR

U.S.S. Emmons *Delivers Gunfire Support, off Omaha Beach, D-day*

Admiral Thomas C. Kinkaid USN

U.S.S. *McDermut*

Night Action, taken from U.S.S. *Pennsylvania*
The nearest line of flashes are gunfire from the U.S. cruisers; the farthest, hits on *Yamashiro* and *Mogami*

The Battle of Surigao Strait

Hit and straddled but still under way

Dead in the water

Note Japanese heavy cruiser on horizon, shooting

Left behind by rest of Taffy 3

Taken from *Kitkun Bay*. These are the only daylight photographs of the Pacific War that show Japanese and U. S. ships on same plate

The Last Fight of Gambier Bay

Rear Admiral Theodore S. Wilkinson USN
Commander Amphibious Force, South Pacific

Admiral Richard L. Conolly USN

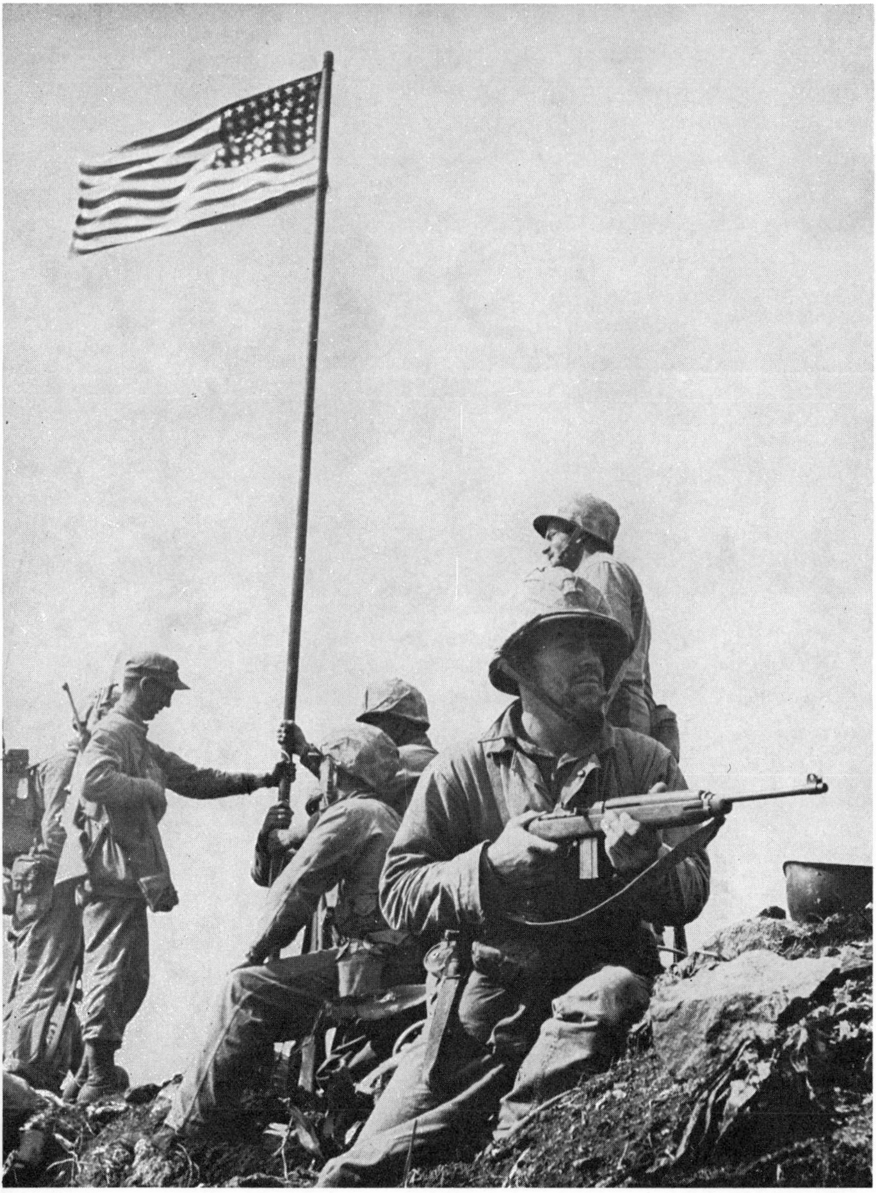

Photo by TSgt. Louis R. Lowery USMC

The First Flag-raising on Mount Suribachi, Iwo Jima

The Marine Corps men grasping the pole are Sgt. H. O. Hansen, Pl. Sgt. E. I. Thomas and 1st Lt. H. B. Shrier. Pfc. J. R. Michaels holds the carbine, Cpl. C. W. Lindberg stands behind

Avengers over the beaches

Kadena Airfield under No. 57

LVTs passing U.S.S. *Tennessee*

L-day at Okinawa

U.S.S. *Laffey*, after hits on 16 April

U.S.S. *Aaron Ward*, after hits on 3 May

Kamikaze Victims at Okinawa

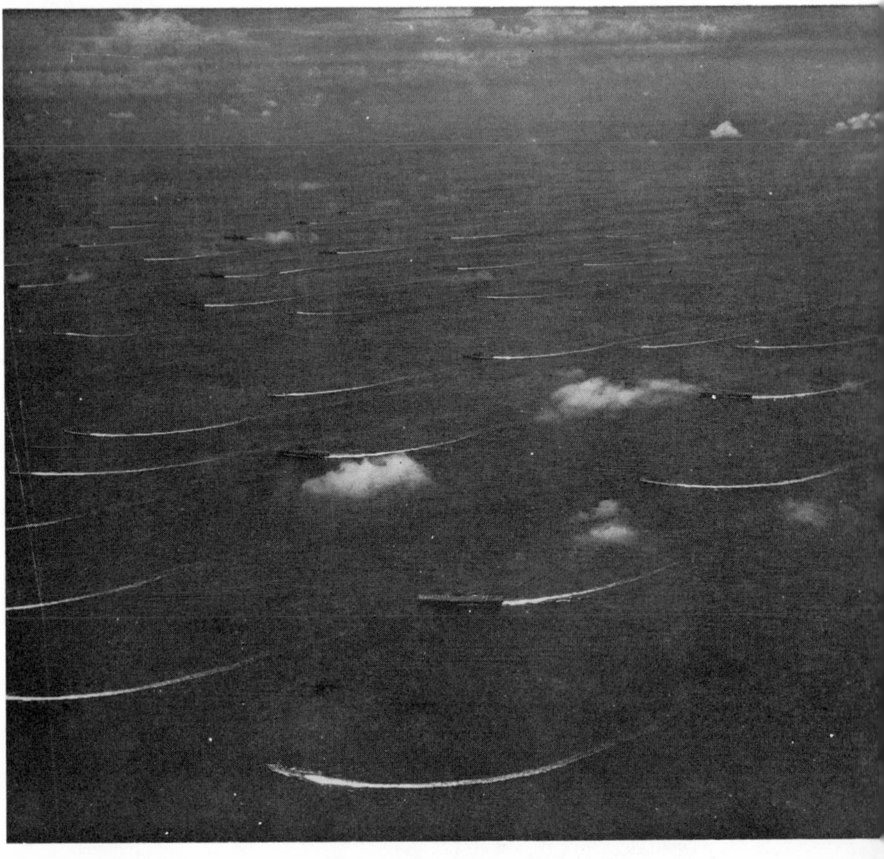

Third Fleet off Coast of Japan, 17 August 1945

every vessel assigned to cross on her own bottom — and there were 931 of them for the American beaches and 1796 for the British — was in her assembly port awaiting the word to go.

Would the capricious June weather of northern Europe allow it to go? Forecasts on Saturday June 3 were unfavorable, even alarming. By 0400 Sunday, when Eisenhower met the generals and admirals at Southwick House, it seemed hopeless. The Supreme Commander then postponed D-day from the 5th to the 6th of June, and vessels which had already started were recalled. At 9 o'clock Sunday evening all top commanders met in Southwick House. The weather chart still looked foul, but the staff meteorologist predicted moderating wind and sea for the 6th. If D-day were postponed further, it would have to be postponed for two weeks, when the tide would be right again for landing; that would never do. So, one hour before midnight 4 June, orders were issued to all ships of both Navies to sail to meet a 6 June D-day, and, at 0415 June 5, General Eisenhower made it definite with the laconic order: "O.K. We'll go."

Almost every one of the thousands of ships and craft was under way by noon June 5. At 1800, off Portland Bill, as far as the eye could reach, the Channel was covered with vessels "fraught with the ministers and instruments of cruel war," the small ones tossing and heaving, the great ones steadily advancing. In Portland itself, as midnight approached, the only assault forces left were the motor torpedo boats, to dash across after daybreak. Portland Bill lighthouse was the point of departure for 925 transport planes carrying 13,000 American paratroops, who preceded the seaborne assault. Groups of 18 aircraft each, flying at about 500 feet, came in with running lights on; as they converged on the darkened lighthouse tower, they blacked out and altered course for the Far Shore, streaming away from the towered headland like the wings on the Victory of Samothrace. Cross-Channel they flew, and at

0136 June 6 began dropping troops in the swampy region behind Utah Beach.

The surface crossing was so well planned, with so many different lanes for the 2727 ships and small craft, that in spite of rough water there were no collisions and few arrived late.

Even more astonishing, the Germans were unaware of the impending invasion. The Allies' secrets never leaked. In the tall, conspicuous lighthouse at Cape Barfleur, the powerful lamp was burning brightly. No Luftwaffe reconnaissance plane had seen anything unusual in the Channel. No German E-boats patrolled — because the local naval commander, Admiral Krancke, considered the weather too foul both for them and for us; and he was easy in his mind because, in his book, the tides were not right for a landing between 4 and 6 June.[5] Not until 0309 June 6 did German search radar pick up anything, although many ships had reached their transport areas an hour earlier. The shore batteries waited until first light, shortly after 0500, when they opened up on destroyers *Corry* and *Fitch*.

To repel any possible invasion, General Dollman's Seventh Army at or near the landing beaches had one armored, two "attack" (fully equipped) infantry divisions, and three "static" or vehicle-less divisions. Six armored and 19 other divisions (the Fifteenth Army) were deployed from the mouth of the Seine to the Pas de Calais. Assuming that these could help, the Germans would outnumber the Allies for at least two weeks; and as standard amphibious doctrine required a three-to-one superiority of attack over defense, the success of Operation NEPTUNE was no foregone conclusion.

Over all German forces was Field Marshal Rommel, "Monty's" old desert antagonist; and over him, Field Marshal von Rundstedt.

[5] The Germans wanted us, and apparently expected us, to land at high water, when the boats would be hung up or blown up by the obstacles; we, naturally, did the contrary.

Rommel believed in those favorite shibboleths of his oriental ally, to "annihilate the enemy at the beachhead," "hurl him into the sea," and so on, and he had more dirty means of doing that than the Japanese ever thought of. First, a line of underwater mines, then all manner of mined obstacles on the beaches designed to trip up landing craft and disembowel men; then the "Atlantic Wall" of casemated and mobile guns, so placed as to enfilade the dry parts of the beaches, with plenty of land mines planted behind them. Hitler supported this water's-edge defense concept of his favorite general — whom he was to liquidate shortly. The Fuehrer, in an impassioned speech to his principal commanders on 20-21 March, declared that the enemy assault must be repelled within a few hours in order to "prevent the reëlection of Roosevelt," who "with luck, would finish up somewhere in jail!" Churchill, too, would be "finished," and the Allies would never be able to launch another invasion.

Thus, D-day caught the Germans in France unready to meet an invasion, and with only one stout leg to their strategic tripod — the army. More than half of that was pinned down in the Pas de Calais because of a successful deception by the British; the creation of a phantom army around Dover. But the Atlantic Wall — that crust of steel and concrete girdled with mined obstacles — inadequate as it proved to be for stopping the American, Canadian and British troops, was the most formidable barrier encountered by any amphibious assault in history. It might even have been a fatal barrier but for the Allies' priceless asset of surprise, which they maintained right up to H-hour of D-day.

3. *The Landings, D-day, 6 June*

The nine-mile stretch of beach on the east coast of the Cotentin (Cherbourg) Peninsula, which we named (and the French still call)

Utah, is featureless: a shelving beach backed by dunes, such as one finds in a thousand places from Canada to Key West. The Germans had not paid as much attention to this — fortunately for General Collins's VII Corps — as to Omaha, or to the British sector; but they had built a concrete wall along the edge of the dunes, planted thousands of underwater mines, and had some sections of beach swept by fields of gunfire.

At 0200 June 6, 34 British and United States minesweepers under a veteran minecraft officer, Commander M. H. Brown RN, began sweeping the transport area ten miles off shore, the fire support areas, and the approach channels for boats and bombardment ships. These mines, of the type that required several sweeps to deactivate, proved to be the most dangerous enemy weapon of the Utah assault; two minecraft, two destroyers, a DE, two LCIs, a PC and three LCTs carrying tanks were sunk by them.

First wave of troops touched down exactly at H-hour, 0630. A curious feature of this landing was that the whole thing "slipped" a mile south of the designated points. A ten-mile boat trip against head wind and sea, and a strong southerly set of current, were responsible. This mistake — which Brigadier General Theodore Roosevelt discovered — was a lucky break, as the "right" beaches were enfiladed by casemated German batteries and the "wrong" ones were lightly defended. Twenty-six assault waves were landed before noon, dumps were quickly established inland; by 1800, over 21,000 troops and 1700 vehicles were ashore, and the big transports were not only unloaded by midnight, but, most of them, back in Portland. The 4th Division, with the essential help of the paratroops who dropped well behind Utah, had reached their first objective line, and suffered only 197 casualties.

A principal factor in breaking down German resistance at Utah was abundant and accurate naval gunfire support, especially on the remote and large-caliber batteries that the assault troops could not get at. This was directed by Rear Admiral Morton L. Deyo

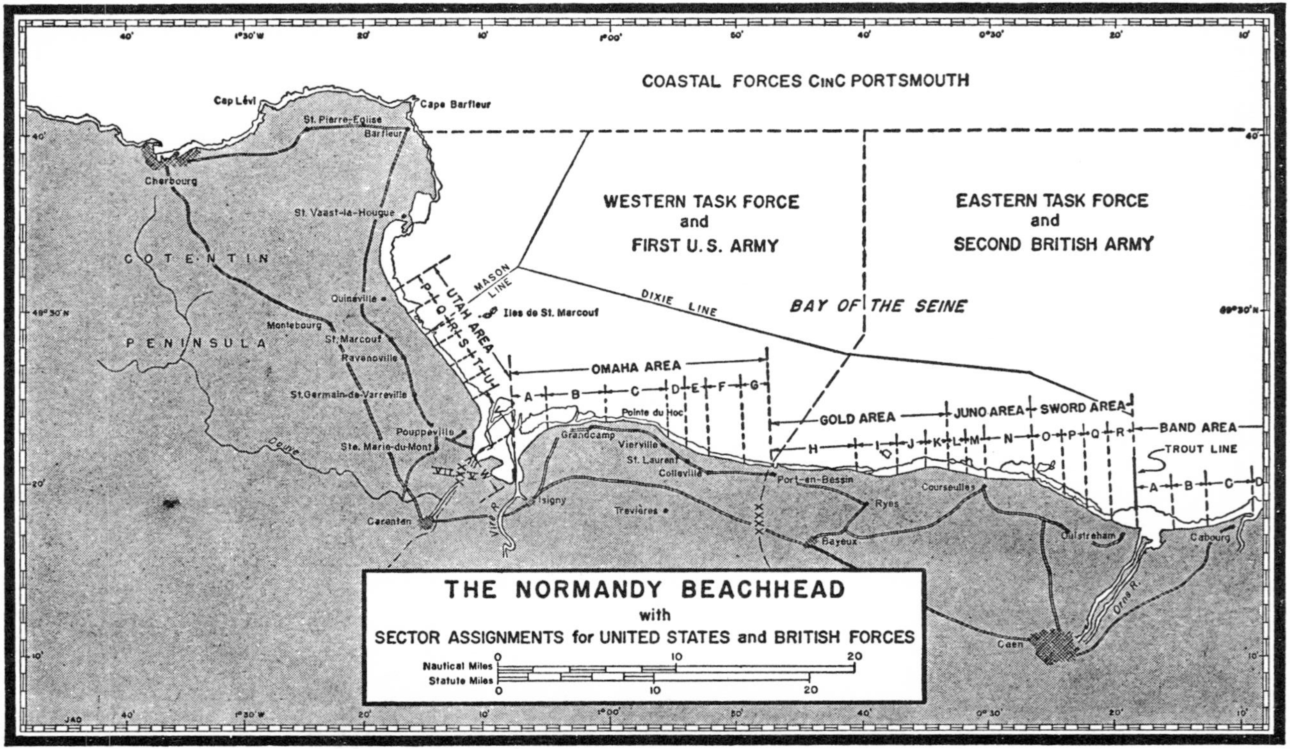
COASTAL FORCES CinC PORTSMOUTH
WESTERN TASK FORCE
and
FIRST U.S. ARMY
EASTERN TASK FORCE
and
SECOND BRITISH ARMY
BAY OF THE SEINE
DIXIE LINE
MASON LINE
UTAH AREA
OMAHA AREA
GOLD AREA
JUNO AREA
SWORD AREA
BAND AREA
TROUT LINE
Cap Lévi
Cape Barfleur
St. Pierre-Eglise
Barfleur
Cherbourg
St. Vaast-la-Hougue
COTENTIN
PENINSULA
Quinéville
Montebourg
St. Marcouf
Ravenoville
St. Germain-de-Varreville
Pouppeville
Ste. Marie-du-Mont
Carentan
Iles de St. Marcouf
Pointe du Hoc
Grandcamp
Vierville
St. Laurent
Colleville
Isigny
Trevières
Port-en-Bessin
Bayeux
Ryes
Courseulles
Ouistreham
Caen
Cabourg
Orne R.
Vire R.
Douve
VII
XXX
XXXX
THE NORMANDY BEACHHEAD
with
SECTOR ASSIGNMENTS for UNITED STATES and BRITISH FORCES
Nautical Miles
Statute Miles
0
10
20

in heavy cruiser *Tuscaloosa*. The flagship, *Nevada*, and H.M.S. *Black Prince* and *Erebus*, for 50 minutes following H-hour, bombarded heavy German batteries north of the beachhead, using air spot. After completing these scheduled shoots, the big ships fired on targets of opportunity on request of shore fire-control parties. The new method of air spotting by land-based fighter planes, devised at Salerno, was used. *Nevada*, that gallant old survivor of Pearl Harbor, even answered a call for gunfire from the paratroops well inland, and received the thanks of General Ridgway.

Very different indeed was the experience of landing at Omaha Beach.[6] This six-mile-long stretch between Pointe de la Percée and Port-en-Bessin was far better defended than Utah, both by fixed defenses and troops; and no American airdrop behind it engaged the attention of the Germans, who were two or three times as numerous as Allied Intelligence had reported. Casualties were staggering, but General Gerow's V Corps United States Army (1st and 29th Divisions) got through, thanks to their own valor, the landing well planned by Admiral Hall, and naval gunfire support rendered by Admiral Bryant's ships.

The coast here trends easterly and takes on a more rugged character than the Utah area of the Cotentin Peninsula. The land is a bold, high plateau which the sea has abruptly chopped off, leaving steep, sandy bluffs, at the foot of which are wide sandy beaches of gentle gradient. According to plan, the troops landed along this coast at or near low water, so that UDTs would have a chance to blow beach obstacles while the flats were dry, and rising tide (which rose to 22 feet on D-day) would make it easier for reinforcements to get in. Thus, the assault echelons, after debarking at low water, had to tramp across a wet beach planted with booby-trapped obstacles. Above the beach was a ruff of "con-

[6] For a fine detailed narrative, see S. L. A. Marshall "First Wave at Omaha Beach" in *Atlantic Monthly* for November 1960.

certina" barbed wire, against an artificial seawall. Having surmounted that, the GI found himself on a level, grassy area 150 to 300 yards wide, heavily mined and devoid of cover. On the inland side of this level shelf was a line of bluffs, through which there were only four exits, deep ravines eroded through the plateau. Each exit was thoroughly covered by gunfire from concealed concrete emplacements which could not be reached by naval guns.

Altogether, the Germans had provided the best imitation of hell for an invading force that American troops had encountered anywhere. Even the Japanese defenses of Tarawa, Peleliu and Iwo Jima are not to be compared with these. Moreover, the protective works for Omaha had hardly been touched before D-day, owing to the imperative need for tactical surprise. Allied air power had concentrated on isolating, not pounding, the beachhead; and the Navy was not given the time to do much damage on D-day morning.

Minesweeping by British and Canadian minecraft began before midnight and was effectively concluded by 0355. The fire support ships, led by 32-year-old *Arkansas* and including two French cruisers, arrived at 0220. The assault elements of the 1st and 29th Divisions — 16 big transports, 205 beaching craft and numerous small craft — arrived half an hour later. By 0430 the initial boat waves were on their way to the beach from the big transports, anchored eleven miles off shore.[7] There was no enemy reaction until 0530, half an hour before sunrise, when a light battery began firing ineffectively at *Arkansas* and several destroyers. For 35 minutes, beginning at 0550, *Texas* and other gunfire support ships worked over the beach exit that led to Vierville; *Arkansas* and H.M.S. *Glasgow* plastered the Les Moulins area; French cruiser *Georges Leygues* and other ships smacked the Saint-Laurent

[7] Admiral Kirk was criticized for placing his transports so far out; the reason he did so was to protect them from coast defense guns on the lofty Pointe du Hoc near the western end of the Omaha area. This point was captured by Lt. Col. Rudder's 2nd Ranger Battalion United States Army on D-day morning, only to find that the dreaded cannon were "Quaker guns" made of telephone poles.

plateau where the military cemetery is now located. All this did some good, but not nearly enough; and the 484 B–24s of VIII Army Air Force, which were supposed to bomb the major enemy strongpoints after the ships lifted their fire, missed the beach altogether and dropped their stuff on crops and cattle three miles inland.

At H-hour, 0630, when the naval bombardment ceased, a new and ominous noise was heard. From Pointe de la Percée to Port-en-Bessin, German automatic weapons and artillery began belching fire on landing craft at the water's edge.

A bloody morning lay ahead. First casualties were the DD (dual drive) amphibious tanks, scheduled to land five minutes ahead of the infantry. These were fitted with "bloomers," canvas water-wings which were supposed to afford enough flotation to enable them to churn ashore if launched from LCTs a mile or more off the beach. On this occasion the bloomers failed to bloom in the rough water, and 27 out of 32 tanks destined for the eastern half of Omaha Beach went straight to the bottom, carrying most of their crews with them. Those for the western part, owing to the good judgment of Captain Lorenzo S. Sabin, were landed on the beach directly from LCTs, but most of them were shot up by German artillery before they could support the American infantry.

As landing craft of the first assault waves grounded and dropped ramps, the GIs came under intense enemy gunfire. They had to wade through 50 to 100 yards of water, then cross 200 to 300 yards of beach, dodging the fixed obstacles, to the protection of the seawall. Some drowned after one wound or a stumble, others were blown to bits by the mines or, if only wounded, lay on the beach until the flood tide drowned them; so many company officers were killed or wounded that survivors, crouching under the seawall, knew not what to do next. Only two companies out of the eight in the first assault wave were on the beaches where they were supposed to be. By 0800 not a man or a vehicle had moved in-

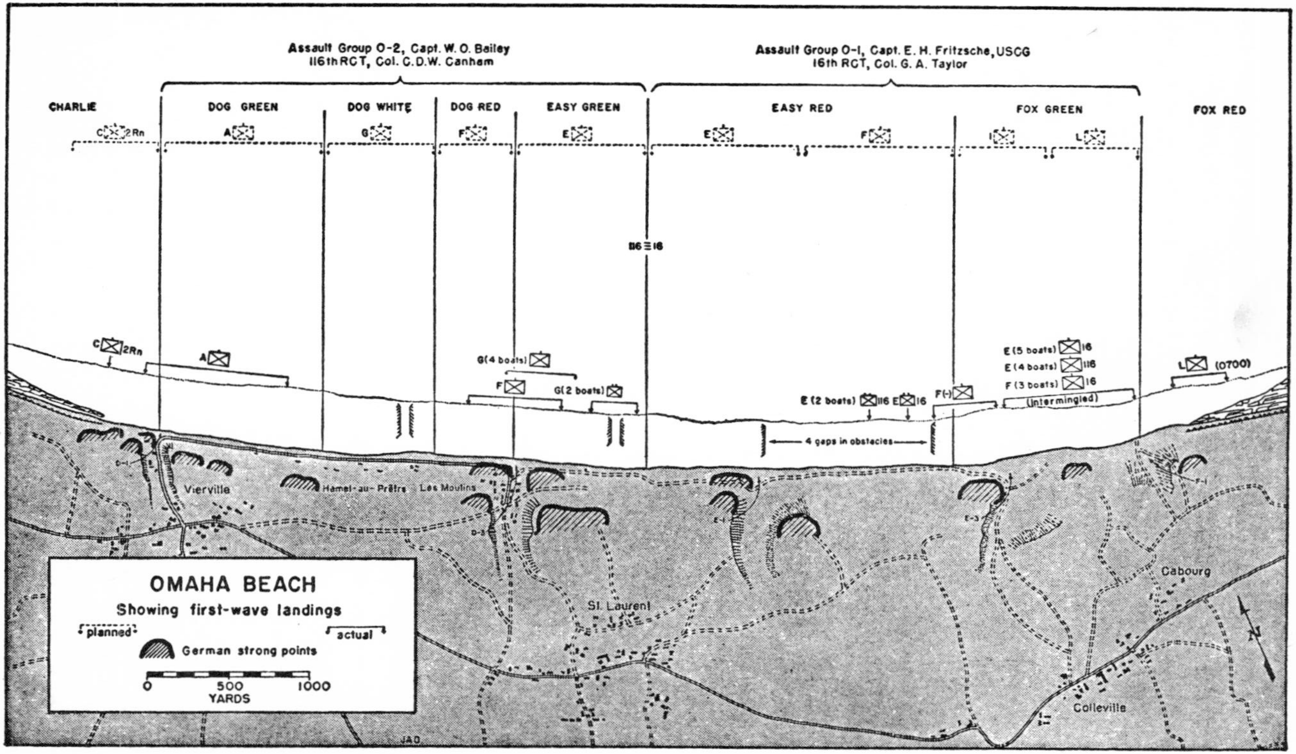

Assault Group O-2, Capt. W. O. Bailey
116th RCT, Col. C.D.W. Canham
Assault Group O-1, Capt. E. H. Fritzsche, USCG
16th RCT, Col. G. A. Taylor
CHARLIE
DOG GREEN
DOG WHITE
DOG RED
EASY GREEN
EASY RED
FOX GREEN
FOX RED
116 ≡ 16
G(4 boats)
G(2 boats)
E (2 boats)
E (5 boats)
E (4 boats)
F (3 boats)
(intermingled)
(0700)
4 gaps in obstacles
Vierville
Hamel-au-Prêtre
Les Moulins
St. Laurent
Cabourg
Colleville
OMAHA BEACH
Showing first-wave landings
planned
actual
German strong points
0 500 1000
YARDS

land in the western sector, and very few had done so in the eastern; and the congestion became so great that at 0830 the head beachmaster ordered no more boats to land until it could be cleared up.

The busiest people in this phase of the assault were the 16 UDTs of seven sailors and five Army Engineers each, trying to blast boat channels through beach obstacles before they became submerged by the rising tide. One team was wiped out by an enemy salvo just as it landed. Another had its charges all set to blow when a direct hit set them off and killed every man but one. Before the flood tide, rising twelve inches every eight minutes, forced them to vacate, these brave men had blown five big channels and three partial ones through the hideous array of murderous obstacles.

Once the assault started, landing and beaching craft crews were completely on their own, with no direction from senior officers; they had to use their own judgment. Neither admirals nor generals could learn what was going on. Three troop-laden LCIs were hit by artillery fire and burned; their survivors had to swim for it. For two hours after the beachmaster suspended landings, about 50 LCTs and LCIs milled about looking for gaps in the obstacles. Two young skippers then broke the stalemate. Lieutenant (jg) S. W. Brinker USNR crashed *LCT-30* through and beached, her automatic weapons blazing at an enemy strongpoint, which shot her up so that she had to be abandoned; but her vehicles got ashore. Lieutenant E. B. Koehler USNR followed with *LCI-554*, but managed to retract after landing his passengers; and after this example the shoreward movement was never interrupted.

Most of the artillery scheduled to land between 0800 and 0900 was boated in dukws, which were unable to cope with the choppy sea. Only five made the beach; hence only one Army battery managed to get into action on D-day. But the place of the drowned artillery was proudly taken by the 5-inch guns of the support destroyers. At 0950 Admiral Bryant called to all gunfire support ships over TBS: "Get on them, men! Get on them! They are raising hell with the men on the beach, and we can't have any more of that. We must stop it!" Magnificently they complied, although hampered by the want of shore fire-control parties with the troops — these had been shot up or their radios drowned out. In their eagerness to help, the destroyers incurred the risk of running aground time and again; several actually did scrape the bottom, but got off. *Frankford, Doyle, Harding, Thompson, Baldwin, McCook* and *Emmons* all got into the act; the first-named fired from shoal water up to 800 yards off the beach, often with but a few inches between her keel and the sand. Captain Sanders led his "cans" this close to shore in order to see profitable targets with the naked eye. The battleships and cruisers, using air spot by pairs of Spitfires as off Utah, took on inland strongpoints and batteries; and *Texas* in the afternoon helped materially to clear one of the beach exits with shellfire. She and "Arky" between them shot off 771 rounds of 14-inch on D-day. "Without that gunfire," wrote the chief of staff of the 1st Division to Admiral Hall, "we positively could not have crossed the beaches."

Around 1100 the situation at Omaha improved. Surviving company officers began leading their men inland and smoking Germans out of their casemates. Enemy artillery fire on the beaches diminished during the afternoon. Engineers bulldozed two new roads inland, and tanks started rumbling along them. Army artillery began to come ashore in strength. By dark the better part of five regimental combat teams were ashore, and the beachhead extended a mile or more from highwater mark.

Admiral Kirk, thinking over D-day ten years later, said, "Our greatest asset was the resourcefulness of the American sailor." Throughout the confusion created by heavy enemy fire on the boats and explosions of mined obstacles, the bluejackets kept their heads, found means to beach (not always on the right beach), retracted, brought in another load under fire, never flinched, never failed. Destroyer sailors risked grounding and being pounded to pieces by shore batteries. Battleship sailors did their best to knock out strongpoints. Minecraft sailors were in there first, sweeping. UDTs, the "naked warriors," sacrificed themselves to help the others. Courage there was in plenty; but the resourcefulness of these young sailors made courage and training count. That evening, when General Gerow set up headquarters on the beach, his first message to General Bradley, still on board *Augusta*, was: "Thank God for the United States Navy!"

Although we cannot tell the story of the Eastern Naval Task Force commanded by Rear Admiral Sir Philip Vian RN in anything like the detail it deserves, we remind the reader that it was an essential part of Operation NEPTUNE-OVERLORD, and a bigger part than that assigned to Admiral Kirk's Western Naval Task Force — a three-division as compared with a two-division landing. All troops concerned were British or Canadian, but many beaching craft of the United States Navy participated, just as British landing craft, minecraft and support ships were used in the American sector.

The British assault area extended from Port-en-Bessin, where Omaha ended, about twenty-five statute miles eastward to Ouistreham at the mouth of the River Orne. The three assault landing beaches (Gold, Juno, and Sword) were separated from one another by reefs which prevented access to the shore.

Landings in this sector, as at Utah, were preceded by a paratroop drop. The 6th Airborne Division British Army dropped during the night of 5-6 June, and seized bridges over the Orne and the Caen Canal.

Because the reefs and the foul ground off the British beaches were bare at low water, it was necessary to postpone H-hour until the flood tide had been running between 60 and 90 minutes. This gift of time was well improved by the Royal Navy to bombard selected strongpoints with high-caliber shell for almost two hours by daylight — four times as long a bombardment as the United States Navy had opportunity to deliver at Utah and Omaha. H.M.S. *Warspite,* veteran of the Battle of Jutland, was particularly effective. Owing to this two-hour pounding of beach defenses and strongpoints, and the fact that only one "static" German division was defending the British area, these landings were a pushover. But elements of a German panzer division were about to be committed, and Caen, which optimists thought might fall on 7 June, would be captured only after more than a month of heavy fighting. The Germans here made their bitterest stand against the invasion, to block the road to Paris. All this was expected, and in accordance with Montgomery's plan to draw upon the British Army the weight of German countereffort, giving the United States Army time to capture Cherbourg.

The Royal Navy kept busy delivering gunfire support in its area, as the United States Navy did off Omaha and Utah. There was not a day and hardly an hour after 6 June when one or more British battleships, cruisers or destroyers were not supporting Sir Miles Dempsey's Second Army. Since the British sector lay close to Le Havre, a German advanced naval base, the British gunfire ships were subjected to frequent night raids by enemy torpedo boats, and lost several ships. At Admiral Ramsay's request, Bomber Command R.A.F. hit Le Havre harbor with 2000 tons of bombs shortly before midnight 14 June. The effects were catastrophic. Three torpedo boats, 10 E-boats, 15 R-boats, several patrol vessels and harbor defense vessels, and 11 other small craft were sunk; others were badly damaged. And at dusk 15 June, the R.A.F. hit Boulogne with a similar raid, sank 25 R-boats and small craft, and damaged 10 others. Thus, within two days, the German surface fleet threatening the Allies in the Bay of the Seine was wiped out. But there were more to come. E-boats were shipped into

Le Havre by rail, 47 one-man "human torpedoes" came out in July and sank three British minecraft; remote-controlled explosive motor boats were employed with some effect. All these "secret weapons" were mere fleabites to the British, annoying them without even delaying the invasion. British coastal craft, aided by American motor torpedo boats, set up a close blockade of Le Havre which squelched that source of nuisance.

These events on the east flank are an interesting commentary on Admiral Mahan's doctrine of the ineffectiveness of special devices and a mosquito fleet against a seagoing navy. The British were shuttling thousands of men and hundreds of ships between the English coast and the Far Shore every day and night, under the noses of the Germans at Le Havre, a city that had land, sea and air communications with Germany. The enemy had plenty of torpedo boats, small craft and secret weapons; but they availed him naught. And his U-boats, which might have raised havoc among the invasion fleet, were kept out of the Channel by a tight air and surface patrol.

4. *Consolidating and Supporting the Beachhead, 7–18 June*

Consolidation of the American beachhead and the beginning of a massive buildup began on 7 June. Although the troops had scanty artillery and tank support from their own elements that day, they enjoyed ready and accurate naval gunfire support, which frustrated the enemy's attempts to counterattack. Behind Utah, Generals Barton and Collins devoted their efforts to cleaning out pockets of resistance and the 4th Division extended its line about two miles to the north. Admiral Deyo's gunfire support group had another busy day: *Nevada* broke up a troop concentration; *Quincy* obliged the Army by smashing a few bridges over the Douvres River; *Tuscaloosa* took on a 155-mm coastal battery near

Saint-Vaast which was straddling destroyer *Jeffers*, and which *Nevada* finally demolished. The same sort of thing went on at Omaha, as the beachhead enlarged.

So well had the airdrops and deception done their work that no German reinforcements reached the American battle area before June 8. By that time, the original defenders had been all but obliterated. These reinforcements afforded the gunfire support ships plenty more shoots during the next six days. Army aviation engineers had a 3500-foot runway good enough for transport planes ready by 2100 June 8. Four full divisions were ashore at Omaha on the 9th, and two at Utah — not counting the paratroops, who were fighting harder than anybody. Six more divisions were landed on the American beaches by 22 June, and the millionth Allied soldier to arrive in France got there on the Fourth of July.

Unloading at Omaha was greatly facilitated by "Mulberry A," an artificial harbor composed of concrete caissons that were towed across the Channel and sunk, enclosing a sheltered harbor as big as Gibraltar's, with three pontoon-section runways where LSTs could unload at any stage of tide. In addition, both Omaha and Utah had a "Gooseberry," a sheltered harbor for small craft created by sinking a line of old ships parallel to the shore. Both were British projects and British built. Those at the American beaches were functioning by 16 June. The aspect of these lonely stretches of beach, where nothing bigger than a small fishing boat had ever landed, was astounding; Omaha's Mulberry A had become the most active port in Europe, with the British Mulberry B a close second.

Leaving it to others to describe the movements of troops ashore, we must record German counterattacks on the naval forces, which stood by for call fire for two weeks. The German Air Force flew up about a thousand aircraft from Germany and Italy, and expended them freely in a vain endeavor to hamper the Allied build-up. Their attacks began on the night of 7-8 June, when they sank destroyer *Meredith* with a glide-bomb, and next day they got a Liberty ship. Within a few days, fighter interception became so well organized that Luftwaffe raids became less frequent.

The German weapon that gave sailors the greatest concern was the mine. One of the most fortunate things that happened to the Allies was the enemy's delay in planting the "oyster" mines that he had recently developed; these lay on the bottom and were exploded by the pressure applied by a ship going over them. Most of the mines that did the damage off the beaches were delayed-action magnetic or sonic mines, laid before D-day. At 0820 June 7, *Susan B. Anthony* exploded one of these while approaching Omaha, and went down quickly. Her troops were rescued by small craft. Next day saw the loss by mines of destroyer escort *Rich* and of destroyer *Glennon*. Up to 3 July, 261 mines were swept in the American sector and 291 in the British.

5. *The Great Storm and the Capture of Cherbourg, 18 June–16 July*

On D-day plus 12, June 18, everything in both sectors was "all tickety-boo," to use a favorite phrase of Field Marshal Montgomery for describing military perfection. By the end of that day 314,514 troops, 41,000 vehicles and 116,000 tons of supplies had been landed over the American beaches; 314,547 troops, 54,000 vehicles and 102,000 tons of supplies over the British beaches. Then Nature intervened with the worst June storm in forty years.

At midnight 18-19 June, a strong wind with heavy rain began to blow on the assault beaches. During the day the wind increased and the sea built up so rapidly that by midafternoon unloading had to stop on Omaha beach. This state of affairs continued for two more days. Heavy surf pounded the beaches, small craft took shelter behind the block-ships, all work stopped, ships anchored off shore dragged anchors and fouled one another, beaching craft were driven ashore, Mulberry A began to break up, and the crash of small craft, dukws, vehicles and derelict units grinding together was heard above the din of war. When the wind abated, on 22 June, the Omaha beaches were a shambles of stranded and wrecked craft, coasting vessels, barges and Mulberry fragments. General Bradley was "appalled by the desolation." Yet, even before the wreckage was surveyed, unloading had to be resumed, since almost nothing had been landed during those three days; it had been necessary to ration ammunition among the troops ashore. Unloading soon recovered momentum, and on 24 June 15,525 troops, 3321 vehicles and 11,562 tons of supplies were landed over the Omaha beaches alone.

Mulberry A was so thoroughly broken up that Admiral Kirk decided to make no attempt to repair it. Mulberry B at Arromanche was far less damaged, owing to its partial protection by the offlying reefs and capes. Most of the "gooseberry" breakwaters of sunken ships at Omaha and Utah held fast.

This storm warned all hands that their hold on Normandy was precarious. Until the Allies could capture Cherbourg, the nearest major port, they would be at the mercy of tricky English Channel weather. "We've *got* to get to Cherbourg in a hurry," was the theme of every staff conference at First Army headquarters. "Fortress Cherbourg" contained a garrison of over 40,000 men. The German commander had been charged by Hitler to make it impregnable. The Fuehrer knew that the Allies must have a port to supply their armies, and thought he could stop the invasion by denying it to them.

By 22 June General Collins's VII Corps, now beefed-up to six divisions, two squadrons of motorized cavalry and two tank battalions, was ready to advance. The three divisions which did most of the fighting lost over 2800 killed and 13,500 wounded in liberating Cherbourg. But it will not detract from the Army's glory to point out that the United States Navy delivered an important Sunday punch on 25 June.

Admiral Deyo commanded the bombardment force, which comprised most of his Utah fire-support ships, together with others from Omaha. They silenced a coast defense battery of 150-mm guns at Querqueville, and delivered carefully air-spotted fire on German strongpoints in the town, into which the American troops were now breaking. The four 280-mm (11-inch) pieces of Battery "Hamburg" east of the city, which had a range of 40,000 yards, were taken under fire by *Texas*, *Arkansas*, and a number of destroyers, two of which were hit, as was *Texas*, none of them lethally. Only one gun of the Hamburg's 4-gun battery was knocked out; but that helped, in conjunction with shoots on other batteries. Both German commanders at Cherbourg, and Admiral Krancke, regarded this "naval bombardment of a hitherto unequaled fierceness" as one of the main factors which led to the surrender of the city next day. A number of isolated forts and units still held out, and the Navy helped mop them up.

Operation NEPTUNE, the amphibious part of OVERLORD, was now concluded. On 25 June Montgomery opened his drive to take Caen, which fell on 9 July. The American First Army, after eleven days' heavy fighting in the *bocage* country, entered Saint-Lô on 18 July. Patton "busted loose" on the 30th, and the rest of the great story of the drive across France and into Germany is the Army's.

The Allied Navies' first task in France was now the clearance of Cherbourg, which the Germans had left a demolished, ruined and booby-trapped port. The inner harbor was a mass of scuttled ships, thickly sown with mines. All cranes and other harbor works which could have been useful were destroyed. Commodore William A. Sullivan and part of his salvage outfit arrived around 1 July, followed by Rear Admiral John Wilkes as Commander United States Naval Bases, France, with a capable staff and a few hundred Seabees. Six British and three American salvage vessels, 20 United States Navy coastal minesweepers, two flotillas of similar British craft and four flotillas of British motor minesweepers were allocated for the clearance. Commodore Sullivan, who had already cleared North African and Italian ports, found German sabotage and demolition to be more spectacular than effective, but their mining of both outer and inner harbors was thorough beyond belief.

The first Allied cargo landed at Cherbourg from lighters on 16 July. By the end of that month, 12 to 14 Liberty ships could be discharged at once, together with six LSTs. By autumn, Cherbourg had become second only to Marseilles as a port of logistic supply to the United States Army in Europe. Proudly the Cherbourgeois refer to their city as the first French port to be recovered, and the starting point of the *chemin de la libération* which led to Paris and the Rhine.

6. *The Invasion of Southern France, 15 April–15 September 1944*

The Southern France amphibious operation — ANVIL, as it was originally called, DRAGOON as Churchill renamed it, because he said he was "dragooned" into it by Roosevelt and Eisenhower — is one of the most controversial of the entire war. The dispute, unlike those over Tarawa and Anzio, is not about how it was carried out — everyone admits that DRAGOON was done perfectly — but whether a different operation, which might have beaten the Russians to the Danube, should not have been substituted, as Churchill ardently desired.

Since the Allies had not sufficient troop-lift or gun power for a simultaneous invasion of both Northern and Southern France, the latter had to be postponed to 15 August. General Eisenhower insisted on this southern invasion for two good reasons. He knew that the armies would need another major port — Marseilles — to handle their logistic supply; and he was right, for Cherbourg could not do it all, and Antwerp was not secured until 1945. In addition, "Ike" wanted General Patch's Seventh United States Army and General de Lattre de Tassigny's First French Army deployed on his southern flank to take part in the invasion of Germany. Churchill and the British Chiefs of Staff opposed the Southern France invasion because many of the troops would have to be taken out of the Italian campaign, Alan Brooke's pet baby; and also because they wanted any amphibious operation in the Mediterranean to be directed to Trieste. From that port at the head of the Adriatic, troops would march through the Ljubljana Gap in the Balkans and reach Budapest and Vienna before the Russians.

All American strategists, planners, generals and admirals, and (naturally) the French, were appalled at the idea of shifting this amphibious assault to Trieste, a thousand miles farther than Marseilles from Gibraltar. Eisenhower rejected it, not once and again but again and again. Hanson Baldwin supports Churchill in denouncing the American refusal to make this switch as a major blunder, assuming that we could have liberated Hungary and Austria ahead of the Russians, and perhaps even have kept Rumania and Bulgaria from going Red. But — could we have? The Ljubljana Gap, narrow, tortuous, dominated by mountain peaks, would have been a tactical cul-de-sac. The railway runs through innumerable tunnels which the Germans, who were there in force, could easily have blown; and the road was a two-lane affair, over which the logistic support of more than two divisions would have been impossible. Moreover, Tito's partisans, had we attempted to march through Yugoslavia, would have joined the Germans against us.[8] At best, the operation could not have started before the

[8] Wilhelm Hoettl, in *The Secret Front* (1954) p. 165 and ff. tells of intercepting a courier from Stalin to Tito *ordering* him to join forces with the Germans if the Allies tried a landing on the Yugoslav coast; and Anthony Pirie in *Operation Bern-*

end of August, when the Russians were already in Bucharest. Thus, an operation which secured Marseilles, brought in a French Army to help liberate their own country, and provided two more armies for the invasion of Germany, if Churchill and Alan Brooke had had their way, would have been sacrificed in favor of a Balkan safari with very slight chance of success.

Throughout this period of indecision, which lasted right down to D-day minus six when Churchill made his final plea for reconsideration, planning for DRAGOON continued at Admiral Hewitt's headquarters on the Naples waterfront, assuming that it would take place. Training and rehearsals were so thorough that, as Admiral Lowry remarked, all hands "could have made the landing without an operation order." That is as it should be in an amphibious operation, and generally was, too, when Admirals Turner, Wilkinson, Kirk or Hewitt were in charge.

Marseilles, the No. 1 objective, and Toulon, were too well protected by 240-mm coast defense batteries to be the targets of a direct assault. Five yellow sand beaches between pineclad rocky headlands were chosen on the coast of Provence for the initial landings, starting at the Îles d'Hyères and extending to Calanque d'Anthéor, bracketing the gulfs of Saint-Tropez and Fréjus. Knowledge of these spots was easy to obtain from French officers at headquarters and from aërial photographs; and the F.F.I., the patriotic French resistance forces which were very active in Provence, provided abundant data on enemy movements and emplacements. These last were formidable, but not in a class with those of Normandy. The Germans made good use of heavy coast artillery and big guns from French warships, emplaced in heavy concrete casemates. Thousands of land mines were planted on the beaches and behind them, with a density found nowhere else but in Normandy. Underwater obstacles were far less formidable

---

hard (1961) p. 91 tells of Gen. Velebit, one of Tito's closest collaborators, going to the German Ambassador at Agram with that very proposal.

than on the northern coast, and the Navy, after its experience there, was better prepared to cope with them. Germany had about 30,000 troops in the assault zone and over 200,000 near enough to be committed, if the coastal defense could manage to hold up the invaders for a few days. A vain hope, indeed.

The Western Naval Task Force was predominantly American in composition as well as in command, but the Royal Navy made a substantial contribution of gunfire support ships, transports, minecraft, tugboats and LCTs. The French Navy used most of its ships that had been in OVERLORD, and several more. The Royal Canadian Navy provided two fast converted transports and several hundred commandos.

As Eighth Fleet included nothing bigger than light cruisers, five battleships (U.S.S. *Nevada, Texas, Arkansas,* H.M.S. *Ramillies,* French *Lorraine*); three heavy cruisers (*Augusta, Quincy, Tuscaloosa*), and many destroyers and beaching craft were sent down from the English Channel. Also, a number of destroyers manned by Polish and Greek sailors, and flying the flags of these countries, were assigned.

The command organization[9] may be represented as follows: —

WESTERN NAVAL TASK FORCE
Vice Admiral H. Kent Hewitt in *Catoctin*
Lieutenant General Alexander M. Patch, Seventh Army
Général de l'Armée de Lattre de Tassigny, II Corps

SITKA FORCE	ALPHA FORCE	DELTA FORCE	CAMEL FORCE
R. Adm. L. A. Davidson	R. Adm. F. J. Lowry	R. Adm. Bertram J. Rodgers	R. Adm. Spencer S. Lewis
U. S. and French Commandos	Maj. Gen. J. W. O'Daniel	Maj. Gen. W. W. Eagles	Maj. Gen. J. E. Dahlquist
(Îles d'Hyères and Rade de Bormes)	3rd Division U. S. Army	45th Division U. S. Army	36th Division U. S. Army
	(Cavalaire and Pampelonne)	(Baie de Bougnon and Golfe St.-Tropez)	(Fréjus, St.-Raphaël, Calanque d'Anthéor)

[9] The statement in Fergusson *The Watery Maze,* that the top Allied Mediterranean commanders, General Maitland Wilson, Admiral Sir John Cunningham and General Ira Eaker, controlled DRAGOON from Ajaccio, is incorrect. These gentlemen simply approved the plan drafted by Admiral Hewitt's and General Patch's staffs, and exercised no control whatsoever over the operation.

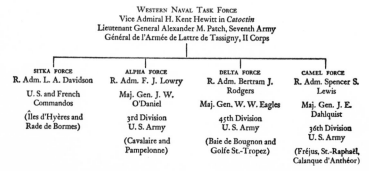

The main landings were preceded by a successful parachute drop from almost 400 planes of a provisional air division U.S. Army, between 0315 and 0515 August 15. There were also Commando raids in the light of a last-quarter moon; one to deceive the Germans (which it didn't do) into believing that the big landings were to be near Toulon, and the other, led in person by Lieutenant Commander Douglas E. Fairbanks, to cut the Corniche road from Cannes (which they failed to do). "Sitka" Force, a double-Commando affair, was more successful. One part seized most of the Îles d'Hyères, and the other, composed of picked men from four nations, blocked the road from Toulon and scared the daylights out of all German troops in the vicinity. Between 0600 and 0730 there was the usual minesweeping, air bombing, and naval bombardment, which proved to be adequate to discourage the defenders.

In this operation, to do away with having to supplicate Army Air Force for air support, Admiral Hewitt had strengthened Western Naval Task Force by two groups of escort carriers: five of the Royal Navy under Rear Admiral Troubridge in H.M.S. *Royalist*, and four of the United States Navy under Rear Admiral Durgin in *Tulagi*. These operated off shore for two weeks without being subjected to a single enemy air or submarine attack. The primary mission of their air groups was to spot for naval gunfire; a secondary one, in which they were highly successful, was to bomb the retiring enemy.

D-day for DRAGOON, 15 August, broke fair, calm and misty. The summits of the Alpes Maritimes could be seen above the haze. Aërial bombing ceased at 0730, to let the Navy deliver the final licks. At that moment the first troop-laden LCVP were speeding down the boat lanes. Fire support destroyers opened a heavy drenching fire on the land behind the beaches. Rocket-equipped LCT spouted missiles onto the beaches themselves. Then compara-

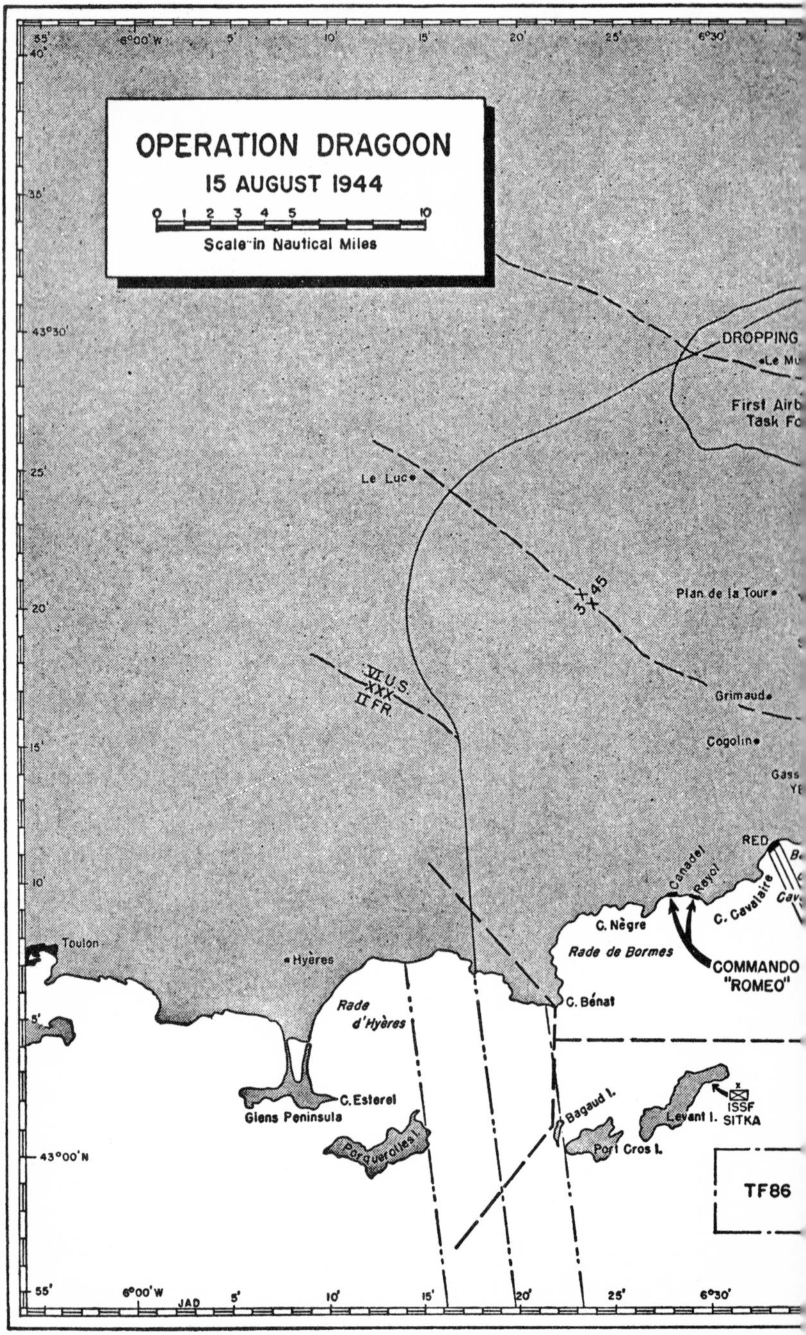

OPERATION DRAGOON
15 AUGUST 1944
0 1 2 3 4 5 10
Scale in Nautical Miles
DROPPING
First Airb
Task Fo
Le Luc
3 X 45
Plan de la Tour
VI U.S.
XXX
II FR.
Grimaud
Cogolin
Toulon
Hyères
Canadel
Rayol
C. Cavalaire
C. Nègre
Rade de Bormes
COMMANDO
"ROMEO"
C. Bénat
Rade d'Hyères
C. Esterel
Giens Peninsula
Porquerolles I.
Bagaud I.
Port Cros I.
Levant I.
ISSF
SITKA
TF86
RED
43°30'
43°00'N
6°00'W
6°30'
JAD

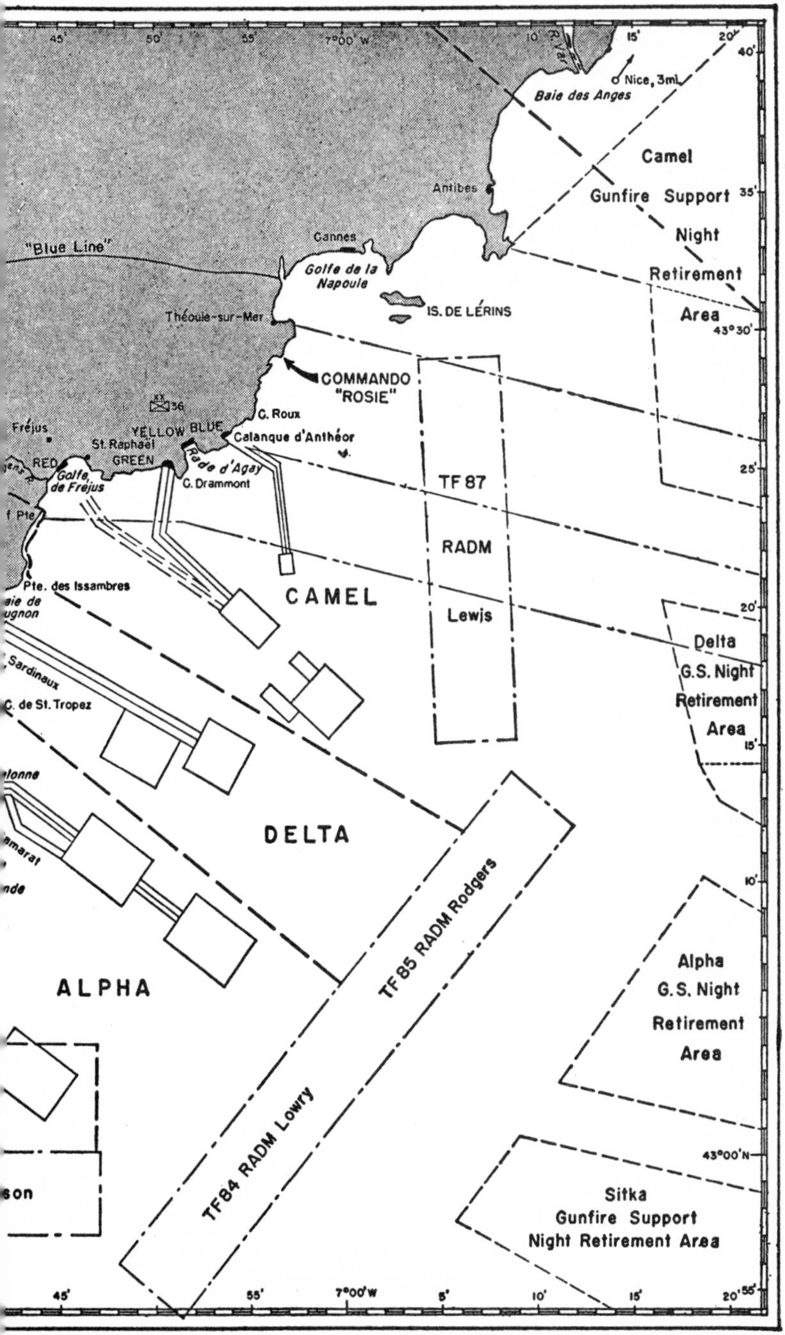

45'
50'
55'
7°00' W
10'
R. Var
15'
20'
40'
Nice, 3mi.
Baie des Anges
Camel
Gunfire Support
Night
Retirement
Area
Antibes
35'
Cannes
"Blue Line"
Golfe de la Napoule
IS. DE LÉRINS
Théoule-sur-Mer
43°30'
COMMANDO "ROSIE"
36
C. Roux
Fréjus
YELLOW
BLUE
St. Raphael
Calanque d'Anthéor
RED
GREEN
Rade d'Agay
Golfe de Fréjus
C. Drammont
TF 87
RADM
Lewis
25'
Pte. des Issambres
CAMEL
20'
Delta
G.S. Night
Retirement
Area
Sardinaux
C. de St. Tropez
15'
DELTA
10'
TF 85 RADM Rodgers
ALPHA
Alpha
G.S. Night
Retirement
Area
TF84 RADM Lowry
43°00'N
son
Sitka
Gunfire Support
Night Retirement Area
45'
55'
7°00'W
5'
10'
15'
20'
55'

tive silence, when one heard only the hum of landing-craft engines. Now the first wave of landing craft began hitting the beaches on the thirty-mile front. One minute after H-hour, at 0801, signals reached Admiral Hewitt that assault troops had landed on one beach after another, all the way from Baie de Cavalaire to Calanque d'Anthéor.

The "Alpha" landings on each side of Cap Camarat were almost too easy; nothing went wrong. By nightfall D-day, some 16,000 men and 2150 vehicles were ashore, and the Germans had been cleared out of this wooded peninsula. Admiral Rodgers found the "Delta" landings a very different problem from conning *Salt Lake City* through the Battle of the Komandorski Islands, but he handled them equally well. Admiral Bryant's strong gunfire support group battered down the principal strongpoints and enabled the troops to make what someone called a "dream landing," before the resort town of Sainte-Maxime. Contre-Amiral Jaujard, who commanded the two French cruisers in the gunfire support group, gave high praise to Admiral Bryant. "By his pluck, his perfect knowledge of his profession and his leadership, he has won our admiration and our gratitude." "Delta" Force unloaded on D-day the contents of all its transports and over a hundred beaching craft, carrying some 33,000 men and 3300 vehicles. No loss of landing or support craft, and no casualties.

"Camel" Force, however, did not find Operation DRAGOON a pushover. It drew the only section of the target coast that was thoroughly mined and well defended, an area extending from Pointe des Issambres to the Golfe de la Napoule, facing Cannes. On its west flank the shores of the Golfe de Fréjus, overlooked by the town of Saint-Raphaël, were badly wanted by the Army. Here, where the sluggish Argens flows into the sea, the French before the war had built a small airfield and seaplane base behind the beach; the only one on the water's edge in Provence. As the Argens valley is a natural invasion route to the interior — had been so used for at least 1500 years — the Germans guessed that we would land there and had prepared a hot reception. Since Intelligence predicted this, Admiral Hewitt's staff selected beaches east of Saint-Raphaël for the initial assault, but postponed landings at the head of the gulf until the afternoon in order to allow time for coast defenses near Saint-Raphaël to be taken out and mines to be swept.

Admiral Deyo's gunfire support group banged away at prearranged targets until 0800, and succeeded in neutralizing many strongpoints. The landings of the 36th Division on Beach Green met with no opposition whatever; Beach Blue, at the head of Calanque d'Anthéor, was a little tougher. After these two points had been taken, the gunfire support ships helped the troops' successful fight to occupy Saint-Raphaël and the rest of the Golfe de Fréjus. On D-day 17,390 troops and 2790 vehicles were landed in the "Camel" area.

The Navy's task in Operation DRAGOON was only half accomplished by the successful landings on 15 and 16 August. Follow-up convoys from Italy, North Africa, Corsica, and even from the United States were scheduled for the next two and a half months; and many of these had to be speeded up, or their composition changed, owing to Seventh Army's requirements in its rapid advance. Admiral Hewitt vested primary control of follow-up convoys in Captain James P. Clay, Comdesron 7. Initially he had 62 escort vessels at his disposal, and by 21 August almost as many more. Captain Clay accelerated the arrival of two French divisions by several days, which enabled General de Lattre de Tassigny to maintain momentum. By the end of 2 September, 190,565 men, 41,534 vehicles, and 219,205 tons of supplies had been landed over the DRAGOON assault beaches. By the 25th, when the last assault beach closed, these figures had been almost doubled.

The Navy also coöperated with the French II Corps, whose

primary mission was to liberate Toulon and Marseilles. Most of the gunfire support ships steamed over to that flank; and a nice job they had to knock out a casemated battery of two 340-mm (13.5-inch) naval guns on Cap Cépet which protected both cities. It took several days' battering by *Nevada*, *Augusta*, *Quincy*, H.M.S. *Ramillies* and French battleship *Lorraine* to do it.

On 28 August Toulon and Marseilles surrendered.

Thus, the great objectives of Operation DRAGOON were secured within two weeks of D-day, and in less than half the time that the planners expected. Although intensive minesweeping and salvage operations were necessary before Marseilles and Toulon could be used, unloading of supplies in the larger port began as early as 3 September; and by the 15th a greater volume of troops and matériel was being discharged in these two harbors than was sent over the assault beaches. On that day, when the Allied troops had reached Lyons, all ground forces in Southern France were incorporated in Lieutenant General J. L. Devers's Sixth Army Group and placed under the operational control of General Eisenhower. By V-E Day (8 May 1945), 4,123,794 long tons of cargo and 905,512 troops had been landed at Marseilles, Toulon and Port de Bouc; the lion's share of them at Marseilles. We must also add the men and matériel landed on the DRAGOON beaches: 380,000 troops, 306,000 tons cargo, 69,312 vehicles and 17,848 tons gasoline to 25 September, when they were closed.

In such wise did Operation DRAGOON justify itself. It may stand as an example of an almost perfect amphibious operation from the point of view of training, timing, Army–Navy–Air Force coöperation, performance and results. But it met no opposition comparable to that which Operation NEPTUNE encountered in Normandy. Moreover, DRAGOON was launched two weeks after the big breakthrough, on a flood tide of victory. Its greatest accomplishment was to swell that tide by an entire Army group, which made the Allied advance into Germany irresistible.

CHAPTER XIV

Leyte

September–December 1944

1. *Pacific Strategy Again*

WE LEFT THE PACIFIC WAR at the end of July 1944, with the Battle of the Philippine Sea won, Saipan, Tinian and Guam secured, and General MacArthur in control of Biak and the New Guinea Vogelkopf, poised to cross the Celebes Sea into Mindanao. But the question whether the liberation of the Philippines should precede or follow the defeat of Japan had not yet been resolved. Whilst both armed services planned to strike Japan repeatedly by sending B–29s "up the ladder of the Bonins," Admiral King and the Navy generally wished to bypass the Philippines, invade Formosa, and then set up a base either on the Chinese mainland or in the Ryukyus for the final assault on Japan. General MacArthur was firmly insistent on liberating the Philippines and using Luzon for the final or semi-final springboard to Japan. He made the strong plea that the United States was honor bound at the earliest possible date to liberate the Philippines, where he had been nourishing resistance forces against the Japanese puppet government; and that if we failed the Filipinos, no Asiatic would ever trust us. He also made the sound strategic argument that loyal Luzon, sealed off by Allied sea power, would be a more suitable base to gather forces for the final assault on Japan than hostile Formosa, which the Japanese could readily reinforce from China.

General MacArthur's strategic plan was sound, even if stripped of its political overtones. From what we learned of the defenses of Formosa after the war, it would have been a very difficult island upon which to obtain a lodgment. And its contemplated use as a steppingstone to the mainland could never have come off, since by the end of 1944 Japan controlled almost the entire coast of China.

The first approach to a decision on this knotty question was made at Pearl Harbor in the last week of July, 1944, at a conference between President Roosevelt, General MacArthur and Admiral Nimitz. In this conference the General not only converted the willing President, but the dubious Admiral Nimitz, to his concept — "Leyte, then Luzon." An understanding was reached, not a decision; but, as in the case of the Mediterranean, when once you put your foot on a strategic ladder it is difficult to get off, unless the enemy throws you off. Admiral King and Rear Admiral Forrest Sherman (Admiral Nimitz's top planner), might still argue in the J.C.S. for bypassing Luzon, and throw ridicule on General MacArthur's contention that Manila could be captured in two weeks after a landing at Lingayen; they lost their case.

At the Quebec Conference, in September 1944, the following timetable was drawn up by the Combined Chiefs of Staff. *September:* MacArthur to take Morotai, Nimitz to take Peleliu. *October:* Nimitz to take Yap in the Carolines, Ulithi a few days later, then to move into Talaud. *November:* MacArthur to occupy Sarangani Bay, Mindanao. *December:* MacArthur and Nimitz in concert to invade Leyte. But it was still left open whether the securing of Leyte would be followed by a landing on Luzon, or on Formosa.

Within a week this timetable was torn up, the plan changed, and the tempo of advance accelerated, owing to Admiral Halsey's carrier raids on the Philippines in September 1944. His *Essex* class carriers steamed up to within sight of shore, pounded Japanese airfields and destroyed the few Japanese planes that they encountered. These carrier strikes dissipated the myth created by

Billy Mitchell-minded airmen to the effect that aircraft carriers could not safely venture within flight distance of enemy airfields, and exposed the enemy's then air weakness in the Philippines. So Halsey sent a message via Nimitz to the Joint Chiefs of Staff, then sitting at Quebec with the British Chiefs of Staff, the President, the Prime Minister, and Mr. Mackenzie King. Halsey recommended that the Peleliu, Morotai, Yap and Mindanao operations be canceled, and that Pacific Fleet and Seventh Fleet make a joint assault on Leyte on 20 October, two months ahead of schedule. The J.C.S. received MacArthur's consent to this acceleration on the night of 15 September; and in an hour and a half they made this decision; MacArthur and Nimitz to invade Leyte on 20 October, and Wilkinson's amphibious force, already embarking to take Peleliu and Yap, to join them after taking Peleliu only.

This sudden change of objectives and of timing was a notable instance of strategic flexibility. The logistic plan, of course, required radical changes, but they were made; and the amphibious assault on Leyte became one of the most successful of the war.

Another important decision at Quebec in September 1944 had to do with participation of the Royal Navy in the Pacific War after the defeat of Germany, which most strategists at that particular moment thought would take place before the end of the year. The British Chiefs of Staff for a year or more had been discussing plans for this participation. Admiral King wished the Royal Navy to operate eastward from the Indian Ocean, recapture Singapore and help puncture the bloated Japanese Empire from the south. This concept was pleasing neither to Churchill nor to the First Sea Lord. They wished the Royal Navy to get into the thick of the fighting alongside the United States Navy as it approached the Japanese home islands. General MacArthur did not want the Royal Navy under his command unless it were in the form of a task force attached to the United States Seventh Fleet, under Admiral Kinkaid. Admiral King did not want the Royal Navy in the Central Pacific at any price; and said so, frankly, creating unnecessary offense. It was not that King was anti-British, or that he disliked sharing the anticipated spoils of a Pacific victory. The root of his objections, purely and simply, was logistics. Ships of the Royal Navy were short-legged — accustomed to putting into a base for replenishment and upkeep about every two or three weeks. American war ships were long-legged — staffed with technicians capable of making extensive repairs at sea, and able to fuel at sea while making twelve to fifteen knots' speed. For the Fast Carrier Forces Pacific Fleet there had been developed a Mobile Service Base of auxiliary craft which provided the fighting ships with everything they needed at sea, from replacement aircraft and spare engines to cigarettes, so that these vessels could, and did, keep the sea literally for months. Since the Royal Navy did not enjoy these facilities, Admiral King feared it would become a drain on us for logistic supply.

President Roosevelt, for the sake of preserving good Anglo-American relations, overruled the Admiral's objections and required American planners to find a place for a British fleet in the final operations against Japan in 1945. That they did; and the United States Pacific Fleet was grateful for Royal Navy support at Okinawa and later.

2. *Preliminaries — Morotai, Peleliu, Formosa Air Battle–15 September–19 October 1944*

Before invading the Philippines, a few islands were considered necessary as advanced bases: Morotai, Peleliu and Ulithi.

Morotai was wanted as a stepping-stone to Mindanao (before the Mindanao invasion had been canceled) and as a base whence the nearby big island of Halmahera, where the Japanese had a large garrison and some eight airfields, could be neutralized. Landings there were carried out on 15 September by units of Admiral Barbey's VII 'Phib, lifting the 31st Infantry Division, with Rear Admiral Russell S. Berkey commanding the support force. They were virtually unopposed. Army Engineers and two airfield construction squadrons of the Royal Australian Air Force moved in, and the first airfield was ready 4 October.

Morotai played an important role in the great operation coming up, because it was the only Allied air base from which short-range fighters and light or medium bombers could be staged up to Leyte. The V A.A.F. used it as a springboard, and had 162 aircraft ready to go in as soon as the airstrip was ready.

On 15 September Vice Admiral Wilkinson's III 'Phib landed on Peleliu, southernmost island but one of the Palau group. This was a very different proposition from Morotai. Admiral Halsey proposed to bypass Peleliu as well as Mindanao, but Admiral Nimitz declined to authorize this because the invasion forces were already at sea, and he felt that the Palaus would be necessary as staging-points for aircraft and ships to Leyte. They did prove useful, though hardly necessary; and, considering that the capture of Peleliu and the adjacent small island of Angaur cost almost as many American lives as the assault on Omaha Beach, it would seem that Cincpac here made one of his rare mistakes.

Wilkinson's III 'Phib, comprising big transports and beaching craft lifting the veteran 1st Marine Division (Major General W. H. Rupertus) was selected for the assault on Peleliu. Naval bombardment of the island began on 12 September and the UDT "frogmen" had plenty of time to work over the reefs off beaches selected for landing, clearing out coral heads, blowing the primitive (compared with the German) antiboat wooden obstacles, and chipping away at the coral to make over the reef for the LVT and berths for the LST.

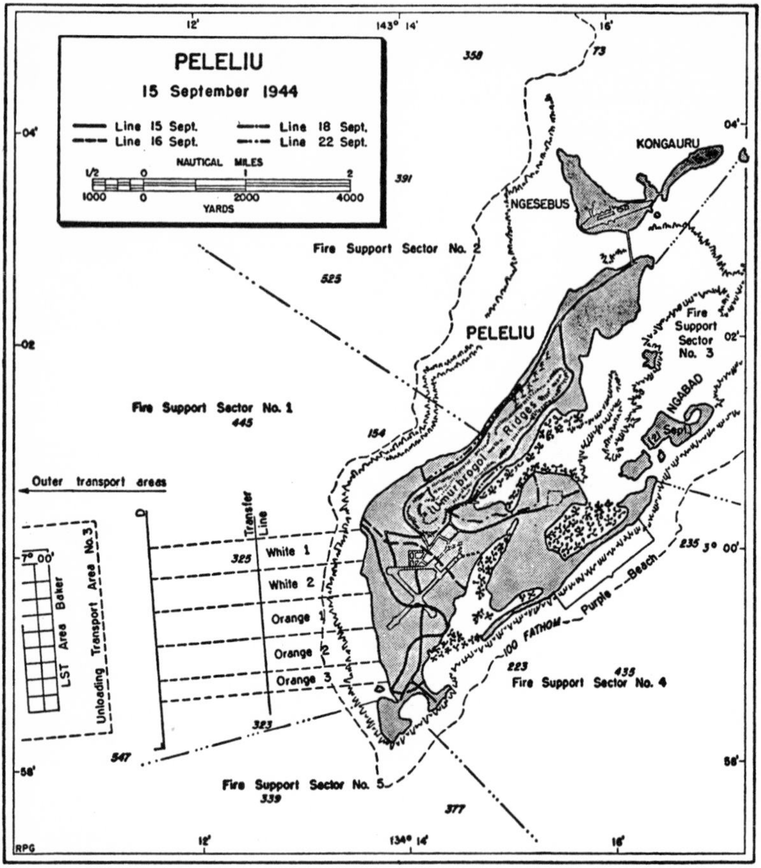

The Japanese defenders under Colonel Nakagawa, numbering 5300 fighting men and as many more construction troops, had no intention of selling Peleliu cheap. Imperial General Headquarters had been giving special attention to defense against amphibious assault. The old tactics of meeting the enemy on the beach had failed everywhere. The new tactics were to prepare a main line of resistance and defensive positions well in the rear of the beaches, place substantial forces in reserve to mount counterattacks at opportune moments, and offer token defense only at the beach. The defenders of Peleliu were the guinea pigs for these new tactics (the reverse of Rommel's on Omaha Beach), which proved hideously successful in prolonging the Iwo Jima and Okinawa operations. Natural caves in the jagged limestone ridges north of the airfield were developed into an interconnected series of underground strongpoints, so strongly protected by sand and concrete as to be almost impervious to aërial bombing or naval bombardment.

Colonel Nakagawa, however, tried both the old and the new. His men so stoutly contested the landings that the Marines lost 210 killed and 900 wounded on D-day, 15 September. By the 18th they had occupied the airfield, but not secured it. Stretching northeasterly from the airfield for two miles was the high Umurbrogol Ridge. Here the Japanese, with the aid of professional miners, had excavated a system of interlocking caves in the soft coral rock, too deep for naval bombardment or air bombing to reach. The Ridge could not be ignored, for several cave entrances overlooked the airfield only a few hundred yards away, and the Japanese were well provided with food, weapons and ammunition. They had to be rooted out or sealed off. The Marines — and a regiment of the 81st Division which was sent to help — would reach a cave mouth after a bloody battle, only to find that it was deserted, or capture a peak and smell cooking being done by cave-dwelling Japanese resting comfortably beneath. The biggest cave, encountered on 27 September, contained more than a thousand Japanese. The only weapon to cope with them was a new long-range flame-thrower, first mounted on LVTs and later on Sherman tanks, which threw a wicked tongue of fire that could penetrate 40 or 50 feet and even lick around a corner. Attrition by this means gradually reduced the enemy.

On the night of 24-25 November occurred the last organized resistance, and Colonel Nakagawa, having done just what the Emperor commanded, committed suicide. His garrison was exterminated, but he had cost the Marines and Army 1950 lives.

Angaur, the two-mile-long island south of Peleliu, wanted for a bomber strip, was captured by the "Wildcat" 81st Division from 1600 die-hard Japanese by 23 October. Kossol Passage, some 60 miles north of Angaur, became a patrol and search base for three squadrons of long-range Mariners, which, with five PBM units equipped for air-sea rescue, arrived on 16-17 September with four tenders. Their searches, extending to 775 miles on October 8, were very useful in the Leyte operation, during which Kossol Passage was extensively used for ships seeking replenishment from service force vessels.

Ulithi Atoll, where Admiral Wilkinson landed an RCT of the 81st Division on 23 September, was wanted for its big, deep lagoon, a perfect fleet base. It was promptly developed as such, and from it sortied on 4-6 October Fast Carrier Forces Pacific Fleet (TF 38) under Halsey and Mitscher: *Enterprise* and eight *Essex* class carriers, eight *Independence* class light carriers, with an ample screen of new battleships, heavy and light cruisers, and destroyers. Shortly before dark 7 October, about 375 miles west of the Marianas, this great carrier task force made rendezvous. The modern age has afforded no marine spectacle comparable to a meeting of these big warships, which have become as beautiful to the modern seaman's eye as a ship of the line to his bell-bottomed forbears. The great flattops, constantly launching and recovering aircraft; the new battleships with their graceful sheer, tossing spray and leaving a boiling wake; the cruisers bristling with antiaircraft guns; the destroyers darting, thrusting and questing for lurking submarines, all riding crested seas of deepest ultramarine; the massy tradewind clouds casting purple shadows — all together composed a picture of mighty naval power. It corresponded to a fleet of ships of the line with their attendant frigates and sloops majestically sailing across the Caribbean in the eighteenth century.

On 12 October began the really big business for Task Force 38: a three-day effort to knock out Japanese air strength on Formosa, and to deny it to the enemy as a staging base toward Leyte. The carriers arrived before dawn at their launching position, 50 to 90 miles east of Formosa. At 0544, an hour before sunrise, the first strike, a fighter sweep to gain command of the air over Formosa and the Pescadores, was launched. Flying weather throughout these three days was perfect. On 12 October no fewer than 1378 sorties were flown on Formosa from all four American carrier groups, followed by 974 on the morning of the 13th. In the afternoon, Japanese planes struck back, making one hit on carrier *Franklin* and a second on cruiser *Canberra*, neither lethal. On the third day, 14 October, when TF 38 made only 146 sorties against Formosa, XX Bomber Command (109 B–29s) carried the ball from China fields. Japanese counterattack crippled but did not sink cruiser *Houston*, and she was towed clear.

The results of this three-day Formosa air battle were over 500 enemy planes destroyed, some twoscore freighters and small craft sunk, and many others damaged; and an enormous destruction of ammunition dumps, hangars, barracks, shops and industrial plants. In the counterattacks, TF 38 engaged nearly a thousand land-based enemy aircraft, and beat off all except those that made the three hits. The cost to the Navy was 79 planes, 64 pilots and crewmen, and a number of seamen killed in the three ships that were hit.

Japanese aircraft losses in the week of 10-17 October were tremendous, but the government consoled itself by the myth — broadcast and stated in official communiqués — that their "eagles" had sunk 11 carriers, 2 battleships and 3 cruisers. Japan was swept by a sudden wave of exhilaration which dispelled the dismay over the loss of the Marianas. The Army even assumed that the American invasion would be given up. Imperial General Headquarters, believing its own propaganda, had actually started planning on that assumption, when the vanguard of American invasion forces for Leyte was sighted off Suluan on 17 October.

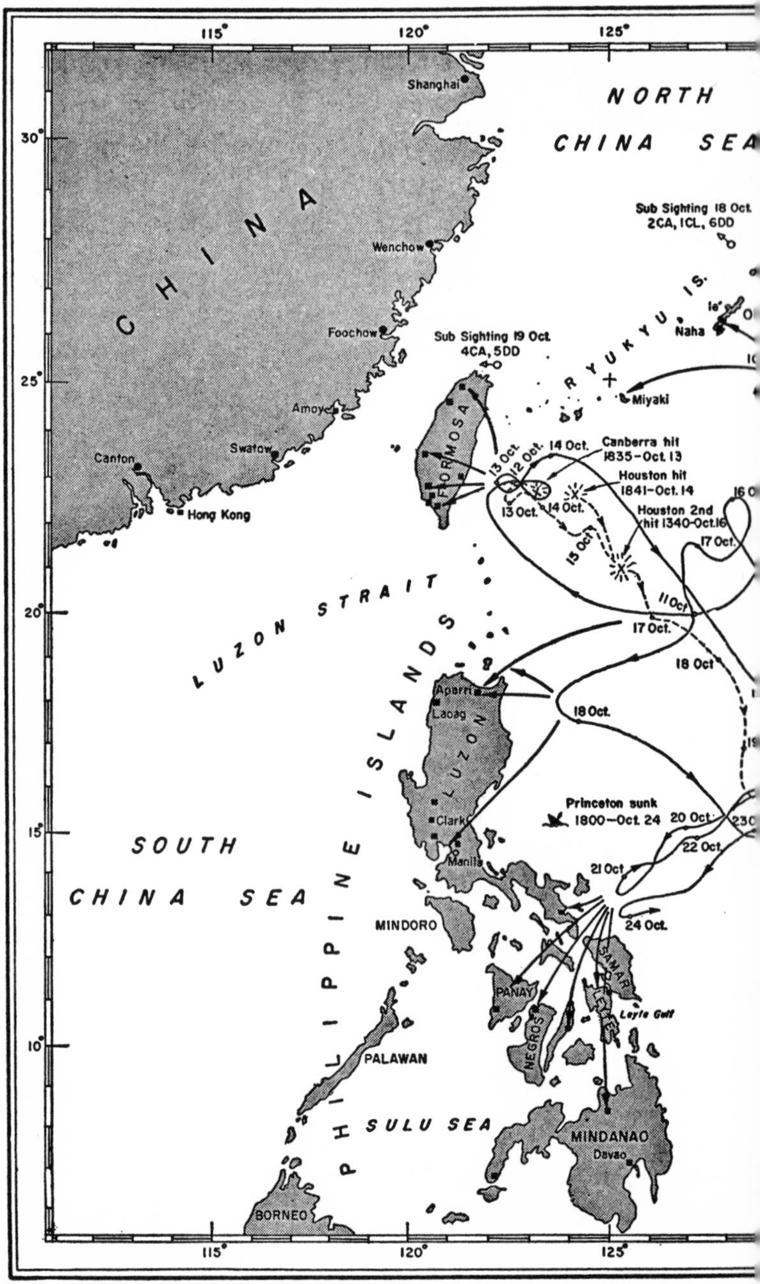
115°
120°
125°
30°
25°
20°
15°
10°
CHINA
Shanghai
Wenchow
Foochow
Amoy
Swatow
Canton
Hong Kong
NORTH CHINA SEA
Sub Sighting 18 Oct. 2CA, 1CL, 6DD
RYUKYU IS.
Naha
Sub Sighting 19 Oct. 4CA, 5DD
Miyaki
FORMOSA
13 Oct.
12 Oct.
14 Oct.
Canberra hit 1835-Oct. 13
Houston hit 1841-Oct. 14
Houston 2nd hit 1340-Oct. 16
13 Oct.
14 Oct.
15 Oct.
17 Oct.
11 Oct.
17 Oct.
18 Oct.
18 Oct.
LUZON STRAIT
PHILIPPINE ISLANDS
Aparri
Laoag
LUZON
Clark
Manila
Princeton sunk 1800-Oct. 24
20 Oct.
22 Oct.
21 Oct.
24 Oct.
SOUTH CHINA SEA
MINDORO
SAMAR
PANAY
LEYTE
Leyte Gulf
NEGROS
PALAWAN
SULU SEA
MINDANAO
Davao
BORNEO

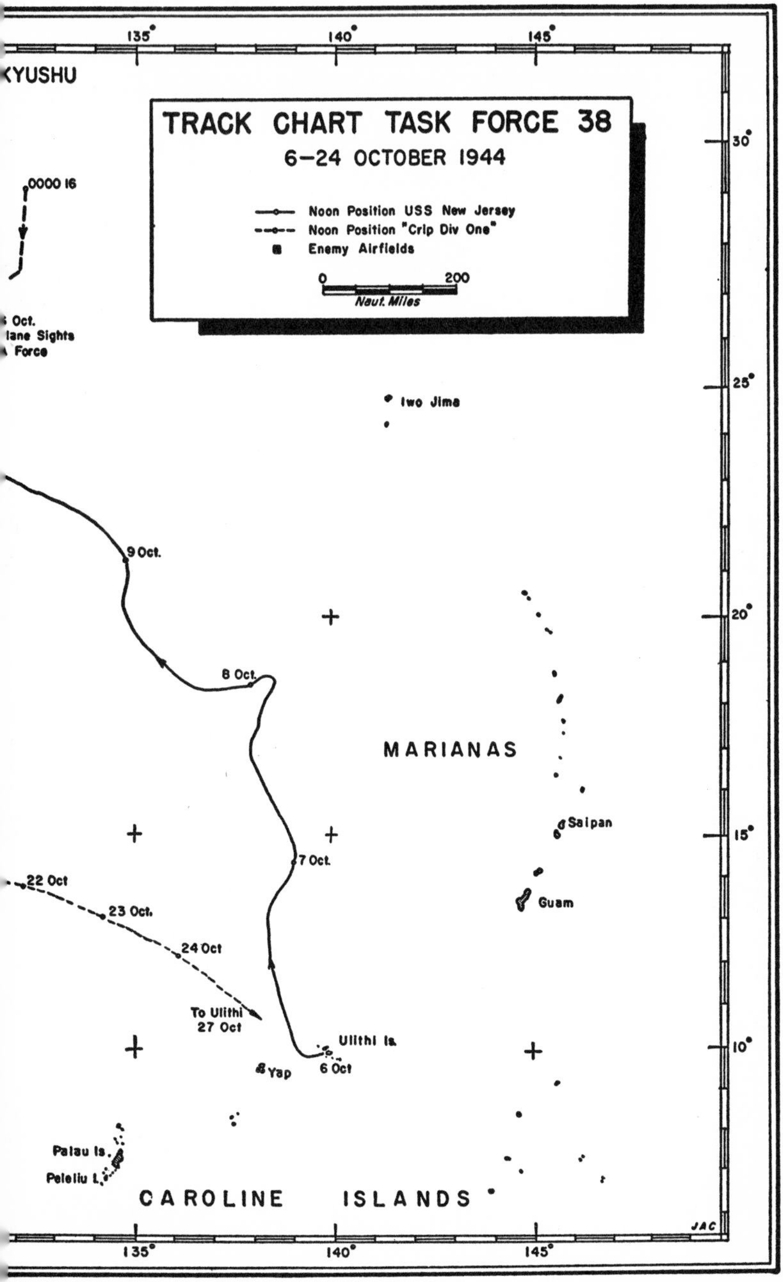
TRACK CHART TASK FORCE 38
6–24 OCTOBER 1944
Noon Position USS New Jersey
Noon Position "Crip Div One"
Enemy Airfields
0
200
Naut. Miles
135°
140°
145°
30°
25°
20°
15°
10°
KYUSHU
0000 16
Oct.
lane Sights
Force
Iwo Jima
9 Oct.
8 Oct.
7 Oct.
MARIANAS
Saipan
Guam
22 Oct
23 Oct.
24 Oct
To Ulithi
27 Oct
Ulithi Is.
6 Oct
Yap
Palau Is.
Peleliu I.
CAROLINE ISLANDS
JAC

Admiral Halsey made a witty reply to these Japanese claims in a message to Admiral Nimitz, and Cincpac promptly released it on the 19th, to the joy of the Navy and the public: —

> ADMIRAL NIMITZ HAS RECEIVED FROM ADMIRAL HALSEY THE COMFORTING ASSURANCE THAT HE IS NOW RETIRING TOWARD THE ENEMY FOLLOWING THE SALVAGE OF ALL THE THIRD FLEET SHIPS RECENTLY REPORTED SUNK BY RADIO TOKYO.

3. *The Leyte Landings, 17–20 October*

The command setup for the invasion of Leyte — which lasted with few changes through the Battle for Leyte Gulf — was not (unfortunately) a unified but a dual one: —

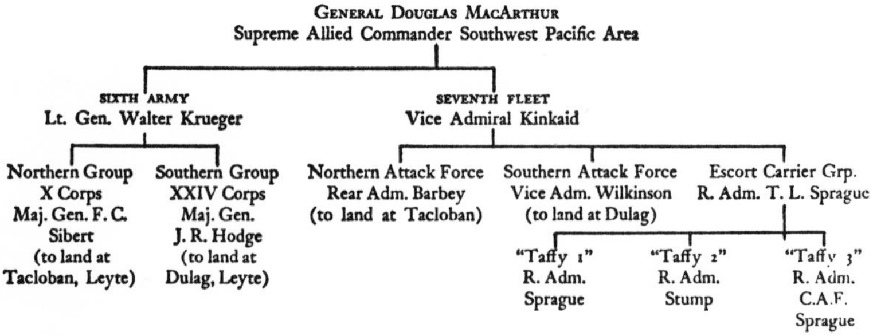

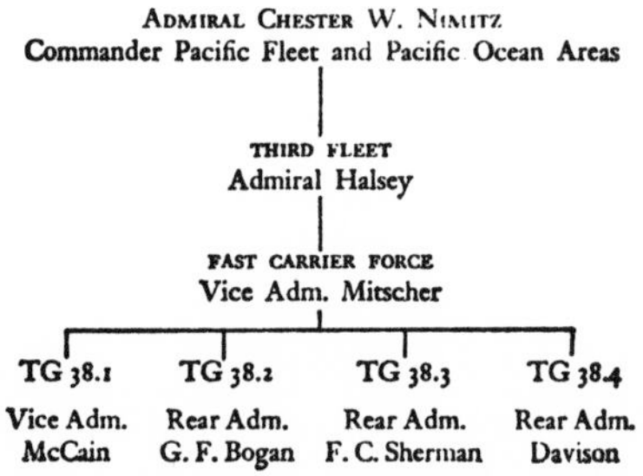

MacArthur and Nimitz had come together at the summit, as it were, and the President did not dare put one over the other.

A large part of Seventh Fleet was "borrowed" for this operation from Third Fleet; Wilkinson's III 'Phib, for instance, was placed under Admiral Kinkaid.

Early in October, General MacArthur's military forces and Admiral Kinkaid's Seventh Fleet began to concentrate at Manus, Hollandia and other places along the coast of New Guinea. Seven hundred and thirty-eight ships were in the attack force; fewer than those that took part in the invasion of Normandy in June, but mounting a heavier striking power.[1] Adding the 17 fleet carriers, six battleships, 17 cruisers and 64 destroyers of TF 38, this made the most powerful naval force ever assembled. But this record would be equaled at Lingayen Gulf in January 1945, and surpassed off Okinawa in April.

On 10 October the northward movement began; slow minecraft which were to sweep safe channels for the transports, in the van. Commander Wayne R. Loud's minesweeping and hydrographic group arrived off Leyte Gulf 17 October and at 0630 began sweeping the approaches to Dinagat and three smaller islands, Calicoan, Suluan and Homonhon, which divided the entrances to Leyte Gulf from the Philippine Sea. Air reconnaissance showed that the enemy had installations on them, probably search radar whose electric feelers would signal the approach of the forces of liberation. They did. At 0750 this Dinagat group was sighted by the Japanese garrison on Suluan, whose commander promptly notified Admiral Toyoda, C. in C. Combined Fleet. He issued the alert for SHO-1, his planned naval battle, at 0809, and ordered important elements of Combined Fleet to get under way at once.

By noon 18 October, all islands commanding the entrances to Leyte Gulf had been secured by the Rangers. Rear Admiral

[1] These comprised 157 combatant ships, 420 amphibious types, 84 patrol, minesweeping and hydrographic types, and 73 service types.

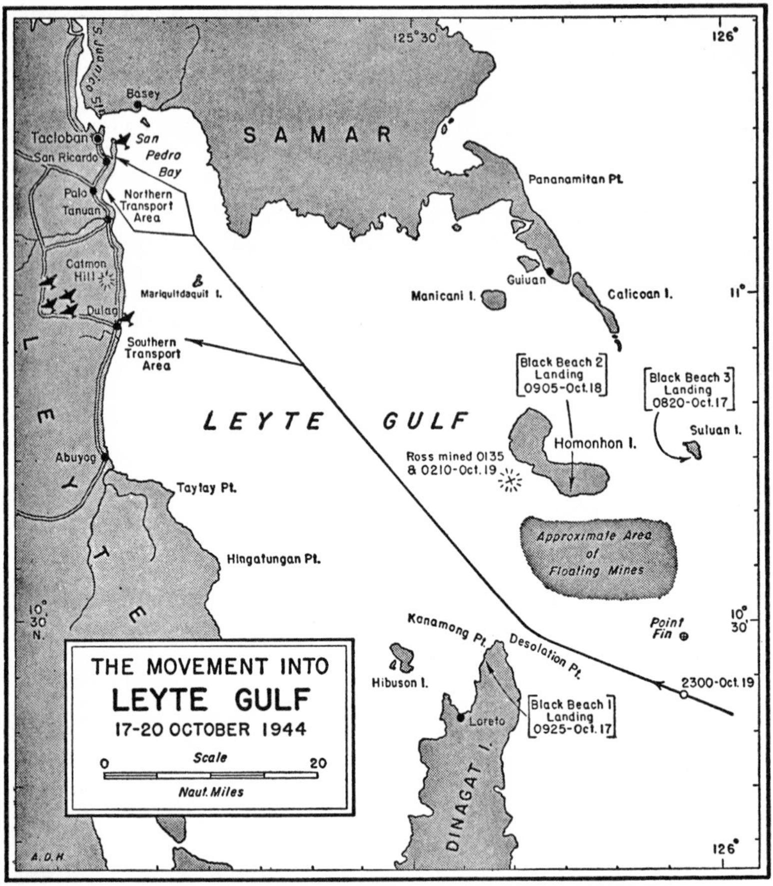

Jesse B. Oldendorf, who commanded the gunfire support ships, then steamed boldly into the Gulf and commenced bombarding the landing beaches to cover operations of the UDTs.

As Assault day (A-day), 20 October, broke, Admiral Wilkinson led the "parade," as he called it, from a rendezvous point 17 miles outside Desolation Point. Admiral Wilkinson's Southern Force was now steaming toward its transport area off Dulag, and Admiral Barbey's Northern Force for its anchorage in San Pedro Bay, as the northern, inside bight of Leyte Gulf is called. A Japanese patrol plane approached to take a look and was shot down. The sun rose out of a yellow haze over Samar, and light spread over the calm green waters of Leyte Gulf. Mist dissolved from the mountains, and the palm-fringed beach, behind which lay the enemy, became clearly visible. In villages and hideouts ashore, Filipinos — and the few Americans who had managed to survive the tragic events of 1941-1942 — peered out through coconut palms at this mighty fleet. Joy filled their hearts, and prayers went up to Heaven; for they knew that the hour of deliverance was at hand.

President Roosevelt, in a message broadcast to the Philippine people that morning, declared: —

> On this occasion of the return of General MacArthur to Philippine soil with our airmen, our soldiers and our sailors, we renew our pledge. We and our Philippine brothers in arms — with the help of Almighty God — will drive out the invader; we will destroy his power to wage war again, and we will restore a world of dignity and freedom — a world of confidence and honesty and peace.

The Leyte Gulf landings were easy, compared with most amphibious operations in World War II — perfect weather, no surf, no mines or underwater obstacles, slight enemy reaction, mostly mortar fire. Admiral Wilkinson's Southern Attack Force landed XXIV Corps on a 5000-yard stretch of beach which began about eleven miles south of the Northern Force left flank. A welcome addition to the amphibious fleet now was the Landing Ship, Medium (LSM), 203 feet long, 900 tons, which had the vehicle capacity of an LCT but was faster, more seaworthy and more comfortable. This Southern landing, too, was relatively uneventful. Dulag was captured by the 7th Division around noon, and the 96th Division drove the Japanese out of their principal strongpoint on "Hill 120" and raised the flag there at 1042, less than an hour and three quarters after the first troops landed.

Liberation of the Philippines was off to a good start.

Dulag and Tacloban airfields fell into American hands on 21 October, and Army Engineers promptly went to work improving them. The 24th Division took Mt. Guinhandang by 0900; and Tacloban itself, with the only docking facilities on Leyte, was captured that day. By midnight, 132,400 men and almost 200,000 tons of supplies and equipment had been landed by the assault echelons of the Northern and Southern Attack Forces, and most of the ships had departed. Now only the three admirals' amphibious force flagships, one AKA, 25 LST and LSM, and 28 Liberty ships, remained in Leyte Gulf. All fire support battleships, cruisers and destroyers were advancing up Surigao Strait to meet the enemy. Lieutenant General Krueger had set up Sixth Army command post ashore, and the amphibious phase of the Leyte operation was over. And the first phase of the great naval Battle for Leyte Gulf had already been fought.

4. *The Battle For Leyte Gulf — Opening Actions, 23–24 October*

As the amphibious vessels completed unloading on the Leyte shore and Sixth Army extended its beachhead, Japanese naval forces were sallying forth to give battle. The four-part Battle for Leyte Gulf [2] that followed comprised every type of naval warfare invented up to that time — heavy and light gunfire; bombing, strafing, rocketing and torpedoing by land-based and carrier-based planes; torpedo attacks by submarines, destroyers and motor torpedo boats. Every naval weapon but the mine was employed by

[2] This official name comprises four naval actions: in the Sibuyan Sea on 24 Oct., Surigao Strait 24-25 Oct., Battle off Samar 25 Oct., and Battle off Cape Engaño 25-26 Oct. 1944. Regarding these as parts of a whole, this was the greatest naval battle of all time. In the Battle of Jutland (1 June 1916), 250 ships (151 British, 99 German) engaged. In the Leyte Battle, 282 ships (216 U.S.N., 2 R.A.N., 64 Japanese) engaged. The air component at Jutland was only 5 seaplanes; at Leyte it was hundreds of planes of all types. Estimates of numbers of officers and men engaged are, U.S.N. and R.A.N., 143,668; Japanese, 42,800. There were more American sailors in this battle than there had been in the entire Navy and Marine Corps in 1938.

both sides, and the Japanese introduced new and deadly air tactics. In every part the action was memorable and decisive, resulting in the destruction of the Japanese Fleet as an effective fighting force. But before victory was won the situation was puzzling, mistakes were made on both sides, and anything might have happened.

Japanese naval ambition to fight a "general decisive battle" with the United States Pacific Fleet was not quenched by the signal defeats sustained at Midway and in the Philippine Sea. Imperial General Headquarters expected its enemy to invade the Philippines, but was uncertain which island would be the initial target. Consequently, it prepared four SHO plans (SHO meaning Victory), and, as we have seen, Admiral Toyoda activated SHO-1, the plan for a decisive naval action off Leyte, on 18 October after Commander Loud's minesweepers were sighted from Suluan. But owing to lack of tankers to carry fuel north, the Combined Fleet was so widely dispersed — from the Inland Sea of Japan to Lingga Roads off Singapore — that a good week elapsed before it could reach the waters off Leyte. Thus the Japanese Navy missed a great chance to attack the Leyte landings in their "naked" phase when troops were being boated ashore and the Gulf was full of vulnerable shipping.

The Japanese Navy's task organization for SHO-1 is on the next page — the words in italics being the somewhat simplified names given by us to the three principal forces, and place names being the locations of these several forces when Operation SHO-1 was activated.

The general outline of the SHO-1 plan was this: —

Ozawa's Northern Force, built around carriers *Zuikaku*, *Zuiho*, *Chitose* and *Chiyoda*, would decoy Halsey's Third Fleet up north and out of the way. Then Kurita's Force "A" or Center Force, which included super-battleships *Musashi* and *Yamato*, and nine heavy cruisers, would debouch from San Bernardino Strait, at the same time as the Nishimura-Shima Force "C" or Southern

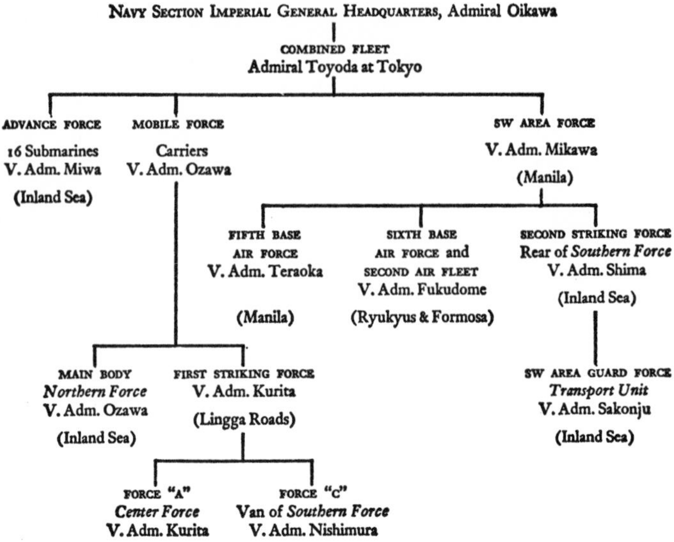

Force debouched from Surigao Strait, to put a pincer on the amphibious ships in Leyte Gulf, destroy them, and then (presumedly) annihilate Halsey. Thus, General MacArthur would be left out on a limb as at Bataan in 1941-1942. This was a typical Japanese strategic plan, employing division, deception, and forces popping out at unexpected places. It required better timing and communications than the Japanese fleet was capable of, but with good luck it might have worked except for starting too late, and *complete lack of air power*. The two Japanese base air forces noted in the above task organization, had not even 200 aircraft available on 22 October, Ozawa's carriers had only 116 planes on board when they sortied from the Inland Sea, and most of these were flown off to land bases before the battle. The Japanese simply did not have time to train new air groups after the destruction wrought by the Spruance-Mitscher forces in the Battle of the Philippine Sea.

Kurita's First Striking Force sortied from Lingga Roads on 18 October and called at Brunei Bay, Borneo, to fuel. On the 20th, it split: the Center Force with the big battleships and most of the heavy cruisers departed at 0800 October 22 for the Sibuyan Sea and San Bernardino Strait, while Nishimura's van of the Southern Force, including two battleships, made for Surigao. At the same time, as an afterthought, Shima's Second Striking Force was ordered south from the Inland Sea to "support and coöperate" with Nishimura. Ozawa's Northern Force, the carriers, sortied from the Inland Sea 20 October, undetected by the United States submarines which had been sent to intercept it.

Kurita's was the first to suffer, in the Palawan Passage between the long island of that name and the reefs that border the South China Sea. In the small hours of 23 October, as Center Force entered Palawan Passage, it encountered U. S. submarines *Darter* (Commander David McClintock) and *Dace* (Commander B. D. M. Claggert). The submarines sent off a contact report to Admiral Halsey — first word any American had of what the enemy was up to — and at 0630 *Darter* got two torpedoes into Kurita's flagship *Atago*, which sank her, and two into *Takao*, which disabled her. *Dace*, shortly after, sank *Maya* in a torpedo attack. *Darter* ran aground on Bonbay Shoal and had to be abandoned, but *Dace* took off all her crew. Kurita proceeded, minus three heavy cruisers. And the submarines' contact reports prepared a heavy reception for him in the Sibuyan Sea.

By noon 24 October three of the Halsey-Mitscher fast carrier groups were deployed on a broad front: Sherman's Group 3 to the northward, Bogan's Group 2 off San Bernardino Strait, Davison's Group 4 about sixty miles off southern Samar.[3] The stage was set for an air-surface engagement, the Battle of the Sibuyan Sea, first

[3] McCain's Group 1 had been sent to Ulithu to refuel, but was promptly recalled, and its planes got into the battle on 25 October.

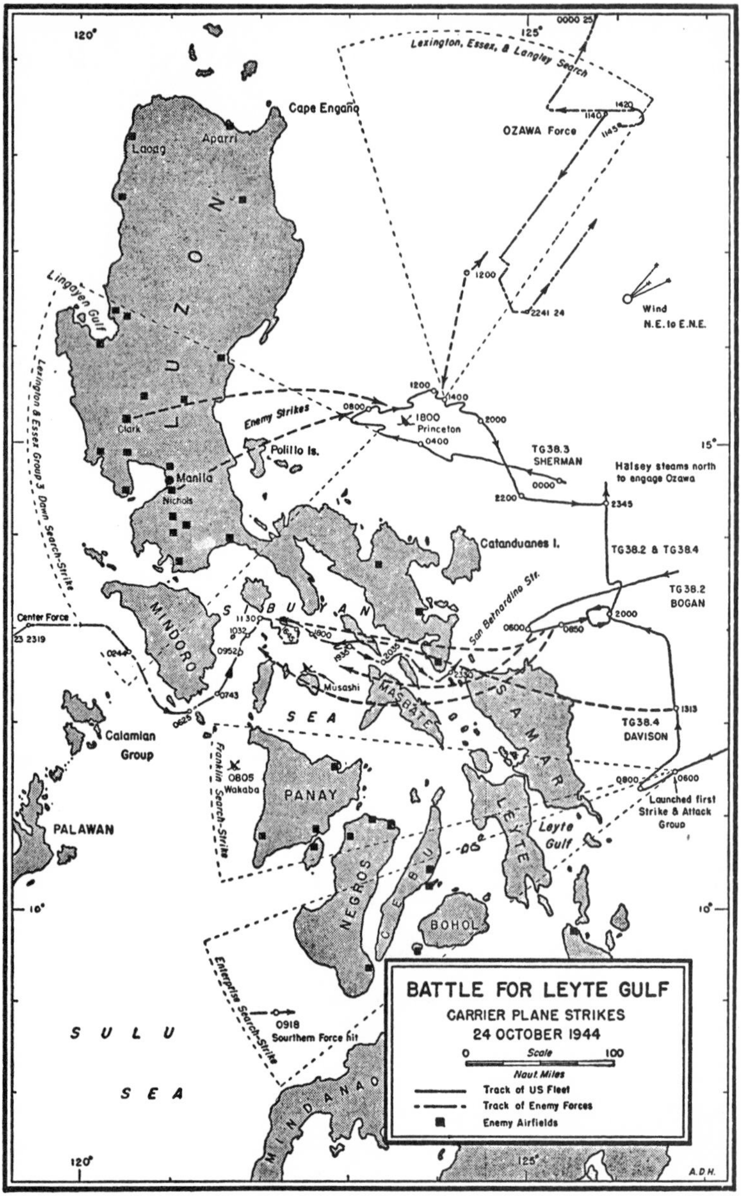
BATTLE FOR LEYTE GULF
CARRIER PLANE STRIKES
24 OCTOBER 1944
Scale
0
100
Naut. Miles
Track of US Fleet
Track of Enemy Forces
Enemy Airfields
Cape Engaño
Aparri
Laoag
LUZON
Lingayen Gulf
Clark
Manila
Nichols
Polillo Is.
Catanduanes I.
Lexington, Essex, & Langley Search
OZAWA Force
Wind
N.E. to E.N.E.
Enemy Strikes
1800
Princeton
TG38.3
SHERMAN
Halsey steams north
to engage Ozawa
TG38.2 & TG38.4
TG38.2
BOGAN
San Bernardino Str.
Lexington & Essex Group 3 Dawn Search-Strike
Center Force
MINDORO
SIBUYAN SEA
Musashi
MASBATE
SAMAR
TG38.4
DAVISON
Launched first
Strike & Attack
Group
Calamian
Group
PALAWAN
Franklin Search-Strike
0805
Wakaba
PANAY
LEYTE
Leyte
Gulf
NEGROS
CEBU
BOHOL
Enterprise Search-Strike
0918
Southern Force hit
SULU SEA
MINDANAO
120°
125°
15°
10°
A.D.H.

of the four major engagements that constitute the Battle for Leyte Gulf. But before Mitscher's planes could strike Kurita's ships, Japanese land-based planes attacked Admiral Frederick Sherman's TG 38.3. Most of them were intercepted and shot down, but one "Judy" made a lucky hit which went through several decks of light carrier *Princeton*, exploded the torpedoes stowed below, and did her in. Cruiser *Birmingham*, which had closed the carrier to help fight fires, was badly damaged by a tremendous explosion of *Princeton*'s torpedo stowage, but eventually was saved.

While *Princeton* was vainly struggling for survival, some 259 sorties of Mitscher's planes were wreaking vengeance on Kurita's ships in the Sibuyan Sea. Kurita had no combat air patrol — Base Force being too heavily engaged in counterattacking TF 38 — and super-battleship *Musashi*, after taking 19 torpedo and 17 bomb hits from *Intrepid*, *Cabot*, *Essex*, *Lexington*, *Franklin* and *Enterprise* aircraft, rolled over and went down at 1935, with great loss of men. Other ships received hits, but all except heavy cruiser *Myoko* were able to proceed. Moreover, the milling around, and evasive courses of Kurita's Center Force in this attack, which lasted intermittently most of the day, delayed the SHO-1 timetable by seven hours. It was no longer possible for Kurita to rendezvous with Nishimura and Shima inside Leyte Gulf at break of day, even if the last two got through; and neither did.

5. *The Battle of Surigao Strait, 24–25 October*

Both parts of the Southern Force (Admiral Nishimura's Force "C" or Van) comprising battleships *Fuso* and *Yamashiro*, heavy cruiser *Mogami* and four destroyers, and Admiral Shima's Second Striking Force or Rear, comprising two heavy cruisers, a light cruiser and four destroyers, were sighted by carrier planes before noon 24 October. Vice Admiral Kinkaid, Commander Seventh Fleet, correctly estimated that Southern Force would try to penetrate Leyte Gulf via Surigao Strait that night, and took measures accordingly. At 1443 he ordered Rear Admiral Jesse B. Oldendorf, who commanded all Seventh Fleet fire support ships at the Leyte landings, to prepare to meet the enemy.

Oldendorf disposed of his force of overwhelming strength with deadly effectiveness, remembering the old California gambler's adage, "Never give a sucker a chance." A Battle Line of six battleships, five of them survivors of Pearl Harbor, together with four heavy cruisers (one, *Shropshire*, of the Royal Australian Navy) and four light cruisers, under Rear Admirals Hayler and Berkey, were so disposed as to cross the fifteen-mile-wide waters between Leyte and Hibuson Island, where Surigao Strait debouches into Leyte Gulf. Two destroyer divisions, under Captains McManes and Coward, were to thrust down the Strait to deliver torpedo attacks, while a third under Captain Smoot was to follow up, and a fourth to stand by Battle Line. Thirty-nine motor torpedo boats, under Lieutenant Commander R. A. Leeson, were sent south to patrol the entire strait, and its approach via the Mindanao Sea.

For want of night-flying, radar-equipped patrol planes, these PTs were the "eyes of the fleet." Their orders were to report all contacts, surface or air, visual or radar, and attack independently. The boats lay-to on station, so as to leave no wake. The sea in the Strait was smooth and glassy, just what they wanted. The atmosphere was clear until a quartering moon set shortly after midnight; then the sky became partly overcast and the night went pitch-black. There were not many rain squalls; it was a fairly dry night for the eastern Philippines. On such a night as this the Pacific Fleet had swapped punches with the enemy in Ironbottom Sound, up the Slot, and off Empress Augusta Bay. But it had never before been so well prepared, with a flock of PTs to intercept, three destroyer squadrons to deliver torpedo attacks and a Battle Line to cap the enemy's column.

Since the Japanese Southern Force was really two independent groups which had no tactical connection, we may follow the ill fortune of the first before turning to the better luck of the second. Vice Admiral Nishimura's van, which included the two battleships, was supposed to arrive in Leyte Gulf before dawn at the same time as Kurita's Center Force. This timing was essential to the success of SHO-1 battle plan. Whether Nishimura imagined he could get through Surigao Strait without a fight, we do not know; but any hope he may have had of joining Kurita in a merry massacre of amphibious craft and transports, which he believed to be present in great numbers, must have vanished around 1830 October 24 when he received a signal from Kurita that he had been delayed by the air battle of the Sibuyan Sea. Nishimura, nevertheless, maintained course and speed, and felt confirmed in this decision around 1900 by an order from Admiral Toyoda: "All forces will dash to the attack." He made no attempt to wait for Shima's rear to catch up with him, probably reflecting that his best chance of penetrating the Gulf lay under cover of darkness, since he had no aircraft to protect him after dawn.

First contact of the Battle of Surigao Strait came at 2236 October 24, when *PT-131*, operating off Bohol, picked up Nishimura's battleships on her radar, and, with the other two boats in her patrol, closed to attack. At four minutes before midnight they were taken under gunfire by destroyer *Shigure* and driven off with some loss; but not before they got off a contact report to Admiral Oldendorf. It was the same story for fifty miles across Mindanao Sea and up the Strait. Nishimura encountered successive PT patrols, each three-boat section observed gun flashes of the previous fight, made contact itself, attempted to get off a report (and sometimes did), attacked with torpedoes (all of which missed), became brightly illuminated by enemy searchlights, came under brisk gunfire, and retired under a smoke screen. They neither stopped nor confused the enemy, but they performed an indispensable service in alerting Admiral Oldendorf.

At six minutes past midnight the moon set — the last moon that Nishimura and most of his sailors were destined to see. After chasing off the last PT attack at 0213, Nishimura steamed quietly along for three quarters of an hour; then he ran into something more serious than motor torpedo boats — Captain Jesse G. Coward's Desron 54.

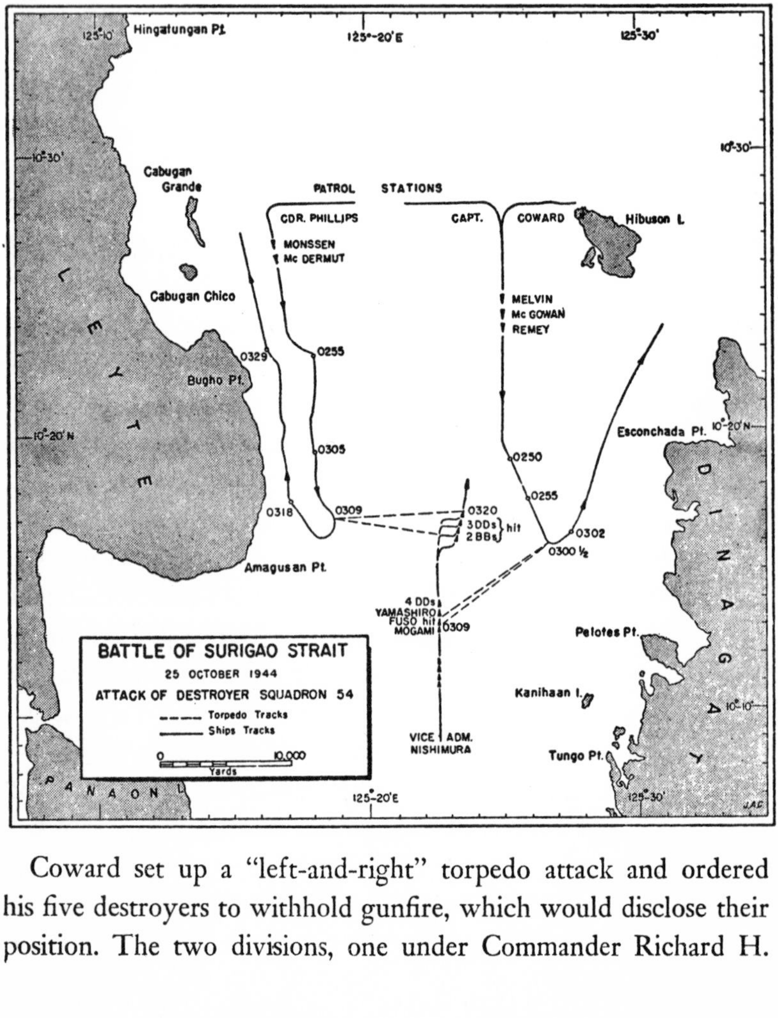

Coward set up a "left-and-right" torpedo attack and ordered his five destroyers to withhold gunfire, which would disclose their position. The two divisions, one under Commander Richard H.

Phillips and the other under Coward himself, started south at 0230 and picked up Nishimura on the radar 15 minutes later. Southern Force van was in single column. Four destroyers led, next came Nishimura's flagship, battleship *Yamashiro*, then, at one-kilometer intervals, *Fuso* and *Mogami*. At 0300 Coward's division (*Remey*, *McGowan*, *Melvin*) commenced launching torpedoes, at ranges of 8200 to 9300 yards. They got one into battleship *Fuso*, which sheered out of column and began to burn and explode. Phillips's flagship *McDermut* had the distinction of torpedoing three destroyers, of which *Yamagumo* blew up and sank, *Michishio* started on her way to the bottom, and *Asagumo*'s bow was knocked off. *Monssen* made a torpedo hit on *Yamashiro* which forced the flooding of two magazines, but failed to stop her. All five American destroyers retired unhurt.

Ten minutes after the Japanese ships had taken these blows, they were subjected to a similar attack from the west side of the Strait by Captain McManes's Desron 24 (*Hutchins*, flag). His ships sank disabled *Michishio* and *Killen* scored a second torpedo hit on *Yamashiro*.

During both destroyer attacks, Nishimura continued to steam stolidly along, neither taking evasive action nor paying attention to the knocked-out ships. His one object, it seems, was to break into Leyte Gulf, being ignorant of the massive forces Admiral Oldendorf had deployed across the entrance to stop him. These amounted to a left flank of three heavy and two light cruisers, a right flank of one heavy and two light cruisers, a line of six battleships, and another destroyer squadron. It was a War College game board setup. The enemy column, now reduced to battleship *Yamashiro*, cruiser *Mogami* and destroyer *Shigure*, made a very short vertical to a very broad T, but Oldendorf was about to cap it, as Togo had done to Rozhdestvenski in 1905 at the Battle of Tsushima Strait, an action which thousands of naval officers had since hoped to emulate.

At 0323, American radar screens began to register the enemy disposition. Oldendorf, whose cruisers were two or three miles nearer the enemy than the battleships, ordered all to open fire at 0351. Two minutes later, *Yamashiro* slowed to 12 knots, but continued on her northerly course, firing at visible targets, since she had no fire control radar. Nishimura was steaming boldly into a terrific concentration of gunfire, supported feebly by *Mogami* astern and *Shigure* on his starboard quarter. His last message, to *Fuso* at 0352, asked that sinking battleship to come along at top speed.

West Virginia, *Tennessee* and *California*, equipped with the newest Mark-8 fire control radar, were responsible for most of Battle Line's action. *West Virginia* opened fire at 0353, range 22,800 yards. These three battlewagons got off 225 rounds of 14-inch armor-piercing shells, fired in six-gun salvos so as to conserve their limited supply. The other three, equipped with Mark-3 fire control radar, had difficulty finding a target. *Maryland* picked up the enemy by ranging on *West Virginia*'s splashes and got off 48 rounds. *Mississippi* fired a single salvo and *Pennsylvania*, with a primitive type of radar, never fired.

While the elusive and lucky *Shigure* dodged salvos, receiving but one hit during the action, *Yamashiro* and *Mogami* were being battered by every size projectile from the light cruisers' 6-inch up to *Maryland*'s and *West Virginia*'s 16-inch AP. They gamely returned fire; *Mogami* until 0355, when her skipper decided to retire; *Yamashiro* until after 0400. The doomed battlewagon directed her 14-inch fire at the nearest group, "Count" Berkey's right flank cruisers, and fired her secondary battery fire at retiring destroyers; she made hits only on destroyer *Albert W. Grant*.

At 0400, when eight bells marked the end of this eventful mid-watch, the battle began to reach a climax. *Yamashiro*, which had been zigzagging in a northerly direction during the last ten minutes, firing doggedly, straightened out on a W by S course. She was burning so brightly that even her 5-inch mounts stood out against flames which seemed to arise from her entire length. *Shigure* turned south to retire; *Mogami*, which had already done so, launched torpedoes at 0401, which missed. A minute later a salvo from cruiser *Portland* exploded on the cruiser's bridge, killing the C.O. and all officers present; other hits were scored in engine and firerooms and *Mogami* slowed almost to a stop. Captain Roland Smoot's Desron 56, having advanced into the fray, launched 13 torpedoes at *Yamashiro* at 0404, and it was two from *Newcomb* which achieved the battleship's ruin.

The American Battle Line changed course from ESE to W by simultaneous turns, and as this maneuver closed the battleships' range, their volume of fire became even greater and more accurate.

"Most beautiful sight I ever witnessed," reported Captain Smoot; "The arched line of tracers in the darkness looked like a continual stream of lighted railroad cars going over a hill." But this show did not long continue. At 0409 Admiral Oldendorf, receiving word that *Albert W. Grant* was being hit by "friendlies," ordered Cease Fire, in order to give Smoot's destroyers a chance to retire. Nishimura and the officers and men of *Yamashiro* must have regarded this cease-fire as God's gift to them and the Emperor. In spite of the punishment their battleship had been taking, she increased speed to 15 knots, turned 90 degrees left, and began to retire southward. But she had less than ten minutes to live. At 0411½ *Newcomb*'s two torpedoes exploded in her, and eight minutes later, as her list increased to 45 degrees, the C.O. ordered Abandon Ship and she sank, taking down the Admiral and all but a few members of the crew.[4]

Mississippi's one salvo, fired at *Yamashiro* just after Admiral Oldendorf ordered Cease Fire, concluded this major phase of the

[4] Lieut. S. Ezaki, the senior survivor, interviewed in 1961, insists that it was the four torpedo hits that sank his ship; the shell hits merely hastened her end.

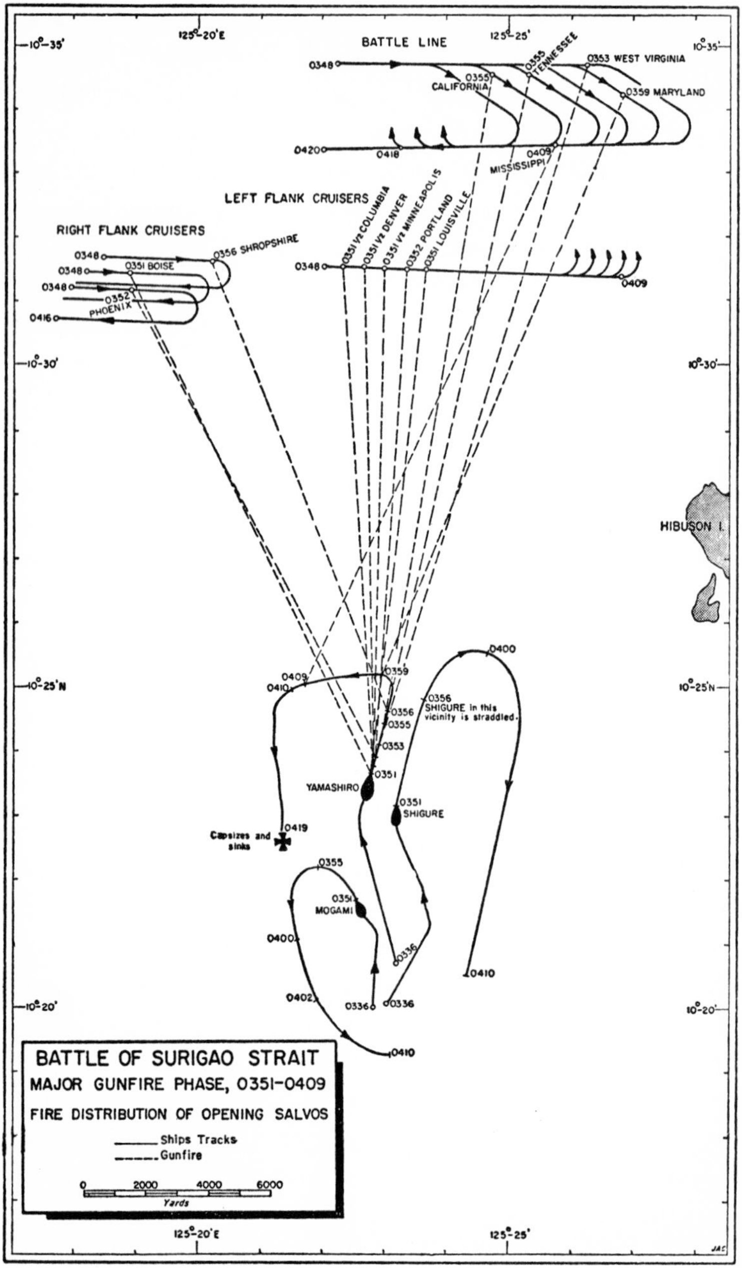

BATTLE OF SURIGAO STRAIT
MAJOR GUNFIRE PHASE, 0351-0409
FIRE DISTRIBUTION OF OPENING SALVOS

battle. Silence followed, as if to honor the passing of the tactics which had so long been foremost in naval warfare. The Battles of Lowestoft, Beachy Head, the Capes of the Chesapeake, Trafalgar, Santiago, Tsushima, Jutland, every major naval action of the past three centuries, had been fought by classic line-of-battle tactics. In the unearthly silence that followed the roar of Oldendorf's 14-inch and 16-inch guns in Surigao Strait, one could imagine the ghosts of all great admirals, from Raleigh and De Ruyter to Togo and Jellicoe, standing at attention to salute the passing of the kind of naval warfare that they all understood. For in those opening minutes of the morning watch of 25 October 1944, Battle Line became as obsolete as the row-galley tactics of Salamis and Syracuse.

Admiral Nishimura's van was done for, all but limping *Mogami* and lively *Shigure;* but Admiral Shima's rear group had not yet put in an appearance. As his column was rounding the southern point of Panaon Island to enter Surigao Strait, light cruiser *Abukuma* was hit by a torpedo from *PT–137* and fell out of formation. Although he passed the burning hulks of some of Nishimura's ships, Shima still thought, at 0420, that he was hastening to the support of what was left of the van. Observing two ships on his radar screen — probably *Louisville* and a left flank cruiser — he ordered *Nachi* and *Ashigara* to attack with torpedoes. They turned east and fired eight torpedoes each. No hits were made, and two of the torpedoes were later recovered on Hibuson Island.

This futile action was Shima's only contribution to the battle. Possessed of unusual discretion for a Japanese admiral, he now decided to retire "temporarily" and await developments. In so doing, *Nachi* collided with *Mogami*, which, miraculously, had managed to turn up enough speed to fall in with Shima's column. *Shigure* followed suit.

The pursuit phase of the battle commenced at 0432 when Admiral Oldendorf started south through the Strait, with his left flank cruisers, screened by Captain Smoot's destroyers. Day was now breaking. In the gray half-light, one could just see the high, verdure-clad shores of Dinagat and Leyte Islands. Filipinos had been gazing seaward all night, wondering what the flashes meant, trusting they were ships of the hated *Hapon* Navy going down. Small groups of Japanese survivors began swimming ashore, to find a reception committee ready with sharp knives and bolos. On board the United States ships, everyone who could be spared topside came up for a breath of cool morning air, a look-around, and a discussion as to whether any of "them bastards" were still afloat. It was good that morning to be alive and with a deck under your feet, in Surigao Strait.

Louisville, *Portland* and *Denver* caught up with *Mogami* around 0530 and added several hits to her collection. But, although the Japanese cruiser appeared to be "burning like a city block," the last of her nine lives was not yet expended. She even drove off two PT attacks after sunrise, and turned up high speed. And "Oley" — who, as his chief of staff "Rafe" Bates frequently reminded him, might have to fight another battle with Kurita's Center Force that very morning — decided to retire at 0537 to keep out of Japanese torpedo water. He turned south again at 0617, and half an hour later sent Bob Hayler with *Denver* and *Columbia* "to polish off enemy cripples." They sank destroyer *Asagumo*, whose bow had been knocked off by Coward's torpedo attack, and then retired.

Admiral T. L. Sprague's escort carriers, which were to bear the brunt of the Battle off Samar, joined in the pursuit as early as 0545. Three hours later, 17 of their Avengers found Shima's retreating rear in the Mindanao Sea, and finally disposed of *Mogami*. Light cruiser *Abukuma*, slowed by a PT torpedo, put in temporarily at Dapitan but was sunk at noon the following day by bombers of the V and XIII Army Air Forces based on Noemfoor and Biak. Shima's two heavies and four destroyers made good their escape. *Shigure,* sole survivor of Nishimura's van, made Brunei Bay safely.

In no battle of the entire war did the United States Navy make so nearly a complete sweep as in that of Surigao Strait, or at so little cost — 39 men killed and 114 wounded, most of them in *Albert W. Grant.* But in no other battle except Halsey's off Cape Engaño, that same day, did the United States Navy enjoy such overwhelming power. The tactical dispositions and battle plan of Admiral Oldendorf were perfect, using his mighty force to best advantage. On the Japanese side, the only alleviating circumstances were the stubborn bravery of *Yamashiro* and *Mogami,* and the intelligent discretion of Vice Admiral Shima in retiring.

6. *The Battle off Samar, 25 October*

One of the strangest incidents in this or any modern war occurred on 25 October, 40 miles off Paninihian Point, Island of Samar, about fifteen minutes after sunrise. An escort carrier group known by its code name "Taffy 3," under Rear Admiral Clifton A. F. Sprague in *Fanshaw Bay*, having launched routine patrols to cover the ships in Leyte Gulf, had secured from General Quarters, and the deck crews were eating breakfast. At 0645 lookouts observed antiaircraft fire to the northward. What could that possibly be? At 0646 the flagship's radar screen showed something odd. One minute later the pilot of a plane on antisubmarine patrol reported that he was being fired upon by a force of battleships, cruisers and destroyers at a position some twenty miles' distant. "Check identification!" yelled Admiral Sprague to air plot. But before verification of this astonishing contact could be obtained, sailors on lookout sighted the unmistakable tall masts of Japanese battleships and

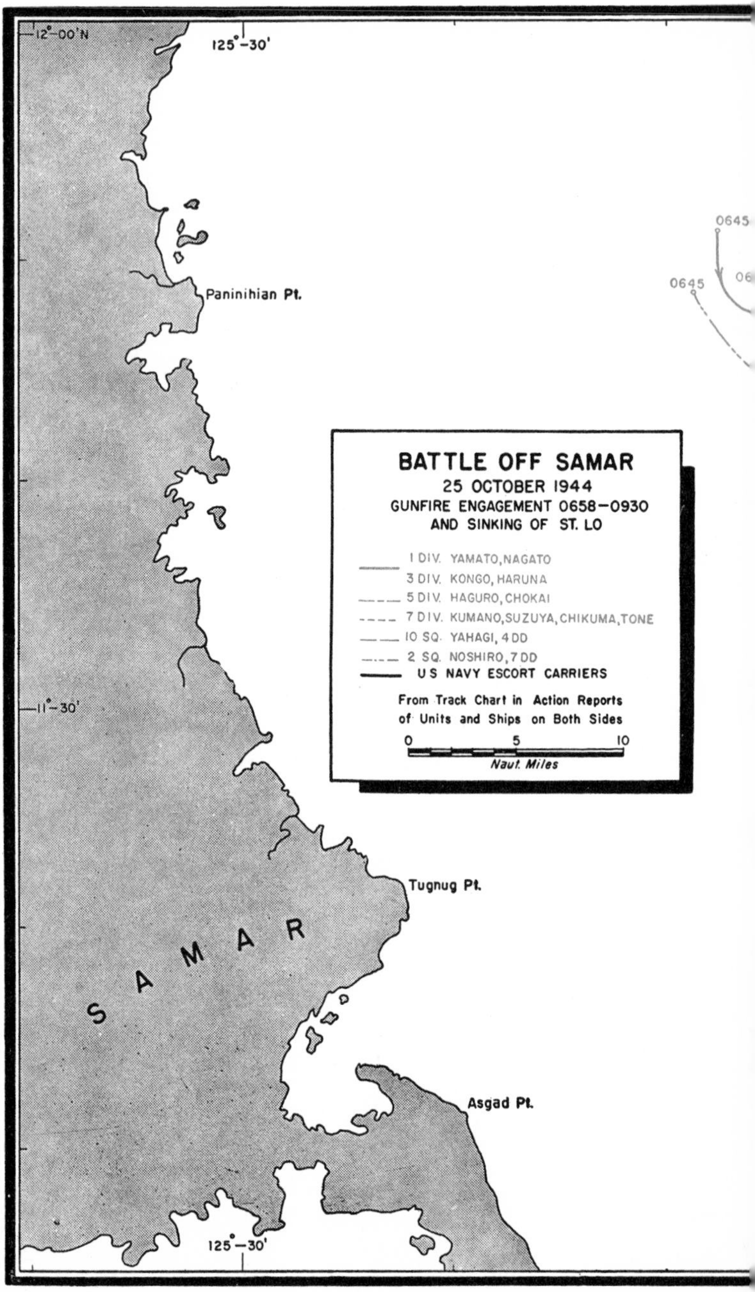

12°-00'N
125°-30'
Paninihian Pt.
0645
0645
06
BATTLE OFF SAMAR
25 OCTOBER 1944
GUNFIRE ENGAGEMENT 0658-0930
AND SINKING OF ST. LO
1 DIV. YAMATO, NAGATO
3 DIV. KONGO, HARUNA
5 DIV. HAGURO, CHOKAI
7 DIV. KUMANO, SUZUYA, CHIKUMA, TONE
10 SQ. YAHAGI, 4 DD
2 SQ. NOSHIRO, 7 DD
U S NAVY ESCORT CARRIERS
From Track Chart in Action Reports
of Units and Ships on Both Sides
0
5
10
Naut. Miles
11°-30'
Tugnug Pt.
S A M A R
Asgad Pt.
125°-30'

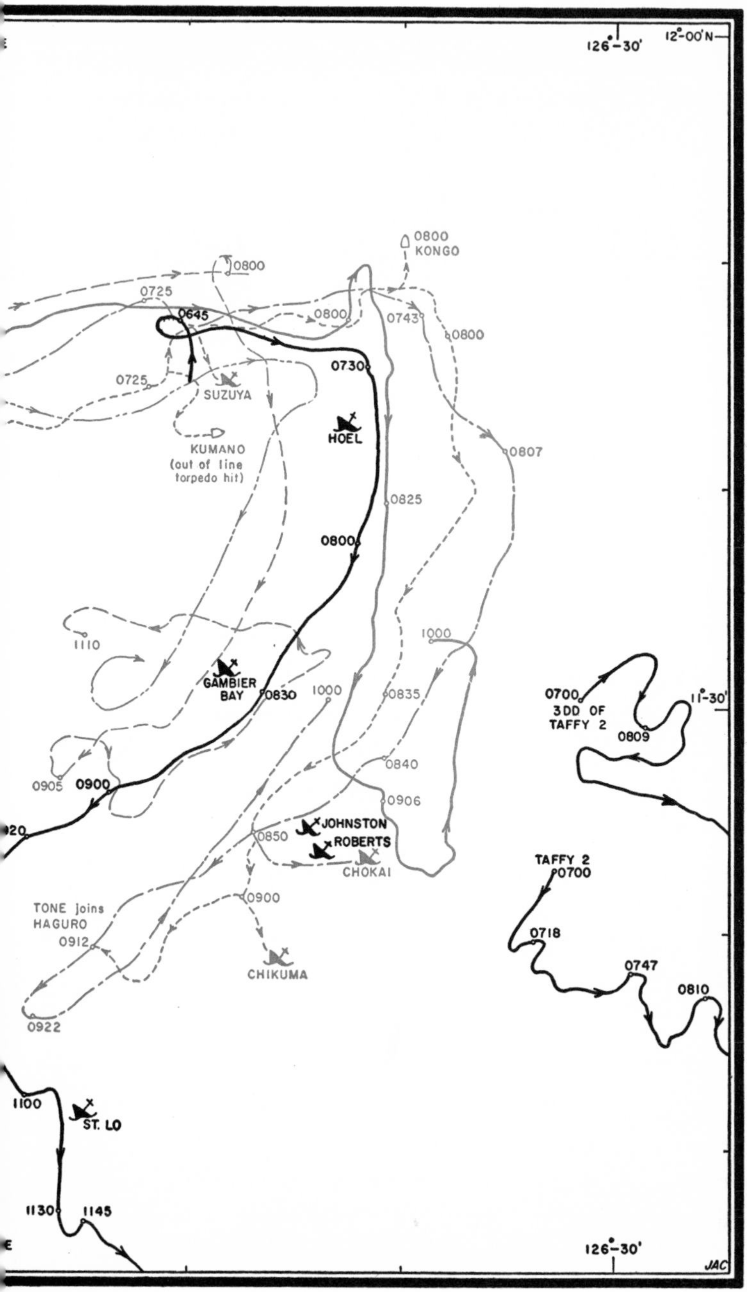

126°-30'
12°-00'N
0800
KONGO
0800
0725
0645
0800
0743
0800
0730
0725
SUZUYA
HOEL
KUMANO
(out of line
torpedo hit)
0807
0825
0800
1110
1000
GAMBIER
BAY
0830
1000
0835
0700
3DD OF
TAFFY 2
0809
11°-30'
0905
0900
0840
0906
JOHNSTON
0850
ROBERTS
CHOKAI
TAFFY 2
0700
0900
TONE joins
HAGURO
0912
0718
CHIKUMA
0747
0810
0922
1100
ST. LO
1130
1145
126°-30'
JAC

cruisers pricking up over the northwestern horizon. At 0648 these ships opened fire, and a minute later splashes from their shells began rising all around Taffy 3.

It was Admiral Kurita's powerful Center Force. He was every bit as surprised as Sprague. He thought he had run smack into Mitscher's Task Force 38.

How could this formidable fleet have covered 125 to 150 miles from *inside* San Bernardino Strait, down along the ocean shore of Samar, in the last seven hours — undetected by ship, search plane or coastwatcher?

Admiral Halsey was informed by a night-search plane from *Independence* that Kurita's Center Force would sortie from San Bernardino Strait. Sightings on it heading that way reached the Admiral as late as 2120 October 24. But he simply did not care. Estimating that his carrier pilots' exaggerated reports of their sinkings in the Battle of the Sibuyan Sea were correct, he assumed that Center Force "could no longer be considered a serious menace to Seventh Fleet," in or outside Leyte Gulf, and did not even warn Kinkaid to watch out. By the time Halsey received the night-sighting reports, his Third Fleet — less McCain's TG 38.1 sent south to fuel — was high-tailing north, hellbent after Ozawa's Northern Force. That was exactly what the Japanese wanted it to do. Halsey might have spared one carrier group and Admiral Lee's Battle Line (*New Jersey*, *Iowa*, *Washington*, *Massachusetts*, *Alabama*) to guard San Bernardino Strait; but he left not even a picket destroyer. That is why Kurita's Center Force was able to debouch unseen into the Philippine Sea at 0030 October 25, and steam south unseen off the Samar shore, until intercepted by Clifton Sprague's escort carriers. And that is why Taffy 3, composed of six escort carriers with no guns bigger than 5-inch, screened by three destroyers and four destroyer escorts, had to fight Kurita's four battleships, six heavy cruisers and numerous destroyers.

Taffy 3 was supported by the aircraft of two other groups of nearly the same strength: Rear Admiral Thomas L. Sprague's Taffy 1, which was operating well to the southward off Mindanao, and Rear Admiral Felix B. Stump's Taffy 2, off the entrance to Leyte Gulf. The total plane complement of these 16 carriers was 235 fighter planes (Hellcats and Wildcats) and 143 Avenger torpedo planes; and it was they, in addition to Clifton Sprague's skillful tactics, and the intrepid attacks by his screen, which enabled him to win this battle against an overwhelming surface and gunfire superiority. But few of these planes were available at the moment of surprise. Taffy 1 had already launched a strike group to pursue Japanese ships fleeing from Surigao Strait; all carriers had launched planes for routine patrol, or for odd jobs such as delivering cans of fresh water to the troops on Leyte.

The Battle off Samar, thus unexpectedly joined at 0648, was the most remarkable of the Pacific war, since the tactics had to be improvised. Prewar training prepared the United States Navy to fight battles such as Surigao Strait; but there was no preparation, no doctrine, for a force of "baby flattops" fighting a battle fleet such as Kurita's. Their training was all for supporting amphibious operations by strikes, C.A.P., and antisubmarine patrol, not for bearing the brunt of a major battle. Rear Admiral Clifton A. F. Sprague, known as "Ziggy" in the Navy, an able and conscientious officer forty-eight years old, had commanded fleet carrier *Wasp* in the Battle of the Philippine Sea, but now he faced a unique challenge.

Weather gave the escort carriers their first break. Wind blew from the eastern quadrant, permitting them to steer away from the enemy while launching planes, and rain squalls afforded occasional cover. Clifton Sprague, knowing very well what a pickle he was in, acted with cool and correct decision. He turned Taffy 3 due east, upped speed to the flattop maximum of 17½ knots, ordered every plane to be launched and to attack, and broadcast an urgent plea for assistance. Admirals Tom Sprague and Felix Stump responded quickly; but Taffy 1 lay 130 miles distant; could the planes get there in time?

Kurita fumbled from the moment the battle joined. His staff told him that the escort carriers were fleet carriers, the destroyers cruisers, and the DEs destroyers. At the moment of impact, he was changing the disposition of Center Force from cruising to antiaircraft formation; he should promptly have formed Battle Line with his fast, powerful ships and committed light forces to torpedo attack. Instead, he ordered General Attack — every ship for itself — which threw his force into confusion and made the battle a helter-skelter affair, ships committed piecemeal and defeated piecemeal, just as the Japanese Army was wont to do ashore.

Clifton Sprague formed his six carriers into a rough circle 2500 yards in diameter, his screen patrolling outside the engaged sector, as Japanese salvos edged closer and closer. At 0706, to quote his Action Report, "The enemy was closing with disconcerting rapidity and the volume and accuracy of fire was increasing. At this point it did not appear that any of our ships could survive another five minutes of the heavy-caliber fire being received." His task unit being faced by "the ultimate in desperate circumstances," he saw that counteraction was urgently required. He ordered all escorts to a torpedo attack. And, also at 0706, compassionate providence sent a rain squall, under which the carriers, in conjunction with the smoke that they and the escorts were making, were protected for about fifteen minutes. During this respite the Admiral decided to bear around to the south and southwest, in order to bring his disposition nearer to the hoped-for help from Leyte Gulf. But no help appeared. Admiral Oldendorf, his ammunition depleted by the night battle, had to replenish from supply ships in Leyte Gulf; and by the time he was ready to sortie it was too late to reach the flattops. Sprague's tactics were risky, since they invited the enemy to take the inside track, but they proved to be correct. Kurita was so obsessed with keeping the weather gauge that, instead of cutting corners, he maintained course until he was due north of the carriers, and then bore down. And most of his ships, repeatedly dodging air and torpedo attacks, could not catch up. The Japanese admiral was sadly bewildered by the way everything we had afloat or airborne went baldheaded for him.

Clifton Sprague ordered Taffy 3 screen to counterattack the Japanese heavy ships at 0716, after the escort carriers had entered the rain squall. The three destroyers were *Hoel*, flying the pennant of Commander W. D. Thomas, and *Heermann* and *Johnston* — all 2100-tonners of the *Fletcher* class. *Johnston* was already counterattacking. Her skipper, Commander Ernest E. Evans, was a fighting Cherokee of the same breed as "Jocko" Clark — short, barrel-chested, loud of voice, a born leader. As soon as the Japanese ships were sighted he had ordered all boilers to be lighted, called all hands to General Quarters,[4] and passed the word, "Prepare to attack major portion of Japanese Fleet." As *Johnston* sheered out to lay a smoke screen, she commenced firing at a range of 18,000 yards. Closing to within 10,000 yards of a heavy cruiser column, she launched torpedoes and got one hit on *Kumano*. The Japanese flag officer on board shifted to *Suzuya*, which had already been slowed down by air bombing, and both cruisers dropped astern and out of the battle.

About 0730, *Johnston* took three 14-inch and three 6-inch shell hits. "It was like a puppy being smacked by a truck," recalled her senior surviving officer. The after fireroom and engine room were knocked out; all power to the after 5-inch guns was lost. A rain squall gave her ten minutes to repair damage. At this stage of the battle confusion reigned supreme. *Johnston*, having

[4] The sailors called *Johnston* "G. Q. Johnny," owing to her frequent General Quarters signals.

expended all torpedoes, used manually-controlled 5-inch gunfire against battleship *Kongo;* and, as if this were not enough, she played the major part in frustrating Kurita's destroyer attack on the carriers. After that, said the survivor, "We were in a position where all the gallantry and guts in the world could not save us." Three cruisers and several destroyers, overtaking her in her slowed-down situation, poured in an avalanche of shells and she went dead in the water. Commander Evans ordered Abandon Ship at 0950. The same Japanese destroyer squadron whose attack on the carriers she had thwarted, now made a running circle around her, shooting rapidly. At 1010 she rolled over and began to sink. A destroyer closed to give her the *coup de grâce*. A swimming survivor saw the Japanese skipper on her bridge salute as *Johnston* took the final plunge.

Hoel and *Heermann* were fighting just as vigorously, their skippers' one object being to inflict maximum damage on the enemy in the hope of diverting major-caliber fire from the carriers. *Heermann* (Commander A. T. Hathaway) at one point was engaging four battleships. She was too nimble for them to hit but her spread of six torpedoes caused the mighty *Yamato* to reverse course for ten minutes, which took those 18.1-inch guns out of the fight. *Hoel* (Commander L. S. Kintberger), with one engine and three 5-inch guns knocked out, was not so lucky. She took over 40 hits, even 16-inch, which went right through her hull without exploding, but knocked her so full of holes that at 0855 she rolled over and sank. Her crew, wrote her C.O., "performed their duties cooly and efficiently until their ship was shot from under them."

In the second torpedo attack Clifton Sprague ordered, at 0742, the three destroyer escorts of his screen also took part. *Samuel B. Roberts* was sunk, after exchanging gunfire with several heavy cruisers. Here is the tribute of her C.O., Lieutenant Commander R. W. Copeland USNR, to his men, one which may apply equally well to the entire screen:

> To witness the conduct of the average enlisted man on board this vessel . . . with an average of less than one year's service, would make any man proud to be an average American. The crew were informed over the loudspeaker system at the beginning of the action of the C.O.'s estimate of the situation: i.e., a fight against overwhelming odds from which survival could not be expected, during which time we would do what damage we could. In the face of this knowledge the men zealously manned their stations . . . and fought and worked with such calmness, courage, and efficiency that no higher honor could be conceived than to command such a group.

For two hours after 0743, when they emerged from the rain squall, the six escort carriers of Taffy 3 were making best speed of 17½ knots around an irregular arc, subtended by a chord almost parallel to the coast of Samar. Their own planes, helped by many from Taffy 2 and Taffy 1, were continually attacking the Japanese with bombs, torpedoes, machine-gun bullets and making dry runs when they ran out of ammunition. Kurita's ships were capable of twice the speed of Sprague's, but their frequent evasive maneuvers to escape destroyers' torpedoes and carrier-plane attacks canceled the advantage; while the flattops, except for some quick salvo-chasing, plodded steadily along. Hence the enemy's main body never appreciably closed range. The three Japanese battleships still advancing at 0820 were astern of the carriers, slowly firing salvos with armor-piercing projectiles which, if they hit, failed to detonate on the thin-skinned flattops. The heavy cruisers were much more deadly: they made thirteen 8-inch hits on *Kalinin Bay*, and she was the only carrier hit by a battleship; heroic efforts of damage control kept her in formation. Boatswains' crews worked in five feet of water to plug holes below the waterline. Black gang worked knee-deep in oil, choked by the stench of burning rubber and threatened by scalding steam, to repair ruptures in the power plant. Main steering control conked out and quartermasters steered the ship by hand from far down in her bowels, like helmsmen in the ancient Spanish galleons.

Aircraft for the most part made individual attacks, as they were too hastily armed and launched to be coördinated. Avengers used torpedoes as long as torpedoes lasted; when these gave out they armed with bombs — even little 100-pounders — and made dry runs to divert the Japanese gunners. Lieutenant Commander Edward J. Huxtable, Air Group Commander in *Gambier Bay*, guided his Avenger for two hours through the flak to make dry runs, once flying down a line of heavy cruisers to divert them from their course and throw off their gunfire for a few precious minutes. The Wildcat pilots strafed topsides or ran interference for an Avenger; and they too made dry runs. Lieutenant Paul G. Garrison USNR made ten such out of a total of twenty. Since the carriers were now scudding and could not afford to luff up to recover, when aircraft ran out of fuel they had to land on a carrier of Stump's Taffy 2 about 25 miles away, or the more distant Tacloban field, Leyte, which Army Engineers had providentially made usable. There they refueled, picked up 500-pound bombs and flew out to sea to attack again.

The battle reached a crisis when Kurita's four remaining heavy cruisers *Chikuma*, *Tone*, *Haguro* and *Chokai*, more enterprising than his battlewagons, pulled ahead on the port quarter of the carriers and closed range. *Chikuma* began a steady pounding of *Gambier Bay*, from which even attacks by the intrepid *Johnston* and *Heermann* did not divert her. The escort carrier, after a salvo-chasing snake dance lasting 25 minutes, began to take 8-inch hits, and dropped astern. The other three heavies, light cruiser *Noshiro*, and a Japanese destroyer now concentrated on *Gambier Bay*. As she began to sink Captain Vieweg gave the order Abandon Ship. *Chikuma* continued to pound her at short range, and at 0907 she capsized and went down.

On to the southwestward plunged the other five American flattops. *White Plains* fired her single 5-inch guns at each cruiser which closed within 18,000 yards, and made at least six hits on

Chokai. "Hold on a little longer, boys," sang out Chief Gunner's Mate Jenkins. "We're sucking 'em into 40-mm range!" And they almost did, or would have, but for an attack on that heavy cruiser by four Avengers led by Commander R. L. Fowler of *Kitkun Bay*'s air group. These planes scored ten hits and had the satisfaction of seeing *Chokai* go down. Next, *Chikuma* was sunk by a well coördinated Wildcat-Avenger attack from Felix Stump's Taffy 2; and down she went. Clifton Sprague's harried and beset carriers, now threatened by high-caliber battleship fire as well as by *Haguro* and *Tone*, saw to their amazement both heavy cruisers break off their pursuit. A moment later a signalman on the bridge of *Fanshaw Bay* yelled "Goddammit, boys, they're getting away!" The entire Center Force was retiring.

Kurita had ordered the break-off at 0911. The air and destroyer attacks had cost his force three heavy cruisers.[5] His communications were so bad that he never knew how near *Tone* and *Haguro* had closed the flattops. At that time, he intended merely to reassemble his dispersed and disorganized force, ascertain damage, and resume the march to Leyte Gulf. But the more he thought it over, the less he liked the prospect, and the better he relished the idea of going home the way he came. Center Force had been battered for three days — by submarines on the 23rd, fast carrier aircraft on the 24th, and in the battle just over. Kurita and his staff were so muddled as to estimate that the escort carriers were making 30 knots (instead of their maximum of 17.5) so that it would be impossible to catch them. "I knew you were scared," said another admiral to Clifton Sprague after reading this postwar statement by Kurita, "but I didn't know you were *that* scared!"

Kurita had already received a radio signal from Admiral Shima indicating that Southern Force, with which he was expected to coöperate, was all washed up. So he figured that his prospects in Leyte Gulf were both thin and grim. American transports and

[5] Including *Suzuya,* which was going down.

amphibious craft would have departed by the time he could get there; he feared massive land-based air attacks from Tacloban Field on Leyte Gulf, and heavy carrier-based air attacks from TF 38, and he did not care to fight Oldendorf's victorious gunfire force (which lay outside the entrance to Leyte Gulf waiting for him until 1300), in order to sink maybe a few LSTs and sprinkle shellfire on American troops ashore. A fresh air attack by 70 Wildcats and Avengers from Taffys 2 and 3, which came in on Center Force at 1230, and made hits on battleship *Nagato* and heavy cruiser *Tone*, helped Kurita to make up his mind to retire. At 1236 he signaled C. in C. Combined Fleet at Tokyo that he was heading for San Bernardino Strait.

Kurita's retirement did not end this day's battle for the escort carriers. While Clifton Sprague's Taffy 3 was fighting to the northward, Tom Sprague's Taffy 1 was receiving the dubious honor of first target of the Kamikaze Corps. Postponing to next chapter a description of this formidable suicide club, we may note here that *Santee* was crashed by a member at 0740, and hit by a torpedo from submarine *I–56* at 0756; but these converted-tanker flattops were tough, and by eight bells *Santee* was making over 16 knots. Sister *Suwannee* received a second kamikaze shortly after, but was able to resume flight operations at 1009. Taffy 3's turn came at 1050 when she hoped that the battle was over. One crashed Rear Admiral Ofstie's flagship *Kitkun Bay* but bounced into the sea; two that made for *Fanshaw Bay* were shot down; two were exploded by antiaircraft fire when diving at *White Plains* and *Kitkun Bay;* two crashed *Kalinin Bay* but inflicted comparatively little damage. But one broke through the flight deck of *St. Lo*, burst into flames, exploded the bombs and torpedoes on the hangar deck, and sank her.

An hour later, Kurita's Center Force was attacked by aircraft from Admiral McCain's TG 38.1. Admiral Halsey, at Kinkaid's urgent request, had ordered this. McCain, fueling when he got the word, turned up flank speed and commenced launching at 1030 when distant 335 miles from Kurita. This was one of the longest-range carrier plane attacks of the war; too long, for Avengers could not carry heavy bombs or torpedoes that far, and they suffered considerable loss without inflicting additional damage.

By noon the Battle off Samar was over. It had been a glorious but expensive victory: two escort carriers, two destroyers and a destroyer escort sunk; several other ships badly damaged, and heavy casualties: —

	Killed & Missing	*Wounded*
Taffy 1 Ships' Crews	283	136
Taffy 3 Ships' Crews	792	768
Aviators, all escort carriers	43	9
Aviators, TG 38.1	12	0
TOTAL	1130	913

Kurita's successful retirement was small consolation for the complete failure of his mission. His defeat was due, in last analysis, to the indomitable spirit of the escort carriers, their screen, and their aviators. It was they who stopped the most powerful gunfire force which Japan had sent to sea since the Battle of Midway.

7. *The Battle off Cape Engaño, 25 October*

All day 24 October Admiral Halsey's Third Fleet search planes were eagerly looking for Admiral Ozawa's Northern Force, and Ozawa was equally anxious to be seen, in order to carry out his mission to bait Halsey up north out of Kurita's way. Yet the Japanese were unable to get themselves sighted until 1540.

Ozawa's Northern Force comprised four carriers with 116 planes on board; the two "hermaphrodites" *Hyuga* and *Ise*, battleships whose superstructures had been shorn abaft the stack to make a short flight deck, but carried no planes; three light cruisers, nine destroyers and a tanker unit. They sortied from Bungo Suido, Inland Sea, on 20 October. During the forenoon watch on the 24th they located a group of Mitscher's TF 38, and at 1145 Ozawa launched a 76-plane strike on Frederick Sherman's TG 38.3. It accomplished nothing. Some planes were splashed, 15 to 20 landed on Luzon fields, and the 29 which returned on board were all that Ozawa had during the battle.[6] Halsey received his search planes' contact reports on Ozawa around 1700; and at 2022, as we have seen, ordered his entire Third Fleet — less McCain's TG 38.1, which had been sent away to fuel — up north. Admiral Mitscher in *Lexington*, next in command under Admiral Halsey in *New Jersey*, had 64 ships and 787 planes (401 fighters, 214 dive-bombers, 171 torpedo-bombers)[7] opposed to Ozawa's 17 ships and 29 aircraft. Surely, enough for him to have spared Lee's Battle Line, or part of it, to guard San Bernardino Strait; but Japanese carriers gave Halsey blood in the eye, and he was taking no chances of letting one guilty flattop escape.

Rendezvous of the three American carrier groups was made around midnight at lat. 14°28′ N, long. 125°30′ E, off central Luzon. All three proceeded north in company, *Independence* sending five night fliers ahead to search. Around 0220 October 25 they sighted the two groups into which Ozawa had divided Northern Force: one under Rear Admiral Matsuda with the two hermaphrodites, a light cruiser and four destroyers; the rest of the force under Ozawa himself. They were then about 200 miles E by N of Cape Engaño, Luzon.

At 0430 October 25 Mitscher (O.T.C. from now on) ordered all carriers to arm a deckload immediately and be prepared to launch at earliest light. Throughout morning watch, deck crews

[6] Apparently the 40 other planes on board had also been flown ashore.

[7] Exclusive of the complement of *Princeton*, sunk that day; but many of her surviving planes had been received on board the other carriers.

were arming and spotting planes and aviators were either taking a last nap or eating an early breakfast. Not since the Battle of the Philippine Sea in June had these air groups had a crack at enemy carriers. This was what they had been looking and praying for. And the new battleships were longing for some good floating targets to test the power and accuracy of their main batteries.

First strike reached the enemy around 0800. Helldivers first, strafing fighter planes next as the dive-bombers overshot, and Avengers last, releasing torpedoes from 700 to 1000 feet, at ranges from 1400 to 1600 yards. Commander David McCampbell of the *Essex* Air Group acted as target coördinator. Admiral Ozawa was not taken aback, but there was nothing he could do except use antiaircraft fire, which was brisk and intense. Despite this, carrier *Chitose* and one destroyer were sunk by a cluster of bomb hits, and big *Zuikaku*, veteran of Pearl Harbor, the Coral Sea and the Philippine Sea, took a torpedo which knocked out her communications and caused Ozawa to shift his flag to light cruiser *Oyodo*. A good beginning indeed.

Strike No. 2 was already in the air. Upon its arrival at the target, around 0945, the enemy force presented a picture of wild confusion. *Lexington*'s and *Franklin*'s planes made bomb hits on *Chiyoda*, setting her heavily afire; a third hit disabled her engines. *Hyuga* attempted to take her in tow, but was frustrated by Strike No. 3. *Chiyoda* was abandoned with her crew still on board, and sunk by gunfire of Admiral DuBose's cruisers at 1630.

Strike No. 3, launched around noon from Sherman's TG 38.3 (*Essex*, flag) and Davison's 38.4 (*Franklin*, flag), comprising over 200 aircraft (about 150 of which had been in Strike No. 1), stayed over and around Ozawa's ships for an hour. *Zuikaku*, as a result of three torpedoes which hit her simultaneously, rolled over and went down. *Zuiho*, her flight deck quaintly camouflaged to make her look like a big-gunned battleship from aloft, took a lot of punishment from this strike, and 27 more planes of Strike No. 4

were required to sink her. Strike No. 5, consisting of full deckloads from five carriers, concentrated on *Ise* but got nothing but near-misses and only slightly damaged that tough old hermaphrodite. She threw up remarkably heavy antiaircraft fire, and her C.O., Rear Admiral Nakase, was an expert at evasive manuevering. Strike No. 6, by 36 planes from Davison's group, took off at 1710 and claimed a few hits, but sank nothing more.

After the war, Admiral Ozawa said that the first three strikes did the most damage, and his chief of staff remarked, "I saw all this bombing and thought the American pilot is not so good." He was not too bad — having sunk four carriers and a destroyer with a total of 527 plane sorties, 201 of them fighters. Yet it must be admitted that, blow for blow, the escort carrier planes in the Battle off Samar inflicted more damage than did the aircraft of any two fast carrier groups. A comparison of this battle with that of the Philippine Sea in June suggests that the American fast carrier planes were much better at intercepting enemy aircraft than at hitting ships. The old SBDs did better at Midway than the SB2Cs off Cape Engaño; but Japanese antiaircraft fire had vastly improved since 1942.

Now came the surface part of the battle, and the controversial "Where is TF 34?" incident. Admiral Halsey at 1512 October 24 had organized Task Force 34, including most of his gunfire ships, under Admiral Lee. The dispatch, headed "Battle Plan," named the battleships, cruisers and destroyer divisions which "will be formed as Task Force 34" and "will engage decisively at long ranges." Admirals Kinkaid in Leyte Gulf, Nimitz at Pearl Harbor, and Cooke, deputy C.N.O. in Washington, all misread Halsey's future indicative for present imperative. They assumed that TF 34 was not only set up on paper but detached to guard San Bernardino Strait; and Kinkaid was not informed of the contrary by Halsey until 0705 October 25. From 0822, following the surprise off Samar, Halsey received a series of plain-language pleas from Kinkaid for any kind of assistance, air or surface, that he could spare; and Halsey complied, as we have seen, to the extent of ordering Admiral McCain to belay fueling his TG 38.1 and hasten to strike Kurita's Center Force. But he did not detach Lee's TF 34 to block Kurita's escape, because he wanted to keep all heavy ships for a gunfire battle up north after his aircraft had done their worst.

Admiral Nimitz, also amazed at the surprise off Samar, wanted information and sent a dispatch asking for it. The encoding yeoman at Pearl Harbor, who apparently had been reading "The Charge of the Light Brigade," put in as padding (to throw off possible enemy decrypters), "the world wonders." The decoding yeoman on board *New Jersey*, taking this to be a part of the message, handed it to Admiral Halsey at 1000 in this form:

> FROM CINCPAC ACTION COM THIRD FLEET INFO COMINCH CTF 77 X WHERE IS RPT WHERE IS TASK FORCE THIRTY-FOUR RR THE WORLD WONDERS.[8]

Halsey was furious. He thought that Nimitz was criticizing him, and that, too, before Admirals King and Kinkaid (CTF 77) by making them addressees. He brooded over the supposed insult for almost an hour, then at 1055 ordered the major part of Lee's TF 34 south to help Seventh Fleet, went along himself in *New Jersey*, and picked up Bogan's carrier group en route. It was too late by several hours for them to reach San Bernardino Strait ahead of Kurita. When they arrived at 0100 on the 26th, there was only one crippled destroyer of Center Force outside the Strait. Kurita had got through three hours earlier.

This was a bitter disappointment to Admiral Lee, as to all battleship sailors. Adept at handling battlewagons, as he had proved in the Battle of Guadalcanal, Lee had planned to form Battle Line between Kurita and the Strait, so that the Japanese would be

[8] Potter and Nimitz *The Great Sea War* p. 390n.

forced to fight. What a brawl that would have been — with *Yamato*, *Nagato*, *Kongo* and *Haruna* on one side, and *Iowa*, *New Jersey*, *Massachusetts*, *South Dakota*, *Washington* and *Alabama* on the other! And it proved to be the last opportunity to find out what *Yamato*'s 18.1-inch main battery could do against the 16-inch guns of the *Iowa* class.

When Halsey sent the major part of TF 34 south at 1045, he detached cruisers *Santa Fe*, *Mobile*, *Wichita*, *New Orleans* and nine destroyers to continue northward with the carriers. Mitscher at 1415 ordered this cruiser group, under command of Rear Admiral Laurance T. DuBose, to pursue Ozawa's limping units. They sank abandoned *Chiyoda*, then encountered *Hatsuzuki* and two smaller destroyers in the twilight. *Mobile* opened fire from very long range at 1853. *Hatsuzuki* returned fire and worked up speed to escape. The cruisers pursued at 28 knots, gradually overhauling the group, and at 1915 DuBose sent three destroyers ahead to make a torpedo attack, which slowed up *Hatsuzuki*. The cruisers closed to 6000 yards, illuminated with star shell, brought the destroyer under gunfire, and saw her explode and sink at 2059. She had absorbed a tremendous amount of punishment.

Half an hour later, two *Independence* night flyers sighted Ozawa's ships steaming north at 22 knots abreast of Bashi Channel, the northern entrance to Luzon Strait. A simple calculation showed that even if DuBose pursued at 30 knots he could not overhaul them before daylight, when they would be under the protection of land-based aircraft on Formosa. So he retired. The black gangs in *Oyodo*, *Hyuga*, *Ise* and five destroyers were "pouring it on" to escape. They ran the gantlet of two wolf-packs of Pacific Fleet submarines, whose torpedoes missed (though *Jallao* sank lagging light cruiser *Tama*, earlier bombed), and made harbor in the Ryukyus on 27 October.

Admiral Ozawa had performed his mission of baiting Halsey and saving Kurita, as well as his own force, from annihilation. The

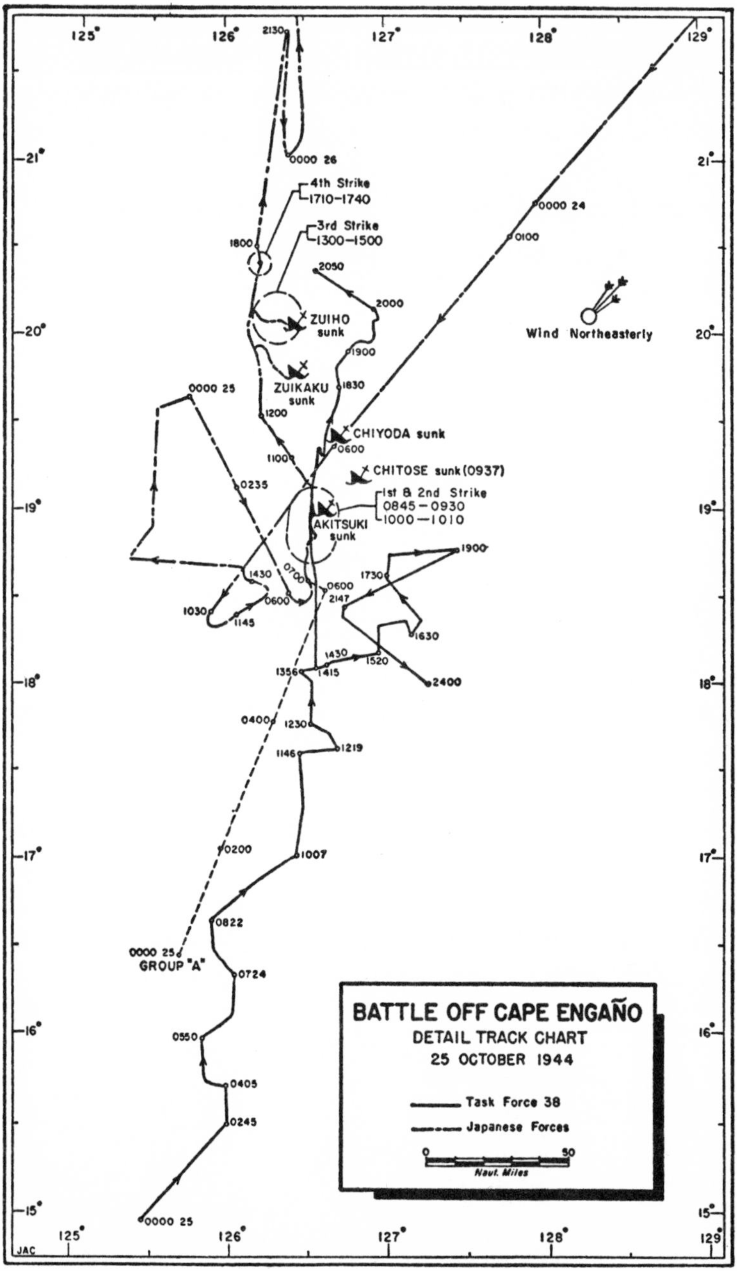

BATTLE OFF CAPE ENGAÑO
DETAIL TRACK CHART
25 OCTOBER 1944
Task Force 38
Japanese Forces
0
50
Naut. Miles
125°
126°
127°
128°
129°
21°
20°
19°
18°
17°
16°
15°
Wind Northeasterly
4th Strike
1710-1740
3rd Strike
1300-1500
1st & 2nd Strike
0845-0930
1000-1010
ZUIHO sunk
ZUIKAKU sunk
CHIYODA sunk
CHITOSE sunk (0937)
AKITSUKI sunk
0000 24
0100
0000 25
0000 26
2130
1800
2050
2000
1900
1830
1200
1100
0600
0235
1430
0700
0600
1030
1145
0600
2147
1730
1900
1630
1430
1356
1415
1520
2400
0400
1230
1219
1146
0200
1007
0822
0000 25
GROUP "A"
0724
0550
0405
0245
0000 25
JAC

antiaircraft fire of his ships, especially *Ise*'s and *Hyuga*'s, was perhaps the most deadly on either side in the Pacific war. Nevertheless, the battle was a "bitter experience," as he admitted. For Ozawa, protagonist of carrier warfare in the Japanese Navy, to be defeated twice in five months, and to be forced to expend his beloved flattops as bait, was bitter indeed. He faced the situation without flinching; and his former enemies, now friends, consider him the ablest Japanese admiral after Yamamoto. What irony that this sacrificial Northern Force should have been superbly handled, tactically; whilst the commanders of the other two, which might have accomplished something positive, fumbled so miserably!

The Battle for Leyte Gulf did not end the war, but it was decisive. And it should be an imperishable part of our national memory. The night action in Surigao Strait is an inspiring example of perfect timing, coördination and almost faultless execution. And the Battle off Samar had no compeer. The story of that action, with its dramatic surprise, the quick thinking and resolute decisions of Clifton Sprague; the little screening vessels feeling for each other through the rain and smoke and, courting annihilation, making individual attacks on battleships and heavy cruisers; naval aviators making dry runs on enemy ships to divert gunfire from their own; the defiant humor and indomitable courage of bluejackets caught in the "ultimate of desperate circumstances," will make the fight of the "Taffys" with Kurita's Center Force forever memorable, forever glorious.

8. *Leyte Secured, 26 October–25 December 1944*

One small section of Combined Fleet which operated on the verge of the battle may be said to have accomplished its mission. This was Vice Admiral Sakonju's Transport Unit. It lost heavy cruiser *Aoba*, torpedoed but not sunk by United States submarine *Bream* outside Manila Bay on 23 October, lost a destroyer next day to plane attack from TF 38, and another destroyer and light cruiser *Kinu* to Tom Sprague's planes on the 26th. But on the day of the big battle, it embarked 2000 troops in destroyer-transports at Cagayan, Mindanao, and landed them next morning at Ormoc on the back of Leyte. That was the beginning of a series of reinforcements by quick, fast thrusts, similar to the Tokyo Expresses at Guadalcanal. They ran 'em in daily, without opposition, until 30 October, when B–24s from Morotai sank an unloaded *Maru* in Ormoc Bay. Two large convoys from Manila were badly bombed on 11 November by planes from three of the fast carrier groups, sinking six destroyers and drowning about 10,000 troops.

Two weeks elapsed before the Japanese could send in more reinforcements. But, before these back-side Leyte convoys were stopped, about 45,000 troops and 10,000 tons of supplies had been landed on the west coast of Leyte, more than 100 per cent increase over what was there on 20 October. The 101,635 American troops ashore by 1 November still outnumbered them, but Japan had some 365,000 troops elsewhere in the Philippines to draw on. The situation bore a distressing resemblance to that on Guadalcanal two years earlier. We had won a great naval battle and secured our sea communications; but without round-the-clock air supremacy it was impossible to prevent the running in of reinforcements by Tokyo Express.

As soon as the Japanese high command caught its breath, it began staging aircraft south into Luzon fields, to harass General Krueger's Sixth Army ashore, and the supply ships constantly coming and going in Leyte Gulf. Admiral Halsey made up for any earlier mistakes through nobly standing by for many days after the big battle, since Army Engineers were unable to get the boggy airstrips on the Leyte beachhead fit to receive Army Air Force until November — and not many planes even then. Admiral Bogan's

TG 38.2 and Admiral Davison's TG 38.4 struck the airfield complex around Manila on 29-30 October; in return, kamikazes crashed carriers *Intrepid*, *Franklin* and *Belleau Wood*, injuring them so badly that they had to retire to Ulithi. Task Force 38 held rendezvous there on 1 November — first rest for the sailors and aviators who had been fighting three days out of four since their last sortie on 6 October.

Upon the departure of the Halsey-Mitscher forces, the air situation over Leyte deteriorated, since troops and ships had for protection only the few Army planes which Tacloban airstrip could accommodate. One destroyer was sunk by a kamikaze and three were damaged by conventional bombers on 1 November. TF 38 was back in the area by 5 November — Bogan's group even earlier — and in two days' strikes on the airfields around Manila they destroyed over 200 enemy planes at the cost of 25 of our own, and a kamikaze crash on *Lexington* which killed 50 and wounded 132 men but did not seriously injure the ship. These efforts brought about a marked improvement in the air situation at Leyte.

On 13-14 November Halsey, at MacArthur's urgent request, resumed air strikes on Luzon. This time he concentrated on reinforcement shipping, sinking a light cruiser, four destroyers and seven *Marus*. Again, on the 25th, *Ticonderoga*'s planes sank heavy cruiser *Kumano* in Dasol Bay and broke up two coastal convoys. The kamikazes then made a really vicious counterattack. Carriers *Intrepid*, *Cabot* and *Essex* were crashed — "Evil I" twice — with a loss of over a hundred men.

This action of 25 November concluded fast carrier support of the Leyte operation, which had begun on 8 October. This support had been prolonged for four weeks after the originally planned date of its termination, owing to the disappointingly slow work on Tacloban airfield. Not counting its two short calls in Ulithi lagoon, TF 38 had been at sea almost continuously for 84 days. The resulting strain on all hands was severe. No ship except *Princeton* had been lost, but five carriers needed extensive repairs. Under these conditions, wrote Admiral Halsey, "further casual strikes did not appear profitable."

In the meantime, General Krueger's Sixth Army had been slashing ahead on Leyte, through foul weather and continual rain. Not since the Guadalcanal and Buna-Gona campaigns had fighting been as arduous as on Leyte. In spite of the victories of 25 October, soldiers, sailors and aviators were dying daily for the liberation of that island.

By December 1, Sixth Army controlled most of Leyte except the San Isidro Peninsula and a semicircular sector with a 12-mile radius from Ormoc. The Japanese still had about 35,000 men on the island, but they could no longer reinforce it, and General Krueger's effective strength had risen to 183,242. His losses up to 2 December were 2260 killed and missing and several thousand laid up from wounds, dysentery, "immersion foot," skin diseases and other ills incident to campaigning in tropical mud. Over 24,000 enemy dead had been counted. It was time to finish.

A preliminary to the finish was a series of destroyer sweeps, commanded by Captains Robert H. Smith and W. M. Cole, into Ormoc Bay and the Camotes Sea, and minesweeping the Canigao Channels between Bohol and Leyte. The PTs got into this, too. There were numerous night and day encounters during the first week of December, in which destroyer *Cooper* was lost after sinking Japanese destroyer *Kuwa;* their rafted survivors drifted together next morning and even conversed in English. There was a shore-to-shore amphibious landing on Ormoc Bay, commanded by Admiral Struble, on 7 December, in which destroyers *Mahan* and *Ward* were sunk by kamikazes. But the 77th Division was landed near Ormoc; and that, as General Krueger commented, "Serving to split the enemy forces and to separate them from their supply base, proved to be the decisive action of the Leyte Operation."

Re-supply echelons now had to be sent from Leyte Gulf through Surigao Strait into Leyte; and the one on 11-12 December under Captain J. D. Murphy took a bad beating from kamikazes, losing destroyer *Reid;* and *Caldwell* was twice crashed but not sunk.

The shore fighting, of which we have no space to tell, culminated in the capture of Palompon on Christmas Day. General MacArthur, congratulating General Krueger on the event, said: "This closes a campaign that has had few counterparts in the utter destruction of the enemy's forces with a maximum conservation of our own. It has been a magnificent performance on the part of all concerned." Next day, the General declared, "The Leyte-Samar campaign can now be regarded as closed, except for minor mopping-up operations." These "minor" operations went on until 5 May 1945; but General MacArthur was unconsciously corroborated by General Yamashita, who, on Christmas Day from his headquarters at Manila, notified General Suzuki on Leyte that he had written off that island as a loss and had decided to concentrate on the defense of Luzon, shedding "tears of remorse" for the tens of thousands of his countrymen who must fight to the death on Leyte.

On the American side, mopping-up operations were conducted under Commanding General Eighth Army, Lieutenant General Robert L. Eichelberger, veteran of the Papuan campaign. General Hodge's XXIV Corps remained to finish the job. All naval supporting forces were withdrawn for the Mindoro and Lingayen operations; the Engineer Special Brigade craft did whatever convoy work was required.

The outstanding tactical lesson of the Battle for Leyte Gulf is the utter helplessness of a modern fleet without air support. That is why "jeep carriers" and their thin screen were able, off Samar, to defeat a powerful fleet of battleships and heavy cruisers. Spruance's victory in June and Halsey's October strikes on Formosa were responsible for the accelerated assault on Leyte, catching Japanese air forces at their lowest ebb. If the original timetable for that assault (20 December) had been strictly maintained, Ozawa would have had new air groups trained, and the Japanese Navy could have put up a far better fight. Halsey was responsible for the accelerated timetable; so let us, in retrospect, remember that strategic inspiration of the grand old admiral, and forget his mistake on the fateful night of 24–25 October, which was fully compensated by the gallantry of Kinkaid's escort carrier groups next morning.

CHAPTER XV

The Philippines and Submarine Operations

13 December 1944 to 15 August 1945

1. *Mindoro*

THREE WEEKS BEFORE the Battle of Leyte Gulf, on 3 October 1944, the Joint Chiefs of Staff decided to liberate Manila and Luzon. That was as General MacArthur had always wished. Admiral King long held out for taking Formosa, which would "put the cork in the bottle" of the South China Sea, isolate Japan, and provide an advanced air and naval base for the final assault. But the Army estimated that at least nine divisions would be required to capture even a part of Formosa; and, owing to involvement in Europe, it could not get nine divisions. However, the five divisions in Leyte should be ready for another amphibious operation before the end of 1944; and these, it was thought, would be enough to invade Luzon. The J.C.S. put the landings at Lingayen Bay, Luzon, on the program for 20 December, ordered Admiral Nimitz to invade Iwo Jima on 20 January 1945, and the Ryukyus on 1 March.

It was impossible to keep to this timetable, largely because of the prolonged Japanese resistance on Leyte, and their revived air power with kamikaze tactics. Admiral Kinkaid finally persuaded General MacArthur to postpone Lingayen to 9 January 1945.

Mindoro was considered an essential stepping-stone to Luzon, where Army Engineers could build airfields to help cover Lingayen convoys and landings. Rear Admiral Arthur D. Struble was appointed commander of the Visayan Attack Force, to bring up 12,000 combat troops, 10,000 A.A.F. and 6000 service troops from Leyte Gulf. Everyone knew that this was going to be a bold and dangerous thrust, since a score of Japanese airfields were within easy range of the route to Mindoro. Accordingly an escort carrier group was attached in wide support, as the one means of protecting the convoy during hours when the A.A.F. at Leyte could not be overhead.

The approach from Leyte Gulf was very eventful. Shortly before 1500 December 13, as the convoy was about to round the southern cape of Negros into the Sulu Sea, a kamikaze sneaked in low from astern and crashed cruiser *Nashville* on her port side abaft Admiral Struble's cabin. Fires immediately broke out; flag bridge, combat information center and communications office were wrecked. No fewer than 133 officers and men — including the Admiral's and the commanding General's chiefs of staff — were killed, and 190 were wounded. Two hours later, a kamikaze crashed destroyer *Haraden* and she too had to return to Leyte. For next day the Japanese prepared an attack by 186 planes on the Visayan Attack Force, but missed owing to an assumption that it was aiming to land on Negros or Panay instead of Mindoro.

The mission of Admiral Struble and General Dunckel was to establish a perimeter embracing the village of San José in southwestern Mindoro, there to begin airstrip construction. The landings on 15 December were uneventful, since there were only a few hundred Japanese troops on Mindoro, and none in that part of the island. But an amphibious landing is only the first step in an overseas operation. Supplying the men with food, clothing and matériel is a great effort, especially where, as in Mindoro, an airfield has to be built promptly. The resupply echelons for Mindoro provided the Kamikaze Corps with rich targets for three weeks. The Corps sank three LST en route to Mindoro, two at the beachhead, and five Liberty ships. Not since the Anzio operation had the Navy experienced so much difficulty supporting an amphibious operation after the initial landing.

By Christmas Eve Army P–38s were operating from the new San José airfield. But a Japanese bombardment force commanded by Rear Admiral Kimura, including heavy cruiser *Ashigara,* light cruiser *Oyodo,* and six destroyers, was on its way to break up the landings. This was all that the Japanese Navy could assemble after the destruction it had sustained in the Battle for Leyte Gulf. Admiral Toyoda may have intended to use his new 27,000-ton carrier *Unryu* in this raid, but she did not survive long enough. On 19 December, as she was steaming southerly toward Formosa Strait, submarine *Redfish* intercepted her in the East China Sea in broad daylight, scored two torpedo hits and had the satisfaction of seeing her go down.

Kimura's force was reported on 26 December by a Leyte-based Liberator, and the entire strength of the V A.A.F. at Mindoro — 92 fighters, 13 B–25s and a few P–61s — took the air to meet the enemy. The situation looked much like that in Empress Augusta Bay on the night of 1-2 November 1943, but with no "Tip" Merrill in sight. The only Allied naval vessels near the beachhead were a score of motor torpedo boats under Lieutenant Commander N. Burt Davis, who also had to protect the merchant ships present. Planes and PTs in concert did a beautiful job, diverting the attention of Japanese gunners so that their shore bombardment went wild. *PT–223,* commanded by Lieutenant (jg) Harry E. Griffin USNR, sank the new destroyer *Kiyoshimo,* and both PTs and planes damaged so many other ships that Kimura put about for home in the early hours of 27 December.

Mindoro was a tough little operation from start to finish, because we lacked complete control of the air, but it was well worth the effort. Army air forces based on Mindoro could not waft the Navy into Lingayen Gulf unmolested, but they may well have saved that bloody passage from becoming a mass slaughter.

2. *The Kamikazes and Lingayen Landings, 1–12 January 1945*

What was this Kamikaze Corps, whose sacrificial crashes had already caused so much agony? It was a special air corps organized by Rear Admiral Arima in 1944 to meet a desperate situation for Japanese air power. The air groups of the Imperial Navy had been largely wiped out in the Battle of the Philippine Sea and land-based aircraft too were in short supply. A new tactical situation had been created by the growing competence of American fighter planes at interception, and by the American invention of a proximity-armed fuse for antiaircraft shells. After the United States Navy had been liberally furnished with these fuses, which exploded a shell automatically when near enough to an attacking plane, it became nearly impossible for a conventional bomber to get near enough to a ship to hit her. Hence the Kamikaze Corps. The name (meaning "Heavenly Wind") came from a famous historical event. In 1570 an Emperor of China organized a huge amphibious force for the invasion of Japan, and there was little preparation to resist him. But the gods sent a Heavenly Wind in the shape of a typhoon which scattered and destroyed the Chinese Fleet.

The new tactics for aircraft were to crash an enemy ship, set it on fire by the spread of gasoline, and explode it with the bombs. The pilot had to be expended, but this sort of sacrifice appealed to the Japanese temperament and thousands of young men volunteered for a duty certain to be fatal to themselves, but expectantly fatal to the United States Navy. These tactics had the additional advantage that obsolete types of aircraft, like biplanes and the Val with nonretractable landing gear, could be used; that the pilots needed very little training, and that even if a pilot were killed by a proximity-fused shell before he crashed, the momentum of the plane would usually take it to the target. The first organized kamikaze attack was the one on escort carriers *Santee* and *Suwannee* on 25 October during the Battle off Samar, which we have already related. And, as we have seen, the kamikazes enjoyed considerable success on convoys plying between Leyte Gulf and Mindoro in December 1944. But their full fury was first unleashed against the expedition proceeding to Lingayen, and at the beachhead itself, in early January 1945.

The Luzon Attack Force included most of the ships which had taken part in the Leyte invasion. Vice Admiral Kinkaid commanded it in AGC *Wasatch*, with Lieutenant General Walter Krueger, Commanding General Sixth Army, on board. There were two main amphibious groups, comprising big transport types and beaching craft, commanded respectively by Vice Admiral Barbey and Vice Admiral Wilkinson. Vice Admiral Oldendorf commanded the bombardment and fire support group of battleships, heavy cruisers and destroyers; Rear Admiral Berkey had a close covering group of light cruisers and destroyers; Rear Admiral Durgin (veteran of Operation DRAGOON) the escort carriers; Commander W. R. Loud a minesweeping group of 22 large and 42 small minecraft.

Admiral Oldendorf in battleship *California* took charge of all operations en route to Lingayen Gulf, and until Admiral Kinkaid arrived with the amphibious forces. "Oley" had 6 battleships, 6 cruisers, 19 destroyers, 12 escort carriers screened by 20 destroyers and destroyer escorts, a big minesweeping group, 10 destroyer transports carrying the underwater demolition teams, and 11 LCI gunboats. These made rendezvous at Leyte Gulf on New Year's

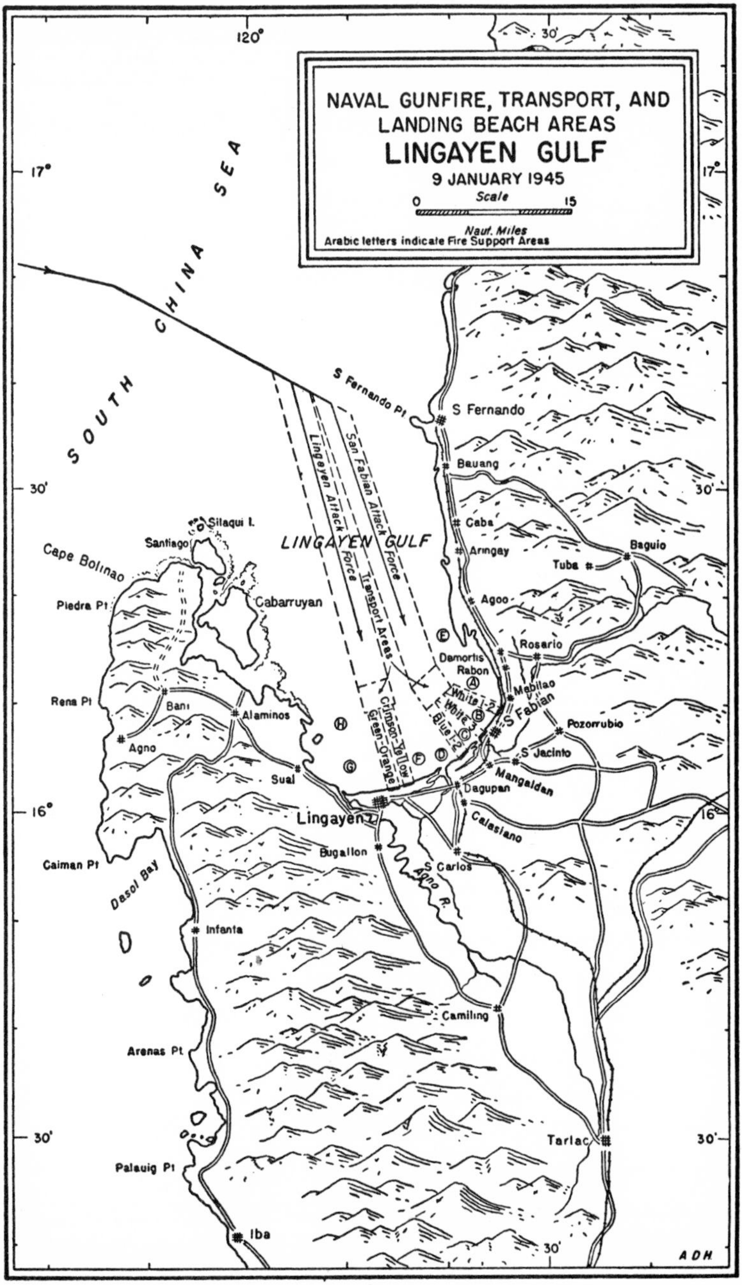

NAVAL GUNFIRE, TRANSPORT, AND
LANDING BEACH AREAS
LINGAYEN GULF
9 JANUARY 1945
Scale
0
15
Naut. Miles
Arabic letters indicate Fire Support Areas
120°
30'
17°
30'
16°
SOUTH CHINA SEA
LINGAYEN GULF
Lingayen Attack Force
San Fabian Attack Force
Transport Areas
Crimson-Yellow
Green-Orange
White 1-2
White 3
Blue 1-2
S Fernando Pt
S Fernando
Bauang
Caba
Aringay
Agoo
Baguio
Tuba
Rosario
Damortis
Rabon
Mabilao
S Fabian
Pozorrubio
S Jacinto
Mangaldan
Dagupan
Calasiano
S Carlos
Agno R.
Bugallon
Lingayen
Sual
Alaminos
Bani
Agno
Silaqui I.
Santiago
Cape Bolinao
Cabarruyan
Piedra Pt
Rena Pt
Caiman Pt
Dasol Bay
Infanta
Camiling
Arenas Pt
Tarlac
Palauig Pt
Iba
A
B
C
D
E
F
G
H
ADH

Day, formed cruising disposition, and passed through Surigao Strait, scene of Admiral Oldendorf's recent victory, into the Sulu Sea. Heavy fighter cover from the CVEs and Tacloban knocked down most of the 120 Japanese planes from Luzon committed against this convoy; but, on 4 January, a kamikaze crashed escort carrier *Ommaney Bay* and sank her, with a loss of 100 men. A severe attack of 16-plus kamikazes developed next day. Cruisers *Louisville* and H.M.A.S. *Australia*, escort carrier *Manila Bay* and destroyer escort *Stafford* were crashed, but survived.

The operation plan for the Lingayen landings called for a three-day interval between Oldendorf's arrival and that of the amphibious forces, to allow plenty of time for minesweeping and shore bombardment. These were three hellish days for ships present. At noon 6 January, when battleship *New Mexico* was bombarding the shore, she was crashed on the port wing of her navigating bridge by a Japanese plane already in flames. The C.O., Captain R. W. Fleming, Lieutenant General Herbert Lumsden (Winston Churchill's liaison officer at General MacArthur's headquarters) and his aide, and *Time* magazine correspondent William Chickering, were instantly killed. There were 26 other fatalities and 87 men wounded; but *New Mexico* continued shooting. Destroyer *Walke*, attacked by four planes in rapid succession, knocked down two, but a third crashed the bridge. The C.O., Commander George F. Davis, drenched with the plane's gasoline, burned like a torch. Sailors smothered the flames and he conned his ship, exhorting all to save her; and, still on his feet, saw his guns in local control destroy a fourth kamikaze. Then, when the safety of his ship was assured, he consented to be carried below. But his burns were too terrible to be borne, and a few hours later he died.

Minesweeper *Long* was crashed and sunk; *Southard* and destroyers *Barton* and *Allen M. Sumner* were crashed but survived. *California* took one at the base of her foremast. A kamikaze crashed the main deck of light cruiser *Columbia* (Captain M. E.

Curts) at top speed. Plane, pilot and engine penetrated the deck and the bomb went through two more decks before exploding. Several fires blazed up, but prompt flooding of magazines saved the ship from a major explosion. Within an hour all fires were out, and at 1828 her forward 20-mm gunners shot the tail off a plane trying to crash H.M.A.S. *Australia.* Despite flooded compartments and loss of two main battery turrets, *Columbia* completed her fire support assignments. *Australia* received a crash at 1734, adding another 14 killed and 26 wounded to her already high casualties of the previous day. But, like her neighbor "The Gem of the Ocean," she kept on shooting. Heavy cruiser *Louisville* was too heavily damaged by a crash abreast the bridge structure to do that, and the flag officer on the bridge, Rear Admiral Theodore E. Chandler, was frightfully burned by the flaming gasoline. He helped handle a fire hose and took his turn with the enlisted men for first aid; but as the flames had scorched his lungs every effort to save him failed, and next day he died. Thirty-one shipmates went with him, and 56 more were wounded; but for an ample supply of blood plasma most of those, too, would have perished.

Not only Admiral Oldendorf but all responsible officers off Lingayen were seriously concerned when they contemplated the results of this 6th day of January, three days before the landings. It was the worst blow to the United States Navy since the Battle of Tassafaronga in November 1942, and the more difficult to bear because the recent naval victory at Leyte Gulf had made men believe that Japan was licked. With the kamikazes she had sprung a tactical surprise which would cost the Allied armed forces dear.

Next day, while bombardment and minesweeping continued, was not so bad; but minecrafts *Hovey* and *Palmer* were crashed and sunk. On the 8th, H.M.A.S. *Australia*, favorite target of the kamikazes, took a third and a fourth crash, but still carried on.

The approach of the two amphibious forces, Barbey's for San

Fabian and Wilkinson's for Lingayen, was comparatively uneventful. Seven ships, including cruiser *Boise* with General MacArthur on board, were attacked, Admiral Ofstie's flagship *Kitkun Bay*, was disabled, but none were sunk.

As S-day, 9 January, dawned over Lingayen Bay, ships could be seen in every direction. At 0700 the combatant ships began hurling high explosives at supposed enemy installations. A few minutes after 0700 a kamikaze crashed *Columbia* and added 92 more casualties to her list; but her valiant crew quenched the fires and resumed bombardment half an hour after the hit. The landings were virtually unopposed.

A hot night followed in the Gulf, as the Japanese pulled what we called the suicide boat out of their bag of tricks. Port Sual, protected by a point of land stretching down from the north, was the concealed anchorage for 70 of these 18½-foot plywood motor boats. Each carried two 260-pound depth charges, one light machine gun and a few hand grenades, with a crew of two or three men, to destroy Allied shipping. They managed to sink two LCIs and to damage four LSTs, but were so severely shot up themselves by destroyers *Philip* and *Leutze* and other intended victims as to be incapable of further operations.

The Lingayen landings were a terrible ordeal for all hands, not excepting troops in the transports and other auxiliaries. Here is an extract from the diary of Lieutenant G. R. Cassels-Smith in transport *Harris* for 11 January:

"Two more burials at sea this evening — that makes four who have died so far and there are several more who may die. They are so badly burned or mangled that they are really better off dead. The doctors . . . are always amazed at the remarkable bravery and fortitude of those wounded men. They never complain and are pathetically grateful for everything that is done for them. The enlisted men of the crew are wonderful too. They labor under a terrific strain unloading hundreds of tons of cargo, then stand their watches at the guns all night without sleep, and then donate their blood to the wounded and volunteer their services to help feed the helpless by hand."

On 10 January, convoys began to depart, the Lingayen airstrip was ready for emergency landings, and Rear Admiral Conolly's Reinforcement Group brought up another infantry division. The kamikazes returned on the 12th to damage DE *Belknap* in Lingayen Gulf, and four Liberty ships in a returning convoy. A crash next morning on escort carrier *Salamaua*, which failed to sink her, was the last successful kamikaze attack in Philippine waters. For the Japanese had expended almost every aircraft they had in the Philippines, excepting 47 units which Admiral Fukudome evacuated to Formosa. Ground crews were forced to join the infantry defending Luzon, and surviving pilots flew north as best they could. After 15 January only ten Japanese planes were left on the entire island of Luzon. For the Allies the kamikazes now seemed but a horrible dream. Unfortunately, like other bad dreams, this one was to recur.

3. *Luzon Secured, 13 January–30 June*

Generals MacArthur and Krueger and their staffs went ashore 13 January; and from then on the story of the campaign that captured Manila and all Luzon, except the mountains to which General Yamashita retreated, is largely the Army's story.

Seventh Fleet still had plenty to do. With the help of Halsey, Admiral Kinkaid set out to secure a difficult sea lane, the Mindoro-Lingayen line, upon which the success of the Luzon campaign and the lives of thousands of American soldiers depended. They were unnecessarily anxious about a possible Japanese naval attack on this line, similar to the one on Mindoro in December. The

Japanese Navy was now incapable of anything like that. Nevertheless, Admiral Halsey made a memorable incursion into the South China Sea, with almost his entire Third Fleet, on 10-20 January. It was a bold and beautifully handled operation, underlining the ability of our fast carriers to take fire power anywhere and supply themselves from the floating service force at sea. The sought-for Japanese warships were not there; but TF 38 planes sank 44 vessels, mostly of the merchant marine, totaling 132,700 tons. Very few of our own planes were lost. The carrier planes took another crack at Formosa on their way out; and here the kamikazes again showed their hands, crashing but not sinking *Langley*, *Ticonderoga* and a destroyer.

Third Fleet support of the Luzon campaign is impressive. During January some 300,000 tons of enemy shipping was sunk or destroyed, and the number of aircraft destroyed exceeded 500. The cost to the United States was 201 carrier aircraft, 167 pilots and aircrewmen, and 205 sailors who were killed in the kamikaze crashes of 21 January. As Halsey wrote, "The outer defenses of the Japanese Empire no longer include Burma and the Netherlands East Indies; those countries are now isolated outposts, and their products are no longer available to the Japanese war machine except with staggering and prohibitive losses en route." In *New Jersey* he arrived at Ulithi on the afternoon of 25 January and two days later Admiral Spruance assumed command of the Fleet, which under him was numbered the Fifth. He had a wonderful reputation to live up to, and that he did.

On 12 January 1945 MacArthur, now a five-star General of the Army, called Admirals Kinkaid and Wilkinson and General Krueger to a conference on board *Boise*, off the beachhead. He stressed the urgency of occupying Manila as early as possible in order to free the Allied prisoners and internees, who were slowly starving to death. He emphasized that our losses so far had been small and predicted that the enemy would evacuate Manila rather

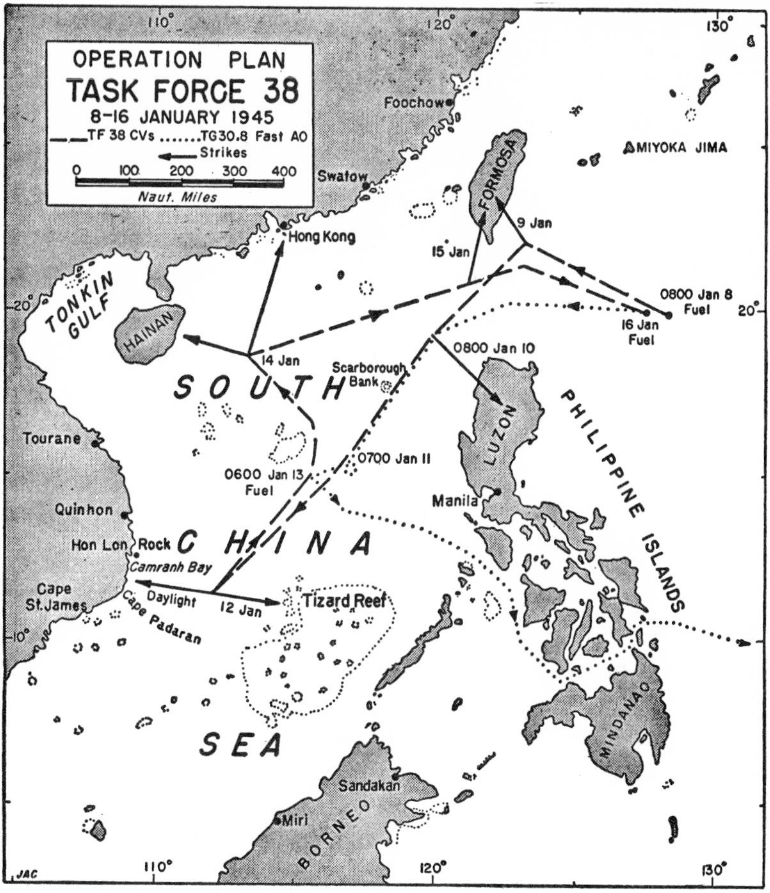

than defend it. Such indeed was General Yamashita's intention, but his orders were not carried out.

The advance on Manila was slow; by 29 January, after two weeks' progress, XIV Corps had only reached San Fernando. The Navy then lent a hand by landing XI Corps on beaches forty-five miles across the mountains from that town; a landing formidable in size, but uncontested. Admiral Struble was pleased to find the area already in friendly hands, with American and Philippine flags displayed by the natives. Indeed, everywhere in the Philippines the Americans were received as liberators and with touchingly enthusiastic demonstrations.

Admiral Fechteler's group of VII 'Phib landed the 11th Airborne Division at Nasugbu, Batangas Province, on the last day of January. This operation was ordered by the General to establish a line of advance on Manila from the southwest. Except for a little trouble from Japanese midget torpedo boats, it was uncontested.

On 1 February the 1st Cavalry Division, covered by Marine Corps aircraft, spearheaded a XIV Corps dash to Manila. On the 3rd they broke into the suburbs, liberating over 5000 Allied internees and prisoners of war. General Yamashita had ordered Manila to be evacuated, but Rear Admiral Iwabachi, commanding a naval base there of 20,000 troops, declined to obey and fought to the bitter end, fanatically defending Manila from house to house. In this month-long battle the Japanese defense forces were wiped out almost to a man; but the beautiful city was wrecked, and Intramuros, the Spanish walled town, was reduced to rubble. Not until 4 March was the city cleared of Japanese. By that time it was a more complete picture of destruction than Cologne, Hamburg or the City of London.

At least it was free. Even before the fighting ended, General MacArthur caused a provisional assembly of Filipino notables to be summoned to Malacañan Place — where his father, General Arthur MacArthur, had lived when military governor — and in their presence declared the Commonwealth of the Philippines to be permanently reëstablished. "My country has kept the faith," he said; "your capital city, cruelly punished though it be, has regained its rightful place — citadel of democracy in the East."

There were still about 1400 Japanese troops on Bataan and 5000 on "The Rock," Corregidor. It took a shore-to-shore amphibious operation from Subic Bay, under Admiral Struble, to take Mariveles (15 February) against considerable opposition, and a parachute drop next day to get a foothold on Corregidor. The Japanese there used a maze of tunnels and caves and had to be dug out or sealed in. For ten days, Desdiv 46 (Captain R. W. Cavenagh in *Converse*) kept two ships on station to support the troops ashore. The destroyers moved in to half a mile from the beach, and, spotted from ashore, shot up pillboxes and fired directly into the mouths of caves full of Japanese. "We were so close," wrote the division commander, "that we could see the Japs get up and run between salvos." By 26 February The Rock was again in American hands, and General MacArthur on 2 March presided over an impressive flag-raising on the island, which he had left under such different circumstances almost three years earlier. Caballo Island held out until 15 April.

Since 9 March Commodore William A. Sullivan had been working on the problem of clearing Manila Harbor of hundreds of sunken ships. He had done this for at least five harbors in Europe, but Manila was the worst, the Japanese being more efficient demolitioners than the Germans. With the aid of the Army Engineers' Special Brigade, two battalions of Seabees, and several salvage ships and minecraft, Sullivan raised some wrecks, destroyed others, and, for future action, buoyed many more. Minesweepers *Scuffle* and *Cable*, with 15 YMS under Lieutenant Eric A. Johnson USNR, worked the harbor and bay; they swept 615 square miles of water and destroyed 584 mines. By 1 May, 350 of the sunken vessels had been removed and the waterfront was progressively cleared until, in mid-August, 24 Liberty ships could berth simultaneously.

For Sixth Army the campaign for the liberation of Luzon had lasted 173 days, during which it lost 8297 killed or missing and had 29,557 wounded. Losses to the U.S. and Australian Navies in the Luzon campaign, mostly due to kamikaze attack, were more than 2000. On 30 June General Eichelberger's Eighth Army took over from Krueger's Sixth the mission of destroying the rest of the

Japanese troops, holed up in the mountains. General Yamashita and about 50,500 men finally surrendered after the close of hostilities on 15 August.

4. *Liberation of the Central and Southern Philippines, 28 February–22 July*

General of the Army Douglas MacArthur was not satisfied with the liberation of Leyte, Samar and Luzon. He felt obligated to expel the enemy from the entire Archipelago. His plan of February 1945 envisaged two series of operations: the Visayas and Mindanao, to be liberated by Seventh Fleet and Eighth Army; Borneo and Java to be liberated by Seventh Fleet and the Australian Army.

The Joint Chiefs of Staff did not see eye to eye with the General in these plans. At the Yalta Conference in February 1945, General Marshall told the British that he did not contemplate employing major United States forces to mop up in the Philippines or the Dutch islands; he assumed that the Filipino guerillas and the newly activated Army of the Philippine Commonwealth could take care of the rest of their country, and that Anglo-Australian forces would cover the N.E.I. But, as Seventh Fleet and Eighth Army were not required for the invasion of Iwo Jima and Okinawa, the J.C.S. simply permitted MacArthur to do as he chose, up to a point.

Herein strategic mistakes were made both by MacArthur and the J.C.S. The General could, as it turned out, have used his leapfrog strategy to bypass the Visayas and Mindanao. The Filipinos in these islands were not suffering greatly at the hands of the Japanese garrisons, which were now cut off from reinforcement and would have surrendered anyway at the end of the war. The forces used to liberate the Visayas and Mindanao could have been thrown immediately into Java and Sumatra, where the Dutch colonists were suffering acutely and the Japanese were cannily nourishing Sukarno's independence movement. Even if General MacArthur did not choose to put the Netherlands East Indies first, the J.C.S. should have found him the necessary shipping when he did propose to do it. But nobody then expected the Pacific war to end with a big bang in August.

At the Quebec Conference of September 1944, the Combined Chiefs of Staff predicted that it would take eighteen months after the defeat of Germany to procure the unconditional surrender of Japan. Actually it took only a little more than three months. It was assumed that we would have to invade Kyushu in October, Honshu in January 1946, and then fight the Japanese on their own soil; so there would be plenty of time to liberate Indonesia. MacArthur presented to the C.C.S. in February 1945 a plan to do it in June. But the C.C.S. fiddled around with this plan until August, when it was too late; MacArthur then had all he could attend to with the occupation of Japan. Not until a full month after the surrender did Allied warships even put in at Batavia (renamed Jakarta), and in the meantime the country was given over to rabid nationalists who, unlike the Filipinos, had no training in self-government.

It may also be observed that Admiral Lord Mountbatten, the Allied commander in Southeast Asia, was ready and eager to liberate Indonesia early in 1945, but could not get at it while the Japanese controlled Singapore and the Strait of Malacca. Admiral King was eager to have Admiral Sir Bruce Fraser's Pacific Fleet help MacArthur and the Australians do the job, but this was vetoed by Churchill. For prestige reasons he wanted the Royal Navy to be "in at the death" of Japan, alongside the United States Navy. That it was, and very helpfully too; but King had the right idea. It was far more important for the future to liberate Indonesia and set up a stable government there before the war's end than to help American forces to capture Okinawa and bombard Japan.

Amphibious operations in the Southern Philippines and Borneo were conducted by General Eichelberger's Eighth Army, and by Rear Admiral Barbey's VII 'Phib. They followed the pattern established in 1944 — preliminary air bombing and naval bombardment, assault troops landing from APDs and beaching craft, Japanese retiring to the jungle and having to be rooted out. VII 'Phib by this time had been divided into groups, of which the 8th, commanded in succession by Rear Admirals W. M. Fechteler and Albert G. Noble; the 6th, commanded by Rear Admiral Forrest B. Royal; and the 9th, commanded by Rear Admiral Struble, did most of the work. Rear Admirals Berkey and Ralph S. Riggs commanded the covering and support groups, comprising two or three light cruisers such as *Denver*, *Phoenix*, H.M.A.S. *Ho-*

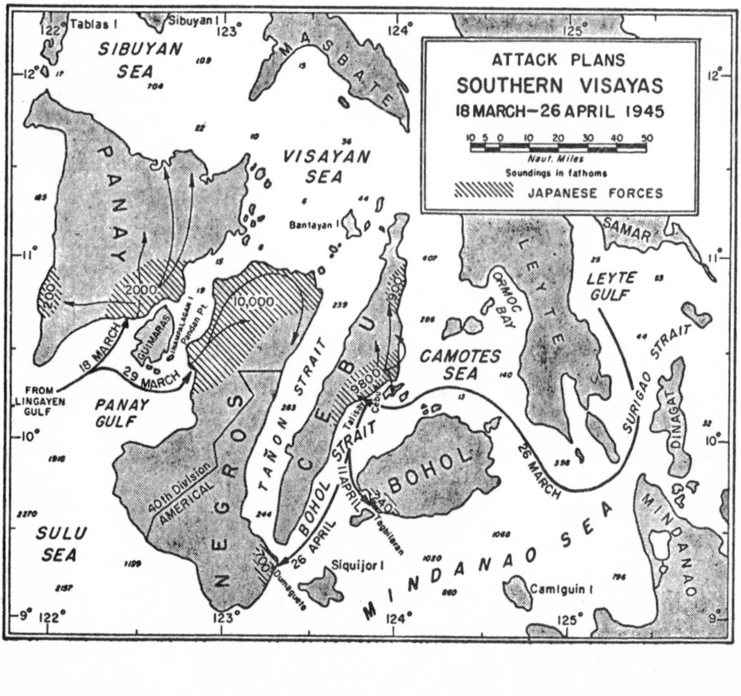

bart, and a number of destroyers. Motor torpedo boats also were very active and useful. The Japanese were able to commit but few and ineffective air forces, from the Netherlands East Indies and Malaya, and no kamikazes; hence these assaults were relatively easy. Rooting out the Japanese defenders from the mountains and jungles was another matter — that cost Eighth Army thousands of casualties.

These ten Southern Philippines and Borneo operations may be represented briefly in tabular form: —

SUMMARY OF OPERATIONS IN SOUTHERN PHILIPPINES AND BORNEO, 1945

		Major Units Engaged		*Commanders*			
Target	*D-day 1945*	*Naval*	*Military*	*Naval Attack Group*	*Covering Group*	*Military*	*Objective Secured 1945*
Palawan	28 Feb.	8th 'Phib Group	41st Div.	Fechteler	Riggs	Haney	22 April
Zamboanga	10 Mar.	6th 'Phib Group	41st Div.	Royal	Riggs	Doe	15 August
Panay, W. Negros	18 Mar.	9th 'Phib Group	40th Div.	Struble	Riggs	Brush	4 June
Cebu	26 Mar.	TG 78.2	Americal	Sprague	Berkey	Arnold	18 April
Bohol	11 Apr.	TU 78.3.3	164th Inf.	Deutermann	none	Arnold	20 April
S.E. Negros	26 Apr.	TU 78.3.3	164th Inf.	Deutermann	none	Arnold	12 June
Mindanao	17 Apr.	8th 'Phib Group	X Corps	Noble	Riggs	Sibert	15 Aug.
Tarakan	1 May	TG 78.1	Aus. I Corps	Royal	Berkey	Morshead	30 May
Brunei Bay	10 June	TG 78.1	9th Aus. Div.	Royal	Berkey	Wootten	1 July
Balikpapan	1 July	8th 'Phib Group	7th Aus. Div.	Noble	Riggs	Milford	22 July

5. *Submarine Operations, 1942–1943*

The United States submarine was destined to be one of the most devastating weapons in the Pacific. General Tojo, after the war, said that the destruction of her merchant marine was one of three factors that defeated Japan, the other two being leapfrog strategy and fast carrier operations. We have already noted the principal instances in which submarines supported the Fleet — especially in the Battles of Midway and of the Philippine Sea — but have said little about their steady, unremitting attrition of the enemy merchant marine. Nearly one third of all Japanese combatant ships destroyed and nearly two thirds of merchant tonnage sunk was the work of United States submarines.

These operated under Commander Submarines Pacific Fleet at Pearl Harbor, and Commander Submarines Southwest Pacific at Fremantle and Brisbane, Australia. Comsubpac, during the greater part of the war, was Vice Admiral Charles A. Lockwood; his opposite numbers were Captain John Wilkes, and Rear Admiral Ralph W. Christie from March 1943. Each exercised full administrative control, but only a limited operational control over his boats[1] once they were committed to an operation. The admirals did not attempt to carry on daily conversations with their boats over radio as Grossadmiral Doenitz did with his U-boats; partly because they wished to give the skippers maximum initiative, and partly because radio transmissions are apt to help the enemy locate a submarine. The submarine service was almost a navy in itself, manned exclusively by volunteers and commanded by ambitious and intelligent young officers.

The American concept of submarine operation, dictated by our few and far-between bases, required that they be capable of self-sustained cruising for long periods over great distances. We had nothing resembling the German milch cows. Thus the Navy entered the war with a preponderance of large fleet-type submarines, of greater endurance, reliability and comfort than the smaller types favored by European powers. These rugged vessels displaced in the neighborhood of 1500 tons. Variations from this mean tonnage were the older and smaller S-boats of 800 to 1100 tons, which were mostly retired by late 1943, and *Argonaut*, *Narwhal* and *Nautilus*, which ran up to 2700 tons' displacement. The average fleet-type submarine was manned by a crew of 7 officers and 70 men. It had a cruising range of 10,000 miles and carried supplies for 60 days. Surface speed was 20 knots; submerged speed 9 knots. Underwater

[1] United States submarines are traditionally referred to as "boats," not "ships," supposedly because the original ones were only boat size.

endurance at 2½ knots was 48 hours. Power on the surface was derived from a diesel-electric engine and motor combination; storage batteries furnished juice to the electric motors when submerged. During 1942 the installation of both air-search and surface-search radars greatly increased the effectiveness of American submarines. Their initial armament consisted of six to ten 21-inch torpedo tubes, one 3-inch 50-caliber deck gun and two .50-caliber machine guns — more deck guns were added later. About 18 spare torpedoes were carried. Initially all torpedoes were propelled by turbines, operated by hot gases resulting from the combustion of a jet of alcohol and compressed air mixed with steam. Later in the war, electric torpedoes, valuable for the absence of the telltale wake, were introduced. The warheads were loaded with TNT, later with the more powerful torpex, and were supposed to detonate whether the torpedo struck a target or passed close to the magnetic field of a metallic hull.

Unfortunately, for reasons explained in Chapter I, American torpedoes at the beginning of the war had grave defects in the depth-control mechanism and the exploder. These did not come to light until the war was well along. The first defect caused the torpedo to run ten feet deeper than set, usually so far under a ship's hull that the magnetic feature was not activated. The contact exploder was a detonating mechanism fitted into the warhead before launching. Its firing pin, supposed to function under physical impact, proved too fragile to stand up under a good, square, 90-degree hit; normally it would set off the charge only if the warhead hit a ship at an acute angle. Thus, the best shooting was rewarded by duds, and submarines returned from war patrols with sad tales of hearing as many as nine torpedoes go bang against the hull of a Japanese ship, without a single one exploding. Admiral Nimitz in June 1943 ordered the magnetic mechanism to be used no longer; and Admiral Lockwood, by conducting a series of tests with torpedoes against the cliffs of Kohoolawe Island, found out what the trouble was with the exploder and fitted stouter firing pins. But it was not until September 1943 that United States submarines had dependable torpedoes.

Before the war, United States and Japanese doctrine of submarine employment was identical — to use the boats primarily to destroy enemy warships. In practice the United States Navy, apart from special missions and supporting a fleet offensive, employed its boats as the Germans did, to reduce the enemy merchant marine. But the Japanese I-boats, which were as big as ours and almost as numerous initially, and which mounted far more powerful torpedoes, rigidly concentrated on sinking enemy warships. They were fairly successful at this in 1942, as we have seen; but as American antisubmarine doctrine improved they seldom got in a shot. For instance, the 16 Japanese submarines which were deployed before and during the Battle of Leyte Gulf managed to sink but one vessel, a destroyer escort. And much of Japan's submarine potential was wastefully diverted to special missions. They made long cruises to conduct nuisance bombardments, as on Midway, Johnston and Canton Islands and (in 1942) the coasts of Vancouver Island and Oregon. They carried scouting aircraft great distances to make reconnaissance flights of no value. But the mortal blow to a successful undersea war was the Japanese Army's discovery that submarines were useful to carry supplies to bypassed garrisons. Thenceforth more and more were pulled off patrols to serve isolated Army garrisons with rice and bullets. By 1943 the United States Navy was able to stop convoying merchant ships in the Pacific and employ escort vessels to better purpose.[2]

Equally strange, and verging on the idiotic, was Japan's failure as an island nation to protect her own merchant marine lifeline. This can be explained only by the assumption that the Japanese

[2] According to Masanori Ito *The End of the Imperial Japanese Navy* (1962) p. 182, Japan had 64 submarines in Dec. 1941 and built 126 during the war, but by the time of the Battle for Leyte Gulf she had only 32 operational. These figures do not include midgets.

war lords refused to face the fact that they might have to wage a defensive war. By the same token, the Japanese Navy in 1942-43 decided to construct twenty aircraft carriers, which are of no use in defensive strategy, and to convert a *Yamato* class battleship hull to the super-carrier *Shinano*. From the same materials they could have built hundreds of destroyers and smaller escort vessels. Not until the end of 1943 was an escort fleet organized, and it never amounted to much. The Japanese ended the war with the same antisubmarine equipment that they had at the beginning — not very accurate depth charges and aircraft bombs; and they never solved the largely mathematical problem of where to drop a depth charge to do damage. They had no method of assessing anti-submarine attacks, and smugly assumed that they were sinking a United States submarine whenever they attacked one. They did manage to sink a good many, as our chart indicates, but never enough to win.

The changing pattern of submarine tactics was illustrated by *Tarpon*'s cruise. Near Tokyo Bay on the night of 1 February 1943, she picked up a radar contact, ran it down on the surface and sank an 11,000-ton *Maru* without using her periscope. In darkness on the 8th she picked up a radar contact, chased it on the surface, and using radar ranges and periscope sighting put four hits into 17,000-ton *Tatsuta Maru*, and that pride of the Japanese merchant marine went to the bottom.

For the entire year 1943 the score by United States submarines in the Pacific was 22 warships and 296 *Marus*, the merchant loss amounting to 1,335,240 gross tons. Since Japanese shipyards had produced a little over half a million tons of new shipping in 1943 and captured or salvaged about 100,000 tons more, the net loss was 718,000 tons. The United States Submarine Force that year lost 15 boats and 1129 officers and men, a heavy toll indeed; yet the three submarine commands in the Pacific, based at Pearl Harbor, Brisbane and Fremantle, had 75 boats on their rolls on New

UNITED STATES
SUBMARINE LOSSES
IN THE WESTERN PACIFIC
KNOWN POSITION
ESTIMATED POSITION
0 5 10 15 20
Scale in Nautical Miles
at Mid Latitude
KAMCHATKA
S—44 Oct.'43
HERRING June'44
ALBACORE Nov.'44
GOLET June'44
POMPANO Aug.'43
RUNNER June '43
PICKEREL Apr.'43
WAHOO Oct.'43
BONEFISH June'45
HONSHU
SCAMP Nov'44
ESCOLAR Oct.'44
SCORPION Jan.'44
CHINA
TRIGGER Mar.'45
KETE Mar.'45
SWORDFISH Jan.'45
GRAYBACK Feb.'44
TANG Oct.'44
SNOOK Apr.'45
TROUT Feb.'44
SHARK II Oct'44
GRAYLING Sept'43
GUDGEON May'44
HARDER Aug.'44
SEALION Dec.'41
GROWLER Nov.'44
PHILIPPINES
CISCO Sept.'43
DARTER Oct.'44
ROBALO July'44
BARBEL Feb.'45
LAGARTO May'45
GRENADIER Apr.'43
FLIER Aug.'44
TULLIBEE Mar.'44
SCULPIN Nov.'43
CORVINA Nov.'43
CAPELIN Dec.'43
SEAWOLF Oct.'44
TRITON Mar.'43
SHARK I Feb.'42
SUMATRA
BORNEO
NEW GUINEA
GRAMPUS Mar.'43
AMBERJACK Feb.'43
PERCH Mar.'42
S-36 Jan.'42
JAVA
BULLHEAD Aug.'45
ARGONAUT Jan.'43
S—39 Aug.'42
AUSTRALIA
JAD
100° 110° 120° 130°E 140° 150° 160°
60° 50° 40° 30° 20° 10°N 0° 10°S 20° 30° 40°

Year's Day 1944, as against 53 on 1 January 1943. And these 75 were almost all fleet submarines, as most of the aged S-boats had been retired to training centers. In the same twelvemonth, Japan lost 23 submarines.

General MacArthur kept contact with Filipino guerillas and unsurrendered members of his army, by Fremantle-based submarines. During the period 8 February 1943 to 5 March 1944, 19 such missions were performed, seven by the big 2700-ton *Narwhal*, which was especially assigned to this work, and others by fleet submarines. These carried important contact men, such as Lieutenant Commander C. Parsons, to the guerillas, together with arms, money, munitions, radio sets and miscellaneous supplies. *Narwhal* on one voyage took 90 tons to Mindanao and Samar and, on another, evacuated 32 civilians from Panay. These missions were of inestimable value in obtaining intelligence of enemy ship and troop movements, supplying guerilla forces with munitions and medicaments, and counteracting Japanese propaganda to the effect that America had forgotten the Philippines.

In May 1943 *Tautog* received a special assignment to land two pro-Allied Javanese agents on the Celebes. Both were pious Mohammedans, which created difficulties not anticipated by the *Submarine Officer's Manual.* Spam, ice cream, fried eggs and other staple submariners' food were tabu; canned tuna fish and salmon had to be provided; and the navigator acquired a new duty of giving his passengers four times daily the course for Mecca. Thus history came full circle; for the science of celestial navigation evolved from this necessity that all Sons of the Prophet were under, to project their prayers in the right direction.

The vicissitudes of a submariner's life are illustrated by the loss of *Sculpin* (Commander Fred Connaway), which was stationed between Truk and Ponape during the Gilberts operation to report Japanese fleet movements. On the night of 18-19 November 1943

Sculpin sighted a fast enemy convoy and at dawn attempted to attack it, submerged, but was detected and forced deep. When she surfaced an hour later, she was immediately forced down and depth-charged by destroyer *Yamagumo.* When the diving officer tried to bring her to periscope depth the depth gauge stuck at 125 feet and *Sculpin* broached. As *Yamagumo* roared in to attack, the submarine dove deep but 18 depth charges followed her down. The explosions threw the boat out of control, distorted her pressure hull, started leaks, jammed her rudders and diving planes. As a desperate expedient Commander Connaway ordered, "Blow all ballast!" and then, as *Sculpin* rose from the depths, gave the signal for gunfire action: "Battle Surface!" *Sculpin*'s one 4-inch and two 20-mm guns had no chance to fight off a Japanese destroyer with six 5.1-inch guns, torpedo tubes and numerous automatic weapons. She took one lethal hit in the main induction valves. A second, penetrating the conning tower, killed the C.O., his exec., and the gunnery officer. The senior surviving officer ordered Abandon Ship. All vents were opened and *Sculpin* dove for the last time. Captain John P. Cromwell, a passenger on board, and a dozen others rode her down, Cromwell deliberately sacrificing his life because he was familiar with operation plans and feared lest information be extorted from him by torture. Forty-two of *Sculpin*'s crew were picked up by *Yamagumo* and with the exception of one wounded man, who was thrown overboard, were taken to Truk, where they were transferred to escort carriers *Chuyo* and *Unyo.* En route to Japan *Chuyo* fell victim to a torpedo attack by United States submarine *Sailfish,* and only one of the prisoners survived. He and 20 prisoners in *Unyo* were forced to work in the copper mines at Ashio until released at the end of the war.

6. *Submarine Operations, 1944–1945*

On 1 January 1944 the Japanese still had 300,000 more tanker tonnage than on 7 December 1941; United States submarines made a special effort to correct this. That month eight more enemy tankers were downed, one to a Navy carrier plane and the other seven to submarines. Greater misfortunes overtook the Japanese oiler fleet next month. The 17 February carrier strike on Truk put five tankers totaling 52,183 tons under the surface; and then along came submarine *Jack* (Commander Thomas M. Dykers), "Jack the Tanker Killer," as she was known in the submarine fleet. In the South China Sea at 0338 February 19, Dykers made a radar contact on an enemy convoy of five tankers and three escorts. In a series of attacks that lasted all day and almost until midnight *Jack* sank four of them, totaling over 20,000 tons.

Grayback (Commander John A. Moore), patrolling between Luzon and Formosa, was lost with all hands on 27 February 1944 after sinking 11,500 more tons of shipping. Probably an enemy plane was responsible. *Trout,* the veteran boat which had carried gold out of Corregidor early in the war, was on her eleventh patrol with Lieutenant Commander Albert H. Clark as skipper when, on 29 February, SSE of Okinawa, she picked up a Japanese convoy carrying troops from Korea to reinforce the Marianas. She damaged a new 11,500-ton transport and sank a 9245-tonner which contained 4124 troops and a crew of 105, half of whom went down with the ship. In the flurry of depth-charge attacks that followed, *Trout* was lost with all hands.

Sandlance (Commander Malcolm E. Garrison) on her maiden voyage patrolled in rough waters. En route Pearl Harbor to the Aleutians in February 1944, she encountered two tempests within four days and, when surfaced, quickly became sheathed in ice, which she could slough off only by submerging. Arriving on station off Paramushiro 24 February, *Sandlance* found herself completely surrounded by drift ice. The temperature dropped so that the sea water froze over the periscope in a film of ice. Despite these difficulties, Commander Garrison conned his boat along the Kuriles and Hokkaido, knocking off a freighter on 28 February and another on 3 March, evading all attacks by patrol craft and planes. Eventually he entered the Japan current, and water temperature promptly rose from barely freezing to 70° F. *Sandlance* passed Honshu and down along the Bonins. During the midwatch 13 March, when his sound operator reported echoes, Garrison brought his boat to periscope depth to view a "sight beautiful to behold — worth the past four weeks of battling typhoons, blizzards and ice-fields. We were completely surrounded by ships." He had run into a second Marianas-bound Japanese reinforcement convoy. A full moon enabled him to select the best targets, light cruiser *Tatsuta* and a large freighter. At 0310 *Sandlance* shot two torpedoes at each, then swung 180 degrees and fired her last two "fish" at a second *Maru*. In a jiffy she was surrounded by wildly depth-charging escorts which could not locate her. Garrison coolly kept his boat at periscope depth for 15 minutes to watch developments. In that time he observed that *Tatsuta* was sinking and that the first *Maru* was burning, decks awash; and he saw the victim of his Parthian shot go down rapidly, bow first. The destroyers then forced him down and kept him down for 18½ hours; after which, with all torpedoes expended, *Sandlance* shaped a course to Pearl Harbor, where Pacific Fleet submariners enjoyed a little recreation between patrols.

By April 1944 the scorekeepers in Washington concluded that the Japanese Navy must be getting short of destroyers, since it had lost 64, and few new ones had been built. Admiral King decided that it was time to decrease the small number left. On 13 April he issued an order to Pacific Fleet submarines to give enemy destroyers No. 2 priority as targets, after capital ships but ahead of transports, tankers and freighters.

United States submariners hardly needed this to persuade them to turn on their traditional enemies. *Albacore* had already sunk *Sazanami; Skipjack* had sunk *Suzukaze* in January; *Guardfish* put *Umikaze* down for keeps and *Pogy* sank *Minekaze* in the East China Sea in February; *Tautog* sank *Shirakumo* off Hokkaido 16 March and *Redfin* disposed of *Akigumo* in April, all before Admiral King issued his order. And the very day that he did, *Harder* (Commander Samuel D. Dealey), after a long duel with *Ikazuchi* off the Marianas, was able to add another good phrase to the book of traditional United States Navy sayings: "Range 900 yards. Commenced firing. Expended four torpedoes and one Jap Destroyer."

In the meantime Rear Admiral Christie's Southwest Pacific submarines, based at Fremantle, were finding good hunting in the Sulu and Celebes Seas. A convoy carrying an infantry division to reinforce the Japanese positions on the Vogelkop lost three transports to *Gurnard* (Commander Charles H. Andrews), and thousands of soldiers were drowned; this discouraged the relief of Biak. *Lapon* and *Raton* made a good bag in the South China Sea in May, 1944. *Rasher* (Commander Henry G. Munson) hit the jackpot on 18 August, sinking escort carrier *Taiyo*, which had been used to furnish C.A.P. for the big battleships.

Southwest Pacific submarines continued to keep Filipino guerillas informed and supplied, evacuating marooned Americans and endangered Filipinos on the return passage. *Angler* (Lieutenant Commander R. I. Olsen) was ordered to rescue "about 20" Filipinos, on whom the Japanese were closing, from a point on the coast of Panay. When Olsen surfaced off the rendezvous on 20 March 1944, he was informed that 58 men, women and children had been assigned to him as passengers. After hiding from the Japanese in the jungle for over two years, many of these unfortunate people were sick and all were undernourished, dirty and lousy; many had tropical ulcers and one woman was expecting a baby. But a submariner is never nonplussed. The entire crew of *Angler*, during the 12-day run to Darwin, was berthed in the after-battery compartment, male passengers in the forward torpedo room, and women and children in the after torpedo room. It was on this passage that the bluejackets felt that they had "seen everything" when a nursing mother, after smoking a large cigar while nursing her infant, let the suckling take a few drags at it, after he had finished feeding. Food had to be strictly rationed, but all passengers were landed without a casualty.

In June 1944, when the Battle of the Philippine Sea was over, more submarines were released for the pursuit of Japanese merchant shipping, and the area which Comsubpac named "Convoy College" — extending across the East China Sea from Luzon Strait to Formosa and the coast of China — became the scene of great destruction. The "Mickey Finns" (*Guardfish, Piranha, Thresher*, and *Apogon*), a wolf-pack under command of Captain W. V. O'Regan, were the first "freshmen" to cross this watery campus, and their five-day semester cost the Japanese some 41,000 more tons of merchant shipping.

A night battle fought in Luzon Strait during the early hours of 31 July 1944, between *Steelhead, Parche* and *Hammerhead* and a big convoy, accounted for a tanker, two transports and two passenger-cargo ships, totaling over 39,000 tons. By this time, Saipan being secured, tender *Holland* moved up there to afford the submarines a forward fueling and repair base 3600 miles west of Pearl Harbor. With hunting grounds restricted by the westward advance of American sea power, and Japanese shipping accordingly canalized to the narrow seas, convoys became larger and hunting more profitable.

The first day of September found Subpac boats vigorously and successfully combing waters around Formosa. Captain E. R. Swinburne's wolf-pack, *Barb, Tunny* and *Queenfish*, was enjoying a profitable term in Convoy College, whose campus extended from Pratas Reef south to Swatow through Luzon Strait to long. 130° East. A transport, a 10,000-ton tanker and a destroyer escort fell to their bag. Commander G. R. Donaho's pack, consisting of *Picuda, Redfish* and *Spadefish,* on 8 September, east of Formosa, sank three or four merchant ships out of a single convoy. By the time Donaho had concluded his patrol, on 21 September, he had eliminated 64,456 tons of enemy shipping, the highest wolf-pack score so far. A third wolf-pack in this scholarly area during September was Commander T. B. Oakley's: *Growler, Pampanito* and *Sealion II.* During the night of 11-12 September they picked up a Singapore-Japan convoy of nine ships with seven escorts, about halfway between Hainan and Cape Bojeador, Luzon. After *Growler* had blown up frigate *Hirado, Sealion* at 0524 torpedoed three ships, one of which, unfortunately, had on board 1350 English and Australian prisoners of war. In the meantime *Growler* at 0653 sank destroyer *Shikinami,* after which the convoy turned and fled toward Hong Kong. But *Pampanito* hung on all day 12 September and at 2240 sank a tanker and 10,509-ton *Kachidoki Maru,* in which were 750 prisoners. The Japanese escorts picked up their own survivors next day but left the prisoners struggling in the water. Many managed to survive by clinging to wreckage, and some were rescued by the submarines.

In October 1944, 68 United States submarines sank 320,906 tons of Japanese merchant shipping, the highest monthly score of the war; and almost one third of it consisted of tankers. In November 214,506 more tons were sunk.

In early October, a bold raid into the Formosa Channel was performed by Commander Richard H. O'Kane in U.S.S. *Tang.* This was her fifth war patrol. After safely weathering a typhoon on 6 October, *Tang* threaded an enemy mine field between Formosa and the Sakashima Gunto and passed close aboard the northern extremity of Formosa. At 0400 October 11, she finished off her first victim, a small, heavily loaded diesel freighter. That night, close to the shore, another small freighter was sunk. *Tang* now steered for Turnabout Island off Haitan, the landmark where, for thousands of years, shipping northbound through Formosa Strait had changed course for Foochow. Shortly after midnight 23-24 October a convoy for the Philippines — four deeply laden freighters carrying planes, a transport with crated planes piled high on deck, a destroyer, and several small escort vessels — headed right for *Tang*. O'Kane maneuvered his boat inside the screen to a firing position where the ships seemed to overlap, bow and stern, on both sides of her. In a few minutes three freighters were floating torches. The unhit freighter and the transport promptly converged on *Tang* with intent to ram.

Tang, under a shower of small-arms fire, slipped between the converging stems of these two ships and had the humorous satisfaction of seeing them collide after she had escaped. O'Kane headed north to relax for a few hours, surfaced before dawn 24 October, then turned in again toward Turnabout.

After dark, the biggest convoy anyone on board had ever seen was tracked close to the jagged coast of Fukien; and, as *Tang* closed, the Japanese escort commander obligingly illuminated his charges with a large searchlight, revealing two big transports and several tankers. These O'Kane selected as preferred targets, and sank one. *Tang* then turned to fire three stern torpedoes at a tanker astern of the first victim, at ranges of 600-700 yards. The tanker was nicely hit and blew up, scattering burning gasoline over the Formosa Channel.

After putting five miles between himself and the milling escorts, O'Kane slowed down to check his two remaining torpedoes. Both appeared to be in order, so *Tang* returned to the scene of her recent exploits to fire her 23rd and 24th torpedoes. The last, launched at about 0200 October 25, broached, porpoised, reversed course, and within half a minute struck the submarine abreast her after torpedo room, and exploded. *Tang* immediately sank by the stern and hit the bottom 30 fathoms down. Sailors in the control room succeeded in closing the conning tower hatch, leveled off the boat by flooding tanks, and destroyed secret publications by burning. Thirty officers and men reached an escape position in the forward torpedo room, where smoke from the burning documents as well as lack of oxygen knocked half of them out. Enemy escorts were depth-charging all about but failed to discover the motionless sunken boat. At 0600 October 25 thirteen men, the only ones still strong enough to make the attempt, started leaving the escape trunk. Eight reached the surface through 160 feet of water. Five of them, together with O'Kane, an officer and two sailors who floated off topside when she sank, were the sole survivors. These men were picked up by an escort vessel and given fairly good treatment, according to Japanese standards. They were liberated at the close of the war.

Bold fight-back tactics saved *Salmon* of Commander Harlfinger's pack from becoming a victim of enemy escorts off the southern cape of Kyushu on the night of 30 October. After she had sent two torpedoes into a tanker, four screening Japanese frigates forced her down, depth charges damaged her hull, and sent clocks, gauges and other detachable objects hurtling about her compartments. Commander H. K. Nauman decided that his only chance was to fight it out with gunfire. Surfacing at 2030, *Salmon* enjoyed a precious respite which gave the skipper and crew time to correct her list, plug holes, pump bilges and get the engines turning up 16 knots. Around 2200 one Japanese frigate began jabbing at *Salmon* like a dog attacking a bear, closing repeatedly to bark and retire. After this had happened several times, and the other frigates began to show signs of closing, Commander Nauman felt ready to take the offensive. *Salmon* attacked the frigate that had been dogging her, passing parallel on opposite course only 50 yards distant, raking topsides clear, knocking all the fight out of the Japanese and scaring away the other escorts. She then ducked into a rain squall, repaired battle damage, and made Saipan safely.

American submarines hotly pursued enemy shipping in November, but found fewer targets. The enemy had become more wary. Singapore-Japan convoys no longer followed the west coast of Luzon but hugged the western shore of the South China Sea, even as close as a mile or two. This month, however, brought rich increase in the bag of combatant ships. Four submarines dogged a big convoy carrying an infantry regiment from Manchuria to Luzon, sinking two troop-filled transports; then (by *Picuda*, Commander O. O. Underwood) escort carrier *Jinyo*. *Sealion II* (Commander G. T. Reich) sank destroyer *Urakaze* and tough old battleship *Kongo* north of Formosa.

Archerfish (Commander J. F. Enright) made the biggest single kill of the submarine war on 29 November: the new 59,000-ton carrier *Shinano*. This leviathan, converted from a *Yamato*-class battleship hull, had taken over four years to build. Provided with a 30-cm thick steel flight deck over a layer of concrete, she should have survived any amount of bombing, and her compartmentation was so complete that she was supposed to be unsinkable. Screened by three destroyers, *Shinano* sailed from Tokyo Bay on her maiden cruise at 1800 November 28. Only two hours later, Enright made radar contact and dogged her, making 20 knots, until 0300 when she presented a perfect target at 1400 yards' range. *Archerfish* launched six torpedoes, four of which exploded on the carrier, whose skipper, believing her unsinkable, maintained speed and course for some eight hours. She then rolled over and sank, taking down most of her crew. *Shinano* was surely the shortest-lived big warship in history.

On 9 December at 0134 *Redfish* (Commander L. D. McGregor), west of Kyushu, got two hits on 24,000-ton carrier *Junyo*. She was the carrier whose planes had bombed Dutch Harbor in

1942, and damaged battleship *South Dakota* in the Battle of the Santa Cruz Islands, and which had survived the Battle of the Philippine Sea. She was now so badly damaged as to be out of the war. *Redfish* was really in the money; on 19 December she had a crack at another carrier, new 17,500-ton *Unryu*, escorted by three destroyers. The group conveniently zigged toward *Redfish*, which at 1635 fired a spread of four torpedoes. One hit the carrier aft, stopping her dead and causing her to burst into flame. While destroyers milled about, dropping depth charges indiscriminately, Commander McGregor reloaded his tubes and at 1650 fired a torpedo which hit just abaft the carrier's island. *Unryu* went down within twenty minutes. Her escorts gave *Redfish* some heavy jolts from a cluster of depth charges, but she escaped by lying on the bottom until dark.

Admiral Halsey's foray into the South China Sea in mid-January 1945 almost completely halted Japanese ship movements in those waters. But Rear Admiral James Fife, who had just relieved Admiral Christie as Commander Submarines Southwest Pacific, was taking no chance of missing anything. He maintained about 20 boats in that sea, and around Borneo. On 24 January 1945 one of them scored well. *Blackfin*, Commander W. L. Kitch, picked up a convoy, made a surface approach and one hit, which sank destroyer *Shigure*, miraculous survivor of many battles, including Surigao Strait.

Blackfin's exploit was emulated by *Pargo* (Commander D. B. Bell) off the coast of Indochina on 19 February. A night torpedo attack on a zigzagging destroyer was followed by a tremendous explosion which tore the destroyer apart. That was the end of *Nokaze*, the 39th and last Japanese destroyer to be destroyed by an American submarine. *Flasher* (Commanders R. I. Whitaker and G. W. Grider), the same month, completed her sixth war patrol, establishing a record for tonnage sunk by any United States submarine — 21 ships totaling over 100,000 tons.

So much for the last operations of Southwest Pacific Submarines, whose main base had now been moved up to Subic Bay, Luzon. It was much the same story — growing scarcity of targets — for Pacific Fleet Submarines, now mostly operating from Guam. Small escort vessels, coastal Marus and the like were the usual victims, but *Balao* (Commander R. K. R. Worthington), operating in the Yellow Sea on 19 March, bagged a 10,413-ton transport.

One of the most successful and carefully planned submarine offensives of the war was Operation BARNEY, the invasion of the Sea of Japan — the only remaining body of water where enemy shipping still moved freely. This project of Admiral Lockwood's completed the ring around Japan by shutting her off from the Asian mainland. A wolf-pack under Commander E. T. Hydeman in *Sea Dog*, known as "Hydeman's Hellcats," was selected for the first penetration of the Sea of Japan. Sailing from Guam on 27 May, these nine submarines headed for the Strait of Tsushima. En route Hellcat *Tinosa* picked up ten survivors from a B-29 which had splashed south of Kyushu; but when the rescued aviators learned of this boat's mission they expressed a unanimous desire to return to their rubber raft and wait for a different rescue! *Tinosa* and her eight sister boats passed through Tsushima Strait on 5-6 June. After reaching their assigned patrol stations on the 9th, they began knocking 'em off — in eleven days, 27 merchantmen for a total of 57,000 tons. The Hellcats made their exit by La Pérouse Strait, between Hokkaido and Sakhalin; but without *Bonefish*, which had mysteriously perished. Admiral Lockwood followed up this foray, and six more submarines operated in the Sea of Japan until V-J Day.

During the waning months of the war, the aircraft lifeguard service by submarines was an even greater contribution to victory than the destruction of enemy shipping. This system, originally set up during the Gilbert Islands operation in November 1943 in order to rescue downed aviators from carrier strikes, had picked up no fewer than 224 airmen by the end of 1944. By the close of that year, when the air effort had became one of the principal offensive elements against Japan, and B–29s were striking the Japanese home islands, it was necessary to step up lifeguard service. For each B–29 mission against Japan at least three submarines, and usually more, were stationed along the flight route and near the targets to pick up aviators who were forced to ditch. During the eight months that the Pacific war lasted in 1945, 86 different submarines rescued a total of 380 aviators. They were not the only means of air-sea rescue. Toward the end of the war there was no point on the B–29 route that could not be reached by a "Dumbo" rescue plane in half an hour, or by a destroyer or submarine in three hours. When the last B–29 strike on Japan was made on 14 August, the air-sea rescue team on station consisted of 14 submarines, 21 Navy seaplanes, nine Dumbos and five ships.

Merchant tonnage owned by Japan declined from about 6 million tons at the beginning of the war to about 2.5 million on 1 December 1944, despite the addition of some 800,000 tons by conquest early in the war, and 3.3 million tons of new construction. At the end of the war she had only 1.8 million tons left in her merchant marine, mostly small wooden vessels in the Inland Sea. United States forces were responsible for the sinking of 2117 Japanese merchant vessels of 8 million tons during the entire war. Of this destruction, submarines accounted for 60 per cent, aircraft 30 per cent, mines and surface ships 10 per cent. Other Allied forces, mainly British and Dutch submarines, sent another 73 merchant ships of 211,664 tons to the bottom. And United States submarines accounted for 201 of the 686 Japanese warships sunk during the war.

JAPANESE TONNAGE SUNK BY UNITED STATES SUBMARINES

Last 4 Months of 1943, 1944, and First 8 Months of 1945

1943	*Number of Warships*	*Displacement*	*Number of Marus*	*Gross Tons*
Sept.	3	3,085	31	135,540
Oct.	–	——	26	128,088
Nov.	4	3,992	47	228,313
Dec.	3	22,120	33	130,097
1944				
Jan.	3	9,230	53	285,672
Feb.	4	12,092	52	252,016
Mar.	5	8,322	29	121,213
Apr.	9	12,203	24	98,199
May	6	6,960	54	236,700
June	11	76,570	44	189,611
July	8	15,689	40	220,089
Aug.	11	41,089	45	232,028
Sept.	7	26,905	48	152,505
Oct.	9	27,662	66	320,906
Nov.	18	125,877	56	214,506
Dec.	13	43,047	18	81,206
1945				
Jan.	8	5,703	27	96,165
Feb.	9	7,085	19	47,878
Mar.	4	3,086	37	89,859
Apr.	12	13,336	32	67,725
May	5	4,550	24	31,222
June	7	12,582	48	83,418
July	11	7,896	18	28,488
Aug.	4	3,900	6	18,297

CHAPTER XVI

Iwo Jima and Okinawa

February–August 1945

1. *The Assault on Iwo Jima, 19 February 1945*

THE JOINT CHIEFS OF STAFF on 3 October 1944 issued a directive to General MacArthur and Admiral Nimitz, in pursuance of which the operations described in this chapter were carried out: —

1. Admiral Nimitz, after providing covering and support forces for the liberation of Luzon, will occupy one or more positions in the Bonins-Volcano Group, target date 20 January 1945, and one or more positions in the Ryukyus, target date 1 March 1945.
2. General MacArthur will provide support for subsequent occupation of the Ryukyus by Admiral Nimitz's forces.

The strategic concept herein was to secure island bases for a final assault on Japan. Tokyo, Saipan, and Formosa make an isosceles triangle with legs 1500 miles long. The eastern leg, Saipan-Tokyo, was about to be used by B–29 Superforts to bomb the Japanese homeland; but a halfway house was wanted, and Iwo Jima alone fitted the bill. Formosa having been rejected as too difficult to capture, the western angle of the strategic triangle was shifted to Okinawa in the Ryukyus, several hundred miles nearer to Japan and less stoutly defended. Owing to the unexpectedly prolonged and bitter defense of Leyte and Luzon, target dates in the 3 October directive could not be kept, and this gave the Japanese another month to make Iwo Jima almost impregnable.

The Iwo Jima operation was placed first because it was expected to be easier than Okinawa. The same Pacific Fleet would have to cover and support both, while Seventh Fleet and Amphibious Force were engaged in covering and liberating the Southern Philippines, as described in our previous chapter.

Iwo Jima, central island of the Volcano group of the Nanpo Shoto or Bonin Islands, was uninhabited except by the Japanese garrison. Shaped like a bloated pear, Iwo is only 4½ miles long and 2½ miles wide. The inactive volcanic crater of Mount Suribachi rises 550 feet above sea level. The northern part of the island is a plateau with rocky, inaccessible shores, but beaches extend from the base of Mount Suribachi for more than two miles north and east. These beaches, the land between them, and a good part of the terrain are deeply covered with brown volcanic ash and black cinders which look like sand, but are so much lighter than sand that walking is difficult and running almost impossible. This grim island, which cost us so dear to wrest from the enemy, was wanted for one thing only: to provide for emergency landings of the B–29s on their bombing missions from the Marianas to Tokyo (which began 24 November 1944), and to base fighter planes for their escort, since no fighter plane could fly the entire distance.

Iwo Jima underwent the most prolonged and also the most disappointing air bombing and naval bombardment of any Pacific island. The VII Army Air Force (Major General Willis H. Hale) raided it ten times in August, 22 times in September, 16 times in October. On 8 December it began daily strikes. Three heavy cruisers (*Chester*, flag) under Rear Admiral Allan E. Smith, bombarded Iwo on 8, 24 and 27 December and 5 and 25 January. Chichi and Haha Jima were also pounded in order to prevent reinforcements from reaching Iwo — but they did. For two weeks from 31 January VII A.A.F. bombed the island night and day, and the B–29s bombed it twice. Some 6800 tons of bombs and 22,000 rounds of shell from 5-inch up to 16-inch were aimed at Iwo Jima before the invasion.

Unfortunately, Iwo's defenses were of such a nature that neither air bombing nor naval bombardment, no matter how prolonged, could neutralize them. The slopes of Mount Suribachi contained a labyrinth of dug-in gun positions for artillery, mortars and machine guns. These were accompanied by elaborate cave and tunnel systems to provide living quarters and storage space for weapons. From the volcano's rim, everything that went on all over the island could be observed. The main feature of the bulbous part of the island was an intricate network of excavated caves, connected by deep tunnels. In some places there were five levels of these caves, each with several entrances, and most served the double purpose of protecting men and positioning weapons. A mortar could be set up at a cave or tunnel mouth, fired and then withdrawn out of sight. Many of the surface positions were so cleverly prepared that they were impossible to spot until they opened up, or until the protective camouflage was blown away by gunfire.

This system, an elaboration of the new Japanese defense tactics first revealed at Peleliu, followed a battle plan drawn up by Lieutenant General Tadamichi Kuribayashi in September 1944. He was to "transform the central island into a fortress." When the landings took place, the garrison must aim at "gradual depletion of enemy attack forces, and even if the situation gets out of hand, defend a corner of the island to the death." What happened is a lesson in the value of speed in securing strategic objectives. We could have walked into Iwo in September, right after securing the Marianas; but at that time the J.C.S. was still arguing over "What next?" The original target date of 20 January would have been far better than the actual one of 19 February, but Sixth Army's pace in taking Leyte dictated the month's postponement.

The Japanese Navy's only contribution to the defense of Iwo Jima was in the form of submarines bearing the "human torpedoes"

— directed by one swimmer — which they called *kaiten*. An initial success of this gimmick, sinking a fleet oiler in Ulithi Lagoon on 20 November, was not repeated. A *kaiten* unit composed of three I-boats sailed for Iwo Jima 22 February. One ran afoul of destroyer escort *Finnegan* (Lieutenant Commander H. Huffman USNR), when escorting a convoy from Iwo Jima to Saipan, and was sunk.

In preparation for protecting the Iwo operation from submarine attack, escort carriers *Anzio* (Captain G. C. Montgomery) and *Tulagi* (Captain J. C. Cronin) were made nuclei of hunter-killer antisubmarine units, similar to those which had done such good work against U-boats in the Atlantic. *Anzio*'s planes sank one *kaiten*-bearing submarine a few miles west of Iwo Jima. The third reached Iwo waters, but was kept down by destroyers for over 48 hours, almost suffocating the crew, and then returned to base. Another, after a frustrating cruise around Iwo, constantly harassed by antisubmarine craft, was recalled. It seems odd that the Japanese Navy had not learned, from our S-boats' lack of success in stopping their original invasion of the Philippines, that submarines are no good against an amphibious operation which has plenty of alert escorts.

During the last three days before Iwo D-day there took place a series of carrier-borne air strikes over and around Tokyo. These were laid on not only as a shield for Iwo Jima, but to destroy enemy planes and reduce Japanese capability for launching air attacks. They were successful in both objects, delivering a powerful two days' attack on Tokyo airfields and aircraft plants on 16-17 February — but this did nothing to reduce the defenses of Iwo Jima.

This was a Fifth Fleet show, with the same Spruance-Turner-Mitscher team that won Saipan and the Philippine Sea. Major General Harry Schmidt commanded the Marines. Pre-landing activities at the objective were under Rear Admiral William H. P. Blandy. "Spike" Blandy was the sanguine Celtic type, with a humorous Irish mouth overhung by a large red nose. As Chief of the Bureau of Ordnance his quick mind, grasp of essentials and driving energy had served the Navy well, especially in developing and manufacturing the Swedish Bofors and the Swiss Oerlikon as the 40-mm and 20-mm antiaircraft weapons. And he had commanded an amphibious group at Saipan. Blandy now had a fair-sized fleet: eight battleships, including four which had helped cover the invasion of France; five heavy cruisers, and a flock of destroyers. They bombarded Iwo vigorously on 16 and 17 February, evoking no reply from the defenders until seven LCI gunboats, advancing in line abreast to cover the underwater demolition teams, drew a torrent of gunfire. All were hit and one was sunk, with an aggregate loss of 76 men; but they stuck to it and recovered the "frogmen," who, after all this fuss, had discovered no underwater obstacles or mines. Another day's bombardment followed on the 18th.

D-day, 19 February, opened with the heaviest pre-H-hour bombardment of World War II, by "Spike" Blandy's ships. "Kelly" Turner ordered "Land the Landing Force" at 0645. H-hour was easily met. Iwo was shrouded in the dust and smoke created by the bombardment, but weather conditions were almost perfect. The operation looked like a pushover. Optimists predicted that the island would be secured in four days, but the Marines were skeptical. A chaplain on one of the transports had printed on cards, and distributed to each Marine, the words of Sir Jacob Astley's famous prayer before the Battle of Edgehill in 1642, which well fitted the mood of United States Marines three centuries later: —

> O Lord! Thou knowest how busy I must be this day:
> If I forget Thee, do not Thou forget me.

At one minute short of H-hour naval gunfire shifted to targets about 200 yards inland, at 0902 it moved another 200 yards inland and thereafter formed a modified rolling barrage ahead of the troops, constantly adjusted to conform to their actual rate of advance. This barrage was fired by the secondary batteries of the heavy ships, to each of which was assigned a shore fire-control party with the troops.

At 0830 the first assault wave, consisting of 68 LVT(A), the amphtrac tanks, left the line of departure. It hit the beach almost precisely at H-hour, 0900. Within the next twenty-three minutes the remaining assault waves landed on schedule, and at 0944 twelve LSMs, carrying medium tanks, beached.

Up to the point of actually touching down, everything went off like a parade. Then trouble started. The LVT(A)s found their way blocked by the first terrace, which rose as high as fifteen feet. The volcanic ash and cinders afforded poor traction, and men of the first wave were slowed down to a walk. A few amphtracs advanced through breaches blasted by naval gunfire, some backed into the water and fired their turrets at inland targets; but many bogged down on the beach. The volume and accuracy of enemy mortar fire increased heavily. A situation developed somewhat similar to the one at Omaha Beach, but here there was not even a sea wall for protection to the troops, who found it virtually impossible to advance in the face of withering fire.

General Kuribayashi's static defense now began to show itself. His troops cozily sat out the naval bombardment. As soon as gunfire lifted they returned to their well-protected positions and opened up on the advancing troops. As the volume of enemy fire on the Marines increased, the gunfire of supporting ships off shore stepped up. *Santa Fe* was the star of the fire support cruisers. She laid almost continuous 5-inch and 6-inch shellfire within 200 yards of the battalion on the left flank of the 5th Division, with the result that hardly a shot was fired by the enemy from the base of Mount Suribachi, commanding their line of advance. *Nevada* became the sweetheart of the Marine Corps. Her skipper, Captain H. L. ("Pop") Grosskopf, an old gunnery officer, had set out to make his battleship the best fire support ship in the Fleet, and did.

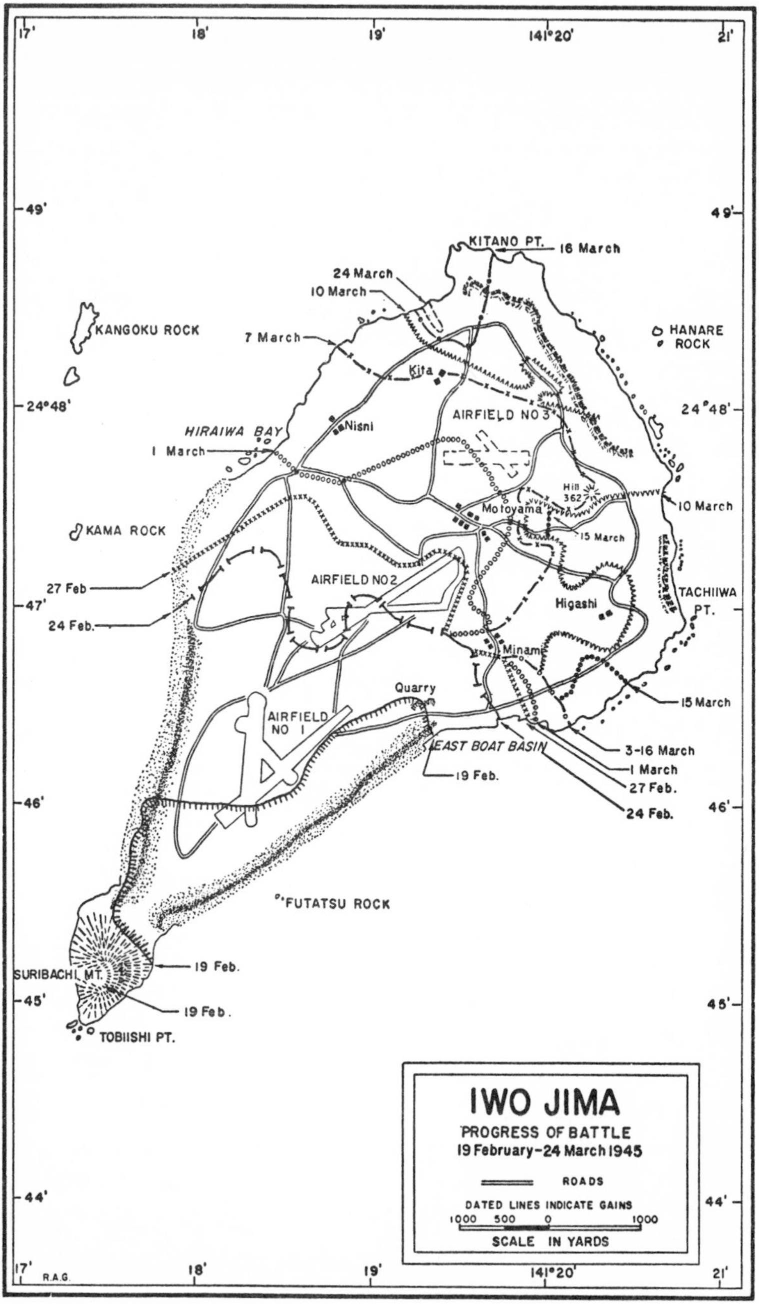
IWO JIMA
PROGRESS OF BATTLE
19 February–24 March 1945
ROADS
DATED LINES INDICATE GAINS
1000 500 0 1000
SCALE IN YARDS
KITANO PT.
16 March
24 March
10 March
7 March
KANGOKU ROCK
HANARE ROCK
Kita
Nisni
AIRFIELD NO 3
HIRAIWA BAY
1 March
Hill 362
Motoyama
10 March
15 March
KAMA ROCK
27 Feb
24 Feb.
AIRFIELD NO 2
Higashi
TACHIIWA PT.
Minami
15 March
Quarry
AIRFIELD NO 1
EAST BOAT BASIN
3-16 March
1 March
27 Feb.
24 Feb.
19 Feb.
FUTATSU ROCK
19 Feb.
SURIBACHI MT.
19 Feb.
TOBIISHI PT.
17'
18'
19'
141°20'
21'
49'
24°48'
47'
46'
45'
44'
R.A.G.

Nevada, when firing her assigned rolling barrage about 0925, found that her secondary battery could not penetrate a concrete blockhouse and turned over the job to her main battery. This damaged a hitherto undisclosed blockhouse behind the beach, blasting away its sand cover and leaving it naked and exposed. At 1100 when this blockhouse again became troublesome the battleship used armor-piercing shells, which took it completely apart. At 1512 *Nevada* observed a gun firing from a cave in the high broken ground east of the beaches. Using direct fire, she shot two rounds of 14-inch, scoring a direct hit in the mouth of the cave, blowing out the side of the cliff and completely destroying the gun. One could see it drooping over the cliff edge "like a half-extracted tooth hanging on a man's jaw."

Approximately 30,000 troops were landed on D-day. There were 2420 casualties, including 519 killed or missing in action; and 47 more died of wounds. The beachhead established fell far short of the planned phase line, but it already contained six infantry regiments, as many artillery battalions and two tank battalions.

Darkness finally closed D-day, a day such as Iwo had never seen since it arose a hissing volcano from the ocean. The Marines dug themselves in where night overtook them. Gunfire support ships moved out to night withdrawal areas, leaving only *Santa Fe* and ten destroyers to supply star shell illumination and harassing fire on enemy positions. The expected big counterattack never came off; banzai charges were no part of General Kuribayashi's plan. He intended to conserve his man power, knowing that American sea and air power had closed all hope of reinforcement, and that it was hopeless to try to drive the Marines into the sea. But he intended to fight for every yard of ground, and did.

2. *Iwo Jima Secured, 20 February–16 March*

The reduction and capture of Iwo Jima is a story of yard-by-yard advance against a tough, resourceful enemy who allowed no let-up, and who used his terrain to extract the maximum price in blood. The Marines, advancing in the open with little natural shelter, had to fight their way against an enemy burrowed underground and protected from everything but a direct hit. It was a costly and exhausting grind, calling for higher qualities of courage, initiative and persistence than a campaign full of charges, countercharges and spectacular incidents that maintain morale. It was like being under the lash of a relentless desert storm, from which there was no shelter, day or night; but this storm lasted six weeks and rained steel, not sand. General Holland Smith said that "Iwo Jima was the most savage and the most costly battle in the history of the Marine Corps." And Admiral Nimitz observed that on Iwo "uncommon valor was a common virtue."

A pattern for the island campaign was promptly cut out. For daytime direct support, each Marine battalion had attached to it one or more destroyers with a liaison officer on board, and a Navy shore fire-control party stayed with it ashore. At daybreak the heavy support ships closed the island to fire a preliminary bombardment on targets selected by divisional and regimental commanders the evening before. After the Marines jumped off, the ships stood by for deep support on targets designated by the troops' shore fire-control parties or by spotting planes. A special feature of gunfire support during the first week was the LCI mortar unit. With their shallow draft these LCI(M)s could work close inshore, often in a position to shoot up gullies at enemy targets invisible to the Marines.

Escort carrier planes acted as winged workhorses of this campaign. While Task Force 58 raided Tokyo and Okinawa, the "jeeps," almost within sight of Mount Suribachi, fed out call-bombing and rocketing missions, and provided C.A.P. and anti-submarine patrol, from before D-day to 9 March. "The daily task of providing air support," observed their commander, Admiral Durgin, "is not broken even for replenishing and refueling. It is a continual grind from dawn to dark each day."

Owing to Iwo's distance from Japanese air bases, the Navy there was not much bothered by kamikazes. One, however, crashed *Saratoga* about 35 miles NW of Iwo on 21 February, and five more attacked, adding a bomb to her collection. She lost 42 planes burned, jettisoned or splashed, 123 men killed and 192 wounded, but she was able to steam under her own power to a West Coast yard. It took a "friendly" atomic bomb at Bikini to put much-bopped old "Sara" down for keeps. Also on the evening of 21 February, escort carrier *Bismarck Sea* was crashed by a kamikaze starting gasoline fires and explosions that did her in and killed 218 of her crew. Simultaneously, several Japanese torpedo-bombers attacked escort carrier *Lunga Point*. All torpedoes missed but one plane skidded across the flight deck with propeller chewing up the planking, and plunged into the sea. The damage was slight and nobody but the pilot was killed. These, together with hits on net cargo ship *Keokuk* and *LST–477*, make up the total enemy aircraft damage in the Iwo Jima operation. It seemed a good omen for Okinawa, but it was not.

On 23 February came the successful scaling of Mount Suribachi. Colonel Harry ("the Horse") Liversedge sent a 40-man detachment from the 28th Marine Regiment, commanded by 1st Lieutenant H. G. Schreier, to scale the volcano. As they scrambled over the rim of the crater they were challenged by the last Japanese survivors on the opposite edge, and a hot little fight developed. Before it ended, at 1020, a Marine picked up a length of iron pipe, lashed to it a small American flag that he had brought in his pocket, and raised it. This flag was too small to be seen through the fog of battle, but already a bigger one was coming up, a battle ensign from *LST–779*, which had beached near the base. A Marine carried it up the mountain, and an Associated Press photographer arrived in time to take the famous picture of the second flag-raising.

Beginning 25 February the Marines made slow but steady progress, gradually pushing the Japanese into the northern part of the island. The final drive was made three divisions abreast. On 4 March the former Japanese airfield, improved and extended by Seabees, received its first call from a B–29, returning from Japan low on gasoline. General Schmidt announced Iowa Jima secured on 16 March, and operation completed on the 26th. But there was plenty of ground fighting between these two dates, and even later. General Kuribayashi's radio informed Chichi Jima on the 21st: "We have not eaten or drunk for five days. But our fighting spirit is still high." It was indeed. His men continued to do all the mischief they could. On 26 March, before dawn, about 350 Japanese tried to brawl their way through an A.A.F. and Seabee camp, killing 53 and wounding 119 American officers and men before being annihilated themselves.

General Schmidt closed his command post 27 March and the 3rd Marine Division departed. The 147th Infantry Regiment U. S. Army, which had been arriving since 21 March, now took over responsibility for mopping-up and garrison duty.

Down to 1800 March 27, the Marine Corps and Navy casualties incurred in capturing Iwo Jima were as follows: —

	MARINE CORPS		NAVY
	Officers	*Men*	*Officers and Men*
Killed in action	215	4,339	363
Died of wounds	60	1,271	70
Missing, presumed dead	3	43	448
Wounded in action	826	16,446	1,917
Combat fatigue casualties	46	2,602	?

Up to and including 26 March the count of Japanese killed and sealed up in caves was 20,703, and only 216 had been taken prisoner. It was then estimated that only 100 to 300 of the enemy were left alive on the island. This proved to be far too optimistic. The Army netted 867 more prisoners in April and May, during which time 1602 more Japanese were killed. Isolated pockets held out even longer in various parts of the island.

The United States Marines conducted this, one of the toughest battles in their entire history, with exemplary endurance, skill and valor. And it was not a spectacular battle, but one of steady slugging against a relentless enemy. Battle casualties amounted to 30 per cent of the entire landing force, and 75 per cent in the infantry regiments of the 4th and 5th Divisions. The Seabees, who began to land on D-day and to restore the No. 1 airstrip five days later, and 7600 of whom were on the island 20 April, did the major work in making Iwo Jima useful to the Army Air Force. By the end of the war about 2400 B–29 landings had been made on the island, carrying crews of many thousand men.

There is no doubt that the capture of Iwo Jima became a major contribution to victory over Japan. One B–29 pilot said, "Whenever I land on this island, I thank God and the men who fought for it."

3. *The Approach to Okinawa, 9–31 March*

Okinawa in the Ryukyus, a name unknown to the vast majority of Americans before 1945, signifies an island where American forces seem destined to remain until the cold war waxes hot or the Communist menace fades. Under an earlier name, "The Great Loochoo," Okinawa became well known to Americans when, in that happy era before "imperialism" and "colonialism" became pejorative words, Commodore Matthew C. Perry was sailing about the Orient. In 1853 the Commodore raised the American flag near Shuri on one of the hills that cost us so dear to capture in 1945. He forced the King of the Ryukyus to sign a treaty guaranteeing friendly treatment to American ships, and even established a temporary coaling station at Naha harbor. Japan only took over the group in 1879 and the Okinawans have never been completely assimilated to the Japanese.

In 1945 the island, with a small rural economy, was overpopulated with almost half a million people. The countryside, with steep limestone hills, umbrella-topped pines, small cultivated fields and patches of woodland, recalls those Italian landscapes seen through the windows of Tuscan and Sienese paintings; but neither tower nor dome breaks the skyline. The soft limestone structure of the island lent itself to a deep, prolonged defense such as General Kuribayashi's on Iwo Jima.

Planning for this massive Operation ICEBERG, described by British observers as "the most audacious and complex enterprise yet undertaken by the American amphibious forces," began with a Cincpac-Cincpoa staff study dated 25 October 1944. The detailed operation plan of Vice Admiral Turner was issued on 9 February 1945.

Admirals Spruance, Mitscher and Turner, and Lieutenant General Simon Bolivar Buckner USA, commanding Tenth Army, were the

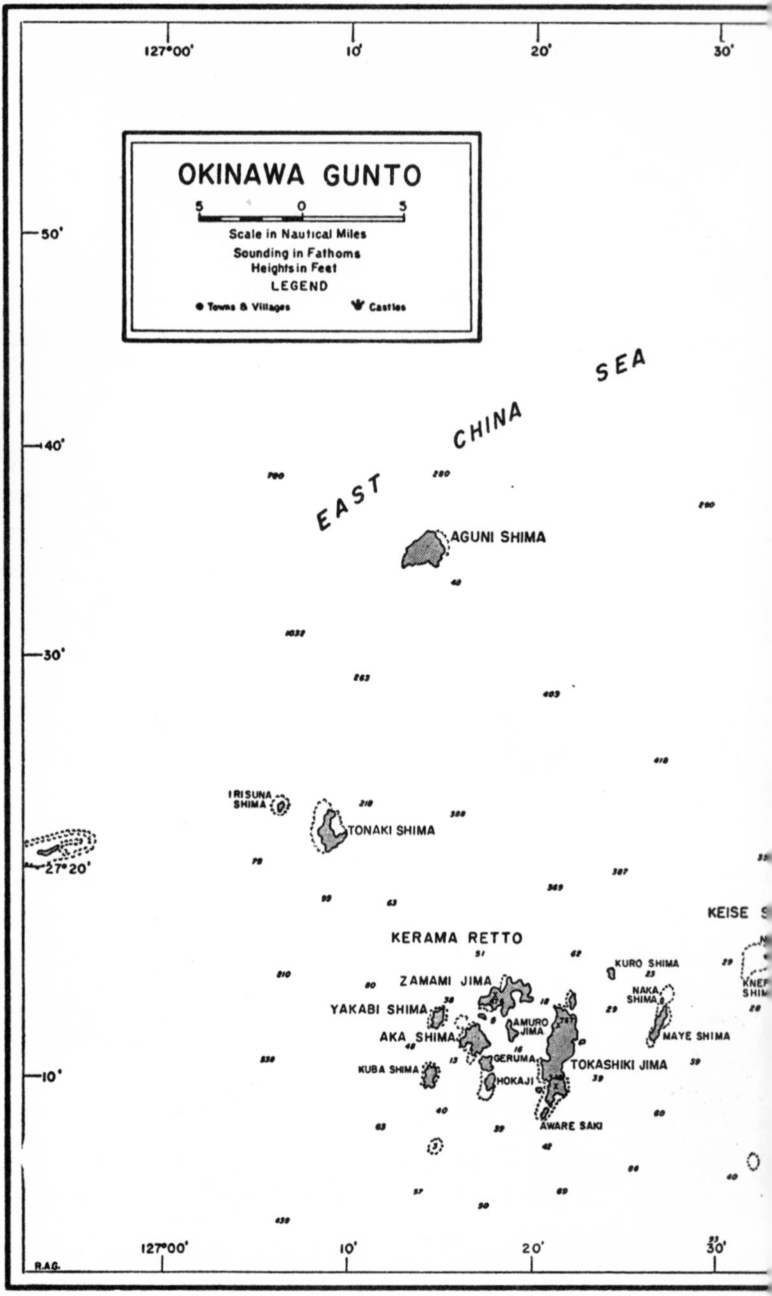

OKINAWA GUNTO
Scale in Nautical Miles
Sounding in Fathoms
Heights in Feet
LEGEND
Towns & Villages
Castles
EAST CHINA SEA
AGUNI SHIMA
IRISUNA SHIMA
TONAKI SHIMA
KERAMA RETTO
ZAMAMI JIMA
YAKABI SHIMA
AKA SHIMA
KUBA SHIMA
AMURO JIMA
GERUMA
HOKAJI
TOKASHIKI JIMA
AWARE SAKI
KURO SHIMA
NAKA SHIMA
MAYE SHIMA
KEISE
127°00'
10'
20'
30'
50'
40'
30'
27°20'
10'
R.A.G.

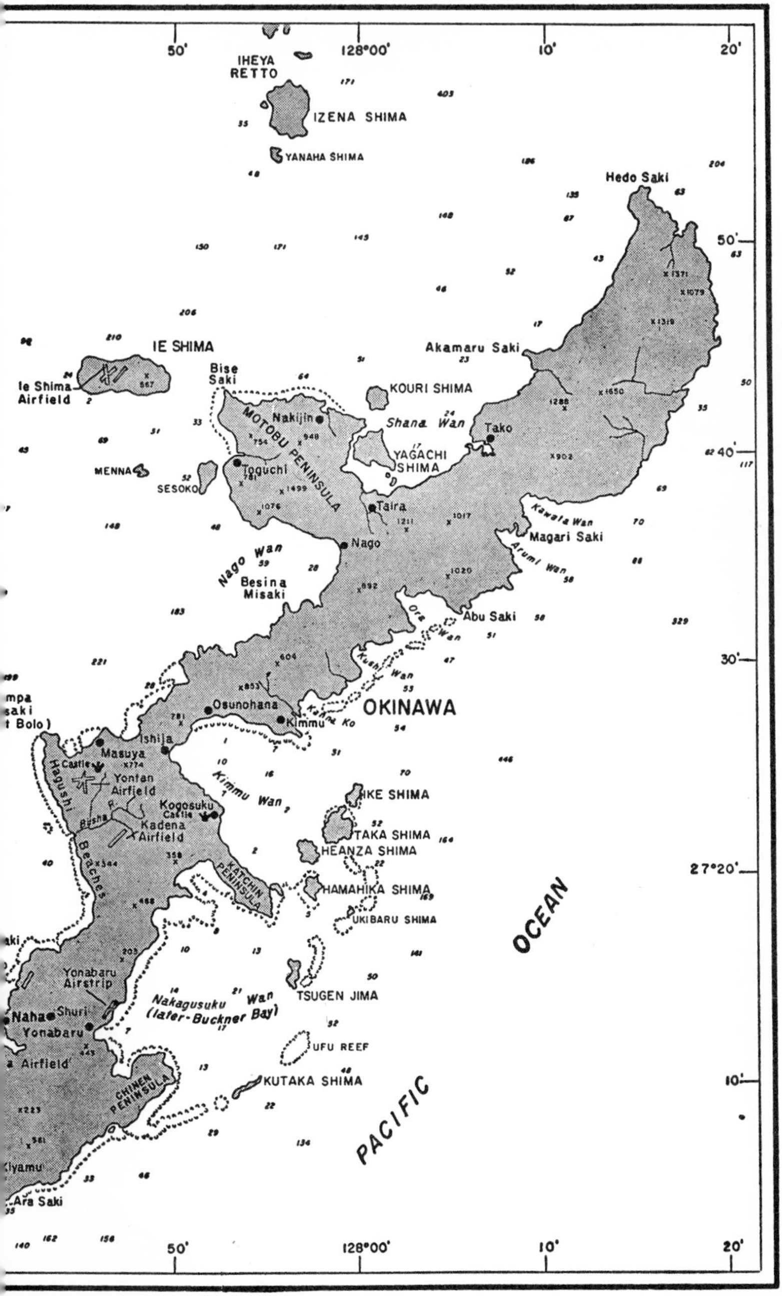
50'
128°00'
10'
20'
IHEYA RETTO
IZENA SHIMA
YANAHA SHIMA
Hedo Saki
50'
IE SHIMA
Ie Shima Airfield
Akamaru Saki
Bise Saki
KOURI SHIMA
MOTOBU PENINSULA
Nakijin
Shana Wan
Tako
YAGACHI SHIMA
40'
MENNA
SESOKO
Toguchi
Taira
Kawala Wan
Magari Saki
Nago
Nago Wan
Arumi Wan
Besina Misaki
Abu Saki
Ora Wan
Kushi Wan
30'
OKINAWA
Osunohana
Kimmu
Kimmu Wan
Ishija
Masuya
Castle
Yontan Airfield
Hagushi
IKE SHIMA
Kogosuku Castle
Kadena Airfield
TAKA SHIMA
HEANZA SHIMA
27°20'
Beaches
KATCHIN PENINSULA
HAMAHIKA SHIMA
UKIBARU SHIMA
OCEAN
Yonabaru Airstrip
TSUGEN JIMA
Nakagusuku Wan (later-Buckner Bay)
Naha
Shuri
Yonabaru
UFU REEF
Airfield
CHINEN PENINSULA
KUTAKA SHIMA
10'
PACIFIC
Ara Saki
50'
128°00'
10'
20'

four principal commanders. Tenth Army was a powerful invasion force, comprising III 'Phib Corps (Major General Roy S. Geiger) of three Marine divisions, and XXIV Army Corps (Major General John R. Hodge USA) of four infantry divisions with a fifth in reserve — a total of about 172,000 combatant and 115,000 service troops.

D-day for Okinawa was set for 1 April 1945. Planners and commanders were highly apprehensive of what enemy air might do to us before we could secure our own airfields on Okinawa. For the Japanese had several airfields there and in the nearby islands, airdromes 150 miles away in the Amami Gunto, about 230 miles away on the Sakishima Gunto, and 65 airfields on Formosa, as well as 55 on Kyushu. Since no other operation would be going on at the time except in the southern Philippines, the enemy could concentrate an estimated 2000 to 3000 planes on the expeditionary force, and employ kamikaze tactics, which is exactly what Imperial General Headquarters planned to do. The island commander, Lieutenant General Mitsuru Ushijima, who had 77,000 to 100,000 troops in his garrison, was ordered to employ the same defense-in-depth tactics as at Iwo Jima.

Air power was not one-sided. Even before the bloody scroll of the Iwo Jima campaign was completely unrolled, the B-29s had begun a series of air raids, with incendiary bombs, on large urban areas of Japan. These, in the words of the Japanese collaborators to General MacArthur's *Historical Report*, "rocked the nation to its very foundations." The attack on the night of 9-10 March, in particular, was "indescribably horrifying." Well over 250,000 houses were destroyed, rendering more than a million persons homeless, and 83,793 people were burned to death. Compared with these, the results of fast carrier raids on Japan on 18-21 March were unimportant; and the kamikazes got in some good licks on *Wasp*, *Yorktown* and *Franklin*. The first-named lost 101 dead and 269 wounded, but continued her flight operations; *Franklin* (Captain Leslie H. Gehres) was very badly damaged, had to be towed clear by heavy cruiser *Pittsburgh* (Captain John E. Gingrich) and lost 724 killed and 265 wounded. *Franklin* was in much worse shape than old *Lexington* in the Coral Sea or old *Yorktown* at Midway; but the outstanding skill, heroism and stamina of damage control parties enabled her to make the 12,000-mile voyage to New York with only one stop.

Neither *Franklin* nor many other ships crashed by kamikazes off Okinawa could have been saved but for the firefighting schools and improved technique instituted by the Navy 1942-1943. The initial impulse came from the New York City fire department, which interested Rear Admiral Edward L. Cochrane, Chief of the Bureau of Ships, in a new "fog nozzle," which atomized water to a fine spray and quenched a blaze much more quickly than a solid stream could do. New York and Boston fire-fighters trained over 260 officer instructors and established schools with mock-up ships at every continental naval base. The damage control party of every new warship was trained at one of these before going to sea. The major object of this instruction was to "get the fear of fire out of the sailor"; to teach him that, if properly equipped with fire mask and helmet, handling an all-purpose nozzle and applicator, he could boldly advance to the source of a blaze and not get hurt. All ships were equipped with 160-pound handy-billies, and the destroyers and larger types with 500-pound mobile pumps, each operated by its own gas engine. Portable oxyacetylene steel-cutting outfits and rescue breathing-apparatus were provided. A foamite system was placed at every hundred feet of a carrier's deck. Foam generators in destroyers were moved topside. Salvage vessels (ARS) were especially fitted out to help fight fires in other ships.

Japanese authorities admit that losses from these carrier raids were "staggering": 161 out of 193 aircraft committed shot down, in addition to an indeterminate number destroyed on the ground. These losses, luckily for us, prevented heavy participation by Japanese air forces in the defense of Okinawa until 6 April.

Two naval bombardment forces were brought up to the Ryukyus eight days before the landings, in order to give Okinawa and the vicinity a complete working-over. Admiral Blandy's amphibious support force of escort carriers, minecraft, light gunboats and the like, and Admiral Deyo's bombardment group of battleships and cruisers, were given this job. Also under Blandy's command was a complete attack group, lifting an infantry division, to take the Kerama Retto, a cluster of small islands 15 miles west of Okinawa. This preliminary operation was the idea of Admiral Turner, in order to secure the Kerama roadstead before the main show, as an advanced naval base for fueling, repairs and ammunition replenishment. The Kerama Retto landings, which would have been considered a major amphibious operation in 1942, went off like clockwork, and the group was secured on the 27th.

Between 28 March and 8 April, seven fleet tankers and three station tankers issued 940,000 barrels of fuel oil and 203,000 barrels of diesel, together with large quantities of lube oil and avgas, to 277 ships. Inside the roadstead, despite frequent air alerts, one had a feeling of security, like having a roof over your head in an air raid. As Rear Admiral Allan Smith wrote, Kerama "gave a firmness to the Okinawa tactical situation . . . We were there to stay, with a place to tow damaged ships, look after survivors, replenish and refuel, drop an anchor."

Aye, drop an anchor! For that boon alone, sailors blessed Kelly Turner, whose bright thought made it possible.

4. *The Okinawa Landings, 1 April 1945*

L-day, as D-day for Okinawa was called, came on Easter Sunday, 1 April. It was preceded by five days of naval bombardment and air bombing. The five-to-six-mile-long strip of Hagushi beaches had been chosen for the landings because they gave ready access to two landing fields, Yontan and Kadena, and it seemed inconceivable that the enemy would abandon these without a fight. For aught we knew, the Japanese were holed up immediately behind the beaches, ready to give the boys hell when they stepped ashore. These beaches were bisected by Bisha River, which flows into the sea between two outthrusting limestone bluffs. The cliff faces were honeycombed with caves and tunnels from which the landing beaches could have been enfiladed by gunfire. Behind every beach was a thick six- to ten-foot-high sea wall of masonry and concrete. Both airfields were dominated by tunneled and fortified hills. It looked as if landing on the Hagushi beaches would be as bloody an affair as Omaha, and that the three days allowed in the operation plan would be too little time for capturing the airfields.

Everyone was wrong. What they thought to be difficult proved to be easy, and after the easy part was over the tough fighting began.

The Paschal sun rose over heavy, low-lying clouds around 0640 April 1. It was a beautiful morning, perfect for an amphibious operation: calm sea, just enough offshore wind to blow the smoke away and to float the varicolored banners of the control craft. As the sun rose over the clouds it cast a peachlike glow over the water and on the multitude of ships, some painted solid gray, some with striped Atlantic Ocean camouflage. These last had not had time to change clothes, as it were, having been hustled more than halfway around the world to meet Okinawa L-day.

At 0600 Vice Admiral Turner in *Eldorado* took over from Rear Admiral Blandy the command of all forces afloat except the fast carriers. After wresting one position after another from the enemy, Turner was in fine fettle. He had just been attacked in the American press for wasting lives at Iwo Jima and compared unfavorably with General MacArthur, but little he cared for that. He was still the same driving, swearing, sweating "Kelly" whose head could conceive more new ideas and retain more detail than any other flag officer in the Navy. His complicated landing plan could hardly go wrong, based as it was on two years' combat experience.

In order not to overwhelm the reader with detail, yet do justice to the magnitude and complexity of this last amphibious operation of the war, I shall describe one quarter part of it, the landing of one infantry division by boats and craft of Transport Group "Dog," Commodore M. O. Carlson. "Dog" formed half of the Southern Attack Force, which was commanded by Rear Admiral "Jimmie" Hall of Normandy fame. His job was to land Major General Hodge's XXIV Corps. The "Dog" transports, which had the 7th Infantry Division on board, were to land it on a front of 3000 yards, the so-called Orange and Purple beaches.

Very early the big attack transports (*Harris*, flag) heave-to about seven and a half miles off shore. Beaching craft proceed to an area four miles nearer, control craft mark the line of departure 4000 yards off shore, and 17 "specialist" beaching craft (supply, water, hospital, and so on) together with LSD *Epping Forest* carrying boated tanks in her womb, heave-to seaward of the LSTs. Each control craft displays a banner of the same color as the beach, with vertical stripes to distinguish between Nos. 1 and 2 of the same color. This is carried out consistently. Every boat wave's guide flies a pennant of similar color and design, and each landing craft

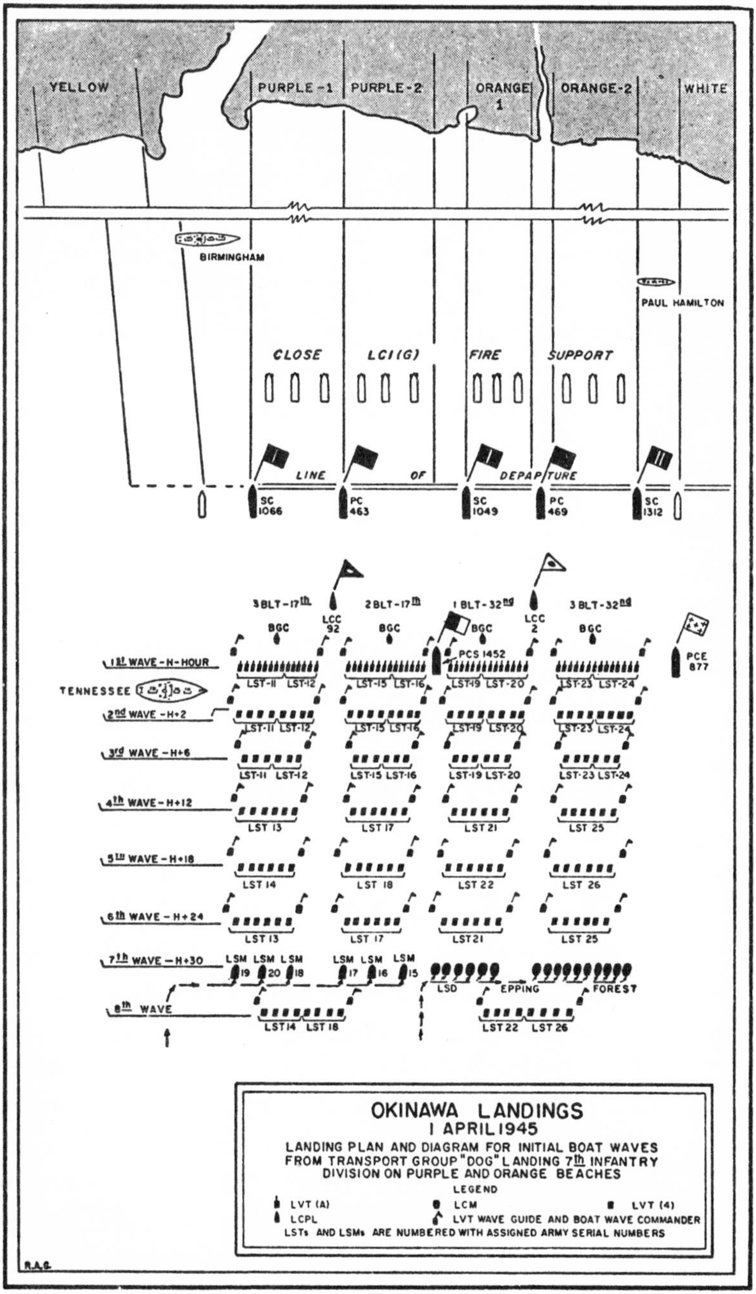
YELLOW
PURPLE-1
PURPLE-2
ORANGE 1
ORANGE-2
WHITE
BIRMINGHAM
PAUL HAMILTON
CLOSE LCI(G) FIRE SUPPORT
LINE OF DEPARTURE
SC 1066
PC 463
SC 1049
PC 469
SC 1312
3 BLT-17th
2 BLT-17th
1 BLT-32nd
3 BLT-32nd
LCC 92
LCC 2
BGC
PCS 1452
PCE 877
1st WAVE - H-HOUR
TENNESSEE
2nd WAVE - H+2
3rd WAVE - H+6
4th WAVE - H+12
5th WAVE - H+18
6th WAVE - H+24
7th WAVE - H+30
8th WAVE
LST-11 LST-12
LST-15 LST-16
LST-19 LST-20
LST-23 LST-24
LST 13
LST 17
LST 21
LST 25
LST 14
LST 18
LST 22
LST 26
LSM 19
LSM 20
LSM 18
LSM 17
LSM 16
LSM 15
LSD EPPING FOREST
LST 14 LST 18
LST 22 LST 26
OKINAWA LANDINGS
1 APRIL 1945
LANDING PLAN AND DIAGRAM FOR INITIAL BOAT WAVES FROM TRANSPORT GROUP "DOG" LANDING 7th INFANTRY DIVISION ON PURPLE AND ORANGE BEACHES
LEGEND
LVT (A)
LCM
LVT (4)
LCPL
LVT WAVE GUIDE AND BOAT WAVE COMMANDER
LSTs AND LSMs ARE NUMBERED WITH ASSIGNED ARMY SERIAL NUMBERS
R.A.C.

of the initial waves has it painted topside. First wave ashore sets up corresponding beach markers about ten feet high, brightly painted on canvas.

Battleship *Tennessee* (Captain John B. Heffernan) with Rear Admiral Deyo embarked, and cruiser *Birmingham* (Captain H. D. Power) with Rear Admiral Bertram J. Rodgers embarked, close to 1900 yards from the beach. En route, a Japanese dive-bomber makes for them but is splashed just astern of *Birmingham*, whose crew, in view of their earlier experiences, are pleasantly surprised at their escape.[1] At 0640 the naval bombardment opens, and continues intermittently until 0735, when it is raised to allow carrier-based planes to play their part. The sound of naval cannon is stilled, but the air is filled with the drone of airplane motors, the rolling rumble of exploding bombs, and the sharp, unmistakable crack of rocket fire.

At 0800 the cry goes up, "Here they come!" In the van are 12 LCI gunboats, moving in perfect alignment at a deliberate three knots in order not to outdistance the LVTs. They pass around the battleships and open fire, their 3-inch guns rattling like old-time musketry. In ten minutes' time three boat waves, each flanked by flag-flying guide boats, have swept around Battleship *Tennessee*'s bow and stern, re-forming on her landward side directly under her guns, which are shooting 14-inch, 5-inch and 40-mm projectiles over the men's heads. The troops in green coveralls and camouflaged helmets gaze curiously at the battleship's flashing guns. The LCI(G)s are now close to the shore; their gunfire sounding like a roll of drums. Just as the fourth wave passes *Tennessee*, planes come in for their last pre-landing strafing and rocket fire, making a noise like a gigantic cotton sheet being ripped apart. The fifth

[1] Kamikazes also attacked the "Demonstration Group" under Rear Admiral Jerauld Wright, which laid on a fake landing at the southern end of Okinawa to distract the enemy. Two crashed an LST and transport *Hinsdale*, killing 40 sailors and Marines.

boat wave passes, troops standing on the after deck to see "what goes on." And a marvelous sight it is, these waves of landing craft extending parallel to the coast as far as the eye can see, all moving with a precise deliberation that well represents the stout though anxious hearts that they are carrying.

At 0828 word arrives that the first wave is 75 yards from the beach. Admiral Deyo orders Cease Fire. The LCI gunboats have halted outside the reef over which amphtracs of Wave 2 are already crawling to begin their last dash through the lagoon. At 0832 comes word, "First wave has hit the beach!" Waves 2 and 3 are on the reef, 4 and 5 take off from Line of Departure; others are forming up as far as you can view seaward.

As *Tennessee* winds ship, in order to give her starboard secondary battery a chance to shoot, the first signs of enemy opposition appear. Plumes of white water rise up between her and the beach. A mortar battery on the bluffs of the Bisha River is trying to get the range, but never does. Sixth wave is composed of LCVPs whose troops will have to be transferred to retracting LVTs to cross the reef. Seventh wave includes six landing ships, medium (LSM) for the Purple beaches. These little sisters to the LST are camouflaged by great blobs of green, yellow and brown paint, which light up to a modernist fantasy when seen in echelon; yet there is also something curiously medieval about them. Nearly amidships rises a tall, cylindrical pilothouse like the turret of a castle, with round ports; and the numerous gadgets which crown the turret have the effect of battlements protecting the helmeted sailors. Can it be a coincidence that the control craft for Purple 1 is numbered 1066? As the LSMs pass, their bow gates are already open, ready to disgorge the newest amphibious vehicle, a medium Sherman tank supported by pontoons. Nine centuries of warfare and military architecture seem to come to a focus off the beaches of Okinawa.

Nine o'clock. The sun has burned away the mist, disclosing an almost solid mass of transports to seaward, beaches swarming with amphtracs and men, troops moving through cornfields toward the tableland, landing craft forming waves, earlier waves retracting. Tanks can be seen swarming up the slope, orange and purple beach markers are clearly visible, landing craft bearing bulldozers and cranes pass; one is labeled PRESS in large white letters. Wind and sea have made up; no whitecaps yet but enough chop so that landing craft pitch and throw spray.

At 1100 word reached *Tennessee* that the Marines in the northern sector had taken Yontan airfield, and that the troops in the Army sector were on Kadena. All hands were stunned by the lack of opposition. Where are the Japanese? What is wrong with their elaborate installations? . . . No one knew the answer. Officers looked at one another and shook their heads. The big joke that morning was the word passed by some Corps humorist: "The Marines are going so fast that they have already contacted the Russians coming up the other side of Okinawa!"

Throughout the afternoon unloading on the beaches continued unopposed, and at 1600 Admiral Turner reported that about 50,000 troops had been landed. The big transports were then withdrawn seaward for the night, and while they were retiring, *Alpine* and *Achernar* were crashed by kamikazes, losing 21 men killed. But they were able to discharge the undamaged part of their cargoes next day before retiring for repairs.

Altogether, this Easter Sunday saw the most successful amphibious landing of the war — not so much owing to our own foolproof plan and tactics as to the enemy's decision to retire from the beach area. What could be his idea?

5. Yamato *and the Fast Carriers, 6–12 April*

The answer is that General Ushijima was rigorously applying the defense-in-depth tactics laid down by his superiors, and practiced at Iwo Jima, for opposing a landing force of superior strength. The idea was to "lure" the enemy into a position where he could not be supported by naval gunfire, and then wipe him out. The General concentrated most of his troops on the southern quarter of the island; hence the Marines, who were given the northern three quarters to conquer, overran that part easily. For several days General Hodge's XXIV Corps felt its way south, and not for a week did the real land battle begin.

In the meantime the Navy had effectively sealed off the big island from any possible reinforcement — there would be no Tokyo Express to Okinawa. The enemy did try one desperate surface lunge at the amphibious forces, but Task Force 58 dealt effectively with that sacrificial sortie.

United States submarines *Threadfin* and *Hackleback*, on the evening of 6 April, reported a sizeable force debouching from Bungo Suido, the southern entrance to the Inland Sea. It consisted of *Yamato*, light cruiser *Yahagi* and eight destroyers. Their objective, in concert with the opening day of Operation TEN-GO — the massed kamikaze attack — was to knock off whatever ships the kamikazes left afloat. They were not expected to return, and only four destroyers did so; *Yamato* had only fuel enough for a one-way trip, and *Yahagi* had food for only five days. But their magazines were fairly bursting with ammunition; *Yamato* had over 1000 rounds for her main battery. This mammoth battlewagon, which had been through the Battles of Midway, the Philippine Sea and Leyte Gulf with little damage and still less effect, was 863 feet long and displaced 72,908 tons when fully laden. Her main battery consisted of nine 460-mm (18.1-inch) guns which threw a projectile weighing 3200 pounds and had a maximum range of 42,000 meters (22½ miles). Her complement was 2767 officers and men. She had radar and 150 antiaircraft and machine guns. Four turbine engines, developing 150,000 horse power, gave her a maximum speed of 27.5 knots. This surprising ratio of speed to weight was attained by a unique hull design. *Yamato* was a very beautiful ship, with a graceful sheer to her flush deck, unbroken from stem to stern, and a stream-lined mast and stack. She and her sister *Musashi* (sunk in the Battle of the Philippine Sea) would have inaugurated a new standard for battleship construction — as H.M.S. *Dreadnought* had done forty years earlier — if air and missile power had not doomed the big-gunned capital ship. So this last sortie of *Yamato* has a sentimental interest for all sailors. When she went down, five centuries of naval warfare ended.

This "Special Surface Attack Force," as it was called, under the command of Vice Admiral Seiichi Ito, sailed through the Inland Sea. It sortied from Bungo Suido at 2000, naked of air cover. That rendered this forlorn hope of the Japanese Navy completely hope-less. With exceedingly bad judgment, the now unified Japanese air command hurled all available fighter planes against the amphibi-ous forces around Okinawa, and at Task Force 58, instead of covering *Yamato*.

Mitscher's fast carriers were in fine shape and vast strength, despite the recent crashes which had sent *Franklin*, *Wasp* and *Sara-toga* home for repairs. He was in *Lexington*, while Spruance flew his flag in *New Mexico* of the bombardment and fire-support group. Both admirals expected *Yamato* to sortie, and assumed that she would approach through the East China Sea, which we dared not enter owing to the mines, and make a night run to Okinawa. Consequently she might escape notice of the TF 58 search planes, operating from east of Okinawa. But Spruance prepared to get her one way or another. The submarines' report of her coming out of the Inland Sea on the evening of 6 April enabled Mitscher to get three of his task groups up north within striking position, and to fly searches at dawn. An *Essex* plane at 0823 April 7 flushed *Yamato* and her consorts after she passed through Van Diemen Strait, making 22 knots, and working west in the hope of keeping out of carrier planes' range. As soon as he heard this, Spruance signaled to Mitscher "You take them," and he did. At the same time he ordered Admiral Deyo's bombardment force to prepare for a surface action northwest of Okinawa, in case the Japanese broke through the air barrier. So, at 1530 April 7, out lumbered the old battlewagons, none too cheerfully; Deyo's chief of staff "Rafe" Bates taking care to point out that *Yamato*'s guns had a range of 45,000 yards as compared with 37,000 for *Tennessee*'s main battery.

But by that time *Yamato* was no more.

It was a mizzling day with low overcast, ideal for air attack. Two tender-based PBMs from Okinawa shadowed the Japanese force for five hours, sending valuable information to Mitscher and coaching-in the carrier plane strikes. The first of these struck at 1232 April 7. Within ten minutes, *Yamato* had received two bombs and one torpedo hit, one destroyer was sunk and the light cruiser knocked out. Between 1300 and 1417 the force was under almost continuous air attack. Antiaircraft gunners, for want of practice, were unable to shoot down more than half a dozen of the American planes which piled in one after the other, in deuces and treys, bombing and torpedoing, reducing *Yamato*'s topsides to a shambles, knocking out every gun. Ensign Yoshida, a survivor, has vividly described the scene in the final attack, when her list had increased to 35 degrees: —

I could hear the Captain vainly shouting, "Hold on, men! Hold on, men!" . . . I heard the exec. report . . . "Correction of list hopeless!" . . . Men were jumbled together in disorder on the deck, but a group of staff officers squirmed out of the pile and crawled over to the Com-

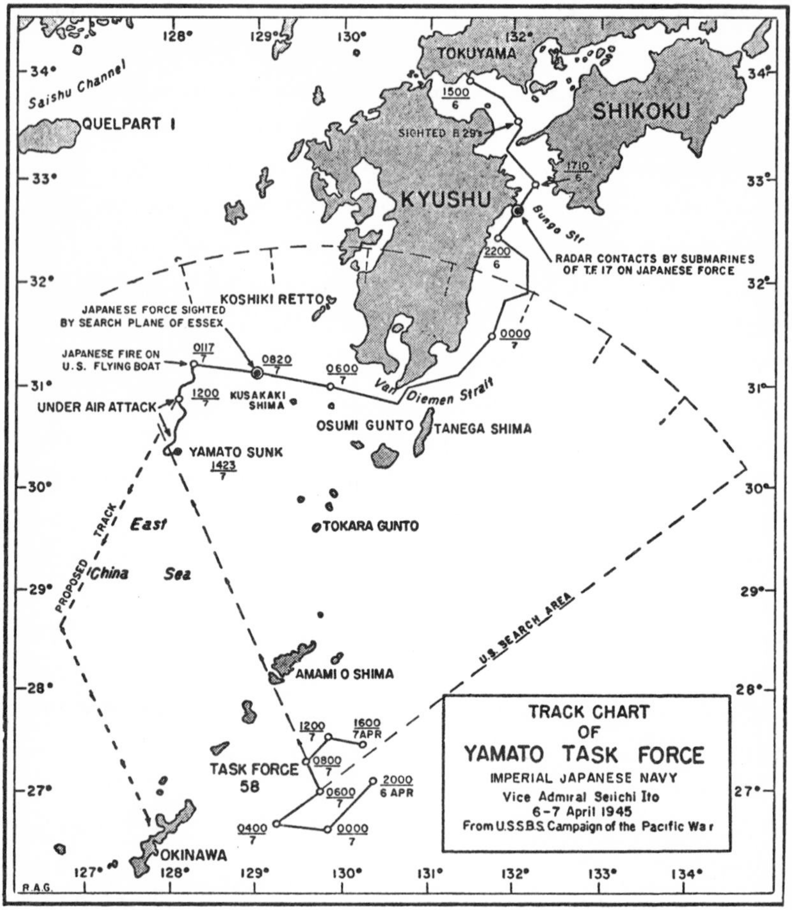

mander in Chief for a final conference. [Admiral Ito] struggled to his feet. His chief of staff then arose and saluted. A prolonged silence followed during which they regarded each other solemnly. The deck was nearly vertical and *Yamato's* battle flag was almost touching the billowing waves. . . . Shells of the big guns skidded and bumped across the deck of the ammunition room, crashing against the bulkhead and kindling the first of a series of explosions. [At 1423] the ship slid under completely, [followed by] the blast, rumble, and shock of compartments bursting from air pressure and exploding magazines already submerged.

Light cruiser *Yahagi* proved almost as tough as the battleship, taking 12 bomb and seven torpedo hits before going down. Four destroyers were sunk or scuttled; four others, damaged, managed to get back to Sasebo. *Yamato* alone lost 2488 officers and men, and the other ships, 1167. Our losses, including those from a kamikaze crash on carrier *Hancock* at noon, were about 15 airplanes and 84 sailors and aviators.

So, farewell to the battlewagons! Japan had only one left, *Haruna*, shortly to be taken apart by air bombing. Most of those of the United States and Royal Navies were still prancing about with the carriers, unconscious that they too would soon be headed for the boneyard; although one would be honored as the scene of Japanese surrender. But not another battleship was ever built. Their long day was now closing, the roar of the big guns would never again be heard, because weapons a thousand times as destructive were to take their place.

A Japanese aviator rescued from the sea boasted to his captors in *Hancock* that they would all be killed by a second massed kamikaze attack on 11 April. So TF 58 got ready for them. True enough, *Missouri* was crashed once, *Enterprise* twice, and destroyer *Kidd* once; but they suffered comparatively slight damage.

Since 26 March the Royal Navy's Pacific Fleet contingent, including carriers *Indomitable*, *Victorious*, *Illustrious* and *Indefatigable*, under Vice Admiral Sir Bernard Rawlings in H.M.S. *King George V*, was performing a useful mission of covering the Sakashima Gunto, pounding down airfields, and intercepting Japanese planes from Formosa. In so doing the British carriers were proving the value of steel decks, which American naval architects had rejected on account of their weight. A kamikaze crashing a steel flattop crumpled up like a scrambled egg, and did no damage beyond its immediate vicinity; but a kamikaze crashing an American wooden deck started serious fires and its bombs penetrated the ship's interior. On the other hand, the Royal Navy carriers were short on fuel capacity and had to retire to refuel every week or so. During that time Admiral Durgin had to send four of his escort carriers from off Okinawa to take the places of the British off Sakashima Gunto. This pattern of wide support by the British carrier forces continued throughout the Okinawa campaign.

6. *The Ordeal of the Radar Pickets, 6–12 April*

The peculiar prolonged hazard to the Navy during this Okinawa campaign was the kamikaze. A series of massed kamikaze attacks, for the first of which *Yamato* was supposed to mop up, were laid on between 6 April and 22 June, constituting Operation TEN-GO. Prior to and in between these *kikusui* (floating chrysanthemum) massed attacks, as the Japanese called them, there were individual kamikaze exploits. Besides those already noted on the landing day, the following were successful during 2-5 April: destroyer transport *Dickerson* was crashed on her bridge, killing her skipper, Lieutenant Commander Ralph E. Lounsbury USNR, the exec., and 52 more officers and men, and she had to be scuttled. Transports *Telfair*, *Goodhue* and *Henrico* were crashed; and the last-named lost the division commander, the skipper, two Army colonels and 45 other sailors and soldiers. The ship survived, but she was out of the war.

Admiral Turner's screening plan for protecting the expeditionary force in and around Okinawa was unusually comprehensive. He set up two antisubmarine destroyer screens, an inner and an outer, a destroyer screen to cover possible approaches of surface raids, a "flycatcher screen" to catch suicide motor boats, and, most important, the radar picket screen, composed primarily of destroyer types[2] but supported by LCI(G)s and other small craft. These

[2] Destroyer types include DDs, DEs, DMs (DDs converted to minecraft) and APDs, destroyer transports.

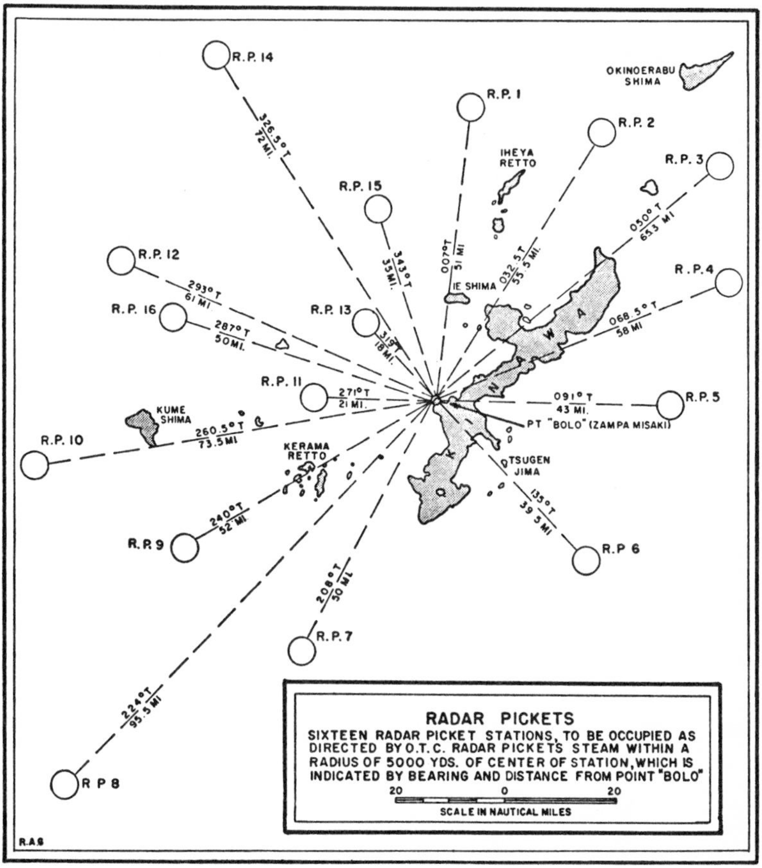

radar picket stations were the posts of greatest danger. They were disposed around Okinawa at distances of between fifteen and one hundred miles from land, so as to pick up flights of approaching enemy planes and, with the aid of C.A.P., to intercept them. From 26 March on, each station was kept by a destroyer type with a fighter-director team on board. This controlled the C.A.P., maintained all day by Admiral Durgin's escort carrier planes. The picket vessel patrolled night and day within 5000 yards of her station, and when bogeys appeared on her radar screen, the fighter-director officer vectored out C.A.P. to intercept. By this means a large proportion of enemy planes approaching Okinawa was shot down before they reached the island, and our forces engaged in landing, unloading or fire support were given timely warning of an air raid. Hundreds of sailors lost their lives and about a score of ships and craft were sunk rendering this service.

The fast carrier forces, too, had their radar pickets; and the casualties to these, while less serious than to those around Okinawa (because more difficult for enemy planes to locate), were formidable. They are included in this table of ten *kikusui* attacks which constituted the better part of Operation TEN-GO.

Attack No.	*Date*	*No. of Planes*		*U. S. Ships*	*Damaged*	
		Kamikaze	*Other*[3]	*Sunk*	*A*	*B*[4]
1	6-7 April	355	341	6	10	7
2	12-13 April	185	195	2	3	6
3	15-16 April	165	150	1	4	2
4	27-28 April	115	100	1	3	1
5	3-4 May	125	110	6	4	2
6	10-11 May	150	125	0	4	0
7	23-25 May	165	150	3	5	1
8	27-29 May	110	100	1	5	2
9	3-7 June	50	40	0	2	1
10	21-22 June	45	40	1	3	1
	TOTAL	1465	1351	21	43	23

Counting all planes in these mass attacks, together with individual kamikaze attacks not included in the table, over 3000 sacrificial sorties were launched against American naval forces in the Okinawan campaign. In addition there were hundreds of attacks by conventional dive-bombers and torpedo planes. The total number

[3] Data in this column (after No. 2) are estimates.

[4] A, scrapped or decommissioned as result of damage, or repairs incomplete at end of war; B, out of action for over 30 days. The complete table, including ships sunk or damaged between *kikusui* attacks and by causes other than air, will be found in my *History of United States Naval Operations in World War II* Vol. XIV: *Victory in the Pacific* pp. 390-392.

of Japanese aircraft involved is not known, but the Japanese Navy counts 3700 sorties by Navy planes, including fighter escorts and conventional bombers. The sorties of Army planes, if in the same proportion to Navy as in the *kikusui* attacks, would add some 2600 more. A book might well be written about each of the six greater *kikusui* attacks, with inspiring details of heroism and suffering on the part of the crashed ships' crews. We shall have to content ourselves here with samples only.

In the first and biggest *kikusui* attack, to which no fewer than 355 kamikazes were committed, destroyers *Leutze* and *Newcomb* bore the brunt. In quick succession one kamikaze crashed *Newcomb*'s after stack, a second was splashed, and a third, carrying a large bomb, crashed her amidships, gouging deep into her bowels with a tremendous explosion that cut off all remaining sources of power and blew both engine rooms and the after fireroom into a mass of rubble. "With intentions of polishing us off," wrote her skipper, Commander I. E. McMillian, "a fourth plane raced toward *Newcomb* from the port beam and although under fire by her forward batteries came through to crash into the forward stack, spraying the entire amidships section of *Newcomb*, which was a raging conflagration, with a fresh supply of gasoline." Flames shot up hundreds of feet, followed by a thick pall of smoke and spray which so completely covered the destroyer that sailors in nearby battleships thought that she had gone down.

Destroyer *Leutze*, closing rapidly to render assistance to *Newcomb*, observed with astonishment that she was still holding together. A solid mass of flame swept from bridge to No. 3 gun, but her valiant skipper and crew showed no intention of abandoning ship. Lieutenant Leon Grabowsky, C.O. of *Leutze*, gallantly risked his ship to help her sister, closed her weather side ten minutes after the first crash and passed hose lines on board to help fight fires. Then a fifth plane approached, heading for *Newcomb*'s bridge. One of her 5-inch guns, fired in local control, made a hit which tilted the plane just enough so that it slid athwartship and on to *Leutze*'s fantail, where it exploded, jamming the rudder.

Now *Leutze* too was in trouble. While one of her repair parties continued fighting fires on board *Newcomb*, two others checked flooding on their own ship and jettisoned topside weights. Seventeen compartments laid open to the sea by the Japanese bomb let in so much water that *Leutze* began to settle. Destroyer *Beale*, fire hoses streaming, now closed the disengaged side of *Newcomb*, and *Leutze* signaled, "Am pulling away, in serious danger of sinking." But minesweeper *Defense* (Lieutenant Commander Gordon Abbott USNR), already damaged by two kamikaze hits shortly after 1800, towed *Leutze* to Kerama Retto. Both destroyers had to be scrapped; they were lucky to lose only 47 men killed or missing.

These ships belonged to the gunfire support screen. Radar picket destroyers fared even worse. *Bush* (Commander R. E. Westholm), on radar picket station No. 1, and *Colhoun* (Commander G. R. Wilson), on station No. 2, were the first to be encountered by "floating chrysanthemums" flying southwest along the Nansei Shoto. Advance elements of the massed air attack heckled them all through the midwatch and *Colhoun* was subjected to eleven bombing attacks, all of which missed, between 0230 and 0600 April 6. The forenoon watch was fairly quiet. Around 1500, 40 to 50 planes flew down from the north, stacked at various altitudes between 500 and 20,000 feet, and began orbiting and attacking *Bush*, while about 12 others went after *Cassin Young* at station No. 3, next to the eastward.

Bush shot down two Vals and drove off two more. Thirteen minutes later a Jill was sighted heading low for her. Fire was opened at a range of 7000 yards. The plane jinked and wove at an altitude of 10 to 35 feet above the water; and although every gun on the destroyer was firing, it kept coming and crashed between the two stacks. The bomb exploded in the forward engine room, killing every man there and in the two firerooms. Flooding started immediately and *Bush* took a 10-degree list, but escaping steam smothered the fires and power was regained as the auxiliary diesel generator cut in. Handy-billies were used to control the flooding, the wounded were treated on the fantail or in the ward-room, and, although the ship had gone dead, everyone expected to save her. All hands cheered when a C.A.P. of four planes appeared overhead.

Colhoun, learning by radio that *Bush* needed help, began to close at 35 knots, bringing along her C.A.P. for the short time it could remain. At 1635 she closed *Bush*, apparently foundering. She signaled a support craft, LCS–64, to rescue the crew and tried to interpose herself between the sinking ship and a flight of about 15 Japanese planes. They approached, and one went for *Bush* at 1700. Commander Westholm ordered about 150 of his men fighting fires topside to jump overboard for self-protection, and trailed knotted lines for them to climb on board again. All his 5-inch guns that would bear were jammed in train, but his 40-mm guns opened fire. *Colhoun* shot every gun she had at an approaching Zeke, which splashed midway between the two ships. Another was hit by a 5-inch shell at 4000 yards, and caught fire. *Colhoun*'s guns Nos. 1, 2 and 3 were quickly trained on a third diving at her starboard bow, and the first salvo hit him square on the nose; he splashed 50 yards abeam. Just then Commander Wilson received a report that a fourth Zeke was about to crash his port bow. Too late he ordered full left rudder. The plane, already aflame, hit *Colhoun*'s main deck, killing the gun crews of two 40-mm mounts. Its bomb exploded in the after fireroom, killing everyone there and rupturing the main steamline in the forward engine room. A quick decision by the engineer officer to open the cross-connection valve enabled *Colhoun* to maintain a speed of 15 knots. She was already getting fires under control when the fifth attack within 11 minutes came in. Two kamikazes were splashed but a third crashed, blowing a great hole below the waterline and breaking the ship's keel. While the damage control parties were working, and three 5-inch guns were being fired manually, a sixth attack came in. Two planes were splashed but a third and a fourth crashed *Bush*, killing all the wounded in the wardroom and starting a fierce fire. Still, neither C.O. would give up his ship. At 1800 a kamikaze crashed *Colhoun*, already so badly damaged that this additional misfortune did not make things much worse.

It was now dark. At 1830 a big swell rocked *Bush*, whose structure was now so weak that she jackknifed and slid to the bottom. Commander Wilson of *Colhoun* now decided to abandon his ship. At 1900 *Cassin Young* closed to take off survivors and recover swimmers, and then sank *Colhoun* by gunfire. *LCS–64*, a fleet tug, and a PC, did their best to rescue *Bush*'s swimmers, and those in floater nets and rubber life rafts; but complete darkness had set in, a high, crested sea had made up, and very many were drowned. *Bush* lost 94 officers and men out of 307 on board. *Colhoun*, owing to *Cassin Young*'s prompt rescue work, lost only 35 killed or missing.

There was air-surface action all around Okinawa that afternoon and evening of 6 April. Destroyer *Emmons*, an LST and two Victory ships carrying ammunition were sunk. Six other destroyer types were crashed. Every one of these put up a good fight; most of them splashed four to six kamikazes before one got in. The massed attacks petered out on 7 April, but total casualties to the ships sunk and badly damaged in this No. 1 *kikusui* assault were 466 killed and 568 wounded. And it must be remembered that most of the wounded in these attacks were horribly burned. They suffered excruciating agony until given first aid; for a man blown overboard, hours might elapse until a pharmacist's mate could relieve him. The medical officers did wonders if the wounded survived long enough to receive attention. And many men in rear hospitals, who looked like mummies under their bandages, breathing through a tube and being fed intravenously while their bodies healed, were cured by virtue of new methods of treating burns.

Japanese losses were equally heavy — 355 kamikazes, none of which returned, and 341 conventional bombers, an uncounted number of which were shot down; but if the enemy could keep up attrition at this rate, the objects of Operation TEN-GO would be attained. Some destroyer officers insisted that a pilot bent on crashing could not be stopped by anything smaller than 5-inch shell, and that under the existing system of gunfire control, it was impossible to knock down planes in one-two-three order. Radar picket duty could be as suicidal for the picketing sailors as for the attacking Japanese, unless two or more destroyers were placed at each station and C.A.P. were provided at dawn and dusk, which the escort carrier planes were unable to do. But an encouraging factor was the prompt buildup of a land-based air force. Yontan and Kadena fields were no beds of roses for tired airmen. Japanese artillery shelled them daily; strafers and bombers paid frequent visits. Yet, by the evening of 8 April, 82 Marine Corsairs and seven night fighters were based on Yontan field, and more were brought up within a day or two by escort carriers. Of this number, 41 were already available for C.A.P.; in another week if all went well these would be increased to 144. The land-based night fighters could not be used for C.A.P. before 14 April, as their radar and calibration gear had not yet been unloaded. So the holes in the Fleet's air cover, at dawn and dusk, were not yet filled. Close support duties for Operation ICEBERG tied down TF 58 until well into June; it got away only to sink *Yamato* and strike Kyushu airfields.

The reserve infantry division, the 27th, was landed on 9-10 April, bringing the total number of American troops ashore up to 160,000. Really tough ground fighting now began. The troops were now up against lines that the enemy intended to defend, the edge of a complicated and heavily fortified region across the three-mile-wide waist of the island, from a point south of the beaches to the Nakagusuku Wan. This area included pillboxes with steel doors impervious to flame-throwers. And Japanese artillery fire was increasing in volume and accuracy.

On 12 April opened the second *kikusui* attack, of 185 kamikazes and 195 other planes. It was bad but far less destructive than the first. Radar picket station No. 1, where Captain C. A. Buchanan was O.T.C. in destroyer *Purdy*, first took the rap. On station No. 4 destroyer *Mannert L. Abele* (Commander A. E. Parker) had the dubious honor of being sunk by the first *baka* bomb seen by our forces in action. This little horror was a one-way glider with three rockets as boosters, only 20 feet long with a wing span of 16½ feet and a warhead carrying 2645 pounds of tri-nitro-anisol. *Baka* arrived in the combat area slung under the belly of a two-engined bomber. Its pilot had an umbilical communication with the bomber's pilot, who released him near the target. The suicide pilot had to pull out of a vertical dive into a glide toward the victim, if necessary increasing speed by the rockets to over 500 knots. The small size and tremendous speed of *baka* made it the worst threat to our ships that had yet appeared, almost equivalent to the guided missiles that the Germans were shooting at London.

This initial *baka* attack was well timed. At about 1445 April 12, *Abele* was crashed by a Zeke which penetrated the after engine room. Its bomb exploded, breaking the keel and the shafts, and *Abele* went dead in the water and lost power. About one minute later, in came a *baka* at 500 knots. It hit the ship on her starboard side beneath the forward stack, penetrated No. 1 fireroom, and exploded. The ship's midship section disintegrated, bow and stern parted, and *Abele* went down so quickly that five minutes later there was nothing on the surface where she had been except wreckage and survivors, who were being bombed and strafed by other Japanese planes. Fortunately, their picket station was also manned by two LSM(R)s which closed to pick up survivors and rescued all the destroyer's crew but 79.

On that same day destroyer *Zellars* and battleship *Tennessee* were crashed, but carried on.

Friday, 13 April, broke bright and clear, but in every other respect it was a Black Friday. Just as first light dawned over Okinawa, devastating news came over ships' loudspeakers: —

"Attention! Attention! All hands! President Roosevelt is dead. Repeat, our Supreme Commander, President Roosevelt, is dead."

Half an hour after the morning watch came on duty, Franklin D. Roosevelt had breathed his last. "We were stunned," recorded one bluejacket in attack transport *Montrose*. "Few of us spoke, or even looked at each other. We drifted apart, seeming instinctively to seek solitude. Many prayed, and many shed tears." In no section of the American people was the President so beloved as in the Navy. Bluejackets went about their duties sadly, officers looked anxious, mess attendants appeared as if they had lost their only friend. The question frequently asked of officers, "What will become of us now?" indicated that sailors had looked to Franklin Delano Roosevelt as their champion in peace, their leader in battle, and their guarantee of a better world after victory.

Radio Tokyo reported the President's death simply and decently; but Hitler, in his Berlin bunker, received the news with maniac glee, thinking it would end the war.

Under Harry Truman, now President of the United States, the war effort did not slacken for a moment.

7. *Ordeal by* Kikusui, *16 April–28 May*

On 16 April hell broke loose again in the third *kikusui* attack, 165 planes strong. Destroyer *Laffey* (Commander Frederick J. Becton), in radar picket station No. 1, was the first to catch it, at 0827. Probably no ship has ever survived an attack of the intensity that she experienced. The kamikazes came in from every quarter of the compass. C.A.P. accounted for a number outside the ship's gun range, and boldly flew into the orbit of her gunfire to intercept. During a period of 80 minutes, in 22 separate attacks, *Laffey* was hit by six kamikazes and four bombs, as well as being near-missed by a bomb and by a seventh kamikaze which splashed close aboard. Her guns, fired in local control after the director was knocked out, splashed eight would-be crashers. *Laffey* lost 31 men killed and 72 wounded in this memorable action, well described by Admiral Joy as standing out "above the outstanding." But the ship lived. Towed into Hagushi roadstead, she was patched up and proceeded to the new repair base at Guam under her own power.

Radar picket destroyer *Pringle* was sunk in this attack with a loss of 65 killed and 110 wounded; four others were badly damaged, and out in Task Force 58 *Intrepid* took her usual beating, losing ten killed and 87 wounded.

The little island of Ie Shima, west of northern Okinawa, wanted for land-based search radar, was invaded 16 April by a landing force of the 77th Division, and secured on the 21st. It was here that the beloved war correspondent Ernie Pyle was killed by machine-gun fire when closely following the troops.

After the 16 April attack, radar pickets had a respite of twelve days while the Japanese were readying more "floating chrysanthemums." The fourth *kikusui* attack of 115 kamikazes was spread over 27 and 28 April. One ammunition ship was sunk, one transport and two destroyer types were badly damaged, and the fully lighted hospital ship *Comfort* was crashed, with a loss of six Army nurses, seven wounded patients and 23 others killed and 52, including four nurses, wounded.

Ashore there was bitter fighting during the last week of April, forcing the Japanese back to another series of caves and entrenchments. Each line of defense was stubbornly held by the Japanese until the sheer weight of attack penetrated and forced abandonment. Then the process was repeated. The battle for Okinawa was the toughest and most prolonged of any in the Pacific war since Guadalcanal.

"Naval gunfire," state the Army historians, "was employed longer and in greater quantities in the battle of Okinawa than in any other in history. It supported the ground troops and complemented the artillery from the day of the landing until action moved to the extreme southern tip of the island, where the combat area was so restricted that there was a danger of shelling American troops." [5] Night illumination with star shell, delivered by destroyers, was also a great help to the troops, thwarting Japanese tactics of infiltration and night attack. *Mississippi*, whose special assignment was the demolition of Shuri Castle (where Commodore Perry had been entertained in 1853) fired 2289 rounds of 14-inch and 6650 rounds of 5-inch in six weeks' duty off Okinawa.

The fifth *kikusui* attack, on 3-4 May, proved to be one of the worst. Destroyer *Luce* was crashed and sunk at radar picket station No. 12. Station No. 1, manned by two destroyers, three LCI(L) and *LSM(R)-194*, really had it. *Morrison*, crashed by two Zekes simultaneously, and immediately after by two antique wood-and-canvas biplanes, had to be abandoned in a hurry and lost 159 officers and men, over half her complement, besides some 100 wounded. The other destroyer, *Ingraham*, was crashed but survived; the rocket LSM was crashed and sunk. Total losses to

[5] R. E. Appleman and others *Okinawa: The Last Battle* p. 253.

the fifth attack were two destroyers, two LSM and 370 officers and men. The sixth big attack, of 150 kamikazes on 10-11 May, more powerful than the fifth, did even greater damage. *Bunker Hill* caught it in TF 58, losing almost 400 officers and men killed; destroyer *Hugh W. Hadley* at radar picket station No. 15 beat off almost as many attacks as had *Laffey*. She lost 28 killed and 67 wounded, including her C.O., Commander Byron J. Mullaney, who survived long enough to write an eloquent report on the performance of his ship's company: —

> No captain of a man of war had a crew who fought more valiantly against such overwhelming odds. Who can measure the degree of courage of men who stand up to their guns in the face of diving planes that destroy them? . . . I know of no record of a destroyer's crew fighting for one hour and thirty-five minutes against overwhelming aircraft attacks and destroying twenty-three planes. My crew accomplished their mission and displayed outstanding fighting abilities.

The seventh *kikusui* attack on 23-25 May, of 165 kamikazes, was mostly beaten off by the radar pickets but some planes penetrated the fire support area, where they sank destroyer transports *Bates* and *Barry* and *LSM-135*, and knocked out five more vessels. The eighth, on 27-29 May, the last to which more than a hundred planes were committed, knocked out *Braine* and *Anthony* and sank *Drexler* at picket stations 5 and 15, with heavy casualties — 290 killed and 207 wounded.

Few missiles or weapons have ever spread such flaming terror, such torturing burns, such searing death, as did the kamikaze in his self-destroying onslaughts on the radar picket and other ships. And naval history has few parallels to the sustained courage, resourcefulness and fighting spirit that the crews of these vessels displayed day after day after day in the battle for Okinawa.

8. *Okinawa Secured, 29 May–3 July*

The eighth *kikusui* attack coincided with the relief of Admiral Spruance by Admiral Halsey on 27 May, when Fifth Fleet again became Third Fleet, and TF 58, TF 38. Since 17 March the fast carrier forces had been at sea dishing it out and taking the rap, exposed to the threat of air attack day and night. With a count so far of 90 ships sunk or damaged badly enough to be out of action for more than a month, this operation had proved to be the most costly naval campaign of the war. Throughout the ordeal Admiral Spruance clung tenaciously to the principle that Okinawa must be secured. He never flinched, and no more did the officers and men of his command. A less serene and courageous man might, before reaching this point, have asked "Is this island worth the cost? Is there no better way to defeat Japan?" But no such doubts or questions ever even occurred to Raymond A. Spruance.

After two months of bitter fighting on the big island, a company of Marines on 29 May captured the shell of Shuri Castle. Naha, the capital, had already been occupied. At the outset of the final push, General Buckner was killed by Japanese artillery. The two last *kikusui* attacks, on 3-7 and 21-22 June, were small and relatively undestructive.

On 21 June, when Tenth Army drove through to the southernmost point of Okinawa, it could be announced that organized resistance had ceased. General Ushijima committed suicide next day.

Base development began by Seabee battalions soon after L-day. Buckner Bay (formerly Nakagasuku Wan) and Kimmu Wan were transformed into seaports, with docks and other cargo handling facilities. New airfields and a seaplane base were built on the eastern side of Okinawa, and airfields on Ie Shima. The face of the island was changed more than it had been for thousands of years, by multi-lane roads, traffic circles, water points, quonset villages, tank farms, storage dumps and hospitals. And by the end of the war in mid-August, base development had progressed to the point where Okinawa could well have performed its original purpose of serving as an advance base for the invasion of Japan proper.

Although your historian himself has been under kamikaze attack, and witnessed the hideous forms of death and torture inflicted by that weapon, words fail him to do justice to the sailors who met it so courageously. Men on radar picket station, to survive, not only had to strike down the flaming terror of the kamikazes roaring out of the blue like thunderbolts of Zeus; they were under constant strain and intense discomfort. In order to supply high steam pressure to build up full speed rapidly in a destroyer, its superheaters, built only for intermittent use, had to be lighted for three and four days' running. For days and even nights on end, the crew had to stand general quarters while the ship was kept "buttoned up." Men had to keep in readiness for the instant reaction and split-second timing necessary to riddle a plane bent on sacrificial death. Sleep became the rarest commodity and choicest luxury, like water to a shipwrecked mariner.

The capture of Okinawa cost the United States Navy 34 naval vessels and craft sunk, 368 damaged, over 4900 sailors killed or missing in action, and over 4800 wounded. Tenth Army lost 7613 killed or missing in action and 31,800 wounded. Sobering as it is to record such losses, the sacrifice of these men is brightened by our knowledge that the capture of Okinawa helped to bring Japanese leaders to face the inevitable surrender.

As Winston Churchill put it, in a message of 22 June to President Truman, "This battle [is] among the most intense and famous of military history. . . . We make our salute to all your troops and their commanders engaged."

CHAPTER XVII

The End of the War

November 1944–September 1945

1. *The U-Boats' Comeback and Defeat, November 1944–May 1945*

THE FEELING OF SECURITY from U-boats which had long existed on the Eastern Sea Frontier of the United States was dissipated by several incidents in the fall of the year 1944.

U–1230 landed on the Maine coast a German and a renegade American who had been given a thorough course of training in Nazi sabotage schools. This big snorkel-equipped submarine shaped a course for Mount Desert Rock, where it escaped the notice of fishermen, coastal pickets and air patrol, steamed into Frenchmans Bay on the calm night of 29 November and debarked the spies in a rubber boat. Landing at Hancock Point, they were observed by a smart lad who notified the police; trailed by F.B.I. agents to New York, they were there picked up. *U–1230* sank a Canadian steamer, 44 members of whose crew died in the icy waters of the Bay of Fundy, and then took up weather-reporting duties.

During December large numbers of U-boats began leaving their Baltic and Norwegian bases, to discover that with snorkel they could operate successfully in coastal waters. They appeared off the East Coast of Britain and in the Western Approaches. Taking advantage of currents and unfavorable sound conditions in shallow waters, they often eluded the antisubmarine vessels and did a good deal of damage. Their active range also extended into the English Channel. Around 10 January 1945 the snorkelers moved into the Irish Sea, where they sank several merchantmen and a British escort carrier. This activity became of great concern to the Allied high command. In spite of the repeated bombing of German plants where U-boats were built, the Germans had so cleverly dispersed production as to raise their average monthly output, December-March, to 27 U-boats, greater than it had been since 1942. By 1 February at least 25 snorkelers were moving into British coastal waters; and this was the first time since 1941 that shipping in the narrow seas had been so troubled. The Admiralty had to deploy over 400 escort vessels and 800 Coastal Command planes to deal with these boats. They sank 51 ships of 253,000 tons in the Atlantic from January through April 1945. The German Army was collapsing under Russian, American and British advances into Germany, but Doenitz was trying to do as much damage as possible before he and the gods of Nazidom passed into the twilight. The snorkel blitz was his counterpart to the kamikaze — a weapon that could only postpone, but could not possibly prevent, Allied victory.

The Royal Navy, assisted by Coastal Command — which now included several United States Navy Liberator squadrons — had to cope with this offensive in the narrow seas, and finally brought to book most of the snorkelers abroad. The R. A. F. and A. A. F. Bomber Commands helped by destroying 24 more in German harbors in March and April.

Four snorkelers moved across the Atlantic early in the New Year. All were sunk by the persistence of hunter-killer groups composed of destroyers and DEs. But this was not Doenitz's final effort in the Western Atlantic.

Early in 1945, tales of the captured spies from *U–1230* and other intelligence items, created a serious apprehension that U-boats were preparing to launch attacks on East Coast cities with robot rocket bombs such as those then falling on London. Admiral Jonas Ingram, who had relieved Admiral Ingersoll as Cinclant, feeling that the American public was becoming too complacent, created a sensation by announcing this unpleasant possibility. Doenitz was indeed planning a final blitz on the Eastern Sea Frontier, but the six 740-ton snorkel U-boats which made up this Group "Seewolf" carried no secret or unconventional weapons. In fact he had none; and in late March 1945, when he dispatched these boats from their Norwegian bases, armies under Eisenhower and Zhukov were battering their way into the heart of the Reich.

Doenitz however, had the satisfaction of giving Cinclant and Tenth Fleet a big scare. Admiral Ingram, who as commander in Brazilian waters had successfully barred the Atlantic Narrows to German raiders and U-boats, tried similar tactics here. He organized a Barrier Force of twenty destroyer escorts to maintain a 120-mile picket line along the meridian which passes between Fayal and Flores, supported by an escort carrier with a screen of DEs, cruising forty to fifty miles to the westward. The first barrier, with Commander Morgan H. Harris USNR commanding the picket line, and Captain Kenneth Craig as C.O. of the *Croatan* carrier group, was set up in exceedingly rough weather on 11 April. *Frost* and *Stanton*, skillful hunters from the carrier screen, sank *U-1235* and *U-880* in a fog-mull on the night of 15-16 April. A second night attack in heavy fog on 21 April by DEs *Carter* and *Neal A. Scott* sank *U-518*. The "creeping" tactics which enabled these destroyer escorts to make kills on foggy nights were worked out by Commander F. D. Giambattista, who had commanded the screen of *Croatan* when that carrier's C.O. was a great U-boat hunter — Captain John P. W. Vest.

The *Croatan* group was now relieved by one built around *Bogue*, commanded by Captain George J. Dufek. A third, of which *Core* (Captain R. S. Purvis) was the nucleus, operated near by. It was still so foggy that aircraft could give no help; five out of six boats of Group "Seewolf" were destroyed by DEs. But one of these gallant little ships was sacrificed in the effort. On 24 April *Frederick C. Davis* detected *U-546* trying to slip through the screen to get *Bogue*, and when hunting it was herself torpedoed and sunk, with great loss of life. The U-boat, after being intensively hunted, hedgehogged and depth-charged for 12 hours, came up fighting, and was then sunk by *Flaherty*'s gunfire, helped by that of three other DEs. And on 6 May *U-881* was sunk by DE *Farquhar*.

These destroyer escorts did their designers and their crews proud in the last months of the war. The final battle in the Western Atlantic was the sinking of snorkeler *U-853* by DE *Atherton* and frigate *Moberly*, off Block Island on 6 May, a few hours before Germany surrendered.

Doenitz's most formidable aces in the hole, the new Type XXI, XXIII and XXVI U-boats, never got into this war. Type XXI was a 1500-tonner with diesel-electric engines, new and powerful batteries, and a beautifully streamlined hull so that she could make 17½ knots submerged. No. XXIII was the same. The first boat of Type XXI was launched in April 1944 on Hitler's birthday, and 119 units were completed before the end of the war; but they were so badly built that they had to be recalled after their training cruises, even during initial war patrols, for extensive repairs and alterations. Only three of these actually departed on combat missions, too late to accomplish anything. An even greater menace was Type XXVI, the "Walter boat," powered by a hydrogen-peroxide turbine which required no air, and capable of steaming 158 miles submerged at 25 knots. Three of these were completed before the end of the war but never got to sea. Fortunate indeed that the war in Europe ended when it did; for a couple of hundred U-boats of these new types might have ruptured Allied sea communications and prolonged the struggle into 1946.

On 30 April 1945, before Group "Seawolf" had been liquidated,

Hitler died a coward's death in his Berlin bunker. Deserted at the last by all top Nazis trying to save their skins, the Fuehrer designated his loyal C. in C. Navy, Grossadmiral Doenitz, as his successor. On 4 May Doenitz had his first surrender offer in the hands of Field Marshal Montgomery, and ordered every German warship at sea to stop fighting and give up, or return to port. The surrender papers were signed at Rheims at 0241 May 7 Central Europe time, Russia signing next day, which is the official V-E day.

The total number of U-boats sunk by Allied forces or lost by marine casualty during the war was 781, together with some 32,000 officers and men. The German submarine fleet sank 2575 Allied and neutral merchant ships, totaling 14.5 million tons.[1] The sailors killed or drowned in these ships numbered just under 30,000 for the British merchant marine alone; and to this we must add at least 15,000 American merchant mariners, passengers, and sailors of the warships sunk.

Of the 398 U-boats still in commission, 217 were destroyed by their own crews. Most of the others began popping up all over the Narrow Seas, off Iceland and Gibraltar, and off the East Coast of the United States, flying the black flag of surrender as Admiral Burrough RN, acting for General Eisenhower, ordered them to do. "They surfaced above their handiwork, in hatred or in fear: sometimes snarling their continued rage, sometimes accepting thankfully a truce they had never offered to other ships, other sailors." [2] They broadcast their positions and were escorted into port with a prize crew on board to prevent scuttling. Of four submarines thus brought into Portsmouth, New Hampshire, *U–234* was a 1600-tonner en route to Tokyo with a German technical mission. The skipper of *U–234* gave permission to two Japanese officer passengers

[1] Italian submarines (of which 85 were lost) sank 94 ships of 532,393.
[2] Nicholas Monsarrat *The Cruel Sea* (1951) p. 501.

to commit suicide before he surrendered; but to his disgust they dosed themselves with luminal instead of performing the traditional *seppuku*, and died slowly and ignobly. Two diehard skippers sailed their boats all the way to Buenos Aires, where they expected to obtain asylum; instead they were surrendered by the Argentine government to the United States Navy.

On 28 May 1945 the Admiralty and C.N.O. issued a joint announcement that convoys were abolished, and that all merchant ships "at night will burn navigation lights at full brilliancy and need not darken ship." This did not, of course, apply to the Pacific; but to sailors in the North and South Atlantic, the Arctic and the Indian Oceans, it meant that the war was really over, and completely won.

There is no denying that the submarine was the greatest threat to Allied victory over the Axis. Doenitz was a competent tactician, and he fought clean; for all his adulation of Hitler, he was a good, solid German and a great leader. The morale of the U-boat crews, which had broken down badly in World War I, kept high to the very end in 1945. But his "integral tonnage concept," which he defends as sound strategy, was a failure. The graph of Allied and neutral merchant ship losses was overtaken by that of new construction in July 1943, and the two never again converged. Doenitz's idea that a ton of shipping lost to the Allies, no matter where or how employed, gained that much to Germany, was unsound; in order to make a score he (fortunately for us) sent to the South Atlantic and Indian Oceans U-boats which, to have decisive effect, should have been hurled at the transatlantic troop and merchant convoys, bridges of ships between the Old World and the New. Admiral Lord Cunningham declared that "Doenitz was probably the most dangerous enemy Britain has had to face since

De Ruyter," a compliment indeed from this great Sea Lord. Admiral King, I think, would have considered Admiral Yamamoto our most competent enemy, with Doenitz a good second.

One boon Doenitz lacked which his enemies enjoyed was a close coöperation with air forces and scientists. It was the unbeatable combination of surface and air power and scientific research that enabled the British and American antisubmarine forces to win. Quantity also entered into it; "more and better of everything" — more and better escorts, more and better planes, better training, improved and vastly more numerous weapons, finally smothered the U-boats. But let us never forget that the initial successes and surprises effected by the U-boats fell not far short of rendering Germany invincible on the seas, while her armies were carrying everything before them on the continent of Europe.

2. *Last Actions in the Pacific, 10 July–15 August*

In Admiral Nimitz's plan of 15 May 1945, Admiral Halsey's Third Fleet was given the mission to "attack Japanese naval and air forces, shipping, shipyards and coastal objectives," as well as to "cover and support Ryukyus forces." On 1 July, after organized resistance on Okinawa had ceased, Task Force 38 sortied from Leyte Gulf to operate close to Japan; and there it stayed until Japan surrendered. The first strikes against Tokyo took place on 10 July. These took the Japanese by surprise, and surprised our pilots too, since they encountered no opposition from the air, very little antiaircraft fire, and grounded planes were well hidden and cunningly camouflaged. For the Japanese were husbanding aircraft to be used in mass kamikaze attacks on the amphibious assault on Kyushu which never came off, thanks to the atomic bomb.

On 14 and 15 July TF 38 planes struck hitherto untouched targets in Honshu and Hokkaido. They completely disrupted the Aomori-Hakodate car ferry system, which carried the coal trade across Tsugaru Strait.

Simultaneously with the air strikes, and for the first time, a naval gunfire force bombarded a major installation within the home islands of Japan. This was the iron works at Kamaishi, one of the seven plants of the Japan Iron Company. Rear Admiral John F. Shafroth commanded the bombardment unit, which comprised battleships *South Dakota, Indiana* and *Massachusetts*, two heavy cruisers and nine destroyers. This bombardment caused a loss of the equivalent of two and one half months of coke production and one month of pig iron production.

On 16 July another task unit under Rear Admiral Oscar Badger, comprising battleships *Iowa, Missouri* and *Wisconsin*, two light cruisers and eight destroyers, bombarded the Nihon Steel Company and the Wanishi Ironworks at Muroran, Hokkaido. This was conducted at exceedingly long range, around midnight, in a heavy overcast and rain which precluded plane spot or illumination. A record number of 16-inch shell was expended. Astern of Admiral Badger's unit steamed H.M.S. *King George V* and two British destroyers, to bombard a plant about eight miles north of the city. The damage resulting from this bombardment cannot be isolated from what was inflicted by B–29s in June and again on 19 July; but the cumulative effect was to cut production almost to zero, and to interrupt rail service, electricity and water supply.

By the end of July the Japanese surface and air navies were knocked out or impotent; but, just as German U-boats swarmed into the Western Atlantic up to the very end of the war, so Japanese submarines continued active in the Western Pacific, and they were much more successful than the U-boats.

The final Japanese naval offensive comprised six I-boats, each carrying six *kaiten* one-man midget submarines, better known as the "human torpedoes." A *kaiten* from *I-53* on 24 July sank destroyer escort *Underhill* when escorting a convoy, with a loss of 112 officers and men. Most disastrous was the loss of heavy cruiser *Indianapolis* (Captain Charles B. McVay), when steaming unescorted across the Philippine Sea to join a training unit off Leyte Gulf. Shortly before midnight 29 July she was torpedoed and sunk by *I-58*. Out of 1199 men on board, some 800 got into the water or into life rafts alive; but, owing to carelessness on the part of authorities ashore, the nonarrival of the cruiser was not noted; the report of an Army aircraft pilot who saw Very lights fired from Captain McVay's life rafts was neglected; and an intercepted contact report from the I-boat's skipper to Tokyo was dismissed as Japanese boasting. The floating survivors were sighted by a Navy plane 84 hours after their ship had gone down, and only 316 were rescued alive.

From this tale of routine stupidity and unnecessary suffering it is pleasant to return to the big carriers. Probably the largest logistics operation ever performed on the high seas was the refueling and replenishment of TF 38 on 21-22 July, along lat. 30° N and between longs. 147° and 142° E. Rear Admiral Beary's floating service force provided the flattops and their screen with 6369 tons of ammunition, 379,157 barrels of fuel oil, 1635 tons of stores and provisions, 99 replacement aircraft and 412 replacements of officers and men.

Replenishment completed 23 July, TF 38 proceeded to launching points for entering the Inland Sea. These strikes, delivered on 24 and 28 July, were among the heaviest of the war and the most destructive of shipping. At Kure and Kobe most of the heavy ships still left to the Imperial Navy were moored in coves and difficult of access to bombers, which nevertheless scored heavily on warships that had been slugging it out with the United States Navy since 1942. Battleships *Haruna*, *Ise* and *Hyuga*, veterans of numerous fights, and battle-scarred heavy cruisers *Tone* and *Aoba*,

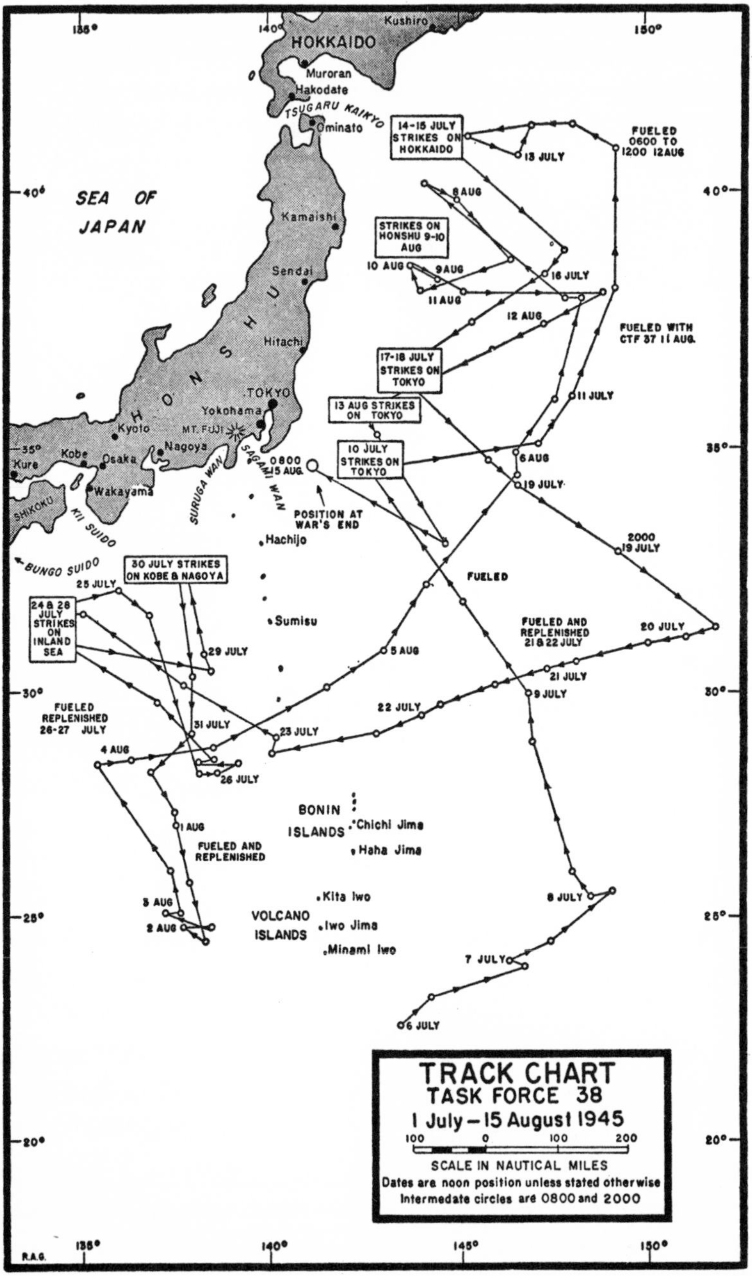

TRACK CHART
TASK FORCE 38
1 July—15 August 1945
SCALE IN NAUTICAL MILES
Dates are noon position unless stated otherwise
Intermedate circles are 0800 and 2000
HOKKAIDO
Kushiro
Muroran
Hakodate
TSUGARU KAIKYO
Ominato
SEA OF JAPAN
Kamaishi
Sendai
HONSHU
Hitachi
TOKYO
Yokohama
MT. FUJI
Kyoto
Nagoya
Kobe
Osaka
Kure
Wakayama
SHIKOKU
KII SUIDO
BUNGO SUIDO
SURUGA WAN
SAGAMI WAN
Hachijo
Sumisu
BONIN ISLANDS
Chichi Jima
Haha Jima
VOLCANO ISLANDS
Kita Iwo
Iwo Jima
Minami Iwo
14-15 JULY STRIKES ON HOKKAIDO
13 JULY
FUELED 0600 TO 1200 12AUG
STRIKES ON HONSHU 9-10 AUG
8 AUG
10 AUG
9AUG
11 AUG
16 JULY
12 AUG
FUELED WITH CTF 37 11 AUG.
17-18 JULY STRIKES ON TOKYO
13 AUG STRIKES ON TOKYO
11 JULY
10 JULY STRIKES ON TOKYO
0800 15 AUG.
POSITION AT WAR'S END
6 AUG
19 JULY
2000 19 JULY
FUELED
30 JULY STRIKES ON KOBE & NAGOYA
25 JULY
24 & 28 JULY STRIKES ON INLAND SEA
29 JULY
5 AUG
FUELED AND REPLENISHED 21 & 22 JULY
20 JULY
21 JULY
9 JULY
22 JULY
FUELED REPLENISHED 26-27 JULY
31 JULY
23 JULY
4 AUG
26 JULY
1 AUG
FUELED AND REPLENISHED
3 AUG
2 AUG
8 JULY
7 JULY
6 JULY
R.A.G.

were now so heavily damaged that they settled on the bottom and were abandoned. Strikes on the new aircraft carriers *Amagi* and *Katsuragi*, and on *Ryuho*, put them out of business.

In mid-forenoon watch 15 August, Admiral Halsey received orders from Cincpac ordering the Navy to "cease all offensive operations against Japan." Commander Third Fleet then broke his four-starred admiral's flag and celebrated the end of the fighting by ordering flagship *Missouri* to blow her whistle and sound her siren for a full minute, at 1100. Yet, even while this informal paean of victory was sounding and starry flags were blossoming on every flag officer's ship, a number of enemy planes, whose pilots had not been ordered to cease fire, approached to attack TF 38. All were shot down or driven off by Combat Air Patrol.

The fighting ended so abruptly that peace was difficult to accept, and the Allied Navies in Japanese waters took no chance of the surrender being a ruse. Air search, antisubmarine patrol and C.A.P. continued on wartime basis, and every ship maintained full defensive alert until 2 September, when the formal surrender was signed on board battleship *Missouri*.

3. *The Atomic Bombs, 6–9 August*

The Koiso cabinet, which had replaced General Tojo's as a result of the loss of Saipan, was itself replaced 7 April 1945 by Baron Suzuki's cabinet, with Shigenori Togo as foreign minister. Both men were advocates of a speedy peace, and both knew that the Emperor expected them to bring it about; but as they held office at the sufferance of the Army, they had to continue making die-hard pronouncements.

The American experimental atomic bomb was exploded on 16 July in New Mexico, at a time when President Truman, Winston

Churchill and the Combined Chiefs of Staff were meeting in Potsdam. The use of the bomb against Japan as soon as possible, without warning, had already been recommended to the President by a committee of high officials and top atomic scientists. And on 25 July the President issued the directive.

In the meantime, Suzuki and other Japanese statesmen were playing with the idiotic notion of getting out of the war through the friendly mediation of Stalin, who had already decided to go in on the other side. Anything to save face! Everyone in the government knew that the war was lost, and that the B–29s were capable of wiping out one Japanese city after another. But nothing was done to prepare the people for the inevitable. On the contrary, Suzuki issued a statement that the loss of Okinawa "improved Japan's strategic position," and dealt America a "severe spiritual blow." "Peace agitators" were threatened in official broadcasts, efforts were made to increase war production, a program of building underground shelters was announced to protect the people from air bombing, and of stockpiling food to render them self-sufficient.

All these foolish calculations were upset by the Potsdam Declaration of 26 July by Truman, Churchill and Chiang Kai-shek, stating conditions under which Japan could end the war. The essential ones were: surrender of all conquests made since 1895; Japan not to be "destroyed as a nation, but stern justice shall be meted out to all war criminals"; "Freedom of speech, of religion, and of thought, as well as respect for the fundamental human rights, shall be established"; Allied occupation of Japan, to be withdrawn "as soon as these objectives have been accomplished, and there has been established a peacefully inclined and responsible government." The Japanese government was called upon "to proclaim now the unconditional surrender of all Japanese armed forces," the alternative being "prompt and utter destruction."

Still, the Suzuki government could not bring itself to face facts and accept the inevitable. One little word at that point could have averted the horror of Hiroshima, since the President's directive to use the bomb could not be executed for at least a week, and at any time could be countermanded. Truman and Secretary Byrnes listened eagerly for that word; but all that came from Suzuki was a silly statement that the Potsdam Declaration was unworthy of notice.

B–29 "Enola Gay" was commanded by Colonel Paul W. Tibbets; Captain William S. Parsons, a naval ordnance expert, went along to make the final adjustments to the bomb. She took off from Tinian at 0245 August 6 and toggled out the bomb over Hiroshima, headquarters of the Japanese Second Army, at 0915.

A new chapter then opened in the history of warfare, and a new challenge to mankind to avert his own destruction.

4. *The Surrender of Japan, 10 August–2 September*

Even after the second atomic bomb was exploded over Nagasaki on 9 August, the same day that Russia declared war on Japan, members of the Imperial Conference, the highest authority in Japan, tried to evade surrender. Admiral Toyoda, the Navy chief of staff; General Umezu, the Army chief of staff; and General Anami, the war minister, all insisted not only that guarantees be given of the Emperor's inviolability, but that there be no military occupation of Japan, no disarming of Japanese troops overseas, no trial of war criminals except by Japanese courts. Foreign Minister Togo pointed out that they could never get Allied consent to such conditions. At a second meeting of the Conference, which lasted until 0230 August 10, the Emperor intervened. He it was who decided, provisionally, to surrender according to the Potsdam terms. That decision was sent to the Allied governments via Switzerland at 0700, and was accepted by them.

Even then there was shuffling of feet among the war lords

in Tokyo; understandably it was a terrible shock to military men with their long tradition of victory to accept defeat short of annihilation. At a third Imperial Conference, opened at 1100 August 14, Anami, Umezu and Toyoda urged the Emperor to fight "one last battle" for the defense of Japan itself, to save national honor. The Emperor then spoke the thoughts that he had long held. Continuing the war would merely result in additional destruction; the nation would be reduced to ashes. The Allied reply to his note of 0700 August 10 indicating positively that he was to continue to reign, showed evidence "of the peaceful and friendly intentions of the enemy." It was the Imperial desire that his ministers of state accept it. They must at once prepare an Imperial rescript broadcasting this decision directly to the people.

The deed was done. At 1449 August 14 (East Longitude date) Radio Tokyo flashed the Emperor's decision around the world. The official notification reached President Truman at 1550 August 14, West Longitude date. He announced it from the White House at 1900 the same day, and declared a two-day holiday of jubilation.

It was a very near thing. That night a military plot to seize the Emperor and impound his recording of the Imperial rescript (which was to be broadcast on the 15th) was narrowly averted. Attempts were made to assassinate Suzuki and others. But the Emperor's message to his people went out in the morning. It ended on the dignified note, "We charge you, Our loyal subjects, to carry out faithfully Our will." Even after the Emperor's will had been made public, it was touch and go whether the Japanese actually would surrender. Hirohito had to send members of the Imperial family to the principal Army commands to ensure compliance. Prince Takamatsu was just in time to make the Atsugi airfield available for the first occupation forces on 26 August, and to keep the kamikazes grounded — they were boasting that they would crash *Missouri* when she entered Tokyo Bay. If these elements had had their way, the war would have been resumed with the Allies feeling that the Japanese were hoplessly treacherous, and with a savagery on both sides that is painful to contemplate.

When these facts and events of the Japanese surrender are known and weighed, it will become evident that the atomic bomb was the keystone of a very fragile arch. Certainly the war would have gone on, and God knows for how long, if the bomb had not been dropped. It has been argued that the maritime blockade would have strangled Japanese economy, and that the B–29s and naval bombardment would have destroyed her principal cities and forced a surrender without benefit of atomic fission. I do not think that anyone acquainted with the admirable discipline and tenacity of the Japanese people can believe this. If their Emperor had told them to fight to the last man, they would have fought to the last man, suffering far, far greater losses and injuries than those inflicted by the atomic bombs.

The probable effects of the projected invasions of Kyushu and Honshu (Operations OLYMPIC and CORONET) in the fall and winter of 1945-1946, and of a desperate hand-to-hand, place-to-place defense of Japan, stagger the imagination. It is simply not true that Japan had no military capability left in mid-August. She had plenty of ammunition; the United States Army after the war found thousands of tons holed up in Hokkaido alone. She had over a million men under arms in the home islands. Although 2550 kamikaze planes had been expended, 5350 were still left, together with as many more ready for orthodox use, and 5000 young men were training for the Kamikaze Corps. All aircraft were to be dispersed on small grass strips in Kyushu, Shikoku and western Honshu, and in underground hangars and caves, to be readied for kamikaze crashes on the Allied amphibious forces invading Kyushu. It requires no prophetic sense to foresee the horrible losses that would have been inflicted on our invading forces, even before they got ashore. After accepting these losses there would have been protracted battles on Japanese soil, which would have cost each side very many more lives, and created a bitterness which even time could hardly have healed. Moreover, Russia would have been a full partner in this final campaign, Japan would have been divided like Germany, and so completely prostrate that the Communists would have had little difficulty in taking over the country.

President Truman announced that General of the Army Douglas MacArthur would be Supreme Commander of the Allied Powers (SCAP) for the surrender and occupation of Japan. This set in motion the wheels of an occupation which rolled smoothly but not quite so fast as that of Germany. For the Imperial government was intact and the Japanese Army, still undefeated, was in a position to resist any premature attempt of the Allies to take over. General MacArthur, who understood the situation perfectly, was responsible for the sequence of events which gave time for the Emperor's commands to reach all his armed forces, as well as time for his own command to prepare the first landings of occupation troops. On 15 August the General directed the Japanese government by radio to order "immediate cessation of hostilities" and to send "a competent representative" by air to Manila to receive instructions for the formal surrender and the reception of occupation forces. An Imperial order went out at 1600 16 August "to the entire Armed Forces to cease fire immediately." This, it will be observed, was thirty hours after Admiral Nimitz had ordered all United States forces to cease fire.

Admiral Halsey decided to anchor major units of Third Fleet in Sagami Wan, under the shadow of Mount Fuji. His own flagship *Missouri*, H.M.S. *Duke of York* wearing the flag of Admiral Sir Bruce Fraser RN, and other ships of Third Fleet and of the British Pacific Fleet, entered Sagami Wan 27 August and proceeded to selected berths. From the anchorage, the sun appeared that evening to set directly into the crater of Mount Fuji. It seemed symbolic — a dismal setting of that sun which had risen triumphant over Oahu on 7 December 1941.

On 29 August, Admiral Nimitz arrived by air, and next morning landings began at the Japanese forts guarding the entrance to Tokyo Bay and at Yokosuka naval base. General MacArthur arrived by air at Atsugi airfield the same day, and set off for Yokohama, where final arrangements were made for the formal signing of the instrument of surrender, at 0900 September 2. General MacArthur, having obtained his wish, the prior occupation of Japan, yielded to Admiral Nimitz the choice of place. Battleship *Missouri* (Captain S. S. Murray), became the scene of the ceremony. She anchored in Tokyo Bay about four and a half miles from Commodore Perry's old anchorage, and on a bulkhead overlooking the ceremony was displayed the 31-star flag that Perry carried into Tokyo Bay in 1853. There were now anchored in that Bay 258 warships of all types from battleship to beaching craft, representing the Allied nations which had been at war with Japan. Most of the aircraft carriers remained outside in order to launch planes at the appropriate moment of this "V-J Day."

Sunday, 2 September, dawned with scattered clouds that dissipated during the morning. The "Mighty Mo," as the bluejackets called her, was especially rigged for the occasion. At Morning Colors the flag that had flown over the Capitol in Washington on 7 December 1941 was raised on the battleship's flagstaff. Destroyer *Buchanan* closed her starboard side at 0803 to deliver high-ranking officers and Allied representatives. When Fleet Admiral Nimitz came on board at 0805, his five-starred flag was broken at the main, Admiral Halsey having shifted his four-starred flag to *Iowa*. General MacArthur's flag was promptly broken alongside that of Admiral Nimitz.

At 0856 the Japanese delegation, lifted from Yokohama in destroyer *Lansdowne*, mounted the starboard gangway. They were headed by the Foreign Minister, Mamoru Shigemitsu, followed by

General Umezu, the diehard chief of the Army general staff, to sign on behalf of Imperial General Headquarters; Rear Admiral S. Tomioka, chief Navy planner for Imperial General Headquarters, and other representatives of the Foreign Office, the Army and the Navy. The civilians were in formal morning dress with top hats, in contrast to the ill-fitting uniforms of the military members and to the khaki uniforms with open-neck shirts worn by the United States Navy and Army officers. Sideboys were stationed and the Japanese delegation were piped on board. As they arrived on deck, their faces expressing no emotion, complete silence fell over the assembled multitude.

Immediately abaft the table on which the documents lay stood representatives of the Allied Nations to sign for their respective governments. On their right and under *Missouri's* No. 2 turret stood a score of flag and general officers of the United States who had taken a leading part in the war against Japan. The atmosphere was frigid. The Japanese, performing an act unprecedented in their country's history, preserved their dignity. After three or four minutes had elapsed, General MacArthur appeared with Admirals Nimitz and Halsey. The General took his place before the microphones to open the ceremony. At his side were Lieutenant General Jonathan M. Wainwright USA, who had surrendered the Philippines in 1942, and Lieutenant General Sir Arthur E. Percival, who had surrendered Singapore the same year. Both had been flown from prison camps in Manchuria. General MacArthur made a short speech stating the purpose of the occasion, concluding with a ringing expression of hope for the future: —

> It is my earnest hope — indeed the hope of all mankind — that from this solemn occasion a better world shall emerge out of the blood and carnage of the past, a world founded upon faith and understanding, a world dedicated to the dignity of man and the fulfillment of his most cherished wish for freedom, tolerance and justice.

Mr. Kase of the Foreign office was profoundly moved by the General's words. It transformed the battleship's quarterdeck, he recorded, "into an altar of peace."

Appropriately, it was Foreign Minister Shigemitsu who, after a year's quiet working for peace, first signed the instrument of surrender at 0904 September 2, officially ending the war. It had lasted exactly 1364 days, 5 hours and 44 minutes from the attack on Pearl Harbor. General Umezu, who in contrast to Shigemitsu had held out for fighting to the last, signed next for Japan. General MacArthur signed the acceptance for all Allied powers; then came the individual signers for each of the nations that had been at war with Japan: the United States (for which Admiral Nimitz signed), Great Britain, Russia, Australia, Canada, France, The Netherlands, and New Zealand.

After all had signed, General MacArthur spoke a final word:

"Let us pray that peace be now restored to the world and that God will preserve it always."

As the formalities came to an end, at 0925, the sun broke through, and a flight of 450 carrier aircraft, together with several hundred of the Army Air Force, swept over *Missouri* and her sister ships.

That Sunday evening Admirals Halsey and Wilkinson attended an impressive sunset ceremony held by Admiral Sir Bruce Fraser on board flagship H.M.S. *Duke of York*, anchored not far from *Missouri.* The flags of all Allies, flying from the signal yards, were handsomely lowered in unison as massed bands from all British ships present played the music of Ellerton's sunset hymn: —

The day thou gavest, Lord, is ended,
The darkness falls at thy behest;
To thee our morning hymns ascended,
Thy praise shall sanctify our rest.

So be it, Lord; thy throne shall never,
  Like earth's proud empires, pass away:
Thy kingdom stands, and grows for ever,
  Till all thy creatures own thy sway.

Nothing could have been more appropriate to the occasion than this Sunday evening hymn to the "Author of Peace and Lover of Concord." The familiar words and music, floating over the now calm waters of the Bay to American and British bluejackets, touched the mystic chords of memory, reminding all hands of the faith that had sustained them through travail and sacrifice. It made sailors feel that their Navies had achieved something more than a military victory.

They were right. If victory over Japan meant anything beyond a change in the balance of power, it meant that eternal values and immutable principles, which had come down to us from ancient Hellas, had been reaffirmed and reëstablished. Often these principles are broken, often these values are lost to sight when people are struggling for power or survival; but to them man must return, and does return, in order to enjoy his Creator's greatest gifts — life, liberty and the pursuit of happiness.

CHAPTER XVIII

Conclusion

IN CONCLUSION, your historian may be allowed a few estimates and remarks on how the United States Navy conducted itself in this, the greatest of all wars in which it has ever been engaged.

On the whole, gloriously. But certain faults and lapses must be remembered, if we are to maintain high standards and meet the challenge of the atomic age. The Navy was caught unprepared mentally for the attack on Pearl Harbor, largely owing to routine and lack of imagination in the higher echelons. It was caught unprepared, both materially and technically, to cope with the U-boat menace — despite benefit of British experience in over two years of antisubmarine war. The Navy's fighter planes and torpedo-bombers were inferior to those of the Japanese, whose night-fighting tactics were superior to ours until mid-1943. Although certain strategists in the United States Navy anticipated the use of aircraft carriers to project striking power deep into enemy-held waters, too many envisaged this war as a succession of Jutlands, to be decided by big guns on battleships. Consequently our gunfire became highly effective, but warships greater than destroyers had no torpedo tubes. Torpedoes themselves underwent no development between wars, and the testing of those we had was so inefficient and misleading that United States submarines long had the mortification of making hit after hit with no explosion to follow. The destroyers, fortunately, retained their torpedoes, but the tactical employment of destroyers for surface action was inferior to that of the Japanese prior to the Battle of Vella Gulf in 1943.

Although the *Iowa* class battleships never had a chance at a long-range gunfire battle (and what a beauty there would have been off San Bernardino Strait had Halsey released Lee in time!) the accuracy and efficiency of our naval gunfire was a great asset in the war. Gunfire support almost opened a new dimension to amphibious operations. Antiaircraft fire, helped by the proximity-fused shell, became so deadly that the Japanese were forced to adopt suicide tactics. Although aircraft bombing tolled the bell for long-range battleship action, naval gunfire will always be wanted to cover amphibious landings, which are likely to be necessary as long as there is war.

The United States Navy quickly adopted and developed the English invention of radar; but it was not until well into 1943 that officers generally appreciated its capabilities and limitations, and made best use of it. Nevertheless, the prior possession of radar turned out to be a great asset.

In antisubmarine warfare it was long before the United States Navy caught up with its teacher, the Royal Navy of Great Britain. But we made full use both of British experience and the contributions of American scientists and mathematicians. This was only the second war that the Navy fought as part of a coalition, and its relations with the British and Royal Canadian Navies were far closer and more effective than in World War I. In the Pacific the United States Navy, owing to its overwhelming strength, called the tune, but was loyally followed by the smaller Navies of three British Commonwealths.

Admiral Ernest J. King was the Navy's principal architect of victory. A stern sailor of commanding presence, vast sea-knowledge, and keen strategic sense, he was so insistent on maintaining the independence of the Navy, not only from our great Ally but from the Army, that he seemed at times to be anti-British and anti-Army. Neither was true; but King's one mistaken idea was his steady opposition to "mixed groups" from different Navies in the same task force; an idea strengthened by the unfortunate experience of the

ABDA command. Mixed groups were of necessity adopted on the convoy routes, with American, Canadian and even an occasional Free French or Polish destroyer in the same escort unit, and they worked well; whilst in the Pacific, ships of the Royal Australian and New Zealand Navies operated perfectly with those of the United States. All three services of the same country worked well on one team in forward areas where the real fighting went on. The in-fighting between services and the disputes between British and American representatives were largely confined to Washington, London or wherever the Combined Chiefs of Staff met.

We may, however, concede to Admiral King a few prejudices, for he was undoubtedly the best naval strategist and organizer in our history. His insistence on limited offensives in the Pacific to keep the Japanese off balance, his successful efforts to provide more and more escorts for convoys, his promotion of the escort carrier antisubmarine groups, his constant backing of General Marshall to produce a firm date for Operation OVERLORD from the reluctant British; his insistence on the dual approach to Japan, are but a few of the many decisions that prove his genius. King's strategy for the final defeat of Japan — the Formosa and China Coast approach, rather than the Luzon-Okinawa route — was overruled; but may well, in the long run, have been better than MacArthur's, which was adopted. King was also defeated in his many attempts to interest the Royal Navy in a Southeast Asia comeback; and in this he was right. The liberation of Malaya before the war's end would have spared the British Empire a long battle with local Communists and would have provided at least a more orderly transfer of sovereignty in the Netherlands East Indies.

After King, Nimitz was our greatest naval strategist and leader, and, as Cincpac-Cincpoa, he had, after King, the biggest responsibility. Nimitz engineered, as it were, the Battles of the Coral Sea and Midway; patiently but stubbornly he held out for the dual approach to Japan. He proposed the bold plan to go right into Kwajalein after securing the Gilberts, and he put it across, contrary to the advice of others. He made only two possible mistakes in the war — detaching Admiral Kinkaid prematurely from his South Pacific task force, and rejecting Halsey's proposal that Peleliu be bypassed. Nimitz probably inspired a greater personal loyalty than did any other admiral in the war. Every commanding officer, when his ship, no matter how small, put in at Pearl Harbor, was encouraged to call on Nimitz at the Cincpac-Cincpoa headquarters in Makalapa and express his views. Knowing that the finest test of a commanding officer is (in Churchill's words) "the quality of his effort," and that mistakes in battle are inevitable, Nimitz was slow to relieve any commanding officer who failed; he believed in the adage that every dog should be allowed two bites. It may be conceded that he allowed one bite too many to certain task force commanders before he relieved them; but it was fortunate for the cause that he allowed two bites to Kelly Turner, who turned out to be a practitioner of amphibious warfare second to none.

In the same web-footed class with Turner were Wilkinson and Barbey in the Pacific, and Hewitt and Kirk in the Atlantic and the Mediterranean. The last two, having to deal with high officers of the Royal Navy who were more used to ordering subordinates than conferring with equals, had to double as diplomats. Ingersoll and Ingram became very competent commanders of the Atlantic Fleet. There was an immense amount of talent in the lower echelons of flag rank. Rear Admirals Hall, Deyo, Conolly, Joy, Fechteler, Blandy, Low, McMorris, Merrill, Denebrink, DuBose, to mention only a few, were fully equal to exercising even higher commands which seniority denied to them. Of these who were killed in action or as a result of it, we remember Kidd, Scott, Callaghan, Mullinnix, Chandler, and Royal.

When we come to the admirals who commanded at sea, and who directed a great battle, there was no one to equal Spruance. Always calm, always at peace with himself, Spruance had that ability which marks the great captain to make correct estimates and the right decisions in a fluid battle situation. He was bold and aggressive when the occasion demanded offensive tactics; cautious when pushing his luck too far might have lost the fruits of victory. Spruance in the Battle of Midway, with his instinct for the enemy's jugular vein — his carriers — deciding to launch planes at the right moment, retiring at night when further persistence would have risked an encounter with Yamamoto's massed gunfire, was superb; there is no other word for it. Spruance in the Battle of the Philippine Sea, overriding Mitscher the carrier expert in letting the enemy planes come at him instead of going in search of them, won the second most decisive battle of the Pacific war. And, off Okinawa, Spruance never faltered in face of the destruction wrought by the kamikazes. It is regrettable that, owing to Spruance's innate modesty and his refusal to create an image of himself in the public eye, he was never properly appreciated.

Halsey, the public's favorite in the Navy, will always remain a controversial figure, but none can deny that he was a great leader; one with the true "Nelson touch." His appointment as Commander South Pacific Force at the darkest moment of the Guadalcanal campaign lifted the hearts of every officer and bluejacket. He hated the enemy with an unholy wrath, and turned that feeling into a grim determination by all hands to hit hard, again and again, and win. His proposal to step up the Leyte operation by two months was a stroke of strategic genius which undoubtedly shortened the Pacific war. Unfortunately, in his efforts to build public morale in America and Australia, Halsey did what Spruance refused to do — built up an image of himself as an exponent of Danton's famous principle, "Audacity, more audacity, always audacity." That was the real reason for his fumble in the Battle for Leyte Gulf. For his inspiring leadership in 1942-1943, his generosity to others, his capacity for choosing the right men for his staff, Halsey well earned his five stars, and his place among the Navy's immortals.

Admiral Kinkaid, after being allowed one "bite" — the loss of *Hornet* in the Battle of the Santa Cruz Islands — rose to be one of our greatest seamen as Commander Seventh Fleet. He had a difficult role to play as head of "MacArthur's Navy," since that great general, for all his genius, at first imperfectly understood the limitation and capabilities of sea power. But he learned from Kinkaid. In the Battle for Leyte Gulf Kinkaid had an unfortunate position in the chain of command, under MacArthur but unable to control Halsey; within these limitations he acquitted himself very well, and is entitled to no small part of the glory reaped by Oldendorf in Surigao Strait and Clifton Sprague off Samar.

In a special category of excellence are the flag officers of fleet carriers, with Mitscher *facile princeps*. Under him, McCain, Reeves, Bogan, Clark, Frederick Sherman and Radford showed qualities of greatness; and the Battle off Samar proved that the escort carrier admirals, the two Spragues and Felix Stump, were in no way inferior. And we must not forget two great chiefs of staff, Burke and Carney.

Above all these sailors was the Commander in Chief, Franklin D. Roosevelt — a remarkable leader indeed. Unlike Winston Churchill, Roosevelt never imagined himself to be a strategist. In general he followed the advice of the Joint Chiefs of Staff, which included King, Marshall, and his own chief of staff, wise old Admiral Leahy. Thrice at least he went over their heads — refusing to redeploy American forces into the Pacific in 1942, insisting that Guadalcanal must be reinforced and held at all costs, and inviting a British fleet to participate in the Okinawa campaign. He also threw his influence in favor of MacArthur's desire to liberate Leyte and Luzon against the Navy's wish to bypass them. He was a tower of strength to Marshall, King and Eisenhower against insistent British pressure to postpone OVERLORD and shift DRAGOON from Marseilles to Trieste. The Navy was his favorite service — I heard him once, in true regal style, refer to it as "my Navy" — and he did his utmost to build it up and improve its efficiency both before and during the war.

In operations, there were several things that the Navy did superlatively well. Instigated by the Marines, it studied and developed the technique of amphibious warfare well before 1939. In this important branch the United States Navy was behind the Japanese but ahead of the Royal Navy when war broke; but the Japanese, thrown on the defensive, had no chance to practise amphibious warfare after the Java campaign, and the Royal Navy, thanks largely to Mountbatten's combined operations unit, caught up with us in Sicily and Normandy. In carrier warfare the United States Navy was supreme, because it successfully resisted (as the Royal Navy had not) the efforts of the Army to obtain control over all combatant planes, and because admirals like Mitscher and McCain made constant efforts to improve carrier tactics and profited by early mistakes. In order to service the fast carrier forces and enable them to keep the sea, fighting, for many weeks on end, the Navy devised the at-sea logistics system, one of the principal instruments of victory. For this, credit is primarily due to Admirals Calhoun and Beary, and Commodores Gray and Carter.

The planning of operations, too, was very well done, even though it often had to be done in a hurry. The supreme planning job of the war was that for Operation NEPTUNE-OVERLORD, in which British and Americans both took part; but for purely United States Navy operations, the top planners — "Savvy" Cooke on King's staff and Forrest Sherman on Nimitz's — deserve a special accolade. Kelly Turner was an amazingly meticulous, thorough and accurate planner for his own amphibious operations, and oversaw every detail himself. Once Turner gave the word "Land the Landing Force!" everything went like clockwork; one felt that anybody could have done it, not knowing the immense amount of skill and thought which had gone into the plan. Wilkinson was Turner's peer in the Central, as Barbey in the Southwest Pacific. Foul-ups (which the Navy called by a harsher word) had always been expected in amphibious operations, even when uncontested, and it was a tribute to our new tactics that the Japanese finally decided not to contest these operations, but to hole up and sell their lives dear.

One feels particular admiration for the officers of the destroyers, the "tin cans" which operated in every theater of the war. They not only had to be first-rate seamen and ship handlers, but men of science to assimilate the new techniques of antisubmarine warfare and air defense. Although overwhelmed with paper work, these young officers maintained something of the port and swagger of the oldtime frigate skipper; they were good for a lark ashore as for a fight at sea. In every theater and every kind of operation, as we have abundantly seen, destroyers were the indispensable component. Whether in convoy duty or in a hunter-killer group in the Atlantic, or supporting amphibious operations, delivering torpedo attacks in a night battle, or taking the rap from kamikazes off Okinawa, the men who manned these ships proved themselves to be the most versatile and courageous of sea warriors. It is no wonder that so many have risen to high command in the new Navy.

Equally admirable were the submariners, an even more scientific and specialized branch of the Navy, and their great leaders, Admirals Lockwood, Christie and Fife. Owing to wartime secrecy, they seldom received public credit; this was the true "silent service." The submarines not only dogged the Japanese merchant navy to its death and sank more than their share of warships; in both oceans they scouted in advance of amphibious landings, and in the Pacific they maintained contact with Philippine patriots. The submarines lost an even greater proportion of their numbers than did the brave naval aviators. And the "boats" named after fishes, whose exploits we have told all too briefly, were immediate ancestors of the nuclear-powered, polaris-armed underwater warships which have become the prime protectors of the free world.

Let us also remember the "small boys" — the gunboats, minecraft, destroyer escorts, PTs, beaching and other lettered craft, even the lowly "yard-birds" and small cutters. These, largely officered by reservists, were forced to perform functions and make long voyages for which they had not been designed. The production of thousands of these in wartime, the training of them at special schools set up for that purpose, the operation of them under the most hazardous conditions, are beyond praise; but we may not forget that when the war involved us the Navy was woefully deficient in escorts and small craft, and should resolve never to be caught short again.

On 1 July 1940 the Navy had only 13,162 officers and 744,824 enlisted men; on 31 August 1945 it had 316,675 officers and 2,935,695 enlisted men. Similar figures for the Marine Corps are 1819 officers and 26,545 enlisted men in 1940; 36,851 officers and 427,017 enlisted men at the end of the war.[2] In spite of this immense dilution of all ranks and ratings, the Navy did a superlative job in making fighting sailors out of young Americans fresh out of school, farm, or minor shore jobs, teaching them the manifold skills necessary to operate and fight a modern warship, pride in their ships, courage to face the most hideous form of death, by burning.

The vastly expanded American merchant marine, too, deserves high praise for its world-wide operations, which were indispensable to support of the Navy, the Army, and our Allies. Merchant mariners and the Naval Armed Guards on the ships showed exemplary courage in convoy duty, in actions with German raiders and U-boats, and in replenishing the Fleet off Okinawa under constant threat of kamikaze attack. We must never forget that, since one of the main functions of a navy is to protect trade and communications both in peace and in war, it can never function properly without a strong and efficient merchant marine, or without the know-how of master mariners and seamen.

So, thanks to all; and, no matter what the atomic age brings, America will always need sailors and ships and shipborne aircraft to preserve her liberty, her communications with the free world, even her existence. If the deadly missiles with their apocalyptic warheads are ever launched at America, the Navy will still be out on blue water fighting for her, and the nation or alliance that survives will be the one that retains command of the oceans.

[2] To these should be added 8399 women officers and 73,685 enlisted women (the "Waves"); 813 officers and 17,350 enlisted women Marines, and 10,968 nurses, all at the end of the war.

Index

Names of Combatant Ships in SMALL CAPITALS
Names of Lettered Combatant Ships such as LSTs, and of Merchant Ships, in *Italics*

F

I

O

T

U

Example

Ben purchases a home on January 1, 2008, and rents it for 2 years. On January 1, 2010, Ben moves into the home and uses it as his personal residence from January 1, 2010, through December 31, 2012. He moves out of the home on December 31, 2012, and rents the home for another year, from January 1, 2013, through December 31, 2013, at which time the home is sold. The amount of gain associated with the rental of the home for the period of January 1, 2009, through December 31, 2009, is a period of nonqualified use and will not qualify for the gain exclusion. However, all of the gain associated with the rental of the home from January 1, 2008, through December 31, 2008, will qualify for the exclusion, since this period of rental occurred before January 1, 2009. In addition, all of the gain related to the rental of the home from January 1, 2013, through December 31, 2013, will also qualify for the gain exclusion since this rental occurred within the 5-year period ending on the date the property was sold, and the rental occurred after the last date Ben used the property as his principal residence. If Ben's gain on the sale of the home was $270,000, $45,000 of the gain would not qualify for the exclusion [$270,000 × (12 months of nonqualified use ÷ 72 months of ownership of the property)]. Thus $225,000 of the gain would be excluded from income, and $45,000 of the gain would be subject to tax.

Depreciation after May 6, 1997. If you were entitled to take depreciation deductions because you used your home for business purposes or as rental property, you cannot exclude the part of your gain equal to any depreciation allowed or allowable as a deduction for periods after May 6, 1997. If you can show by adequate records or other evidence that the depreciation allowed was less than the amount allowable, then you may limit the amount of gain recognized to the depreciation allowed. See Publication 544 for more information.

TAXALERT

Explanation

As described earlier in the section *Periods of Nonqualified Use*, any gain taxable because of depreciation claimed on the property after May 6, 1997, is not taken into account in determining the gain allocated to nonqualified use. See *Example 1*.

Property used partly for business or rental. If you used property partly as a home and partly for business or to produce rental income, see Publication 523.

TAXALERT

A significant provision in the IRS regulations says that no allocation of gain is required where the personal and business portions of the property are within the same dwelling unit. Until those regulations were issued, many taxpayers had refrained from claiming a home office deduction out of concern that any gain allocable to the home office portion of their residence would not qualify for exclusion. IRS regulations now provide that all gain on a later sale of the residence will be eligible for exclusion except for depreciation adjustments for periods after May 6, 1997.

Example

You own a four-unit apartment house. You live in one unit and rent three units. You sell the apartment house for cash. Your records show the following:

Apartment house	
Cost	$80,000
Capital improvements	20,000
Subtotal	$100,000
Minus: Depreciation (on three rented units only)	(40,000)
Adjusted basis	$60,000
Selling price	$120,000
Selling expense	8,000

Because one-fourth of the apartment building is your home, you figure the gain on each portion of the property as follows:

	Personal (1/4)	Rental (3/4)
1) Selling price	$30,000	$90,000
2) Selling expense	(2,000)	(6,000)
3) Amount realized (adjusted sales price) [(1) minus (2)]	$28,000	$84,000
4) Basis (including improvements)	$25,000	$75,000
5) Depreciation	-0-	40,000
6) Adjusted basis [(4) minus (5)]	$25,000	$35,000
7) Gain [(3) minus (6)]	$3,000	$49,000
Next you figure out your taxable gain:		
8) Depreciation allowed/allowable	-0-	$40,000
9) Gain less depreciation [(7) minus (8)]	$3,000	$9,000
10) Maximum exclusion (prorated)	$62,500	$187,500
11) Gain excluded (lesser of 9, 10)	$3,000	$9,000
12) Taxable gain [(7) minus (11)]	-0-	$40,000

The gain of $40,000 on the three-fourths of the building that was rental property is subject to tax in the year of sale. This gain is reported on Form 4797, Gains and Losses from Sales or Exchanges of Assets Used in a Trade or Business and Involuntary Conversions. The gain on the one-fourth that was your home is excluded.

TAXSAVER

Improvements to rental property. If improvements have been made solely to rental units, their cost should be specifically allocated to the rental part of the property. This allocation will decrease the gain on the business portion of the property, which is taxable in the year of sale.

Keep detailed records of improvements. Be careful to specify whether the improvements were made exclusively to either the business or the personal portion of the residence, or whether they improved the residence as a whole.

Example

Jane Smith purchases a two-family house. The two units in the house are identical. Jane rents one out and uses the other as her personal residence. The house costs $80,000–$20,000 for the land and $60,000 ($30,000 per unit) for the building. Jane remodels the kitchen in the rental unit. The job costs $10,000, which is added to the basis of the rental unit, increasing it to $40,000. Once the unit is rented, depreciation may be claimed on this $40,000 basis.

When the property is sold, the selling price must be apportioned between the business and personal portions of the residence. If, at the time of sale, the adjusted basis of the rental unit, including the amount allocated to land, is $28,000, and if $60,000 of the selling price is allocated to the rental unit, there would be a taxable gain of $32,000. Without the $10,000 kitchen expense, the adjusted basis would be only $18,000, increasing the currently taxable gain to $42,000.

Explanation

The apportionment of the selling price between the business and personal portions of a house should be based on the relative fair market value of each portion. Substantial improvements made to each portion of the property should be considered in determining the amount of the selling price that is allocated to each part.

Consequently, the allocation of the sales price, as well as the allocation of the cost of the improvements, may affect the amount of gain to be deferred or taxed on the sale of property used partly as your principal home. Evidence to support a particular allocation of the sales price can include a real estate broker's appraisal or the negotiated terms of the sales contract.

Reporting the Sale

Do not report the 2011 sale of your main home on your tax return unless:

- You have a gain and do not qualify to exclude all of it,
- You have a gain and choose not to exclude it, or
- You have a loss and received Form 1099-S.

If you have any taxable gain on the sale of your main home that cannot be excluded, report the entire gain on Form 8949 and Schedule D (Form 1040). Report the sales price in column (e) and the cost basis in column (f) on Form 8949 and mark box (C). The gain is reported in column (h) of line 3 or line 10 of Schedule D, as short-term or long-term capital gain depending on how long you owned the home. If you qualify for an exclusion, show it on the line directly below the line on which you report the gain. Enter "Section 121 exclusion" in column (a) of that line on Form 8949 and show the amount of the exclusion in column (g) as a loss (in parentheses).

If you have a loss on the sale of your main home for which you received a Form 1099-S, you must report the loss on Form 8949 and Schedule D even though the loss is not deductible. Report the transaction on line 1 of Form 8949 and mark box (C). Complete columns (a) through (f) and enter the loss in column (g) as an adjustment to gain or loss.

If you used the home for business or to produce rental income, you may have to use Form 4797 to report the sale of the business or rental part (or the sale of the entire property if used entirely for business or rental). See *Business Use or Rental of Home* in Publication 523 and the Instructions for Form 4797.

Installment sale. Some sales are made under arrangements that provide for part or all of the selling price to be paid in a later year. These sales are called "installment sales." If you finance the buyer's purchase of your home yourself instead of having the buyer get a loan or mortgage from a bank, you probably have an installment sale. You may be able to report the part of the gain you cannot exclude on the installment basis.

Use Form 6252, Installment Sale Income, to report the sale. Enter your exclusion on line 15 of Form 6252.

Seller-financed mortgage. If you sell your home and hold a note, mortgage, or other financial agreement, the payments you receive in most cases consist of both interest and principal. You must separately report as interest income the interest you receive as part of each payment. If the buyer of your home uses the property as a main or second home, you must also report the name, address, and social security number (SSN) of the buyer on line 1 of Schedule B (Form 1040A or 1040). The buyer must give you his or her SSN, and you must give the buyer your SSN. Failure to meet these requirements may result in a $50 penalty for each failure. If either you or the buyer does not have and is not eligible to get an SSN, see *Social Security Number* in chapter 1.

More information. For more information on installment sales, see Publication 537, *Installment Sales*.

Special Situations

The situations that follow may affect your exclusion.

Sale of home acquired in a like-kind exchange. You cannot claim the exclusion if:

- You acquired your home in a like-kind exchange (also known as a section 1031 exchange) or your basis in your home is determined by reference to the basis of the home in the hands of the person who acquired the property in a like-kind exchange (for example, you received the home from that person as a gift), and
- You sold the home during the 5-year period beginning with the date your home was acquired in the like-kind exchange.

Gain from a like-kind exchange is not taxable at the time of the exchange. This means that gain will not be taxed until you sell or otherwise dispose of the property you receive. To defer gain from a like-kind exchange, you must have exchanged business or investment property for business or investment property of a like kind. For more information about like-kind exchanges, see Publication 544, *Sales and Other Dispositions of Assets*.

Home relinquished in a like-kind exchange. If you use your main home partly for business or rental purposes and then exchange the home for another property, see Publication 523.

TAXSAVER

Under an IRS ruling you can take advantage of both the principal residence gain exclusion and the deferral of gain in a like-kind exchange. For example, assume that you convert your home into rental property after you had owned it and lived in it for 3 years. The cost basis of your home when you exchange it 2 years later is $400,000 but its value is $1 million. (We won't consider depreciation in this example.) You exchange it for another rental property worth $1 million. Your total gain on the exchange is $600,000 ($1 million less $400,000). You can exclude $250,000 of that gain since you meet the ownership and use tests at the date of sale. The balance of the gain ($600,000 – $250,000, or $350,000) is not currently taxable if the like-kind exchange meets the requirements of the tax law. Your adjusted basis in the new home is the carryover basis from the first residence ($400,000). The excluded gain will increase the basis of the new property so your cost basis in that property will be $650,000 ($400,000 plus $250,000).

Expatriates. You cannot claim the exclusion if the expatriation tax applies to you. The expatriation tax applies to certain U.S. citizens who have renounced their citizenship (and to certain long-term residents who have ended their residency). For more information about the expatriation tax, see chapter 4 of Publication 519, *U.S. Tax Guide for Aliens*.

Home destroyed or condemned. If your home was destroyed or condemned, any gain (for example, because of insurance proceeds you received) qualifies for the exclusion.

Any part of the gain that cannot be excluded (because it is more than the maximum exclusion) can be postponed under the rules explained in:

- Publication 547, in the case of a home that was destroyed, or
- Publication 544, chapter 1, in the case of a home that was condemned.

Sale of remainder interest. Subject to the other rules in this chapter, you can choose to exclude gain from the sale of a remainder interest in your home. If you make this choice, you cannot choose to exclude gain from your sale of any other interest in the home that you sell separately.

Exception for sales to related persons. You cannot exclude gain from the sale of a remainder interest in your home to a related person. Related persons include your brothers, sisters, half-brothers, half-sisters, spouse, ancestors (parents, grandparents, etc.), and lineal descendants (children, grandchildren, etc.). Related persons also include certain corporations, partnerships, trusts, and exempt organizations.

TAXALERT

Starting January 1, 2013, the Health Care and Education Reconciliation Act of 2010 imposes a 3.8% tax on gain from the sale of real estate, including residential and investment real estate. The money received from the tax will be allocated to the Medicare Trust Fund. The tax will not apply to you if your adjusted gross income is $200,000 ($250,000 if married filing jointly) or less. The tax is applied on the gain from the sale of real estate after the exclusion of gain on your main home. If your entire gain is excluded, then you do not have to pay the tax. The calculation can be complex and does not take effect until 2013; however, because the law applies to all forms of real estate, you should consider the application of the law to your situation and consult your tax advisor.

Recapturing (Paying Back) a Federal Mortgage Subsidy

If you financed your home under a federally subsidized program (loans from tax-exempt qualified mortgage bonds or loans with mortgage credit certificates), you may have to recapture all or part of the benefit you received from that program when you sell or otherwise dispose of your home. You recapture the benefit by increasing your federal income tax for the year of the sale. You may have to pay this recapture tax even if you can exclude your gain from income under the rules discussed earlier; that exclusion does not affect the recapture tax.

Loans subject to recapture rules. The recapture applies to loans that:

1. Came from the proceeds of qualified mortgage bonds, or
2. Were based on mortgage credit certificates.

The recapture also applies to assumptions of these loans.

When recapture applies. Recapture of the federal mortgage subsidy applies only if you meet both of the following conditions.

- Within the first 9 years after the date you close your mortgage loan, you sell or otherwise dispose of your home at a gain.
- Your income for the year of disposition is more than that year's adjusted qualifying income for your family size for that year (related to the income requirements a person must meet to qualify for the federally subsidized program).

When recapture does not apply. Recapture does not apply in any of the following situations.

- Your mortgage loan was a qualified home improvement loan (QHIL) of not more than $15,000 used for alterations, repairs, and improvements that protect or improve the basic livability or energy efficiency of your home.
- Your mortgage loan was a QHIL of not more than $150,000 in the case of a QHIL used to repair damage from Hurricane Katrina to homes in the hurricane disaster area; a QHIL funded by a qualified mortgage bond that is a qualified Gulf Opportunity Zone Bond; or a QHIL for an owner-occupied home in the Gulf Opportunity Zone (GO Zone), Rita GO Zone, or Wilma GO Zone. For more information, see Publication 4492, *Information for Taxpayers Affected by Hurricanes Katrina, Rita, and Wilma*. Also see Publication 4492-B, *Information for Affected Taxpayers in the Midwestern Disaster Areas*.
- The home is disposed of as a result of your death.
- You dispose of the home more than 9 years after the date you closed your mortgage loan.
- You transfer the home to your spouse, or to your former spouse incident to a divorce, where no gain is included in your income.
- You dispose of the home at a loss.
- Your home is destroyed by a casualty, and you replace it on its original site within 2 years after the end of the tax year when the destruction happened (within 5 years if the home was in the Hurricane Katrina disaster area and was destroyed by reason of the hurricane after August 24, 2005). If your home was located in the Kansas disaster area, one of the Midwestern disaster areas, or another federally declared disaster area, see *Replacement Period* in Publication 547.
- You refinance your mortgage loan (unless you later meet the conditions listed previously under *When recapture applies*).

Notice of amounts. At or near the time of settlement of your mortgage loan, you should receive a notice that provides the federally subsidized amount and other information you will need to figure your recapture tax.

How to figure and report the recapture. The recapture tax is figured on Form 8828. If you sell your home and your mortgage is subject to recapture rules, you must file Form 8828 even if you do not owe a recapture tax. Attach Form 8828 to your Form 1040. For more information, see Form 8828 and its instructions.

Recapturing (Paying Back) the First-Time Homebuyer Credit

Recapture of 2008 first-time homebuyer credit. If you claimed the first-time homebuyer credit in 2008, and you sold the home or the home stopped being your main home in 2011, you generally must repay the unrecaptured balance of the credit. You repay the credit by including it as additional tax on the return for the year your home stops being your main home. For details, see chapter 37.

TAXALERT

In 2008, Congress provided first-time homebuyers a refundable tax credit that was equivalent to an interest-free loan equal to 10% of the purchase of a home (up to a maximum credit of $7,500; $3,750 for a married person filing a separate return). This provision applies to homes purchased after April 8, 2008, and before January 1, 2009. This refundable tax credit is required to be repaid over a 15-year period in 15 equal installments. (The credit essentially functions as an interest-free loan to you from the Federal government.) The repayment period began in 2010.

Example

You bought a home on June, 10, 2008, and claimed the full credit of $7,500 on your 2008 tax return. One-fifteenth of $7,500, or $500, would be treated as additional tax on your tax return for 2010 and successive years, until it is fully paid back in 2024.

The following are exceptions to the requirement to repay the credit for homes purchased in 2008:

- If you sell the home to someone who is not related to you, the repayment in the year of sale is limited to the amount of gain on the sale. When figuring the gain, reduce the adjusted basis of the home by the amount of the credit you did not repay.
- If the home is destroyed, condemned, or disposed of under threat of condemnation, and you acquire a new main home within 2 years of the event, you continue to pay the installments over the remainder of the 15-year repayment period.
- If, as part of a divorce settlement, the home is transferred to a spouse or former spouse, the spouse who receives the home is responsible for making all subsequent installment payments.
- If you die, any remaining annual installments are not due. If you filed a joint return and then you die, your surviving spouse would be required to repay his or her half of the remaining repayment amount.

Recapture of first-time homebuyer credit for purchases in 2009 or 2010. If you claimed the 2009 or 2010 first-time homebuyer credit when you purchased your home, the credit is not required to be repaid unless your home ceases to be your main home within 36 months of the date of purchase. See the Instructions for Form 5405 for details on the exceptions that apply.

EXPLANATION

If you purchased the home after 2008, you generally must repay the credit if, during the 36-month period beginning on the purchase date and after the year for which you claim the credit, you dispose of the home or it ceases to be your main home. This includes situations where you sell the home, you convert the entire home to business or rental property, the home is destroyed, condemned, or disposed of under threat of condemnation, or the lender forecloses on the mortgage.

You repay the credit by including it as additional tax on the return for the year you dispose of the home or it ceases to be your main home. However, if the home is destroyed, condemned, or disposed of under threat of condemnation, and you do not acquire a new home within 2 years of the event, you must repay the entire repayment amount with the return for the year in which the 2-year period ends.

If you and your spouse claim the credit on a joint return, each spouse is treated as having been allowed half of the credit for purposes of repaying the credit.

The following are exceptions to the repayment rule:

- If you sell the home to someone who is not related to you (see the instructions to Form 5405 for the definition of related parties), the repayment in the year of sale is limited to the amount of gain on the sale. The amount of the credit in excess of the gain does not have to be repaid. When figuring the gain, reduce the adjusted basis of the home by the amount of the credit.
- If the home is destroyed, condemned, or disposed of under threat of condemnation, you do not have to repay the credit if you purchase a new main home within 2 years of the event and you own and use it as your new main home during the remainder of the 36-month period.
- If, as part of a divorce settlement, the home is transferred to a spouse or former spouse, the spouse who receives the home is responsible for repaying the credit if, during the 36-month period beginning on the purchase date, he or she disposes of the home or it ceases to be his or her main home and none of the other exceptions apply.
- Members of the uniformed services or Foreign Service and employees of the intelligence community do not have to repay the credit if, after 2008, they sell the home or the home ceases to be their main home because they received government orders to serve on qualified official extended duty (see the instructions for Form 5405, line 12, beginning on page 4, for more information).
- If you die, repayment of the credit is not required. If you claimed the credit on a joint return and then you die, your surviving spouse would be required to repay his or her half of the credit if, during the 36-month period beginning on the purchase date, he or she disposes of the home or it ceases to be his or her main home and none of the other exceptions apply.

Chapter 16

Reporting gains and losses

ey.com/EYTaxGuide

Note

IRS Publication 17 (*Your Federal Income Tax*) has been updated by Ernst & Young LLP for 2011. Dates and dollar amounts shown are for 2011. Underlined type is used to indicate where IRS text has been updated. Places where text has been removed are indicated by the sentence: *Text intentionally omitted*.

ey.com/EYTaxGuide

Ernst & Young LLP will update the *Ernst & Young Tax Guide 2012* website with relevant taxpayer information as it becomes available. You can also sign up for email alerts to let you know when changes have been made.

Introduction

One of the best ways to save tax dollars is to generate long-term capital gains: profits you make from the sale of assets such as stocks, bonds, and real estate. To qualify for long-term capital gains treatment, you have to hold a capital asset for more than 1 year.

The tax benefit of generating long-term capital gains is substantial. Under current tax law, the top tax rate applicable to most long-term capital gains is 15% (it's 0% for taxpayers who are in the 10% or 15% tax brackets for ordinary taxable income). These favorable capital gains rates are applicable through 2012. Unless Congress takes action, beginning in 2013, the long-term capital gain rate will rise to 20%. Even with this increase, you can achieve substantial tax savings by generating capital gains in lieu of ordinary income. Your net capital gain equals net long-term capital gains less net short-term capital losses. A 28% rate applies to collectibles held over 12 months; a 25% rate applies to real estate gains to the extent of depreciation.

The rate differences between ordinary income and capital gains have a profound effect on tax planning and investing. This chapter will provide you with examples of how the rules work. It also provides advice on year-end planning.

What's New

100% exclusion of gain on qualified small business stock. You may be able to exclude from income up to 100% of your gain from the sale or trade of qualified small business stock you acquired after September 27, 2010, and before January 1, 2012, if you hold the stock for more than 5 years.

Basis reporting on Form 1099-B. Starting for 2011, if the stock you sold during the year was acquired after 2010, your broker will also be generally required to report on Form 1099-B your basis in the shares sold and whether any capital gain or loss was short-term or long-term. (For stock purchased and sold during 2011, any gain or loss will be classified as short-term since the securities have been held for less than a year.) The requirements to report basis and holding period (i.e., short- or long-term) will be expanded during 2012 and 2013 to cover other types of securities, such as sales of mutual fund shares, stock acquired in connection with a dividend reinvestment plan, bonds, commodity contracts, and options on securities. On the other hand, brokers are not required to report basis or holding period for any securities acquired before 2011. See chapter 13, *Basis of property*, for more information.

TAXALERT

Until April 1, 2011, there were two ways to calculate the cost basis of mutual fund shares—the single-category method and the double-category method. In general, the single-category method groups in one category all shares regardless of holding period; that is, the basis of each share is the total adjusted basis of all shares at the time of disposition divided by the total shares. The double-category method divides all shares by their holding period. The average cost for each category is calculated and the shareholder can specify from which category shares are sold. As of April 1, 2011, the double-category method has been eliminated. If you have been using the double-category method for the cost basis of your mutual fund shares acquired before April. 1, 2011, you can continue to use that method only for sales before that date.

Tax Breaks and Deductions You Can Use Checklist

Lower Tax Rate on Long-Term Capital Gains. Generally, the gain realized from the sale of a capital asset is treated as a long-term capital gain if the property has been held more than one year (i.e., at least one year and a day) as of the date it is sold. The top tax rate on long-term capital gains is 15%, while the top rate on short-term capital gains and ordinary income is 35%. Therefore, if compatible with your investment goals, you should try to generate long-term capital gains, rather than short-term capital gains or ordinary income. For more information, see Reporting Capital Gains and Losses, later.

Specific Identification of Share Lots or Bonds Sold. Being able to specifically identify share lots and/or bonds sold provides you with the greatest opportunity to manage the amount of a gain or loss generated, as well as whether that gain or loss is treated as long-term or short-term. For more information, see Determination of cost basis and holding period, later.

TAXALERT

Generally, noncorporate taxpayers may exclude 50% of the gain from the sale of certain small business stock acquired at original issue and held for more than 5 years. For stock acquired after February 17, 2009, and before September 28, 2010, the exclusion is increased to 75%. (At the time of sale, however, 28% of the excluded gain is treated as a tax preference item subject to the alternative minimum tax (AMT)).

Two tax laws (including the Act that extended the so-called Bush tax cuts) enacted in 2010 increased the exclusion to 100% for stock acquired at original issue after September 27, 2010, and before January 1, 2012, if the qualified stock has been held at least five years. There is also no AMT preference item attributable for that sale.

For more information, see *Gain on qualified small business stock*, later in this chapter.

TAXALERT

When a C corporation elects to become an S corporation, all gains that are built-in at the time of the election are taxed if they were recognized during the first 10 years of S corporation status. Under the American Recovery and Reinvestment Tax Act of 2009, the built-in gain holding period changed from 10 to 7 years, and under the Small Business Jobs Act of 2010, the built-in gain holding period was further reduced from 7 to 5 years for taxable years beginning in 2011. Unless Congress changes the law, the holding period will increase back to 10 years for taxable years beginning in 2012 and thereafter.

For more information, see Table 16-1, later in this chapter.

This chapter discusses how to report capital gains and losses from sales, exchanges, and other dispositions of investment property on Form 8949 and Schedule D (Form 1040). The discussion includes the following topics.

- How to report short-term gains and losses.
- How to report long-term gains and losses.
- How to figure capital loss carryovers.
- How to figure your tax on a net capital gain.
- An illustrated example of how to complete Form 8949 and Schedule D.

If you sell or otherwise dispose of property used in a trade or business or for the production of income, see Publication 544, *Sales and Other Dispositions of Assets*, before completing Schedule D.

Useful Items

You may want to see:

Publication

- □ **537** Installment Sales
- □ **544** Sales and Other Dispositions of Assets
- □ **550** Investment Income and Expenses

Form (and Instructions)

- □ **Schedule D (Form 1040)** Capital Gains and Losses
- □ **8949** Sales and Other Dispositions of Capital Assets
- □ **4797** Sales of Business Property
- □ **6252** Installment Sale Income
- □ **8582** Passive Activity Loss Limitations

TAXALERT

Beginning with the 2011 tax year, the IRS is requiring brokers to report adjusted cost basis in addition to gross proceeds for covered securities and also to report whether the related gain or loss is long-term or short-term. Covered securities are securities that are purchased or acquired on or after the following legislation effective dates:

Equities. Equity securities are covered securities if they are purchased or acquired on or after January 1, 2011.

Mutual funds and dividend reinvestment plan (DRP) shares. These types of investments are covered if they are purchased or acquired on or after January 1, 2012.

Other specified securities, including fixed income and options. Investments in this category will be covered if purchased or acquired on or after January 1, 2013.

Non-covered securities are those purchased or acquired before the effective dates.

TAXALERT

In connection with the new basis reporting requirements, the IRS has introduced a new Form 8949 to report investment asset sales including stocks and mutual funds reported on Form 1099-B. Sales details are longer directly reported on Schedule D but rather on Form 8949. Use a different copy of Form 8949 for each of the following conditions:

1. Basis was reported on Form 1099-B
2. Basis was NOT reported on Form 1099-B.
3. Sale not reported on Form 1099-B

The totals from each Form 8949 flow to Schedule D and onward to Form 1040

Reporting Capital Gains and Losses

Report capital gains and losses from sales of stock and mutual funds on Form 8949 and Schedule D (Form 1040). Enter your sales and trades of stocks, bonds, etc. (if not reported on Form 4684, 4797, 6252, 6781, or 8824) on Form 8949 Part I or Part II and Schedule D line 1, 2 or 3 of Part I or line 8, 9 or 10 of Part II, as appropriate. The new Form 8949 is where you report the actual transactions. The totals are carried from here to Schedule D. Similar to Schedule D, Form 8949, Sales and Other Dispositions of Capital Assets, breaks the sales into long- and short-term sales. Form 8949 also separates the assets by how the sale is reported: (A) on 1099-B with a cost basis, (B) 1099-B without a cost basis, and (C) sales with no 1099-B. Only one reporting type is allowed per Form 8949. Therefore you may have to prepare three Forms 8949 that carry to one Schedule D. Include all transactions even if you did not receive a Form 1099-B, Proceeds From Broker and Barter Exchange Transactions, or Form 1099-S, Proceeds From Real Estate Transactions (or substitute statement). *Text intentionally omitted.*

EXPLANATION

Characterizing your gain or loss. When you sell or dispose of property, you must determine whether your gain or loss is capital or ordinary. Only capital gains and capital losses are reported on Form 8949 and Schedule D, while ordinary gains and losses are reported elsewhere. This distinction is significant because (1) you can use capital losses to offset gains only to the extent of capital gains plus $3,000, and (2) net capital gains may be subject to a lower tax rate than ordinary income. Any unused capital losses can be carried over to the next year.

Example

Assume that Alan has $12,000 of capital losses and $4,000 of capital gains in 2011. Alan can deduct only $7,000 of his capital losses in 2011, which is equal to his $4,000 of capital gains plus $3,000. The remaining $5,000 of losses ($12,000 gross losses minus $7,000 of losses used) may be carried over and used in later years, subject to the $3,000 limitation. If Alan's losses were ordinary, he could have used all of them in 2011 unless subject to other limitations by special provisions of the Internal Revenue Code.

EXPLANATION

Determining your capital gains rate. The capital gains rate depends on the type of property sold, the holding period prior to sale, and your overall income level. Short-term capital gains are subject to your ordinary income rates. Net capital gains are the excess of (1) net long-term capital gains over (2) net short-term capital losses.

Example

Erik bought 3,000 shares of ABC Company on April 1, 2005, when the price of the stock was $20 per share. On May 1, 2011, he sold all of his ABC holdings for $25 per share, realizing a profit of $15,000. Erik files a joint return showing his wife with a combined taxable income that places him in the 35% tax bracket. Because he held the ABC stock for more than 12 months, Erik is eligible for the favorable capital gain tax rates. As a 35% taxpayer, his long-term capital gain on ABC stock would be taxed at 15%.

TAXPLANNER

Long-term capital gains vs. ordinary income. The difference between the top marginal rate of 35% and the top rate on net capital gains of 15% is significant–a 20% difference. Unless Congress takes action, the top marginal rate in 2013 will increase to 39.6% and the top rate on capital gains will increase to 20%, a difference of 19.6% between the two rates. In either year, since the capital gain rate is still much lower than ordinary rates, you should try to generate long-term capital gains whenever possible. It should be noted, however, that the tax law recharacterizes gains from certain conversion transactions into ordinary income. See later in this chapter for an explanation of conversion transactions.

Example

Nancy is in the 35% marginal tax bracket for 2011 and the 39.6% bracket for 2013 and has the following unrealized capital gains and losses:

Stock A: Unrealized short-term capital gain	$10,000
Stock B: Unrealized long-term capital loss	($13,000)
Stock C: Unrealized long-term capital gain	$15,000

Assume that Nancy sells all three stocks in 2011. Nancy will compute her net capital gain for the year as follows:

Net long-term capital gain	$2,000
Net short-term capital gain	$10,000
Total gains	$12,000

Nancy has a net capital gain of $12,000. Nancy will pay $300 of tax on her net long-term capital gain ($2,000 × 15%) and $3,500 on her short-term capital gains, which are taxed at her regular 35% rate ($10,000 × 35%). Thus, Nancy will pay a total tax of $3,800 ($300 + $3,500) on her capital gains.

Assume instead that Nancy sells stocks A and B in 2011 but waits until 2013 to sell stock C.

Nancy will have a net long-term capital loss of $3,000 for 2011 ($10,000 gain on stock A, less $13,000 loss on stock B). Nancy will be allowed to offset the $3,000 capital loss against her ordinary income, giving her a $1,050 tax saving for 2011.

Nancy will also have a $15,000 net long-term capital gain in 2013 from the sale of stock C. This will represent a net capital gain subject to the maximum 20% rate on net capital gains. Nancy will pay $3,000 of tax in 2013 on her net capital gain ($15,000 × 20%).

By using tax planning, Nancy's total liability on her capital gains would be $1,950 ($3,000 for 2013, less $1,050 of tax savings in 2011). As compared to the $3,800 of tax liability without tax planning, Nancy has saved $1,850. Furthermore, Nancy also delayed the payment of the tax by waiting until 2013 to trigger some of her gains.

The tax savings to Nancy may be small relative to the investment ramifications of holding stock C for a longer period. Nancy must therefore balance the potential tax savings against her overall investment strategy.

Explanation

A capital gain or loss results from (1) the sale or exchange of a capital asset or (2) net Section 1231 gains being treated as a capital gain.

Almost everything you own and use for personal purposes or investment purposes is a capital asset. For example, stocks, bonds, jewelry, and household furnishings generally are all capital assets. Most properties held in a business (e.g., inventory, accounts receivable, machinery) are not capital assets. See chapter 14, *Sale of property*, for a further elaboration on what constitutes a capital asset.

A net Section 1231 gain is also treated as a capital gain, while a net Section 1231 loss is treated as an ordinary loss. A Section 1231 gain or loss is any gain or loss from the sale or exchange of real property or depreciable personal property used in your trade or business and held by you for more than 1 year. Any depreciation recapture must be separately computed on the sale of depreciable property and reported as ordinary income. Thus, the portion of the gain that is considered depreciation recapture is ordinary income, rather than a Section 1231 gain. The computation of depreciation recapture is discussed in more detail at the end of this chapter.

Section 1231 gains also include recognized gains on the involuntary conversion of (1) property used in a trade or a business and held for more than 1 year, and (2) any capital asset held for more than 1 year and held in connection with a trade or a business or a transaction entered into for profit. Net involuntary conversion losses on these properties are not Section 1231 losses but are deductible as ordinary losses. An involuntary conversion is the loss of property resulting from destruction (complete or partial), theft, seizure, requisition, or condemnation. An involuntary conversion also includes the sale or exchange of property under the threat or imminence of seizure, requisition, or condemnation.

For more information, see Publication 544, *Sales and Other Dispositions of Assets*.

Tax treatment of gains and losses. Once the disposition is properly classified, you can determine whether your gains and losses will be considered ordinary, capital, or nondeductible.

Losses on the sale of personal-use property (e.g., a family car) cannot be used to offset capital gains. These losses are not reported on your income tax return. Capital gains on the sale of personal-use property are taxable, however, and are reported on Schedule D.

You must aggregate all of your Section 1231 gains and losses during the year to determine the tax treatment of these items. Net Section 1231 gains are treated as capital, while net Section 1231 losses are treated as ordinary. Under a special look-back rule, if you have a net Section 1231 gain in 2011, the gain will be treated as ordinary income to the extent of any Section 1231 losses in the preceding 5 years (which were not previously used to recharacterize gains). Remember, any gain resulting in depreciation recapture is ordinary income and as a result is not considered in these computations. Fill out Form 4797 to report these items. Ordinary gains and losses are generally included in gross income. The capital gain portion is reported on Schedule D.

Capital gains and losses reported on Schedule D are further classified under long-term and short-term. Net Section 1231 gains are long-term. For other classifications, see the discussion in chapter 14, *Sale of property*.

TAXALERT

Recharacterizing capital gains. The Internal Revenue Code contains a provision that recharacterizes capital gains from certain conversion transactions as ordinary income. The purpose of this provision is to prohibit taxpayers from taking advantage of the favorable tax rate on capital gains by entering into transactions that are, in effect, loans, but that, because of their form, generate capital gains. In a conversion transaction, the taxpayer is in the economic position of a lender, and substantially all of the taxpayer's return is attributable to the amount of time the investment is held. In order to be a conversion transaction, a transaction must satisfy at least one of the following four criteria: (1) the transaction consists of the acquisition of property by the taxpayer and a substantially contemporaneous agreement to sell the same or substantially identical property in the future; (2) the transaction is a straddle (see chapter 14, *Sale of property*); (3) the transaction is one that is marketed or sold to the taxpayer on the basis that it would have the economic characteristics of a loan but the interest-like return would be taxed as capital gain; or (4) the transaction is described in regulations promulgated by the Secretary of the Treasury.

Be sure to add all sales price entries on Schedule D in column (e) of lines 1, 2 and 3. *Text intentionally omitted.* Also add all sales price entries on Schedule D in column (e) of lines 8, 9 and 10. *Text intentionally omitted.* Then add the following amounts reported to you for 2011 on Forms 1099-B and Forms 1099-S (or on substitute statements):

- Proceeds from transactions involving stocks, bonds, and other securities, and
- Gross proceeds from real estate transactions (other than the sale of your main home if you had no taxable gain) not reported on another form or schedule.

If this total is more than the total of lines 1, 2 and 3 and 8, 9 and 10 of Schedule D, attach a statement to your return explaining the difference.

Installment sales. You cannot use the installment method to report a gain from the sale of stock or securities traded on an established securities market. You must report the entire gain in the year of sale (the year in which the trade date occurs).

TAXALERT

Date of installment payments. For purposes of the dates that determine when capital gains are taxed, the date you receive an installment payment is relevant, not the actual date of sale.

Passive activity gains and losses. If you have gains or losses from a passive activity, you may also have to report them on Form 8582. In some cases, the loss may be limited under the passive activity rules. Refer to Form 8582 and its separate instructions for more information about reporting capital gains and losses from a passive activity.

EXPLANATION

The gain or loss realized upon the sale or disposition of an interest in a passive activity must be combined with other items of income, expense, gain, or loss from investments in passive activities in order to determine the amount of passive activity losses that will be deductible on Form 1040. See chapter 12, *Other income*, for more information.

TAXPLANNER

Passive capital gains. If you generate a passive capital gain, you will be allowed to deduct passive losses to the extent of the passive gain as explained above. In addition, that passive capital gain can still be offset by capital losses on Schedule D.

Form 1099-B transactions. If you sold property, such as stocks, bonds, or certain commodities, through a broker, you should receive Form 1099-B or an equivalent statement from the broker. Use the Form 1099-B or the equivalent statement to complete Form(s) 8949 and Schedule D.

Report the gross proceeds shown in box 2 of Form 1099-B as the gross sales price in column (e) of either line 1 or line 3 of Form 8949 with either box (A), (B) or (C) marked as appropriate. However, if the broker advises you, in box 2 of Form 1099-B, that gross proceeds (gross sales price) less commissions and option premiums were reported to the IRS, enter that net sales price in column (e) of either line 1 or line 3 of Form(s) 8949, whichever applies.

If the net sales price is entered in column (e), do not include the commissions and option premiums in column (f).

If the Form 1099-B includes cost basis in box 3, report the cost basis shown in box 3 as the cost or other basis in column (f) of either line 1 or line 3 on Form 8949 and check box (A).

EXPLANATION

Form 1099-B will only include cost basis information in box 3 if the securities sold are covered securities. In 2011, the term covered securities only includes equity securities that were purchased or acquired on or after January 1, 2011. Include the amount reported in box 3 on Form 8949, column (f), and check box (A). If Form 1099-B, box 3, is blank, you should complete column (f) with the appropriate cost basis from your records and check box (B) on the Form 8949. Since the implementation of the new basis reporting rules will occur over a three-year period, you may receive multiple Forms 1099-B from the broker for the same account. Make sure to examine all Forms 1099-B carefully to ensure all transactions are reported on Form 8949.

Form 1099-CAP transactions. If a corporation in which you own stock has had a change in control or a substantial change in capital structure, you should receive Form 1099-CAP or an equivalent statement from the corporation. Use the Form 1099-CAP or equivalent statement to figure the gain to report on Schedule D (Form 1040). You cannot claim a loss on Schedule D (Form 1040) as a result of this transaction.

Report the aggregate amount received shown in box 2 of Form 1099-CAP as the gross sales price in column (e) of either line 1 or line 3 of Form 8949, whichever applies.

Form 1099-S transactions. If you sold or traded reportable real estate, you generally should receive from the real estate reporting person a Form 1099-S showing the gross proceeds.

"Reportable real estate" is defined as any present or future ownership interest in any of the following:

- Improved or unimproved land, including air space,
- Inherently permanent structures, including any residential, commercial, or industrial building,
- A condominium unit and its accessory fixtures and common elements, including land, and
- Stock in a cooperative housing corporation (as defined in section 216 of the Internal Revenue Code).

A "real estate reporting person" could include the buyer's attorney, your attorney, the title or escrow company, a mortgage lender, your broker, the buyer's broker, or the person acquiring the biggest interest in the property.

Your Form 1099-S will show the gross proceeds from the sale or exchange in box 2. Follow the instructions for Schedule D to report these transactions and include them on Form 8949, line 1 or 3, as appropriate. However, report like-kind exchanges on Form 8824 instead.

It is unlawful for any real estate reporting person to separately charge you for complying with the requirement to file Form 1099-S.

Nominees. If you receive gross proceeds as a nominee (that is, the gross proceeds are in your name but actually belong to someone else), report on Form 8949, lines 1 and 3, only the proceeds that belong to you. Then add the following amounts reported to you for 2011 on Forms 1099-B and 1099-S (or substitute statements) that you are not reporting on another form or schedule included with your return:

1. Proceeds from transactions involving stocks, bonds, and other securities, and
2. Gross proceeds from real estate transactions (other than the sale of your main home if you are not required to report it).

If the total of (1) and (2) is more than the total of Form 8949 lines 2 and 4, attach a statement to your return explaining the reason for the difference.

EXPLANATION

Amounts reported to you on Form 1099-B are also reported to the IRS. The IRS matches the amounts reported on Forms 1099-B to your return to make sure you reported all of your security sales. The amounts reported on Forms 1099-B should equal the sum of the amounts on Form(s) 8949, lines 2 and 4, columns (e) and (f), if applicable. If not, you will probably receive a letter from the IRS asking you to explain the difference. If the amounts are different, you should attach a schedule to your return explaining why.

TAXORGANIZER

Documents you need for Form(s) 8949 and Schedule D. Taxpayers who sell stocks, bonds, or other property through a broker should maintain the following documentation in order to facilitate the completion of Form(s) 8949 and Schedule D:

- Confirmations received from the broker documenting all sales transactions executed. These can be used to ensure the accuracy of any Forms 1099-B received.
- Confirmations received from the broker documenting all purchase transactions executed. These will be needed to calculate any gains or losses realized upon the sale of the property. The confirmations will also be needed to determine if any gains or losses are long term or short term.

TAXPLANNER

Real property tax. The person reporting a real estate transaction is also responsible for including on Form 1099-S the portion of any real property tax that is property allocable to the purchaser. Thus, property tax allocable from the date of sale to year-end is reported on Form 1099-S. Note that if the purchaser agrees to pay the taxes the seller owed on the new home (up to the date of sale), these taxes are not treated as taxes paid by the purchaser but instead are treated as part of the purchaser's cost. Accordingly, these amounts are not included on Form 1099-S as real property tax allocable to the purchaser. Instead, these amounts are included on Form 1099-S as part of the seller's proceeds.

File Form 1099-B or Form 1099-S with the IRS. If you received gross proceeds as a nominee in 2011, you must file a Form 1099-B or Form 1099-S for those proceeds with the IRS. Send the Form 1099-B or Form 1099-S with a Form 1096, Annual Summary and Transmittal of U.S. Information Returns, to your Internal Revenue Service Center by February 28, 2012 (April 2, 2012, if you file Form 1099-B or Form 1099-S electronically). Give the actual owner of the proceeds Copy B of the Form 1099-B or Form 1099-S by February 15, 2012. On Form 1099-B, you should be listed as the "Payer." The other owner should be listed as the "Recipient." On Form 1099-S, you should be listed as the "Filer." The other owner should be listed as the "Transferor." You do not, however, have to file a Form 1099-B or Form 1099-S to show proceeds for your spouse. For more information about the reporting requirements and the penalties for failure to file (or furnish) certain information returns, see the General Instructions for Certain Information Returns (Forms 1098, 1099, 3921, 3922, 5498, and W-2G). If you are filing electronically see Publication 1220.

Sale of property bought at various times. If you sell a block of stock or other property that you bought at various times, report the short-term gain or loss from the sale on one line in Part I of Form 8949 and the long-term gain or loss on one line in Part II. Write "Various" in column (c) for the "Date acquired." See the *Comprehensive Example* later in this chapter.

Sale expenses. Add to your cost or other basis any expense of sale such as brokers' fees, commissions, state and local transfer taxes, and option premiums. Enter this adjusted amount in column (f) of either Part I or Part II of Form(s) 8949, whichever applies, unless you reported the net sales price amount in column (e).

For more information about adjustments to basis, see chapter 13.

EXPLANATION

Most property you own and use for personal purposes or for pleasure, such as your house, furniture, and car, falls under the heading of capital asset. A gain on the sale of this kind of property is treated as a capital gain, but no loss is recognized for income tax purposes unless the property was used for business or investment purposes. If you realize a loss on property used for both business and personal purposes, the portion of the loss that is allocated to the business portion of the property may be deductible.

Short-term gains and losses. Capital gain or loss on the sale or trade of investment property held 1 year or less is a short-term capital gain or loss. You report it in Part I of Form(s) 8949 and Part I of Schedule D. If the amount you report in column (g) of Form(s) 8949 or column (h) of Schedule D is a loss, show it in parentheses.

You combine your share of short-term capital gain or loss from partnerships, S corporations, and fiduciaries, and any short-term capital loss carryover, with your other short-term capital gains and losses to figure your net short-term capital gain or loss on line 7 of Schedule D.

Long-term gains and losses. A capital gain or loss on the sale or trade of investment property held more than 1 year is a long-term capital gain or loss. You report it in Part II of Form(s) 8949 and Part II of Schedule D. If the amount you report in column (g) of Form(s) 8949 or column (h) of Schedule D is a loss, show it in parentheses.

EXPLANATION

The shortest length of time that qualifies for long-term status is 1 year plus 1 day. Your holding period begins on the day after you buy the property and includes the day you sell it.

Example

Donald pays $1,000 for Corporation X stock on August 2, 2010. His holding period begins on August 3, 2010. Donald sells the stock on August 2, 2011, for $1,500. His holding period runs from August 3, 2010 (the day after he purchased the stock), through August 2, 2011 (the day he sold the stock). Donald has a short-term capital gain of $500 because he has held the stock for exactly 1 year.

Assume instead that Donald sells the stock on August 3, 2011. His holding period runs from August 3, 2010, through August 3, 2011. His holding period is now in excess of 1 year (1 year and 1 day), so Donald's gain will be long term.

You also report the following in Part II of Schedule D:

- Undistributed long-term capital gains from a mutual fund (or other regulated investment company) or real estate investment trust (REIT),
- Your share of long-term capital gains or losses from partnerships, S corporations, and fiduciaries,
- All capital gain distributions from mutual funds and REITs not reported directly on line 10 of Form 1040A or line 13 of Form 1040, and
- Long-term capital loss carryovers.

EXPLANATION

Dividends from mutual funds, which are technically known as **regulated investment companies**, are frequently composed of a combination of long-term capital gains and ordinary income. The nature of the gain is determined by how long the mutual fund has held the underlying property that generates the income, not how long you have held the mutual fund shares. Consequently, you may have a long-term capital gain, although you have held the mutual fund shares for less than the required long-term holding period.

Determination of cost basis and holding period. Mutual fund shares may be acquired on various dates, in various quantities, and at various prices. Some individuals may purchase shares through participation in dividend reinvestment or payroll deduction plans. Shares may also be sold on a periodic basis. As a result, individuals often encounter difficulty in determining their cost basis and hence gain or loss on the sale of their mutual fund shares. Prior to April 1, 2011, four methods could be used by mutual fund shareholders to determine the cost basis of shares sold. They are:

1. The specific identification method
2. The FIFO (first in, first out) method
3. The single-category method using the average approach
4. The double-category method using the average approach

Effective April 1, 2011, the double-category method using the average approach was eliminated by the IRS. Taxpayers formally using this method must re-calculate basis as of April 1, 2011, for identical shares regardless of holding period.

The specific identification method. In order to specifically identify the shares sold, the following requirements must be met:

1. Specific instructions to the broker or agent must be given by the customer, indicating the particular shares to be sold. These instructions must be given at the time of sale or transfer.
2. Written *confirmation* of this request must be received from the broker or agent within a reasonable time after the sale.

The individual shareholder bears the burden of proof that he or she owned and chose to sell the specific shares at the time of sale.

TAXPLANNER

Managing gains and losses. The specific identification method provides an investor with the greatest opportunity to manage his or her reported gain or loss. For example, if a shareholder has other capital losses during the year and wishes to generate capital gains, he or she can specifically identify those shares acquired at the *lowest prices* as the shares being sold. One problem with this method, particularly with mutual funds, is the inability of transfer agents to confirm, in writing, specific shares sold to the shareholder.

Explanation

The FIFO method. Under the FIFO (first in, first out) method, the basis of shares acquired first represents the cost of the shares sold. In other words, the oldest shares held by the taxpayer are considered to be the first sold. The FIFO method is also a default method. If specific identification procedures are not or cannot be followed and the average basis approach (discussed below) is not elected, then the FIFO method will apply.

TAXSAVER

Trap for the unwary. In a rising market, the FIFO method generally produces the greatest gain (and least loss) and hence, generally, the most tax.

Explanation

The single- and double-category methods using the average approach. The average basis method must be elected by the individual shareholder by attaching a statement to his or her income tax return for each year the choice applies. The election must indicate whether the single-category method or the double-category method (discussed below) is being used. Once the election is made, it must continue to be used for *all* accounts in the same mutual fund. The average method permits the taxpayer to calculate his or her gain or loss based on the average price paid for the shares.

With the single-category method, all shares are included in a single category; that is, the basis of each share is the total adjusted basis of all shares at the time of disposition divided by the total shares. In determining the holding period (long- or short-term), the shares disposed of are considered to be those shares acquired *first* (using a FIFO-type method, discussed earlier).

With the double-category method, all shares in an account are separated into two categories:

1. Short-term: shares held for 1 year or less
2. Long-term: shares held more than 1 year

The average cost for each category is calculated; that is, the basis of each share in a category is the total adjusted basis of all shares in that category divided by the total shares in that category. The shareholder can specify from which category shares are sold. The custodian or agent must confirm this to the shareholder in writing. If no selection is made, the shares in the long-term category are deemed to be sold first. After a share has been held for more than 1 year, it must be transferred from the short-term to the long-term category.

TAXPLANNER

Since the IRS eliminated the double category method for all mutual fund sales occurring on or after April 1, 2011, taxpayers must recalculate the basis of all identical shares regardless of holding period. For mutual fund sales prior to April 1, 2011, the double category method can still be used to calculate the basis, and the single category method must be used prospectively for sales.

TAXPLANNER

Under the new basis reporting rules, brokers are required to track adjusted cost basis for mutual fund and DRP shares acquired on or after January 1, 2012. Brokers must track adjusted cost basis in accordance with their default method unless a taxpayer notifies the broker in writing to elect a different method. As the broker is not required to inform you of their default method, you can contact your broker to find out their elected default method and their procedures for you as the shareowner to utilize another method.

EXPLANATION

Mutual fund dividends. If an individual who purchases shares in a mutual fund receives a capital gain distribution and then sells the shares at a loss within 6 months after purchase, the loss is treated as a *long-term* capital loss to the extent of the capital gain distribution received. Just as important, you may have to pay taxes on a capital gain distribution when you have not had a profit on your investment.

Example

You pay $10,000 for ABC Mutual Fund on June 30. On July 1, ABC Mutual Fund pays you a long-term capital gain distribution of $1,000. The same day, the value of your ABC shares drops to $9,000. You haven't made any money on your investment, but you still have to pay a tax on the capital gain distribution.

TAXSAVER

When to generate losses. If at the end of the year you find that you have only short-term capital gains, you might consider generating capital losses by selling assets that have declined in value. Short-term gains are taxed as ordinary income, but you can avoid paying tax on them by offsetting them against both short-term and long-term losses. However, if you sell stock or securities at a loss and then acquire substantially identical securities within 30 days before or 30 days after the sale, your loss may be disallowed in the year of sale. The purpose of this "wash sale" rule is to prevent taxpayers from generating losses on securities when the taxpayers are economically still in the same position after the sale.

Explanation

Sales or load charges. When a person invests in a mutual fund, he or she may be subject to a sales or load charge, which is similar to a commission. When shares are sold or redeemed, the sales or load charge is generally taken into account as part of the purchaser's basis for purposes of computing gain or loss on the sale.

If an investor exchanges shares in a mutual fund for shares in the same "family" or complex of funds, an additional sales or load charge may be waived or reduced if the investor acquires a reinvestment right (i.e., the right to acquire stock of one or more mutual funds without the payment of all or part of the standard load charge) on the original purchase. If such an exchange occurs within 90 days of the original purchase of mutual fund shares, the original sales or load charge will not be included as basis in determining the gain or loss on the exchange. This rule only applies to the extent that the additional sales or load charge is waived or reduced on the exchange. To the extent that the sales or load charge is not treated as basis in computing gain or loss, such a charge will be taken into account on shares subsequently sold.

Example

On February 1, 2011, Kurt Norton purchased 100 shares of mutual fund A for $110, which included a $10 sales or load charge. On February 22, 2011, Kurt exchanged these shares for 50 shares of mutual fund B, worth $115. Mutual fund B is in the same family as mutual fund A. The sales or load charge of $10 on Kurt's purchase of mutual fund B was waived. Kurt's gain or loss on the exchange is computed as follows:

Sales price of mutual fund A	$115
Cost basis of mutual fund A	(100)
Gain (loss)	$15

The sales or load charge of $10 on the purchase of mutual fund A did not affect the taxable gain or loss on the exchange but will become part of the basis of mutual fund B.

For more about mutual funds see chapter 39, *Mutual funds*.

The result after combining these items with your other long-term capital gains and losses is your net long-term capital gain or loss (line 15 of Schedule D).

Capital gain distributions only. You do not have to file Schedule D if both the following are true.

- The only amounts you would have to report on Schedule D are capital gain distributions from box 2a of Form 1099-DIV (or substitute statement).
- You do not have an amount in box 2b, 2c, or 2d of any Form 1099-DIV (or substitute statement).

If both the above statements are true, report your capital gain distributions directly on line 13 of Form 1040 and check the box on line 13. Also use the Qualified Dividends and Capital Gain Tax Worksheet in the Form 1040 instructions to figure your tax.

You can report your capital gain distributions on line 10 of Form 1040A, instead of on Form 1040, if both the following are true.

- None of the Forms 1099-DIV (or substitute statements) you received have an amount in box 2b, 2c, or 2d.
- You do not have to file Form 1040 for any other capital gains or losses.

Total net gain or loss. To figure your total net gain or loss, combine your net short-term capital gain or loss (line 7) with your net long-term capital gain or loss (line 15). Enter the result on Schedule D, Part III, line 16. If your losses are more than your gains, see *Capital Losses*, next. If both lines 15 and 16 are gains and line 43 of Form 1040 is more than zero, see *Capital Gain Tax Rates*, later.

Table 16-1. **What Is Your Maximum Capital Gain Rate?**

IF your net capital gain is from ...	**THEN your maximum capital gain rate is ...**
a collectibles gain	28%
an eligible gain on qualified small business stock minus the section 1202 exclusion	28%
an unrecaptured section 1250 gain	25%
other gain[1] and the regular tax rate that would apply is 25% or higher	15%
other gain[1] and the regular tax rate that would apply is lower than 25%	0%

[1]Other gain means any gain that is not collectibles gain, gain on qualified small business stock, or 550 unrecaptured section 1250 gain.

TAXALERT

Prior to enactment of the American Recovery and Reinvestment Tax Act of 2009, when a C corporation elected to become an S corporation, all gains that were built-in at the time of the election (or were attributable to property received by the S corporation from a C corporation in a transaction when basis carried over) were taxed if they were recognized during the first 10 years of S corporation status. The built-in gains tax is assessed at the highest corporate rate, currently 35%. This tax does not include gains that were created after the election or offset by losses.

The 2009 law reduces the built-in gain holding period from 10 to 7 years for tax years that begin in 2009 and 2010, thereby reducing the period when S corporation shareholders may distribute built-in gains.

The Small Business Jobs Act of 2010 further reduces the built-in gain holding period from 7 to 5 years for taxable years beginning in 2011. Unless Congress changes the law, the holding period will increase back to 10 years for taxable years beginning in 2012 and thereafter.

Capital Losses

If your capital losses are more than your capital gains, you can claim a capital loss deduction. Report the deduction on line 13 of Form 1040, enclosed in parentheses.

EXAMPLES

Example 1

You have capital gains and losses for the year as follows:

	Short-term	Long-term
Gains	$700	$400
Losses	800	2,000

Your net deductible capital loss is $1,700, which you figure as follows:

Short-term capital losses	$800	
Less: Short-term capital gains	(700)	
Net short-term capital loss		$100
Long-term capital losses	$2,000	
Less: Long-term capital gains	(400)	
Net long-term capital loss		$1,600
Net deductible capital loss		$1,700

Your deduction is limited to the lesser of $3,000 ($1,500 if married filing separately) or your capital loss of $1,700.

Example 2

You have a net long-term capital loss of $1,600 and a net short-term capital gain of $450. Your deductible capital loss is $1,150 ($1,600 – $450).

Limit on deduction. Your allowable capital loss deduction, figured on Schedule D, is the lesser of:

- $3,000 ($1,500 if you are married and file a separate return), or
- Your total net loss as shown on line 16 of Schedule D.

You can use your total net loss to reduce your income dollar for dollar, up to the $3,000 limit.

Capital loss carryover. If you have a total net loss on line 16 of Schedule D that is more than the yearly limit on capital loss deductions, you can carry over the unused part to the next year and treat it as if you had incurred it in that next year. If part of the loss is still unused, you can carry it over to later years until it is completely used up.

When you figure the amount of any capital loss carryover to the next year, you must take the current year's allowable deduction into account, whether or not you claimed it and whether or not you filed a return for the current year.

When you carry over a loss, it remains long term or short term. A long-term capital loss you carry over to the next tax year will reduce that year's long-term capital gains before it reduces that year's short-term capital gains.

Figuring your carryover. The amount of your capital loss carryover is the amount of your total net loss that is more than the lesser of:

1. Your allowable capital loss deduction for the year, or
2. Your taxable income increased by your allowable capital loss deduction for the year and your deduction for personal exemptions.

If your deductions are more than your gross income for the tax year, use your negative taxable income in computing the amount in item (2).

Complete the Capital Loss Carryover Worksheet in the Instructions for Schedule D or Publication 550 to determine the part of your capital loss for 2011 that you can carry over to 2012.

Example. Bob and Gloria sold securities in 2011. The sales resulted in a capital loss of $7,000. They had no other capital transactions. Their taxable income was $26,000. On their joint 2011 return, they can deduct $3,000. The unused part of the loss, $4,000 ($7,000 – $3,000), can be carried over to 2012.

If their capital loss had been $2,000, their capital loss deduction would have been $2,000. They would have no carryover.

Use short-term losses first. When you figure your capital loss carryover, use your short-term capital losses first, even if you incurred them after a long-term capital loss. If you have not reached the limit on the capital loss deduction after using the short-term capital losses, use the long-term capital losses until you reach the limit.

EXPLANATION

A net loss may be carried forward until it is exhausted or until the taxpayer dies. This carryforward may be used to reduce your tax when you have a capital gain sometime in the future. Even if you do not have future gains, the carryforward loss may be used to offset taxable income up to $3,000 per year.

Decedent's capital loss. A capital loss sustained by a decedent during his or her last tax year (or carried over to that year from an earlier year) can be deducted only on the final income tax return filed for the decedent. The capital loss limits discussed earlier still apply in this situation. The decedent's estate cannot deduct any of the loss or carry it over to following years.

TAXPLANNER

If the decedent filed a joint return in the year of death, the surviving spouse may offset gains recognized after the decedent's death but before the end of the tax year against the decedent's capital loss carryforward. Therefore, if the surviving spouse has assets that have appreciated in value, he or she should consider selling them in the year of the decedent's death. For a further discussion of this point, see chapter 43, *Decedents: Dealing with the death of a family member*.

Joint and separate returns. If you and your spouse once filed separate returns and are now filing a joint return, combine your separate capital loss carryovers. However, if you and your spouse once filed a joint return and are now filing separate returns, any capital loss carryover from the joint return can be deducted only on the return of the spouse who actually had the loss.

Capital Gain Tax Rates

The tax rates that apply to a net capital gain are generally lower than the tax rates that apply to other income. These lower rates are called the maximum capital gain rates.

The term "net capital gain" means the amount by which your net long-term capital gain for the year is more than your net short-term capital loss.

For 2011, the maximum capital gain rates are 0%, 15%, 25%, or 28%. See Table 16-1 for details.

TAXPLANNER

Long-term investment strategies. Investment strategies that emphasize capital appreciation over current income can significantly enhance your after-tax portfolio returns. For example, "buy-and-hold" investors may want to keep growth-oriented investments outside of tax-deferred accounts to benefit from the capital gains tax relief. Long-term gains in a tax-deferred account are taxed at ordinary income rates—currently as high as 35%—when withdrawn. Outside a tax-deferred account, those same long-term gains would be taxed at the more favorable capital gains rate. In addition, new investments in tax-deferred variable annuities will require much longer holding periods to outperform "comparable" investments held in a taxable account. Although mutual funds have not—with some notable exceptions—historically paid considerable attention to the impact of taxes on shareholder returns, more fund families are developing "tax-managed" funds that seek to minimize taxable distributions to shareholders.

To take advantage of the 0% and 15% rates, you should specifically identify shares of securities and/or mutual funds held more than 12 months prior to executing the sale. For tax purposes, the selling instructions given to the broker or fund representative must be in writing. Confirmation of the instructions should be kept in your personal files.

High-income taxpayers who have the option of deferring current compensation may be better off paying tax currently and reinvesting the after-tax proceeds in assets expected to appreciate over the long term. This may apply, for example, in the case of a corporate executive with significant nonqualified stock option holdings where the current option spread—and, thus, the associated current tax liability—is small but the outlook for the company's stock price is favorable.

Tip

If you figure your tax using the maximum capital gain rates and the regular tax computation results in a lower tax, the regular tax computation applies.

Example. All of your net capital gain is from selling collectibles, so the capital gain rate would be 28%. Because you are single and your taxable income is $25,000, none of your taxable income will be taxed above the 15% rate. The 28% rate does not apply.

Investment interest deducted. If you claim a deduction for investment interest, you may have to reduce the amount of your net capital gain that is eligible for the capital gain tax rates. Reduce it by the amount of the net capital gain you choose to include in investment income when figuring the limit on your investment interest deduction. This is done on the Schedule D Tax Worksheet or the Qualified Dividends and Capital Gain Tax Worksheet. For more information about the limit on investment interest, see *Interest Expenses* in chapter 3 of Publication 550.

TAXPLANNER

Net capital gains. Net capital gains are not included in "investment income" for purposes of determining a taxpayer's deduction for investment interest expense. However, you can elect to include capital gains as investment income. This election can be made for all or just a portion of your capital gains. In addition, you can make one election for regular tax purposes and another for alternative minimum tax purposes. If you make such an election, you must reduce the amount of capital gains that are otherwise eligible for the maximum capital gain tax rate by the amount included as investment income. The same election is available for qualified dividends that are taxed at capital gains rates and are also otherwise not considered to be investment income. See chapter 8, *Dividends and other corporate distributions*, for more details.

Collectibles gain or loss. This is gain or loss from the sale or trade of a work of art, rug, antique, metal (such as gold, silver, and platinum bullion), gem, stamp, coin, or alcoholic beverage held more than 1 year.

Collectibles gain includes gain from sale of an interest in a partnership, S corporation, or trust due to unrealized appreciation of collectibles.

Gain on qualified small business stock. If you realized a gain from qualified small business stock that you held more than 5 years, you generally can exclude up to 50% of your gain from income. The exclusion can be up to 75% for stock acquired after February 17, 2009 (100% for stock acquired after September 27, 2010), and before January 1, 2012. The exclusion can be up to 60% for certain empowerment zone business stock. The eligible gain minus your section 1202 exclusion is a 28% rate gain. See *Gains on Qualified Small Business Stock* in chapter 4 of Publication 550.

EXPLANATION

The amount of gain eligible for the exclusion is limited to the greater of ten times the taxpayer's basis in the stock or $10 million of gain from stock in that corporation. Qualifying small business stock is from a C corporation with gross assets that do not exceed $50 million (including the proceeds received from the issuance of the stock). The corporation must also meet a specific active business requirement.

TAXALERT

The American Recovery and Reinvestment Act increases the gain exclusion to 75% for stock that is issued after February 16, 2009, and before September 28, 2010. Although the 28% tax rate applicable to a sale of qualified small business stock (QSBS) remains the same, this 2009 law does, however, lower the effective tax rate on gains realized for regular tax purposes 7% (to 28% tax rate × 25% gain subject to tax and to 12.88% for AMT purposes). The 75% exclusion also applies to QSBS of empowerment zone businesses. For more information, consult your tax advisor.

TAXALERT

The 2010 Tax Relief Act temporarily increased the amount of the exclusion to 100% of the gain from the sale of qualified small business stock (QSBS) that is acquired at original issue after September 27, 2010, and before January 1, 2012, and held for at least 5 years. Therefore, there is no regular tax or alternative minimum tax imposed on the sale of such QSBS. The 100% exclusion also applies to QSBS of empowerment zone businesses.

TAXSAVER

For sales of qualified small business stock acquired before February 17, 2009, and after December 31, 2011, individuals can exclude from income 50% of the gain resulting from the sale that was purchased at original issue and had been held for at least 5 years. The gain eligible for exclusion is capped at the greater of 10 times the basis in the stock or $10 million. The remaining gain is taxed at a maximum rate of 28%.

The maximum tax rate is effectively 14%, as half of the gain is excluded and the other half is taxed at a 28% rate. However, for alternative minimum tax (AMT) purposes (see chapter 31, *How to figure your tax*), 7% of the amount excluded from gross income is an AMT preference item and is added back to taxable income to arrive at alternative minimum taxable income. For a taxpayer subject to AMT, the effective maximum rate is 14.98%. The additional 0.98% results from the 7% add back of the excluded gain taxed at a 28% rate.

Unrecaptured section 1250 gain. Generally, this is any part of your capital gain from selling section 1250 property (real property) that is due to depreciation (but not more than your net section 1231 gain), reduced by any net loss in the 28% group. Use the Unrecaptured Section 1250 Gain Worksheet in the Schedule D instructions to figure your unrecaptured section 1250 gain. For more information about section 1250 property and section 1231 gain, see chapter 3 of Publication 544.

EXPLANATION

Computing depreciation recapture. If you sell property at a gain, you must generally compute the portion of your gain that is depreciation recapture. Depreciation recapture is treated as ordinary income. The portion of the gain that is not depreciation recapture is treated as a Section 1231 gain. Unrecaptured Section 1250 gain on the sale of Section 1231 assets is subject to either the 15% maximum rate or, if the gain is attributable to adjustments in the basis of real estate, the 25% maximum rate. Complete Form 4797 to determine the amount of your gain that is depreciation recapture.

Sale of depreciable personal property. The depreciation recapture rules for depreciable personal property are relatively simple, compared to the rules for real property. Depreciation recapture is the lesser of (1) the gain recognized or (2) depreciation taken on the property since 1961. Note that, under these rules, if depreciable personal property is sold at less than its original cost, the full gain will inevitably be depreciation recapture.

Example

In 2006, Alan bought personal property that he used in his trade for $5,000. Alan sold the property for $2,500 in 2011. He had already taken $3,662 in depreciation. Alan computes his gain or loss as follows:

Sales price	$2,500
Purchase price	5,000
Less: Depreciation taken	(3,662)
Adjusted basis	1,338
Gain on sale	$1,162

Alan's gain on the sale is $1,162, which is less than the $3,662 of depreciation he had taken on the property. Therefore, his depreciation recapture is $1,162. Because this represents the full gain on the sale, no portion of the gain is treated as a Section 1231 gain and all of it will be treated as ordinary income.

Assume instead that the property had appreciated and that Alan sold the property for $6,000:

Sales price	$6,000
Adjusted basis (computed above)	(1,338)
Gain on sale	$4,662

Because the depreciation Alan took on the property ($3,662) is less than the gain on the sale ($4,662), Alan reports the $3,662 depreciation taken as depreciation recapture. The remaining $1,000 of his gain ($4,662 – $3,662) is treated as a Section 1231 gain.

Explanation

Sale of depreciable real estate. The depreciation recapture rules relating to the sale of real estate are quite complex. These rules depend on (1) when you placed the property in service, (2) what method of depreciation was used, and (3) whether the property was residential rental property or held for business use. It should be noted that no depreciation recapture should occur for real property acquired after 1986 because straight-line depreciation is the only method available for such property.

Residential real property acquired after 1980 and before 1987. Any gain on the sale of *residential real property* is ordinary income if the deductions taken under the accelerated ACRS method of depreciation exceed the depreciation allowed under the 15-year straight-line method of depreciation. However, any gain you incur in excess of the amount you have to recapture is treated as a capital gain. For property acquired after March 15, 1984, the ACRS period is 18 years, and for property acquired after May 8, 1985, the ACRS period is 19 years.

Tax computation using maximum capital gains rates. Use the Qualified Dividends and Capital Gain Tax Worksheet or the Schedule D Tax Worksheet (whichever applies) to figure your tax if you have qualified dividends or net capital gain. You have net capital gain if Schedule D, lines 15 and 16, are both gains.

Schedule D Tax Worksheet. You must use the Schedule D Tax Worksheet in the Schedule D instructions to figure your tax if:

- You have to file Schedule D, and
- Schedule D, line 18 (28% rate gain) or line 19 (unrecaptured section 1250 gain), is more than zero.

See Comprehensive Example, later, for an example of how to figure your tax using the Schedule D Tax Worksheet.

Qualified Dividends and Capital Gain Tax Worksheet. If you do not have to use the Schedule D Tax Worksheet (as explained above) and any of the following apply, use the Qualified Dividends and Capital Gain Tax Worksheet in the instructions for Form 1040 or Form 1040A (whichever you file) to figure your tax.

- You received qualified dividends. (See *Qualified Dividends* in chapter 8.)
- You do not have to file Schedule D and you received capital gain distributions. (See *Capital gain distributions only*, earlier.)
- Schedule D, lines 15 and 16, are both more than zero.

Alternative minimum tax. These capital gain rates are also used in figuring alternative minimum tax.

Comprehensive Example

Emily Jones is single and, in addition to wages from her job, she has income from stocks and other securities. For the 2011 tax year, she had the following capital gains and losses, which she reports on Forms 8949 and Schedule D. Her filled-in Forms 8949 and Schedule D are shown at the end of this example.

28% Rate Gain Worksheet for Emily Jones—Line 18 *Keep for Your Records*

1. Enter the total of all collectibles gain or (loss) from items you reported on line 8, column (f), of Schedules D and D-1	1.	0
2. Enter as a positive number the amount of any section 1202 exclusion you reported on lines 8, 9, and 10, in column (g), of Schedules D and D-1, for which you excluded 50% of the gain, plus ⅔ of any section 1202 exclusion you reported on lines 8, 9, or 10, in column (g), of Schedules D and D-1, for which you excluded 60% of the gain	2.	1,500
3. Enter the total of all collectibles gain or (loss) from Form 4684, line 4 (but only if Form 4684, line 15, is more than zero); Form 6252; Form 6781, Part II; and Form 8824	3.	
4. Enter the total of any collectibles gain reported to you on: • Form 1099-DIV, box 2d; • Form 2439, box 1d; and • Schedule K-1 from a partnership, S corporation, estate, or trust.	4.	
5. Enter your long-term capital loss carryovers from Schedule D, line 14, and Schedule K-1 (Form 1041), box 11, code C	5.	(500)
6. If Schedule D, line 7, is a (loss), enter that (loss) here. Otherwise, enter -0-	6.	(550)
7. Combine lines 1 through 6. If zero or less, enter -0-. If more than zero, also enter this amount on Schedule D, line 18	7.	450

Capital gains and losses—Forms 8949 and Schedule D. Emily sold stock in two different companies that she held for less than a year. In June, she sold 100 shares of Trucking Co. stock that she bought in February. She had an adjusted basis of $1,150 in the stock and sold it for $400, for a loss of $750. In July, she sold 25 shares of Computer Co. stock that she bought in June. She had an adjusted basis in the stock of $2,000 and sold it for $2,500, for a gain of $500. She reports these short-term transactions on line 1 in Part I of Form 8949, checking box (A) which flows to line 1 in Part I of Schedule D.

Emily had other stock sales that she reports as long-term transactions on line 3 in Part II of Form 8949, checking box (B) which flows to line 9 in Part II of Schedule D.

In June, she sold 500 shares of Furniture Co. stock for $5,000. She bought 100 of those shares in 1998, for $1,000. She bought 100 more shares in 2000 for $2,200, and an additional 300 shares in 2003 for $1,500. Her total basis in the stock is $4,700. She has a $300 ($5,000 − $4,700) gain on this sale. She enters this transaction on Form 8949 Part II line 3, and the gain on this sale flows to column (h) of line 9 on Schedule D.

In December, she sold 20 shares of Toy Co. stock for $4,100. This was qualified small business stock that she bought in September 2005. Her basis is $1,100, so she has a $3,000 gain. She enters this transaction on Form 8949 Part II line 2, and the gain flows to column (h) of line 9 on Schedule D. Because she held the stock more than 5 years, she has a $1,500 section 1202 exclusion. She claims the exclusion by entering $1,500 as a loss in column (g). She also enters the exclusion as a positive amount on line 2 of the 28% Rate Gain Worksheet.

She received a Form 1099-B (not shown) from her broker for each of these transactions. The entries shown in box 2 of these forms total $12,000 and box 3 totals $3,150.

Reconciliation of Forms 1099-B. Emily makes sure that the total of the amounts reported in column (e) of lines 2 and 4 of Forms 8949 is not less than the total of the amounts shown on the Forms 1099-B she received from her broker. For 2011, the total of lines 2 and 4 of Forms 8949 is $12,000, which is the same amount reported by the broker on Forms 1099-B (not shown).

Capital loss carryover from 2010. Emily has a capital loss carryover to 2011 of $800, of which $300 is short-term capital loss, and $500 is long-term capital loss. She enters these amounts on lines 6 and 14 of Schedule D. She also enters the $500 long-term capital loss carryover on line 5 of the 28% Rate Gain Worksheet.

She kept the completed Capital Loss Carryover Worksheet in her 2010 edition of Publication 550 (not shown), so she could properly report her loss carryover for the 2011 tax year without refiguring it.

Tax computation. Because Emily has gains on both lines 15 and 16 of Schedule D, she checks the "Yes" box on line 17 and goes to line 18. On line 18 she enters $450 from line 7 of the 28% Rate Gain Worksheet. Because line 18 is greater than zero, she checks the "No" box on line 20 and uses the Schedule D Tax Worksheet to figure her tax.

After entering the gain from line 16 on line 13 of her Form 1040, she completes the rest of Form 1040 through line 43. She enters the amount from that line, $30,000, on line 1 of the Schedule D Tax Worksheet. After filling out the rest of that worksheet, she figures her tax as $4,034. This is less than the tax she would have figured without the capital gain tax rates, $4,079.

Schedule D Tax Worksheet

Keep for Your Records

Complete this worksheet only if line 18 or line 19 of Schedule D is more than zero. Otherwise, complete the Qualified Dividends and Capital Gain Tax Worksheet in the Instructions for Form 1040, line 44 (or in the Instructions for Form 1040NR, line 42) to figure your tax.

Exception: Do not use the Qualified Dividends and Capital Gain Tax Worksheet **or** this worksheet to figure your tax if:

- Line 15 or line 16 of Schedule D is zero or less **and** you have no qualified dividends on Form 1040, line 9b (or Form 1040NR, line 10b); **or**
- Form 1040, line 43 (or Form 1040NR, line 41) is zero or less.

Instead, see the instructions for Form 1040, line 44 (or Form 1040NR, line 42).

1. Enter your taxable income from Form 1040, line 43 (or Form 1040NR, line 41). (However, if you are filing Form 2555 or 2555-EZ (relating to foreign earned income), enter instead the amount from line 3 of the Foreign Earned Income Tax Worksheet in the Instructions for Form 1040, line 44) . . . **1.** 30,000
2. Enter your qualified dividends from Form 1040, line 9b (or Form 1040NR, line 10b) . . . **2.** ______
3. Enter the amount from Form 4952 (used to figure investment interest expense deduction), line 4g . . . **3.** ______
4. Enter the amount from Form 4952, line 4e* . . . **4.** ______
5. Subtract line 4 from line 3. If zero or less, enter -0- . . . **5.** ______
6. Subtract line 5 from line 2. If zero or less, enter -0-** . . . **6.** ______
7. Enter the **smaller** of line 15 or line 16 of Schedule D . . . **7.** 750
8. Enter the **smaller** of line 3 or line 4 . . . **8.** ______
9. Subtract line 8 from line 7. If zero or less, enter -0-** . . . **9.** 750
10. Add lines 6 and 9 . . . **10.** 750
11. Add lines 18 and 19 of Schedule D** . . . **11.** 450
12. Enter the **smaller** of line 9 or line 11 . . . **12.** 450
13. Subtract line 12 from line 10 . . . **13.** 300
14. Subtract line 13 from line 1. If zero or less, enter -0- . . . **14.** 29,700
15. Enter:
    - $34,000 if single or married filing separately;
    - $68,000 if married filing jointly or qualifying widow(er); or
    - $45,550 if head of household . . . **15.** 34,000
16. Enter the **smaller** of line 1 or line 15 . . . **16.** 30,000
17. Enter the **smaller** of line 14 or line 16 . . . **17.** 29,700
18. Subtract line 10 from line 1. If zero or less, enter -0- . . . **18.** 29,250
19. Enter the **larger** of line 17 or line 18 . . . ▶ **19.** 29,700
20. Subtract line 17 from line 16. This amount is taxed at 0% . . . ▶ **20.** 300

    If lines 1 and 16 are the same, skip lines 21 through 33 and go to line 34. Otherwise, go to line 21.
21. Enter the **smaller** of line 1 or line 13 . . . **21.** ______
22. Enter the amount from line 20 (if line 20 is blank, enter -0-) . . . **22.** ______
23. Subtract line 22 from line 21. If zero or less, enter -0- . . . ▶ **23.** ______
24. Multiply line 23 by 15% (.15) . . . **24.** ______

    If Schedule D, line 19, is zero or blank, skip lines 25 through 30 and go to line 31. Otherwise, go to line 25.
25. Enter the **smaller** of line 9 above or Schedule D, line 19 . . . **25.** ______
26. Add lines 10 and 19 . . . **26.** ______
27. Enter the amount from line 1 above . . . **27.** ______
28. Subtract line 27 from line 26. If zero or less, enter -0- . . . **28.** ______
29. Subtract line 28 from line 25. If zero or less, enter -0- . . . ▶ **29.** ______
30. Multiply line 29 by 25% (.25) . . . **30.** ______

    If Schedule D, line 18, is zero or blank, skip lines 31 through 33 and go to line 34. Otherwise, go to line 31.
31. Add lines 19, 20, 23, and 29 . . . **31.** ______
32. Subtract line 31 from line 1 . . . **32.** ______
33. Multiply line 32 by 28% (.28) . . . **33.** ______
34. Figure the tax on the amount on **line 19.** If the amount on line 19 is less than $100,000, use the Tax Table to figure the tax. If the amount on line 19 is $100,000 or more, use the Tax Computation Worksheet . . . **34.** 4,034
35. Add lines 24, 30, 33, and 34 . . . **35.** 4,034
36. Figure the tax on the amount on **line 1.** If the amount on line 1 is less than $100,000, use the Tax Table to figure the tax. If the amount on line 1 is $100,000 or more, use the Tax Computation Worksheet . . . **36.** 4,079
37. **Tax on all taxable income (including capital gains and qualified dividends).** Enter the **smaller** of line 35 or line 36. Also include this amount on Form 1040, line 44 (or Form 1040NR, line 42). (If you are filing Form 2555 or 2555-EZ, do not enter this amount on Form 1040, line 44. Instead, enter it on line 4 of the Foreign Earned Income Tax Worksheet in the Form 1040 instructions) . . . **37.** 4,034

*If applicable, enter instead the smaller amount you entered on the dotted line next to line 4e of Form 4952.

**If you are filing Form 2555 or 2555-EZ, see the footnote in the Foreign Earned Income Tax Worksheet in the Instructions for Form 1040, line 44, before completing this line.

Form **8949**

Department of the Treasury
Internal Revenue Service (99)

Sales and Other Dispositions of Capital Assets

► See Instructions for Schedule D (Form 1040).
► Attach to Schedule D to list your transactions for lines 1, 2, 3, 8, 9, and 10.

OMB No. 1545-0074

2011

Attachment Sequence No. **12A**

Name(s) shown on return: **Emily Jones**

Your social security number: **111-00-1111**

Part I **Short-Term Capital Gains and Losses—Assets Held One Year or Less**

Note. Please round and use whole dollars on this form.

Check the box below that describes the transactions listed on this page.

Caution. Check only one box. If you have more than one type of transaction, complete a separate Form 8949 for each type.

☑ **(A)** Short-term gains and losses (Form 1099-B, box 3, shows basis)
☐ **(B)** Short-term gains and losses (Form 1099-B, box 3, does not show basis)
☐ **(C)** Short-term gains and losses (Form 1099-B not received)

1 (a) Description of property (Example: 100 sh. XYZ Co.)	(b) Code	(c) Date acquired (Mo., day, yr.)	(d) Date sold (Mo., day, yr.)	(e) Sales price (see instructions)	(f) Cost or other basis (see instructions)	(g) Adjustments to gain or loss
100 sh. Trucking Co.		2-11-11	6-10-11	400	1,150	
25 sh. Computer Co.		6-30-11	7-29-11	2,500	2,000	
2 **Totals.** Add the amounts in columns (e) and (f). Also, combine the amounts in column (g). Enter here and include on Schedule D, line 1 (if box A above is checked), line 2 (if box B above is checked), or line 3 (if box C above is checked) . . . . ►			2	2,900	3,150	0

For Paperwork Reduction Act Notice, see your tax return instructions. Cat. No. 37768Z Form **8949** (2011)

Name(s) shown on return. Do not enter name and social security number if shown on other side.
Emily Jones

Your social security number
111-00-1111

Part II **Long-Term Capital Gains and Losses—Assets Held More Than One Year**

Note. Please round and use whole dollars on this form.

Check the box below that describes the transactions listed on this page.

Caution. Check only one box. If you have more than one type of transaction, complete a separate Form 8949 for each type.

☐ **(A)** Long-term gains and losses (Form 1099-B, box 3, shows basis)
☑ **(B)** Long-term gains and losses (Form 1099-B, box 3, does not show basis)
☐ **(C)** Long-term gains and losses (Form 1099-B not received)

3 **(a)** Description of property (Example: 100 sh. XYZ Co.)	**(b)** Code	**(c)** Date acquired (Mo., day, yr.)	**(d)** Date sold (Mo., day, yr.)	**(e)** Sales price (see instructions)	**(f)** Cost or other basis (see instructions)	**(g)** Adjustments to gain or loss
500 sh. Furniture Co.		VARIOUS	6-30-11	5,000	4,700	
20 sh. Toy Co.		9-28-05	12-15-11	4,100	1,100	(1,500)
4 Totals. Add the amounts in columns (e) and (f). Also, combine the amounts in column (g). Enter here and include on Schedule D, line 8 (if box A above is checked), line 9 (if box B above is checked), or line 10 (if box C above is checked) . . . . ▶ 4				9,100	5,800	(1,500)

Form **8949** (2011)

SCHEDULE D (Form 1040)

Department of the Treasury Internal Revenue Service (99)

Capital Gains and Losses

▶ Attach to Form 1040 or Form 1040NR. ▶ See Instructions for Schedule D (Form 1040).
▶ Use Form 8949 to list your transactions for lines 1, 2, 3, 8, 9, and 10.

OMB No. 1545-0074

2011

Attachment Sequence No. 12

Name(s) shown on return	Your social security number
Emily Jones	**111-00-1111**

Part I Short-Term Capital Gains and Losses—Assets Held One Year or Less

Note: Please round and use whole dollars on this form.	**(e)** Sales price from Form(s) 8949, line 2, column (e)	**(f)** Cost or other basis from Form(s) 8949, line 2, column (f)	**(g)** Adjustments to gain or loss from Form(s) 8949, line 2, column (g)	**(h) Gain or (loss)** Combine columns (e), (f), and (g)
1 Short-term totals from all Forms 8949 with box A checked in Part I	**2,900**	(**3,150**)		**(250)**
2 Short-term totals from all Forms 8949 with box B checked in Part I		( )		
3 Short-term totals from all Forms 8949 with box C checked in Part I		( )		

4 Short-term gain from Form 6252 and short-term gain or (loss) from Forms 4684, 6781, and 8824 .	4	
5 Net short-term gain or (loss) from partnerships, S corporations, estates, and trusts from Schedule(s) K-1	5	
6 Short-term capital loss carryover. Enter the amount, if any, from line 8 of your **Capital Loss Carryover Worksheet** in the instructions	6	(**300**)
7 **Net short-term capital gain or (loss).** Combine lines 1 through 6 in column (h)	7	**(550)**

Part II Long-Term Capital Gains and Losses—Assets Held More Than One Year

Note: Please round and use whole dollars on this form.	**(e)** Sales price from Form(s) 8949, line 4, column (e)	**(f)** Cost or other basis from Form(s) 8949, line 4, column (f)	**(g)** Adjustments to gain or loss from Form(s) 8949, line 4, column (g)	**(h) Gain or (loss)** Combine columns (e), (f), and (g)
8 Long-term totals from all Forms 8949 with box A checked in Part II		( )		
9 Long-term totals from all Forms 8949 with box B checked in Part II	**9,100**	(**5,800**)	**(1,500)**	**(1,800)**
10 Long-term totals from all Forms 8949 with box C checked in Part II		( )		

11 Gain from Form 4797, Part I; long-term gain from Forms 2439 and 6252; and long-term gain or (loss) from Forms 4684, 6781, and 8824	11	
12 Net long-term gain or (loss) from partnerships, S corporations, estates, and trusts from Schedule(s) K-1	12	
13 Capital gain distributions. See the instructions	13	
14 Long-term capital loss carryover. Enter the amount, if any, from line 13 of your **Capital Loss Carryover Worksheet** in the instructions	14	(**500**)
15 **Net long-term capital gain or (loss).** Combine lines 8 through 14 in column (h). Then go to Part III on the back	15	**1,300**

For Paperwork Reduction Act Notice, see your tax return instructions. Cat. No. 11338H **Schedule D (Form 1040) 2011**

Part III **Summary. Note:** Please round and use whole dollars on this form.

16	Combine lines 7 and 15 and enter the result	16	750
	• If line 16 is a **gain**, enter the amount from line 16 on Form 1040, line 13, or Form 1040NR, line 14. Then go to line 17 below. • If line 16 is a **loss**, skip lines 17 through 20 below. Then go to line 21. Also be sure to complete line 22. • If line 16 is **zero**, skip lines 17 through 21 below and enter -0- on Form 1040, line 13, or Form 1040NR, line 14. Then go to line 22.		
17	Are lines 15 and 16 **both** gains? ☑ **Yes.** Go to line 18. ☐ **No.** Skip lines 18 through 21, and go to line 22.		
18	Enter the amount, if any, from line 7 of the **28% Rate Gain Worksheet** in the instructions ▶	18	450
19	Enter the amount, if any, from line 18 of the **Unrecaptured Section 1250 Gain Worksheet** in the instructions ▶	19	
20	Are lines 18 and 19 **both** zero or blank? ☐ **Yes.** Complete Form 1040 through line 43, or Form 1040NR through line 41. Then complete the **Qualified Dividends and Capital Gain Tax Worksheet** in the instructions for Form 1040, line 44 (or in the instructions for Form 1040NR, line 42). **Do not** complete lines 21 and 22 below. ☑ **No.** Complete Form 1040 through line 43, or Form 1040NR through line 41. Then complete the **Schedule D Tax Worksheet** in the instructions. **Do not** complete lines 21 and 22 below.		
21	If line 16 is a loss, enter here and on Form 1040, line 13, or Form 1040NR, line 14, the **smaller** of: • The loss on line 16 or • ($3,000), or if married filing separately, ($1,500) **Note.** When figuring which amount is smaller, treat both amounts as positive numbers.	21	( )
22	Do you have qualified dividends on Form 1040, line 9b, or Form 1040NR, line 10b? ☐ **Yes.** Complete Form 1040 through line 43, or Form 1040NR through line 41. Then complete the **Qualified Dividends and Capital Gain Tax Worksheet** in the instructions for Form 1040, line 44 (or in the instructions for Form 1040NR, line 42). ☐ **No.** Complete the rest of Form 1040 or Form 1040NR.		

Schedule D (Form 1040) 2011

Part 4

Adjustments to income

ey.com/EYTaxGuide

The four chapters in this part discuss six of the adjustments to income that you can deduct in figuring your adjusted gross income. These chapters cover:

- Contributions you make to traditional individual retirement arrangements (IRAs) (chapter 17)
- Alimony you pay (chapter 18)
- Educator expenses, student loan interest, and tuition and fees you pay (chapter 19)
- Moving expenses you pay (chapter 20)

Other adjustments to income are discussed in other parts of this or other publications. For details, see the table on the next page.

Other adjustments to income

Use this table to find information about other adjustments to income not covered in this part of the publication.

IF you are looking for more information about the deduction for...	THEN see...
Certain business expenses of reservists, performing artists, and fee-basis officials	chapter 27.
Contributions to a health savings account	Publication 969, *Health Savings Accounts and Other Tax-Favored Health Plans*.
Moving expenses	chapter 20.
One-half of self-employment tax	chapter 23.
Self-employed health insurance	chapter 22.
Payments to self-employed SEP, SIMPLE, and qualified plans	Publication 560, *Retirement Plans for Small Business*.
Penalty on the early withdrawal of savings	chapter 7.
Contributions to an Archer MSA	chapter 22.
Reforestation amortization or expense	chapter 9 of Publication 535, *Business Expenses*.
Contributions to Internal Revenue Code section 501(c)(18)(D) pension plans	Publication 525, *Taxable and Nontaxable Income*.
Expenses from the rental of personal property	chapter 12.
Certain required repayments of supplemental unemployment benefits (sub-pay)	chapter 12.
Foreign housing costs	chapter 4 of Publication 54, *Tax Guide for U.S. Citizens and Resident Aliens Abroad*.
Jury duty pay given to your employer	chapter 12.
Contributions by certain chaplains to Internal Revenue Code section 403(b) plans	Publication 517, *Social Security and Other Information for Members of the Clergy and Religious Workers*.
Attorney fees and certain costs for actions involving certain unlawful discrimination claims or awards to whistleblowers	Publication 525.
Domestic production activities deduction	Form 8903.

Chapter 17

Individual retirement arrangements (IRAs)

ey.com/EYTaxGuide

Note

IRS Publication 17 (*Your Federal Income Tax*) has been updated by Ernst & Young LLP for 2011. Dates and dollar amounts shown are for 2011. Underlined type is used to indicate where IRS text has been updated. Places where text has been removed are indicated by the sentence: *Text intentionally omitted*.

ey.com/EYTaxGuide

Ernst & Young LLP will update the *Ernst & Young Tax Guide 2012* website with relevant taxpayer information as it becomes available. You can also sign up for email alerts to let you know when changes have been made.

Introduction

There are two basic types of individual retirement arrangements (IRAs) discussed in this chapter: traditional IRAs and Roth IRAs. Each has different eligibility requirements and characteristics.

- **Traditional IRAs:** If you are not eligible for your employer's qualified retirement plan(s), or you are eligible but your income does not exceed specified limits, your contributions to a traditional IRA are deductible. Otherwise, you can only make nondeductible contributions to the IRA. Your maximum annual contribution is the lesser of $5,000 ($6,000 if you're age 50 by the end of the year) or your taxable compensation. (This limit applies on a combined basis to your traditional [whether deductible or not deductible] and Roth contributions.) You defer paying taxes on the income earned by the funds held in your IRA until withdrawal. How distributions from traditional IRAs are taxed at the time of withdrawal depends on whether your contribution was deductible or nondeductible. Where all the contributions to the traditional IRA were deductible, all of the distribution is taxable. Where some or all of the contributions to the traditional IRA were nondeductible, the pro rata portion of the distribution that is attributable to your nondeductible contributions is not taxable.
- **Roth IRAs:** If your income is below specified levels, you can make nondeductible contributions to a Roth IRA. Although contributions are not deductible, distributions from your Roth IRA account, including income and any gains, are tax free if the distribution meets certain requirements. Like a traditional IRA, the maximum amount you can contribute to a Roth IRA in 2011 is limited to the lesser of $5,000 ($6,000 if you're age 50 by the end of the year) or the amount of your taxable compensation. Your maximum allowable contribution to the Roth IRA may be further reduced depending on the amount of your modified adjusted gross income and your filing status.

This chapter also discusses the simplified employee pension IRA (SEP IRA) and the Savings Incentive Match Plans for Employees (SIMPLE IRA). These are employer-sponsored plans that are established using IRAs. The SEP IRA and the SIMPLE IRA have different contribution limits, both from each other and from traditional and Roth IRAs.

Tax Breaks and Deductions You Can Use Checklist

Individual Retirement Arrangements (IRAs). IRAs come in several different "flavors"–traditional IRA, Roth IRA, SIMPLE IRA, and SEP IRA. Each type of IRA has different eligibility requirements and characteristics–all offer tax benefits of one variety or another.

- ***Traditional IRA.*** There are two types of contributions to traditional IRAs–deductible and nondeductible. If you meet the eligibility standards for the year, the amount you contribute is deductible when contributed. If you don't meet the eligibility standards for the year because of your income level and your employer provides a retirement plan, you can still contribute, but the amount is not deductible (nondeductible IRA). You may establish separate IRAs for deductible and nondeductible contributions or combine them into one IRA. The income you accumulate in a traditional IRA account is not taxed until you take a withdrawal. This is true whether the earnings are on deductible or nondeductible contributions. However, when you take a distribution, whether the original contribution was deductible or nondeductible, makes a difference. Where all the contributions to the traditional IRA were deductible, all of the distribution is taxable. Where some or all of the contributions to the traditional IRA were nondeductible, the pro rata portion of the distribution that is attributable to your nondeductible contributions is not taxable.

  In 2011, you can contribute up to the lesser of

What's New for 2011

Due date for contributions and withdrawals. Contributions can be made to your IRA for a year at any time during the year or by the due date for filing your return for that year, not including extensions. Because April 15, 2012, falls on a Sunday, and Emancipation Day, Monday, April 16, 2012, is a legal holiday in the District of Columbia, the due date for making contributions for 2011 to your IRA is April 17, 2012. See *When Can Contributions Be Made?*

There is a 6% excise tax on excess contributions not withdrawn by the due date (including extensions) for your return. You will not have to pay the 6% tax if any 2011 excess contributions are withdrawn by the due date of your return (including extensions). See *Excess Contributions* under *What Acts Result in Penalties or Additional Taxes?*

Modified AGI limit for traditional IRA contributions increased. For 2011, if you were covered by a retirement plan at work, your deduction for contributions to a traditional IRA is reduced (phased out) if your modified AGI is:

- More than $90,000 but less than $110,000 for a married couple filing a joint return or a qualifying widow(er),
- More than $56,000 but less than $66,000 for a single individual or head of household, or
- Less than $10,000 for a married individual filing a separate return.

If you either lived with your spouse or file a joint return, and your spouse was covered by a retirement plan at work, but you were not, your deduction is phased out if your modified AGI is more than $169,000 but less than $179,000. If your modified AGI is $179,000 or more, you cannot take a deduction for contributions to a traditional IRA. See *How Much Can You Deduct?* later.

Modified AGI limit for Roth IRA contributions increased. For 2011, your Roth IRA contribution limit is reduced (phased out) in the following situations.

- Your filing status is married filing jointly or qualifying widow(er) and your modified AGI is at least $169,000. You cannot make a Roth IRA contribution if your modified AGI is $179,000 or more.
- Your filing status is single, head of household, or married filing separately and you did not live with your spouse at any time in 2010 and your modified AGI is at least $107,000. You cannot make a Roth IRA contribution if your modified AGI is $122,000 or more.
- Your filing status is married filing separately, you lived with your spouse at any time during the year, and your modified AGI is more than -0-. You cannot make a Roth IRA contribution if your modified AGI is $10,000 or more.

See *Can You Contribute to a Roth IRA?* later.

Text intentionally omitted.

Qualified charitable distributions (QCDs). Tax-free treatment of distributions from traditional and Roth IRAs for charitable purposes has been extended through December 31, 2011, with the following special rule. For qualified charitable distributions (QCDs) made during January 2011, you can elect to have the distribution deemed to have been made on December 31, 2010. If you make this election, the QCD will count toward your 2010 exclusion limit of $100,000, as well as your 2010 minimum required distribution. QCDs are discussed further later in this chapter.

Text intentionally omitted.

What's New for 2012

Modified AGI limit for traditional IRA contributions increased. For 2012, if you are covered by a retirement plan at work, your deduction for contributions to a traditional IRA is reduced (phased out) if your modified AGI is:

- More than $91,000 but less than $111,000 for a married couple filing a joint return or a qualifying widow(er),
- More than $57,000 but less than $67,000 for a single individual or head of household, or
- Less than $10,000 for a married individual filing a separate return.

If you either live with your spouse or file a joint return, and your spouse is covered by a retirement plan at work, but you are not, your deduction is phased out if your modified AGI is more than $170,000 but less than $180,000. If your modified AGI is $180,000 or more, you cannot take a deduction for contributions to a traditional IRA.

Modified AGI limit for Roth IRA contributions increased. For 2012, your Roth IRA contribution limit is reduced (phased out) in the following situations.

- Your filing status is married filing jointly or qualifying widow(er) and your modified AGI is at least $169,000. You cannot make a Roth IRA contribution if your modified AGI is $179,000 or more.
- Your filing status is single, head of household, or married filing separately and you did not live with your spouse at any time in 2012 and your modified AGI is at least $107,000. You cannot make a Roth IRA contribution if your modified AGI is $122,000 or more.
- Your filing status is married filing separately, you lived with your spouse at any time during the year, and your modified AGI is more than -0-. You cannot make a Roth IRA contribution if your modified AGI is $10,000 or more.

TAXALERT

IRA contribution limits. The IRA contribution limit is adjusted annually for inflation. For 2011, however, the IRA contribution limit is unchanged from 2010 because inflation was not large enough to trigger an increase in the contribution limit. As of the date this book was published, the IRS had not yet announced the IRA contribution limits for 2012. Check ey.com/EYTaxGuide for updates.

Reminders

Contributions to both traditional and Roth IRAs. For information on your combined contribution limit if you contribute to both traditional and Roth IRAs, see *Roth IRAs and traditional IRAs* under *How Much Can Be Contributed?* later.

Statement of required minimum distribution. If a minimum distribution is required from your IRA, the trustee, custodian, or issuer that held the IRA at the end of the preceding year must either report the amount of the required minimum distribution to you, or offer to calculate it for you. The report or offer must include the date by which the amount must be distributed. The report is due January 31 of the year in which the minimum distribution is required. It can be provided with the year-end fair market value statement that you normally get each year. No report is required for IRAs of owners who have died.

IRA interest. Although interest earned from your IRA is generally not taxed in the year earned, it is not tax-exempt interest. Tax on your traditional IRA is generally deferred until you take a distribution. Do not report this interest on your tax return as tax-exempt interest.

Form 8606. To designate contributions as nondeductible, you must file Form 8606, Nondeductible IRAs.

Disaster-related tax relief. Special rules apply to the use of retirement funds (including IRAs) by qualified individuals who suffered an economic loss as a result of:

- The storms that began on May 4, 2007, in the Kansas disaster area, or
- The severe storms in the Midwestern disaster areas in 2008.

For more information on these special rules see *Tax Relief for Kansas Disaster Area* and *Tax Relief for Midwestern Disaster Areas* in chapter 4 of Publication 590.

TAXSAVER

Retirement savings through IRAs. Wealth can build up much faster in an IRA or other tax-deferred retirement plan than in a savings account or other non-tax-exempt investment. Because you do not have to pay income tax as your earnings accumulate within the IRA or plan, your investments compound in value more quickly. A person in the 28% tax bracket, for example, could end up with 1.7 times more money after tax on a $5,000 deductible IRA contribution held for 20 years than if he or she did not make the contribution. If the person's marginal tax rate drops to 15% in retirement, he or she could have 2 times more money after tax.

Example

If in 2011 you invested $5,000 in an IRA that earns 10% per year, it will be worth $24,219 in 2031 after all taxes are paid if you are in the 28% bracket. If in 2031 you retire and drop into the 15% tax bracket and take a distribution, your original $5,000 investment will be worth $28,592 after all taxes are paid.

$5,000 ($6,000 if you're age 50 by the end of the year) or the amount of your taxable compensation to a traditional IRA. (This is a combined limit with the Roth IRA.) You may also be eligible to deduct all or a portion of the contribution. The deduction is allowed as an adjustment in arriving at your adjusted gross income. Therefore, deducting your IRA contributions reduces your income subject to tax regardless of whether you itemize deductions. Three factors determine the extent to which you may deduct your contribution: the amount of your modified adjusted gross income; your filing status; and whether you are covered by a retirement plan at work.

For more information on figuring the deductible portion of your contribution to a traditional IRA, see *How Much Can You Deduct?* later in this chapter.

- ***Roth IRA.*** You can receive income accumulated within a Roth IRA account completely tax-free and penalty-free if certain conditions are met. In comparison, the income built up inside a traditional IRA is eventually subject to income tax at ordinary income tax rates as distributions are received.

To qualify as a tax-free and penalty-free distribution, generally, the Roth IRA must have been established more than five years earlier and the distribution is received after you reach age 59½,

Tip

The term "50 or older" is used several times in this chapter. It refers to an IRA owner who is age 50 or older by the end of the tax year.

made because you are disabled, made to a beneficiary following your death, or made to pay up to $10,000 (lifetime limit) of certain qualified first-time homebuyer amounts. Roth IRAs also have the advantage that there is no age at which minimum distributions must commence while you are alive.

Like with a traditional IRA, the maximum amount you can contribute to a Roth IRA in 2011 is limited to the lesser of $5,000 ($6,000 if you're age 50 by the end of the year) or the amount of your taxable compensation. Your maximum allowable contribution may be further reduced depending on the amount of your modified adjusted gross income and your filing status. No portion of your contribution to a Roth IRA is deductible.

See Roth IRAs, later in this chapter, for more information.

- ***SIMPLE IRA.*** If you work for a small employer, your employer may be eligible to establish a SIMPLE IRA account for you. This is a plan similar to a 401(k) plan, but with lower limits on both the amount of contributions the employer can make and the salary deferrals you can make, compared to a 401(k) plan. Your employer will also be required to make a matching contribution of either 2% or 3% of your annual compensation to your SIMPLE account, depending on the terms of the plan adopted by your employer. Under a SIMPLE IRA, the contributions for you are made to your IRA rather than to an employer trust. You may also be able to establish a SIMPLE IRA if you are self-employed. Generally, the annual contributions and accumulated income are not

However, if you do not have an IRA, the $5,000 you receive in 2011 is subject to tax immediately. If you are in the 28% bracket, you are left with only $3,600. Investing that $3,600 in 2011 in a non-IRA investment earning 10%, remaining in the 28% bracket until you retire, and being in the 15% bracket when you retire, will leave you with only $14,461 in 2031 after taxes.

Note: The highest tax bracket in 2011 is 35%. As of the date this book was published, this reduced top individual rate is scheduled to expire after December 31, 2012. Therefore, the savings resulting from an IRA may be different than indicated in this example. Also, the results will be different for a contribution to a non-deductible IRA or to a Roth IRA.

An individual retirement arrangement (IRA) is a personal savings plan that gives you tax advantages for setting aside money for your retirement.

This chapter discusses the following topics.

- The rules for a traditional IRA (any IRA that is not a Roth or SIMPLE IRA).
- The Roth IRA, which features nondeductible contributions and tax-free distributions.

Simplified Employee Pensions (SEPs) and Savings Incentive Match Plans for Employees (SIMPLEs) are not discussed in this chapter. For more information on these plans and employees' SEP IRAs and SIMPLE IRAs that are part of these plans, see Publications 560 and 590.

For information about contributions, deductions, withdrawals, transfers, rollovers, and other transactions for 2011, see Publication 590.

Useful Items

You may want to see:

Publication

- □ **560** Retirement Plans for Small Business
- □ **590** Individual Retirement Arrangements (IRAs)

Form (and Instructions)

- □ **5329** Additional Taxes on Qualified Plans (including IRAs) and Other Tax-Favored Accounts
- □ **8606** Nondeductible IRAs

TAXPLANNER

Self-employed persons often overlook the benefits available to them from establishing an IRA. The only requirement for contributing to an IRA is that you have not reached age 70½ (note: this does not apply to Roth IRAs) and have earned income, which includes income from your business, provided that your personal efforts create a major portion of the business income. Therefore, a self-employed person could establish both a Keogh plan and an IRA. For more information on retirement plans for the self-employed, see chapter 10, *Retirement plans, pensions, and annuities.*

TAXSAVER

You are a sole proprietor and you hire your spouse or child to perform bona fide services, such as bookkeeping, as an employee. Assuming that the family member works in a genuine employment relationship, the salary paid is compensation for personal services and should be included in the family member's gross income. The family member's salary is a deductible expense to you. This gross income would entitle that family member to make a contribution to an IRA of up to $5,000 (or, if a non-spouse with less than $5,000 income, up to the non-spouse's actual income).

Your spouse's wages constitute wages subject to social security tax, so this strategy may not work to your advantage.

Be prepared to defend the genuine employment relationship of your spouse if the IRS should question it.

Traditional IRAs

In this chapter the original IRA (sometimes called an ordinary or regular IRA) is referred to as a "traditional IRA." A traditional IRA is any IRA that is not a Roth IRA or a SIMPLE IRA. Two advantages of a traditional IRA are:

- You may be able to deduct some or all of your contributions to it, depending on your circumstances, and
- Generally, amounts in your IRA, including earnings and gains, are not taxed until they are distributed.

Who Can Open a Traditional IRA?

You can open and make contributions to a traditional IRA if:

- You (or, if you file a joint return, your spouse) received taxable compensation during the year, and
- You were not age 70½ by the end of the year.

What is compensation? Generally, compensation is what you earn from working. Compensation includes wages, salaries, tips, professional fees, bonuses, and other amounts you receive for providing personal services. The IRS treats as compensation any amount properly shown in box 1 (Wages, tips, other compensation) of Form W-2, Wage and Tax Statement, provided that amount is reduced by any amount properly shown in box 11 (Nonqualified plans).

Scholarship and fellowship payments are compensation for this purpose only if shown in box 1 of Form W-2.

Compensation also includes commissions and taxable alimony and separate maintenance payments.

Self-employment income. If you are self-employed (a sole proprietor or a partner), compensation is the net earnings from your trade or business (provided your personal services are a material income-producing factor) reduced by the total of:

- The deduction for contributions made on your behalf to retirement plans, and
- The deduction allowed for one-half of your self-employment taxes.

Compensation includes earnings from self-employment even if they are not subject to self-employment tax because of your religious beliefs.

Nontaxable combat pay. For IRA purposes, if you were a member of the U.S. Armed Forces, your compensation includes any non-taxable combat pay you receive.

TAXSAVER

Taxpayers can now count tax-free combat pay when determining whether they qualify to contribute to either a traditional or Roth IRA. Before this change, part of the Heroes Earned Retirement Opportunities (HERO) Act enacted in 2006, members of the military whose earnings came entirely from tax-free combat pay were generally barred from using IRAs to save for retirement because they had only combat pay, which did not count as earnings for purposes of establishing an IRA.

What is not compensation? Compensation does not include any of the following items.

- Earnings and profits from property, such as rental income, interest income, and dividend income.
- Pension or annuity income.
- Deferred compensation received (compensation payments postponed from a past year).
- Income from a partnership for which you do not provide services that are a material income-producing factor.
- Conservation Reserve Program (CRP) payments reported on Schedule SE (Form 1040), line 1(b).
- Any amounts (other than combat pay) you exclude from income, such as foreign earned income and housing costs.

EXPLANATION

For purposes of figuring your contribution to your IRA, compensation includes sales commissions, net income from your business, and partnership income that is subject to self-employment tax. Business and partnership income must be reduced by any contributions to a Keogh or SEP plan you make. Compensation does not include nontaxable amounts (other than combat pay), deferred compensation, severance pay, or pension distributions. If you have multiple sources of self-employment income and/or partnership income subject to self-employment tax, all gains and losses from these sources must be aggregated for purposes of computing compensation from self-employment. If the result is a gain, it is added to your wages, possibly permitting you

taxable until you take distributions.

The maximum limits on annual contributions to a SIMPLE IRA are substantially greater than for either a traditional or Roth IRA. In 2011, the limit is $11,500 ($14,000 if you are over age 50 by the end of the year). This is less than if your employer had established a 401(k) plan, and is coordinated with any amounts deferred to a 401(k) plan or a salary reduction simplified employee pension (SARSEP) plan of another employer. (New SARSEPS were prohibited after December 31, 1996.)

For more information on SIMPLE plans, see Savings Incentive Match Plans for Employees (SIMPLE), later in this chapter.

- ***SEP IRA.*** Employers may also establish a SEP IRA. In this structure, like the SIMPLE IRA, your employer makes contributions for you to your IRA. In most cases, there are only employer contributions to the SEP; however, before 1997 small employers were able to establish SARSEPs to accept elective deferrals. Employers who established a SARSEP before 1997 can continue to use them for both old and new employees as long as they had 25 or fewer employees in the prior year. The SEP contribution is made to a traditional IRA. The salary deferral limits are the same as for 401(k) plans ($16,500 in 2011, plus $5,500 if you have attained age 50 by the end of the 2011 calendar year). The limit is coordinated with any amounts deferred to a 401(k) plan or SIMPLE IRA of another employer.

Rollovers to a Traditional IRA. You can make a tax-free transfer of money or property you receive from a qualified retirement plan, including a traditional IRA, into a traditional IRA. This tax-free rollover must generally be accomplished by the 60th day after the day you first received the distribution. In addition, if the rollover is from one traditional IRA account into another traditional IRA account, you can only perform the rollover once per year with respect to each separate IRA account you own. You can also make a direct rollover from a qualified retirement plan to a traditional IRA. In this case, the one-time rule does not apply. For more information, see *Can You Move Retirement Plan Assets?* later.

Converting a Traditional IRA to a Roth IRA. You can convert assets held in a traditional IRA account into a Roth IRA. If you make the conversion, you will have to pay income tax on any portion of the distribution of the traditional IRA that had not been previously taxed. Converting to a Roth IRA may be more beneficial than leaving the assets in a traditional IRA if you plan on leaving the money invested for a long period of time. For more information, see *Converting From Any Traditional IRA to a Roth IRA*, later.

Converting a Qualified Retirement Plan to a Roth IRA. You can convert investments held in a qualified retirement plan (i.e., 401(k)), 403(b) tax-sheltered annuities, and government plans under Section 457 into a Roth IRA. If you make the conversion, you will have to pay income tax on any portion of the distribution of the qualified plan that had not been previously taxed. However, the conversion from a qualified employer plan

to make a larger deductible contribution to your IRA. If the result of your self-employment activities is a loss, however, you need not account for it in determining your IRA contribution eligibility. Income earned outside the United States is compensation to the extent that it is taxable in the United States (other than combat pay). Your foreign earned income must be adjusted for any foreign income exclusion. For more information, see chapter 41, *U.S. citizens working abroad: Tax treatment of foreign earned income.*

When and How Can a Traditional IRA Be Opened?

You can open a traditional IRA at any time. However, the time for making contributions for any year is limited. See *When Can Contributions Be Made*, later.

You can open different kinds of IRAs with a variety of organizations. You can open an IRA at a bank or other financial institution or with a mutual fund or life insurance company. You can also open an IRA through your stockbroker. Any IRA must meet Internal Revenue Code requirements.

Kinds of traditional IRAs. Your traditional IRA can be an individual retirement account or annuity. It can be part of either a simplified employee pension (SEP) or an employer or employee association trust account.

EXPLANATION

The basic difference between individual retirement arrangements and individual retirement annuities lies in the type of investment and the method of funding it. An individual retirement arrangement is generally a type of trust with varied investments, such as stocks, bonds, savings accounts, certificates of deposit, credit union accounts, common trust funds, and real estate, among other things. An individual retirement annuity is an investment in an insurance contract.

TAXPLANNER

Self-directed IRAs. If you want to actively manage your IRA investments, you may consider setting up a self-directed IRA. To do so, without having to obtain preapproval from the IRS, you may use Form 5305, a model trust form, and Form 5305-A, a model custodial account agreement. However, keep in mind that even if you use these model forms, you still will have to find a financial institution to administer your account.

TAXPLANNER

In deciding whether or not to create a self-directed IRA, keep in mind that an investment in the following collectibles is not allowed by an IRA:

- Artworks
- Coins (unless state issued, U.S. minted gold, and silver coins of 1 ounce or less)
- Stamps
- Gems
- Antiques
- Rugs
- Alcoholic beverages
- Metals (except for certain types of bullion traded on a contract market)

How Much Can Be Contributed?

There are limits and other rules that affect the amount that can be contributed to a traditional IRA. These limits and other rules are explained below.

Community property laws. Except as discussed later under *Spousal IRA limit*, each spouse figures his or her limit separately, using his or her own compensation. This is the rule even in states with community property laws.

Brokers' commissions. Brokers' commissions paid in connection with your traditional IRA are subject to the contribution limit.

TAXALERT

Under an IRS letter ruling, if you pay a so-called wrap fee for the management of your IRA, that fee is not subject to the contribution limit even if it also covers the cost of commissions. A wrap fee is typically based on a percentage of the assets under management.

may take place only if there is a "distributable event," such as separation from your employer or, under some plans, attaining age 59½.

Trustees' fees. Trustees' administrative fees are not subject to the contribution limit.

Qualified reservist repayments. If you are (or were) a member of a reserve component and you were ordered or called to active duty after September 11, 2001, you may be able to contribute (repay) to an IRA amounts equal to any qualified reservist distributions you received. You can make these repayment contributions even if they would cause your total contributions to the IRA to be more than the general limit on contributions. To be eligible to make these repayment contributions, you must have received a qualified reservist distribution from an IRA or from a section 401(k) or 403(b) plan or similar arrangement.

For more information, see *Qualified reservist repayments* under *How Much Can Be Contributed?* in chapter 1 of Publication 590.

Caution

Contributions on your behalf to a traditional IRA reduce your limit for contributions to a Roth IRA. (See Roth IRAs, later.)

General limit. For 2011, the most that can be contributed to your traditional IRA generally is the smaller of the following amounts.

- $5,000 ($6,000 if you are 50 or older).
- Your taxable compensation (defined earlier) for the year.

This is the most that can be contributed regardless of whether the contributions are to one or more traditional IRAs or whether all or part of the contributions are nondeductible. (See *Nondeductible Contributions*, later.) Qualified reservist repayments do not affect this limit.

Example 1. Betty, who is 34 years old and single, earned $24,000 in 2011. Her IRA contributions for 2011 are limited to $5,000.

Example 2. John, an unmarried college student working part time, earned $3,500 in 2011. His IRA contributions for 2011 are limited to $3,500, the amount of his compensation.

Spousal IRA limit. For 2011, if you file a joint return and your taxable compensation is less than that of your spouse, the most that can be contributed for the year to your IRA is the smaller of the following amounts.

1. $5,000 ($6,000 if you are 50 or older).
2. The total compensation includible in the gross income of both you and your spouse for the year, reduced by the following two amounts.
   a. Your spouse's IRA contribution for the year to a traditional IRA.
   b. Any contribution for the year to a Roth IRA on behalf of your spouse.

This means that the total combined contributions that can be made for the year to your IRA and your spouse's IRA can be as much as $10,000 ($11,000 if only one of you is 50 or older, or $12,000 if both of you are 50 or older).

EXAMPLES

Example 1

A wife holds a job that pays over $10,000 and her husband does not hold a job. The two spouses file a joint return and neither has attained age 50. They may contribute up to a total of $10,000 to IRAs. They may split the contribution between the husband's and wife's accounts in any way they wish, as long as no more than $5,000 is allocated to either account. For example, if they decided to make a total contribution of $7,000 they could put $5,000 in the wife's IRA and $2,000 in the husband's.

Example 2

The working wife dies during the year after earning over $10,000. The nonworking husband is allowed to put $5,000 in his spousal IRA for the year, as long as he files a joint return with his deceased wife. A payment cannot be made to the decedent's IRA for the year of death after she dies.

You should disregard community property laws when you are determining if you are eligible to make payments to an IRA for your nonworking spouse. Thus, your nonworking spouse is not considered to have earned half your income.

When Can Contributions Be Made?

As soon as you open your traditional IRA, contributions can be made to it through your chosen sponsor (trustee or other administrator). Contributions must be in the form of money (cash, check, or money order). Property cannot be contributed.

Contributions must be made by due date. Contributions can be made to your traditional IRA for a year at any time during the year or by the due date for filing your return for that year, not including extensions.

Age 70½ rule. Contributions cannot be made to your traditional IRA for the year in which you reach age 70½ or for any later year.

You attain age 70½ on the date that is 6 calendar months after the 70th anniversary of your birth. If you were born on or before June 30, 1941, you cannot contribute for 2011 or any later year.

Designating year for which contribution is made. If an amount is contributed to your traditional IRA between January 1 and April 17, you should tell the sponsor which year (the current year or the previous year) the contribution is for. If you do not tell the sponsor which year it is for, the sponsor can assume, and report to the IRS, that the contribution is for the current year (the year the sponsor received it).

Filing before a contribution is made. You can file your return claiming a traditional IRA contribution before the contribution is actually made. Generally, the contribution must be made by the due date of your return, not including extensions.

Contributions not required. You do not have to contribute to your traditional IRA for every tax year, even if you can.

TAXPLANNER

You can make your 2011 IRA contribution as late as April 17, 2012. (The due date is actually April 17, 2012, because April 15, 2012, falls on Sunday, and the following day, April 16, is the Emancipation Day holiday in the District of Columbia, which is observed as a legal holiday.) However, funding your IRA as early as possible maximizes your ending balance (assuming positive earnings throughout the year). For example, assume you have 20 years until retirement; make the maximum $10,000 contribution for you and your spouse, and the account earns 8% each year. If you make your contributions at year end, your ending IRA balance will be $457,620. If you make your contributions at the beginning of the year, your ending account balance will be $494,230, an increase of $36,610.

If you don't have available funds to make an IRA contribution by December 31, 2011, you may be able to generate the cash by filing your tax return early in 2012, taking the deduction for the contribution, and using your tax refund (if any) to make the contribution when it's received prior to April 17, 2012, the latest date on which contributions may be made for 2011. Caution must be taken to ensure the contribution is made timely if a deduction is taken on the 2011 tax return.

If you do not have the cash available to make your 2011 IRA contribution by April 17, 2012, the deadline for 2011 contributions, you could "borrow" money by distributing part or all of an existing IRA (IRA 1) to yourself and use the money to make your 2011 IRA contribution to another IRA account (IRA 2). You would have to complete the rollover to IRA 2 within 60 days of the withdrawal from IRA 1. If you do not come up with the funds to complete the rollover to IRA 2, you would be subject to income tax and possibly the 10% penalty for early withdrawal. This approach only helps if you have a very short-term cash shortage and know you will have the needed cash within 60 days of the distribution. *Note:* You may only roll over an IRA fund to a new IRA once in a 12-month period.

For more information about *Rollovers*, see the discussion later in this chapter.

TAXPLANNER

Direct deposit of tax refunds into an IRA account. You can choose to have the IRS directly deposit your tax refund into your IRA account(s) (and/or your spouse's IRA account(s) if you file a joint tax return). Use Form 8888 to instruct the IRS to make a direct deposit to the IRA.

(You can also use Form 8888 to instruct the IRS to directly deposit your tax refund in up to three accounts. In addition to an IRA, an account can be a checking, savings, or health savings account (HSA), an Archer MSA, or Coverdell education savings account. You cannot have your refund deposited into more than one account if you file Form 8379, Injured Spouse Allocation.)

To have the IRS directly deposit your tax refund into your IRA account, you must establish the IRA at a bank or other financial institution before you request direct deposit. You must also notify the trustee of your account of the year to which the deposit is to be applied. If you do not, the trustee can assume the deposit is for the year during which you are filing the return. For example, if you file your 2011 return during 2012 and do not notify the trustee in advance, the trustee can assume the deposit into your IRA is for 2012. If you designate your deposit to be for 2011, you must verify that the deposit was actually made to the account by the original due date of the return, without regard to extensions. If the deposit was not made into your account by April 17, 2012, the deposit is not an IRA contribution for 2011 and you must file an amended return and reduce any IRA deduction and any retirement savings contribution credit you claimed.

How Much Can You Deduct?

Generally, you can deduct the lesser of:

- The contributions to your traditional IRA for the year, or
- The general limit (or the spousal IRA limit, if it applies).

However, if you or your spouse was covered by an employer retirement plan, you may not be able to deduct this amount. See *Limit If Covered by Employer Plan*, later.

Trustees' fees. Trustees' administrative fees that are billed separately and paid in connection with your traditional IRA are not deductible as IRA contributions. However, they may be deductible as a miscellaneous itemized deduction on Schedule A (Form 1040). See chapter 28.

Brokers' commissions. Brokers' commissions are part of your IRA contribution and, as such, are deductible subject to the limits.

Full deduction. If neither you nor your spouse was covered for any part of the year by an employer retirement plan, you can take a deduction for total contributions to one or more traditional IRAs of up to the lesser of:

- $5,000 ($6,000 if you are 50 or older in 2011).
- 100% of your compensation.

This limit is reduced by any contributions made to a 501(c)(18) plan on your behalf.

Spousal IRA. In the case of a married couple with unequal compensation who file a joint return, the deduction for contributions to the traditional IRA of the spouse with less compensation is limited to the lesser of the following amounts.

1. $5,000 ($6,000 if you are 50 or older in 2011).
2. The total compensation includible in the gross income of both spouses for the year reduced by the following three amounts.
   a. The IRA deduction for the year of the spouse with the greater compensation.
   b. Any designated nondeductible contribution for the year made on behalf of the spouse with the greater compensation.
   c. Any contributions for the year to a Roth IRA on behalf of the spouse with the greater compensation.

This limit is reduced by any contributions to a 501(c)(18) plan on behalf of the spouse with the lesser compensation.

Note. If you were divorced or legally separated (and did not remarry) before the end of the year, you cannot deduct any contributions to your spouse's IRA. After a divorce or legal separation, you can deduct only contributions to your own IRA. Your deductions are subject to the rules for single individuals.

Covered by an employer retirement plan. If you or your spouse was covered by an employer retirement plan at any time during the year for which contributions were made, your deduction may be further limited. This is discussed later under *Limit If Covered by Employer Plan*. Limits on the amount you can deduct do not affect the amount that can be contributed. See *Nondeductible Contributions*, later.

Are You Covered by an Employer Plan?

The Form W-2 you receive from your employer has a box used to indicate whether you were covered for the year. The "Retirement plan" box should be checked if you were covered.

Reservists and volunteer firefighters should also see *Situations in Which You Are Not Covered*, later.

Tip

You may be eligible to claim a credit for contributions to your traditional IRA. For more information, see chapter 37.

If you are not certain whether you were covered by your employer's retirement plan, you should ask your employer.

TAXPLANNER

We recommend that you check your Form W-2 to ensure that the coverage status is accurate. The rules used to determine if you are covered by an employer's plan will depend on the type of plan maintained by your employer. If you are not sure what type of plan your employer maintains, you should ask your employer. The information may also be found in the Summary Plan Description, which can be obtained from your employer. You test eligibility to participate in your employer's plan based on the plan year ending with or within the tax year. Generally, you will be considered covered if:

1. Your employer maintains a defined benefit pension plan and you meet the plan's eligibility requirements.
2. Your employer maintains a defined contribution money purchase plan, you meet the plan's eligibility requirements, and your employer is required to make a contribution to your account.
3. Your employer maintains a profit-sharing plan and makes a contribution that is allocated to your account or allocates a forfeiture to your account, or you make any contribution with respect to a plan year ending with or within your tax year.
4. Your employer maintains a 401(k), a SEP, or a 403(b) plan, and for the plan year ending with or within your tax year, you elect to defer any compensation.

Example

Assume that you first became eligible to participate in your employer's profit-sharing plan on July 2, 2011. Your employer makes a contribution for the plan year ending on June 30, 2012. You will not be considered an active participant until 2012, since that is the first tax year during which an allocation was made to your account.

Federal judges. For purposes of the IRA deduction, federal judges are covered by an employer retirement plan.

For Which Year(s) Are You Covered?

Special rules apply to determine the tax years for which you are covered by an employer plan. These rules differ depending on whether the plan is a defined contribution plan or a defined benefit plan.

Tax year. Your tax year is the annual accounting period you use to keep records and report income and expenses on your income tax return. For almost all people, the tax year is the calendar year.

Defined contribution plan. Generally, you are covered by a defined contribution plan for a tax year if amounts are contributed or allocated to your account for the plan year that ends with or within that tax year.

A defined contribution plan is a plan that provides for a separate account for each person covered by the plan. Types of defined contribution plans include profit-sharing plans, stock bonus plans, and money purchase pension plans.

Defined benefit plan. If you are eligible to participate in your employer's defined benefit plan for the plan year that ends within your tax year, you are covered by the plan. This rule applies even if you:

- Declined to participate in the plan,
- Did not make a required contribution, or
- Did not perform the minimum service required to accrue a benefit for the year.

A defined benefit plan is any plan that is not a defined contribution plan. Defined benefit plans include pension plans and annuity plans.

No vested interest. If you accrue a benefit for a plan year, you are covered by that plan even if you have no vested interest in (legal right to) the accrual.

Situations in Which You Are Not Covered

Unless you are covered under another employer plan, you are not covered by an employer plan if you are in one of the situations described below.

Social security or railroad retirement. Coverage under social security or railroad retirement is not coverage under an employer retirement plan.

Benefits from a previous employer's plan. If you receive retirement benefits from a previous employer's plan, you are not covered by that plan.

Reservists. If the only reason you participate in a plan is because you are a member of a reserve unit of the armed forces, you may not be covered by the plan. You are not covered by the plan if both of the following conditions are met.

1. The plan you participate in is established for its employees by:
   a. The United States,
   b. A state or political subdivision of a state, or
   c. An instrumentality of either (a) or (b) above.
2. You did not serve more than 90 days on active duty during the year (not counting duty for training).

Volunteer firefighters. If the only reason you participate in a plan is because you are a volunteer firefighter, you may not be covered by the plan. You are not covered by the plan if both of the following conditions are met.

1. The plan you participate in is established for its employees by:
   a. The United States,
   b. A state or political subdivision of a state, or
   c. An instrumentality of either (a) or (b) above.
2. Your accrued retirement benefits at the beginning of the year will not provide more than $1,800 per year at retirement.

Limit If Covered by Employer Plan

If either you or your spouse was covered by an employer retirement plan, you may be entitled to only a partial (reduced) deduction or no deduction at all, depending on your income and your filing status.

Your deduction begins to decrease (phase out) when your income rises above a certain amount and is eliminated altogether when it reaches a higher amount. These amounts vary depending on your filing status.

To determine if your deduction is subject to phaseout, you must determine your modified adjusted gross income (AGI) and your filing status. See *Filing status* and *Modified adjusted gross income (AGI)*, later. Then use Table 17-1 or 17-2 to determine if the phaseout applies.

Social security recipients. Instead of using Table 17-1 or Table 17-2, use the worksheets in Appendix B of Publication 590 if, for the year, all of the following apply.

- You received social security benefits.
- You received taxable compensation.
- Contributions were made to your traditional IRA.
- You or your spouse was covered by an employer retirement plan.

Use those worksheets to figure your IRA deduction, your nondeductible contribution, and the taxable portion, if any, of your social security benefits.

Table 17-1. **Effect of Modified AGI[1] on Deduction if You Are Covered by Retirement Plan at Work**

If you are covered by a retirement plan at work, use this table to determine if your modified AGI affects the amount of your deduction.

IF your filing status is...	AND your modified AGI is...	THEN you can take...
single or **head of household**	$56,000 or less	a full deduction.
	more than $56,000 but less than $66,000	a partial deduction.
	$66,000 or more	no deduction.
married filing jointly or **qualifying widow(er)**	$90,000 or less	a full deduction.
	more than $90,000 but less than $110,000	a partial deduction.
	$110,000 or more	no deduction.
married filing separately[2]	less than $10,000	a partial deduction.
	$10,000 or more	no deduction.

[1] Modified AGI (adjusted gross income). See *Modified adjusted gross income (AGI)*.

[2] If you did not live with your spouse at any time during the year, your filing status is considered Single for this purpose (therefore, your IRA deduction is determined under the "Single" column).

Table 17-2. **Effect of Modified AGI[1] on Deduction if You Are NOT Covered by Retirement Plan at Work**

If you are not covered by a retirement plan at work, use this table to determine if your modified AGI affects the amount of your deduction.

IF your filing status is...	AND your modified AGI is...	THEN you can take...
single, head of household, or **qualifying widow(er)**	any amount	a full deduction.
married filing jointly or separately with a spouse who ***is not*** covered by a plan at work	any amount	a full deduction.
married filing jointly with a spouse who ***is*** covered by a plan at work	$169,000 or less	a full deduction.
	more than $169,000 but less than $179,000	a partial deduction.
	$179,000 or more	no deduction.
married filing separately with a spouse who ***is*** covered by a plan at work[2]	less than $10,000	a partial deduction.
	$10,000 or more	no deduction.

[1] Modified AGI (adjusted gross income). See Modified adjusted gross income (AGI).
[2] You are entitled to the full deduction if you did not live with your spouse at any time during the year.

Deduction phaseout. If you were covered by an employer retirement plan and you did not receive any social security retirement benefits, your IRA deduction may be reduced or eliminated depending on your filing status and modified AGI as shown in Table 17-1.

If your spouse is covered. If you are not covered by an employer retirement plan, but your spouse is, and you did not receive any social security benefits, your IRA deduction may be reduced or eliminated entirely depending on your filing status and modified AGI as shown in Table 17-2.

Filing status. Your filing status depends primarily on your marital status. For this purpose, you need to know if your filing status is single or head of household, married filing jointly or qualifying widow(er), or married filing separately. If you need more information on filing status, see chapter 2.

Lived apart from spouse. If you did not live with your spouse at any time during the year and you file a separate return, your filing status, for this purpose, is single.

EXAMPLE

Joe and Mary are both employed. During 2011, Mary's compensation was $80,000, and she was not covered by her employer's retirement plan. Joe's compensation was $35,000, and he was covered by his employer's plan. If Joe and Mary file a joint return, Mary can claim a deduction for an IRA contribution since she is not covered by her employer's retirement plan. However, Joe cannot claim an IRA contribution deduction. If Joe and Mary didn't live together at all during the year and file separate returns, Joe could deduct an IRA contribution of $5,000 (subject to the adjusted gross income limitation), while Mary could deduct $5,000, since she is not covered by her employer's plan.

If they lived together for part of the year and file separate returns, neither can make a deductible IRA contribution.

Caution

Do not assume that your modified AGI is the same as your compensation. Your modified AGI may include income in addition to your compensation (discussed earlier), such as interest, dividends, and income from IRA distributions.

Modified adjusted gross income (AGI). How you figure your modified AGI depends on whether you are filing Form 1040 or Form 1040A. If you made contributions to your IRA for 2011 and received a distribution from your IRA in 2011, see Publication 590.

Form 1040. If you file Form 1040, refigure the amount on the page 1 "adjusted gross income" line without taking into account any of the following amounts.

- IRA deduction.
- Student loan interest deduction.
- Qualified tuition and fees deduction.
- Domestic production activities deduction.
- Foreign earned income exclusion.
- Foreign housing exclusion or deduction.

- Exclusion of qualified savings bond interest shown on Form 8815, Exclusion of Interest From Series EE and I U.S. Savings Bonds Issued After 1989 (For Filers With Qualified Higher Education Expenses).
- Exclusion of employer-provided adoption benefits shown on Form 8839, Qualified Adoption Expenses.

This is your modified AGI.

Text intentionally omitted.

Form 1040A. If you file Form 1040A, refigure the amount on the page 1 "adjusted gross income" line without taking into account any of the following amounts.

- IRA deduction.
- Student loan interest deduction.
- Tuition and fees deduction.
- Exclusion of qualified savings bond interest shown on Form 8815.

This is your modified AGI.

Both contributions for 2011 and distributions in 2011. If all three of the following apply, any IRA distributions you received in 2011 may be partly tax free and partly taxable.

- You received distributions in 2011 from one or more traditional IRAs.
- You made contributions to a traditional IRA for 2011.
- Some of those contributions may be nondeductible contributions.

If this is your situation, you must figure the taxable part of the traditional IRA distribution before you can figure your modified AGI. To do this, you can use Worksheet 1-5, Figuring the Taxable Part of Your IRA Distribution, in Publication 590.

If at least one of the above does not apply, figure your modified AGI using Worksheet 17-1 on this page.

How to figure your reduced IRA deduction. You can figure your reduced IRA deduction for either Form 1040 or Form 1040A by using the worksheets in chapter 1 of Publication 590. Also, the instructions for Form 1040 and Form 1040A include similar worksheets that you may be able to use instead.

Reporting Deductible Contributions

If you file Form 1040, enter your IRA deduction on line 32 of that form. If you file Form 1040A, enter your IRA deduction on line 17. You cannot deduct IRA contributions on Form 1040EZ.

Nondeductible Contributions

Although your deduction for IRA contributions may be reduced or eliminated, contributions can be made to your IRA up to the general limit or, if it applies, the spousal IRA limit. The difference between your total permitted contributions and your IRA deduction, if any, is your nondeductible contribution.

Example. Mike is 28 years old and single. In 2011, he was covered by a retirement plan at work. His salary was $57,312. His modified AGI was $68,000. Mike made a $5,000 IRA contribution for 2011. Because he was covered by a retirement plan and his modified AGI was over $66,000, he

Worksheet 17-1. **Figuring Your Modified AGI** *Keep for Your Records*

Use this worksheet to figure your modified adjusted gross income for traditional IRA purposes.

1.	Enter your adjusted gross income (AGI) from Form 1040, line 38; or Form 1040A, line 22, figured without taking into account the amount from Form 1040, line 32; or Form 1040A, line 17	**1.**	________
2.	Enter any student loan interest deduction from Form 1040, line 33; or Form 1040A, line 18..........	**2.**	________
3.	Enter any tuition and fees deduction from Form 1040, line 34; or Form 1040A, line 19	**3.**	________
4.	Enter any domestic production activities deduction from Form 1040, line 35	**4.**	________
5.	Enter any foreign earned income and/or housing exclusion from Form 2555, line 45; or Form 2555-EZ, line 18	**5.**	________
6.	Enter any foreign housing deduction from Form 2555, line 50	**6.**	________
7.	Enter any excludable savings bond interest from Form 8815, line 14	**7.**	________
8.	Enter any excluded employer-provided adoption benefits from Form 8839, line 26	**8.**	________
9.	Add lines 1 through 7. This is your **Modified AGI** for traditional IRA purposes	**9.**	________

cannot deduct his $5,000 IRA contribution. He must designate this contribution as a nondeductible contribution by reporting it on Form 8606, as explained next.

EXPLANATION

The chief advantage of nondeductible IRA contributions is that since the income compounds on a tax-deferred basis, the ending balance will be substantially larger under an IRA than in a taxable account. In deciding whether to make nondeductible contributions, you should compare the IRA's estimated rate of return over time against the estimated rate of return of other investments, such as tax-exempt municipal bonds and annuity contracts, and after-tax rates of return on taxable investments. You must also consider the expected tax effect when you begin taking distributions (i.e., whether you expect to be in a lower tax bracket when you receive distributions). In most cases, if you are eligible, you will be better off making a contribution to a Roth IRA than to a non-deductible IRA. The taxation of IRA distributions is discussed later.

Form 8606. To designate contributions as nondeductible, you must file Form 8606.

You do not have to designate a contribution as nondeductible until you file your tax return. When you file, you can even designate otherwise deductible contributions as nondeductible.

You must file Form 8606 to report nondeductible contributions even if you do not have to file a tax return for the year.

Failure to report nondeductible contributions. If you do not report nondeductible contributions, all of the contributions to your traditional IRA will be treated as deductible contributions when withdrawn. All distributions from your IRA will be taxed unless you can show, with satisfactory evidence, that nondeductible contributions were made.

Penalty for overstatement. If you overstate the amount of nondeductible contributions on your Form 8606 for any tax year, you must pay a penalty of $100 for each overstatement, unless it was due to reasonable cause.

Penalty for failure to file Form 8606. You will have to pay a $50 penalty if you do not file a required Form 8606, unless you can prove that the failure was due to reasonable cause.

Caution

A Form 8606 is not used for the year that you make a rollover from a qualified retirement plan to a traditional IRA and the rollover includes nontaxable amounts. In those situations, a Form 8606 is completed for the year you take a distribution from that IRA. See Form 8606 *under* Distributions Fully or Partly Taxable, *later.*

EXPLANATION

The law subjecting taxpayers to a $50 fine for failure to file Form 8606 applies retroactively to 1987. If you should have filed Form 8606 for a prior tax year but failed to do so, you should consider amending your return. See chapter 1, *Filing information*, for additional details regarding amending your return.

Tax on earnings on nondeductible contributions. As long as contributions are within the contribution limits, none of the earnings or gains on contributions (deductible or nondeductible) will be taxed until they are distributed. See *When Can You Withdraw or Use IRA Assets*, later.

Cost basis. You will have a cost basis in your traditional IRA if you made any nondeductible contributions. Your cost basis is the sum of the nondeductible contributions to your IRA minus any withdrawals or distributions of nondeductible contributions.

Inherited IRAs

If you inherit a traditional IRA, you are called a beneficiary. A beneficiary can be any person or entity the owner chooses to receive the benefits of the IRA after he or she dies. Beneficiaries of a traditional IRA must include in their gross income any taxable distributions they receive.

Inherited from spouse. If you inherit a traditional IRA from your spouse, you generally have the following three choices. You can:

1. Treat it as your own IRA by designating yourself as the account owner.
2. Treat it as your own by rolling it over into your IRA, or to the extent it is taxable, into a:
   a. Qualified employer plan,
   b. Qualified employee annuity plan (section 403(a) plan),
   c. Tax-sheltered annuity plan (section 403(b) plan), or
   d. Deferred compensation plan of a state or local government (section 457 plan).
3. Treat yourself as the beneficiary rather than treating the IRA as your own.

Treating it as your own. You will be considered to have chosen to treat the IRA as your own if:

- Contributions (including rollover contributions) are made to the inherited IRA, or
- You do not take the required minimum distribution for a year as a beneficiary of the IRA.

You will only be considered to have chosen to treat the IRA as your own if:

- You are the sole beneficiary of the IRA, and
- You have an unlimited right to withdraw amounts from it.

However, if you receive a distribution from your deceased spouse's IRA, you can roll that distribution over into your own IRA within the 60-day time limit, as long as the distribution is not a required distribution, even if you are not the sole beneficiary of your deceased spouse's IRA.

TAXPLANNER

If you are the beneficiary of a deceased employee's IRA or other eligible retirement plan (such as a qualified pension, profit-sharing, stock bonus, Section 403(b) or Section 457 plan), and are not the employee's surviving spouse (surviving spouses have additional options), you may be able to roll over a distribution from the plan tax free to an IRA you specifically set up to receive the distribution. To qualify as an eligible rollover distribution, the distribution must be a direct trustee-to-trustee transfer completed within 60 days of the distribution. The IRA receiving the distribution is treated as an inherited IRA. For more information, see *What if You Inherit an IRA* in Publication 590, *Individual Retirement Arrangements (IRAs)*.

Inherited from someone other than spouse. If you inherit a traditional IRA from anyone other than your deceased spouse, you cannot treat the inherited IRA as your own. This means that you cannot make any contributions to the IRA. It also means you cannot roll over any amounts into or out of the inherited IRA. However, you can make a trustee-to-trustee transfer as long as the IRA into which amounts are being moved is set up and maintained in the name of the deceased IRA owner for the benefit of you as beneficiary.

For more information, see the discussion of *inherited IRAs* under *Rollover From One IRA Into Another,* later.

Can You Move Retirement Plan Assets?

You can transfer, tax free, assets (money or property) from other retirement plans (including traditional IRAs) to a traditional IRA. You can make the following kinds of transfers.

- Transfers from one trustee to another.
- Rollovers.
- Transfers incident to a divorce.

Transfers to Roth IRAs. Under certain conditions, you can move assets from a traditional IRA or from a designated Roth account to a Roth IRA. You can also move assets from a qualified retirement plan to a Roth IRA. See *Can You Move Amounts Into a Roth IRA?* under *Roth IRAs*, later.

Trustee-to-Trustee Transfer

A transfer of funds in your traditional IRA from one trustee directly to another, either at your request or at the trustee's request, is not a rollover. Because there is no distribution to you, the transfer is tax free. Because it is not a rollover, it is not affected by the 1-year waiting period required between rollovers, discussed later under *Rollover From One IRA Into Another*. For information about direct transfers to IRAs from retirement plans other than IRAs, see Publication 590.

Rollovers

Generally, a rollover is a tax-free distribution to you of cash or other assets from one retirement plan that you contribute (roll over) to another retirement plan. The contribution to the second retirement plan is called a "rollover contribution."

EXPLANATION

When you receive a property distribution (e.g., shares of stock) from your IRA or a qualified employer plan, you may roll over the property received into an IRA. You are also permitted to sell the property and roll over the sale proceeds into an IRA. You may not retain the property distribution and roll over the property's cash equivalent.

Note. An amount rolled over tax free from one retirement plan to another is generally includible in income when it is distributed from the second plan.

Kinds of rollovers to a traditional IRA. You can roll over amounts from the following plans into a traditional IRA:

- A traditional IRA,
- An employer's qualified retirement plan for its employees,
- A deferred compensation plan of a state or local government (section 457 plan), or
- A tax-sheltered annuity plan (section 403(b) plan).

Treatment of rollovers. You cannot deduct a rollover contribution, but you must report the rollover distribution on your tax return as discussed later under *Reporting rollovers from IRAs* and under *Reporting rollovers from employer plans*.

Kinds of rollovers from a traditional IRA. You may be able to roll over, tax free, a distribution from your traditional IRA into a qualified plan. These plans include the federal Thrift Savings Fund (for federal employees), deferred compensation plans of state or local governments (section 457 plans), and tax-sheltered annuity plans (section 403(b) plans). The part of the distribution that you can roll over is the part that would otherwise be taxable (includible in your income). Qualified plans may, but are not required to, accept such rollovers.

Time limit for making a rollover contribution. You generally must make the rollover contribution by the 60th day after the day you receive the distribution from your traditional IRA or your employer's plan.

The IRS may waive the 60-day requirement where the failure to do so would be against equity or good conscience, such as in the event of a casualty, disaster, or other event beyond your reasonable control. For more information, see Publication 590.

Extension of rollover period. If an amount distributed to you from a traditional IRA or a qualified employer retirement plan is a frozen deposit at any time during the 60-day period allowed for a rollover, special rules extend the rollover period. For more information, see Publication 590.

More information. For more information on rollovers, see Publication 590.

Rollover From One IRA Into Another

You can withdraw, tax free, all or part of the assets from one traditional IRA if you reinvest them within 60 days in the same or another traditional IRA. Because this is a rollover, you cannot deduct the amount that you reinvest in an IRA.

Waiting period between rollovers. Generally, if you make a tax-free rollover of any part of a distribution from a traditional IRA, you cannot, within a 1-year period, make a tax-free rollover of any later distribution from that same IRA. You also cannot make a tax-free rollover of any amount distributed, within the same 1-year period, from the IRA into which you made the tax-free rollover.

The 1-year period begins on the date you receive the IRA distribution, not on the date you roll it over into an IRA.

Example. You have two traditional IRAs, IRA-1 and IRA-2. You make a tax-free rollover of a distribution from IRA-1 into a new traditional IRA (IRA-3). You cannot, within 1 year of the distribution from IRA-1, make a tax-free rollover of any distribution from either IRA-1 or IRA-3 into another traditional IRA.

However, the rollover from IRA-1 into IRA-3 does not prevent you from making a tax-free rollover from IRA-2 into any other traditional IRA. This is because you have not, within the last year, rolled over, tax free, any distribution from IRA-2 or made a tax-free rollover into IRA-2.

Exception. For an exception for distributions from failed financial institutions, see Publication 590.

Partial rollovers. If you withdraw assets from a traditional IRA, you can roll over part of the withdrawal tax free and keep the rest of it. The amount you keep will generally be taxable (except for the part that is a return of nondeductible contributions). The amount you keep may be subject to the 10% additional tax on early distributions, discussed later under *What Acts Result in Penalties or Additional Taxes*.

Required distributions. Amounts that must be distributed during a particular year under the required distribution rules (discussed later) are not eligible for rollover treatment.

Inherited IRAs. If you inherit a traditional IRA from your spouse, you generally can roll it over, or you can choose to make the inherited IRA your own. See *Treating it as your own*, earlier.

Not inherited from spouse. If you inherit a traditional IRA from someone other than your spouse, you cannot roll it over or allow it to receive a rollover contribution. You must withdraw the IRA assets within a certain period. For more information, see Publication 590.

TAXALERT

The rules are different depending on whether you inherit as a spouse or you inherit as a nonspouse, such as a child. The surviving spouse may treat the IRA as his or her own for all purposes and the minimum distribution requirements generally apply as if it were the surviving spouse's IRA. If you inherit a traditional IRA from anyone other than your deceased spouse, you cannot treat the inherited IRA as your own. This means that you cannot make any contributions to the IRA. Nor can you roll over any amounts into or out of the inherited IRA. However, you can make a trustee-to-trustee transfer as long as the IRA into which amounts are being moved is set up and maintained in the name of the deceased IRA owner for the benefit of you as beneficiary. You will not be taxed on the transfer but you must start taking distributions under the rules for distributions to beneficiaries. For more information, see *What if You Inherit an IRA* in Publication 590, *Individual Retirement Arrangements (IRAs)*.

Reporting rollovers from IRAs. Report any rollover from one traditional IRA to the same or another traditional IRA on lines 15a and 15b, Form 1040, or lines 11a and 11b, Form 1040A.

Enter the total amount of the distribution on Form 1040, line 15a, or Form 1040A, line 11a. If the total amount on Form 1040, line 15a, or Form 1040A, line 11a, was rolled over, enter zero on Form 1040, line 15b, or Form 1040A, line 11b. If the total distribution was not rolled over, enter the taxable portion of the part that was not rolled over on Form 1040, line 15b, or Form 1040A, line 11b. Put "Rollover" next to Form 1040, line 15b, or Form 1040A, line 11b. See the forms instructions.

If you rolled over the distribution into a qualified plan (other than an IRA) or you make the rollover in 2012, attach a statement explaining what you did.

Rollover From Employer's Plan Into an IRA

You can roll over into a traditional IRA all or part of an eligible rollover distribution you receive from your (or your deceased spouse's):

- Employer's qualified pension, profit-sharing or stock bonus plan,
- Annuity plan,
- Tax-sheltered annuity plan (section 403(b) plan), or
- Governmental deferred compensation plan (section 457 plan).

A qualified plan is one that meets the requirements of the Internal Revenue Code.

TAXPLANNER

Income tax withholding may apply to distributions made from qualified employer plans. Withholding at a rate of 20% is required on a distribution unless it is transferred directly from your former employer's qualified plan to an IRA trustee or another employer's qualified plan.

The withholding rules do not apply to distributions from IRAs (or simplified employee pensions [SEPs]). However, if you wish to roll over a qualified plan distribution to an IRA, be sure to transfer the amount directly from your employer's plan to an IRA trustee or another employer plan. Otherwise, 20% of the distribution will be withheld while 100% of the taxable distribution must be rolled over within 60 days to avoid taxation on the taxable amount not rolled over (i.e., the 20% withheld is not exempt from tax unless an equal amount is rolled over timely). If you don't have the money to cover the 20% shortage, income taxes (and possibly a 10% penalty) will be due on the amount not rolled over.

For further information, see chapter 10, *Retirement plans, pensions, and annuities*.

Eligible rollover distribution. Generally, an eligible rollover distribution is any distribution of all or part of the balance to your credit in a qualified retirement plan except the following.

1. A required minimum distribution (explained later under *When Must You Withdraw IRA Assets? (Required Minimum Distributions)*.
2. A hardship distribution.
3. Any of a series of substantially equal periodic distributions paid at least once a year over:
   a. Your lifetime or life expectancy,
   b. The lifetimes or life expectancies of you and your beneficiary, or
   c. A period of 10 years or more.
4. Corrective distributions of excess contributions or excess deferrals, and any income allocable to the excess, or of excess annual additions and any allocable gains.
5. A loan treated as a distribution because it does not satisfy certain requirements either when made or later (such as upon default), unless the participant's accrued benefits are reduced (offset) to repay the loan.

Tip

Any nontaxable amounts that you roll over into your traditional IRA become part of your basis (cost) in your IRAs. To recover your basis when you take distributions from your IRA, you must complete Form 8606 for the year of the distribution. See Form 8606 *under* Distributions Fully or Partly Taxable, *later.*

6. Dividends on employer securities.
7. The cost of life insurance coverage.

EXPLANATION

You may withdraw the balance in your IRA and reinvest it in another IRA with no tax consequences if the money is reinvested within 60 days after the funds are received. This type of rollover may be done only once in a 1-year period. This rule applies to each separate IRA you own.

Example

You have two or more IRAs. You can roll over a single distribution from each or all of them to a new IRA or to another existing IRA within a 1-year period (i.e., only once for each IRA). For example, you can do one 60-day rollover from your first IRA and one 60-day rollover from your other IRA, but you cannot do two 60-day rollovers from your first IRA. Trustee-to-trustee transfers do not count as a rollover for this purpose and are unlimited.

TAXALERT

The 60-day rule described above applies to the day you receive the distribution, not the day the distribution is made. Therefore, if you receive the distribution in the mail, you have 60 days from the date you received it in the mail to roll the funds into a new account, regardless of the date the check was cut.

TAXPLANNER

If you transfer funds directly between trustees of your IRA and you never actually control or use the account assets, you may transfer your account as often as you like.

All or part of a lump-sum distribution from a qualified employer benefit plan may be transferred to an IRA. You may affect a partial rollover—and be taxed at ordinary income rates—only on the portion of the money not reinvested within 60 days. As mentioned earlier, withholding at a rate of 20% is required on a qualified employer plan distribution unless it is transferred directly from your employer to the trustee of an IRA.

TAXPLANNER

A partial distribution from a qualified plan is eligible for rollover treatment as long as it is not:

1. A required minimum distribution (e.g., for individuals who have attained age 70½);
2. A distribution that is part of a series of substantially equal payments that are received at least annually over life, life expectancy, or a period of at least 10 years;
3. A hardship distribution;
4. A return of excess contributions, excess aggregate contributions, or excess deferrals;
5. A loan treated as a distribution because it does not satisfy certain requirements either when made or later (such as upon default), unless the participant's accrued benefits are reduced (offset) to repay the loan;
6. Dividends on employer securities; or
7. Payment for life insurance coverage.

TAXPLANNER

Not all distributions from qualified employer benefit plans may be rolled over into an IRA. IRAs are specifically prohibited from investing in life insurance contracts. Therefore, if your employer plan distributes to you both cash and a life insurance policy, the value of the life insurance policy (except for your contributions) is currently taxable to you. If this is the case, you should consider rolling over the life insurance contract into another qualified pension, profit-sharing, or stock bonus plan that allows investments in life insurance contracts. You can also cash in the life insurance policy and roll over the proceeds.

TAXPLANNER

A court has held that a tax-free rollover can be made only if the employer's plan and trust are tax-exempt when the distribution is made. In this particular case, the IRS retroactively revoked the tax-exempt status of the trust. This made the distribution retroactively ineligible for a rollover.

The IRS believes that once you have made a rollover, you cannot change your mind and report the distribution as taxable income. However, you could replicate this effect by taking a distribution from the IRA to which you rolled the prior distribution. You could also transfer it to a Roth IRA, which would mean you would pay tax upon the transfer to the Roth but not when the transferred amount (and earnings thereon) are distributed from the Roth IRA (as long as the requirements for a tax-free, qualified distribution are met).

You may roll over a lump-sum distribution from a former spouse's IRA or employee plan that was transferred to you by a divorce decree or written agreement incident to the divorce.

TAXALERT

The IRS has the ability to waive the 60-day rule where there are extenuating circumstances, such as a casualty, disaster, or an egregious error by a financial institution. In certain circumstances the waiver may be automatic; in others you may have to file a request with the IRS. The IRS has been relatively sympathetic to taxpayers and has issued a number of waiver rulings in recent years.

Rollover by nonspouse beneficiary. A direct transfer from a deceased employee's qualified pension, profit-sharing or stock bonus plan, annuity plan, tax-sheltered annuity (section 403(b)) plan, or governmental deferred compensation (section 457) plan to an IRA set up to receive the distribution on your behalf can be treated as an eligible rollover distribution if you are the designated beneficiary of the plan and not the employee's spouse. The IRA is treated as an inherited IRA. For more information about inherited IRAs, see *Inherited IRAs*, earlier.

Reporting rollovers from employer plans. Enter the total distribution (before income tax or other deductions were withheld) on Form 1040, line 16a, or Form 1040A, line 12a. This amount should be shown in box 1 of Form 1099-R. From this amount, subtract any contributions (usually shown in box 5 of Form 1099-R) that were taxable to you when made. From that result, subtract the amount that was rolled over either directly or within 60 days of receiving the distribution. Enter the remaining amount, even if zero, on Form 1040, line 16b, or Form 1040A, line 12b. Also, enter "Rollover" next to Form 1040, line 16b, or Form 1040A, line 12b.

Transfers Incident to Divorce

If an interest in a traditional IRA is transferred from your spouse or former spouse to you by a divorce or separate maintenance decree or a written document related to such a decree, the interest in the IRA, starting from the date of the transfer, is treated as your IRA. The transfer is tax free. For detailed information, see Publication 590.

Converting From Any Traditional IRA to a Roth IRA

Allowable conversions. You can withdraw all or part of the assets from a traditional IRA and reinvest them (within 60 days) in a Roth IRA. The amount that you withdraw and timely contribute (convert) to the Roth IRA is called a conversion contribution. If properly (and timely) rolled over, the 10% additional tax on early distributions will not apply.

TAXALERT

Prior to 2010, only taxpayers with modified AGI of less than $100,000 and whose filing status was anything other than married filing separate were eligible to convert tax-deferred savings accounts, such as traditional IRAs, to Roth IRAs. Beginning with 2010, these restrictions have been lifted, and anyone can make the conversion to a Roth IRA.

Required distributions. You cannot convert amounts that must be distributed from your traditional IRA for a particular year (including the calendar year in which you reach age 70½) under the required distribution rules (discussed later).

Income. You must include in your gross income distributions from a traditional IRA that you would have had to include in income if you had not converted them into a Roth IRA. These amounts are normally included in income on your return for the year that you converted them from a traditional IRA to a Roth IRA. *Text intentionally omitted.* You do not include in gross income any part of a distribution from a traditional IRA that is a return of your basis, as discussed later.

You must file Form 8606 to report 2011 conversions from traditional, SEP, or SIMPLE IRAs to a Roth IRA in 2011 (unless you recharacterized the entire amount) and to figure the amount to include in income.

If you must include any amount in your gross income, you may have to increase your withholding or make estimated tax payments. See chapter 4.

Recharacterizations

You may be able to treat a contribution made to one type of IRA as having been made to a different type of IRA. This is called recharacterizing the contribution. More detailed information is in Publication 590.

How to recharacterize a contribution. To recharacterize a contribution, you generally must have the contribution transferred from the first IRA (the one to which it was made) to the second IRA in a trustee-to-trustee transfer. If the transfer is made by the due date (including extensions) for your tax return for the year during which the contribution was made, you can elect to treat the contribution as having been originally made to the second IRA instead of to the first IRA. If you recharacterize your contribution, you must do all three of the following.

- Include in the transfer any net income allocable to the contribution. If there was a loss, the net income you must transfer may be a negative amount.
- Report the recharacterization on your tax return for the year during which the contribution was made.
- Treat the contribution as having been made to the second IRA on the date that it was actually made to the first IRA.

No deduction allowed. You cannot deduct the contribution to the first IRA. Any net income you transfer with the recharacterized contribution is treated as earned in the second IRA.

Required notifications. To recharacterize a contribution, you must notify both the trustee of the first IRA (the one to which the contribution was actually made) and the trustee of the second IRA (the one to which the contribution is being moved) that you have elected to treat the contribution as having been made to the second IRA rather than the first. You must make the notifications by the date of the transfer. Only one notification is required if both IRAs are maintained by the same trustee. The notification(s) must include all of the following information.

- The type and amount of the contribution to the first IRA that is to be recharacterized.
- The date on which the contribution was made to the first IRA and the year for which it was made.
- A direction to the trustee of the first IRA to transfer in a trustee-to-trustee transfer the amount of the contribution and any net income (or loss) allocable to the contribution to the trustee of the second IRA.
- The name of the trustee of the first IRA and the name of the trustee of the second IRA.
- Any additional information needed to make the transfer.

Reporting a recharacterization. If you elect to recharacterize a contribution to one IRA as a contribution to another IRA, you must report the recharacterization on your tax return as directed by Form 8606 and its instructions. You must treat the contribution as having been made to the second IRA.

When Can You Withdraw or Use IRA Assets?

There are rules limiting use of your IRA assets and distributions from it. Violation of the rules generally results in additional taxes in the year of violation. See *What Acts Result in Penalties or Additional Taxes*, later.

Contributions returned before the due date of return. If you made IRA contributions in 2011, you can withdraw them tax free by the due date of your return. If you have an extension of time to file your return, you can withdraw them tax free by the extended due date. You can do this if, for each contribution you withdraw, both of the following conditions apply.

- You did not take a deduction for the contribution.
- You withdraw any interest or other income earned on the contribution. You can take into account any loss on the contribution while it was in the IRA when calculating the amount that must be withdrawn. If there was a loss, the net income earned on the contribution may be a negative amount.

Note. To calculate the amount you must withdraw, see Publication 590.

Earnings includible in income. You must include in income any earnings on the contributions you withdraw. Include the earnings in income for the year in which you made the contributions, not in the year in which you withdraw them.

Early distributions tax. The 10% additional tax on distributions made before you reach age 59½ does not apply to these tax-free withdrawals of your contributions. However, the distribution of interest or other income must be reported on Form 5329 and, unless the distribution qualifies as an exception to the age 59½ rule, it will be subject to this tax.

Caution

Generally, except for any part of a withdrawal that is a return of nondeductible contributions (basis), any withdrawal of your contributions after the due date (or extended due date) of your return will be treated as a taxable distribution. Excess contributions can also be recovered tax free as discussed under What Acts Result in Penalties or Additional Taxes, *later.*

TAXPLANNER

Withdrawals from IRAs before age 59½ to pay educational expenses. Withdrawals from an IRA are not subject to the 10% early distribution additional tax, if for the year of withdrawal you have paid sufficient (i.e., in excess of the withdrawal) qualified higher education expenses for yourself, your spouse, or for your or your spouse's children or grandchildren. This exception does not apply if you use the money to pay for expenses you incurred in a different year.

Qualifications and income limits. There are no specific income limits restricting the use of this provision.

When Must You Withdraw IRA Assets? (Required Minimum Distributions)

You cannot keep funds in a traditional IRA indefinitely. Eventually they must be distributed. If there are no distributions, or if the distributions are not large enough, you may have to pay a 50% excise tax on the amount not distributed as required. See *Excess Accumulations (Insufficient Distributions)*, later. The requirements for distributing IRA funds differ depending on whether you are the IRA owner or the beneficiary of a decedent's IRA.

Required minimum distribution. The amount that must be distributed each year is referred to as the required minimum distribution.

Required distributions not eligible for rollover. Amounts that must be distributed (required minimum distributions) during a particular year are not eligible for rollover treatment.

IRA owners. If you are the owner of a traditional IRA, you must generally start receiving distributions from your IRA by April 1 of the year following the year in which you reach age 70½. April 1 of the year following the year in which you reach age 70½ is referred to as the required beginning date.

Distributions by the required beginning date. You must receive at least a minimum amount for each year starting with the year you reach age 70½ (your 70½ year). If you do not (or did not) receive that minimum amount in your 70½ year, then you must receive distributions for your 70½ year by April 1 of the next year.

If an IRA owner dies after reaching age 70½, but before April 1 of the next year, no minimum distribution is required because death occurred before the required beginning date.

Distributions after the required beginning date. The required minimum distribution for any year after the year you turn 70½ must be made by December 31 of that later year.

Caution

Even if you begin receiving distributions before you attain age 70½, you must begin calculating and receiving required minimum distributions by your required beginning date.

TAXPLANNER

Explanation

The purpose of an IRA is to provide retirement income. Therefore, when you reach age 70½, you are expected to begin withdrawing the proceeds in your IRA rather than continue to let the funds accumulate and use the IRA as a tool to build your estate. If you don't withdraw the minimum amounts yearly, a 50% nondeductible tax is levied on the amount of the minimum payment left in your IRA.

You must start receiving minimum payments from your IRA by April 1 of the year after the year in which you reach age 70½. Unlike the qualified plan rule for non-5% owners, there is no delay because you are still working.

It is only your first distribution (the distribution for the year you reach age 70½) that may be delayed until April 1 of the following year. The second distribution must be made by December 31 of the same year. The doubling of distributions will have an effect on your tax liability.

Generally, the minimum distribution is based on the joint life expectancy of both you and a survivor who is assumed to be no more than 10 years younger (see IRS Publication 590 or chapter 10 for the appropriate life expectancy table). Alternatively, if your spouse is more than 10 years younger than you, and your spouse is the sole beneficiary of your IRA, the minimum distribution is based on your and your spouse's actual joint life expectancy (see IRS Publication 590 for the appropriate life expectancy table). Using this alternate method will result in a lower minimum distribution than the general method due to using a longer life expectancy.

It's worth noting that your IRA fund may continue to grow, even if you are taking the required distributions. For example, if the table used indicates a life expectancy of 20 years, you must withdraw only one-twentieth (5%) of your IRA funds in that year. If the funds in your IRA are earning income at the rate of 10%, your account will continue to grow. You may not make additional annual contributions after you attain age 70½. However, this rule does not prevent you from making contributions to a new or existing Roth IRA if you meet the income standards. There are no minimum distribution requirements from a Roth IRA while you are alive. Because there are such requirements for qualified plans, including Roth 401(k) plans, and the income limit has been removed on Roth conversions, you should consult with your tax advisor about rolling over qualified plan accounts to a Roth IRA. Remember that if you roll over a qualified plan account to a Roth IRA, you may pay tax immediately.

TAXALERT

Once distributions are required, a minimum distribution must be made each year based on the age of the IRA owner and, where relevant, his or her spouse using the appropriate life expectancy or annuity table.

Example

Jack Jones, who is single, attains age 70½ years old on May 1, 2011. He has an IRA with a December 31, 2010, balance of $80,000. By looking at tables published by the IRS, he finds that his life expectancy for purposes of his IRA distributions is 26.5 years. This is the life expectancy for a person who is 71, which he will be during 2011. To figure his minimum distribution, he divides the amount in his IRA by 26.5. He must receive a distribution of $3,019 prior to April 1, 2012, to avoid a penalty. If Jack was married, he would use the same life expectancy table as long as his wife isn't 10 or more years younger than him. If she was, Jack would use a different table. For example, if Jack's wife is age 60 when he attains age 70½, he would use a life expectancy of 27.2 years, providing for a required minimum distribution of $2,941.

TAXPLANNER

You are always permitted to take more out of your IRA than the required minimum distribution. However, while the distribution will reduce the balance on which the following year's required minimum distribution is calculated, you cannot get "advance credit" to offset the minimum distribution requirement in that following year.

TAXPLANNER

The rules for determining required minimum distributions for beneficiaries depend on whether the beneficiary is the sole beneficiary of an individual. The rules for individuals are explained below. If the owner's beneficiary is not an individual (for example, the owner's estate), see IRS Publication 590.

Surviving spouse. If you are a surviving spouse who is the sole beneficiary of your deceased spouse's IRA, you may elect to be treated as the owner and not the beneficiary. If you elect to be treated as the owner, you determine the required minimum distribution (if any) as if you were the owner beginning with the year you elect or are deemed to be the owner. However, if you become the owner in the year your deceased spouse died, you are not required to determine the required minimum distribution for that year using your life; rather, you can take the deceased owner's required minimum distribution for that year (to the extent it was not already distributed to the owner before his or her death).

Taking balance within 5 years. A beneficiary who is an individual may be required to take the entire account by the end of the fifth year following the year of the owner's death. If this rule applies, no distribution is required for any year before that fifth year.

Owner died on or after required beginning date. If the owner died on or after his or her required beginning date, and you are the designated beneficiary, you generally must base required minimum distributions for years after the year of the owner's death on the longer of your single life expectancy, or the owner's life expectancy.

Owner died before required beginning date. If the owner died before the required beginning date, base required minimum distributions for years after the year of the owner's death generally on your single life expectancy.

Generally, the designated beneficiary is determined on September 30 of the calendar year following the calendar year of the IRA owner's death. In order to be a designated beneficiary, an individual must be a beneficiary as of the date of death. Any person who was a beneficiary on the date of the owner's death, but is not a beneficiary on September 30 of the calendar year following the calendar year of the owner's death (because, for example, he or she disclaimed entitlement or received his or her entire benefit), will not be taken into account in determining the designated beneficiary.

See IRS Publication 590 for further guidance and examples. However, these rules are quite complex and you should seek tax advice.

TAXPLANNER

There are no minimum required distributions for a Roth IRA during the life of the account owner (see *Roth IRAs* for more details).

TAXPLANNER

Keogh plans. The same withdrawal techniques described earlier in the TaxPlanners may be used with a Keogh plan, a retirement arrangement that self-employed people may set up.

TAXPLANNER

Employer stock bonus plans and company profit-sharing plans. The main attraction of having your employer put some of your compensation into a stock bonus plan or a company profit-sharing plan is that you are not currently taxed on the contributions to or the earnings in the plan. In addition, these plans have certain advantages that IRAs do not:

1. Borrowing is permitted if the loan is repaid within 5 years.
2. A lump-sum distribution may qualify for 10-year averaging for those born before January 2, 1936.
3. Minimum distributions from the employer's plan can be deferred if you continue to work for that employer after age 70½.
4. The contribution limits are higher.

Beneficiaries. If you are the beneficiary of a decedent's traditional IRA, the requirements for distributions from that IRA generally depend on whether the IRA owner died before or after the required beginning date for distributions.

More information. For more information, including how to figure your minimum required distribution each year and how to figure your required distribution if you are a beneficiary of a decedent's IRA, see Publication 590.

Are Distributions Taxable?

In general, distributions from a traditional IRA are taxable in the year you receive them.

Exceptions. Exceptions to distributions from traditional IRAs being taxable in the year you receive them are:

- Rollovers,
- Qualified charitable distributions, discussed later,
- Tax-free withdrawals of contributions, discussed earlier, and
- The return of nondeductible contributions, discussed later under *Distributions Fully or Partly Taxable*.

Caution

Although a conversion of a traditional IRA is considered a rollover for Roth IRA purposes, it is not an exception to the rule that distributions from a traditional IRA are taxable in the year you receive them. Conversion distributions are includible in your gross income subject to this rule and the special rules for conversions explained in Publication 590.

Text intentionally omitted.

EXPLANATION

IRA distributions are taxed in a manner similar to annuities. If you do not make nondeductible contributions, all distributions from a traditional IRA are taxed as ordinary income. You may not use special 10-year averaging on a lump-sum distribution from your IRA, even if the account is a rollover from a qualified plan. If you made nondeductible contributions, a portion of the distribution may be excludable from income. The excludable amount is computed as follows:

$$\frac{\text{Undistributed Nondeductible Contributions}}{\text{Total of All IRA Balances}} \times \text{Distribution Amount}$$

Example

Assume that Mary has one IRA to which she made a $2,000 nondeductible contribution and that her total account balance is $20,000. In 2011, she takes a $5,000 distribution. Her tax-free amount is:

$2,000 / $20,000 × $5,000 = $500

TAXORGANIZER

Undistributed nondeductible contributions are obtained from the last Form 8606 you filed. Therefore, make sure you always keep the most recent copy in your files.

TAXPLANNER

Money that you withdraw from your IRA is treated as a distribution to you and may trigger the 10% penalty that is imposed on premature distributions. However, it is possible to "borrow" temporarily from your IRA by taking a distribution and rolling over the funds to the same or to a new IRA within 60 days. That money is not considered premature distributions. You may not contribute any money you earn on it during those 60 days to your IRA account, nor may you reduce the amount you must roll over by any losses during those 60 days.

Qualified charitable distributions (QCDs). A qualified charitable distribution (QCD) is a nontaxable distribution made directly by the trustee of your IRA (other than a SEP or SIMPLE IRA) to an organization eligible to receive tax-deductible contributions. You must be at least age 70½ when the distribution is made. Your total QCDs for the year cannot be more than $100,000. If you file a joint return, your spouse can also have a QCD of up to $100,000. However, the amount of the QCD is limited to the amount of the distribution that would otherwise be included in income. If your IRA includes nondeductible contributions, the distribution is first considered to be paid out of otherwise taxable income. For more information see Publication 590.

Caution. *You cannot claim a charitable contribution deduction for any QCD not included in your income.*

TAXALERT

The December 2010 tax law that extended the so-called Bush tax cuts also extended a provision through December 31, 2011, which allows a person who is 70½ or older to take a distribution from an IRA, contribute it to a charity, and not recognize any income. (The distribution must be made directly by the IRA trustee to the charity and not to the individual.) This exclusion is limited to $100,000 for each year. The opportunity to exclude the otherwise taxable portion of an IRA distribution that is donated to charity through a qualified charitable distribution lowers your adjusted gross income (AGI). A smaller AGI in turn shrinks the various limitations based on a percentage of AGI that are applied to reduce the amount of personal exemptions and certain deductions and credits you may be allowed.

Unless Congress acts, this provision expires after 2011. For updated information on this and any other tax law changes that occur after this book was published, see our website, *ey.com/EYTaxGuide*.

Ordinary income. Distributions from traditional IRAs that you include in income are taxed as ordinary income.

No special treatment. In figuring your tax, you cannot use the 10-year tax option or capital gain treatment that applies to lump-sum distributions from qualified retirement plans.

Distributions Fully or Partly Taxable

Distributions from your traditional IRA may be fully or partly taxable, depending on whether your IRA includes any nondeductible contributions.

Fully taxable. If only deductible contributions were made to your traditional IRA (or IRAs, if you have more than one), you have no basis in your IRA. Because you have no basis in your IRA, any distributions are fully taxable when received. See *Reporting taxable distributions on your return*, later.

Partly taxable. If you made nondeductible contributions or rolled over any after-tax amounts to any of your traditional IRAs, you have a cost basis (investment in the contract) equal to the amount of those contributions. These nondeductible contributions are not taxed when they are distributed to you. They are a return of your investment in your IRA.

TAXALERT

1. The occurrence of a prohibited transaction causes the entire amount in your individual retirement account to be treated as distributed and therefore taxable to you. For instance, if you lend yourself the money in your IRA, the entire amount in the account is then currently taxable to you (see *Prohibited Transactions*, following).
2. The pledging of an IRA causes the portion pledged to be treated as distributed. For example, if you have an IRA with a value of $7,500 that you pledge as security for a $5,000 bank loan, you are taxed on the $5,000.
3. The pledging of an IRA annuity causes the entire account to be treated as distributed.

Only the part of the distribution that represents nondeductible contributions and rolled over after-tax amounts (your cost basis) is tax free. If nondeductible contributions have been made or after-tax amounts have been rolled over to your IRA, distributions consist partly of nondeductible contributions (basis) and partly of deductible contributions, earnings, and gains (if there are any). Until all of your basis has been distributed, each distribution is partly nontaxable and partly taxable.

Form 8606. You must complete Form 8606 and attach it to your return if you receive a distribution from a traditional IRA and have ever made nondeductible contributions or rolled over after-tax amounts to any of your traditional IRAs. Using the form, you will figure the nontaxable distributions for 2011 and your total IRA basis for 2011 and earlier years.

Note. If you are required to file Form 8606, but you are not required to file an income tax return, you still must file Form 8606. Send it to the IRS at the time and place you would otherwise file an income tax return.

Distributions reported on Form 1099-R. If you receive a distribution from your traditional IRA, you will receive Form 1099-R, Distributions From Pensions, Annuities, Retirement or Profit-Sharing Plans, IRAs, Insurance Contracts, etc., or a similar statement. IRA distributions are shown in boxes 1 and 2a of Form 1099-R. A number or letter code in box 7 tells you what type of distribution you received from your IRA.

TAXORGANIZER

Keep Form 1099-R with your records to substantiate IRA distributions and federal income tax withholding.

Withholding. Federal income tax is withheld from distributions from traditional IRAs unless you choose not to have tax withheld. See chapter 4.

EXPLANATION

You may elect at any time not to have taxes withheld on the distribution. Before electing not to withhold, however, you must review your withholdings from other sources and estimated payments. See chapter 4, *Tax withholding and estimated tax*, for the rules relating to underpayment penalties.

IRA distributions delivered outside the United States. In general, if you are a U.S. citizen or resident alien and your home address is outside the United States or its possessions, you cannot choose exemption from withholding on distributions from your traditional IRA.

Reporting taxable distributions on your return. Report fully taxable distributions, including early distributions, on Form 1040, line 15b, or Form 1040A, line 11b (no entry is required on Form 1040, line 15a, or Form 1040A, line 11a). If only part of the distribution is taxable, enter the total amount on Form 1040, line 15a, or Form 1040A, line 11a, and the taxable part on Form 1040, line 15b, or Form 1040A, line 11b. You cannot report distributions on Form 1040EZ.

What Acts Result in Penalties or Additional Taxes?

The tax advantages of using traditional IRAs for retirement savings can be offset by additional taxes and penalties if you do not follow the rules.

There are additions to the regular tax for using your IRA funds in prohibited transactions. There are also additional taxes for the following activities.

- Investing in collectibles.
- Making excess contributions.
- Taking early distributions.
- Allowing excess amounts to accumulate (failing to take required distributions).

There are penalties for overstating the amount of nondeductible contributions and for failure to file a Form 8606, if required.

Prohibited Transactions

Generally, a prohibited transaction is any improper use of your traditional IRA by you, your beneficiary, or any disqualified person.

Disqualified persons include your fiduciary and members of your family (spouse, ancestor, lineal descendent, and any spouse of a lineal descendent).

The following are examples of prohibited transactions with a traditional IRA.

- Borrowing money from it.
- Selling property to it.
- Receiving unreasonable compensation for managing it.
- Using it as security for a loan.
- Buying property for personal use (present or future) with IRA funds.

Effect on an IRA account. Generally, if you or your beneficiary engages in a prohibited transaction in connection with your traditional IRA account at any time during the year, the account stops being an IRA as of the first day of that year.

Effect on you or your beneficiary. If your account stops being an IRA because you or your beneficiary engaged in a prohibited transaction, the account is treated as distributing all its assets to you at their fair market values on the first day of the year. If the total of those values is more than your basis in the IRA, you will have a taxable gain that is includible in your income. For information on figuring your gain and reporting it in income, see *Are Distributions Taxable*, earlier. The distribution may be subject to additional taxes or penalties.

Taxes on prohibited transactions. If someone other than the owner or beneficiary of a traditional IRA engages in a prohibited transaction, that person may be liable for certain taxes. In general, there is a 15% tax on the amount of the prohibited transaction and a 100% additional tax if the transaction is not corrected.

More information. For more information on prohibited transactions, see Publication 590.

EXPLANATION

The rules relating to prohibited transactions are designed to prevent the manipulation of IRA funds by the person who has set the funds aside for his or her retirement.

Investment in Collectibles

If your traditional IRA invests in collectibles, the amount invested is considered distributed to you in the year invested. You may have to pay the 10% additional tax on early distributions, discussed later.

Collectibles. These include:

- Artworks,
- Rugs,
- Antiques,
- Metals,
- Gems,
- Stamps,
- Coins,
- Alcoholic beverages, and
- Certain other tangible personal property.

Exception. Your IRA can invest in one, one-half, one-quarter, or one-tenth ounce U.S. gold coins, or one-ounce silver coins minted by the Treasury Department. It can also invest in certain platinum coins and certain gold, silver, palladium, and platinum bullion.

EXPLANATION

Although an investment in tangible property, such as artworks, precious metals or gems, antiques, or alcoholic beverages, is not technically a prohibited transaction, the cost of the item is treated as a distribution from your IRA. The amount is included in your income and may be subject to the 10% premature distribution penalty tax.

This rule is designed to prevent you from directing your IRA to invest in property that the trustee could conceivably allow you to keep in your home for your personal enjoyment (e.g., art for display on your home or office walls).

In order to help sell U.S. and state-issued gold and silver coins, Congress removed the penalty for such coins acquired after October 1, 1986.

Excess Contributions

Generally, an excess contribution is the amount contributed to your traditional IRA(s) for the year that is more than the smaller of:

- The maximum deductible amount for the year. For 2011, this is $5,000 ($6,000 if you are 50 or older), or
- Your taxable compensation for the year.

EXAMPLE

You contribute $10,000 to IRAs you have set up for you and your nonworking spouse. You put $5,050 into your account and $4,950 into your spouse's account. There is a $50 excess contribution to your account. Only $9950 ($5,000 + $4,950) can be contributed and deducted on your joint income tax return. In order to obtain the full $10,000 contribution, you can withdraw the $50 excess contribution from your account and put it into your spouse's account. This must be done no later than April 17, 2012. (The due date is actually April 17, 2012, because April 15, 2012, falls on Sunday, and the following day, April 16, is the Emancipation Day holiday in the District of Columbia, which is observed as a legal holiday.)

Tax on excess contributions. In general, if the excess contributions for a year are not withdrawn by the date your return for the year is due (including extensions), you are subject to a 6% tax. You must pay the 6% tax each year on excess amounts that remain in your traditional IRA at the end of your tax year. The tax cannot be more than 6% of the combined value of all your IRAs as of the end of your tax year.

Excess contributions withdrawn by due date of return. You will not have to pay the 6% tax if you withdraw an excess contribution made during a tax year and you also withdraw interest or other income earned on the excess contribution. You must complete your withdrawal by the date your tax return for that year is due, including extensions.

How to treat withdrawn contributions. Do not include in your gross income an excess contribution that you withdraw from your traditional IRA before your tax return is due if both the following conditions are met.

- No deduction was allowed for the excess contribution.
- You withdraw the interest or other income earned on the excess contribution.

You can take into account any loss on the contribution while it was in the IRA when calculating the amount that must be withdrawn. If there was a loss, the net income you must withdraw may be a negative amount.

How to treat withdrawn interest or other income. You must include in your gross income the interest or other income that was earned on the excess contribution. Report it on your return for the year in which the excess contribution was made. Your withdrawal of interest or other income may be subject to an additional 10% tax on early distributions, discussed later.

EXPLANATION

Excess contributions you withdraw before the due date of the return are not subject to the 6% excise tax, provided that the full amount of income attributable to the excess contribution is also distributed. The income portion of the distribution is then included in your income in the year in which the excess contribution was made. The withdrawn income may be subject to the 10% tax on premature distributions (see *Early Distributions*, following).

Excess contributions withdrawn after due date of return. In general, you must include all distributions (withdrawals) from your traditional IRA in your gross income. However, if the following conditions are met, you can withdraw excess contributions from your IRA and not include the amount withdrawn in your gross income.

- Total contributions (other than rollover contributions) for 2011 to your IRA were not more than $5,000 ($6,000 if you are 50 or older).
- You did not take a deduction for the excess contribution being withdrawn.

The withdrawal can take place at any time, even after the due date, including extensions, for filing your tax return for the year.

EXPLANATION

Excess payments may also be adjusted by deducting the correct amount in the current year and applying the excess to the following year's contribution.

Example

If you mistakenly contributed $5,500 to your IRA in 2010, when you were entitled to only a $5,000 contribution, you may reduce your 2011 contribution by the excess $500. If you are entitled to a $5,000 contribution in 2011, you should then contribute no more than $4,500 that year. To make this application work, you must deduct only $5,000 for 2010–not the actual $5,500 you contributed. Although you are still subject to the 6% tax on the $500 excess contribution in 2011, if you reduce the following year's contribution to $4,500, there is no excess contribution remaining in your IRA and no tax would be imposed for 2011.

You would receive a $5,000 deduction for 2011 consisting of the $4,500 you actually contributed in 2011 plus the excess contribution from 2010.

Excess contribution deducted in an earlier year. If you deducted an excess contribution in an earlier year for which the total contributions were not more than the maximum deductible amount for that year ($2,000 for 2001 and earlier years, $3,000 for 2002 through 2004 ($3,500 if you were age 50 or older), $4,000 for 2005 ($4,500 if you were age 50 or older), $4,000 for 2006 or 2007 ($5,000 if you were age 50 or older), $5,000 for 2008 through 2010 ($6,000 if you were age 50 or older)), you can still remove the excess from your traditional IRA and not include it in your gross income. To do this, file Form 1040X for that year and do not deduct the excess contribution on the amended return. Generally, you can file an amended return within 3 years after you filed your return, or 2 years from the time the tax was paid, whichever is later.

Excess due to incorrect rollover information. If an excess contribution in your traditional IRA is the result of a rollover and the excess occurred because the information the plan was required to give you was incorrect, you can withdraw the excess contribution. The limits mentioned above are increased by the amount of the excess that is due to the incorrect information. You will have to amend your return for the year in which the excess occurred to correct the reporting of the rollover amounts in that year. Do not include in your gross income the part of the excess contribution caused by the incorrect information.

Early Distributions

You must include early distributions of taxable amounts from your traditional IRA in your gross income. Early distributions are also subject to an additional 10% tax. See the discussion of Form 5329 under *Reporting Additional Taxes*, later, to figure and report the tax.

Early distributions defined. Early distributions generally are amounts distributed from your traditional IRA account or annuity before you are age 59½.

> **TAXPLANNER**
>
> If you are fortunate enough to have sufficient income without taking any distributions from your IRA, you may wish to postpone withdrawing money from your IRA as long as possible. Distributions do not have to begin until April 1 of the calendar year following the year in which you reach age 70½. See *Required Distributions*, earlier.

Age 59½ rule. Generally, if you are under age 59½, you must pay a 10% additional tax on the distribution of any assets (money or other property) from your traditional IRA. Distributions before you are age 59½ are called early distributions.

The 10% additional tax applies to the part of the distribution that you have to include in gross income. It is in addition to any regular income tax on that amount.

Exceptions. There are several exceptions to the age 59½ rule. Even if you receive a distribution before you are age 59½, you may not have to pay the 10% additional tax if you are in one of the following situations.

- You have unreimbursed medical expenses that are more than 7.5% of your adjusted gross income.
- The distributions are not more than the cost of your medical insurance.
- You are disabled.
- You are the beneficiary of a deceased IRA owner.
- You are receiving distributions in the form of an annuity.
- The distributions are not more than your qualified higher education expenses.
- You use the distributions to buy, build, or rebuild a first home.
- The distribution is due to an IRS levy of the qualified plan.
- The distribution is a qualified reservist distribution.

Most of these exceptions are explained in Publication 590.

Note. Distributions that are timely and properly rolled over, as discussed earlier, are not subject to either regular income tax or the 10% additional tax. Certain withdrawals of excess contributions after the due date of your return are also tax free and therefore not subject to the 10% additional tax. (See *Excess contributions withdrawn after due date of return*, earlier.) This also applies to transfers incident to divorce, as discussed earlier.

> **TAXPLANNER**
>
> The life annuity exception may be beneficial if you retire before age 55, your employer's plan does not provide for a life annuity, and you don't want to pay the penalty and taxes on the distribution, but you need supplemental income. You will not be subject to the penalty if the plan distribution is rolled over into an IRA and then distributed as part of a series of substantially equal periodic payments (made no less frequently than annually) over your life expectancy or the joint life expectancies of you and a beneficiary.
>
> Note that, using the life annuity exception, you would not be making a single withdrawal. Rather, you would effectively be receiving an annuity in which the payments will be substantially equal. Modifying the payments before you reach age 59½, or, in any event, within 5 years of the date of the first payment, will result in the imposition of the 10% penalty tax that would have applied absent the exception, plus interest. The only exception is if you switch once from the amortization or the annuity factor method to the straight life expectancy method.
>
> The IRS has identified three methods available for determining whether distributions from an IRA are considered to be "substantially equal periodic payments."
>
> 1. The "straight life expectancy" method: To use this method, you divide the balance in the individual retirement account at the end of each year by the owner's life expectancy or joint and survivor life expectancy, as determined from tables published by the IRS. Under this method, distributions may vary from year to year due to:
>   a. account balance changes resulting from earnings and distributions during the year, and
>   b. changes in the owner's life expectancy as the owner gets older.

2. The amortization method: This method involves determining an annuity payment based on the balance in the individual retirement account, the beneficiary's life expectancy, and an assumed interest rate. Under this method, you would essentially be able to choose among various distribution amounts: IRS rules allow you to select from several interest rate assumptions and between two published life expectancy tables. However, once the annuity amount has been determined, it will not change from year to year.
3. The annuity factor method: This method involves determining an annuity payment by dividing the balance in the individual retirement account by an annuity factor derived from a reasonable mortality table using a reasonable rate of interest. As under the amortization method, once determined, the annuity amount will not change.

TAXALERT

Note that the substantially equal periodic payment exception (described previously) is applied on an IRA-by-IRA basis. Therefore, an IRA owner who wants the flexibility in the future to increase the annual withdrawal amounts can divide an existing IRA into several IRAs before distributions begin. Substantially equal periodic distributions could be taken prior to age 59½ from only one of the IRAs. In the future, if additional payments are needed, distributions could be taken from one or more of the other IRAs.

Taxpayers have the ability to make a one-time switch from either the amortization method or annuity factor method to the straight life expectancy method. The one-time switch may be beneficial if you are locked into a fixed payment under either the amortization or annuity factor methods and your account has dropped in value. By using the one-time switch to the straight life expectancy method, a new lower payment can be calculated based on the lower account balance. You should consult your tax advisor for additional details.

The straight life expectancy method (method 1, described earlier) is the easiest to use but will result in the smallest annual distribution. The amortization and annuity factor methods result in larger distributions and are more difficult to compute, respectively, than the straight life expectancy method.

Since the rules regarding substantially equal periodic payments are complex and substantial penalties apply for failure to comply, you should consult your tax advisor when planning to take early distributions from your IRA(s).

Receivership distributions. Early distributions (with or without your consent) from savings institutions placed in receivership are subject to this tax unless one of the exceptions listed earlier applies. This is true even if the distribution is from a receiver that is a state agency.

Additional 10% tax. The additional tax on early distributions is 10% of the amount of the early distribution that you must include in your gross income. This tax is in addition to any regular income tax resulting from including the distribution in income.

Nondeductible contributions. The tax on early distributions does not apply to the part of a distribution that represents a return of your non-deductible contributions (basis).

TAXALERT

Distributions received from an IRA by members of the National Guard and Reserves, called to active duty for a period in excess of 179 days or for an indefinite period after September 11, 2001, are not subject to the 10% additional tax. (This exemption from the 10% additional tax also applies to distributions received from 401(k), 403(b), and similar plans. See chapter 10, *Retirement plans, pensions, and annuities*.) The distribution received may otherwise be subject to ordinary income tax in the year received. See *Distributions Fully or Partly Taxable*, earlier.

A refund or credit of the 10% early withdrawal tax previously paid on distributions that qualify for exemption from this penalty tax may be obtained.

Any portion of such distributions may be contributed into an IRA account anytime within the 2-year period following the end of the period of active duty. The dollar limitations otherwise applicable to contributions to IRAs do not apply to any contribution made pursuant to the provision. No deduction is allowed for any contribution made under the provision.

TAXALERT

Although amounts contributed back into an IRA cannot be deducted, such amounts do not reduce the maximum amount that you can otherwise contribute during the year to your IRA based on your earnings.

TAXPLANNER

If you are eligible for this provision, consider rolling over a prior distribution and filing an amended return for a refund of tax or any penalty you paid.

More information. For more information on early distributions, see Publication 590.

Excess Accumulations (Insufficient Distributions)

You cannot keep amounts in your traditional IRA indefinitely. Generally, you must begin receiving distributions by April 1 of the year following the year in which you reach age 70½. The required minimum distribution for any year after the year in which you reach age 70½ must be made by December 31 of that later year.

Tax on excess. If distributions are less than the required minimum distribution for the year, you may have to pay a 50% excise tax for that year on the amount not distributed as required.

Request to waive the tax. If the excess accumulation is due to reasonable error, and you have taken, or are taking, steps to remedy the insufficient distribution, you can request that the tax be waived. If you believe you qualify for this relief, attach a statement of explanation and complete Form 5329 as instructed under *Waiver of tax* in the Instructions for Form 5329.

Exemption from tax. If you are unable to take required distributions because you have a traditional IRA invested in a contract issued by an insurance company that is in state insurer delinquency proceedings, the 50% excise tax does not apply if the conditions and requirements of Revenue Procedure 92-10 are satisfied.

TAXALERT

If you cannot receive required distributions from your IRA because your insurance company is in state insurer delinquency proceedings, consult a tax advisor to see if you can avoid the 50% excise tax.

More information. For more information on excess accumulations, see Publication 590.

Reporting Additional Taxes

Generally, you must use Form 5329 to report the tax on excess contributions, early distributions, and excess accumulations. If you must file Form 5329, you cannot use Form 1040A or Form 1040EZ.

Filing a tax return. If you must file an individual income tax return, complete Form 5329 and attach it to your Form 1040. Enter the total additional taxes due on Form 1040, line 58.

Not filing a tax return. If you do not have to file a tax return but do have to pay one of the additional taxes mentioned earlier, file the completed Form 5329 with the IRS at the time and place you would have filed your Form 1040. Be sure to include your address on page 1 and your signature and date on page 2. Enclose, but do not attach, a check or money order payable to the United States Treasury for the tax you owe, as shown on Form 5329. Enter your social security number and "2011 Form 5329" on your check or money order.

Form 5329 not required. You do not have to use Form 5329 if either of the following situations exist.

- Distribution code 1 (early distribution) is correctly shown in box 7 of Form 1099-R. If you do not owe any other additional tax on a distribution, multiply the taxable part of the early distribution by 10% and enter the result on Form 1040, line 58. Put "No" to the left of the line to indicate that you do not have to file Form 5329. However, if you owe this tax and also owe any other additional tax on a distribution, do not enter this 10% additional tax directly on your Form 1040. You must file Form 5329 to report your additional taxes.

- If you rolled over part or all of a distribution from a qualified retirement plan, the part rolled over is not subject to the tax on early distributions.

Roth IRAs

Regardless of your age, you may be able to establish and make nondeductible contributions to a retirement plan called a Roth IRA.

Contributions not reported. You do not report Roth IRA contributions on your return.

What Is a Roth IRA?

A Roth IRA is an individual retirement plan that, except as explained in this chapter, is subject to the rules that apply to a traditional IRA (defined earlier). It can be either an account or an annuity. Individual retirement accounts and annuities are described in Publication 590.

To be a Roth IRA, the account or annuity must be designated as a Roth IRA when it is opened. A deemed IRA can be a Roth IRA, but neither a SEP IRA nor a SIMPLE IRA can be designated as a Roth IRA.

Unlike a traditional IRA, you cannot deduct contributions to a Roth IRA. But, if you satisfy the requirements, qualified distributions (discussed later) are tax free. Contributions can be made to your Roth IRA after you reach age 70½ and you can leave amounts in your Roth IRA as long as you live.

When Can a Roth IRA Be Opened?

You can open a Roth IRA at any time. However, the time for making contributions for any year is limited. See When Can You Make Contributions, later under *Can You Contribute to a Roth IRA?*

Can You Contribute to a Roth IRA?

Tip

You may be eligible to claim a credit for contributions to your Roth IRA. For more information, see chapter 37.

Generally, you can contribute to a Roth IRA if you have taxable compensation (defined later) and your modified AGI (defined later) is less than:

- $179,000 for married filing jointly or qualifying widow(er),
- $122,000 for single, head of household, or married filing separately and you did not live with your spouse at any time during the year, or
- $10,000 for married filing separately and you lived with your spouse at any time during the year.

Is there an age limit for contributions? Contributions can be made to your Roth IRA regardless of your age.

Can you contribute to a Roth IRA for your spouse? You can contribute to a Roth IRA for your spouse provided the contributions satisfy the spousal IRA limit (discussed in How Much Can Be Contributed under *Traditional IRAs*), you file jointly, and your modified AGI is less than $179,000.

Compensation. Compensation includes wages, salaries, tips, professional fees, bonuses, and other amounts received for providing personal services. It also includes commissions, self-employment income, nontaxable combat pay, military differential pay, and taxable alimony and separate maintenance payments.

Modified AGI. Your modified AGI for Roth IRA purposes is your adjusted gross income (AGI) as shown on your return modified as follows.

1. Subtract the following.
   a. Roth IRA conversions included on Form 1040, line 15b, or Form 1040A, line 11b.
   b. Roth IRA rollovers from qualified retirement plans included on Form 1040, line 16b, or Form 1040A, line 12b.
2. Add the following deductions and exclusions:
   a. Traditional IRA deduction,
   b. Student loan interest deduction,
   c. Tuition and fees deduction,
   d. Domestic production activities deduction,
   e. Foreign earned income exclusion,
   f. Foreign housing exclusion or deduction,
   g. Exclusion of qualified savings bond interest shown on Form 8815, and
   h. Exclusion of employer-provided adoption benefits shown on Form 8839.

You can use Worksheet 17-2 to figure your modified AGI.

Worksheet 17-2. **Modified Adjusted Gross Income for Roth IRA Purposes** *Keep for Your Records*

Use this worksheet to figure your modified adjusted gross income for Roth IRA purposes.

1.	Enter your adjusted gross income from Form 1040, line 38; or Form 1040A, line 22	**1.** ______
2.	Enter any income resulting from the conversion of an IRA (other than a Roth IRA) to a Roth IRA, a rollover from a qualified retirement plan to a Roth IRA, and a minimum required distribution from an IRA (for conversions and rollovers from qualified retirement plans only)	**2.** ______
3.	Subtract line 2 from line 1	**3.** ______
4.	Enter any traditional IRA deduction from Form 1040, line 32; or Form 1040A, line 17	**4.** ______
5.	Enter any student loan interest deduction from Form 1040, line 33; or Form 1040A, line 18	**5.** ______
6.	Enter any tuition and fees deduction from Form 1040, line 34; or Form 1040A, line 19	**6.** ______
7.	Enter any domestic production activities deduction from Form 1040, line 35	**7.** ______
8.	Enter any foreign earned income and/or housing exclusion from Form 2555, line 45; or Form 2555-EZ, line 18	**8.** ______
9.	Enter any foreign housing deduction from Form 2555, line 50	**9.** ______
10.	Enter any excludable savings bond interest from Form 8815, line 14	**10.** ______
11.	Enter any excluded employer-provided adoption benefits from Form 8839, line 23	**11.** ______
12.	Add the amounts on lines 3 through 11	**12.** ______
13.	Enter: • $179,000 if married filing jointly or qualifying widow(er) • $10,000 if married filing separately and you lived with your spouse at any time during the year • $122,000 for all others	**13.** ______

Is the amount on line 12 more than the amount on line 13?

If yes, then see the Note below.

If no, then the amount on line 12 is your modified AGI for Roth IRA purposes.

Note. If the amount on line 12 is more than the amount on line 13 and you have other income or loss items, such as social security income or passive activity losses, that are subject to AGI-based phaseouts, you can refigure your AGI solely for the purpose of figuring your modified AGI for Roth IRA purposes. When figuring your modified AGI for conversion purposes, refigure your AGI without taking into account any income from conversions or minimum required distributions from IRAs. (If you receive social security benefits, use *Worksheet 1* in *Appendix B* of Publication 590 to refigure your AGI.) Then go to list item (2) under *Modified AGI* or line 3 above in *Worksheet 17-2* to refigure your modified AGI. If you do not have other income or loss items subject to AGI-based phaseouts, your modified AGI for Roth IRA purposes is the amount on line 12.

Text intentionally omitted.

How Much Can Be Contributed?

The contribution limit for Roth IRAs generally depends on whether contributions are made only to Roth IRAs or to both traditional IRAs and Roth IRAs.

Roth IRAs only. If contributions are made only to Roth IRAs, your contribution limit generally is the lesser of the following amounts.

- $5,000 ($6,000 if you are 50 or older in 2011).
- Your taxable compensation.

However, if your modified AGI is above a certain amount, your contribution limit may be reduced, as explained later under Contribution limit reduced.

Roth IRAs and traditional IRAs. If contributions are made to both Roth IRAs and traditional IRAs established for your benefit, your contribution limit for Roth IRAs generally is the same as your limit would be if contributions were made only to Roth IRAs, but then reduced by all contributions for the year to all IRAs other than Roth IRAs. Employer contributions under a SEP or SIMPLE IRA plan do not affect this limit.

This means that your contribution limit is generally the lesser of the following amounts.

- $5,000 ($6,000 if you are 50 or older in 2011) minus all contributions (other than employer contributions under a SEP or SIMPLE IRA plan) for the year to all IRAs other than Roth IRAs.
- Your taxable compensation minus all contributions (other than employer contributions under a SEP or SIMPLE IRA plan) for the year to all IRAs other than Roth IRAs.

However, if your modified AGI is above a certain amount, your contribution limit may be reduced, as explained next under *Contribution limit reduced.*

Contribution limit reduced. If your modified AGI is above a certain amount, your contribution limit is gradually reduced. Use Table 17-3 to determine if this reduction applies to you.

Figuring the reduction. If the amount you can contribute to your Roth IRA is reduced, see Publication 590 for how to figure the reduction.

Tip

You can make contributions for 2011 by the due date (not including extensions) for filing your 2011 tax return.

When Can You Make Contributions?

You can make contributions to a Roth IRA for a year at any time during the year or by the due date of your return for that year (not including extensions).

EXPLANATION

Roth IRAs

Roth IRAs are tax-free retirement savings vehicles. By permitting tax-free withdrawals, contributions made early in your working life receive the greatest tax benefit.

Example 1

John is 25 years old on January 1, 2011. On January 1 of each year, he contributes $5,000 to a Roth IRA. The account earns 8% per year. John retires on January 1, 2051, at age 65 (immediately after he makes his last Roth IRA contribution). He will have accumulated $1,403,905 toward retirement–all available tax free.

Example 2

Jim is also 25 years old on January 1, 2011. Rather than make his $5,000 Roth contribution on January 1 of each year, he waits until April 15 of the next year to make his contribution. His account also earns 8% per year. In order to retire with the same amount as John, he must wait until April 15, 2052, to retire. Alternatively, if he retires on January 1, 2051, he will only have accumulated $1,260,948 toward retirement–$142,957 less than John.

Table 17-3. **Effect of Modified AGI on Roth IRA Contribution**

This table shows whether your contribution to a Roth IRA is affected by the amount of your modified adjusted gross income (modified AGI).

IF you have taxable compensation and your filing status is...	AND your modified AGI is...	THEN...
married filing jointly, or **qualifying widow(er)**	less than $169,000	you can contribute up to $5,000 ($6,000 if you are 50 or older in 2011).
	at least $169,000 but less than $179,000	the amount you can contribute is reduced as explained under *Contribution limit reduced* in Publication 590.
	$179,000 or more	you cannot contribute to a Roth IRA.
married filing separately and you lived with your spouse at any time during the year	zero (-0-)	you can contribute up to $5,000 ($6,000 if you are 50 or older in 2011).
	more than zero (-0-) but less than $10,000	the amount you can contribute is reduced as explained under *Contribution limit reduced* in Publication 590.
	$10,000 or more	you cannot contribute to a Roth IRA.
single, head of household, or **married filing separately** and you did not live with your spouse at any time during the year	less than $107,000	you can contribute up to $5,000 ($6,000 if you are 50 or older in 2011).
	at least $107,000 but less than $122,000	the amount you can contribute is reduced as explained under *Contribution limit reduced* in Publication 590.
	$122,000 or more	you cannot contribute to a Roth IRA.

> ***Example 3***
> Mary is 16 years old and earns wages of $5,000 in 2011. Her father gifts her $5,000, which she uses to open a Roth IRA on December 31, 2011. If the account earns 8% per year, it will be worth approximately $235,000 (tax free) if she retires at age 66.

What If You Contribute Too Much?

A 6% excise tax applies to any excess contribution to a Roth IRA.

Excess contributions. These are the contributions to your Roth IRAs for a year that equal the total of:

1. Amounts contributed for the tax year to your Roth IRAs (other than amounts properly and timely rolled over from a Roth IRA or properly converted from a traditional IRA or rolled over from a qualified retirement plan, as described later) that are more than your contribution limit for the year, plus
2. Any excess contributions for the preceding year, reduced by the total of:
   a. Any distributions out of your Roth IRAs for the year, plus
   b. Your contribution limit for the year minus your contributions to all your IRAs for the year.

Withdrawal of excess contributions. For purposes of determining excess contributions, any contribution that is withdrawn on or before the due date (including extensions) for filing your tax return for the year is treated as an amount not contributed. This treatment applies only if any earnings on the contributions are also withdrawn. The earnings are considered to have been earned and received in the year the excess contribution was made.

Applying excess contributions. If contributions to your Roth IRA for a year were more than the limit, you can apply the excess contribution in one year to a later year if the contributions for that later year are less than the maximum allowed for that year.

Can You Move Amounts Into a Roth IRA?

You may be able to convert amounts from either a traditional, SEP, or SIMPLE IRA into a Roth IRA. You may be able to roll amounts over from a qualified retirement plan to a Roth IRA. You may be able to recharacterize contributions made to one IRA as having been made directly to a different IRA. You can roll amounts over from a designated Roth account or from one Roth IRA to another Roth IRA.

Conversions

You can convert a traditional IRA to a Roth IRA. The conversion is treated as a rollover, regardless of the conversion method used. Most of the rules for rollovers, described earlier under Rollover From One IRA Into Another under *Traditional IRAs*, apply to these rollovers. However, the 1-year waiting period does not apply.

> ***TAXALERT***
> Beginning in 2010, taxpayers at all income levels, including those who are married filing separately, are permitted to roll over ("convert") a traditional IRA (and/or an employer qualified retirement plan) into a Roth IRA. The amount distributed is taxable income at the time of the distribution, except to the extent it includes nontaxable amounts (e.g., after-tax contributions). Investment earnings and growth in a traditional IRA (and an employer qualified retirement plan other than a Roth 401(k)) grow tax deferred so that when funds are ultimately withdrawn, they are taxable to the participant. But investments held inside a Roth IRA grow tax free and therefore future withdrawals are not taxed, provided the funds are not withdrawn until age 59½ and five years from the date of conversion. (Tax-free distributions may also be made under other circumstances [e.g., disability].)

> ***TAXSAVER***
> **Roth IRA Conversions in 2011.** The anticipated increase in individual income tax rates beginning in 2013 enhances the potential tax benefits of converting a traditional IRA to a Roth IRA in 2011. Converting a traditional IRA to a Roth IRA is a taxable event and taxpayers should consider whether the prospect of higher tax rates scheduled to take effect in 2013 may result in higher taxes being paid on conversion income if they wait to convert the IRA until 2013 rather than opting to accelerate the income recognized to 2011 and paying the tax at 2011 tax rates.

For taxpayers expecting to pay the alternative minimum tax (AMT) in 2011 at its 28% marginal rate (see Alternative Minimum Tax, in chapter 31, *How to figure your tax*, for more information on how the AMT is calculated) but the regular income tax in 2012 and 2013 at a higher marginal rate (the top rate is scheduled to rise to 39.6% in 2013 and later years), making the Roth conversion entirely in 2011 rather than waiting until 2012 or 2013 may result in lower taxes paid overall. These taxpayers may also be able to further enhance the benefit of a Roth conversion by delaying their state income tax payments related to the Roth IRA conversion until early 2012, as they may obtain a state income tax deduction benefit against their regular tax in 2012. Such a state income tax deduction benefit would not be available if the amounts are paid in 2011 when they are subject to the AMT.

TAXALERT

Late in 2010, Congress passed the Small Business Jobs Act of 2010, containing a provision that allows 401(k), 403(b), and governmental 457(b) plans to permit participants to roll their pre-tax account balances into a designated Roth account within the same plan. Under prior law, these distributions could only be rolled over (after taxation) to a Roth IRA. Rollovers to a designated Roth account are only allowed, however, in the event of a permitted distributable event such as separation from service or attaining age 59½.

Just like a conversion to a Roth IRA, the amount rolled over is includible in taxable income except to the extent it includes a return of after-tax contributions. This new provision offers eligible taxpayers another option for converting pre-tax amounts held inside their 401(k), 403(b), and/or 457(b) plans to a Roth account.

Conversion methods. You can convert amounts from a traditional IRA to a Roth IRA in any of the following ways.

- ***Rollover.*** You can receive a distribution from a traditional IRA and roll it over (contribute it) to a Roth IRA within 60 days after the distribution.
- ***Trustee-to-trustee transfer.*** You can direct the trustee of the traditional IRA to transfer an amount from the traditional IRA to the trustee of the Roth IRA.
- ***Same trustee transfer.*** If the trustee of the traditional IRA also maintains the Roth IRA, you can direct the trustee to transfer an amount from the traditional IRA to the Roth IRA.

Same trustee. Conversions made with the same trustee can be made by redesignating the traditional IRA as a Roth IRA, rather than opening a new account or issuing a new contract.

Text intentionally omitted.

TAXPLANNER

You can choose to change a Roth Conversion IRA back into a regular IRA and once again convert the regular IRA back into a Roth IRA. Generally, you can only do this once in a calendar year. Such a change can be beneficial in a situation where you converted a regular IRA into a Roth IRA at a time when stock market values were high and then they subsequently dropped significantly. You can avoid paying tax on the "vanished" profits by recharacterizing the Roth IRA as a regular IRA and then converting back to a Roth IRA the following year if stock values stay low.

The Roth IRA conversion rules—including trying to roll over only basis to a Roth IRA, splitting one IRA into several Roth IRAs and recharacterizing one or more of your IRAs—are complex. You should consult with your tax advisor before the initial conversion.

TAXPLANNER

Even if you're past the age when required minimum distributions (RMDs) from traditional IRAs have begun, you can still convert the IRA to a Roth IRA and pay taxes currently, but you then eliminate the requirement to make additional lifetime distributions from the account. *Note:* You cannot roll over the current year RMD to a Roth IRA as part of a conversion.

TAXPLANNER

Partial conversions are permissible. You can also convert one or more separate IRAs. However, in determining the tax consequences of a partial conversion–whether from a single IRA or separate accounts–normal IRA distribution rules apply. Thus, the tax consequences depend on the value of all IRAs, as well as your total nondeductible contributions to all IRAs.

Example

Suppose you have two IRAs, each with a current value of $50,000. One was funded entirely with deductible contributions, while the other was funded entirely with nondeductible contributions totaling $20,000. If you converted either IRA in full, you would recognize $40,000 of income. Note that this result occurs regardless of the IRA converted.

Value of IRA converted		$50,000
Total nondeductible contributions	$20,000 (a)	
Percentage of the total value of all IRAs converted	50% (b)	
Nondeductible contributions deemed rolled over (a) × (b)		($10,000)
Gross income inclusion		($40,000)

TAXPLANNER

Whether to convert or not can be a perplexing issue. It depends on many factors, such as your income tax bracket at the time of conversion versus your tax bracket in the future (e.g., during retirement), investment rates of return, your age and life expectancy, whether you have sufficient funds outside of your IRA with which to pay the taxes attributable to the conversion, and to what extent you'll need the funds in your IRA during retirement (versus accumulating wealth primarily for your heirs). Like many complex financial decisions, it pays to run the numbers. Consult with your financial advisor about whether a Roth IRA conversion makes sense for you.

Rollover from a qualified retirement plan into a Roth IRA. You can roll over into a Roth IRA all or part of an eligible rollover distribution you receive from your (or your deceased spouse's):

- Employer's qualified pension, profit-sharing or stock bonus plan,
- Annuity plan,
- Tax-sheltered annuity plan (section 403(b) plan), or
- Governmental deferred compensation plan (section 457 plan).

Any amount rolled over is subject to the same rules for converting a traditional IRA into a Roth IRA. Also, the rollover contribution must meet the rollover requirements that apply to the specific type of retirement plan.

Income. You must include in your gross income distributions from a qualified retirement plan that you would have had to include in income if you had not rolled them over into a Roth IRA. You do not include in gross income any part of a distribution from a qualified retirement plan that is a return of contributions (after-tax contributions) to the plan that were taxable to you when paid.

These amounts are normally included in income on your return for the year you rolled them over from the employer plan to a Roth IRA. *Text intentionally omitted.*

For more information, see *Rollover From Employer's Plan Into a Roth IRA* in chapter 2 of Publication 590.

Caution

If you must include any amount in your gross income, you may have to increase your withholding or make estimated tax payments. See Publication 505, Tax Withholding and Estimated Tax.

Converting from a SIMPLE IRA. Generally, you can convert an amount in your SIMPLE IRA to a Roth IRA under the same rules explained earlier under <u>*Converting From Any Traditional IRA to a Roth IRA*</u>.

However, you cannot convert any amount distributed from the SIMPLE IRA during the 2-year period beginning on the date you first participated in any SIMPLE IRA plan maintained by your employer.

More information. For more detailed information on conversions, see Publication 590.

TAXALERT

Legislation passed by Congress in 2008 allows qualified airline employees to contribute any portion of an airline payment received from a commercial airline carrier involved in bankruptcy proceedings to a Roth IRA within 180 days of receiving the payment or by June 23, 2009, whichever is later. The contribution is treated as a qualified rollover contribution and, therefore, is included in your gross income to the extent the payment would be included were it not part of the rollover contribution. The modified adjusted gross income limits that generally apply to Roth IRA contributions (for 2011: under $122,000 for single filers; under $179,000 for married filing jointly) do not apply to airline payments. Nor is the rollover amount limited by the annual contribution limits to Roth IRAs (for 2011: $5,000; $6,000 for those age 50 or older). Also, any reduction in the airline payment on account of employment taxes is disregarded when figuring the amount of the airline payment that can be contributed to a Roth IRA. For more information, see *Rollover of Airline Payments*, in chapter 2 of Publication 590, *Individual Retirement Arrangements (IRAs)*.

Rollover From a Roth IRA

You can withdraw, tax free, all or part of the assets from one Roth IRA if you contribute them within 60 days to another Roth IRA. Most of the rules for rollovers, explained earlier under Rollover From One IRA Into Another under *Traditional IRAs*, apply to these rollovers.

Rollover from designated Roth account. A rollover from a designated Roth account can only be made to another designated Roth account or to a Roth IRA.

Are Distributions Taxable?

You do not include in your gross income qualified distributions or distributions that are a return of your regular contributions from your Roth IRA(s). You also do not include distributions from your Roth IRA that you roll over tax free into another Roth IRA. You may have to include part of other distributions in your income. See Ordering rules for distributions, later.

What are qualified distributions? A qualified distribution is any payment or distribution from your Roth IRA that meets the following requirements.

1. It is made after the 5-year period beginning with the first taxable year for which a contribution was made to a Roth IRA set up for your benefit, and
2. The payment or distribution is:
   a. Made on or after the date you reach age 59½,
   b. Made because you are disabled,
   c. Made to a beneficiary or to your estate after your death, or
   d. To pay up to $10,000 (lifetime limit) of certain qualified first-time homebuyer amounts. See Publication 590 for more information.

Additional tax on distributions of conversion and certain rollover contributions within 5-year period. If, within the 5-year period starting with the first day of your tax year in which you convert an amount from a traditional IRA or roll over an amount from a qualified retirement plan to a Roth IRA, you take a distribution from a Roth IRA, you may have to pay the 10% additional tax on early distributions. You generally must pay the 10% additional tax on any amount attributable to the part of the amount converted or rolled over (the conversion or rollover contribution) that you had to include in income. A separate 5-year period applies to each conversion and rollover. See Ordering rules for distributions, later, to determine the amount, if any, of the distribution that is attributable to the part of the conversion or rollover contribution that you had to include in income.

Additional tax on other early distributions. Unless an exception applies, you must pay the 10% additional tax on the taxable part of any distributions that are not qualified distributions. See Publication 590 for more information.

Ordering rules for distributions. If you receive a distribution from your Roth IRA that is not a qualified distribution, part of it may be taxable. There is a set order in which contributions (including conversion contributions and rollover contributions from qualified retirement plans) and earnings are considered to be distributed from your Roth IRA. Regular contributions are distributed first. See Publication 590 for more information.

Must you withdraw or use Roth IRA assets? You are not required to take distributions from your Roth IRA at any age. The minimum distribution rules that apply to traditional IRAs do not apply to Roth IRAs while the owner is alive. However, after the death of a Roth IRA owner, certain of the minimum distribution rules that apply to traditional IRAs also apply to Roth IRAs.

TAXPLANNER

There are no required minimum distributions (RMDs) for a Roth IRA during the life of the account owner. This means that your account can stay intact for as long as you live, allowing investment earnings to grow on a tax-free basis. In addition, if you're married, your spouse–if named the beneficiary of the account–can "step into your shoes" (e.g., by establishing a Roth IRA rollover account) and continue to defer distributions during the remainder of his or her lifetime.

Following your death (or the death of your surviving spouse if he or she were named the account beneficiary and rolled over the account after your death), the normal postmortem RMD rules would apply (see *Required Distributions*, earlier). Since there is technically no required beginning date for making RMDs from a Roth IRA during your life, the schedule of required distributions after your death would be determined by your designated beneficiary, who can receive distributions over his or her remaining life expectancy, so long as the first RMD is made by December 31 in the year following the year of your death. The ability to delay distributions until after your death, and then have the account gradually distributed tax free to heirs over their lifetimes, creates a valuable way to transfer wealth from one generation to another.

More information. For more detailed information on Roth IRAs, see Publication 590.

Simplified Employee Pensions (SEPs)

A simplified employee pension is a written plan that allows an employer to make contributions toward an employee's retirement without becoming involved in more complex retirement plans. If you are self-employed, you can contribute to your own SEP.

For 2011, the SEP rules permit an employer to contribute and deduct each year to each participating employee's SEP up to 25% of the employee's compensation, up to $245,000, or $49,000, whichever is less. If you are self-employed, special rules apply when figuring the maximum deduction for these contributions. In determining the percentage limit on contributions, compensation is net earnings from self-employment, taking into account the contributions to the SEP.

TAXSAVER

Even if your employer makes contributions to a SEP for your account, you can make contributions to your own IRA. The IRA deduction rules, previously discussed, apply to any amounts you contribute to your IRA.

TAXSAVER

A self-employed person can claim a deduction to a SEP as long as the contribution is made by the due date of the return, including extensions. Even if you failed to set up a plan by December 31, you can still establish a SEP after the end of the year and make a timely payment.

TAXALERT

SEPs permitting salary reduction contributions could not be established after 1996, although SEPs that allowed elective deferrals before 1997 (SARSEPs) can continue to do so.

Savings Incentive Match Plans for Employees (SIMPLE)

Your employer can establish a type of retirement plan called the savings incentive match plan for employees. In general, employers with 100 or fewer employees earning at least $5,000 and who do not maintain another employer-sponsored retirement plan are eligible to set up SIMPLE plans. SIMPLE plans, which are not subject to some of the complicated rules that apply to other types of retirement plans, can be adopted as an IRA or as a part of a 401(k) plan. All employees who earn more than $5,000 a year must be eligible to participate, and self-employed individuals may also participate in SIMPLE plans. In general, contributions to a SIMPLE plan are not taxable until withdrawn.

The employer generally must either match elective employee contributions dollar for dollar up to 3% of compensation or make a "nonelective" contribution of 2% of compensation on behalf of each eligible employee. No other contributions may be made to a SIMPLE account. Contributions to a SIMPLE account generally are deductible by the employer; however, matching contributions are deductible only if made by the due date (including extensions) of the employer's tax return.

TAXALERT

The limit on maximum annual elective deferrals to a SIMPLE plan are:

Year	Regular Amount	"Catch-up"* Amount
2006	$10,000	$12,500
2007	10,500	13,000
2008	10,500	13,000
2009	11,500	14,000
2010	11,500	14,000
2011	11,500**	14,000**

*For taxpayers who reach age 50 before the end of the plan year.
**Adjusted for inflation in $500 increments.

Employers are given a 2-year grace period to maintain a SIMPLE plan once they are no longer eligible to establish one.

Chapter 18
Alimony

ey.com/EYTaxGuide

Note

IRS Publication 17 (*Your Federal Income Tax*) has been updated by Ernst & Young LLP for 2011. Dates and dollar amounts shown are for 2011. Underlined type is used to indicate where IRS text has been updated. Places where text has been removed are indicated by the sentence: *Text intentionally omitted*.

ey.com/EYTaxGuide

Ernst & Young LLP will update the *Ernst & Young Tax Guide 2012* website with relevant taxpayer information as it becomes available. You can also sign up for email alerts to let you know when changes have been made.

Introduction

This chapter discusses alimony and child support and the complicated tax rules and regulations that apply.

Designing a divorce decree, a separation agreement, or a support decree is rarely an easy task. Marital settlements are so diverse and so complex that no two situations are the same. One common element, however, is likely to be the payment of *alimony*. Alimony is an amount subject to one of these settlement agreements that is not considered *child support* or a property settlement, and that meets certain specific tests. If certain circumstances are met, alimony is a deduction from gross income for the spouse who pays it and included in the income of the spouse who receives it.

Alimony may take many different forms. The payment by one spouse of the other spouse's share of mortgage and other costs for jointly owned property may be considered alimony. The payment of life insurance premiums on policies irrevocably assigned to a spouse may also be considered alimony. Alimony may even include the payment of medical and dental expenses. This chapter discusses what should and should not be considered an alimony payment.

The Deficit Reduction Act of 1984 completely restructured the alimony rules. The old rules still apply to alimony payments made under pre-1985 divorce and separation agreements, unless those agreements have been specifically modified. For related information, refer to Dependency exemption (see chapter 3, *Personal exemptions and dependents*), the child care credit (see chapter 33, *Child and dependent care credit*), Head of household status (see chapter 2, *Filing status*), the Earned income credit, and the Retirement savings credit (for both, see chapter 37, *Other credits including the earned income credit*).

What's New

Limit on personal exemptions ended. For 2010 and 2011, you will no longer lose part of your deduction for personal exemptions, regardless of the amount of your adjusted gross income.

TAXPLANNER

The repeal of this limitation on personal exemptions also applies for 2012. After 2012, the old phaseout rule is scheduled to return in full force unless Congress intervenes. For updated information on these proposals and any other tax law changes that occur after this book was published, see our website, *ey.com/EYTaxGuide.*

This chapter discusses the rules that apply if you pay or receive alimony. It covers the following topics.

- What payments are alimony.
- What payments are not alimony, such as child support.
- How to deduct alimony you paid.
- How to report alimony you received as income.
- Whether you must recapture the tax benefits of alimony. Recapture means adding back in your income all or part of a deduction you took in a prior year.

Tax Breaks and Deductions You Can Use Checklist

Deducting Alimony Payments. You can deduct payments you make in cash to your spouse or former spouse under a divorce or separation agreement if those payments meet the definition of alimony under the tax law. This deduction is allowed as an adjustment in figuring your adjusted gross income; therefore, it reduces your taxable income even if you do not itemize deductions.

Alimony includes payments made directly to your spouse or former spouse as well as to a third party on behalf of your former spouse. Your former spouse will have to include these alimony payments in income. For more information on what payments do and do not qualify as deductible alimony, see *Instruments Executed After 1984*, later.

Deducting Mortgage Payments and Other Housing Costs Paid on a Home Jointly Owned Following Divorce or Separation. If the terms of a divorce or separation agreement require you to pay the entire amount of each mortgage payment (both principal and interest) and/or other housing expenses, such as real estate taxes, property insurance, and utilities, and the payments otherwise meet the tax law definition of alimony, then you may be able to deduct half of the housing costs as alimony. Your former spouse will have to include these alimony payments in income. Although amounts paid on your "half" of the property cannot be deductible as alimony, you may be able to deduct mortgage interest and real estate taxes if you itemize deductions. For more information, see *Expenses of a home*, later.

Alimony is a payment to or for a spouse or former spouse under a divorce or separation instrument. It does not include voluntary payments that are not made under a divorce or separation instrument.

Alimony is deductible by the payer and must be included in the spouse's or former spouse's income. Although this chapter is generally written for the payer of the alimony, the recipient can use the information to determine whether an amount received is alimony.

To be alimony, a payment must meet certain requirements. Different requirements generally apply to payments under instruments executed after 1984 and to payments under instruments executed before 1985. This chapter discusses the rules for payments under instruments executed after 1984. If you need the rules for payments under pre-1985 instruments, get and keep a copy of the 2004 version of Publication 504. That was the last year the information on pre-1985 instruments was included in Publication 504.

Use Table 18-1 in this chapter as a guide to determine whether certain payments are considered alimony.

Definitions. The following definitions apply throughout this chapter.

Spouse or former spouse. Unless otherwise stated, the term "spouse" includes former spouse.

Divorce or separation instrument. The term "divorce or separation instrument" means:

- A decree of divorce or separate maintenance or a written instrument incident to that decree,
- A written separation agreement, or
- A decree or any type of court order requiring a spouse to make payments for the support or maintenance of the other spouse. This includes a temporary decree, an interlocutory (not final) decree, and a decree of alimony *pendente lite* (while awaiting action on the final decree or agreement).

Useful Items

You may want to see:

Publication

- □ **504** Divorced or Separated Individuals

General Rules

The following rules apply to alimony regardless of when the divorce or separation instrument was executed.

Payments not alimony. Not all payments under a divorce or separation instrument are alimony. Alimony does not include:

- Child support,
- Noncash property settlements,
- Payments that are your spouse's part of community income as explained under *Community Property* in Publication 504,
- Payments to keep up the payer's property, or
- Use of the payer's property.

EXPLANATION

Other Payments Not Deductible as Alimony

Do not deduct as alimony the following:

1. Any payment not required by the decree or agreement
2. Any payment that does not arise out of the marital relationship but that is required by the decree or agreement, such as repayment of a loan to your spouse
3. Any payment you make before the decree or agreement
4. Any payment you agreed to make before the decree or agreement and paid later
5. Any payment you make after your former spouse's remarriage
6. Any payment you make after your divorced spouse's death, even though required by the decree or agreement
7. Any payment you make that is part of a property settlement

Payments to a third party. Cash payments, checks, or money orders to a third party on behalf of your spouse under the terms of your divorce or separation instrument can be alimony, if they otherwise qualify. These include payments for your spouse's medical expenses, housing costs (rent,

Table 18-1. **Alimony Requirements (Instruments Executed After 1984)**

Payments ARE alimony if all of the following are true:	**Payments are NOT alimony if any of the following are true:**
Payments are required by a divorce or separation instrument.	Payments are not required by a divorce or separation instrument.
Payer and recipient spouse do not file a joint return with each other.	Payer and recipient spouse file a joint return with each other.
Payment is in cash (including checks or money orders).	Payment is: • Not in cash, • A noncash property settlement, • Spouse's part of community income, or • To keep up the payer's property.
Payment is not designated in the instrument as not alimony.	Payment is designated in the instrument as not alimony.
Spouses legally separated under a decree of divorce or separate maintenance are not members of the same household.	Spouses legally separated under a decree of divorce or separate maintenance are members of the same household.
Payments are not required after death of the recipient spouse.	Payments are required after death of the recipient spouse.
Payment is not treated as child support.	Payment is treated as child support.
These payments are deductible by the payer and includible in income by the recipient.	*These payments are neither deductible by the payer nor includible in income by the recipient.*

utilities, etc.), taxes, tuition, etc. The payments are treated as received by your spouse and then paid to the third party.

EXPLANATION

The ownership of a life insurance policy must be assigned to your former spouse before you may deduct the premiums you pay as alimony. In addition, your former spouse must be the irrevocable beneficiary of the policy. Your children may be irrevocable contingent beneficiaries.

If your children are the beneficiaries of a life insurance policy and your former spouse is a contingent beneficiary, you still control the policy. The premiums you pay are not considered alimony.

For the premiums to be considered alimony, your former spouse's benefit from the life insurance policy must be measurable in dollars. If your former spouse would benefit from the policy only under certain contingencies, the economic advantage cannot be measured and your premiums would not be considered alimony.

Life insurance premiums. Alimony includes premiums you must pay under your divorce or separation instrument for insurance on your life to the extent your spouse owns the policy.

Payments for jointly-owned home. If your divorce or separation instrument states that you must pay expenses for a home owned by you and your spouse or former spouse, some of your payments may be alimony.

Mortgage payments. If you must pay all the mortgage payments (principal and interest) on a jointly-owned home, and they otherwise qualify as alimony, you can deduct one-half of the total payments as alimony. If you itemize deductions and the home is a qualified home, you can claim half of the interest in figuring your deductible interest. Your spouse must report one-half of the payments as alimony received. If your spouse itemizes deductions and the home is a qualified home, he or she can claim one-half of the interest on the mortgage in figuring deductible interest.

Taxes and insurance. If you must pay all the real estate taxes or insurance on a home held as tenants in common, you can deduct one-half of these payments as alimony. Your spouse must report

Deducting Mortgage Payments and Other Housing Costs Paid on a Home Owned by Your Former Spouse Following Divorce or Separation. If the terms of a divorce or separation agreement require you to pay the mortgage payments and/or other housing expenses, such as real estate taxes, property insurance, and utilities, on the home owned by your former spouse, and the payments otherwise meet the tax law definition of alimony, you may be able to deduct these payments as alimony. Your former spouse will have to include these alimony payments in income. For more information, see Expenses of a home, later.

Deducting Mortgage Payments and Other Housing Costs Paid on a Home You Own and That Is Lived in Rent-Free by Your Former Spouse Following Divorce or Separation. Because you own the home and the debts are yours, you cannot deduct the mortgage or real estate tax payments you make as alimony. Nor are you allowed to claim the fair rental value of your spouse's use of the home as alimony. However, you can deduct qualifying mortgage interest and real estate taxes paid if you itemize deductions.

While mortgage and real estate tax payments do not qualify as deductible alimony, payments you make for utilities on behalf of a former spouse who is entitled to occupy your home under the terms of a divorce or separation agreement can be deducted as alimony. Your former spouse will have to include these utility payments in income. For more information, see Expenses of a home, later.

one-half of these payments as alimony received. If you and your spouse itemize deductions, you can each claim one-half of the real estate taxes and none of the home insurance.

If your home is held as tenants by the entirety or joint tenants, none of your payments for taxes or insurance are alimony. But if you itemize deductions, you can claim all of the real estate taxes and none of the home insurance.

Other payments to a third party. If you made other third-party payments, see Publication 504 to see whether any part of the payments qualifies as alimony.

Instruments Executed After 1984

The following rules for alimony apply to payments under divorce or separation instruments executed after 1984.

Exception for instruments executed before 1985. There are two situations where the rules for instruments executed after 1984 apply to instruments executed before 1985.

1. A divorce or separation instrument executed before 1985 and then modified after 1984 to specify that the after-1984 rules will apply.
2. A temporary divorce or separation instrument executed before 1985 and incorporated into, or adopted by, a final decree executed after 1984 that:
   a. Changes the amount or period of payment, or
   b. Adds or deletes any contingency or condition.

For the rules for alimony payments under pre-1985 instruments not meeting these exceptions, see the 2004 revision of Publication 504 on the IRS website at www.irs.gov.

Example 1. In November 1984, you and your former spouse executed a written separation agreement. In February 1985, a decree of divorce was substituted for the written separation agreement. The decree of divorce did not change the terms for the alimony you pay your former spouse. The decree of divorce is treated as executed before 1985. Alimony payments under this decree are not subject to the rules for payments under instruments executed after 1984.

Example 2. Assume the same facts as in Example 1 except that the decree of divorce changed the amount of the alimony. In this example, the decree of divorce is not treated as executed before 1985. The alimony payments are subject to the rules for payments under instruments executed after 1984.

EXPLANATION

For divorce decrees and separation agreements executed after 1984 (and, in certain cases, decrees or agreements executed before 1985 which have been modified), payments may not be deductible, even if there is a legal obligation to make them. Payments would be deductible only if all the other requirements were fulfilled. See *Alimony requirements*, later.

TAXPLANNER

Don't overlook the opportunity to use the new rules on an old divorce.

Example

Bob and Mary were divorced in 1982, with Mary agreeing to pay Bob $2,000 per month in qualifying alimony payments. Mary was a stockbroker earning top dollars in 1982. Bob had never had a full-time job. In 2011, Mary's fortunes are not so rosy, whereas Bob is a top Los Angeles real estate broker.

Bob and Mary could agree that, in 2011, Mary will pay less money to Bob but that it won't be considered alimony. If Mary's marginal tax bracket has dropped to 15% and Bob's tax bracket is 35%, Mary could pay Bob as little as 65% of what her normal payment is ($1,300), and both would win. If Mary were to pay Bob $2,000 in alimony, and take the associated deduction, her after-tax out-of-pocket expense would be $1,700. Bob would reflect $2,000 in income, which would equate to $1,300 after tax. Thus, if they would agree to a $1,300 payment, Bob would receive the same amount in after-tax dollars, but Mary would come out ahead.

Alimony requirements. A payment to or for a spouse under a divorce or separation instrument is alimony if the spouses do not file a joint return with each other and all the following requirements are met.

- The payment is in cash.
- The instrument does not designate the payment as not alimony.

- The spouses are not members of the same household at the time the payments are made. This requirement applies only if the spouses are legally separated under a decree of divorce or separate maintenance.
- There is no liability to make any payment (in cash or property) after the death of the recipient spouse.
- The payment is not treated as child support.

Each of these requirements is discussed next.

Cash payment requirement. Only cash payments, including checks and money orders, qualify as alimony. The following do not qualify as alimony.

- Transfers of services or property (including a debt instrument of a third party or an annuity contract).
- Execution of a debt instrument by the payer.
- The use of the payer's property.

TAXALERT

Actual payment of the alimony must be made in order to take the deduction. A recent court decision stated that the taxpayer was not entitled to alimony deductions for years that he did not make alimony payments. The state court ordered the taxpayer to make payments that would have constituted alimony had they been made but the taxpayer made no payments. It was not enough that the taxpayer's property was subject to a lien to secure the alimony and the subject property was later sold and placed in a trust to satisfy the obligation.

TAXPLANNER

According to the IRS, an annuity contract given to a spouse is a transfer of property and not a cash payment. Therefore, the spouse transferring the annuity contract is not entitled to a deduction for alimony. The spouse receiving the annuity contract has the same investment cost as the spouse transferring it. The only taxable income to the receiving spouse would be the amounts received in excess of cost.

If you are the alimony payer and want to ensure a tax deduction, use the distributions from the annuity contract to make future alimony payments rather than transfer the annuity contract to your spouse.

Payments to a third party. Cash payments to a third party under the terms of your divorce or separation instrument can qualify as cash payments to your spouse. See *Payments to a third party* under *General Rules,* earlier.

Also, cash payments made to a third party at the written request of your spouse may qualify as alimony if all the following requirements are met.

- The payments are in lieu of payments of alimony directly to your spouse.
- The written request states that both spouses intend the payments to be treated as alimony.
- You receive the written request from your spouse before you file your return for the year you made the payments.

EXPLANATION

Medical and dental expenses. If you paid your spouse's medical and dental expenses under a decree or agreement, you may deduct them as alimony. However, a payment of unusually large medical expenses in a given year might trigger excess front-loading rules. The result could be that you lose the deduction for payments under the recapture rules (see a discussion of recapture rules later), even though they are required as part of the divorce or separation agreement.

Your spouse must report these payments as alimony received and may include them as medical expenses if he or she is itemizing deductions.

Note: The spouse who pays the medical bills saves tax by claiming the amounts as alimony rather than as medical expenses. Alimony is fully deductible from adjusted gross income (AGI), whether or not the payer itemizes deductions. For medical expenses, only those exceeding 7.5% of AGI are deductible (or those exceeding 10% of AGI for alternative minimum tax purposes).

TAXSAVER

If you pay medical insurance premiums on behalf of a former spouse, you may be entitled to an additional deduction. Your former spouse may be able to deduct those payments as medical expenses.

Example

A husband who had not been directly ordered by the courts to carry medical insurance for his former wife but who was ordered to pay her reasonable medical expenses was allowed to deduct premiums paid as alimony. (He could not deduct the premiums as a medical expense.) His former wife had to include the amount that her former husband paid for the insurance premiums as income. Both parties treated the premiums and any actual medical expenses paid that were not reimbursed by insurance payments as alimony.

Note: The husband may have created a larger deduction for alimony by taking out an insurance policy on his former wife, since he may deduct the cost of the premiums (his out-of-pocket cost) whether or not his former wife incurs any actual medical expenses. Conversely, the former wife may pay a tax on an amount from which she derives no direct benefit.

Payments designated as not alimony. You and your spouse can designate that otherwise qualifying payments are not alimony. You do this by including a provision in your divorce or separation instrument that states the payments are not deductible as alimony by you and are excludable from your spouse's income. For this purpose, any instrument (written statement) signed by both of you that makes this designation and that refers to a previous written separation agreement is treated as a written separation agreement (and therefore a divorce or separation instrument). If you are subject to temporary support orders, the designation must be made in the original or a later temporary support order.

Your spouse can exclude the payments from income only if he or she attaches a copy of the instrument designating them as not alimony to his or her return. The copy must be attached each year the designation applies.

Spouses cannot be members of the same household. Payments to your spouse while you are members of the same household are not alimony if you are legally separated under a decree of divorce or separate maintenance. A home you formerly shared is considered one household, even if you physically separate yourselves in the home.

You are not treated as members of the same household if one of you is preparing to leave the household and does leave no later than 1 month after the date of the payment.

Exception. If you are not legally separated under a decree of divorce or separate maintenance, a payment under a written separation agreement, support decree, or other court order may qualify as alimony even if you are members of the same household when the payment is made.

EXPLANATION

Separated and living apart. The courts have traditionally held that spouses living under the same roof are not separated. However, some courts have looked to the facts and circumstances surrounding each case to determine whether or not spouses living in the same house who seldom see each other and who incur duplicate living expenses are, in fact, separated. The Appeals Courts have been reluctant to deal with the highly personalized questions that must be asked to determine whether or not the parties are truly living apart.

Liability for payments after death of recipient spouse. If any part of payments you make must continue to be made for any period after your spouse's death, that part of your payments is not alimony, whether made before or after the death. If all of the payments would continue, then none of the payments made before or after the death are alimony.

The divorce or separation instrument does not have to expressly state that the payments cease upon the death of your spouse if, for example, the liability for continued payments would end under state law.

Example. You must pay your former spouse $10,000 in cash each year for 10 years. Your divorce decree states that the payments will end upon your former spouse's death. You must also pay your former spouse or your former spouse's estate $20,000 in cash each year for 10 years. The death of your spouse would not terminate these payments under state law.

The $10,000 annual payments may qualify as alimony. The $20,000 annual payments that do not end upon your former spouse's death are not alimony.

Substitute payments. If you must make any payments in cash or property after your spouse's death as a substitute for continuing otherwise qualifying payments before the death, the otherwise qualifying payments are not alimony. To the extent that your payments begin, accelerate, or increase because of the death of your spouse, otherwise qualifying payments you made may be treated as payments that were not alimony. Whether or not such payments will be treated as not alimony depends on all the facts and circumstances.

Example 1. Under your divorce decree, you must pay your former spouse $30,000 annually. The payments will stop at the end of 6 years or upon your former spouse's death, if earlier.

Your former spouse has custody of your minor children. The decree provides that if any child is still a minor at your spouse's death, you must pay $10,000 annually to a trust until the youngest child reaches the age of majority. The trust income and corpus (principal) are to be used for your children's benefit.

These facts indicate that the payments to be made after your former spouse's death are a substitute for $10,000 of the $30,000 annual payments. Of each of the $30,000 annual payments, $10,000 is not alimony.

Example 2. Under your divorce decree, you must pay your former spouse $30,000 annually. The payments will stop at the end of 15 years or upon your former spouse's death, if earlier. The decree provides that if your former spouse dies before the end of the 15-year period, you must pay the estate the difference between $450,000 ($30,000 × 15) and the total amount paid up to that time. For example, if your spouse dies at the end of the tenth year, you must pay the estate $150,000 ($450,000 – $300,000).

These facts indicate that the lump-sum payment to be made after your former spouse's death is a substitute for the full amount of the $30,000 annual payments. None of the annual payments are alimony. The result would be the same if the payment required at death were to be discounted by an appropriate interest factor to account for the prepayment.

TAXALERT

A court decision denied an alimony deduction because the taxpayer was required to make payments to his children in the same amount as the alimony if his ex-wife died. The agreement stated that the alimony payments ended at death; however, the alimony was set up as installment payments and if the ex-wife died before all payments were made, the remaining payments were to be paid to the children. Although no post-death payments were actually made, the alimony deduction was still disallowed.

Child support. A payment that is specifically designated as child support or treated as specifically designated as child support under your divorce or separation instrument is not alimony. The amount of child support may vary over time. Child support payments are not deductible by the payer and are not taxable to the recipient.

Specifically designated as child support. A payment will be treated as specifically designated as child support to the extent that the payment is reduced either:

- On the happening of a contingency relating to your child, or
- At a time that can be clearly associated with the contingency.

A payment may be treated as specifically designated as child support even if other separate payments are specifically designated as child support.

TAXPLANNER

Since child support payments are considered fixed, any reductions in child support that are not part of the original decree or a subsequent court-approved modified divorce decree are considered reductions in alimony, not child support. Therefore, be sure to have the court approve any child support reductions so that you can continue to deduct the full alimony payments.

Example

After a taxpayer remarried, his son from his previous marriage began to live with him. The taxpayer and his former wife agreed that, as a result, his child support payments should be eliminated. Even though both former spouses agreed that the payment reductions applied to child support, the courts held that they applied to alimony because the taxpayer and his former spouse did not obtain a modification of their divorce decree in court.

Contingency relating to your child. A contingency relates to your child if it depends on any event relating to that child. It does not matter whether the event is certain or likely to occur. Events relating to your child include the child's:

- Becoming employed,
- Dying,
- Leaving the household,
- Leaving school,
- Marrying, or
- Reaching a specified age or income level.

Clearly associated with a contingency. Payments that would otherwise qualify as alimony are presumed to be reduced at a time clearly associated with the happening of a contingency relating to your child only in the following situations.

- The payments are to be reduced not more than 6 months before or after the date the child will reach 18, 21, or local age of majority.
- The payments are to be reduced on two or more occasions that occur not more than 1 year before or after a different one of your children reaches a certain age from 18 to 24. This certain age must be the same for each child, but need not be a whole number of years.

In all other situations, reductions in payments are not treated as clearly associated with the happening of a contingency relating to your child.

Either you or the IRS can overcome the presumption in the two situations just described. This is done by showing that the time at which the payments are to be reduced was determined independently of any contingencies relating to your children. For example, if you can show that the period of alimony payments is customary in the local jurisdiction, such as a period equal to one-half of the duration of the marriage, you can overcome the presumption and may be able to treat the amount as alimony.

EXPLANATION

Child Support in Agreements Executed Before 1985

Child support amounts may not be inferred for payments made under agreements executed before 1985 and not revised. You may not assume that portions of the alimony payments are used by a former spouse for support of a child. The U.S. Supreme Court has held that payments are not treated as child support payments unless they are expressly designated as such in the governing document.

Child Support in Agreements Executed After 1984

Child support amounts *may* be inferred for payments made under agreements executed or revised after 1984, even if such payments are not specifically earmarked. However, such payments will be reduced upon certain contingencies related to the child. Such contingencies would include the child attaining a certain age or income level, dying, marrying, leaving school, leaving the spouse's household, or getting a job.

Payments that are reduced at a time that can clearly be associated with a contingency will be treated as child support. For example, if a payment was to stop at a certain calendar date that just happened to be the child's nineteenth birthday, that payment would be considered child support.

The parent who has custody of the child is entitled to take the dependency exemption for the child, as long as the parents themselves could have claimed the exemption had they filed a joint return. This will not apply if

1. There is a multiple support agreement in effect specifying who gets the exemption.
2. The custodial parent relinquishes the exemption in writing (using language in IRS Form 8332).
3. There is an executed, pre-1985 divorce or separation agreement in effect that provides that the noncustodial parent who also furnishes at least $600 of child support can claim the exemption.

Note: The custodial parent is still entitled to claim the dependent care credit, even if he or she relinquishes the dependency exemption to the noncustodial parent.

A parent can deduct medical expenses that he or she paid directly for a child's benefit, even though the dependency exemption for the child is claimed by the other parent. This is the case as long as a multiple-support agreement is not in effect.

TAXALERT

If the divorce decree or separation agreement went into effect after 1984 and before 2009, the noncustodial parent can still attach pages from the decree or agreement to the tax return in support of the exemption taken on the return. However, for any divorce decree or separation agreement executed after 2008, Form 8332 must be used.

Beginning in 2009, new rules apply to allow the custodial parent to revoke a release of claim to exemption that was previously released to the noncustodial parent on Form 8332. The revocation is effective the year following the year the custodial parent provides the noncustodial parent with written notice of revocation. For example, if the custodial parent provided notice of revocation to the noncustodial parent in 2010, the earliest tax year the revocation can be effective is the tax year beginning in 2011.

For more information, see chapter 3, *Personal exemptions and dependents*.

How To Deduct Alimony Paid

You can deduct alimony you paid, whether or not you itemize deductions on your return. You must file Form 1040. You cannot use Form 1040A or Form 1040EZ.

Enter the amount of alimony you paid on Form 1040, line 31a. In the space provided on line 31b, enter your spouse's social security number.

If you paid alimony to more than one person, enter the social security number of one of the recipients. Show the social security number and amount paid to each other recipient on an attached statement. Enter your total payments on line 31a.

Caution

If you do not provide your spouse's social security number, you may have to pay a $50 penalty and your deduction may be disallowed.

EXPLANATION

Even if the validity of a divorce decree is questioned, your former spouse must include periodic payments that you make under such a divorce decree in income. You may also deduct the payments as alimony. A divorce decree is valid for tax purposes until a court having proper jurisdiction declares it invalid.

The IRS generally recognizes a state court as having proper jurisdiction if that court has personal jurisdiction over the parties involved or if that court has jurisdiction over the subject matter of the action.

Example 1

In the process of separating, a taxpayer and spouse entered into a support agreement under a state court. The taxpayer later obtained a Mexican divorce that said nothing about the support agreement. The state considered the divorce to be valid. Even though the Mexican divorce decree made no mention of the support payments, the payments were considered alimony because the original state support agreement had never been invalidated.

Example 2

A taxpayer who obtained a Mexican divorce was later sued by his former spouse for support payments and for a legal separation under state law. The state court granted the former spouse the support payments. The Mexican divorce was not recognized by the state, but the payments were considered to be alimony.

How To Report Alimony Received

Report alimony you received as income on Form 1040, line 11. You cannot use Form 1040A or Form 1040EZ.

Caution

You must give the person who paid the alimony your social security number. If you do not, you may have to pay a $50 penalty.

Recapture Rule

If your alimony payments decrease or terminate during the first 3 calendar years, you may be subject to the recapture rule. If you are subject to this rule, you have to include in income in the third year part of the alimony payments you previously deducted. Your spouse can deduct in the third year part of the alimony payments he or she previously included in income.

The 3-year period starts with the first calendar year you make a payment qualifying as alimony under a decree of divorce or separate maintenance or a written separation agreement. Do not include any time in which payments were being made under temporary support orders. The second and third years are the next 2 calendar years, whether or not payments are made during those years.

The reasons for a reduction or termination of alimony payments that can require a recapture include:

- A change in your divorce or separation instrument,
- A failure to make timely payments,
- A reduction in your ability to provide support, or
- A reduction in your spouse's support needs.

When to apply the recapture rule. You are subject to the recapture rule in the third year if the alimony you pay in the third year decreases by more than $15,000 from the second year or the alimony you pay in the second and third years decreases significantly from the alimony you pay in the first year.

TAXSAVER

If the payments are spread out equally over the 3 years, they are all deductible. Also, when determining the timing of making extraordinary payments, consider making them in year 3 rather than year 2. This will prevent the payments in year 3 from declining by more than $15,000 from the payments in year 2.

When you figure a decrease in alimony, do not include the following amounts.

- Payments made under a temporary support order.
- Payments required over a period of at least 3 calendar years that vary because they are a fixed part of your income from a business or property, or from compensation for employment or self-employment.
- Payments that decrease because of the death of either spouse or the remarriage of the spouse receiving the payments before the end of the third year.

TAXPLANNER

Determining the post-separation years is critical in order to apply the recapture rules properly. The first year is the first calendar year in which the taxpayer pays alimony or maintenance payments to the former spouse. This is not necessarily the year the spouses physically separate or even the year in which a final decree of divorce is entered. It may also not be the year payments are first made, if those payments do not qualify as alimony or separate maintenance payments. The second and third years are the next two succeeding calendar years.

Example

A divorce decree is entered in October 2011 and it calls for Henry to pay to Wilma alimony payments beginning in November 2011. However, Henry and Wilma occupy the same household until March 2012. Their cohabitation prevents the payments from being treated as deductible alimony, and so 2011 cannot be the first year.

Figuring the recapture. You can use Worksheet 1 in Publication 504 to figure recaptured alimony.

TAXPLANNER

Example 1

Henry pays $42,000 alimony to Wilma in the first and second years. In the third year, Henry pays Wilma alimony of $20,000. In the third year, Henry must recapture $7,000, the amount by which the excess of the second year payments over the third year payments ($42,000 - $20,000 = $22,000) exceeds the $15,000 floor ($22,000 - $15,000 = $7,000). Wilma has a corresponding $7,000 deduction.

Example 2

Henry pays $42,000 alimony to Wilma in the first year. In the second year, Henry pays $12,000, and in the third year, he pays $8,000. The average alimony for the second and third years is $10,000 [($12,000 + $8,000)/2]. The alimony paid in the first year exceeds this amount by $32,000 ($42,000 - $10,000). This excess of the amount over the floor is $17,000 ($32,000 - $15,000). Henry must recapture this amount as gross income in the third year. Wilma has a corresponding deduction.

Example 3
Henry pays $60,000 alimony to Wilma in the first year. In the second year, Henry pays $24,000, and in the third year, he pays $6,000. Two computations are required to determine the recapture. Under the first computation, Henry must recapture $3,000, the amount by which the excess of the second-year payments over the third-year payments ($24,000 - $6,000 = $18,000) exceeds the floor ($18,000 - $15,000). Then, the second computation is made, but in doing so, $3,000 is subtracted from the payments of the second year. So, from $60,000 is subtracted the sum of the average of the adjusted second-year payment and the third-year amount of $13,500 [(21,000 + 6000)/2] plus the $15,000 floor. The amount recaptured in the second computation is $31,500 ($60,000 - $28,500). The total amount of recapture from both computations is $34,500 ($3,000 + $31,500).

Including the recapture in income. If you must include a recapture amount in income, show it on Form 1040, line 11 ("Alimony received"). Cross out "received" and enter "recapture." On the dotted line next to the amount, enter your spouse's last name and social security number.

Deducting the recapture. If you can deduct a recapture amount, show it on Form 1040, line 31a ("Alimony paid"). Cross out "paid" and enter "recapture." In the space provided, enter your spouse's social security number.

Other Alimony Issues and Rules

Explanation

Transfer of property. If property is transferred in settlement of marital rights, the spouse making the transfer does not recognize either gain or loss on the transfer, whether the property has appreciated or declined in value. The transfer is treated like a gift, and the spouse receiving the property takes the basis of the transferring spouse. This is true even if the spouse receiving the property pays cash and the transaction is cast in the form of a sale.

The following are exceptions to the nonrecognition rules:

1. Transfer of an installment note to a trust will cause the deferred gain to be recognized
2. Transfer of property subject to liabilities in excess of basis will cause the excess to be recognized

TAXPLANNER

The transfer between spouses of a note receivable that arose from an installment sale will not be considered a disposition for purposes of accelerating the reporting of previously deferred income. Instead, the recipient of the installment note will have the same tax posture as the spouse who made the transfer.

Explanation

Transfer of business property. The law is silent on the status of unrealized income from normal business accounts receivable that may be transferred. There is no recapture of investment tax credit or depreciation on the transfer of business property. The spouse making the transfer must provide permanent records of cost basis, accumulated depreciation, holding period, and investment-credit recapture potential to the other spouse. There is no penalty for failure to do so, however.

TAXALERT

There is a special property transfer provision for tax years beginning after December 31, 2004. Any disallowed losses due to the cost basis of business property are carried over to the spouse or former spouse in a tax-free transfer of S corporation stock incident to divorce. Under prior law, the losses suspended due to basis limitations could not be transferred.

TAXPLANNER

A spouse who is to receive property with a tax basis substantially less than its current value should carefully evaluate the tax consequences of disposing of it. The recipient may be subject to tax from recapture of investment tax credit and depreciation and should obtain the advice of competent counsel on such matters.

Example

As part of the divorce property settlement, Kyle gives Mary a computer that he used for 4 years in his sole proprietorship business. Kyle paid $5,000 for the computer, claimed investment credit on it, and claimed depreciation of $3,950. Since the computer ceased to be business property when it was given to Mary, she must recapture part of the investment credit claimed by Kyle. Further, Mary must pay ordinary income tax on her profit if she sells the computer for more than $1,050. See chapter 16, *Reporting gains and losses*, and chapter 37, *Other credits including the earned income credit.*

Explanation

Trust property. If income-producing property is placed in trust to pay alimony, the alimony payments are not included in or deducted from income. This rule applies whether the alimony payments are made out of the trust income or principal. Trust distributions must be reported as income by your spouse. If your obligation to pay alimony is stated in a divorce decree, other court order, or written separation agreement, your spouse reports the distributions as alimony on line 11 of Form 1040. If your obligation is not so stated, your spouse reports the income distributions as income received from a trust on Schedule E (Form 1040).

You may also set up a trust to pay both alimony and child support. If your former spouse remarries and you are no longer required to pay alimony, the trust may continue disbursing monies for child support.

TAXPLANNER

If a trust that is set up to disburse alimony payments holds municipal bonds, the distributions to the former spouse are nontaxable to the extent that they are attributable to the trust's municipal bond income. Also, if the distributions from the trust exceed the trust's income, the excess distribution of trust principal is not taxable.

Explanation

Insurance, endowment, or annuity. If an insurance or endowment policy or an annuity contract is purchased to discharge alimony or support called for in a divorce decree, the payer does not include in, or deduct from, income payments made under the contract. The recipient must include the payments in income.

Annulments. Generally, state laws blur the distinction between a divorce and an annulment. The rules on alimony often apply to an annulment decree as well as to a divorce decree. You should examine the law of the state in which you reside to determine if this is the case.

Example

In New York, a marriage was annulled due to the wife's insanity. The husband was required to provide for her care and maintenance. Since under the general rules of law the annulment would be considered a divorce, the husband's payments were treated as alimony.

TAXPLANNER

Expenses of a home. If part of an alimony award is used to pay such expenses as real estate taxes, insurance, mortgage payments, or utilities for a home owned by a divorced couple, the facts in each case determine the amount deductible by one spouse and includible by the other spouse. Two facts to consider are the type of ownership and the kinds of expenses that must be paid. The spouse making the payments will only be entitled to a deduction if he or she has an ownership interest in the home. However, in each case, the payments must cover a period of more than 10 years or otherwise qualify as periodic payments if made pursuant to a pre-1985 agreement.

Ownership

You should check your state law, ownership documents, and your divorce decree to determine what type of ownership you have.

1. **Joint tenants or tenants by the entirety.** You and your former spouse own a home jointly as tenants by the entirety or joint tenants with a right of survivorship. You are both jointly and individually responsible for the entire mortgage balance. If your divorce decree states that your former spouse is to pay the mortgage (principal and interest) on the property from money that he or she receives from you as support, then your former spouse must include one-half of each principal and interest payment as income from alimony, and you may deduct one-half of each principal and interest payment as alimony.

   Your former spouse may also deduct one-half of the interest if he or she itemizes deductions on Schedule A (Form 1040). If you itemize your deductions, it is not clear how your share of the interest should be handled. It may be deductible under the home mortgage rules if your children live there and you are not already deducting interest on two personal residences. Or it might be considered investment interest, since as far as you are concerned, the property is now just an investment. Lastly, it could be personal interest and therefore not deductible.
2. **Tenants in common.** If you and your former spouse own a home as **tenants in common**, your former spouse owns half of the property. Therefore, you may deduct as alimony amounts you pay on your former spouse's half of the property for principal, interest, insurance, and taxes. Your former spouse must include these amounts in income.

   If your former spouse itemizes deductions on Schedule A (Form 1040), he or she may deduct as taxes and interest the part you paid for real estate taxes and interest on your former spouse's half of the property. He or she may not deduct amounts for insurance. Insurance is a nondeductible personal expense.

   Amounts you paid on your half of the property are not deductible as alimony, nor are they includible in income by your former spouse. If you itemize your deductions on Schedule A (Form 1040), you may deduct the part you pay for real estate taxes and interest on your half of the property. You may not deduct insurance payments on your half of the property.
3. **Your former spouse owns the home.** If the home is owned by your former spouse, and under a decree or agreement you pay the real estate taxes, mortgage payments, and insurance premiums on it, you may deduct these payments as alimony. Your former spouse must include these payments in income.

   If your former spouse itemizes deductions on Schedule A (Form 1040), he or she may deduct the part of each payment that is for taxes and interest on the mortgage.
4. **You own the home.** If the home you own is lived in rent-free by your former spouse, you may not deduct your mortgage payments or the fair rental value of the home as alimony. However, if you itemize your deductions, you may deduct on Schedule A (Form 1040) any real estate taxes and interest you pay on the property.

Rent. If, under a divorce or separate maintenance decree or written separation agreement, you must pay rent to a third-party lessor to provide housing for your spouse or former spouse, you may deduct the rent payments as alimony. Your former spouse must include these payments in income.

Utilities. If your former spouse is the one who has the right to use the home, regardless of the type of ownership, you may deduct as alimony the amount you pay for utilities under a decree or agreement. Your former spouse must include these amounts in income.

Property ownership. There are many consequences of property ownership that must be considered in a divorce settlement. Any payments made pursuant to a divorce decree by you for the mortgage, property taxes, insurance, and so on are considered alimony only if the house belongs to your former spouse. If you transfer your interest in the property to your children, payments to cover their portion of the mortgage payments would be treated as child support, not alimony.

Sale of property. If you sell property that you and your spouse own jointly, you must report your share of the recognized gain or loss on your income tax return for the year of the sale. Your share of the gain or loss is determined by your state law governing ownership of property. For more information on how to report the gain or loss, see IRS Publication 544.

Example

John and Mary owned a home that cost them $150,000. In their divorce, the court decree holds that Mary can remain in the home until their son, who is 10 years old, reaches 18. Mary must pay rent to John for using his half of the house. In 2011, the house is sold and John and Mary together receive $250,000.

Upon sale of the home, Mary is subject to tax on the gain on the home sale. Assuming she meets the requirements, she can exclude up to $250,000 of her portion of the total gain. See chapter 15, *Selling your home*.

John was a landlord during the rental years and probably claimed related expenses and depreciation on his tax return. If the rent charged was reasonable, John could deduct any losses, subject to the restrictions on passive activities.

Upon sale, John is subject to tax on his entire portion of the gain.

TAXPLANNER

Other aspects of obtaining a divorce. IRS Publication 504, *Divorced or Separated Individuals,* examines more closely some of the tax aspects of obtaining a divorce, including the tax treatment of costs incurred in working out a settlement.

Court costs and legal fees related to the divorce are not deductible. However, the portion of these fees attributable to obtaining alimony is deductible as an itemized deduction, since it is an expense associated with the production of income. Any additional costs incurred to obtain alimony are also deductible, as are costs for tax advice.

Be sure to have itemized invoices for professional services. Deductible items should be specifically listed on any bill. You may claim only the deductible portion of your own legal expenses. You may not deduct the legal expenses of your spouse. Those expenses also may not be considered alimony payments.

A portion of your legal fees may give rise to a tax benefit, even though the fees are not paid for obtaining alimony or tax advice. For example, if a portion of your legal fees may be allocated to obtaining property, the tax basis of the property should be increased by the amount of the allocated fees. If the property is business property, you will have larger depreciation deductions and a smaller gain if the property is sold.

There are several additional aspects that you should consider in a year in which you become divorced:

1. **Revising Form W-4.** Form W-4 should be changed if you are no longer able to claim as many withholding allowances due to your change in marital status. This may occur because you no longer file a joint return with your former spouse. It also may occur if you are not entitled to a dependency exemption for one or more of your children. When you revise your Form W-4, your employer adjusts your tax withholding to reflect the changes in your marital status or number of dependents.
2. **Estimated taxes on alimony.** If you are receiving alimony, you may be required to make estimated tax payments, since alimony is not covered by withholding. (See chapter 4, *Tax withholding and estimated tax*.)
3. **Allocating joint estimated tax payments between you and your former spouse.** If you and your former spouse are divorced during the year and have been making joint estimated tax payments, the payments you have already made may be applied to either person's separate return or may be divided between you, as the two of you see fit. If no allocation can be agreed on, the estimated payments should be applied between the separate returns in proportion to the taxes due on each.

   Example

   Your return shows a tax liability of $5,100. Your former spouse's return shows a tax liability of $2,300. You would be entitled to apply 69% [$5,100 ÷ ($5,100 + $2,300)] of your total joint estimated payments against your tax liability.
4. **Retirement plans.** An employee's interest in a qualified retirement plan can be allocated between a current and a former spouse by a qualified domestic relations order. Benefits so allocated are taxed to the current and former spouses when the payments are actually received.

   If the benefits are received by anyone other than the employee or the current or former spouses, the benefits are taxed to the employee, not the recipient.
5. **Federal income taxes withheld.** Taxes withheld from your income are treated the same way as the income that generates them. If salary is split equally between you and your spouse because of community property rules, then the tax withholding is also divided evenly between the two of you.
6. **Alimony and your IRA.** All taxable alimony or separate maintenance payments received by an individual under a decree of divorce or separate maintenance are treated as eligible compensation for making IRA contributions. See chapter 17, *Individual retirement arrangements (IRAs),* for details.
7. **Stock options.** If you transfer nonqualified stock options you received from your employer to your spouse in a divorce, there would be no tax at that time. When the options are exercised your spouse will be taxed on the difference between the exercise price of the option and the value of the stock.

Chapter 19

Education-related adjustments

ey.com/EYTaxGuide

Note

IRS Publication 17 (*Your Federal Income Tax*) has been updated by Ernst & Young LLP for 2011. Dates and dollar amounts shown are for 2011. Underlined type is used to indicate where IRS text has been updated. Places where text has been removed are indicated by the sentence: *Text intentionally omitted*.

ey.com/EYTaxGuide

Ernst & Young LLP will update the *Ernst & Young Tax Guide 2012* website with relevant taxpayer information as it becomes available. You can also sign up for email alerts to let you know when changes have been made.

Introduction

This chapter discusses the education-related adjustments you can deduct in figuring your adjusted gross income (AGI). These include certain educator expenses and interest paid on qualified student loans, as well as certain amounts paid for tuition and other expenses. Students and teachers alike will find this information interesting, relevant, and, hopefully, money-saving as well. In addition to these education adjustments that can lower your AGI, and, ultimately, your tax bill, you may also be eligible for education credits to offset your tax. See chapter 36, *Education credits and other education tax benefits.*

This chapter discusses the education-related adjustments you can deduct in figuring your adjusted gross income.

This chapter covers the educator expense deduction, student loan interest deduction, and the tuition and fees deduction.

TAXSAVER

Chapter 36, *Education credits and other education tax benefits,* discusses other education-related items that you may be able to claim.

Useful Items

You may want to see:

Publication

- □ **970** Tax Benefits for Education

Educator Expenses

If you were an eligible educator, you can deduct up to $250 of qualified expenses you paid during the year as an adjustment to gross income, rather than as a miscellaneous itemized deduction. If you and your spouse are filing jointly and both of you were eligible educators, the maximum deduction is $500. However, neither spouse can deduct more than $250 of his or her own qualified expenses. You may be able to deduct expenses that are more than the $250 (or $500) limit as a miscellaneous itemized deduction on Schedule A (Form 1040), line 21.

Tax Breaks and Deductions You Can Use Checklist

Educator Expenses Deduction. If you were a teacher, instructor, counselor, principal, or aide for any grade(s) between kindergarten and 12th grade during the year, you can deduct up to $250 of qualified expenses you paid during 2011 for books, supplies, equipment (including computer equipment, software, and other related services), and other materials used in the classroom. This deduction is allowed as an adjustment in figuring your adjusted gross income; therefore, it reduces your taxable income even if you do not itemize deductions. For more information, see *Educator Expenses*, later.

Student Loan Interest Deduction. You may be able to deduct up to $2,500 in interest you paid in 2011 on a qualified student loan used for higher education. This deduction reduces the amount of your income subject to tax, regardless of whether or not you itemize deductions. To qualify for the deduction, your modified adjusted gross income in 2011 must be less than $75,000 ($150,000 if you file a joint return) and you cannot file a return as married filing separately nor be claimed as a dependent on the tax return of another person. For more information, see *Student Loan Interest Deduction*, later.

Tuition and Fees Deduction. You may be able to deduct qualified education expenses you paid during 2011 for tuition and fees at a college, university, or other qualifying postsecondary education institution. This deduction for tuition and fees is allowed as an adjustment in figuring your AGI; therefore, it reduces your taxable income even if you do not itemize

TAXALERT

In December 2010, President Obama signed legislation that extended the availability of the $250 adjustment you can deduct from your gross income (to figure your AGI) for expenses paid or incurred through the end of 2011 for books, qualifying supplies, and equipment (including computer equipment, software, and service) by elementary and secondary school teachers and other eligible school professionals. Unless Congress acts, this adjustment will expire and not be available after 2011. For updated information on this and any other tax law changes that occur after this book was published, see our website, ey.com/EYTaxGuide.

Eligible Educator. An eligible educator is a kindergarten through grade 12 teacher, instructor, counselor, principal, or aide who worked in a school for at least 900 hours during a school year.

Qualified Expenses. Qualified expenses include ordinary and necessary expenses paid in connection with books, supplies, equipment (including computer equipment, software, and services), and other materials used in the classroom. An ordinary expense is one that is common and accepted in your educational field. A necessary expense is one that is helpful and appropriate for your profession as an educator. An expense does not have to be required to be considered necessary.

Qualified expenses do not include expenses for home schooling or for nonathletic supplies for courses in health or physical education.

You must reduce your qualified expenses by the following amounts.

- Excludable U.S. series EE and I savings bond interest from Form 8815. See *Figuring the Tax-Free Amount* in chapter 10 of Publication 970.
- Nontaxable distribution of earnings from a qualified tuition program (QTP). See *Figuring the Taxable Portion of a Distribution* in chapter 8 of Publication 970.
- Nontaxable distribution of earnings from a Coverdell education savings account. See *Figuring the Taxable Portion of a Distribution* in chapter 7 of Publication 970.
- Any reimbursements you received for these expenses that were not reported to you in Box 1 of your Form W-2.

How the deduction is claimed. To claim the deduction, enter the allowable amount on Form 1040, line 23, or Form 1040A, line 16.

TAXALERT

Ordinary and necessary educator expenses that do not qualify for the $250 adjustment may be deductible as a miscellaneous itemized deduction subject to the 2% limitation. For more information on this itemized deduction, see *Educator Expenses* in chapter 29, *Miscellaneous deductions*.

Student Loan Interest Deduction

Generally, personal interest you pay, other than certain mortgage interest, is not deductible on your tax return. However, if your modified adjusted gross income (MAGI) is less than $75,000 ($150,000 if filing a joint return) there is a special deduction allowed for paying interest on a student loan (also known as an education loan) used for higher education. For most taxpayers, MAGI is the adjusted gross income as figured on their federal income tax return before subtracting any deduction for student loan interest. This deduction can reduce the amount of your income subject to tax by up to $2,500 in 2011. Table 19-1 summarizes the features of the student loan interest deduction.

Student Loan Interest Defined

Student loan interest is interest you paid during the year on a qualified student loan. It includes both required and voluntary interest payments.

Qualified Student Loan

This is a loan you took out solely to pay qualified education expenses (defined later) that were:

- For you, your spouse, or a person who was your dependent (defined in chapter 3) when you took out the loan,

Table 19-1. **Student Loan Interest Deduction at a Glance**

Do not rely on this table alone. Refer to the text for more details.

Feature	Description
Maximum benefit	You can reduce your income subject to tax by up to $2,500.
Loan qualifications	Your student loan: • must have been taken out solely to pay qualified education expenses, and • cannot be from a related person or made under a qualified employer plan.
Student qualifications	The student must be: • you, your spouse, or your dependent, and • enrolled at least half-time in a degree program.
Time limit on deduction	You can deduct interest paid during the remaining period of your student loan.
Phaseout	The amount of your deduction depends on your income level.

deductions. The maximum deduction is $4,000 if your modified adjusted gross income (MAGI) is less than $65,000 ($130,000 if you are married filing jointly). The maximum available deduction shrinks to $2,000 if your MAGI is over $65,000 ($130,000 if filing jointly) and below $80,000 ($160,000 if filing jointly). No deduction is available if your MAGI exceeds $80,000 ($160,000 if filing jointly). The deduction is also unavailable—regardless of your MAGI—if your filing status for 2011 is married filing separately or you can be claimed as a dependent on the tax return of another person. In addition, deduction is disallowed if you or anyone else claims an American opportunity credit or lifetime learning credit with respect to the same student. See *Tuition and Fees Deduction*, later.

- Paid or incurred within a reasonable period of time before or after you took out the loan, and
- For education provided during an academic period for an eligible student.

Loans from the following sources are not qualified student loans.

- A related person.
- A qualified employer plan.

Exceptions. For purposes of the student loan interest deduction, the following are exceptions to the general rules for dependents.

- An individual can be your dependent even if you are the dependent of another tax payer.
- An individual can be your dependent even if the individual files a joint return with a spouse.
- An individual can be your dependent even if the individual had gross income for the year that was equal to or more than the exemption amount for the year ($3,700 for 2011).

Reasonable period of time. Qualified education expenses are treated as paid or incurred within a reasonable period of time before or after you take out the loan if they are paid with the proceeds of student loans that are part of a federal postsecondary education loan program.

Even if not paid with the proceeds of that type of loan, the expenses are treated as paid or incurred within a reasonable period of time if both of the following requirements are met.

- The expenses relate to a specific academic period.
- The loan proceeds are disbursed within a period that begins 90 days before the start of that academic period and ends 90 days after the end of that academic period.

If neither of the above situations applies, the reasonable period of time usually is determined based on all the relevant facts and circumstances.

Academic period. An academic period includes a semester, trimester, quarter, or other period of study (such as a summer school session) as reasonably determined by an educational institution. In the case of an educational institution that uses credit hours or clock hours and does not have academic terms, each payment period can be treated as an academic period.

Eligible student. This is a student who was enrolled at least half-time in a program leading to a degree, certificate, or other recognized educational credential.

Enrolled at least half-time. A student was enrolled at least half-time if the student was taking at least half the normal full-time work load for his or her course of study.

The standard for what is half of the normal full-time work load is determined by each eligible educational institution. However, the standard may not be lower than any of those established by the Department of Education under the Higher Education Act of 1965.

Related person. You cannot deduct interest on a loan you get from a related person. Related persons include:

- Your spouse,
- Your brothers and sisters,

- Your half brothers and half sisters,
- Your ancestors (parents, grandparents, etc.),
- Your lineal descendants (children, grandchildren, etc.), and
- Certain corporations, partnerships, trusts, and exempt organizations.

Qualified employer plan. You cannot deduct interest on a loan made under a qualified employer plan or under a contract purchased under such a plan.

Qualified Education Expenses

For purposes of the student loan interest deduction, these expenses are the total costs of attending an eligible educational institution, including graduate school. They include amounts paid for the following items.

- Tuition and fees.
- Room and board.
- Books, supplies, and equipment.
- Other necessary expenses (such as transportation).

The cost of room and board qualifies only to the extent that it is not more than the greater of:

- The allowance for room and board, as determined by the eligible educational institution, that was included in the cost of attendance (for federal financial aid purposes) for a particular academic period and living arrangement of the student, or
- The actual amount charged if the student is residing in housing owned or operated by the eligible educational institution.

Eligible educational institution. An eligible educational institution is any college, university, vocational school, or other postsecondary educational institution eligible to participate in a student aid program administered by the Department of Education. It includes virtually all accredited public, nonprofit, and proprietary (privately owned profit-making) postsecondary institutions.

Certain educational institutions located outside the United States also participate in the U.S. Department of Education's Federal Student Aid (FSA) programs.

For purposes of the student loan interest deduction, an eligible educational institution also includes an institution conducting an internship or residency program leading to a degree or certificate from an institution of higher education, a hospital, or a health care facility that offers postgraduate training.

An educational institution must meet the above criteria only during the academic period(s) for which the student loan was incurred. The deductibility of interest on the loan is not affected by the institution's subsequent loss of eligibility.

Tip

The educational institution should be able to tell you if it is an eligible educational institution.

Adjustments to qualified education expenses. You must reduce your qualified education expenses by certain tax-free items (such as the tax-free part of scholarships and fellowships). See chapter 4 of Publication 970 for details.

Include as Interest

In addition to simple interest on the loan, certain loan origination fees, capitalized interest, interest on revolving lines of credit, and interest on refinanced student loans can be student loan interest if all other requirements are met.

Loan origination fee. In general, this is a one-time fee charged by the lender when a loan is made. To be deductible as interest, the fee must be for the use of money rather than for property or services (such as commitment fees or processing costs) provided by the lender. A loan origination fee treated as interest accrues over the life of the loan.

Capitalized interest. This is unpaid interest on a student loan that is added by the lender to the outstanding principal balance of the loan.

Interest on revolving lines of credit. This interest, which includes interest on credit card debt, is student loan interest if the borrower uses the line of credit (credit card) only to pay qualified education expenses. See *Qualified Education Expenses*, earlier.

Interest on refinanced student loans. This includes interest on both:

- Consolidated loans—loans used to refinance more than one student loan of the same borrower, and
- Collapsed loans—two or more loans of the same borrower that are treated by both the lender and the borrower as one loan.

Voluntary interest payments. These are payments made on a qualified student loan during a period when interest payments are not required, such as when the borrower has been granted a deferment or the loan has not yet entered repayment status.

Do Not Include as Interest

You cannot claim a student loan interest deduction for any of the following items.

- Interest you paid on a loan if, under the terms of the loan, you are not legally obligated to make interest payments.
- Loan origination fees that are payments for property or services provided by the lender, such as commitment fees or processing costs.
- Interest you paid on a loan to the extent payments were made through your participation in the National Health Service Corps Loan Repayment Program (the "NHSC Loan Repayment Program") or certain other loan repayment assistance programs. For more information, see *Student Loan Repayment Assistance* in chapter 5 of Publication 970.

Caution

If you refinance a qualified student loan for more than your original loan and you use the additional amount for any purpose other than qualified education expenses, you cannot deduct any interest paid on the refinanced loan.

Can You Claim the Deduction

Generally, you can claim the deduction if all four of the following requirements are met.

- Your filing status is any filing status except married filing separately.
- No one else is claiming an exemption for you on his or her tax return.
- You are legally obligated to pay interest on a qualified student loan.
- You paid interest on a qualified student loan.

Interest paid by others. If you are the person legally obligated to make interest payments and someone else makes a payment of interest on your behalf, you are treated as receiving the payments from the other person and, in turn, paying the interest. See chapter 4 of Publication 970 for more information.

No Double Benefit Allowed

You cannot deduct as interest on a student loan any amount that is an allowable deduction under any other provision of the tax law (for example, home mortgage interest).

TAXPLANNER

You can deduct interest paid on a student loan for your dependent only if:

- The person for whom you took the loan was a dependent when you took out the loan,
- You are legally obligated to make the interest payments, and
- You actually made the payments during the tax year. You are not considered to have made student loan interest payments actually made by your dependent, regardless of whether your dependent is legally liable for the loan.

How Much Can You Deduct

Your student loan interest deduction for 2011 is generally the smaller of:

- $2,500, or
- The interest you paid in 2011.

However, the amount determined above is phased out (gradually reduced) if your MAGI is between $60,000 and $75,000 ($120,000 and $150,000 if you file a joint return). You cannot take a student loan interest deduction if your MAGI is $75,000 or more ($150,000 or more if you file a joint return). For details on figuring your MAGI, see chapter 4 of Publication 970.

How Do You Figure the Deduction

Generally, you figure the deduction using the Student Loan Interest Deduction Worksheet in the Form 1040 or Form 1040A instructions. However, if you are filing Form 2555, 2555-EZ, or 4563, or you are excluding income from sources within Puerto Rico, you must complete Worksheet 4-1 in chapter 4 of Publication 970.

To help you figure your student loan interest deduction, you should receive Form 1098-E, Student Loan Interest Statement. Generally, an institution (such as a bank or governmental agency) that received interest payments of $600 or more during 2011 on one or more qualified student loans must send Form 1098-E (or acceptable substitute) to each borrower by January 31, 2012.

For qualified student loans taken out before September 1, 2004, the institution is required to include on Form 1098-E only payments of stated interest. Other interest payments, such as certain loan origination fees and capitalized interest, may not appear on the form you receive. However, if you pay qualifying interest that is not included on Form 1098-E, you can also deduct those amounts. For information on allocating payments between interest and principal, see chapter 4 of Publication 970.

To claim the deduction, enter the allowable amount on Form 1040, line 33, or Form 1040A, line 18.

Tuition and Fees Deduction

You may be able to deduct qualified education expenses paid during the year for yourself, your spouse, or your dependent(s). You cannot claim this deduction if your filing status is married filing separately or if another person can claim an exemption for you as a dependent on his or her tax return. The qualified expenses must be for higher education, as explained later under *What Expenses Qualify*.

The tuition and fees deduction can reduce the amount of your income subject to tax by up to $4,000.

Table 19-2 summarizes the features of the tuition and fees deduction.

TAXALERT

In December 2010, President Obama signed legislation that extended the availability of the adjustment you can deduct from your gross income (to figure your AGI) for qualified tuition and fees through the end of 2011. Unless Congress acts, this adjustment will expire and not be available after 2011. For updated information on this and any other tax law changes that occur after this book was published, see our website, *ey.com/EYTaxGuide*.

Can You Claim the Deduction

The following rules will help you determine if you can claim the tuition and fees deduction.

Who Can Claim the Deduction

Generally, you can claim the tuition and fees deduction if all three of the following requirements are met.

1. You paid qualified education expenses of higher education.
2. You paid the education expenses for an eligible student.
3. The eligible student is yourself, your spouse, or your dependent for whom you claim an exemption (defined in chapter 3) on your tax return.

Qualified education expenses are defined under *What Expenses Qualify*. Eligible students are defined later under *Who Is an Eligible Student*.

Who Cannot Claim the Deduction

You cannot claim the tuition and fees deduction if any of the following apply.

- Your filing status is married filing separately.
- Another person can claim an exemption for you as a dependent on his or her tax return. You cannot take the deduction even if the person does not actually claim that exemption.
- Your modified adjusted gross income (MAGI) is more than $80,000 ($160,000 if filing a joint return).
- You (or your spouse) were a nonresident alien for any part of the year and the nonresident alien did not elect to be treated as a resident alien for tax purposes. More information on nonresident aliens can be found in Publication 519, *US Tax Guide for Aliens*.
- You or anyone else claims an American opportunity or lifetime learning credit with respect to expenses of the student for whom the qualified education expenses were paid.

What Expenses Qualify

The tuition and fees deduction is based on qualified education expenses you pay for yourself, your spouse, or a dependent for whom you claim an exemption on your tax return. Generally, the deduction is allowed for qualified education expenses paid in 2011 in connection with enrollment at an institution of higher education during 2011 or for an academic period (defined earlier under *Student Loan Interest Deduction*) beginning in 2011 or in the first 3 months of 2012.

Payments with borrowed funds. You can claim a tuition and fees deduction for qualified education expenses paid with the proceeds of a loan. Use the expenses to figure the deduction for the

Table 19-2. **Tuition and Fees Deduction at a Glance**

Do not rely on this table alone. Refer to the text for more details.

Question	**Answer**
What is the maximum benefit?	You can reduce your income subject to tax by up to $4,000.
Where is the deduction taken?	As an adjustment to income on Form 1040, line 34, or Form 1040A, line 19.
For whom must the expenses be paid?	A student enrolled in an eligible educational institution who is either: • you, • your spouse, or • your dependent for whom you claim an exemption.
What tuition and fees are deductible?	Tuition and fees required for enrollment or attendance at an eligible postsecondary educational institution, but not including personal, living, or family expenses, such as room and board.

year in which the expenses are paid, not the year in which the loan is repaid. Treat loan payments sent directly to the educational institution as paid on the date the institution credits the student's account.

Student withdraws from class(es). You can claim a tuition and fees deduction for qualified education expenses not refunded when a student withdraws.

Qualified Education Expenses

For purposes of the tuition and fees deduction, qualified education expenses are tuition and certain related expenses required for enrollment or attendance at an eligible educational institution.

Eligible educational institution. An eligible educational institution is any college, university, vocational school, or other postsecondary educational institution eligible to participate in a student aid program administered by the U.S. Department of Education. It includes virtually all accredited public, nonprofit, and proprietary (privately owned profit-making) postsecondary institutions. The educational institution should be able to tell you if it is an eligible educational institution.

Certain educational institutions located outside the United States also participate in the U.S. Department of Education's Federal Student Aid (FSA) programs.

Related expenses. Student-activity fees and expenses for course-related books, supplies, and equipment are included in qualified education expenses only if the fees and expenses must be paid to the institution as a condition of enrollment or attendance.

No Double Benefit Allowed

You cannot do any of the following.

- Deduct qualified education expenses you deduct under any other provision of the law, for example, as a business expense.
- Deduct qualified education expenses for a student on your income tax return if you or anyone else claims an American opportunity or lifetime learning credit for that same student for the same year.
- Deduct qualified education expenses that have been used to figure the tax-free portion of a distribution from a Coverdell education savings account (Coverdell ESA) or a qualified tuition program (QTP). For a QTP, this applies only to the amount of tax-free earnings that were distributed, not to the of contributions to the program. See *Figuring the Taxable Portion of a Distribution* in chapter 7 (Coverdell ESA) and chapter 8 (QTP) of Publication 970.
- Deduct qualified education expenses that have been paid with tax-free interest on U.S. savings bonds (Form 8815). See *Figuring the Tax-Free Amount* in chapter 10 of Publication 970.
- Deduct qualified education expenses that have been paid with tax-free educational assistance such as a scholarship, grant, or employer-provided educational assistance. See the following section on *Adjustments to qualified education expenses.*

Adjustments to qualified education expenses. If you pay qualified education expenses with certain tax-free funds, you cannot claim a deduction for those amounts. You must reduce the qualified education expenses by the amount of any tax-free educational assistance and refunds you received.

Tax-free educational assistance. This includes:

- The tax-free part of scholarships and fellowships (see chapter 1 of Publication 970),
- Pell grants (see chapter 1 of Publication 970),
- Employer-provided educational assistance (see chapter 12 of Publication 970),
- Veterans' educational assistance (see chapter 1 of Publication 970), and
- Any other nontaxable (tax-free) payments (other than gifts or inheritance) received as educational assistance.

Refunds. Qualified education expenses do not include expenses for which you, or someone else who paid qualified education expenses on behalf of a student, receive a refund. (For information on expenses paid by a dependent student or third party, see *Who Can Claim a Dependent's Expenses*, later.)

If a refund of expenses paid in 2011 is received before you file your tax return for 2011, simply reduce the amount of the expenses paid by the amount of the refund received. If the refund is received after you file your 2011 tax return, see *When Must the Deduction Be Repaid (Recaptured)*, in chapter 6 of Publication 970.

You are considered to receive a refund of expenses when an eligible educational institution refunds loan proceeds to the lender on behalf of the borrower. Follow the above instructions according to when you are considered to receive the refund.

Amounts that do not reduce qualified education expenses. Do not reduce qualified education expenses by amounts paid with funds the student receives as:

- Payment for services, such as wages,
- A loan,
- A gift,
- An inheritance, or
- A withdrawal from the student's personal savings.

Do not reduce the qualified education expenses by any scholarship or fellowship reported as income on the student's tax return in the following situations.

- The use of money is restricted to costs of attendance (such as room and board) other than qualified education expenses.
- The use of money is not restricted and is used to pay education expenses that not are not qualified (such as room and board).

Expenses That Do Not Qualify

Qualified education expenses do not include amounts paid for:

- Insurance
- Medical expenses (including student health fees)
- Room and board
- Transportation, or
- Similar personal, living, or family expenses.

This is true even if the amount must be paid to the institution as a condition of enrollment or attendance.

Sports, games, hobbies, and noncredit courses. Qualified education expenses generally do not include expenses that relate to any course of instruction or other education that involves sports, games or hobbies, or any noncredit course. However, if the course of instruction or other education is part of the student's degree program, these expenses can qualify.

Comprehensive or bundled fees. Some eligible educational institutions combine all of their fees for an academic period into one amount. If you do not receive, or do not have access to, an allocation showing how much you paid for qualified education expenses and how much you paid for personal expenses, such as those listed above, contact the institution. The institution is required to make this allocation and provide you with the amount you paid (or were billed) for qualified education expenses on Form 1098-T, Tuition Statement. See *How Do You Figure the Deduction*, later, for more information about Form 1098-T.

Who Is an Eligible Student

For purposes of the tuition and fees deduction, an eligible student is a student who is enrolled in one or more courses at an eligible educational institution (defined earlier). The student must have either a high school diploma or a General Educational Development (GED) credential.

Table 19-3. **Who Can Claim a Dependent's Expenses**

Do not rely on this table alone. See Who Can Claim a Dependent's Expenses *in chapter 6 of Publication 970.*

IF your dependent is an eligible student and you...	**AND...**	**THEN...**
claim an exemption for your dependent	**you** paid all qualified expenses for your dependent	only **you** can deduct the qualified education expenses that you paid. Your dependent cannot take a deduction.
claim an exemption for your dependent	**your dependent** paid all qualified education expenses	**no one** is allowed to take a deduction.
do not claim an exemption for your dependent but are **eligible** to	**you** paid all qualified expenses for your dependent	**no one** is allowed to take a deduction.
do not claim an exemption for your dependent but are **eligible** to	**your dependent** paid all qualified education expenses	**no one** is allowed to take a deduction.
are **not** eligible to claim an exemption for your dependent	**you** paid all qualified expenses for your dependent	only your **dependent** can deduct the amount you paid. The amount you paid is treated as a gift to your dependent.
are **not** eligible to claim an exemption for your dependent	**your dependent** paid all qualified education expenses	only your **dependent** can take a deduction.

Who Can Claim a Dependent's Expenses

Generally, in order to claim the tuition and fees deduction for qualified education expenses for a dependent, you must:

- Have paid the expenses, and
- Claim an exemption for the student as a dependent.

Table 19-3 summarizes who can claim the deduction.

How Much Can You Deduct

The maximum tuition and fees deduction is $4,000, $2,000, or $0, depending on the amount of your MAGI. For details on figuring your MAGI, see chapter 6 of Publication 970.

How Do You Figure the Deduction

Figure the deduction using Form 8917.

To help you figure your tuition and fees deduction, you should receive Form 1098-T, Tuition Statement. Generally, an eligible educational institution (such as a college or university) must send Form1098-T (or acceptable substitute) to each enrolled student by February 1, 2012.

To claim the deduction, enter the allowable amount on Form 1040, line 34, or Form 1040A, line 19, and attach your completed Form 8917.

TAXPLANNER

While eligible taxpayers can claim a deduction in 2011 for up to $4,000 of qualified higher education expenses, qualified expenses must be incurred in connection with an academic term which began in 2011 or which will begin during the first 3 months of 2012. To be an eligible taxpayer in 2011, you must meet a number of requirements and must not have adjusted gross income in excess of $65,000 if single or $130,000 if married filing jointly to claim the $4,000 deduction. You may claim a deduction for up to $2,000 of qualified expenses if your adjusted gross income is more than $65,000 but not more than $80,000 if single, or more than $130,000 but not more than $160,000 if married filing jointly.

Chapter 20

Moving expenses

ey.com/EYTaxGuide

Note

ey.com/EYTaxGuide

Ernst & Young LLP will update the *Ernst & Young Tax Guide 2012* website with relevant taxpayer information as it becomes available. You can also sign up for email alerts to let you know when changes have been made.

Introduction

Moving expenses are deducted from your gross income in arriving at your adjusted gross income (AGI). This can be advantageous, since you do not have to complete Schedule A-Itemized Deductions in order to receive the benefit of this deduction.

But, in general, most expenses connected with a move are not deductible. For example, meals bought in connection with a move, expenses related to searching for a residence or living in temporary quarters, and expenses incurred in selling, purchasing, or leasing a residence in connection with a move are not deductible expenses.

The good news about moving expenses is that you usually may deduct them if you move because you change jobs. The not-so-good news is that, because no two moves are alike, there are several tests you must meet in order to claim the deductions. Disagreements with the IRS over moving expenses are frequent.

If you are interested in deducting as much of your move as possible, the first rule you should follow is to keep adequate records of all your moving-related expenditures. Receipts, plus a log of your activities, will generally suffice. The other ins and outs of moving expenses are detailed in this chapter.

What's New

Standard mileage rate. For 2011, the standard mileage rate for the cost of operating your car as part of a deductible move was 19 cents per mile from January 1, 2011 through June 30, 2011, and 23.5 cents per mile from July 1, 2011 through December 31, 2011. See *Travel by car* under *Deductible Moving Expenses.*

Reminder

Change of address. If you change your mailing address, be sure to notify the IRS using Form 8822, Change of Address. Mail it to the Internal Revenue Service Center for your old address. Addresses for the Service Centers are on the back of the form.

This chapter explains the deduction of certain expenses of moving to a new home because you changed job locations or started a new job. It includes the following topics.

- Who can deduct moving expenses.
- What moving expenses are deductible.
- What moving expenses are not deductible.
- How a reimbursement affects your moving expense deduction.

- How and when to report moving expenses.
- Special rules for members of the Armed Forces.

You may be able to deduct moving expenses whether you are self-employed or an employee. Your expenses generally must be related to starting work at your new job location. However, certain retirees and survivors may qualify to claim the deduction even though they are not starting work at a new job location. See *Who Can Deduct Moving Expenses*.

Moves to locations outside the United States. This chapter does not discuss moves outside the United States. If you are a United States citizen or resident alien who moved outside the United States or its possessions because of your job or business, see Publication 521, *Moving Expenses*, for special rules that apply to your move.

Useful Items

You may want to see:

Publication

- □ **521** Moving Expenses

Form (and Instructions)

- □ **3903** Moving Expenses
- □ **8822** Change of Address

Who Can Deduct Moving Expenses

You can deduct your moving expenses if you meet all three of the following requirements.

1. Your move is closely related to the start of work.
2. You meet the distance test.
3. You meet the time test.

After you have read these rules, you may want to use Figure 20-B to help you decide if you can deduct your moving expenses.

Different rules may apply if you are a member of the Armed Forces or a retiree or survivor moving to the United States. These rules are discussed later in this chapter.

Related to Start of Work

Your move must be closely related, both in time and in place, to the start of work at your new job location.

Closely related in time. You can generally consider moving expenses incurred within 1 year from the date you first reported to work at the new location as closely related in time to the start of work. It is not necessary that you arrange to work before moving to a new location, as long as you actually do go to work.

If you do not move within 1 year of the date you begin work, you ordinarily cannot deduct the expenses unless you can show that circumstances existed that prevented the move within that time.

Example. Your family moved more than a year after you started work at a new location. You delayed the move for 18 months to allow your child to complete high school. You can deduct your moving expenses.

EXPLANATION

You must make the actual move within a year of starting a new job, unless circumstances prevent you from doing so. Not moving your family so that your child may complete high school in the same school is an acceptable reason, but not moving because you haven't sold your home is not. Good intentions are not enough.

Closely related in place. You can generally consider your move closely related in place to the start of work if the distance from your new home to the new job location is not more than the distance from your former home to the new job location. If your move does not meet this requirement, you may still be able to deduct moving expenses if you can show that:

1. You are required to live at your new home as a condition of your employment, or
2. You will spend less time or money commuting from your new home to your new job location.

Tax Breaks and Deductions You Can Use Checklist

Moving Expenses. If you meet certain requirements, you can deduct reasonable expenses of moving your household goods and personal effects and for traveling to your new home. The deduction for moving expenses is an adjustment in figuring your adjusted gross income; therefore, it reduces your taxable income even if you do not itemize deductions. For more information on the types of expenses that qualify as deductible moving expenses, see *Deductible Moving Expenses*, later.

Deductions for moving expenses will be allowed if you meet three general requirements:

Related to the Start of Work: The move is made within a year of starting your new job and the distance from your new home to the location of your new job is less than the distance from your former home to the new job location;

Distance Test: Your new job location is at least 50 miles farther from your former home than the location of your old job was from your former home; and

Time Test: You must work full time for at least 39 weeks during the first 12 months after you arrive in the general area where your new job is located. If you are self-employed, you must also work for a total of at least 78 weeks during the first 24 months.

For more information on these requirements, as well as exceptions and variations to them, see *Who Can Deduct Moving Expenses*.

EXPLANATION

Assume that your new home is 60 miles from your new job but that your former home was only 55 miles from your new job. If you want to deduct your moving expenses, you must give the IRS an acceptable reason why you now drive farther than you would have if you hadn't moved. An acceptable reason might be that from your new home you are able to use a freeway or a commuter train or bus that saves you time and/or money, whereas before you had to drive across town on local streets all the way to work.

Home defined. Your home means your main home (residence). It can be a house, apartment, condominium, houseboat, house trailer, or similar dwelling. It does not include other homes owned or kept up by you or members of your family. It also does not include a seasonal home, such as a summer beach cottage. Your former home means your home before you left for your new job location. Your new home means your home within the area of your new job location.

Retirees or survivors. You may be able to deduct the expenses of moving to the United States or its possessions even though the move is not related to the start of work at a new job location. You must have worked outside the United States or be a survivor of someone who did. See *Retirees or Survivors Who Move to the United States*, later.

Distance Test

Your move will meet the distance test if your new main job location is at least 50 miles farther from your former home than your old main job location was from your former home. For example, if your old main job location was 3 miles from your former home, your new main job location must be at least 53 miles from that former home. You can use Worksheet 20-1 to see if you meet this test.

The distance between a job location and your home is the shortest of the more commonly traveled routes between them. The distance test considers only the location of your former home. It does not take into account the location of your new home. See Figure 20-A.

Example. You moved to a new home less than 50 miles from your former home because you changed main job locations. Your old main job location was 3 miles from your former home. Your new main job location is 60 miles from that home. Because your new main job location is 57 miles farther from your former home than the distance from your former home to your old main job location, you meet the distance test.

EXPLANATION

The key is that your new job location must be at least 50 miles farther from your former home than your old job location. The IRS doesn't care how far away you live from your new office in absolute terms. To be able to deduct moving expenses, your new job has to be 50 miles farther from your former home than your old job used to be.

Worksheet 20-1. **Distance Test**

Note. Members of the armed forces may not have to meet this test. See *Members of the Armed Forces*.

1. Enter the number of miles from your old home to your new workplace. . . . . 1. _______miles

2. Enter the number of miles from your old home to your old workplace. . . . . 2. _______miles

3. Subtract line 2 from line 1. If zero or less, enter -0- . . . . 3. _______miles

4. Is line 3 at least 50 miles?

☐ Yes. You meet this test.
☐ No. You do not meet this test. You cannot deduct your moving expenses.

Figure 20-A. **Ilustration of Distance Test**

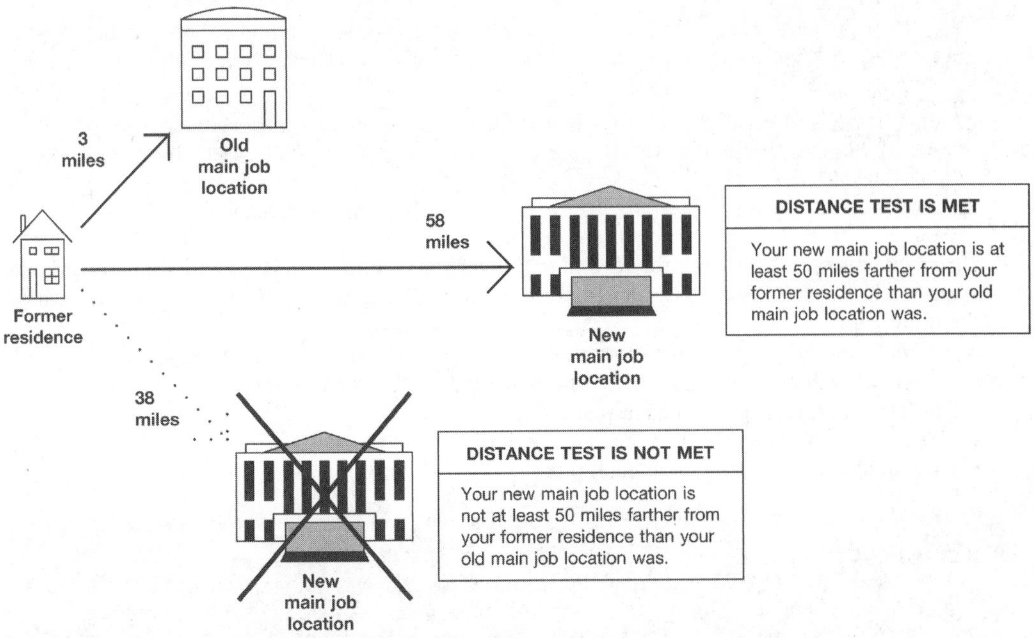
3 miles
Old main job location
58 miles
DISTANCE TEST IS MET
Your new main job location is at least 50 miles farther from your former residence than your old main job location was.
Former residence
New main job location
38 miles
DISTANCE TEST IS NOT MET
Your new main job location is not at least 50 miles farther from your former residence than your old main job location was.
New main job location

> ***Example***
> Even though you may now live 55 miles from your office, the fact that your office is only 45 miles more from your old home than it used to be means that you will not be able to deduct your moving expenses.
>
> You can tell whether you meet the distance test simply by subtracting the total miles from your old home to the old job from the total miles from the old home to the new job. The difference must be 50 miles or greater.

First job or return to full-time work. If you go to work full time for the first time, your place of work must be at least 50 miles from your former home to meet the distance test.

If you go back to full-time work after a substantial period of part-time work or unemployment, your place of work must also be at least 50 miles from your former home.

> ***TAXSAVER***
> First-time job seekers, such as high school and college graduates, and people reentering the labor force after a substantial period of unemployment may deduct moving expenses.
>
> You must move from a former principal home to a new principal home, which means that you must have a principal home from which to move. According to one court, a college graduate could not deduct his expenses to move to his new job location because his student residence was not his principal home.
>
> ***Explanation***
> Two months of unemployment is not long enough to qualify as a substantial period of unemployment. If you had only a brief break in employment, you must meet the same distance requirement that you would if you had been working continuously.

Armed Forces. If you are in the Armed Forces and you moved because of a permanent change of station, you do not have to meet the distance test. See *Members of the Armed Forces*, later.

Main job location. Your main job location is usually the place where you spend most of your working time. If there is no one place where you spend most of your working time, your main job location is the place where your work is centered, such as where you report for work or are otherwise required to "base" your work.

EXPLANATION

Your principal place of work is usually the place where you spend the most time working. An employee's principal place of work is the employer's plant, office, shop, store, or other property.

Example

A member of a railroad crew spends most of his working time aboard a train. His principal place of work is his home terminal, station, or other central point where he reports in, checks out, or receives instructions.

Union members. If you work for several employers on a short-term basis and you get work under a union hall system (such as a construction or building trades worker), your main job location is the union hall.

More than one job. If you have more than one job at any time, your main job location depends on the facts in each case. The more important factors to be considered are:

- The total time you spend at each place,
- The amount of work you do at each place, and
- How much money you earn at each place.

EXAMPLE

A consultant working on an assignment in Detroit—a city that was not his main job location—was allowed by the Tax Court to deduct moving expenses when, at the request of his employer, he moved from Canton, Ohio, to Dallas, Texas, even though he continued the consulting assignment in Detroit. The Tax Court's rationale was that Detroit was only a temporary place of work and that the moving expenses arose from a shift from one principal place of work—Canton—to another—Dallas.

Time Test

To deduct your moving expenses, you also must meet one of the following two time tests.

1. The time test for employees.
2. The time test for self-employed persons.

Both of these tests are explained below. See Table 20-1 for a summary of these tests.

Time Test for Employees

If you are an employee, you must work full time for at least 39 weeks during the first 12 months (39-week test) after you arrive in the general area of your new job location. Full-time employment depends on what is usual for your type of work in your area.

For purposes of this test, the following four rules apply.

1. You count only your full-time work as an employee, not any work you do as a self-employed person.
2. You do not have to work for the same employer for all 39 weeks.
3. You do not have to work 39 weeks in a row.
4. You must work full time within the same general commuting area for all 39 weeks.

EXPLANATION

The courts have held that mere enrollment in an employment registry does not by itself constitute full-time employment.

Example

A registered nurse moved to California, where she enrolled with a nursing registry that facilitated the employment of nurses. Even though it may be the customary method to obtain a job in a hospital in California, the mere enrollment in the registry does not establish the taxpayer as a full-time employee.

Temporary absence from work. You are considered to have worked full time during any week you are temporarily absent from work because of illness, strikes, lockouts, layoffs, natural disasters, or similar causes. You are also considered to have worked full time during any week you are absent from work for leave or vacation provided for in your work contract or agreement.

Table 20-1. **Satisfying the Time Test for Employees and Self-Employed Persons**

IF you are...	THEN you satisfy the time test by meeting the...
an employee	39-week test for employees.
both self-employed and an employee, but unable to satisfy the 39-week test for employees	78-week test for self-employed persons.
both self-employed and an employee at the same time	78-week test for self-employed persons or the 39-week test for an employee. Your principal place of work determines which test applies.
self-employed	78-week test for self-employed persons.

EXAMPLE

A government employee moved to Washington, D.C., from Honolulu but took a temporary leave of absence from her job to go to Texas to continue her studies. The Tax Court ruled that she could not deduct her moving expenses to Washington, D.C., since her location during the time of her leave was not in the "general location" of her new workplace.

A person on leave is still considered to be a full-time employee and must meet the distance requirements as though he or she were actually working at his or her new business location. In this example, the employee would have had to remain in Washington, D.C., for the required 39 weeks in the year (see below) following her move from Honolulu for her moving expenses to have been deductible.

Seasonal work. If your work is seasonal, you are considered to be working full time during the off-season only if your work contract or agreement covers an off-season period of less than 6 months. For example, a school teacher on a 12-month contract who teaches on a full-time basis for more than 6 months is considered to have worked full time for the entire 12 months.

EXPLANATION

According to the IRS, a seasonal employee under contract for less than 39 weeks of work does not meet the 39-week test unless the contract is extended and the employee actually works the required additional time or is prevented from doing so involuntarily, for example, because of illness, natural disaster, or a similar cause.

Time Test for Self-Employed Persons

If you are self-employed, you must work full time for at least 39 weeks during the first 12 months and for a total of at least 78 weeks during the first 24 months (78-week test) after you arrive in the general area of your new job location.

For purposes of the time test for self-employed persons, the following three rules apply.

1. You count any full-time work you do either as an employee or as a self-employed person.
2. You do not have to work for the same employer or be self-employed in the same trade or business for the 78 weeks.
3. You must work within the same general commuting area for all 78 weeks.

Self-employment. You are self-employed if you work as the sole owner of an unincorporated business or as a partner in a partnership carrying on a business. You are not considered self-employed if you are semiretired, are a part-time student, or work only a few hours each week.

Full-time work. You can count only those weeks during which you work full time as a week of work. Whether you work full time during any week depends on what is usual for your type of work in your area.

For example, you are a self-employed dentist and maintain office hours 4 days a week. You are considered to perform services full time if maintaining office hours 4 days a week is not unusual for other self-employed dentists in your area.

If you were both an employee and self-employed, see Table 20-1 for the requirements.

Joint Return

If you are married, file a joint return, and both you and your spouse work full time, either of you can satisfy the full-time work test. However, you cannot add the weeks your spouse worked to the weeks you worked to satisfy that test.

> ***TAXSAVER***
>
> If you file separate returns, each person must meet the time test individually and deduct only his or her own expenses.
>
> The time test may be met by either spouse if a joint return is filed. However, weeks worked by both husband and wife cannot be added together to meet the time test.
>
> If you and your spouse are living together, and if both of you have been working full-time but one of you loses your job, you obtain the maximum tax benefits by filing a joint return. This is the case even if you reside in a **community property** state. Moving expenses paid by both husband and wife may be aggregated and are deductible in full.

Time test not yet met. You can deduct your moving expenses on your 2011 tax return even though you have not yet met the time test by the date your 2011 return is due. You can do this if you expect to meet the 39-week test in 2012, or the 78-week test in 2012 or 2013. If you deduct moving expenses but do not meet the time test in 2012 or 2013, you must either:

1. Report your moving expense deduction as other income on your Form 1040 for the year you cannot meet the test, or
2. Amend your 2011 return.

If you do not deduct your moving expenses on your 2011 return and you later meet the time test, you can file an amended return for 2011 to take the deduction.

Example. You arrive in the general area of your new job location September 10, 2011. You deduct moving expenses on your 2011 return, the year of the move, even though you have not met the time test by the date your return is due. If you do not meet the 39-week test during the 12-month period following your arrival in the general area of your new job location, you must either:

1. Report your moving expense deduction as other income on your Form 1040 for 2012, or
2. Amend your 2011 return.

Exceptions to the Time Test

You do not have to meet the time test if one of the following applies.

1. You are in the Armed Forces and you moved because of a permanent change of station. See Members of the Armed Forces, later.
2. Your main job location was outside the United States and you moved to the United States because you retired. See Retirees or Survivors Who Move to the United States, later.
3. You are the survivor of a person whose main job location at the time of death was outside the United States. See Retirees or Survivors Who Move to the United States, later.
4. Your job at the new location ends because of death or disability.
5. You are transferred for your employer's benefit or laid off for a reason other than willful misconduct. For this exception, you must have obtained full-time employment and you must have expected to meet the test at the time you started the job.

> ***EXPLANATION***
>
> The courts have held and the IRS agrees that if, after moving for job-related purposes, you are fired or laid off, involuntarily lose your job (for other than willful misconduct), or are required to move again by your employer before the 39 weeks are up, you are still able to deduct your moving expenses. Death and disability also exempt a taxpayer from the 39-week requirement. However, if you voluntarily take a leave of absence—even if employment benefits continue—you may not count the leave period toward the 39 weeks.
>
> ***Example***
>
> A taxpayer who terminated his employment voluntarily after working in his new location only 37 weeks (even though he did so in order to start a different job elsewhere) was not allowed the deduction for his original moving costs.

TAXSAVER

Since you have 2 years to fulfill the time requirement, you should assume that you will meet it and deduct moving expenses in the year in which you incur them. Even if you expect to incur more moving expenses later, do not wait to deduct those that you already have incurred. Any later expenses that qualify may be deducted in a subsequent year.

If you fail to meet the time test later, you may either file an amended return and repay any tax due along with interest or report as income the amount you previously deducted. In some cases, the 2-year period may be extended.

Example

A woman was allowed to deduct moving expenses incurred 30 months after her transfer because she waited until her child finished school before moving her family. The IRS rule is: You have to demonstrate that there is a good reason for the delay.

Members of the Armed Forces

If you are a member of the Armed Forces on active duty and you move because of a permanent change of station, you do not have to meet the distance and time tests, discussed earlier. You can deduct your unreimbursed moving expenses.

A permanent change of station includes:

- A move from your home to your first post of active duty,
- A move from one permanent post of duty to another, and
- A move from your last post of duty to your home or to a nearer point in the United States. The move must occur within 1 year of ending your active duty or within the period allowed under the Joint Travel Regulations.

Spouse and dependents. If a member of the Armed Forces dies, is imprisoned, or deserts, a permanent change of station for the spouse or dependent includes a move to:

- The place of enlistment,
- The member's, spouse's, or dependent's home of record, or
- A nearer point in the United States.

If the military moves you and your spouse and dependents to or from separate locations, the moves are treated as a single move to your new main job location.

More information. For more information on moving expenses for members of the Armed Forces, and instructions for completing Form 3903, see *Members of the Armed Forces* in Publication 521.

EXPLANATION

If an Armed Forces member's family can't move to his or her new permanent location, the cost of moving the family to a new location is still deductible.

An Armed Forces member's family may deduct expenses for a move to the foreign country to which the service member is transferred, even if the family obtains only 90-day tourist visas. The IRS recognizes the family as being part of the Armed Forces member's household, residing with him or her before and after the move.

In general, a dislocation allowance received by Armed Forces personnel is excludable from wages.

Retirees or Survivors Who Move to the United States

If you are a retiree who was working abroad or a survivor of a decedent who was working abroad and you move to the United States or one of its possessions, you do not have to meet the time test, discussed earlier. However, you must meet the requirements discussed below under Retirees who were working abroad or Survivors of decedents who were working abroad.

United States defined. For this section of this chapter, the term "United States" includes the possessions of the United States.

Retirees who were working abroad. You can deduct moving expenses for a move to a new home in the United States when you permanently retire. However, both your former main job location and your former home must have been outside the United States.

Caution

If you are living in the United States, retire, and then move and remain retired, you cannot claim a moving expense deduction for that move.

Permanently retired. You are considered permanently retired when you cease gainful full-time employment or self-employment. If, at the time you retire, you intend your retirement to be permanent, you will be considered retired though you later return to work. Your intention to retire permanently may be determined by:

1. Your age and health,
2. The customary retirement age for people who do similar work,
3. Whether you receive retirement payments from a pension or retirement fund, and
4. The length of time before you return to full-time work.

EXPLANATION

A retiree may deduct the cost of moving back to a residence in the United States without having to be employed on returning. Although there is no timetable for the move specified in the law, it must be "in connection with the bona fide retirement of an individual." Moving expenses incurred after a lengthy delay following retirement may not be deductible.

Survivors of decedents who were working abroad. If you are the spouse or the dependent of a person whose main job location at the time of death was outside the United States, you can deduct moving expenses if the following five requirements are met.

1. The move is to a home in the United States.
2. The move begins within 6 months after the decedent's death. (When a move begins is described later.)
3. The move is from the decedent's former home.
4. The decedent's former home was outside the United States.
5. The decedent's former home was also your home.

When a move begins. A move begins when one of the following events occurs.

1. You contract for your household goods and personal effects to be moved to your home in the United States, but only if the move is completed within a reasonable time.
2. Your household goods and personal effects are packed and on the way to your home in the United States.
3. You leave your former home to travel to your new home in the United States.

Deductible Moving Expenses

If you meet the requirements discussed earlier under <u>*Who Can Deduct Moving Expenses*</u>, you can deduct the reasonable expenses of:

1. Moving your household goods and personal effects (including in-transit or foreign-move storage expenses), and
2. Traveling (including lodging but not meals) to your new home.

Caution

You cannot deduct any expenses for meals.

Reasonable expenses. You can deduct only those expenses that are reasonable for the circumstances of your move. For example, the cost of traveling from your former home to your new one should be by the shortest, most direct route available by conventional transportation. If, during your trip to your new home, you stop over, or make side trips for sightseeing, the additional expenses for your stopover or side trips are not deductible as moving expenses.

TAXPLANNER

Qualified moving expenses not paid or reimbursed by your employer will be allowed as a deduction in calculating your adjusted gross income. Moving expenses paid for by your employer directly or through reimbursement will be excludable from your gross income and wages for income and employment tax purposes, unless you actually deducted the expenses in a prior taxable year.

Travel by car. If you use your car to take yourself, members of your household, or your personal effects to your new home, you can figure your expenses by deducting either:

1. Your actual expenses, such as gas and oil for your car, if you keep an accurate record of each expense, or
2. The standard mileage rate of 19 cents per mile from January 1, 2011 through June 30, 2011 and 23.5 cents per mile from July 1, 2011 through December 31, 2011.

Whether you use actual expenses or the standard mileage rate to figure your expenses, you can deduct parking fees and tolls you paid in moving. You cannot deduct any part of general repairs, general maintenance, insurance, or depreciation for your car.

EXPLANATION

For 2011, the standard mileage rate for moving expenses is 19 cents per mile from January 1, 2011, to June 30, 2011, and 23.5 cents per mile from July 1, 2011, to December 31, 2011, and the mileage rate for business expenses is 51 cents per mile for January 1, 2011, through June 30, 2011, and 55.5 cents per mile for July 1, 2011, through December 31, 2011.

The IRS has resisted any attempt to include depreciation of an automobile as a moving expense, maintaining that depreciation does not apply to a personal automobile.

Member of household. You can deduct moving expenses you pay for yourself and members of your household. A member of your household is anyone who has both your former and new home as his or her home. It does not include a tenant or employee, unless that person is your dependent.

EXPLANATION

The costs of moving dependent children who do not reside with the parents before the move are not deductible, even if the parents and children move to the new location simultaneously. The reason is that the children were not members of the former household.

Location of move. There are different rules for moving within or to the United States than for moving outside the United States. This chapter only discusses moves within or to the United States. The rules for moves outside the United States can be found in Publication 521.

Household Goods and Personal Effects

You can deduct the cost of packing, crating, and transporting your household goods and personal effects and those of the members of your household from your former home to your new home. For purposes of moving expenses, the term "personal effects" includes, but is not limited to, movable personal property that the taxpayer owns and frequently uses.

If you use your own car to move your things, see *Travel by car*, earlier.

You can deduct any costs of connecting or disconnecting utilities required because you are moving your household goods, appliances, or personal effects.

You can deduct the cost of shipping your car and household pets to your new home.

You can deduct the cost of moving your household goods and personal effects from a place other than your former home. Your deduction is limited to the amount it would have cost to move them from your former home.

Caution

You cannot deduct the cost of moving furniture you buy on the way to your new home.

EXPLANATION

Moving furniture that was in storage at the time of the move is deductible as long as the actual cost of moving it does not exceed what the cost of moving it would have been had the furniture been located at your former home.

Example

You are a resident of North Carolina and have been in college pursuing a degree for the last 4 years. Because of the small size of your apartment, you stored some of your furniture with your parents in Georgia.

You get a job in Washington, D.C. It costs you $1,100 to move the furniture from Georgia to Washington, D.C. If the furniture in Georgia had been shipped from North Carolina, your former home, it would have cost only $600. You may deduct only $600 of the $1,100 charge.

Note: If you lived in a dormitory or other rented quarters in North Carolina but you went home to Georgia for the summers, were considered an out-of-state or nonresident student in North Carolina, and otherwise maintained most of the major elements of residency (voting, automobile registration, charge accounts, etc.) in Georgia, you could argue that Georgia was your former home. In that case, all moving expenses would be deductible.

EXPLANATION

A yacht is not considered a part of your household goods or personal effects. The rationale given by the courts is that Congress intended moving expenses to cover only items that you must move from your old home to a new location. To be deductible as a moving expense, an item must be, according to the courts, "intimately associated" with your home. A yacht is not.

However, the courts have upheld the deductibility of costs associated with moving a sailboat that the taxpayer owned for 4 years and frequently used. The taxpayer proved that he was "intimately associated" with the boat. This "intimate association" enabled the boat to be characterized as a "personal effect," thereby making all expenses associated with moving it deductible.

Storage expenses. You can include the cost of storing and insuring household goods and personal effects within any period of 30 consecutive days after the day your things are moved from your former home and before they are delivered to your new home.

Travel Expenses

You can deduct the cost of transportation and lodging for yourself and members of your household while traveling from your former home to your new home. This includes expenses for the day you arrive.

You can include any lodging expenses you had in the area of your former home within one day after you could no longer live in your former home because your furniture had been moved.

You can deduct expenses for only one trip to your new home for yourself and members of your household. However, all of you do not have to travel together or at the same time. If you use your own car, see *Travel by car*, earlier.

EXPLANATION

The courts allowed the cost of an escort as a moving expense when a taxpayer's mobile home broke down en route–the breakdown was attributable solely to the move. The charge for moving a mobile home by a professional mover is deductible. However, the replacement cost of tires for the mobile home does not qualify as a deductible moving expense. The reason is that new tires are essentially capital improvements.

TAXALERT

Travel expenses from your former home to your new home are only deductible as moving expenses when incurred after obtaining employment in the area to which you are moving. However, some travel expenses related to your job search, prior to obtaining employment, may be deductible. See *Job Search Expenses* in chapter 29, *Miscellaneous deductions*, for additional details.

Nondeductible Expenses

You cannot deduct the following items as moving expenses.

- Any part of the purchase price of your new home.

EXPLANATION

No deduction is allowed for the costs of selling your former home (or settling an unexpired lease) and purchasing your new home (or the acquisition of a new lease).

- Car tags.
- Driver's license.
- Expenses of buying or selling a home.
- Expenses of getting or breaking a lease.
- Home improvements to help sell your home.
- Loss on the sale of your home.

EXPLANATION

Under no circumstances is a loss on the sale of your personal residence deductible as a moving expense, or as any other kind of expense, even if the move forced you to sell at a loss. However, if any portion of your home was used for income-producing purposes, then the portion of the loss allocable to such use may be deductible. For more information see chapter 15, *Selling your home*.

Although you may not deduct property taxes and interest as moving expenses, you may claim them as itemized deductions.

- Losses from disposing of memberships in clubs.
- Meal expenses.
- Mortgage penalties.
- Pre-move house-hunting expenses.
- Real estate taxes.
- Refitting of carpets and draperies.
- Return trips to your former residence.
- Security deposits (including any given up due to the move).
- Storage charges except those incurred in transit and for foreign moves.
- Temporary living expenses.

EXPLANATION

Many moving costs represent real economic losses to you but are not deductible as moving expenses when you are computing your taxable income. These nondeductible moving costs are simply considered personal expenses, whether or not you are reimbursed for them. If you itemize your deductions, you might be able to deduct some costs that are not deductible as moving expenses.

Mortgage penalties that are loan prepayment penalties are usually deductible as interest. Real estate taxes are deductible. In many states, automobile tags are deductible as personal property taxes.

You may not deduct the cost of buying new drapes.

House-hunting trips and temporary housing expenses are not deductible. Also, the cost of meals incurred in connection with a move are not deductible. In addition, expenses associated with the purchase, sale, or lease of a residence are not deductible.

Example 1

The IRS has ruled that the costs associated with the transfer of a U.S. government employee were not deductible, since the employee initiated the transfer, even when the transfer was in the interest of the government. The transfer must be a requirement of the employer and not merely for the benefit of the employee.

Example 2

A taxpayer replaced carpeting and drapes at her newly leased apartment because of her husband's allergies. The costs were for the comfort of the taxpayer rather than moving expenses. A deduction was not allowed.

No double deduction. You cannot take a moving expense deduction and a business expense deduction for the same expenses. You must decide if your expenses are deductible as moving expenses or as business expenses. For example, expenses you have for travel, meals, and lodging while temporarily working at a place away from your regular place of work may be deductible as business expenses if you are considered away from home on business. Generally, your work at a single location is considered temporary if it is realistically expected to last (and does in fact last) for 1 year or less. See *Temporary Assignment or Job* in chapter 27 for information on deducting your expenses.

TAXSAVER

If you are denied a deduction for moving expenses on the grounds that the move is only temporary (generally a year or less), you may still deduct your expenses for travel, meals, and lodging while away from home as business expenses.

Example

A professor who went on a 10-month sabbatical for postdoctoral research training could not deduct the expense of moving his household and personal goods. He could, however, deduct his traveling expenses, as well as the cost of his meals and lodging, while away.

TAXPLANNER

If you are a nonresident alien temporarily in the United States earning taxable income for performing personal services, you can also deduct moving expenses to the United States if you meet both the time test and the distance test, explained earlier in this chapter. However, if you deduct moving expenses to the United States, you cannot also deduct travel expenses while temporarily away from your foreign home because moving expenses are based on a change of your principal place of business.

How and When To Report

This section explains how and when to report your moving expenses and any reimbursements or allowances you received for your move.

Form 3903. Use Form 3903 to figure your moving expense deduction.

Caution

You cannot deduct moving expenses on Form 1040EZ or Form 1040A.

Where to deduct. Deduct your moving expenses on line 26 of Form 1040. The amount of moving expenses you can deduct is shown on line 5 of Form 3903.

Reimbursements. If you receive a reimbursement for your moving expenses, how you report this amount and your expenses depends on whether the reimbursement is paid to you under an accountable plan or a nonaccountable plan.

For more information on reimbursements, see Publication 521.

TAXSAVER

When your employer buys your home. If your employer purchases your former residence, the real estate commission that is avoided is not income to you, although the gain on the sale of the residence is taxed as a capital gain, subject to the capital gain exclusion rules, discussed in chapter 15, *Selling your home*.

Any reimbursement by your employer for a loss on the sale of your home must be included in your income. You may not deduct the loss on your home, though you may deduct the amount attributable to the real estate commission, if any, as a selling expense.

If your employer purchases your former home from you at fair market value and there is a subsequent decline in its worth, the loss is sustained by your employer. The home's drop in value does not affect you.

If your employer purchases your former home from you at more than fair market value, the excess is ordinary taxable income to you and not capital gain. You cannot exclude that excess from your income, even if you purchased a new home for more than you got in total for the old one.

Explanation

Some employers use third-party relocation service companies to buy your home from you. If the third party pays any direct home-selling costs that are normally imposed on the seller by local law and/or custom, then you will be treated as having received taxable income.

Example

An employer agreed to pay home-selling costs but required that the employee repay them if he terminated employment within a stipulated period of time. The IRS held that an enforceable debt was created and that the employee had taxable income to report when the debt was canceled (or not paid). The employer must report the income on Form W-2.

When To Deduct Expenses

You may have a choice of when to deduct your moving expenses and report any reimbursement.

Expenses not reimbursed. If you were not reimbursed, deduct your allowable moving expenses either in the year you incurred them or in the year you paid them.

Example. In December 2010, your employer transferred you to another city in the United States, where you still work. You are single and were not reimbursed for your moving expenses. In 2010, you paid for moving your furniture and you deducted these expenses on your 2010 tax return. In January 2011, you paid for travel to the new city. You can deduct these additional expenses on your 2011 tax return.

Figure 20-B. **Can You Deduct Expenses for a Non-Military Move Within the United States?**[1]

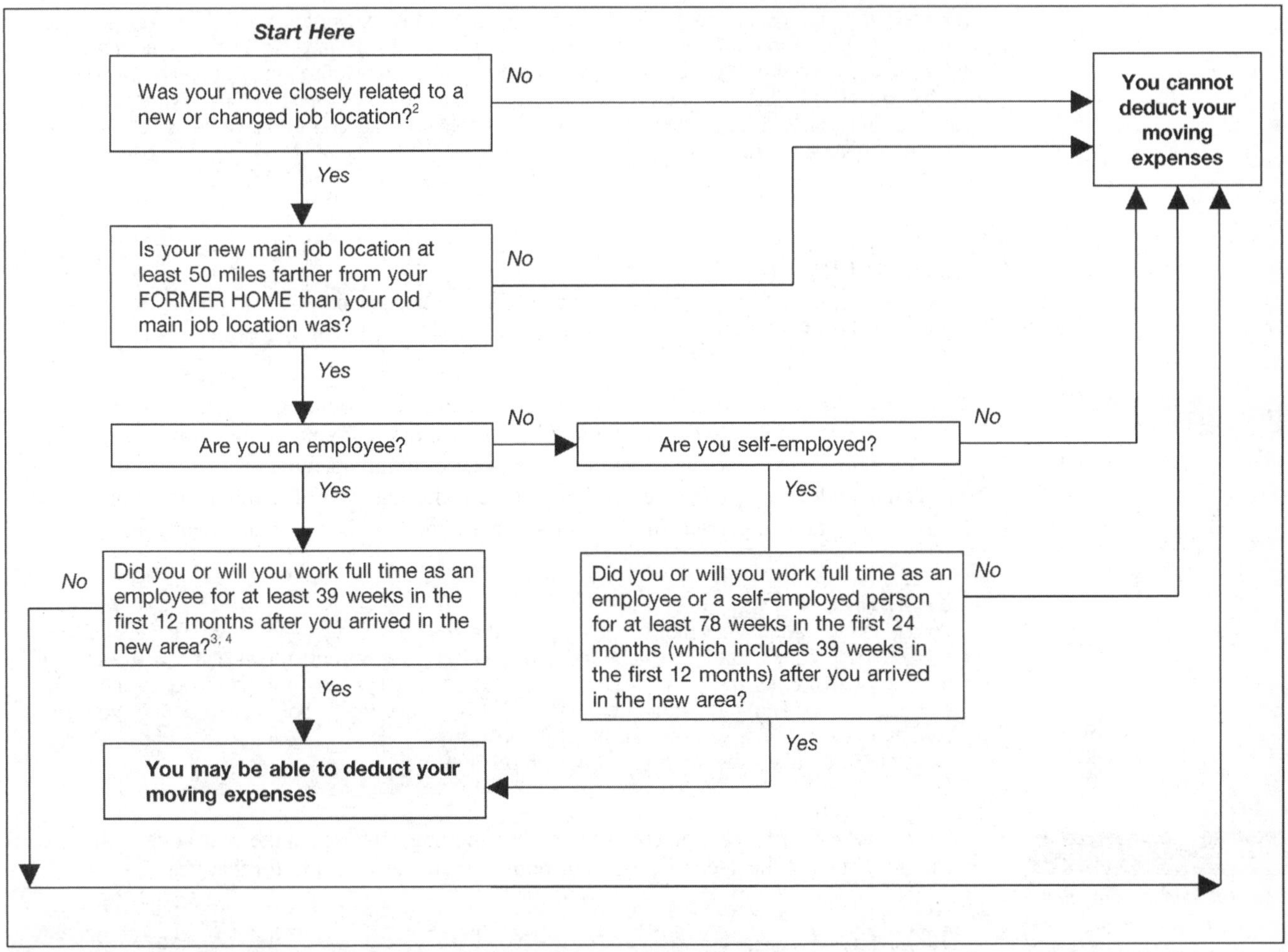

Start Here
Was your move closely related to a new or changed job location?[2]
No
You cannot deduct your moving expenses
Yes
Is your new main job location at least 50 miles farther from your FORMER HOME than your old main job location was?
No
Yes
Are you an employee?
No
Are you self-employed?
No
Yes
Yes
Did you or will you work full time as an employee for at least 39 weeks in the first 12 months after you arrived in the new area?[3, 4]
No
Did you or will you work full time as an employee or a self-employed person for at least 78 weeks in the first 24 months (which includes 39 weeks in the first 12 months) after you arrived in the new area?
No
Yes
Yes
You may be able to deduct your moving expenses

[1] Military persons should see *Members of the Armed Forces* for special rules that apply to them.

[2] Your move must be closely related to the start of work at your new job location. See *Related to Start of Work.*

[3] If you deduct expenses and do not meet this test later, you must either file an amended tax return or report your moving expense deduction as other income. See *Time test not yet met.*

[4] If you become self-employed during the first 12 months, answer YES if your time as a full-time employee added to your time as a self-employed person equals or will equal at least 78 weeks in the first 24 months (including 39 weeks in the first twelve months) after you arrived in the new area.

Expenses reimbursed. If you are reimbursed for your expenses, you may be able to deduct your expenses either in the year you incurred them or in the year you paid them. If you use the cash method of accounting, you can choose to deduct the expenses in the year you are reimbursed even though you paid the expenses in a different year.

If you are reimbursed for your expenses in a year after you paid the expenses, you may want to delay taking the deduction until the year you receive the reimbursement. If you do not choose to delay your deduction until the year you are reimbursed and you deduct moving expenses that will be reimbursed, you must include the reimbursement in your income.

EXPLANATION

Your employer may give you a flat amount of money to cover all your moving expenses, some of which may not be deductible. The IRS says that the employer must apply the reimbursement first to the deductible moving expenses that are not subject to withholding and then deduct withholding and social security tax from the remainder.

TAXPLANNER

If your move is a result of a qualified assignment by your employer for one year or less, and you receive reimbursement for your daily expenses (or a per diem allowance), your reimbursement for moving expenses may not be fully tax-free to you. Though your flight, hotel, and meal costs while traveling for business may be considered tax-free, the reimbursement from your employer for costs associated with the movement of household goods and storage would be fully taxable to you when received.

TAXALERT

Be sure to take into account reimbursement for nondeductible expenses when you are figuring your **estimated tax** payments.

Choosing when to deduct. If you use the cash method of accounting, which is used by most individuals, you can choose to deduct moving expenses in the year your employer reimburses you if:

1. You paid the expenses in a year before the year of reimbursement, or
2. You paid the expenses in the year immediately after the year of reimbursement but by the due date, including extensions, for filing your return for the reimbursement year.

TAXSAVER

You generally deduct your moving expenses in the year in which you pay them. However, if you receive a reimbursement in one year and don't pay the expenses until the next year, you still may deduct the expenses in the earlier year, as long as you pay them before the due date, including extensions, for filing your return for the year of reimbursement. You should deduct your expenses in the year in which you will save the most taxes.

Report your moving expense deduction on Form 3903.

Caution

You cannot deduct any moving expenses for which you received a reimbursement that was not included in your income. (Reimbursements are discussed in Publication 521.)

How to make the choice. You choose to deduct moving expenses in the year you received reimbursement by taking the deduction on your return, or amended return, for that year.

TAXORGANIZER

Records you should keep:

Receipts for:

- Professional mover's fees
- Rental of moving truck and/or equipment
- Storage and insurance of household goods and personal effects
- Cost of lodging while traveling from former home to new home
- Parking fees and tolls during move
- Mileage for use of car or actual expenses (gas and oil) while traveling from former home to new home

Part 5

Standard deduction and itemized deductions

ey.com/EYTaxGuide

After you have figured your adjusted gross income, you are ready to subtract the deductions used to figure taxable income. You can subtract either the standard deduction or itemized deductions. Itemized deductions are deductions for certain expenses that are listed on Schedule A (Form 1040). The ten chapters in this part discuss the standard deduction and each itemized deduction. See chapter 21 for the factors to consider when deciding whether to subtract the standard deduction or itemized deductions.

GENERALLY TAKE THE STANDARD DEDUCTION IF:

- Your standard deduction is more than the total itemized deductions you can claim (chapter 21, *Standard deduction,* and chapters 22 through 29, *Miscellaneous deductions.*

YOU GENERALLY CANNOT TAKE THE STANDARD DEDUCTION IF:

- You are filing a tax return with a short tax year,
- You were a nonresident or a dual-status alien during the year (chapter 21, *Standard deduction*), or
- You are married filing separately, and your spouse itemizes deductions.

ITEMIZE YOUR DEDUCTIONS IF:

- You cannot take the standard deduction (chapter 21, *Standard deduction*),
- You had large uninsured medical and dental expenses (chapter 22, *Medical and dental expenses*),
- You paid taxes and interest on your home (chapter 23, *Taxes you may deduct,* and chapter 24, *Interest expense*),
- You made large charitable contributions (chapter 25, *Contributions*),
- You had large uninsured casualty or theft losses (chapter 26, *Casualty and theft losses*),
- You had employee business expenses (chapter 27, *Car expenses and other employee business expenses*),
- You had employee educational expenses (chapter 28, *Tax benefits for work-related education*), or
- You had various miscellaneous expenses (chapter 29, *Miscellaneous deductions*),

and

- Your total itemized deductions are more than the standard deduction you can claim (chapter 21, *Standard deduction*).

Chapter 21
Standard deduction

ey.com/EYTaxGuide

Note

IRS Publication 17 (*Your Federal Income Tax*) has been updated by Ernst & Young LLP for 2011. Dates and dollar amounts shown are for 2011. Underlined type is used to indicate where IRS text has been updated. Places where text has been removed are indicated by the sentence: *Text intentionally omitted.*

ey.com/EYTaxGuide

Ernst & Young LLP will update the *Ernst & Young Tax Guide 2012* website with relevant taxpayer information as it becomes available. You can also sign up for email alerts to let you know when changes have been made.

Introduction

Taxpayers who do not itemize their deductions are eligible for the standard deduction. However, you should determine whether itemizing deductions or taking the applicable standard deduction produces greater tax savings. In determining the amount of your standard deduction, you must consider many factors, including filing status, age, blindness, unearned income, and whether or not someone is claiming you as an exemption. Higher deductions are allowed if you or your spouse is over age 65 or is totally or partially blind. On the other hand, if another taxpayer can claim you as a dependent, your standard deduction may be limited. This chapter includes a useful worksheet that will help you figure out what your standard deduction is.

What's New

Standard deduction increased. The standard deduction for some taxpayers who do not itemize their deductions on Schedule A of Form 1040 is higher in 2011 than it was in 2010. The amount depends on your filing status. *Text intentionally omitted.*

Text intentionally omitted.

TAXALERT

The basic standard deduction amount for married couples filing joint returns is twice the basic standard deduction for single returns. This mitigates the so-called marriage penalty, where a married couple filing a joint return pays more in taxes than two single individuals with the same income.

This chapter discusses the following topics.

- How to figure the amount of your standard deduction.
- The standard deduction for dependents.
- Who should itemize deductions.

Most taxpayers have a choice of either taking a standard deduction or itemizing their deductions. If you have a choice, you can use the method that gives you the lower tax.

The standard deduction is a dollar amount that reduces the amount of income on which you are taxed. It is a benefit that eliminates the need for many taxpayers to itemize actual deductions, such as medical expenses, charitable contributions, and taxes, on Schedule A of Form 1040. The standard deduction is higher for taxpayers who:

- Are 65 or older, or
- Are blind. *Text intentionally omitted.*

Tip

You benefit from the standard deduction if your standard deduction is more than the total of your allowable itemized deductions.

Persons not eligible for the standard deduction. Your standard deduction is zero and you should itemize any deductions you have if:

- Your filing status is married filing separately, and your spouse itemizes deductions on his or her return,

Tax Breaks and Deductions You Can Use Checklist

Standard Deduction. A standard deduction is allowed for every taxpayer who does not itemize deductions. An additional standard deduction is allowed for taxpayers who are blind or age 65 or older. Generally, you would use the standard deduction only if it's more than the total of the deductions you would otherwise itemize.

Itemizing Even When the Standard Deduction Is Higher. Sometimes it may make sense to elect to itemize your deductions even when your standard deduction is higher. That may be the case if you're subject to the alternative minimum tax (AMT) (see chapter 31, *How to figure your tax*) since the standard deduction must be added back in full when calculating the AMT. You might have a lower overall tax if your itemized deductions consist of amounts which are allowed for AMT purposes, such as charitable contributions and mortgage interest. Another reason to itemize might be for state tax purposes. To make this election you check the box at the bottom of Schedule A (Form 1040).

- You are filing a tax return for a short tax year because of a change in your annual accounting period, or
- You are a nonresident or dual-status alien during the year. You are considered a dual-status alien if you were both a nonresident and resident alien during the year.

Note. If you are a nonresident alien who is married to a U.S. citizen or resident alien at the end of the year, you can choose to be treated as a U.S. resident. (See Publication 519, *U.S. Tax Guide for Aliens*.) If you make this choice, you can take the standard deduction.

EXPLANATION

Married persons who file separate returns must be consistent in claiming the standard deduction or itemizing deductions. If one spouse itemizes deductions, the other spouse must also itemize deductions and cannot claim the standard deduction.

Example

Mike and Denise are married. Each of them has a very successful business, and this year they plan to file separate income tax returns. Denise is very detail-oriented and keeps accurate records of all her itemized deductions. Mike has never cared much for what he considers tedious accounting, and would be happy to avoid this chore by claiming the standard deduction on his return ($5,800 in 2011 for a married taxpayer filing separately). If Denise itemizes deductions on her 2011 return, however, Mike will not be eligible to claim the standard deduction.

TAXPLANNER

You cannot forgo an otherwise allowable dependent exemption in order to increase that dependent's standard deduction.

Text intentionally omitted.

Standard Deduction Amount

The standard deduction amount depends on your filing status, whether you are 65 or older or blind, and whether an exemption can be claimed for you by another taxpayer. *Text intentionally omitted.* Generally, the standard deduction amounts are adjusted each year for inflation. Use Worksheet 21-1 to figure your standard deduction amount.

Decedent's final return. The amount of the standard deduction for a decedent's final tax return is the same as it would have been had the decedent continued to live. However, if the decedent was not 65 or older at the time of death, the higher standard deduction for age cannot be claimed.

EXPLANATION

A tax return filed for a decedent through the date of death is not considered a short tax year, so the decedent is entitled to the full standard deduction.

Example

John Thomas dies on June 15, 2011. John's final tax return will cover the period from January 1 through June 15.

The full amount of the standard deduction may be claimed on John's final return.

Caution

If an exemption for you can be claimed on another person's return (such as your parents' return), your standard deduction maybe limited. See Standard Deduction for Dependents, *later.*

Higher Standard Deduction for Age (65 or Older)

If you do not itemize deductions, you are entitled to a higher standard deduction if you are age 65 or older at the end of the year. You are considered 65 on the day before your 65th birthday. Therefore, you can take a higher standard deduction for 2011 if you were born before January 2, 1947.

Higher Standard Deduction for Blindness

If you are blind on the last day of the year and you do not itemize deductions, you are entitled to a higher standard deduction. You qualify for this benefit if you are totally or partly blind.

Partly blind. If you are partly blind, you must get a certified statement from an eye doctor or registered optometrist that:

- You cannot see better than 20/200 in the better eye with glasses or contact lenses, or
- Your field of vision is not more than 20 degrees.

If your eye condition will never improve beyond these limits, the statement should include this fact. You must keep the statement in your records.

If your vision can be corrected beyond these limits only by contact lenses that you can wear only briefly because of pain, infection, or ulcers, you can take the higher standard deduction for blindness if you otherwise qualify.

Spouse 65 or Older or Blind

You can take the higher standard deduction if your spouse is age 65 or older or blind and:

- You file a joint return, or
- You file a separate return and can claim an exemption for your spouse because your spouse had no gross income and an exemption for your spouse could not be claimed by another taxpayer.

Caution

You cannot claim the higher standard deduction for an individual other than yourself and your spouse.

TAXSAVER

Itemizing vs. standard deduction. In calculating your taxable income, you generally should use the larger of your itemized deductions or your standard deduction. By doing some planning, it may be possible to use the standard deduction in some years and to itemize deductions in others.

Example

In December 2011, Bill and Barbara Chapman add up their itemized deductions for 2011 and find that the total is only $8,000. At that time, they receive an annual real estate tax bill for $1,450, which can be paid anytime before January 31, 2012. A religious organization that the Chapmans are affiliated with is also requesting a $2,150 contribution for its building fund. If the Chapmans make both expenditures in 2011, they will receive no tax benefit from these tax-deductible expenditures because their itemized deductions would total $11,600, the same as their standard deduction. If they make the expenditures in 2012, they might generate more than the standard deduction for that year. Postponing would be a better strategy.

TAXALERT

Be cautious when determining whether to make expenditures in one year or another since they may be added back to your income when calculating alternative minimum taxable (AMT) income. Expenditures such as state income taxes, real estate taxes, and personal property taxes are not allowed in determining your alternative minimum taxable income and could subject you to AMT. See Alternative Minimum Tax in chapter 31, *How to figure your tax*.

TAXPLANNER

If you would not obtain a benefit from claiming an itemized deduction this year (because your total itemized deductions will be less than the standard deduction available for the year), you may be able to obtain a benefit from claiming that item in the following year. Review this carefully or speak with your tax advisor before proceeding because only certain itemized deductions may be deferred.

Text intentionally omitted.

Examples

The following examples illustrate how to determine your standard deduction using Worksheet 21-1.

Example 1. Larry, 46, and Donna, 33, are filing a joint return for 2011. Neither is blind, and neither can be claimed as a dependent. *Text intentionally omitted.* They decide not to itemize their deductions. Because they are married filing jointly, they enter $11,600 on line 1 of Worksheet 21-1. They check the "No" box on line 2, so they also enter $11,600 on lines 4 and 6. Their standard deduction is $11,600.

Example 2. The facts are the same as in Example 1 except that Larry is blind at the end of 2011, so he and Donna enter $1,150 on line 5 of Worksheet 21-1. They then enter $12,750 ($11,600 + $1,150) on line 6, so their standard deduction is $12,750.

Example 3. Bill and Lisa are filing a joint return for 2011. Both are over age 65. Neither is blind, and neither can be claimed as a dependent. *Text intentionally omitted.* They do not itemize deductions, so they use Worksheet 21-1. Because they are married filing jointly, they enter $11,600 on line 1. They check the "No" box on line 2, so they also enter $11,600 on line 4. Because they are both over age 65, they enter $2,300 ($1,150 × 2) on line 5. They enter $13,900 ($11,600 + $2,300) on line 6, so their standard deduction is $13,900.

Text intentionally omitted.

Standard Deduction for Dependents

The standard deduction for an individual for whom an exemption can be claimed on another person's tax return is generally limited to the greater of:

- $950, or
- The individual's earned income for the year + $300 (but not more than the regular standard deduction amount, generally $5,800).

However, the standard deduction may be higher if the individual is 65 or older or blind. *Text intentionally omitted.*

If an exemption for you (or your spouse if you are filing jointly) can be claimed on someone else's return, use Worksheet 21-1 to determine your standard deduction.

EXPLANATION

Although the reduction in the standard deduction available to your dependent children is well publicized, the reduction for dependent parents is not so well known.

Example

Assume that your 61-year-old widowed mother has $6,850 of interest income. If she is not your dependent, she has no tax liability. Her $5,800 standard deduction plus her $3,700 personal exemption eliminate her taxable income. As your dependent, her standard deduction drops to $950 and she loses her personal exemption entirely. Her taxable income would be $5,900 and her tax would be $590. You might pay less tax because of the additional $3,700 dependent exemption, but no one will benefit from the remaining unused standard deduction of $4,850 ($5,800 – $950).

Earned income defined. Earned income is salaries, wages, tips, professional fees, and other amounts received as pay for work you actually perform.

For purposes of the standard deduction, earned income also includes any part of a scholarship or fellowship grant that you must include in your gross income. See *Scholarships and fellowships* in chapter 12 for more information on what qualifies as a scholarship or fellowship grant.

Example 1. Michael is single. His parents claim an exemption for him on their 2011 tax return. He has interest income of $780 and wages of $150. *Text intentionally omitted.* He has no itemized deductions. Michael uses Worksheet 21-1 to find his standard deduction. Because he is single, he enters $5,800 on line 1. He checks the "Yes" box on line 2, enters $950 on line 3, and also enters $950 (the smaller of line 1 and line 3) on line 4. He leaves lines 5 blank and enters $950 on line 6. His standard deduction is $950.

Example 2. Joe, a 22-year-old full-time college student, is claimed on his parents' 2011 tax return. Joe is married and files a separate return. His wife does not itemize deductions on her separate return. Joe has $1,500 in interest income and wages of $3,800. *Text intentionally omitted.* He has no itemized deductions. Joe finds his standard deduction by using Worksheet 21-1. Because he is married filing a separate return, he enters $5,800 on line 1. He checks the "Yes" box on line 2, enters $4,100 ($3,800 + $300) on line 3, and also enters $4,100 (the smaller of line 1 and line 3) on line 4. He leaves lines 5 blank and enters $4,100 on line 6. His standard deduction is $4,100.

Example 3. Amy, who is single, is claimed on her parents' 2011 return. She is 18 years old and blind. She has interest income of $1,300 and wages of $2,900. *Text intentionally omitted.* She has no itemized deductions. Amy finds her standard deduction by using Worksheet 21-1. Because she is single, she enters $5,800 on line 1. She checks the "Yes" box on line 2, enters $3,200 ($2,900 + $300) on line 3, and also enters $3,200 (the smaller of line 1 and line 3) on line 4. Because she is blind, she enters $1,450 on line 5. She enters $4,650 ($3,200 + $1,450) on line 6. Her standard deduction is $4,650.

Who Should Itemize

You should itemize deductions if your total deductions are more than the standard deduction amount. Also, you should itemize if you do not qualify for the standard deduction, as discussed earlier under <u>*Persons not eligible for the standard deduction*</u>.

You should first figure your itemized deductions and compare that amount to your standard deduction to make sure you are using the method that gives you the greater benefit.

When to itemize. You may benefit from itemizing your deductions on Schedule A (Form 1040) if you:

- Do not qualify for the standard deduction, or the amount you can claim is limited,
- Had large uninsured medical and dental expenses during the year,
- Paid interest and taxes on your home,
- Had large unreimbursed employee business expenses or other miscellaneous deductions,
- Had large uninsured casualty or theft losses,
- Made large contributions to qualified charities, or
- Have total itemized deductions that are more than the standard deduction to which you otherwise are entitled.

These deductions are explained in chapters 22-29.

If you decide to itemize your deductions, complete Schedule A and attach it to your Form 1040. Enter the amount from Schedule A, line 29, on Form 1040, line 40.

Electing to itemize for state tax or other purposes. Even if your itemized deductions are less than the amount of your standard deduction, you can elect to itemize deductions on your federal return rather than take the standard deduction. You may want to do this, for example, if the tax benefit of being able to itemize your deductions on your state tax return is greater than the tax benefit you lose on your federal return by not taking the standard deduction. To make this election, you must check the box on line 30 of Schedule A.

TAXPLANNER

Another reason to itemize even when your deductions are less than the standard deduction may apply if you are subject to the alternative minimum tax (AMT). The entire standard deduction is disallowed for AMT purposes. If you instead itemize your deductions, some of those deductions, such as charitable contributions or mortgage interest, may reduce your AMT and therefore your tax bill. You make the election to itemize by checking the box on line 30 of Schedule A. For more information about the AMT, see the special section in <u>chapter 31</u>, *How to figure your tax.*

Changing your mind. If you do not itemize your deductions and later find that you should have itemized—or if you itemize your deductions and later find you should not have—you can change your return by filing Form 1040X, Amended U.S. Individual Income Tax Return. See <u>*Amended Returns and Claims for Refund*</u> in chapter 1 for more information on amended returns.

Married persons who filed separate returns. You can change methods of taking deductions only if you and your spouse both make the same changes. Both of you must file a consent to assessment for any additional tax either one may owe as a result of the change.

You and your spouse can use the method that gives you the lower total tax, even though one of you may pay more tax than you would have paid by using the other method. You both must use the same method of claiming deductions. If one itemizes deductions, the other should itemize because he or she will not qualify for the standard deduction. See <u>*Persons not eligible for the standard deduction*</u>, earlier.

Worksheet 21-1. **2011 Standard Deduction Worksheet**

Caution. Do not complete this worksheet if you expect your spouse to itemize on a separate return or you expect to be a dual-status alien. In either case, your standard deduction will be zero.		
1.	Enter the amount shown below for your filing status. • Single or married filing separately – $5,800 • Married filing jointly or Qualifying widow(er) – $11,600 • Head of household – $8,500	1. ______
2.	Can you (or your spouse if filing jointly) be claimed as a dependent on someone else's return? ☐ **No.** Skip line 3; enter the amount from line 1 on line 4. ☐ **Yes.** Go to line 3.	
3.	Is your **earned income*** more than $650? ☐ **Yes.** Add $300 to your earned income. Enter the total. ☐ **No.** Enter $950	3. ______
4.	Enter the **smaller** of line 1 or line 3	4. ______
5.	Were you (or your spouse if filing jointly) born before January 2, 1947, or blind? ☐ **No.** Go to line 6. ☐ **Yes.** Check if: a. **You** were ☐ Born before January 2, 1947 ☐ Blind b. **Your spouse** was ☐ Born before January 2, 1947 ☐ Blind c. **Total boxes checked in 5a and 5b** ☐ Multiply $1,150 ($1,450 if single or head of household) by the number in the box on line 5c	5. ______
6.	Standard deduction. Add lines 4 and 5 and enter here and on Worksheet 1, line 2	6. ______
***Earned income** *includes wages, salaries, tips, professional fees, and other compensation received for personal services you performed. It also includes any amount received as a scholarship that you must include in your income. Reduce your earned income by your expected deduction for self-employment tax* (Form 1040, line 27).		

Chapter 22
Medical and dental expenses

ey.com/EYTaxGuide

Note

IRS Publication 17 (*Your Federal Income Tax*) has been updated by Ernst & Young LLP for 2011. Dates and dollar amounts shown are for 2011. Underlined type is used to indicate where IRS text has been updated. Places where text has been removed are indicated by the sentence: *Text intentionally omitted.*

ey.com/EYTaxGuide

Ernst & Young LLP will update the *Ernst & Young Tax Guide 2012* website with relevant taxpayer information as it becomes available. You can also sign up for email alerts to let you know when changes have been made.

Introduction

Deductible medical expenses include payments for the diagnosis, cure, mitigation, treatment, and prevention of disease. Payments with respect to any part or function of the body are allowed, as are payments for the prevention or alleviation of mental illness. You may include even your cab or bus fare to the doctor's office. But you may not include expenditures that are merely beneficial to your general health or purely cosmetic medical procedures—like vacation costs or hair transplants, for example.

While almost any medical expense qualifies for the deduction, your medical expenses must total more than 7.5% of your adjusted gross income before you can take any deduction. In other words, someone with an adjusted gross income of $30,000 in 2011 has to have more than $2,250 of medical expenses before he or she may deduct any of them.

What's New

Standard mileage rate. The standard mileage rate allowed for operating expenses for a car when you use it for medical reasons is 19 cents per mile from January 1, 2011, through June 30, 2011. The rate is 23.5 cents per mile for July 1, 2011, through December 31, 2011. See *Transportation* under *What Medical Expenses Are Includible.*

COBRA Premium Assistance. If you involuntarily lost your job after August 31, 2008, and before June 1, 2010, you may qualify for a 65% reduction in premiums for COBRA continuation coverage for up to 15 months. There are also special rules for individuals who lost their health coverage because of a reduction in working hours. The premium reduction is not included in your gross income. You cannot claim the health coverage tax credit for any month that you receive this premium. Also, certain TAA-eligible and PBGC recipients qualify for an extension of COBRA benefits.

For more information, see Publication 502, *Medical and Dental Expenses*.

Tax Breaks and Deductions You Can Use Checklist

Medical and Dental Expenses. The tax law allows you to deduct the medical and dental expenses you incurred, but only to the extent the total is more than 7.5% of your adjusted gross income. Because of this limit, it's important to make sure that you've taken into account all the amounts you paid. Table 22-1, *Medical and Dental Expenses Checklist*, shows many common (and not so common) expenses which qualify for this deduction.

Smoking-Cessation Programs. Amounts that you pay to participate in a smoking-cessation program and for prescribed drugs designed to alleviate nicotine withdrawal are deductible expenses for medical care. However, nonprescription nicotine gum and certain nicotine patches aren't deductible.

Weight-Loss Programs. The amount you pay for a weight-loss program is a deductible medical expense if the program is undertaken as treatment for a disease diagnosed by a physician. The disease can be obesity itself or another disease, such as hypertension or heart disease, for which the doctor directs you to lose weight. You should get a written diagnosis before starting the program. Deductible expenses include fees paid to join the program and to attend periodic meetings. However, the cost of low-calorie food that you eat in place of your regular diet isn't deductible.

Laser Eye Surgery. Laser surgery to correct your vision is deductible as a medical expense, even though it may not be covered by your medical insurance. It is not considered to be cosmetic surgery, the cost of which is not deductible.

TAXALERT

The COBRA premium subsidy is not included in your income. However, the subsidy is phased out for certain high-income individuals. The way it works is that if your income is over a certain amount, your tax liability is increased if you received the subsidy. The phaseout impacts individuals whose modified adjusted gross income exceeds $125,000, or $250,000 for those filing joint returns. Your tax liability is increased, to achieve repayment of a portion of the subsidy, if your modified adjusted gross income is between $125,000 and $145,000, or $250,000 and $290,000 for those filing joint returns. If your modified adjusted gross income exceeds $145,000, or $290,000 for those filing joint returns, the full amount of the subsidy must be repaid as an additional tax. There is no additional tax for individuals with modified adjusted gross income less than these income levels.

TAXPLANNER

There is much more information about the COBRA subsidy, including questions and answers for employers, and for employees or former employees, on the *COBRA* pages of www.irs.gov.

TAXSAVER

Some people who are eligible for the COBRA subsidy also qualify for the health coverage tax credit (HCTC) and may want to choose the HCTC benefit, instead. Until February 12, 2011, the HCTC paid 80% of health insurance premiums for you, your spouse, and other qualifying family members. After February 12, 2011, the credit decreased to 65%. For more information about the HCTC, see *HCTC: Eligibility Requirements and How to Receive the HCTC* on www.irs.gov.

This chapter will help you determine the following.

- **What medical expenses are.**
- **What expenses you can include this year.**
- **How much of the expenses you can deduct.**
- **Whose medical expenses you can include.**
- **What medical expenses are includible.**
- **How to treat reimbursements.**
- **How to report the deduction on your tax return.**
- **How to report impairment-related work expenses.**
- **How to report health insurance costs if you are self-employed.**

Useful Items

You may want to see:

Publication

- □ **502** Medical and Dental Expenses
- □ **969** Health Savings Accounts and Other Tax-Favored Health Plans

Form (and Instructions)

- □ **Schedule A (Form 1040)** Itemized Deductions

What Are Medical Expenses?

Medical expenses are the costs of diagnosis, cure, mitigation, treatment, or prevention of disease, and the costs for treatments affecting any part or function of the body. These expenses include payments for legal medical services rendered by physicians, surgeons, dentists, and other medical practitioners. They include the costs of equipment, supplies, and diagnostic devices needed for these purposes.

Medical care expenses must be primarily to alleviate or prevent a physical or mental defect or illness. Do not include expenses that are merely beneficial to general health, such as vitamins or a vacation.

Medical expenses include the premiums you pay for insurance that covers the expenses of medical care, and the amounts you pay for transportation to get medical care. Medical expenses also include amounts paid for qualified long-term care services and limited amounts paid for any qualified long-term care insurance contract.

TAXALERT

Marijuana and other controlled substances. The IRS has ruled that the cost of marijuana or any other federally controlled substance, even if recommended by a physician in a state whose laws permit such purchase and use, is not deductible. The U.S. Supreme Court has upheld this ruling.

Sex Change Operations. The IRS previously ruled that costs for gender reassignment surgery (and related medications, treatments, and transportation) may not be deducted as medical expenses. However, in February 2010, the U.S. Tax Court held that hormone therapy and sex reassignment surgery were not cosmetic and allowed a taxpayer's deductions for those costs. On the other hand, the U.S. Tax Court disallowed the deduction for a taxpayer's breast augmentation surgery because it was cosmetic surgery directed at improving appearance. The ruling was a partial victory for both the taxpayer and the IRS.

Breast-Feeding Supplies. Breast pumps and other lactation supplies are now tax deductible as medical expenses. In February 2011, the IRS reversed its long-held position prohibiting a medical expense deduction for such supplies. Amounts reimbursed for these expenses under flexible spending arrangements, Archer medical savings accounts, health reimbursement arrangements, or health savings accounts are not income to the taxpayer.

Cosmetic Surgery. Cosmetic surgery, such as plastic surgery (not resulting from an accident or birth defect), and other treatments, such as tooth whitening, is not deductible as a medical expense.

What Expenses Can You Include This Year?

You can include only the medical and dental expenses you paid this year, regardless of when the services were provided. If you pay medical expenses by check, the day you mail or deliver the check generally is the date of payment. If you use a "pay-by-phone" or "online" account to pay your medical expenses, the date reported on the statement of the financial institution showing when payment was made is the date of payment. If you use a credit card, include medical expenses you charge to your credit card in the year the charge is made, not when you actually pay the amount charged.

TAXPLANNER

Timing your medical expenses. Medical expenses don't usually lend themselves to tax planning. However, because a medical deduction is available only in the year of payment, you may be able to maximize your deduction if you can control the timing of your payment.

To determine the most beneficial year of payment, you need to assess your situation prior to the end of the year. If it is clear that your current-year medical expenses will not exceed the nondeductible floor–7.5% of your adjusted gross income–try to defer payment of any medical bills until after year-end. You may be able to salvage a deduction next year.

If you can schedule major or minor surgery in nonemergency cases, you should compare this year's medical deductions with what they are liable to be next year to choose the more beneficial time. It is the date of payment–not the date of surgery–that determines the year in which you may deduct the expense. Remember, putting the charge on a credit card counts as payment at that time.

If you suspect that your adjusted gross income is going to drop substantially next year, defer the payment of medical bills. However, if you think your adjusted gross income is going to skyrocket next year, pay those bills now and try to salvage a deduction.

Exception

Prepaid medical expenses generally are not deductible until the year of treatment.

Separate returns. If you and your spouse live in a noncommunity property state and file separate returns, each of you can include only the medical expenses you actually paid. Any medical expenses paid out of a joint checking account in which you and your spouse have the same interest are considered to have been paid equally by each of you, unless you can show otherwise.

Community property states. If you and your spouse live in a community property state and file separate returns, any medical expenses paid out of community funds are divided equally. Each of you should include half the expenses. If medical expenses are paid out of the separate funds of one spouse, only the spouse who paid the medical expenses can include them. If you live in a community property state, are married, and file a separate return, see Publication 555, *Community Property*.

How Much of the Expenses Can You Deduct?

You can deduct on Schedule A (Form 1040) only the amount of your medical and dental expenses that is more than 7.5% of your AGI (Form 1040, line 38).

In this chapter, the term "7.5% limit" is used to refer to 7.5% of your AGI. The phrase "subject to the 7.5% limit" is also used. This phrase means that you must subtract 7.5% (.075) of your AGI from your medical expenses to figure your medical expense deduction.

Example. Your AGI is $40,000, 7.5% of which is $3,000. You paid medical expenses of $2,500. You cannot deduct any of your medical expenses because they are not more than 7.5% of your AGI.

TAXPLANNER

If your spouse's medical expenses exceed yours. You should consider filing separate returns whenever the medical expenses of either spouse substantially exceed those of the other spouse. Compute and compare your tax liability if you and your spouse were to file jointly with the potential tax liability if you were to file separately before deciding which filing status to choose.

Whose Medical Expenses Can You Include?

You can generally include medical expenses you pay for yourself as well as those you pay for someone who was your spouse or your dependent either when the services were provided or when you paid for them. There are different rules for decedents and for individuals who are the subject of multiple support agreements. See *Support claimed under a multiple support agreement,* later.

Yourself

You can include medical expenses you paid for yourself.

Spouse

You can include medical expenses you paid for your spouse. To include these expenses, you must have been married either at the time your spouse received the medical services or at the time you paid the medical expenses.

Example 1. Mary received medical treatment before she married Bill. Bill paid for the treatment after they married. Bill can include these expenses in figuring his medical expense deduction even if Bill and Mary file separate returns.

If Mary had paid the expenses, Bill could not include Mary's expenses on his separate return. Mary would include the amounts she paid during the year in her separate return. If they filed a joint return, the medical expenses both paid during the year would be used to figure their medical expense deduction.

Example 2. This year, John paid medical expenses for his wife Louise, who died last year. John married Belle this year and they file a joint return. Because John was married to Louise when she received the medical services, he can include those expenses in figuring his medical expense deduction for this year.

Dependent

You can include medical expenses you paid for your dependent. For you to include these expenses, the person must have been your dependent either at the time the medical services were provided or at the time you paid the expenses. A person generally qualifies as your dependent for purposes of the medical expense deduction if both of the following requirements are met.

1. The person was a qualifying child (defined later) or a qualifying relative (defined later), and
2. The person was a U.S. citizen or national, or a resident of the United States, Canada, or Mexico. If your qualifying child was adopted, see *Exception for adopted child,* next.

You can include medical expenses you paid for an individual that would have been your dependent except that:

1. He or she received gross income of $3,700 or more in 2011,
2. He or she filed a joint return for 2011, or
3. You, or your spouse if filing jointly, could be claimed as a dependent on someone else's 2011 return.

Exception for adopted child. If you are a U.S. citizen or U.S. national and your adopted child lived with you as a member of your household for 2011, that child does not have to be a U.S. citizen or national or a resident of the United States, Canada, or Mexico.

Qualifying Child

A qualifying child is a child who:

1. Is your son, daughter, stepchild, foster child, brother, sister, stepbrother, stepsister, half brother, half sister, or a descendant of any of them (for example, your grandchild, niece, or nephew),
2. Was:
   a. Under age 19 at the end of 2011 and younger than you (or your spouse, if filing jointly),
   b. Under age 24 at the end of 2011, a full-time student, and younger than you (or your spouse, if filing jointly), or
   c. Any age and permanently and totally disabled,
3. Lived with you for more than half of 2011,
4. Did not provide over half of his or her own support for 2011, and
5. Did not file a joint return, other than to claim a refund.

> ***TAXPLANNER***
>
> **If you pay medical expenses for others.** If you pay medical expenses on behalf of someone other than yourself, your spouse, or your dependent and your payment is made directly to the provider of the medical service, the payment is not deductible for income tax purposes. However, your payment will not be considered a gift to the individual either. An unlimited gift tax exclusion is available for qualifying medical expenses paid on any individual's behalf directly to the provider of the medical service. This exclusion is also available for transfers that would otherwise be subject to the generation-skipping transfer (GST) tax. For more information about gift tax and the GST tax, see chapter 44, *Estate and gift tax planning*.
>
> ***Example***
>
> A grandparent pays medical expenses directly to the hospital on a grandchild's behalf. The payments will reduce the grandparent's taxable estate and will not be subject to gift tax or GST tax. This could result in significant tax savings. You should consult your tax advisor if you are interested in pursuing this type of tax planning.

Adopted child. A legally adopted child is treated as your own child. This includes a child lawfully placed with you for legal adoption.

You can include medical expenses that you paid for a child before adoption if the child qualified as your dependent when the medical services were provided or when the expenses were paid.

If you pay back an adoption agency or other persons for medical expenses they paid under an agreement with you, you are treated as having paid those expenses provided you clearly substantiate that the payment is directly attributable to the medical care of the child.

But if you pay the agency or other person for medical care that was provided and paid for before adoption negotiations began, you cannot include them as medical expenses.

> **Tip**
>
> *You may be able to take an adoption credit for other expenses related to an adoption. See the Instructions for Form 8839, Qualified Adoption Expenses, for more information.*

Child of divorced or separated parents. For purposes of the medical and dental expenses deduction, a child of divorced or separated parents can be treated as a dependent of both parents. Each parent can include the medical expenses he or she pays for the child, even if the other parent claims the child's dependency exemption, if:

1. The child is in the custody of one or both parents for more than half the year,
2. The child receives over half of his or her support during the year from his or her parents, and
3. The child's parents:
   a. Are divorced or legally separated under a decree of divorce or separate maintenance,
   b. Are separated under a written separation agreement, or
   c. Lived apart at all times during the last 6 months of the year.

This does not apply if the child's exemption is being claimed under a multiple support agreement (discussed later).

Qualifying Relative

A qualifying relative is a person:

1. Who is your:
   a. Son, daughter, stepchild, foster child, or a descendant of any of them (for example, your grandchild),
   b. Brother, sister, half brother, half sister, or a son or daughter of either of them,

   c. Father, mother, or an ancestor or sibling of either of them (for example, your grandmother, grandfather, aunt, or uncle),
   d. Stepbrother, stepsister, stepfather, stepmother, son-in-law, daughter-in-law, father-in-law, mother-in-law, brother-in-law, or sister-in-law, or
   e. Any other person (other than your spouse) who lived with you all year as a member of your household if your relationship did not violate local law,
2. Who was not a qualifying child (see *Qualifying Child* earlier) of any other person for 2011, and
3. For whom you provided over half of the support in 2011. But see *Child of divorced or separated parents,* earlier, and *Support claimed under a multiple support agreement,* next.

Support claimed under a multiple support agreement. If you are considered to have provided more than half of a qualifying relative's support under a multiple support agreement, you can include medical expenses you pay for that person. A multiple support agreement is used when two or more people provide more than half of a person's support, but no one alone provides more than half.

For rules regarding what expenses you can include this year, see *What Expenses Can You Include This Year?,* earlier.

Any medical expenses paid by others who joined you in the agreement cannot be included as medical expenses by anyone. However, you can include the entire unreimbursed amount you paid for medical expenses.

Example. You and your three brothers each provide one-fourth of your mother's total support. Under a multiple support agreement, you treat your mother as your dependent. You paid all of her medical expenses. Your brothers reimbursed you for three-fourths of these expenses. In figuring your medical expense deduction, you can include only one-fourth of your mother's medical expenses. Your brothers cannot include any part of the expenses. However, if you and your brothers share the nonmedical support items and you separately pay all of your mother's medical expenses, you can include the unreimbursed amount you paid for her medical expenses in your medical expenses.

Decedent

Medical expenses paid before death by the decedent are included in figuring any deduction for medical and dental expenses on the decedent's final income tax return. This includes expenses for the decedent's spouse and dependents as well as for the decedent.

The survivor or personal representative of a decedent can choose to treat certain expenses paid by the decedent's estate for the decedent's medical care as paid by the decedent at the time the medical services were provided. The expenses must be paid within the 1-year period beginning with the day after the date of death. If you are the survivor or personal representative making this choice, you must attach a statement to the decedent's Form 1040 (or the decedent's amended return, Form 1040X) saying that the expenses have not been and will not be claimed on the estate tax return.

Amended returns and claims for refund are discussed in chapter 1.

Caution

Qualified medical expenses paid before death by the decedent are not deductible if paid with a tax-free distribution from any Archer MSA, Medicare Advantage MSA, or health savings account.

What if you pay medical expenses of a deceased spouse or dependent? If you paid medical expenses for your deceased spouse or dependent, include them as medical expenses on your Form 1040 in the year paid, whether they are paid before or after the decedent's death. The expenses can be included if the person was your spouse or dependent either at the time the medical services were provided or at the time you paid the expenses.

What Medical Expenses Are Includible?

Use Table 22-1 below, as a guide to determine which medical and dental expenses you can include on Schedule A (Form 1040).

This table does not include all possible medical expenses. To determine if an expense not listed can be included in figuring your medical expense deduction, see *What Are Medical Expenses?,* earlier.

Table 22-1. **Medical and Dental Expenses Checklist** See Publication 502 for more information for these and other expenses.

You can include:	You cannot include:
• Bandages • Birth control pills prescribed by your doctor • Body scan • Capital expenses for equipment or improvements to your home needed for medical care (see the worksheet in Publication 502) • Diagnostic devices • Expenses of an organ donor • Eye surgery—to promote the correct function of the eye • Fertility enhancement, certain procedures • Guide dogs or other animals aiding the blind, deaf, and disabled • Hospital services fees (lab work, therapy, nursing services, surgery, etc.) • Lead-based paint removal • Legal abortion • Legal operation to prevent having children such as a vasectomy or tubal ligation • Long-term care contracts, qualified • Meals and lodging provided by a hospital during medical treatment • Medical services fees (from doctors, dentists, surgeons, specialists, and other medical practitioners) • Medicare Part D premiums • Medical and hospital insurance premiums • Oxygen equipment and oxygen • Part of life-care fee paid to retirement home designated for medical care • Physical examination • Pregnancy test kit • Prescription medicines (prescribed by a doctor) and insulin • Psychiatric and psychological treatment • Social security tax, Medicare tax, FUTA, and state employment tax for worker providing medical care (see *Wages for nursing services*, below) • Special items (artificial limbs, false teeth, eye-glasses, contact lenses, hearing aids, crutches, wheelchair, etc.) • Special education for mentally or physically disabled persons • Stop-smoking programs • Transportation for needed medical care • Treatment at a drug or alcohol center (includes meals and lodging provided by the center) • Wages for nursing services • Weight-loss, certain expenses for obesity	• Baby sitting and childcare • Bottled water • Contributions to Archer MSAs (see Publication 969) • Diaper service • Expenses for your general health (even if following your doctor's advice) such as— – Health club dues – Household help (even if recommended by a doctor) – Social activities, such as dancing or swimming lessons – Trip for general health improvement • Flexible spending account reimbursements for medical expenses (if contributions were on a pre-tax basis) • Funeral, burial, or cremation expenses • Health savings account payments for medical expenses • Illegal operation or treatment • Life insurance or income protection policies, or policies providing payment for loss of life, limb, sight, etc. • Maternity clothes • Medical insurance included in a car insurance policy covering all persons injured in or by your car • Medicine you buy without a prescription • Nursing care for a healthy baby • Prescription drugs you brought in (or ordered shipped) from another country, in most cases • Nutritional supplements, vitamins, herbal supplements, "natural medicines," etc., unless recommended by a medical practitioner as a treatment for a specific medical condition diagnosed by a physician • Surgery for purely cosmetic reasons • Toothpaste, toiletries, cosmetics, etc. • Teeth whitening • Weight-loss expenses not for the treatment of obesity or other disease

TAXPLANNER

If the IRS challenges your deduction. In case the IRS challenges your deduction of medical expenses, you should keep the following information in order to support your claim for medical expenses incurred:

- Receipts and canceled checks evidencing payment of medical expenses
- A permanent record of the name and address of the provider of medical care, the amount of the expenses, and the date paid
- Documentation that the expense was to obtain medical treatment, that medicine was prescribed, and that the expense was incurred on a doctor's recommendation

After reviewing the checklist, you may still be wondering whether a particular expense is deductible or not. The most comprehensive listing of items that you may and may not include when figuring your medical expenses appears in Publication 502, *Medical and Dental Expenses*.

Examples

Here are more examples of items that have been held to be deductible:

- An annual physical examination and diagnostic testing. You do not have to be ill for these expenses to be deductible.
- A full-body electronic scan
- A pregnancy test kit
- A wig, if it is essential to your mental health and not just for enhancing your personal appearance

- Cosmetic surgery that is medically necessary (meaningfully promotes the proper function of the body or prevents or treats illness or disease) or needed to correct a deformity related to an injury, disease, or congenital abnormality and not just for enhancing personal appearance
- Special diet food that is necessary and prescribed by a doctor to the extent that the cost exceeds the amount spent for normal nutritional needs
- Orthopedic shoes in excess of the cost of normal shoes
- Fees paid to someone to accompany and guide a blind person
- Costs attributable to a dog or other animal that assists individuals with physical disabilities
- Fees paid for a note taker for a deaf person
- Legal fees to obtain guardianship over a mental patient who has refused to accept therapy voluntarily
- Fees paid for childbirth preparation classes if instruction relates to obstetrical care
- Costs of a weight loss program for treatment of a specific disease, such as hypertension or obesity
- Costs of a wheelchair lift and its installation in a van
- Reasonable costs for home modifications or improvements to accommodate a handicapped person's condition when incurred for the purpose of medical care or directly related to medical care
- Legal fees necessary to authorize medical treatment for mental illness
- Expenses incurred for radial keratotomy (i.e., eye surgery to correct nearsightedness)

TAXSAVER

Weight loss programs. The IRS has ruled that individuals who suffer from specific physician-diagnosed diseases, such as obesity and hypertension, may deduct, as a medical expense, uncompensated costs of participation in weight loss programs. Costs associated with weight loss programs to improve general health and appearance are not deductible. Whether the cost of the program is deductible or not, the costs of low-calorie foods purchased while in the program are not deductible.

TAXSAVER

Physical and dental exams. The cost of periodic physical and dental exams can be included as a deductible medical expense. Usually, these expenses are too small to be deductible because only expenses over 7.5% of your adjusted gross income can be deducted. However, in years where other medical expenses have been incurred, the inclusion of these expenses in calculating your medical expense deduction can lead to tax savings.

TAXSAVER

Drugs that may be obtained without a prescription (aspirin, cold remedies, skin ointments, etc.) are not deductible, even though they may be recommended or prescribed by a physician.

Before 2011, the cost of an over-the-counter medicine or drug was reimbursable from an employer-sponsored health plan (such as a flexible savings account, health reimbursement arrangement, or Archer Medical Savings Account). But, beginning in 2011, such reimbursements are no longer allowed for such medications unless a prescription is obtained. The change does not affect insulin, even if purchased without a prescription, or other health care expenses such as medical devices, eyeglasses, contact lenses, co-pays, and deductibles.

TAXPLANNER

Medical fees and school tuition. Some schools include a fee for medical care in the amount charged for tuition. Because you may deduct only the amount allocated to medical care if it is separately stated, an itemized bill should be requested.

Explanation
Whether or not an expense is deductible is determined by the nature of the services rendered, not by the qualifications and/or experience of the person rendering them. For example, the services do not necessarily need to be performed by a nurse, as long as the services rendered are generally considered nursing services. These include services connected with caring for the patient's condition, such as giving medication or changing bandages, as well as bathing and grooming the patient.

Examples
The courts allowed deductions for payments to a daughter for the care of her arthritic mother to the extent that they were for medical care.

In another instance, the courts allowed a deduction for the compensation paid to a "personal attendant" who was not a registered or a practical nurse. The deduction was permitted because the invalid was recovering from surgery and was in need of constant attendance.

TAXPLANNER
Two choices, one deduction. An expense may qualify for more than one tax benefit. For instance, a payment may qualify for the childcare credit (see chapter 33, *Child and dependent care credit*), or it may be considered a medical expense. However, the same expense generally may not be used for both benefits. You should analyze each benefit based on your marginal tax rate and your medical expense deduction limitation (7.5% of adjusted gross income) to determine how best to classify the expense.

TAXSAVER
Capital expenses. You may include in medical expenses all or part of the amounts you pay for special equipment installed in your home, or for improvements, if the main reason for the purchase is for medical care. The amount of your medical expense deduction will depend on the extent to which the equipment or improvement has increased the value of the property. To the extent a capital improvement adds value to your home, it increases the cost basis of your home. Any amount paid above the added value is currently deductible as a medical expense. A U.S. District Court held that this deduction is available in the year the home becomes habitable. So if a home is built over a period of years, the amount paid over the added value is all deductible in the year you can move into it, making it easier to get above the 7.5% adjusted gross income (AGI) threshold.

Example
You have a heart ailment. On your doctor's advice, you install an elevator in your home so that you will not need to climb stairs. The elevator costs $2,000. According to competent appraisals, the elevator increases the value of your home by $1,400. The $600 difference is a medical expense. However, you may include the total cost of $2,000 in medical expenses if the elevator does not increase the value of your home.

TAXSAVER
Appraisals. The cost of an appraisal obtained to determine the increase in value of your home is deductible, but not as a medical expense. The appraisal cost is an expense associated with the determination of your tax liability and can be included as a miscellaneous itemized deduction. See chapter 29, *Miscellaneous deductions.*

Explanation
Operating and upkeep expenses. If a capital expense qualifies as a medical expense, amounts paid for operation or upkeep also qualify as medical expenses, as long as the medical reason for the capital expense still exists. These expenses are medical expenses even if none or only part of the original expense was deductible.

Example
Assume the same facts as in the previous example, except that the elevator increased the value of your home by $2,000. In this case, you are not entitled to a medical deduction for the cost of the elevator. However, the costs of electricity to operate the elevator and repairs to maintain it are deductible, as long as the medical reason for the elevator exists.

Exception

An exception to the general rule exists for expenditures incurred to accommodate the condition of a physically handicapped person that generally do not increase the value of a personal residence. These expenses are deductible in full as a medical expense. Examples of expenses made for the primary purpose of accommodating a personal residence to the handicapped condition of a taxpayer, the taxpayer's spouse, or dependents who reside there include:

- Construction of entrance or exit ramps to the residence
- Widening doorways at entrances or exits to the residence
- Widening or otherwise modifying hallways and interior doorways
- Installing railings, support bars, or other modifications to bathrooms
- Lowering or making other modifications to kitchen cabinets and equipment
- Altering the location or otherwise modifying electrical outlets and fixtures
- Installing porch lifts and other forms of lifts (an elevator, however, may also add to the fair market value of the residence, and any deduction would have to be decreased to that extent)
- Modifying fire alarms, smoke detectors, and other warning systems
- Modifying stairs
- Adding handrails or grab bars, whether or not in bathrooms
- Modifying hardware on doors
- Modifying areas in front entrance and exit doorways
- Grading of ground to provide access to the residence

According to the IRS, other similar expenditures may also be incurred in accommodating a personal residence to the handicapped condition of a taxpayer or a dependent. However, only reasonable costs for accommodating a handicapped person's condition will be considered incurred for the purpose of medical care. Additional costs attributable to personal desires are not deductible.

Example

You are physically handicapped and confined to a wheelchair. You incur expenses to widen doorways and lower kitchen cabinets in your residence to permit access by you. These expenses are deductible, subject to the 7.5% threshold discussed earlier.

TAXPLANNER

Medically related capital improvements. If you have to make a medically related capital improvement, you should request a written recommendation from your doctor. In addition, obtain a reliable written appraisal from a real estate appraiser or a valuation expert. Be prepared to prove to what extent the value of your property was or was not increased.

TAXPLANNER

Swimming pools. It is often difficult to obtain a medical deduction for the installation of a swimming pool. The IRS has held that swimming pools generally fall within the category of recreational or luxury items and will look at various facts when it is determining the deduction for the cost of a swimming pool, including:

- Whether the primary purpose of the pool is for medical care
- Whether the expenditure is related to medical care
- Whether the pool does more than serve the convenience and/or comfort of the taxpayer
- You should contact your tax advisor if you intend to install a swimming pool for medical reasons.

Insurance Premiums

You can include in medical expenses insurance premiums you pay for policies that cover medical care. Medical care policies can provide payment for treatment that includes:

- Hospitalization, surgical services, X-rays,
- Prescription drugs and insulin,
- Dental care,
- Replacement of lost or damaged contact lenses, or
- Long-term care (subject to additional limitations). See *Qualified Long-term Care Insurance Contracts* in Publication 502.

If you have a policy that provides payments for other than medical care, you can include the premiums for the medical care part of the policy if the charge for the medical part is reasonable. The cost of the medical part must be separately stated in the insurance contract or given to you in a separate statement.

Note. When figuring the amount of insurance premiums you can include in medical expenses on Schedule A, do not include any health coverage tax credit advance payments shown in box 1 of Form 1099-H, *Health Coverage Tax Credit (HCTC) Advance Payments*.

TAXALERT

You can treat premiums paid for qualified long-term care insurance as a deductible medical expense subject to dollar limits based on your age at the close of the taxable year.

Age	Annual deductible limit
40 or less	$340
Over 40 but not more than 50	640
Over 50 but not more than 60	1,270
Over 60 but not more than 70	3,390
Over 70	4,240

Explanation

Amounts you pay to receive medical care from a health maintenance organization (HMO) are treated as medical insurance premiums.

TAXSAVER

Cafeteria plans. Employees who pay all or part of their medical insurance premiums via employer plans should ask their employer to investigate a flexible spending arrangement, which is sometimes referred to as a cafeteria plan.

Example

You are in the 28% tax bracket, and you pay $2,000 to cover your medical insurance premiums. Because medical expenses are deductible only if they exceed 7.5% of your adjusted gross income, chances are that you are not able to deduct your payments for medical insurance.

If your company offers medical insurance as part of a cafeteria plan, you may opt to have your wages reduced by $2,000 under a salary reduction plan to cover the cost of the insurance. The cut in wages reduces your income tax, producing a federal tax savings in this case of $560. Additional tax savings may also be enjoyed because of lower state income taxes and reduced FICA taxes.

Employer-sponsored health insurance plan. Do not include in your medical and dental expenses any insurance premiums paid by an employer-sponsored health insurance plan unless the premiums are included in box 1 of your Form W-2. Also, do not include any other medical and dental expenses paid by the plan unless the amount paid is included in box 1 of your Form W-2.

Example. You are a federal employee participating in the premium conversion plan of the Federal Employee Health Benefits (FEHB) program. Your share of the FEHB premium is paid by making a pre-tax reduction in your salary. Because you are an employee whose insurance premiums are paid with money that is never included in your gross income, you cannot deduct the premiums paid with that money.

Long-term care services. Contributions made by your employer to provide coverage for qualified long-term care services under a flexible spending or similar arrangement must be included in your income. This amount will be reported as wages in box 1 of your Form W-2.

Health reimbursement arrangement (HRA). If you have medical expenses that are reimbursed by a health reimbursement arrangement, you cannot include those expenses in your medical expenses. This is because an HRA is funded solely by the employer.

Retired public safety officers. If you are a retired public safety officer, do not include as medical expenses any health or long-term care premiums that you elect to have paid with tax-free distributions from your retirement plan. This applies only to distributions that would otherwise be included in income.

Medicare A. If you are covered under social security (or if you are a government employee who paid Medicare tax), you are enrolled in Medicare A. The payroll tax paid for Medicare A is not a medical expense.

If you are not covered under social security (or were not a government employee who paid Medicare tax), you can voluntarily enroll in Medicare A. In this situation you can include the premiums you paid for Medicare A as a medical expense.

Medicare B. Medicare B is supplemental medical insurance. Premiums you pay for Medicare B are a medical expense. Check the information you received from the Social Security Administration to find out your premium.

Medicare D. Medicare D is a voluntary prescription drug insurance program for persons with Medicare A or B. You can include as a medical expense premiums you pay for Medicare D.

Prepaid insurance premiums. Premiums you pay before you are age 65 for insurance for medical care for yourself, your spouse, or your dependents after you reach age 65 are medical care expenses in the year paid if they are:

- Payable in equal yearly installments, or more often, and
- Payable for at least 10 years, or until you reach age 65 (but not for less than 5 years).

Unused sick leave used to pay premiums. You must include in gross income cash payments you receive at the time of retirement for unused sick leave. You also must include in gross income the value of unused sick leave that, at your option, your employer applies to the cost of your continuing participation in your employer's health plan after you retire. You can include this cost of continuing participation in the health plan as a medical expense.

If you participate in a health plan where your employer automatically applies the value of unused sick leave to the cost of your continuing participation in the health plan (and you do not have the option to receive cash), do not include the value of the unused sick leave in gross income. You cannot include this cost of continuing participation in that health plan as a medical expense.

Meals and Lodging

You can include in medical expenses the cost of meals and lodging at a hospital or similar institution if a principal reason for being there is to get medical care. See *Nursing home*, later.

You may be able to include in medical expenses the cost of lodging not provided in a hospital or similar institution. You can include the cost of such lodging while away from home if all of the following requirements are met.

- The lodging is primarily for and essential to medical care.
- The medical care is provided by a doctor in a licensed hospital or in a medical care facility related to, or the equivalent of, a licensed hospital.
- The lodging is not lavish or extravagant under the circumstances.
- There is no significant element of personal pleasure, recreation, or vacation in the travel away from home.

The amount you include in medical expenses for lodging cannot be more than $50 for each night for each person. You can include lodging for a person traveling with the person receiving the medical care. For example, if a parent is traveling with a sick child, up to $100 per night can be included as a medical expense for lodging. Meals are not included.

EXAMPLES

Example 1

A businessman who became ill while out of town was allowed to deduct the costs of his meals and hotel room when, due to a shortage of hospital rooms, he was required to move into a hotel. He had not recovered sufficiently to return home. The courts found that the test of deductibility was not the nature of the institution (i.e., whether it was a hospital or a similar institution) but the condition of the individual and the nature of the services.

Example 2

The parents of a mentally ill son rented an apartment to be close to the son's clinic. They were not allowed to deduct its costs because no care was received in the apartment, and the apartment had not been altered in any way to facilitate their son's treatment. Therefore, the court held that the parents had not incurred any expenses for their son's care in the apartment.

Nursing home. You can include in medical expenses the cost of medical care in a nursing home, home for the aged, or similar institution, for yourself, your spouse, or your dependents. This includes the cost of meals and lodging in the home if a principal reason for being there is to get medical care.

Do not include the cost of meals and lodging if the reason for being in the home is personal. You can, however, include in medical expenses the part of the cost that is for medical or nursing care.

Transportation

Include in medical expenses amounts paid for transportation primarily for, and essential to, medical care. You can include:

- Bus, taxi, train, or plane fares, or ambulance service,
- Transportation expenses of a parent who must go with a child who needs medical care,
- Transportation expenses of a nurse or other person who can give injections, medications, or other treatment required by a patient who is traveling to get medical care and is unable to travel alone, and
- Transportation expenses for regular visits to see a mentally ill dependent, if these visits are recommended as a part of treatment.

TAXALERT

The IRS has ruled that transportation costs and registration fees for attending a medical conference on a chronic disease suffered by a dependent are deductible medical expenses. The cost of meals and lodging cannot be deducted.

Explanation

Although the IRS has repeatedly denied any deduction for commuting expenses to get to one's place of work—even for disabled individuals—under certain circumstances, a deduction may be permitted for transportation required for medical reasons.

Example

If, at your doctor's advice, you take a job for the purposes of occupational therapy, you may deduct your commuting expenses. Because the employment is prescribed therapy, the expense of going to and from work is incurred in the course of obtaining occupational therapy and thus is deductible as medical transportation.

Explanation

The courts have, however, allowed a deduction for the costs of meals as well as lodging and transportation between a taxpayer's home and the out-of-state clinic where treatment was obtained, when the trip was made for medical reasons. The meals were considered to be part of the transportation costs. In addition, because the taxpayer's husband had to accompany his spouse on the trip, his food costs en route were also deductible.

The expenses of a move to a different climate may be deductible if the principal purpose of the move is to alleviate an illness.

TAXALERT

The Tax Court has ruled that a couple could not deduct depreciation as a medical expense for a modified van in which they transported their disabled son, who had spina bifida. The court said that depreciation is not a medical expense. They did allow the cost of necessary modifications to the van.

Car expenses. You can include out-of-pocket expenses, such as the cost of gas and oil, when you use your car for medical reasons. You cannot include depreciation, insurance, general repair, or maintenance expenses.

If you do not want to use your actual expenses for 2011, you can use a standard medical mileage rate of 19 cents a mile from January 1, 2011, through June 30, 2011, and 23.5 cents per mile from July 1, 2011, through December 31, 2011.

You can also include parking fees and tolls. You can add these fees and tolls to your medical expenses whether you use actual expenses or use the standard mileage rate.

Example. Bill Jones drove 2,800 miles for medical reasons during the first 6 months of the year. He spent $500 for gas, $30 for oil, and $100 for tolls and parking. He wants to figure the amount he can include in medical expenses both ways to see which gives him the greater deduction.

He figures the actual expenses first. He adds the $500 for gas, the $30 for oil, and the $100 for tolls and parking for a total of $630.

He then figures the standard mileage amount. He multiplies the 2,800 miles by 19 cents a mile for a total of $532. He then adds the $100 in tolls and parking for a total of $632.

Bill includes the $632 of car expenses with his other medical expenses for the year because the $632 is more than the $630 he figured using actual expenses.

Transportation expenses you cannot include. You cannot include in medical expenses the cost of transportation expenses in the following situations.

- Going to and from work, even if your condition requires an unusual means of transportation.
- Travel for purely personal reasons to another city for an operation or other medical care.
- Travel that is merely for the general improvement of one's health.
- The costs of operating a specially equipped car for other than medical reasons.

Disabled Dependent Care Expenses

Some disabled dependent care expenses may qualify as either:

- Medical expenses or
- Work-related expenses for purposes of taking a credit for dependent care. (See chapter 33.)

You can choose to apply them either way as long as you do not use the same expenses to claim both a credit and a medical expense deduction.

EXPLANATION

Special care for persons with disabilities. The costs of sending a person with a mental or physical disability to a special school or home, including certain advance payments for lifetime care, may be included in medical expenses. See Publication 502, *Medical and Dental Expenses*, for more information about medical care expenses for a person with disabilities. Enter the amount you paid for special care on line 1, Schedule A (Form 1040).

The distinguishing characteristic of a special school is the content of its curriculum, which must be designed to enable the student to compensate for or overcome a disability in order to prepare him or her for future normal education and living. Thus, any expenses for therapy that helps your child's adaptation are deductible medical expenses. In addition, the expenses of your child's schooling at a "special school" for mentally or physically disabled individuals are deductible (including the cost of an ordinary education) if the resources of the school are the reason for your child's presence and the educational services provided are rendered only as an incident to the medical care provided. For instance, schools that provide special services for children with mental and/or physical disabilities, such as schools for the teaching of Braille or lip reading, are special schools because the primary purpose of the schools is alleviating or treating a physical disability. Similarly, schools with special programs for treating severe learning, mental, psychological, or emotional disorders or dyslexia are special schools. The curriculum of a special school may include some ordinary education, but this must be incidental to the primary purpose of the school.

If a person with disabilities attends a school that is not a special school, only those costs that are specifically attributable to medical care are deductible expenses. A school that offers small classes and individual attention does not qualify as a special school.

Example

In addition to the regular tuition for a private school, the parents of a disabled child paid a special fee for a language development program designed to help students with learning disabilities. Although no deduction was allowed for the regular tuition, the cost of the special course was deductible as a medical expense.

However, if an ordinary school is willing to develop a special program that meets your child's needs, the school will qualify as a special school, since the determination of whether a school is a special school is made on the basis of your child's curriculum, not the curriculum of the school as a whole.

How Do You Treat Reimbursements?

You can include in medical expenses only those amounts paid during the taxable year for which you received no insurance or other reimbursement.

Insurance Reimbursement

You must reduce your total medical expenses for the year by all reimbursements for medical expenses that you receive from insurance or other sources during the year. This includes payments from Medicare.

Even if a policy provides reimbursement for only certain specific medical expenses, you must use amounts you receive from that policy to reduce your total medical expenses, including those it does not provide reimbursement for.

Example. You have insurance policies that cover your hospital and doctors' bills but not your nursing bills. The insurance you receive for the hospital and doctors' bills is more than their charges. In figuring your medical deduction, you must reduce the total amount you spent for medical care by the total amount of insurance you received, even if the policies do not cover some of your medical expenses.

Health reimbursement arrangement (HRA). A health reimbursement arrangement is an employer-funded plan that reimburses employees for medical care expenses and allows unused amounts to be carried forward. An HRA is funded solely by the employer and the reimbursements for medical expenses, up to a maximum dollar amount for a coverage period, are not included in your income.

Other reimbursements. Generally, you do not reduce medical expenses by payments you receive for:

- Permanent loss or loss of use of a member or function of the body (loss of limb, sight, hearing, etc.) or disfigurement to the extent the payment is based on the nature of the injury without regard to the amount of time lost from work, or
- Loss of earnings.

You must, however, reduce your medical expenses by any part of these payments that is designated for medical costs. See How Do You Figure and Report the Deduction on Your Tax Return, later.

For how to treat damages received for personal injury or sickness, see Damages for Personal Injuries, later.

You do not have a medical deduction if you are reimbursed for all of your medical expenses for the year.

Excess reimbursement. If you are reimbursed more than your medical expenses, you may have to include the excess in income. You may want to use Figure 22-A to help you decide if any of your reimbursement is taxable.

Figure 22-A. **Is Your Excess Medical Reimbursement Taxable?**

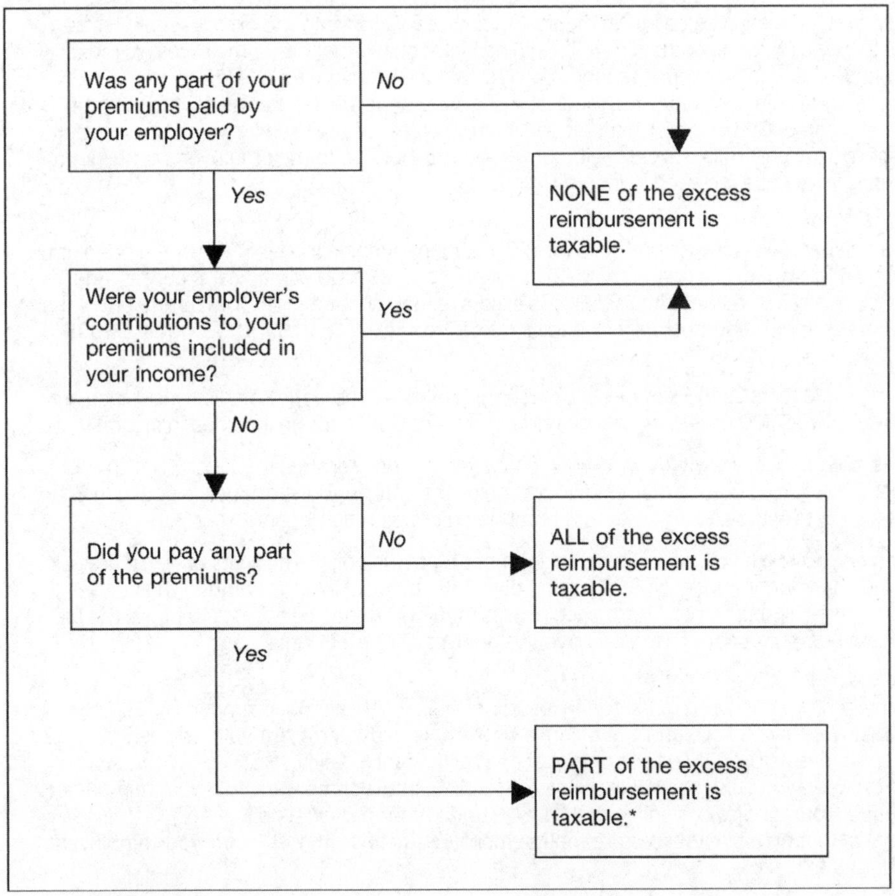

*See Premiums paid by you and your employer in this chapter.

Premiums paid by you. If you pay either the entire premium for your medical insurance or all of the costs of a plan similar to medical insurance and your insurance payments or other reimbursements are more than your total medical expenses for the year, you have an excess reimbursement. Generally, you do not include the excess reimbursement in your gross income.

Premiums paid by you and your employer. If both you and your employer contribute to your medical insurance plan and your employer's contributions are not included in your gross income, you must include in your gross income the part of your excess reimbursement that is from your employer's contribution.

EXPLANATION

You can figure the percentage of the excess reimbursement you must include in gross income using the following formula.

$$\frac{\text{Amount paid by employer}}{\text{Total annual cost of policy}} = \text{Percent of excess reimbursement that is taxable}$$

Example

You are covered by your employer's medical insurance policy. The annual premium is $2,000. Your employer pays $600 of that amount and the balance of $1,400 is taken out of your wages. The part of any excess reimbursement you receive under the policy that is from your employer's contributions is figured as follows:

$$\frac{\$600}{\$2000} = 30\%$$

You must include in your gross income 30% (.30) of any excess reimbursement you received for medical expenses under the policy.

Insurance reimbursements. Reimbursements from insurance or other sources received during the year in which the medical expense is paid reduce the medical deduction to the extent of the reimbursement.

If total reimbursements exceed total medical expenses for the year, the excess reimbursement may have to be included in income. The determining factor of whether or not the excess reimbursement has to be included in income depends on who paid the premium for the insurance policy.

If you pay the entire premium for medical insurance, none of the excess reimbursement is includible in income. On the other hand, if you share the cost of the premium with, for example, your employer, the part of the excess reimbursement attributable to the employer's contribution to the premium must be included in income.

Example 1

John's annual medical insurance premium is $3,000. John's employer pays $900 of the premium, and John pays $2,100 of the premium. In 2011, John incurs $5,000 of medical expenses, and his insurance company reimburses him $5,500, an excess reimbursement of $500. The amount of the excess reimbursement that must be included in John's income is $150 ($900/$3,000 × $500).

Example 2

Assume the same facts as in Example 1, except John pays for the entire medical insurance premium himself. The $500 excess insurance reimbursement would not be included in income.

Premiums paid by your employer. If your employer or your former employer pays the total cost of your medical insurance plan and your employer's contributions are not included in your income, you must report all of your excess reimbursement as other income.

More than one policy. If you are covered under more than one policy, the costs of which are paid by both you and your employer, you must first divide the medical expense among the policies to figure the excess reimbursement from each policy. Then divide the policy costs to figure the part of any excess reimbursement that is from your employer's contribution.

Example

You are covered by your employer's health insurance policy. The annual premium is $1,200.

Your employer pays $300, and the balance of $900 is deducted from your wages. You also paid the entire premium ($250) for a personal health insurance policy.

During the year, you paid medical expenses of $3,600. In the same year, you were reimbursed $2,400 under your employer's policy and $1,600 under your personal policy.

You figure the part of any excess reimbursement you receive that is from your employer's contribution as follows:

Step 1.

Reimbursement from employer's policy	$2,400
Reimbursement from your policy	1,600
Total reimbursement	**$4,000**
Amount of medical expenses from your policy [($1,600 ÷ $4,000) × $3,600 total medical expenses]	$1,440
Amount of medical expenses from your employer's policy [($2,400 – $4,000) ÷ $3,600 total medical expenses]	2,160
Total medical expenses	**$3,600**
Excess reimbursement from your employer's policy ($2,400 – $2,160)	$240

Step 2.

Because both you and your employer contributed to the cost of this policy, you must divide the cost to determine the excess reimbursement from your employer's contribution.

Employer's contribution in relation to the annual cost of the policy ($300 ÷ $1,200)	25%
Amount to report as other income on line 21, Form 1040 (25% × $240)	**$60**

See Publication 502 to figure the amount of the excess reimbursement you must include in gross income.

Reimbursement in a later year. If you are reimbursed in a later year for medical expenses you deducted in an earlier year, you generally must report the reimbursement as income up to the amount you previously deducted as medical expenses.

However, do not report as income the amount of reimbursement you received up to the amount of your medical deductions that did not reduce your tax for the earlier year. For more information about the recovery of an amount that you claimed as an itemized deduction in an earlier year, see *Itemized Deduction Recoveries* in chapter 12.

EXAMPLE

John pays $1,800 and his employer pays $600 toward the $2,400 annual premium for health insurance policy No. 1. Additionally, John pays the entire premium, $500, for health insurance policy No. 2. During 2011, John paid $7,200 of medical expenses and in the same year was reimbursed $5,000 under the first policy and $3,000 under the second policy.

The portion of excess reimbursement attributable to the employer's contribution is computed as follows:

Reimbursement from policy No. 1	$5,000
Reimbursement from policy No. 2	3,000
Total reimbursement	**$8,000**
Amount of reimbursed medical expenses from policy No. 1 ($5,000/$8,000 × $7,200 total medical expenses)	$4,500
Amount of reimbursed medical expenses from policy No. 2 ($3,000/$8,000 × $7,200 total medical expenses)	2,700
Total medical expenses	**$7,200**
Excess reimbursement from policy No. 1 ($5,000 – $4,500)	$500

The employer's contribution to the annual cost of policy No. 1 is 25% ($600/$2,400). Consequently, John must include $125 in income for 2011 ($500 × 25%).

None of the excess reimbursement from policy No. 2, $300 ($3,000 - $2,700), must be included in income, because John paid the entire premium of the policy.

Medical expenses not deducted. If you did not deduct a medical expense in the year you paid it because your medical expenses were not more than 7.5% of your AGI, or because you did not itemize deductions, do not include the reimbursement up to the amount of the expense in income. However, if the reimbursement is more than the expense, see *Excess reimbursement,* earlier.

Example. Last year, you had medical expenses of $500. You cannot deduct the $500 because it is less than 7.5% of your AGI. If, in a later year, you are reimbursed for any of the $500 in medical expenses, you do not include the amount reimbursed in your gross income.

Damages for Personal Injuries

If you receive an amount in settlement of a personal injury suit, part of that award may be for medical expenses that you deducted in an earlier year. If it is, you must include that part in your income in the year you receive it to the extent it reduced your taxable income in the earlier year. See *Reimbursement in a Later Year,* discussed under *How Do You Treat Reimbursements,* earlier.

Future medical expenses. If you receive an amount in settlement of a damage suit for personal injuries, part of that award may be for future medical expenses. If it is, you must reduce any future medical expenses for these injuries until the amount you received has been completely used.

How Do You Figure and Report the Deduction on Your Tax Return?

Once you have determined which medical expenses you can include, you figure and report the deduction on your tax return.

What Tax Form Do You Use?

You figure your medical expense deduction on lines 1–4 of Schedule A, Form 1040. You cannot claim medical expenses on Form 1040A, or Form 1040EZ. If you need more information on itemized deductions or you are not sure if you can itemize, see chapters 20 and 29.

Enter the amount you paid for medical and dental expenses on line 1, Schedule A (Form 1040). This should be your expenses that were not reimbursed by insurance or any other sources.

You can deduct only the amount of your medical and dental expenses that is more than 7.5% of your AGI shown on line 38, Form 1040. For an example, see the partial Schedule A, later.

Impairment-Related Work Expenses

If you are a person with a disability, you can take a business deduction for expenses that are necessary for you to be able to work. If you take a business deduction for these impairment-related work expenses, they are not subject to the 7.5% limit that applies to medical expenses.

You have a disability if you have:

- A physical or mental disability (for example, blindness or deafness) that functionally limits your being employed, or
- A physical or mental impairment (for example, a sight or hearing impairment) that substantially limits one or more of your major life activities, such as performing manual tasks, walking, speaking, breathing, learning, or working.

Impairment-related expenses defined. Impairment-related expenses are those ordinary and necessary business expenses that are:

- Necessary for you to do your work satisfactorily,
- For goods and services not required or used, other than incidentally, in your personal activities, and
- Not specifically covered under other income tax laws.

Where to report. If you are self-employed, deduct the business expenses on the appropriate form (Schedule C, C-EZ, E, or F) used to report your business income and expenses.

If you are an employee, complete Form 2106, Employee Business Expenses, or Form 2106-EZ, Unreimbursed Employee Business Expenses. Enter on Schedule A (Form 1040), line 28, that part of the amount on Form 2106, line 10, or Form 2106-EZ, line 6, that is related to your impairment. Enter the amount that is unrelated to your impairment on Schedule A (Form 1040), line 21. Your impairment-related work expenses are not subject to the 2%-of-adjusted-gross-income limit that applies to other employee business expenses.

Example. You are blind. You must use a reader to do your work. You use the reader both during your regular working hours at your place of work and outside your regular working hours away from your place of work. The reader's services are only for your work. You can deduct your expenses for the reader as business expenses.

SCHEDULE A (Form 1040) Department of the Treasury Internal Revenue Service (99)	Itemized Deductions ▶ Attach to Form 1040. ▶ See Instructions for Schedule A (Form 1040).	OMB No. 1545-0074 2011 Attachment Sequence No. 07
Name(s) shown on Form 1040 Bill and Helen Jones		Your social security number 000-00-0000

Medical and Dental Expenses	**Caution.** Do not include expenses reimbursed or paid by others.				
	1 Medical and dental expenses (see page A-1)	1	3,434		
	2 Enter amount from Form 1040, line 38 [2] 33,000				
	3 Multiply line 2 by 7.5% (.075)	3	2,475		
	4 Subtract line 3 from line 1. If line 3 is more than line 1, enter -0-			4	959

TAXSAVER

While most miscellaneous itemized deductions are only allowed to the extent that the aggregate of such deductions exceeds 2% of your adjusted gross income, "impairment-related work expenses" are not subject to this limitation.

Example 1

You are confined to a wheelchair. Sometimes you must go out of town on business. Your friend or spouse goes with you to help with such things as carrying your luggage or getting up steps. You do not pay your helper a salary, but you do pay for your helper's travel, meals, and lodging while on such trips. You have learned how to take care of yourself and to do your job in your hometown without a helper. Because the expenses for the transportation, meals, and lodging of your helper are directly related to doing your job, you may deduct them as miscellaneous deductions on Form 1040.

Example 2

Assume the same facts as in Example 1, except you are dependent on your friend's help at home as well as while traveling on business. The expenses of the friend are medical expenses, not business expenses.

If, in Example 2, your spouse goes with you on the out-of-town business trips, you may deduct as medical expenses only the out-of-pocket costs for your spouse's transportation. Expenses for your spouse's meals and lodging are not deductible.

Health Insurance Costs for Self-Employed Persons

If you were self-employed and had a net profit for the year, you may be able to deduct, as an adjustment to income, amounts paid for medical and qualified long-term care insurance on behalf of yourself, your spouse, and *(text intentionally omitted)* your children who were under age 27 at the end of 2011, even if the child was not your dependent. For this purpose, you were self-employed if you were a general partner (or a limited partner receiving guaranteed payments) or you received wages from an S corporation in which you were more than a 2% shareholder.

TAXALERT

If you are self-employed and have a net profit for the year, you can deduct up to 100% of the amount you pay for health insurance on behalf of yourself, your spouse, and children under the age of 27 as of the end of 2011, even if they are not dependents. A child includes your son, daughter, stepchild, adopted child, or foster child. A foster child is any child placed with you by an authorized placement agency or by judgment, decree, or other order of any court of competent jurisdiction. This deduction cannot be greater than your net earnings from your trade or business.

You may also be able to deduct premiums if you received wages from an S corporation in which you were more than a 2% shareholder. Eligible premiums will be shown in box 14 of your W-2.

TAXALERT

For 2010 only, you were allowed to reduce your self-employment income by the amount of the self-employed health insurance deduction for purposes of calculating self-employment tax for 2010. This is not available for 2011. See Schedule SE, Self-Employment Tax, for more information.

The insurance plan must be established under your trade or business and the deduction cannot be more than your earned income from that trade or business.

You cannot deduct payments for medical insurance for any month in which you were eligible to participate in a health plan subsidized by your employer, your spouse's employer, or, *(text intentionally omitted)* an employer of your dependent or your child under age 27 at the end of 2011. You cannot deduct payments for a qualified long-term care insurance contract for any month in which you were eligible to participate in a long-term care insurance plan subsidized by your employer or your spouse's employer.

Medicare premiums you voluntarily pay to obtain insurance that is similar to qualifying private health insurance can be used to figure the deduction. If you previously filed a return without using Medicare premiums to figure the deduction, you can file an amended return to refigure the deduction. For more information, see Form 1040X, Amended U.S. Individual Income Tax Return.

If you qualify to take the deduction, use the Self-Employed Health Insurance Deduction Worksheet in the Form 1040 instructions to figure the amount you can deduct. But if any of the following applies, do not use that worksheet.

- You had more than one source of income subject to self-employment tax.
- You file Form 2555, Foreign Earned Income, or Form 2555-EZ, Foreign Earned Income Exclusion.
- You are using amounts paid for qualified long-term care insurance to figure the deduction.

If you cannot use the worksheet in the Form 1040 instructions, use the worksheet in Publication 535, *Business Expenses*, to figure your deduction.

Note. When figuring the amount you can deduct for insurance premiums, do not include any advance payments shown in box 1 of Form 1099-H, Health Coverage Tax Credit (HCTC) Advance Payments. Also, if you are claiming the health coverage tax credit, subtract the amount shown on Form 8885, line 4, from the total insurance premiums you paid.

Also, do not include amounts paid for health insurance coverage with retirement plan distributions that were tax-free because you are a retired public safety officer.

Where to report. You take this deduction on Form 1040, line 29. If you itemize your deductions and do not claim 100% of your self-employed health insurance on line 29, include any remaining premiums with all other medical care expenses on Schedule A (Form 1040), subject to the 7.5% limit. See chapter 6 of Publication 535, *Business Expenses*, for more information.

TAXORGANIZER

Records you should keep:

- Receipts and canceled checks evidencing payment of medical expenses
- A permanent record of the name and address of the provider of medical care, the amount of the expenses, and the date paid
- Documentation that the expense was to obtain medical treatment, that medicine was prescribed, and that the expense was incurred on a doctor's recommendation

Chapter 23

Taxes you may deduct

ey.com/EYTaxGuide

Note

IRS Publication 17 (*Your Federal Income Tax*) has been updated by Ernst & Young LLP for 2011. Dates and dollar amounts shown are for 2011. Underlined type is used to indicate where IRS text has been updated. Places where text has been removed are indicated by the sentence: *Text intentionally omitted*.

ey.com/EYTaxGuide

Ernst & Young LLP will update the *Ernst & Young Tax Guide 2012* website with relevant taxpayer information as it becomes available. You can also sign up for email alerts to let you know when changes have been made.

Introduction

You have been allowed to deduct taxes you pay—other than your federal income tax—ever since the nation's income tax was first enacted. The underlying theory is that taxes are an involuntary expenditure and therefore should be deducted from an individual's gross income. But there is a practical consideration as well: The payment of state and local taxes makes it more difficult for an individual to meet the federal tax bill.

For tax year 2011, you can also choose to deduct your state and local *sales* taxes instead of deducting state and local income taxes. This choice is especially meaningful for people who live in states that impose no state income tax, such as Alaska, Florida, Nevada, South Dakota, Texas, Washington, and Wyoming. However, unless Congress acts, this deduction is set to expire at the end of 2011.

Taxes you pay to a foreign government may also be deducted. These and other taxes that you may deduct from your federal income tax are described in this chapter.

Prior to 2010, itemized deductions were subject to certain limitations if your adjusted gross income exceeded certain amounts (for 2009, this amount was $166,800; $83,400 if married filing separately). But the itemized deduction phaseout has been temporarily repealed and higher-income taxpayers do not have to reduce their total itemized deductions for 2011 or 2012. However, unless Congress acts, the old phaseout rule is scheduled to return beginning in 2013.

What's New

Itemized deductions phaseout not in effect for 2011. For 2011, taxpayers with adjusted gross income above a certain amount will not lose part of their deduction for itemized deductions.

TAXALERT

As it was in 2010, for tax years 2011 and 2012 the itemized deduction phaseout is repealed and higher-income taxpayers will not have to reduce their total itemized deductions based on an adjusted gross income (AGI) limitation. (Limitations on specific itemized deductions such as medical expenses, miscellaneous deductions, and casualty losses still apply.) After 2012, the old phaseout rule, which limited the amount of your itemized deductions if your adjusted gross income exceeded certain amounts, returns.

Deduction for general sales taxes extended. The deduction for state and local general sales taxes that you can elect to take as an itemized deduction on Schedule A (Form 1040) instead of state and local income taxes was extended through 2011.

Tax Breaks and Deductions You Can Use Checklist

Taxes You May Deduct. You can claim most of the taxes you pay to state and local governments as itemized deductions. These include income or sales taxes (you have to choose between these), real estate taxes, and certain personal property taxes.

Sales Taxes. You can elect to deduct either your state and local income taxes or state and local sales taxes paid in 2011, but not both. If you decide to deduct your sales taxes, you can calculate the amount using IRS-provided tables based on your income and where you live. Alternatively, you can base your deduction on the actual sales taxes you paid. In that case, you should retain all your records of taxable purchases for the year. The availability of the deduction for state and local sales taxes expires at the end of 2011 unless Congress acts to extend it.

TAXALERT

The option to deduct state and local sales taxes expires at the end of 2011 unless Congress acts to extend it.

This chapter discusses which taxes you can deduct if you itemize deductions on Schedule A (Form 1040). It also explains which taxes you can deduct on other schedules or forms and which taxes you cannot deduct.

This chapter covers the following topics.

- Income taxes (federal, state, local, and foreign).
- General sales taxes (state and local).
- Real estate taxes (state, local, and foreign).
- Personal property taxes (state and local).
- Taxes and fees you cannot deduct.

Use Table 23-1 as a guide to determine which taxes you can deduct.

The end of the chapter contains a section that explains which forms you use to deduct different types of taxes.

Business taxes. You can deduct certain taxes only if they are ordinary and necessary expenses of your trade or business or of producing income. For information on these taxes, see Publication 535, *Business Expenses*.

State or local taxes. These are taxes imposed by the 50 states, U.S. possessions, or any of their political subdivisions (such as a county or city), or by the District of Columbia.

Indian tribal government. An Indian tribal government recognized by the Secretary of the Treasury as performing substantial government functions will be treated as a state for purposes of claiming a deduction for taxes. Income taxes, real estate taxes, and personal property taxes imposed by that Indian tribal government (or by any of its subdivisions that are treated as political subdivisions of a state) are deductible.

General sales taxes. These are taxes imposed at one rate on retail sales of a broad range of classes of items.

Foreign taxes. These are taxes imposed by a foreign country or any of its political subdivisions.

Useful Items

You may want to see:

Publication

- □ **514** Foreign Tax Credit for Individuals
- □ **530** Tax Information for Homeowners

Form (and Instructions)

- □ **Schedule A (Form 1040)** Itemized Deductions
- □ **Schedule E (Form 1040)** Supplemental Income and Loss
- □ **1116** Foreign Tax Credit

Tests To Deduct Any Tax

The following two tests must be met for you to deduct any tax.

- The tax must be imposed on you.
- You must pay the tax during your tax year.

The tax must be imposed on you. Generally, you can deduct only taxes imposed on you.

Generally, you can deduct property taxes only if you are an owner of the property. If your spouse owns the property and pays the real estate taxes, the taxes are deductible on your spouse's separate return or on your joint return.

You must pay the tax during your tax year. If you are a cash basis taxpayer, you can deduct only those taxes you actually paid during your tax year. If you pay your taxes by check, the day you mail or deliver the check is the date of payment, provided the check is honored by the financial institution. If you use a pay-by-phone account (such as a credit card or electronic funds withdrawal), the date reported on the statement of the financial institution showing when payment was made is the date of payment. If you contest a tax liability and are a cash basis taxpayer, you can deduct the tax

Table 23-1. **Which Taxes Can You Deduct?**

Type of Tax	You Can Deduct	You Cannot Deduct
Fees and Charges	Fees and charges that are expenses of your trade or business or of producing income.	Fees and charges that are not expenses of your trade or business or of producing income, such as fees for driver's licenses, car inspections, parking, or charges for water bills (see *Taxes and Fees You Cannot Deduct*). Fines and penalties.
General Sales Taxes *Text intentionally omitted.*	State and local general sales taxes, including compensating use taxes. *Text intentionally omitted.*	State and local income taxes if you choose to deduct state and local general sales taxes. *Text intentionally omitted.*
Income Taxes	State and local income taxes if higher than state and local sales tax. Foreign income taxes. Employee contributions to state funds listed under *Contributions to state benefit funds*.	Federal income taxes. Employee contributions to private or voluntary disability plans.
Other Taxes	Taxes that are expenses of your trade or business. Taxes on property producing rent or royalty income. Occupational taxes. See chapter 28. One-half of self-employment tax paid.	Federal excise taxes, such as tax on gasoline, that are not expenses of your trade or business or of producing income. Per capita taxes.
Personal Property Taxes	State and local personal property taxes.	Customs duties that are not expenses of your trade or business or of producing income.
Real Estate Taxes	State and local real estate taxes. Foreign real estate taxes. Tenant's share of real estate taxes paid by cooperative housing corporation.	Foreign real estate taxes, if you take the standard deduction and the real property is not used in your trade or business or does not produce rental income. Real estate taxes that are treated as imposed on someone else (see *Division of real estate taxes between buyers and sellers*). Taxes for local benefits (with exceptions). See *Real Estate-Related Items You Cannot Deduct*. Trash and garbage pickup fees (with exceptions). See *Real Estate-Related Items You Cannot Deduct*. Rent increase due to higher real estate taxes. Homeowners' association charges.

only in the year you actually pay it (or transfer money or other property to provide for satisfaction of the contested liability). See Publication 538, *Accounting Periods and Methods*, for details.

If you use an accrual method of accounting, see Publication 538 for more information.

Income Taxes

This section discusses the deductibility of state and local income taxes (including employee contributions to state benefit funds) and foreign income taxes.

State and Local Income Taxes

You can deduct state and local income taxes. However, you can elect to deduct state and local general sales taxes instead of state and local income taxes. But you cannot deduct both taxes in the same year.

Exception. You cannot deduct state and local income taxes you pay on income that is exempt from federal income tax, unless the exempt income is interest income. For example, you cannot deduct the part of a state's income tax that is on a cost-of-living allowance exempt from federal income tax.

TAXALERT

The option to deduct state and local sales taxes expires at the end of 2011 unless Congress acts to extend it.

Text intentionally omitted.

What To Deduct

Your deduction may be for withheld taxes, estimated tax payments, or other tax payments as follows.

Withheld taxes. You can deduct state and local income taxes withheld from your salary in the year they are withheld. For 2011, these taxes will be shown in boxes 17 and 19 of your Form W-2. You may also have state or local income tax withheld on Form W-2G (box 14), Form 1099-MISC (box 16), or Form 1099-R (boxes 12 and 15).

Estimated tax payments. You can deduct estimated tax payments you made during the year to a state or local government. However, you must have a reasonable basis for making the estimated tax payments. Any estimated state or local tax payments that are not made in good faith at the time of payment are not deductible. For example, you made an estimated state income tax payment. However, the estimate of your state tax liability shows that you will get a refund of the full amount of your estimated payment. You had no reasonable basis to believe you had any additional liability for state income taxes and you cannot deduct the estimated tax payment.

Refund applied to taxes. You can deduct any part of a refund of prior-year state or local income taxes that you chose to have credited to your 2011 estimated state or local income taxes. Do not reduce your deduction by either of the following items.

- Any state or local income tax refund (or credit) you expect to receive for 2011.
- Any refund of (or credit for) prior-year state and local income taxes you actually received in 2011.

However, part or all of this refund (or credit) may be taxable. See *Refund (or credit) of state or local income taxes*, later.

EXPLANATION

Generally, all state, county, city, and municipal income taxes are deductible in the year in which you pay them—including the state and local taxes applicable to interest income that is not taxable at the federal level.

Example

You have the following income:

Salary	$18,000
Municipal bond income (exempt from federal tax but taxable by your state)	$2,000
Total income	$20,000

If your state income tax is $1,000, then 10%, or $100, is attributable to the federally exempt income. Nevertheless, you may deduct the entire $1,000 on your federal return.

TAXALERT

Municipal bonds. Municipal bonds issued by your state frequently are not subject to your state's income tax, whereas obligations for other states usually are subject to the state tax. Municipal bonds issued by Puerto Rico, Guam, Virgin Islands, Northern Mariana Islands, and American Samoa are exempt from state income tax for all investors regardless of their state of residence.

Be sure to use your effective state rate after the federal tax benefit when you are deciding between investing in a state tax-exempt municipal bond or an obligation that is subject to your state's tax.

TAX PLANNER

Deducting expenses. If you deduct an expense when you pay it rather than when the expense is incurred, as most people do, you may deduct the following:

1. State income tax withheld from salary in 2011
2. State **estimated tax** payments made in 2011 for 2011
3. Fourth-quarter state estimated tax payment for 2010 made in January 2011

4. State income tax paid with your 2010 state income tax return filed in 2011
5. State income tax paid in 2011 with a request for a filing extension for your 2010 state income tax return
6. Additional state income tax paid in 2011 as a result of an **audit** or an amended return.

In most states, the fourth-quarter estimated tax payment is due in January of the following year. A January 2012 payment for the last quarter of 2011 is deductible on your 2012 return. If, however, the payment is made by December 31, 2011, it is deductible on your 2011 return. If you can accelerate your payment by a few weeks, you can accelerate your **deduction** for state income taxes by a full year.

TAXALERT

Taxpayers have been denied deductions when state estimated tax payments made on December 31 were substantially in excess of their actual tax liability. To be assured of a deduction, you must be able to prove that the tax payment was based on a reasonable estimate of your actual tax bill. Also, be sure not to prepay your state taxes if you're in an alternative minimum tax position. See chapter 31, *How to figure your tax*.

TAXORGANIZER

You should keep canceled checks for payments of state estimated income tax (or any deductible tax) in order to support your claim for deductible taxes.

Separate federal returns. If you and your spouse file separate state, local, and federal income tax returns, you each can deduct on your federal return only the amount of your own state and local income tax that you paid during the tax year.

Joint state and local returns. If you and your spouse file joint state and local returns and separate federal returns, each of you can deduct on your separate federal return a part of the total state and local income taxes paid during the tax year. You can deduct only the amount of the total taxes that is proportionate to your gross income compared to the combined gross income of you and your spouse. However, you cannot deduct more than the amount you actually paid during the year. You can avoid this calculation if you and your spouse are jointly and individually liable for the full amount of the state and local income taxes. If so, you and your spouse can deduct on your separate federal returns the amount you each actually paid.

Joint federal return. If you file a joint federal return, you can deduct the total of the state and local income taxes both of you paid.

TAXPLANNER

If you plan on filing a joint state return with your spouse and separate federal returns, and if you are both jointly and individually liable for the full amount of the state tax, the state tax should be paid, to the extent possible, by the person in the higher separate federal income tax bracket. (For advice on filing jointly or separately, see chapter 2, *Filing status*.)

Contributions to state benefit funds. As an employee, you can deduct mandatory contributions to state benefit funds withheld from your wages that provide protection against loss of wages. For example, certain states require employees to make contributions to state funds providing disability or unemployment insurance benefits. Mandatory payments made to the following state benefit funds are deductible as state income taxes on Schedule A (Form 1040), line 5a.

- Alaska Unemployment Compensation Fund.
- California Nonoccupational Disability Benefit Fund.
- New Jersey Nonoccupational Disability Benefit Fund.
- New Jersey Unemployment Compensation Fund.
- New York Nonoccupational Disability Benefit Fund.
- Pennsylvania Unemployment Compensation Fund.
- Rhode Island Temporary Disability Benefit Fund.
- Washington State Supplemental Workmen's Compensation Fund.

Caution

Employee contributions to private or voluntary disability plans are not deductible.

Refund (or credit) of state or local income taxes. If you receive a refund of (or credit for) state or local income taxes in a year after the year in which you paid them, you may have to include the refund in income on Form 1040, line 10, in the year you receive it. This includes refunds resulting from taxes that were overwithheld, applied from a prior year return, not figured correctly, or figured again because of an amended return. If you did not itemize your deductions in the previous year, do not include the refund in income. If you deducted the taxes in the previous year, include all or part of the refund on Form 1040, line 10, in the year you receive the refund. For a discussion of how much to include, see Recoveries in chapter 12.

EXPLANATION

If you received a refund of taxes that you paid in an earlier year, such as 2009 or 2010, do not use that refund to reduce your deduction for taxes that you paid during 2011.

However, if you receive a refund of taxes in the same year in which you paid the taxes, you would use the refund to reduce your deduction for taxes.

Example

You paid $4,000 of estimated state income taxes for 2010 in four equal payments. You made your fourth payment in January 2011. You were not subject to state income tax withholding in 2010. In 2011, you received a $400 tax refund based on your 2010 state income tax return. One hundred dollars (25% of $400) of the refund is attributable to your 2011 payment. Your deduction for state and local income taxes paid in 2011 includes $900 ($1,000 - $100) plus any other payments you made during 2011 and any amount withheld during 2011. The amount of your state tax refund to be reported as income in 2011 would be $300 ($400 - $100).

TAXSAVER

Reducing the amount of the reported refund will reduce your adjusted gross income. If your adjusted gross income is lower, you may benefit from greater itemized deductions.

TAXPLANNER

If you subtract part of the refund from your other tax payments, the income reported by you will not match the amount reported to the IRS by the state on Form 1099-G. You may then receive a notice proposing an additional assessment of tax. You may avoid the notice by attaching an explanation to your return.

Explanation

An overpayment of state income tax that is to be credited against the estimated state tax for the following year is treated as though it were refunded to you. The overpayment may then be deducted as an estimated tax payment.

Example

Your 2010 state return showed an overpayment of $500, which you indicated was to be credited against your 2011 state estimated tax declaration. In addition, you made three quarterly state estimated tax payments of $500 each during 2011. On your 2011 Form 1040, you report a tax refund of $500 on line 10 and a deduction on Schedule A of $2,000.

TAXORGANIZER

When you receive your Form 1099-G from your state or local government, keep it as documentation of your refund.

Foreign Income Taxes

Generally, you can take either a deduction or a credit for income taxes imposed on you by a foreign country or a U.S. possession. However, you cannot take a deduction or credit for foreign income taxes paid on income that is exempt from U.S. tax under the foreign earned income exclusion or the foreign housing exclusion. For information on these exclusions, see Publication 54, *Tax Guide for U.S. Citizens and Resident Aliens Abroad.* For information on the foreign tax credit, see Publication 514.

EXPLANATION

If you have income from foreign sources, you may be required to pay foreign taxes on that income, or foreign taxes may be withheld on that income before you receive it.

TAXALERT

Since 2007, certain categories of income have been eliminated for purposes of computing the foreign tax credit limit. Income that previously fell into these eliminated categories will fall in either the passive income category or the general limitation income category. For more information, see chapter 37, *Other credits including the earned income credit,* and Publication 514, *Foreign Tax Credit for Individuals.*

TAXPLANNER

Credit for foreign taxes. It is usually better to take a credit for foreign taxes than to deduct them as itemized deductions. Credits reduce your U.S. tax on a dollar-for-dollar basis, whereas a deduction just reduces the amount of income subject to tax. However, if your foreign tax credit is limited and must be carried over to future years, you may want to consider taking a deduction now instead of waiting for a credit. See chapter 41, *U.S. citizens working abroad: Tax treatment of foreign earned income,* for more information on foreign tax credit limitations. The following example shows how a credit is usually more advantageous.

Example

You and your spouse had **adjusted gross income** of $90,000 in 2011, $20,000 of which was from foreign sources. You file a joint return and have no **dependents.** You had to pay $2,000 in foreign income taxes on interest income received from sources within a foreign country. If your itemized deductions are otherwise $11,700, your added deduction for the foreign income tax reduces your U.S. tax by $500. If, however, you choose to claim a credit for the $2,000 foreign tax, your U.S. tax is reduced by the full $2,000. Therefore, you have an additional tax benefit of $1,500 by taking the credit.

TAXORGANIZER

Your qualified payee statements (including Form 1099-INT, Form 1099-DIV, Schedule K-1 (Form 1041), Schedule K-1 (Form 1065-B), Schedule K-1 (Form 1120S), or similar substitute statements) should show amounts of foreign taxes paid on foreign passive income.

General Sales Taxes

TAXALERT

The option to deduct state and local sales taxes expires at the end of 2011 unless Congress acts to extend it.

You can elect to deduct state and local general sales taxes, instead of state and local income taxes, as an itemized deduction on Schedule A (Form 1040), line 5b. Generally, you can use either your actual expenses or the state and local sales tax tables to figure your sales tax deduction.

Actual expenses. Generally, you can deduct the actual state and local general sales taxes (including compensating use taxes) if the tax rate was the same as the general sales tax rate. However, sales taxes on food, clothing, medical supplies, and motor vehicles are deductible as a general sales tax even if the tax rate was less than the general sales tax rate. If you paid sales tax on a motor vehicle at a rate higher than the general sales tax rate, you can deduct only the amount of tax that you would have paid at the general sales tax rate on that vehicle. If you use the actual expenses method, you must have receipts to show the general sales taxes paid.

Optional sales tax tables. Instead of using your actual expenses, you can figure your state and local general sales tax deduction using the state and local sales tax tables in the Instructions for Schedule A (Form 1040). You may also be able to add the state and local general sales taxes paid on certain specified items, such as motor vehicles (purchased or leased), aircraft, boats, homes (including mobile and prefabricated homes) and home building materials. Your applicable table amount is based on the state where you live, your income, and the number of exemptions claimed on your tax return. Your income is your adjusted gross income plus any nontaxable items such as the following.

- Tax-exempt interest.
- Veterans' benefits.
- Nontaxable combat pay.
- Workers' compensation.
- Nontaxable part of social security and railroad retirement benefits.
- Nontaxable part of IRA, pension, or annuity distributions, excluding rollovers.
- Public assistance payments.

If you lived in different states during the same tax year, you must prorate your applicable table amount for each state based on the days you lived in each state. See the instructions for Schedule A (Form 1040), line 5, for details.

TAXSAVER

The election to deduct sales tax makes sense if your sales taxes are greater than your income taxes. To prove your actual sales taxes, if you don't use the Optional State Sales Tax Table amounts in the Instructions for Schedule A (Form 1040), you have to keep track of all your purchases during the year. Even if you use the Optional State Sales Tax Table amounts, you may also be able to add the state and local general sales taxes paid on certain specified items such as a motor vehicle, boat, or home. This deduction is especially useful for people who live in states with no income taxes, such as Florida, Nevada, and Texas.

Real Estate Taxes

Deductible real estate taxes are any state, local, or foreign taxes on real property levied for the general public welfare. You can deduct these taxes only if they are based on the assessed value of the real property and charged uniformly against all property under the jurisdiction of the taxing authority.

Deductible real estate taxes generally do not include taxes charged for local benefits and improvements that increase the value of the property. They also do not include itemized charges for services (such as trash collection) assessed against specific property or certain people, even if the charge is paid to the taxing authority. For more information about taxes and charges that are not deductible, see *Real Estate-Related Items You Cannot Deduct*, later.

Tenant-shareholders in a cooperative housing corporation. Generally, if you are a tenant-stockholder in a cooperative housing corporation, you can deduct the amount paid to the corporation that represents your share of the real estate taxes the corporation paid or incurred for your dwelling unit. The corporation should provide you with a statement showing your share of the taxes. For more information, see *Special Rules for Cooperatives* in Publication 530.

EXPLANATION

Generally, you may deduct only those real estate taxes assessed against property that you own.

Examples

No deduction was allowed for real estate taxes when:

- A taxpayer paid, under court order, real estate taxes on his aunt's house, in which he resided.
- A guarantor paid real estate taxes on foreclosed property.
- The executor of an estate paid real estate taxes on a residence belonging to the estate, which she was occupying.
- A tenant-shareholder in a cooperative housing corporation paid his proportionate share of real estate taxes levied on recreational facilities owned and maintained by another corporation.

- A husband paid real estate taxes on property previously transferred to his wife. He had guaranteed payment if his wife defaulted but was not otherwise obligated. He will not be able to claim a deduction unless his wife actually defaults.
- The Tax Court held that a couple could not claim deductions for real property taxes paid by the husband for property owned by the S corporations that the couple owned.
- The Tax Court has held that sons could not deduct real estate taxes they paid on a house owned by their father and uncle because they did not have a beneficial interest in the property under California law.
- You may, however, deduct real estate taxes when you have a beneficial interest in property, if the payment is made to protect that interest.

TAXORGANIZER

Real estate documents you need. You should keep a copy of your real estate tax bill in order to support your claim for the real estate tax deduction. Also, if you purchased a new house during the year, you should keep the closing statement. Typically, the closing statement will show the amount of taxes you paid to the seller at the time of the purchase.

Division of real estate taxes between buyers and sellers. If you bought or sold real estate during the year, the real estate taxes must be divided between the buyer and the seller.

The buyer and the seller must divide the real estate taxes according to the number of days in the real property tax year (the period to which the tax is imposed relates) that each owned the property. The seller is treated as paying the taxes up to, but not including, the date of sale. The buyer is treated as paying the taxes beginning with the date of sale. This applies regardless of the lien dates under local law. Generally, this information is included on the settlement statement provided at the closing.

If you (the seller) cannot deduct taxes until they are paid because you use the cash method of accounting, and the buyer of your property is personally liable for the tax, you are considered to have paid your part of the tax at the time of the sale. This lets you deduct the part of the tax to the date of sale even though you did not actually pay it. However, you must also include the amount of that tax in the selling price of the property. The buyer must include the same amount in his or her cost of the property.

You figure your deduction for taxes on each property bought or sold during the real property tax year as follows.

Worksheet 23-1. **Figuring Your Real Estate Tax Deduction** *Keep for Your Records*

1. Enter the total real estate taxes for the real property tax year	
2. Enter the number of days in the real property tax year that you owned the property	
3. Divide line 2 by 365 (for leap years, divide line 2 by 366).	
4. Multiply line 1 by line 3. This is your deduction. Enter it on Schedule A (Form 1040), line 6	

Note. Repeat steps 1 through 4 for each property you bought or sold during the real property tax year. Your total deduction is the sum of the line 4 amounts for all of the properties.

Real estate taxes for prior years. Do not divide delinquent taxes between the buyer and seller if the taxes are for any real property tax year before the one in which the property is sold. Even if the buyer agrees to pay the delinquent taxes, the buyer cannot deduct them. The buyer must add them to the cost of the property. The seller can deduct these taxes paid by the buyer. However, the seller must include them in the selling price.

Examples. The following examples illustrate how real estate taxes are divided between buyer and seller.

Example 1. Dennis and Beth White's real property tax year for both their old home and their new home is the calendar year, with payment due August 1. The tax on their old home, sold on May 7, was $620. The tax on their new home, bought on May 3, was $732. Dennis and Beth are considered to have paid a proportionate share of the real estate taxes on the old home even though they did not actually pay them to the taxing authority. On the other hand, they can claim only a proportionate share of the taxes they paid on their new property even though they paid the entire amount.

Dennis and Beth owned their old home during the real property tax year for 126 days (January 1 to May 6, the day before the sale). They figure their deduction for taxes on their old home as follows.

Worksheet 23-1. **Figuring Your Real Estate Tax Deduction–Taxes on Old Home**

1. Enter the total real estate taxes for the real property tax year	$620
2. Enter the number of days in the real property tax year that you owned the property.	126
3. Divide line 2 by 365 (for leap years, divide line 2 by 366).	.3452
4. Multiply line 1 by line 3. This is your deduction. Enter it on Schedule A (Form 1040), line 6	$214

Since the buyers of their old home paid all of the taxes, Dennis and Beth also include the $214 in the selling price of the old home. (The buyers add the $214 to their cost of the home.)

Dennis and Beth owned their new home during the real property tax year for 243 days (May 3 to December 31, including their date of purchase). They figure their deduction for taxes on their new home as follows.

Worksheet 23-1. **Figuring Your Real Estate Tax Deduction–Taxes on New Home**

1. Enter the total real estate taxes for the real property tax year	$732
2. Enter the number of days in the real property tax year that you owned the property.	243
3. Divide line 2 by 365 (for leap years, divide line 2 by 366).	.6658
4. Multiply line 1 by line 3. This is your deduction. Enter it on Schedule A (Form 1040), line 6	$487

Since Dennis and Beth paid all of the taxes on the new home, they add $245 ($732 paid less $487 deduction) to their cost of the new home. (The sellers add this $245 to their selling price and deduct the $245 as a real estate tax.)

Dennis and Beth's real estate tax deduction for their old and new homes is the sum of $214 and $487, or $701. They will enter this amount on Schedule A (Form 1040), line 6.

Example 2. George and Helen Brown bought a new home on May 3, 2011. Their real property tax year for the new home is the calendar year. Real estate taxes for 2010 were assessed in their state on January 1, 2011. The taxes became due on May 31, 2011, and October 31, 2011.

The Browns agreed to pay all taxes due after the date of purchase. Real estate taxes for 2010 were $680. They paid $340 on May 31, 2011, and $340 on October 31, 2011. These taxes were for the 2010 real property tax year. The Browns cannot deduct them since they did not own the property until 2011. Instead, they must add $680 to the cost of their new home.

In January 2012, the Browns receive their 2011 property tax statement for $752, which they will pay in 2012. The Browns owned their new home during the 2011 real property tax year for 243 days (May 3 to December 31). They will figure their 2012 deduction for taxes as follows.

Worksheet 23-1. **Figuring Your Real Estate Tax Deduction–Taxes on New Home**

1. Enter the total real estate taxes for the real property tax year	$752
2. Enter the number of days in the real property tax year that you owned the property.	243
3. Divide line 2 by 365 (for leap years, divide line 2 by 366).	.6658
4. Multiply line 1 by line 3. This is your deduction. Claim it on Schedule A (Form 1040), line 6	$501

The remaining $251 ($752 paid less $501 deduction) of taxes paid in 2012, along with the $680 paid in 2011, is added to the cost of their new home.

Because the taxes up to the date of sale are considered paid by the seller on the date of sale, the seller is entitled to a 2011 tax deduction of $931. This is the sum of the $680 for 2009 and the $251 for the 123 days the seller owned the home in 2011. The seller must also include the $931 in the selling price when he or she figures the gain or loss on the sale. The seller should contact the Browns in January 2012 to find out how much real estate tax is due for 2011.

Form 1099-S. For certain sales or exchanges of real estate, the person responsible for closing the sale (generally the settlement agent) prepares Form 1099-S, Proceeds From Real Estate Transactions, to report certain information to the IRS and to the seller of the property. Box 2 of the form is for the gross proceeds from the sale and should include the portion of the seller's real estate tax liability that the buyer will pay after the date of sale. The buyer includes these taxes in the cost basis of the property, and the seller both deducts this amount as a tax paid and includes it in the sales price of the property.

For a real estate transaction that involves a home, any real estate tax the seller paid in advance but that is the liability of the buyer appears on Form 1099-S, box 5. The buyer deducts this amount as a real estate tax, and the seller reduces his or her real estate tax deduction (or includes it in income) by the same amount. See *Refund (or rebate)*, later.

EXPLANATION

Frequently, when property is sold, the amount of the real estate taxes for the "real property tax year" is not yet known, so an allocation is made on the closing statement at the time of sale based on the tax bill for the preceding year.

If the actual real estate tax bill for the real property tax year is greater than the amount used in the original allocation, the seller is entitled to a deduction greater than that shown on the real estate closing statement. The difference between the deductible amount and the amount allocated on the closing statement is considered additional proceeds of the sale.

The buyer is entitled to deduct his or her allocable share of the actual bill. The excess of the amount that he or she pays over (1) the deductible amount and (2) the amount paid or received at the closing is added to the cost of the property.

TAXPLANNER

When to deduct real estate taxes. If the real estate taxes are actually paid after the year of the sale, the seller may deduct his or her share of the taxes either in the year of the sale or in the year in which the tax is paid, whichever produces the greatest tax advantage.

The situation is slightly different for the buyer. If the buyer is liable for payment of the tax, he or she may deduct his or her allocated share of the tax only in the year in which the payment is made. If the seller is liable for payment of the tax, the buyer may deduct his or her allocated share either in the year of the sale or in the year of payment.

Taxes placed in escrow. If your monthly mortgage payment includes an amount placed in escrow (put in the care of a third party) for real estate taxes, you may not be able to deduct the total amount placed in escrow. You can deduct only the real estate tax that the third party actually paid to the taxing authority. If the third party does not notify you of the amount of real estate tax that was paid for you, contact the third party or the taxing authority to find the proper amount to show on your return.

TAXPLANNER

When to accelerate a tax payment. Most lenders arrange for payment of taxes out of escrow accounts on the tax due date. When the due date is shortly after the end of the calendar year, it may be advantageous to accelerate the payment in order to get the deduction for payment a year earlier. The benefits of this strategy may be reduced or eliminated due to the alternative minimum tax, which does not provide for a deduction of real estate taxes.

Example

Real estate taxes of $1,200 for the year 2011 become due and payable on February 1, 2012. The taxpayer made monthly escrow payments of $100 each during 2011. If the taxes were paid from the escrow account on the February 1, 2012, due date, the $1,200 is a 2012 deduction. However, if the taxes were paid by December 31, 2011, the $1,200 is a 2011 deduction.

TAXORGANIZER

Escrow statements. Be sure to keep your yearly escrow statement, which should indicate the amount of real estate taxes paid from the escrow account.

Tenants by the entirety. If you and your spouse held property as tenants by the entirety and you file separate federal returns, each of you can deduct only the taxes each of you paid on the property.

Divorced individuals. If your divorce or separation agreement states that you must pay the real estate taxes for a home owned by you and your spouse, part of your payments may be deductible as alimony and part as real estate taxes. See *Taxes and insurance* in chapter 18 for more information.

Ministers' and military housing allowances. If you are a minister or a member of the uniformed services and receive a housing allowance that you can exclude from income, you still can deduct all of the real estate taxes you pay on your home.

Refund (or rebate). If you received a refund or rebate in 2011 of real estate taxes you paid in 2011, you must reduce your deduction by the amount refunded to you. If you received a refund or rebate in 2011 of real estate taxes you deducted in an earlier year (either as an itemized deduction or an increase to your standard deduction), you generally must include the refund or rebate in income in the year you receive it. However, the amount you include in income is limited to the amount of the deduction that reduced your tax in the earlier year. For more information, see *Recoveries* in chapter 12.

Real Estate-Related Items You Cannot Deduct

Payments for the following items generally are not deductible as real estate taxes.

- Taxes for local benefits.
- Itemized charges for services (such as trash and garbage pickup fees).
- Transfer taxes (or stamp taxes).
- Rent increases due to higher real estate taxes.
- Homeowners' association charges.

Taxes for local benefits. Deductible real estate taxes generally do not include taxes charged for local benefits and improvements tending to increase the value of your property. These include assessments for streets, sidewalks, water mains, sewer lines, public parking facilities, and similar improvements. You should increase the basis of your property by the amount of the assessment.

Local benefit taxes are deductible only if they are for maintenance, repair, or interest charges related to those benefits. If only a part of the taxes is for maintenance, repair, or interest, you must be able to show the amount of that part to claim the deduction. If you cannot determine what part of the tax is for maintenance, repair, or interest, none of it is deductible.

Caution

Taxes for local benefits may be included in your real estate tax bill. If your taxing authority (or mortgage lender) does not furnish you a copy of your real estate tax bill, ask for it. You should use the rules above to determine if the local benefit tax is deductible. Contact the taxing authority if you need additional information about a specific charge on your real estate tax bill.

EXPLANATION

Real property taxes are deductible if they are levied for the welfare of the general public and are levied at a proportionate rate against all property within the taxing jurisdiction. Real property taxes should be distinguished from assessments paid for local benefits, such as repair of streets, sidewalks, sewers, curbs, gutters, and other improvements that tend to benefit specific properties. Assessments of this type generally are not deductible.

A property owner often has the option of paying a special assessment in one payment or spreading the assessment over a period of years. In either case, the assessment itself is not deductible. However, payment of certain special assessments may increase the tax basis of your home. (See chapter 13, *Basis of property*, for a full discussion of this matter.) If an assessment on business or investment property is paid in installments, any interest charged is deductible. If the property is personal rather than business property, the interest would not be deductible. See chapter 24, *Interest expense*.

The IRS and the courts have held that the following are deductible as real property taxes:

- Assessments for the repair and resurfacing of streets, but not the lengthening or widening of them
- Wheeling, West Virginia, police and fire department charges imposed on owners of buildings and tangible personal property

If you pay real estate taxes this year but you are not itemizing your deductions, see chapter 13, *Basis of property*.

Different rules apply to real estate taxes paid during the period in which you are making improvements intended for business use. These rules are discussed in chapter 24, *Interest expense*.

Itemized charges for services. An itemized charge for services assessed against specific property or certain people is not a tax, even if the charge is paid to the taxing authority. For example, you cannot deduct the charge as a real estate tax if it is:

- A unit fee for the delivery of a service (such as a $5 fee charged for every 1,000 gallons of water you use),
- A periodic charge for a residential service (such as a $20 per month or $240 annual fee charged to each homeowner for trash collection), or
- A flat fee charged for a single service provided by your government (such as a $30 charge for mowing your lawn because it was allowed to grow higher than permitted under your local ordinance).

Exception. Service charges used to maintain or improve services (such as trash collection or police and fire protection) are deductible as real estate taxes if:

- The fees or charges are imposed at a like rate against all property in the taxing jurisdiction,
- The funds collected are not earmarked; instead, they are commingled with general revenue funds, and
- Funds used to maintain or improve services are not limited to or determined by the amount of these fees or charges collected.

Caution

You must look at your real estate tax bill to determine if any nondeductible itemized charges, such as those listed above, are included in the bill. If your taxing authority (or mortgage lender) does not furnish you a copy of your real estate tax bill, ask for it.

EXPLANATION

If the cost of providing certain services, such as garbage collection or sanitary measures, is paid for out of the general real estate tax fund, the entire amount of your real estate tax bill is deductible. If, however, the amount charged for such services is separately stated or paid into a specific fund, that amount is not deductible.

Transfer taxes (or stamp taxes). Transfer taxes and similar taxes and charges on the sale of a personal home are not deductible. If they are paid by the seller, they are expenses of the sale and reduce the amount realized on the sale. If paid by the buyer, they are included in the cost basis of the property.

Rent increase due to higher real estate taxes. If your landlord increases your rent in the form of a tax surcharge because of increased real estate taxes, you cannot deduct the increase as taxes.

Homeowners' association charges. These charges are not deductible because they are imposed by the homeowners' association, rather than the state or local government.

Text intentionally omitted.

Personal Property Taxes

Personal property tax is deductible if it is a state or local tax that is:

- Charged on personal property,
- Based only on the value of the personal property, and
- Charged on a yearly basis, even if it is collected more or less than once a year.

A tax that meets the above requirements can be considered charged on personal property even if it is for the exercise of a privilege. For example, a yearly tax based on value qualifies as a personal property tax even if it is called a registration fee and is for the privilege of registering motor vehicles or using them on the highways.

If the tax is partly based on value and partly based on other criteria, it may qualify in part.

Example. Your state charges a yearly motor vehicle registration tax of 1% of value plus 50 cents per hundredweight. You paid $32 based on the value ($1,500) and weight (3,400 lbs.) of your car. You can deduct $15 (1% × $1,500) as a personal property tax because it is based on the value. The remaining $17 ($.50 × 34), based on the weight, is not deductible.

EXPLANATION

Most state automobile license fees are not based on the value of the automobile and, therefore, are not deductible as personal property taxes.

Taxes and Fees You Cannot Deduct

Many federal, state, and local government taxes are not deductible because they do not fall within the categories discussed earlier. Other taxes and fees, such as federal income taxes, are not deductible because the tax law specifically prohibits a deduction for them. See Table 23-1.

Taxes and fees that are generally not deductible include the following items.

- ***Employment taxes.*** This includes social security, Medicare, and railroad retirement taxes withheld from your pay. However, one-half of self-employment tax you pay is deductible. In addition, the social security and other employment taxes you pay on the wages of a household worker may be included in medical expenses that you can deduct or child care expenses that allow you to claim the child and dependent care credit. For more information, see chapters 21 and 32.
- ***Estate, inheritance, legacy, or succession taxes.*** However, you can deduct the estate tax attributable to income in respect of a decedent if you, as a beneficiary, must include that income in your gross income. In that case, deduct the estate tax as a miscellaneous deduction that is not subject to the 2%-of-adjusted-gross-income limit. For more information, see Publication 559, *Survivors, Executors, and Administrators*.
- ***Federal income taxes.*** This includes income taxes withheld from your pay.
- ***Fines and penalties.*** You cannot deduct fines and penalties paid to a government for violation of any law, including related amounts forfeited as collateral deposits.
- ***Gift taxes.***

TAXALERT

Gift taxes may, in certain cases, be added to the basis of the property gifted.

- ***License fees.*** You cannot deduct license fees for personal purposes (such as marriage, driver's, and dog license fees).
- ***Per capita taxes.*** You cannot deduct state or local per capita taxes.
- *Text intentionally omitted.*

EXPLANATION

Other taxes that are not deductible include the following:

1. Federal and state excise taxes on telephone service
2. Federal gasoline taxes
3. Federal excise taxes on tobacco products and alcoholic beverages
4. Federal excise taxes on automobiles with low gas mileage (the "gas guzzler" tax)
5. Foreign taxes on income earned by U.S. citizens and U.S. **resident aliens** who qualify for the foreign **earned income** exclusion
6. Passport fees
7. Occupancy taxes
8. Penalties assessed as taxes

Many taxes and fees other than those listed above are also nondeductible, unless they are ordinary and necessary expenses of a business or income producing activity. For other nondeductible items, see *Real Estate-Related Items You Cannot Deduct*, earlier.

Where To Deduct

You deduct taxes on the following schedules.

State and local income taxes. These taxes are deducted on Schedule A (Form 1040), line 5a if higher than sales taxes. This is true even if your only source of income is from business, rents, or royalties.

General sales taxes. Sales taxes are deducted on Schedule A (Form 1040), line 5b. You must check box b on line 5. If you elect to deduct sales taxes, you cannot deduct state and local income taxes.

TAXALERT

The option to deduct state and local sales taxes expires at the end of 2011 unless Congress acts to extend it.

Foreign income taxes. Generally, income taxes you pay to a foreign country or U.S. possession can be claimed as an itemized deduction on Schedule A (Form 1040), line 8, or as a credit against your U.S. income tax on Form 1040, line 47. To claim the credit, you may have to complete and attach Form 1116. For more information, see chapter 37, the Form 1040 instructions, or Publication 514.

Real estate taxes and personal property taxes. These taxes are deducted on Schedule A (Form 1040), lines 6 and 7, respectively, unless they are paid on property used in your business, in which case they are deducted on Schedule C, Schedule C-EZ, or Schedule F (Form 1040). Taxes on property that produces rent or royalty income are deducted on Schedule E (Form 1040).

Text intentionally omitted.

Self-employment tax. Deduct one-half of your self-employment tax on Form 1040, line 27.

Other taxes. All other deductible taxes are deducted on Schedule A (Form 1040), line 8.

Chapter 24

Interest expense

ey.com/EYTaxGuide

Introduction

Interest expense is the amount of money you pay for the use of borrowed money. Depending on the use of the borrowed funds, certain types of interest expense may be deducted from your income.

To calculate your deduction, you must first separate your borrowings into five categories: (1) amounts used for investments generating portfolio income (interest, dividends, etc.), (2) amounts used for investment in passive activities (see chapter 12, *Other income*), (3) amounts used to purchase or improve a personal residence, (4) amounts used in an active trade or business, and (5) amounts used for personal reasons. Remember that no portion of your personal interest expense is deductible.

The interest paid on the other four categories of borrowings are subject to different rules regarding deductibility. This chapter will explain those rules and how to account for the use of your borrowings.

Prior to 2010, itemized deductions were subject to certain limitations if your adjusted gross income exceeded certain amounts (for 2009, this amount was $166,800; $83,400 if married filing separately). But the itemized deduction phaseout has been temporarily repealed and higher-income taxpayers do not have to reduce their total itemized deductions for 2011 or 2012. Unless Congress acts, the old phaseout rule is scheduled to return beginning in 2013.

What's New

Extended provisions. The following provisions have been extended and will apply for 2011.

- Your itemized deductions are not limited because of your adjusted gross income.
- Premiums paid for mortgage insurance are deductible as qualified residence interest.

Text intentionally omitted.

TAXPLANNER

You can take an itemized deduction in 2011 for the cost of mortgage insurance premiums you paid on a qualified personal residence. The deduction is phased out by 10% for each $1,000 by which your adjusted gross income (AGI) exceeds $100,000. Therefore, the deduction is unavailable for a taxpayer with AGI over $109,000. See the section on *Mortgage Insurance Premiums* later in this chapter for more information.

Unless Congress acts, this deduction will expire and be unavailable after 2011. For updated information on this and any other tax law changes that occur after this book was published, see our website, *ey.com/EYTaxGuide*.

Note

IRS Publication 17 (*Your Federal Income Tax*) has been updated by Ernst & Young LLP for 2011. Dates and dollar amounts shown are for 2011. Underlined type is used to indicate where IRS text has been updated. Places where text has been removed are indicated by the sentence: *Text intentionally omitted.*

ey.com/EYTaxGuide

Ernst & Young LLP will update the *Ernst & Young Tax Guide 2012* website with relevant taxpayer information as it becomes available. You can also sign up for email alerts to let you know when changes have been made.

This chapter discusses what interest expenses you can deduct. Interest is the amount you pay for the use of borrowed money.

The following are types of interest you can deduct as itemized deductions on Schedule A (Form 1040).

- Home mortgage interest, including certain points and mortgage insurance premiums.
- Investment interest.

This chapter explains these deductions. It also explains where to deduct other types of interest and lists some types of interest you cannot deduct.

Use Table 24-1 to find out where to get more information on various types of interest, including investment interest.

EXPLANATION

Loan payments generally are divided between principal and interest. In the absence of any specific division, partial payments are presumed to apply first to interest and then to principal. However, if a single payment is made in full settlement of an outstanding debt, the payment is first applied to the remaining principal balance and then to interest.

Interest paid to a related person is deductible, as long as it is paid for a bona fide debt. For example, parents may deduct interest paid on amounts borrowed from their minor children if the interest is otherwise deductible. If the borrower is not legally liable for the debt, or if there is no intent for the loan to be repaid, it is not a bona fide debt and interest payments are not deductible.

To deduct interest that you pay, the interest must be your liability. When two or more persons are jointly liable for the payment of interest, the person actually making the interest payment is entitled to the entire deduction.

It is not necessary to have a fixed percentage interest rate applied to the money that you have borrowed for the interest to be deducted. What is necessary is that the amount of interest paid can be definitely determined. It is usually based on a written agreement between the lender and the borrower. Low-interest and interest-free loans, which were once popular between family members, now have severe limitations applied to them. See chapter 7, *Interest income*.

Tax Breaks and Deductions You Can Use Checklist

Interest Expense. Interest you pay on certain types of loans–business loans, investment loans, and mortgages–is deductible. Interest on personal loans is not. If you're paying high, nondeductible interest on credit card debt, consider paying it off with a home equity loan. See *The benefits of home equity loans.*

Alternative Minimum Tax. Although home equity loan interest is deductible on loans up to $100,000 for regular tax purposes, it is not deductible for AMT purposes unless the loan is used for buying, constructing, or improving your main or second home. Consider the AMT before you take out such a loan. See chapter 31, *How to figure your tax*, for more details on the AMT.

Useful Items

You may want to see:

Publication

- □ **936** Home Mortgage Interest Deduction
- □ **550** Investment Income and Expenses

Home Mortgage Interest

Generally, home mortgage interest is any interest you pay on a loan secured by your home (main home or a second home). The loan may be a mortgage to buy your home, a second mortgage, a line of credit, or a home equity loan.

You can deduct home mortgage interest if all the following conditions are met.

- You file Form 1040 and itemize deductions on Schedule A (Form 1040).
- The mortgage is a secured debt on a qualified home in which you have an ownership interest. (Generally, your mortgage is a secured debt if you put your home up as collateral to protect the interest of the lender. The term "qualified home" means your main home or second home. For details, see Publication 936.)

Both you and the lender must intend that the loan be repaid.

EXPLANATION

To be fully deductible as home mortgage interest, the interest must be on a debt that is secured by property that is a qualified residence. A qualified residence is property that is owned by you and used as a principal or second residence. A residence may, among other things, be a house, a cooperative apartment, a condominium, a house trailer, or a houseboat. To be considered a qualified residence, a houseboat must include basic living accommodations, including sleeping space, a toilet, and cooking facilities.

TAXPLANNER

You may treat a home currently under construction as a qualified home for a period of up to 24 months if it becomes a qualifying residence as of the time that it is ready for occupancy.

Amount Deductible

In most cases, you can deduct all of your home mortgage interest. How much you can deduct depends on the date of the mortgage, the amount of the mortgage, and how you use the mortgage proceeds.

Fully deductible interest. If all of your mortgages fit into one or more of the following three categories at all times during the year, you can deduct all of the interest on those mortgages. (If any one mortgage fits into more than one category, add the debt that fits in each category to your other debt in the same category.)

The three categories are as follows:

1. Mortgages you took out on or before October 13, 1987 (called grandfathered debt).

EXPLANATION

All mortgage indebtedness existing on October 13, 1987 (grandfathered debt), is treated as acquisition indebtedness, regardless of the amount. The interest on this indebtedness is fully deductible.

Individuals who refinanced and increased their mortgage indebtedness before October 14, 1987, may have greater interest deductions than those individuals who waited until later because new or refinanced indebtedness is limited in amount, as explained in this chapter.

Example 1

When you are refinancing pre-October 14, 1987, mortgage debt, the amount that exceeds the existing debt does not qualify as grandfathered debt. The excess may be treated as home acquisition or home equity indebtedness, but the total qualifying indebtedness cannot exceed the fair market value of the residence. Grandfathered debt refinanced after October 13, 1987, generally retains its status as grandfathered debt only for the remaining term of the original debt.

Example 2

An original mortgage note incurred prior to October 14, 1987, to purchase a qualified residence had been reduced to $100,000 in 2011, when the value of the residence was $175,000. If this mortgage is refinanced, $100,000 of the new mortgage note is treated as grandfathered debt. Up to $75,000 may be treated as home acquisition or home equity indebtedness. If the indebtedness exceeds the value of the residence ($175,000), the excess must be allocated in accordance with the use of the excess amount.

2. Mortgages you took out after October 13, 1987, to buy, build, or improve your home (called home acquisition debt), but only if throughout 2011 these mortgages plus any grandfathered debt totaled $1 million or less ($500,000 or less if married filing separately).

EXPLANATION

This limitation applies only to loans incurred to purchase, construct, or improve a home.

TAXPLANNER

Is your loan large enough? When you are purchasing or constructing a home, consider your future financial needs carefully. The original loan can never be refinanced to increase the amount available for this limitation.

If you believe that you will need money for personal uses in the near future, you may want to increase the original mortgage at the time of acquisition or improvement to meet those future needs. Otherwise, if you later obtain a home equity loan, the interest on only $100,000 of the loan ($50,000 if married filing separately) is deductible as mortgage interest.

Additionally, interest paid on a home equity loan where the loan proceeds were used for personal use, and not for home improvements, is not deductible under the alternative minimum tax rules (see chapter 31, *How to figure your tax*).

3. Mortgages you took out after October 13, 1987, other than to buy, build, or improve your home (called home equity debt), but only if throughout 2011 these mortgages totaled $100,000 or less ($50,000 or less if married filing separately) and totaled no more than the fair market value of your home reduced by (1) and (2).

EXPLANATION

Guidance issued by the IRS in late 2010 explains that indebtedness incurred by a taxpayer to acquire, construct, or substantially improve a qualified residence may be deductible as home equity indebtedness to the extent that the debt exceeds $1 million. This means, for example, that a taxpayer taking a mortgage loan of $1.2 million may deduct the interest paid on $1 million as acquisition indebtedness used to acquire the residence, and may also deduct the interest paid on $100,000 of the remaining $200,000 of acquisition indebtedness as home equity indebtedness. Any interest paid on indebtedness in excess of $1.1 million continues to be nondeductible personal interest.

TAXSAVER

The benefits of home equity loans. Many taxpayers are taking home equity loans as a means of paying off their credit card balances, automobile loans, and other types of consumer expenditures. There are two major benefits of home equity borrowing:

1. Interest on up to $100,000 of home equity loans ($50,000 if married filing separately) is tax deductible for federal income tax purposes, whereas personal interest is not.
2. Home equity loans are less expensive than other types of credit. For example, the rate for home equity loans may be 7% or less. In comparison, the interest rates for credit cards and unsecured personal loans can exceed 18%.

Although home equity loans present several benefits, you should remember that if you are unable to pay off the loan, your house is in jeopardy—not the items that you purchased with the borrowed funds. In addition, not all home equity debt interest is deductible for alternative minimum tax purposes.

The dollar limits for the second and third categories apply to the combined mortgages on your main home and second home.

See *Part II* of Publication 936 for more detailed definitions of grandfathered, home acquisition, and home equity debt.

You can use Figure 24-A to check whether your home mortgage interest is fully deductible.

EXPLANATION

According to the IRS, the fair market value of your home cannot be less than the adjusted purchase price on the last day of the taxable year.

Example

John Joyce purchases a home in August 2011 for $150,000. He makes improvements costing $10,000 to the home during 2011, but these improvements add only $5,000 to the value of the home.

Although the value of the home at the end of 2011 is only $155,000, John is allowed to use $160,000, the cost of the home plus improvements, as the fair market value.

TAXSAVER

If your mortgage is above the limit. If part of your mortgage is in excess of the qualified mortgage limitation and you have investments that produce taxable income, you could sell some of your investments and use the proceeds to reduce your mortgage principal, in order to meet the qualified mortgage limitation. You could then borrow funds to repurchase the investment. Interest paid on this new loan would be traceable to the purchase of the new investment and therefore deductible as investment interest expense, subject to the investment income limitations discussed later in this chapter.

Remember to consider transaction costs of switching investments, including taxable gain or loss on the sale of securities, the capital loss limitation rule, and the "wash sale" rule discussed in chapter 14, *Sale of property*, and chapter 16, *Reporting gains and losses*. For additional information, consult your tax advisor.

Figure 24-A. **Is My Home Mortgage Interest Fully Deductible?**
(Instructions: Include balances of **ALL** mortgages secured by your main home and second home.)

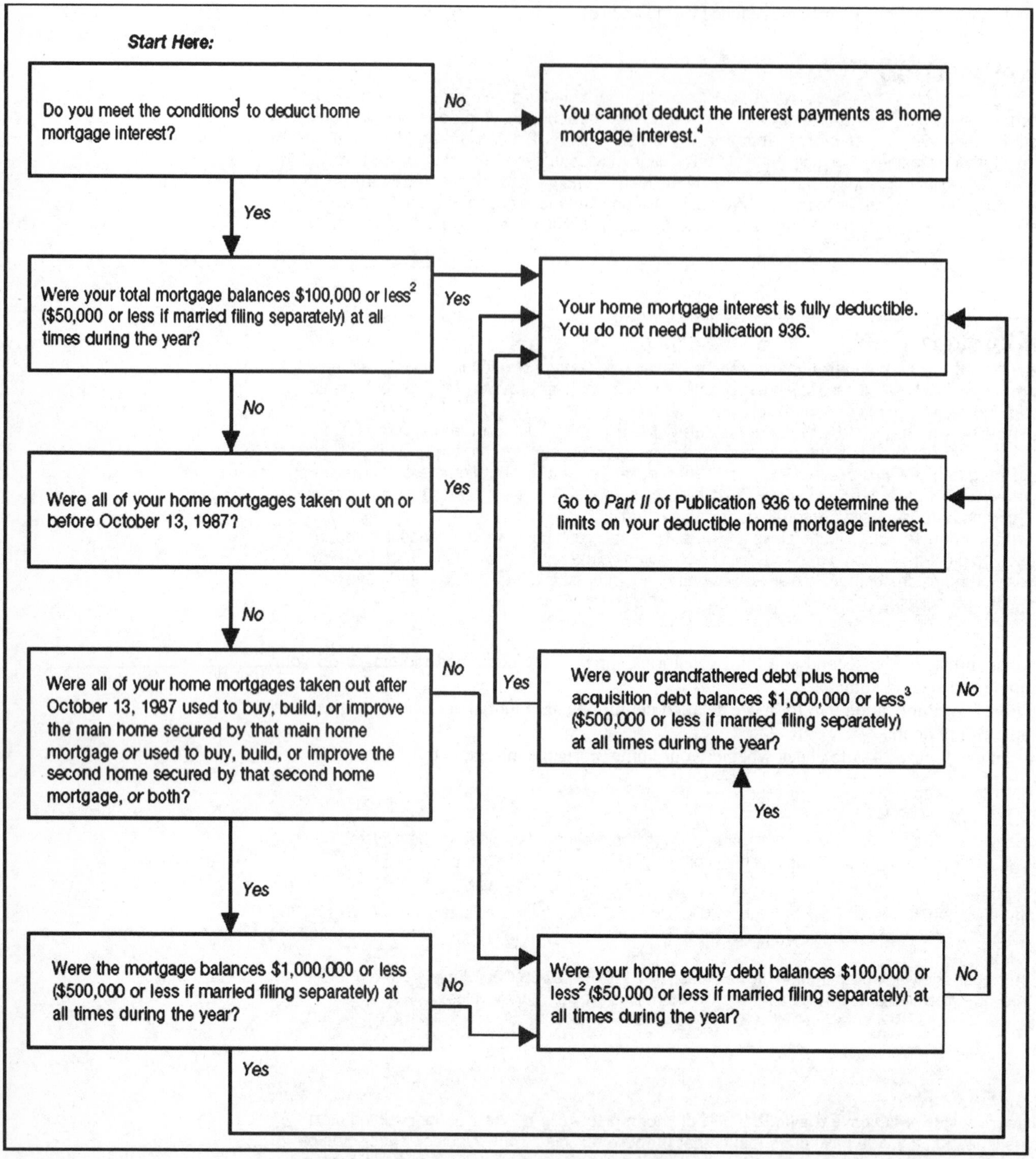

[1]You must itemize deductions on Schedule A (Form 1040). The loan must be a secured debt on a qualified home. See Home Mortgage Interest.
[2]If all mortgages on your main or second home exceed the home's fair market value, a lower limit may apply. See *Home equity debt limit* under *Home Equity Debt* in *Part II* of Publication 936.
[3]Amounts over the $1,000,000 limit ($500,000 if married filing separately) qualify as home equity debt if they are not more than the total home equity debt limit. See Publication 936 for more information about grandfathered debt, home acquisition debt, and home equity debt.
[4]See Table 24-1 for where to deduct other types of interest payments.

EXPLANATION

A second home may also be a qualified residence. A second home may be one that you do not occupy, a home that you occupy part of the year, or a home that you rent out. If the home is rented out, it is subject to the use requirements relating to vacation homes. It qualifies as your home only if you used it more than the greater of:

1. 14 days, or
2. 10% of the number of days during the year that it was rented at a fair rental or held out for sale.

If a dwelling is not rented at any time during the year, it may be treated as a qualified residence, even if it is not used by you. For this purpose, the IRS states that "rented" includes holding the residence out for rental or for resale.

Example

Mary owns a vacation home in northern Michigan. Because of business pressures, she is unable to use the home in 2010 or 2011 and lists the home for sale on October 31, 2011.

The house qualifies as a residence in 2010. It is not considered her residence in 2011, because Mary did not use the house for more than the greater of 14 days or 10% of the number of days it was held out for sale (10% × 61 days = 6 days).

TAXPLANNER

If, in the earlier example, members of Mary's family use the home for 15 days in 2011, she will be considered to have used it for the same period of time and the home will be considered her residence. Members of Mary's family include her brothers and sisters, husband, children and grandchildren, and parents and grandparents.

TAXPLANNER

If you own more than two homes, you may not deduct interest on the mortgages secured by more than two of these homes during any one year as home mortgage interest. You must include your main residence as one of the homes. You may choose any one of your other homes as a qualified residence and may change this choice for each tax year. However, you cannot choose to treat one home as a second residence for part of a year and another home as a second residence for the remainder of the year if both of these homes were owned by you during the entire year and neither home was your main residence during that year.

Limits on deduction. You cannot fully deduct interest on a mortgage that does not fit into any of the three categories listed above. If this applies to you, see *Part II* of Publication 936 to figure the amount of interest you can deduct.

Special Situations

This section describes certain items that can be included as home mortgage interest and others that cannot. It also describes certain special situations that may affect your deduction.

Late payment charge on mortgage payment. You can deduct as home mortgage interest a late payment charge if it was not for a specific service performed in connection with your mortgage loan.

EXPLANATION

The Tax Court in one case broadly interpreted the phrase *specific services* and ruled that a taxpayer was not allowed to deduct late charges on a home mortgage loan as mortgage interest. The Court determined in that case that the late charges related to the specific service of collecting the late payment. Furthermore, the formula used in calculating the late charge did not resemble standard interest computations, because the late charge was the same whether the payment was 1 day or 1 year late.

Mortgage prepayment penalty. If you pay off your home mortgage early, you may have to pay a penalty. You can deduct that penalty as home mortgage interest provided the penalty is not for a specific service performed or cost incurred in connection with your mortgage loan.

Sale of home. If you sell your home, you can deduct your home mortgage interest (subject to any limits that apply) paid up to, but not including, the date of sale.

Example. John and Peggy Harris sold their home on May 7. Through April 30, they made home mortgage interest payments of $1,220. The settlement sheet for the sale of the home showed $50 interest for the 6-day period in May up to, but not including, the date of sale. Their mortgage interest deduction is $1,270 ($1,220 + $50).

Prepaid interest. If you pay interest in advance for a period that goes beyond the end of the tax year, you must spread this interest over the tax years to which it applies. You can deduct in each year only the interest that qualifies as home mortgage interest for that year. However, there is an exception that applies to points, discussed later.

EXAMPLES

Example 1

When Dan borrowed $10,000 on a mortgage on November 3, 2011, he prepaid 16 months of interest ($1,600). The $1,600 of prepaid interest is considered to be paid, and therefore deductible, equally over the 16-month period ($100 per month). Dan should deduct $200 in 2011, $1,200 in 2012, and $200 in 2013.

Example 2

On March 25, Eric signed a mortgage note for $12,000 and agreed to repay it in 12 equal installments, beginning on April 29. Interest of $960 was subtracted from the face value of the note, and Eric received $11,040. If Eric uses the cash method of accounting, as most people do, interest is considered to be paid in 12 installments of $80 each ($960 ÷ 12). Eric may deduct $720 ($80 × 9 months) for the first year and $240 ($80 × 3 months) in the following year.

No deduction is permitted for the interest if payment for an installment period is not made. Therefore, if Eric were to miss two installment payments in the first year, he could deduct only $560 ($80 × 7 months).

Mortgage interest credit. You may be able to claim a mortgage interest credit if you were issued a mortgage credit certificate (MCC) by a state or local government. Figure the credit on Form 8396, Mortgage Interest Credit. If you take this credit, you must reduce your mortgage interest deduction by the amount of the credit.

For more information on the credit, see chapter 37.

Ministers' and military housing allowance. If you are a minister or a member of the uniformed services and receive a housing allowance that is not taxable, you can still deduct your home mortgage interest.

Mortgage assistance payments. If you qualify for mortgage assistance payments for lower-income families under section 235 of the National Housing Act, part or all of the interest on your mortgage may be paid for you. You cannot deduct the interest that is paid for you.

No other effect on taxes. Do not include these mortgage assistance payments in your income. Also, do not use these payments to reduce other deductions, such as real estate taxes.

Divorced or separated individuals. If a divorce or separation agreement requires you or your spouse or former spouse to pay home mortgage interest on a home owned by both of you, the payment of interest may be alimony. See the discussion of *Payments for jointly-owned home* in chapter 18.

Redeemable ground rents. If you make annual or periodic rental payments on a redeemable ground rent, you can deduct them as mortgage interest.

Payments made to end the lease and to buy the lessor's entire interest in the land are not deductible as mortgage interest. For more information, see Publication 936.

Nonredeemable ground rents. Payments on a nonredeemable ground rent are not mortgage interest. You can deduct them as rent if they are a business expense or if they are for rental property.

Reverse mortgages. A reverse mortgage is a loan where the lender pays you (in a lump sum, a monthly advance, a line of credit, or a combination of all three) while you continue to live in your home. With a reverse mortgage, you retain title to your home. Depending on the plan, your reverse mortgage becomes due with interest when you move, sell your home, reach the end of a pre-selected loan period, or die. Because reverse mortgages are considered loan advances and not income, the amount you receive is not taxable. Any interest (including original issue discount) accrued on a reverse mortgage is not deductible until the loan is paid in full. Your deduction may be limited because a reverse mortgage loan generally is subject to the limit on *Home Equity Debt* discussed in Publication 936.

Rental payments. If you live in a house before final settlement on the purchase, any payments you make for that period are rent and not interest. This is true even if the settlement papers call them interest. You cannot deduct these payments as home mortgage interest.

Mortgage proceeds invested in tax-exempt securities. You cannot deduct the home mortgage interest on grandfathered debt or home equity debt if you used the proceeds of the mortgage to buy securities or certificates that produce tax-free income. "Grandfathered debt" and "home equity debt" are defined earlier under *Amount Deductible.*

Refunds of interest. If you receive a refund of interest in the same tax year you paid it, you must reduce your interest expense by the amount refunded to you. If you receive a refund of interest you deducted in an earlier year, you generally must include the refund in income in the year you receive it. However, you need to include it only up to the amount of the deduction that reduced your tax in the earlier year. This is true whether the interest overcharge was refunded to you or was used to reduce the outstanding principal on your mortgage.

If you received a refund of interest you overpaid in an earlier year, you generally will receive a Form 1098, Mortgage Interest Statement, showing the refund in box 3. For information about Form 1098, see *Form 1098, Mortgage Interest Statement,* later.

For more information on how to treat refunds of interest deducted in earlier years, see *Recoveries* in chapter 12.

EXAMPLE

During 2011, Andrea paid $2,000 in interest on her adjustable rate mortgage. On December 31, 2011, a $200 interest refund for 2011 was credited to her account. Andrea's net deduction for interest on her loans is $1,800 ($2,000 paid minus $200 refunded).

Refunds of interest paid must be included in income if they represent a return of interest deducted in a prior year. If you receive a refund in 2011 for interest paid in 2010 and *did not itemize* your deductions in 2010, the refund *should not be included* in your 2011 income. If you receive the refund in 2011 and *you did itemize* your deductions in 2010, the refund is generally included in your 2011 income to the extent the deduction reduced your tax in 2010.

Points

The term "points" is used to describe certain charges paid, or treated as paid, by a borrower to obtain a home mortgage. Points may also be called loan origination fees, maximum loan charges, loan discount, or discount points.

A borrower is treated as paying any points that a home seller pays for the borrower's mortgage. See *Points paid by the seller,* later.

EXPLANATION

Usually, for federally regulated mortgage loans, points will be designated on the Uniform Settlement Statement (also known as Form HUD-1) as "loan origination fee," "loan discount," "discount points," or simply "points."

General Rule

You generally cannot deduct the full amount of points in the year paid. Because they are prepaid interest, you generally deduct them ratably over the life (term) of the mortgage. See *Deduction Allowed Ratably,* next.

For exceptions to the general rule, see *Deduction Allowed in Year Paid,* later.

EXPLANATION

Deducting points. Generally, taxpayers are prohibited from deducting prepaid interest in the year of payment. Rather, they must capitalize the prepaid interest and deduct it ratably over the life of the loan.

However, as discussed later, an exception exists for taxpayers who buy, build, or improve their principal residences and pay "points" in order to obtain a lower interest rate on their loans. The term "points" is a fee paid by the borrower that is like prepaid interest. To be deductible, the charge must represent interest paid for the use of money and must be paid before the time for which it represents a charge for the use of the money. Furthermore, the home must be the taxpayer's principal residence. You should note that the IRS has ruled that you can elect not to currently deduct points and to amortize them over the life of a loan. Such an election may be advantageous if the deduction does not benefit you in the year of purchase (e.g., you're not itemizing your deductions).

Deduction Allowed Ratably

If you do not meet the tests listed under *Deduction Allowed in Year Paid*, later, the loan is not a home improvement loan, or you choose not to deduct your points in full in the year paid, you can deduct the points ratably (equally) over the life of the loan if you meet all the following tests.

1. You use the cash method of accounting. This means you report income in the year you receive it and deduct expenses in the year you pay them. Most individuals use this method.
2. Your loan is secured by a home. (The home does not need to be your main home.)
3. Your loan period is not more than 30 years.
4. If your loan period is more than 10 years, the terms of your loan are the same as other loans offered in your area for the same or longer period.
5. Either your loan amount is $250,000 or less, or the number of points is not more than:
   a. 4, if your loan period is 15 years or less, or
   b. 6, if your loan period is more than 15 years.

Deduction Allowed in Year Paid

You can fully deduct points in the year paid if you meet all the following tests. (You can use Figure 24-B as a quick guide to see whether your points are fully deductible in the year paid.)

1. Your loan is secured by your main home. (Your main home is the one you ordinarily live in most of the time.)
2. Paying points is an established business practice in the area where the loan was made.
3. The points paid were not more than the points generally charged in that area.
4. You use the cash method of accounting. This means you report income in the year you receive it and deduct expenses in the year you pay them. (If you want more information about this method, see *Accounting Methods* in chapter 1.)
5. The points were not paid in place of amounts that ordinarily are stated separately on the settlement statement, such as appraisal fees, inspection fees, title fees, attorney fees, and property taxes.
6. The funds you provided at or before closing, plus any points the seller paid, were at least as much as the points charged. The funds you provided do not have to have been applied to the points. They can include a down payment, an escrow deposit, earnest money, and other funds you paid at or before closing for any purpose. You cannot have borrowed these funds from your lender or mortgage broker.
7. You use your loan to buy or build your main home.
8. The points were computed as a percentage of the principal amount of the mortgage.
9. The amount is clearly shown on the settlement statement (such as the Settlement Statement, Form HUD-1) as points charged for the mortgage. The points may be shown as paid from either your funds or the seller's.

Note. If you meet all of these tests, you can choose to either fully deduct the points in the year paid, or deduct them over the life of the loan.

Home improvement loan. You can also fully deduct in the year paid points paid on a loan to improve your main home, if tests (1) through (6) are met.

Figure 24-B. **Are My Points Fully Deductible This Year?**

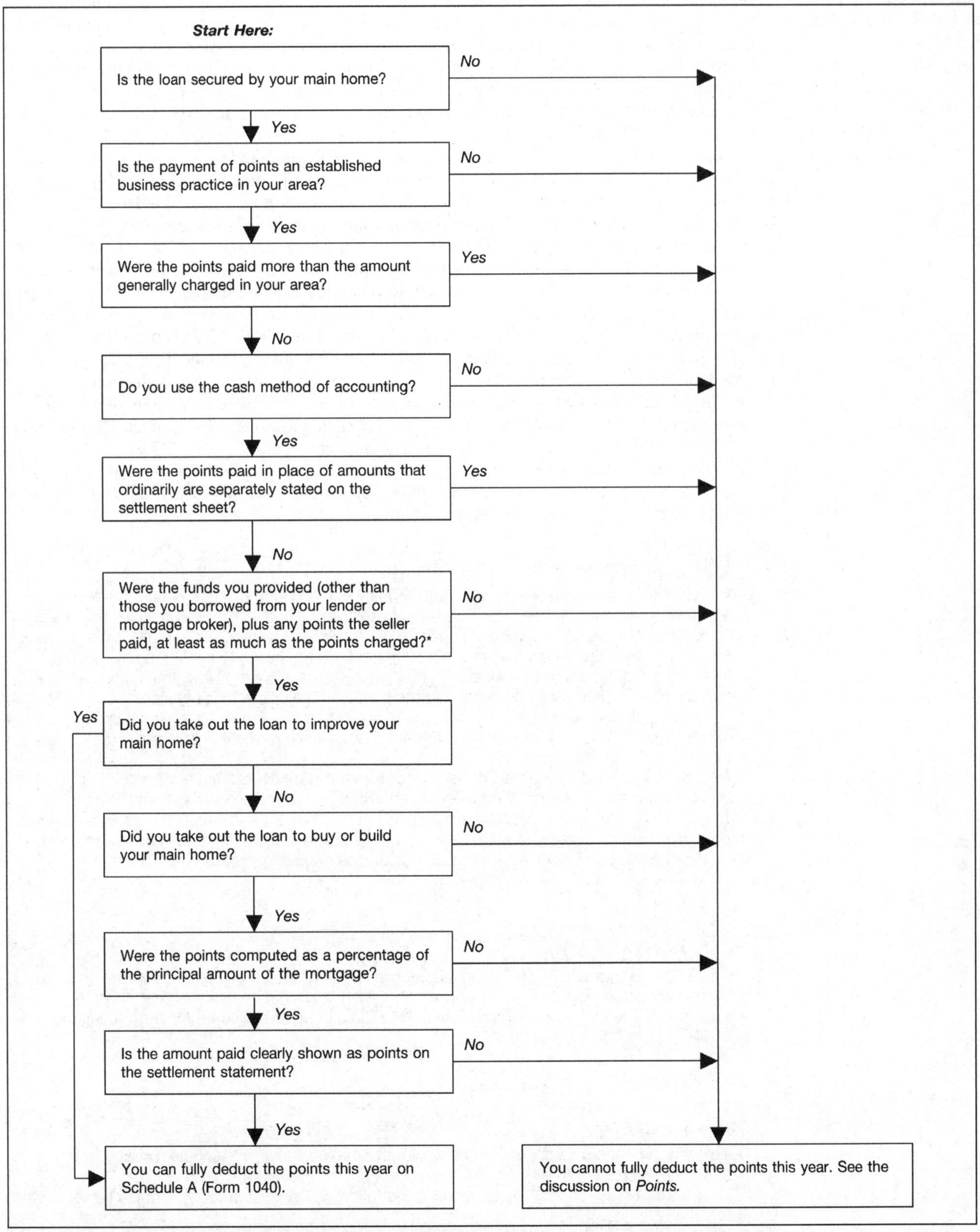

*The funds you provided do not have to have been applied to the points. They can include a down payment, an escrow deposit, earnest money, and other funds you paid at or before closing for any purpose.

Caution

Second home. *You cannot fully deduct in the year paid points you pay on loans secured by your second home. You can deduct these points only over the life of the loan.*

Refinancing. Generally, points you pay to refinance a mortgage are not deductible in full in the year you pay them. This is true even if the new mortgage is secured by your main home.

However, if you use part of the refinanced mortgage proceeds to improve your main home and you meet the first 6 tests listed under *Deduction Allowed in Year Paid,* earlier, you can fully deduct the part of the points related to the improvement in the year you paid them with your own funds. You can deduct the rest of the points over the life of the loan.

Example 1. In 1996, Bill Fields got a mortgage to buy a home. In 2011, Bill refinanced that mortgage with a 15-year $100,000 mortgage loan. The mortgage is secured by his home. To get the new loan, he had to pay three points ($3,000). Two points ($2,000) were for prepaid interest, and one point ($1,000) was charged for services, in place of amounts that ordinarily are stated separately on the settlement statement. Bill paid the points out of his private funds, rather than out of the proceeds of the new loan. The payment of points is an established practice in the area, and the points charged are not more than the amount generally charged there. Bill's first payment on the new loan was due July 1. He made six payments on the loan in 2011 and is a cash basis taxpayer.

Bill used the funds from the new mortgage to repay his existing mortgage. Although the new mortgage loan was for Bill's continued ownership of his main home, it was not for the purchase or improvement of that home. He cannot deduct all of the points in 2011. He can deduct two points ($2,000) ratably over the life of the loan. He deducts $67 [($2,000 ÷ 180 months) × 6 payments] of the points in 2011. The other point ($1,000) was a fee for services and is not deductible.

Example 2. The facts are the same as in *Example 1,* except that Bill used $25,000 of the loan proceeds to improve his home and $75,000 to repay his existing mortgage. Bill deducts 25% ($25,000 ÷ $100,000) of the points ($2,000) in 2011. His deduction is $500 ($2,000 × 25%).

Bill also deducts the ratable part of the remaining $1,500 ($2,000 − $500) that must be spread over the life of the loan. This is $50 [($1,500 ÷ 180 months) × 6 payments] in 2011. The total amount Bill deducts in 2011 is $550 ($500 + $50).

EXPLANATION

According to the IRS, points paid when you refinance an existing mortgage must be deducted ratably over the life of the new loan. They are not fully deductible in the year in which they were paid because they were not paid in connection with the improvement or purchase of a home, even though the original loan met the requirements for deductibility. However, points paid on a refinanced mortgage are fully deductible in the year paid to the extent the additional loan proceeds are used for home improvement and the points are paid with funds you provide. If only a portion of the loan proceeds is used for home improvement, then only a corresponding portion of the points is fully deductible in the year paid. The balance of the points is deducted ratably over the life of the loan.

However, an Eighth Circuit Court decision allowed a full immediate deduction for points paid by taxpayers in obtaining a permanent mortgage on their home, the proceeds of which were used to pay off a short-term, 3-year mortgage with a balloon payment and a recently obtained home improvement loan secured by a second mortgage. The court indicated that the permanent mortgage obtained was sufficiently "in connection with" the original purchase of the home.

TAXALERT

The IRS has disagreed with this court decision and still argues that points paid for a loan to refinance a mortgage on a taxpayer's principal residence are not deductible. Therefore, the IRS will not follow the decision outside of the Eighth Circuit (Arkansas, Iowa, Minnesota, Missouri, Nebraska, North Dakota, and South Dakota).

TAXPLANNER

Before you refinance. Before you refinance your home mortgage, you should consider both tax and financial factors.

For the interest to remain fully deductible, the following tax-related factors should be considered:

- Whether the term of the mortgage should be extended beyond the original term.
- In general, the total of all mortgage balances should not exceed the lesser of the fair market value of the house or $1.1 million ($1 million acquisition debt and $100,000

home equity debt) or, if married filing separately, $550,000. However, see previous discussion of refinanced grandfather debt if you have a pre-October 14, 1987, mortgage. Other limitations may also apply. See limits on the deduction of mortgage interest, discussed previously in this chapter.

- When a loan is either refinanced or paid off, the remaining balance points being amortized on the old loan (the one being refinanced) can be taken as an itemized deduction.

Example

On January 1, 2006, Tom refinanced and paid $3,000 in points for a 15-year loan. He was taking a deduction for $200 each year for the points paid ($3,000 ÷ 15 years). He again refinanced in 2011 at a lower interest rate. The balance of the points from the original refinanced loan ($2,000) can be deducted in 2011 since the loan was paid off.

The financial factors you may also want to consider include the following:

- If there are refinancing costs, you should determine how many months it would take to recoup these costs. To do so, divide the total amount of estimated refinancing costs (deductible and nondeductible) by the anticipated reduction in your monthly mortgage payment (i.e., the difference between your existing monthly payment of principal and interest and the new monthly payment). If you will recover your refinancing costs before you sell your home, then refinancing may be a smart thing to do.
- You should evaluate whether the current value of the after-tax savings from a lower interest rate exceeds the up-front cost of refinancing. Specifically, consider such factors as taxes, present value, and opportunity costs (lost income on funds used to pay refinancing charges). Software programs and financial calculators available on many financial institution websites can assist you in evaluating whether it may be beneficial to refinance. You may also want to consult your tax advisor.
- If refinancing extends the life of your payments you also need to evaluate the total interest cost.

Example

If you are in your 10th year of a 30-year mortgage, you may be paying more interest in the long term if you refinance to a new 30-year mortgage, even if the interest rate is lower. Typically interest amounts are higher in the beginning years of a loan and more of your payment goes toward interest rather than principal in the beginning years.

Special Situations

This section describes certain special situations that may affect your deduction of points.

Original issue discount. If you do not qualify to either deduct the points in the year paid or deduct them ratably over the life of the loan, or if you choose not to use either of these methods, the points reduce the issue price of the loan. This reduction results in original issue discount, which is discussed in chapter 4 of Publication 535.

Amounts charged for services. Amounts charged by the lender for specific services connected to the loan are not interest. Examples of these charges are:

- Appraisal fees,
- Notary fees, and
- Preparation costs for the mortgage note or deed of trust.

You cannot deduct these amounts as points either in the year paid or over the life of the mortgage.

TAXPLANNER

Pointers about points. To get a deduction for points, make sure that the loan document clearly establishes that the points were not paid for any specific services that the lender performed or agreed to perform in connection with the borrower's account under the loan contract. Charges should be separately itemized on the financing and settlement statements.

Points paid by the seller. The term "points" includes loan placement fees that the seller pays to the lender to arrange financing for the buyer.

Treatment by seller. The seller cannot deduct these fees as interest. But they are a selling expense that reduces the amount realized by the seller. See chapter 15 for information on selling your home.

Treatment by buyer. The buyer reduces the basis of the home by the amount of the seller-paid points and treats the points as if he or she had paid them. If all the tests under *Deduction Allowed* *in Year Paid*, earlier, are met, the buyer can deduct the points in the year paid. If any of those tests are not met, the buyer deducts the points over the life of the loan.

For information about basis, see chapter 13.

EXPLANATION

Points paid by the seller, including those charged to the seller, in connection with the buyer's home mortgage loan are considered points paid by the buyer. Therefore, points paid by the seller may be fully deductible by the buyer in the year paid (see previous section, *Points*). As a reminder, your basis in the home needs to be reduced by the amount of seller-paid points.

Funds provided are less than points. If you meet all the tests in *Deduction Allowed in Year Paid*, earlier, except that the funds you provided were less than the points charged to you (test (6)), you can deduct the points in the year paid, up to the amount of funds you provided. In addition, you can deduct any points paid by the seller.

Example 1. When you took out a $100,000 mortgage loan to buy your home in December, you were charged one point ($1,000). You meet all the tests for deducting points in the year paid, except the only funds you provided were a $750 down payment. Of the $1,000 charged for points, you can deduct $750 in the year paid. You spread the remaining $250 over the life of the mortgage.

Example 2. The facts are the same as in *Example 1*, except that the person who sold you your home also paid one point ($1,000) to help you get your mortgage. In the year paid, you can deduct $1,750 ($750 of the amount you were charged plus the $1,000 paid by the seller). You spread the remaining $250 over the life of the mortgage. You must reduce the basis of your home by the $1,000 paid by the seller.

Excess points. If you meet all the tests in *Deduction Allowed in Year Paid*, earlier, except that the points paid were more than generally paid in your area (test (3)), you deduct in the year paid only the points that are generally charged. You must spread any additional points over the life of the mortgage.

Mortgage ending early. If you spread your deduction for points over the life of the mortgage, you can deduct any remaining balance in the year the mortgage ends. However, if you refinance the mortgage with the same lender, you cannot deduct any remaining balance of spread points. Instead, deduct the remaining balance over the term of the new loan.

A mortgage may end early due to a prepayment, refinancing, foreclosure, or similar event.

Example. Dan paid $3,000 in points in 2000 that he had to spread out over the 15-year life of the mortgage. He deducts $200 in points per year. Through 2010, Dan has deducted $2,200 of the points.

Dan prepaid his mortgage in full in 2011. He can deduct the remaining $800 of points in 2011.

Limits on deduction. You cannot fully deduct points paid on a mortgage unless the mortgage fits into one of the categories listed earlier under *Fully deductible interest*. See Publication 936 for details.

Mortgage Insurance Premiums

You can treat amounts you paid during 2011 for qualified mortgage insurance as home mortgage interest. The insurance must be in connection with home acquisition debt and the insurance contract must have been issued after 2006.

Qualified mortgage insurance. Qualified mortgage insurance is mortgage insurance provided by the Department of Veterans Affairs, the Federal Housing Administration, or the Rural Housing Service, and private mortgage insurance (as defined in section 2 of the Homeowners Protection Act of 1998 as in effect on December 20, 2006).

Mortgage insurance provided by the Department of Veterans Affairs is commonly known as a funding fee. If provided by the Rural Housing Service, it is commonly known as a guarantee fee. These fees can be deducted fully in 2011 if the mortgage insurance contract was issued in 2011. Contact the mortgage insurance issuer to determine the deductible amount if it is not reported in box 4 of Form 1098.

Special rules for prepaid mortgage insurance. Generally, if you paid premiums for qualified mortgage insurance that are allocable to periods after the close of the tax year, such premiums are treated as paid in the period to which they are allocated. You must allocate the premiums over the shorter of the stated term of the mortgage or 84 months, beginning with the month the insurance was obtained. No deduction is allowed for the unamortized balance if the mortgage is satisfied before its term. This paragraph does not apply to qualified mortgage insurance provided by the Department of Veterans Affairs or the Rural Housing Service. See the Example below.

Example. Ryan purchased a home in May of 2010 and financed the home with a 15-year mortgage. Ryan also prepaid all of the $9,240 in private mortgage insurance required at the time of closing in May. Since the $9,240 in private mortgage insurance is allocable to periods after 2010, Ryan must allocate the $9,240 over the shorter of the life of the mortgage or 84 months. Ryan's adjusted gross income (AGI) for 2010 is $76,000. Ryan can deduct $880 ($9,240 ÷ 84 × 8 months) for qualified mortgage insurance premiums in 2010. For 2011, Ryan can deduct $1,320 ($9,240 ÷ 84 × 12 months) if his AGI is $100,000 or less.

In this example, the mortgage insurance premiums are allocated over 84 months, which is shorter than the life of the mortgage of 15 years (180 months).

Limit on deduction. If your adjusted gross income on Form 1040, line 38, is more than $100,000 ($50,000 if your filing status is married filing separately), the amount of your mortgage insurance premiums that are otherwise deductible is reduced and may be eliminated. See *Line 13* in the instructions for Schedule A (Form 1040) and complete the *Qualified Mortgage Insurance Premiums Deduction Worksheet* to figure the amount you can deduct. If your adjusted gross income is more than $109,000 ($54,500 if married filing separately), you cannot deduct your mortgage insurance premiums.

TAXALERT

The deduction for mortgage insurance premiums is available only for premiums paid or accrued through 2011 on insurance contracts issued after December 31, 2006, and before January 1, 2012. No deduction for mortgage insurance premiums is available after 2011 unless Congress acts to extend it. In addition, no deduction is allowed for taxpayers with adjusted gross income over $109,000 ($54,500 if you're married filing separately).

Form 1098, Mortgage Interest Statement

If you paid $600 or more of mortgage interest (including certain points and mortgage insurance premiums) during the year on any one mortgage, you generally will receive a Form 1098 or a similar statement from the mortgage holder. You will receive the statement if you pay interest to a person (including a financial institution or a cooperative housing corporation) in the course of that person's trade or business. A governmental unit is a person for purposes of furnishing the statement.

The statement for each year should be sent to you by January 31 of the following year. A copy of this form will also be sent to the IRS.

TAXORGANIZER

When you receive Form 1098, the form which lists your mortgage interest and applicable points paid during the year, keep it with your other important tax documents.

Explanation

An individual who "takes back" a mortgage indebtedness when selling a residence is not required to prepare a Form 1098 or otherwise notify the debtor of the amount of interest paid. He or she must include the interest income on his or her tax return as seller-financed mortgage interest income and report the payer's name and amount received.

The statement will show the total interest you paid during the year, any mortgage insurance premiums you paid, and if you purchased a main home during the year, it also will show the deductible points paid during the year, including seller-paid points. However, it should not show any interest that was paid for you by a government agency.

As a general rule, Form 1098 will include only points that you can fully deduct in the year paid. However, certain points not included on Form 1098 also may be deductible, either in the year paid or over the life of the loan. See Points, earlier, to determine whether you can deduct points not shown on Form 1098.

Prepaid interest on Form 1098. If you prepaid interest in 2011 that accrued in full by January 15, 2012, this prepaid interest may be included in box 1 of Form 1098. However, you cannot deduct the prepaid amount for January 2012 in 2011. (See *Prepaid interest*, earlier.) You will have to figure the interest that accrued for 2012 and subtract it from the amount in box 1. You will include the interest for January 2012 with the other interest you pay for 2012. See *How To Report*, later.

Refunded interest. If you received a refund of mortgage interest you overpaid in an earlier year, you generally will receive a Form 1098 showing the refund in box 3. See *Refunds of interest*, earlier.

Mortgage insurance premiums. The amount of mortgage insurance premiums you paid during 2011 may be shown in box 4 of Form 1098. See *Mortgage Insurance Premiums*, earlier.

TAXALERT

The deduction for mortgage insurance premiums is available only for premiums paid or accrued through 2011 on insurance contracts issued between 2007 and 2011. In addition, no deduction is allowed for taxpayers with adjusted gross income over $109,000 ($54,500 if you're married filing separately).

Investment Interest

This section discusses interest expenses you may be able to deduct as an investor.

If you borrow money to buy property you hold for investment, the interest you pay is investment interest. You can deduct investment interest subject to the limit discussed later. However, you cannot deduct interest you incurred to produce tax-exempt income. Nor can you deduct interest expenses on straddles.

Investment interest does not include any qualified home mortgage interest or any interest taken into account in computing income or loss from a passive activity.

Investment Property

Property held for investment includes property that produces interest, dividends, annuities, or royalties not derived in the ordinary course of a trade or business. It also includes property that produces gain or loss (not derived in the ordinary course of a trade or business) from the sale or trade of property producing these types of income or held for investment (other than an interest in a passive activity). Investment property also includes an interest in a trade or business activity in which you did not materially participate (other than a passive activity).

Partners, shareholders, and beneficiaries. To determine your investment interest, combine your share of investment interest from a partnership, S corporation, estate, or trust with your other investment interest.

Allocation of Interest Expense

If you borrow money for business or personal purposes as well as for investment, you must allocate the debt among those purposes. Only the interest expense on the part of the debt used for investment purposes is treated as investment interest. The allocation is not affected by the use of property that secures the debt.

Limit on Deduction

Generally, your deduction for investment interest expense is limited to the amount of your net investment income.

You can carry over the amount of investment interest that you could not deduct because of this limit to the next tax year. The interest carried over is treated as investment interest paid or accrued in that next year.

You can carry over disallowed investment interest to the next tax year even if it is more than your taxable income in the year the interest was paid or accrued.

Net Investment Income

Determine the amount of your net investment income by subtracting your investment expenses (other than interest expense) from your investment income.

Investment income. This generally includes your gross income from property held for investment (such as interest, dividends, annuities, and royalties). Investment income does not include Alaska Permanent Fund dividends. It also does not include qualified dividends or net capital gain unless you choose to include them.

Choosing to include qualified dividends. Investment income generally does not include qualified dividends, discussed in chapter 8. However, you can choose to include all or part of your qualified dividends in investment income.

You make this choice by completing Form 4952, line 4g, according to its instructions.

If you choose to include any amount of your qualified dividends in investment income, you must reduce your qualified dividends that are eligible for the lower capital gains tax rates by the same amount.

Choosing to include net capital gain. Investment income generally does not include net capital gain from disposing of investment property (including capital gain distributions from mutual funds). However, you can choose to include all or part of your net capital gain in investment income.

You make this choice by completing Form 4952, line 4g, according to its instructions.

If you choose to include any amount of your net capital gain in investment income, you must reduce your net capital gain that is eligible for the lower capital gains tax rates by the same amount.

Tip

Before making either choice, consider the overall effect on your tax liability. Compare your tax if you make one or both of these choices with your tax if you do not.

EXPLANATION

Qualified dividends are not treated as "investment income" for purposes of determining the limitation on the deductibility of investment interest expense, unless you elect to treat the dividends as not eligible for the favorable capital gains rates.

TAXPLANNER

While it may be possible to borrow in order to acquire dividend-paying stocks, it will be necessary to analyze your entire portfolio to determine if the interest expense deduction will be limited due to insufficient investment income from other sources.

Explanation

A deduction is allowed for interest paid on indebtedness incurred to purchase or hold investment property. Investment property includes any property producing interest, dividends, annuities, royalties, or certain gains.

Example

Suppose you borrow money to purchase both taxable securities and tax-free investments (such as state municipal bonds). The interest income from the tax-free bonds is not taxable. Accordingly, the interest expense paid on the loan allocable to the tax-free bonds is not deductible. And the interest income from the tax-free bonds, since it is not taxable, does not count as investment income for purposes of calculating the limitation.

Explanation

The amount of investment interest that may be deducted is limited to the amount of investment income less allowable expenses, other than interest, that are directly connected with the production of investment income. Investment income does not include qualified dividends or long-term capital gains unless you make an election to treat them as not eligible for the favorable capital gains rates. The allowable expenses include those expenses that are deducted on your tax return, after the 2% of adjusted gross income limitation on miscellaneous deductions. (For more information, see chapter 29, *Miscellaneous deductions*.)

If the investment interest paid exceeds investment income, the excess may be carried forward to offset investment income in future years.

No deduction is allowed for interest paid on indebtedness incurred to hold obligations that are exempt from federal taxation.

Example 1

In 2011, Lorraine borrows $83,000 to purchase White Company securities. During the same year, she earns $30,000 of net investment income and incurs $10,000 of interest expense on her loan. Lorraine can deduct the $10,000 interest expense as investment interest on Schedule A (Form 1040).

Example 2

George and Lisa Salazar, who file a joint return, have the following income and deductions in 2011:

Salary	$30,000
Interest income from a state municipal bond	500
Interest income	20,000
Short-term capital gain	5,000
Adjusted gross income	$55,000
Investment advisory fees	$2,000
Investment interest expense	$31,000

Their deduction for investment interest is figured as follows:

Investment income	$25,000
Direct investment expense ($2,000 – 2% of $55,000)	(900)
Net investment income ($25,000 – $900)	$24,100
Investment interest deduction	$24,100

The $6,900 ($31,000 – $24,100) of investment interest expense that is not allowed as a deduction in 2011 may be carried forward to 2012.

TAXALERT

Net long-term capital gains from the disposition of investment property and qualified dividends are not treated as investment income for purposes of computing the limitation on investment interest deductions. You may, however, elect to include net long-term capital gain and qualified dividend amounts in investment income for this purpose if you also reduce by the same amount the net long-term capital gain and qualified dividends that are eligible for the special maximum capital gains rates. Short-term capital gains may still be included in the computation of investment income. For an additional discussion of reporting gains and losses, see chapter 16, *Reporting gains and losses*.

Explanation

The 2% limitation on miscellaneous deductions applies first to deductions other than investment expenses.

Example

In Example 2, if George and Lisa Salazar also had tax preparation fees of $500, the $1,100 (2% limitation) would reduce this amount first. The remainder, $600, would then reduce the investment expense, leaving $1,400 to be subtracted from investment income.

Explanation

Deduct interest on margin accounts on Schedule A (Form 1040) for the year in which you paid it. Interest on these accounts is considered paid when the broker is paid or when the interest becomes available to the broker through your account.

Deduct interest on money borrowed to buy a money market certificate on Schedule A (Form 1040). You must include the total interest you earn on the certificate in your income.

Example

You deposited $5,000 with a bank and borrowed another $5,000 from the same bank to make up the $10,000 minimum deposit required to buy a 6-month money market certificate. The certificate earned $250 at maturity in 2011, but you received only $100, which represents the $250 you earned minus $150 interest charged on your $5,000 loan. The bank gives you a Form 1099-INT, Statement of Recipients of Interest Income, showing the $250 interest you earned. The bank also gives you a statement showing that you paid $150 interest for 2011. You must include the $250 in your income. You may deduct $150 on Schedule A (Form 1040) if you itemize your deductions.

TAXPLANNER

The amount that you forfeit to a bank or a savings institution as a penalty for premature withdrawal of funds from an account is deductible from your gross income in figuring your adjusted gross income. You need not itemize to get this deduction.

Investment income of child reported on parent's return. Investment income includes the part of your child's interest and dividend income that you choose to report on your return. If the child does not have qualified dividends, Alaska Permanent Fund dividends, or capital gain distributions, this is the amount on line 6 of Form 8814, Parents' Election To Report Child's Interest and Dividends.

Child's qualified dividends. If part of the amount you report is your child's qualified dividends, that part (which is reported on Form 1040, line 9b) generally does not count as investment income. However, you can choose to include all or part of it in investment income, as explained under *Choosing to include qualified dividends*, earlier.

Your investment income also includes the amount on Form 8814, line 12 (or, if applicable, the reduced amount figured next under *Child's Alaska Permanent Fund dividends*).

Child's Alaska Permanent Fund dividends. If part of the amount you report is your child's Alaska Permanent Fund dividends, that part does not count as investment income. To figure the amount of your child's income that you can consider your investment income, start with the amount on Form 8814, line 6. Multiply that amount by a percentage that is equal to the Alaska Permanent Fund dividends divided by the total amount on Form 8814, line 4. Subtract the result from the amount on Form 8814, line 12.

Child's capital gain distributions. If part of the amount you report is your child's capital gain distributions, that part (which is reported on Schedule D, line 13, or Form 1040, line 13) generally does not count as investment income. However, you can choose to include all or part of it in investment income, as explained in *Choosing to include net capital gain*, earlier.

Your investment income also includes the amount on Form 8814, line 12 (or, if applicable, the reduced amount figured under *Child's Alaska Permanent Fund dividends*, earlier).

Investment expenses. Investment expenses are your allowed deductions (other than interest expense) directly connected with the production of investment income. Investment expenses that are included as a miscellaneous itemized deduction on Schedule A (Form 1040), are allowable deductions after applying the 2% limit that applies to miscellaneous itemized deductions. Use the smaller of:

- The investment expenses included on Schedule A (Form 1040), line 23, or
- The amount on Schedule A, line 27.

Losses from passive activities. Income or expenses that you used in computing income or loss from a passive activity are not included in determining your investment income or investment expenses (including investment interest expense). See Publication 925, *Passive Activity and At-Risk Rules*, for information about passive activities.

Form 4952

Use Form 4952, Investment Interest Expense Deduction, to figure your deduction for investment interest.

Exception to use of Form 4952. You do not have to complete Form 4952 or attach it to your return if you meet all of the following tests.

- Your investment interest expense is not more than your investment income from interest and ordinary dividends minus any qualified dividends.
- You do not have any other deductible investment expenses.
- You have no carryover of investment interest expense from 2010.

If you meet all of these tests, you can deduct all of your investment interest.

More Information

For more information on investment interest, see *Interest Expenses* in chapter 3 of Publication 550.

Items You Cannot Deduct

Some interest payments are not deductible. Certain expenses similar to interest also are not deductible. Nondeductible expenses include the following items.

- Personal interest (discussed later).
- Service charges (however, see *Other Expenses* in chapter 29).
- Annual fees for credit cards.
- Loan fees.
- Credit investigation fees.
- Interest to purchase or carry tax-exempt securities.

EXPLANATION

While the general rule is that interest paid on a debt incurred to purchase or carry tax-exempt obligations is not deductible, this does not mean that if you hold tax-exempt obligations, all interest expense deductions are disallowed. The courts have consistently held that there must be a sufficiently direct relationship between the incurring of the debt and the carrying of the tax-exempt obligation before the interest is disallowed. However, if you have significant interest expense and municipal bond income, you may lose your investment interest deductions.

The IRS has ruled that a direct relationship between debt and the purchase of tax-exempt obligations exists when the debt proceeds are used for, and are directly traceable to, the purchase of tax-exempts. A direct relationship between debt and the carrying of tax-exempt obligations exists when tax-exempts are used as collateral for a loan.

If only part of a debt you have is related to the holding of tax-exempt obligations, only that part of the interest paid is disallowed.

Example

Barry and Tricia borrow $10,000 from a bank and invest $2,500 of the proceeds in tax-exempt obligations. In this case, 25% ($2,500 × $10,000) of the interest they pay on the loan is not deductible as investment interest.

TAXPLANNER

Don't worry about whether or not you use debt to acquire or carry tax-exempt obligations if your investment in tax-exempts is "insubstantial." The IRS defines "insubstantial" as being less than 2% of the average adjusted basis of your portfolio investments and business assets.

Penalties. You cannot deduct fines and penalties paid to a government for violations of law, regardless of their nature.

TAXPLANNER

If you used borrowed funds to pay interest. To get an interest deduction when you use borrowed funds to pay interest, you need to be careful in structuring the transaction. Generally, the IRS says that meeting an interest obligation by giving a new note or increasing the amount due on an old note does not constitute payment. A deduction would be allowed only when the renewed note is paid. If, however, you borrow the money to pay the interest from a *different creditor*, the interest deduction would be allowed.

Nevertheless, the Tax Court allowed an interest deduction when the purpose of the second loan was not limited to the payment of interest on the first loan and the taxpayer showed that he could have paid the interest with other funds. You can't be too cautious in this area. Borrow from a second lender whenever possible.

TAXPLANNER

Margin interest. Stockbrokers charge you interest on a margin account–an account in which you place the money you have borrowed from your broker to purchase stocks or bonds. For the interest to be deductible, there must be a subsequent payment to your broker in cash. Alternatively, you may specifically allocate proceeds from dividends, interest, or stock sales to cover the interest. Merely charging the account does not constitute payment.

Personal Interest

Personal interest is not deductible. Personal interest is any interest that is not home mortgage interest, investment interest, business interest, or other deductible interest. It includes the following items.

- Interest on car loans (unless you use the car for business).
- Interest on federal, state, or local income tax.
- Finance charges on credit cards, retail installment contracts, and revolving charge accounts incurred for personal expenses.
- Late payment charges by a public utility.

Tip

You may be able to deduct interest you pay on a qualified student loan. For details, see Publication 970, Tax Benefits for Education.

TAXPLANNER

When you are faced with the necessity of purchasing both a house and a large-ticket consumer item (e.g., a car), you should consider the tax nature of the debt, particularly the value of the deductible interest on acquisition debt compared to loans that are repaid with nondeductible interest. Your future plans to purchase consumer items should play an important role in your mortgage and other financing decisions. In addition, if you plan ahead, you can avoid the additional costs of refinancing your mortgage or taking out a home equity loan in order to make your consumer purchases.

Example 1

Suppose you plan to finance the purchase of a car next year. If you take out a longer-term mortgage with lower payments than you might otherwise have done, you can apply the difference to your car payments. This will enable you to reduce the term of your car loan, which most likely will be financed at a higher rate than your mortgage and paid for with nondeductible interest.

Example 2

You are considering purchasing a new house and a new car within a relatively short time period. You may want to decrease your down payment on the house so that there will be extra cash available for a down payment on the car. By making a larger down payment on the car, your nondeductible interest, the interest paid on the car loan, will be less. Conversely, by decreasing your down payment on the house, you gain a tax benefit in the form of higher mortgage interest deductions.

EXPLANATION

Student loan interest deduction. You can claim a deduction for interest paid on qualified education loans that include indebtedness incurred for your benefit or the benefit of your spouse, or any dependent at the time the indebtedness is incurred. Qualified loans also include refinancings or consolidations of the original loans. You can claim this deduction whether or not you itemize your deductions.

The deduction is allowed only for interest paid on a qualified education loan. No deduction is allowed for individuals claimed as dependents on another taxpayer's return for the tax year. The maximum deduction is $2,500 in 2011.

The deduction is phased out for individual single taxpayers with modified adjusted gross income (AGI) in 2011 of $60,000–$75,000 and for couples filing jointly with modified AGI of $120,000–$150,000.

TAXSAVER

What loans cannot include in order to qualify. Education loans include loans covering both tuition and room and board. However, loans cannot include educational expenses that are paid through amounts from an employer educational assistance program or from amounts withdrawn from a Coverdell education savings account or qualified tuition programs. It is unclear how students or the IRS will be able to separate these expenses from the total loans received and payments made on those loans.

The U.S. Treasury is authorized to require lenders to report to borrowers the amount that constitutes deductible student loan interest. The government has also devised a method for borrowers to certify to lenders that loan proceeds are being used to pay for qualified educational expenses.

As with the education tax credits, this deduction is another factor to consider in determining whether or not a working student should be claimed as a dependent. Parents with income above the income thresholds cannot claim this deduction.

For further information about claiming the student loan interest deduction, see student loan interest deduction in chapter 19, *Education-related adjustments*.

Explanation

Interest you pay on loans acquired to purchase life insurance is also personal interest and generally is not deductible under current law. In addition, when a taxpayer borrows against his or her 401(k) plan account, the interest paid back to the plan is also generally not deductible.

TAXPLANNER

If you have loans outstanding for personal purposes, consider paying off these loans and substituting a different form of indebtedness.

Example

You have a $5,000 indebtedness on your credit card account. The funds were used for various personal purposes, and the interest is not deductible. You also have a $5,000 certificate of deposit (CD) that matures in 2011. Use the $5,000 from the maturity of the CD to pay off the credit card indebtedness. If you wish, you may borrow new funds for investment in a new CD. The interest on the new borrowings will be investment interest. The rules for deducting investment interest expense are more lenient than those for personal interest. Be sure to calculate the amount you would earn after taxes on such a borrowing or investment.

Allocation of Interest

If you use the proceeds of a loan for more than one purpose (for example, personal and business), you must allocate the interest on the loan to each use. However, you do not have to allocate home mortgage interest if it is fully deductible, regardless of how the funds are used.

You allocate interest (other than fully deductible home mortgage interest) on a loan in the same way as the loan itself is allocated. You do this by tracing disbursements of the debt proceeds to specific uses. For details on how to do this, see chapter 4 of Publication 535.

EXPLANATION

There are five types of interest expense, each of which has different limitations on deductibility:

1. Personal interest is not deductible (except for a limited amount of student loan interest described earlier in this chapter). Personal interest generally includes interest on credit card debts and on automobile loans. If you have to incur debt, try to make the debt related to either trade or business interest, investment interest, passive activity interest, or qualified residence interest.
2. Trade or business interest is fully deductible. Generally, it is interest on debt that relates to your trade or business. However, trade or business interest is not deductible if it is in connection with the trade or business of performing services as an employee.
3. Investment interest deductions may be limited because the deduction cannot exceed your net investment income for the taxable year. Any excess investment interest that is not deductible in the taxable year may be deducted in following years.
4. Passive activity interest is interest that is used to offset passive activity income. Generally, a passive activity is any interest in a real estate or other activity in which you do not materially participate. For tax purposes, you are considered a material participant if you are involved in the operations of the activity on a regular, continuous, and substantial basis. For additional discussion, see chapter 12, *Other income*.
5. Interest on a debt secured by a qualified residence is deductible within the limitations discussed earlier in this chapter.

TAXSAVER

When interest on debt used for investment exceeds investment income, the remaining investment interest may be deducted if it is qualified residence interest.

Example

In 2011, you purchase corporate bonds for $200,000, using a 6% home equity loan. Your investment income is $5,000.

Interest on your home equity loan	$12,000
Interest on portion of loan up to $100,000	(6,000)
Balance investment interest expense	$6,000
Deductible investment interest equal to investment income	(5,000)
Investment interest expense carried over to 2012	$1,000

TAXSAVER

Interest on debt used for a passive activity is subject to the same deduction rules as other passive activity expenses.

Example 1

Phil borrowed money to purchase a one-fourth interest in a partnership that manages an apartment building. In 2011, Phil paid $16,000 interest on the loan. His share of income and expenses was $60,000 and $40,000, respectively. Phil's passive income is $4,000 ($60,000 – $40,000 – $16,000). If his share of the partnership's expenses had been $50,000 instead of $40,000, Phil's $16,000 in interest expense would have resulted in a passive loss of $6,000 ($60,000 – $50,000 – $16,000). This loss can be carried over to future years in which there is additional passive income or when the investment is sold.

Example 2

Karen Pan has the following income and expenses in 2011:

Wages	$79,000
Interest	18,000
Short-term capital gain from sale of stock	2,000
Long-term capital gain taxed at 15%	1,000
Adjusted gross income (AGI)	$100,000
Investment interest expense	$21,000
Investment fees	$2,500
Unreimbursed employee expenses	$1,000

Karen's total miscellaneous itemized deductions are $3,500 ($2,500 + $1,000). After considering the 2% floor limitation, her allowable miscellaneous itemized deductions are $1,500 [$3,500 – (2% × $100,000 AGI)]. Therefore, Karen's net investment income is $18,500 [($18,000 + $2,000) – $1,500]. Because the long-term capital gain is taxed at 15%, it is not considered investment income. Karen could elect to treat the gain as ordinary income and would then be allowed to treat the $1,000 as investment income. Note that, in computing the allowable deductions, the noninvestment expenses were disallowed before the investment expenses.

EXPLANATION

The proceeds of loans, other than qualified mortgage loans, which were used for mixed purposes must be allocated to each applicable category.

Example

Joan borrows $100,000 on September 1, 2011, at an interest rate of 12% and deposits the funds in one checking account. Joan uses the money to purchase investment securities ($30,000 on September 1), a personal automobile ($30,000 on October 1), and equipment for her business ($40,000 on November 1). Joan pays interest of $1,000 at the end of each month.

Under the allocation rules, the interest on the loan is considered investment interest unless the proceeds are traceable to other purposes. The allocation is made as follows:

	Investment interest		Personal interest		Business interest	
September	100%	$1,000	–		–	
October	70%	700	30%	$300	–	
November	30%	300	30%	300	40%	$400
December	30%	300	30%	300	40%	400
Total		$2,300		$900		$800

When repayments of the debt are made, the repayment amounts are allocated first to nondeductible personal expenditures, then to investment and passive activity expenditures, and then to business expenditures.

TAXSAVER

The accounting for interest expense on loans used for mixed purposes is extremely complex.

To simplify your tax records, establish separate loan and bank accounts for each category of expenditure.

TAXSAVER

Interest on a qualified mortgage loan is not required to be allocated and is fully deductible when paid.

Although borrowing against your residence may ensure deductibility of the interest expense, the residence serves as collateral on the loan and may be foreclosed in the event of default.

As a reminder, interest paid on a home equity loan where the proceeds are not used to buy, build, or improve your home is not deductible under the Alternative Minimum Tax rules.

How To Report

You must file Form 1040 to deduct any home mortgage interest expense on your tax return. Where you deduct your interest expense generally depends on how you use the loan proceeds. See Table 24-1 for a summary of where to deduct your interest expense.

Home mortgage interest and points. Deduct the home mortgage interest and points reported to you on Form 1098 on Schedule A (Form 1040), line 10. If you paid more deductible interest to the financial institution than the amount shown on Form 1098, show the larger deductible amount on line 10. Attach a statement explaining the difference and print "See attached" next to line 10.

Deduct home mortgage interest that was not reported to you on Form 1098 on Schedule A (Form 1040), line 11. If you paid home mortgage interest to the person from whom you bought your home, show that person's name, address, and taxpayer identification number (TIN) on the dotted lines next to line 11. The seller must give you this number and you must give the seller your TIN. A Form W-9, Request for Taxpayer Identification Number and Certification, can be used for this purpose. Failure to meet any of these requirements may result in a $50 penalty for each failure. The TIN can be either a social security number, an individual taxpayer identification number (issued by the Internal Revenue Service), or an employer identification number. See *Social Security Number* in chapter 1 for more information about TINs.

Table 24-1. **Where To Deduct Your Interest Expense**

IF you have...	**THEN deduct it on...**	**AND for more information go to...**
deductible student loan interest	Form 1040, line 33, or Form 1040A, line 18	Publication 970.
deductible home mortgage interest and points reported on Form 1098	Schedule A (Form 1040), line 10	Publication 936.
deductible home mortgage interest not reported on Form 1098	Schedule A (Form 1040), line 11	Publication 936.
deductible points not reported on Form 1098	Schedule A (Form 1040), line 12	Publication 936.
deductible mortgage insurance premiums	Schedule A (Form 1040), line 13	Publication 936.
deductible investment interest (other than incurred to produce rents or royalties)	Schedule A (Form 1040), line 14	Publication 550.
deductible business interest (non-farm)	Schedule C or C-EZ (Form 1040)	Publication 535.
deductible farm business interest	Schedule F (Form 1040)	Publications 225 and 535.
deductible interest incurred to produce rents or royalties	Schedule E (Form 1040)	Publications 527 and 535.
personal interest	not deductible.	

TAXALERT

Seller-financed mortgages. If you pay interest on a seller-financed mortgage, you are required to include the following information on line 11 of Schedule A (Form 1040):

- The seller's social security number or identification number
- The seller's name and address

You must also provide the seller with your social security or identification number. Obviously, the best time to exchange this information is at the closing. However, this rule also applies to prior agreements. If you do not have the seller's identification number, or have not provided the seller with your social security number, you should meet the requirements as soon as possible to reduce the potential for penalties.

If you can take a deduction for points that were not reported to you on Form 1098, deduct those points on Schedule A (Form 1040), line 12.

Deduct mortgage insurance premiums on Schedule A (Form 1040), line 13.

More than one borrower. If you and at least one other person (other than your spouse if you file a joint return) were liable for and paid interest on a mortgage that was for your home, and the other person received a Form 1098 showing the interest that was paid during the year, attach a statement to your return explaining this. Show how much of the interest each of you paid, and give the name and address of the person who received the form. Deduct your share of the interest on Schedule A (Form 1040), line 11, and print "See attached" next to the line. Also, deduct your share of any qualified mortgage insurance premiums on Schedule A (Form 1040), line 13.

Similarly, if you are the payer of record on a mortgage on which there are other borrowers entitled to a deduction for the interest shown on the Form 1098 you received, deduct only your share of the interest on Schedule A (Form 1040), line 10. You should let each of the other borrowers know what his or her share is.

TAXALERT

Unmarried borrowers and Tenants in Common. If you own your home and took out a mortgage jointly with another individual who is not your spouse, you will generally only receive one Form 1098, Mortgage Interest Statement. The social security number of the first person listed on the mortgage loan will most likely be the one shown on the Form 1098 issued by your lender. Because the IRS matches informational tax forms, such as the Form 1098, with actual returns filed, you should report the allocated interest carefully to avoid confusion and unnecessary inquiries from the IRS. The individual whose social security number appears on the Form 1098 should report all of the interest paid on Schedule A, line 10, *Home mortgage interest and points reported to you on Form 1098,* and should report on the same line a negative (off-setting) interest amount representing the co-borrower's share. The co-borrower should report his or her share of the mortgage interest paid on Schedule A, line 11, *Home mortgage interest not reported to you on Form 1098,* and attach a statement noting the name, address, and social security number of the person who was named on Form 1098.

Mortgage proceeds used for business or investment. If your home mortgage interest deduction is limited, but all or part of the mortgage proceeds were used for business, investment, or other deductible activities, see Table 24-1. It shows where to deduct the part of your excess interest that is for those activities.

Investment interest. Deduct investment interest, subject to certain limits discussed in Publication 550, on Schedule A (Form 1040), line 14.

Amortization of bond premium. There are various ways to treat the premium you pay to buy taxable bonds. See *Bond Premium Amortization* in Publication 550.

TAXSAVER

Premiums on taxable bonds. There are various ways to treat the premium you pay to buy taxable bonds. You may deduct amortizable bond premiums directly from interest income. This could be beneficial whether or not you itemize your deductions.

Explanation

Premiums on tax-exempt bonds. You must amortize the premium and reduce the basis of tax-exempt bonds. However, you may not deduct the amortized premium. See Publication 535, *Business Expenses*.

Market discounts. You may be able to deduct only some of the interest expense incurred to acquire or carry marketable bonds with market discounts. For debt obligations issued after July 18, 1984, the interest expense deduction will be limited to the sum of:

- Interest income from marketable bonds
- The interest expense in excess of interest income in (1) and accrued market discount

The disallowed interest expense is deferred until the bond is sold or matures and is deducted then. The interest limitation does not apply to tax-exempt obligations purchased before May 1, 1993, U.S. savings bonds, obligations with a maturity of 1 year or less, and certain installment obligations.

Example

Sam acquires a $100,000, 9% interest-bearing bond for $90,000 on January 2, 2011. The bond was originally issued at face value in 2002. It matures in 2021, 10 years after Sam purchased it. Sam borrowed money to acquire the bond. In 2011, Sam paid $10,200 in interest on the debt. The allowable interest deduction for the year is figured as follows:

a. Interest expense	$10,200
b. Interest income ($100,000 × 9%)	(9,000)
c. Net interest expense	$1,200
d. Accrued market discount ($10,000 ÷ 10 yrs.)	(1,000)
e. Net interest expense in excess of accrued market discount	$200

Total allowable interest expense is $9,200 [(b) + (e)]. The remaining $1,000 will be allowed as a deduction in the year in which the bond matures or is sold.

Sam may elect to include the accrued market discount in income for the tax years to which it's attributable, thus allowing all interest expense to be deductible. If Sam makes this election, it will apply to all market discount bonds he acquires.

See the discussion in this chapter regarding limitations on the deduction of investment interest.

Income-producing rental or royalty interest. Deduct interest on a loan for income-producing rental or royalty property that is not used in your business in Part I of Schedule E (Form 1040).

Example. You rent out part of your home and borrow money to make repairs. You can deduct only the interest payment for the rented part in Part I of Schedule E (Form 1040). Deduct the rest of the interest payment on Schedule A (Form 1040) if it is deductible home mortgage interest.

Chapter 25
Contributions

ey.com/EYTaxGuide

Note

IRS Publication 17 (*Your Federal Income Tax*) has been updated by Ernst & Young LLP for 2011. Dates and dollar amounts shown are for 2011. Underlined type is used to indicate where IRS text has been updated. Places where text has been removed are indicated by the sentence: *Text intentionally omitted*.

ey.com/EYTaxGuide

Ernst & Young LLP will update the *Ernst & Young Tax Guide 2012* website with relevant taxpayer information as it becomes available. You can also sign up for email alerts to let you know when changes have been made.

Introduction

Americans give billions of dollars to charity each year. One explanation for that generosity may be that the federal government encourages charitable giving. It has long been the policy of the government to allow individuals tax deductions for charitable contributions they make. In effect, by allowing a deduction which reduces your taxable income (and therefore your tax), Uncle Sam is contributing part of every dollar you give to charity.

Even so, there are lots of rules governing charitable contributions, and it's important that you know them. This chapter tells you how to maximize your allowable charitable deductions and minimize your taxes. You'll learn why, for example, you might want to consider giving shares of stock instead of cash to your favorite charity. Just as important, the chapter tells you how to document your contributions.

Prior to 2010, itemized deductions were subject to certain limitations if your adjusted gross income exceeded certain amounts (for 2009, this amount was $166,800; $83,400 if married filing separately). But the itemized deduction phaseout has been temporarily repealed and higher-income taxpayers do not have to reduce their total itemized deductions for 2011 or 2012. Unless Congress acts, the old phaseout rule is scheduled to return beginning in 2013.

Tax Breaks and Deductions You Can Use Checklist

Contributions of Property. If you have capital gain property that you've held for more than a year, and you want to make a charitable contribution, you're usually better off donating that property rather than cash. That's because you get a market value deduction for capital gain property and you don't have to recognize any gain as income. You can always use the cash to buy back the property with a higher basis. See *Giving Property That Has Increased in Value*, later in this chapter.

Donating a Used Car to Charity. If you donate a used car to charity, you should remember that the amount of the deduction you will be allowed to claim may be subject to special limitations. For cars worth over $500, the deduction will be the amount for which the charity actually sells the car, if it sells the car without materially improving it or using it in its operations. So in many cases, you won't know the amount of your deduction until the charity has sold the car and reported the sale proceeds to you.

Contributions of Time. You can't deduct the value of the time you contribute to charity but you can deduct any out-of-pocket expenses you incurred as a result of your volunteering, such as mileage or the cost of uniforms. See *Out-of-Pocket Expenses in Giving Services*, later in this chapter.

Substantiating Your Charitable Contributions. Properly substantiating charitable contributions is critical—the IRS can, and will, disallow your deduction if you don't have the necessary documentation.

What's New

Text intentionally omitted. **Extended provisions.** The following provisions have been extended and will apply for 2011.

- Special rules for qualified charitable distributions from IRAs.
- The special deduction limit for qualified conservation contributions.

Text intentionally omitted.

TAXALERT

Contributions of real property made for conservation purposes. Through the end of 2011, the charitable deduction limit for qualified conservation contributions is 50% of the excess of the taxpayer's adjusted gross income (AGI) over the amount of all other allowable charitable contributions. If the individual making the contribution was a qualified farmer or rancher, the limitation is further increased to 100%.

The higher deduction limits for qualified conservation contributions expire at the end of 2011 unless Congress acts to extend them. Otherwise, the limit for qualified conservation contributions made after 2011 drops to 30%. For updated information on this and any other tax law changes that occur after this book was published, see our website, *ey.com/EYTaxGuide*. See the section on *Qualified Conservation Contribution*, later in this chapter, for more information.

Tax-free distributions from IRAs for charity. Through the end of 2011, an IRA owner age 70½ or older can take up to $100,000 in distributions from his or her IRA accounts (other than an SEP or SIMPLE IRA), contribute them to charity through a direct transfer received from the IRA trustee, and not recognize any income. Therefore, if all the requirements are met, a "Qualified Charitable Distribution" is nontaxable, but you cannot claim a charitable contribution deduction for it. See *Qualified charitable distributions (QCDs)* in chapter 17, *Individual retirement arrangements (IRAs)*.

Unless Congress acts, beginning in 2012, this exclusion of qualified charitable IRA distributions is not available. For updated information on this and any other tax law changes that occur after this book was published, see our website, *ey.com/EYTaxGuide*.

This chapter explains how to claim a deduction for your charitable contributions. It discusses the following topics.

- Organizations that are qualified to receive deductible charitable contributions.
- The types of contributions you can deduct.
- How much you can deduct.
- What records to keep.
- How to report your charitable contributions.

A charitable contribution is a donation or gift to, or for the use of, a qualified organization. It is voluntary and is made without getting, or expecting to get, anything of equal value.

Form 1040 required. To deduct a charitable contribution, you must file Form 1040 and itemize deductions on Schedule A. The amount of your deduction may be limited if certain rules and limits explained in this chapter apply to you.

Useful Items

You may want to see:

Publication

- □ **78** Cumulative List of Organizations
- □ **526** Charitable Contributions
- □ **561** Determining the Value of Donated Property

Form (and Instructions)

- □ **Schedule A (Form 1040)** Itemized Deductions
- □ **8283** Noncash Charitable Contributions

Organizations That Qualify To Receive Deductible Contributions

You can deduct your contributions only if you make them to a qualified organization. To become a qualified organization, most organizations other than churches and governments, as described below, must apply to the IRS.

Types of Qualified Organizations

Generally, only the five following types of organizations can be qualified organizations.

1. A community chest, corporation, trust, fund, or foundation organized or created in or under the laws of the United States, any state, the District of Columbia, or any possession of the United States (including Puerto Rico). It must be organized and operated only for one or more of the following purposes.
   a. Religious.
   b. Charitable.
   c. Educational.
   d. Scientific.
   e. Literary.
   f. The prevention of cruelty to children or animals.

   Certain organizations that foster national or international amateur sports competition also qualify.
2. War veterans' organizations, including posts, auxiliaries, trusts, or foundations, organized in the United States or any of its possessions.
3. Domestic fraternal societies, orders, and associations operating under the lodge system.
   Note. Your contribution to this type of organization is deductible only if it is to be used solely for charitable, religious, scientific, literary, or educational purposes, or for the prevention of cruelty to children or animals.
4. Certain nonprofit cemetery companies or corporations.
   Note. Your contribution to this type of organization is not deductible if it can be used for the care of a specific lot or mausoleum crypt.
5. The United States or any state, the District of Columbia, a U.S. possession (including Puerto Rico), a political subdivision of a state or U.S. possession, or an Indian tribal government or any of its subdivisions that perform substantial government functions.
   Note. To be deductible, your contribution to this type of organization must be made solely for public purposes.

All contributions must be substantiated, but contributions of $250 or more require a written receipt from the charity that meets specific requirements. A deduction for a cash contribution of any amount to charity will not be allowed unless the donor has a bank record or a receipt or a written communication from the charitable organization that shows the name of the charity, as well as the date and the amount of the contribution. Maintaining your own written log of cash contributions will no longer be sufficient substantiation. If you donate property valued at more than $500, you must file Form 8283.

Tip

You can ask any organization whether it is a qualified organization, and most will be able to tell you. Or you can check IRS Publication 78, which lists most qualified organizations. You may find Publication 78 in your local library's reference section. Or you can find it on the Internet at www.irs.gov/app/pub-78. *You can also call the IRS at 1-877-829-5500 to find out if an organization is qualified. (For TTY/TDD help, call 1-800-829-4059.)*

EXAMPLES

Contributions to the following U.S. and political subdivisions have been allowed:

- Contributions to the National Park Foundation
- Money donated to a state by an individual to defray expenses of hosting a governor's conference
- Contributions to a state for a parade incidental to a presidential inauguration

The IRS has ruled that the following are *not deductible* as contributions:

- Payments made to a state hospital for the purpose of reimbursing the state for the care of a person confined in the hospital do not constitute contributions made to a state for exclusively public purposes.
- The amount spent by a tenant for additions or improvements to government-owned housing is not deductible as a charitable contribution. Such amounts represent a nondeductible personal, living, or family expense.

Examples. The following list gives some examples of qualified organizations.

- Churches, a convention or association of churches, temples, synagogues, mosques, and other religious organizations.
- Most nonprofit charitable organizations such as the Red Cross and the United Way.
- Most nonprofit educational organizations, including the Boy (and Girl) Scouts of America, colleges, museums, and daycare centers if substantially all the child care provided is to enable individuals (the parents) to be gainfully employed and the services are available to the general public. However, if your contribution is a substitute for tuition or other enrollment fee, it is not deductible as a charitable contribution, as explained later under *Contributions You Cannot Deduct*.
- Nonprofit hospitals and medical research organizations.
- Utility company emergency energy programs, if the utility company is an agent for a charitable organization that assists individuals with emergency energy needs.
- Nonprofit volunteer fire companies.
- Public parks and recreation facilities.
- Civil defense organizations.

Certain foreign charitable organizations. Under income tax treaties with Canada, Israel, and Mexico, you may be able to deduct contributions to certain Canadian, Israeli, or Mexican charitable organizations. Generally, you must have income from sources in that country. For additional information on the deduction of contributions to Canadian charities, see Publication 597, *Information on the United States–Canada Income Tax Treaty*. If you need more information on how to figure your contribution to Mexican and Israeli charities, see Publication 526.

EXPLANATION

Any organization can tell you if it is a qualified organization.

Generally, charitable contributions must be made to organizations to be deductible. However, the courts have upheld contributions made to certain individuals on the grounds that the contribution was made to him or her as an agent for the organization. Consider the following cases in which deductions were allowed:

- An individual established a scholarship fund consisting of a personal checking account. Recipients were picked by school principals on the basis of need and scholastic merit. Each check was signed by the donor and made payable jointly to the scholar and the school. The donor was not involved in the selection process.
- A host family acting as a caretaker for an individual under a Department of Public Welfare/Medical Assistance Program is entitled to deduct as a charitable contribution any unreimbursed out-of-pocket expenses incurred in supporting a participant.
- A taxpayer directed his bank to send a check to a specifically named missionary. He instructed the bank to inform the missionary that the check was for Presbyterian mission work. The Tax Court held that this was really a contribution to the church through the missionary as an agent for the church.

Exception

The Supreme Court ruled that funds transferred by parents directly to their sons while they served as unpaid missionaries were not charitable contributions "for the use of" the church, even though the funds were requested by the church.

Contributions You Can Deduct

Generally, you can deduct your contributions of money or property that you make to, or for the use of, a qualified organization. A gift or contribution is "for the use of" a qualified organization when it is held in a legally enforceable trust for the qualified organization or in a similar legal arrangement. The contributions must be made to a qualified organization and not set aside for use by a specific person.

If you give property to a qualified organization, you generally can deduct the fair market value of the property at the time of the contribution. See *Contributions of Property*, later in this chapter.

Your deduction for charitable contributions is generally limited to 50% of your adjusted gross income, but in some cases 20% and 30% limits may apply. See *Limits on Deductions*, later.

Table 25-1 lists some examples of contributions you can deduct and some that you cannot deduct.

EXPLANATION

Fair market value generally is the price that property would sell for on the open market. It takes into account many factors that affect the value of property on the date of the contribution.

Example

If you give used clothing to the Salvation Army, the fair market value is the price that typical buyers actually pay for clothing of this age, condition, style, and use. Usually, such items are worth far less than what you paid for them.

TAXPLANNER

Determining fair market value. A valuable tool for determining fair market value is IRS Publication 561, *Determining the Value of Donated Property*. The publication helps donors and appraisers determine the value of property given to qualified organizations and includes the kind of information you must have to support the charitable deduction you claim on your return.

Table 25-1. **Examples of Charitable Contributions—A Quick Check**

Use the following lists for a quick check of contributions you can or cannot deduct. See the rest of this chapter for more information and additional rules and limits that may apply.

Deductible As Charitable Contributions	**Not Deductible As Charitable Contributions**
Money or property you give to: • Churches, synagogues, temples, mosques, and other religious organizations • Federal, state, and local governments, if your contribution is solely for public purposes (for example, a gift to reduce the public debt) • Nonprofit schools and hospitals • Public parks and recreation facilities • Salvation Army, Red Cross, CARE, Goodwill Industries, United Way, Boy Scouts, Girl Scouts, Boys and Girls Clubs of America, etc. • War veterans groups • Charitable organizations listed in Publication 78 • Expenses paid for a student living with you, sponsored by a qualified organization • Out-of-pocket expenses when you serve a qualified organization as a volunteer	Money or property you give to: • Civic leagues, social and sports clubs, labor unions, and chambers of commerce • Foreign organizations (except certain Canadian, Israeli, and Mexican charities) • Groups that are run for personal profit • Groups whose purpose is to lobby for law changes • Homeowners' associations • Individuals • Political groups or candidates for public office • Cost of raffle, bingo, or lottery tickets • Dues, fees, or bills paid to country clubs, lodges, fraternal orders, or similar groups • Tuition • Value of your time or services • Value of blood given to a blood bank

A sale or purchase of similar property reasonably close to the date of your contribution is usually the best indication of fair market value. Replacement cost and opinions of experts are also valid methods for determining value.

IRS Publication 561 discusses pitfalls to be avoided in determining the value of donated property. Some pitfalls and how to avoid them are the following:

1. The best evidence of fair market value depends on actual transactions, not on some artificial estimate.
2. Do not consider unexpected events occurring after your donation of property in making the valuation. Generally, you should only consider facts known at the time of the gift.
3. Past events are not necessarily reliable in predicting future earnings and fair market value. For example, a taxpayer contributes all rights in a patent to a charitable organization. The patent has a history of high earnings, but the current trend reflects declining earnings. In this case, more emphasis should be placed on the earnings trend rather than on the earnings history.

The cost of an appraisal is not deductible as a charitable contribution, but it may be claimed as a miscellaneous itemized deduction.

A description of property for which a deduction of more than $500 is claimed must be attached to your return along with Form 8283. Additionally, you are required to obtain a qualified appraisal for certain noncash donations. A qualified appraisal must be made by an independent party. The charity or any person or entity related to the charity cannot render the appraisal. Appraisals are required for the donation of property with a claimed value in excess of $5,000. If you make gifts of two or more items of similar property during the year, the claimed value of all of those items will be added together in determining whether the $5,000 limit is exceeded. For contributions of property in excess of $500,000 the appraisal must be attached to your return.

The appraisal may not be made by the organization receiving the gift, the party from whom the taxpayer acquired the property, the taxpayer, or certain persons related to any of these persons.

The appraisal fee cannot be based on a percentage of the appraised value of the gift.

Form 8283, containing an acknowledgment of receipt of the property by the receiving organization and a certification by the appraiser, must be filed with the tax return on which the deduction is taken.

Special Rules and Limitations: The appraisal rules may be different for certain types of property. In general, the above appraisal rules do not apply to contributions of intellectual property (e.g., patents, copyrights, trademarks, etc.), certain stock in trade or inventory held for sale in the normal course of business, publicly traded securities, and certain "qualified vehicles" (i.e., motor vehicles, boats, and airplanes).

TAXALERT

Donations of Vehicles–SPECIAL RULES

Under the American Jobs Creation Act of 2004 and under guidance issued by the IRS in 2005, donations of vehicles are subject to additional requirements and limitations. In general, to be fully deductible, the charity must either (1) use the vehicle in a significant way in performing its regularly conducted activities (known as "significant intervening use"), (2) materially improve the vehicle's condition (e.g., through major repairs that significantly increase the vehicle's value–minor repairs, routine maintenance, and cleaning are not considered material improvements), or (3) give or sell the vehicle to a needy individual for a price significantly below its fair market value (FMV) in furtherance of the organization's charitable purpose of relieving the poor, distressed, or underprivileged who are in need of transportation. If the charity sells the vehicle without any significant intervening use or material improvement, the deduction cannot exceed the gross proceeds received by the charity from the sale. In other words, if the charity sells the vehicle, your deduction will be limited to its sales proceeds.

You can't take a deduction of more than $500 for a contribution of a motor vehicle, boat, or airplane unless it is substantiated by a contemporaneous (i.e., within 30 days of the contribution, or sale if the vehicle is sold) written acknowledgment by the charity receiving the gift which contains:

1. The name and taxpayer identification number of the donor,
2. The vehicle identification number or similar number, and
3. Certification of use in one of the following forms:
   i. If the vehicle is to be used or improved by the charity: a certification of the intended use or material improvement of the vehicle and the intended duration of the use, and a certification that the vehicle will not be sold before the completion of such use or improvement.
   ii. If the vehicle is sold without intervening use or improvement: a certification that the vehicle was sold in an arm's-length transaction between unrelated parties, the gross proceeds from the sale, and a statement that the deductible amount may not exceed the amount of such gross proceeds.
   iii. If the vehicle is given or sold to a needy individual for a price significantly below its FMV: a certification that the vehicle was given or sold to a needy individual at a price significantly below its FMV in furtherance of the organization's charitable purpose of relieving the poor, distressed or underprivileged who are in need of transportation.

The charity will use Form 1098-C for this purpose.

Examples

Example 1. As part of its regularly conducted activities, an organization delivers meals to needy individuals. The use requirement would be met if the organization actually used a donated qualified vehicle to deliver food to the needy. Use of the vehicle to deliver meals substantially furthers a regularly conducted activity of the organization. However, the use also must be significant, which depends on the nature, extent, and frequency of the use. If the organization used the vehicle only once or a few times to deliver meals, the use would not be considered significant. If the organization used the vehicle to deliver meals every day for one year, the use would be considered significant. If the organization drove the vehicle 10,000 miles while delivering meals, such use likely would be considered significant. However, use of a vehicle in such an activity for one week or for several hundreds of miles generally would not be considered a significant use.

Example 2. An organization uses a donated qualified vehicle to transport its volunteers. The use would not be significant merely because a volunteer used the vehicle over a brief period of time to drive to or from the organization's premises. On the other hand, if at the time the organization accepts the contribution of a qualified vehicle, the organization intends to use the vehicle as a regular and ongoing means of transport for volunteers of the organization, and such vehicle is so used, then the significant use test likely would be met.

Example 3. The following example is a general illustration of the provision. A taxpayer makes a charitable contribution of a used automobile in good running condition and that needs no immediate repairs to a charitable organization that operates an elder care facility. The charitable organization accepts the vehicle and immediately provides the donor a written acknowledgment containing the name and TIN of the donor, the vehicle identification number, a certification that it intends to retain the vehicle for a year or longer to transport the facility's residents to community and social events and deliver meals to the needy, and a certification that the vehicle will not be transferred in exchange for money, other property, or services before completion of such use by the organization. A few days after receiving the vehicle, the charitable organization commences to use the vehicle three times a week to transport some of its residents to various community events, and twice a week to deliver food to needy individuals. The organization continues to regularly use the vehicle for these purposes for approximately one year and then sells the vehicle.

Under the provision, the charity's use of the vehicle constitutes a significant intervening use prior to the sale by the organization, and the donor's deduction is not limited to the gross proceeds received by the organization.

Intellectual Property

Due to the inherent difficulties in valuing intellectual property, such as patents, copyrights, trademarks, trade names, trade secrets, know-how, software, similar property, or applications or registrations of such property, the American Jobs Creation Act of 2004 contained significant revisions to the rules for deducting contributions of intellectual property, effective for contributions made after June 3, 2004. Under these rules, the deduction for a contribution of intellectual property is generally limited to the lesser of the taxpayer's basis in the property or the fair market value of the property.

Further, you would be allowed to deduct additional amounts in the year of contribution or in subsequent tax years based on a specified percentage of the "qualified donee income" received or accrued by the charitable recipient for the contributed property. Qualified donee income is only the income properly allocable to the intellectual property itself, rather than to the activity in which such property is used.

If you make a qualified intellectual property contribution, the deduction allowed for each tax year ending on or after the date of the contribution is increased by the applicable percentage of qualified income for the contribution that is properly allocable to that year. The amount of the additional deduction allowed per year phases out over the 12 years following the contribution.

The calculation of the charitable contribution deduction is very complex. You should consult your tax advisor if you're considering donating intellectual property to charity.

TAXALERT

Accurate assessments. It is very important to get an accurate assessment of donated property because you may be liable for a special penalty if you overstate its value. You may be liable for the penalty if the value claimed on your return is more than 150% (200% for tax returns filed before August 18, 2006) of the correct amount.

The penalty is 20% of the tax underpayment attributable to the overvaluation and may increase to 40% if the value claimed is 200% (400% for tax returns filed before August 18, 2006) or more of the correct amount.

Contributions From Which You Benefit

If you receive a benefit as a result of making a contribution to a qualified organization, you can deduct only the amount of your contribution that is more than the value of the benefit you receive. Also, see Contributions From Which You Benefit under *Contributions You Cannot Deduct,* later.

If you pay more than fair market value to a qualified organization for merchandise, goods, or services, the amount you pay that is more than the value of the item can be a charitable contribution. For the excess amount to qualify, you must pay it with the intent to make a charitable contribution.

Example 1. You pay $65 for a ticket to a dinner-dance at a church. All of the proceeds of the function go to the church. The ticket to the dinner-dance has a fair market value of $25. When you buy your ticket, you know that its value is less than your payment. To figure the amount of your charitable contribution, you subtract the value of the benefit you receive ($25) from your total payment ($65). You can deduct $40 as a contribution to the church.

Example 2. At a fund-raising auction conducted by a charity, you pay $600 for a week's stay at a beach house. The amount you pay is no more than the fair rental value. You have not made a deductible charitable contribution.

Athletic events. If you make a payment to, or for the benefit of, a college or university and, as a result, you receive the right to buy tickets to an athletic event in the athletic stadium of the college or university, you can deduct 80% of the payment as a charitable contribution.

If any part of your payment is for tickets (rather than the right to buy tickets), that part is not deductible. In that case, subtract the price of the tickets from your payment. 80% of the remaining amount is a charitable contribution.

Example 1. You pay $300 a year for membership in an athletic scholarship program maintained by a university (a qualified organization). The only benefit of membership is that you have the right to buy one season ticket for a seat in a designated area of the stadium at the university's home football games. You can deduct $240 (80% of $300) as a charitable contribution.

Example 2. The facts are the same as in Example 1 except that your $300 payment included the purchase of one season ticket for the stated ticket price of $120. You must subtract the usual price of a ticket ($120) from your $300 payment. The result is $180. Your deductible charitable contribution is $144 (80% of $180).

EXCEPTIONS

A deduction for a charitable contribution was not permitted in the following instances:

- A person contributed a computer to a university, and the donor reserved the right to use the computer for 12 weeks per year.
- A person released frontage to a county for widening a road in order to obtain the required approval by the county planning commission of the development plan for certain lots prior to their sale. (However, the cost of the frontage is part of the total cost basis of the remaining property for determining the gain or loss on the sale of the property.)
- The amount paid by a taxpayer to purchase building bonds issued by a church was not a gift made to the church. However, if the taxpayer had subsequently given the bonds to the church, he would have been entitled to a charitable deduction for their fair market value at the time of the gift.
- A person made contributions to a nonprofit organization formed by parents of pupils attending a private school. The organization provided school bus transportation for members' children. The contributions served a private rather than a public interest.
- A taxpayer paid a fee to a nonprofit corporation for the privilege of taking up residence in a home operated by the corporation. This fee, along with a required entrance fee, entitled the taxpayer to lifetime care in the home. The fee represented a personal expense.

Caution

Even if the ticket or other evidence of payment indicates that the payment is a "contribution," this does not mean you can deduct the entire amount. If the ticket shows the price of admission and the amount of the contribution, you can deduct the contribution amount.

Charity benefit events. If you pay a qualified organization more than fair market value for the right to attend a charity ball, banquet, show, sporting event, or other benefit event, you can deduct only the amount that is more than the value of the privileges or other benefits you receive.

If there is an established charge for the event, that charge is the value of your benefit. If there is no established charge, your contribution is that part of your payment that is more than the reasonable value of the right to attend the event. Whether you use the tickets or other privileges has no effect on the amount you can deduct. However, if you return the ticket to the qualified organization for resale, you can deduct the entire amount you paid for the ticket.

Example. You pay $40 to see a special showing of a movie for the benefit of a qualified organization. Printed on the ticket is "Contribution—$40." If the regular price for the movie is $8, your contribution is $32 ($40 payment − $8 regular price).

EXPLANATION

The IRS requires that charities determine the fair market value of benefits offered in exchange for contributions in advance of the solicitation and state in the solicitation, as well as in the receipt, tickets, or other documents, what portion of the contribution is deductible. The charity may advise donors that the full amount of a contribution is deductible if any of the following applies:

- The fair market value of all the benefits received in conjunction with the contribution is not more than the lesser of 2% of the payment or $95.
- The contribution is at least $47.50, and the only benefits received in connection with the payment are token items, such as bookmarks, calendars, key chains, mugs, posters, and T-shirts bearing the organization's name or logo (i.e., low-cost articles with a cost not in excess of $9.50).
- The charity distributes unordered items to patrons. The distributed item must be accompanied by a request for a contribution and by a statement that the item can be retained whether or not a contribution is made. The aggregate cost per patron of these items cannot exceed $9.50.

Example

In 2011, a nonprofit broadcast organization sends its patrons a listener's guide for 1 year in return for a contribution of $47.50 or more. The cost of the production and distribution of the listener's guide is $8 per year per patron, and its fair market value is $10. The listener's guide is not available to nonmembers by paid subscription or through newsstand sales. Because the cost of the listener's guide is $8 and it is received in return for a contribution of $47.50 or more, the broadcast organization may advise its patrons that the full amount of the payment is a deductible contribution. However, if the cost of the publication exceeds $9.50, the charitable organization would be required to inform its patrons of the amount by which they should reduce their charitable deductions.

Membership fees or dues. You may be able to deduct membership fees or dues you pay to a qualified organization. However, you can deduct only the amount that is more than the value of the benefits you receive. You cannot deduct dues, fees, or assessments paid to country clubs and other social organizations. They are not qualified organizations.

Certain membership benefits can be disregarded. Both you and the organization can disregard certain membership benefits you get in return for an annual payment of $75 or less to the qualified organization. The benefits that can be disregarded are:

1. Any rights or privileges, other than those discussed under *Athletic events*, earlier, that you can use frequently while you are a member, such as:
   a. Free or discounted admission to the organization's facilities or events,
   b. Free or discounted parking,
   c. Preferred access to goods or services, and
   d. Discounts on the purchase of goods and services.
2. Admission, while you are a member, to events that are open only to members of the organization, if the organization reasonably projects that the cost per person (excluding any allocated overhead) is not more than $9.60.

Token items. You can deduct your entire payment to a qualified organization as a charitable contribution if both of the following are true.

- You get a small item or other benefit of token value.
- The qualified organization correctly determines that the value of the item or benefit you received is not substantial and informs you that you can deduct your payment in full.

Written statement. A qualified organization must give you a written statement if you make a payment to it that is more than $75 and is partly a contribution and partly for goods or services. The statement must tell you that you can deduct only the amount of your payment that is more than the value of the goods or services you received. It must also give you a good faith estimate of the value of those goods or services.

The organization can give you the statement either when it solicits or when it receives the payment from you.

Exception. An organization will not have to give you this statement if one of the following is true.

1. The organization is:
   a. The type of organization described in (5) under *Types of Qualified Organizations*, earlier, or
   b. Formed only for religious purposes, and the only benefit you receive is an intangible religious benefit (such as admission to a religious ceremony) that generally is not sold in commercial transactions outside the donative context.
2. You receive only items whose value is not substantial as described under *Token items*, earlier.
3. You receive only membership benefits that can be disregarded, as described earlier.

Expenses Paid for Student Living With You

You may be able to deduct some expenses of having a student live with you. You can deduct qualifying expenses for a foreign or American student who:

1. Lives in your home under a written agreement between you and a qualified organization as part of a program of the organization to provide educational opportunities for the student,
2. Is not your relative or dependent, and
3. Is a full-time student in the twelfth or any lower grade at a school in the United States.

For additional information, see *Expenses Paid for Student Living With You* in Publication 526.

Mutual exchange program. You cannot deduct the costs of a foreign student living in your home under a mutual exchange program through which your child will live with a family in a foreign country.

Tip

You can deduct up to $50 a month for each full calendar month the student lives with you. Any month when conditions (1) through (3) above are met for 15 days or more counts as a full month.

EXPLANATION

The deduction is limited to amounts that you actually spend for the well-being of the student during the taxable year while the student is a member of the household and a full-time student. Amounts you pay for the student's books, tuition, food, clothing, transportation, medical and dental care, and entertainment qualify for the deduction. Depreciation on your home, the fair market value of lodging at your home, or similar items are not considered an amount spent by you and are not deductible.

If you are compensated or reimbursed for the costs of having a student live with you, you may not take a deduction for any part of these costs.

Out-of-Pocket Expenses in Giving Services

Although you cannot deduct the value of your services given to a qualified organization, you may be able to deduct some amounts you pay in giving services to a qualified organization. The amounts must be:

- Unreimbursed,
- Directly connected with the services,
- Expenses you had only because of the services you gave, and
- Not personal, living, or family expenses.

EXPLANATION

Unreimbursed out-of-pocket expenses incurred in rendering services to qualified charities are considered contributions made "to" the charitable entities rather than "for the use of" the charitable entities, and, as such, the deduction may be subject to the 50% limit rather than the 30% limit. See *Limits on Deductions*, later, to determine if further limitations apply.

Table 25-2 contains questions and answers that apply to some individuals who volunteer their services.

Conventions. If you are a chosen representative attending a convention of a qualified organization, you can deduct unreimbursed expenses for travel and transportation, including a reasonable amount for meals and lodging, while away from home overnight in connection with the convention. However, see *Travel*, later.

You cannot deduct personal expenses for sightseeing, fishing parties, theater tickets, or nightclubs. You also cannot deduct transportation, meals and lodging, and other expenses for your spouse or children.

Table 25-2. **Volunteers' Questions and Answers**

If you do volunteer work for a qualified organization, the following questions and answers may apply to you. All of the rules explained in this chapter also apply. See, in particular, *Out-of-Pocket Expenses in Giving Services*.

Question	Answer
I do volunteer work 6 hours a week in the office of a qualified organization. The receptionist is paid $10 an hour to do the same work I do. Can I deduct $60 a week for my time?	No, you cannot deduct the value of your time or services.
The office is 30 miles from my home. Can I deduct any of my car expenses for these trips?	Yes, you can deduct the costs of gas and oil that are directly related to getting to and from the place where you are a volunteer. If you don't want to figure your actual costs, you can deduct 14 cents for each mile.
I volunteer as a Red Cross nurse's aide at a hospital. Can I deduct the cost of uniforms that I must wear?	Yes, you can deduct the cost of buying and cleaning your uniforms if the hospital is a qualified organization, the uniforms are not suitable for everyday use, and you must wear them when volunteering.
I pay a babysitter to watch my children while I do volunteer work for a qualified organization. Can I deduct these costs?	No, you cannot deduct payments for child care expenses as a charitable contribution, even if they are necessary so you can do volunteer work for a qualified organization. (If you have child care expenses so you can work for pay, see chapter 32.)

You cannot deduct your expenses in attending a church convention if you go only as a member of your church rather than as a chosen representative. You can deduct unreimbursed expenses that are directly connected with giving services for your church during the convention.

Uniforms. You can deduct the cost and upkeep of uniforms that are not suitable for everyday use and that you must wear while performing donated services for a charitable organization.

Foster parents. You may be able to deduct as a charitable contribution some of the costs of being a foster parent (foster care provider) if you have no profit motive in providing the foster care and are not, in fact, making a profit. A qualified organization must designate the individuals you take into your home for foster care.

You can deduct expenses that meet both of the following requirements.

1. They are unreimbursed out-of-pocket expenses to feed, clothe, and care for the foster child.
2. They must be mainly to benefit the qualified organization.

EXPLANATION

You may deduct reasonable, unreimbursed out-of-pocket expenses you spend for underprivileged children to attend athletic events, movies, or dinners. It must be part of an event sponsored on behalf of a qualifying organization. Expenses for yourself are not deductible.

Unreimbursed expenses that you cannot deduct as charitable contributions may be considered support provided by you in determining whether you can claim the foster child as a dependent. For details, see chapter 3.

Example. You cared for a foster child because you wanted to adopt her, not to benefit the agency that placed her in your home. Your unreimbursed expenses are not deductible as charitable contributions.

TAXALERT

Although you cannot claim a charitable deduction for your unreimbursed expenses, you may be entitled to a tax credit for certain qualified adoption expenses (see Form 8839).

Car expenses. You can deduct unreimbursed out-of-pocket expenses, such as the cost of gas and oil, that are directly related to the use of your car in giving services to a charitable organization. You cannot deduct general repair and maintenance expenses, depreciation, registration fees, or the costs of tires or insurance.

If you do not want to deduct your actual expenses, you can use a standard mileage rate of 14 cents a mile to figure your contribution.

You can deduct parking fees and tolls whether you use your actual expenses or the standard mileage rate.

You must keep reliable written records of your car expenses. For more information, see *Car expenses* under *Records To Keep,* later.

Travel. Generally, you can claim a charitable contribution deduction for travel expenses necessarily incurred while you are away from home performing services for a charitable organization only if there is no significant element of personal pleasure, recreation, or vacation in the travel. This applies whether you pay the expenses directly or indirectly. You are paying the expenses indirectly if you make a payment to the charitable organization and the organization pays for your travel expenses.

The deduction for travel expenses will not be denied simply because you enjoy providing services to the charitable organization. Even if you enjoy the trip, you can take a charitable contribution deduction for your travel expenses if you are on duty in a genuine and substantial sense throughout the trip. However, if you have only nominal duties, or if for significant parts of the trip you do not have any duties, you cannot deduct your travel expenses.

Example 1. You are a troop leader for a tax-exempt youth group and you help take the group on a camping trip. You are responsible for overseeing the setup of the camp and for providing adult supervision for other activities during the entire trip. You participate in the activities of the group and really enjoy your time with them. You oversee the breaking of camp and you help transport the group home. You can deduct your travel expenses.

Example 2. You sail from one island to another and spend 8 hours a day counting whales and other forms of marine life. The project is sponsored by a charitable organization. In most circumstances, you cannot deduct your expenses.

Example 3. You work for several hours each morning on an archaeological dig sponsored by a charitable organization. The rest of the day is free for recreation and sightseeing. You cannot take a charitable contribution deduction even though you work very hard during those few hours.

Example 4. You spend the entire day attending a charitable organization's regional meeting as a chosen representative. In the evening you go to the theater. You can claim your travel expenses as charitable contributions, but you cannot claim the cost of your evening at the theater.

Daily allowance (per diem). If you provide services for a charitable organization and receive a daily allowance to cover reasonable travel expenses, including meals and lodging while away from home overnight, you must include in income the amount of the allowance that is more than your deductible travel expenses. You can deduct your necessary travel expenses that are more than the allowance.

Deductible travel expenses. These include:

- Air, rail, and bus transportation,
- Out-of-pocket expenses for your car,
- Taxi fares or other costs of transportation between the airport or station and your hotel,
- Lodging costs, and
- The cost of meals.

Because these travel expenses are not business-related, they are not subject to the same limits as business-related expenses. For information on business travel expenses, see Travel Expenses in chapter 27.

Contributions You Cannot Deduct

There are some contributions you cannot deduct, such as those made to specific individuals and those made to nonqualified organizations. (See *Contributions to Individuals* and *Contributions to Nonqualified Organizations*, next.) There are others you can deduct only part of, as discussed later under *Contributions From Which You Benefit*.

Contributions to Individuals

You cannot deduct contributions to specific individuals, including the following.

- Contributions to fraternal societies made for the purpose of paying medical or burial expenses of deceased members.
- Contributions to individuals who are needy or worthy. This includes contributions to a qualified organization if you indicate that your contribution is for a specific person. But you can deduct a contribution that you give to a qualified organization that in turn helps needy or worthy individuals if you do not indicate that your contribution is for a specific person.

  Example. You can deduct contributions for flood relief, hurricane relief, or other disaster relief to a qualified organization. However, you cannot deduct contributions earmarked for relief of a particular individual or family.
- Payments to a member of the clergy that can be spent as he or she wishes, such as for personal expenses.
- Expenses you paid for another person who provided services to a qualified organization.

  Example. Your son does missionary work. You pay his expenses. You cannot claim a deduction for your son's unreimbursed expenses related to his contribution of services.
- Payments to a hospital that are for a specific patient's care or for services for a specific patient. You cannot deduct these payments even if the hospital is operated by a city, a state, or other qualified organization.

TAXPLANNER

Direct contributions to needy individuals. Direct contributions to needy or worthy individuals are not deductible. But, if you can show that the economic benefit derived by the specific individual to whom your contribution is directed is less than the contribution to the organization in whose care the individual is placed, the excess may be deductible.

Example

An individual made a contribution to a school for crippled children that her son attended. The donor required that a portion of her contribution be used to purchase a wheelchair for the exclusive use of her son. She was allowed a deduction for a charitable contribution for the amount by which the contribution exceeded the cost of the wheelchair. (The cost of the wheelchair may qualify as a medical expense.)

Contributions to Nonqualified Organizations

You cannot deduct contributions to organizations that are not qualified to receive tax-deductible contributions, including the following.

1. Certain state bar associations if:
   a. The state bar is not a political subdivision of a state,
   b. The bar has private, as well as public, purposes, such as promoting the professional interests of members, and
   c. Your contribution is unrestricted and can be used for private purposes.
2. Chambers of commerce and other business leagues or organizations (but see chapter 29).
3. Civic leagues and associations.
4. Communist organizations.
5. Country clubs and other social clubs.
6. Foreign organizations other than:
   a. A U.S. organization that transfers funds to a charitable foreign organization if the U.S. organization controls the use of the funds or if the foreign organization is only an administrative arm of the U.S. organization, or

EXAMPLE

A contribution to the U.S. Red Cross is deductible, even though some portion of the contribution may be used outside the United States. If you make a contribution to a U.S. organization directing that it be sent to a foreign charitable organization to be used abroad, a deduction may not be allowed because the real recipient is not a domestic organization.

   b. Certain Canadian, Israeli, or Mexican charitable organizations. See *Certain foreign charitable organizations* under *Organizations That Qualify To Receive Deductible Contributions,* earlier.

EXPLANATION

The Canadian, Mexican, and Israeli tax treaties provide that contributions to charitable organizations (other than charitable contributions to a college or a university at which you or a member of your family is or was enrolled) are subject to the U.S. percentage limits on charitable contributions, applied to your income from sources in each of these countries.

7. Homeowners' associations.
8. Labor unions (but see chapter 29).
9. Political organizations and candidates.

Contributions From Which You Benefit

If you receive or expect to receive a financial or economic benefit as a result of making a contribution to a qualified organization, you cannot deduct the part of the contribution that represents the value of the benefit you receive. See *Contributions From Which You Benefit* under *Contributions You Can Deduct,* earlier. These contributions include the following.

- Contributions for lobbying. This includes amounts that you earmark for use in, or in connection with, influencing specific legislation.
- Contributions to a retirement home that are clearly for room, board, maintenance, or admittance. Also, if the amount of your contribution depends on the type or size of apartment you will occupy, it is not a charitable contribution.

- Costs of raffles, bingo, lottery, etc. You cannot deduct as a charitable contribution amounts you pay to buy raffle or lottery tickets or to play bingo or other games of chance. For information on how to report gambling winnings and losses, see chapters 12 and 29.
- Dues to fraternal orders and similar groups. However, see *Membership fees or dues*, earlier, under *Contributions You Can Deduct*.
- Tuition, or amounts you pay instead of tuition, even if you pay them for children to attend parochial schools or qualifying nonprofit day-care centers. You also cannot deduct any fixed amount you may be required to pay in addition to the tuition fee to enroll in a private school, even if it is designated as a "donation."

EXPLANATION

Tuition-type payments disguised as a charitable contribution are not deductible. Certain rules have been established by the IRS to determine whether an item is a tuition payment or a charitable contribution.

No deduction for a charitable contribution is allowed if at least one of the following conditions exists:

1. A contract under which a taxpayer agrees to make a "contribution," and that contract contains provisions ensuring the admission of the taxpayer's child;
2. A plan allowing taxpayers either to pay tuition or to make "contributions" in exchange for schooling;
3. The designation of a contribution for the direct benefit of a particular child;
4. The otherwise unexplained denial of admission or readmission to a school of children of taxpayers who are financially able but who do not contribute.

Other factors that are considered in deciding if a contribution is deductible include the following:

1. The absence of a significant tuition charge;
2. Substantial or unusual pressure to contribute applied to parents of students;
3. Contribution appeals made as part of the admissions or enrollment process;
4. The absence of significant potential sources of revenue for operating the school other than contributions by parents of students;
5. The contribution amounts are the same for all families or are paid pursuant to published guidelines for donations.

Value of Time or Services

You cannot deduct the value of your time or services, including:

- Blood donations to the Red Cross or to blood banks, and
- The value of income lost while you work as an unpaid volunteer for a qualified organization.

TAXPLANNER

Services to a charitable organization. If you contribute your services to a charitable organization, you are not permitted to take a charitable deduction for the value of your time or services. However, you are entitled to take a charitable deduction if you acquire the right to services to be performed by another and then gratuitously transfer that right to the charity.

Example

You purchase a series of six golf lessons from a local golf professional. Because you are unable to use the lessons, you donate them to your church for use in their raffle. The cost of the six lessons is deductible as a charitable contribution.

Personal Expenses

You cannot deduct personal, living, or family expenses, such as the following items.

- The cost of meals you eat while you perform services for a qualified organization unless it is necessary for you to be away from home overnight while performing the services.
- Adoption expenses, including fees paid to an adoption agency and the costs of keeping a child in your home before adoption is final (but see *Adoption Credit* in chapter 37, and the instructions for Form 8839, Qualified Adoption Expenses). You also may be able to claim an exemption for the child. See *Adopted child* in chapter 3.

Appraisal Fees

Fees that you pay to find the fair market value of donated property are not deductible as contributions (but see chapter 29).

Contributions of Property

If you contribute property to a qualified organization, the amount of your charitable contribution is generally the fair market value of the property at the time of the contribution. However, if the property has increased in value, you may have to make some adjustments to the amount of your deduction. See *Giving Property That Has Increased in Value*, later.

EXPLANATION

If you permit a charitable organization to use your property without charge (or at a minimal rate), no charitable deduction is allowed.

TAXSAVER

The IRS, however, will allow charitable deductions for the cost of operation, maintenance, and repair of property directly related to the charitable organization's use of the property.

If you donate the use of your yacht to the church for use in their raffle, no income tax deduction is allowed for the rental value or other value of the donated use. Direct operating costs, such as fuel, used in connection with the donated use are allowable as a charitable contribution.

For information about the records you must keep and the information you must furnish with your return if you donate property, see *Records To Keep* and *How To Report*, later.

TAXPLANNER

Some of the rules for reporting contributions of certain noncash property were changed by 2004 tax legislation. The 2004 law extends to all C corporations the requirement previously and currently applicable to an individual, closely held corporation, personal service corporation, partnership, or S corporation, that the donor must obtain a qualified appraisal of the property if the deduction claimed exceeds $5,000. (A C corporation is generally a business entity owned by shareholders and treated as a separate tax entity.) In addition, the law provides that if the amount of the contribution of property exceeds $500,000, the donor (whether an individual, partnership, or corporation) must attach a qualified appraisal to the tax return. ***Note that these rules apply to contributions made after June 3, 2004.***

Clothing and household items. You cannot take a deduction for clothing or household items you donate unless the clothing or household items are in good used condition or better.

Exception. You can take a deduction for a contribution of an item of clothing or household item that is not in good used condition or better if you deduct more than $500 for it and include a qualified appraisal of it with your return.

Household items. Household items include:

- Furniture and furnishings,
- Electronics,
- Appliances,
- Linens, and
- Other similar items.

Household items do not include:

- Food,
- Paintings, antiques, and other objects of art,
- Jewelry and gems, and
- Collections.

Cars, boats, and airplanes. The following rules apply to any donation of a qualified vehicle.

A qualified vehicle is:

- A car or any motor vehicle manufactured mainly for use on public streets, roads, and highways,
- A boat, or
- An airplane.

Deduction more than $500. If you donate a qualified vehicle to a qualified organization and you claim a deduction of more than $500, you can deduct the smaller of:

- The gross proceeds from the sale of the vehicle by the organization, or

- The vehicle's fair market value on the date of the contribution. If the vehicle's fair market value was more than your cost or other basis, you may have to reduce the fair market value to figure the deductible amount, as described under *Giving Property That Has Increased in Value*, later.

Form 1098-C. You must attach to your return Copy B of the Form 1098-C, Contributions of Motor Vehicles, Boats, and Airplanes (or other statement containing the same information as Form 1098-C), you received from the organization. The Form 1098-C (or other statement) will show the gross proceeds from the sale of the vehicle.

If you e-file your return, you must (a) attach Copy B of Form 1098-C to Form 8453 and mail the forms to the IRS, or (b) include Copy B of Form 1098-C as a pdf attachment if your software program allows it.

If you do not attach Form 1098-C (or other statement), you cannot deduct your contribution. You must get Form 1098-C (or other statement) within 30 days of the sale of the vehicle. But if exception 1 or 2 (described next) applies, you must get Form 1098-C (or other statement) within 30 days of your donation.

Filing deadline approaching and still no Form 1098-C. If the filing deadline is approaching and you still do not have a Form 1098-C, you have two choices.

- Request an automatic 6-month extension of time to file your return. You can get this extension by filing Form 4868, Application for Automatic Extension of Time to File U.S. Individual Income Tax Return. For more information, see chapter 1.
- File the return on time without claiming the deduction for the qualified vehicle. After receiving the Form 1098-C, file an amended return, Form 1040X, claiming the deduction. Attach Copy B of Form 1098-C (or other statement) to the amended return. For more information about amended returns, see chapter 1.

Exceptions. There are two exceptions to the rules just described for deductions of more than $500.

Exception 1—vehicle used or improved by organization. If the qualified organization makes a significant intervening use of or material improvement to the vehicle before transferring it, and you claim a deduction of more than $500, you generally can deduct the vehicle's fair market value at the time of the contribution. But if the vehicle's fair market value was more than your cost or other basis, you may have to reduce the fair market value to get the deductible amount, as described under *Giving Property That Has Increased in Value*, later. The Form 1098-C (or other statement) will show whether this exception applies.

Exception 2—vehicle given or sold to needy individual. If the qualified organization will give the vehicle, or sell it for a price well below fair market value, to a needy individual to further the organization's charitable purpose, and you claim a deduction of more than $500, you generally can deduct the vehicle's fair market value at the time of the contribution. But if the vehicle's fair market value was more than your cost or other basis, you may have to reduce the fair market value to get the deductible amount, as described under *Giving Property That Has Increased in Value*, later. The Form 1098-C (or other statement) will show whether this exception applies.

This exception does not apply if the organization sells the vehicle at auction. In that case, you cannot deduct the vehicle's fair market value.

Example. Anita donates a used car to a qualified organization. She bought it 3 years ago for $9,000. A used car guide shows the fair market value for this type of car is $6,000. However, Anita gets a Form 1098-C from the organization showing the car was sold for $2,900. Neither exception 1 nor exception 2 applies. If Anita itemizes her deductions, she can deduct $2,900 for her donation. She must attach Form 1098-C and Form 8283 to her return.

Deduction $500 or less. If the qualified organization sells the vehicle for $500 or less and exceptions 1 and 2 do not apply, you can deduct the smaller of:

- $500, or
- The vehicle's fair market value on the date of the contribution. But if the vehicle's fair market value was more than your cost or other basis, you may have to reduce the fair market value to get the deductible amount, as described under *Giving Property That Has Increased in Value*, later.

If the vehicle's fair market value is at least $250 but not more than $500, you must have a written statement from the qualified organization acknowledging your donation. The statement must contain the information and meet the tests for an acknowledgment described under *Deductions of At Least $250 But Not More Than $500* under *Records To Keep*, later.

Partial interest in property. Generally, you cannot deduct a charitable contribution of less than your entire interest in property.

Right to use property. A contribution of the right to use property is a contribution of less than your entire interest in that property and is not deductible. For exceptions and more information, see *Partial Interest in Property Not in Trust* in Publication 561.

EXPLANATION

This rule does not apply to a contribution of a partial interest in property if that interest is your entire interest in the property, such as an income interest.

Nevertheless, there are some situations in which you may claim a deduction for a charitable contribution that is less than your entire interest in the property.

1. **Undivided part of your entire interest.** A contribution of an undivided part of your entire interest in property must consist of a part of each and every substantial interest or right you own in the property and must extend over the entire term of your interest in the property.
   Example 1
   If you own 100 acres of land and give 50 acres to a qualified organization, you may deduct the charitable contribution.
2. **Remainder interest in a personal home or farm.** You may take a charitable deduction for a gift to a qualified organization of a remainder interest in a personal home or a farm if the gift is irrevocable.
   Example 2
   If you transfer a remainder interest in your home to your church but keep the right to live there for life, you may take a deduction for the value of the remainder interest transferred.
3. **Valuation of a partial interest in property.** The amount of the deduction for a charitable contribution of a partial interest in property is the fair market value of the partial interest at the time of the contribution. If the contribution is a remainder interest in real property, **depreciation** (figured on the **straight-line** method) and **depletion** of the property must be taken into account in determining its value. This future value must be further discounted at a rate set by the government. The rate is published each month, and you may use the rate for the month in which the contribution is made or, if you elect, the rate in either of the preceding 2 months. You should use the rate that produces the largest charitable deduction.

TAXPLANNER

If a fractional interest in an item of tangible personal property (e.g., a painting or other artwork) is donated after August 17, 2006, the tax law requires that charities receiving property must take complete ownership of the item within 10 years of when the contribution was made or the date of death of the donor, whichever is first. In addition, the charity must have (1) taken possession of the item at least once during the 10-year period as long as the donor remains alive, and (2) used the item for the organization's exempt purpose. Failure to comply with these requirements results in the recapture of all tax benefits the donor previously recognized plus interest and the imposition of a 10% penalty.

TAXPLANNER

No deduction is allowed for the value of an interest in property transferred in trust unless the donor's entire interest is contributed to a qualified organization or unless the interest is an income interest or a remainder interest. A deduction for a charitable contribution of an income interest in property made by a transfer in trust is allowed if the income interest is either a guaranteed **annuity** interest or a unitrust interest. A **unitrust** interest is the irrevocable right to receive payment of a fixed percentage of the net fair market value of the trust **assets** determined on a yearly basis, while an annuity interest is a right to receive a fixed percentage of the initial fair market value of the transferred assets.

A deduction for a charitable contribution of a remainder interest in trust is allowed if the trust is (1) a **pooled income fund,** (2) a charitable remainder annuity trust, or (3) a charitable remainder unitrust.

The use of these trusts may be very beneficial both to the individual and to the individual's favorite charity. Individuals with substantial wealth should consult their tax and legal advisors about using these mechanisms.

> **TAXALERT**
>
> **Charitable remainder trusts.** A special rule applies to charitable remainder trusts that requires that the present value of the amount passing to a charity and the amount of the charitable deduction be no less than 10% of the fair market value of property contributed to the trust. Also, the annual annuity percentage of the charitable remainder trust cannot exceed 50%. Please consult your tax advisor regarding these special rules.

Future interests in tangible personal property. You may be able to deduct the value of a charitable contribution of a future interest in tangible personal property only after all intervening interests in and rights to the actual possession or enjoyment of the property have either expired or been turned over to someone other than yourself, a related person, or a related organization.

Tangible personal property. This is any property, other than land or buildings, that can be seen or touched. It includes furniture, books, jewelry, paintings, and cars.

Future interest. This is any interest that is to begin at some future time, regardless of whether it is designated as a future interest under state law.

> **EXPLANATION**
>
> The amount of the deduction is the value of the future interest when you and the related person no longer have an interest in the tangible personal property. When these interests end, the deduction is allowed to you, even if there are other outstanding interests that must end before the future interest is realized by the qualified organization.
>
> ***Example***
>
> In 2011, you transferred a painting to your daughter to use and enjoy for life. When your daughter dies, the painting will go to the local art museum. If your daughter irrevocably transfers her life interest to an unrelated person in a later year, you may take a charitable deduction in that year, but not sooner. The amount of your deduction is the value of the future interest in the painting at the time of the transfer to the unrelated person.

Determining Fair Market Value

This section discusses general guidelines for determining the fair market value of various types of donated property. Publication 561 contains a more complete discussion.

Fair market value is the price at which property would change hands between a willing buyer and a willing seller, neither having to buy or sell, and both having reasonable knowledge of all the relevant facts.

Used clothing and household items. Generally, the fair market value of used clothing and household goods is far less than its original cost.

For used clothing, you should claim as the value the price that buyers of used items actually pay in used clothing stores, such as consignment or thrift shops. See *Household Goods* in Publication 561 for information on the valuation of household goods, such as furniture, appliances, and linens.

Example. Dawn Greene donated a coat to a thrift store operated by her church. She paid $300 for the coat 3 years ago. Similar coats in the thrift store sell for $50. The fair market value of the coat is reasonably determined to be $50. Dawn's donation is limited to $50.

Cars, boats, and airplanes. If you contribute a car, boat, or airplane to a charitable organization, you must determine its fair market value. Certain commercial firms and trade organizations publish used car pricing guides, commonly called "blue books," containing complete dealer sale prices or dealer average prices for recent model years. The guides may be published monthly or seasonally and for different regions of the country. These guides also provide estimates for adjusting for unusual equipment, unusual mileage, and physical condition. The prices are not "official" and these publications are not considered an appraisal of any specific donated property. But they do provide clues for making an appraisal and suggest relative prices for comparison with current sales and offerings in your area.

Example. You donate a used car in poor condition to a local high school for use by students studying car repair. A used car guide shows the dealer retail value for this type of car in poor condition is $1,600. However, the guide shows the price for a private party sale of the car is only $750. The fair market value of the car is considered to be $750.

Large quantities. If you contribute a large number of the same item, fair market value is the price at which comparable numbers of the item are being sold.

Giving Property That Has Decreased in Value

If you contribute property with a fair market value that is less than your basis in it, your deduction is limited to its fair market value. You cannot claim a deduction for the difference between the property's basis and its fair market value.

> **TAXPLANNER**
>
> If investment property that you are planning to donate has declined in value, you may wish to consider selling it and giving the proceeds to the charitable organization. By following this strategy, you get the deduction (subject to limitations) for the capital loss, as well as the deduction for the charitable cash gift.

Giving Property That Has Increased in Value

If you contribute property with a fair market value that is more than your basis in it, you may have to reduce the fair market value by the amount of appreciation (increase in value) when you figure your deduction.

Your basis in property is generally what you paid for it. See chapter 13 if you need more information about basis.

Different rules apply to figuring your deduction, depending on whether the property is:

- Ordinary income property, or
- Capital gain property.

Ordinary income property. Property is ordinary income property if its sale at fair market value on the date it was contributed would have resulted in ordinary income or in short-term capital gain. Examples of ordinary income property are inventory, works of art created by the donor, manuscripts prepared by the donor, and capital assets (defined in chapter 14) held 1 year or less.

Amount of deduction. The amount you can deduct for a contribution of ordinary income property is its fair market value minus the amount that would be ordinary income or short-term capital gain if you sold the property for its fair market value. Generally, this rule limits the deduction to your basis in the property.

Example. You donate stock that you held for 5 months to your church. The fair market value of the stock on the day you donate it is $1,000, but you paid only $800 (your basis). Because the $200 of appreciation would be short-term capital gain if you sold the stock, your deduction is limited to $800 (fair market value minus the appreciation).

> **EXPLANATION**
>
> **Ordinary income property.** If, on the date it was contributed, the sale of the property would have resulted in ordinary income or a short-term capital gain to the donor, it is ordinary income property. Examples of ordinary income property include inventory, letters, and memoranda given by the person who prepared them (or the person for whom they were prepared) and any property that was acquired and held for 1 year or less.
>
> **Example**
>
> You contribute inventory to your church with a fair market value of $20,000 and a cost of $8,000. Because the inventory is property that had previously been held for sale in the ordinary course of business, you would have recognized ordinary income of $12,000 had the property been sold. Therefore, your contribution of $20,000 is reduced by $12,000. Your deduction is limited to $8,000.

Capital gain property. Property is capital gain property if its sale at fair market value on the date of the contribution would have resulted in long-term capital gain. It includes capital assets held more than 1 year, as well as certain real property and depreciable property used in your trade or business and, generally, held more than 1 year.

Amount of deduction — general rule. When figuring your deduction for a gift of capital gain property, you generally can use the fair market value of the gift.

Exceptions. In certain situations, you must reduce the fair market value by any amount that would have been long-term capital gain if you had sold the property for its fair market value. Generally, this means reducing the fair market value to the property's cost or other basis.

EXAMPLE

An individual purchased stock in 1983 for $1,000. He contributed it to his church in 2011, at which time it was worth $20,000. His charitable contribution deduction is $20,000, the fair market value at the date of the contribution.

EXPLANATION

You usually may deduct a gift of capital gain property at its fair market value. However, your deduction is limited to your adjusted basis in the property in the following instances:

1. If the capital gain property (other than qualified appreciated stock) is contributed to certain private foundations. (A private foundation generally receives only small or no contributions from the general public.)

   Contributions to private foundations. Contributions of qualified appreciated stock to private foundations are deductible at full market value subject to the 20% limitation, discussed later. If, on the date of contribution, market quotes are readily available and the sale of the stock would result in a long-term capital gain, it is qualified appreciated stock. An example would be shares of Microsoft that qualify for long-term capital gain treatment.
2. If you choose the 50% limit instead of the special 30% limit, discussed later (see *Limit on Deductions*, later).
3. If the property contributed is **tangible personal property** that is put to an unrelated use by the charity, that is, a use that is unrelated to the purpose or function of the charitable organization for which it was granted its tax-exempt status.

Example

If a painting you contribute to an educational institution is placed in the organization's library for display and study by art students, the use is not an unrelated use. But, if the painting is sold and the proceeds are used by the organization for educational purposes, the use is unrelated and your deduction is limited to the painting's cost.

TAXPLANNER

Before you donate a gift of tangible personal property, attempt to determine whether the use will be related to the charitable organization's exempt function. In such circumstances, ask the charitable organization to prepare a statement of intended use and retain it in your tax return file.

TAXSAVER

If you donate appreciated securities that you have held for more than a year, not only can you take a deduction based on the fair market value of the securities, but you will also avoid paying tax on the appreciation. Consequently, the cost of your contribution is reduced by the tax deduction you claim and the tax you avoided by not selling the property. In most cases, the charity does not incur any tax when it sells the property. Be careful, though, if the securities are the subject of a tender offer or other purchase agreement. The Tax Court has ruled that a gift of securities subject to such an agreement will result in income to the donor for the gain.

Example

You own stock worth $1,000. When you bought the stock more than a year ago, it cost you $100. If you sell the stock and donate the $1,000 to your favorite charity, you incur capital gains tax—possibly as much as $135, depending on what tax bracket you're in. If you contribute the stock directly to the charity, the $900 gain is not subject to tax.

TAXSAVER

To get the maximum tax benefit from a contribution of appreciated property, be sure that the property qualifies for long-term capital gain treatment if it is sold.

Example

You purchased stock for $1,000 on January 6, 2010. The stock was donated to your church on January 4, 2011, at which time it was worth $3,000. Because the $2,000 of appreciation would have been a short-term capital gain if you had sold the stock, your deduction is limited to $1,000. If, however, you had waited to make your donation to the church until January 7, 2011, and the stock was still worth $3,000, you would have been able to deduct $3,000.

TAXALERT

You can recognize a charitable contribution for the full fair market value of appreciated property for both regular and alternative minimum tax purposes.

TAXALERT

A tax law enacted in 2006 provides that the tax benefit you realize from claiming a charitable contribution deduction of more than $5,000 for the fair market value of appreciated tangible personal property will be reduced if the charitable recipient disposes of this property within three years of the date of the contribution. This rule applies to contributions made after September 1, 2006.

If the disposition occurs in the tax year of the donor in which the contribution is made, the donor's deduction generally would be basis and not fair market value. If the disposition occurs in a subsequent year, the donor would include as ordinary income for its tax year in which the disposition occurs an amount equal to the excess (if any) of (1) the amount of the deduction previously claimed by the donor as a charitable contribution with respect to such property, over (2) the donor's basis in such property at the time of the contribution.

No adjustment of the tax benefit is required if the charitable organization submits written certification to the IRS that either (1) certifies that the use of the property by the organization was related to the purpose or function constituting the basis for the organization's exemption, and describes how the property was used and how such use furthered such purpose or function or (2) states the intended use of the property by the organization at the time of the contribution and certifies that such use became impossible or infeasible to implement. A copy of the certification must be provided to the donor of the property.

Bargain sales. A bargain sale of property (a sale or exchange for less than the property's fair market value) to a qualified organization is partly a charitable contribution and partly a sale or exchange. A bargain sale may result in a taxable gain.

EXPLANATION

A bargain sale is the sale of property to a charitable organization at a price less than the property's fair market value (FMV). For tax purposes, this transaction is made up of two components: (1) a sale and (2) a gift. You can claim a charitable contribution deduction for the gift component. You will also have to recognize capital gain income attributable to the profit earned on the sale component. The calculation of the taxable gain on the bargain sale requires that you properly allocate your tax basis in the property between the sale and charitable gift components.

The following example illustrates these rules: Susan purchased property three years ago for $3,000. She sold the property to her favorite charity for $6,000 when the FMV of the property was $10,000.

Property:	FMV	$10,000
	Adjusted basis	$ 3,000
	Sold to ABC Charity for	$ 6,000

The gift component that qualifies for a charitable contribution deduction is $4,000 ($10,000 FMV minus price at which the property was sold to the charity of $6,000).

The calculation of the basis allocated to the sale component is determined using the following formula:

$$\frac{\text{Sale price}}{\text{FMV}} \times \text{Adjusted basis}$$

In this example, the tax basis attributable to the sale is $1,800 [($6,000 sale price ÷ $10,000 FMV) × $3,000 adjusted basis]. The taxable gain is $4,200 ($6,000 sale price less $1,800 basis allocated to the sale component). The gain is long-term capital gain since the sale occurred more than one year after the property had been acquired.

More information. For more information on donated appreciated property, see *Giving Property That Has Increased in Value* in Publication 526.

When To Deduct

You can deduct your contributions only in the year you actually make them in cash or other property (or in a later carryover year, as explained later under Carryovers). This applies whether you use the cash or an accrual method of accounting.

Time of making contribution. Usually, you make a contribution at the time of its unconditional delivery.

Checks. A check that you mail to a charity is considered delivered on the date you mail it.

Credit card. Contributions charged on your credit card are deductible in the year you make the charge.

Pay-by-phone account. If you use a pay-by-phone account, the date the financial institution pays the amount is the date you make a contribution.

Stock certificate. A gift to a charity of a properly endorsed stock certificate is completed on the date of mailing or other delivery to the charity or to the charity's agent. However, if you give a stock certificate to your agent or to the issuing corporation for transfer to the name of the charity, your gift is not completed until the date the stock is transferred on the books of the corporation.

Promissory note. If you issue and deliver a promissory note to a charitable organization as a contribution, it is not a contribution until you make the note payments.

Option. If you grant an option to buy real property at a bargain price to a charitable organization, you cannot take a deduction until the organization exercises the option.

Borrowed funds. If you make a contribution with borrowed funds, you can deduct the contribution in the year you make it, regardless of when you repay the loan.

Limits on Deductions

If your total contributions for the year are 20% or less of your adjusted gross income, you do not need to read this section. The limits discussed in this section do not apply to you.

The amount of your deduction for charitable contributions is limited to 50% of your adjusted gross income and may be limited to 30% or 20% of your adjusted gross income, depending on the type of property you give and the type of organization you give it to.

If your contributions are more than any of the limits that apply, see Carryovers, later.

50% Limit

This limit applies to the total of all charitable contributions you make during the year. This means that your deduction for charitable contributions cannot be more than 50% of your adjusted gross income for the year.

Generally, the 50% limit is the only limit that applies to gifts to organizations listed below under 50% limit organizations. But there is one exception. A special 30% limit also applies to these gifts if they are gifts of capital gain property for which you figure your deduction using fair market value without reduction for appreciation. (See Special 30% Limit for Capital Gain Property, later.)

50% limit organizations. You can ask any organization whether it is a 50% limit organization and most will be able to tell you. Or you may check IRS Publication 78 or call the IRS at 1-877-829-5500 (TTY/TDD 1-800-829-4059).

The following is a partial list of the types of organizations that are 50% limit organizations.

- Churches and conventions or associations of churches.
- Educational organizations with a regular faculty and curriculum that normally have a regularly enrolled student body attending classes on site.

- Hospitals and certain medical research organizations associated with these hospitals.
- Publicly supported charities.

30% Limit

A 30% limit applies to the following gifts.

- Gifts to all qualified organizations other than 50% limit organizations. This includes gifts to veterans' organizations, fraternal societies, nonprofit cemeteries, and certain private nonoperating foundations.
- Gifts for the use of any organization.

However, if these gifts are of capital gain property, they are subject to the 20% limit, described later, rather than the 30% limit.

Student living with you. Amounts you spend on behalf of a student living with you are subject to the 30% limit. These amounts are considered a contribution for the use of a qualified organization. See Expenses Paid for Student Living With You, earlier.

Special 30% Limit for Capital Gain Property

A special 30% limit applies to gifts of capital gain property to 50% limit organizations. (For gifts of capital gain property to other organizations, see 20% Limit, later.) However, the special 30% limit does not apply when you choose to reduce the fair market value of the property by the amount that would have been long-term capital gain if you had sold the property. Instead, only the 50% limit applies.

Two separate 30% limits. This special 30% limit for capital gain property is separate from the other 30% limit. Therefore, the deduction of a contribution subject to one 30% limit does not reduce the amount you can deduct for contributions subject to the other 30% limit. However, the total you deduct cannot be more than 50% of your adjusted gross income.

Example. Your adjusted gross income is $50,000. During the year, you gave capital gain property with a fair market value of $15,000 to a 50% limit organization. You do not choose to reduce the property's fair market value by its appreciation in value. You also gave $10,000 cash to a qualified organization that is not a 50% limit organization. The $15,000 gift of property is subject to the special 30% limit. The $10,000 cash gift is subject to the other 30% limit. Both gifts are fully deductible because neither is more than the 30% limit that applies ($15,000 in each case) and together they are not more than the 50% limit ($25,000).

For more information, see the rules for electing the 50% limit for capital gain property under *How To Figure Your Deduction When Limits Apply* in Publication 526.

20% Limit

This limit applies to all gifts of capital gain property to or for the use of qualified organizations (other than gifts of capital gain property to 50% limit organizations).

EXPLANATION

An organization can tell you whether contributions to it qualify for the 50%, 30%, or 20% limit. Contributions to any charitable organization are limited to 50% of your adjusted gross income. This includes a gift of an income interest in trust to a charitable organization.

How to figure your deduction. To figure your deduction, first you consider gifts to charitable organizations that qualify for the 50% limit. Second, you consider gifts to which the 20% and 30% limits apply. Third, you consider gifts of capital gain property to which the special 30% limit for capital gain property applies.

Example 1

Your adjusted gross income is $50,000 for 2011. On September 1, 2011, you gave your church $2,000 cash plus land with a fair market value of $30,000 and a basis to you of $10,000. You had held the land for investment for more than 1 year. You also gave $5,000 cash to a private foundation to which the 30% limit applies. Because your allowable contributions–$32,000 ($2,000 + $30,000)–to an organization to which the 50% limit applies are more than $25,000 (50% of $50,000), your deductions subject to the 30% limit are not allowable. The $2,000 cash donated to the church is considered first. The deduction for the gift of land does not have to be reduced by the appreciation in value and is limited to $15,000 (30% × $50,000). The unused part ($15,000) may be carried over for 5 years. Therefore, in 2011, your deduction is limited to $17,000 ($2,000 + $15,000). The $5,000 contribution to the private foundation may also be carried over for 5 years.

Example 2
Your 2011 adjusted gross income was $50,000. During the year, you gave $5,000 cash to a private foundation, to which the 30% limit applies. You made no other charitable contributions. The entire $5,000 is deductible, because 30% of $50,000 is greater than $5,000.

TAXPLANNER
Contributions of inventory property that was acquired during the taxable year in which the gift was made are not subject to the percentage limitation rules. The cost of these items is claimed as part of the cost of goods sold.

TAXPLANNER
To ease the restrictions on charitable contribution limitations, you may consider making a series of smaller gifts over several years rather than one or two large gifts per year.

Qualified Conservation Contribution

The special 30% limit does not apply to qualified conservation contributions (QCCs). Instead, a 50% limit applies. For qualified farmers and ranchers, QCCs are deductible up to 100% of adjusted gross income. See Publication 526 for details.

TAXALERT
Through the end of 2011, the charitable deduction limit for qualified conservation contributions is 50% of the excess of the taxpayer's adjusted gross income (AGI) over the amount of all other allowable charitable contributions. If the individual making the contribution is a qualified farmer or rancher, the limitation is further increased to 100%. The higher deduction limits for qualified conservation contributions expires at the end of 2011 unless Congress acts to extend them. Otherwise, the limit for qualified conservation contributions made after 2011 drops to 30%. For updated information on this and any other tax law changes that occur after this book was published, see our website, *ey.com/EYTaxGuide*.

Explanation
Qualified conservation contribution. A qualified conservation contribution is a contribution of a qualified real property interest to a qualified organization to be used only for conservation purposes. A qualified real property interest consists of any of the following interests in real property:

1. Your entire interest in real estate other than a mineral interest (subsurface oil, gas, or other minerals, and the right of access to these minerals).
2. A remainder interest.
3. A restriction (granted in perpetuity) on the use that may be made of the real property.

A qualified organization is a governmental unit, a publicly supported charitable, religious, scientific, literary, educational, etc., organization, or an organization that is controlled by, and operated for the exclusive benefit of, a governmental unit or a publicly supported charity. The organization also must have a commitment to protect the conservation purposes of the donation and must have the resources to enforce the restrictions.

Your contribution must be made only for one of the following conservation purposes:

- Preserving land areas for outdoor recreation by, or for the education of, the general public.
- Protecting a relatively natural habitat of fish, wildlife, or plants, or a similar ecosystem.
- Preserving open space, including farmland and forest land, if it yields a significant public benefit. It must be either for the scenic enjoyment of the general public or under a clearly defined federal, state, or local governmental conservation policy.
- Preserving a historically important land area or a certified historic structure.

For further information, see the section on *Qualified Conservation Contribution*, earlier.

Carryovers

You can carry over your contributions that you are not able to deduct in the current year because they exceed your adjusted-gross-income limits. You can deduct the excess in each of the next 5 years until it is used up, but not beyond that time. For more information, see *Carryovers* in Publication 526.

EXPLANATION

For contributions made to private nonoperating foundations that are in excess of 30% of your adjusted gross income, or 20% for capital gain property, you may continue to deduct the excess in each of the next 5 years until it is used up.

You may not carry over gifts to certain veterans' organizations, fraternal societies, and nonprofit cemetery companies to which the 20% limit applies.

For other contributions in excess of the percentage limitations, you may deduct the amount carried over in the following year to the extent that it is not more than the applicable percentage of your adjusted gross income for that year less the amount donated to qualified organizations during that year. In other words, current-year contributions are considered before prior-year carryovers. The excess can be carried over for 5 years.

The carryover amounts retain their respective limitation percentages in the carryover year.

Excess contributions can be carried over only to subsequent returns of the person who made the gift. If the person who made the gift dies, the carryover is lost.

Example 1

You had adjusted gross income of $20,000 in 2010. During the year, you contributed $11,000 cash to your church.

You deducted $10,000 in 2010 (50% of $20,000) and carried over $1,000. In 2011, you had adjusted gross income of $20,000 and contributed $9,000 during the year. You can deduct the entire amount that you carried over from 2010. However, if you had contributed $9,500 during 2011, you could deduct only $500 of the $1,000 you carried over, carrying over the balance of $500 to 2012.

Example 2

Your adjusted gross income for 2010 and 2011 is $50,000 and $20,000, respectively. During 2010, you contributed long-term capital gain property valued at $25,000 to your church. In 2010, you deducted $15,000 (30% of $50,000) and carried over $10,000. In 2011, however, your carryover deduction is limited to 30% of $20,000, or $6,000; the remaining $4,000 will have to be carried over to 2012.

EXPLANATION

If a gift of long-term capital gain property subject to the 30% limitation is made and, for some unforeseen reasons, cannot be utilized entirely in the current year or in carryover years, you may elect to reduce its value by 100% of the gain and deduct the lower net value of the gift under the 50% limitation.

Example

Julia Walsh makes a contribution of long-term capital gain property that cost her $40,000 and now has a fair market value of $50,000. Julia dies during the taxable year. Her adjusted gross income on her final return is $80,000.

Without the election mentioned above, Julia's deduction would be limited to $24,000 (30% × $80,000). However, if the value of the property is reduced by $10,000 to Julia's cost, the deduction is increased to $40,000 (50% × $80,000).

Records To Keep

You must keep records to prove the amount of the contributions you make during the year. The kind of records you must keep depends on the amount of your contributions and whether they are:

- Cash contributions,
- Noncash contributions, or
- Out-of-pocket expenses when donating your services.

TAXORGANIZER

If the IRS raises questions. In case the IRS questions your charitable contribution deductions, you should keep the following information to support your claim for charitable contribution deductions:

- Canceled checks evidencing payments of charitable contributions.
- Receipts (letters or other written communication) from the charitable organization showing the name of the organization, the date of the contribution, and the amount of the contribution. The IRS allows the use of e-mail receipts.
- Other reliable written records that include the information described above (records may be considered reliable if they were made at or near the time of the contribution, were regularly kept by you, or in the case of small donations, you have emblems, buttons, or other tokens that are regularly given to persons making small cash contributions).
- Copies of appraisals (if you are claiming a deduction in excess of $5,000) or other determinations of the market value of the contribution.

Note. An organization generally must give you a written statement if it receives a payment from you that is more than $75 and is partly a contribution and partly for goods or services. (See *Contributions From Which You Benefit* under *Contributions You Can Deduct,* earlier.) Keep the statement for your records. It may satisfy all or part of the recordkeeping requirements explained in the following discussions.

Cash Contributions

Cash contributions include those paid by cash, check, electronic funds transfer, credit card, or payroll deduction.

You cannot deduct a cash contribution, regardless of the amount, unless you keep one of the following.

1. A bank record that shows the name of the qualified organization, the date of the contribution, and the amount of the contribution. Bank records may include:
   a. A canceled check,
   b. A bank or credit union statement, or
   c. A credit card statement.
2. A receipt (or a letter or other written communication) from the qualified organization showing the name of the organization, the date of the contribution, and the amount of the contribution.
3. The payroll deduction records described next.

TAXALERT

A deduction for a cash contribution of any amount will not be allowed unless you have a bank record, such as a canceled check, a receipt, or a written communication from the charitable organization that shows the name of the charity, as well as the date and amount of the contribution. This means that cash contributions to a church collection plate, for example, will not be deductible unless you get a receipt from the church with date and amount details.

Text intentionally omitted.

Payroll deductions. If you make a contribution by payroll deduction, you must keep:

1. A pay stub, Form W-2, or other document furnished by your employer that shows the date and amount of the contribution, and
2. A pledge card or other document prepared by or for the qualified organization that shows the name of the organization.

If your employer withheld $250 or more from a single paycheck, see *Contributions of $250 or More*, next.

Contributions of $250 or More

You can claim a deduction for a contribution of $250 or more only if you have an acknowledgment of your contribution from the qualified organization or certain payroll deduction records.

If you made more than one contribution of $250 or more, you must have either a separate acknowledgment for each or one acknowledgment that lists each contribution and the date of each contribution and shows your total contributions.

TAXALERT

Written acknowledgments. You are required to obtain a contemporaneous written acknowledgment from any charitable organization to which a contribution of $250 or more is made in order to deduct that contribution. Contemporaneous for this purpose means that you must obtain the written acknowledgment on or before the earlier of (1) the date on which your 2011 return is actually filed or (2) the due date for the return, including extensions. An e-mail receipt qualifies as a written acknowledgment.

A canceled check does not constitute adequate substantiation for a cash contribution of the amount. The written acknowledgment will have to state the amount of cash and a description (but not the value) of any property other than cash contributed. It must also state whether the charitable organization provided any goods or services in consideration for the contribution, and, if so, a description and good faith estimate of the value of goods or services provided. If the goods or services provided as consideration for the contribution consist solely of intangible religious benefits, a statement to that effect will have to be included in the written acknowledgment.

Note that the primary responsibility lies with you, not the charitable organization, to request and maintain the required substantiation in your records.

For any contribution over $75 for which the charity provides goods or services, such as a dinner, the charity must provide a statement to the donor that reports the estimated value of the goods or services received by the donor in exchange for the contribution. A payment to a charity is deductible only to the extent that it exceeds the value of any goods or services received in return.

TAXPLANNER

Separate payments. In general, separate payments are not combined for purposes of the substantiation requirement. Therefore, you could deduct separate contributions of less than $250 from each paycheck or make monthly payments to a charity without running afoul of the requirement. However, you could not, for example, simply write multiple checks on the same day in order to avoid substantiation. Similarly, separate payments made at different times with respect to different fundraising events are not totaled in order to determine whether the charity must inform the donor of the value of any benefit received in return for a donation in excess of $75.

Amount of contribution. In figuring whether your contribution is $250 or more, do not combine separate contributions. For example, if you gave your church $25 each week, your weekly payments do not have to be combined. Each payment is a separate contribution.

If contributions are made by payroll deduction, the deduction from each paycheck is treated as a separate contribution.

If you made a payment that is partly for goods and services, as described earlier under *Contributions From Which You Benefit*, your contribution is the amount of the payment that is more than the value of the goods and services.

Acknowledgment. The acknowledgment must meet these tests.

1. It must be written.
2. It must include:
   a. The amount of cash you contributed,
   b. Whether the qualified organization gave you any goods or services as a result of your contribution (other than certain token items and membership benefits),
   c. A description and good faith estimate of the value of any goods or services described in (b) (other than intangible religious benefits), and
   d. A statement that the only benefit you received was an intangible religious benefit, if that was the case. The acknowledgment does not need to describe or estimate the value of an intangible religious benefit. An intangible religious benefit is a benefit that generally is not sold in commercial transactions outside a donative (gift) context. An example is admission to a religious ceremony.
3. You must get it on or before the earlier of:
   a. The date you file your return for the year you make the contribution, or
   b. The due date, including extensions, for filing the return.

If the acknowledgment does not show the date of the contribution, you must also have a bank record or receipt, as described earlier, that does show the date of the contribution. If the acknowledgment does show the date of the contribution and meets the other tests just described, you do not need any other records.

Payroll deductions. If you make a contribution by payroll deduction and your employer withheld $250 or more from a single paycheck, you must keep:

1. A pay stub, Form W-2, or other document furnished by your employer that shows the amount withheld as a contribution, and
2. A pledge card or other document prepared by or for the qualified organization that shows the name of the organization and states the organization does not provide goods or services in return for any contribution made to it by payroll deduction.

A single pledge card may be kept for all contributions made by payroll deduction regardless of amount as long as it contains all the required information.

If the pay stub, Form W-2, pledge card, or other document does not show the date of the contribution, you must also have another document that does show the date of the contribution. If the pay stub, Form W-2, pledge card, or other document does show the date of the contribution, you do not need any other records except those just described in (1) and (2).

Noncash Contributions

For a contribution not made in cash, the records you must keep depend on whether your deduction for the contribution is:

1. Less than $250,
2. At least $250 but not more than $500,
3. Over $500 but not more than $5,000, or
4. Over $5,000.

Amount of deduction. In figuring whether your deduction is $500 or more, combine your claimed deductions for all similar items of property donated to any charitable organization during the year.

If you received goods or services in return, as described earlier in *Contributions From Which You Benefit*, reduce your contribution by the value of those goods or services. If you figure your deduction by reducing the fair market value of the donated property by its appreciation, as described earlier in *Giving Property That Has Increased in Value*, your contribution is the reduced amount.

Deductions of Less Than $250

If you make any noncash contribution, you must get and keep a receipt from the charitable organization showing:

1. The name of the charitable organization,
2. The date and location of the charitable contribution, and
3. A reasonably detailed description of the property.

You are not required to have a receipt where it is impractical to get one (for example, if you leave property at a charity's unattended drop site).

Tip

A letter or other written communication from the charitable organization acknowledging receipt of the contribution and containing the information in (1), (2), and (3) will serve as a receipt.

Additional records. You must also keep reliable written records for each item of donated property. Your written records must include the following information.

- The name and address of the organization to which you contributed.
- The date and location of the contribution.
- A description of the property in detail reasonable under the circumstances. For a security, keep the name of the issuer, the type of security, and whether it is regularly traded on a stock exchange or in an over-the-counter market.
- The fair market value of the property at the time of the contribution and how you figured the fair market value. If it was determined by appraisal, keep a signed copy of the appraisal.
- The cost or other basis of the property if you must reduce its fair market value by appreciation. Your records should also include the amount of the reduction and how you figured it. If you choose the 50% limit instead of the special 30% limit on certain capital gain property, you must keep a record showing the years for which you made the choice, contributions for the current year to which the choice applies, and carryovers from preceding years to which the choice applies. See *How To Figure Your Deduction When Limits Apply* in Publication 526 for information on how to make the capital gain property election.
- The amount you claim as a deduction for the tax year as a result of the contribution, if you contribute less than your entire interest in the property during the tax year. Your records must include the amount you claimed as a deduction in any earlier years for contributions of other interests in this property. They must also include the name and address of each organization to which you contributed the other interests, the place where any such tangible property is

located or kept, and the name of any person in possession of the property, other than the organization to which you contributed.
- The terms of any conditions attached to the gift of property.

Deductions of At Least $250 But Not More Than $500

If you claim a deduction of at least $250 but not more than $500 for a noncash charitable contribution, you must get and keep an acknowledgment of your contribution from the qualified organization. If you made more than one contribution of $250 or more, you must have either a separate acknowledgment for each or one acknowledgment that shows your total contributions.

The acknowledgment must contain the information in items (1) through (3) listed under *Deductions of Less Than $250*, earlier, and your written records must include the information listed in that discussion under *Additional records*.

The acknowledgment must also meet these tests.

1. It must be written.
2. It must include:
   a. A description (but not necessarily the value) of any property you contributed,
   b. Whether the qualified organization gave you any goods or services as a result of your contribution (other than certain token items and membership benefits), and
   c. A description and good faith estimate of the value of any goods or services described in (b). If the only benefit you received was an intangible religious benefit (such as admission to a religious ceremony) that generally is not sold in a commercial transaction outside the donative context, the acknowledgment must say so and does not need to describe or estimate the value of the benefit.
3. You must get it on or before the earlier of:
   a. The date you file your return for the year you make the contribution, or
   b. The due date, including extensions, for filing the return.

Deductions Over $500

You are required to give additional information if you claim a deduction over $500 for noncash charitable contributions. See *Records To Keep* in Publication 526 for more information.

EXPLANATION

A receipt is not required if you deposit property at a charity's unattended drop site unless you claim that the property is worth more than $250. However, you must maintain a written record of the contribution, listing the items contributed and the date and location of the contribution.

You are required to file Form 8283, Noncash Charitable Contributions, if you claim a deduction of over $500 for noncash contributions. Additionally, there are special rules for noncash contributions in excess of $5,000 and $500,000, as well as donations of vehicles, discussed previously in this chapter.

For contributions having a fair market value of more than $500 but not more than $5,000, the donor must provide the following information:

- The name and address of the charitable organization
- The description of the donated property
- The date of the contribution
- The date it was acquired by the donor
- How it was acquired by the donor
- The donor's cost or adjusted basis (except for publicly traded securities or property held for more than 12 months)
- The fair market value of the contribution
- The method used to determine the fair market value (e.g., appraisal, thrift shop value, catalog, market quote, or comparable sales)

Form 8283 must be filed with the tax return on which the deduction is taken.

For contributions in excess of $500,000 you must attach a copy of the qualified appraisal to your return.

TAXALERT

Through the end of 2011, the charitable deduction limit for qualified conservation contributions is 50% of the excess of the taxpayer's adjusted gross income (AGI) over the amount of all other allowable charitable contributions. If the individual making the contribution was a qualified farmer or rancher, the limitation is further increased to 100%. Unless Congress acts, beginning in 2012, the deduction limit drops to 30% of AGI for all taxpayers. For updated information on this and any other tax law changes that occur after this book was published, see our website, ey.com/EYTaxGuide. See the section on *Qualified Conservation Contribution*, earlier, for more information.

Qualified conservation contributions of capital gain property are subject to the limit of 50% of adjusted gross income and have a 15-year carryover. The Tax Relief, Unemployment Insurance Reauthorization, and Job Creation Act of 2010 retroactively restored the liberalized deduction rules for qualified conservation contributions and extended them through tax years beginning in 2011.

Out-of-Pocket Expenses

If you render services to a qualified organization and have unreimbursed out-of-pocket expenses related to those services, the following three rules apply.

1. You must have adequate records to prove the amount of the expenses.
2. You must get an acknowledgment from the qualified organization that contains:
   a. A description of the services you provided,
   b. A statement of whether or not the organization provided you any goods or services to reimburse you for the expenses you incurred,
   c. A description and a good faith estimate of the value of any goods or services (other than intangible religious benefits) provided to reimburse you, and
   d. A statement that the only benefit you received was an intangible religious benefit, if that was the case. The acknowledgment does not need to describe or estimate the value of an intangible religious benefit (defined earlier under *Acknowledgment*).
3. You must get the acknowledgment on or before the earlier of:
   a. The date you file your return for the year you make the contribution, or
   b. The due date, including extensions, for filing the return.

Car expenses. If you claim expenses directly related to use of your car in giving services to a qualified organization, you must keep reliable written records of your expenses. Whether your records are considered reliable depends on all the facts and circumstances. Generally, they may be considered reliable if you made them regularly and at or near the time you had the expenses.

Your records must show the name of the organization you were serving and the date each time you used your car for a charitable purpose. If you use the standard mileage rate of 14 cents a mile, your records must show the miles you drove your car for the charitable purpose. If you deduct your actual expenses, your records must show the costs of operating the car that are directly related to a charitable purpose.

See *Car expenses* under *Out-of-Pocket Expenses in Giving Services,* earlier, for the expenses you can deduct.

How To Report

Report your charitable contributions on Schedule A (Form 1040).

If your total deduction for all noncash contributions for the year is over $500, you must also file Form 8283. See *How To Report* in Publication 526 for more information.

Chapter 26

Nonbusiness casualty and theft losses

ey.com/EYTaxGuide

Note

IRS Publication 17 (*Your Federal Income Tax*) has been updated by Ernst & Young LLP for 2011. Dates and dollar amounts shown are for 2011. Underlined type is used to indicate where IRS text has been updated. Places where text has been removed are indicated by the sentence: *Text intentionally omitted.*

ey.com/EYTaxGuide

Ernst & Young LLP will update the *Ernst & Young Tax Guide 2012* website with relevant taxpayer information as it becomes available. You can also sign up for email alerts to let you know when changes have been made.

Introduction

Almost anytime something you own is stolen, damaged, or destroyed in an accident or by an act of nature and you are not compensated by insurance, you are eligible for a tax deduction. The loss need not be connected in any way to your trade or business, and it may include such personal items as jewelry, furs, and antiques. That's small comfort if everything you own has been demolished in a terrible earthquake or a devastating hurricane, but it's something.

In order to claim a casualty loss deduction, you must first prove that the casualty occurred. The most difficult task is substantiating the value of the property you have lost. That gorgeous necklace that your grandmother gave you may be worth a substantial amount, but, unless you can prove it, you're going to have a difficult time claiming a tax deduction if it is stolen. (Of course, even if you can prove the value, your deduction is generally limited to your cost basis.) Recordkeeping and documentation are extremely important.

No matter how good your records are, you must itemize your deductions and pass two general limitations on the amount of your casualty and theft loss. First, for personal use losses that occurred in 2011 you may not deduct the first $100 of any loss. Second and more significant, you are able to deduct personal casualty and theft losses only when the total amount you lost in any year—reduced by $100 per casualty—exceeds 10% of your adjusted gross income (AGI).

This chapter spells out which casualty losses are deductible. You'll also learn about the details that should be considered in deciding when to take your deduction. The rules for deducting business losses are different. They are also discussed in this chapter. Most importantly, this chapter discusses the records and other evidence you need to support any claim that you make.

What's New

Qualified disaster relief payments received by victims of March 2011 Japan earthquake and tsunami are excludable from gross income. The earthquake and tsunami in Japan in March 2011 has been designated a qualified disaster for federal tax purposes. Recipients of qualified disaster relief payments related to this disaster are allowed to exclude such payments from income on their tax returns.

Text intentionally omitted.

This chapter explains the tax treatment of personal (not business or investment related) casualty losses, theft losses, and losses on deposits.

The chapter also explains the following topics.

- How to figure the amount of your loss.
- How to treat insurance and other reimbursements you receive.
- The deduction limits.
- When and how to report a casualty or theft.

EXPLANATION

This chapter includes a discussion on what to do if a loss is partly business and partly personal. For example, if your basement flooded and damage occurred to both personal property and business property in your home office located in the basement, the loss would be partly business and partly personal. See *Property Used Partly for Business and Partly for Personal Purposes*, later in this chapter.

This chapter also discusses the special rules for disaster area losses.

Forms to file. When you have a casualty or theft, you have to file Form 4684. You will also have to file one or more of the following forms.

- Schedule A (Form 1040), Itemized Deductions
- Schedule D (Form 1040), Capital Gains and Losses

Text intentionally omitted.

EXPLANATION

For details on which form to use, see *How to Report Gains and Losses*, later in this chapter.

Condemnations. For information on condemnations of property, see *Involuntary Conversions* in chapter 1 of Publication 544.

Workbook for casualties and thefts. Publication 584 is available to help you make a list of your stolen or damaged personal-use property and figure your loss. It includes schedules to help you figure the loss on your home, its contents, and your motor vehicles.

TAXPLANNER

Publication 584-B, *Business Casualty, Disaster, and Theft Loss Workbook,* is available to help you make a list of your stolen or damaged business or income-producing property and figure your loss.

Other sources of information. For information on a casualty or theft loss of business or income-producing property, see Publication 547.

Useful Items

You may want to see:

Publication

- □ **544** Sales and Other Dispositions of Assets
- □ **547** Casualties, Disasters, and Thefts
- □ **584** Casualty, Disaster, and Theft Loss Workbook (Personal-Use Property)

Form (and Instructions)

- □ **Schedule A (Form 1040)** Itemized Deductions
- □ **Schedule D (Form 1040)** Capital Gains and Losses

Text intentionally omitted.

- □ **4684** Casualties and Thefts

Tax Breaks and Deductions You Can Use Checklist

Casualty and Theft Losses. You can claim an itemized deduction for personal losses from fires, storms, car accidents, and similar "sudden, unexpected, or unusual" events, as well as losses from theft. These losses are deductible only to the extent they exceed $100 per occurrence in 2011 and 10% of your adjusted gross income. If the loss occurred in a federally declared disaster area, you can elect to claim the loss on your prior year's return, with certain restrictions.

Victims of Federally Declared Disasters. Special tax law provisions may help taxpayers and businesses recover from the impact of a disaster, especially when the federal government declares their location to be a major disaster area. Depending on the circumstances, the IRS may grant additional time to file returns and pay taxes. Both individuals and businesses in a federally declared disaster area can get a faster refund by claiming losses related to the disaster on the tax return for the previous year, usually by filing an amended return. Search "Disaster Assistance" on *www.irs.gov* for the latest information regarding tax law provisions related to disaster relief. Generally, you must deduct a casualty loss in the year it occurred. However, if you incurred a casualty loss in a federally declared disaster area during 2011, the tax law allows you to claim that loss on your 2010 tax return or an amended return for 2010, instead of claiming the loss on your 2011 return. If you do so, the loss is treated as having occurred in 2010. Claiming a federally declared disaster loss incurred in 2011

EXPLANATION

Other useful publications and references include:

Publication

- □ **584-B** Business Casualty, Disaster, and Theft Loss Workbook
- □ **2194** Disaster Losses Kit for Individuals
- □ **2194-B** Disaster Losses Kit for Businesses

on your 2010 return or amended return may result in a lower tax or produce or increase a cash refund. You should compare the tax savings you may recognize from claiming such a disaster loss on your 2011 return versus 2010.

Casualty

A casualty is the damage, destruction, or loss of property resulting from an identifiable event that is sudden, unexpected, or unusual.

- A sudden event is one that is swift, not gradual or progressive.
- An unexpected event is one that is ordinarily unanticipated and unintended.
- An unusual event is one that is not a day-to-day occurrence and that is not typical of the activity in which you were engaged.

Deductible losses. Deductible casualty losses can result from a number of different causes, including the following.

- Car accidents (but see Nondeductible losses, next, for exceptions).

EXPLANATION

Damage resulting from faulty but not intentionally reckless driving is a casualty loss. Damage incurred while an automobile was operated by an unauthorized person is also a casualty loss.

The following are examples of casualty losses involving automobiles:

- The loss of an automobile that fell through the ice while the taxpayer was ice fishing
- Damage to an automobile starter caused by a child who pressed the starter button while the automobile's engine was operating

- Earthquakes.
- Fires (but see Nondeductible losses, next, for exceptions).
- Floods.
- Government-ordered demolition or relocation of a home that is unsafe to use because of a disaster as discussed under *Disaster Area Losses* in Publication 547.
- Mine cave-ins.
- Shipwrecks.
- Sonic booms.
- Storms, including hurricanes and tornadoes.
- Terrorist attacks.
- Vandalism.
- Volcanic eruptions.

EXPLANATION

Losses caused by a person's own negligence are deductible, as are losses that occur even though they could have been foreseen or prevented. The courts have also allowed casualty loss deductions in the following cases:

Animals and insects

- Damage caused by a mass attack of southern pine beetles capable of destroying a tree in 5 to 10 days
- Death of a horse by swallowing the lining of a hat

Drought

- Cracking of foundation walls due to soil shrinkage
- Death of trees and plants within 3 to 4 months as a result of extraordinary drought

Earthquakes and landslides

- Collapse of a garage wall due to subsoil hydraulic action
- Damage caused by a mine cave-in (a deduction was allowed even though the landslide was reasonably foreseeable)

Household
- Damage from corrosive drywall
- Bursting of hot water boiler caused by air obstruction in water pipes
- Damage to furniture dropped 16 floors by movers
- Damage caused by a flood due to faulty construction (however, the cost of repairing the defect was not deductible)
- Septic tank

Lightning
- Any damage by lightning

Personal belongings
- Damage to a diamond ring inadvertently dropped in a kitchen garbage disposal
- Damage to a ring caused by a husband slamming a car door on his wife's finger

Storms
- Damage to an artificial beach due to abnormal rains
- Damage to a home by ice and snow
- Damage to a beach house that was caused by a hurricane but was not discovered until 2 years later, when the floorboards and porch buckled (the loss was deductible in the year in which the damage was discovered)
- Property damage due to unusually high water levels caused by storms

Trees, shrubs, and landscaping
- Damage caused by accidental application of chemical weed killer to a lawn
- Damage to trees caused by blizzards and snowstorms
- Loss of trees, shrubs, and grass due to fire
- Damage by a tractor plowing the ground

Vandalism
- Damage to household appliances caused by vandals who broke into a house under construction
- Damage and destruction of art objects by vandals

Nondeductible losses. A casualty loss is not deductible if the damage or destruction is caused by the following.
- Accidentally breaking articles such as glassware or china under normal conditions.
- A family pet (explained below).
- A fire if you willfully set it or pay someone else to set it.
- A car accident if your willful negligence or willful act caused it. The same is true if the willful act or willful negligence of someone acting for you caused the accident.
- Progressive deterioration (explained later).

Family pet. Loss of property due to damage by a family pet is not deductible as a casualty loss unless the requirements discussed earlier under <u>*Casualty*</u> are met.

Example. Your antique oriental rug was damaged by your new puppy before it was housebroken. Because the damage was not unexpected and unusual, the loss is not deductible as a casualty loss.

Progressive deterioration. Loss of property due to progressive deterioration is not deductible as a casualty loss. This is because the damage results from a steadily operating cause or a normal process, rather than from a sudden event. The following are examples of damage due to progressive deterioration.
- The steady weakening of a building due to normal wind and weather conditions.
- The deterioration and damage to a water heater that bursts. However, the rust and water damage to rugs and drapes caused by the bursting of a water heater does qualify as a casualty.

EXPLANATION

The following also do *not* qualify as casualty losses: damage from faulty construction that caused walls and floors to settle, dry rot to a wooden sloop, and the decline in value of a piece of land affected by gradual deterioration. However, the breaking up of a driveway caused by weather conditions over a 4-month period has been allowed.

- Most losses of property caused by droughts. To be deductible, a drought-related loss generally must be incurred in a trade or business or in a transaction entered into for profit.

EXPLANATION

A water well that ran dry because of a drought may not be deducted as a casualty loss. The courts have also disallowed deductions for casualty losses in the following cases:

Animals and insects

- Damage to shrubs eaten by a horse
- Damage to an antique vase by a cat
- Damage to a fur coat by moths
- Loss of a valuable dog that strayed off

Automobiles

- Damage to a fuel pump and muffler caused by high stones in a road (the taxpayer was unable to prove that it was more than wear and tear)
- Damage caused by a tire blowout due to overloading
- Damage caused by exposure to salt water
- The forced sale of an automobile due to divorce
- Damage caused by potholes in the road
- Payment in settlement of a wrongful death claim stemming from an automobile accident

Earthquakes and landslides

- Any additional loss in value due to buyer resistance (a deduction is allowed only for physical damage)

Household items

- Sale of household items by a storage company (the sale was not an unexpected occurrence)

Personal belongings

- The loss of a ring from the owner's finger
- The accidental disposal of tissues in which two rings were wrapped
- The accidental dropping of eyeglasses or a watch
- The loss of baggage and contents in transit as a result of a shipwreck
- The snapping of a propeller on a yacht that was not the result of a shipwreck or other casualty

Trees, shrubs, and landscaping

- Damage to trees from Dutch elm disease (the disease is progressive and not sudden or unexpected)
- The gradual suffocation of a root system over a 16-month period
- Damage to palm trees caused by lethal yellowing

- Termite or moth damage.
- The damage or destruction of trees, shrubs, or other plants by a fungus, disease, insects, worms, or similar pests. However, a sudden destruction due to an unexpected or unusual infestation of beetles or other insects may result in a casualty loss.

EXPLANATION

The following are also not considered casualty losses: damage to trees and plants caused by moths, damage caused by rat infestation, the death of a horse from colic, and the loss of livestock due to disease.

Damage from corrosive drywall. Under a special procedure, you may be able to claim a casualty loss deduction for amounts you paid to repair damage to your home and household appliances that resulted from corrosive drywall. For details, see Publication 547.

EXPLANATION

The special procedure for deducting amounts to repair damage from corrosive drywall is effective for returns filed after September 29, 2010 (including amended returns). "Corrosive drywall" is identified as problem drywall under the two-step identification method published by the Consumer Product Safety Commission (CPSC) and the Department of Housing and Urban Development (HUD) in interim guidance dated January 28, 2010, as revised by the CPSC and HUD. Revised identification guidance and remediation guidelines are available at *www.cpsc.gov/info/drywall/InterimIDGuidance012810.pdf.* Incidents of corrosive drywall largely involve homes built in 2006 and 2007. A record number of new homes were built during this time period, largely as a result of the hurricanes in 2004 and 2005 that destroyed or damaged many homes.

The amount of the loss allowed under the special procedure for corrosive drywall is as follows:

- If a claim for reimbursement is not pending and is not intended to be filed, you can claim a loss for all unreimbursed amounts paid during the year to repair the damage from corrosive drywall to your personal residence and household appliances (otherwise if a reimbursement claim is pending or intended to be filed, the loss is limited to 75% of the unreimbursed amounts paid in the tax year).
- If you have been fully reimbursed before filing a return for the year the loss was sustained, you cannot claim a loss.

Refer to Publication 547 and Revenue Procedure 2010-36 for additional details related to reporting such claim.

Theft

A theft is the taking and removing of money or property with the intent to deprive the owner of it. The taking of property must be illegal under the laws of the state where it occurred and it must have been done with criminal intent. You do not need to show a conviction for theft.

EXPLANATION

A theft loss is deducted in the year of discovery, not the year of the theft, unless they both occur in the same year. If, in the year of discovery, an insurance claim exists and there is a reasonable expectation of recovering the cost of the asset from the insurance company, no deduction is permitted. Losses on securities which resulted from malfeasance of officers or directors—such as in the case of Enron—are not considered theft losses. Instead the loss is treated as a capital loss.

Theft includes the taking of money or property by the following means.

- Blackmail.
- Burglary.
- Embezzlement.
- Extortion.
- Kidnapping for ransom.
- Larceny.
- Robbery.

EXAMPLES

- A taxpayer from New York was allowed a deduction for a theft loss for money given to fortune-tellers. Under New York law, fortune-telling is a crime. The taxpayer's testimony and receipts were sufficient proof of the amounts paid to the fortune-tellers.
- A moving company placed an individual's belongings in storage until a price dispute could be resolved. A court ruled that because there was a reasonable likelihood that the individual would recover his property, no theft loss was allowed.

The taking of money or property through fraud or misrepresentation is theft if it is illegal under state or local law.

Decline in market value of stock. You cannot deduct as a theft loss the decline in market value of stock acquired on the open market for investment if the decline is caused by disclosure of accounting fraud or other illegal misconduct by the officers or directors of the corporation that issued the stock. However, you can deduct as a capital loss the loss you sustain when you sell or exchange the stock or the stock becomes completely worthless. You report a capital loss on Schedule D (Form 1040). For more information about stock sales, worthless stock, and capital losses, see chapter 4 of Publication 550.

Mislaid or lost property. The simple disappearance of money or property is not a theft. However, an accidental loss or disappearance of property can qualify as a casualty if it results from an identifiable event that is sudden, unexpected, or unusual. Sudden, unexpected, and unusual events are defined earlier.

Example. A car door is accidentally slammed on your hand, breaking the setting of your diamond ring. The diamond falls from the ring and is never found. The loss of the diamond is a casualty.

EXPLANATION

Another type of loss you may experience is seizure, requisition, or condemnation. For example, the government might seize your home in order to build a new highway. For further discussion, see chapter 13, *Basis of property*, and chapter 14, *Sale of property*.

Losses from Ponzi-type investment schemes. If you had a loss from a Ponzi-type investment scheme, see:

- Revenue Ruling 2009-9, 2009-14 I.R.B. 735 (available at *www.irs.gov/irb/2009-14_IRB/ar07.html*).
- Revenue Procedure 2009-20, 2009-14 I.R.B. 749 (available at *www.irs.gov/irb/2009-14_IRB/ar11.html*).

These losses are deductible as theft losses of income-producing property on your tax return for the year the loss was discovered. You figure the deductible loss in Section B of Form 4684. If you qualify to use Revenue Procedure 2009-20 and you choose to follow the procedures in Revenue Procedure 2009-20, you also must complete Appendix A of that procedure and write "Revenue Procedure 2009-20" across the top of Form 4684. For more information, see the above revenue ruling and revenue procedure.

TAXALERT

In a change to its long-standing position, the IRS ruled (Revenue Ruling 2009-9) that losses suffered in a Ponzi scheme (for example, the multibillion dollar fraud perpetrated by Bernard Madoff and his investment company) are not subject to the restrictions generally applicable to personal theft losses. Therefore, losses from a Ponzi scheme are not reduced by 10% of adjusted gross income (AGI) plus $100. (Like personal theft losses generally, Ponzi scheme losses are also not subject to the 2%-of-AGI limitation on miscellaneous itemized deductions—see chapter 29, *Miscellaneous deductions*.)

The IRS has also offered victims of Ponzi schemes an option to claim a significant portion of their potential theft loss deduction (the deduction can range from 75% up to 95% of the total potential loss, depending upon the taxpayer's recovery efforts) in the year of discovery. This is available for losses discovered after 2007. Under existing regulations and case law, a claim for reimbursement of a theft loss typically bars a current deduction if there is a reasonable prospect for recovery for any portion of the claim.

The rules are very complex. Consult with your tax advisor if you have suffered losses from a Ponzi scheme.

Loss on Deposits

A loss on deposits can occur when a bank, credit union, or other financial institution becomes insolvent or bankrupt. If you incurred this type of loss, you can choose one of the following ways to deduct the loss.

- As a casualty loss.
- As an ordinary loss.
- As a nonbusiness bad debt.

EXPLANATION

For more information see *Special Treatment for Losses on Deposits in Insolvent or Bankrupt Financial Institutions* in the instructions for Form 4684.

Casualty loss or ordinary loss. You can choose to deduct a loss on deposits as a casualty loss or as an ordinary loss for any year in which you can reasonably estimate how much of your deposits you have lost in an insolvent or bankrupt financial institution. The choice is generally made on the return you file for that year and applies to all your losses on deposits for the year in that particular financial institution. If you treat the loss as a casualty or ordinary loss, you cannot treat the same amount of the loss as a nonbusiness bad debt when it actually becomes worthless. However, you can take a nonbusiness bad debt deduction for any amount of loss that is more than the estimated amount you deducted as a casualty or ordinary loss. Once you make this choice, you cannot change it without permission from the Internal Revenue Service.

If you claim an ordinary loss, report it as a miscellaneous itemized deduction on Schedule A (Form 1040), line 23. The maximum amount you can claim is $20,000 ($10,000 if you are married filing separately) reduced by any expected state insurance proceeds. Your loss is subject to the 2%-of-adjusted-gross-income limit. You cannot choose to claim an ordinary loss if any part of the deposit is federally insured.

EXPLANATION

If you choose to treat the loss as a 2011 casualty loss, it is subject to $100 per event and 10% of your adjusted gross income limitations (see *Deduction Limits,* later).

Example

In 2011, Molly had an adjusted gross income of $25,000 and a loss on deposits of $7,500.

Casualty loss (minus $100 floor)	$7,400
Less: 10% of AGI (10% × $25,000)	(2,500)
Itemized deduction	$4,900

For 2011, Molly would have a $4,900 itemized deduction with no further tax deduction in the following tax year related to this deposit.

Nonbusiness bad debt. If you do not choose to deduct the loss as a casualty loss or as an ordinary loss, you must wait until the year the actual loss is determined and deduct the loss as a nonbusiness bad debt in that year.

EXPLANATION

A nonbusiness bad debt arises from loans between an individual and those not connected with the individual's business. If you elect to treat the loss as a nonbusiness bad debt, the loss is treated as a short-term capital loss. Capital losses, net of capital gains, are subject to the $3,000 ($1,500 for married persons filing separately) capital loss limitation in any 1 year, with any excess over the annual limit being deductible in following tax years. See chapter 16, *Reporting gains and losses,* for a further explanation of the limitations regarding the deductibility of capital losses.

Example

If Molly chose to treat her loss on deposits as a nonbusiness bad debt, she would have a $3,000 loss in 2011, a $3,000 loss in 2012, and a $1,500 loss in 2013, assuming no other capital gains or losses in these years. Her total allowable loss is $7,500.

How to report. The kind of deduction you choose for your loss on deposits determines how you report your loss. If you choose:

- Casualty loss—report it on Form 4684 first and then on Schedule A (Form 1040).
- Ordinary loss—report it on Schedule A (Form 1040) as a miscellaneous itemized deduction.
- Nonbusiness bad debt—report it on Schedule D (Form 1040).

More information. For more information, see *Special Treatment for Losses on Deposits in Insolvent or Bankrupt Financial Institutions* in the Instructions for Form 4684 or *Deposit in Insolvent or Bankrupt Financial Institution* in Publication 550.

EXPLANATION

Deducted loss recovered. If you recover an amount you deducted as a loss in an earlier year, you may have to include the amount recovered in your income for the year of recovery. If any part of the original deduction did not reduce your tax in the earlier year, you do not have to include that part of the recovery in your income. For more information, see *Recoveries* in Publication 525.

Proof of Loss

To deduct a casualty or theft loss, you must be able to prove that you had a casualty or theft. You also must be able to support the amount you take as a deduction.

Casualty loss proof. For a casualty loss, your records should show all the following.

- The type of casualty (car accident, fire, storm, etc.) and when it occurred.
- That the loss was a direct result of the casualty.
- That you were the owner of the property or, if you leased the property from someone else, that you were contractually liable to the owner for the damage.
- Whether a claim for reimbursement exists for which there is a reasonable expectation of recovery.

Theft loss proof. For a theft loss, your records should show all the following.

- When you discovered that your property was missing.
- That your property was stolen.
- That you were the owner of the property.
- Whether a claim for reimbursement exists for which there is a reasonable expectation of recovery.

Records

It is important that you have records that will prove your deduction. If you do not have the actual records to support your deduction, you can use other satisfactory evidence to support it.

TAXPLANNER

Proving a theft took place. For a loss from theft to be deductible, you must be able to prove that a theft has taken place. Therefore, if you think a theft may have occurred, you should file a report with the police and attach a copy of the police report to your return. The report should tell of any evidence of breaking and entering and of any witness to the removal of the property. It is not necessary that the police investigate the alleged incident.

Supporting evidence. If you are going to claim a deduction for a casualty or theft loss, it is important that you gather as much supporting evidence as possible. Newspaper clippings about a storm, police reports, and insurance reports may all be helpful in proving the nature of the casualty or theft and when it occurred. You have the burden of proof to establish that a casualty occurred and that your loss was a direct result of the casualty.

Examples

- The Tax Court disallowed a casualty loss deducted for flood damage because the taxpayer failed to corroborate his testimony or provide reliable substantiation of the amount of loss, such as an inventory of damaged personal items and receipts for repairs to his residence.
- The Tax Court denied the amount of a casualty loss deduction that exceeded the insurance estimate for hurricane damage because the handwritten receipt for repairs appeared suspect to the IRS and insufficient to support the taxpayer's claim.
- A taxpayer was disallowed a casualty loss deduction relating to the alleged theft of rental equipment from the taxpayer's van. The rental invoices submitted for proof of the deduction were considered inadmissible by the Court since they were provided on the day of the trial and were not for the same year the taxpayer claimed the deduction.

Explanation

If there is no positive proof that a theft occurred, all details and evidence should be presented. If evidence points to a theft, the Tax Court has allowed a deduction. However, if the evidence points to a mysterious (unexplained) disappearance, deductions may be disallowed.

If the property is leased. Losses are deductible only by the owner of the property, unless the property is leased and the lessee is obligated to repair casualty damage to the property.

Examples

- If you purchase an automobile for your son or daughter and put the title to the automobile in the child's name, any casualty or theft loss is deductible by the child–not by you.
- If you damage another person's property, you may not deduct any payments you make to restore or replace that property.
- Members of social clubs may not deduct an assessment to repair hurricane damage to club property.
- Tenant-stockholders of a cooperative housing corporation (co-op) may not deduct an allocable share of the assessment to fix a collapsed retaining wall on a co-op's grounds.

Figuring a Loss

Figure the amount of your loss using the following steps.

1. Determine your adjusted basis in the property before the casualty or theft.
2. Determine the decrease in fair market value of the property as a result of the casualty or theft.

3. From the smaller of the amounts you determined in (1) and (2), subtract any insurance or other reimbursement you received or expect to receive.

EXPLANATION

Calculate your loss, taking into consideration any reimbursements you may receive. Your loss is limited to the lesser of your cost or the reduction in fair market value.

Proof of the amount of a casualty loss is as important as proving the existence of the casualty. There are numerous court cases in which the taxpayers have shown the existence of a casualty but failed to establish a loss amount and were therefore denied a casualty loss deduction.

Example 1

A ruby ring valued at $5,000 is stolen from your house. The ring was purchased by your grandfather in 1950 for $500 and was handed down through two generations by means of nontaxable gifts. The amount of the loss is limited to $500, the cost of the ring to your grandfather.

Example 2

A homeowner was not entitled to a casualty loss deduction resulting from hurricane damage to trees located on his property, since a real estate agent's appraisal was not accepted as adequate proof of decline in the fair market value of the property. Thus, the decrease in the fair market value of the property as a result of the casualty was zero.

TAXPLANNER

Establishing the amount of your loss may be difficult, but the time you spend documenting the loss may be of great value in reducing your tax. You should make a list of all stolen, lost, damaged, or destroyed items as soon after the theft, disaster, or casualty as possible. IRS Publication 584, *Disaster and Casualty Loss Workbook,* may be useful. It has schedules to help you calculate a loss on your home and its contents and on your automobile, van, truck, or motorcycle.

It is equally important to retain records that help you establish the adjusted basis of valuable property. In other words, you should keep as supporting documentation receipts and documents establishing the original purchase price, costs of improvements, portions sold, or earlier losses in the value of the property.

In one court opinion, a taxpayer was denied a casualty loss deduction because she failed to establish either her basis in or the fair market value of the property.

Determining the decrease in market value of household items and personal belongings is often difficult. A certain percentage of the original cost of an item has often been used both by the IRS and by the courts to determine the fair market value of a particular item. Therefore, if you can produce evidence of the original cost of the items that were lost or damaged, you may help your case.

The IRS has provided methods that may be used to figure the deduction for a casualty loss of personal-use residential real property and personal belongings damaged, destroyed, or stolen as a result of storms and other federally declared disasters. See Publication 547, *Casualties, Disasters, and Thefts,* for more information.

For personal-use property and property used in performing services as an employee, apply the deduction limits, discussed later, to determine the amount of your deductible loss.

Gain from reimbursement. If your reimbursement is more than your adjusted basis in the property, you have a gain. This is true even if the decrease in the FMV of the property is smaller than your adjusted basis. If you have a gain, you may have to pay tax on it, or you may be able to postpone reporting the gain. See Publication 547 for more information on how to treat a gain from a reimbursement for a casualty or theft.

EXPLANATION

In addition to Publication 547, see *Insurance and Other Reimbursements,* later.

Leased property. If you are liable for casualty damage to property you lease, your loss is the amount you must pay to repair the property minus any insurance or other reimbursement you receive or expect to receive.

EXPLANATION

Business or income-producing property. If you have business or income-producing property, such as rental property, and it is stolen or completely destroyed, the decrease in fair market value is not considered. Your loss is figured as follows: Your adjusted basis in the property minus any salvage value minus any insurance or other reimbursement you receive or expect to receive.

Decrease in Fair Market Value

Fair market value (FMV) is the price for which you could sell your property to a willing buyer when neither of you has to sell or buy and both of you know all the relevant facts.

The decrease in FMV used to figure the amount of a casualty or theft loss is the difference between the property's fair market value immediately before and immediately after the casualty or theft.

FMV of stolen property. The FMV of property immediately after a theft is considered to be zero, since you no longer have the property.

Example. Several years ago, you purchased silver dollars at face value for $150. This is your adjusted basis in the property. Your silver dollars were stolen this year. The FMV of the coins was $1,000 just before they were stolen, and insurance did not cover them. Your theft loss is $150.

EXPLANATION

Your theft loss is $150, the lesser of the adjusted basis in the property ($150) or the decrease in fair market value of the property ($1,000).

Recovered stolen property. Recovered stolen property is your property that was stolen and later returned to you. If you recovered property after you had already taken a theft loss deduction, you must refigure your loss using the smaller of the property's adjusted basis (explained later) or the decrease in FMV from the time just before it was stolen until the time it was recovered. Use this amount to refigure your total loss for the year in which the loss was deducted.

If your refigured loss is less than the loss you deducted, you generally have to report the difference as income in the recovery year. But report the difference only up to the amount of the loss that reduced your tax. For more information on the amount to report, see *Recoveries* in chapter 12.

EXAMPLE

Your personal automobile is stolen. You paid $27,000 for it, and, on the day it was stolen, it had a fair market value of $15,500. Several days later, your automobile is found damaged and abandoned. The fair market value is reduced to $13,000 because of the damage. Your loss is $2,500. The decrease in market value ($15,500 – $13,000) is less than your cost of $27,000. Therefore, your deduction is limited to $2,500.

Figuring Decrease in FMV—Items To Consider

To figure the decrease in FMV because of a casualty or theft, you generally need a competent appraisal. However, other measures can also be used to establish certain decreases.

Appraisal. An appraisal to determine the difference between the FMV of the property immediately before a casualty or theft and immediately afterward should be made by a competent appraiser. The appraiser must recognize the effects of any general market decline that may occur along with the casualty. This information is needed to limit any deduction to the actual loss resulting from damage to the property.

Several factors are important in evaluating the accuracy of an appraisal, including the following.

- The appraiser's familiarity with your property before and after the casualty or theft.
- The appraiser's knowledge of sales of comparable property in the area.
- The appraiser's knowledge of conditions in the area of the casualty.
- The appraiser's method of appraisal.

Tip

You may be able to use an appraisal that you used to get a federal loan (or a federal loan guarantee) as the result of a federally declared disaster to establish the amount of your disaster loss. For more information on disasters, see Disaster Area Losses, *in Publication 547.*

EXPLANATION

An appraisal obtained for the purpose of getting a loan of federal funds or a loan guarantee from the federal government as a result of a disaster could also be used to establish the amount of a disaster loss. Consult your tax advisor to be certain you comply with IRS guidelines.

Appraisal fee. The appraisal fee is not a part of the casualty or theft loss. It is an expense in determining your tax liability. You can deduct it as a miscellaneous deduction subject to the 2%-of-adjusted-gross-income limit on Schedule A (Form 1040). See *Costs of photographs and appraisals*. For information about miscellaneous deductions, see chapter 29, *Miscellaneous deductions*.

TAXSAVER

If you have property appraised because you have a casualty loss and the loss turns out not to be deductible because it does not exceed 10% of your adjusted gross income (see *10% Rule*, under *Deduction Limits*, later), the cost of the appraisal is still deductible as a miscellaneous deduction subject to the 2%-of-adjusted-gross-income limit on Schedule A (Form 1040).

Cost of cleaning up or making repairs. The cost of repairing damaged property is not part of a casualty loss. Neither is the cost of cleaning up after a casualty. But you can use the cost of cleaning up or making repairs after a casualty as a measure of the decrease in FMV if you meet all the following conditions.

- The repairs are actually made.
- The repairs are necessary to bring the property back to its condition before the casualty.
- The amount spent for repairs is not excessive.
- The repairs take care of the damage only.
- The value of the property after the repairs is not, due to the repairs, more than the value of the property before the casualty.

EXPLANATION

Courts have held that cleanup expenses are deductible in the following circumstances:

- Replanting of damaged trees necessary to restore the property to its approximate value before the casualty
- Removing destroyed or damaged trees and shrubs, less any salvage value received
- Replacing a windstorm-damaged carport

Note: Losses must be reduced by the $100 deductible limit and any money paid by an insurance company (see *$100 Rule*, under Deduction Limits, later).

TAXSAVER

Damaged trees. If a casualty occurs that damages or destroys trees or shrubs on your residential property and you do not plan to repair or replace them, make sure that the appraiser's valuation documenting the decrease in the value of the property considers the estimated cleanup costs.

TAXSAVER

If the fair market value of your property is decreased. If the repairs do not bring the property back to its condition before the casualty, it may be that the decrease in fair market value is greater than the cost of the repairs. The greater loss is deductible.

Example

As a result of a boating accident, the fair market value of your boat drops from $6,000 to $2,500. You originally paid $5,000 for the boat. You spend $2,000 on repairs, which actually increase the market value of the boat to $4,800. Nevertheless, you are entitled to a deduction of $3,500, which is the decrease in market value as a result of the casualty ($6,000 – $2,500).

Landscaping. The cost of restoring landscaping to its original condition after a casualty may indicate the decrease in FMV. You may be able to measure your loss by what you spend on the following.

- Removing destroyed or damaged trees and shrubs minus any salvage you receive.
- Pruning and other measures taken to preserve damaged trees and shrubs.
- Replanting necessary to restore the property to its approximate value before the casualty.

EXPLANATION

The IRS takes the position that ornamental trees and shrubbery are an integral part of the real property and have no separate value. Therefore, the loss from damage to landscaping is measured by the decline in the fair market value of the entire property, not of an individual tree.

This treatment generally works to your advantage. If you originally planted the trees, your basis in them is probably substantially less than the decline in their fair market value. However, because the trees are regarded as an integral part of the property, your basis for figuring your loss is not just your basis for the trees but your basis for the entire property.

Example

You purchased a lot 10 years ago for $12,000 and spent $2,000 for shrubs and saplings. The entire property is now worth $20,000. A fire destroys all of the now mature shrubs and trees and reduces the market value of the property to $11,000. You are entitled to a deduction of $9,000. Even though you paid only $2,000 for the trees, you paid $14,000 for the entire property. Because the decline in value of $9,000 is less than your basis of $14,000, you may deduct the entire decrease in fair market value.

TAXSAVER

Storm damage. After a storm, damaged or fallen mature trees are often replaced with saplings. You should argue that the replacements–the saplings–are worth less than the fallen trees and a loss greater than the cost of the saplings should be allowed.

Car value. Books issued by various automobile organizations that list your car may be useful in figuring the value of your car. You can use the book's retail values and modify them by such factors as mileage and the condition of your car to figure its value. The prices are not official, but they may be useful in determining value and suggesting relative prices for comparison with current sales and offerings in your area. If your car is not listed in the books, determine its value from other sources. A dealer's offer for your car as a trade-in on a new car is not usually a measure of its true value.

TAXSAVER

A few resources that can assist you with determining the value of your car are Kelley Blue Book (*www.kbb.com*), NADA (*www.nada.com*), and Edmunds (*www.edmunds.com*).

Figuring Decrease in FMV—Items Not To Consider

You generally should not consider the following items when attempting to establish the decrease in FMV of your property.

Cost of protection. The cost of protecting your property against a casualty or theft is not part of a casualty or theft loss. The amount you spend on insurance or to board up your house against a storm is not part of your loss.

If you make permanent improvements to your property to protect it against a casualty or theft, add the cost of these improvements to your basis in the property. An example would be the cost of a dike to prevent flooding.

EXPLANATION

Burglar alarms. The costs of protecting your property against potential casualty are not deductible. This includes such items as burglar alarms and smoke detectors.

Exception. You cannot increase your basis in the property by, or deduct as a business expense, any expenditures you made with respect to qualified disaster mitigation payments. See *Disaster Area Losses* in Publication 547.

Related expenses. Any incidental expenses you have due to a casualty or theft, such as expenses for the treatment of personal injuries, for temporary housing, or for a rental car, are not part of your casualty or theft loss.

TAXSAVER

Incidental expenses may be deductible as business expenses if the damaged or stolen property is business property.

However, money spent for temporary lodging at a hotel or an apartment while your residence is being repaired or rebuilt, the cost of water purchased due to well contamination, the cost of putting up a fence around a fire-damaged residence, and the towing of an automobile to a garage for repairs are all personal expenses that may not be deducted.

Replacement cost. The cost of replacing stolen or destroyed property is not part of a casualty or theft loss.

EXAMPLE

You bought a new chair 4 years ago for $300. In April, a fire destroyed the chair. You estimate that it would cost $500 to replace it. If you had sold the chair before the fire, you estimate that you could have received only $100 for it because it was 4 years old. The chair was not insured. Your loss, before limitations, is $100, the fair market value of the chair before the fire. It is not $500, the replacement cost.

Sentimental value. Do not consider sentimental value when determining your loss. If a family portrait, heirloom, or keepsake is damaged, destroyed, or stolen, you must base your loss on its FMV.

Decline in market value of property in or near casualty area. A decrease in the value of your property because it is in or near an area that suffered a casualty, or that might again suffer a casualty, is not to be taken into consideration. You have a loss only for actual casualty damage to your property. However, if your home is in a federally declared disaster area, see *Disaster Area Losses* in Publication 547.

EXPLANATION

Taxpayers have been unable to take deductions for such things as a decline in market value of a house because it is near a newly opened highway or because of the stigma of a previous fire. There must be actual physical damage to the property that is the immediate and direct result of a casualty. However, a court case has held that an owner could deduct as a casualty loss the decrease in fair market value due to permanent buyer resistance resulting from changes made to the neighborhood following a flood.

Costs of photographs and appraisals. Photographs taken after a casualty will be helpful in establishing the condition and value of the property after it was damaged. Photographs showing the condition of the property after it was repaired, restored, or replaced may also be helpful.

Appraisals are used to figure the decrease in FMV because of a casualty or theft. See Appraisal, earlier, under *Figuring Decrease in FMV—Items To Consider,* for information about appraisals.

The costs of photographs and appraisals used as evidence of the value and condition of property damaged as a result of a casualty are not a part of the loss. You can claim these costs as a miscellaneous itemized deduction subject to the 2%-of-adjusted-gross-income limit on Schedule A (Form 1040). For information about miscellaneous deductions, see chapter 29.

TAXORGANIZER

Photographs or videotapes of your home and its contents may be useful in other ways as well. First, they may provide evidence of value before the casualty. Recent photos, or tapes, for example, may be used to prove that the property was in good condition prior to the casualty. Second, they may assist you in determining what items are missing or were destroyed in a fire or theft. People often do not have an accurate inventory of household items. Photos or tapes serve as useful reminders.

The photographs or videotapes should be updated annually and kept outside your house, preferably in a safe-deposit box. They may be even more important in dealing with your insurance claim than they are in helping you with the IRS.

Adjusted Basis

Adjusted basis is your basis in the property (usually cost) increased or decreased by various events, such as improvements and casualty losses. For more information, see chapter 13.

TAXPLANNER

Separate computations. Generally, if a single casualty or theft involves more than one item of property, you must figure the loss on each item separately; then combine the losses to determine the total loss from that casualty or theft.

Exception for personal-use real property. In figuring a casualty loss on personal-use real property, the entire property (including any improvements, such as buildings, trees, and shrubs) is treated as one item.

Figure the loss using the smaller of the following:

- The decrease in fair market value of the entire property
- The adjusted basis of the entire property

Insurance and Other Reimbursements

If you receive an insurance payment or other type of reimbursement, you must subtract the reimbursement when you figure your loss. You do not have a casualty or theft loss to the extent you are reimbursed.

If you expect to be reimbursed for part or all of your loss, you must subtract the expected reimbursement when you figure your loss. You must reduce your loss even if you do not receive payment until a later tax year. See *Reimbursement Received After Deducting Loss*, later.

Failure to file a claim for reimbursement. If your property is covered by insurance, you must file a timely insurance claim for reimbursement of your loss. Otherwise, you cannot deduct this loss as a casualty or theft loss. However, this rule does not apply to the portion of the loss not covered by insurance (for example, a deductible).

Example. You have a car insurance policy with a $1000 deductible. Because your insurance did not cover the first $1000 of an auto collision, the $1000 would be deductible (subject to the deduction limits discussed later). This is true even if you do not file an insurance claim, because your insurance policy would never have reimbursed you for the deductible.

EXPLANATION

You do not have to report a gain that results from a reimbursement that exceeds your basis in the lost, damaged, or destroyed property if you use the entire reimbursement to purchase property that is either similar or related in use to the original property. Instead, the recognition of the gain is postponed until the replacement property is sold. Your basis in the replacement property is its cost minus any postponed gain. With a home, the gain may not be taxable under the rules for exclusion of gain on home sales (see the rules discussed in chapter 15, *Selling your home*).

You are allowed a certain amount of time to select and purchase the replacement property. This time period begins on the day of the casualty or theft and ends 2 years after the close of the tax year in which the reimbursement is received (4 years for a federally declared disaster area). Thus, if your house was robbed on August 1, 2008, and your insurance company reimbursed you for your loss on June 1, 2009, you would have until December 31, 2011, to repair or replace the damaged goods. If the cost of the replacement property is less than the reimbursement received, the unspent part of the reimbursement must be recognized as a gain.

Types of Reimbursements

The most common type of reimbursement is an insurance payment for your stolen or damaged property. Other types of reimbursements are discussed next. Also see the Instructions for Form 4684.

Employer's emergency disaster fund. If you receive money from your employer's emergency disaster fund and you must use that money to rehabilitate or replace property on which you are claiming a casualty loss deduction, you must take that money into consideration in computing the casualty loss deduction. Take into consideration only the amount you used to replace your destroyed or damaged property.

Example. Your home was extensively damaged by a tornado. Your loss after reimbursement from your insurance company was $10,000. Your employer set up a disaster relief fund for its employees. Employees receiving money from the fund had to use it to rehabilitate or replace their damaged or destroyed property. You received $4,000 from the fund and spent the entire amount on repairs to your home. In figuring your casualty loss, you must reduce your unreimbursed loss ($10,000) by the $4,000 you received from your employer's fund. Your casualty loss before applying the deduction limits discussed later is $6,000.

EXPLANATION

If you have use and occupancy insurance for your business and are reimbursed for loss of business income, it does not reduce your casualty or theft loss. However, the reimbursement is considered income and is taxed in the same way as your other business income.

Cash gifts. If you receive excludable cash gifts as a disaster victim and there are no limits on how you can use the money, you do not reduce your casualty loss by these excludable cash gifts. This applies even if you use the money to pay for repairs to property damaged in the disaster.

Example. Your home was damaged by a hurricane. Relatives and neighbors made cash gifts to you that were excludable from your income. You used part of the cash gifts to pay for repairs to your home. There were no limits or restrictions on how you could use the cash gifts. Because it was an excludable gift, the money you received and used to pay for repairs to your home does not reduce your casualty loss on the damaged home.

Insurance payments for living expenses. You do not reduce your casualty loss by insurance payments you receive to cover living expenses in either of the following situations.

- You lose the use of your main home because of a casualty.
- Government authorities do not allow you access to your main home because of a casualty or threat of one.

Inclusion in income. If these insurance payments are more than the temporary increase in your living expenses, you must include the excess in your income. Report this amount on Form 1040, line 21. However, if the casualty occurs in a federally declared disaster area, none of the insurance payments are taxable. See *Qualified disaster relief payments,* under *Disaster Area Losses* in Publication 547.

A temporary increase in your living expenses is the difference between the actual living expenses you and your family incurred during the period you could not use your home and your normal living expenses for that period. Actual living expenses are the reasonable and necessary expenses incurred because of the loss of your main home. Generally, these expenses include the amounts you pay for the following.

- Rent for suitable housing.
- Transportation.
- Food.
- Utilities.
- Miscellaneous services.

Normal living expenses consist of these same expenses that you would have incurred but did not because of the casualty or the threat of one.

Example. As a result of a fire, you vacated your apartment for a month and moved to a motel. You normally pay $525 a month for rent. None was charged for the month the apartment was vacated. Your motel rent for this month was $1,200. You normally pay $200 a month for food. Your food expenses for the month you lived in the motel were $400. You received $1,100 from your insurance company to cover your living expenses. You determine the payment you must include in income as follows.

1) Insurance payment for living expenses		$1,100
2) Actual expenses during the month you are unable to use your home because of fire	1,600	
3) Normal living expenses	725	
4) Temporary increase in living expenses: Subtract line 3 from line 2		875
5) Amount of payment includible in income: Subtract line 4 from line 1		$ 225

Tax year of inclusion. You include the taxable part of the insurance payment in income for the year you regain the use of your main home or, if later, for the year you receive the taxable part of the insurance payment.

Example. Your main home was destroyed by a tornado in August 2009. You regained use of your home in November 2010. The insurance payments you received in 2009 and 2010 were $1,500 more than the temporary increase in your living expenses during those years. You include this amount in income on your 2010 Form 1040. If, in 2011, you receive further payments to cover the living expenses you had in 2009 and 2010, you must include those payments in income on your 2011 Form 1040.

Disaster relief. Food, medical supplies, and other forms of assistance you receive do not reduce your casualty loss unless they are replacements for lost or destroyed property.

Disaster unemployment assistance payments are unemployment benefits that are taxable.

Generally, disaster relief grants and qualified disaster mitigation payments made under the Robert T. Stafford Disaster Relief and Emergency Assistance Act or the National Flood Insurance Act (as in effect on April 15, 2005) are not includible in your income. See *Disaster Area Losses* in Publication 547.

Tip

Qualified disaster relief payments you receive for expenses you incurred as a result of a federally declared disaster are not taxable income to you. For more information, see Disaster Area Losses *in Publication 547.*

Reimbursement Received After Deducting Loss

If you figured your casualty or theft loss using your expected reimbursement, you may have to adjust your tax return for the tax year in which you receive your actual reimbursement. This section explains the adjustment you may have to make.

Actual reimbursement less than expected. If you later receive less reimbursement than you expected, include that difference as a loss with your other losses (if any) on your return for the year in which you can reasonably expect no more reimbursement.

Example. Your personal car had an FMV of $2,000 when it was destroyed in a collision with another car in 2010. The accident was due to the negligence of the other driver. At the end of 2010, there was a reasonable prospect that the owner of the other car would reimburse you in full. You did not have a deductible loss in 2010.

In January 2011, the court awarded you a judgment of $2,000. However, in July it became apparent that you will be unable to collect any amount from the other driver. You can deduct the loss in 2011 subject to the limits discussed later.

TAXPLANNER

Even though there is no formal IRS ruling, many IRS auditors tend to disallow any deduction for the unreimbursed amount if you are fully insured and settle your claim with the insurance carrier for less than the amount of the loss by signing a proof of loss statement. The proof of loss statement sets the value of the loss between you and the insurance company. Generally, the IRS auditor will only allow a deduction of the unreimbursed loss if he or she is convinced that you have attempted all reasonable remedies against the insurer.

Actual reimbursement more than expected. If you later receive more reimbursement than you expected after you claimed a deduction for the loss, you may have to include the extra reimbursement in your income for the year you receive it. However, if any part of the original deduction did not reduce your tax for the earlier year, do not include that part of the reimbursement in your income. You do not refigure your tax for the year you claimed the deduction. For more information, see Recoveries in chapter 12.

EXAMPLE

Last year, a hurricane destroyed your motorboat. Your loss was $3,000, and you estimated that your insurance would cover $2,500 of it. Because you did not itemize deductions on your return last year, you could not deduct the loss. When the insurance company reimburses you for the loss, you do not report any of the reimbursement as income. This is true even if it is for the full $3,000 because you did not deduct the loss on your return. The loss did not reduce your tax.

Caution

If the total of all the reimbursements you receive is more than your adjusted basis in the destroyed or stolen property, you will have a gain on the casualty or theft. If you have already taken a deduction for a loss and you receive the reimbursement in a later year, you may have to include the gain in your income for the later year. Include the gain as ordinary income up to the amount of your deduction that reduced your tax for the earlier year. See Publication 547 for more information on how to treat a gain from the reimbursement of a casualty or theft.

Actual reimbursement same as expected. If you receive exactly the reimbursement you expected to receive, you do not have to include any of the reimbursement in your income and you cannot deduct any additional loss.

Example. In December 2011, you had a collision while driving your personal car. Repairs to the car cost $950. You had $100 deductible collision insurance. Your insurance company agreed to reimburse you for the rest of the damage. Because you expected a reimbursement from the insurance company, you did not have a casualty loss deduction in 2011.

Due to the $100 rule (discussed later under <u>*Deduction Limits*</u>), you cannot deduct the $100 you paid as the deductible. When you receive the $850 from the insurance company in 2012, do not report it as income.

EXAMPLE

A taxpayer suffered a casualty loss from vandalism and filed a claim with her insurance company in the year of the loss. The insurance company denied any liability for the damage. Consequently, the taxpayer filed suit against the insurance company. A court held that the taxpayer could not deduct the loss in the year in which it was incurred, because a reasonable possibility of recovery still existed. No deduction was allowed while the suit against the insurance company was still pending.

Single Casualty on Multiple Properties

Personal property. Personal property is any property that is not real property. If your personal property is stolen or is damaged or destroyed by a casualty, you must figure your loss separately for each item of property. Then combine these separate losses to figure the total loss from that casualty or theft.

Example. A fire in your home destroyed an upholstered chair, an oriental rug, and an antique table. You did not have fire insurance to cover your loss. (This was the only casualty or theft you had during the year.) You paid $750 for the chair and you established that it had an FMV of $500 just before the fire. The rug cost $3,000 and had an FMV of $2,500 just before the fire. You bought the table at an auction for $100 before discovering it was an antique. It had been appraised at $900 before the fire. You figure your loss on each of these items as follows:

	Chair	Rug	Table
1) Basis (cost)	$750	$3,000	$100
2) FMV before fire	$500	$2,500	$900
3) FMV after fire	–0–	–0–	–0–
4) Decrease in FMV	$500	$2,500	$900
5) Loss (smaller of (1) or (4))	$500	$2,500	$100
6) **Total loss**			**$3,100**

Real property. In figuring a casualty loss on personal-use real property, treat the entire property (including any improvements, such as buildings, trees, and shrubs) as one item. Figure the loss using the smaller of the adjusted basis or the decrease in FMV of the entire property.

Example. You bought your home a few years ago. You paid $160,000 ($20,000 for the land and $140,000 for the house). You also spent $2,000 for landscaping. This year a fire destroyed your home. The fire also damaged the shrubbery and trees in your yard. The fire was your only casualty or theft loss this year. Competent appraisers valued the property as a whole at $200,000 before the fire, but only $30,000 after the fire. (The loss to your household furnishings is not shown in this example. It would be figured separately on each item, as explained earlier under Personal property) Shortly after the fire, the insurance company paid you $155,000 for the loss. You figure your casualty loss as follows:

1) Adjusted basis of the entire property (land, building, and landscaping)	$162,000
2) FMV of entire property before fire	$200,000
3) FMV of entire property after fire	30,000
4) Decrease in FMV of entire property	$170,000
5) Loss (smaller of (1) or (4))	$162,000
6) Subtract insurance	155,000
7) **Amount of loss after reimbursement**	**$7,000**

Deduction Limits

After you have figured your casualty or theft loss, you must figure how much of the loss you can deduct. If the loss was to property for your personal use or your family's use, there are two limits on the amount you can deduct for your casualty or theft loss.

1. You must reduce each casualty or theft loss by $100 ($100 rule).
2. You must further reduce the total of all your casualty or theft losses by 10% of your adjusted gross income (10% rule).

You make these reductions on Form 4684.

These rules are explained next and Table 26-1 summarizes how to apply the $100 rule and the 10% rule in various situations. For more detailed explanations and examples, see Publication 547.

Property used partly for business and partly for personal purposes. When property is used partly for personal purposes and partly for business or income-producing purposes, the casualty or theft loss deduction must be figured separately for the personal-use part and for the business or income-producing part. You must figure each loss separately because the $100 rule and the 10% rule apply only to the loss on the personal-use part of the property.

Table 26-1. **How To Apply the Deduction Limits for Personal-Use Property**

		$100 Rule	**10% Rule**
General Application		You must reduce each casualty or theft loss by $100 when figuring your deduction. Apply this rule after you have figured the amount of your loss.	You must reduce your total casualty or theft loss by 10% of your adjusted gross income. Apply this rule after you reduce each loss by $100 (the $100 rule).
Single Event		Apply this rule only once, even if many pieces of property are affected.	Apply this rule only once, even if many pieces of property are affected.
More Than One Event		Apply to the loss from each event.	Apply to the total of all your losses from all events.
More Than One Person—With Loss From the Same Event (other than a married couple filing jointly)		Apply separately to each person.	Apply separately to each person.
Married Couple—With Loss From the Same Event	Filing Jointly	Apply as if you were one person.	Apply as if you were one person.
	Filing Separately	Apply separately to each spouse.	Apply separately to each spouse.
More Than One Owner (other than a married couple filing jointly)		Apply separately to each owner of jointly owned property.	Apply separately to each owner of jointly owned property.
Text intentionally omitted.			

EXPLANATION

Business or income-producing property. A loss on business property, property that earns you rent or royalty income, or other income-producing property is not subject to either the $100 rule or the 10% rule. For business or income-producing property, you must figure your loss separately for each item that is stolen, damaged, or destroyed. If casualty damage occurs both to a building and to trees on the same piece of property, the loss is measured separately for each.

Total loss of business or income-producing property. If you have business or income-producing property that is completely lost because of a casualty or theft, your deductible loss is your basis in the property minus any salvage value and minus any insurance or other reimbursement you receive or expect to receive. It does not matter what the decrease in fair market value is.

Example

You owned machinery that you used in your business. The machinery had an adjusted basis of $25,000 when it was completely destroyed by fire. Its fair market value just before the fire was $20,000. Because this was business property, and because it was completely destroyed, your deductible loss is your adjusted basis in the machinery, $25,000, decreased by salvage value and by any insurance or other reimbursement. Fair market value is not considered when you are figuring your loss, even though it is less than your basis in the machinery.

Explanation

Partial loss of business or income-producing property. If business or income-producing property is damaged but not completely destroyed in a casualty, the loss is the decrease in value because of the casualty or your adjusted basis in the property, whichever is less. From this amount (the lesser of your adjusted basis or the decrease in value), you must subtract any insurance or other reimbursement you receive or expect to receive.

TAXSAVER

If your car is stolen. If your automobile is stolen or destroyed, you may be able to deduct more than the value listed in one of the various books issued or websites sponsored by automobile organizations. If you use the automobile for business, you must make a separate calculation of the business and personal portions of the loss. This may produce a larger loss.

Example

Blair Hunt's automobile, which cost $8,000, is stolen. The "blue book"—one of the books published by automobile organizations—values his automobile at $5,000. Blair used the automobile for business 40% of the time and deducted $800 of depreciation expense.

	Business portion	Personal portion
Value before theft	$2,000	$3,000
Value after theft	-0-	-0-
Decrease in value	$2,000	$3,000
Adjusted basis:		
Original cost	$3,200	$4,800
Depreciation	(800)	-0-
Adjusted basis	$2,400	$4,800

Blair's casualty loss before the $100 limitation is $5,400, computed as follows:

Business portion—adjusted basis	$2,400
Personal portion—the lower of the decrease in value or the adjusted basis	3,000
Total	$5,400

TAXSAVER

By reporting the business loss on Schedule C (if self-employed), you can reduce your self-employment income and, hence, your self-employment tax.

$100 Rule

After you have figured your casualty or theft loss on personal-use property, you must reduce that loss by $100. This reduction applies to each total casualty or theft loss. It does not matter how many pieces of property are involved in an event. Only a single $100 reduction applies.

Example. A hailstorm damages your home and your car. Determine the amount of loss, as discussed earlier, for each of these items. Since the losses are due to a single event, you combine the losses and reduce the combined amount by $100.

Single event. Generally, events closely related in origin cause a single casualty. It is a single casualty when the damage is from two or more closely related causes, such as wind and flood damage caused by the same storm.

EXPLANATION

A single casualty may also damage two or more pieces of property, such as a hailstorm that damages both your home and your car parked in your driveway.

10% Rule

You must reduce the total of all your casualty or theft losses on personal-use property by 10% of your adjusted gross income. Apply this rule after you reduce each loss by $100. *Text intentionally omitted.* For more information, see the Form 4684 instructions. If you have both gains and losses from casualties or thefts, see Gains and losses, later in this discussion.

TAXSAVER

Generally, you must deduct a casualty loss in the year it occurred. However, if you incurred a casualty loss in a federally declared disaster area during 2011, the tax law allows you to claim that loss on your 2010 tax return or an amended return for 2010 instead of claiming the loss on your 2011 return. If you do so, the loss is treated as having occurred in 2010. Claiming a federally declared disaster loss incurred in 2011 on your 2010 tax return may result in a lower tax or produce or increase a cash refund. You should compare the tax savings you would recognize from claiming such a disaster loss on your 2011 return versus 2010.

Example 1. In June, you discovered that your house had been burglarized. Your loss after insurance reimbursement was $2,000. Your adjusted gross income for the year you discovered the theft is $29,500. You first apply the $100 rule and then the 10% rule. Figure your theft loss deduction as follows.

1) Loss after insurance	$2,000
2) Subtract $100	100
3) Loss after $100 rule	$1,900
4) Subtract 10% × $29,500 AGI	2,950
5) **Theft loss deduction**	–0–

You do not have a theft loss deduction because your loss after you apply the $100 rule ($1,900) is less than 10% of your adjusted gross income ($2,950).

EXPLANATION

More than one loss. If you have more than one casualty or theft loss during your tax year, reduce each loss by any reimbursement and by $100. Then you must reduce the total of all your losses by 10% of your adjusted gross income.

Example 2. In March, you had a car accident that totally destroyed your car. You did not have collision insurance on your car, so you did not receive any insurance reimbursement. Your loss on the car was $1,800. In November, a fire damaged your basement and totally destroyed the furniture, washer, dryer, and other items stored there. Your loss on the basement items after reimbursement was $2,100. Your adjusted gross income for the year that the accident and fire occurred is $25,000. You figure your casualty loss deduction as follows.

	Car	Basement
1) Loss	$1,800	$2,100
2) Subtract $100 per incident	100	100
3) Loss after $100 rule	$1,700	$2,000
4) Total loss		$3,700
5) Subtract 10% × $25,000 AGI		2,500
6) **Casualty loss deduction**		**$1,200**

Caution

Casualty or theft gains do not include gains you choose to postpone. See Publication 547 for information on the postponement of gain.

Gains and losses. If you had both gains and losses from casualties or thefts to personal-use property, you must compare your total gains to your total losses. Do this after you have reduced each loss by any reimbursements and by $100, but before you have reduced the losses by 10% of your adjusted gross income.

Losses more than gains. If your losses are more than your recognized gains, subtract your gains from your losses and reduce the result by 10% of your adjusted gross income. The rest, if any, is your deductible loss from personal-use property.

EXAMPLE

Your theft loss after reducing it by reimbursements and by $100 is $2,700. Your casualty gain is $700. Because your loss is more than your gain, you must reduce your $2,000 net loss ($2,700 – $700) by 10% of your adjusted gross income.

Gains more than losses. If your recognized gains are more than your losses, subtract your losses from your gains. The difference is treated as capital gain and must be reported on Schedule D (Form 1040). The 10% rule does not apply to your gains.

EXAMPLES

Example 1

Your theft loss after reducing it by reimbursements and by $100 is $600. Your casualty gain is $1,600. Because your gain is more than your loss, you must report the $1,000 net gain ($1,600 – $600) on Schedule D.

Example 2

During 2011, a storm completely destroyed your summer cottage, resulting in a casualty gain of $5,000 after you were reimbursed by your insurance company. Later in the year, your home was broken into on two separate occasions. Jewelry, silverware, and other items of personal property were stolen each time. The loss (after applying the $100 rule) on the first theft was $900 and on the second theft was $4,000. Your 2011 adjusted gross income is $25,000.

1) Loss on first theft	$ 900
2) Plus loss on second theft	4,000
3) Total losses	$4,900
4) Gain on cottage	5,000
5) Net gain for 2010	**$100**

The $100 gain will be reported on Form 4684. See Insurance and Other Reimbursements, regarding recognition of gains, discussed earlier.

When To Report Gains and Losses

Gains. If you receive an insurance or other reimbursement that is more than your adjusted basis in the destroyed or stolen property, you have a gain from the casualty or theft. You must include this gain in your income in the year you receive the reimbursement, unless you choose to postpone reporting the gain as explained in Publication 547.

If you have a loss, see Table 26-2.

Table 26-2. **When To Deduct a Loss**

IF you have a loss...	THEN deduct it in the year...
from a casualty,	the loss occurred.
in a federally declared disaster area,	the disaster occurred or the year immediately before the disaster.
from a theft,	the theft was discovered.
on a deposit treated as a:	
• casualty,	• a reasonable estimate can be made.
• bad debt,	• deposits are totally worthless.
• ordinary loss,	• a reasonable estimate can be made.

Losses. Generally, you can deduct a casualty loss that is not reimbursable only in the tax year in which the casualty occurred. This is true even if you do not repair or replace the damaged property until a later year.

You can deduct theft losses that are not reimbursable only in the year you discover your property was stolen.

If you are not sure whether part of your casualty or theft loss will be reimbursed, do not deduct that part until the tax year when you become reasonably certain that it will not be reimbursed.

EXPLANATION

The Tax Court denied a casualty loss deduction for a car that was totaled while stalled on the highway since the taxpayer admitted to an unresolved claim for damages with the insurance company and she was also not able to support the car's adjusted tax basis. The Court held that the taxpayer must establish the amount of the loss before a casualty loss deduction can be claimed.

Loss on deposits. If your loss is a loss on deposits in an insolvent or bankrupt financial institution, see *Loss on Deposits*, earlier.

Disaster Area Loss

You generally must deduct a casualty loss in the year it occurred. However, if you have a casualty loss from a federally declared disaster that occurred in an area warranting public or individual assistance (or both), you can choose to deduct the loss on your tax return or amended return for either of the following years.

- The year the disaster occurred.
- The year immediately preceding the year the disaster occurred.

See the Form 4684 instructions. *Text intentionally omitted.*

TAXPLANNER

If you are not in need of an immediate tax refund, you may want to wait to file until near the April 17 deadline (tax deadline is April 17, 2012, for 2011 tax returns). By waiting, you may be able to determine which tax year provides greater tax savings from the deduction and to choose that year to claim the loss. For more information, consult your tax advisor.

Explanation

A loss in a federally declared disaster area may be deducted on the tax return for the year in which the disaster occurs or in the immediately preceding tax year if certain requirements are met. First, the loss must have been from a disaster in an area that the President says needs federal assistance. Second, the tax return for the preceding year must be amended by the date it is due (with extensions), or, if that date has already passed, by the date the tax return for the year of the disaster is due (without extensions). Generally, you would have until April 17, 2012, to amend a 2010 return to report a 2011 disaster loss. An amended return is filed on Form 1040X. A listing of federal disaster areas may be obtained from your newspaper, from local officials, or from the Federal Emergency Management Agency's website (www.fema.gov/disasters).

TAXPLANNER

To determine whether you should claim the disaster loss on your current year's return or on your return for the preceding year, you should calculate the tax effects of claiming the loss in both years. Once you make a choice, it becomes irrevocable 90 days after you file your return.

TAXSAVER

Generally, you must deduct a casualty loss in the year it occurred. However, if you incurred a casualty loss in a federally declared disaster area during 2011, the tax law allows you to claim that loss on your 2010 tax return or an amended return for 2010 instead of claiming the loss on your 2011 return. If you do so, the loss is treated as having occurred in 2010. You should compare the tax savings you may recognize from claiming such a disaster loss on your 2011 return versus 2010.

Gains. Special rules apply if you choose to postpone reporting gain on property damaged or destroyed in a federally declared disaster area. For those special rules, see Publication 547.

Postponed tax deadlines. The IRS may postpone for up to 1 year certain tax deadlines of taxpayers who are affected by a federally declared disaster. The tax deadlines the IRS may postpone include those for filing income and employment tax returns, paying income and employment taxes, and making contributions to a traditional IRA or Roth IRA.

If any tax deadline is postponed, the IRS will publicize the postponement in your area by publishing a news release, revenue ruling, revenue procedure, notice, announcement, or other guidance in the Internal Revenue Bulletin (IRB).

Who is eligible. If the IRS postpones a tax deadline, the following taxpayers are eligible for the postponement.

- Any individual whose main home is located in a covered disaster area (defined next).
- Any business entity or sole proprietor whose principal place of business is located in a covered disaster area.
- Any individual who is a relief worker affiliated with a recognized government or philanthropic organization who is assisting in a covered disaster area.
- Any individual, business entity, or sole proprietorship whose records are needed to meet a postponed tax deadline, provided those records are maintained in a covered disaster area. The main home or principal place of business does not have to be located in the covered disaster area.
- Any estate or trust that has tax records necessary to meet a postponed tax deadline, provided those records are maintained in a covered disaster area.
- The spouse on a joint return with a taxpayer who is eligible for postponements.
- Any individual, business entity, or sole proprietorship not located in a covered disaster area, but whose records necessary to meet a postponed tax deadline are located in the covered disaster area.
- Any individual visiting the covered disaster area who was killed or injured as a result of the disaster.
- Any other person determined by the IRS to be affected by a federally declared disaster.

Covered disaster area. This is an area of a federally declared disaster in which the IRS has decided to postpone tax deadlines for up to 1 year.

Abatement of interest and penalties. The IRS may abate the interest and penalties on underpaid income tax for the length of any postponement of tax deadlines.

More information. For more information, see *Disaster Area Losses* in Publication 547.

How To Report Gains and Losses

Use Form 4684 to report a gain or a deductible loss from a casualty or theft. If you have more than one casualty or theft, use a separate Form 4684 to determine your gain or loss for each event. Combine the gains and losses on one Form 4684. Follow the form instructions as to which lines to fill out. In addition, you must use the appropriate schedule to report a gain or loss. The schedule you use depends on whether you have a gain or loss.

If you have a:	Report it on:
Gain	Schedule D (Form 1040)
Loss	Schedule A (Form 1040)

Text intentionally omitted.

Adjustments to basis. If you have a casualty or theft loss, you must decrease your basis in the property by any insurance or other reimbursement you receive, and by any deductible loss. Amounts you spend to restore your property after a casualty increase your adjusted basis. See *Adjusted Basis* in chapter 13 for more information.

Net operating loss (NOL). If your casualty or theft loss deduction causes your deductions for the year to be more than your income for the year, you may have an NOL. You can use an NOL to lower your tax in an earlier year, allowing you to get a refund for tax you have already paid. Or, you can use it to lower your tax in a later year. You do not have to be in business to have an NOL from a casualty or theft loss. For more information, see Publication 536, *Net Operating Losses (NOLs) for Individuals, Estates, and Trusts*.

TAXPLANNER

If your loss exceeds your income. If your casualty loss exceeds your income, you should fill out Form 1045, Application for Tentative Refund, to see whether you have a net operating loss. When filling out this form, treat your casualty losses as business deductions rather than nonbusiness deductions. If your casualty loss results in a net operating loss, then your net operating loss can be carried back to prior years to offset your taxable income, and you may get a refund of prior-year taxes.

For example, a 2011 net operating loss caused by a casualty loss can be carried back first to 2008; any remaining loss should be carried back to 2009, and into 2010. If any loss still remains, it can be carried forward for the next 20 years. Alternatively, you may elect on your 2011 tax return not to carry back your net operating loss but carry it forward only. You should compare the refund available from a carryback to the expected tax benefits in the future in order to determine whether you should make the election. This is a very complex area. Affected taxpayers should consult a professional tax advisor.

TAXORGANIZER

Records you should keep:

- Documentation of date, time, and place of occurrence of the casualty or theft
- Police reports
- Insurance reports including evidence of amount of reimbursement, if any
- Original receipts (if applicable)
- Repair bills
- Form 1099 (if applicable)
- Any appraisals or valuations supporting property value immediately before and after the casualty or theft
- An inventory and/or supporting pictures or video of all household items before casualty or theft
- An inventory of stolen, lost, damaged, or destroyed items
- Pictures or video of damaged items (if any)
- Any type of supporting evidence such as newspaper clippings about a storm
- Electronic backup set of records (bank statements, tax returns, insurance policies, etc.) kept in a safe place away from the original set

Chapter 27

Car expenses and other employee business expenses

ey.com/EYTaxGuide

Note

IRS Publication 17 (*Your Federal Income Tax*) has been updated by Ernst & Young LLP for 2011. Dates and dollar amounts shown are for 2011. Underlined type is used to indicate where IRS text has been updated. Places where text has been removed are indicated by the sentence: *Text intentionally omitted.*

ey.com/EYTaxGuide

Ernst & Young LLP will update the *Ernst & Young Tax Guide 2012* website with relevant taxpayer information as it becomes available. You can also sign up for email alerts to let you know when changes have been made.

Introduction

If you are traveling on business and your employer does not reimburse your expenses, you may deduct many of them on your income tax return. If you use your automobile partly for business purposes, you may be able to deduct some of your operating expenses. If you entertain a business associate at a restaurant or sporting event, you may be able to deduct that expense, too. Within strict limits, business gifts are also deductible.

You must be able to prove the business purpose, as well as the amount of the expense, to claim a deduction for employee expenses. All expenses should be substantiated with receipts and records indicating the time, place, and business nature of the expense. This chapter explains business-related expenses for travel, transportation, entertainment, and gifts that you may deduct on your income tax return. It also discusses the reporting and recordkeeping requirements for these expenses.

What's New

Standard mileage rate. For 2011, the standard mileage rate for the cost of operating your car for business use is 51 cents per mile from January 1, 2011, through June 30, 2011, and 55.5 cents per mile from July 1, 2011, through December 31, 2011.

TAXALERT

Beginning in 2011, the business standard mileage rate can be used for vehicles used for hire, such as taxicabs.

Car expenses and use of the standard mileage rate are explained under *Transportation Expenses*, later.

TAXSAVER

You may also benefit from deducting the standard mileage rate for costs to operate your car for charitable, medical, or moving purposes. The rate to operate your car for medical reasons or as part of a deductible move in 2011 is 19 cents per mile from January 1, 2011, through June 30, 2011, and 23.5 cents per mile from July 1, 2011, through December 31, 2011. (See chapter 22, *Medical and dental expenses*.) Also, the standard mileage rate for charitable purposes in 2011 is 14 cents per mile. (See chapter 25, *Contributions*.)

Depreciation limits on cars, trucks, and vans. For 2011, the first-year limit on the total section 179 deduction, special depreciation allowance, and depreciation deduction for cars remains at $11,060 ($3,060 if you elect not to claim the special depreciation allowance). For trucks and vans the first-year limit has increased to $11,260 ($3,260 if you elect not to claim the special depreciation allowance). For more information see *Depreciation limits* in Publication 463.

TAXALERT

For 2011, you can exclude up to $230 per month of employer-provided parking, commuter vehicle transportation, and transit passes even if you choose it instead of cash or your employer reduces your compensation to provide the parking. The $230 is indexed for inflation.

You may be able to deduct the ordinary and necessary business-related expenses you have for:

- **Travel,**
- **Entertainment,**
- **Gifts, or**
- **Transportation.**

An ordinary expense is one that is common and accepted in your trade or business. A necessary expense is one that is helpful and appropriate for your business. An expense does not have to be required to be considered necessary.

This chapter explains the following.

- What expenses are deductible.
- How to report your expenses on your return.
- What records you need to prove your expenses.
- How to treat any expense reimbursements you may receive.

EXPLANATION

All employee-related expenses and certain transportation expenses are classified as miscellaneous itemized deductions. Included in this category are expenses incurred by employees that are fully or partially reimbursed or not reimbursed at all by their employer. Also included are any expenses for traveling away from home or for transportation.

Only the total of all miscellaneous itemized expenses (including those mentioned previously, as well as those discussed in chapter 29, *Miscellaneous deductions*) over 2% of a taxpayer's adjusted gross income can be deducted.

Who does not need to use this chapter. If you are an employee, you will not need to read this chapter if all of the following are true.

Tax Breaks and Deductions You Can Use Checklist

Employee Business Expenses. You can deduct any expenses you incur which are directly related to your employment. But these expenses are only deductible to the extent that, when combined with your other miscellaneous itemized deductions, they exceed 2% of your adjusted gross income (AGI). That's one of the reasons why you should try to get your employer to pay for these expenses on a pre-tax basis.

Qualified transportation fringe benefits. For 2011, you can exclude from your gross income certain qualified transportation fringe benefits received from your employer up to specified dollar amounts. Qualified transportation fringe benefits include: (1) transportation in a commuter highway vehicle (such as a van) between your home and workplace, (2) transit pass, (3) qualified parking, or (4) qualified bicycle commuting reimbursement. The exclusion for commuter vehicle transportation, qualified parking, and transit pass fringe benefits cannot be more than $230 a month. The exclusion for qualified bicycle commuting is discussed immediately below. If the benefits have a value that is more than these limits, the excess must be included in your income. You are not entitled to these exclusions if the reimbursement is made under a compensation reduction agreement. See *Transportation* in chapter 5, *Wages, salaries, and other earnings*, for more information.

Qualified bicycle commuting reimbursement. You may be able to exclude from your gross income reimbursements from your employer for reasonable expenses of qualified bicycle commuting. Reasonable expenses include the purchase of a bicycle and bicycle improvements, repair, and storage. These are considered reasonable expenses as long as the bicycle is regularly used for travel between the employee's residence and place of employment. The exclusion for a calendar year is $20 multiplied by the number of qualified bicycle commuting months during the year. A qualified bicycle commuting month is any month you use the bicycle regularly for a substantial portion of the travel between your residence and place of employment and you do not receive any of the other qualified transportation fringe benefits.

Tip

If you meet these conditions and your employer included reimbursements on your Form W-2 in error, ask your employer for a corrected Form W-2.

- You fully accounted to your employer for your work-related expenses.
- You received full reimbursement for your expenses.
- Your employer required you to return any excess reimbursement and you did so.
- There is no amount shown with a code "L" in box 12 of your Form W-2, Wage and Tax Statement.

If you meet all of these conditions, there is no need to show the expenses or the reimbursements on your return. See *Reimbursements*, later, if you would like more information on reimbursements and accounting to your employer.

Useful Items

You may want to see:

Publication

- □ **463** Travel, Entertainment, Gift, and Car Expenses
- □ **535** Business Expenses
- □ **1542** Per Diem Rates

Form (and Instructions)

- □ **Schedule A (Form 1040)** Itemized Deductions
- □ **Schedule C (Form 1040)** Profit or Loss From Business
- □ **Schedule C-EZ (Form 1040)** Net Profit From Business
- □ **Schedule F (Form 1040)** Profit or Loss From Farming
- □ **Form 2106** Employee Business Expenses
- □ **Form 2106-EZ** Unreimbursed Employee Business Expenses

Travel Expenses

If you temporarily travel away from your tax home, you can use this section to determine if you have deductible travel expenses. This section discusses:

- Traveling away from home,
- Tax home,
- Temporary assignment or job, and
- What travel expenses are deductible.

It also discusses the standard meal allowance, rules for travel inside and outside the United States, and deductible convention expenses.

Travel expenses defined. For tax purposes, travel expenses are the ordinary and necessary expenses (defined earlier) of traveling away from home for your business, profession, or job.

You will find examples of deductible travel expenses in Table 27-1.

EXAMPLES

Example 1

The courts held that a stockholder of a corporation could not deduct the expense of operating his personal automobile while performing services for the corporation. The stockholder was not an employee or officer of the corporation. He was not reimbursed for his expenses. The courts held that the stockholder's interest in the corporation was too remote for the expense to be an ordinary business expense.

Example 2

A government employee was allowed to deduct unreimbursed expenses incurred in the use of his private airplane for business purposes. He was also allowed to depreciate the business portion of the airplane's use.

TAXPLANNER

For you to deduct a business expense, a board resolution or a policy statement from the company that employs you should indicate that you may have to incur certain expenses for which you will not be reimbursed in order for you to fulfill your job.

Table 27-1. **Travel Expenses You Can Deduct**

This chart summarizes expenses you can deduct when you travel away from home for business purposes.

IF you have expenses for...	THEN you can deduct the cost of...
transportation	travel by airplane, train, bus, or car between your home and your business destination. If you were provided with a ticket or you are riding free as a result of a frequent traveler or similar program, your cost is zero. If you travel by ship, see *Luxury Water Travel* and *Cruise ships* (under *Conventions*) in Publication 463 for additional rules and limits.
taxi, commuter bus, and airport limousine	fares for these and other types of transportation that take you between: • The airport or station and your hotel, and • The hotel and the work location of your customers or clients, your business meeting place, or your temporary work location.
baggage and shipping	sending baggage and sample or display material between your regular and temporary work locations.
car	operating and maintaining your car when traveling away from home on business. You can deduct actual expenses or the standard mileage rate as well as business-related tolls and parking. If you rent a car while away from home on business, you can deduct only the business-use portion of the expenses.
lodging and meals	your lodging and meals if your business trip is overnight or long enough that you need to stop for sleep or rest to properly perform your duties. Meals include amounts spent for food, beverages, taxes, and related tips. See Meals and Incidental Expenses for additional rules and limits.
cleaning	dry cleaning and laundry.
telephone	business calls while on your business trip. This includes business communication by fax machine or other communication devices.
tips	tips you pay for any expenses in this chart.
other	other similar ordinary and necessary expenses related to your business travel. These expenses might include transportation to or from a business meal, public stenographer's fees, computer rental fees, and operating and maintaining a house trailer.

TAXPLANNER

You are able to deduct only 50% of most business meal and entertainment costs. Other allowable unreimbursed entertainment expenses will be grouped with certain other of your miscellaneous itemized deductions. You will be allowed a tax deduction to the extent that all these deductions exceed 2% of your adjusted gross income.

Traveling Away From Home

You are traveling away from home if:

- Your duties require you to be away from the general area of your tax home (defined later) substantially longer than an ordinary day's work, and
- You need to sleep or rest to meet the demands of your work while away from home.

This rest requirement is not satisfied by merely napping in your car. You do not have to be away from your tax home for a whole day or from dusk to dawn as long as your relief from duty is long enough to get necessary sleep or rest.

Example 1. You are a railroad conductor. You leave your home terminal on a regularly scheduled round-trip run between two cities and return home 16 hours later. During the run, you have 6 hours off at your turnaround point where you eat two meals and rent a hotel room to get necessary sleep before starting the return trip. You are considered to be away from home.

Example 2. You are a truck driver. You leave your terminal and return to it later the same day. You get an hour off at your turnaround point to eat. Because you are not off to get necessary sleep and the brief time off is not an adequate rest period, you are not traveling away from home.

Members of the Armed Forces. If you are a member of the U.S. Armed Forces on a permanent duty assignment overseas, you are not traveling away from home. You cannot deduct your expenses for meals and lodging. You cannot deduct these expenses even if you have to maintain a home in the United States for your family members who are not allowed to accompany you overseas. If you are transferred from one permanent duty station to another, you may have deductible moving expenses, which are explained in Publication 521, *Moving Expenses*.

A naval officer assigned to permanent duty aboard a ship that has regular eating and living facilities has a tax home aboard ship for travel expense purposes.

Tax Home

To determine whether you are traveling away from home, you must first determine the location of your tax home.

Generally, your tax home is your regular place of business or post of duty, regardless of where you maintain your family home. It includes the entire city or general area in which your business or work is located.

If you have more than one regular place of business, your tax home is your main place of business. See Main place of business or work, later.

If you do not have a regular or a main place of business because of the nature of your work, then your tax home may be the place where you regularly live. See No main place of business or work, later.

If you do not have a regular or a main place of business or post of duty and there is no place where you regularly live, you are considered an itinerant (a transient) and your tax home is wherever you work. As an itinerant, you cannot claim a travel expense deduction because you are never considered to be traveling away from home.

Main place of business or work. If you have more than one place of business or work, consider the following when determining which one is your main place of business or work.

- The total time you ordinarily spend in each place.
- The level of your business activity in each place.
- Whether your income from each place is significant or insignificant.

Example. You live in Cincinnati where you have a seasonal job for 8 months each year and earn $40,000. You work the other 4 months in Miami, also at a seasonal job, and earn $15,000. Cincinnati is your main place of work because you spend most of your time there and earn most of your income there.

No main place of business or work. You may have a tax home even if you do not have a regular or main place of business or work. Your tax home may be the home where you regularly live.

Factors used to determine tax home. If you do not have a regular or main place of business or work, use the following three factors to determine where your tax home is.

1. You perform part of your business in the area of your main home and use that home for lodging while doing business in the area.
2. You have living expenses at your main home that you duplicate because your business requires you to be away from that home.
3. You have not abandoned the area in which both your historical place of lodging and your claimed main home are located; you have a member or members of your family living at your main home; or you often use that home for lodging.

If you satisfy all three factors, your tax home is the home where you regularly live. If you satisfy only two factors, you may have a tax home depending on all the facts and circumstances. If you satisfy only one factor, you are an itinerant; your tax home is wherever you work and you cannot deduct travel expenses.

EXAMPLE

After a taxpayer's employment in Cape Canaveral, Florida, was terminated, the taxpayer obtained temporary contract jobs in Virginia, Florida, North Carolina, Vermont, and Alabama. The Tax Court rejected the IRS assertion that the taxpayer had no tax home and allowed deductions for travel, meals, and lodging because he maintained a "tax home" in Cape Canaveral. The court noted that such deductions were allowed because the taxpayer returned to his Cape Canaveral home during periods of unemployment, and the taxpayer had a valid business purpose for maintaining his permanent address.

Example. You are single and live in Boston in an apartment you rent. You have worked for your employer in Boston for a number of years. Your employer enrolls you in a 12-month executive training program. You do not expect to return to work in Boston after you complete your training.

During your training, you do not do any work in Boston. Instead, you receive classroom and on-the-job training throughout the United States. You keep your apartment in Boston and return to it frequently. You use your apartment to conduct your personal business. You also keep up your community contacts in Boston. When you complete your training, you are transferred to Los Angeles.

You do not satisfy factor (1) because you did not work in Boston. You satisfy factor (2) because you had duplicate living expenses. You also satisfy factor (3) because you did not abandon your apartment in Boston as your main home, you kept your community contacts, and you frequently returned to live in your apartment. You have a tax home in Boston.

EXPLANATION

According to the IRS, a home is a "regular place of abode in a real and substantial sense." The criteria are as follows:

1. You work in the same vicinity as your claimed abode and use it while doing business.
2. Your living expenses incurred at your claimed abode are duplicated when you're away on business.
3. You (a) have not abandoned the vicinity in which your place of lodging and claimed abode are both located; (b) have a family member or members (marital or lineal) currently residing at your claimed abode; or (c) use the claimed abode frequently.

If you maintain no fixed home, the burden of proof is on you to show the business portion of your daily expenses.

Example 1

You are an outside salesperson with a sales territory covering several states. Your employer's main office is in Newark, New Jersey, but you do not conduct any business there. Your work assignments are temporary, and you have no way of knowing where your future assignments will be located. You have a room in your married sister's house in Dayton, Ohio. You stay there for one or two weekends a year, but you do no work in the area. You do not pay your sister for the use of the room.

You do not satisfy any of the three factors listed earlier. You are a transient and have no tax home.

Example 2

A traveling salesman could not establish Reno, Nevada, as his tax home, even though he maintained a post office box and a bank account there, had dealings with a local stockbroker, bought an automobile there, stored his personal belongings there, and filed an income tax return from the city. He did not maintain a permanent place in Reno but stayed in hotels while he was there. Since no tax home was established, he could deduct only the business portion of his daily expenses. However, no expenses were allowed, since he did not maintain the necessary records.

Example 3

A traveling saleswoman maintained a room in her sister's home at a nominal rent. She worked for an employer in the same city, who paid her a per diem when she was away from that city. She had established a home for travel expense purposes.

Example 4

A college professor held a tenured position at a university located in Texas. While studying for her Ph.D. in Hawaii, she maintained a credit union account, a houseboat on which she paid property taxes, a post office box, and a library card in Texas and also stored almost all of her possessions there. She returned to the university after receiving her degree. The court ruled that her stay was not for an indefinite period, and she was able to deduct her lodging expenses in Hawaii.

Tax home different from family home. If you (and your family) do not live at your tax home (defined earlier), you cannot deduct the cost of traveling between your tax home and your family home. You also cannot deduct the cost of meals and lodging while at your tax home. See Example 1 that follows.

If you are working temporarily in the same city where you and your family live, you may be considered as traveling away from home. See Example 2 later.

Example 1. You are a truck driver and you and your family live in Tucson. You are employed by a trucking firm that has its terminal in Phoenix. At the end of your long runs, you return to your home terminal in Phoenix and spend one night there before returning home. You cannot deduct any expenses you have for meals and lodging in Phoenix or the cost of traveling from Phoenix to Tucson. This is because Phoenix is your tax home.

Example 2. Your family home is in Pittsburgh, where you work 12 weeks a year. The rest of the year you work for the same employer in Baltimore. In Baltimore, you eat in restaurants and sleep in a rooming house. Your salary is the same whether you are in Pittsburgh or Baltimore.

Because you spend most of your working time and earn most of your salary in Baltimore, that city is your tax home. You cannot deduct any expenses you have for meals and lodging there. However, when you return to work in Pittsburgh, you are away from your tax home even though you stay at your family home. You can deduct the cost of your round trip between Baltimore and Pittsburgh. You can also deduct your part of your family's living expenses for meals and lodging while you are living and working in Pittsburgh.

EXAMPLES

Example 1

A famous baseball player was not allowed to deduct expenses for meals and lodging in Los Angeles, California, even though he maintained a home in another state. The court found his tax home to be Los Angeles, since it was his principal place of business.

Example 2

A member of the Marine Corps was stationed in Japan. His family remained in California, since they were not allowed to accompany him to his principal place of duty. The marine was not allowed to deduct travel expenses. His tax home was Japan, his principal place of duty. See *Members of the Armed Forces,* earlier

EXPLANATION

Where you earn the most money is the principal test for deciding where your tax home is.

Example

The IRS required a taxpayer to claim as his tax home a city away from the home in which his family resided. He earned 75% of his income in the city away from his family and 25% of his income in the city where his family lived. Since his tax home was different from his personal residence, he could deduct travel expenses incurred while living with his family.

EXPLANATION

The distance between your residence and your place of employment is not a factor in determining whether expenses away from home are being incurred.

Example

The courts ruled that a taxpayer's personal decision to live a great distance from the location of his permanent employment did not render his meal and lodging expenses deductible. His place of business was his tax home.

Temporary Assignment or Job

You may regularly work at your tax home and also work at another location. It may not be practical to return to your tax home from this other location at the end of each work day.

Temporary assignment vs. indefinite assignment. If your assignment or job away from your main place of work is temporary, your tax home does not change. You are considered to be away from home for the whole period you are away from your main place of work. You can deduct your travel expenses if they otherwise qualify for deduction. Generally, a temporary assignment in a single location is one that is realistically expected to last (and does in fact last) for 1 year or less.

However, if your assignment or job is indefinite, the location of the assignment or job becomes your new tax home and you cannot deduct your travel expenses while there. An assignment or job in a single location is considered indefinite if it is realistically expected to last for more than 1 year, whether or not it actually lasts for more than 1 year.

If your assignment is indefinite, you must include in your income any amounts you receive from your employer for living expenses, even if they are called travel allowances and you account to your employer for them. You may be able to deduct the cost of relocating to your new tax home as a moving expense. See Publication 521 for more information.

EXAMPLES

Example 1

A construction worker who had been regularly employed near his home took a job in a city 250 miles away when construction got very slow in his hometown. He lived in his own trailer at the new job location. The job was expected to last 16 months, after which he planned to return home to his family. He frequently visited his hometown and continued to search for work there. *Previously,* the IRS had ruled that the worker was temporarily away from his home and could deduct his meals and lodging. However, under the most recent ruling, the worker's meals and lodging expenses would not be deductible because the assignment was expected to last longer than a year.

Example 2

A worker sold his residence in his home city, ceased to search for work there, and bought a new home at a new job location. The IRS ruled that the worker's stay was indefinite. He could not deduct the cost of his meals and lodging.

Example 3

A professional hockey player was allowed to deduct the cost of meals and lodging while playing hockey in San Diego, California. The Tax Court ruled that his tax home was in Michigan, where he maintained his house. A limited contract and the seasonal nature of the hockey profession caused the court to classify the San Diego job as temporary.

Example 4

A professional gambler spent equal amounts of time each year in Tampa and Gainesville, Florida; engaged in an equal amount of activity in both places; derived equal amounts of income in both places; and rented an apartment in each location. The court ruled that the activities were not temporary because they were "seasonal and recurring" activities. Therefore, the costs of both apartments were not deductible.

Exception for federal crime investigations or prosecutions. If you are a federal employee participating in a federal crime investigation or prosecution, you are not subject to the 1-year rule. This means you may be able to deduct travel expenses even if you are away from your tax home for more than 1 year, provided you meet the other requirements for deductibility.

For you to qualify, the Attorney General (or his or her designee) must certify that you are traveling:

- For the federal government,
- In a temporary duty status, and
- To investigate or prosecute, or provide support services for the investigation or prosecution of a federal crime.

Determining temporary or indefinite. You must determine whether your assignment is temporary or indefinite when you start work. If you expect an assignment or job to last for 1 year or less, it is temporary unless there are facts and circumstances that indicate otherwise. An assignment or job that is initially temporary may become indefinite due to changed circumstances. A series of assignments to the same location, all for short periods but that together cover a long period, may be considered an indefinite assignment.

EXPLANATION

If employment away from home in a single location is realistically expected to last for more than 1 year, or if there is no realistic expectation that the employment will last for 1 year or less, the employment is indefinite regardless of whether it actually exceeds 1 year.

Employment is temporary if work away from home in a single location is realistically expected to last (and does in fact last) for 1 year or less, in the absence of any facts and circumstances indicating otherwise.

TAXPLANNER

Employment away from home in a single location lasting more than 1 year is not treated as temporary. However, if employment away from home was initially expected to be for 1 year or less, and then expectations changed for it to be for more than 1 year, the employment will be considered temporary up to the point that the time length expectations changed.

Example 1

A taxpayer accepts work in a city 250 miles from the city in which she is regularly employed. She expects the work to be completed in 18 months but in fact completes the work in 10 months. The taxpayer's travel expenses are not deductible because the taxpayer's employment is indefinite. Even though the work actually lasted less than 1 year, the employment is still indefinite because the taxpayer realistically expected the work to last longer than 1 year.

Example 2

The facts are the same except that the taxpayer expects the work to be completed in 9 months. After 8 months, however, the taxpayer is asked to remain for 7 more months (for an actual stay of 15 months). The taxpayer's travel expenses are deductible only during the first 8 months of employment because only during those months did the taxpayer realistically expect the employment to be temporary.

Going home on days off. If you go back to your tax home from a temporary assignment on your days off, you are not considered away from home while you are in your hometown. You cannot deduct the cost of your meals and lodging there. However, you can deduct your travel expenses, including meals and lodging, while traveling between your temporary place of work and your tax home. You can claim these expenses up to the amount it would have cost you to stay at your temporary place of work.

If you keep your hotel room during your visit home, you can deduct the cost of your hotel room. In addition, you can deduct your expenses of returning home up to the amount you would have spent for meals had you stayed at your temporary place of work.

Probationary work period. If you take a job that requires you to move, with the understanding that you will keep the job if your work is satisfactory during a probationary period, the job is indefinite. You cannot deduct any of your expenses for meals and lodging during the probationary period.

What Travel Expenses Are Deductible?

Once you have determined that you are traveling away from your tax home, you can determine what travel expenses are deductible.

You can deduct ordinary and necessary expenses you have when you travel away from home on business. The type of expense you can deduct depends on the facts and your circumstances.

EXPLANATION

Ordinarily, you can deduct expenses that you incurred to produce or collect income, or to manage, conserve, or maintain property held for producing income, only on Schedule A (Form 1040). Therefore, you must itemize your deductions to claim these expenses. See chapter 29, *Miscellaneous deductions*.

To be deductible, an expense must be closely associated with an activity that is expected to produce income or must be incurred maintaining property that is held to produce income. Such expenses are deductible only if you itemize.

Travel and other costs of attending investment seminars are specifically disallowed.

Example 1

Transportation expenses to attend a stockholders' meeting are not deductible, unless you can demonstrate that you played a fairly substantial role in the meeting. Otherwise, it is not clear that the expenses were incurred to produce income.

Example 2

The courts held that an individual who spent his lunch hour at brokerage houses could not deduct his travel expenses because he could not establish the relationship between his visits and his investment activities.

Table 27-1, earlier, summarizes travel expenses you may be able to deduct. You may have other deductible travel expenses that are not covered there, depending on the facts and your circumstances.

Separating costs. If you have one expense that includes the costs of meals, entertainment, and other services (such as lodging or transportation), you must allocate that expense between the cost of meals and entertainment and the cost of other services. You must have a reasonable basis for making this allocation. For example, you must allocate your expenses if a hotel includes one or more meals in its room charge.

Travel expenses for another individual. If a spouse, dependent, or other individual goes with you (or your employee) on a business trip or to a business convention, you generally cannot deduct his or her travel expenses.

Employee. You can deduct the travel expenses of someone who goes with you if that person:

1. Is your employee,
2. Has a *bona fide* business purpose for the travel, and
3. Would otherwise be allowed to deduct the travel expenses.

Business associate. If a business associate travels with you and meets the conditions in (2) and (3) above, you can deduct the travel expenses you have for that person. A business associate is someone with whom you could reasonably expect to actively conduct business. A business associate can be a current or prospective (likely to become) customer, client, supplier, employee, agent, partner, or professional advisor.

Bona fide business purpose. A *bona fide* business purpose exists if you can prove a real business purpose for the individual's presence. Incidental services, such as typing notes or assisting in entertaining customers, are not enough to make the expenses deductible.

Example. Jerry drives to Chicago on business and takes his wife, Linda, with him. Linda is not Jerry's employee. Linda occasionally types notes, performs similar services, and accompanies Jerry to luncheons and dinners. The performance of these services does not establish that her presence on the trip is necessary to the conduct of Jerry's business. Her expenses are not deductible.

Jerry pays $199 a day for a double room. A single room costs $149 a day. He can deduct the total cost of driving his car to and from Chicago, but only $149 a day for his hotel room. If he uses public transportation, he can deduct only his fare.

Records

When you travel away from home on business, you should keep records of all the expenses you have and any advances you receive from your employer. You can use a log, diary, notebook, or any other written record to keep track of your expenses. The types of expenses you need to record, along with supporting documentation, are described in Table 27-2, later.

TAXALERT

The tax law denies a deduction for travel expenses paid or incurred for a spouse, dependent, or other individual accompanying you on business travel, unless certain requirements are met. For the expenses to be deductible, your traveling companion must (1) be a bona fide employee of the person paying or reimbursing the expenses; (2) be traveling for a bona fide business purpose; and (3) have expenses that are otherwise deductible. The denial of the deduction does not apply to expenses that would otherwise qualify as deductible moving expenses.

Meals and Incidental Expenses

You can deduct the cost of meals in either of the following situations.

- It is necessary for you to stop for substantial sleep or rest to properly perform your duties while traveling away from home on business.
- The meal is business-related entertainment.

Business-related entertainment is discussed under *Entertainment Expenses*, later. The following discussion deals only with meals (and incidental expenses) that are not business-related entertainment.

Lavish or extravagant. You cannot deduct expenses for meals that are lavish or extravagant. An expense is not considered lavish or extravagant if it is reasonable based on the facts and circumstances. Expenses will not be disallowed merely because they are more than a fixed dollar amount or take place at deluxe restaurants, hotels, nightclubs, or resorts.

50% limit on meals. You can figure your meal expenses using either of the following methods.

- Actual cost.
- The standard meal allowance.

Both of these methods are explained below. But, regardless of the method you use, you generally can deduct only 50% of the unreimbursed cost of your meals.

TAXALERT

Meal expenses when subject to hours of service limits. Generally, you can deduct only 50% of your business-related meal expenses while traveling away from your tax home for business purposes. However, if you consume the meals during any period when you are subject to the Department of Transportation's hours of service limits, you can deduct 80%.

Individuals subject to the Department of Transportation's hours of service limits include the following persons:

1. Certain air transportation workers (such as pilots, crew, dispatchers, mechanics, and control tower operators) who are under Federal Aviation Administration regulations.
2. Interstate truck operators and bus drivers who are under Department of Transportation regulations.
3. Certain railroad employees (such as engineers, conductors, train crews, dispatchers, and control operations personnel) who are under Federal Railroad Administration regulations.
4. Certain merchant mariners who are under Coast Guard regulations. For more information on business meal expenses, see Publication 463.

If you are reimbursed for the cost of your meals, how you apply the 50% limit depends on whether your employer's reimbursement plan was accountable or nonaccountable. If you are not reimbursed, the 50% limit applies whether the unreimbursed meal expense is for business travel or business entertainment. The 50% limit is explained later under Entertainment Expenses. Accountable and nonaccountable plans are discussed later under Reimbursements.

Actual cost. You can use the actual cost of your meals to figure the amount of your expense before reimbursement and application of the 50% deduction limit. If you use this method, you must keep records of your actual cost.

Standard meal allowance. Generally, you can use the "standard meal allowance" method as an alternative to the actual cost method. It allows you to use a set amount for your daily meals and incidental expenses (M&IE), instead of keeping records of your actual costs. The set amount varies depending on where and when you travel. In this chapter, "standard meal allowance" refers to the federal rate for M&IE, discussed later under Amount of standard meal allowance. If you use the standard meal allowance, you still must keep records to prove the time, place, and business purpose of your travel. See Recordkeeping, later.

Incidental expenses. The term "incidental expenses" means:

- Fees and tips given to porters, baggage carriers, bellhops, hotel maids, stewards or stewardesses and others on ships, and hotel servants in foreign countries,
- Transportation between places of lodging or business and places where meals are taken, if suitable meals can be obtained at the temporary duty site, and
- Mailing costs associated with filing travel vouchers and payment of employer-sponsored charge card billings.

Incidental expenses do not include expenses for laundry, cleaning and pressing of clothing, lodging taxes, or the costs of telegrams or telephone calls.

Incidental expenses only method. You can use an optional method (instead of actual cost) for deducting incidental expenses only. The amount of the deduction is $5 a day. You can use this method only if you did not pay or incur any meal expenses. You cannot use this method on any day that you use the standard meal allowance.

Caution

Federal employees should refer to the Federal Travel Regulations at www.gsa.gov. Find "What GSA Offers" and click on "Regulations: FMR, FTR, FAR" for Federal Travel Regulation (FTR) for changes affecting claims for reimbursement.

TAXALERT

As of the date this book was published, the amount of the standard meal allowance effective after October 1, 2011, had not yet been announced by the IRS. For updated information on this and any other tax law changes that occur after this book was published, see our website, ey.com/EYTaxGuide.

50% limit may apply. If you use the standard meal allowance method for meal expenses and you are not reimbursed or you are reimbursed under a nonaccountable plan, you can generally deduct only 50% of the standard meal allowance. If you are reimbursed under an accountable plan and you are deducting amounts that are more than your reimbursements, you can deduct only 50% of the excess amount. The 50% limit is explained later under Entertainment Expenses. Accountable and nonaccountable plans are discussed later under Reimbursements.

Who can use the standard meal allowance. You can use the standard meal allowance whether you are an employee or self-employed, and whether or not you are reimbursed for your traveling expenses.

Use of the standard meal allowance for other travel. You can use the standard meal allowance to figure your meal expenses when you travel in connection with investment and other income-producing property. You can also use it to figure your meal expenses when you travel for qualifying educational purposes. You cannot use the standard meal allowance to figure the cost of your meals when you travel for medical or charitable purposes.

Caution

There is no optional standard lodging amount similar to the standard meal allowance. Your allowable lodging expense deduction is your actual cost.

Amount of standard meal allowance. The standard meal allowance is the federal M&IE rate. For travel in 2011, the rate for most small localities in the United States is $46 a day.

Most major cities and many other localities in the United States are designated as high-cost areas, qualifying for higher standard meal allowances. Locations qualifying for these rates are listed in Publication 1542 which is available on the Internet at www.irs.gov.

You can also find this information (organized by state) on the Internet at www.gsa.gov. Click on "Per Diem Rates," then select "2011" for the period January 1, 2011–September 30, 2011, and select "2012" for the period October 1, 2011–December 31, 2011. However, you can apply the rates in effect before October 1, 2011, for expenses of all travel within the United States for 2011 instead of the updated rates. You must consistently use either the rates for the first 9 months for all of 2011 or the updated rates for the period of October 1, 2011, through December 31, 2011.

If you travel to more than one location in one day, use the rate in effect for the area where you stop for sleep or rest. If you work in the transportation industry, however, see Special rate for transportation workers, later.

TAXPLANNER

Whether or not you receive meal money from your employer, you may claim the standard meal allowance and therefore minimize your recordkeeping problems. If you are self-employed, you may also claim the standard meal allowance.

Standard meal allowance for areas outside the continental United States. The standard meal allowance rates above do not apply to travel in Alaska, Hawaii, or any other location outside the continental United States. The Department of Defense establishes per diem rates for Alaska, Hawaii, Puerto Rico, American Samoa, Guam, Midway, the Northern Mariana Islands, the U.S. Virgin Islands, Wake Island, and other non-foreign areas outside the continental United States. The Department of State establishes per diem rates for all other foreign areas.

You can access per diem rates for non-foreign areas outside the continental United States at: *www.defensetravel.dod.mil/site/perdiemCalc.cfm*. You can access all other foreign per diem rates at: *www.state.gov/travel/*. Click on "Travel Per Diem Allowances for Foreign Areas" under "Foreign Per Diem Rates," to obtain the latest foreign per diem rates.

Special rate for transportation workers. You can use a special standard meal allowance if you work in the transportation industry. You are in the transportation industry if your work:

- Directly involves moving people or goods by airplane, barge, bus, ship, train, or truck, and
- Regularly requires you to travel away from home and, during any single trip, usually involves travel to areas eligible for different standard meal allowance rates.

If this applies to you, you can claim a standard meal allowance of $59 a day ($65 for travel outside the continental United States).

TAXALERT

As of the date this book was published, the standard meal allowance amounts effective after October 1, 2011, had not yet been announced by the IRS. For updated information on this and any other tax law changes that occur after this book was published, see our website, *ey.com/EYTaxGuide*.

Using the special rate for transportation workers eliminates the need for you to determine the standard meal allowance for every area where you stop for sleep or rest. If you choose to use the special rate for any trip, you must use the special rate (and not use the regular standard meal allowance rates) for all trips you take that year.

Travel for days you depart and return. For both the day you depart for and the day you return from a business trip, you must prorate the standard meal allowance (figure a reduced amount for each day). You can do so by one of two methods.

- Method 1: You can claim ¾ of the standard meal allowance.
- Method 2: You can prorate using any method that you consistently apply and that is in accordance with reasonable business practice.

Example. Jen is employed in New Orleans as a convention planner. In March, her employer sent her on a 3-day trip to Washington, DC, to attend a planning seminar. She left her home in New Orleans at 10 a.m. on Wednesday and arrived in Washington, DC, at 5:30 p.m. After spending two nights there, she flew back to New Orleans on Friday and arrived back home at 8:00 p.m. Jen's employer gave her a flat amount to cover her expenses and included it with her wages.

Under Method 1, Jen can claim 2½ days of the standard meal allowance for Washington, DC: ¾ of the daily rate for Wednesday and Friday (the days she departed and returned), and the full daily rate for Thursday.

Under Method 2, Jen could also use any method that she applies consistently and that is in accordance with reasonable business practice. For example, she could claim 3 days of the standard meal allowance even though a federal employee would have to use Method 1 and be limited to only 2½ days.

Travel in the United States

The following discussion applies to travel in the United States. For this purpose, the United States includes the 50 states and the District of Columbia. The treatment of your travel expenses depends on how much of your trip was business related and on how much of your trip occurred within the United States. See Part of Trip Outside the United States, later.

Trip Primarily for Business

You can deduct all your travel expenses if your trip was entirely business related. If your trip was primarily for business and, while at your business destination, you extended your stay for a vacation, made a personal side trip, or had other personal activities, you can deduct your business-related travel expenses. These expenses include the travel costs of getting to and from your business destination and any business-related expenses at your business destination.

Example. You work in Atlanta and take a business trip to New Orleans in May. On your way home, you stop in Mobile to visit your parents. You spend $1,999 for the 9 days you are away from home for travel, meals, lodging, and other travel expenses. If you had not stopped in Mobile, you would have been gone only 6 days, and your total cost would have been $1,699. You can deduct $1,699 for your trip, including the cost of round-trip transportation to and from New Orleans. The deduction for your meals is subject to the 50% limit on meals mentioned earlier.

Trip Primarily for Personal Reasons

If your trip was primarily for personal reasons, such as a vacation, the entire cost of the trip is a nondeductible personal expense. However, you can deduct any expenses you have while at your destination that are directly related to your business.

A trip to a resort or on a cruise ship may be a vacation even if the promoter advertises that it is primarily for business. The scheduling of incidental business activities during a trip, such as viewing videotapes or attending lectures dealing with general subjects, will not change what is really a vacation into a business trip.

> ***EXPLANATION***
>
> The courts have not allowed expenses to be deducted for trips whose primary purpose is pleasure but whose secondary purpose is the investigation of business rental properties. If the primary purpose of the trip is to search for rental properties, all travel expenses can be deducted.

> ***TAXORGANIZER***
>
> Careful records should be maintained when family members are along on business trips. If a spouse or other family member on a trip serves a business purpose, care should be taken to document that fact. Otherwise, the incremental travel expenses attributed to the additional person may not be deducted. Receipts and a diary of your activities will be of assistance in documenting the purpose of your trip.

Part of Trip Outside the United States

If part of your trip is outside the United States, use the rules described later under *Travel Outside the United States* for that part of the trip. For the part of your trip that is inside the United States, use the rules for travel in the United States. Travel outside the United States does not include travel from one point in the United States to another point in the United States. The following discussion can help you determine whether your trip was entirely within the United States.

Public transportation. If you travel by public transportation, any place in the United States where that vehicle makes a scheduled stop is a point in the United States. Once the vehicle leaves the last scheduled stop in the United States on its way to a point outside the United States, you apply the rules under *Travel Outside the United States*.

Example. You fly from New York to Puerto Rico with a scheduled stop in Miami. You return to New York nonstop. The flight from New York to Miami is in the United States, so only the flight from Miami to Puerto Rico is outside the United States. Because there are no scheduled stops between Puerto Rico and New York, all of the return trip is outside the United States.

Private car. Travel by private car in the United States is travel between points in the United States, even when you are on your way to a destination outside the United States.

Example. You travel by car from Denver to Mexico City and return. Your travel from Denver to the border and from the border back to Denver is travel in the United States, and the rules in this section apply. The rules under *Travel Outside the United States* apply to your trip from the border to Mexico City and back to the border.

Travel Outside the United States

If any part of your business travel is outside the United States, some of your deductions for the cost of getting to and from your destination may be limited. For this purpose, the United States includes the 50 states and the District of Columbia.

How much of your travel expenses you can deduct depends in part upon how much of your trip outside the United States was business related.

See chapter 1 of Publication 463 for information on luxury water travel.

Travel Entirely for Business or Considered Entirely for Business

You can deduct all your travel expenses of getting to and from your business destination if your trip is entirely for business or considered entirely for business.

Travel entirely for business. If you travel outside the United States and you spend the entire time on business activities, you can deduct all of your travel expenses.

Travel considered entirely for business. Even if you did not spend your entire time on business activities, your trip is considered entirely for business if you meet at least one of the following four exceptions.

Exception 1—No substantial control. Your trip is considered entirely for business if you did not have substantial control over arranging the trip. The fact that you control the timing of your trip does not, by itself, mean that you have substantial control over arranging your trip.

You do not have substantial control over your trip if you:

- Are an employee who was reimbursed or paid a travel expense allowance,
- Are not related to your employer, and
- Are not a managing executive.

"Related to your employer" is defined later in this chapter under *Per Diem and Car Allowances*.

A "managing executive" is an employee who has the authority and responsibility, without being subject to the veto of another, to decide on the need for the business travel.

A self-employed person generally has substantial control over arranging business trips.

Exception 2—Outside United States no more than a week. Your trip is considered entirely for business if you were outside the United States for a week or less, combining business and nonbusiness activities. One week means 7 consecutive days. In counting the days, do not count the day you leave the United States, but do count the day you return to the United States.

Exception 3—Less than 25% of time on personal activities. Your trip is considered entirely for business if:

- You were outside the United States for more than a week, and
- You spent less than 25% of the total time you were outside the United States on nonbusiness activities.

For this purpose, count both the day your trip began and the day it ended.

Exception 4—Vacation not a major consideration. Your trip is considered entirely for business if you can establish that a personal vacation was not a major consideration, even if you have substantial control over arranging the trip.

Tip

You do not have to allocate your travel expense deduction if you meet one of the four exceptions listed earlier under Travel considered entirely for business*. In those cases, you can deduct the total cost of getting to and from your destination.*

Travel Primarily for Business

If you travel outside the United States primarily for business but spend some of your time on nonbusiness activities, you generally cannot deduct all of your travel expenses. You can only deduct the business portion of your cost of getting to and from your destination. You must allocate the costs between your business and nonbusiness activities to determine your deductible amount. These travel allocation rules are discussed in chapter 1 of Publication 463.

EXPLANATION

A business day is established if, during any part of the day, you are required to be present at a business-related event. Weekends falling between business days may be considered business days, but if they fall at the end of your business meetings and you remain for personal reasons, they are not business days. Transportation days are business days when you travel to your destination on a direct route.

TAXPLANNER

If, in order to take advantage of lower plane fares, your employer reimburses your travel expenses for staying overnight on Saturday at the end of a business trip, the meals and lodging costs for Saturday can be deducted by your employer and excluded from your income to the extent the costs do not exceed the cost savings. The IRS privately ruled that these travel expenses relating to the Saturday night away are deductible even though the day is spent sightseeing.

Travel Primarily for Personal Reasons

If you travel outside the United States primarily for vacation or for investment purposes, the entire cost of the trip is a nondeductible personal expense. If you spend some time attending brief professional seminars or a continuing education program, you can deduct your registration fees and other expenses you have that are directly related to your business.

Caution

Your appointment or election as a delegate does not, in itself, determine whether you can deduct travel expenses. You can deduct your travel expenses only if your attendance is connected to your own trade or business.

Conventions

You can deduct your travel expenses when you attend a convention if you can show that your attendance benefits your trade or business. You cannot deduct the travel expenses for your family.

If the convention is for investment, political, social, or other purposes unrelated to your trade or business, you cannot deduct the expenses.

Convention agenda. The convention agenda or program generally shows the purpose of the convention. You can show your attendance at the convention benefits your trade or business by comparing the agenda with the official duties and responsibilities of your position. The agenda does not have to deal specifically with your official duties and responsibilities; it will be enough if the agenda is so related to your position that it shows your attendance was for business purposes.

EXPLANATION

To determine whether a trip is primarily for business, the courts have used the following guidelines:

1. The amount of time spent on personal activity compared with the amount of time spent on business activity.
2. The location of the convention (the setting of a convention at a resort does not mean that the expense is disallowed, but a more businesslike setting increases the strength of your case).
3. The attitude of your sponsor toward the purpose of the meeting.

The courts must also be satisfied that the primary purpose of the convention is business related.

Conventions held outside the North American area. See chapter 1 of Publication 463 for information on conventions held outside the North American area.

EXPLANATION

The amount of expenses you incur when you travel on an ocean liner or cruise ship may not be fully deductible. If you attend a convention, seminar, or similar meeting while aboard the cruise ship, you may still deduct up to $2,000 per individual per calendar year if the following requirements are met:

1. The meeting must be directly related to the active conduct of a business.
2. The cruise ship is a vessel registered in the United States
3. All of the cruise ship's ports of call are in the U.S. or U.S. possessions.
4. You attach to your return a written statement signed by you that includes:
   a. The total days of the trip, excluding the days of transportation to and from the cruise ship port;
   b. The number of hours each day that you devoted to scheduled business activities, and
   c. A program of the scheduled business activities of the meeting.
5. You attach to your return a written statement signed by an officer of the organization or group sponsoring the meeting that includes:
   a. A schedule of the business activities of each day of the meeting, and
   b. The number of hours you attended the scheduled business activities.

Example

You attend a business meeting sponsored by your employer held on a U.S. registered cruise ship sailing to Puerto Rico. You spend 6 days on the cruise ship from the time you depart until the time you return. The total cost of the 6-day cruise package is $3,000. You may deduct only $2,000 of the $3,000 costs provided you attach the written statement signed by you and the written statement signed by the officer of your employer as discussed earlier in this chapter.

Entertainment Expenses

You may be able to deduct business-related entertainment expenses you have for entertaining a client, customer, or employee.

You can deduct entertainment expenses only if they are both ordinary and necessary (defined earlier in the *Introduction*) and meet one of the following tests.

- Directly-related test.
- Associated test.

Both of these tests are explained in chapter 2 of Publication 463.

Caution

The amount you can deduct for entertainment expenses may be limited. Generally, you can deduct only 50% of your unreimbursed entertainment expenses. This limit is discussed next.

50% Limit

In general, you can deduct only 50% of your business-related meal and entertainment expenses. (If you are subject to the Department of Transportation's "hours of service" limits, you can deduct 80% of your business-related meal and entertainment expenses. See *Individuals subject to "hours of service" limits*, later.)

The 50% limit applies to employees or their employers, and to self-employed persons (including independent contractors) or their clients, depending on whether the expenses are reimbursed.

Figure 27-A summarizes the general rules explained in this section.

The 50% limit applies to business meals or entertainment expenses you have while:

- Traveling away from home (whether eating alone or with others) on business,
- Entertaining customers at your place of business, a restaurant, or other location, or
- Attending a business convention or reception, business meeting, or business luncheon at a club.

TAXPLANNER

The tax law denies a deduction for amounts paid or incurred for membership in any club organized for business, pleasure, recreation, or other social purpose. However, costs incurred to hold a business-related meeting at such club may be deductible if other conditions discussed earlier are met.

Included expenses. Expenses subject to the 50% limit include:

- Taxes and tips relating to a business meal or entertainment activity,
- Cover charges for admission to a nightclub,
- Rent paid for a room in which you hold a dinner or cocktail party, and
- Amounts paid for parking at a sports arena.

However, the cost of transportation to and from a business meal or a business-related entertainment activity is not subject to the 50% limit.

Application of 50% limit. The 50% limit on meal and entertainment expenses applies if the expense is otherwise deductible and is not covered by one of the exceptions discussed later in this section.

The 50% limit also applies to certain meal and entertainment expenses that are not business related. It applies to meal and entertainment expenses incurred for the production of income, including rental or royalty income. It also applies to the cost of meals included in deductible educational expenses.

When to apply the 50% limit. You apply the 50% limit after determining the amount that would otherwise qualify for a deduction. You first have to determine the amount of meal and entertainment expenses that would be deductible under the other rules discussed in this chapter.

Example 1. You spend $200 for a business-related meal. If $110 of that amount is not allowable because it is lavish and extravagant, the remaining $90 is subject to the 50% limit. Your deduction cannot be more than $45 (.50 × $90).

Example 2. You purchase two tickets to a concert and give them to a client. You purchased the tickets through a ticket agent. You paid $200 for the two tickets, which had a face value of $80 each ($160 total). Your deduction cannot be more than $80 (.50 × $160).

Figure 27-A. **Does the 50% Limit Apply to Your Expenses?**

There are exceptions to these rules. See Exceptions to the 50% Limit.

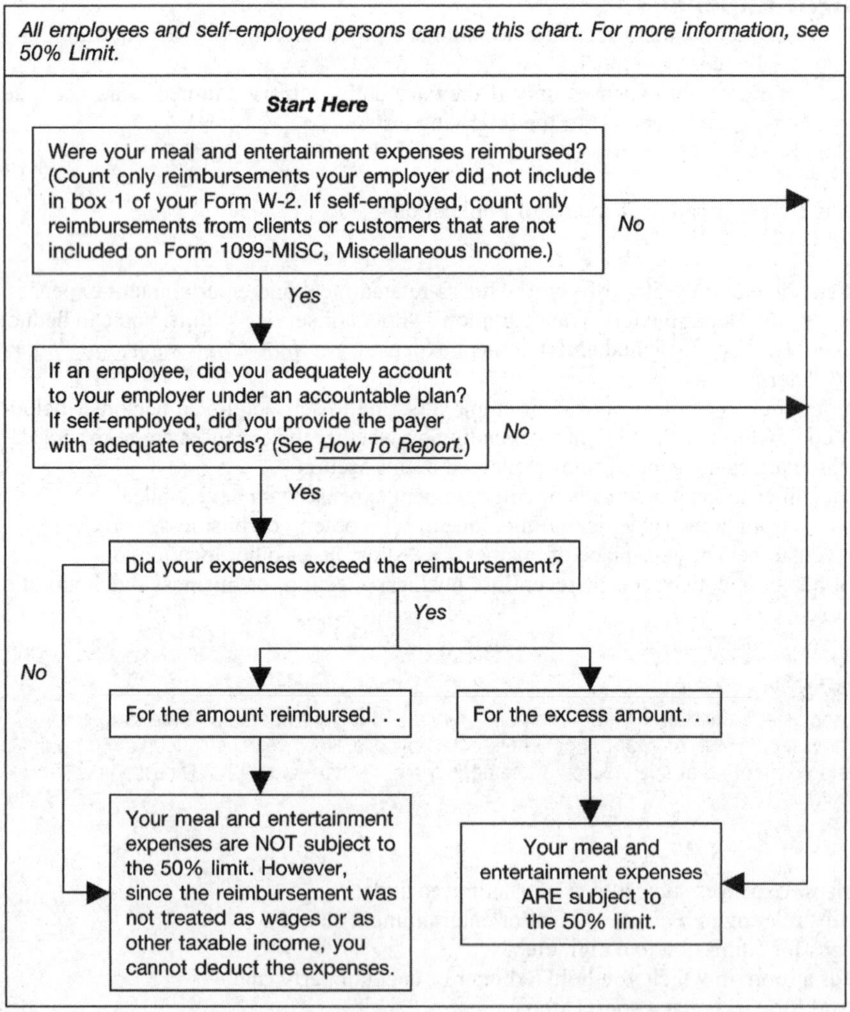

Exceptions to the 50% Limit

Generally, business-related meal and entertainment expenses are subject to the 50% limit. Figure 27-A can help you determine if the 50% limit applies to you.

Your meal or entertainment expense is not subject to the 50% limit if the expense meets one of the following exceptions.

Employee's reimbursed expenses. If you are an employee, you are not subject to the 50% limit on expenses for which your employer reimburses you under an accountable plan. Accountable plans are discussed later under *Reimbursements*.

EXCEPTIONS

Entertainment test exceptions. Expenses incurred in the following situations generally are not subject to the directly related and associated with tests:

- Business meals in surroundings normally considered conducive to a business discussion.
- Recreational and social activities primarily benefiting employees (e.g., company picnics, office Christmas parties, and golf outings).
- Business meetings of employees, stockholders, agents, or directors.
- Attendance at a business meeting of a tax-exempt business league (e.g., a chamber of commerce, a board of trade, or a professional organization).
- Employee entertainment or recreation that is treated as compensation on the employee's income tax return and as wages for withholding purposes.
- Nonemployee entertainment or recreation that is treated as income on the nonemployee's tax return and reported to him or her on an informational return (Form 1099).

Exceptions to the 50% limit. Expenses incurred in the following situations are not subject to the 50% disallowance provision:

- Reimbursed meal or entertainment expenses.
- Employer-paid recreational expenses for employees (e.g., a holiday party).
- Entertainment taxable to the recipient.
- Entertainment expenses made available to the general public.
- Entertainment expenses related to charitable fundraising sports events.

Individuals subject to "hours of service" limits. You can deduct a higher percentage of your meal expenses while traveling away from your tax home if the meals take place during or incident to any period subject to the Department of Transportation's "hours of service" limits. The percentage is 80%.

Individuals subject to the Department of Transportation's "hours of service" limits include the following persons.

- Certain air transportation workers (such as pilots, crew, dispatchers, mechanics, and control tower operators) who are under Federal Aviation Administration regulations.
- Interstate truck operators and bus drivers who are under Department of Transportation regulations.
- Certain railroad employees (such as engineers, conductors, train crews, dispatchers, and control operations personnel) who are under Federal Railroad Administration regulations.
- Certain merchant mariners who are under Coast Guard regulations.

Other exceptions. There are also exceptions for the self-employed, advertising expenses, selling meals or entertainment, and charitable sports events. These are discussed in Publication 463.

What Entertainment Expenses Are Deductible?

This section explains different types of entertainment expenses you may be able to deduct.

Entertainment. Entertainment includes any activity generally considered to provide entertainment, amusement, or recreation. Examples include entertaining guests at nightclubs; at social, athletic, and sporting clubs; at theaters; at sporting events; on yachts; or on hunting, fishing, vacation, and similar trips.

A meal as a form of entertainment. Entertainment includes the cost of a meal you provide to a customer or client, whether the meal is a part of other entertainment or by itself. A meal expense includes the cost of food, beverages, taxes, and tips for the meal. To deduct an entertainment-related meal, you or your employee must be present when the food or beverages are provided.

Caution

You cannot claim the cost of your meal both as an entertainment expense and as a travel expense.

Separating costs. If you have one expense that includes the costs of entertainment and other services (such as lodging or transportation), you must allocate that expense between the cost of entertainment and the cost of other services. You must have a reasonable basis for making this allocation. For example, you must allocate your expenses if a hotel includes entertainment in its lounge on the same bill with your room charge.

Taking turns paying for meals or entertainment. If a group of business acquaintances take turns picking up each others' meal or entertainment checks without regard to whether any business purposes are served, no member of the group can deduct any part of the expense.

EXPLANATION

The courts have held that costs of entertaining fellow employees are not deductible, even though the entertaining may have contributed to high morale and increased productivity.

Lavish or extravagant expenses. You cannot deduct expenses for entertainment that are lavish or extravagant. An expense is not considered lavish or extravagant if it is reasonable considering the facts and circumstances. Expenses will not be disallowed just because they are more than a fixed dollar amount or take place at deluxe restaurants, hotels, nightclubs, or resorts.

Trade association meetings. You can deduct entertainment expenses that are directly related to, and necessary for, attending business meetings or conventions of certain exempt organizations if the expenses of your attendance are related to your active trade or business. These organizations include business leagues, chambers of commerce, real estate boards, trade associations, and professional associations.

Entertainment tickets. Generally, you cannot deduct more than the face value of an entertainment ticket, even if you paid a higher price. For example, you cannot deduct service fees you pay to ticket agencies or brokers or any amount over the face value of the tickets you pay to scalpers.

What Entertainment Expenses Are Not Deductible?

This section explains different types of entertainment expenses you generally may not be able to deduct.

Club dues and membership fees. You cannot deduct dues (including initiation fees) for membership in any club organized for:

- Business,
- Pleasure,
- Recreation, or
- Other social purpose.

This rule applies to any membership organization if one of its principal purposes is either:

- To conduct entertainment activities for members or their guests, or
- To provide members or their guests with access to entertainment facilities.

The purposes and activities of a club, not its name, will determine whether or not you can deduct the dues. You cannot deduct dues paid to:

- Country clubs,
- Golf and athletic clubs,
- Airline clubs,
- Hotel clubs, and
- Clubs operated to provide meals under circumstances generally considered to be conducive to business discussions.

Entertainment facilities. Generally, you cannot deduct any expense for the use of an entertainment facility. This includes expenses for depreciation and operating costs such as rent, utilities, maintenance, and protection.

An entertainment facility is any property you own, rent, or use for entertainment. Examples include a yacht, hunting lodge, fishing camp, swimming pool, tennis court, bowling alley, car, airplane, apartment, hotel suite, or home in a vacation resort.

Out-of-pocket expenses. You can deduct out-of-pocket expenses, such as for food and beverages, catering, gas, and fishing bait, that you provided during entertainment at a facility. These are not expenses for the use of an entertainment facility. However, these expenses are subject to the directly-related and associated tests and to the 50% limit discussed earlier.

Additional information. For more information on entertainment expenses, including discussions of the directly-related and associated tests, see chapter 2 of Publication 463.

EXPLANATION

Although entertaining a client or a business associate often makes sound business sense, entertainment deductions have sometimes been abused. For this reason, Congress has imposed limitations on the deductibility of entertainment expenses. Only 50% of otherwise allowable entertainment expenses are deductible. The 50% disallowance generally applies to all taxpayers, regardless of the nature of the business. Even before the 50% disallowance, entertainment expenses are subject to stringent recordkeeping requirements and must pass one of two tests (see Publication 463 for the specific factors that should be considered):

1. **Directly related test.** The expenditure is directly related to the active conduct of your business.
2. **Associated test.** The expenditure is associated with the active conduct of your business, and the entertainment directly precedes or follows a substantial, bona fide business discussion.

Business meals—those that have a business purpose as opposed to a social and personal one—are not subject to these entertainment rules if they occur in surroundings conducive to business discussion, the taxpayer or an employee of the taxpayer is present when the food or beverages are served, and the expenses are properly substantiated.

Deductions for entertainment or business meals may not be taken if such expenses are considered lavish or extravagant.

Example

State police officers who are required to eat meals while on duty in public places were permitted to deduct expenses for these meals. The court found that the officers were significantly restricted by their employment regarding the time and place they were permitted to eat and that the meals were often subject to business-related interruptions.

EXPLANATION

Entertainment directly related to business. The directly related test is satisfied if all of the following are true:

- You expect to derive income or some other specific business benefit (other than mere goodwill) at some indefinite future time. However, it is not necessary to demonstrate that you actually receive the benefit.
- You actively engage in a business meeting, discussion, or other bona fide business transaction with the person being entertained.
- Your principal purpose of the combined business-entertainment activity is the active conduct of your business. It is not necessary to devote more time to business than to the entertainment to meet this requirement.

Certain entertainment activities generally do not meet the directly related test unless proven otherwise. If you are not present for the entertainment, if the group entertained includes persons other than business associates (such as spouses), or if there are substantial distractions (as may occur in nightclubs, theaters, sporting events, and vacation resorts), your activity may fail the directly related test.

The IRS gives taxpayers some relief from these strict rules when the activity is clearly in a business setting. For example, expenditures made to further your business by providing a hospitality room at a convention are treated as entertainment expenses directly related to business. Additionally, situations in which no meaningful personal or social relationship exists between you and the persons entertained are often considered to have occurred in a business setting. For example, entertaining business and civic leaders at the opening of a new hotel or theatrical production—for the purpose of obtaining business publicity rather than creating or maintaining goodwill—is a deductible entertainment expense directly related to business. Also, entertainment that represents a price rebate on the sale of your products (such as a restaurant owner occasionally providing a free meal to a loyal customer) is also considered a business setting by the IRS.

Example
An attorney paid for the costs of an annual fishing trip with three business associates who were sources of referrals to his law practice. He also used his cabin 75% of the time for entertaining business clients. The attorney could not prove that substantial and bona fide business discussions occurred during the fishing trip or on any of the occasions when business clients used the cabin. He showed that, at most, he had just a generalized expectation of deriving income or other business benefits at some indefinite future time from those entertained. As a result, he was denied deductions for these expenses because they did not meet the directly related test.

EXPLANATION

Entertainment associated with business. If an entertainment expenditure does not meet the directly related requirements, it may still be deductible if it passes the associated test. An entertainment activity passes the associated test only if it satisfies two conditions:

- The activity has a clear business purpose.
- The entertainment directly precedes or follows a substantial, bona fide business discussion.

The desire to obtain new business and the intent to maintain an existing business relationship—goodwill—are objectives that have a clear business purpose. A substantial, bona fide business discussion occurs when you actively engage in a business transaction to obtain some business benefit and the business meeting, negotiation, or discussion is substantial in relation to the entertainment. However, it is not necessary to spend more time on business than on entertainment.

Example
Bonnie McDonald, an independent consultant, spends 4 hours delivering a new management program to a group of executives in her client's New Orleans office. After the meeting, Bonnie takes the group to the French Quarter for dinner and a show. Dixieland jazz is played throughout dinner.

The entertainment passes the associated with test and is therefore deductible (subject to the 50% limitation) because Bonnie is maintaining a business relationship and the entertainment follows a substantial business meeting. The expense would not pass the directly related test because (1) goodwill generally does not qualify and (2) substantial distractions exist.

EXPLANATION

Entertainment directly precedes or follows a substantial business discussion if it occurs on the same day. If the entertainment and business discussion do not occur on the same day, the facts and circumstances of each case determine whether or not the entertainment and the business discussion occur close enough in time so that the expenses can be deducted.

Example
A group of business associates come to Denver and hold substantial discussions with a taxpayer. Entertainment for the business guests on the evening prior to or after the day of the business discussions is generally regarded as directly preceding or following the business discussion. Therefore, 50% of the entertainment expenses are deductible.

EXPLANATION

Deducting goodwill entertainment. Generally, entertaining for goodwill alone is not deductible. However, you may deduct goodwill expenditures when:

- The goodwill occurs during a quiet business lunch or dinner.
- The goodwill precedes or follows a substantial business discussion (i.e., passes the associated with test).

Example 1

Liz Brown, a partner of a management consulting firm, plans a dinner party in a New York City hotel. She invites a number of current and prospective clients. Business is only casually discussed; her main goal is to cultivate goodwill. The expense for the dinner party is not deductible. The goodwill is a clear business purpose, but the dinner is not preceded or followed by a substantial business discussion.

Example 2

After considering the tax cost of the nondeductible goodwill expenses, Liz Brown holds a second dinner party, but she adds a formal presentation, which is substantial in relation to the time spent cultivating goodwill. The costs of the refreshments and dinner qualify as goodwill entertainment, since the entertainment is associated with business and the goodwill (the business purpose) is preceded by a substantial business discussion (the presentation). As a result, 50% of the qualifying expenses are deductible.

EXPLANATION

Out-of-pocket entertaining costs at clubs and lodges. Congress has made it clear that out-of-pocket entertainment costs–that otherwise qualify as "directly related to" or "associated with" business expenses–may still be partially deducted, even if they are incurred at an entertainment facility. Again, 50% of such costs may not be deducted.

An entertainment facility is usually real property, such as a fishing camp, a ski lodge, an apartment, or a hotel suite, but may also include personal property, such as a yacht, an airplane, or an automobile. You may own or rent the facility or just be a member of a club or organization, such as a country club or a sporting group, which provides use of a facility.

Example

Mike Franklin, a sports equipment manufacturer, takes a customer to a hunting lodge on an overnight trip. Immediately after the trip, the customer discusses products and market projections. The discussion ends with the customer placing his semiannual order.

In this instance, 50% of the costs of the meals, hunting rights, drinks in the nightclub, and transportation to and from the lodge are deductible. These costs qualify as entertainment associated with business and followed by a substantial business discussion (i.e., the expenses pass the associated test). Because 50% of the entertainment costs would have been deductible if not incurred at an entertainment facility, they are also deductible even though the hunting lodge is an entertainment facility. These costs are not directly associated with the operation and maintenance of the place. However, the cost of the lodging is associated with the operation and maintenance of the facility. Therefore, the lodging expense, though partially deductible if incurred at a nonentertainment facility (e.g., a hotel instead of the hunting lodge), is not deductible.

EXPLANATION

Deductions for the costs of tickets to cultural, theatrical, or sporting events are severely limited. In addition to meeting the directly related or associated with tests, the allowable portion of the ticket cost is limited to the face value of the ticket. The allowable portion of the ticket cost must be further reduced because only 50% of the allowable expense may be deducted.

Example

You pay a scalper $150 for three tickets to a sporting event. The face value of each ticket is $20. Your deduction is limited to $30 ($20 face value × three tickets × 50%).

EXPLANATION

A similar rule also applies to the cost of luxury skyboxes at sports arenas. Costs for the business use of a suite, an apartment, an automobile, or an airplane are generally deductible. Personal use of an entertainment facility may be considered compensation, and the individual may be subject to tax.

Gift Expenses

If you give gifts in the course of your trade or business, you can deduct all or part of the cost. This section explains the limits and rules for deducting the costs of gifts.

$25 limit. You can deduct no more than $25 for business gifts you give directly or indirectly to each person during your tax year. A gift to a company that is intended for the eventual personal use or benefit of a particular person or a limited class of people will be considered an indirect gift to that particular person or to the individuals within that class of people who receive the gift.

If you give a gift to a member of a customer's family, the gift is generally considered to be an indirect gift to the customer. This rule does not apply if you have a *bona fide*, independent business connection with that family member and the gift is not intended for the customer's eventual use.

If you and your spouse both give gifts, both of you are treated as one taxpayer. It does not matter whether you have separate businesses, are separately employed, or whether each of you has an independent connection with the recipient. If a partnership gives gifts, the partnership and the partners are treated as one taxpayer.

Incidental costs. Incidental costs, such as engraving on jewelry, or packaging, insuring, and mailing, are generally not included in determining the cost of a gift for purposes of the $25 limit.

A cost is incidental only if it does not add substantial value to the gift. For example, the cost of gift wrapping is an incidental cost. However, the purchase of an ornamental basket for packaging fruit is not an incidental cost if the value of the basket is substantial compared to the value of the fruit.

Exceptions. The following items are not considered gifts for purposes of the $25 limit.

1. An item that costs $4 or less and:
   a. Has your name clearly and permanently imprinted on the gift, and
   b. Is one of a number of identical items you widely distribute. Examples include pens, desk sets, and plastic bags and cases.
2. Signs, display racks, or other promotional material to be used on the business premises of the recipient.

EXPLANATION

Business gifts are subject to close scrutiny. The IRS views this area as one of potential abuse. Business gifts are subject to strict substantiation requirements. The date of the gift, description of the gift, your cost, recipient's name, occupation, title or other designation establishing the business relationship between you and the recipient and the business reason for making the gift must be noted in your records to uphold the deduction.

The business gift limitations do not apply to the following types of donations:

- Fellowship grants or scholarships.
- Achievement prizes and awards.
- Death benefits to an employee's survivors.

Examples

The cost of beer offered by a service station owner to entice customers into his service station was allowed as a business gift deduction. The courts held that the expenses were directly related to the active conduct of his business and were incurred to sell additional goods and services.

Wine samples distributed in connection with a public offering of stock were allowed as a business gift subject to the $25 per recipient limitation.

Gift or entertainment. Any item that might be considered either a gift or entertainment generally will be considered entertainment. However, if you give a customer packaged food or beverages you intend the customer to use at a later date, treat it as a gift.

If you give a customer tickets to a theater performance or sporting event and you do not go with the customer to the performance or event, you have a choice. You can treat the cost of the tickets as either a gift expense or an entertainment expense, whichever is to your advantage.

If you go with the customer to the event, you must treat the cost of the tickets as an entertainment expense. You cannot choose, in this case, to treat the cost of the tickets as a gift expense.

TAXPLANNER

It is usually to your advantage to define a particular item as an entertainment expense rather than as a gift. Although entertainment expenses are subject to the 50% limitation, there is no fixed dollar limitation on the deduction, though the expenses must be considered ordinary and necessary.

Transportation Expenses

This section discusses expenses you can deduct for business transportation when you are not traveling away from home as defined earlier under *Travel Expenses*. These expenses include the cost of transportation by air, rail, bus, taxi, etc., and the cost of driving and maintaining your car.

Transportation expenses include the ordinary and necessary costs of all of the following.

- Getting from one workplace to another in the course of your business or profession when you are traveling within the area of your tax home. (Tax home is defined earlier under *Travel Expenses*.)
- Visiting clients or customers.
- Going to a business meeting away from your regular workplace.
- Getting from your home to a temporary workplace when you have one or more regular places of work. These temporary workplaces can be either within the area of your tax home or outside that area.

Transportation expenses do not include expenses you have while traveling away from home overnight. Those expenses are travel expenses, discussed earlier. However, if you use your car while traveling away from home overnight, use the rules in this section to figure your car expense deduction. See *Car Expenses*, later.

Illustration of transportation expenses. Figure 27-B illustrates the rules for when you can deduct transportation expenses when you have a regular or main job away from your home. You may want to refer to it when deciding whether you can deduct your transportation expenses.

Temporary work location. If you have one or more regular work locations away from your home and you commute to a temporary work location in the same trade or business, you can deduct the expenses of the daily round-trip transportation between your home and the temporary location, regardless of distance.

If your employment at a work location is realistically expected to last (and does in fact last) for 1 year or less, the employment is temporary unless there are facts and circumstances that would indicate otherwise.

If your employment at a work location is realistically expected to last for more than 1 year or if there is no realistic expectation that the employment will last for 1 year or less, the employment is not temporary, regardless of whether it actually lasts for more than 1 year.

If employment at a work location initially is realistically expected to last for 1 year or less, but at some later date the employment is realistically expected to last more than 1 year, that employment will be treated as temporary (unless there are facts and circumstances that would indicate otherwise) until your expectation changes. It will not be treated as temporary after the date you determine it will last more than 1 year.

If the temporary work location is beyond the general area of your regular place of work and you stay overnight, you are traveling away from home. You may have deductible travel expenses as discussed earlier in this chapter.

No regular place of work. If you have no regular place of work but ordinarily work in the metropolitan area where you live, you can deduct daily transportation costs between home and a temporary work site outside that metropolitan area.

Generally, a metropolitan area includes the area within the city limits and the suburbs that are considered part of that metropolitan area.

You cannot deduct daily transportation costs between your home and temporary work sites within your metropolitan area. These are nondeductible commuting expenses.

Figure 27-B. **When Are Transportation Expenses Deductible?**

Most employees and self-employed persons can use this chart. (Do not use this chart if your home is your principal place of business. See *Office in the home*.)

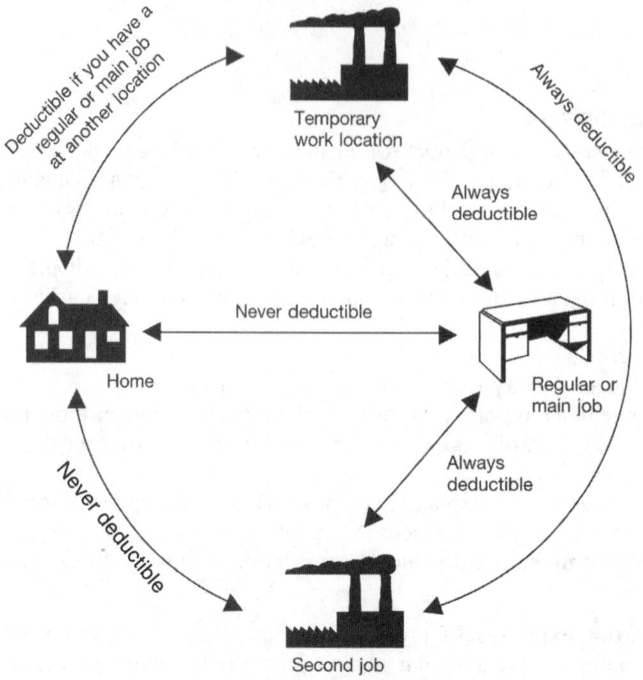

Home: The place where you reside. Transportation expenses between your home and your main or regular place of work are personal commuting expenses.

Regular or main job: Your principal place of business. If you have more than one job, you must determine which one is your regular or main job. Consider the time you spend at each, the activity you have at each, and the income you earn at each.

Temporary work location: A place where your work assignment is realistically expected to last (and does in fact last) one year or less. Unless you have a regular place of business, you can only deduct your transportation expenses to a temporary work location outside your metropolitan area.

Second job: If you regularly work at two or more places in one day, whether or not for the same employer, you can deduct your transportation expenses of getting from one workplace to another. if you do not go directly from your first job to your second job, you can only deduct the transportation expenses of going directly from your first job to your second job. You cannot deduct your transportation expenses between your home and a second job on a day off from main job.

TAXPLANNER

The IRS has ruled that a taxpayer may deduct the expenses of daily transportation between his or her residence and any temporary work site as long as he or she has a regular work site.

Based on this ruling by the IRS, the Tax Court allowed a logger to deduct his expenses of traveling between his residence and various cutting sites because the court held the logger's residence was his regular place of business.

However, in response to this decision by the Tax Court, the IRS issued a ruling that stated that daily transportation expenses incurred in going between a taxpayer's residence and a work location are nondeductible commuting expenses unless one of the following three exceptions applies:

1. A taxpayer may deduct daily transportation expenses incurred in going between the taxpayer's residence and a temporary work location outside the metropolitan area where the taxpayer lives and normally works. However, unless paragraph (2) or (3) below applies, daily transportation expenses incurred in going between the taxpayer's residence and a temporary work location within that metropolitan area are nondeductible commuting expenses.

2. If a taxpayer has one or more regular work locations away from the taxpayer's residence, the taxpayer may deduct daily transportation expenses incurred in going between the taxpayer's residence and a temporary work location in the same trade or business, regardless of the distance.
3. If a taxpayer's residence is the taxpayer's principal place of business (as opposed to a regular place of business), the taxpayer may deduct daily transportation expenses incurred in going between the residence and another work location in the same trade or business, regardless of whether the other work location is regular or temporary and regardless of the distance.

Explanation

It is important to note the difference between a principal place of business and a regular place of business. A principal place of business is determined by a facts and circumstances test. Among the facts and circumstances to be taken into account in determining an individual's principal place of business are the following:

1. The portion of total income from business activities that is attributable to activities at each location.
2. The portion of time spent in business activities in each location.
3. The facilities available to the taxpayer at each location.

The regular place of business standard is less stringent than the principal place of business standard. A regular place of business is defined as any location at which the taxpayer works or performs services on a regular basis.

Two places of work. If you work at two places in one day, whether or not for the same employer, you can deduct the expense of getting from one workplace to the other. However, if for some personal reason you do not go directly from one location to the other, you cannot deduct more than the amount it would have cost you to go directly from the first location to the second.

Transportation expenses you have in going between home and a part-time job on a day off from your main job are commuting expenses. You cannot deduct them.

EXAMPLES

Example 1

A doctor who practiced at a private clinic could not deduct the automobile expenses incurred on his regular and emergency trips between his home and the hospital. Under the hospital rules, the doctor was required to visit the hospital daily, as well as to spend a day on call each month. The court ruled that since the hospital was an integral and regular place of business for the doctor, his travel was a nondeductible commuting expense.

Example 2

A doctor could not deduct the cost of traveling between his office at home and the clinic where he practiced. Although he kept his medical and business records in his office in the home, he didn't see patients there. The court ruled that it was neither a principal business office nor a focal point for his medical practice and disallowed the deduction.

Example 3

A doctor who maintained two separate offices was denied a deduction for the costs of commuting between his residence and the places where he conducted his medical practices. He was, however, permitted to deduct commuting costs between his offices and to the hospital where he made his rounds.

Example 4

A college professor who maintained a home office was not allowed to deduct transportation expenses from his home to the college. The court determined that the focal point of his activities was the college at which he taught.

Exception

A police officer was allowed to claim a deduction for automobile expenses traveling to and from work because he was under orders to consider himself at work from the moment he left home until he returned.

Armed Forces reservists. A meeting of an Armed Forces reserve unit is a second place of business if the meeting is held on a day on which you work at your regular job. You can deduct the expense of getting from one workplace to the other as just discussed under <u>*Two places of work*</u>.

You usually cannot deduct the expense if the reserve meeting is held on a day on which you do not work at your regular job. In this case, your transportation generally is a nondeductible commuting expense. However, you can deduct your transportation expenses if the location of the meeting is temporary and you have one or more regular places of work.

If you ordinarily work in a particular metropolitan area but not at any specific location and the reserve meeting is held at a temporary location outside that metropolitan area, you can deduct your transportation expenses.

If you travel away from home overnight to attend a guard or reserve meeting, you can deduct your travel expenses. These expenses are discussed earlier under Travel Expenses.

If you travel more than 100 miles away from home in connection with your performance of services as a member of the reserves, you may be able to deduct some of your reserve-related travel costs as an adjustment to income rather than as an itemized deduction. See Armed Forces reservists traveling more than 100 miles from home under *Special Rules,* later.

Commuting expenses. You cannot deduct the costs of taking a bus, trolley, subway, or taxi, or of driving a car between your home and your main or regular place of work. These costs are personal commuting expenses. You cannot deduct commuting expenses no matter how far your home is from your regular place of work. You cannot deduct commuting expenses even if you work during the commuting trip.

Example. You sometimes use your cell phone to make business calls while commuting to and from work. Sometimes business associates ride with you to and from work, and you have a business discussion in the car. These activities do not change the trip from personal to business. You cannot deduct your commuting expenses.

Parking fees. Fees you pay to park your car at your place of business are nondeductible commuting expenses. You can, however, deduct business-related parking fees when visiting a customer or client.

Advertising display on car. Putting display material that advertises your business on your car does not change the use of your car from personal use to business use. If you use this car for commuting or other personal uses, you still cannot deduct your expenses for those uses.

Car pools. You cannot deduct the cost of using your car in a nonprofit car pool. Do not include payments you receive from the passengers in your income. These payments are considered reimbursements of your expenses. However, if you operate a car pool for a profit, you must include payments from passengers in your income. You can then deduct your car expenses (using the rules in this chapter).

Hauling tools or instruments. Hauling tools or instruments in your car while commuting to and from work does not make your car expenses deductible. However, you can deduct any additional costs you have for hauling tools or instruments (such as for renting a trailer you tow with your car).

EXAMPLE

A teacher could not deduct the expenses for an automobile she used to carry books and teaching materials to her classes, even though she could not store them at the school. She also used her automobile on days on which she came to school just to attend meetings. It took an hour to drive to school. Getting there by alternative means of transportation took 1½ hours and was very inconvenient. The court concluded that she would have driven even if she didn't have to transport books and that her expenses were merely commuting costs and not deductible.

Union members' trips from a union hall. If you get your work assignments at a union hall and then go to your place of work, the costs of getting from the union hall to your place of work are nondeductible commuting expenses. Although you need the union to get your work assignments, you are employed where you work, not where the union hall is located.

Office in the home. If you have an office in your home that qualifies as a principal place of business, you can deduct your daily transportation costs between your home and another work location in the same trade or business. (See chapter 29 for information on determining if your home office qualifies as a principal place of business.)

Examples of deductible transportation. The following examples show when you can deduct transportation expenses based on the location of your work and your home.

Example 1. You regularly work in an office in the city where you live. Your employer sends you to a 1-week training session at a different office in the same city. You travel directly from your home to the training location and return each day. You can deduct the cost of your daily round-trip transportation between your home and the training location.

Example 2. Your principal place of business is in your home. You can deduct the cost of round-trip transportation between your qualifying home office and your client's or customer's place of business.

Example 3. You have no regular office, and you do not have an office in your home. In this case, the location of your first business contact is considered your office. Transportation expenses between your home and this first contact are nondeductible commuting expenses. Transportation expenses between your last business contact and your home are also nondeductible commuting expenses. Although you cannot deduct the costs of these first and last trips, you can deduct the costs of going from one client or customer to another.

Car Expenses

If you use your car for business purposes, you may be able to deduct car expenses. You generally can use one of the two following methods to figure your deductible expenses.

- Standard mileage rate.
- Actual car expenses.

If you use actual car expenses to figure your deduction for a car you lease, there are rules that affect the amount of your lease payments you can deduct. See *Leasing a car* under *Actual Car Expenses,* later.

In this chapter, "car" includes a van, pickup, or panel truck.

EXPLANATION

Fixed and variable rate. Under certain circumstances, employees' business expenses for car expenses will be deemed substantiated when their employer reimburses such expenses with a mileage allowance different from the standard mileage rates for 2011 (51 cents per mile prior to June 30, 2011; 55.5 cents per mile after June 30, 2011).

TAXPLANNER

A court held that it was sufficient for a salesman to maintain records of personal miles driven only. The difference between his total mileage and his personal mileage represented his business mileage.

The courts have allowed a taxpayer a deduction for depreciation of a car used in business, even though his travel records were not very accurate or complete. Depreciation of a business asset is not subject to the strict record-keeping requirements that other types of travel expenses are. A deduction for depreciation is allowed if you can simply show that the car was used for business.

Rural mail carriers. If you are a rural mail carrier, you may be able to treat the amount of qualified reimbursement you received as the amount of your allowable expense. Because the qualified reimbursement is treated as paid under an accountable plan, your employer should not include the amount of reimbursement in your income.

If your vehicle expenses are more than the amount of your reimbursement, you can deduct the unreimbursed expenses as an itemized deduction on Schedule A (Form 1040). You must complete Form 2106 and attach it to your Form 1040.

A "qualified reimbursement" is the reimbursement you receive that meets both of the following conditions.

- It is given as an equipment maintenance allowance (EMA) to employees of the U.S. Postal Service.
- It is at the rate contained in the 1991 collective bargaining agreement. Any later agreement cannot increase the qualified reimbursement amount by more than the rate of inflation.

See your employer for information on your reimbursement.

Standard Mileage Rate

You may be able to use the standard mileage rate to figure the deductible costs of operating your car for business purposes. For 2011, the standard mileage rate for each mile of business use is 51 cents per mile from January 1, 2011, through June 30, 2011, and 55.5 cents from July 1, 2011, through December 31, 2011.

Tip

You may be entitled to a tax credit for an alternative motor vehicle you place in service during the year. The vehicle must meet certain requirements, and you do not have to use it in your business to qualify for the credit. For more information, see *chapter 37*.

Caution

If you are a rural mail carrier and received a qualified reimbursement, you cannot use the standard mileage rate.

TAXALERT

For 2011, the optional federal standard mileage rates for business, charitable, medical, and moving use of an automobile are:

	January 1-June 30, 2011	July 1-December 31, 2011
Business	51¢	55.5¢
Charitable	14¢	14¢
Medical & Moving	19.5¢	23.5¢

Caution

If you use the standard mileage rate for a year, you cannot deduct your actual car expenses for that year, but see Parking fees and tolls, *later.*

You generally can use the standard mileage rate whether or not you are reimbursed and whether or not any reimbursement is more or less than the amount figured using the standard mileage rate. See *Reimbursements* under *How To Report,* later.

Choosing the standard mileage rate. If you want to use the standard mileage rate for a car you own, you must choose to use it in the first year the car is available for use in your business. Then in later years, you can choose to use either the standard mileage rate or actual expenses.

If you want to use the standard mileage rate for a car you lease, you must use it for the entire lease period. For leases that began on or before December 31, 1997, the standard mileage rate must be used for the entire portion of the lease period (including renewals) that is after 1997.

You must make the choice to use the standard mileage rate by the due date (including extensions) of your return. You cannot revoke the choice. However, in a later year, you can switch from the standard mileage rate to the actual expenses method. If you change to the actual expense method in a later year, but before your car is fully depreciated, you have to estimate the remaining useful life of the car and use straight line depreciation.

Example. Larry is an employee who occasionally uses his own car for business purposes. He purchased the car in 2009, but he did not claim any unreimbursed employee expenses on his 2009 tax return. Because Larry did not use the standard mileage rate the first year the car was available for business use, he cannot use the standard mileage rate in 2011 to claim unreimbursed employee business expenses.

For more information about depreciation included in the standard mileage rate, see the exception in *Methods of depreciation* under *Depreciation Deduction* in chapter 4 of Publication 463.

EXPLANATION

If you select the actual cost method (operating expenses and ACRS or MACRS depreciation expense method), the standard mileage rate may never be used for that automobile. However, if you use the standard mileage rate for the first year, you may switch to the actual cost method, but you then must use a straight-line depreciation rate for the remaining estimated life of the automobile. Generally, actual expenses exceed the amount you may claim by using the standard mileage rate. As long as you keep adequate records, you will probably be better off claiming actual expenses.

Standard mileage rate not allowed. You cannot use the standard mileage rate if you:

- *Text intentionally omitted.*
- Use five or more cars at the same time (as in fleet operations),
- Claimed a depreciation deduction for the car using any method other than straight line depreciation,
- Claimed a section 179 deduction on the car,
- Claimed the special depreciation allowance on the car,
- Claimed actual car expenses after 1997 for a car you leased, or
- Are a rural mail carrier who received a qualified reimbursement. (See *Rural mail carriers,* earlier.)

TAXALERT

Beginning in 2011, the business standard mileage rate can be used for vehicles used for hire, such as taxicabs.

Five or more cars. If you own or lease five or more cars that are used for business at the same time, you cannot use the standard mileage rate for the business use of any car. However, you may be able to deduct your actual expenses for operating each of the cars in your business. See *Actual Car Expenses* in chapter 4 of Publication 463 for information on how to figure your deduction.

You are not using five or more cars for business at the same time if you alternate using (use at different times) the cars for business.

Parking fees and tolls. In addition to using the standard mileage rate, you can deduct any business-related parking fees and tolls. (Parking fees you pay to park your car at your place of work are nondeductible commuting expenses.)

TAXALERT

Employer-provided parking. For 2011, you can exclude up to $230 per month of employer-provided parking, even if you choose it instead of cash or your employer reduces your compensation to provide the parking.

Actual Car Expenses

If you do not use the standard mileage rate, you may be able to deduct your actual car expenses.

Tip

If you qualify to use both methods, you may want to figure your deduction both ways to see which gives you a larger deduction.

Actual car expenses include:

Depreciation	Lease payments	Registration fees
Garage rent	Licenses	Repairs
Gas	Oil	Tires
Insurance	Parking fees	Tolls

Business and personal use. If you use your car for both business and personal purposes, you must divide your expenses between business and personal use. You can divide your expense based on the miles driven for each purpose.

Example. You are a contractor and drive your car 20,000 miles during the year: 12,000 miles for business use and 8,000 miles for personal use. You can claim only 60% (12,000 ÷ 20,000) of the cost of operating your car as a business expense.

EXPLANATION

To claim a deduction for car expenses properly, you must establish that you are entitled to the deduction because the car was used at least partially for business. The deduction will be allowed only to the extent of business use. If you can establish that you are entitled to the deduction but are unable to establish the precise amount of the deduction, the court will apply its own best judgment to make an approximation of the business portion of the expenses.

Example 1

A doctor who is constantly on emergency call may not deduct all of his automobile expenses and depreciation. He must calculate how much of the automobile's use is business and how much is personal. The business portion is deductible.

Example 2

A construction worker who kept a logbook of miles driven but failed to distinguish between business and personal mileage was not allowed to take any deduction.

Example 3

A salesman was able to prove that he used his automobile exclusively for business except for his round-trip to and from work of 16 miles. However, he was unable to establish how many miles were dedicated to business use. The court concluded that his business use was 75% and his personal use was 25%.

Interest on car loans. If you are an employee, you cannot deduct any interest paid on a car loan. This interest is treated as personal interest and is not deductible. However, if you are self-employed and use your car in that business, see chapter 4 of Publication 535.

Tip

If you use a home equity loan to purchase your car, you may be able to deduct the interest. See chapter 24 for more information.

TAXPLANNER

If an employee who owns a home finances the purchase of an automobile through a loan secured by the home, the interest would be fully deductible as home mortgage interest if the employee is within the $100,000 home equity indebtedness rules.

Taxes paid on your car. If you are an employee, you can deduct personal property taxes paid on your car if you itemize deductions. Enter the amount paid on line 7 of Schedule A (Form 1040). (See chapter 23 for more information on taxes.) If you are not an employee, see your form instructions for information on how to deduct personal property taxes paid on your car.

Sales taxes. Generally, sales taxes on your car are part of your car's basis and are recovered through depreciation, discussed later. However, to the extent the car is not used in your trade or business, you can choose to deduct the nonbusiness part of the sales tax deduction on Schedule A (Form 1040). You can only choose to deduct state and local sales taxes as an itemized deduction if you choose not to deduct state and local income taxes.
Text intentionally omitted.

Fines and collateral. You cannot deduct fines you pay and forfeited collateral for traffic violations.

Depreciation and section 179 deductions. Generally, the cost of a car, plus sales tax and improvements, is a capital expense. Because the benefits last longer than 1 year, you generally cannot deduct a capital expense. However, you can recover this cost through the section 179 deduction (the deduction allowed by section 179 of the Internal Revenue Code), special depreciation allowance, and depreciation deductions. Depreciation allows you to recover the cost over more than 1 year by deducting part of it each year. The section 179 deduction, special depreciation allowance, and the depreciation deduction are discussed in more detail in chapter 4 of Publication 463.

Generally, there are limits on these deductions. Special rules apply if you use your car 50% or less in your work or business.

EXPLANATION

Severe limitations on deductions apply on luxury automobiles and automobiles used for both business and personal purposes.

Passenger automobile. The total initial-year depreciation deduction (including section 179 expense) you can take for a passenger automobile (that is not a truck, van, or an electric vehicle) that you use in your business and first place in service in 2011 is $3,060 ($11,060 for automobiles for which the special depreciation allowance applies).

Truck or van. The total initial-year depreciation deduction (including section 179 expense) you can take for a truck or van (such as a minivan or a sports utility vehicle built on a truck chassis) that you use in your business and first place in service in 2011 is higher than for other passenger vehicles. The maximum amount allowable is $3,260 ($11,260 for trucks or vans for which the special depreciation allowance applies).

Caution: *The limits are reduced if the business use of the vehicle is less than 100%.*

Explanation

If qualified business use of a vehicle purchased after 1986 is over 50%, then you can claim 200% declining balance depreciation over a 5-year period. Declining balance depreciation is described in Publication 946, *How to Depreciate Property*. Qualified business use means direct use in your trade or business, including your job. It does not include looking after your investments. However, if you use your automobile more than 50% in your trade or business, you can then use accelerated 5-year depreciation for the part used for looking after your investments.

If qualified business use is 50% or less, depreciation must be calculated on a straight-line basis over 5 years, with a proration of the maximum deduction. Although a 5-year life is used, only a half-year's depreciation is deductible in the first year. The other half-year is not deductible until the sixth year. Again, depreciation in excess of the allowed amounts is carried over to future years to depreciate fully the business portion of the asset.

Example

You buy an automobile in 2011 and use it 60% for business, 10% for looking after your investments, and 30% for personal use. You can deduct 70% of your depreciation, calculated using accelerated depreciation. If you use your automobile only 45% for business and 25% for looking after your investments, you can still deduct 70%, but it must be computed on a straight-line basis.

Caution: *You are allowed to take the accelerated depreciation as long as the asset is used 50% or more for qualified business use. If in any year after the first year, you use this asset less than 50%, you must include in your income the excess depreciation expense taken (i.e., the difference between accelerated and straight-line depreciation expense).*

Leasing a car. If you lease a car, truck, or van that you use in your business, you can use the standard mileage rate or actual expenses to figure your deductible car expense.

Deductible payments. If you choose to use actual expenses, you can deduct the part of each lease payment that is for the use of the vehicle in your business. You cannot deduct any part of a lease payment that is for personal use of the vehicle, such as commuting.

You must spread any advance payments over the entire lease period. You cannot deduct any payments you make to buy a vehicle, even if the payments are called lease payments.

If you lease a car, truck, or van for 30 days or more, you may have to reduce your lease payment deduction by an "inclusion amount." For information on reporting lease inclusion amounts, see *Leasing a Car* in chapter 4 of Publication 463.

TAXPLANNER

If you buy an automobile (for personal use) and finance it, you cannot deduct any of the interest charges. If you finance the car by taking out a home equity loan, the interest may be deductible as home mortgage interest. See chapter 24, *Interest expense*. However, if you are **self-employed** and use your car in your trade or business, you may deduct 100% of the business portion of the interest charges. If you simply use your car as an **employee**, you may pay less tax by leasing a car rather than buying it because you can deduct your lease payments subject to the business use rules discussed elsewhere in this chapter.

Leasing an automobile. Deducting employee business expenses for the cost of a leased automobile is similar to doing so for an automobile you own. You may deduct the portion of the total lease payments that is attributable to business use, using the ratio of business miles to total miles to make the calculation. This deduction represents the depreciation and financing costs. Normal operating costs and maintenance (if not included in the lease) and business parking may also be deducted.

The luxury automobile rules are intended to impose the same unfavorable treatment for leased automobiles as for purchased automobiles. If you lease an automobile for business use, you can deduct the lease payments and operating expenses for that business use. If you lease an automobile and the value exceeds certain levels, you are deemed to have received additional income.

Note: You must recapture a portion of your lease payment deductions and report them as income if your business use of the automobile falls below 50%.

See Publication 463, *Travel, Entertainment, Gift and Car Expenses*, for further details and the tables for computing the lease adjustments.

Sale, Trade-In, or Other Disposition

If you sell, trade in, or otherwise dispose of your car, you may have a taxable gain or a deductible loss. This is true whether you used the standard mileage rate or actual car expenses to deduct the business use of your car. Publication 544 has information on sales of property used in a trade or business, and details on how to report the disposition.

EXPLANATION

Unreimbursed automobile expenses are deductible only as miscellaneous itemized deductions. Employees formerly classified as "outside sales representatives" are also subject to this provision.

As a result, these expenses will be deductible only to the extent that, when aggregated with your other miscellaneous itemized deductions, they exceed 2% of your adjusted gross income.

TAXSAVER

In some cases, you may be able to deduct a greater mileage rate than the IRS customarily permits. For example, the courts have allowed truck drivers who were reimbursed at a greater rate than the standard rate to deduct the greater rate. The truck drivers had kept detailed weekly records of their trucks' operating costs.

TAXSAVER

If you own an expensive business automobile, the standard mileage rate is probably inadequate to cover your operating costs. You should keep detailed records of your total expenses so that you may claim a larger deduction than you would be able to claim by using the standard mileage rate.

Records

If you keep timely and accurate records, you will have support to show the IRS if your tax return is ever examined. You will also have proof of expenses that your employer may require if you are reimbursed under an accountable plan. These plans are discussed later under Reimbursements.

Recordkeeping

If you deduct travel, entertainment, gift, or transportation expenses, you must be able to prove (substantiate) certain elements of the expense. This section discusses the records you need to keep to prove these expenses.

TAXPLANNER

Good recordkeeping is a good business practice and a must for tax purposes. A clear and consistent set of records is the first step in justifying your expense deduction. Reasonable estimates of expenses are no longer acceptable, even if the estimate is moderate in relation to the income generated.

Form 4562, which is used to show your automobile depreciation, specifically asks whether you have evidence to support your business use percentage.

You must maintain adequate records or sufficient evidence, either written or oral, that will corroborate your own statement. Sufficient evidence includes account books, trip sheets, expense reports, appointment calendars, statements of witnesses, and certain accountings to an employer. Contemporaneous logs are no longer required, but a report made at the event would be more credible than records prepared at a later date.

If you are required to turn in the original copies of your receipts and logbooks to your employer, you should make copies for yourself. If the confidentiality of names is a consideration, special arrangements might have to be made with your employer to make necessary information available if and when it is needed.

When records are lost in circumstances beyond your control, such as destruction by fire, flood, earthquake, or other casualty, the IRS is more lenient in accepting reconstructed records and secondary evidence than it is when records are not available because of carelessness or mysterious disappearance.

Example

Travel expense records were lost during a change of residence resulting from marital problems. The court ruled that marital difficulties did not constitute a casualty warranting the use of reconstructed records.

Caution

You cannot deduct amounts that you approximate or estimate.

How To Prove Expenses

Table 27-2 is a summary of records you need to prove each expense discussed in this chapter. You must be able to prove the elements listed across the top portion of the chart. You prove them by having the information and receipts (where needed) for the expenses listed in the first column.

You should keep adequate records to prove your expenses or have sufficient evidence that will support your own statement. You must generally prepare a written record for it to be considered adequate. This is because written evidence is more reliable than oral evidence alone. However, if you prepare a record on a computer it is considered an adequate record.

TAXALERT

Generally, deductions are not allowed for any travel expenses without proper records. However, the IRS issued guidance in September 2009 that states if your employer provides a per diem allowance, your expenses can be "deemed" to be substantiated. The amount "deemed substantiated" is the lesser of the per diem allowance or the federal per diem rate for the locality on the day of travel.

TAXALERT

If you are self-employed or an employee who is not reimbursed for allowable meal and incidental expenses, you may use the lesser of the following to substantiate your deduction:

1. Actual expenses
2. The federal meals and incidental expenses rate for the locality of travel for that day

The amount will be deemed substantiated if you can substantiate the elements of time, place and business purpose of travel for that day.

Table 27-2. **How To Prove Certain Business Expenses**

IF you have expenses for...	THEN you must keep records that show details of the following elements...			
	Amount	**Time**	**Place or Description**	**Business Purpose and Business Relationship**
Travel	Cost of each separate expense for travel, lodging, and meals. Incidental expenses may be totaled in reasonable categories such as taxis, fees and tips, etc.	Dates you left and returned for each trip and number of days spent on business.	Destination or area of your travel (name of city, town, or other designation).	Purpose: Business purpose for the expense or the business benefit gained or expected to be gained. Relationship: N/A
Entertainment	Cost of each separate expense. Incidental expenses such as taxis, telephones, etc., may be totaled on a daily basis.	Date of entertainment. (Also see *Business Purpose.*)	Name and address or location of place of entertainment. Type of entertainment if not otherwise apparent. (Also see *Business Purpose.*)	Purpose: Business purpose for the expense or the business benefit gained or expected to be gained. For entertainment, the nature of the business discussion or activity. If the entertainment was directly before or after a business discussion: the date, place, nature, and duration of the business discussion, and the identities of the persons who took part in both the business discussion and the entertainment activity. Relationship: Occupations or other information (such as names, titles, or other designations) about the recipients that shows their business relationship to you. For entertainment, you must also prove that you or your employee was present if the entertainment was a business meal.
Gifts	Cost of the gift.	Date of the gift.	Description of the gift.	
Transportation	Cost of each separate expense. For car expenses, the cost of the car and any improvements, the date you started using it for business, the mileage for each business use, and the total miles for the year.	Date of the expense. For car expenses, the date of the use of the car.	Your business destination.	Purpose: Business purpose for the expense. Relationship: N/A

TAXALERT

In lieu of using actual expenses, the amount "deemed substantiated" for incidental expenses on a day you can document the time, place, and business purpose of travel will be $5 per day for any locality in the continental United States and localities outside the continental United States, after October 1, 2010.

As of the date this book was published, the amount deemed substantiated after October 1, 2011, had not yet been announced by the IRS. For updated information on this and any other tax law changes that occur after this book was published, see our website, *ey.com/EYTaxGuide*.

What Are Adequate Records?

You should keep the proof you need in an account book, diary, statement of expense, or similar record. You should also keep documentary evidence that, together with your records, will support each element of an expense.

Documentary evidence. You generally must have documentary evidence, such as receipts, canceled checks, or bills, to support your expenses.

Exception. Documentary evidence is not needed if any of the following conditions apply.

- You have meals or lodging expenses while traveling away from home for which you account to your employer under an accountable plan and you use a per diem allowance method that includes meals and/or lodging. (Accountable plans and per diem allowances are discussed later under *Reimbursements*.)
- Your expense, other than lodging, is less than $75.
- You have a transportation expense for which a receipt is not readily available.

TAXALERT

The tax law disallows an otherwise allowable deduction for any expense for traveling, entertainment, gifts, or listed property, unless the expense is substantiated by adequate records. Taxpayers are required to maintain documentary evidence (such as receipts) for (1) any lodging expenditure and (2) any other expenditure of $75 or more.

Adequate evidence. Documentary evidence ordinarily will be considered adequate if it shows the amount, date, place, and essential character of the expense.

For example, a hotel receipt is enough to support expenses for business travel if it has all of the following information.

- The name and location of the hotel.
- The dates you stayed there.
- Separate amounts for charges such as lodging, meals, and telephone calls.

A restaurant receipt is enough to prove an expense for a business meal if it has all of the following information.

- The name and location of the restaurant.
- The number of people served.
- The date and amount of the expense.

If a charge is made for items other than food and beverages, the receipt must show that this is the case.

Canceled check. A canceled check, together with a bill from the payee, ordinarily establishes the cost. However, a canceled check by itself does not prove a business expense without other evidence to show that it was for a business purpose.

TAXPLANNER

You must maintain detailed records and report the required information on your tax return if you wish to claim a deduction for expenses that exceed reimbursements. You must keep these records, even though you do not have to give the completely detailed information to your employer because reimbursements by your employer meet the IRS per diem standards.

Duplicate information. You do not have to record information in your account book or other record that duplicates information shown on a receipt as long as your records and receipts complement each other in an orderly manner.

You do not have to record amounts your employer pays directly for any ticket or other travel item. However, if you charge these items to your employer, through a credit card or otherwise, you must keep a record of the amounts you spend.

Timely-kept records. You should record the elements of an expense or of a business use at or near the time of the expense or use and support it with sufficient documentary evidence. A timely-kept record has more value than a statement prepared later when generally there is a lack of accurate recall.

You do not need to write down the elements of every expense on the day of the expense. If you maintain a log on a weekly basis which accounts for use during the week, the log is considered a timely-kept record.

If you give your employer, client, or customer an expense account statement, it can also be considered a timely-kept record. This is true if you copy it from your account book, diary, statement of expense, or similar record.

Proving business purpose. You must generally provide a written statement of the business purpose of an expense. However, the degree of proof varies according to the circumstances in each case. If the business purpose of an expense is clear from the surrounding circumstances, then you do not need to give a written explanation.

Confidential information. You do not need to put confidential information relating to an element of a deductible expense (such as the place, business purpose, or business relationship) in your account book, diary, or other record. However, you do have to record the information elsewhere at or near the time of the expense and have it available to fully prove that element of the expense.

What if I Have Incomplete Records?

If you do not have complete records to prove an element of an expense, then you must prove the element with:

- Your own written or oral statement, containing specific information about the element, and
- Other supporting evidence that is sufficient to establish the element.

Destroyed records. If you cannot produce a receipt because of reasons beyond your control, you can prove a deduction by reconstructing your records or expenses. Reasons beyond your control include fire, flood, and other casualty.

Separating and Combining Expenses

This section explains when expenses must be kept separate and when expenses can be combined.

Separating expenses. Each separate payment is generally considered a separate expense. For example, if you entertain a customer or client at dinner and then go to the theater, the dinner expense and the cost of the theater tickets are two separate expenses. You must record them separately in your records.

Combining items. You can make one daily entry in your record for reasonable categories of expenses. Examples are taxi fares, telephone calls, or other incidental travel costs. Meals should be in a separate category. You can include tips for meal-related services with the costs of the meals.

Expenses of a similar nature occurring during the course of a single event are considered a single expense. For example, if during entertainment at a cocktail lounge, you pay separately for each serving of refreshments, the total expense for the refreshments is treated as a single expense.

Allocating total cost. If you can prove the total cost of travel or entertainment but you cannot prove how much it cost for each person who participated in the event, you may have to allocate the total cost among you and your guests on a pro rata basis. An allocation would be needed, for example, if you did not have a business relationship with all of your guests.

If your return is examined. If your return is examined, you may have to provide additional information to the IRS. This information could be needed to clarify or to establish the accuracy or reliability of information contained in your records, statements, testimony, or documentary evidence before a deduction is allowed.

How Long To Keep Records and Receipts

You must keep records as long as they may be needed for the administration of any provision of the Internal Revenue Code. Generally, this means you must keep your records that support your deduction (or an item of income) for 3 years from the date you file the income tax return on which the deduction is claimed. A return filed early is considered filed on the due date. For a more complete explanation, see Publication 583, *Starting a Business and Keeping Records*.

EXPLANATION

If you use your automobile less than 50% for business and claim actual expenses, you must keep those records for at least 6 years (i.e., more than the recovery period for straight-line depreciation).

Reimbursed for expenses. Employees who give their records and documentation to their employers and are reimbursed for their expenses generally do not have to keep copies of this information. However, you may have to prove your expenses if any of the following conditions apply.

- You claim deductions for expenses that are more than reimbursements.
- Your expenses are reimbursed under a nonaccountable plan.
- Your employer does not use adequate accounting procedures to verify expense accounts.
- You are related to your employer, as defined later under <u>*Related to employer*</u>.

See the next section, <u>*How To Report*</u>, for a discussion of reimbursements, adequate accounting, and nonaccountable plans.

EXPLANATION

If you have expenses greater than your reimbursement and want to deduct them, you are required to put a statement in your tax return showing the total of all expenses you incurred and all reimbursements you received for that year. This information may be given in broad categories, such as transportation, meals, and lodging while away from home overnight, entertainment expenses, and other business expenses. The statement must show the total of any charges paid or borne directly by your employer through credit cards or any other means. See Records for more details.

Self-employed persons and independent contractors must be able to show that the expenses were directly related to, or associated with, their business.

Example

An accountant was not allowed to deduct expenses incurred at a country club because she failed to indicate the business purpose of the activities that generated the expenses and she did not maintain a detailed record of the persons entertained on each occasion. Lacking any documentation to the contrary, a court concluded that there was a likelihood that the expenses were at least partially personal.

Additional information. Chapter 5 of Publication 463 has more information on recordkeeping, including examples.

How To Report

This section explains where and how to report the expenses discussed in this chapter. It discusses reimbursements and how to treat them under accountable and nonaccountable plans. It also explains rules for independent contractors and clients, fee-basis officials, certain performing artists, Armed Forces reservists, and certain disabled employees. This section ends with an illustration of how to report travel, entertainment, gift, and car expenses on Form 2106-EZ.

EXPLANATION

Employees receiving the standard meal allowance under a nonaccountable plan (discussed later) may claim 50% of the standard meal allowance as a miscellaneous itemized deduction, subject to the 2% limitation. Reimbursements under accountable plans are not included in the employee's taxable compensation. Therefore, such employees receive no deduction, and the 50% limitation applies to the employer's deduction.

Self-employed. You must report your income and expenses on Schedule C or C-EZ (Form 1040) if you are a sole proprietor, or on Schedule F (Form 1040) if you are a farmer. You do not use Form 2106 or 2106-EZ. See your form instructions for information on how to complete your tax return. You can also find information in Publication 535 if you are a sole proprietor, or in Publication 225, *Farmer's Tax Guide*, if you are a farmer.

Both self-employed and an employee. If you are both self-employed and an employee, you must keep separate records for each business activity. Report your business expenses for self-employment on Schedule C, C-EZ, or F (Form 1040), as discussed earlier. Report your business expenses for your work as an employee on Form 2106 or 2106-EZ, as discussed next.

Employees. If you are an employee, you generally must complete Form 2106 to deduct your travel, transportation, and entertainment expenses. However, you can use the shorter Form 2106-EZ instead of Form 2106 if you meet all of the following conditions.

- You are an employee deducting expenses attributable to your job.
- You were not reimbursed by your employer for your expenses (amounts included in box 1 of your Form W-2 are not considered reimbursements).
- If you claim car expenses, you use the standard mileage rate.

For more information on how to report your expenses on Forms 2106 and 2106-EZ, see Completing Forms 2106 and 2106-EZ, later.

Gifts. If you did not receive any reimbursements (or the reimbursements were all included in box 1 of your Form W-2), the only business expense you are claiming is for gifts, and the rules for certain individuals (such as performing artists) discussed later under *Special Rules* do not apply to you, do not complete Form 2106 or 2106-EZ. Instead, claim the amount of your deductible gifts directly on line 21 of Schedule A (Form 1040).

Statutory employees. If you received a Form W-2 and the "Statutory employee" box in box 13 was checked, report your income and expenses related to that income on Schedule C or C-EZ (Form 1040). Do not complete Form 2106 or 2106-EZ.

Statutory employees include full-time life insurance salespersons, certain agent or commission drivers, traveling salespersons, and certain homeworkers.

EXAMPLES

Example 1

John Smith, a salesman working on behalf of a principal, solicits orders from wholesalers and restaurants for merchandise intended for resale. John reports his income and expenses on Schedule C as a statutory employee.

Example 2

An agent-driver engaged in distributing meat, vegetables, bakery goods, beverages (other than milk), or dry cleaning services is classified as a statutory employee.

Caution

If you are entitled to a reimbursement from your employer but you do not claim it, you cannot claim a deduction for the expenses to which that unclaimed reimbursement applies.

EXPLANATION

While you may not claim a deduction for an expense that your employer would reimburse, you may be entitled to a deduction for a work-related expense that you feel was necessary to do your job but that your employer does not reimburse.

Example

You are a technician who works in a laboratory in which your employer requires you to wear a certain type of uniform while on the job. The uniform is unsuitable for street wear. Your employer refuses to reimburse you for the cost of the uniform. You are entitled to deduct the expense on your own income tax return.

Reimbursement for personal expenses. If your employer reimburses you for nondeductible personal expenses, such as for vacation trips, your employer must report the reimbursement as wage income in box 1 of your Form W-2. You cannot deduct personal expenses.

Reimbursements

This section explains what to do when you receive an advance or are reimbursed for any of the employee business expenses discussed in this chapter.

TAXSAVER

If the various requirements discussed later are met, reimbursements are excluded from the employee's gross income for income tax as well as employment tax purposes. Amounts considered paid under a nonaccountable plan are subject to income tax as well as to employment taxes. A tax deduction is allowable as a miscellaneous itemized deduction, subject to applicable limitations, for employee business expenses reimbursed under a nonaccountable plan.

If you received an advance, allowance, or reimbursement for your expenses, how you report this amount and your expenses depends on whether the reimbursement was paid to you under an accountable plan or a nonaccountable plan.

This section explains the two types of plans, how per diem and car allowances simplify proving the amount of your expenses, and the tax treatment of your reimbursements and expenses.

No reimbursement. You are not reimbursed or given an allowance for your expenses if you are paid a salary or commission with the understanding that you will pay your own expenses. In this situation, you have no reimbursement or allowance arrangement, and you do not have to read this section on reimbursements. Instead, see *Completing Forms 2106 and 2106-EZ*, later, for information on completing your tax return.

TAXSAVER

You may claim a deduction for business expenses even if you don't receive specific reimbursements from your employer. You should have your employer supply you with a written document explaining that your compensation plan is based on the expectation that you will incur various travel, transportation, automobile, entertainment, and business gift expenses.

Travel, transportation, automobile expenses, entertainment, business gifts, and other expenses should be reported as miscellaneous deductions on Schedule A of Form 1040.

If you are repeatedly spending money for business expenses, it is probably advantageous for you to make an arrangement with your employer to adjust your salary and/or commission downward and to give you an expense allowance. This could help you justify your deductions if you are subject to an IRS examination.

Reimbursement, allowance, or advance. A reimbursement or other expense allowance arrangement is a system or plan that an employer uses to pay, substantiate, and recover the expenses, advances, reimbursements, and amounts charged to the employer for employee business expenses. Arrangements include per diem and car allowances.

A per diem allowance is a fixed amount of daily reimbursement your employer gives you for your lodging, meal, and incidental expenses when you are away from home on business. (The term "incidental expenses" is defined earlier under *Meals and Incidental Expenses*.) A car allowance is an amount your employer gives you for the business use of your car.

Your employer should tell you what method of reimbursement is used and what records you must provide.

Accountable Plans

To be an accountable plan, your employer's reimbursement or allowance arrangement must include all of the following rules.

1. Your expenses must have a business connection — that is, you must have paid or incurred deductible expenses while performing services as an employee of your employer.
2. You must adequately account to your employer for these expenses within a reasonable period of time.
3. You must return any excess reimbursement or allowance within a reasonable period of time.

See *Adequate Accounting* and *Returning Excess Reimbursements*, later.

EXPLANATION

For a reimbursement or other expense allowance arrangement to be an accountable plan, it must satisfy the substantiation requirement. Generally, for each expense item and for each business use, the employee must report the amount, time, place, and business purpose.

Example 1

An employer proposed to reimburse its district manager's business expenses in lieu of paying additional salary. This would result in a portion of the district manager's salary being recharacterized as paid under a reimbursement or other expense allowance arrangement, and, thus, it would fail the reimbursement requirement. Therefore, the reimbursements would be subject to employment taxes since they would not be paid under an arrangement that is an accountable plan.

Example 2

Where a taxpayer did not substantiate expenses or return excess allowance amounts, such amounts were paid under a nonaccountable plan and, thus, were includible in gross income.

Exception 1

The substantiation requirement for expense amounts related to business meals and lodging can be satisfied by using a per diem allowance. Per diem reimbursements of such expenses are not included in taxable income to the extent of the government rate.

Exception 2

The substantiation requirement for expenses relating to the business use of an employee's private automobile can be satisfied by using the standard mileage rates for 2011 of 51 cents per mile prior to June 30, 2011, and 55.5 cents after June 30, 2011, or the fixed-and-variable-rate allowance. Under the fixed-and-variable-rate allowance method, an employer reimburses an employee's business mileage expenses using a flat rate or a stated schedule of fixed and variable rate payments that incorporates specific rules to approximate the employee's actual automobile expenses.

An excess reimbursement or allowance is any amount you are paid that is more than the business-related expenses that you adequately accounted for to your employer.

The definition of a reasonable period of time depends on the facts and circumstances of your situation. However, regardless of the facts and circumstances of your situation, actions that take place within the times specified in the following list will be treated as taking place within a reasonable period of time.

1. You receive an advance within 30 days of the time you have an expense.
2. You adequately account for your expenses within 60 days after they were paid or incurred.
3. You return any excess reimbursement within 120 days after the expense was paid or incurred.
4. You are given a periodic statement (at least quarterly) that asks you to either return or adequately account for outstanding advances and you comply within 120 days of the statement.

TAXALERT

It is imperative that the substantiation be done and that excess amounts are returned within a reasonable period of time. If the reasonable time requirement is not met, the unsubstantiated or excess amounts are treated as reimbursements under a nonaccountable plan.

Employee meets accountable plan rules. If you meet the three rules for accountable plans, your employer should not include any reimbursements in your income in box 1 of your Form W-2. If your expenses equal your reimbursement, you do not complete Form 2106. You have no deduction since your expenses and reimbursement are equal.

Caution

If your employer included reimbursements in box 1 of your Form W-2 and you meet all the rules for accountable plans, ask your employer for a corrected Form W-2.

Accountable plan rules not met. Even though you are reimbursed under an accountable plan, some of your expenses may not meet all the rules. Those expenses that fail to meet all three rules for accountable plans are treated as having been reimbursed under a nonaccountable plan (discussed later).

TAXPLANNER

A plan providing per diem allowances or mileage allowances that are reasonably calculated not to exceed the employee's expenses will satisfy the requirement for the return of excess reimbursement, even though the employee is not required to return the excess allowance. However, the employee must return the portion of the allowance attributable to unsubstantiated days or miles of travel.

Example

An employee receives a monthly mileage allowance of $204, based on anticipated business miles of 400 per month for months January through June, reimbursed at the rate of 51 cents per mile. The 51-cent-per-mile rate is reasonably calculated not to exceed the employee's expenses. The employee travels and substantiates only 300 business miles. The requirement to return the excess is satisfied if the employee is required to return the $51 (100 miles x 51 cents) advance allowance that is attributable to the 100 unsubstantiated business miles.

Reimbursement of nondeductible expenses. You may be reimbursed under your employer's accountable plan for expenses related to that employer's business, some of which are deductible as employee business expenses and some of which are not deductible. The reimbursements you receive for the nondeductible expenses do not meet rule (1) for accountable plans, and they are treated as paid under a nonaccountable plan.

Example. Your employer's plan reimburses you for travel expenses while away from home on business and also for meals when you work late at the office, even though you are not away from home. The part of the arrangement that reimburses you for the nondeductible meals when you work late at the office is treated as paid under a nonaccountable plan.

Tip

The employer makes the decision whether to reimburse employees under an accountable plan or a nonaccountable plan. If you are an employee who receives payments under a nonaccountable plan, you cannot convert these amounts to payments under an accountable plan by voluntarily accounting to your employer for the expenses and voluntarily returning excess reimbursements to the employer.

Adequate Accounting

One of the rules for an accountable plan is that you must adequately account to your employer for your expenses. You adequately account by giving your employer a statement of expense, an account book, a diary, or a similar record in which you entered each expense at or near the time you had it, along with documentary evidence (such as receipts) of your travel, mileage, and other employee business expenses. (See Table 27-2, earlier, for details you need to enter in your record and documents you need to prove certain expenses.) A per diem or car allowance satisfies the adequate accounting requirement under certain conditions. See *Per Diem and Car Allowances*, later.

You must account for all amounts you received from your employer during the year as advances, reimbursements, or allowances. This includes amounts you charged to your employer by credit card or other method. You must give your employer the same type of records and supporting information that you would have to give to the IRS if the IRS questioned a deduction on your return. You must pay back the amount of any reimbursement or other expense allowance for which you do not adequately account or that is more than the amount for which you accounted.

Per Diem and Car Allowances

If your employer reimburses you for your expenses using a per diem or car allowance, you can generally use the allowance as proof of the amount of your expenses. A per diem or car allowance satisfies the adequate accounting requirements for the amount of your expenses only if all the following conditions apply.

- Your employer reasonably limits payments of your expenses to those that are ordinary and necessary in the conduct of the trade or business.
- The allowance is similar in form to and not more than the federal rate (discussed later).
- You prove the time (dates), place, and business purpose of your expenses to your employer (as explained in Table 27-2) within a reasonable period of time.
- You are not related to your employer (as defined next). If you are related to your employer, you must be able to prove your expenses to the IRS even if you have already adequately accounted to your employer and returned any excess reimbursement.

If the IRS finds that an employer's travel allowance practices are not based on reasonably accurate estimates of travel costs (including recognition of cost differences in different areas for per diem amounts), you will not be considered to have accounted to your employer. In this case, you must be able to prove your expenses to the IRS.

Related to employer. You are related to your employer if:

1. Your employer is your brother or sister, half brother or half sister, spouse, ancestor, or lineal descendant,
2. Your employer is a corporation in which you own, directly or indirectly, more than 10% in value of the outstanding stock, or
3. Certain relationships (such as grantor, fiduciary, or beneficiary) exist between you, a trust, and your employer.

You may be considered to indirectly own stock, for purposes of (2), if you have an interest in a corporation, partnership, estate, or trust that owns the stock or if a member of your family or your partner owns the stock.

The federal rate. The federal rate can be figured using any one of the following methods.

1. For per diem amounts:
   a. The regular federal per diem rate.
   b. The standard meal allowance.
   c. The high-low rate.
2. For car expenses:
   a. The standard mileage rate.
   b. A fixed and variable rate (FAVR).

Regular federal per diem rate. The regular federal per diem rate is the highest amount that the federal government will pay to its employees for lodging, meal, and incidental expenses (or meal and incidental expenses only) while they are traveling away from home in a particular area. The rates are different for different locations. Your employer should have these rates available. (Employers can get Publication 1542 on the Internet, which gives the rates in the continental United States for the current year.)

Tip

For per diem amounts, use the rate in effect for the area where you stop for sleep or rest.

The standard meal allowance. The standard meal allowance (discussed earlier) is the federal rate for meals and incidental expenses (M&IE). The rate for most small localities in the United States is $46 a day. Most major cities and many other localities qualify for higher rates. The rates for all localities within the continental United States are listed in Publication 1542. You can also find this information on the Internet at www.gsa.gov.

You receive an allowance only for meals and incidental expenses when your employer does one of the following.

- Provides you with lodging (furnishes it in kind).
- Reimburses you, based on your receipts, for the actual cost of your lodging.
- Pays the hotel, motel, etc., directly for your lodging.
- Does not have a reasonable belief that you had (or will have) lodging expenses, such as when you stay with friends or relatives or sleep in the cab of your truck.
- Figures the allowance on a basis similar to that used in computing your compensation, such as number of hours worked or miles traveled.

High-low rate. This is a simplified method of computing the federal per diem rate for travel within the continental United States. It elimina tes the need to keep a current list of the per diem rate for each city.

Under the high-low method, the per diem amount for travel during January through September of 2011 is $233 (including $65 for M&IE) for certain high-cost locations. All other areas have a per diem amount of $160 (including $52 for M&IE). (Employers can get Publication 1542 which gives the areas eligible for the $233 per diem amount under the high-low method for all or part of this period.)

Caution

Text intentionally omitted.

TAXALERT

The per diem amounts effective after October 1, 2011, increase from $233 to $242 for high cost areas of travel and from $160 to $163 for any other travel locations within the continental United States. The rate that applies to meals and incidental expenses remains at $65 for high-cost localities and $52 for other locations. The incidental-expense-only per diem rate remains at $5.

Prorating the standard meal allowance on partial days of travel. The standard meal allowance is for a full 24-hour day of travel. If you travel for part of a day, such as on the days you depart and return, you must prorate the full-day M&IE rate. This rule also applies if your employer uses the regular federal per diem rate or the high-low rate.

You can use either of the following methods to figure the federal M&IE for that day.

1. *Method 1*:
   a. For the day you depart, add ¾ of the standard meal allowance amount for that day.
   b. For the day you return, add ¾ of the standard meal allowance amount for the preceding day.
2. *Method 2:* Prorate the standard meal allowance using any method you consistently apply in accordance with reasonable business practice.

The standard mileage rate. This is a set rate per mile that you can use to compute your deductible car expenses. For 2011, the standard mileage rate for the cost of operating your car is 51 cents per mile from January 1, 2011, through June 30, 2011, and 55.5 cents per mile from July 1, 2011, through December 31, 2011.

Fixed and variable rate (FAVR). This is an allowance your employer may use to reimburse your car expenses. Under this method, your employer pays an allowance that includes a combination of payments covering fixed and variable costs, such as a cents-per-mile rate to cover your variable operating costs (such as gas, oil, etc.) plus a flat amount to cover your fixed costs (such as depreciation (or lease payments), insurance, etc.). If your employer chooses to use this method, your employer will request the necessary records from you.

Reporting your expenses with a per diem or car allowance. If your reimbursement is in the form of an allowance received under an accountable plan, the following facts affect your reporting.

- The federal rate.
- Whether the allowance or your actual expenses were more than the federal rate.

The following discussions explain where to report your expenses depending upon how the amount of your allowance compares to the federal rate.

Allowance less than or equal to the federal rate. If your allowance is less than or equal to the federal rate, the allowance will not be included in box 1 of your Form W-2. You do not need to report the related expenses or the allowance on your return if your expenses are equal to or less than the allowance.

However, if your actual expenses are more than your allowance, you can complete Form 2106 and deduct the excess amount on Schedule A (Form 1040). If you are using actual expenses, you must be able to prove to the IRS the total amount of your expenses and reimbursements for the entire year. If you are using the standard meal allowance or the standard mileage rate, you do not have to prove that amount.

Example. Nicole drives 10,000 miles in 2011 for business (5,000 miles before July 1 and 5,000 miles thereafter through the end of the year). Under her employer's accountable plan, she accounts for the time (dates), place, and business purpose of each trip. Her employer pays her a mileage allowance of 40 cents a mile.

Since Nicole's $5,325 expense computed under the standard mileage rate (5,000 × 51 cents for miles prior to June and 5,000 × 55.5 cents for miles after June) is more than her $4,000 reimbursement (10,000 miles × 40 cents), she itemizes her deductions to claim the excess expense. Nicole completes Form 2106 (showing all her expenses and reimbursements) and enters $1,325 ($5,325 – $4,000) as an itemized deduction.

Allowance more than the federal rate. If your allowance is more than the federal rate, your employer must include the allowance amount up to the federal rate in box 12 of your Form W-2. This amount is not taxable. However, the excess allowance will be included in box 1 of your Form W-2. You must report this part of your allowance as if it were wage income.

If your actual expenses are less than or equal to the federal rate, you do not complete Form 2106 or claim any of your expenses on your return.

However, if your actual expenses are more than the federal rate, you can complete Form 2106 and deduct those excess expenses. You must report on Form 2106 your reimbursements up to the federal rate (as shown in box 12 of your Form W-2) and all your expenses. You should be able to prove these amounts to the IRS.

Example. Joe lives and works in Austin. In May his employer sent him to San Diego for 4 days and paid the hotel directly for Joe's hotel bill. The employer reimbursed Joe $75 a day for his meals and incidental expenses. The federal rate for San Diego is $71 a day.

Joe can prove that his actual meal expenses totaled $380. His employer's accountable plan will not pay more than $75 a day for travel to San Diego, so Joe does not give his employer the records that prove that he actually spent $380. However, he does account for the time, place, and business purpose of the trip. This is Joe's only business trip this year.

Joe was reimbursed $300 ($75 × 4 days), which is $16 more than the federal rate of $284 ($71 × 4 days). His employer includes the $16 as income on Joe's Form W-2 in box 1. His employer also enters $284 in box 12 of Joe's Form W-2.

Joe completes Form 2106 to figure his deductible expenses. He enters the total of his actual expenses for the year ($380) on Form 2106. He also enters the reimbursements that were not included in his income ($284). His total deductible expense, before the 50% limit, is $96. After he figures the 50% limit on his un-reimbursed meals and entertainment, he will include the balance, $48, as an itemized deduction on Schedule A (Form 1040).

Returning Excess Reimbursements

Under an accountable plan, you are required to return any excess reimbursement or other expense allowances for your business expenses to the person paying the reimbursement or allowance. Excess reimbursement means any amount for which you did not adequately account within a reasonable period of time. For example, if you received a travel advance and you did not spend all the money on business-related expenses or you do not have proof of all your expenses, you have an excess reimbursement.

"Adequate accounting" and "reasonable period of time" were discussed earlier in this chapter.

Travel advance. You receive a travel advance if your employer provides you with an expense allowance before you actually have the expense, and the allowance is reasonably expected to be no more than your expense. Under an accountable plan, you are required to adequately account to your employer for this advance and to return any excess within a reasonable period of time.

If you do not adequately account for or do not return any excess advance within a reasonable period of time, the amount you do not account for or return will be treated as having been paid under a nonaccountable plan (discussed later).

Unproven amounts. If you do not prove that you actually traveled on each day for which you received a per diem or car allowance (proving the elements described in Table 27-2), you must return this unproved amount of the travel advance within a reasonable period of time. If you do not do this, the unproved amount will be considered paid under a nonaccountable plan (discussed later).

Per diem allowance more than federal rate. If your employer's accountable plan pays you an allowance that is higher than the federal rate, you do not have to return the difference between the two rates for the period you can prove business-related travel expenses. However, the difference will be reported as wages on your Form W-2. This excess amount is considered paid under a nonaccountable plan (discussed later).

Example. Your employer sends you on a 5-day business trip to Phoenix in March 2011 and gives you a $400 ($80 × 5 days) advance to cover your meals and incidental expenses. The federal per diem for meals and incidental expenses for Phoenix is $71. Your trip lasts only 3 days. Under your employer's accountable plan, you must return the $160 ($80 × 2 days) advance for the 2 days you did not travel. For the 3 days you did travel you do not have to return the $27 difference between the allowance you received and the federal rate for Phoenix (($80 – $71) × 3 days). However, the $27 will be reported on your Form W-2 as wages.

Nonaccountable Plans

A nonaccountable plan is a reimbursement or expense allowance arrangement that does not meet one or more of the three rules listed earlier under *Accountable Plans*.

In addition, even if your employer has an accountable plan, the following payments will be treated as being paid under a nonaccountable plan.

- Excess reimbursements you fail to return to your employer.
- Reimbursement of nondeductible expenses related to your employer's business. See *Reimbursement of nondeductible expenses* earlier under *Accountable Plans*.

If you are not sure if the reimbursement or expense allowance arrangement is an accountable or nonaccountable plan, ask your employer.

Reporting your expenses under a nonaccountable plan. Your employer will combine the amount of any reimbursement or other expense allowance paid to you under a nonaccountable plan with your wages, salary, or other pay. Your employer will report the total in box 1 of your Form W-2.

You must complete Form 2106 or 2106-EZ and itemize your deductions to deduct your expenses for travel, transportation, meals, or entertainment. Your meal and entertainment expenses will be subject to the 50% limit discussed earlier under *Entertainment Expenses*. Also, your total expenses will be subject to the 2%-of-adjusted-gross-income limit that applies to most miscellaneous itemized deductions on Schedule A (Form 1040).

Example. Kim's employer gives her $1,000 a month ($12,000 for the year) for her business expenses. Kim does not have to provide any proof of her expenses to her employer, and Kim can keep any funds that she does not spend.

Kim is being reimbursed under a nonaccountable plan. Her employer will include the $12,000 on Kim's Form W-2 as if it were wages. If Kim wants to deduct her business expenses, she must complete Form 2106 or 2106-EZ and itemize her deductions.

Completing Forms 2106 and 2106-EZ

This section briefly describes how employees complete Forms 2106 and 2106-EZ. Table 27-3 explains what the employer reports on Form W-2 and what the employee reports on Form 2106. The instructions for the forms have more information on completing them.

Caution

If you are self-employed, do not file Form 2106 or 2106-EZ. Report your expenses on Schedule C, C-EZ, or F (Form 1040). See the instructions for the form that you must file.

Form 2106-EZ. You may be able to use the shorter Form 2106-EZ to claim your employee business expenses. You can use this form if you meet all the following conditions.

- You are an employee deducting expenses attributable to your job.
- You were not reimbursed by your employer for your expenses (amounts included in box 1 of your Form W-2 are not considered reimbursements).
- If you are claiming car expenses, you use the standard mileage rate.

Car expenses. If you used a car to perform your job as an employee, you may be able to deduct certain car expenses. These are generally figured on Form 2106, Part II, and then claimed on Form 2106, Part I, line 1, Column A. Car expenses using the standard mileage rate can also be figured on Form 2106-EZ by completing Part II and Part I, line 1.

Transportation expenses. Show your transportation expenses that did not involve overnight travel on Form 2106, line 2, Column A, or on Form 2106-EZ, Part I, line 2. Also include on this line business expenses you have for parking fees and tolls. Do not include expenses of operating your car or expenses of commuting between your home and work.

Tip

If line 4 expenses are the only ones you are claiming, you received no reimbursements (or the reimbursements were all included in box 1 of your Form W-2), and the Special Rules *discussed later do not apply to you, do not complete Form 2106 or 2106-EZ. Claim these amounts directly on Schedule A (Form 1040), line 21. List the type and amount of each expense on the dotted lines and include the total on line 21.*

Employee business expenses other than meals and entertainment. Show your other employee business expenses on Form 2106, lines 3 and 4, Column A, or Form 2106-EZ, lines 3 and 4. Do not include expenses for meals and entertainment on those lines. Line 4 is for expenses such as gifts, educational expenses (tuition and books), office-in-the-home expenses, and trade and professional publications.

Meal and entertainment expenses. Show the full amount of your expenses for business-related meals and entertainment on Form 2106, line 5, Column B. Include meals while away from your tax home overnight and other business meals and entertainment. Enter 50% of the line 8, Column B, meal and entertainment expenses on line 9, Column B.

If you file Form 2106-EZ, enter the full amount of your meals and entertainment on the line to the left of line 5 and multiply the total by 50%. Enter the result on line 5.

Hours of service limits. If you are subject to the Department of Transportation's "hours of service" limits, use 80% instead of 50% for meals while away from your tax home.

Reimbursements. Enter on Form 2106, line 7, the amounts your employer (or third party) reimbursed you that were not included in box 1 of your Form W-2. (You cannot use Form 2106-EZ.) This includes any reimbursement reported under code L in box 12 of Form W-2.

Allocating your reimbursement. If you were reimbursed under an accountable plan and want to deduct excess expenses that were not reimbursed, you may have to allocate your reimbursement. This is necessary if your employer pays your reimbursement in the following manner:

- Pays you a single amount that covers meals and/or entertainment, as well as other business expenses, and
- Does not clearly identify how much is for deductible meals and/or entertainment.

You must allocate that single payment so that you know how much to enter on Form 2106, line 7, Column A and Column B.

Example. Rob's employer paid him an expense allowance of $12,000 this year under an accountable plan. The $12,000 payment consisted of $5,000 for airfare and $7,000 for entertainment and car expenses. Rob's employer did not clearly show how much of the $7,000 was for the cost of deductible entertainment. Rob actually spent $14,000 during the year ($5,500 for airfare, $4,500 for entertainment, and $4,000 for car expenses).

Table 27-3. **Reporting Travel, Entertainment, Gift, and Car Expenses and Reimbursements**

IF the type of reimbursement (or other expense allowance) arrangement is under:	THEN the employer reports on Form W-2:	AND the employee reports on Form 2106:*
An accountable plan with:		
Actual expense reimbursement: Adequate accounting made and excess returned.	No amount.	No amount.
Actual expense reimbursement: Adequate accounting and return of excess both required but excess not returned.	The excess amount as wages in box 1.	No amount.
Per diem or mileage allowance up to the federal rate: Adequate accounting made and excess returned.	No amount.	All expenses and reimbursements only if excess expenses are claimed. Otherwise, form is not filed.
Per diem or mileage allowance up to the federal rate: Adequate accounting and return of excess both required but excess not returned.	The excess amount as wages in box 1. The amount up to the federal rate is reported only in box 12–it is not reported in box 1.	No amount.
Per diem or mileage allowance exceeds the federal rate: Adequate accounting up to the federal rate only and excess not returned.	The excess amount as wages in box 1. The amount up to the federal rate is reported only in box 12–it is not reported in box 1.	All expenses (and reimbursement reported on Form W-2, box 12) only if expenses in excess of the federal rate are claimed. Otherwise, form is not required.
A nonaccountable plan with:		
Either adequate accounting or return of excess, or both, not required by plan	The entire amount as wages in box 1.	All expenses.
No reimbursement plan:	The entire amount as wages in box 1.	All expenses.

* You may be able to use Form 2106-EZ. See *Completing Forms 2106 and 2106-EZ*.

Since the airfare allowance was clearly identified, Rob knows that $5,000 of the payment goes in Column A, line 7 of Form 2106. To allocate the remaining $7,000, Rob uses the worksheet from the instructions for Form 2106. His completed worksheet follows.

Reimbursement Allocation Worksheet (keep for your records)		
1.	Enter the total amount of reimbursements your employer gave you that were not reported to you in box 1 of Form W-2	$7,000
2.	Enter the total amount of your expenses for the periods covered by this reimbursement	8,500
3.	Of the amount on line 2, enter your total expense for meals and entertainment	4,500
4.	Divide line 3 by line 2. Enter the result as a decimal (rounded to at least three places)	.529
5.	Multiply line 1 by line 4. Enter the result here and in Column B, line 7	3,703
6.	Subtract line 5 from line 1. Enter the result here and in Column A, line 7	$3,297

On line 7 of Form 2106, Rob enters $8,297 ($5,000 airfare and $3,297 of the $7,000) in Column A and $3,703 (of the $7,000) in Column B.

After you complete the form. After you have completed your Form 2106 or 2106-EZ, follow the directions on that form to deduct your expenses on the appropriate line of your tax return. For most taxpayers, this is line 21 of Schedule A (Form 1040). However, if you are a government official paid on a fee basis, a performing artist, an Armed Forces reservist, or a disabled employee with impairment-related work expenses, see Special Rules, later.

Limits on employee business expenses. Your employee business expenses may be subject to either of the limits described next. These limits are figured in the following order on the specified form.

1. Limit on meals and entertainment. Certain meal and entertainment expenses are subject to a 50% limit. If you are an employee, you figure this limit on line 9 of Form 2106 or line 5 of Form 2106-EZ. See 50% Limit under *Entertainment Expenses,* earlier.

2. Limit on miscellaneous itemized deductions. If you are an employee, deduct employee business expenses (as figured on Form 2106 or 2106-EZ) on line 21 of Schedule A (Form 1040). Most miscellaneous itemized deductions, including employee business expenses, are subject to a 2% limit. This limit is figured on line 26 of Schedule A (Form 1040).

Special Rules

This section discusses special rules that apply to Armed Forces reservists, government officials who are paid on a fee basis, performing artists, and disabled employees with impairment-related work expenses.

Armed Forces reservists traveling more than 100 miles from home. If you are a member of a reserve component of the Armed Forces of the United States and you travel more than 100 miles away from home in connection with your performance of services as a member of the reserves, you can deduct your travel expenses as an adjustment to gross income rather than as a miscellaneous itemized deduction. The amount of expenses you can deduct as an adjustment to gross income is limited to the regular federal per diem rate (for lodging, meals, and incidental expenses) and the standard mileage rate (for car expenses) plus any parking fees, ferry fees, and tolls. The federal rate is explained earlier under Per Diem and Car Allowances. Any expenses in excess of these amounts can be claimed only as a miscellaneous itemized deduction subject to the 2% limit.

Member of a reserve component. You are a member of a reserve component of the Armed Forces of the United States if you are in the Army, Navy, Marine Corps, Air Force, or Coast Guard Reserve, the Army National Guard of the United States, the Air National Guard of the United States, or the Reserve Corps of the Public Health Service.

How to report. If you have reserve-related travel that takes you more than 100 miles from home, you should first complete Form 2106 or Form 2106-EZ. Then include your expenses for reserve travel over 100 miles from home, up to the federal rate, from Form 2106, line 10, or Form 2106-EZ, line 6, in the total on Form 1040, line 24. Subtract this amount from the total on Form 2106, line 10, or Form 2106-EZ, line 6, and deduct the balance as an itemized deduction on Schedule A (Form 1040), line 21.

You cannot deduct expenses of travel that does not take you more than 100 miles from home as an adjustment to gross income. Instead, you must complete Form 2106 or 2106-EZ and deduct those expenses as an itemized deduction on Schedule A (Form 1040), line 21.

Officials paid on a fee basis. Certain fee-basis officials can claim their employee business expenses whether or not they itemize their other deductions on Schedule A (Form 1040).

Fee-basis officials are persons who are employed by a state or local government and who are paid in whole or in part on a fee basis. They can deduct their business expenses in performing services in that job as an adjustment to gross income rather than as a miscellaneous itemized deduction.

If you are a fee-basis official, include your employee business expenses from Form 2106, line 10, or Form 2106-EZ, line 6, on Form 1040, line 24.

Expenses of certain performing artists. If you are a performing artist, you may qualify to deduct your employee business expenses as an adjustment to gross income rather than as a miscellaneous itemized deduction. To qualify, you must meet all of the following requirements.

1. During the tax year, you perform services in the performing arts as an employee for at least two employers.
2. You receive at least $200 each from any two of these employers.
3. Your related performing-arts business expenses are more than 10% of your gross income from the performance of those services.
4. Your adjusted gross income is not more than $16,000 before deducting these business expenses.

Special rules for married persons. If you are married, you must file a joint return unless you lived apart from your spouse at all times during the tax year.

If you file a joint return, you must figure requirements (1), (2), and (3) separately for both you and your spouse. However, requirement (4) applies to your and your spouse's combined adjusted gross income.

Where to report. If you meet all of the above requirements, you should first complete Form 2106 or 2106-EZ. Then you include your performing-arts-related expenses from line 10 of Form 2106 or line 6 of Form 2106-EZ in the total on line 24 of Form 1040.

If you do not meet all of the above requirements, you do not qualify to deduct your expenses as an adjustment to gross income. Instead, you must complete Form 2106 or 2106-EZ and deduct your employee business expenses as an itemized deduction on Schedule A (Form 1040), line 21.

Impairment-related work expenses of disabled employees. If you are an employee with a physical or mental disability, your impairment-related work expenses are not subject to the 2%-of-adjusted-gross-income limit that applies to most other employee business expenses. After you complete Form 2106 or 2106-EZ, enter your impairment-related work expenses from Form 2106, line 10, or Form 2106-EZ, line 6, on Schedule A (Form 1040), line 28, and identify the type and amount of this expense on the dotted line next to line 28. Enter your employee business expenses that are unrelated to your disability from Form 2106, line 10, or Form 2106-EZ, line 6, on Schedule A, line 21.

Impairment-related work expenses are your allowable expenses for attendant care at your workplace and other expenses you have in connection with your workplace that are necessary for you to be able to work. For more information, see chapter 21.

Illustrated Example

Bill Wilson is an employee of Fashion Clothing Co. in Manhattan, NY. In a typical travel week, Bill leaves his home on Long Island on Monday morning and drives to Albany to exhibit the Fashion line for 3 days to prospective customers. Then he drives to Troy to show Fashion's new line of merchandise to Town Department Store, an old customer. While in Troy, he talks with Tom Brown, purchasing agent for Town Department Store, to discuss the new line. He later takes John Smith of Attire Co. out to dinner to discuss Attire Co.'s buying Fashion's new line of clothing.

Bill purchased his car on January 3, 2007. He uses the standard mileage rate for car expense purposes. He records his total mileage, business mileage, parking fees, and tolls for the year. Bill records his expenses and other pertinent information in a travel expense log (not shown). He obtains receipts for his expenses for lodging and for any other expenses of $75 or more.

During the year, Bill drove a total of 25,000 miles of which 20,000 miles were for business (incurred pro rata throughout the year). He answers all the questions in Part II of Form 2106-EZ and figures his car expense to be $10,600 (10,000 × 51 cents per mile through June and 10,000 × 55.5 cents per mile after June).

His total employee business expenses are shown in the following table.

Type of Expense	Amount
Parking fees and tolls	$520
Car expenses	10,600
Meals	3,861
Lodging, laundry, dry cleaning	18,318
Entertainment	3,250
Gifts, education, etc.	650
Total	**$37,199**

Bill received an allowance of $33,000 ($2,750 per month) to help offset his expenses. Bill did not have to account to his employer for the reimbursement, and the $33,000 was included as income in box 1 of his Form W-2.

Because Bill's reimbursement was included in his income and he is using the standard mileage rate for his car expenses, he files Form 2106-EZ with his tax return. His filled-in form is shown on the next page.

TAXORGANIZER

Records you should keep. If you deduct expenses for traveling away from home, you must be able to substantiate the expenses by keeping adequate evidence.

Adequate Evidence. Evidence is ordinarily considered adequate if it shows the amount, date, place, and essential character of the expense.

For example, a hotel receipt is sufficient to prove an expense for business travel if it has all of the following information:

1. The name and location of the hotel
2. The dates of your stay
3. Itemization of separate charges such as lodging, meals, and telephone calls

A restaurant receipt is enough to prove an expense for a business meal if it has all of the following:

1. The name and location of the restaurant
2. The number of people served
3. The date and amount of expense

Generally, you must have documentary evidence, such as receipts, canceled checks, or bills, to support your expenses. A canceled check, together with a bill from the payee, ordinarily establishes the cost. However, a canceled check alone does not prove a business expense without other evidence to show that it was for a business purpose.

Exceptions. Evidence is not needed if:

1. You have meals or lodging expenses while traveling away from home for which you account to your employer under an accountable plan and you use a per diem allowance method that includes meals and/or lodging.
2. Your expense, other than lodging, is less than $75.
3. You have transportation expense for which a receipt is not readily available.

If a charge is made for an item other than food and beverage, the receipt must show that this is the case.

Incomplete Records. If you do not have complete records to prove an element of expense, then you must prove the element by:

1. Your own statement, whether written or oral, that contains specific information about the element, and
2. Other supporting evidence that is sufficient to establish the element.

In addition, it is helpful to keep an account book, diary, or similar record that includes the following:

- Amount of each separate expense,
- Time and place of travel or entertainment,
- Number of days away from home spent on business, and
- Business purpose of the expense.

Form **2106-EZ**

Department of the Treasury
Internal Revenue Service (99)

Unreimbursed Employee Business Expenses

▶ **Attach to Form 1040 or Form 1040NR.**

OMB No. 1545-0074

2011

Attachment Sequence No. **129A**

Your name	Occupation in which you incurred expenses	Social security number
BILL WILSON	SALES	555 00 5555

You Can Use This Form Only if All of the Following Apply.

- You are an employee deducting ordinary and necessary expenses attributable to your job. An ordinary expense is one that is common and accepted in your field of trade, business, or profession. A necessary expense is one that is helpful and appropriate for your business. An expense does not have to be required to be considered necessary.
- You **do not** get reimbursed by your employer for any expenses (amounts your employer included in box 1 of your Form W-2 are not considered reimbursements for this purpose).
- If you are claiming vehicle expense, you are using the standard mileage rate for 2011.

Caution: *You can use the standard mileage rate for 2011* ***only if: (a)*** *you owned the vehicle and used the standard mileage rate for the first year you placed the vehicle in service,* ***or (b)*** *you leased the vehicle and used the standard mileage rate for the portion of the lease period after 1997.*

Part I Figure Your Expenses

1	Complete Part II. Multiply line 8a by 51¢ (.51) for miles driven **before** July 1, 2011, and by 55.5¢ (.555) for miles driven **after** June 30, 2011. Add the amounts , then enter the result here . . .	1	10,600
2	Parking fees, tolls, and transportation, including train, bus, etc., that **did not** involve overnight travel or commuting to and from work . . .	2	520
3	Travel expense while away from home overnight, including lodging, airplane, car rental, etc. **Do not** include meals and entertainment . . .	3	18,318
4	Business expenses not included on lines 1 through 3. **Do not** include meals and entertainment . . .	4	650
5	Meals and entertainment expenses: $ ________ × 50% (.50). (Employees subject to Department of Transportation (DOT) hours of service limits: Multiply meal expenses incurred while away from home on business by 80% (.80) instead of 50%. For details, see instructions.)	5	3,556
6	**Total expenses.** Add lines 1 through 5. Enter here and on **Schedule A (Form 1040), line 21** (or on **Schedule A (Form 1040NR), line 7**). (Armed Forces reservists, fee-basis state or local government officials, qualified performing artists, and individuals with disabilities: See the instructions for special rules on where to enter this amount.) . . .	6	33,644

Part II Information on Your Vehicle. Complete this part **only** if you are claiming vehicle expense on line 1.

7 When did you place your vehicle in service for business use? (month, day, year) ▶ 01 / 03 / 2009

8 Of the total number of miles you drove your vehicle during 2011, enter the number of miles you used your vehicle for:

a Business 20,000 **b** Commuting (see instructions) 2,600 **c** Other 2,400

9 Was your vehicle available for personal use during off-duty hours? . . . ☑ **Yes** ☐ **No**

10 Do you (or your spouse) have another vehicle available for personal use? . . . ☑ **Yes** ☐ **No**

11a Do you have evidence to support your deduction? . . . ☑ **Yes** ☐ **No**

b If "Yes," is the evidence written? . . . ☑ **Yes** ☐ **No**

For Paperwork Reduction Act Notice, see your tax return instructions. Cat. No. 20604Q Form **2106-EZ** (2011)

Chapter 28

Tax benefits for work-related education

ey.com/EYTaxGuide

Note

IRS Publication 17 (*Your Federal Income Tax*) has been updated by Ernst & Young LLP for 2011. Dates and dollar amounts shown are for 2011. Underlined type is used to indicate where IRS text has been updated. Places where text has been removed are indicated by the sentence: *Text intentionally omitted*.

ey.com/EYTaxGuide

Ernst & Young LLP will update the *Ernst & Young Tax Guide 2012* website with relevant taxpayer information as it becomes available. You can also sign up for email alerts to let you know when changes have been made.

Introduction

Educational expenses are generally considered to be personal in nature. The law, however, does recognize that certain educational expenses are necessary for you in your business or as an employee. Deductions may be allowed for these expenses as well as for reasonable expenses incurred in acquiring the education.

It's often difficult to determine if work-related educational expenses are deductible. You do not necessarily have to earn a new degree for such expenses to be claimed. On the other hand, earning a degree doesn't necessarily make the expenses deductible. The expenses do have to meet certain tests. For example, they are deductible if the education either maintains or improves skills required in your trade or business or if the courses are required for you to retain your current job. The expenses are not deductible if they are spent on education that is required for you to meet the minimum educational requirements of your position. In addition, travel as a form of education is not deductible.

This chapter discusses work-related educational expenses. You'll learn that you may be able to deduct not only your fees for educational instruction but also a number of other expenses that you incur because you are simultaneously working and in school.

An employee's work-related educational expenses and other miscellaneous itemized deductions are deductible only to the extent that they exceed 2% of adjusted gross income.

Prior to 2010, itemized deductions were subject to certain limitations if your adjusted gross income exceeded certain amounts (for 2009, this amount was $166,800; $83,400 if married filing separately). But the itemized deduction phaseout has been temporarily repealed and higher-income taxpayers do not have to reduce their total itemized deductions for 2011 or 2012. Unless Congress acts, the old phaseout rule is scheduled to return beginning in 2013. See chapter 47, *Planning ahead for 2012 and beyond*, for more information on the return of the overall phaseout of itemized deductions.

For a discussion of education credits and other education benefits—such as employer-provided educational programs and qualified tuition programs—see chapter 36, *Education credits and other education tax benefits*.

Tax Breaks and Deductions You Can Use Checklist

Work-Related Education. You can deduct the cost of work-related education on your tax return. If you are self-employed, you can take that deduction in calculating your adjusted gross income (AGI); if you're an employee, the cost is a miscellaneous itemized deduction. Your employer can pay or reimburse you for an unlimited amount of that cost on a tax-free basis.

What's New

Standard mileage rate. Generally, If you claim a business deduction for work-related education and you drive your car to and from school, the amount you can deduct for miles driven during 2011 is 51 cents per mile from January 1, 2011, through June 30, 2011, and 55.5 cents per mile from July 1, 2011, through December 31, 2011. For more information, see *Transportation Expenses* under *What Expenses Can Be Deducted.*

TAXALERT

Before 2010, many itemized deductions, including work-related education claimed as miscellaneous itemized deductions, were also subject to other limitations if your adjusted gross income (AGI) exceeded certain amounts. For tax years 2010-2012, the itemized deduction phaseout was repealed and higher-income taxpayers do not have to reduce their total itemized deductions based on an AGI limitation. After 2012, the old phaseout rule returns. See chapter 47, *Planning ahead for 2012 and beyond*, for more information on the return of the overall phaseout of itemized deductions.

This chapter discusses work-related education expenses that you may be able to deduct as business expenses.

To claim such a deduction, you must:

- Be working,
- Itemize your deductions on Schedule A (Form 1040) if you are an employee,
- File Schedule C (Form 1040), Schedule C-EZ (Form 1040), or Schedule F (Form 1040) if you are self-employed, and
- Have expenses for education that meet the requirements discussed under *Qualifying Work-Related Education*.

If you are an employee and can itemize your deductions, you may be able to claim a deduction for the expenses you pay for your work-related education. Your deduction will be the amount by which your qualifying work-related education expenses plus other job and certain miscellaneous expenses is greater than 2% of your adjusted gross income. See chapter 29.

If you are self-employed, you deduct your expenses for qualifying work-related education directly from your self-employment income.

Your work-related education expenses may also qualify you for other tax benefits, such as the American opportunity, and lifetime learning credits (see chapter 36). You may qualify for these other benefits even if you do not meet the requirements listed earlier.

Also, keep in mind that your work-related education expenses may qualify you to claim more than one tax benefit. Generally, you may claim any number of benefits as long as you use different expenses to figure each one.

TAXPLANNER

For example, eligible taxpayers in 2011 may be able to deduct as an adjustment for figuring adjusted gross income (AGI) for up to $4,000 of qualified tuition and related expenses, regardless of whether those expenses would be considered to be work-related. However, this tuition and fees deduction is not available to taxpayers with modified AGI greater than $160,000 if married and filing jointly (or $80,000 single). (See *Tuition and Fees Deduction* in chapter 19, *Education-related adjustments*, for more information.) On the other hand, work-related education expenses deducted as a miscellaneous itemized deduction will be subject to the 2%-of-AGI limitation on miscellaneous itemized deductions. (See chapter 29, *Miscellaneous deductions*, for more information on how the 2% limitation applies.)

TAXALERT

Exclusion for employer-provided educational assistance for graduate education extended. In addition to work-related education expenses that you may be able to deduct or claim an education credit, an employee may be eligible to exclude from gross income up to $5,250 for income and employment tax purposes per year of employer-provided education assistance. For 2011 and 2012, this exclusion is available for qualifying undergraduate and graduate education. For more information, see Publication 970, *Tax Benefits for Education*.

Useful Items

You may want to see:

Publication

- □ **463** Travel, Entertainment, Gift, and Car Expenses
- □ **970** Tax Benefits for Education

Form (and Instructions)

- □ **2106** Employee Business Expenses
- □ **2106-EZ** Unreimbursed Employee Business Expenses
- □ **Schedule A (Form 1040)** Itemized Deductions

Caution

Text intentionally omitted. *Your work-related education expenses may also qualify for the tuition and fees deduction. For more information, go to* www.irs.gov/formspubs. *Also see Publication 970,* Tax Benefits for Education.

Qualifying Work-Related Education

You can deduct the costs of qualifying work-related education as business expenses. This is education that meets at least one of the following two tests.

- The education is required by your employer or the law to keep your present salary, status, or job. The required education must serve a bona fide business purpose of your employer.
- The education maintains or improves skills needed in your present work.

However, even if the education meets one or both of the above tests, it is not qualifying work-related education if it:

- Is needed to meet the minimum educational requirements of your present trade or business, or
- Is part of a program of study that will qualify you for a new trade or business.

You can deduct the costs of qualifying work-related education as a business expense even if the education could lead to a degree.

Use Figure 28-A, later, as a quick check to see if your education qualifies.

Tip

When you figure your taxes, you may want to compare these tax benefits so you can choose the method(s) that give you the lowest tax liability.

EXPLANATION

In order to be deductible, work-related educational expenses must relate to your current occupation.

Example

A college student obtaining employment through his or her college cooperative program or work/study program is not engaged in a trade or a business. His or her college fees are not deductible as a work-related education expense, because they are incurred in preparation for an occupation.

A full-time student does not have a trade or a business and may not deduct the cost of courses toward a college degree, even though the student may be employed full-time during the summer months.

TAXPLANNER

The IRS does not explicitly allow or disallow work-related educational expenses for a semi-retired person. Therefore, it appears that educational expenses to maintain skills are deductible, even though the individual has reduced the scope of his or her trade or business.

An individual who abandons a former profession for a period of years and acquires a new profession may not deduct courses related to resuming his or her original profession.

A fully retired individual is not considered to have a trade or a business and is not entitled to a deduction for work-related educational expenses.

Example

Gaby, an engineer, decides to teach math at a local high school. After teaching for a few years, she decides to resume her former career in engineering. Gaby takes refresher courses at a local college. The costs of these courses are not work-related educational expenses.

Education Required by Employer or by Law

Once you have met the minimum educational requirements for your job, your employer or the law may require you to get more education. This additional education is qualifying work-related education if all three of the following requirements are met.

- It is required for you to keep your present salary, status, or job,
- The requirement serves a business purpose of your employer, and
- The education is not part of a program that will qualify you for a new trade or business.

EXAMPLES

Example 1
As a result of a corporate downsizing policy, you are taking courses to be retrained in another trade or business. If this education qualifies you to enter a new trade or business, even with the same employer, the costs are nondeductible.

Example 2
Your employer is restructuring its workforce. The company has said that additional education is required for you to retain your current job. Because the education serves a business purpose of your employer and is necessary for you to maintain your current position, the additional educational expenses are deductible.

When you get more education than your employer or the law requires, the additional education can be qualifying work-related education only if it maintains or improves skills required in your present work. See *Education To Maintain or Improve Skills*, below.

Example. You are a teacher who has satisfied the minimum requirements for teaching. Your employer requires you to take an additional college course each year to keep your teaching job. If the courses will not qualify you for a new trade or business, they are qualifying work-related education even if you eventually receive a master's degree and an increase in salary because of this extra education.

Education To Maintain or Improve Skills

If your education is not required by your employer or the law, it can be qualifying work-related education only if it maintains or improves skills needed in your present work. This could include refresher courses, courses on current developments, and academic or vocational courses.

Example. You repair televisions, radios, and stereo systems for XYZ Store. To keep up with the latest changes, you take special courses in radio and stereo service. These courses maintain and improve skills required in your work.

EXAMPLES

The following are examples of educational expenses that were deductible because the courses maintained or improved skills:

- A tax attorney attended an out-of-town tax forum. The course was valuable for her in maintaining current knowledge of the tax laws.
- An engineering aide took night courses that improved his skills but were not required by his employer.
- A concert harpist took music lessons. The costs were deductible because she was maintaining or improving her skills.
- A doctor, engaged in the private practice of psychiatry, undertook a program of study and training at an accredited psychoanalytic institute that enabled him to qualify to practice psychoanalysis. The expenditures were deductible because the study and training maintained or improved skills required in the doctor's trade or business and didn't qualify the doctor for a new trade or business.
- A farmer could deduct the cost of a welding course that improved his welding skills. Welding skills were necessary in the farming operation to keep the machinery repaired.
- An ordained minister could deduct the cost of undergraduate courses in psychology, education, and business. The court determined that the courses maintained and improved the skills that he needed to lead a congregation competently: counseling, teaching, and managing the financial affairs of the church.
- An attorney who has already passed the bar and is working as a tax lawyer can deduct the cost of obtaining a master's in laws of taxation (LLM).
- A CPA practicing in the area of taxation can deduct the cost of obtaining a master's in taxation graduate degree provided it is not a requirement for taking the CPA exam.

Maintaining skills vs. qualifying for new job. Education to maintain or improve skills needed in your present work is not qualifying education if it will also qualify you for a new trade or business.

EXAMPLES

- A bookkeeper who was also a tax return preparer returned to school and earned a bachelor's degree in accounting. The degree qualified her to sit for the certified public accounting examination. The costs incurred in earning the degree are not deductible because the courses were intended to obtain a new degree rather than to improve or maintain her skills; the new degree qualified her for a new trade or business.
- A quality control foreman took courses in business law, corporate strategy and business policies, and business finance. The costs were held to be nondeductible because they were only remotely related to his duties.

Education during temporary absence. If you stop working for a year or less in order to get education to maintain or improve skills needed in your present work and then return to the same general type of work, your absence is considered temporary. Education that you get during a temporary absence is qualifying work-related education if it maintains or improves skills needed in your present work.

Example. You quit your biology research job to become a full-time biology graduate student for one year. If you return to work in biology research after completing the courses, the education is related to your present work even if you do not go back to work with the same employer.

Education during indefinite absence. If you stop work for more than a year, your absence from your job is considered indefinite. Education during an indefinite absence, even if it maintains or improves skills needed in the work from which you are absent, is considered to qualify you for a new trade or business. Therefore, it is not qualifying work-related education.

EXPLANATION

While the IRS defines a temporary leave of absence as a period of 1 year or less, the courts have been more lenient, approving deductions for educational expenses for a leave of more than 1 year. The cases turn on whether or not the taxpayer's intention is to reenter the same trade or business, regardless of whether or not it is with a new employer.

Examples

- A manager who quit his job to pursue a 2-year master of business administration program but who expected to reenter the same trade or business was allowed to deduct the cost of his courses.
- A parochial schoolteacher ended her employment to raise a family. Over the next 23 years, she attended several different colleges until she was awarded a bachelor's degree in education. The following fall, she began employment again as a full-time teacher. The court determined that when she left the parochial school, there was no indication that she was on a leave of absence or that she planned to resume teaching in the future. Consequently, the court denied the deduction for the educational expenses.

Education To Meet Minimum Requirements

Education you need to meet the minimum educational requirements for your present trade or business is not qualifying work-related education. The minimum educational requirements are determined by:

- Laws and regulations,
- Standards of your profession, trade, or business, and
- Your employer.

EXAMPLES

You have completed 2 years of a 3-year law school curriculum and are hired by a law firm to do legal research and to perform other functions on a full-time basis. As a condition of employment, you are required to obtain a law degree and to pass the state bar examination. You complete the law school education by attending night classes and take a bar review course in order to prepare for the bar examination. The law courses and the bar review course are considered the minimum educational requirements needed to qualify for your trade or business, and thus the costs of such courses are not deductible. However, courts have held that you may amortize over your life expectancy fees paid to state bar admission authorities.

Caution

You have not necessarily met the minimum educational requirements of your trade or business simply because you are already doing the work.

Once you have met the minimum educational requirements that were in effect when you were hired, you do not have to meet any new minimum educational requirements. This means that if the minimum requirements change after you were hired, any education you need to meet the new requirements can be qualifying education.

Example 1. You are a full-time engineering student. Although you have not received your degree or certification, you work part-time as an engineer for a firm that will employ you as a full-time engineer after you finish college. Although your college engineering courses improve your skills in your present job, they are also needed to meet the minimum job requirements for a full-time engineer. The education is not qualifying work-related education.

Example 2. You are an accountant and you have met the minimum educational requirements of your employer. Your employer later changes the minimum educational requirements and requires you to take college courses to keep your job. These additional courses can be qualifying work-related education because you have already satisfied the minimum requirements that were in effect when you were hired.

Requirements for Teachers

States or school districts usually set the minimum educational requirements for teachers. The requirement is the college degree or the minimum number of college hours usually required of a person hired for that position.

If there are no requirements, you will have met the minimum educational requirements when you become a faculty member. You generally will be considered a faculty member when one or more of the following occurs.

- You have tenure.
- Your years of service count toward obtaining tenure.
- You have a vote in faculty decisions.
- Your school makes contributions for you to a retirement plan other than social security or a similar program.

Example 1. The law in your state requires beginning secondary school teachers to have a bachelor's degree, including 10 professional education courses. In addition, to keep the job, a teacher must complete a fifth year of training within 10 years from the date of hire. If the employing school certifies to the state Department of Education that qualified teachers cannot be found, the school can hire persons with only 3 years of college. However, to keep their jobs, these teachers must get a bachelor's degree and the required professional education courses within 3 years.

Under these facts, the bachelor's degree, whether or not it includes the 10 professional education courses, is considered the minimum educational requirement for qualification as a teacher in your state.

If you have all the required education except the fifth year, you have met the minimum educational requirements. The fifth year of training is qualifying work-related education unless it is part of a program of study that will qualify you for a new trade or business.

Example 2. Assume the same facts as in Example 1 except that you have a bachelor's degree and only six professional education courses. The additional four education courses can be qualifying work-related education. Although you do not have all the required courses, you have already met the minimum educational requirements.

Example 3. Assume the same facts as in Example 1 except that you are hired with only 3 years of college. The courses you take that lead to a bachelor's degree (including those in education) are not qualifying work-related education. They are needed to meet the minimum educational requirements for employment as a teacher.

Example 4. You have a bachelor's degree and you work as a temporary instructor at a university. At the same time, you take graduate courses toward an advanced degree. The rules of the university state that you can become a faculty member only if you get a graduate degree. Also, you can keep your job as an instructor only as long as you show satisfactory progress toward getting this degree. You have not met the minimum educational requirements to qualify you as a faculty member. The graduate courses are not qualifying work-related education.

TAXSAVER

It's possible to maximize an education deduction by carefully limiting pre-employment education to minimum job requirements. Courses taken after employment is secured may then be deductible as maintaining or improving skills.

Example 1
Denise Thomas is starting her final semester of courses that will enable her to be a registered nurse. She needs 6 credit hours of nursing courses to reach the required level of education. In addition to the 6 credit hours, Denise also wants to take an advanced nursing course. To reduce her taxes, Denise should complete the minimum job requirements for nursing. If she takes the advanced nursing course after she qualifies to be a nurse and secures a nursing position, the cost of the advanced nursing course is deductible.

Example 2
Robert Taylor is a recent law school graduate and is considering the pursuit of a full-time graduate law (LLM) program in international law. To qualify for a deduction, Robert should secure employment as a lawyer and complete the minimum requirements for practicing law (i.e., bar admission) before starting any graduate program. After meeting these minimum requirements for practicing law, Robert may begin a graduate law program in international law and deduct the related educational expenses.

Certification in a new state. Once you have met the minimum educational requirements for teachers for your state, you are considered to have met the minimum educational requirements in all states. This is true even if you must get additional education to be certified in another state. Any additional education you need is qualifying work-related education. You have already met the minimum requirements for teaching. Teaching in another state is not a new trade or business.

Example. You hold a permanent teaching certificate in State A and are employed as a teacher in that state for several years. You move to State B and are promptly hired as a teacher. You are required, however, to complete certain prescribed courses to get a permanent teaching certificate in State B. These additional courses are qualifying work-related education because the teaching position in State B involves the same general kind of work for which you were qualified in State A.

Figure 28-A. **Does Your Work-Related Education Qualify?**

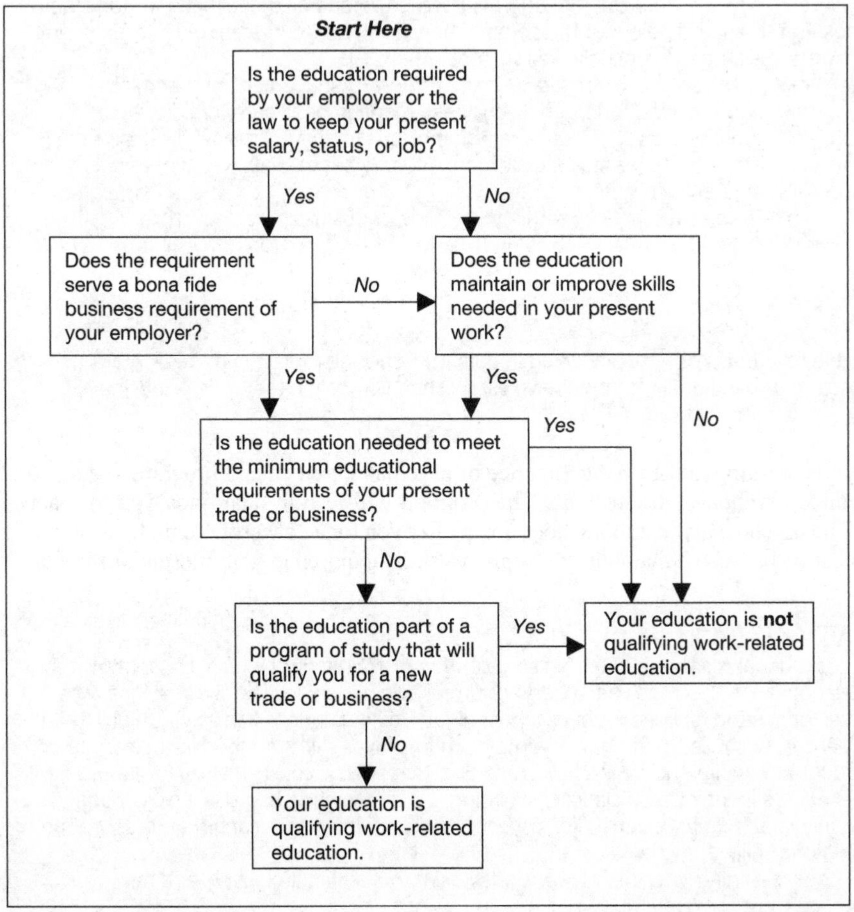

Education That Qualifies You for a New Trade or Business

Education that is part of a program of study that will qualify you for a new trade or business is not qualifying work-related education. This is true even if you do not plan to enter that trade or business.

If you are an employee, a change of duties that involves the same general kind of work is not a new trade or business.

Example 1. You are an accountant. Your employer requires you to get a law degree at your own expense. You register at a law school for the regular curriculum that leads to a law degree. Even if you do not intend to become a lawyer, the education is not qualifying because the law degree will qualify you for a new trade or business.

Example 2. You are a general practitioner of medicine. You take a 2-week course to review developments in several specialized fields of medicine. The course does not qualify you for a new profession. It is qualifying work-related education because it maintains or improves skills required in your present profession.

EXPLANATION

A change of duties is limited to employees. It does not pertain to self-employed individuals.

The IRS defines the phrase "the same general type of work" very narrowly. The burden is on the taxpayer to prove that he or she has not qualified for a new trade or business. However, teachers are generally given more latitude (see the following section, *Teaching and Related Duties*). A deduction as a work-related expense has not been allowed for law school educational expenses, even if they are required by an employer. The courts have specifically disallowed a deduction for law school for employees in the following trades or businesses: accountant, insurance claims adjuster, industrial arts teacher, engineer, probation officer, patent examiner, mathematics teacher, IRS agent, hospital administrator, doctor, philosophy professor, and computer systems analyst.

Exceptions

Nevertheless, the courts have allowed deductions in some special cases:

- A night manager of a supermarket took food management courses at a local university. The courses elevated his rank within the management structure and also qualified him for a day manager position. The court held that the general management progression did not represent a change in business, and the court allowed the deductions.
- An engineer whose duties were changing to include more management and administrative skills took courses and received a degree in business management and administration. The courses were deductible because the education did not qualify him for a new trade or a business but was directly related to his current position. The courses also allowed him to maintain and improve skills required by his employer.
- Costs incurred in becoming a specialist within your trade or business are deductible.

TAXSAVER

You may be able to deduct expenses incurred in gaining a specialty within a trade or a business if the expenses are delayed until after you have established yourself in the trade or business.

Example 3. While working in the private practice of psychiatry, you enter a program to study and train at an accredited psychoanalytic institute. The program will lead to qualifying you to practice psychoanalysis. The psychoanalytic training does not qualify you for a new profession. It is qualifying work-related education because it maintains or improves skills required in your present profession.

EXPLANATION

Payment for psychoanalysis that is required as part of your training to be a psychoanalyst may be a deductible educational expense necessary for professional training. The law specifically permits an itemized deduction for the cost of psychoanalytic training undertaken by psychiatrists as education expenses, because the training maintains or improves skills required in their trade or business and does not qualify them for a new trade or business. The courts have also allowed deductions for expenses incurred by a clinical psychologist in studying to become a psychoanalyst and expenses incurred by a psychiatrist for psychoanalytic training as a condition to accepting the directorship of a child study center.

However, when a psychiatric residency was undertaken to qualify a taxpayer for a new profession, the expenses were not deductible.

Bar or CPA Review Course

Review courses to prepare for the bar examination or the certified public accountant (CPA) examination are not qualifying work-related education. They are part of a program of study that can qualify you for a new profession.

> **EXPLANATION**
>
> Bar review courses are not deductible, even if you are currently practicing in one state and are seeking admission to the bar in another state. However, you may be able to deduct the cost of graduate courses (LLM). See earlier examples under Education To Maintain or Improve Skills and Education To Meet Minimum Requirements.

Teaching and Related Duties

All teaching and related duties are considered the same general kind of work. A change in duties in any of the following ways is not considered a change to a new business.

- Elementary school teacher to secondary school teacher.
- Teacher of one subject, such as biology, to teacher of another subject, such as art.
- Classroom teacher to guidance counselor.
- Classroom teacher to school administrator.

> **EXPLANATION**
>
> If you are an employed teacher who meets the minimum education requirements of one state, you may deduct the cost of required courses to qualify as a teacher in another state. Changing employers and locations is not a significant change of duties and does not create a new trade or business. Likewise, deductions have been allowed for a Canadian teacher taking courses to qualify to teach in the United States. However, the IRS has ruled that the position of elementary school teacher does not involve the same general type of work and is not the same trade or business as a university professor.
>
> ***Example***
>
> Lynn Arnold left her position as an elementary music teacher to obtain a Ph.D. degree in music. After obtaining her degree, she took a job as an assistant professor in the music department of a university. Lynn cannot deduct the expenses of getting her Ph.D.

What Expenses Can Be Deducted

If your education meets the requirements described earlier under *Qualifying Work-Related Education,* you can generally deduct your education expenses as business expenses. If you are not self-employed, you can deduct business expenses only if you itemize your deductions.

You cannot deduct expenses related to tax-exempt and excluded income.

Deductible expenses. The following education expenses can be deducted.

- Tuition, books, supplies, lab fees, and similar items.
- Certain transportation and travel costs.
- Other education expenses, such as costs of research and typing when writing a paper as part of an educational program.

Nondeductible expenses. You cannot deduct personal or capital expenses. For example, you cannot deduct the dollar value of vacation time or annual leave you take to attend classes. This amount is a personal expense.

Unclaimed reimbursement. If you do not claim reimbursement that you are entitled to receive from your employer, you cannot deduct the expenses that apply to the reimbursement.

Example. Your employer agrees to pay your education expenses if you file a voucher showing your expenses. You do not file a voucher, and you do not get reimbursed. Because you did not file a voucher, you cannot deduct the expenses on your tax return.

Transportation Expenses

If your education qualifies, you can deduct local transportation costs of going directly from work to school. If you are regularly employed and go to school on a temporary basis, you can also deduct the costs of returning from school to home.

Temporary basis. You go to school on a temporary basis if either of the following situations applies to you.

1. Your attendance at school is realistically expected to last 1 year or less and does indeed last for 1 year or less.
2. Initially, your attendance at school is realistically expected to last 1 year or less, but at a later date your attendance is reasonably expected to last more than 1 year. Your attendance is temporary up to the date you determine it will last more than 1 year.

Note. If you are in either situation (1) or (2) above, your attendance is not temporary if facts and circumstances indicate otherwise.

Attendance not on a temporary basis. You do not go to school on a temporary basis if either of the following situations apply to you.

1. Your attendance at school is realistically expected to last more than 1 year. It does not matter how long you actually attend.
2. Initially, your attendance at school is realistically expected to last 1 year or less, but at a later date your attendance is reasonably expected to last more than 1 year. Your attendance is not temporary after the date you determine it will last more than 1 year.

Deductible Transportation Expenses

If you are regularly employed and go directly from home to school on a temporary basis, you can deduct the round-trip costs of transportation between your home and school. This is true regardless of the location of the school, the distance traveled, or whether you attend school on nonwork days.

Transportation expenses include the actual costs of bus, subway, cab, or other fares, as well as the costs of using your car. Transportation expenses do not include amounts spent for travel, meals, or lodging while you are away from home overnight.

Example 1. You regularly work in a nearby town, and go directly from work to home. You also attend school every work night for 3 months to take a course that improves your job skills. Since you are attending school on a temporary basis, you can deduct your daily round-trip transportation expenses in going between home and school. This is true regardless of the distance traveled.

Example 2. Assume the same facts as in *Example 1* except that on certain nights you go directly from work to school and then home. You can deduct your transportation expenses from your regular work site to school and then home.

Example 3. Assume the same facts as in *Example 1* except that you attend the school for 9 months on Saturdays, nonwork days. Since you are attending school on a temporary basis, you can deduct your round-trip transportation expenses in going between home and school.

Example 4. Assume the same facts as in *Example 1* except that you attend classes twice a week for 15 months. Since your attendance in school is not considered temporary, you cannot deduct your transportation expenses in going between home and school. If you go directly from work to school, you can deduct the one-way transportation expenses of going from work to school. If you go from work to home to school and return home, your transportation expenses cannot be more than if you had gone directly from work to school.

Using your car. If you use your car (whether you own or lease it) for transportation to school, you can deduct your actual expenses or use the standard mileage rate to figure the amount you can deduct. The standard mileage rate for miles driven during 2011 is 51 cents a mile from January 1, 2011, through June 30, 2011, and 55.5 cents a mile from July 1, 2011, through December 31, 2011. Whichever method you use, you can also deduct parking fees and tolls. See chapter 27 for information on deducting your actual expenses of using a car.

Travel Expenses

You can deduct expenses for travel, meals (see *50% limit on meals*, later), and lodging if you travel overnight mainly to obtain qualifying work-related education.

Travel expenses for qualifying work-related education are treated the same as travel expenses for other employee business purposes. For more information, see chapter 27.

Caution

You cannot deduct expenses for personal activities, such as sightseeing, visiting, or entertaining.

Mainly personal travel. If your travel away from home is mainly personal, you cannot deduct all of your expenses for travel, meals, and lodging. You can deduct only your expenses for lodging and 50% of your expenses for meals during the time you attend the qualified educational activities.

Whether a trip's purpose is mainly personal or educational depends upon the facts and circumstances. An important factor is the comparison of time spent on personal activities with time spent on educational activities. If you spend more time on personal activities, the trip is considered mainly educational only if you can show a substantial nonpersonal reason for traveling to a particular location.

Example 1. John works in Newark, New Jersey. He traveled to Chicago to take a deductible 1-week course at the request of his employer. His main reason for going to Chicago was to take the course.

While there, he took a sightseeing trip, entertained some friends, and took a side trip to Pleasantville for a day.

Since the trip was mainly for business, John can deduct his round-trip airfare to Chicago. He cannot deduct his transportation expenses of going to Pleasantville. He can deduct only the meals (subject to the 50% limit) and lodging connected with his educational activities.

Example 2. Sue works in Boston. She went to a university in Michigan to take a course for work. The course is qualifying work-related education.

She took one course, which is one-fourth of a full course load of study. She spent the rest of the time on personal activities. Her reasons for taking the course in Michigan were all personal.

Sue's trip is mainly personal because three-fourths of her time is considered personal time. She cannot deduct the cost of her round-trip train ticket to Michigan. She can deduct one-fourth of the meals (subject to the 50% limit) and lodging costs for the time she attended the university.

Example 3. Dave works in Nashville and recently traveled to California to take a 2-week seminar. The seminar is qualifying work-related education.

While there, he spent an extra 8 weeks on personal activities. The facts, including the extra 8-week stay, show that his main purpose was to take a vacation.

Dave cannot deduct his round-trip airfare or his meals and lodging for the 8 weeks. He can deduct only his expenses for meals (subject to the 50% limit) and lodging for the 2 weeks he attended the seminar.

TAXSAVER

Through careful planning and documentation, as well as recognition of the stringent tests applied by the courts, it's possible to mix business with pleasure and deduct some or all of your travel expenses. If you travel away from home primarily to obtain education, your expenditures for the education, as well as for travel, meals, and lodging while away from home, are deductible. It is helpful to be able to prove that the location you are visiting is unique and that, if education is involved, the education cannot be obtained elsewhere.

However, if you engage in some personal activity while on the trip, such as sightseeing, social visiting, entertaining, or other recreation, your expenses attributable to those personal activities are nondeductible personal expenses.

If your travel away from home is primarily personal, your expenditures for travel, meals, and lodging (other than meals and lodging during the time spent participating in deductible educational pursuits) are not deductible.

Whether a particular trip is primarily personal or primarily educational depends on all the facts and circumstances of each case, including the time devoted to personal activity as compared with the time devoted to educational pursuits. It is important to maintain good documentation regarding the types of expenses incurred and in what capacity they were incurred.

Example

Shannon, a hair stylist, decides to attend a 4-day workshop on the latest trends of hair coloring and styling that is offered in Tampa, Florida, 400 miles from her home. Her primary purpose in going to Tampa is to take the course, but she also takes a side trip to Orlando (a couple of hours away from Tampa) for 2 days. Shannon's transportation expenses to Tampa are deductible, but her transportation to Orlando is not. Additionally, her expenses for meals and lodging while away from home must be allocated between her educational pursuits and her personal activities. Those expenses that are entirely personal, such as sightseeing in Orlando, are not deductible. The cost of deductible meals must be reduced by 50%.

Cruises and conventions. Certain cruises and conventions offer seminars or courses as part of their itinerary. Even if the seminars or courses are work-related, your deduction for travel may be limited. This applies to:

- Travel by ocean liner, cruise ship, or other form of luxury water transportation, and
- Conventions outside the North American area.

For a discussion of the limits on travel expense deductions that apply to cruises and conventions, see *Luxury Water Travel* and *Conventions* in chapter 1 of Publication 463.

50% limit on meals. You can deduct only 50% of the cost of your meals while traveling away from home to obtain qualifying work-related education. You cannot have been reimbursed for the meals.

Employees must use Form 2106 or Form 2106-EZ to apply the 50% limit.

Travel as Education

You cannot deduct the cost of travel as a form of education even if it is directly related to your duties in your work or business.

Example. You are a French language teacher. While on sabbatical leave granted for travel, you traveled through France to improve your knowledge of the French language. You chose your itinerary and most of your activities to improve your French language skills. You cannot deduct your travel expenses as education expenses. This is true even if you spent most of your time learning French by visiting French schools and families, attending movies or plays, and engaging in similar activities.

> ***EXPLANATION***
>
> The cost of travel is not a deductible educational expense when the educational aspect of a trip is the trip itself. However, if you establish an ordinary and necessary business need for the travel, such as research that can only be done in a specific location or a specific seminar, then a deduction may be allowed for travel expenses.

No Double Benefit Allowed

You cannot do either of the following.

- Deduct work-related education expenses as business expenses if you benefit from these expenses under any other provision of the law, for example, as an education credit (see chapter 36).
- Deduct work-related education expenses paid with tax-free scholarship, grant, or employer-provided educational assistance. See *Adjustments to Qualifying Work-Related Education Expenses*, below.

> ***TAXSAVER***
>
> **Student Loan Interest Expense.** Interest expense of up to $2,500 paid during 2011 on qualified student loans may be deducted from your income to determine your adjusted gross income, if your income is below $60,000; $120,000 if you are married filing jointly. The deduction is unavailable for you if your income is above $75,000; $150,000 if you are married filing jointly. If you qualify, you can take this deduction whether or not the education is work related and even if you do not itemize deductions on Schedule A (Form 1040). For more information on the deduction of student loan interest, see Publication 970 and the section on *Student Loan Interest Deduction* in chapter 19, *Education-related adjustments.*

Adjustments to Qualifying Work-Related Education Expenses

If you pay qualifying work-related education expenses with certain tax-free funds, you cannot claim a deduction for those amounts. You must reduce the qualifying expenses by the amount of any tax-free educational assistance you received.

Tax-free educational assistance includes:

- The tax-free part of scholarships and fellowships (see chapter 1 of Publication 970),
- Pell grants (see chapter 1 of Publication 970),
- Employer-provided educational assistance (see chapter 11 of Publication 970),
- Veterans' educational assistance (see chapter 1 of Publication 970), and
- Any other nontaxable (tax-free) payments (other than gifts or inheritances) received for education assistance.

Amounts that do not reduce qualifying work-related education expenses. Do not reduce the qualifying work-related education expenses by amounts paid with funds the student receives as:

- Payment for services, such as wages,
- A loan,
- A gift,
- An inheritance, or
- A withdrawal from the student's personal savings.

Also, do not reduce the qualifying work-related education expenses by any scholarship or fellowship reported as income on the student's return or any scholarship which, by its terms, cannot be applied to qualifying work-related education expenses.

Reimbursements

How you treat reimbursements depends on the arrangement you have with your employer.

There are two basic types of reimbursement arrangements—accountable plans and nonaccountable plans. You can tell the type of plan you are reimbursed under by the way the reimbursement is reported on your Form W-2.

For information about how to treat reimbursements under both accountable and nonaccountable plans, see *Reimbursements* in chapter 27.

Deducting Business Expenses

Self-employed persons and employees report business expenses differently.

The following information explains what forms you must use to deduct the cost of your qualifying work-related education as a business expense.

Self-Employed Persons

If you are self-employed, you must report the cost of your qualifying work-related education on the appropriate form used to report your business income and expenses (generally Schedule C, C-EZ, or F). If your educational expenses include expenses for a car or truck, travel, or meals, report those expenses the same way you report other business expenses for those items. See the instructions for the form you file for information on how to complete it.

> ***TAXSAVER***
>
> From a tax perspective, it is more beneficial to report educational expenses on Schedules C, C-EZ, or F as appropriate. Reporting expenses on these forms will lower your adjusted gross income (AGI). As a result, the education expenses will not be subject to the 2%-of-AGI limitation on miscellaneous itemized deductions (see *Deductions Subject to the 2% Limit,* in chapter 29, *Miscellaneous deductions).* In addition, reporting the expenses on Schedules C, C-EZ, or F will reduce your self-employment tax.

Employees

If you are an employee, you can deduct the cost of qualifying work-related education only if you:

1. Did not receive any reimbursement from your employer,
2. Were reimbursed under a nonaccountable plan (amount is included in box 1 of Form W-2), or
3. Received reimbursement under an accountable plan, but the amount received was less than your expenses.

If either (1) or (2) applies, you can deduct the total qualifying cost. If (3) applies, you can deduct only the qualifying costs that were more than your reimbursement.

In order to deduct the cost of your qualifying work-related education as a business expense, include the amount with your deduction for any other employee business expenses on Schedule A (Form 1040), line 21. (Special rules for expenses of certain performing artists and fee-basis officials and for impairment-related work expenses are explained later.)

This deduction is subject to the 2%-of-adjusted-gross-income limit that applies to most miscellaneous itemized deductions. See chapter 29.

Form 2106 or 2106-EZ. To figure your deduction for employee business expenses, including qualifying work-related education, you generally must complete Form 2106 or Form 2106-EZ.

Form not required. Do not complete either Form 2106 or Form 2106-EZ if:

- All reimbursements, if any, are included in box 1 of your Form W-2, and
- You are not claiming travel, transportation, meal, or entertainment expenses.

If you meet both of these requirements, enter the expenses directly on Schedule A (Form 1040), line 21. (Special rules for expenses of certain performing artists and fee-basis officials and for impairment-related work expenses are explained below.)

Using Form 2106-EZ. This form is shorter and easier to use than Form 2106. Generally, you can use this form if:

- All reimbursements, if any, are included in box 1 of your Form W-2, and
- You are using the standard mileage rate if you are claiming vehicle expenses.

If you do not meet both of these requirements, use Form 2106.

Performing Artists and Fee-Basis Officials

If you are a qualified performing artist, or a state (or local) government official who is paid in whole or in part on a fee basis, you can deduct the cost of your qualifying work-related education as an adjustment to gross income rather than as an itemized deduction.

Include the cost of your qualifying work-related education with any other employee business expenses on Form 1040, line 24. You do not have to itemize your deductions on Schedule A (Form 1040), and, therefore, the deduction is not subject to the 2%-of-adjusted-gross-income limit. You must complete Form 2106 or 2106-EZ to figure your deduction, even if you meet the requirements described earlier under *Form not required*.

For more information on qualified performing artists, see chapter 6 of Publication 463.

Impairment-Related Work Expenses

If you are disabled and have impairment-related work expenses that are necessary for you to be able to get qualifying work-related education, you can deduct these expenses on Schedule A (Form 1040), line 28. They are not subject to the 2%-of-adjusted-gross-income limit. To deduct these expenses, you must complete Form 2106 or 2106-EZ even if you meet the requirements described earlier under *Form not required*.

For more information on impairment-related work expenses, see chapter 6 of Publication 463.

Recordkeeping

For specific information about keeping records of business expenses, see *Recordkeeping* in chapter 27.

Records

You must keep records as proof of any deduction claimed on your tax return. Generally, you should keep your records for 3 years from the date of filing the tax return and claiming the deduction.

TAXORGANIZER

Records you should keep:

- Job descriptions and other employer-provided materials that would set forth the educational requirements of your job
- Descriptions of educational programs and courses taken
- Tuition statements and canceled checks
- Receipts for books, supplies, lab fees, and the like
- Records of travel, transportation, lodging, and meal expenses related to education and training activity

Chapter 29

Miscellaneous deductions

ey.com/EYTaxGuide

Note

IRS Publication 17 (*Your Federal Income Tax*) has been updated by Ernst & Young LLP for 2011. Dates and dollar amounts shown are for 2011. Underlined type is used to indicate where IRS text has been updated. Places where text has been removed are indicated by the sentence: *Text intentionally omitted*.

ey.com/EYTaxGuide

Ernst & Young LLP will update the *Ernst & Young Tax Guide 2012* website with relevant taxpayer information as it becomes available. You can also sign up for email alerts to let you know when changes have been made

Introduction

This chapter covers a variety of expenses, some of which are deductible on your tax return and some of which are not. Deductible expenses can be broadly broken down into three categories: (1) deductible employee expenses, (2) deductible expenses of producing or collecting income, and (3) other deductible expenses. The general rule is that you may deduct any "ordinary and necessary" expense related to your trade or business, connected with producing or collecting other taxable income, or paid to determine your tax. Note, however, that your deductions may be limited depending on the type of the expense and your income level. (See discussion later regarding *Deductions Subject to the 2% Limit*.)

Nondeductible expenses, by definition, are all expenses that are not deductible. These expenses are typically personal in nature. The nondeductible expenses discussed in this chapter are not all-inclusive, but rather reflect the more common expenses that people may think are (or should be) deductible.

With proper planning, you may be able to deduct more than you think. Be sure to take note of the special comments throughout this chapter with respect to documenting the appropriateness of your deductions. Also, check out the list at the front of the book for *50 of the Most Easily Overlooked Deductions* to be sure you haven't missed anything.

What's New

Limit on itemized deductions. For 2011, the dollar limitations for itemized deductions based on your adjusted gross income do not apply.

TAXALERT

In December 2010, President Obama and Congress agreed to extend the so-called Bush tax cuts. Among the provisions extended, is the continuing repeal of the dollar limitations imposed on itemized deductions based upon your adjusted gross income (AGI) through 2012. Therefore, for 2011 and 2012, higher-income taxpayers are not required to reduce their total itemized deductions based on an AGI limitation. Unless Congress acts, beginning in 2013, the old phaseout rule is scheduled to return in full force. For more information on the phaseout rule scheduled to be restored in 2013, see chapter 30, *Limit on itemized deductions*.

Educator expenses. The deduction for up to $250 of certain educator expenses as an adjustment to income has been extended for 2011. See *Educator Expenses* in this chapter.

Tax Breaks and Deductions You Can Use Checklist

Job-Hunting Expenses. Job-hunting expenses are deductible whether or not you find a new job. For job-search expenses to be deductible, you must be looking for employment in the same trade or business in which you are engaged. Accepting temporary employment in another line of work won't affect your deduction for expenses in searching for permanent employment in your regular line of work. But job-hunting costs aren't deductible if you are looking for a job in a new trade or business, even if you find employment as a result of the search.

IRA Fees. Fees you pay to an IRA custodian are deductible as miscellaneous deductions as long as they are paid from an account other than your IRA account. If they are paid directly from your IRA, you get no deduction and your IRA account is reduced.

Deduction for Estate Tax on Income in Respect of a Decedent. This deduction is missed by many taxpayers. If someone bequeaths taxable income (such as an IRA or nonqualified stock option) to an estate or beneficiary, the recipient is entitled to an income tax deduction for any federal estate tax paid which is allocable to that income. The deduction is not subject to the 2% of adjusted gross income (AGI) floor.

Gambling Losses. Gambling losses can be claimed as a miscellaneous deduction not subject to the 2% of adjusted gross income (AGI) floor. But gambling losses are only deductible to the extent that you have gambling winnings during the same year. If your winnings are over certain specified amounts, they

TAXALERT

In December 2010, President Obama signed legislation that extended the so-called Bush tax cuts. This new tax law extended the availability of the $250 above-the-line deduction for expenses paid or incurred in 2011 for books, qualifying supplies, equipment (including computer equipment, software, and service) by elementary and secondary school teachers and other eligible school professionals. An "above-the-line" deduction is a deduction you take to reduce your gross income in order to calculate your adjusted gross income. For more information on this adjustment to figuring adjusted gross income, see chapter 19, *Education-related adjustments*. Ordinary and necessary educator expenses that do not qualify for the $250 adjustment may be deductible as a miscellaneous itemized deduction subject to the 2% limitation. For more details, see Education Expenses.

Text intentionally omitted.

Standard mileage rate. The 2011 rate for business use of a vehicle is 51 cents per mile for miles driven January 1, 2011 through June 30, 2011, and 55.5 cents per mile for miles driven after June 30, 2011.

This chapter explains which expenses you can claim as miscellaneous itemized deductions on Schedule A (Form 1040). You must reduce the total of most miscellaneous itemized deductions by 2% of your adjusted gross income. This chapter covers the following topics.

- Deductions subject to the 2% limit.
- Deductions not subject to the 2% limit.
- Expenses you cannot deduct.

You must keep records to verify your deductions. You should keep receipts, canceled checks, substitute checks, financial account statements, and other documentary evidence. For more information on recordkeeping, get Publication 552, *Record-keeping for Individuals*.

Useful Items

You may want to see:

Publication

- □ **463** Travel, Entertainment, Gift, and Car Expenses
- □ **529** Miscellaneous Deductions
- □ **535** Business Expenses
- □ **587** Business Use of Your Home (Including Use by Daycare Providers)
- □ **946** How To Depreciate Property

Form (and Instructions)

- □ **Schedule A (Form 1040)** Itemized Deductions
- □ **2106** Employee Business Expenses
- □ **2106-EZ** Unreimbursed Employee Business Expenses

Deductions Subject to the 2% Limit

You can deduct certain expenses as miscellaneous itemized deductions on Schedule A (Form 1040). You can claim the amount of expenses that is more than 2% of your adjusted gross income. You figure your deduction on Schedule A by subtracting 2% of your adjusted gross income from the total amount of these expenses. Your adjusted gross income is the amount on Form 1040, line 38.

Generally, you apply the 2% limit after you apply any other deduction limit. For example, you apply the 50% (or 80%) limit on business-related meals and entertainment (discussed in chapter 27) before you apply the 2% limit.

EXPLANATION

2% limitation. First, you must determine which expenses are deductible. Next, you must calculate the amount that is deductible, taking into account any limitation for certain types of expenses (e.g., 50% for meals and entertainment). The sum of all of your allowable miscellaneous deductions is then reduced by 2% of your adjusted gross income (AGI).

Example

Assume an individual's adjusted gross income is $45,000 in 2011. This person paid $1,500 in 2011 for the preparation of his 2010 income tax returns and also had $200 of unreimbursed business-related meal expenses for 2011. Both of these expenses are deductible. The $1,500 tax preparation fee is fully deductible, whereas only 50% of the $200 meal expense is deductible. Therefore, total miscellaneous deductions are $1,600 ($1,500 + [50% × $200]). However, 2% of the individual's AGI is $900 ($45,000 × 2%), so he is permitted a deduction of only $700 ($1,600 of total allowable deductions reduced by 2% of AGI, or $900).

will be reported to you on Form W-2G, Certain Gambling Winnings. See Gambling Losses Up to the Amount of Gambling Winnings later in this chapter for more information.

Deductions subject to the 2% limit are discussed in the three categories in which you report them on Schedule A (Form 1040).

- Unreimbursed employee expenses (line 21).
- Tax preparation fees (line 22).
- Other expenses (line 23).

Unreimbursed Employee Expenses (Line 21)

Generally, the following expenses are deductible on Schedule A (Form 1040), line 21.

You can deduct only unreimbursed employee expenses that are:

- Paid or incurred during your tax year,
- For carrying on your trade or business of being an employee, and
- Ordinary and necessary.

An expense is ordinary if it is common and accepted in your trade, business, or profession. An expense is necessary if it is appropriate and helpful to your business. An expense does not have to be required to be considered necessary.

EXPLANATION

Unreimbursed employee business expenses. If you are an employee and have business expenses that are either not reimbursed or are more than the amount reimbursed by your employer, you can generally deduct them only as a miscellaneous deduction (subject to the 2% adjusted gross income limit) on Schedule A (Form 1040).

TAXPLANNER

If you can get your employer to reimburse you for what would otherwise be unreimbursed business expenses, in lieu of an equal amount of future salary, you should do so. The reimbursement for those expenses is not included on your Form W-2 as compensation, so your tax liability should be less. You benefit at no additional cost to your employer because reimbursed employee business expenses that you have adequately reported to your employer are deductible by your employer the same as wages. This only works, however, if you give up your right to receive payment in the event you don't incur any business expenses.

Examples of unreimbursed employee expenses are listed next. The list is followed by discussions of additional unreimbursed employee expenses.

- Business bad debt of an employee.
- Education that is work related. (See chapter 28.)
- Legal fees related to your job.
- Licenses and regulatory fees.
- Malpractice insurance premiums.
- Medical examinations required by an employer.
- Occupational taxes.
- Passport for a business trip.
- Subscriptions to professional journals and trade magazines related to your work.
- Travel, transportation, entertainment, and gifts related to your work. (See chapter 27.)

EXPLANATION

Business bad debt of an employee. A business bad debt is a loss from a debt created or acquired in your trade or business, or a loss when there is a very close relationship between the debt and your trade or business when the debt is created (e.g., as an employee, your main motive for creating the debt is a business reason). For example, if an employee makes a bona fide loan to his employer in order to keep his job, and the company fails to pay the debt, the employee has a business bad debt. See Publication 535 for more information on business bad debts.

EXPLANATION

Business travel and entertainment. Generally, only 50% of the amount spent for business meals (including meals away from home on overnight business) and entertainment will be deductible. This limit must be applied before arriving at the amount subject to the 2% of AGI limitation.

TAXALERT

You are not allowed to deduct the travel expenses of family members, even if there is a business purpose for their presence on the trip, unless the family member is also an employee. If your employer reimburses you for travel expenses, the portion of the expense attributable to family members who are not employees of the company may be included in your W-2 income. See chapter 27, *Car expenses and other employee business expenses,* for more information.

TAXALERT

The deduction percentage for meals consumed while away from home by individuals subject to hours of service limitations of the Department of Transportation, such as interstate truck and bus drivers, certain railroad employees, and certain merchant marines, is 80%. (See *Exceptions to the 50% Limit* under *50% Limit* in chapter 27, *Car expenses and other employee business expenses.*) Note that you must apply this percentage before applying the 2% of adjusted gross income (AGI) limitation.

TAXORGANIZER

Records you should keep. Adequate records should be kept for the amount of your travel and entertainment expenses, the time and place they occurred, the business purpose of the expenses, and the business relationship to the persons entertained in order for you to substantiate your deduction.

Explanation

Business gifts. You can deduct no more than $25 for business gifts to any one person per year. See chapter 27, *Car expenses and other employee business expenses,* for more information.

Business Liability Insurance

You can deduct insurance premiums you paid for protection against personal liability for wrongful acts on the job.

Damages for Breach of Employment Contract

If you break an employment contract, you can deduct damages you pay your former employer that are attributable to the pay you received from that employer.

Depreciation on Computers

You can claim a depreciation deduction for a computer that you use in your work as an employee if its use is:

- For the convenience of your employer, and
- Required as a condition of your employment.

EXPLANATION

"For the convenience of your employer" means that your use of the computer is for a substantial business reason of your employer. All facts must be considered in making this determination. The use of your computer during your regular working hours to carry on your employer's business is generally for the convenience of your employer.

"Required as a condition of your employment" means that you cannot properly perform your duties without it. Whether or not you can properly perform your duties without the computer depends on all the facts and circumstances. It is not necessary that your employer explicitly requires you to use your computer. But neither is it sufficient that your employer merely states that your use of this item is a condition of your employment.

Example

You are an engineer with an engineering firm. You occasionally take work home at night rather than work late at the office. You own and use a computer that is similar to the one you use at the office to complete your work at home. Because your use of the computer is not for the convenience of your employer and is not required as a condition of your employment, you cannot claim a deduction.

TAXALERT

Cellular phones and other telecommunication equipment were subject to the same rules applicable to computers. However, the Small Business Jobs Act of 2010 provided that telecommunication equipment, including cell phones, can now be deducted or depreciated like other business property, without the recordkeeping requirements that apply to computers. This provision became effective for tax years ending after December 31, 2009.

TAXALERT

The depreciation method you may use depends on whether your computer is used predominantly (over 50%) for business or personal purposes. See Publication 529 for more information.

TAXALERT

The rules for depreciation of a computer that you use in your work as an employee differ from the rules for depreciation of a computer owned or leased and used only in your home office. See the section later regarding home offices and Publication 529, *Miscellaneous Deductions*, for more information.

TAXPLANNER

Personal computers. Home computers are frequently used for both business and personal purposes. Video games, children's homework, and personal finances are considered personal uses. If you don't have separate personal and business computers, some type of allocation should be made between business use and personal use of the same computer.

The point to remember is that it is difficult to claim a deduction for your home computer. The IRS position is that no deduction will be allowed for a personal computer unless it meets the "for the convenience of your employer" and "required as a condition of your employment" tests described earlier.

TAXORGANIZER

Records you should keep. Adequate records must be maintained to support your business use of the property in order to claim a depreciation expense deduction.

In case the IRS challenges your deductions for depreciation on home computers, you should keep the following information to support your claim for home computer depreciation deductions:

- Documentation from your employer that use of the home computer is required by the employer; and
- A log of time spent using the computer and whether time was for personal or business use.

For details on allowable methods of depreciation, see chapter 9, *Rental income and expenses*. The Section 179 deduction is explained in chapter 38, *Self-employment income: How to file Schedule C*.

For more information about the rules and exceptions to the rules affecting the allowable deductions for a home computer, see Publication 529.

Dues to Chambers of Commerce and Professional Societies
You may be able to deduct dues paid to professional organizations (such as bar associations and medical associations) and to chambers of commerce and similar organizations, if membership helps you carry out the duties of your job. Similar organizations include:

- Boards of trade,
- Business leagues,
- Civic or public service organizations,
- Real estate boards, and
- Trade associations.

Lobbying and political activities. You may not be able to deduct that part of your dues that is for certain lobbying and political activities. See *Dues used for lobbying* under *Lobbying Expenses,* later.

Educator Expenses
In 2011, if you were an eligible educator, you could deduct your qualified education expenses as an adjustment to income up to $250. If your ordinary and necessary educator expenses were over that amount, you could deduct the excess as a miscellaneous itemized deduction subject to the 2% limit. *Text intentionally omitted.*

TAXALERT
In December 2010, President Obama signed legislation that extended the availability of the above-the-line deduction for up to $250 in expenses paid or incurred in 2011 for books, qualifying supplies, and equipment (including computer equipment, software, and service) by elementary and secondary school teachers and other eligible school professionals. This adjustment reduced income subject to tax regardless of whether or not the taxpayer itemized deductions. For more information on this adjustment to figuring adjusted gross income, see chapter 19, *Education-related adjustments*. Ordinary and necessary educator expenses that do not qualify for the $250 adjustment may be deductible as a miscellaneous itemized deduction (as unreimbursed employee business expenses) subject to the 2% limitation if you otherwise itemize your deductions.

Unless Congress acts, this educator expense adjustment of up to $250 will not be available after 2011. Instead, you will only be able to deduct ordinary and necessary educator expenses as a miscellaneous itemized deduction subject to the 2% limitation. For updated information on this and any other tax law changes that occur after this book was published, see our website, *ey.com/EYTaxGuide*.

Home Office
If you use a part of your home regularly and exclusively for business purposes, you may be able to deduct a part of the operating expenses and depreciation of your home.

TAXALERT
Home office deduction. It is now easier for taxpayers to claim a home office deduction. Even if you were not able to claim a home office deduction in prior years and your business use of your home has not changed, you should check again to see if you are able to take a deduction.

Explanation
Individuals claiming home office deductions on Schedule C are required to figure those deductions on Form 8829, Expenses for Business Use of Your Home. However, if you are an employee claiming unreimbursed job-related expenses, use Form 2106, Employee Business Expenses, if applicable, or include the amount directly on Schedule A.

You can claim this deduction for the business use of a part of your home only if you use that part of your home regularly and exclusively:

- As your principal place of business for any trade or business,
- As a place to meet or deal with your patients, clients, or customers in the normal course of your trade or business, or
- In the case of a separate structure not attached to your home, in connection with your trade or business.

EXPLANATION

A home may be a house, an apartment, a condominium, a mobile home, or even a boat. It may also be other structures on the same property as the house you live in, such as a studio, a barn, a greenhouse, or an unattached garage.

The regular and exclusive business use must be for the convenience of your employer and not just appropriate and helpful in your job. Get Publication 587 for more detailed information and a worksheet.

EXPLANATION

A home office deduction will only be allowed if you use your home in connection with a trade or business. All profit-seeking activities are not trades or businesses (e.g., if you invest from home and are not a broker or dealer investing on behalf of clients or are not a "trader," you are not in the business of investing). However, you may take a home office deduction for a trade or business that is not your full-time occupation, as long as all appropriate tests are met (an example would be an attorney who uses his home office for managing rental properties he owns).

Once the trade or business test is met, the remaining tests for qualifying for a home office deduction are:

1. The "principal place of business" test
2. The "regular and exclusive use" test
3. If an employee, the "for the convenience of your employer" test

The deduction is then limited to your gross income from your trade or business.

TAXPLANNER

Principal place of business. Administrative and management activities for your trade or business that are performed exclusively and regularly in your home will qualify your home as your **principal place of business** if you have no other fixed location where you perform substantial administrative or management activities. Activities that are considered administrative or managerial include billing clients, customers, or patients; keeping books and records; ordering supplies; setting up appointments; and writing reports.

In addition, certain administrative and management activities may be performed in other locations and not disqualify your home office as your principal place of business for purposes of meeting the test described earlier. For example, you may hire another person or company to perform your administrative activities, such as computing employee payrolls, at locations other than your home. You may also conduct administrative and management activities at places that are not fixed locations, such as hotel rooms or airports, and you may occasionally conduct minimal administrative and managerial activities at a fixed location outside of your home. Also, performing substantial non-administrative activities outside of your home, such as servicing clients or making sales calls, will not disqualify your home as your principal place of business. And, significantly, you may even have suitable space available to you outside your home for performing administrative and managerial tasks but choose to use your home instead. (Note, however, that if you are an employee, any use of your home must be for the convenience of your employer in order to qualify for the home office deduction.)

Example
Jeff is a self-employed anesthesiologist, working for three different local hospitals. One of the hospitals provides him with a small shared office where he could perform administrative or management activities. However, Jeff prefers to use a room in his home as an office. He regularly and exclusively uses this room to schedule patients, maintain patient logs, bill patients, and read medical journals.

Prior to 2001, Jeff's home office did not qualify as his principal place of business because his most important activity, administering anesthetics, was performed in the hospitals. Under the current rules, Jeff's office qualifies for the home office deduction in 2011 (i.e., his home office will qualify as his principal place of business) because he conducts administrative and managerial activities for his business there and has no other fixed location where these activities take place. Neither the fact that Jeff has available space at the hospital for performing administrative tasks nor the fact that his most important task is performed outside of his home disqualifies his home office as his principal place of business.

Explanation
To qualify for the **regular and exclusive use** test, you must use a specific area of your home only for your trade or business and on a continuing basis. The specific area can be a separate room or any identifiable space (the space does not need to be marked off by a permanent enclosure). Any personal use of the space will cause you to fail the requirements of the exclusive use test. Occasional or incidental use will cause you to fail the regular use test, even if that area of your house is not used for any other purposes.

Exceptions
Note that there is an exception to the regular and exclusive use test if you use part of your home as a daycare facility for children, persons age 65 or older, or individuals who are physically or mentally incapable of caring for themselves. The daycare provider must be licensed or certified under applicable state law, or exempt from licensing, for the exception to apply. There is also an exception to the regular and exclusive use test if you use part of your home to store inventory or product samples. If your home is the principal place of your business, the space used for inventory and sample storage qualifies for the home office deduction as long as it is used regularly, but not necessarily exclusively, for business.

TAXPLANNER
Many home sales operations require a great deal of personal time and attention but produce a minimum of deductible expenses. You should note, however, that the use of space in your home to store inventory or product samples may produce valuable deductions for otherwise underutilized spaces, such as attics and basements. Remember, the storage space must be a specific area that is used as a part of your principal place of business.

TAXSAVER
Daycare providers. Daycare providers who operate businesses in their homes may benefit from a recent IRS ruling. The square footage of a room that is regularly used for daycare and is available throughout the business day will be considered used for daycare for the entire business day. Previously, taxpayers had to take partial days based on the hours of actual business use. The deduction for daycare providers is equal to the total costs of maintaining the home (e.g., electricity, gas, water, trash collection, general maintenance) to provide daycare, multiplied by the following two fractions:

$$\frac{\text{Total square feet available and used regularly each day}}{\text{Total square feet of home}}$$

$$\frac{\text{Total hours each year home used for daycare business}}{\text{Total hours each year (8,760 hours in 2011)}}$$

The resulting deduction is subject to the income limitation, discussed later. IRS Form 8829 will help you work through this calculation.

Example
A daycare provider uses a bedroom (available for child care throughout the business day) for the children's morning and afternoon naps every day. Although the bedroom is not used during every hour of the business day, the total square footage of that room is considered as daycare usage for the entire business day when the total area for business is calculated.

Explanation

If you are an employee and you meet the tests described earlier for the use of your home in your trade or business, you will only qualify for a home office deduction if your use of your home is for the **convenience of your employer** and you do not rent your home office to your employer. It is not sufficient that a home office is helpful to your job; it must be a requirement of your employer. Your home office must also be justified by the nature of your job, which depends on all the facts and circumstances.

How to figure the deduction. To figure the percentage of your home used for business, you may compare the square feet of space used for business to the total square feet in your home. Or, if the rooms in your home are approximately the same size, you may compare the number of rooms used for business to the total number of rooms in your home. You may also use any other reasonable method. Generally, you figure the business part of your expenses by applying the percentage to the total of each expense.

Example

The room in your home that you use for business measures 120 square feet. Your home measures 1,200 square feet. Therefore, you are using one-tenth, or 10%, of the total area for business.

If you use one room for business in a five-room house and the rooms in your home are about the same size, you are using one-fifth, or 20%, of the total area for business.

Basing the deduction on an approximation of the rental costs of comparable office space is not a proper method, according to one court ruling.

Explanation

The general rule is that the expenses you have for maintaining and running your entire home may be taken, in part, as deductions, because they benefit both the business and the personal parts of your home.

If you have purchased your home, you may deduct part of the interest you pay on your home mortgage as a business expense. To figure the business part of your mortgage interest, multiply the mortgage interest by the part of your home used for business. If you rent a home, you may deduct part of the rent you pay using a similar calculation.

If you have a casualty loss (see chapter 26, *Casualty and theft losses)* on your home or other property that you use in business, you may deduct the business part of the loss as a business expense. The amount of the loss that qualifies for a deduction depends on what property is affected. If the loss is sustained on property that you use only in your business, the entire loss is treated as a business deduction. If the loss affects property used for both business and personal purposes, only the business part is a business deduction.

If you use part of your home for business, you may also deduct part of the expenses for utilities and services, such as electricity, gas, trash removal, and cleaning services. Expenses that are related only to your business, such as business long-distance telephone calls and depreciation of office furniture and equipment, are fully deductible.

Likewise, if you use part of your home for business, you may deduct part of your insurance on your home. However, if your insurance premium gives you coverage for a period that extends past the end of your tax year, you may deduct for business only the part of the premium that covers you for the tax year.

Example

If you paid a 2-year premium of $240 on September 1, 2011, only 4 months of the policy are included in your 2011 tax year. Therefore, only four twenty-fourths (1/6) of the premium may be used to figure your deduction in 2011. In 2012, you may use twelve twenty-fourths (1/2), and in 2013 eight twenty-fourths (1/3) would be used to figure your deduction. The premium must then be allocated between business and nonbusiness uses of your home.

Explanation

When it comes to repairs, you may deduct the cost of labor and supplies for the business part of your home. Your own labor, however, is not a deductible expense.

You can deduct part of the cost of painting the outside of your home or repairing the roof based on the percentage of your home used for business. However, you cannot deduct expenses for lawn care and landscaping.

Example

A repair to your furnace benefits the entire home. If 10% of the area of your home is used for business, 10% of the cost of the furnace repair is deductible.

Depreciation. You can deduct depreciation on the part of your home used for business subject to the limit on the deduction previously discussed.

Home leased to employer. If you lease any part of your home to your employer, you cannot claim a home office deduction for that part for any period you use that part of your home to perform services for your employer. However, you may want to see chapter 9, *Rental income and expenses,* as well as Publication 527, *Residential Rental Property,* for information on deducting rental expenses.

Income limitation. Deductions for the business use of your home may not create or add to a business loss. Therefore, if the total gross income for your business exceeds all of your business expenses (both direct business expenses and the expenses you have allocated for the use of a home office), you may deduct all of your expenses. However, if your business expenses exceed your gross business income, your deduction of certain expenses may be limited. You can carry any excess business expenses that are not currently deductible over to the next tax year, assuming that you have income from the business in the next tax year. If you do not have income from the business in the next tax year, the deductions may be carried to any later year in which you have gross income from the business.

Explanation

Your business deductions for the business use of your home are deducted in the following order:

1. The business percentage of the expenses that would otherwise be allowable as deductions, that is, mortgage interest, real estate taxes, and deductible casualty losses.
2. The direct expenses for your business in your home, such as expenses for supplies and compensation, but not the other expenses of the office in your home (such as those listed later in item 3).
3. The other expenses for the business use of your home, such as maintenance, utilities, insurance, and depreciation. Deductions that adjust the basis in your home are taken last.

Example

Peggy Green is an employee who works in her home for the convenience of her employer. She uses 20% of her home regularly and exclusively for this business purpose. In 2011, her gross income, expenses for the business, and computation of the deduction for the business use of her home are as follows:

Gross income from business use of home		$7,500
Minus:		
Business percentage (20% of home use) of mortgage interest and real estate taxes	2,000	
Other business expenses (supplies, transportation, etc.)	5,000	(7,000)
Modified net income		$500
Business use of home expenses		
Maintenance, insurance, utilities (20%)		$800
Depreciation (20%)		700
Total		$1,500
Deduction limited to modified net income		500
Carryover expenses to 2012 (subject to income limitation in 2012)		$1,000

The deduction of $500 is considered to be maintenance, insurance, and utilities. Peggy will not reduce the basis in her home for the $700 of depreciation until that amount is deducted in a future year.

TAXORGANIZER

Records you should keep. If you intend to deduct home office expenses, it is extremely important that you keep adequate records. You should keep records of clients who come to your home, hours worked at home, type of work done at home, and office equipment purchases. Additionally, you should keep track of repairs that can be allocated to your home office. See the Records You Should Keep section at the front of this book for other items that you should keep.

For more information on using your home in your work and how to compute your allowable deduction, see IRS Publication 587, *Business Use of Your Home (Including Use by Day-Care Providers).*

Job Search Expenses

You can deduct certain expenses you have in looking for a new job in your present occupation, even if you do not get a new job. You cannot deduct these expenses if:

- You are looking for a job in a new occupation,
- There was a substantial break between the ending of your last job and your looking for a new one, or
- You are looking for a job for the first time.

TAXPLANNER

If you are a member of the Armed Forces, you may be able to deduct some costs you incur while looking for a new job. Expenses may include travel, resume preparation fees, and outplacement agency fees. See Publication 3, *Armed Forces Tax Guide*, for more information.

EXAMPLES

- A certified public accountant employed by a national accounting firm was permitted to deduct expenses incurred in investigating whether or not he could practice his profession as a **self-employed** person.
- A corporate executive could deduct expenses involved in seeking a position as a corporate executive with another corporation.
- An attorney for a state agency could deduct the costs of taking an examination for a position as an attorney in another city because the new position would be in the same trade or business.
- An unemployed electrician was allowed to deduct transportation costs for going to the union hall to check on potential job opportunities. He was considered to be in the electrical trade, even though he was unemployed at the time.

Employment and outplacement agency fees. You can deduct employment and outplacement agency fees you pay in looking for a new job in your present occupation.

Employer pays you back. If, in a later year, your employer pays you back for employment agency fees, you must include the amount you receive in your gross income up to the amount of your tax benefit in the earlier year. (See Recoveries in chapter 12.)

Employer pays the employment agency. If your employer pays the fees directly to the employment agency and you are not responsible for them, you do not include them in your gross income.

EXPLANATION

Job search expenses and fees are deductible, even if the agency does not find you a suitable job.

Expenses for career counseling are deductible if they are incurred in your effort to find other employment in the same trade or business.

Résumé. You can deduct amounts you spend for preparing and mailing copies of a resume to prospective employers if you are looking for a new job in your present occupation.

Travel and transportation expenses. If you travel to an area and, while there, you look for a new job in your present occupation, you may be able to deduct travel expenses to and from the area. You can deduct the travel expenses if the trip is primarily to look for a new job. The amount of time you spend on personal activity compared to the amount of time you spend in looking for work is important in determining whether the trip is primarily personal or is primarily to look for a new job.

Even if you cannot deduct the travel expenses to and from an area, you can deduct the expenses of looking for a new job in your present occupation while in the area.

You can choose to use the standard mileage rate to figure your car expenses. The 2011 rate for business use of a vehicle is 51 cents per mile for miles driven prior to July 1, 2011 and 55.5 cents per mile for miles driven after June 30, 2011. See chapter 27 for more information.

TAXORGANIZER

Records you should keep. In case the IRS challenges your deduction for job search expenses, you should keep the following information to support your claim for job search expense deductions:

- Evidence of your current occupation at the time the job search expenses were incurred
- Written records, such as a letter from a prospective employer or an employment agency contract, evidencing a search for employment and the nature of the job
- Receipts, canceled checks, credit card slips, plane tickets, and the like evidencing the amount and payment of job search expenses
- Detailed records and evidence of costs, such as automobile mileage, for which a direct payment is not made
- A log allocating the time spent while traveling on personal activities compared to the time spent looking for a job

Licenses and Regulatory Fees

You can deduct the amount you pay each year to state or local governments for licenses and regulatory fees for your trade, business, or profession.

Occupational Taxes

You can deduct an occupational tax charged at a flat rate by a locality for the privilege of working or conducting a business in the locality. If you are an employee, you can claim occupational taxes only as a miscellaneous deduction subject to the 2% limit; you cannot claim them as a deduction for taxes elsewhere on your return.

Repayment of Income Aid Payment

An "income aid payment" is one that is received under an employer's plan to aid employees who lose their jobs because of lack of work. If you repay a lump-sum income aid payment that you received and included in income in an earlier year, you can deduct the repayment.

Research Expenses of a College Professor

If you are a college professor, you can deduct research expenses, including travel expenses, for teaching, lecturing, or writing and publishing on subjects that relate directly to your teaching duties. You must have undertaken the research as a means of carrying out the duties expected of a professor and without expectation of profit apart from salary. However, you cannot deduct the cost of travel as a form of education.

EXPLANATION

Travel as a form of education is never deductible. An example would be a French teacher who, in order to learn more about local customs in France, travels throughout the country. The travel in this case is not for research in writing or publishing and the person did not teach while traveling. Travel as a form of education tends to resemble travel for personal purposes, and the IRS will disallow a deduction for travel expenses as a form of educational expenses. See chapter 28, *Tax benefits for work-related education*, for more information on deductible expenses.

Tools Used in Your Work

Generally, you can deduct amounts you spend for tools used in your work if the tools wear out and are thrown away within 1 year from the date of purchase. You can depreciate the cost of tools that have a useful life substantially beyond the tax year. For more information about depreciation, see Publication 946.

Union Dues and Expenses

You can deduct dues and initiation fees you pay for union membership.

You can also deduct assessments for benefit payments to unemployed union members. However, you cannot deduct the part of the assessments or contributions that provides funds for the payment of sick, accident, or death benefits. Also, you cannot deduct contributions to a pension fund, even if the union requires you to make the contributions.

You may not be able to deduct amounts you pay to the union that are related to certain lobbying and political activities. See *Lobbying Expenses* under *Nondeductible Expenses,* later.

EXPLANATION

A fine paid by a union member is deductible if by not paying the fine the member would be dropped from the union.

If a union contract provides that all employees, regardless of whether or not they are union members, must pay union dues, the nonmembers may also deduct the union dues.

Caution

It is not enough that you wear distinctive clothing. The clothing must be specifically required by your employer. Nor is it enough that you do not, in fact, wear your work clothes away from work. The clothing must not be suitable for taking the place of your regular clothing.

Work Clothes and Uniforms

You can deduct the cost and upkeep of work clothes if the following two requirements are met.

- You must wear them as a condition of your employment.
- The clothes are not suitable for everyday wear.

Examples of workers who may be able to deduct the cost and upkeep of work clothes are: delivery workers, firefighters, health care workers, law enforcement officers, letter carriers, professional athletes, and transportation workers (air, rail, bus, etc.).

Musicians and entertainers can deduct the cost of theatrical clothing and accessories that are not suitable for everyday wear.

However, work clothing consisting of white cap, white shirt or white jacket, white bib overalls, and standard work shoes, which a painter is required by his union to wear on the job, is not distinctive in character or in the nature of a uniform. Similarly, the costs of buying and maintaining blue work clothes worn by a welder at the request of a foreman are not deductible.

Protective clothing. You can deduct the cost of protective clothing required in your work, such as safety shoes or boots, safety glasses, hard hats, and work gloves.

Examples of workers who may be required to wear safety items are: carpenters, cement workers, chemical workers, electricians, fishing boat crew members, machinists, oil field workers, pipe fitters, steamfitters, and truck drivers.

Military uniforms. You generally cannot deduct the cost of your uniforms if you are on full-time active duty in the armed forces. However, if you are an armed forces reservist, you can deduct the unreimbursed cost of your uniform if military regulations restrict you from wearing it except while on duty as a reservist. In figuring the deduction, you must reduce the cost by any nontaxable allowance you receive for these expenses.

If local military rules do not allow you to wear fatigue uniforms when you are off duty, you can deduct the amount by which the cost of buying and keeping up these uniforms is more than the uniform allowance you receive.

You can deduct the cost of your uniforms if you are a civilian faculty or staff member of a military school.

EXPLANATION

The initial expense and the costs of maintaining work clothes and business uniforms are deductible, not only if they must be worn as a condition of employment and they are not suitable for general or personal use but also if they are in fact not used for personal purposes. Taxpayers have been allowed to deduct costs relating to uniforms in the following cases:

- An art teacher deducted the costs of protective smocks.
- An airline clerk deducted the cost of "unfeminine, businesslike" shoes that she was required to wear and, in fact, wore only at work.
- A hospital worker deducted work clothes he kept in a locker at the hospital. He was in frequent contact with contagious persons and never brought the clothing home.
- A private-duty nurse deducted a uniform that served as a mark of her profession and was necessary for patient care.
- A member of the National Ski Patrol was allowed to deduct the cost of the parkas and ski trousers patrol members are required to wear.
- Scoutmasters, Red Cross volunteers, and others who wear uniforms while performing charitable activities may deduct the cost of the uniforms as charitable donations.

Tax Preparation Fees (Line 22)

You can usually deduct tax preparation fees in the year you pay them. Thus, on your 2011 return, you can deduct fees paid in 2011 for preparing your 2010 return. These fees include the cost of tax preparation software programs and tax publications. They also include any fee you paid for electronic filing of your return.

EXPLANATION

You may deduct expenses paid for the determination, collection, or refund of any tax–income tax, estate tax, gift tax, sales tax, or property tax. Fees paid to a consultant to advise you on the tax consequences of a transaction are deductible. If you contest a tax assessment, any fees paid are deductible, even if the defense is unsuccessful. Professional fees incurred in obtaining federal tax rulings are deductible. However, the cost of filing a complaint in court relating to an IRS levy against property is considered a capital expenditure and therefore not deductible.

TAXPLANNER

Business related. Generally, most tax preparation fees are only deductible on Schedule A and are subject to the 2% adjusted gross income floor. However, according to the IRS, business owners can deduct the portion of tax preparation fees relating to a business directly on Schedule C, E, or F (and related business schedules).

TAXORGANIZER

In order to minimize controversy with the IRS over what portion of tax preparation fees applies to each activity, it's best to have your tax advisor give you a detailed breakdown of your bill, indicating the amounts attributable to each activity.

Example

Mark, an individual taxpayer, owns a consulting business and rental property. In 2010, he paid $900 in tax preparation fees, of which $400 was related to the consulting business, $300 to the rental property, and $200 to his individual return. Mark can deduct $400 as a business expense on Schedule C, $300 as a business expense on Schedule E, and $200 as a miscellaneous itemized deduction (subject to the 2%-adjusted-gross-income floor) on Schedule A.

Other Expenses (Line 23)

You can deduct certain other expenses as miscellaneous itemized deductions subject to the 2% limit. On Schedule A (Form 1040), line 23, you can deduct expenses that you pay:

1. To produce or collect income that must be included in your gross income,
2. To manage, conserve, or maintain property held for producing such income, or
3. To determine, contest, pay, or claim a refund of any tax.

You can deduct expenses you pay for the purposes in (1) and (2) above only if they are reasonably and closely related to these purposes. Some of these other expenses are explained in the following discussions.

If the expenses you pay produce income that is only partially taxable, see *Tax-Exempt Income Expenses,* later, under *Nondeductible Expenses.*

EXPLANATION

Deductions have also been allowed for the following:

- Monthly service charges paid to a bank to participate in an automatic investment service plan
- Service charges subtracted from cash dividends before the dividends are reinvested
- Premiums on indemnity bonds posted to secure replacement of lost taxable securities
- Trustee's commission for administering a revocable trust
- Expenses incurred by an official of the National Association of Investment Clubs in attending conventions
- Transportation and parking costs on trips to the taxpayer's stockbroker
- Packing, moving, and storage expenses of condominium furniture when the only tenant the taxpayer could find wanted the unit unfurnished
- Depreciation on a safe used to store securities and other financial certificates
- Expenses incurred in moving the office in which a taxpayer carries on his or her investment activities to a new location
- Postage related to investment activities
- A fee paid to a broker engaged to find another company that could be merged with the taxpayer's closely held company, even though no company was found
- Safe-deposit box rental when the box was used to store Series EE treasury bonds, even though no income is reportable in the tax year because the taxpayer elected to report the appreciation when the bonds matured (see chapter 7, *Interest income*, for details)
- Entertainment expenses in connection with taxable investments
- Investor's payment to a stockholders' committee that sought changes in corporate management
- Travel expenses to a directors' meeting of a director who was also a substantial minority shareholder. (The taxpayer feared that the policies of the majority would endanger his investment. Because the expense was incurred to protect his investment, it was deductible.)
- Costs incurred in a proxy fight opposing management
- Fees paid to an attorney for estate planning (but not for the preparation of a will)

You may deduct a reward paid for the return of business property you have lost.

Example

A man left his briefcase on the train. A deduction was allowed for the reward given and for the cost of the ad offering the reward.

Appraisal Fees

You can deduct appraisal fees if you pay them to figure a casualty loss or the fair market value of donated property.

Casualty and Theft Losses
You can deduct a casualty or theft loss as a miscellaneous itemized deduction subject to the 2% limit if you used the damaged or stolen property in performing services as an employee. First report the loss in Section B of Form 4684, Casualties and Thefts. You may also have to include the loss on Form 4797, Sales of Business Property, if you are otherwise required to file that form. To figure your deduction, add all casualty or theft losses from this type of property included on Form 4684, lines 32 and 38b, or Form 4797, line 18a. For other casualty and theft losses, see chapter 26.

Clerical Help and Office Rent
You can deduct office expenses, such as rent and clerical help, which you have in connection with your investments and collecting the taxable income on them.

Credit or Debit Card Convenience Fees
You can deduct the convenience fee charged by the card processor for paying your income tax (including estimated tax payments) by credit or debit card. The fees are deductible in the year paid.

Depreciation on Home Computer
You can deduct depreciation on your home computer if you use it to produce income (for example, to manage your investments that produce taxable income). You generally must depreciate the computer using the straight line method over the Alternative Depreciation System (ADS) recovery period. But if you work as an employee and also use the computer in that work, see Publication 946.

Excess Deductions of an Estate
If an estate's total deductions in its last tax year are more than its gross income for that year, the beneficiaries succeeding to the estate's property can deduct the excess. Do not include deductions for the estate's personal exemption and charitable contributions when figuring the estate's total deductions. The beneficiaries can claim the deduction only for the tax year in which, or with which, the estate terminates, whether the year of termination is a normal year or a short tax year. For more information, see *Termination of Estate* in Publication 559, *Survivors, Executors, and Administrators*.

Fees to Collect Interest and Dividends
You can deduct fees you pay to a broker, bank, trustee, or similar agent to collect your taxable bond interest or dividends on shares of stock. But you cannot deduct a fee you pay to a broker to buy investment property, such as stocks or bonds. You must add the fee to the cost of the property.

You cannot deduct the fee you pay to a broker to sell securities. You can use the fee only to figure gain or loss from the sale. See the instructions for Schedule D (Form 1040), columns (d) and (e), for information on how to report the fee.

Hobby Expenses
You can generally deduct hobby expenses, but only up to the amount of hobby income. A hobby is not a business because it is not carried on to make a profit. See *Activity not for profit* in chapter 12 under *Other Income.*

Indirect Deductions of Pass-Through Entities
Pass-through entities include partnerships, S corporations, and mutual funds that are not publicly offered. Deductions of pass-through entities are passed through to the partners or shareholders. The partners or shareholders can deduct their share of passed-through deductions for investment expenses as miscellaneous itemized deductions subject to the 2% limit.

Example. You are a member of an investment club that is formed solely to invest in securities. The club is treated as a partnership. The partnership's income is solely from taxable dividends, interest, and gains from sales of securities. In this case, you can deduct your share of the partnership's operating expenses as miscellaneous itemized deductions subject to the 2% limit. However, if the investment club partnership has investments that also produce nontaxable income, you cannot deduct your share of the partnership's expenses that produce the nontaxable income.

Publicly offered mutual funds. Publicly offered mutual funds do not pass deductions for investment expenses through to shareholders. A mutual fund is "publicly offered" if it is:

- Continuously offered pursuant to a public offering,
- Regularly traded on an established securities market, or
- Held by or for at least 500 persons at all times during the tax year.

A publicly offered mutual fund will send you a Form 1099-DIV, Dividends and Distributions, or a substitute form, showing the net amount of dividend income (gross dividends minus investment expenses). This net figure is the amount you report on your return as income. You cannot deduct investment expenses.

Information returns. You should receive information returns from pass-through entities.

Partnerships and S corporations. These entities issue Schedule K-1, which lists the items and amounts you must report and identifies the tax return schedules and lines to use.

Nonpublicly offered mutual funds. These funds will send you a Form 1099-DIV, Dividends and Distributions, or a substitute form, showing your share of gross income and investment expenses. You can claim the expenses only as a miscellaneous itemized deduction subject to the 2% limit.

Investment Fees and Expenses

You can deduct investment fees, custodial fees, trust administration fees, and other expenses you paid for managing your investments that produce taxable income.

Legal Expenses

You can usually deduct legal expenses that you incur in attempting to produce or collect taxable income or that you pay in connection with the determination, collection, or refund of any tax.

You can also deduct legal expenses that are:

- Related to either doing or keeping your job, such as those you paid to defend yourself against criminal charges arising out of your trade or business,
- For tax advice related to a divorce, if the bill specifies how much is for tax advice and it is determined in a reasonable way, or
- To collect taxable alimony.

You can deduct expenses of resolving tax issues relating to profit or loss from business (Schedule C or C-EZ), rentals or royalties (Schedule E), or farm income and expenses (Schedule F) on the appropriate schedule. You deduct expenses of resolving nonbusiness tax issues on Schedule A (Form 1040). See *Tax Preparation Fees,* earlier.

TAXPLANNER

Professional fees. Legal, accounting, and professional fees often have deductible and nondeductible elements. Whether professional fees should be deducted, capitalized, or considered personal expenses depends on the reasons the fees were incurred. To be deductible as a miscellaneous expense on Schedule A, the expense must either be connected to producing income (advising you on your employment, collecting alimony, and the like) or be incurred for a tax-related matter.

TAXSAVER

The law now makes legal and other expenses deductible in calculating adjusted gross income for "civil rights" type lawsuits which are settled or paid after October 22, 2004.

TAXORGANIZER

Records you should keep. To minimize controversy with the IRS over what portion of a professional fee is deductible, it's best to have the professional give you a detailed breakdown of your bill, indicating which portions are tax-deductible.

Loss on Deposits

For information on whether, and if so, how, you may deduct a loss on your deposit in a qualified financial institution, see *Loss on Deposits* in chapter 26.

TAXSAVER

Loss on IRA. If you have a loss on your traditional IRA (or Roth IRA) investment, you can deduct the loss as a miscellaneous itemized deduction subject to the 2% limit, but only when all the amounts in all your traditional IRA (or Roth IRA) accounts have been distributed to you and the total distributions are less than your unrecovered basis. For more information, see Publication 590, *Individual Retirement Arrangements (IRAs).*

Repayments of Income

If you had to repay an amount that you included in income in an earlier year, you may be able to deduct the amount you repaid. If the amount you had to repay was ordinary income of $3,000 or less, the deduction is subject to the 2% limit. If it was more than $3,000, see *Repayments Under Claim of Right* under *Deductions Not Subject to the 2% Limit,* later.

Repayments of Social Security Benefits

For information on how to deduct your repayments of certain social security benefits, see *Repayments More Than Gross Benefits* in chapter 11.

Safe Deposit Box Rent

You can deduct safe deposit box rent if you use the box to store taxable income-producing stocks, bonds, or investment-related papers and documents. You cannot deduct the rent if you use the box only for jewelry, other personal items, or tax-exempt securities.

Service Charges on Dividend Reinvestment Plans

You can deduct service charges you pay as a subscriber in a dividend reinvestment plan. These service charges include payments for:

- Holding shares acquired through a plan,
- Collecting and reinvesting cash dividends, and
- Keeping individual records and providing detailed statements of accounts.

Trustee's Administrative Fees for IRA

Trustee's administrative fees that are billed separately and paid by you in connection with your individual retirement arrangement (IRA) are deductible (if they are ordinary and necessary) as a miscellaneous itemized deduction subject to the 2% limit. For more information about IRAs, see chapter 17.

TAXSAVER

Administrative fees paid to IRA trustees are deductible if the fees are billed to, and paid by, the account owner separate from any IRA contribution. If the trustee takes the fee out of your $5,000 contribution, you then have less money remaining in the IRA account for investment. Because the income in the IRA account accumulates tax-free, the difference in these two amounts–the full $5,000 and the remainder of that sum after fees–compounded annually, becomes significant over the years. For example, if in 2011 you are under age 50, you can contribute up to $5,000 to your IRA. If the trustee's administration fee for the year is $500, and is not billed separately from the annual contribution, you will have an IRA contribution deduction of $5,000 but will not have any deduction for the fee charged and the IRA balance will only be increased by the net $4,500 that remains in the account. However, if the fee is billed and paid separately, your IRA contribution deduction will be $5,000 and your miscellaneous itemized deduction will be $500. The full $5,000 contribution will be added to your IRA account to accumulate tax-free.

Deductions Not Subject to the 2% Limit

You can deduct the items listed below as miscellaneous itemized deductions. They are not subject to the 2% limit. Report these items on Schedule A (Form 1040), line 28.

List of Deductions

Each of the following items is discussed in detail after the list.

- Amortizable premium on taxable bonds.
- Casualty and theft losses from income-producing property.
- Federal estate tax on income in respect of a decedent.
- Gambling losses up to the amount of gambling winnings.
- Impairment-related work expenses of persons with disabilities.
- Loss from other activities from Schedule K-1 (Form 1065-B), box 2.
- Losses from Ponzi-type investment schemes.
- Repayments of more than $3,000 under a claim of right.
- Unrecovered investment in an annuity.

Amortizable Premium on Taxable Bonds

In general, if the amount you pay for a bond is greater than its stated principal amount, the excess is bond premium. You can elect to amortize the premium on taxable bonds. The amortization of the premium is generally an offset to interest income on the bond rather than a separate deduction item.

Part of the premium on some bonds may be a miscellaneous deduction not subject to the 2% limit. For more information, see *Amortizable Premium on Taxable Bonds* in Publication 529, and *Bond Premium Amortization* in chapter 3 of Publication 550, *Investment Income and Expenses*.

TAXORGANIZER

Records You Should Keep. You should keep documentation that shows the date of purchase, face value, and the purchase price of the bond. The types of documents you may want to keep include your broker's confirmation or monthly account statement.

Casualty and Theft Losses of Income-Producing Property

You can deduct a casualty or theft loss as a miscellaneous itemized deduction not subject to the 2% limit if the damaged or stolen property was income-producing property (property held for investment, such as stocks, notes, bonds, gold, silver, vacant lots, and works of art). First, report the loss in Form 4684, Section B. You may also have to include the loss on Form 4797, Sales of Business Property, if you are otherwise required to file that form. To figure your deduction, add all casualty or theft losses from this type of property included on Form 4684, lines 32 and 38b, or Form 4797, line 18a. For more information on casualty and theft losses, see chapter 26.

TAXALERT

Some taxpayers had attempted to take the position that losses from stock which resulted from corporate malfeasance, such as was the case with Enron or WorldCom, could be deducted as theft losses not subject to the 2% of AGI disallowance. The IRS has ruled that this position is incorrect. Because there was no direct relationship between shareholders and the executives of these companies there was no "theft." Instead, the losses would have to be claimed as capital losses subject to the $3,000 annual limit on such losses.

Caution

You cannot reduce your gambling winnings by your gambling losses and report the difference. You must report the full amount of your winnings as income and claim your losses (up to the amount of winnings) as an itemized deduction. Therefore, your records should show your winnings separately from your losses.

Federal Estate Tax on Income in Respect of a Decedent

You can deduct the federal estate tax attributable to income in respect of a decedent that you as a beneficiary include in your gross income. Income in respect of the decedent is gross income that the decedent would have received had death not occurred and that was not properly includible in the decedent's final income tax return. See Publication 559 for more information.

TAXALERT

Distributions to a beneficiary from an IRA or employer pension plan are common forms of income in respect of a decedent. If the decedent's estate owed federal estate tax on these amounts, the beneficiary may be entitled to claim this income tax deduction.

Records

Diary of winnings and losses. *You must keep an accurate diary or similar record of your losses and winnings. Your diary should contain at least the following information.*

- *The date and type of your specific wager or wagering activity.*
- *The name and address or location of the gambling establishment.*
- *The names of other persons present with you at the gambling establishment.*
- *The amount(s) you won or lost.*

See Publication 529 for more information.

Gambling Losses Up to the Amount of Gambling Winnings

You must report the full amount of your gambling winnings for the year on Form 1040, line 21. You deduct your gambling losses for the year on Schedule A (Form 1040), line 28. You cannot deduct gambling losses that are more than your winnings.

TAXORGANIZER

Records you should keep. For specific wagering transactions, you can use the following items to support your winnings and losses:

Keno: Copies of the keno tickets you purchased that were validated by the gambling establishment, copies of your casino credit records, and copies of your casino check-cashing records.

Slot machines: A record of the machine number and all winnings by date and time the machine was played.

Table games (twenty-one [blackjack], craps, poker, baccarat, roulette, wheel of fortune, etc.): The number of the table at which you were playing and casino credit card data indicating whether the credit was issued in the pit or at the cashier's cage.

Bingo: A record of the number of games played, cost of tickets purchased, and amounts collected on winning tickets. Supplemental records include any receipts from the casino, parlor, etc.

Racing (horse, harness, dog, etc.): A record of the races, amounts of wagers, amounts collected on winning tickets, and amounts lost on losing tickets. Supplemental records include unredeemed tickets and payment records from the racetrack.

Lotteries: A record of ticket purchases, dates, winnings, and losses. Supplemental records include unredeemed tickets, payment slips, and winnings statements.

TAXPLANNER

The cost of transportation, meals, and lodging related to gambling is not tax deductible.

Impairment-Related Work Expenses

If you have a physical or mental disability that limits your being employed, or substantially limits one or more of your major life activities, such as performing manual tasks, walking, speaking, breathing, learning, and working, you can deduct your impairment-related work expenses.

Impairment-related work expenses are ordinary and necessary business expenses for attendant care services at your place of work and for other expenses in connection with your place of work that are necessary for you to be able to work.

Self-employed. If you are self-employed, enter your impairment-related work expenses on the appropriate form (Schedule C, C-EZ, E, or F) used to report your business income and expenses.

Loss From Other Activities From Schedule K-1 (Form 1065-B), Box 2

If the amount reported in Schedule K-1 (Form 1065-B), box 2, is a loss, report it on Schedule A (Form 1040), line 28. It is not subject to the passive activity limitations.

Repayments Under Claim of Right

If you had to repay more than $3,000 that you included in your income in an earlier year because at the time you thought you had an unrestricted right to it, you may be able to deduct the amount you repaid or take a credit against your tax. See *Repayments* in chapter 12 for more information.

Unrecovered Investment in Annuity

A retiree who contributed to the cost of an annuity can exclude from income a part of each payment received as a tax-free return of the retiree's investment. If the retiree dies before the entire investment is recovered tax free, any unrecovered investment can be deducted on the retiree's final income tax return. See chapter 10 for more information about the tax treatment of pensions and annuities.

Nondeductible Expenses

Examples of nondeductible expenses are listed next. The list is followed by discussions of additional nondeductible expenses.

List of Nondeductible Expenses

- Broker's commissions that you paid in connection with your IRA or other investment property.
- Burial or funeral expenses, including the cost of a cemetery lot.
- Capital expenses.
- Fees and licenses, such as car licenses, marriage licenses, and dog tags.
- Hobby losses, but see *Hobby Expenses,* earlier.
- Home repairs, insurance, and rent.
- Illegal bribes and kickbacks—See *Bribes and kickbacks* in chapter 11 of Publication 535.
- Losses from the sale of your home, furniture, personal car, etc.
- Personal disability insurance premiums.
- Personal, living, or family expenses.
- The value of wages never received or lost vacation time.

EXPLANATION

Expenses of a general search or preliminary investigation of a business or investment by an individual taxpayer are generally nondeductible.

Exception

While funeral and burial expenses may not be deducted on your personal income tax return, they may be deducted on your federal estate tax return (Form 706). Contributions to a not-for-profit cemetery company may be deductible as charitable contributions.

Adoption Expenses

You cannot deduct the expenses of adopting a child, but you may be able to take a credit for those expenses. See chapter 37.

Campaign Expenses

You cannot deduct campaign expenses of a candidate for any office, even if the candidate is running for reelection to the office. These include qualification and registration fees for primary elections.

Legal fees. You cannot deduct legal fees paid to defend charges that arise from participation in a political campaign.

Check-Writing Fees on Personal Account

If you have a personal checking account, you cannot deduct fees charged by the bank for the privilege of writing checks, even if the account pays interest.

Club Dues

Generally, you cannot deduct the cost of membership in any club organized for business, pleasure, recreation, or other social purpose. This includes business, social, athletic, luncheon, sporting, airline, hotel, golf, and country clubs.

You cannot deduct dues paid to an organization if one of its main purposes is to:

- Conduct entertainment activities for members or their guests, or
- Provide members or their guests with access to entertainment facilities.

Dues paid to airline, hotel, and luncheon clubs are not deductible.

EXPLANATION

No deduction is allowed for club dues if the club is organized for business, pleasure, recreation, or social purposes. These clubs include any organization whose principal purpose is the entertainment of its members or guests. The character of an organization is determined by its purposes and activities, not by its name. For example, no deduction is allowed for dues paid to country clubs, airline clubs, and hotel clubs.

The IRS has specified, however, that some club dues will continue to be deductible under the regular business-use rules. For example, dues paid to trade associations, bar and medical associations, and civic organizations–such as Rotary clubs or Kiwanis clubs–will continue to be deductible as long as the principal purpose of these organizations is not to conduct entertainment activities for their members.

TAXSAVER

Meals and entertainment. Specific business expenses, such as meals and entertainment that occur at a club, are deductible to the extent that they otherwise satisfy the standard for deductibility. For details, see chapter 27, *Car expenses and other employee business expenses*.

Commuting Expenses

You cannot deduct commuting expenses (the cost of transportation between your home and your main or regular place of work). If you haul tools, instruments, or other items, in your car to and from work, you can deduct only the additional cost of hauling the items such as the rent on a trailer to carry the items.

EXPLANATION

Commuting to a temporary work site can be a deductible expense. A work assignment is temporary if the individual has the expectation that it will last less than one year, and it actually does last for one year or less. If you have a regular place of business away from home, then travel expenses from home to a temporary work site are deductible, regardless of the distance.

An individual who has no regular place of business outside the home (or a home office), but who works at several locations within a metropolitan area, can deduct travel expenses to a temporary work site outside the metropolitan area. However, many people commute as many as 2 hours or more one way. Therefore, the IRS interpretation of a "metropolitan area" is expanding.

Another increasingly common scenario is an individual who loses his full-time job due to downsizing or outsourcing and subsequently works for several different employers on a part-time basis. This individual has no regular place of business. It is not clear whether his travel to a temporary work site outside the metropolitan area is deductible. A strict interpretation of the rules would indicate that such travel is deductible, because a regular business location is not a consideration. However, the IRS may argue that he has merely extended his personal commute, because he is working for a different employer in each location.

TAXSAVER

If you drive to a location close to home to perform a bona fide job function and then drive to your regular work location, the second leg of the trip is deductible. See chapter 27, *Car expenses and other employee business expenses,* for details.

Example

An accountant drives to the local IRS office to represent clients and then goes to his office downtown later that day. The second leg of his travel is deductible.

TAXORGANIZER

Records you should keep:

- Purchase price of car
- Monthly lease payments on car
- Gas receipts
- Toll receipts
- Receipts for repairs and maintenance
- Log showing the date of the trip, beginning mileage, ending mileage, and purpose of the trip
- Receipts for personal property tax and interest expense on car

You should keep a written record of expenses and dates incurred to verify deductibility.

Fines or Penalties

You cannot deduct fines or penalties you pay to a governmental unit for violating a law. This includes an amount paid in settlement of your actual or potential liability for a fine or penalty (civil or criminal). Fines or penalties include parking tickets, tax penalties, and penalties deducted from teachers' paychecks after an illegal strike.

EXPLANATION

Although state taxes are deductible when itemizing your deductions, the penalties and interest related to the underpayment or late payment of taxes are not deductible.

Health Spa Expenses

You cannot deduct health spa expenses, even if there is a job requirement to stay in excellent physical condition, such as might be required of a law enforcement officer.

Home Security System

You cannot deduct the cost of a home security system as a miscellaneous deduction. However, you may be able to claim a deduction for a home security system as a business expense if you have a home office. See *Home Office* under *Unreimbursed Employee Expenses,* earlier, and *Security System* under *Deducting Expenses* in Publication 587.

Investment-Related Seminars

You cannot deduct any expenses for attending a convention, seminar, or similar meeting for investment purposes.

Life Insurance Premiums

You cannot deduct premiums you pay on your life insurance. You may be able to deduct, as alimony, premiums you pay on life insurance policies assigned to your former spouse. See chapter 18 for information on alimony.

Lobbying Expenses

You generally cannot deduct amounts paid or incurred for lobbying expenses. These include expenses to:

- Influence legislation,
- Participate or intervene in any political campaign for, or against, any candidate for public office,
- Attempt to influence the general public, or segments of the public, about elections, legislative matters, or referendums, or
- Communicate directly with covered executive branch officials in any attempt to influence the official actions or positions of those officials.

Lobbying expenses also include any amounts paid or incurred for research, preparation, planning, or coordination of any of these activities.

Dues used for lobbying. If a tax-exempt organization notifies you that part of the dues or other amounts you pay to the organization are used to pay nondeductible lobbying expenses, you cannot deduct that part. See *Lobbying Expenses* in Publication 529 for information on exceptions.

Lost or Mislaid Cash or Property

You cannot deduct a loss based on the mere disappearance of money or property. However, an accidental loss or disappearance of property can qualify as a casualty if it results from an identifiable event that is sudden, unexpected, or unusual. See chapter 26.

Example. A car door is accidentally slammed on your hand, breaking the setting of your diamond ring. The diamond falls from the ring and is never found. The loss of the diamond is a casualty.

Lunches with Co-workers

You cannot deduct the expenses of lunches with co-workers, except while traveling away from home on business. See chapter 27 for information on deductible expenses while traveling away from home.

Meals While Working Late

You cannot deduct the cost of meals while working late. However, you may be able to claim a deduction if the cost of meals is a deductible entertainment expense, or if you are traveling away from home. See chapter 27 for information on deductible entertainment expenses and expenses while traveling away from home.

Personal Legal Expenses

You cannot deduct personal legal expenses such as those for the following.

- Custody of children.
- Breach of promise to marry suit.
- Civil or criminal charges resulting from a personal relationship.
- Damages for personal injury, except for certain unlawful discrimination and whistleblower claims.
- Preparation of a title (or defense or perfection of a title).
- Preparation of a will.
- Property claims or property settlement in a divorce.

You cannot deduct these expenses even if a result of the legal proceeding is the loss of income-producing property.

Political Contributions

You cannot deduct contributions made to a political candidate, a campaign committee, or a newsletter fund. Advertisements in convention bulletins and admissions to dinners or programs that benefit a political party or political candidate are not deductible.

Professional Accreditation Fees

You cannot deduct professional accreditation fees such as the following.

- Accounting certificate fees paid for the initial right to practice accounting.
- Bar exam fees and incidental expenses in securing initial admission to the bar.
- Medical and dental license fees paid to get initial licensing.

Professional Reputation

You cannot deduct expenses of radio and TV appearances to increase your personal prestige or establish your professional reputation.

Relief Fund Contributions

You cannot deduct contributions paid to a private plan that pays benefits to any covered employee who cannot work because of any injury or illness not related to the job.

Residential Telephone Service

You cannot deduct any charge (including taxes) for basic local telephone service for the first telephone line to your residence, even if it is used in a trade or business.

Stockholders' Meetings

You cannot deduct transportation and other expenses you pay to attend stockholders' meetings of companies in which you own stock but have no other interest. You cannot deduct these expenses even if you are attending the meeting to get information that would be useful in making further investments.

EXPLANATION

The courts have allowed deductions for stockholders' meetings when the shareholders' interests are more extensive. Consider the following:

- A shareholder who went to a meeting to present a resolution that management stop diluting shareholder equity was entitled to deduct his travel expenses. (See chapter 27, *Car expenses and other employee business expenses.*)
- A court held that an investor's travel expenses to an investment convention were deductible because (1) the trip was part of a rationally planned, systematic investigation of business operations; (2) the costs were reasonable in relation to the size of the investment and the value of the information expected; (3) there was no disguised personal motive for the trip; and (4) there was evidence of practical application of the information obtained on the trip.
- Nevertheless, if a person owns only a very small interest in a large corporation and cannot reasonably expect that his or her attendance at a stockholders' meeting would affect his or her income or investment, the deduction of travel expenses probably would not be allowed.

Tax-Exempt Income Expenses

You cannot deduct expenses to produce tax-exempt income. You cannot deduct interest on a debt incurred or continued to buy or carry tax-exempt securities.

If you have expenses to produce both taxable and tax-exempt income, but you cannot identify the expenses that produce each type of income, you must divide the expenses based on the amount of each type of income to determine the amount that you can deduct.

Example. During the year, you received taxable interest of $4,800 and tax-exempt interest of $1,200. In earning this income, you had total expenses of $500 during the year. You cannot identify the amount of each expense item that is for each income item. Therefore, 80% ($4,800/$6,000) of the expense is for the taxable interest and 20% ($1,200/$6,000) is for the tax-exempt interest. You can deduct, subject to the 2% limit, expenses of $400 (80% of $500).

Travel Expenses for Another Individual

You generally cannot deduct travel expenses you pay or incur for a spouse, dependent, or other individual who accompanies you (or your employee) on business or personal travel. See chapter 27 for more information on deductible travel expenses.

Voluntary Unemployment Benefit Fund Contributions

You cannot deduct voluntary unemployment benefit fund contributions you make to a union fund or a private fund. However, you can deduct contributions as taxes if state law requires you to make them to a state unemployment fund that covers you for the loss of wages from unemployment caused by business conditions.

Wristwatches

You cannot deduct the cost of a wristwatch, even if there is a job requirement that you know the correct time to properly perform your duties.

EXPLANATION

The courts have found the following to be nondeductible expenses:

- Amounts paid to guard a personal residence against burglary attempts
- The cost of a home security system installed to protect a collector's stamps and coins. (The IRS reasoned that the activity was an investment activity and not a regular trade or business; consequently, the expense did not meet the home office rules, discussed earlier in this chapter.)
- Payments for general advice pertaining to a family trust
- Legal fees for defending a libel suit arising from the purchase of the taxpayer's residence

TAXALERT

The cost of specific legal advice on the disposition of a stock is not deductible as a miscellaneous expense on Schedule A but must be treated as a selling expense and an increase to your basis.

TAXORGANIZER

Records you should keep:

- Legal fees itemizing services performed
- Tax preparation fees that allocate amounts between Schedules A, C, and E
- Financial account statements that indicate investment fees
- Logs substantiating the use of property (i.e., a home computer, an automobile) for both business and personal purposes
- Home office expenses and the calculation to allocate total expenses between business and personal use
- Evidence of job search expenses
- For miscellaneous deductions, taxpayers' records should demonstrate (1) why the expense is deductible due to its relationship to the production or collection of income or the determination of tax, and (2) that the expense is clearly incurred in support of that deductible purpose

Chapter 30
Limit on itemized deductions

ey.com/EYTaxGuide

Note

ey.com/EYTaxGuide
Ernst & Young LLP will update the *Ernst & Young Tax Guide 2012* website with relevant taxpayer information as it becomes available. You can also sign up for email alerts to let you know when changes have been made.

Introduction

The tax law limits the amount of certain itemized deductions that individuals can use to reduce their taxable income. For example, the threshold for deducting medical and dental expenses is 7.5% of adjusted gross income (AGI) (see chapter 22, *Medical and dental expenses*), certain miscellaneous deductions are limited to those in excess of 2% of adjusted gross income (see chapter 29, *Miscellaneous deductions*), and home mortgage interest expense is subject to various limitations (see chapter 24, *Interest expense*).

Prior to 2010, the tax law also imposed an additional "overall" limitation on the deductibility of a certain group of itemized deductions. (In 2009, the phaseout on this group of itemized deductions was 1% of the amount of your AGI in excess of $166,800; $83,400 if married filing separately. But not more than 26.67% of these otherwise allowable deductions were disallowed.)

For 2011 (as well as 2010 and 2012), however, the "overall" itemized deduction limitation (or phaseout), is repealed altogether. Higher-income taxpayers will not have to reduce their total itemized deductions based on their AGI. Unless Congress acts, the old phaseout rules are scheduled to be fully reinstated beginning in 2013.

TAXALERT

Overall phaseout of itemized deductions scheduled to resume in 2013. Under the tax law scheduled to take effect in 2013, the phaseout on itemized deductions will be 3% of the amount of your AGI in excess of the applicable thresholds (For 2009, the threshold was $166,800 [$83,400 if married filing separately]. The amounts applicable to 2013 will be indexed for inflation.) No more than 80% of these otherwise allowable deductions will be phased out.

Itemized deductions that will be again subject to this limitation include taxes, home mortgage interest, charitable contributions, and miscellaneous itemized deductions. This limitation will be applied after you have used any other limitations that exist in the law, such as the AGI limitation for charitable contributions and the mortgage interest expense limitations. However, medical expenses, casualty and theft losses, investment interest expense, and deductible gambling losses are not subject to this rule.

Example 1

Martin and Judy Stone file a joint income tax return for 2013. They have an adjusted gross income of $350,500. The Stones' only itemized deductions are $20,000 of home mortgage interest and $8,000 of real estate taxes. Because both of these itemized deductions are subject to the overall limitation, their total deductions of $28,000 must be reduced by $5,511. $5,511 is the smaller of either 3% of $183,700 (the amount by which AGI exceeds $166,800–assuming the threshold in 2013 is the same as it was for 2009), or 80% of $28,000 ($22,400). They may reduce their taxable income by total itemized deductions of $22,489 ($28,000 – $5,511).

Example 2

Assume the same facts as *Example 1*, except that the Stones live in a downtown apartment, and their only itemized deduction is $28,000 of otherwise allowable investment interest expense. Because investment interest expense is not subject to the 3% limitation, the entire $28,000 will be deductible.

President Obama has proposed raising the applicable threshold amount beginning in 2013 to $250,000 for married taxpayers filing jointly and $200,000 for single taxpayers (both adjusted for inflation from 2009 values). In addition, the annual threshold would be increased each year for inflation. For updated information on this and any other tax law changes that occur after this book was published, see our website, *ey.com/EYTaxGuide*.

TAXSAVER

Since the overall limitation on itemized deductions is repealed for 2011 and 2012 but scheduled to be restored in 2013, higher-income taxpayers may consider accelerating itemized deductions that would be subject to the phaseout in 2013 to 2012. Rather than losing the tax benefit from such deductions altogether, these deductions could reduce their 2012 tax bill. But if you consider accelerating your itemized deductions, you need to weigh all the ramifications. For example, how much would prepaying such items strain your available financial resources? You should also monitor potential legislative changes to these phaseout rules that may be enacted in the near future. Affected taxpayers should see their tax advisor for assistance.

Part 6

Figuring your taxes and credits

ey.com/EYTaxGuide

The seven chapters in this part explain how to figure your tax and how to figure the tax of certain children who have more than $1,900 of investment income. They also discuss tax credits that, unlike deductions, are subtracted directly from your tax and reduce your tax, dollar for dollar. Chapter 37 discusses the earned income credit and how you may be able to get part of the credit paid to you in advance throughout the year.

Chapter 31

How to figure your tax

ey.com/EYTaxGuide

Note

IRS Publication 17 (*Your Federal Income Tax*) has been updated by Ernst & Young LLP for 2011. Dates and dollar amounts shown are for 2011. Underlined type is used to indicate where IRS text has been updated. Places where text has been removed are indicated by the sentence: *Text intentionally omitted*.

ey.com/EYTaxGuide

Ernst & Young LLP will update the *Ernst & Young Tax Guide 2012* website with relevant taxpayer information as it becomes available. You can also sign up for email alerts to let you know when changes have been made.

Introduction

This chapter explains how to calculate your tax liability under all three available tax forms—Form 1040EZ, Form 1040A, and Form 1040. It will help you decide which of the forms to file.

In particular, you should review the section of this chapter on the alternative minimum tax to determine if that tax may apply to you.

What's New

Personal Exemption amount increased for 2011. The personal exemption amount for tax years beginning in 2011 is increased to $3,700.

TAXALERT

Prior to 2010, personal exemptions were subject to certain limitations if your adjusted gross income (AGI) exceeded certain amounts. But the phaseout of personal exemptions has been temporarily repealed and higher-income taxpayers do not have to reduce their total personal exemptions for 2011 or 2012. Unless Congress acts, the old phaseout rule is scheduled to return beginning in 2013.

Standard Deduction amount increased. The personal standard deduction amount for tax years beginning in 2011 is increased to $5,800 for unmarried taxpayers, $11,600 if married filing jointly or a surviving spouse, $8,500 if filing as head of household, and $5,800 if married filing separately.

Alternative Minimum Tax (AMT) exemption amount increased. For 2011, the AMT exemption amount is increased to $48,450 ($74,450 if married filing jointly or a qualifying widow(er); $37,225 if married filing separately).

AMT exemption amount for a child increased. The AMT exemption amount for a child whose unearned income is taxed at the parent's tax rate has increased to $6,800.

TAXALERT

In recent years, Congress has repeatedly enacted temporary measures (typically called an "AMT patch") that significantly raised the applicable AMT exemption amounts above the level that last applied in 2000. In December 2010, the President and Congress agreed to extend the so-called Bush tax cuts. Under this new tax law, the AMT exemption for 2011 was also increased as follows:

- $74,450 (up from $72,450 in 2010) for married couples filing jointly and surviving spouses;
- $48,450 (up from $47,450 in 2010) for other unmarried individuals; and,
- $37,225 (up from $36,225 in 2010) for married individuals filing separate returns.

Tax Breaks and Deductions You Can Use Checklist

The Alternative Minimum Tax (AMT). If you have large amounts of certain deductions, such as personal exemptions; state and local income taxes, sales taxes or real estate taxes; interest on certain home equity loans; and miscellaneous itemized deductions, or have certain types of income such as income from the exercise of an incentive stock option, you must consider the impact of the AMT. Many taxpayers cannot avoid the AMT because of the size of their family or where they live. Others may be able to plan to minimize its impact.

The exemption phases out at higher levels of alternative minimum taxable income (AMTI). For 2011, the exemptions fully phase out at: $447,800 of AMTI for married couples filing jointly and surviving spouses; $306,300 for other unmarried individuals; and $223,900 for married individuals filing separately. This increases the income range in which AMT taxpayers would be subject to a marginal tax rate of as high as 22% on capital gains and qualified dividends.

Absent any future legislation to change the AMT exemption once again, the 2012 AMT exemption amounts will revert to the levels that existed before 2001: $45,000 for married couples filing jointly and surviving spouses, $33,750 for other unmarried individuals, and $22,500 for married individuals filing separately. Such lower exemption amounts will result in substantially more taxpayers subject to the AMT in 2012. For updated information on this and any other tax law changes that occur after this book was published, see our website, ey.com/EYTaxGuide.

After you have figured your income and deductions as explained in *Parts One* through *Five,* your next step is to figure your tax. **This chapter discusses:**

- **The general steps you take to figure your tax,**
- **An additional tax you may have to pay called the alternative minimum tax, and**
- **The conditions you must meet if you want the IRS to figure your tax.**

TAXPLANNER

As described later in more detail in the TaxAlert on "How the AMT works," the AMT structure requires taxpayers to "add back" certain preference and adjustment items to arrive at AMT income, subject to tax at the 26% or 28% minimum tax rates. Under prior law, one of the preference items was tax-exempt interest on certain bonds issued for private activities.

Tax legislation enacted in 2009, however, provides that interest received on tax-exempt private activity bonds issued in 2009 and 2010 is not an AMT preference item. You should consult with your investment advisor to see how the new provision may have affected the interest rate on private activity bonds issued during this 2-year period (issuers may have been able to issue bonds with a somewhat lower interest rate than they otherwise would have had to do when interest paid was treated as a preference item), as well as the effect on market pricing for new and previously issued bonds. Interest received on private activity bonds issued prior to 2009 and after 2010 is counted as an AMT preference.

Figuring Your Tax

Your income tax is based on your taxable income. After you figure your income tax and any alternative minimum tax, subtract your tax credits and add any other taxes you may owe. The result is your total tax. Compare your total tax with your total payments to determine whether you are entitled to a refund or owe additional tax.

This section provides a general outline of how to figure your tax. You can find step-by-step directions in the Instructions for Forms 1040EZ, 1040A, and 1040. If you are unsure of which tax form you should file, see *Which Form Should I Use?* in chapter 1.

Tax. Most taxpayers use either the Tax Table or the Tax Computation Worksheet to figure their income tax. However, there are special methods if your income includes any of the following items.

- A net capital gain. (See chapter 16.)
- Qualified dividends taxed at the same rates as a net capital gain. (See chapters 8 and 16.)
- Lump-sum distributions. (See chapter 10.)
- Farming or fishing income. (See Schedule J (Form 1040), Income Averaging for Farmers and Fishermen.)
- Investment income over $1,900 for certain children. (See chapter 32.)
- Parents' election to report child's interest and dividends. (See chapter 32.)
- Foreign earned income exclusion or the housing exclusion. (See Form 2555, Foreign Earned Income, or Form 2555-EZ, Foreign Earned Income Exclusion, and the Foreign Earned Income Tax Worksheet in the Form 1040 Instructions.)

Credits. After you figure your income tax and any alternative minimum tax (discussed later), determine your tax credits. This chapter does not explain whether you are eligible for these credits. You can find that information in chapters 33 through 37 and your form instructions. See the following table for credits you may be able to subtract from your income tax.

Credits

For information on:	See chapter:
Adoption	37
Alternative motor vehicle	37
Alternative fuel vehicle refueling property	37
Child and dependent care	33
Child tax credit	35
Credit to holders of tax credit bonds	37
Education	36
Elderly or disabled	34
Electric vehicle credits	37
Foreign tax	37
Mortgage interest	37
Prior year minimum tax	37
Residential energy	37
Retirement savings contributions	37

Some credits (such as the earned income credit) are not listed above because they are treated as payments. See *Payments,* later.

There are other credits that are not discussed in this publication. These include the following credits.

- General business credit, which is made up of several separate business-related credits. These generally are reported on Form 3800, General Business Credit, and are discussed in chapter 4 of Publication 334, *Tax Guide for Small Business*.
- Empowerment zone and renewal community employment credit. See Form 8844.
- District of Columbia first-time homebuyer credit. See Form 8859.
- Credit for alcohol used as fuel. See Form 6478.
- Renewable electricity, refined coal, and Indian coal production credit for electricity and refined coal produced at facilities placed in service after October 22, 2004, and Indian coal produced at facilities placed in service after August 8, 2005. See Form 8835, Part II.
- Work opportunity credit. See Form 5884.
- Credit for employer social security and Medicare taxes paid on certain employee tips. See Form 8846.

Other taxes. After you subtract your tax credits, determine whether there are any other taxes you must pay. This chapter does not explain these other taxes. You can find that information in other chapters of this publication and your form instructions. See the following table for other taxes you may need to add to your income tax.

Other Taxes

For information on:	See chapter:
Additional taxes on qualified retirement plans and IRAs	10, 17
Advance earned income credit payments	37
Household employment taxes	33
Recapture of an education credit	36
Social security and Medicare tax on wages	5
Social security and Medicare tax on tips	6
Uncollected social security and Medicare tax on tips	6

Another tax you may have to pay, the alternative minimum tax, is discussed later in this chapter.

There are other taxes that are not discussed in this publication. These include the following items.

1. *Self-employment tax.* You must figure this tax if either of the following applies to you (or your spouse if you file a joint return).
   a. Your net earnings from self-employment from other than church employee income were $400 or more. The term "net earnings from self-employment" may include certain nonemployee compensation and other amounts reported to you on Form 1099-MISC, Miscellaneous Income. If you received a Form 1099-MISC, see the *Instructions for Recipients* on the back. Also see the Instructions for Schedule SE (Form 1040), Self-Employment Tax; and Publication 334, *Tax Guide for Small Business*.
   b. You had church employee income of $108.28 or more.

2. *Recapture taxes.* You may have to pay these taxes if you previously claimed an investment credit, a District of Columbia first-time homebuyer credit, a low-income housing credit, a new markets credit, a qualified plug-in electric vehicle credit, an alternative motor vehicle credit, a credit for employer-provided child care facilities, an Indian employment credit, or other credits listed in the instructions for Form 1040, line 60. For more information, see the instructions for Form 1040, line 60.
3. *Section 72(m)(5) excess benefits tax.* If you are (or were) a 5% owner of a business and you received a distribution that exceeds the benefits provided for you under the qualified pension or annuity plan formula, you may have to pay this additional tax. See *Tax on Excess Benefits* in chapter 4 of Publication 560, *Retirement Plans for Small Business* (SEP, SIMPLE, and Qualified Plans).
4. *Uncollected social security and Medicare tax on group-term life insurance.* If your former employer provides you with more than $50,000 of group-term life insurance coverage, you must pay the employee part of social security and Medicare taxes on those premiums. The amount should be shown in box 12 of your Form W-2 with codes M and N.
5. *Tax on golden parachute payments.* This tax applies if you received an "excess parachute payment" (EPP) due to a change in a corporation's ownership or control. The amount should be shown in box 12 of your Form W-2 with code K. See the instructions for Form 1040, line 60.
6. *Tax on accumulation distribution of trusts.* This applies if you are the beneficiary of a trust that accumulated its income instead of distributing it currently. See the Instructions for Form 4970, Tax on Accumulation Distribution of Trusts.
7. *Additional tax on HSAs or MSAs.* If amounts contributed to, or distributed from, your health savings account or medical savings account do not meet the rules for these accounts, you may have to pay additional taxes. See Publication 969, *Health Savings Accounts and Other Tax-Favored Health Plans*; Form 8853, Archer MSAs and Long-Term Care Insurance Contracts; Form 8889, Health Savings Accounts (HSAs); and Form 5329, Additional Taxes on Qualified Plans (Including IRAs) and Other Tax-Favored Accounts.
8. *Additional tax on Coverdell ESAs.* This applies if amounts contributed to, or distributed from, your Coverdell ESA do not meet the rules for these accounts. See Publication 970, *Tax Benefits for Education*, and Form 5329.
9. *Additional tax on qualified tuition programs.* This applies to amounts distributed from qualified tuition programs that do not meet the rules for these accounts. See Publication 970 and Form 5329.
10. *Excise tax on insider stock compensation from an expatriated corporation.* You may owe a 15% excise tax on the value of non-statutory stock options and certain other stock-based compensation held by you or a member of your family from an expatriated corporation or its expanded affiliated group in which you were an officer, director, or more-than-10% owner. For more information, see the instructions for Form 1040, line 60.
11. *Additional tax on income you received from a nonqualified deferred compensation plan that fails to meet certain requirements.* This income should be shown in Form W-2, box 12, with code Z, or in Form 1099-MISC, box 15b. For more information, see the instructions for Form 1040, line 60.
12. *Interest on the tax due on installment income from the sale of certain residential lots and timeshares.* For more information, see the instructions for Form 1040, line 60.
13. *Interest on the deferred tax on gain from certain installment sales with a sales price over $150,000.* For more information, see the instructions for Form 1040, line 60.

Payments. After you determine your total tax, figure the total payments you have already made for the year. Include credits that are treated as payments. This chapter does not explain these payments and credits. You can find that information in other chapters of this publication and your form instructions. See the following table for amounts you can include in your total payments.

Payments

For information on:	See chapter:
Child tax credit (additional)	35
Earned income credit	37
Estimated tax paid	4

Excess social security and RRTA tax withheld	37
Federal income tax withheld	4
First-time homebuyer credit	37
Health coverage tax credit	37
Regulated investment company credit	37
Refundable credit for prior-year minimum tax	37
Tax paid with extension	1

Another credit that is treated as a payment is the credit for federal excise tax paid on fuels. This credit is for persons who have a nontaxable use of certain fuels, such as diesel fuel and kerosene. It is claimed on Form 1040, line 70. See Form 4136, Credit for Federal Tax Paid on Fuels.

Refund or balance due. To determine whether you are entitled to a refund or owe additional tax, compare your total payments with your total tax. If you are entitled to a refund, see your form instructions for information on having it directly deposited into one or more of your accounts instead of receiving a paper check.

EXPLANATION

For information on how to elect to pay your 2011 tax in installments, see Amount You Owe in chapter 1, *Filing information.*

Alternative Minimum Tax

This section briefly discusses an additional tax you may have to pay.

The tax law gives special treatment to some kinds of income and allows special deductions and credits for some kinds of expenses. Taxpayers who benefit from the law in these ways may have to pay at least a minimum amount of tax through an additional tax. This additional tax is called the alternative minimum tax (AMT).

TAXALERT

In recent years, an increasing number of taxpayers have been subject to the alternative minimum tax (AMT). Indeed, absent legislation that extends the increased AMT personal exemption amounts that will expire at the end of 2011, over 25% of all individual taxpayers will be subject to the AMT in 2012.

Begun in 1970, the AMT was originally intended to ensure the "rich" paid at least some minimum amount of tax. Until recently the vast majority of taxpayers were not subject to the AMT. But the reduction in regular income tax rates in 2001 and 2003 without a corresponding reduction in AMT rates caused more people to become subject to this tax.

How the AMT works: The simplest way to understand the AMT is to think of it as a separate tax system with its own allowable deductions and exclusions, many of which are different from those allowed for regular income tax purposes. Thus, although it is in many ways parallel to the "regular income tax" computation, some of the applicable rules are different. You first calculate your regular income tax as you always have, then you calculate your tax under the AMT system and pay the greater of the two amounts. The following are some of the more common items treated differently under the two tax systems that can affect your exposure to AMT:

- State and local income and sales taxes
- Real estate and personal property taxes
- Large medical and dental expenses
- Miscellaneous itemized deductions (subject to the 2% of AGI floor)
- Interest expense from a mortgage or home equity loan that is not used for the purpose of acquiring, constructing, or improving a principal residence or "second home"
- The "spread" on the exercise of incentive stock options (ISOs)
- Deductions for personal exemptions
- The standard deduction

Most of these items consist of deductions that are allowed in computing your regular income tax liability but are not allowed when you figure your AMT. Take, for example, state and local income, sales, and real estate taxes that you pay. They are allowable as a deduction against your income for regular tax purposes but not for AMT. (You'll find a more detailed explanation of how to figure your AMT later in this section.)

TAXALERT

If your deduction for state taxes is unusually high—for example, perhaps you made a large payment with your 2010 state tax return when you filed in April 2011, or perhaps you have substantial state tax withholding during 2011 on your regular income—you should take a closer look at the possibility of being subject to the AMT.

Example

The Smiths have two children and gross wages totaling $250,000. Their itemized deductions consist of state and local income taxes and real estate taxes totaling $22,500 and mortgage interest of $20,000 (all related to the acquisition of their principal residence). Assume the Smiths have no interest, dividend, or capital gain income. Their regular tax will be $42,026. However, since the AMT is $45,654 the Smith's will pay the higher of the two taxes effectively denying them some of their deductions for taxes paid and personal exemptions.

TAXPLANNER

The AMT can not only affect the amount of tax you pay, but it can also potentially affect the most tax-efficient way to invest your money.

For example, if part of your investment portfolio consists of municipal bond holdings, beware. Interest paid on private activity bonds issued before 2009 and after 2010 is a preference item that can make it more likely that you will be subject to AMT. Generally, you earn a higher yield on such private activity bonds than other municipals. However, if you're subject to the AMT, your effective yield on these bonds will be slashed. If you're not sure what type of municipal bonds you have, ask your investment advisor. On the other hand, a tax law enacted in early 2009 provides that interest received on tax-exempt private activity bonds issued in 2009 and 2010 is not an AMT preference item. In 2011, long-term capital gains and qualifying dividends are subject to the same maximum rate, 15%, for AMT purposes as they are for regular tax purposes. But because these items of income are included in AMTI, which could reduce your allowable AMT exemption, the actual marginal AMT rate could be as high as 22%. Before deciding to invest in securities that generate these types of income, you should consider the effect of the AMT. Tax and investment planning is further complicated by tax rate increases scheduled to take effect beginning in 2013 with the expiration of the so-called Bush tax cuts, and the forthcoming additional 3.8% Medicare tax on investment income received by higher income taxpayers that was enacted as part of the 2010 comprehensive health care reform legislation. See chapter 47, *Planning ahead for 2012 and beyond,* for a discussion of tax changes that are scheduled to take effect beginning in 2013. For updated information on this and any other tax law changes that occur after this book was published, see our website, *ey.com/EYTaxGuide*.

Example

Consider the Smiths again in the earlier example. Assume that in addition to their other income ($250,000 in gross wages), the Smiths had a long-term capital gain in 2011 of $50,000. At first blush, you might expect that their federal tax bill would increase by about $7,500 (15% long-term capital gain rate on $50,000, assuming no state income tax). However, because they are subject to AMT, the additional tax burden is actually $11,000.

This estimate does not include any additional state income tax. Considering that most states do impose income taxes on capital gains, the Smiths would be liable for additional state tax. If, say, the Smiths lived in a state with an 8% tax rate, after taking into account the state tax itself, there would be a total of $15,000 of federal and state taxes attributable to a long-term gain of $50,000!

You may have to pay the AMT if your taxable income for regular tax purposes, combined with certain adjustments and tax preference items, is more than a certain amount. See Form 6251, Alternative Minimum Tax—Individuals.

TAXALERT

In recent years, Congress has repeatedly enacted temporary measures (typically called an "AMT patch") that significantly raised the applicable exemption amounts above the level that last applied in 2000. In December 2010, the President and Congress agreed to extend the so-called Bush tax cuts. Under this new tax law, the AMT exemption for 2011 was increased as follows:

- $74,450 for married couples filing jointly and surviving spouses;
- $48,450 for other unmarried individuals; and
- $37,225 for married individuals filing separate returns.

The exemption phases out at higher levels of alternative minimum taxable income (AMTI). The exemptions fully phase out at $447,800 of AMTI for married couples filing jointly and surviving spouses; $306,300 for other unmarried individuals; and $223,900 for married individuals filing separately. This increases the income range in which AMT taxpayers would be subject to a marginal tax rate of as high as 22% on capital gains and qualified dividends.

Absent any future legislation to "patch" the AMT exemption once again, the 2012 AMT exemption amounts will revert to the levels that existed before 2001: $45,000 for married couples filing jointly and surviving spouses, $33,750 for other unmarried individuals, and $22,500 for married individuals filing separately. Such lower exemption amounts will result in substantially more taxpayers subject to the AMT in 2012. For updated information on this and any other tax law changes that occur after this book was published, see our website, ey.com/EYTaxGuide.

Explanation

Individuals, trusts, and estates must pay the alternative minimum tax (AMT) if it exceeds their regular tax liability for the year. The amount subject to the AMT will be determined by adding a number of preference items to your taxable income and making various adjustments to your regular taxable income. This amount is reduced by the exemption amounts, and the balance is subject to the following AMT rates:

Rate	Married filing separately	All other filers
26%	Up to $87,500 over exemption amount	Up to $175,000 over exemption amount
28%	Greater than $87,500 over exemption amount	Greater than $175,000 over exemption amount

	Exemption amount	
Filing status	**Base amount**	**Less 25% of the amount by which AMTI* exceeds**
Single	$48,450	$112,500
Married filing jointly, surviving spouses	74,450	150,000
Married filing separately, estates and trusts	37,225	75,000

*Alternative minimum taxable income

TAXPLANNER

The chart below should provide you with a better understanding of whether you might be affected by the AMT. Look at where your taxable income falls–then see how much you would need to have in preferences and adjustments (state and local taxes, personal exemptions, miscellaneous itemized deductions, standard deduction, etc.) to see whether you'd be subject to the AMT. For example, say you have ordinary taxable income of $100,000, claim four personal exemptions at $3,700 each ($14,800 in total), and take the standard deduction of $11,600. Your total preferences are $26,400 and you'd be subject to the AMT.

Regular	Adjustments & preferences needed to trigger AMT	
taxable income	**Joint**	**Single**
$50,000	34,817	22,514
100,000	15,437	19,613
150,000	10,794	12,670
200,000	2,418	7,725
300,000	0*	2,010

*At this income level, because a taxpayer filing jointly would have at least two personal exemptions, no additional adjustments would be needed to trigger AMT.

Analysis assumes ordinary income, no capital gains or qualifying dividends.

Explanation

Once your alternative minimum taxable income (AMTI) increases above a certain level, your AMT exemption begins to phase out.

If you are married and filing a joint return, for every dollar that your AMTI exceeds $150,000 ($112,500 for single filers), you lose $.25 of your exemption until it's totally phased out at $447,800 in 2011 (for single taxpayers it's totally phased out at $306,300).

TAXALERT

AMT exemption for a child subject to the "kiddie tax." For purposes of calculating AMT, the exemption applicable to a child subject to the kiddie tax is limited to the sum of (1) the child's earned income for the taxable year, plus (2) $6,800. For more information on the kiddie tax, see chapter 32, *Tax on investment income of certain children*.

Adjustments and tax preference items. The more common adjustments and tax preference items include:

- Addition of personal exemptions,
- Addition of the standard deduction (if claimed),
- Addition of itemized deductions claimed for state and local taxes, certain interest, most miscellaneous deductions, and part of medical expenses,
- Subtraction of any refund of state and local taxes included in gross income,
- Changes to accelerated depreciation of certain property,
- Difference between gain or loss on the sale of property reported for regular tax purposes and AMT purposes,
- Addition of certain income from incentive stock options,
- Change in certain passive activity loss deductions,

EXPLANATION

Besides accounting for tax preference items, certain adjustments (increases or decreases) must be made to taxable income to arrive at alternative minimum taxable income. The adjustments are as follows:

1. An alternative depreciation deduction (using less accelerated methods and longer depreciable lives) is substituted for the regular tax depreciation deduction for real and personal property and certified pollution control facilities placed in service after 1986 and before 1999. Recomputations are done in the aggregate; that is, the amount of the adjustment is not determined on a property-by-property basis. Note: This adjustment does not apply if you have elected to apply the alternative depreciation system (ADS) for regular tax purposes. For tax years beginning in or after 1999, the recovery periods over which property is depreciated are the same for regular and AMT purposes.
2. Mining exploration and development costs must be amortized over 10 years using the straight-line method.
3. The percentage-of-completion method of accounting must be used for long-term contracts entered into on or after March 1, 1986. Certain small construction contracts entered into on or after June 21, 1988, must use separate, simplified procedures for cost allocations in the percentage of completion calculation.
4. An alternative tax net operating loss deduction replaces the regular net operating loss deduction.
5. The treatment of itemized deductions is modified as follows:
   - Medical expenses are deductible only to the extent that they exceed 10% (instead of 7.5%) of the taxpayer's adjusted gross income.
   - State, local, and foreign real property, sales and income taxes, and state and local personal property taxes are deductible for AMT purposes only if they are deductible for regular tax purposes in computing adjusted gross income. Note: These are taxes related to business, rental property, and farming that are deducted on Schedules C, E, or F.

- Investment interest is deductible to the extent of net investment income that is adjusted for amounts relating to tax-exempt interest earned on certain private-activity bonds.
- Home mortgage interest is allowed as a deduction for AMT purposes. However, the definition of such interest is narrower than that of "qualified residence interest" for regular tax purposes. Refinanced home mortgage interest that is applicable to any mortgage in excess of the outstanding mortgage before refinancing is not deductible unless the excess was used for home improvements.
- No deduction is allowed for miscellaneous itemized deductions subject to the 2%-of-adjusted gross income limit.

6. No deduction is allowed for the standard deduction.
7. Circulation expenditures and research/experimental costs must be amortized over 3- and 10-year periods, respectively.
8. Deductions for passive farm losses are denied, except to the extent that the taxpayer is insolvent or the activity is disposed of during the year.
9. Rules limiting passive loss deductions also apply to the AMT, except that (a) otherwise disallowed losses are reduced by the amount by which the taxpayer is insolvent, and (b) all AMT adjustments and preferences are taken into consideration in computing income and/or losses from passive activities.
10. For beneficiaries of estates and trusts, the difference between a distribution included in income for regular tax and the AMT income shown on Schedule K-1 must be taken into account.
11. For property disposed of during the year, the gain or loss is refigured to take into consideration the impact that AMT adjustments, such as depreciation, have on the taxpayer's basis in the property.
12. For partners in partnerships and shareholders in S corporations, the income or loss is refigured to take into account AMT adjustments.
13. In exercising an incentive stock option (ISO), the taxpayer needs to adjust for the difference between the option price and the fair market value at the time the option is exercised. In calculating the AMT gain or loss on the subsequent sale of the ISO stock, the AMT basis in the stock is the sum of the option price paid and the AMT adjustment included in alternative minimum taxable income when the ISO was exercised.

TAXALERT

Incentive stock options present a unique AMT trap. While the "spread"–the difference between the fair market value of the stock at the time the option is exercised and the exercise price–is not taxable for regular tax purposes, it is for the AMT. The larger the "spread," the more likely you will be liable for AMT.

In addition, you compute your "basis" (generally the amount you paid) for stock bought with incentive stock options one way for regular tax purposes and another way for figuring your AMT. Your basis for regular tax purposes will generally be the exercise price of the options. The basis for AMT will usually be the fair market value of the shares when exercised, assuming you held the shares more than one year from the date you exercised your option. Figuring your basis is more complicated if you sell the shares within a year of exercising your options. You should consult your tax advisor.

If matters weren't complicated enough, the amount of AMT attributable to an incentive stock option can be credited against your regular tax liability in a future year. So, should your regular tax liability exceed your AMT tax calculation in a subsequent year, you can apply the credit against the difference between the two.

Example

In 2011 Martin and Fern Burns have $125,000 of ordinary income and $19,500 of itemized deductions–$2,500 of state income taxes, $2,000 of real estate taxes, and $15,000 of mortgage interest. They have no dependents. Their regular tax would be $16,781. They would not be subject to the AMT since that amount ($9,243) would be less than their regular tax.

Now suppose that in 2011 Fern exercised 1,000 incentive stock options (ISOs) that had an exercise price of $10 a share and that the stock was worth $45 a share at the time of exercise. That results in a total spread of $35,000 (1,000 × $35) that has to be added back in calculating AMT. The Burns, AMT for 2011 would be $18,343, an additional tax of $1,562. But all is not lost. Since the additional $1,562 in AMT liability was a result of the ISO exercise, that amount can be carried forward to a future year and credited against their tax to the extent their regular tax exceeds their AMT in that future year.

Let's say that in 2013 Fern sells the stock she got from the ISO exercise for $50 a share. The basis of the stock for regular tax purposes is $10 a share, so she has a regular long-term capital gain of $40,000 (1,000 × $40). But her basis for AMT purposes is $45 a share—the value of the stock on the date of exercise—for an AMT long-term capital gain of $5,000 (1,000 × $5). So in calculating her AMT in 2013 she would reflect a negative adjustment on Form 6251 of $35,000.

Explanation

The law provides a credit against the regular tax for all or a portion of the AMT you paid in previous years. The credit is the AMT attributable to deferral, rather than exclusion, items. Deferral items such as accelerated depreciation or the spread on incentive stock option (ISO), are those that have the effect of reducing your regular taxable income relative to alternative minimum taxable income in early years, but the situation reverses over time. Thus, the same total of deductions is eventually allowed under both tax systems.

When you pay AMT as a result of deferral preferences or adjustments, the law gives you a credit that can be used to reduce your regular tax liability in the future. This avoids double taxation on the same income. In addition to this credit, a tax law passed in 2008 also permits refunds for "old," unused AMT credits even though these additional credits do not reduce your regular tax liability for the year you claim them. Indeed, you may be able to claim a refund in excess of your entire tax for the year. For 2011, this applies to unused minimum tax credits from 2007. The AMT refundable credit is available through 2012. For more information, see *AMT refundable credit* in chapter 37, *Other credits including the earned income credit.*

Exclusion preferences, such as certain tax-exempt interest income, reduce your regular taxable income permanently. Because these preferences never reverse in the future, you are not given a credit for AMT paid. The AMT credit is carried forward indefinitely from the year of payment and cannot be carried back.

- Addition of certain depletion that is more than the adjusted basis of the property,
- Addition of part of the deduction for certain intangible drilling costs, and

TAXSAVER

To avoid treating excess intangible drilling costs as a tax preference item, you may elect to capitalize and amortize these expenses over a 10-year period in your regular tax calculation.

- Addition of tax-exempt interest on certain private activity bonds.

TAXALERT

Tax legislation enacted in 2009 provides that interest received on tax-exempt private activity bonds issued in 2009 and 2010 is not an AMT preference item. You should consult with your investment advisor to see how this provision may have affected the interest rate on private activity bonds issued during this two-year period (issuers may have been able to issue bonds with a somewhat lower interest rate than they otherwise would have had to do when interest paid was treated as a preference item), as well as the effect on market pricing for new and previously issued bonds.

TAXALERT

If you plan to make a substantial gift of appreciated property (e.g., stock) to a charity, there is no adjustment to consider for the alternative minimum tax (AMT). You are able to recognize a charitable contribution deduction for the full fair market value of appreciated long-term capital gain property for both regular and AMT purposes (subject to adjusted gross income limitations).

Example

The following example demonstrates how you would calculate your regular tax and your AMT for calendar year 2011 assuming your filing status is married filing jointly.

	Regular tax	Alternative minimum tax
Salary	$150,000	$150,000
Interest	11,000	11,000
Long-term capital gains (15%)	80,000	80,000
Net passive losses	(25,000)	(25,000)
Passive losses disallowed by Tax Reform Act of 1986	25,000	25,000
Adjusted gross income	$241,000	$241,000
State taxes	(30,000)	n/a*
Charitable contributions	(50,000)	(50,000)
Interest expense–principal residence	(27,000)	(27,000)
Exemptions (4)	(14,800)	n/a
Tax adjustment items:		
Incentive stock options	n/a	25,000
Alternative taxable income before exemption	n/a	$189,000
Exemption ($74,450 less 25% of alternative taxable income in excess of $150,000)	n/a	($64,700)
Taxable income	$119,200	$124,300
Tax due	$12,564	$19,048

*n/a means "not applicable."

Because your regular tax is less than your AMT, you must pay the AMT of $19,048.

The $30,000 you paid in state income tax was not allowed as a deduction from alternative minimum taxable income. Because deductions are based on actual payments made during the calendar year, good planning would require minimizing your state income taxes and your miscellaneous deductions to the extent that you are able in a year when it is possible you will be subject to the AMT.

TAXPLANNER

Even if you have benefited from the tax preference items that generally subject you to the AMT, you may avoid the AMT by controlling the timing of certain transactions. The trick is not to exceed the amount exempt from the AMT for a given year. If you know that you will be subject to the AMT this year, and provided your current AMT situation is due to exclusion items, you should consider realizing income this year that otherwise would be realized next year so that it is taxed at 26% or 28% rather than at a higher rate next year. Likewise, consider deferring deductions, especially those that are not deductible for AMT purposes.

The $74,450 exemption for joint returns is phased out beginning at $150,000 of alternative minimum taxable income. For unmarried taxpayers, the exemption amount is $48,450, and it is phased out beginning at $112,500. You lose $1 of exemption for every $4 over the base amount. Consequently, the exemption amount is completely phased out at $447,800 for joint returns and $306,300 for unmarried taxpayers.

More information. For more information about the AMT, see the instructions for Form 1040, line 45, and Form 6251.

Tax Figured by IRS

If you file by April 17, 2012, you can have the IRS figure your tax for you on Form 1040EZ, Form 1040A, or Form 1040.

If the IRS figures your tax and you paid too much, you will receive a refund. If you did not pay enough, you will receive a bill for the balance. To avoid interest or the penalty for late payment, you must pay the bill within 30 days of the date of the bill or by the due date for your return, whichever is later.

> **TAXPLANNER**
>
> If you make a preliminary calculation and see that you owe money to the IRS, you might consider waiting until the April due date (the due date is actually April 17, 2012, because April 15, 2012, falls on Sunday, and the following day, April 16, is the Emancipation Day holiday in the District of Columbia, which is observed as a legal holiday) to file your return and letting the IRS figure your tax. It will take the IRS some time to process your return and compute your tax. You will not have to come up with the money you owe until 30 days after the IRS sends you a bill. You will not have to pay any interest if you pay within 30 days of receiving your bill.

When the IRS cannot figure your tax. The IRS cannot figure your tax for you if any of the following apply.

1. You want your refund directly deposited into your accounts.
2. You want any part of your refund applied to your 2011 estimated tax.
3. You had income for the year from sources other than wages, salaries, tips, interest, dividends, taxable social security benefits, unemployment compensation, IRA distributions, pensions, and annuities.
4. Your taxable income is $100,000 or more.
5. You itemize deductions.
6. You file any of the following forms.
   a. Form 2555, Foreign Earned Income.
   b. Form 2555-EZ, Foreign Earned Income Exclusion.
   c. Form 4137, Social Security and Medicare Tax on Unreported Tip Income.
   d. Form 4970, Tax on Accumulation Distribution of Trusts.
   e. Form 4972, Tax on Lump-Sum Distributions.
   f. Form 6198, At-Risk Limitations.
   g. Form 6251, Alternative Minimum Tax—Individuals.
   h. Form 8606, Nondeductible IRAs.
   i. Form 8615, Tax for Certain Children Who Have Investment Income of More Than $1,900.
   j. Form 8814, Parents' Election To Report Child's Interest and Dividends.
   k. Form 8839, Qualified Adoption Expenses.
   l. Form 8853, Archer MSAs and Long-Term Care Insurance Contracts.
   m. Form 8889, Health Savings Accounts (HSAs).
   n. Form 8919, Uncollected Social Security and Medicare Tax on Wages.
   o. Form 8930, Qualified Disaster Recovery Assistance Retirement Plan Distributions and Repayments.

Filing the Return

After you complete the line entries for the tax form you are filing, fill in your name and address. Enter your social security number in the space provided. If you are married, enter the social security numbers of you and your spouse even if you file separately. Complete the "Third Party Designee" area of the return if you would like another person to discuss your return with the IRS. Sign and date your return and enter your occupation(s). If you are filing a joint return, both you and your spouse must sign it. Enter your daytime phone number in the space provided.

Attach a copy of each of your Forms W-2 to your return. Also attach any Form 1099-R you received that has withholding tax in box 4.

Mail your return to the Internal Revenue Service Center for the area where you live. A list of Service Center addresses is shown near the end of this publication.

> **TAXPLANNER**
>
> You may have an alternative to mailing your tax return to the IRS Service Center. See chapter 45, *Everything you need to know about e-filing*, for information on electronic filing.

Form 1040EZ Line Entries

Read lines 1 through 9 and fill in the lines that apply to you. Do not complete lines 10 through 12. If you are filing a joint return, use the space to the left of line 6 to separately show your taxable income and your spouse's taxable income.

Payments. Enter any federal income tax withheld on line 7. Federal income tax withheld is shown on Form W-2, box 2.

Earned income credit. If you can take this credit, as discussed in chapter 37, the IRS can figure it for you. Enter "EIC" in the space to the left of line 8a. Enter the nontaxable combat pay you elect to include in earned income on line 8b.

If your credit for any year after 1996 was reduced or disallowed by the IRS, you may also have to file Form 8862, Information To Claim Earned Income Credit After Disallowance, with your return. For details, see the Form 1040EZ Instructions.

Form 1040A Line Entries

Read lines 1 through 27 and fill in the lines that apply to you. If you are filing a joint return, use the space to the left of the entry space for line 27 to separately show your taxable income and your spouse's taxable income. Do not complete line 28. Complete lines 29 through 33 and 36 through 40 if they apply to you. Do not fill in lines 30, 38a, and 40 if you want the IRS to figure the credits shown on those lines. Also, enter any write-in information that applies to you in the space to the left of line 41. Do not complete lines 34, 35, 41, and 42 through 46.

Payments. Enter any federal income tax withheld that is shown on Form W-2, box 2, or the appropriate box of Form 1099, on line 36. Enter any estimated tax payments you made on line 37.

Credit for child and dependent care expenses. If you can take this credit, as discussed in chapter 33, complete Form 2441, Child and Dependent Care Expenses, and attach it to your return. Enter the amount of the credit on line 29. The IRS will not figure this credit.

Credit for the elderly or the disabled. If you can take this credit, as discussed in chapter 34, attach Schedule R (Form 1040), Credit for the Elderly or the Disabled. Enter "CFE" in the space to the left of line 30. The IRS will figure this credit for you. On Schedule R, check the box in Part I for your filing status and age. Complete Part II and Part III, lines 11 and 13, if they apply.

Earned income credit. If you can take this credit, as discussed in chapter 37, the IRS will figure it for you. Enter "EIC" to the left of the entry space for line 38a. Enter the nontaxable combat pay you elect to include in earned income on line 38b. If you have a qualifying child, you must fill in Schedule EIC, Earned Income Credit, and attach it to your return.

If your credit for any year after 1996 was reduced or disallowed by the IRS, you may also have to file Form 8862, Information To Claim Earned Income Credit After Disallowance, with your return. For details, see the Form 1040A Instructions.

Form 1040 Line Entries

Read lines 1 through 43 and fill in the lines that apply to you. Do not complete line 44.

If you are filing a joint return, use the space under the words "Adjusted Gross Income" on line 37 on the front of your return to separately show your taxable income and your spouse's taxable income.

Read lines 45 through 71. Fill in the lines that apply to you, but do not fill in lines 54, 61, and 72. Also, do not complete line 55 and lines 73 through 77. Do not fill in line 53, box "c," if you are completing Schedule R, and 64a if you want the IRS to figure the credits shown on those lines.

Fill in any forms or schedules asked for on the lines you completed, and attach them to your return.

Payments. Enter any federal income tax withheld that is shown on Form W-2, box 2, or the appropriate box of Form 1099, on line 62. Enter any estimated tax payments you made on line 63.

Credit for child and dependent care expenses. If you can take this credit, as discussed in chapter 33, complete Form 2441 and attach it to your return. Enter the amount of the credit on line 48. The IRS will not figure this credit.

Credit for the elderly or the disabled. If you can take this credit, as discussed in chapter 34, attach Schedule R to your return, check box "c" and enter "CFE" on the line next to line 53. The IRS will figure the credit for you. On Schedule R check the box in Part I for your filing status and age. Complete Part II and Part III, lines 11 and 13, if they apply.

Earned income credit. If you can take this credit, as discussed in chapter 37, the IRS will figure it for you. Enter "EIC" on the dotted line next to Form 1040, line 64a. Enter the nontaxable combat pay you elect to include in earned income on line 64b. If you have a qualifying child, you must fill in Schedule EIC and attach it to your return.

If your credit for any year after 1996 was reduced or disallowed by the IRS, you may also have to file Form 8862 with your return. For details, see the Form 1040 Instructions.

TAXORGANIZER

Records you should keep:

- *W-2:* Wages, salaries, tips; allocated tips; advance EIC payments; dependent care benefits; adoption benefits; employer contributions to a medical savings account
- *W-2G:* Gambling winnings
- *K-1:* Partner's share of income, deductions, credits, etc.
- *1098:* Mortgage interest; points; refund of overpaid interest
- *1098-E:* Student loan interest
- *1099-A:* Acquisition or abandonment of secured property
- *1099-B:* Stocks and bonds; bartering; futures contracts
- *1099-C:* Canceled debt
- *1099-DIV:* Ordinary dividends; total capital gains distributions; nontaxable distributions; investment expenses; foreign tax paid
- *1099-G:* Unemployment compensation; state or local income tax refund; taxable grants; agriculture payments
- *1099-INT:* Interest income; early withdrawal penalty; interest on U.S. savings bonds and Treasury obligations
- *1099-LTC:* Long-term care and accelerated death benefits
- *1099-MISC:* Rents; royalties; other income (prizes, awards); nonemployee compensation
- *1099-MSA, 1099-HSA:* Distributions from medical savings accounts and health savings accounts
- *1099-OID:* Original issue discount; other periodic interest; early withdrawal penalty
- *1099-PATR:* Patronage dividends and other distributions from a cooperative; credits; patron's AMT adjustment
- *1099-R:* Distributions from IRAs; distributions from pensions, annuities; capital gain
- *1099-S:* Gross proceeds from real estate transactions; buyer's part of real estate tax

Chapter 32

Tax on investment income of certain children

ey.com/EYTaxGuide

Note

IRS Publication 17 (*Your Federal Income Tax*) has been updated by Ernst & Young LLP for 2011. Dates and dollar amounts shown are for 2011. Underlined type is used to indicate where IRS text has been updated. Places where text has been removed are indicated by the sentence: *Text intentionally omitted*.

ey.com/EYTaxGuide

Ernst & Young LLP will update the *Ernst & Young Tax Guide 2012* website with relevant taxpayer information as it becomes available. You can also sign up for email alerts to let you know when changes have been made.

Introduction

There's nothing easy about bringing up children these days, and that applies to their tax returns as well. It is enormously complicated to determine the correct tax and fill out a proper tax return for children under certain ages who have unearned income.

Unearned income of children under certain ages is taxed at the marginal rate of their parents, as if the parents had received the income, rather than at the child's lower rate. This is commonly referred to as the "kiddie tax." The affected ages are:

- Under age 18 by the end of 2011;
- Age 18 by the end of 2011 if the child's earned income is not over one-half of their support; or,
- Over age 18 and under age 24 by the end of 2011 if the child was a full-time student and if the child's earned income is not over one-half of their support

Because most parents have a higher marginal tax rate than their children, these rules generally eliminate the benefits of transferring income-producing assets, such as stocks or bonds, to your minor children in order for the income to be taxed at the children's lower marginal rate.

The following are additional complications:

1. A child may not claim a personal exemption for himself or herself if he or she is eligible to be claimed on a parent's return.
2. A child's unearned income falls under special rules. The child can use $950 of his or her standard deduction to offset unearned income. The next $950 of unearned income is taxed at the child's tax rate. The balance of a child's unearned income will be taxed at the parent's marginal tax rate; this is accomplished by including the child's income on the parent's return (use Form 8814) OR by filing a tax return for the child (attach Form 8615).
3. If a child also has earned income, his or her tax return gets more complicated still. The earned income can increase his or her allowable standard deduction.

This chapter will help you sort through all the complications. Here's hoping that, while you're muddling through it, your children will be out having fun.

TAXPLANNER

The rules for taxing a child's investment income will impact parents who are considering transferring money to their children. You should carefully evaluate the types of assets you want to transfer to your children.

Tax Breaks and Deductions You Can Use Checklist

The Kiddie Tax. The kiddie tax rules apply to a child who has more than a prescribed amount of unearned (investment) income for the tax year—$1,900 for 2011—and whose age is:

- Under 18 years old by the end of 2011;
- 18 years old by the end of 2011 if the child's earned income is not greater than one-half of the support the child receives; and,
- Between 19 and 23 by the end of 2011 if a full-time student and if the child's earned income is not greater than one-half of the support the child receives.

Basically, the rules take the investment income of the child above this amount (called "net unearned income") and tax it at the parent's (higher) tax rate. So while you can still save some tax by shifting unearned income (up to $1,900 in 2011) to children who are subject to the kiddie tax, substantial tax savings aren't available.

You should consider investments for your child that generate little or no taxable income until your child "grows out" of the reach of the kiddie tax. For example, if the choice is between a growth-oriented mutual fund and an income-oriented mutual fund, it is clearly a better idea from a tax perspective to transfer the growth-oriented fund to the child. No current income tax will be due since the fund is focused on capital appreciation, not income distribution.

Then any accumulated gain could be realized after the child is no longer subject to the kiddie tax and instead pays tax at his or her own tax rate.

Also consider a 529 plan (qualified tuition programs) to build college savings. The investment income earned in the 529 plan accumulates tax-free and there is no tax for withdrawals if used to pay qualified higher education expenses. See the section on *Qualified Tuition Programs* in Publication 970, *Tax Benefits for Education,* for further information about 529 plans.

This chapter discusses the following two rules that may affect the tax on investment income of certain children.

1. If the child's interest and dividend income (including capital gain distributions) total less than $9,500, the child's parent may be able to choose to include that income on the parent's return rather than file a return for the child. (See *Parent's Election To Report Child's Interest and Dividends,* later.)
2. If the child's interest, dividends, and other investment income total more than $1,900, part of that income may be taxed at the parent's tax rate instead of the child's tax rate. (See *Tax for Certain Children Who Have Investment Income of More Than $1,900,* later.)

For these rules, the term "child" includes a legally adopted child and a stepchild. These rules apply whether or not the child is a dependent.

TAXALERT

For 2011, the first $950 of income of a child subject to the kiddie tax will generally not be subject to tax, and the next $950 will be taxable at the child's own bracket. Unearned income in excess of $1,900 will be taxed to the child at the parent's tax rate.

EXPLANATION

For the 2011 tax year, "under age 19" means that the child has not reached age 19 by January 1, 2012. If your child reached age 19 at any time during 2011 (and they are not a full-time student), this chapter will not apply.

TAXSAVER

The tax benefit of transferring investment property to your children is limited, however, some advantages still exist. First, keep in mind that the first $1,900 in 2011 in investment income is taxed at a very low rate. Second, the child will eventually no longer be subject to the kiddie tax and will instead pay tax using his or her own tax bracket (which will probably be lower than yours). Third, if the property appreciates in value while your child is subject to the kiddie tax, the appreciation will not complicate your tax situation.

Useful Items

You may want to see:

Publication

- □ **929** Tax Rules for Children and Dependents

Form (and Instructions)

- □ **8615** Tax for Certain Children Who Have Investment Income of More Than $1,900
- □ **8814** Parents' Election To Report Child's Interest and Dividends

Which Parent's Return To Use

If a child's parents are married to each other and file a joint return, use the joint return to figure the tax on the child's investment income. The tax rate and other return information from that return are used to figure the child's tax as explained later under *Tax for Certain Children Who Have Investment Income of More Than $1,900.*

Parents Who Do Not File a Joint Return

For parents who do not file a joint return, the following discussions explain which parent's tax return must be used to figure the tax.

Only the parent whose tax return is used can make the election described under *Parent's Election To Report Child's Interest and Dividends.*

Parents are married. If the child's parents file separate returns, use the return of the parent with the greater taxable income.

Parents not living together. If the child's parents are married to each other but not living together, and the parent with whom the child lives (the custodial parent) is considered unmarried, use the return of the custodial parent. If the custodial parent is not considered unmarried, use the return of the parent with the greater taxable income.

For an explanation of when a married person living apart from his or her spouse is considered unmarried, see *Head of Household* in chapter 2.

Parents are divorced. If the child's parents are divorced or legally separated, and the parent who had custody of the child for the greater part of the year (the custodial parent) has not remarried, use the return of the custodial parent.

Custodial parent remarried. If the custodial parent has remarried, the stepparent (rather than the noncustodial parent) is treated as the child's other parent. Therefore, if the custodial parent and the stepparent file a joint return, use that joint return. Do not use the return of the noncustodial parent.

If the custodial parent and the stepparent are married, but file separate returns, use the return of the one with the greater taxable income. If the custodial parent and the stepparent are married but not living together, the earlier discussion under *Parents not living together* applies.

EXPLANATION

When both parents have custody of a child with unearned income, the custodial parent is the parent with custody for the greater portion of the calendar year.

Parents never married. If a child's parents have never been married to each other, but lived together all year, use the return of the parent with the greater taxable income. If the parents did not live together all year, the rules explained earlier under *Parents are divorced* apply.

Widowed parent remarried. If a widow or widower remarries, the new spouse is treated as the child's other parent. The rules explained earlier under *Custodial parent remarried* apply.

Parent's Election To Report Child's Interest and Dividends

You may be able to elect to include your child's interest and dividend income (including capital gain distributions) on your tax return. If you do, your child will not have to file a return.

You can make this election only if all the following conditions are met.

- Your child was under age 19 (or under age 24 if a full-time student) at the end of the year.
- Your child had income only from interest and dividends (including capital gain distributions and Alaska Permanent Fund dividends).
- The child's gross income was less than $9,500.
- The child is required to file a return unless you make this election.
- The child does not file a joint return for the year.
- No estimated tax payment was made for the year, and no overpayment from the previous year (or from any amended return) was applied to this year under your child's name and social security number.
- No federal income tax was taken out of your child's income under the backup withholding rules.
- You are the parent whose return must be used when applying the special tax rules for children. (See *Which Parent's Return To Use,* earlier.)

These conditions are also shown in Figure 32-A.

Figure 32-A. **Can You Include Your Child's Income On Your Tax Return?**

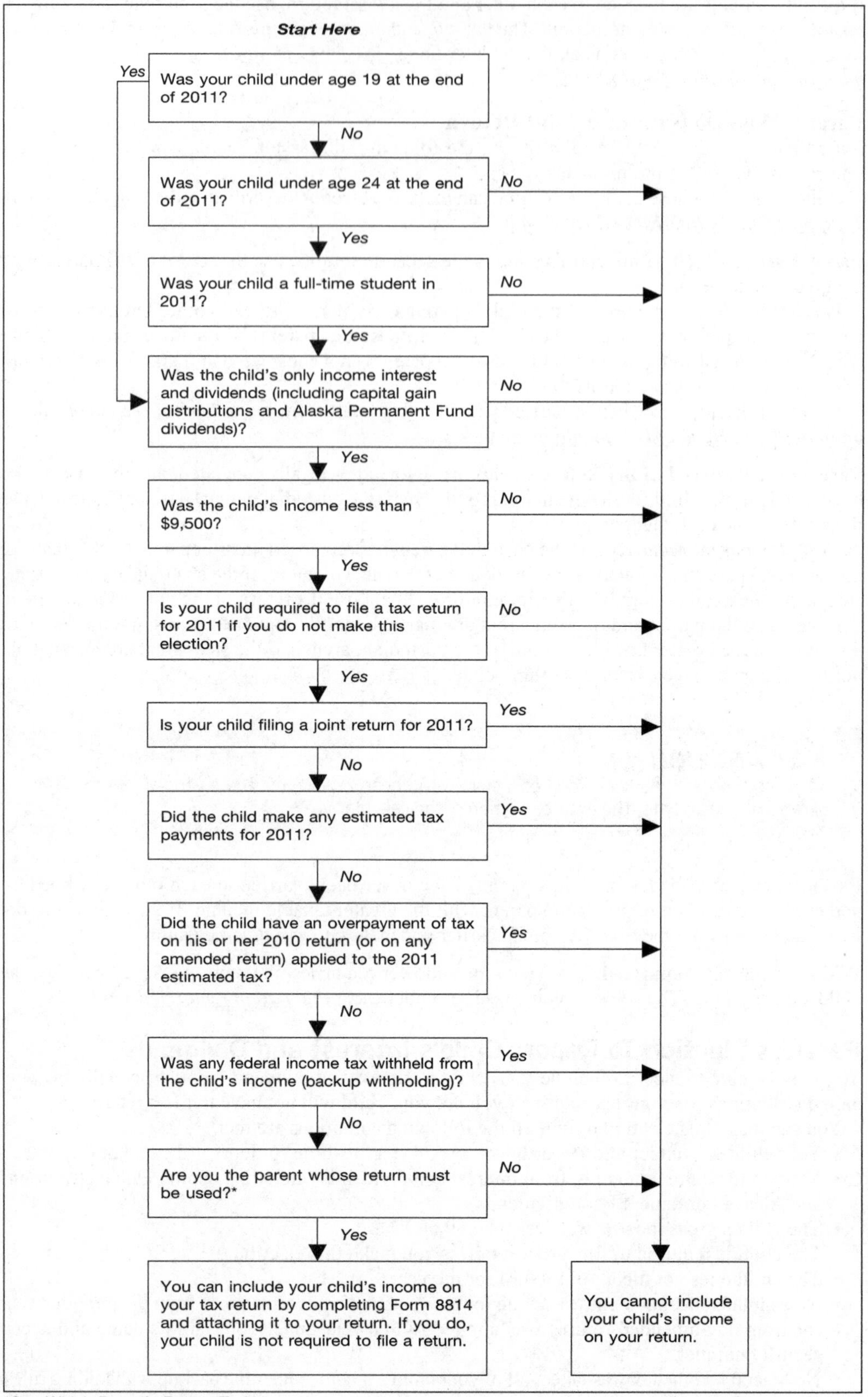
Start Here
Was your child under age 19 at the end of 2011?
Yes
No
Was your child under age 24 at the end of 2011?
No
Yes
Was your child a full-time student in 2011?
No
Yes
Was the child's only income interest and dividends (including capital gain distributions and Alaska Permanent Fund dividends)?
No
Yes
Was the child's income less than $9,500?
No
Yes
Is your child required to file a tax return for 2011 if you do not make this election?
No
Yes
Is your child filing a joint return for 2011?
Yes
No
Did the child make any estimated tax payments for 2011?
Yes
No
Did the child have an overpayment of tax on his or her 2010 return (or on any amended return) applied to the 2011 estimated tax?
Yes
No
Was any federal income tax withheld from the child's income (backup withholding)?
Yes
No
Are you the parent whose return must be used?*
No
Yes
You can include your child's income on your tax return by completing Form 8814 and attaching it to your return. If you do, your child is not required to file a return.
You cannot include your child's income on your return.

*See *Which Parent's Return To Use*

Certain January 1 birthdays. A child born on January 1, 1993, is considered to be age 19 at the end of 2011. You cannot make this election for such a child unless the child was a full-time student.

A child born on January 1, 1988, is considered to be age 24 at the end of 2011. You cannot make this election for such a child.

Full-time student. A full-time student is a child who during some part of each of any 5 calendar months of the year was enrolled as a full-time student at a school, or took a full-time, on-farm training course given by a school or a state, county, or local government agency. A school includes a technical, trade, or mechanical school. It does not include an on-the-job training course, correspondence school, or school offering courses only through the Internet.

How to make the election. Make the election by attaching Form 8814 to your Form 1040. (If you make this election, you cannot file Form 1040A or Form 1040EZ.) Attach a separate Form 8814 for each child for whom you make the election. You can make the election for one or more children and not for others.

Effect of Making the Election

The federal income tax on your child's income may be more if you make the Form 8814 election.

Rate may be higher. If your child received qualified dividends or capital gain distributions, you may pay up to $95 more tax if you make this election instead of filing a separate tax return for the child. This is because the tax rate on the child's income between $950 and $1,900 is 10% if you make this election. However, if you file a separate return for the child, the tax rate may be as low as 0% (zero percent) because of the preferential tax rates for qualified dividends and capital gain distributions.

> ***TAXSAVER***
> Most individuals will not want to elect to file Form 8814, because, as the IRS notes, in some cases it could result in more total tax. In addition, you may be required to pay more in state income taxes if this election is made.

Deductions you cannot take. By making the Form 8814 election, you cannot take any of the following deductions that the child would be entitled to on his or her return.

- The additional standard deduction if the child is blind.
- The deduction for a penalty on an early withdrawal of your child's savings.
- Itemized deductions (such as your child's investment expenses or charitable contributions).

> ***TAXSAVER***
> If you use Form 8814 to add your child's income to yours, the increased adjusted gross income may reduce the benefit of certain items on your return, such as any itemized deductions for medical expenses, casualty and theft losses, certain miscellaneous expenses, your deduction for IRA contributions (see chapter 17, *Individual retirement arrangements (IRAs)*), and your ability to claim the favorable $25,000 rental loss allowance under the passive activity rules (see chapter 12, *Other income*). Finally, adding your child's income to yours also may increase your state and local tax liability. Consider this election carefully before filing Form 8814.

Reduced deductions or credits. If you use Form 8814, your increased adjusted gross income may reduce certain deductions or credits on your return including the following.

- Deduction for contributions to a traditional individual retirement arrangement (IRA).
- Deduction for student loan interest.
- Itemized deductions for medical expenses, casualty and theft losses, and certain miscellaneous expenses.
- *Text intentionally omitted.*
- *Text intentionally omitted.*
- Credit for child and dependent care expenses.
- Child tax credit.
- Education tax credits.
- Earned income credit.

- *Text intentionally omitted.*
- First-time homebuyer credit.

Penalty for underpayment of estimated tax. If you make this election for 2011 and did not have enough tax withheld or pay enough estimated tax to cover the tax you owe, you may be subject to a penalty. If you plan to make this election for 2012, you may need to increase your federal income tax withholding or your estimated tax payments to avoid the penalty. See chapter 4 for more information.

Figuring Child's Income

Use Form 8814, Part I, to figure your child's interest and dividend income to report on your return. Only the amount over $1,900 is added to your income. The amount over $1,900 is shown on Form 8814, line 6. Unless the child's income includes qualified dividends or capital gain distributions (discussed next), the same amount is shown on Form 8814, line 12. Include the amount from Form 8814, line 12, on Form 1040, line 21. Enter "Form 8814" on the dotted line next to line 21. If you file more than one Form 8814, include the total amounts from line 12 of all your Forms 8814 on Form 1040, line 21.

Capital gain distributions and qualified dividends. If your child's dividend income included any capital gain distributions, see *Capital gain distributions* under *Figuring Child's Income* in Part 2 of Publication 929. If your child's dividend income included any qualified dividends, see *Qualified dividends* under *Figuring Child's Income* in Part 2 of Publication 929.

Figuring Additional Tax

Use Form 8814, Part II, to figure the tax on the $1,900 of your child's interest and dividends that you do not include in your income. This tax is added to the tax figured on your income.

This additional tax is the smaller of:

1. 10% × (your child's gross income – $950), or
2. $95.

Include the amount from line 15 of all your Forms 8814 in the total on Form 1040, line 44. Check box a on Form 1040, line 44.

Illustrated Example

David and Linda Parks are married and will file separate tax returns for 2011. Their only child, Philip, is 8. Philip received a Form 1099-INT showing $1,650 taxable interest income and a Form 1099-DIV showing $1,150 ordinary dividends. All the dividends were qualified dividends. His parents decide to include that income on one of their returns so they will not have to file a return for Philip.

First, David and Linda each figure their taxable income (Form 1040, line 43) without regard to Philip's income. David's taxable income is $56,700 and Linda's is $74,300. Because her taxable income is greater, Linda can elect to include Philip's income on her return. See *Which Parent's Return To Use*, earlier.

On Form 8814 (see illustrated form), Linda enters her name and social security number, then Philip's name and social security number. She enters Philip's taxable interest income, $1,650, on line 1a. Philip had no tax-exempt interest income, so she leaves line 1b blank. She enters Philip's ordinary dividends, $1,150, on line 2a. All of Philip's ordinary dividends were qualified dividends, so Linda also enters $1,150 on line 2b. Philip did not have any capital gain distributions, so she leaves line 3 blank.

Linda adds lines 1a and 2a and enters the result, $2,800, on line 4. Because Philip had qualified dividends, Linda must complete lines 7 through 11 of Form 8814. She includes the amount from line 9 of Form 8814 ($370) on lines 9a and 9b of her Form 1040. On the dotted lines next to lines 9a and 9b, she enters "Form 8814–$370."

Linda includes $530 in the total on line 21 of her Form 1040 (not illustrated) and in the space next to that line writes "Form 8814–$530." Adding that amount, plus the $370 of qualified dividends, to her income increases each of the amounts on lines 22, 37, 38, 41, and 43 of her Form 1040 by $900. Linda is not claiming any deductions that are affected by the increase to her income. Therefore, her revised taxable income on line 43 is $75,200 ($74,300 + $370 + $530).

On Form 8814, Linda subtracts the $950 shown on line 13 from the $2,800 on line 4 and enters the result, $1,850, on line 14. Because that amount is not less than $950, she enters $95 on line 15. This is the tax on the first $1,900 of Philip's income, which Linda did not have to add to her income. She must add this additional tax to the tax figured on her revised taxable income.

Form **8814**			

Form **8814**
Department of the Treasury
Internal Revenue Service (99)

**Parents' Election To Report
Child's Interest and Dividends**
▶ See instructions.
▶ **Attach to parents' Form 1040 or Form 1040NR.**

OMB No. 1545-0074
2011
Attachment
Sequence No. **40**

Name(s) shown on your return	Your social security number
Linda Parks	111-00-1111

Caution. The federal income tax on your child's income, including qualified dividends and capital gain distributions, may be less if you file a separate tax return for the child instead of making this election. This is because you cannot take certain tax benefits that your child could take on his or her own return. For details, see **Tax benefits you cannot take** in the instructions.

A Child's name (first, initial, and last)	B Child's social security number
Philip Parks	000-00-0000

C If more than one Form 8814 is attached, check here . ▶ ☐

Part I	**Child's Interest and Dividends To Report on Your Return**			

1a	Enter your child's **taxable** interest. If this amount is different from the amounts shown on the child's Forms 1099-INT and 1099-OID, see the instructions	**1a**	1650	
b	Enter your child's **tax-exempt** interest. **Do not** include this amount on line 1a	**1b**		
2a	Enter your child's ordinary dividends, including any Alaska Permanent Fund dividends. If your child received any ordinary dividends as a nominee, see the instructions	**2a**	1150	
b	Enter your child's qualified dividends included on line 2a. See the instructions	**2b**	1150	
3	Enter your child's capital gain distributions. If your child received any capital gain distributions as a nominee, see the instructions	**3**		
4	Add lines 1a, 2a, and 3. If the total is $1,900 or less, skip lines 5 through 12 and go to line 13. If the total is $9,500 or more, **do not** file this form. Your child **must** file his or her own return to report the income	**4**	2800	
5	Base amount .	**5**	1,900	00
6	Subtract line 5 from line 4 .	**6**	900	
	If both lines 2b and 3 are zero or blank, skip lines 7 through 10, enter -0- on line 11, and go to line 12. Otherwise, go to line 7.			
7	Divide line 2b by line 4. Enter the result as a decimal (rounded to at least three places)	**7**	.411	
8	Divide line 3 by line 4. Enter the result as a decimal (rounded to at least three places)	**8**	.	
9	Multiply line 6 by line 7. Enter the result here. See the instructions for where to report this amount on your return	**9**	370	
10	Multiply line 6 by line 8. Enter the result here. See the instructions for where to report this amount on your return	**10**		
11	Add lines 9 and 10 .	**11**	370	
12	Subtract line 11 from line 6. Include this amount in the total on Form 1040, line 21, or Form 1040NR, line 21. In the space next to line 21, enter "Form 8814" and show the amount. If you checked the box on line C above, see the instructions. Go to line 13 below	**12**	530	

Part II	**Tax on the First $1,900 of Child's Interest and Dividends**			

13	Amount not taxed .	**13**	950	00
14	Subtract line 13 from line 4. If the result is zero or less, enter -0-	**14**	1850	
15	**Tax.** Is the amount on line 14 less than $950? ☐ **No.** Enter $95 here and see the **Note** below. ☐ **Yes.** Multiply line 14 by 10% (.10). Enter the result here and see the **Note** below.	**15**	95	

Note. If you checked the box on line C above, see the instructions. Otherwise, include the amount from line 15 in the tax you enter on Form 1040, line 44, or Form 1040NR, line 42. Be sure to check box **a** on Form 1040, line 44, or Form 1040NR, line 42.

For Paperwork Reduction Act Notice, see your tax return instructions. Cat. No. 10750J Form **8814** (2011)

The tax on her $75,200 revised taxable income, figured using the Qualified Dividends and Capital Gain Tax Worksheet in the Form 1040 instructions, is $15,042. She adds $95, and enters the $15,137 total on Form 1040, line 44, and checks box a.

Linda attaches Form 8814 to her Form 1040.

Tax for Certain Children Who Have Investment Income of More Than $1,900

If a child's interest, dividends, and other investment income total more than $1,900, part of that income may be taxed at the parent's tax rate instead of the child's tax rate. If the parent does not or cannot choose to include the child's income on the parent's return, use Form 8615 to figure the child's tax. Attach the completed form to the child's Form 1040 or Form 1040A.

When Form 8615 must be filed. Form 8615 must be filed for a child if all of the following statements are true.

1. The child's investment income was more than $1,900.
2. The child is required to file a return for 2011.
3. The child either:
   a. Was under age 18 at the end of the year,
   b. Was age 18 at the end of the year and did not have earned income that was more than half of his or her support, or
   c. Was a full-time student over age 18 and under age 24 at the end of the year and did not have earned income that was more than half of his or her support.
4. At least one of the child's parents was alive at the end of 2011.
5. The child does not file a joint return for 2011.

These conditions are also shown in Figure 32-B.

Earned income. Earned income includes wages, tips, and other payments received for personal services performed. It does not include investment income as defined later in this chapter.

Support. Your child's support includes all amounts spent to provide the child with food, lodging, clothing, education, medical and dental care, recreation, transportation, and similar necessities. To figure your child's support, count support provided by you, your child, and others. However, a scholarship received by your child is not considered support if your child is a full-time student. See chapter 3 for details about support.

Certain January 1 birthdays. Use the following chart to determine whether certain children with January 1 birthdays meet condition 3 under *When Form 8615 must be filed.*

IF a child was born on...	THEN, at the end of 2011, the child is considered to be...
January 1, 1994	18*
January 1, 1993	19**
January 1, 1988	24***

*This child is not **under** age 18. The child meets condition 3 only if the child did not have earned income that was more than half of the child's support.
**This child meets condition 3 only if the child was a full-time student who did not have earned income that was more than half of the child's support.
***Do not use Form 8615 for this child.

Providing Parental Information (Form 8615, lines A–C)

On Form 8615, lines A and B, enter the parent's name and social security number. (If the parents filed a joint return, enter the name and social security number listed first on the joint return.) On line C, check the box for the parent's filing status.

See *Which Parent's Return To Use* at the beginning of this chapter for information on which parent's return information must be used on Form 8615.

Parent with different tax year. If the parent and the child do not have the same tax year, complete Form 8615 using the information on the parent's return for the tax year that ends in the child's tax year.

Figure 32-B. **Do You Have To Use Form 8615 To Figure Your Child's Tax?**

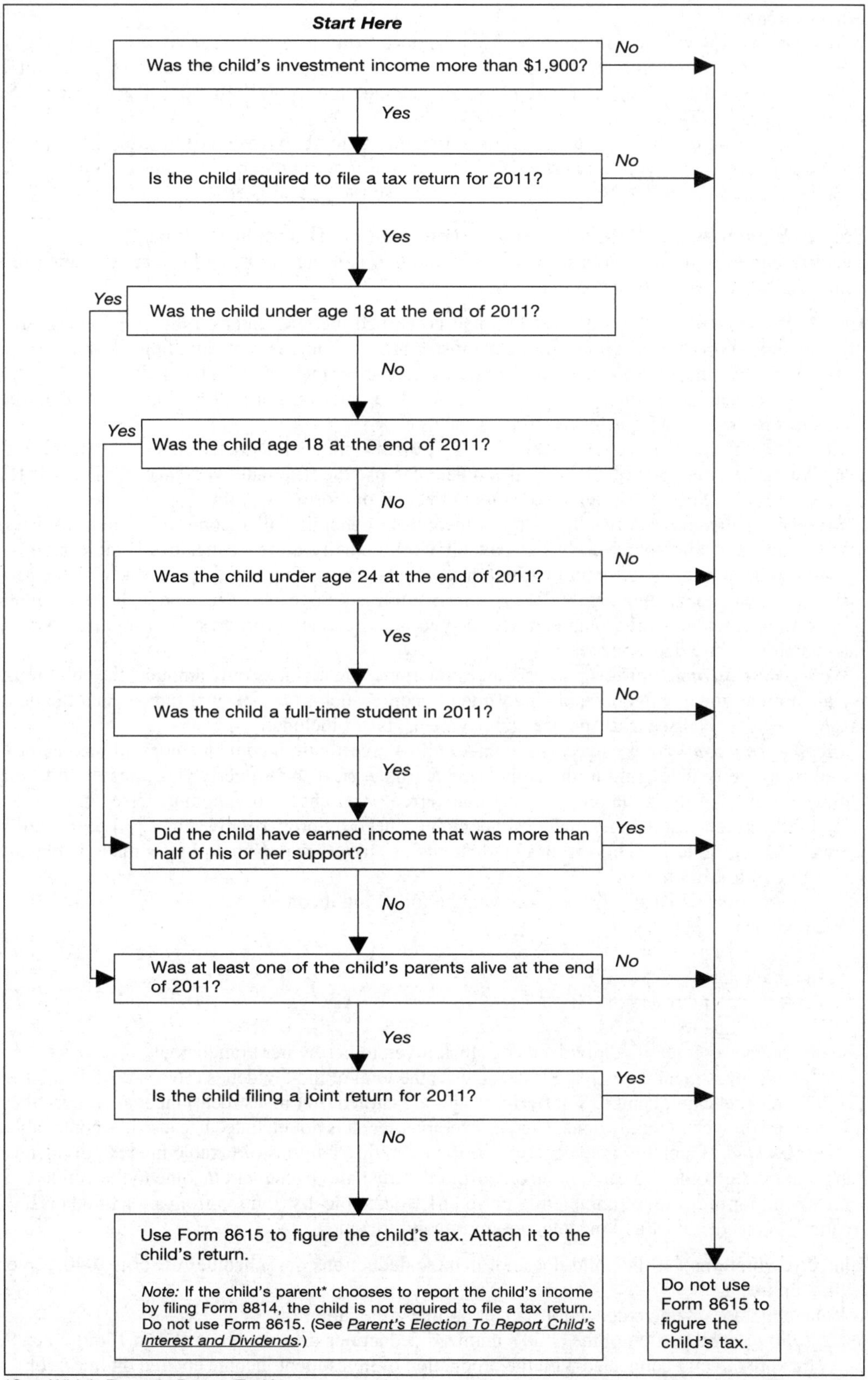

Start Here
Was the child's investment income more than $1,900?
Is the child required to file a tax return for 2011?
Was the child under age 18 at the end of 2011?
Was the child age 18 at the end of 2011?
Was the child under age 24 at the end of 2011?
Was the child a full-time student in 2011?
Did the child have earned income that was more than half of his or her support?
Was at least one of the child's parents alive at the end of 2011?
Is the child filing a joint return for 2011?
Use Form 8615 to figure the child's tax. Attach it to the child's return.
Note: If the child's parent* chooses to report the child's income by filing Form 8814, the child is not required to file a tax return. Do not use Form 8615. (See Parent's Election To Report Child's Interest and Dividends.)
Do not use Form 8615 to figure the child's tax.
Yes
No

*See *Which Parent's Return To Use*

Parent's return information not known timely. If the information needed from the parent's return is not known by the time the child's return is due (usually April 15), you can file the return using estimates.

You can use any reasonable estimate. This includes using information from last year's return. If you use an estimated amount on Form 8615, enter "Estimated" on the line next to the amount.

When you get the correct information, file an amended return on Form 1040X, Amended U.S. Individual Income Tax Return.

Instead of using estimates, you can get an automatic 6-month extension of time to file if, by the date your return is due, you file Form 4868, Application for Automatic Extension of Time To File U.S. Individual Income Tax Return. Extensions are discussed in chapter 1.

Step 1. Figuring the Child's Net Investment Income (Form 8615, Part I)

The first step in figuring a child's tax using Form 8615 is to figure the child's net investment income. To do that, use Form 8615, Part I.

Line 1 (investment income). If the child had no earned income, enter on this line the adjusted gross income shown on the child's return. Adjusted gross income is shown on Form 1040, line 38, or Form 1040A, line 22. Form 1040EZ cannot be used if Form 8615 must be filed.

If the child had earned income, figure the amount to enter on Form 8615, line 1, by using the worksheet in the instructions for the form.

However, if the child has excluded any foreign earned income or deducted either a loss from self-employment or a net operating loss from another year, use the Alternate Worksheet for Form 8615, Line 1, in Publication 929 to figure the amount to enter on Form 8615, line 1.

Investment income defined. Investment income is generally all income other than salaries, wages, and other amounts received as pay for work actually done. It includes taxable interest, dividends (including capital gain distributions), capital gains, the taxable part of social security and pension payments, and certain distributions from trusts. Investment income includes amounts produced by assets the child obtained with earned income (such as interest on a savings account into which the child deposited wages).

Nontaxable income. For this purpose, investment income includes only amounts the child must include in total income. Nontaxable investment income, such as tax-exempt interest and the nontaxable part of social security and pension payments, is not included.

Income from property received as a gift. A child's investment income includes all income produced by property belonging to the child. This is true even if the property was transferred to the child, regardless of when the property was transferred or purchased or who transferred it.

A child's investment income includes income produced by property given as a gift to the child. This includes gifts to the child from grandparents or any other person and gifts made under the Uniform Gift to Minors Act.

Example. Amanda Black, age 13, received the following income.

- Dividends — $600
- Wages — $2,100
- Taxable interest — $1,200
- Tax-exempt interest — $100
- Net capital gains — $100

The dividends were qualified dividends on stock given to her by her grandparents.

Amanda's investment income is $1,900. This is the total of the dividends ($600), taxable interest ($1,200), and net capital gains ($100). Her wages are earned (not investment) income because they are received for work actually done. Her tax-exempt interest is not included because it is nontaxable.

Trust income. If a child is the beneficiary of a trust, distributions of taxable interest, dividends, capital gains, and other investment income from the trust are investment income to the child.

However, for purposes of completing Form 8615, a taxable distribution from a qualified disability trust is considered earned income, not investment income.

Line 2 (deductions). If the child does not itemize deductions on Schedule A (Form 1040), enter $1,900 on line 2.

If the child does itemize deductions, enter on line 2 the larger of:

1. $950 plus the portion of the child's itemized deductions on Schedule A (Form 1040), line 29, that are directly connected with the production of investment income entered on line 1, or
2. $1,900.

Directly connected. Itemized deductions are directly connected with the production of investment income if they are for expenses paid to produce or collect taxable income or to manage, conserve, or maintain property held for producing income. These expenses include custodian fees and service charges, service fees to collect taxable interest and dividends, and certain investment counsel fees.

These expenses are added to certain other miscellaneous itemized deductions on Schedule A (Form 1040). Only the amount greater than 2% of the child's adjusted gross income can be deducted. See chapter 29 for more information.

EXPLANATION

Directly connected itemized deductions also include any investment interest expense deducted on the child's return that relates to debt incurred to finance the investments that produced the unearned income.

Example 1. Roger, age 12, has investment income of $8,000, no other income, no adjustments to income, and itemized deductions of $300 (net of the 2% limit) that are directly connected with his investment income. His adjusted gross income is $8,000, which is entered on Form 1040, line 38, and on Form 8615, line 1. Line 2 is $1,900 because that is more than the sum of $950 and his directly-connected itemized deductions of $300.

Example 2. Eleanor, age 8, has investment income of $16,000 and an early withdrawal penalty of $100. She has no other income. She has itemized deductions of $1,050 (net of the 2% limit) that are directly connected with the production of her investment income. Her adjusted gross income, entered on line 1, is $15,900 ($16,000 − $100). The amount on line 2 is $2,000. This is the larger of:

1. $950 plus the $1,050 of directly connected itemized deductions, or
2. $1,900.

TAXSAVER

Children with investment income. If your child is subject to the kiddie tax and has investment income and you are in the top income bracket, you may want to consider altering his or her investment strategy if it is financially appropriate. Because a child with over $1,900 in unearned income will be taxed at his or her parent's rate, it might be advisable to seek out deferred or tax-exempt income.

An example of deferred income might be generated by an investment in a growth-oriented stock or mutual fund. Such an investment may not pay high current dividends, and the realization of any appreciation in value may be deferred by holding the investment until the child is no longer subject to the kiddie tax. Tax-exempt income may be generated by municipal bonds.

Line 3. Subtract line 2 from line 1 and enter the result on this line. If zero or less, do not complete the rest of the form. However, you must still attach Form 8615 to the child's tax return. Figure the tax on the child's taxable income in the normal manner.

Line 4 (child's taxable income). Enter on line 4 the child's taxable income from Form 1040, line 43, or Form 1040A, line 27.

However, if the child files Form 2555 or 2555-EZ to claim the foreign earned income exclusion or housing exclusion, see the Form 8615 instructions.

Line 5 (net investment income). A child's net investment income cannot be more than his or her taxable income. Enter on Form 8615, line 5, the smaller of line 3 or line 4. This is the child's net investment income.

If zero or less, do not complete the rest of the form. However, you must still attach Form 8615 to the child's tax return. Figure the tax on the child's taxable income in the normal manner.

Step 2. Figuring Tentative Tax at the Parent's Tax Rate (Form 8615, Part II)

The next step in completing Form 8615 is to figure a tentative tax on the child's net investment income at the parent's tax rate. The tentative tax at the parent's tax rate is the difference between the tax on the parent's taxable income figured with the child's net investment income (plus the net investment income of any other child whose Form 8615 includes the tax return information of that parent) and the tax figured without it.

When figuring the tentative tax at the parent's tax rate, do not refigure any of the exclusions, deductions, or credits on the parent's return because of the child's net investment income. For example, do not refigure the medical expense deduction.

Figure the tentative tax on Form 8615, lines 6 through 13.

Note. If the child or parent has any capital gains or losses, get Publication 929 for help in completing Form 8615, Part II.

Line 6 (parent's taxable income). Enter on line 6 the parent's taxable income from Form 1040, line 43, or Form 1040A, line 27.

If the Foreign Earned Income Tax Worksheet (in the Form 1040 instructions) was used to figure the parent's tax, enter the amount from line 3 of that worksheet instead of the parent's taxable income.

Line 7 (net investment income of other children). If the tax return information of the parent is also used on any other child's Form 8615, enter on line 7 the total of the amounts from line 5 of all the other children's Forms 8615. Do not include the amount from line 5 of the Form 8615 being completed.

Example. Paul and Jane Persimmon have three children, Sharon, Jerry, and Mike, who must attach Form 8615 to their tax returns. The children's net investment income amounts on line 5 of their Forms 8615 are:

- Sharon — $800
- Jerry — $600
- Mike — $1,000

Line 7 of Sharon's Form 8615 will show $1,600, the total of the amounts on line 5 of Jerry's and Mike's Forms 8615.

Line 7 of Jerry's Form 8615 will show $1,800 ($800 + $1,000).

Line 7 of Mike's Form 8615 will show $1,400 ($800 + $600).

Other children's information not available. If the net investment income of the other children is not available when the return is due, either file the return using estimates or get an extension of time to file. See *Parent's return information not known timely,* earlier.

Line 11 (tentative tax). Subtract line 10 from line 9 and enter the result on this line. This is the tentative tax.

If line 7 is blank, skip lines 12a and 12b and enter the amount from line 11 on line 13. Also skip the discussion for lines 12a and 12b that follows.

Lines 12a and 12b (dividing the tentative tax). If an amount is entered on line 7, divide the tentative tax shown on line 11 among the children according to each child's share of the total net investment income. This is done on lines 12a, 12b, and 13. Add the amount on line 7 to the amount on line 5 and enter the total on line 12a. Divide the amount on line 5 by the amount on line 12a and enter the result, as a decimal, on line 12b.

Example. In the earlier example under *Line 7 (net investment income of other children),* Sharon's Form 8615 shows $1,600 on line 7. The amount entered on line 12a is $2,400, the total of the amounts on lines 5 and 7 ($800 + $1,600). The decimal on line 12b is .333, figured as follows and rounded to three places.

$$\frac{\$800}{\$2{,}400} = .333$$

Step 3. Figuring the Child's Tax (Form 8615, Part III)

The final step in figuring a child's tax using Form 8615 is to determine the larger of:

1. The total of:
   a. The child's share of the tentative tax based on the parent's tax rate, plus
   b. The tax on the child's taxable income in excess of net investment income, figured at the child's tax rate, or
2. The tax on the child's taxable income, figured at the child's tax rate.

This is the child's tax. It is figured on Form 8615, lines 14 through 18.

Alternative minimum tax. A child may be subject to alternative minimum tax (AMT) if he or she has certain items given preferential treatment under the tax law. See *Alternative Minimum Tax* in chapter 31.

For more information on who is liable for AMT and how to figure it, see Form 6251, Alternative Minimum Tax—Individuals. For information on special limits that apply to a child who files Form 6251, see *Alternative Minimum Tax* in Publication 929.

Illustrated Example

The following example includes a completed Form 8615. Form 1040A is not shown.

John and Laura Brown have one child, Sara. She is 13 and has $2,800 taxable interest income and $1,500 earned income. She does not itemize deductions. John and Laura file a joint return with John's name and social security number listed first. They claim three exemptions, including an exemption for Sara, on their return.

Because Sara is under age 18 and has more than $1,900 investment income, part of her income may be subject to tax at her parents' rate. A completed Form 8615 must be attached to her return.

Sara's father, John, fills out Sara's return for her. He completes her Form 1040A through line 27, then begins completing her Form 8615.

John enters his name and social security number on Sara's Form 8615 because his name and number are listed first on the joint return he and Laura are filing. He checks the box for married filing jointly.

He enters Sara's investment income, $2,800, on line 1. Sara does not itemize deductions, so John enters $1,900 on line 2. He enters $900 ($2,800 – $1,900) on line 3.

Sara's taxable income on her Form 1040A, line 27, is $2,500. This is her total income ($4,300) minus her standard deduction ($1,800). Her standard deduction is limited to the amount of her earned income plus $300. John enters $2,500 on line 4.

John compares lines 3 and 4 and enters the smaller amount, $900, on line 5.

John enters $48,000 on line 6. This is the taxable income from line 43 of John and Laura's joint Form 1040 return. Sara is an only child, so line 7 is blank. He adds line 5 ($900), line 6 ($48,000), and line 7 (blank), and enters $48,900 on line 8.

Using the column for married filing jointly in the Tax Table, John finds the tax on $48,900. He enters the tax, $6,489, on line 9. He enters $6,354 on line 10. This is the tax from line 44 of John and Laura's Form 1040. He enters $135 on line 11 ($6,489 – $6,354).

Because line 7 is blank, John skips lines 12a and 12b and enters $135 on line 13.

John subtracts line 5 ($900) from line 4 ($2,500) and enters the result, $1,600, on line 14. Using the column for single filing status in the Tax Table, John finds the tax on $1,600 and enters this tax, $161, on line 15. He adds lines 13 ($135) and 15 ($161) and enters $296 on line 16.

Using the column for single filing status in the Tax Table, John finds the tax on $2,500 (line 4) and enters this tax, $251, on line 17.

John compares lines 16 and 17 and enters the larger amount, $296, on line 18 of Sara's Form 8615. He also enters that amount on line 28 of Sara's Form 1040A.

John also completes Schedule B (Form 1040A or 1040) for Sara.

TAXORGANIZER

Records you should keep:

You should retain documentation for the following items:

- 1099-INT or 1099-OID: Child's interest income.
- 1099-DIV: Child's dividend investment income; child's capital gain investment income.
- W-2: Child's earned income; child's estimated tax payments for the year (if any).

Form **8615**

Department of the Treasury
Internal Revenue Service (99)

Tax for Certain Children Who Have Investment Income of More Than $1,900

▶ Attach only to the child's Form 1040, Form 1040A, or Form 1040NR.
▶ See separate instructions.

OMB No. 1545-0074
2011
Attachment Sequence No. **33**

Child's name shown on return	Child's social security number
Sara L. Brown	117-00-1111

Before you begin: If the child, the parent, or any of the parent's other children for whom Form 8615 must be filed must use the Schedule D Tax Worksheet or has income from farming or fishing, see **Pub. 929,** Tax Rules for Children and Dependents. It explains how to figure the child's tax using the **Schedule D Tax Worksheet** or **Schedule J** (Form 1040).

A Parent's name (first, initial, and last). **Caution:** *See instructions before completing.*	**B** Parent's social security number
John J. Brown	007-00-0001

C Parent's filing status (check one):
☐ Single ☑ Married filing jointly ☐ Married filing separately ☐ Head of household ☐ Qualifying widow(er)

Part I Child's Net Investment Income

1	Enter the child's investment income (see instructions)	1	2,800
2	If the child **did not** itemize deductions on **Schedule A** (Form 1040 or Form 1040NR), enter $1,900. Otherwise, see instructions	2	1,900
3	Subtract line 2 from line 1. If zero or less, **stop;** do not complete the rest of this form but **do** attach it to the child's return	3	900
4	Enter the child's **taxable income** from Form 1040, line 43; Form 1040A, line 27; or Form 1040NR, line 41. If the child files Form 2555 or 2555-EZ, see the instructions	4	2,500
5	Enter the **smaller** of line 3 or line 4. If zero, **stop;** do not complete the rest of this form but **do** attach it to the child's return	5	900

Part II Tentative Tax Based on the Tax Rate of the Parent

6	Enter the parent's **taxable income** from Form 1040, line 43; Form 1040A, line 27; Form 1040EZ, line 6; Form 1040NR, line 41; or Form 1040NR-EZ, line 14. If zero or less, enter -0-. If the parent files Form 2555 or 2555-EZ, see the instructions			6	48,000
7	Enter the total, if any, from Forms 8615, line 5, of **all other** children of the parent named above. **Do not** include the amount from line 5 above			7	
8	Add lines 5, 6, and 7 (see instructions)			8	48,900
9	Enter the tax on the amount on line 8 based on the **parent's** filing status above (see instructions). If the Qualified Dividends and Capital Gain Tax Worksheet, Schedule D Tax Worksheet, or Schedule J (Form 1040) is used to figure the tax, check here ▶ ☐			9	6,489
10	Enter the parent's tax from Form 1040, line 44; Form 1040A, line 28, minus any alternative minimum tax; Form 1040EZ, line 10; Form 1040NR, line 42; or Form 1040NR-EZ, line 15. **Do not** include any tax from **Form 4972** or **8814** or any tax from recapture of an education credit. If the parent files Form 2555 or 2555-EZ, see the instructions. If the Qualified Dividends and Capital Gain Tax Worksheet, Schedule D Tax Worksheet, or Schedule J (Form 1040) was used to figure the tax, check here ▶ ☐			10	6,354
11	Subtract line 10 from line 9 and enter the result. If line 7 is blank, also enter this amount on line 13 and go to **Part III**			11	135
12a	Add lines 5 and 7	12a			
b	Divide line 5 by line 12a. Enter the result as a decimal (rounded to at least three places)			12b	× .
13	Multiply line 11 by line 12b			13	135

Part III Child's Tax—If lines 4 and 5 above are the same, enter -0- on line 15 and go to line 16.

14	Subtract line 5 from line 4	14	1,600		
15	Enter the tax on the amount on line 14 based on the **child's** filing status (see instructions). If the Qualified Dividends and Capital Gain Tax Worksheet, Schedule D Tax Worksheet, or Schedule J (Form 1040) is used to figure the tax, check here ▶ ☐			15	161
16	Add lines 13 and 15			16	296
17	Enter the tax on the amount on line 4 based on the **child's** filing status (see instructions). If the Qualified Dividends and Capital Gain Tax Worksheet, Schedule D Tax Worksheet, or Schedule J (Form 1040) is used to figure the tax, check here ▶ ☐			17	251
18	Enter the **larger** of line 16 or line 17 here and on the **child's** Form 1040, line 44; Form 1040A, line 28; or Form 1040NR, line 42. If the child files Form 2555 or 2555-EZ, see the instructions			18	296

For Paperwork Reduction Act Notice, see your tax return instructions. Cat. No. 64113U Form **8615** (2011)

Chapter 33
Child and dependent care credit

ey.com/EYTaxGuide

Note

IRS Publication 17 (*Your Federal Income Tax*) has been updated by Ernst & Young LLP for 2011. Dates and dollar amounts shown are for 2011. Underlined type is used to indicate where IRS text has been updated. Places where text has been removed are indicated by the sentence: *Text intentionally omitted*.

ey.com/EYTaxGuide

Ernst & Young LLP will update the *Ernst & Young Tax Guide 2012* website with relevant taxpayer information as it becomes available. You can also sign up for email alerts to let you know when changes have been made.

Introduction

A credit that directly reduces your taxes is available for certain child and dependent care expenses that enable you to work. The credit may be as much as $1,050 if you have one qualifying individual or $2,100 if you have more than one qualifying individual. The credit is designed to help ease the tax burden of persons who must work and who also have the responsibility for the care of children or disabled dependents and spouses.

In general, to claim this credit, you must pay someone (other than a dependent) to care for a qualifying individual so that you can work or look for work. You must also have earned income from your work during the year and must have maintained a home for yourself and the qualifying individual for more than one-half of the year. This chapter spells out all the details.

Reminders

Taxpayer identification number needed for each qualifying person. You must include on line 2 of Form 2441 the name and taxpayer identification number (generally the social security number) of each qualifying person. See *Taxpayer identification number* under *Qualifying Person Test*, later.

You may have to pay employment taxes. If you pay someone to come to your home and care for your dependent or spouse, you may be a household employer who has to pay employment taxes. Usually, you are not a household employer if the person who cares for your dependent or spouse does so at his or her home or place of business. See *Employment Taxes for Household Employers*, later.

EXPLANATION

See chapter 40, *What to do if you employ domestic help*, for additional information.

This chapter discusses the credit for child and dependent care expenses and covers the following topics.

- Tests you must meet to claim the credit.
- How to figure the credit.
- How to claim the credit.
- Employment taxes you may have to pay as a household employer.

Tax Breaks and Deductions You Can Use Checklist

Child and Dependent Care Credit. The tax law allows you a credit against your tax if you pay child and dependent care expenses under certain circumstances. For an expense to qualify for the credit, it must be an "employment-related" expense, meaning that it must enable you and your spouse to work or look for work, and it must be for the care of your child, stepchild, or foster child, or your brother or sister or stepsibling (or a descendant of any of these) who is under 13, lives in your home for over half the year, and does not provide over half of his or her own support for the year. You may also be eligible for the credit if you pay for the care of your spouse or dependent who is physically or mentally incapable of caring for himself or herself and lives with you for over half the year. To claim the credit, you and your spouse must file a joint return. Further, you must include the social security number of the qualifying individual and the caregiver's name, address, and social security number (or ID number if it's a daycare center or nursery school) on the form for Child and Dependent Care expenses (Form 2441). A daycare center must be in compliance with state and local regulations.

Earned Income Test. If married, both you and your spouse must have earned income to be eligible to claim the child and dependent care credit. However, a nonworking spouse who cannot physically or mentally care for himself, or a spouse who is a full-time student for at least 5 months of the year is considered to have earned income.

You may be able to claim the credit if you pay someone to care for your dependent who is under age 13 or for your spouse or dependent who is not able to care for himself or herself. The credit can be up to 35% of your expenses. To qualify, you must pay these expenses so you can work or look for work.

Dependent care benefits. If you received any dependent care benefits from your employer during the year, you may be able to exclude from your income all or part of them. You must complete Part III of Form 2441 before you can figure the amount of your credit. See Dependent Care Benefits under *How To Figure the Credit,* later.

Useful Items

You may want to see:

Publication

- □ **501** Exemptions, Standard Deduction, and Filing Information
- □ **503** Child and Dependent Care Expenses
- □ **926** Household Employer's Tax Guide

Form (and Instructions)

- □ **2441** Child and Dependent Care Expenses
- □ **Schedule H (Form 1040)** Household Employment Taxes
- □ **W-7** Application for IRS Individual Taxpayer Identification Number
- □ **W-10** Dependent Care Provider's Identification and Certification

Tests To Claim the Credit

To be able to claim the credit for child and dependent care expenses, you must file Form 1040 or Form 1040A, not Form 1040EZ, and meet all the following tests.

1. The care must be for one or more qualifying persons who are identified on the form you use to claim the credit. (See *Qualifying Person Test.*)
2. You (and your spouse if filing jointly) must have earned income during the year. (However, see *Rule for student-spouse or spouse not able to care for self* under *Earned Income Test*, later.)
3. You must pay child and dependent care expenses so you (and your spouse if filing jointly) can work or look for work. (See *Work-Related Expense Test,* later.)
4. You must make payments for child and dependent care to someone you (and your spouse) cannot claim as a dependent. If you make payments to your child, he or she cannot be your dependent and must be age 19 or older by the end of the year. You cannot make payments to:
   a. Your spouse, or
   b. The parent of your qualifying person if your qualifying person is your child and under age 13.

   (See *Payments to Relatives or Dependents* under *Work-Related Expense Test,* later.)
5. Your filing status must be single, head of household, qualifying widow(er) with dependent child, or married filing jointly. You must file a joint return if you are married, unless an exception applies to you. (See *Joint Return Test,* later.)
6. You must identify the care provider on your tax return. (See *Provider Identification Test,* later.)
7. If you exclude or deduct dependent care benefits provided by a dependent care benefits plan, the total amount you exclude or deduct must be less than the dollar limit for qualifying expenses (generally, $3,000 if one qualifying person was cared for or $6,000 if two or more qualifying persons were cared for). (If two or more qualifying persons were cared for, the amount you exclude or deduct will always be less than the dollar limit, since the amount you can exclude or deduct is limited to $5,000. See Reduced Dollar Limit under *How To Figure the Credit,* later.)

These tests are presented in Figure 33-A and are also explained in detail in this chapter.

EXPLANATION

If a child turned 13 during the year, the child is a qualifying person only for the part of the year he was under age 13.

Example

Jan's child is a qualifying individual because she is a qualifying child who has not attained age 13. However, on March 20, Jan's child turns 13. Jan's child is a qualifying individual from January 1 through March 19.

Figure 33-A. **Can You Claim the Credit?**

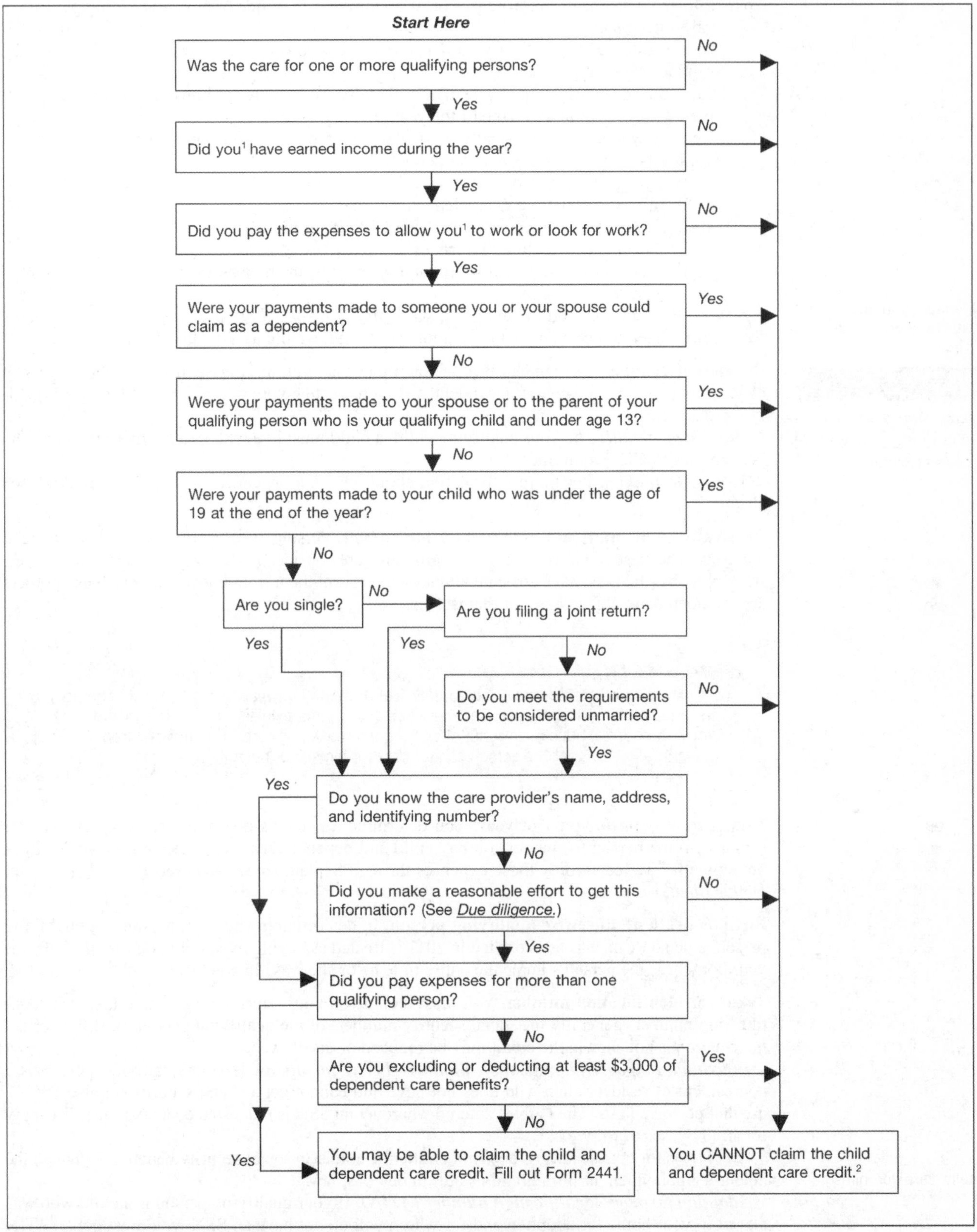

[1]This also applies to your spouse, unless your spouse was disabled or a full-time student.

[2] If you had expenses that met the requirements for 2010, except that you did not pay them until 2011, you may be able to claim those expenses in 2011. See *Expenses not paid until the following year* under *How To Figure the Credit.*

Qualifying Person Test

Your child and dependent care expenses must be for the care of one or more qualifying persons.

A qualifying person is:

1. Your qualifying child who is your dependent and who was under age 13 when the care was provided (but see *Note* later),
2. Your spouse who was not physically or mentally able to care for himself or herself and lived with you for more than half the year, or
3. A person who was not physically or mentally able to care for himself or herself, lived with you for more than half the year, and either:
   a. Was your dependent, or
   b. Would have been your dependent except that:
      i. He or she received gross income of $3,700 or more,
      ii. He or she filed a joint return, or
      iii. You, or your spouse if filing jointly, could be claimed as a dependent on someone else's 2011 return.

Note. If you are divorced or separated, see *Child of divorced or separated parents or parents living apart,* later, to determine which parent may treat the child as a qualifying person.

Caution

This credit should not be confused with the child tax credit discussed in chapter 35.

Dependent defined. A dependent is a person, other than you or your spouse, for whom you can claim an exemption. To be your dependent, a person must be your qualifying child (or your qualifying relative).

Qualifying child. To be your qualifying child, a child must live with you for more than half the year and meet other requirements.

More information. For more information about who is a dependent or a qualifying child, see chapter 3.

Physically or mentally not able to care for oneself. Persons who cannot dress, clean, or feed themselves because of physical or mental problems are considered not able to care for themselves. Also, persons who must have constant attention to prevent them from injuring themselves or others are considered not able to care for themselves.

EXPLANATION

For a person to be considered disabled, physical or mental incapacity must prevent the person from caring for himself or herself. The mere inability to engage in any substantial gainful activity, perform the normal household functions of a homemaker, or care for minor children does not necessarily establish that the person cannot care for himself or herself.

Person qualifying for part of year. You determine a person's qualifying status each day. For example, if the person for whom you pay child and dependent care expenses no longer qualifies on September 16, count only those expenses through September 15. Also see *Yearly Limit* under *Dollar Limit,* later.

Birth or death of otherwise qualifying person. In determining whether a person is a qualifying person, a person who was born or died in 2011 is treated as having lived with you for all of 2011 if your home was the person's home the entire time he or she was alive in 2011.

Taxpayer identification number. You must include on your return the name and taxpayer identification number (generally the social security number) of the qualifying person(s). If the correct information is not shown, the credit may be reduced or disallowed.

Individual taxpayer identification number (ITIN) for aliens. If your qualifying person is a nonresident or resident alien who does not have and cannot get a social security number (SSN), use that person's ITIN. The ITIN is entered wherever an SSN is requested on a tax return. To apply for an ITIN, see Form W-7.

An ITIN is for tax use only. It does not entitle the holder to social security benefits or change the holder's employment or immigration status under U.S. law.

Adoption taxpayer identification number (ATIN). If your qualifying person is a child who was placed in your home for adoption and for whom you do not have an SSN, you must get an ATIN for the child. File Form W-7A, Application for Taxpayer Identification Number for Pending U.S. Adoptions.

Child of divorced or separated parents or parents living apart. Even if you cannot claim your child as a dependent, he or she is treated as your qualifying person if:

- The child was under age 13 or was not physically or mentally able to care for himself or herself,
- The child received over half of his or her support during the calendar year from one or both parents who are divorced or legally separated under a decree of divorce or separate maintenance, are separated under a written separation agreement, or lived apart at all times during the last 6 months of the calendar year,
- The child was in the custody of one or both parents for more than half the year, and
- You were the child's custodial parent (the parent with whom the child lived for the greater part of 2011).

The noncustodial parent cannot treat the child as a qualifying person even if that parent is entitled to claim the child as a dependent under the special rules for a child of divorced or separated parents.

EXPLANATION

To take the credit, you do not necessarily have to claim the child as a dependent. If you have custody of the child even though you have signed a statement that entitles your ex-spouse to the child's dependency exemption, you may still claim the credit. To receive the credit, however, you must write your child's name on line 2 of Form 2441. To avoid questions from the IRS, you may want to attach to your tax return a copy of the signed statement authorizing the release of your dependency claim.

Example

Charles and Katherine Collins are divorced and share custody of their 3-year-old son, Dieter. Dieter lives 10 months a year with Katherine and attends a daycare center while his mother works. Charles and Katherine provide all of Dieter's support. Dieter is a qualifying person, since he is under age 13, is in the custody of his parents for more than half the year, and receives more than half his support from his parents. He is a qualifying person for Katherine and not Charles, because Katherine has custody of him for a longer period than does Charles. Dieter is a qualifying person for Katherine, even if she has released her right to claim him as a dependent to Charles.

In no case may two taxpayers filing separate returns claim separate tax credits for the same qualifying individual.

Earned Income Test

To claim the credit, you (and your spouse if filing jointly) must have earned income during the year.

Earned income. Earned income includes wages, salaries, tips, other taxable employee compensation, and net earnings from self-employment. A net loss from self-employment reduces earned income. Earned income also includes strike benefits and any disability pay you report as wages.

Generally, only taxable compensation is included. However, you can elect to include nontaxable combat pay in earned income. If you are filing a joint return and both you and your spouse received nontaxable combat pay, you can each make your own election. You should figure your credit both ways and make the election if it gives you a greater tax benefit.

Members of certain religious faiths opposed to social security. Certain income earned by persons who are members of certain religious faiths that are opposed to participation in Social Security Act programs and have an IRS-approved form that exempts certain income from social security and Medicare taxes may not be considered earned income for this purpose. See *Earned Income Test* in Publication 503.

Not earned income. Earned income does not include:

- Pensions and annuities,
- Social security and railroad retirement benefits,
- Workers' compensation,
- Interest and dividends,
- Unemployment compensation,
- Scholarship or fellowship grants, except for those reported on a Form W-2 and paid to you for teaching or other services,
- Nontaxable workfare payments,

- Child support payments received by you,
- Income of nonresident aliens that is not effectively connected with a U.S. trade or business, or
- Any amount received for work while an inmate in a penal institution.

Rule for student-spouse or spouse not able to care for self. Your spouse is treated as having earned income for any month that he or she is:

1. A full-time student, or
2. Physically or mentally not able to care for himself or herself. (Your spouse also must live with you for more than half the year.)

Figure the earned income of the nonworking spouse described under (1) or (2) above as explained under Earned Income Limit, later.

This rule applies to only one spouse for any one month. If, in the same month, both you and your spouse do not work and are either full-time students or not physically or mentally able to care for yourselves, only one of you can be treated as having earned income in that month.

Full-time student. You are a full-time student if you are enrolled at a school for the number of hours or classes that the school considers full time. You must have been a full-time student for some part of each of 5 calendar months during the year. (The months need not be consecutive.)

School. The term "school" includes high schools, colleges, universities, and technical, trade, and mechanical schools. A school does not include an on-the-job training course, correspondence school, or school offering courses only through the Internet.

EXAMPLE

Ben Winston and Sarah Winston are married and file a joint return. Sarah works full-time. Ben was a full-time student from January through May and from September through December. Their 6-year-old son attends a daycare center while Ben is in school. Since Ben was a full-time student during at least 5 months of the year, the minimum required by the IRS, he is considered to have worked each of the 9 months he was a full-time student.

Assume the same facts, except that both Ben and Sarah were full-time students for 9 months during the year. Only one of them may be considered as having worked during the months they were students. They would not be able to claim a credit for child care expenses.

Assume instead that while Ben and Sarah were full-time students, Ben also held a part-time job. Both may now be considered as having worked during the 9 months they were students–Ben because he was working and Sarah because she was a full-time student. They may claim a credit for child care expenses.

Work-Related Expense Test

Child and dependent care expenses must be work-related to qualify for the credit. Expenses are considered work-related only if both of the following are true.

- They allow you (and your spouse if filing jointly) to work or look for work.
- They are for a qualifying person's care.

Working or Looking for Work

To be work-related, your expenses must allow you to work or look for work. If you are married, generally both you and your spouse must work or look for work. Your spouse is treated as working during any month he or she is a full-time student or is not physically or mentally able to care for himself or herself.

Your work can be for others or in your own business or partnership. It can be either full time or part time.

Work also includes actively looking for work. However, if you do not find a job and have no earned income for the year, you cannot take this credit. See Earned Income Test, earlier.

An expense is not considered work-related merely because you had it while you were working. The purpose of the expense must be to allow you to work. Whether your expenses allow you to work or look for work depends on the facts.

Example 1. The cost of a babysitter while you and your spouse go out to eat is not normally a work-related expense.

Example 2. You work during the day. Your spouse works at night and sleeps during the day. You pay for care of your 5-year-old child during the hours when you are working and your spouse is sleeping. Your expenses are considered work-related.

Volunteer work. For this purpose, you are not considered to be working if you do unpaid volunteer work or volunteer work for a nominal salary.

EXAMPLES

Example 1

Susan McMorris is single. She began looking for a job in November 2011. Prior to this time, she had not worked. While looking for a job, she paid a sitter to watch her 2-year-old daughter. She finally found a job in February 2012. Her child care expenses during November and December 2011 were $125. Since Susan did not have income from work in 2011, she may not claim a credit for her child care expenses for that year.

Assume the same facts, except that Susan had worked until October 2011 when she was laid off and began looking for a new job. In this instance, she did have income from work during the year, so she may claim a credit for her child care expenses incurred while looking for work.

Example 2

Missy Angelle works 12 hours per week as an unpaid volunteer in the local library. She pays a sitter to watch her 3-year-old twins while she is working. Since she is not compensated for her work, she may not claim a credit for her child care expenses.

If Missy were paid $15 per week for her services in the library, she still could not claim a credit for her child care expenses because her work is for a nominal salary. What is considered a nominal salary is determined by the facts and circumstances of each situation. As a general rule, however, if you are working for less than the minimum wage, you are probably working for a nominal salary.

Work for part of year. If you work or actively look for work during only part of the period covered by the expenses, then you must figure your expenses for each day. For example, if you work all year and pay care expenses of $250 a month ($3,000 for the year), all the expenses are work-related. However, if you work or look for work for only 2 months and 15 days during the year and pay expenses of $250 a month, your work-related expenses are limited to $625 (2½ months × $250).

Temporary absence from work. You do not have to figure your expenses for each day during a short, temporary absence from work, such as for vacation or a minor illness, if you have to pay for care anyway. Instead, you can figure your credit including the expenses you paid for the period of absence.

An absence of 2 weeks or less is a short, temporary absence. An absence of more than 2 weeks may be considered a short, temporary absence, depending on the circumstances.

Example. You pay a nanny to care for your 2-year-old son and 4-year-old daughter so you can work. You become ill and miss 4 months of work but receive sick pay. You continue to pay the nanny to care for the children while you are ill. Your absence is not a short, temporary absence, and your expenses are not considered work-related.

Part-time work. If you work part-time, you generally must figure your expenses for each day. However, if you have to pay for care weekly, monthly, or in another way that includes both days worked and days not worked, you can figure your credit including the expenses you paid for days you did not work. Any day when you work at least 1 hour is a day of work.

Example 1. You work 3 days a week. While you work, your 6-year-old child attends a dependent care center, which complies with all state and local regulations. You can pay the center $150 for any 3 days a week or $250 for 5 days a week. Your child attends the center 5 days a week. Your work-related expenses are limited to $150 a week.

Example 2. The facts are the same as in *Example 1* except the center does not offer a 3-day option. The entire $250 weekly fee may be a work-related expense.

TAXPLANNER

There is an exception to the requirement to allocate expenses for short, temporary absences. If you are gainfully employed, you are not required to allocate expenses during a short, temporary absence from work, such as for vacation or minor illness, provided that the caregiving arrangement requires the taxpayer to pay for care during the absence. An absence of 2 consecutive calendar weeks is considered a short, temporary absence. Whether an absence longer than 2 consecutive calendar weeks is a short, temporary absence is determined based on all the facts and circumstances.

Care of a Qualifying Person

To be work-related, your expenses must be to provide care for a qualifying person.

You do not have to choose the least expensive way of providing care. The cost of a paid care provider may be an expense for the care of a qualifying person even if another care provider is available at no cost.

Expenses are for the care of a qualifying person only if their main purpose is the person's well-being and protection.

Expenses for household services qualify if part of the services is for the care of qualifying persons. See *Household services*, later.

Expenses not for care. Expenses for care do not include amounts you pay for food, lodging, clothing, education, and entertainment. However, you can include small amounts paid for these items if they are incident to and cannot be separated from the cost of caring for the qualifying person.

Education. Expenses for a child in nursery school, pre-school, or similar programs for children below the level of kindergarten are expenses for care. Expenses to attend kindergarten or a higher grade are not expenses for care. Do not use these expenses to figure your credit. However, expenses for before-school or after-school care of a child in kindergarten or a higher grade may be expenses for care. Summer school and tutoring programs are expenses not for care.

EXPLANATION

You can use the total cost of schooling prior to kindergarten only if the cost of schooling is incidental to and cannot be separated from the cost of the child's care. The IRS says that the cost of kindergarten does not qualify for the credit because it is primarily for educational purposes.

Example 1. You take your 3-year-old child to a nursery school that provides lunch and educational activities as a part of its preschool childcare service. The lunch and educational activities are incident to the childcare, and their cost cannot be separated from the cost of care. You can count the total cost when you figure the credit.

Example 2. You place your 10-year-old child in a boarding school so you can work full time. Only the part of the boarding school expense that is for the care of your child is a work-related expense. You can count that part of the expense in figuring your credit if it can be separated from the cost of education. You cannot count any part of the amount you pay the school for your child's education.

Care outside your home. You can count the cost of care provided outside your home if the care is for your dependent under age 13 or any other qualifying person who regularly spends at least 8 hours each day in your home.

Dependent care center. You can count care provided outside your home by a dependent care center only if the center complies with all state and local regulations that apply to these centers.

A dependent care center is a place that provides care for more than six persons (other than persons who live there) and receives a fee, payment, or grant for providing services for any of those persons, even if the center is not run for profit.

EXPLANATION

If a care center has six or fewer individuals enrolled on the day on which you enroll a qualified person, you may presume that it is not a dependent care center for the tax year. You may also presume that if a center was not a dependent care center in the prior year and has six or fewer individuals enrolled on January 1, it will not be considered a dependent care center during the current year.

As the IRS text notes, if care is provided by a dependent care center, the center must meet local and state regulations for your expenses to qualify for the credit. For example, most states stipulate the maximum permissible ratio of children to adult workers in a daycare center. You may wish to inquire at a center if it meets all state and local regulations. Ask to see a copy of the center's most recent certification from the proper authorities. However, if care is provided by a center that is not a dependent care center, the center need not meet local and state regulations for your expenses to qualify for the credit.

Camp. The cost of sending your child to an overnight camp is not considered a work-related expense. The cost of sending your child to a day camp may be a work-related expense, even if the camp specializes in a particular activity, such as computers or soccer.

Transportation. If a care provider takes a qualifying person to or from a place where care is provided, that transportation is for the care of the qualifying person. This includes transportation by bus, subway, taxi, or private car. However, transportation not provided by a care provider is not for the care of a qualifying person. Also, if you pay the transportation cost for the care provider to come to your home, that expense is not for care of a qualifying person.

Fees and deposits. Fees you paid to an agency to get the services of a care provider, deposits you paid to an agency or pre-school, application fees, and other indirect expenses are work-related expenses if you have to pay them to get care, even though they are not directly for care. However, a forfeited deposit is not for the care of a qualifying person if care is not provided.

Example 1. You paid a fee to an agency to get the services of the nanny who cares for your 2-year-old daughter while you work. The fee you paid is a work-related expense.

Example 2. You placed a deposit with a pre-school to reserve a place for your 3-year-old child. You later sent your child to a different pre-school and forfeited the deposit. The forfeited deposit is not for care and so is not a work-related expense.

Household services. Expenses you pay for household services meet the work-related expense test if they are at least partly for the well-being and protection of a qualifying person.

Household services are ordinary and usual services done in and around your home that are necessary to run your home. They include the services of a housekeeper, maid, or cook. However, they do not include the services of a chauffeur, bartender, or gardener. See *Household Services* in Publication 503 for more information.

TAXPLANNER

Allocating expenses. There are no hard-and-fast rules that govern when an allocation is reasonable or when the expense for other services is small in relation to the total expense. The facts and circumstances of each case are the determining factors. Use your best judgment. If you must make an allocation, you should document how the allocation is made. If you decide that an allocation is not necessary, you should also document the basis for your decision. A note in your personal records should be sufficient.

In this chapter, the term housekeeper refers to any household employee whose services include the care of a qualifying person.

Taxes paid on wages. The taxes you pay on wages for qualifying child and dependent care services are work-related expenses. See Employment Taxes for Household Employers, later.

Payments to Relatives or Dependents

You can count work-related payments you make to relatives who are not your dependents, even if they live in your home. However, do not count any amounts you pay to:

1. A dependent for whom you (or your spouse if filing jointly) can claim an exemption,
2. Your child who was under age 19 at the end of the year, even if he or she is not your dependent,
3. A person who was your spouse any time during the year, or
4. The parent of your qualifying person if your qualifying person is your child and under age 13.

EXAMPLE

Edward McKenzie lives with his daughter Stacy and cares for his granddaughter Melissa after school while Stacy is at work. Stacy pays her father $300 per month and cannot claim him as a dependent. These payments qualify as work-related expenses for Stacy.

Assume, instead, that Stacy pays her other daughter, Sarah, $150 per month to look after Melissa, Sarah's sister. Sarah turns 19 during the year and can be claimed as a dependent by Stacy. Stacy's payments to Sarah are not qualified work-related expenses.

Joint Return Test

Generally, married couples must file a joint return to take the credit. However, if you are legally separated or living apart from your spouse, you may be able to file as Head of Household and still take the credit. However, you cannot use the filing status Married Filing Separately if you plan to claim the credit.

Legally separated. You are not considered married if you are legally separated from your spouse under a decree of divorce or separate maintenance. You may be eligible to take the credit on your return using Head of Household filing status.

Married and living apart. You are not considered married and are eligible to take the credit if all the following apply.

1. You file a return apart from your spouse.
2. Your home is the home of a qualifying person for more than half the year.
3. You pay more than half the cost of keeping up your home for the year.
4. Your spouse does not live in your home for the last 6 months of the year.

EXAMPLE

Cole and Christine Lee separated in April. They are not legally separated at the end of the year and plan to file separate returns. Their two children lived with Christine for the entire year, and she provided more than half the costs of maintaining her household for the year. Christine may claim a credit on her separate return.

Assume, instead, that Cole and Christine were separated in August. Since Cole lived in Christine's home during part of the last 6 months of the year, a joint return must be filed to claim the credit.

Costs of keeping up a home. The costs of keeping up a home normally include property taxes, mortgage interest, rent, utility charges, home repairs, insurance on the home, and food eaten at home.

The costs of keeping up a home do not include payments for clothing, education, medical treatment, vacations, life insurance, transportation, or mortgage principal.

They also do not include the purchase, permanent improvement, or replacement of property. For example, you cannot include the cost of replacing a water heater. However, you can include the cost of repairing a water heater.

Death of spouse. If your spouse died during the year and you do not remarry before the end of the year, you generally must file a joint return to take the credit. If you do remarry before the end of the year, the credit can be claimed on your deceased spouse's own return.

Provider Identification Test

You must identify all persons or organizations that provide care for your child or dependent. Use Part I of Form 2441 to show the information.

Note. If you did not have a qualifying person and any care providers for 2011, and you are filing Form 2441 only to report taxable income in Part III, enter "none" in line 1, column (a).

Information needed. To identify the care provider, you must give the provider's:

1. Name,
2. Address, and
3. Taxpayer identification number.

If the care provider is an individual, the taxpayer identification number is his or her social security number or individual taxpayer identification number. If the care provider is an organization, then it is the employer identification number (EIN).

You do not have to show the taxpayer identification number if the care provider is a tax-exempt organization (such as a church or school). In this case, enter "Tax-Exempt" in the space where the tax form calls for the number.

If you cannot provide all of the information or if the information is incorrect you must be able to show that you used due diligence (discussed later) in trying to furnish the necessary information.

Getting the information. You can use Form W-10 to request the required information from the care provider. If you do not use Form W-10, you can get the information from one of the other sources listed in the instructions for Form W-10 including:

1. A copy of the provider's social security card,
2. A copy of the provider's completed Form W-4 if he or she is your household employee,
3. A copy of the statement furnished by your employer if the provider is your employer's dependent care plan, or
4. A letter or invoice from the provider if it shows the information.

EXPLANATION

Also see Records You Need in chapter 40, *What to do if you employ domestic help*, if the care provider does not have a social security number.

TAXORGANIZER

Keep Form W-10 with your tax records to substantiate the name, address, and taxpayer identification number(s) of your daycare provider(s). If Form W-10 is not used, keep any other documents that substantiate the required information.

Records

You should keep this information with your tax records. Do not send Form W-10 (or other document containing this information) to the Internal Revenue Service.

Due diligence. If the care provider information you give is incorrect or incomplete, your credit may not be allowed. However, if you can show that you used due diligence in trying to supply the information, you can still claim the credit.

You can show due diligence by getting and keeping the provider's completed Form W-10 or one of the other sources of information listed earlier. Care providers can be penalized if they do not provide this information to you or if they provide incorrect information.

Provider refusal. If the provider refuses to give you their identifying information, you should report whatever information you have (such as the name and address) on the form you use to claim the credit. Enter "See Attached Statement" in the columns calling for the information you do not have. Then attach a statement explaining that you requested the information from the care provider, but the provider did not give you the information. Be sure to write your name and social security number on this statement. The statement will show that you used due diligence in trying to furnish the necessary information.

U.S. citizens and resident aliens living abroad. If you are living abroad, your care provider may not have, and may not be required to get, a U.S. taxpayer identification number (for example, an SSN or EIN). If so, enter "LAFCP" (Living Abroad Foreign Care Provider) in the space for the care provider's taxpayer identification number.

How To Figure the Credit

Your credit is a percentage of your work-related expenses. Your expenses are subject to the earned income limit and the dollar limit. The percentage is based on your adjusted gross income.

Figuring Total Work-Related Expenses

To figure the credit for 2011 work-related expenses, count only those you paid by December 31, 2011.

Expenses prepaid in an earlier year. If you pay for services before they are provided, you can count the prepaid expenses only in the year the care is received. Claim the expenses for the later year as if they were actually paid in that later year.

EXAMPLE

Martha Winters paid $1,800 in November 2011 to the daycare center her son attends. The payment was for the 6-month period from November 2011 through April 2012. She may use $600 (2/6 × $1,800) of this payment in calculating her credit for 2011. This amount represents payment for services rendered in November and December 2011. She may use $1,200 (4/6 × $1,800) of this payment in 2012. This amount represents payment for services rendered in January through April 2012.

Tip

If you had expenses in 2011 that you did not pay until 2012, you cannot count them when figuring your 2011 credit. You may be able to claim a credit for them on your 2012 return.

Expenses not paid until the following year. Do not count 2010 expenses that you paid in 2011 as work-related expenses for 2011. You may be able to claim an additional credit for them on your 2011 return, but you must figure it separately. See *Payments for previous year's expenses* under *Amount of Credit* in Publication 503.

TAXPLANNER

The general rule is that expenses used in computing your child care credit are included in figuring your tax for the year in which the expenses are paid or for the year in which the services are provided, whichever is later. However, regardless of when they are paid, expenses are subject to the dollar limitation for the year in which the services are provided. You may not reap an additional tax advantage by paying your expenses in a year that is different from the one in which the services are provided. See *Amount of Credit* and *Worksheet A* in IRS Publication 503, *Child and Dependent Care Expenses.*

Example

Bernadette Dryden, who is divorced and files a separate return, paid $300 in January 2011 for care provided for her daughter in November and December 2010. Her adjusted gross income and earned income in 2010 were $25,000, and she paid $1,200 for work-related expenses in 2010. Bernadette may increase her 2011 child care credit by $90 (as calculated in Column A, following:

	Column A	Column B
1) 2010 qualified expenses paid in 2010	$1,200	$3,000
2) 2010 qualified expenses paid in 2011	300	300
3) Total qualified 2010 expenses	$1,500	$3,300
4) Limitation for one qualifying person	$3,000	$3,000
5) Earned income limitation	25,000	25,000
6) Smallest of lines 3, 4, and 5	1,500	3,000
7) Child care expenses used in calculating 2010 credit	(1,200)	(3,000)
8) 2010 expenses carried over to 2011	$300	-0-
9) Credit percentage applicable for 2010 adjusted gross income	30%	30%
10) Increase in 2011 credit (line 8 × line 9)	$90	-0-

Bernadette should attach a statement to her 2011 return, showing the name and taxpayer identification number of her daughter (for whom she paid the prior year's expenses) and the calculation in Column A as support for her inclusion of $90 on line 9, Form 2441. She should write "CPYE" and the amount of the additional credit in the dotted line next to line 9 on Form 2441 and should increase line 9 by this amount.

Assume, instead, that Bernadette paid $3,000 in work-related expenses during 2010. No increase in her 2011 credit is available (see Column B, earlier), since the maximum amount of expenses for 2010 is already used in calculating the credit. She receives no benefit for the $300 paid in 2011, as she would have received no benefit if it had been paid in 2010.

Expenses reimbursed. If a state social services agency pays you a nontaxable amount to reimburse you for some of your child and dependent care expenses, you cannot count the expenses that are reimbursed as work-related expenses.

Example. You paid work-related expenses of $3,000. You are reimbursed $2,000 by a state social services agency. You can use only $1,000 to figure your credit.

Medical expenses. Some expenses for the care of qualifying persons who are not able to care for themselves may qualify as work-related expenses and also as medical expenses. You can use them either way, but you cannot use the same expenses to claim both a credit and a medical expense deduction.

If you use these expenses to figure the credit and they are more than the earned income limit or the dollar limit, discussed later, you can add the excess to your medical expenses. However, if you use your total expenses to figure your medical expense deduction, you cannot use any part of them to figure your credit.

EXAMPLE

During the year, you pay $3,350 to a private-duty nurse for the care of your physically handicapped dependent daughter, who is not able to care for herself. These expenses are for work done in your home and qualify as medical expenses. Your earned income for the year is $25,000. Because your work-related expenses are for one qualifying person, you may take a maximum of $3,000 of these expenses into account in figuring your tax credit. You may treat the remaining $350 as a medical expense.

TAXORGANIZER

Keep copies of receipts and canceled checks to document the amount of dependent care expenses that you paid for the year. The fact that you have provided these to your employer's plan may not be sufficient without such records.

Dependent Care Benefits

If you receive dependent care benefits, your dollar limit for purposes of the credit may be reduced. See <u>*Reduced Dollar Limit,*</u> later. But, even if you cannot take the credit, you may be able to take an exclusion or deduction for the dependent care benefits.

Caution

Amounts excluded from your income under your employer's dependent care benefits plan cannot be used to claim a medical expense deduction.

Dependent care benefits. Dependent care benefits include:

1. Amounts your employer paid directly to either you or your care provider for the care of your qualifying person while you work,
2. The fair market value of care in a daycare facility provided or sponsored by your employer, and
3. Pre-tax contributions you made under a dependent care flexible spending arrangement.

Your salary may have been reduced to pay for these benefits. If you received benefits as an employee, they should be shown in box 10 of your Form W-2. See <u>*Statement for employee,*</u> later. Benefits you received as a partner should be shown in box 13 of your Schedule K-1 (Form 1065) with code O. Enter the amount of these benefits on the first line of Part III of Form 2441.

Exclusion or deduction. If your employer provides dependent care benefits under a qualified plan, you may be able to exclude these benefits from your income. Your employer can tell you whether your benefit plan qualifies. To claim the exclusion, you must complete Part III of Form 2441. You cannot use Form 1040EZ.

If you are self-employed and receive benefits from a qualified dependent care benefit plan, you are treated as both employer and employee. Therefore, you would not get an exclusion from wages. Instead, you would get a deduction on Form 1040, Schedule C, line 14; Schedule E, line 19 or 28; or Schedule F, line 15. To claim the deduction, you must use Form 2441.

The amount you can exclude or deduct is limited to the smallest of:

1. The total amount of dependent care benefits you received during the year,
2. The total amount of qualified expenses you incurred during the year,
3. Your earned income,
4. Your spouse's earned income, or
5. $5,000 ($2,500 if married filing separately). See <u>*Earned Income Limit,*</u> below.

The definition of earned income for the exclusion or deduction is the same as the definition used when figuring the credit except that earned income for the exclusion or deduction does not include any dependent care benefits you receive. For details or if you or your spouse had nontaxable combat pay, see the instructions for Form 2441.

TAXSAVER

If your employer provides dependent care benefits, you will see them reported on your W-2 in Box 10. These benefits reduce your expenses available for the child care credit.

For example, if your employer excluded $1,000 from your income for dependent care, you would only be allowed to use $2,000 to claim the credit.

Child care expenses paid during 2011	$3,000
Less: Employer-provided benefits	(1,000)
Maximum expenses available for the credit	$2,000

To ensure that you get the greater tax savings, you should carefully consider the impact of a reduction in income as compared to the value of the credit. Generally, as long as the credit amount is not greater than the taxpayer's tax liability, those with lower levels of adjusted gross income will benefit more from the dependent care credit than from a dependent care benefit reduction to taxable income.

EXPLANATION

If you incur expenses for more than one qualifying person, you can still claim a credit if your employer has reduced your income by the full $5,000 and you have been reimbursed the full $5,000. See Reduced Dollar Limit, later. But your credit will be based on a maximum of $1,000 of expenses ($6,000 less $5,000) since your expenses must be reduced by the amount of any reimbursement.

Statement for employee. Your employer must give you a Form W-2 (or similar statement) showing in box 10 the total amount of dependent care benefits provided to you during the year under a qualified plan. Your employer will also include any dependent care benefits over $5,000 in your wages shown on your Form W-2 in box 10.

Effect of exclusion. If you exclude dependent care benefits from your income, the amount of the excluded benefits:

1. Is not included in your work-related expenses, and
2. Reduces the dollar limit, discussed later.

Earned Income Limit

The amount of work-related expenses you use to figure your credit cannot be more than:

1. Your earned income for the year if you are single at the end of the year, or
2. The smaller of your or your spouse's earned income for the year if you are married at the end of the year.

Earned income is defined under Earned Income Test, earlier.

Tip

For purposes of item (2), use your spouse's earned income for the entire year, even if you were married for only part of the year.

TAXPLANNER

At year-end, if you are self-employed, you should review your income and expenses for the year. To the extent it is possible, income and expenses for the remaining part of the year should be timed to take maximum advantage of the dependent care credit.

Separated spouse. If you are legally separated or married and living apart from your spouse (as described under Joint Return Test, earlier), you are not considered married for purposes of the earned income limit. Use only your income in figuring the earned income limit.

Surviving spouse. If your spouse died during the year and you file a joint return as a surviving spouse, you are not considered married for purposes of the earned income limit. Use only your income in figuring the earned income limit.

Community property laws. You should disregard community property laws when you figure earned income for this credit.

EXAMPLE

Durwood and Sheila Dupuis are married and live in a community property state. Durwood earns $52,000 as an engineer, while Sheila earns $15,000 as a teaching assistant. Under community property laws, each is considered to have earned half the other's compensation, and is considered to bring in $33,500 [(50% × $52,000) + (50% × $15,000)]. Community property laws are disregarded, however, for the purpose of calculating this tax credit. Under the Earned Income Limit test, Durwood has $52,000 of earned income and Sheila has $15,000.

Student-spouse or spouse not able to care for self. Your spouse who is either a full-time student or not able to care for himself or herself is treated as having earned income. His or her earned income for each month is considered to be at least $250 if there is one qualifying person in your home, or at least $500 if there are two or more.

Spouse works. If your spouse works during that month, use the higher of $250 (or $500) or his or her actual earned income for that month.

Spouse qualifies for part of month. If your spouse is a full-time student or not able to care for himself or herself for only part of a month, the full $250 (or $500) still applies for that month.

Both spouses qualify. If, in the same month, both you and your spouse are either full-time students or not able to care for yourselves, only one spouse can be considered to have this earned income of $250 (or $500) for that month.

TAXALERT

As stated under the Qualifying Person Test, if the dependent for whom you have work-related expenses is disabled for only part of a month, the total work-related expenses are limited to that part of the month.

Example 1

David and Donna are married and file a joint return. Because of an accident, David is incapable of self-care for the entire tax year. To keep working, Donna pays a neighbor $2,000 to take care of him. Donna's adjusted gross income is $29,000. The entire amount is earned income. They figure their credit on the smallest of the following amounts:

1) Total work-related expenses	$2,000
2) Donna's earned income	$29,000
3) Income considered earned by David (12 x $250)	$3,000
Allowable credit (28% of $2,000)	$560

Example 2

Carlos works and keeps up a home for himself, his wife, Diana, and their two children (both under age 13). Carlos has adjusted gross income of $35,000. The entire amount is earned income.

Diana is a full-time student at State University from January 4 through June 10. She does not return to school after June 10.

They paid a neighbor $600 per month from January 4 to June 10 (total $3,600) to care for their two children in her home while the children were not in school.

They figure the credit on the smallest of the following amounts:

1) Total work-related expenses	$3,600
2) Carlos's earned income	$35,000
3) Income considered earned by Diana (6 x $500)	$3,000
Allowable credit (25% of $3,000)	$750

Dollar Limit

There is a dollar limit on the amount of your work-related expenses you can use to figure the credit. This limit is $3,000 for one qualifying person, or $6,000 for two or more qualifying persons.

Yearly limit. The dollar limit is a yearly limit. The amount of the dollar limit remains the same no matter how long, during the year, you have a qualifying person in your household. Use the $3,000 limit if you paid work-related expenses for the care of one qualifying person at any time during the year. Use $6,000 if you paid work-related expenses for the care of more than one qualifying person at any time during the year.

Tip

If you paid work-related expenses for the care of two or more qualifying persons, the $6,000 limit does not need to be divided equally among them. For example, if your work-related expenses for the care of one qualifying person are $3,200 and your work-related expenses for another qualifying person are $2,800, you can use the total, $6,000, when figuring the credit.

EXAMPLE

Wendy Ackal employs a full-time housekeeper to care for her two children while she works. Her older child turned 13 years old during the year. The dollar limit on her work-related expenses is $6,000, since at some time during the year she had two qualifying persons.

Assume the same facts, except that Wendy has only one child, Paris, who turned 13 years old on August 31. The dollar limit on her work-related expenses is $3,000. Only her expenses through August 31 may be used. The limit is the maximum amount that may be used in calculating the credit. If her actual expenses through August are less than $3,000, she must use that amount in calculating her tax credit.

Reduced Dollar Limit

If you received dependent care benefits that you exclude or deduct from your income, you must subtract that amount from the dollar limit that applies to you. Your reduced dollar limit is figured in Part III of Form 2441. See Dependent Care Benefits, earlier, for information on excluding or deducting these benefits.

Example. George is a widower with one child and earns $24,000 a year. He pays work-related expenses of $2,900 for the care of his 4-year-old child and qualifies to claim the credit for child and dependent care expenses. His employer pays an additional $1,000 under a dependent care benefit plan. This $1,000 is excluded from George's income.

Although the dollar limit for his work-related expenses is $3,000 (one qualifying person), George figures his credit on only $2,000 of the $2,900 work-related expenses he paid. This is because his dollar limit is reduced as shown next.

George's Reduced Dollar Limit

1)	Maximum allowable expenses for one qualifying person	$3,000
2)	Minus: Dependent care benefits George excludes from income	−1,000
3)	Reduced dollar limit on expenses George can use for the credit	$2,000

Amount of Credit

To determine the amount of your credit, multiply your work-related expenses (after applying the earned income and dollar limits) by a percentage. This percentage depends on your adjusted gross income shown on Form 1040, line 38, or Form 1040A, line 22. The following table shows the percentage to use based on adjusted gross income.

IF your adjusted gross income is:		THEN the
Over	But not over	percentage is:
$ 0	$15,000	35%
15,000	17,000	34%
17,000	19,000	33%
19,000	21,000	32%
21,000	23,000	31%
23,000	25,000	30%
25,000	27,000	29%
27,000	29,000	28%
29,000	31,000	27%
31,000	33,000	26%
33,000	35,000	25%
35,000	37,000	24%
37,000	39,000	23%
39,000	41,000	22%
41,000	43,000	21%
43,000	No limit	20%

EXAMPLES

Example 1

Karl Dryden is single, has adjusted gross income of $23,500, and has $1,800 in qualified expenses for 2011. The credit available to him is $540 (30% × $1,800).

Assume, instead, that Karl has adjusted gross income of $28,500. Now his available tax credit is $504 (28% × $1,800).

Example 2

Joni Morris has a tax liability of $730 before credits and a potential child care credit of $1,050. She may use $730 of the child care credit to bring her tax liability to zero. The excess credit of $320 is effectively lost. It may not be refunded, carried forward to a future year, or carried back to a prior year.

How To Claim the Credit

To claim the credit, you can file Form 1040 or Form 1040A. You cannot claim the credit on Form 1040EZ.

Form 1040 or 1040A. You must complete Form 2441 and attach it to your Form 1040 or 1040A. Enter the credit on Form 1040, line 48, or Form 1040A, line 29. An example of a filled-in Form 2441 is shown at the end of this chapter.

Limit on credit. The amount of credit you can claim is limited to your regular tax (after reduction by any allowable foreign tax credit) plus your alternative minimum tax, if any. For more information, see the Instructions for Form 2441.

> ***EXPLANATION***
> In December 2010, the President and Congress agreed to extend the so-called Bush tax cuts. This new tax law included a provision that extended the ability for individuals to offset their entire regular and AMT tax liabilities in 2011 (and 2010) with personal nonrefundable tax credits (including the child and dependent care credit).

Tax credit not refundable. You cannot get a refund for any part of the credit that is more than this limit.

Recordkeeping. You should keep records of your work-related expenses. Also, if your dependent or spouse is not able to care for himself or herself, your records should show both the nature and the length of the disability. Other records you should keep to support your claim for the credit are described earlier under *Provider Identification Test*.

> ***TAXORGANIZER***
> Your records of work-related expenses may be either canceled checks or cash receipt tickets. A note in your files recording the nature and length of a person's disability should be sufficient documentation in most cases.

Employment Taxes for Household Employers

If you pay someone to come to your home and care for your dependent or spouse, you may be a household employer. If you are a household employer, you will need an employer identification number (EIN) and you may have to pay employment taxes. If the individuals who work in your home are self-employed, you are not liable for any of the taxes discussed in this section. Self-employed persons who are in business for themselves are not household employees. Usually, you are not a household employer if the person who cares for your dependent or spouse does so at his or her home or place of business.

If you use a placement agency that exercises control over what work is done and how it will be done by a babysitter or companion who works in your home, the worker is not your employee. This control could include providing rules of conduct and appearance and requiring regular reports. In this case, you do not have to pay employment taxes. But, if an agency merely gives you a list of sitters and you hire one from that list, and pay the sitter directly, the sitter may be your employee.

If you have a household employee, you may be subject to:

1. Social security and Medicare taxes,
2. Federal unemployment tax, and
3. Federal income tax withholding.

Social security and Medicare taxes are generally withheld from the employee's pay and matched by the employer. Federal unemployment (FUTA) tax is paid by the employer only and provides for payments of unemployment compensation to workers who have lost their jobs. Federal income tax is withheld from the employee's total pay if the employee asks you to do so and you agree.

For more information on a household employer's tax responsibilities, see Publication 926 and Schedule H (Form 1040) and its instructions.

State employment tax. You may also have to pay state unemployment tax. Contact your state unemployment tax office for information. You should also find out whether you need to pay or collect other state employment taxes or carry workers' compensation insurance. A list of state employment tax agencies, including addresses and phone numbers, is in Publication 926.

> ***EXPLANATION***
> Also, see chapter 40, *What to do if you employ domestic help.*

Example

The following example shows how to figure the credit for child and dependent care expenses for two children when employer-provided dependent care benefits are involved. The filled-in draft Form 2441 is shown at the end of this chapter.

Illustrated example. Joan Thomas is divorced and has two children, ages 3 and 9. She works at ACME Computers. Her adjusted gross income (AGI) is $29,000, and the entire amount is earned income.

Joan's younger child (Susan) stays at her employer's on-site childcare center while she works. The benefits from this childcare center qualify to be excluded from her income. Her employer reports the value of this service as $3,000 for the year. This $3,000 is shown on her Form W-2 in box 10, but is not included in taxable wages in box 1.

A neighbor cares for Joan's older child (Seth) after school, on holidays, and during the summer. Joan pays her neighbor $2,400 for this care.

Joan figures her credit on Form 2441 as follows.

1) Work-related expenses Joan paid	$ 2,400
2) Dollar limit (2 or more qualified individuals)	$ 6,000
3) Minus: Dependent care benefits excluded from Joan's income	–3,000
4) Reduced dollar limit	$ 3,000
5) Lesser of expenses paid ($2,400) or dollar limit ($3,000)	$ 2,400
6) Percentage for AGI of $29,000 (28%)	.28
7) Multiply the amount on line 5 by the percentage on line 6 ($2,400 × .28)	$ 672
8) Enter the tax liability limit from Form 2441, line 10	$ 940
9) Credit (Enter the smaller of line 7 or line 8)	$ 672

EXPLANATION

Note: The dollar limit for two or more qualifying persons ($6,000) is reduced by the amount of excluded benefits, as discussed earlier under Reduced Dollar Limit.

TAXORGANIZER

Records you should keep:

Keep copies of receipts and canceled checks to document the amount of dependent care expenses that you paid for the year.

Keep Form W-10 with your tax records to substantiate the name, address, and taxpayer identification number(s) of your daycare provider(s). If Form W-10 is not used, keep any other documents that substantiate the required daycare provider information.

If your dependent or spouse is disabled, your records should contain the description and the length of the disability.

Form **2441**

Department of the Treasury
Internal Revenue Service (99)

Child and Dependent Care Expenses

► Attach to Form 1040, Form 1040A, or Form 1040NR.

► See separate instructions.

1040 / 1040A / 1040NR / 2441

OMB No. 1545-0074

2011

Attachment Sequence No. 21

Name(s) shown on return: Joan Thomas

Your social security number: 559-00-3436

Part I **Persons or Organizations Who Provided the Care**—You **must** complete this part.
(If you have more than two care providers, see the instructions.)

1 (a) Care provider's name	(b) Address (number, street, apt. no., city, state, and ZIP code)	(c) Identifying number (SSN or EIN)	(d) Amount paid (see instructions)
Pat Green	12 Ash Avenue Hometown, TX 75240	240-00-3811	2,400
ACME Computers	(See W-2)		

Did you receive **dependent care benefits?**
- **No** ► Complete only Part II below.
- **Yes** ► Complete Part III on the back next.

Caution. If the care was provided in your home, you may owe employment taxes. If you do, you cannot file Form 1040A. For details, see the instructions for Form 1040, line 59a, or Form 1040NR, line 58a.

Part II **Credit for Child and Dependent Care Expenses**

2 Information about your **qualifying person(s).** If you have more than two qualifying persons, see the instructions.

(a) Qualifying person's name — First	Last	(b) Qualifying person's social security number	(c) **Qualified expenses** you incurred and paid in 2011 for the person listed in column (a)
Seth	Thomas	559-00-1234	2,400
Sarah	Thomas	559-00-5678	

3 Add the amounts in column (c) of line 2. **Do not** enter more than $3,000 for one qualifying person or $6,000 for two or more persons. If you completed Part III, enter the amount from line 31 . . . **3** 2,400

4 Enter your **earned income**. See instructions . . . **4** 29,000

5 If married filing jointly, enter your spouse's earned income (if your spouse was a student or was disabled, see the instructions); **all others**, enter the amount from line 4 . . . **5** 29,000

6 Enter the **smallest** of line 3, 4, or 5 . . . **6** 2,400

7 Enter the amount from Form 1040, line 38; Form 1040A, line 22; or Form 1040NR, line 37. . . . **7** 29,000

8 Enter on line 8 the decimal amount shown below that applies to the amount on line 7

If line 7 is: Over	But not over	Decimal amount is	If line 7 is: Over	But not over	Decimal amount is
$0	15,000	.35	$29,000	31,000	.27
15,000	17,000	.34	31,000	33,000	.26
17,000	19,000	.33	33,000	35,000	.25
19,000	21,000	.32	35,000	37,000	.24
21,000	23,000	.31	37,000	39,000	.23
23,000	25,000	.30	39,000	41,000	.22
25,000	27,000	.29	41,000	43,000	.21
27,000	29,000	.28	43,000	No limit	.20

8 X. 28

9 Multiply line 6 by the decimal amount on line 8. If you paid 2010 expenses in 2011, see the instructions . . . **9** 672

10 Tax liability limit. Enter the amount from the Credit Limit Worksheet in the instructions. . . . **10** 940

11 **Credit for child and dependent care expenses.** Enter the **smaller** of line 9 or line 10 here and on Form 1040, line 48; Form 1040A, line 29; or Form 1040NR, line 46 . . . **11** 672

For Paperwork Reduction Act Notice, see your tax return instructions. Cat. No. 11862M Form **2441** (2011)

Part III Dependent Care Benefits

12	Enter the total amount of **dependent care benefits** you received in 2011. Amounts you received as an employee should be shown in box 10 of your Form(s) W-2. **Do not** include amounts reported as wages in box 1 of Form(s) W-2. If you were self-employed or a partner, include amounts you received under a dependent care assistance program from your sole proprietorship or partnership . . .			12	3,000
13	Enter the amount, if any, you carried over from 2010 and used in 2011 during the grace period. See instructions . . .			13	
14	Enter the amount, if any, you forfeited or carried forward to 2012. See instructions . . .			14	( )
15	Combine lines 12 through 14. See instructions . . .			15	3,000
16	Enter the total amount of **qualified expenses** incurred in 2011 for the care of the **qualifying person(s)** . . .	16	5,400		
17	Enter the **smaller** of line 15 or 16 . . .	17	3,000		
18	Enter your **earned income.** See instructions . . .	18	29,000		
19	Enter the amount shown below that applies to you. • If married filing jointly, enter your spouse's earned income (if your spouse was a student or was disabled, see the instructions for line 5). • If married filing separately, see instructions. • All others, enter the amount from line 18.	19	29,000		
20	Enter the **smallest** of line 17, 18, or 19 . . .	20	3,000		
21	Enter $5,000 ($2,500 if married filing separately **and** you were required to enter your spouse's earned income on line 19) . . .	21	5,0000		
22	Is any amount on line 12 from your sole proprietorship or partnership? (Form 1040A filers go to line 25.) ☐ **No.** Enter -0-. ☐ **Yes.** Enter the amount here . . .			22	-0-
23	Subtract line 22 from line 15 . . .	23	3,000		
24	**Deductible benefits.** Enter the **smallest** of line 20, 21, or 22. Also, include this amount on the appropriate line(s) of your return. See instructions . . .			24	-0-
25	**Excluded benefits. Form 1040 and 1040NR filers:** If you checked "No" on line 22, enter the smaller of line 20 or 21. Otherwise, subtract line 24 from the smaller of line 20 or line 21. If zero or less, enter -0-. **Form 1040A filers:** Enter the **smaller** of line 20 or line 21 . . .			25	3,000
26	**Taxable benefits. Form 1040 and 1040NR filers:** Subtract line 25 from line 23. If zero or less, enter -0-. Also, include this amount on Form 1040, line 7; or Form 1040NR, line 8. On the dotted line next to Form 1040, line 7; or Form 1040NR, line 8, enter "DCB." **Form 1040A filers:** Subtract line 25 from line 15. Also, include this amount on Form 1040A, line 7. In the space to the left of line 7, enter "DCB" . . .			26	-0-

To claim the child and dependent care credit, complete lines 27 through 31 below.

Line	Description	Box	Amount
27	Enter $3,000 ($6,000 if two or more qualifying persons) . . .	27	6,000
28	**Form 1040 and 1040NR filers:** Add lines 24 and 25. **Form 1040A filers:** Enter the amount from line 25 . . .	28	3,000
29	Subtract line 28 from line 27. If zero or less, **stop.** You cannot take the credit. **Exception.** If you paid 2010 expenses in 2011, see the instructions for line 9 . . .	29	3,000
30	Complete line 2 on the front of this form. **Do not** include in column (c) any benefits shown on line 28 above. Then, add the amounts in column (c) and enter the total here . . .	30	2,400
31	Enter the **smaller** of line 29 or 30. Also, enter this amount on line 3 on the front of this form and complete lines 4 through 11 . . .	31	2,400

Form **2441** (2011)

Chapter 34

Credit for the elderly or the disabled

ey.com/EYTaxGuide

Note

IRS Publication 17 (*Your Federal Income Tax*) has been updated by Ernst & Young LLP for 2011. Dates and dollar amounts shown are for 2011. Underlined type is used to indicate where IRS text has been updated. Places where text has been removed are indicated by the sentence: *Text intentionally omitted*.

ey.com/EYTaxGuide

Ernst & Young LLP will update the *Ernst & Young Tax Guide 2012* website with relevant taxpayer information as it becomes available. You can also sign up for email alerts to let you know when changes have been made.

Introduction

When Congress passed legislation giving the elderly a tax credit, the idea was to provide a measure of tax relief for older citizens who were not receiving adequate amounts of social security or other nontaxable *pensions*. Consequently, if you or your spouse is 65 years old or older, you may be entitled to a credit of as much as $1,125 against your tax.

Taxpayers under 65 years of age who are permanently and totally disabled may also be eligible for the credit.

In general, if you file as a *single* individual, you do not qualify for the tax credit if (1) you receive nontaxable social security or other nontaxable pensions of $5,000 or more, (2) your *adjusted gross income* is $17,500 or more, or (3) your tax is zero.

This chapter tells you specifically if you are eligible for the credit for the elderly and, if so, how you may claim it—whether you are single or married.

If you qualify, you may be able to reduce the tax you owe by taking the credit for the elderly or the disabled which is figured on Schedule R (Form 1040A or Form 1040).

This chapter explains the following.

- Who qualifies for the credit for the elderly or the disabled.
- How to figure the credit.

You may be able to take the credit for the elderly or the disabled if:

- You are age 65 or older, or
- You retired on permanent and total disability and have taxable disability income.

Useful Items

You may want to see:

Publication

- □ **524** Credit for the Elderly or the Disabled
- □ **554** Tax Guide for Seniors
- □ **967** The IRS Will Figure Your Tax

Form (and Instruction)

- □ **Schedule R (Form 1040A or 1040)** Credit for the Elderly or the Disabled

EXPLANATION

See chapter 11, *Social security and equivalent railroad retirement benefits,* for a discussion of how social security and equivalent railroad retirement benefits are taxed.

Tax Breaks and Deductions You Can Use Checklist

Credit for the Elderly or Disabled. Someone who is 65 or older, or is under 65 and who retired with a permanent and total disability and receives taxable disability income, can claim a credit equal to 15% of a specific amount. That amount equals an initial (or base) amount–generally $3,750, $5,000, or $7,500, depending on age and filing status–reduced by nontaxable social security benefits and certain other nontaxable payments received. The base amount must also be reduced by half of adjusted gross income in excess of certain minimum levels. The maximum credit is $1,125, on a joint return where both spouses qualify and no reductions apply. Because of the low base amounts only people with very small amounts of income can claim the credit.

Tip

You can take the credit only if you file Form 1040 or Form 1040A. You cannot take the credit if you file Form 1040EZ.

Are You Eligible for the Credit?

You can take the credit for the elderly or the disabled if you meet both of the following requirements.

- You are a qualified individual.
- Your income is not more than certain limits.

You can use Figure 34-A and Figure 34-B as guides to see if you are eligible for the credit.

Use Figure 34-A first to see if you are a qualified individual. If you are, go to Figure 34-B to make sure your income is not too high to take the credit.

Qualified Individual

You are a qualified individual for this credit if you are a U.S. citizen or resident alien, and either of the following applies.

1. You were age 65 or older at the end of 2011.
2. You were under age 65 at the end of 2011 and all three of the following statements are true.
   a. You retired on permanent and total disability (explained later).
   b. You received taxable disability income for 2011.
   c. On January 1, 2011, you had not reached mandatory retirement age (defined later under *Disability income*).

EXPLANATION

To qualify for the credit, you cannot have reached your employer's mandatory retirement age before the beginning of the year. The reason for the requirement is that any amount received from your employer after you have reached mandatory retirement age is not disability income.

Age 65. You are considered to be age 65 on the day before your 65th birthday. Therefore, if you were born on January 1, 1947, you are considered to be age 65 at the end of 2011.

U.S. Citizen or Resident Alien

You must be a U.S. citizen or resident alien (or be treated as a resident alien) to take the credit. Generally, you cannot take the credit if you were a nonresident alien at any time during the tax year.

Exceptions. You may be able to take the credit if you are a nonresident alien who is married to a U.S. citizen or resident alien at the end of the tax year and you and your spouse choose to treat you as a U.S. resident alien. If you make that choice, both you and your spouse are taxed on your worldwide incomes.

If you were a nonresident alien at the beginning of the year and a resident alien at the end of the year, and you were married to a U.S. citizen or resident alien at the end of the year, you may be able to choose to be treated as a U.S. resident alien for the entire year. In that case, you may be allowed to take the credit.

For information on these choices, see chapter 1 of Publication 519, *U.S. Tax Guide for Aliens*.

EXPLANATION

For more information about resident and nonresident aliens, see chapter 42, *Foreign citizens living in the United States.*

Married Persons

Generally, if you are married at the end of the tax year, you and your spouse must file a joint return to take the credit. However, if you and your spouse did not live in the same household at any time during the tax year, you can file either joint or separate returns and still take the credit.

EXAMPLES

Example 1

Don and Sylvia Fitch are both past the age of 65 and are married at year's end, but they have been living apart since May. They must file a joint return to claim the credit. Next year, if they remain married and live apart for the entire year, they may file separate returns and claim the credit.

Example 2

Sam and Leah Wilkins are married at year's end and have lived apart for the entire year. Leah is 63 years old and receives a disability pension from her former employer. Sam is 69 years old. They may file separate returns, and each may claim a credit, since both meet the basic tests for eligibility.

Figure 34-A. **Are You a Qualified Individual?**

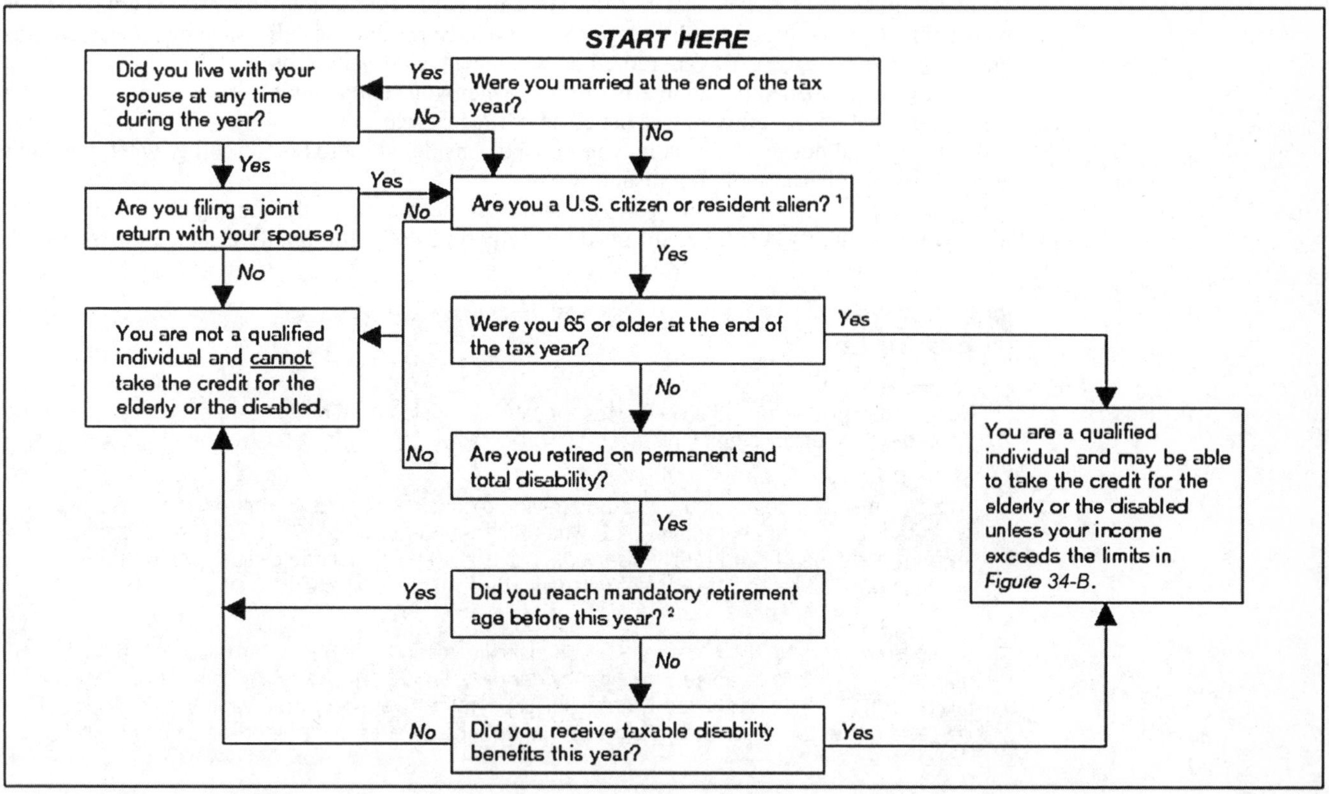

[1] If you were a nonresident alien at any time during the tax year and were married to a U.S. citizen or resident alien at the end of the tax year, see *U.S. Citizen or Resident Alien* under *Qualified Individual.* If you and your spouse choose to treat you as a U.S. resident alien, answer "Yes" to this question.

[2] Mandatory retirement age is the age set by your employer at which you would have been required to retire, had you not become disabled.

Figure 34-B. **Income Limits**

IF your filing status is ...	**THEN even if you qualify (see *Figure 34-A*), you CANNOT take the credit if ...** Your adjusted gross income (AGI)* is equal to or more than ...	**OR the total of your nontaxable social security and other nontaxable pension(s) is equal to or more than ...**
single, head of household, or qualifying widow(er) with dependent child	$17,500	$5,000
married filing a joint return and both spouses qualify in *Figure 34-A*	$25,000	$7,500
married filing a joint return and only one spouse qualifies in *Figure 34-A*	$20,000	$5,000
married filing a separate return	$12,500	$3,750

*AGI is the amount on Form 1040A, line 22, or Form 1040, line 38.

Head of household. You can file as head of household and qualify to take the credit, even if your spouse lived with you during the first 6 months of the year, if you meet all the tests. See <u>Head of Household</u> in chapter 2 for the tests you must meet.

Under Age 65

If you are under age 65 at the end of 2011, you can qualify for the credit only if you are retired on permanent and total disability (discussed next) and have taxable disability income (discussed later under *Disability income*). You are retired on permanent and total disability if:

- You were permanently and totally disabled when you retired, and
- You retired on disability before the close of the tax year.

Even if you do not retire formally, you may be considered retired on disability when you have stopped working because of your disability.

If you retired on disability before 1977, and were not permanently and totally disabled at the time, you can qualify for the credit if you were permanently and totally disabled on January 1, 1976, or January 1, 1977.

EXAMPLES

Example 1

Ray Russell is 62 years old and receives a disability pension from his former employer. He is eligible for the disability credit if he meets the other tests.

Example 2

Fritz Hartman retired at age 60 and is receiving a pension from his former employer. Fritz was not disabled when he retired. In 2011, when Fritz was 62 years old, he was in an accident that left him permanently and totally disabled. Fritz is not eligible for the disability credit in 2011, because when he retired, he was not permanently and totally disabled.

Example 3

Joelle Bowes retired in 1976 at age 25 on disability, even though she was not at the time permanently and totally disabled. However, by January 1, 1977, she was permanently and totally disabled. In 2011, she is still receiving disability payments from her former employer and has not yet reached her employer's mandatory retirement age. Joelle is eligible for the credit in 2011.

Permanent and total disability. You are permanently and totally disabled if you cannot engage in any substantial gainful activity because of your physical or mental condition. A physician must certify that the condition has lasted or can be expected to last continuously for 12 months or more, or that the condition can be expected to result in death. See *Physician's statement,* later.

Substantial gainful activity. Substantial gainful activity is the performance of significant duties over a reasonable period of time while working for pay or profit, or in work generally done for pay or profit. Full-time work (or part-time work done at your employer's convenience) in a competitive work situation for at least the minimum wage conclusively shows that you are able to engage in substantial gainful activity.

Substantial gainful activity is not work you do to take care of yourself or your home. It is not unpaid work on hobbies, institutional therapy or training, school attendance, clubs, social programs, and similar activities. However, doing this kind of work may show that you are able to engage in substantial gainful activity.

The fact that you have not worked for some time is not, of itself, conclusive evidence that you cannot engage in substantial gainful activity.

EXPLANATION

The facts and circumstances of your particular situation determine whether you are able to "engage in substantial gainful activity" for purposes of claiming the credit. No strict rule governs every case. The most important question to remember is "Did you hold a job that paid at least the minimum wage?" This can mean any job, not just the job you held before your disability.

Sheltered employment. Certain work offered at qualified locations to physically or mentally impaired persons is considered sheltered employment. These qualified locations are in sheltered workshops, hospitals, and similar institutions, homebound programs, and Department of Veterans Affairs (VA) sponsored homes.

Compared to commercial employment, pay is lower for sheltered employment. Therefore, one usually does not look for sheltered employment if he or she can get other employment. The fact that one has accepted sheltered employment is not proof of that person's ability to engage in substantial gainful activity.

Physician's statement. If you are under age 65, you must have your physician complete a statement certifying that you were permanently and totally disabled on the date you retired. You can use the statement in the instructions for Schedule R.

You do not have to file this statement with your Form 1040 or Form 1040A, but you must keep it for your records.

Veterans. If the Department of Veterans Affairs (VA) certifies that you are permanently and totally disabled, you can substitute VA Form 21-0172, Certification of Permanent and Total Disability, for the physician's statement you are required to keep. VA Form 21-0172 must be signed by a person authorized by the VA to do so. You can get this form from your local VA regional office.

Physician's statement obtained in earlier year. If you got a physician's statement in an earlier year and, due to your continued disabled condition, you were unable to engage in any substantial gainful activity during 2011, you may not need to get another physician's statement for 2011. For a detailed explanation of the conditions you must meet, see the instructions for Part II of Schedule R. If you meet the required conditions, check the box on line 2 of Part II of Schedule R.

If you checked box 4, 5, or 6 in Part I of Schedule R, enter in the space above the box on line 2 in Part II the first name(s) of the spouse(s) for whom the box is checked.

Disability income. If you are under age 65, you must also have taxable disability income to qualify for the credit. Disability income must meet both of the following requirements.

- It must be paid under your employer's accident or health plan or pension plan.
- It must be included in your income as wages (or payments instead of wages) for the time you are absent from work because of permanent and total disability.

Payments that are not disability income. Any payment you receive from a plan that does not provide for disability retirement is not disability income. Any lump-sum payment for accrued annual leave that you receive when you retire on disability is a salary payment and is not disability income.

For purposes of the credit for the elderly or the disabled, disability income does not include amounts you receive after you reach mandatory retirement age. Mandatory retirement age is the age set by your employer at which you would have had to retire, had you not become disabled.

EXAMPLES

Example 1

Melissa Lee retired in June at age 55 with a total and permanent disability. At retirement, she received a $5,000 payment for accrued vacation and sick-leave days. The amount is not disability income, since it is not paid to her as wages or in lieu of wages because of her permanent and total disability.

Example 2

Adam LeBleu turned 62 years old on September 9, 2011. He had retired several years earlier as a result of a total and permanent disability. He has received disability payments from his employer since retirement. His former employer's mandatory retirement age is 62. As a result, any amount Adam receives after he reaches the age of 62 will not be disability income.

Income Limits

To determine if you can claim the credit, you must consider two income limits. The first limit is the amount of your adjusted gross income (AGI). The second limit is the amount of nontaxable social security and other nontaxable pensions you received. The limits are shown in Figure 34-B.

If both your AGI and nontaxable pensions are less than the income limits, you may be able to claim the credit. See *Figuring the Credit Yourself*, later.

Caution

If either your AGI or your nontaxable pensions are equal to or more than the income limits, you cannot take the credit.

Credit Figured for You

You can figure the credit yourself, or the Internal Revenue Service (IRS) will figure it for you. See *Figuring the Credit Yourself* next.

TAXALERT

With the aid of this book, you should not have to rely on the IRS to calculate your credit. Although the IRS routinely checks the arithmetic on a return, it too can make computational errors. Also, as noted in chapter 31, *How to figure your tax,* you must still provide certain information to enable the IRS to calculate the credit. Therefore, our advice is to give the calculation of your credit a try.

If you choose to have the IRS figure the credit for you, read the following discussion for the form you will file (Form 1040 or 1040A).

If you want the IRS to figure your tax, see chapter 31.

Form 1040. If you want the IRS to figure your credit, see *Form 1040 Line Entries* under *Tax Figured by IRS* in chapter 31.

Form 1040A. If you want the IRS to figure your credit, see *Form 1040A Line Entries* under *Tax Figured by IRS* in chapter 31.

Figuring the Credit Yourself

If you figure the credit yourself, fill out the front of Schedule R. Next, fill out Part III of Schedule R. If you file Form 1040A, enter the amount from Schedule R, line 22, on line 30. If you file Form 1040, include the amount from Schedule R, line 22, on line 53, check box c, and enter "Sch R" on the line next to that box.

There are five steps in Part III to determine the amount of your credit:

1. Determine your initial amount (lines 10–12).
2. Determine the total of any nontaxable social security and certain other nontaxable pensions and disability benefits you received (lines 13a, 13b, and 13c).
3. Determine your excess adjusted gross income (lines 14–17).
4. Determine the total of Steps 2 and 3 (line 18).
5. Determine your credit (lines 19–22).

These steps are discussed in more detail next.

Step 1. Determine Initial Amount

To figure the credit, you must first determine your initial amount using lines 10 through 12. See Table 34-1. Your initial amount is on line 12.

Initial amounts for persons under age 65. If you are a qualified individual under age 65, your initial amount cannot be more than your taxable disability income.

Table 34-1. **Initial Amounts**

IF your filing status is ...	**THEN enter on line 10 of Schedule R...**
single, head of household, or **qualifying widow(er)** with dependent child and, by the end of 2011, you were	
• 65 or older	$5,000
• under 65 and retired on permanent and total disability[1]	$5,000
married filing a joint return and by the end of 2011	
• both of you were 65 or older	$7,500
• both of you were under 65 and one of you retired on permanent and total disability[1]	$5,000
• both of you were under 65 and both of you retired on permanent and total disability[2]	$7,500
• one of you was 65 or older, and the other was under 65 and retired on permanent and total disability[3]	$7,500
• one of you was 65 or older, and the other was under 65 and not retired on permanent and total disability	$5,000
married filing a separate return and you did not live with your spouse at any time during the year and, by the end of 2011, you were	
• 65 or older	$3,750
• under 65 and retired on permanent and total disability[1]	$3,750

[1]Amount cannot be more than the taxable disability income.

[2]Amount cannot be more than your combined taxable disability income.

[3]Amount is $5,000 plus the taxable disability income of the spouse under age 65, but not more than $7,500.

EXAMPLES

Example 1

Ben Winston, who is 59 years old and single, retired during the year because of a total and permanent physical disability. He received $4,300 in income during the year from his prior employer because of his disability. He received no other income. The initial amount Ben uses in calculating his credit is $4,300.

If Ben had received $6,900 in disability income, his initial amount would be $5,000.

Example 2

David Jefferson is 72 years old and files a joint return with his wife, Donna. Donna is 63 years old and is permanently and totally disabled. She received $3,000 from her previous employer because of her disability. The initial amount they use in calculating their credit is $7,500, which is the lesser of (1) the $7,500 initial amount for married couples filing joint returns or (2) $5,000 plus the $3,000 disability income received by the person under the age of 65.

Step 2. Total Certain Nontaxable Pensions and Benefits

Step 2 is to figure the total amount of nontaxable social security and certain other nontaxable payments you received during the year. You must reduce your initial amount by these payments.

Enter these nontaxable payments on line 13a or 13b, and total them on line 13c. If you are married filing a joint return, you must enter the combined amount of nontaxable payments both you and your spouse receive.

Nontaxable payments. Include the following nontaxable payments in the amounts you enter on lines 13a and 13b.

Tip

Worksheets are provided in the instructions for Forms 1040 and 1040A to help you determine if any of your social security benefits (or equivalent railroad retirement benefits) are taxable.

EXAMPLES

Example 1

Tony and Sheila are married and file a joint return. He is 69 years old and she is 64, and each receives $1,000 in nontaxable social security benefits. The initial amount used to figure their credit is $5,000, since only Tony is 65 years of age or older. This initial amount must be reduced by the $2,000 in nontaxable social security benefits that they received during the year. Next year, when Sheila becomes 65 years old, their initial amount will rise to $7,500.

Example 2

Gail Goodson retired in January 2011 at age 62 because of a permanent disability and collected $4,600 from her former employer as a disability pension. She also received $3,600 in nontaxable social security benefits in 2011. Gail is single, and her adjusted gross income is less than $7,500. Gail must subtract the nontaxable social security income from her disability income in computing the adjusted initial amount. Her credit is $150 [15% × ($4,600 – $3,600)].

- Nontaxable social security payments. This is the nontaxable part of the benefits shown in box 5 of Form SSA-1099, Social Security Benefit Statement, which includes disability benefits, before deducting any amounts withheld to pay premiums on supplementary Medicare insurance, and before any reduction because of benefits received under workers' compensation. (Do not include a lump-sum death benefit payment you may receive as a surviving spouse, or a surviving child's insurance benefit payments you may receive as a guardian.)
- Nontaxable railroad retirement pension payments treated as social security. This is the nontaxable part of the benefits shown in box 5 of Form RRB-1099, Payments by the Railroad Retirement Board.
- Nontaxable pension or annuity payments or disability benefits that are paid under a law administered by the Department of Veterans Affairs (VA). (Do not include amounts received as a pension, annuity, or similar allowance for personal injuries or sickness resulting from active service in the armed forces of any country or in the National Oceanic and Atmospheric Administration, or the Public Health Service, or as a disability annuity under section 808 of the Foreign Service Act of 1980.)
- Pension or annuity payments or disability benefits that are excluded from income under any provision of federal law other than the Internal Revenue Code. (Do not include amounts that are a return of your cost of a pension or annuity. These amounts do not reduce your initial amount.)

Caution

You should be sure to take into account all of the nontaxable amounts you receive. These amounts are verified by the IRS through information supplied by other government agencies.

EXPLANATION

Do not reduce the initial amount used to figure your credit by any of the following:

- Amounts that are treated as a return of your cost of an annuity or a pension
- Veterans Administration service-connected disability compensation
- Payments from accident or health insurance policies
- Basic or supplementary Medicare benefits
- Death compensation paid by the Veterans Administration to the surviving spouse of a veteran who died from sickness or injury incurred in active service
- Life insurance payments received when the insured person dies

Step 3. Determine Excess Adjusted Gross Income

You also must reduce your initial amount by your excess adjusted gross income. Figure your excess adjusted gross income on lines 14–17.

You figure your excess adjusted gross income as follows:

1. Subtract from your adjusted gross income (Form 1040, line 38, or Form 1040A, line 22) the amount shown for your filing status in the following list.
   a. $7,500 if you are single, a head of household, or a qualifying widow(er),
   b. $10,000 if you are married filing a joint return, or
   c. $5,000 if you are married filing a separate return and you and your spouse did not live in the same household at any time during the tax year.
2. Divide the result of (1) by 2.

EXAMPLES

Example 1

Raymond is over age 65 and single, with $8,900 in adjusted gross income, which is in excess of the $7,500 allowed for his single filing status. He must reduce his initial amount by $700 (one-half of the $1,400 difference between $8,900 and $7,500). Raymond also receives $1,000 in nontaxable social security payments. The adjusted initial amount he uses to compute his credit is $3,300, calculated as follows:

Initial amount	$5,000
Less:	
Nontaxable social security	(1,000)
Excess adjusted gross income [1/2($8,900 – $7,500)]	(700)
Adjusted initial amount	$3,300
Tentative credit (15% of $3,300)	$495

Note: 15% times the adjusted initial amount is the method you use in calculating your tentative credit.

Example 2

Horace and Prudence are married, both are over age 65, and they file a joint return. Their adjusted gross income for the year is $12,000. They receive $1,750 in nontaxable social security. Their adjusted initial amount used to figure their credit is $4,750, calculated as follows:

Initial amount	$7,500
Less:	
Nontaxable social security	(1,750)
Excess adjusted gross income [1/2 ($12,000 – $10,000)]	(1,000)
Adjusted initial amount	$4,750
Tentative credit (15% of $4,750)	$713

Step 4. Determine the Total of Steps 2 and 3

To determine if you can take the credit, you must add (on line 18) the amounts you figured in Step 2 and Step 3.

IF the total of Steps 2 and 3 is ...	THEN ...
equal to or more than the amount in Step 1	you **cannot** take the credit.
less than the amount in Step 1	you **can** take the credit.

Step 5. Determine Your Credit

If you can take the credit, subtract the amount determined in Step 4 (line 18) from the amount determined in Step 1 (line 12) and multiply the result by 15%.

In certain cases, the amount of your credit may be limited. See *Limit on credit,* later.

> ***EXPLANATION***
>
> In summary, you may not claim the credit for the elderly and disabled if (1) your nontaxable social security and other nontaxable pensions or (2) 50% of your excess adjusted gross income or (3) the sum of (1) and (2) equals or exceeds your initial amount.
>
> A simple way to compute your credit is as follows:
>
> - Subtract from your initial amount the sum of your nontaxable social security income, other nontaxable pensions, and your excess adjusted gross income.
> - Multiply the amount from step 1 by 15%. This is your credit for the year.

Example. You are 66 years old and your spouse is 64. Your spouse is not disabled. You file a joint return on Form 1040. Your adjusted gross income is $14,630. Together you received $3,200 from social security, which was nontaxable. You figure the credit as follows:

Applying the 5 Step Process		**Amount**
1) Initial amount		$5,000
2) Total of social security and other nontaxable pensions	$3,200	
3) Excess adjusted gross income ($14,630 − $10,000) ÷ 2	2,315	
4) Add line 2 and line 3		5,515
5) Subtract line 4 from line 1 (Do not enter less than -0-)		-0-

You cannot take the credit because your nontaxable social security (line 2) plus your excess adjusted gross income (line 3) is more than your initial amount (line 1).

Limit on credit. The amount of credit you can claim is generally limited to the amount of your tax. For more information, see the instructions for Part III, Schedule R.

Example

The following example illustrates the credit for the elderly or the disabled. The initial amount is taken from Table 34-1, shown earlier.

James Davis is 58 years old. In 2004 he retired on permanent and total disability, and he is still permanently and totally disabled. He got the required physician's statement in 2004, and kept it with his tax records. His physician signed on line B of the statement. This year James checks the box in Part II of Schedule R. He does not need to get another statement for 2011.

He received the following income for the year:

Nontaxable social security	$1,500
Interest (taxable)	100
Taxable disability pension	11,400

James' adjusted gross income is $11,500 ($11,400 + $100). He figures the credit on Schedule R as follows:

1) Initial amount		$5,000
2) Taxable disability pension		11,400
3) Smaller of (1) or (2)		5,000
4) Nontaxable social security benefits	$1,500	
5) Excess adjusted gross income ($11,500 – $7,500) ÷ 2	2,000	
6) Add lines 4 and 5		3,500
7) Subtract line 6 from line 3 (Do not enter less than -0-)		1,500
8) Multiply line 7 by 15% (.15)		225
9) Enter the amount from the Credit Limit Worksheet in the Schedule R instructions		216
10) Credit (Enter the smaller of line 8 or line 11)		$216

He enters $216 on line 30 of Form 1040A. The Schedule R for James Davis is not shown.

Chapter 35
Child tax credit

ey.com/EYTaxGuide

Introduction

The child tax credit is a credit of up to $1,000 for each qualifying child under age 17. A qualifying child (defined in greater detail in chapter 3, *Personal exemptions and dependents*) is an individual for whom the taxpayer can claim a dependency exemption and who is the child, stepchild, or eligible foster child of the taxpayer or is a brother, sister, stepbrother, or stepsister of the taxpayer or a descendant of any of these relatives ("brother" and "sister" include a brother or sister by half-blood). That means a "qualifying child" doesn't necessarily have to be your child!

The child tax credit is phased out depending on your adjusted gross income and the number of qualifying children. While the child tax credit is nonrefundable, meaning the credit is limited to the amount of the tax liability on the return, there are certain cases in which you may be able to receive a refund when the child tax credit exceeds your tax liability. This refundable portion of the child tax credit is called the additional child tax credit.

The child tax credit is the largest tax code provision benefiting families with children. Be careful not to confuse the child tax credit with the credit for child and dependent care expenses, which is explained in chapter 33, *Child and dependent care credit*.

Note

IRS Publication 17 (*Your Federal Income Tax*) has been updated by Ernst & Young LLP for 2011. Dates and dollar amounts shown are for 2011. Underlined type is used to indicate where IRS text has been updated. Places where text has been removed are indicated by the sentence: *Text intentionally omitted*.

ey.com/EYTaxGuide
Ernst & Young LLP will update the *Ernst & Young Tax Guide 2012* website with relevant taxpayer information as it becomes available. You can also sign up for email alerts to let you know when changes have been made.

TAXALERT

In December 2010, the President and Congress agreed to extend the so-called Bush tax cuts. Among the provisions extended was the "enhanced" child tax credit as it existed in 2010. This extension is available for 2011 and 2012.

The child tax credit is a credit that may reduce your tax by as much as $1,000 for each of your qualifying children.

The additional child tax credit is a credit you may be able to take if you are not able to claim the full amount of the child tax credit.

This chapter explains the following.

- Who is a qualifying child.
- How much is the credit.
- How to claim the credit.
- Why you should check your tax withholding.

If you have no tax. Credits, such as the child tax credit or the credit for child and dependent care expenses, are used to reduce tax. If your tax on Form 1040, line 46, or Form 1040A, line 28, is zero, do not figure the child tax credit because there is no tax to reduce. However, you may qualify for the additional child tax credit on line 65 (Form 1040) or line 42 (Form 1040A).

Caution

The child tax credit and the additional child tax credit should not be confused with the child and dependent care credit discussed in chapter 33.

Useful Items

You may want to see:

Publication

- ☐ **972** Child Tax Credit

Form (and Instructions)

- ☐ **8812** Additional Child Tax Credit
- ☐ **W-4** Employee's Withholding Allowance Certificate

Qualifying Child

A qualifying child for purposes of the child tax credit is a child who:

1. Is your son, daughter, stepchild, foster child, brother, sister, stepbrother, stepsister, or a descendant of any of them (for example, your grandchild, niece, or nephew),
2. Was under age 17 at the end of 2011,
3. Did not provide over half of his or her own support for 2011,
4. Lived with you for more than half of 2011 (see <u>*Exceptions to time lived with you*</u> below),
5. Is claimed as a dependent on your return, and
6. Was a U.S. citizen, a U.S. national, or a resident of the United States. If the child was adopted, see <u>*Adopted child*</u> below.

For each qualifying child you must check the box on Form 1040 or Form 1040A, line 6c, column (4).

Example. Your son turned 17 on December 30, 2011. He is a citizen of the United States and you claimed him as a dependent on your return. He is not a qualifying child for the child tax credit because he was not under age 17 at the end of 2011.

Exceptions to time lived with you. A child is considered to have lived with you for all of 2011 if the child was born or died in 2011 and your home was this child's home for the entire time he or she was alive. Temporary absences for special circumstances, such as for school, vacation, medical care, military service, or detention in a juvenile facility, count as time the child lived with you.

There are also exceptions for kidnapped children and children of divorced or separated parents. For details, see <u>*Residency Test*</u> in chapter 3.

Qualifying child of more than one person. A special rule applies if your qualifying child is the qualifying child of more than one person. For details, see <u>*Special Rule for Qualifying Child of More Than One Person*</u> in chapter 3.

Adopted child. An adopted child is always treated as your own child. An adopted child includes a child lawfully placed with you for legal adoption.

If you are a U.S. citizen or U.S. national and your adopted child lived with you all year as a member of your household in 2010, that child meets condition (6) above to be a qualifying child for the child tax credit.

Tax Breaks and Deductions You Can Use Checklist

Child Tax Credit. A tax credit of up to $1,000 is available for every eligible child you have who is under the age of 17. A credit is much better than a deduction; it reduces your tax liability dollar for dollar, while a deduction only reduces your taxable income. The actual credit you can claim depends on your modified adjusted gross income (MAGI). Once your MAGI exceeds $110,000 (married, filing jointly); $75,000 (single, head of household, or qualifying widow(er)); or $55,000 (married, filing separately) you have to reduce the credit you can claim.

Additional Child Tax Credit. You may be entitled to a refundable child tax credit if you meet certain requirements. A refundable credit means that you can actually get money back from the IRS if the credit is more than your tax liability. You should file Form 8812 to claim the credit. See <u>*Additional Child Tax Credit*</u>, later.

Amount of Credit

The maximum amount you can claim for the credit is $1,000 for each qualifying child.

Limits on the Credit

You must reduce your child tax credit if either (1) or (2) applies.

1. The amount on line 46, Form 1040, or line 28, Form 1040A, is less than the credit. If this amount is zero, you cannot take this credit because there is no tax to reduce. But you may be able to take the additional child tax credit. See <u>*Additional Child Tax Credit*</u>, later.
2. Your modified adjusted gross income (AGI) is above the amount shown below for your filing status.
   a. Married filing jointly – $110,000.
   b. Single, head of household, or qualifying widow(er) – $75,000.
   c. Married filing separately – $55,000.

EXPLANATION

The maximum child credit you may claim is equal to $1,000 multiplied by the number of qualifying children you have. However, if your adjusted gross income (AGI) is greater than a specified amount, then there are limitations on the amount of child tax credit that you may claim. The amount of the credit allowable is reduced (but not below zero) by $50 for each $1,000 (or part of that amount) by which your AGI exceeds the threshold amounts. The threshold amounts for 2011 are $75,000 for single filers and head of household, $110,000 for couples filing jointly, and $55,000 for married persons filing separately.

Modified AGI. For purposes of the child tax credit, your modified AGI is your AGI plus the following amounts that may apply to you.

- Any amount excluded from income because of the exclusion of income from Puerto Rico. On the dotted line next to Form 1040, line 38, enter the amount excluded and identify it as "EPRI." Also attach a copy of any Form(s) 499R-2/W-2PR to your return.
- Any amount on line 45 or line 50 of Form 2555, Foreign Earned Income.
- Any amount on line 18 of Form 2555-EZ, Foreign Earned Income Exclusion.
- Any amount on line 15 of Form 4563, Exclusion of Income for Bona Fide Residents of American Samoa.

If you do not have any of the above, your modified AGI is the same as your AGI.

AGI. YourAGI is the amount on Form 1040, line 38, or Form 1040A, line 22.

Claiming the Credit

To claim the child tax credit, you must file Form 1040 or Form 1040A. You cannot claim the child tax credit on Form 1040EZ. You must provide the name and identification number (usually a social security number) on your tax return for each qualifying child.

If you are filing Form 1040, answer the *Questions* in your form instructions for line 51, Form 1040, to find out which child tax credit worksheet you can use to figure the credit.

If you answer "Yes" to question 1 or 2 in your Form 1040 instructions, you must complete the child tax credit worksheet in Publication 972. Otherwise, you can use the Child Tax Credit Worksheet in your Form 1040 or Form 1040A instructions. (See *Example,* later.)

TAXSAVER

The child tax credit can offset taxes imposed by the alternative minimum tax calculation.

Additional Child Tax Credit

This credit is for certain individuals who get less than the full amount of the child tax credit. The additional child tax credit may give you a refund even if you do not owe any tax.

How to claim the additional child tax credit. To claim the additional child tax credit, follow the steps below.

1. Make sure you figured the amount, if any, of your child tax credit. See *Claiming the Credit,* earlier.
2. If you answered "Yes" on line 9 or line 10 of the Child Tax Credit Worksheet in the Form 1040 or Form 1040A instructions, or line 13 of the Child Tax Credit Worksheet in Publication 972, use Form 8812 to see if you can take the additional child tax credit.
3. If you have an additional child tax credit on line 13 of Form 8812, carry it to Form 1040, line 65, or Form 1040A, line 42.

EXPLANATION

The refundable portion of the additional child tax credit has two different methods of calculation depending on the number of children the taxpayer is claiming. For families with three qualifying children or fewer, the refundable portion of the child tax credit is the smaller of the unused portion or 15% of the taxpayer's earned income over $3,000. For families with four or more qualifying children, the refundable portion of the child tax credit is the smaller of the unused portion or the larger of either 15% of the taxpayer's earned income over $3,000 or the sum of Social Security and Medicare taxes paid less the earned income credit.

Checking Your Withholding

The child tax credit decreases your tax. You can check your tax withholding by using Publication 919, *How Do I Adjust My Tax Withholding.*

If you are having too much tax withheld, and you prefer to have the money during the year, you may be able to decrease your withholding. You do this by completing a new Form W-4 and giving it to your employer.

Example

Amy Brown files as head of household and has two dependent children under age 17. The children are qualifying children for purposes of the child tax credit. Amy's only income is her salary of $30,450. Amy chooses to itemize her deductions and files Form 1040. Her AGI, shown on line 38 of her Form 1040, is $30,450. This is her taxable earned income.

Amy does not file Form 2555, 2555-EZ, or 4563. She does not exclude income from Puerto Rico. Her modified AGI is $30,450.

Amy's tax, shown on line 46 of her Form 1040, is $1,108. She claims a $225 credit for child and dependent care expenses on line 48. She claims a $2,082 earned income credit on line 64a. She has no other credits.

After answering the *Questions* in the Form 1040 instructions for line 51, she completes the child tax credit worksheet to figure her child tax credit of $883. Amy's completed questions and child tax credit worksheet are shown later.

Amy reads the *TIP* in the worksheet and finds that she may be able to take the additional child tax credit. See <u>*Additional Child Tax Credit*</u> and Amy's completed Form 8812, later.

Filled-in Questions for Amy Brown
(Page references are to the Form 1040 instructions.)

Questions **Who Must Use Pub. 972**

Pub. 972

1. Are you claiming any of the following credits?

- Mortgage interest credit, Form 8396.
- Adoption credit, Form 8839.
- Residental energy efficient property credit, Form 5695, Part II.

☐ **Yes.** STOP You must use Pub. 972 to figure your child tax credit. You will also need the form(s) listed above for any credit(s) you are claiming.

☑ **No.** Continue

2. Are you excluding income from Puerto Rico or are you filing any of the following forms?

- Form 2555 or 2555-EZ (relating to foreign earned income).
- Form 4563 (exclusion of income for residents of American Samoa).

☐ **Yes.** STOP You must use Pub. 972 to figure your credit.

☑ **No.** Use the worksheet on pages 43 and 44 to figure your credit.

Child Tax Credit Worksheet—Line 51

Keep for Your Records

CAUTION

- To be a qualifying child for the child tax credit, the child must be your dependent, **under age 17** at the end of 2011, and meet all the conditions in Steps 1 through 3 on page 15.
- **Do not** use this worksheet if you answered "Yes" to question 1 or 2 on page 40. Instead, use Pub. 972.

Part 1

1. Number of qualifying children: 2 × $1,000. Enter the result. — **1** 2,000

2. Enter the amount from Form 1040, line 38. — **2** 30,450

3. Enter the amount shown below for your filing status. — **3** 75,000
   - Married filing jointly — $110,000
   - Single, head of household, or qualifying widow(er) — $75,000
   - Married filing separately — $55,000

4. Is the amount on line 2 more than the amount on line 3? — **4**

   ☑ **No.** Leave line 4 blank. Enter -0- on line 5.

   ☐ **Yes.** Subtract line 3 from line 2.
   If the result is not a multiple of $1,000, increase it to the next multiple of $1,000. For example, increase $425 to $1,000, increase $1,025 to $2,000, etc.

5. Multiply the amount on line 4 by 5% (.05). Enter the result. — **5** -0-

6. Is the amount on line 1 more than the amount on line 5?

   ☐ **No.** STOP
   You cannot take the child tax credit on Form 1040, line 51. You also cannot take the additional child tax credit on Form 1040, line 65. Complete the rest of your Form 1040.

   ☑ **Yes.** Subtract line 5 from line 1. Enter the result. *Go to Part 2 on the next page.* — **6** 2,000

Before you begin Part 2: √ Figure the amount of any credits you are claiming on Form 5695, Part I; Form 8834, Part I; Form 8910; Form 8936; or Schedule R.

Part 2

7. Enter the amount from Form 1040, line 46. **7** 1,108

8. Add the following amounts from:

Form 1040, line 47 ________

Form 1040, line 48 + 225

Form 1040, line 49 + ________

Form 1040, line 50 + ________

Form 5695, line 11 + ________

Form 8834, line 22 + ________

Form 8910, line 21 + ________

Form 8936, line 14 + ________

Schedule R, line 22 + ________ Enter the total. **8** 225

9. Are the amounts on lines 7 and 8 the same?

☐ **Yes.** STOP

You cannot take this credit because there is no tax to reduce. However, you may be able to take the **additional child tax credit.** See the **TIP** below.

☑ **No.** Subtract line 8 from line 7. **9** 883

10. Is the amount on line 6 more than the amount on line 9?

☑ **Yes.** Enter the amount from line 9. Also, you may be able to take the **additional child tax credit.** See the **TIP** below.

☐ **No.** Enter the amount from line 6.

This is your child tax credit. **10** 883

Enter this amount on Form 1040, line 51.

1040

TIP You may be able to take the **additional child tax credit** on Form 1040, line 65, if you answered "Yes" on line 9 **or** line 10 above.

- First, complete your Form 1040 through lines 64a and 64b.
- Then, use Form 8812 to figure any additional child tax credit.

Form **8812** Department of the Treasury Internal Revenue Service (99)

Additional Child Tax Credit

Complete and attach to Form 1040, Form 1040A, or Form 1040NR.

OMB No. 1545-0074 | **2011** | Attachment Sequence No. **47**

1040 / 1040A / 1040NR → 8812

Name(s) shown on return	Your social security number
Amy Brown	012-00-5678

Part I — All Filers

Line	Description			Line	Amount
1	**1040 filers:** Enter the amount from line 6 of your Child Tax Credit Worksheet (see the Instructions for Form 1040, line 51). **1040A filers:** Enter the amount from line 6 of your Child Tax Credit Worksheet (see the Instructions for Form 1040A, line 33). **1040NR filers:** Enter the amount from line 6 of your Child Tax Credit Worksheet (see the Instructions for Form 1040NR, line 48). If you used Pub. 972, enter the amount from line 8 of the Child Tax Credit Worksheet in the publication.			1	2,000
2	Enter the amount from Form 1040, line 51, Form 1040A, line 33, or Form 1040NR, line 48			2	883
3	Subtract line 2 from line 1. If zero, **stop**; you cannot take this credit			3	1,117
4a	Earned income (see instructions on back)	4a	30,450		
b	Nontaxable combat pay (see instructions on back) 4b				
5	Is the amount on line 4a more than $3,000? ☐ **No.** Leave line 5 blank and enter -0- on line 6. ☒ **Yes.** Subtract $3,000 from the amount on line 4a. Enter the result	5	27,450		
6	Multiply the amount on line 5 by 15% (.15) and enter the result			6	4,118
	Next. Do you have three or more qualifying children? ☒ **No.** If line 6 is zero, stop; you cannot take this credit. Otherwise, skip Part II and enter the **smaller** of line 3 or line 6 on line 13. ☐ **Yes.** If line 6 is equal to or more than line 3, skip Part II and enter the amount from line 3 on line 13. Otherwise, go to line 7.				

Part II — Certain Filers Who Have Three or More Qualifying Children

Line	Description			Line	Amount
7	Withheld social security and Medicare taxes from Form(s) W-2, boxes 4 and 6. If married filing jointly, include your spouse's amounts with yours. If you worked for a railroad, see instructions on back	7			
8	**1040 filers:** Enter the total of the amounts from Form 1040, lines 27 and 57, plus any taxes that you identified using code "UT" and entered on line 60. **1040A filers:** Enter -0-. **1040NR filers:** Enter the total of the amounts from Form 1040NR, lines 27 and 55, plus any taxes that you identified using code "UT" and entered on line 59.	8			
9	Add lines 7 and 8	9			
10	**1040 filers:** Enter the total of the amounts from Form 1040, lines 64a and 69. **1040A filers:** Enter the total of the amount from Form 1040A, line 38a, plus any excess social security and tier 1 RRTA taxes withheld that you entered to the left of line 41 (see instructions on back). **1040NR filers:** Enter the amount from Form 1040NR, line 65.	10			
11	Subtract line 10 from line 9. If zero or less, enter -0-			11	
12	Enter the **larger** of line 6 or line 11			12	
	Next, enter the **smaller** of line 3 or line 12 on line 13.				

Part III — Additional Child Tax Credit

Line	Description	Line	Amount
13	**This is your additional child tax credit**	13	1,117

Enter this amount on Form 1040, line 65, Form 1040A, line 39, or Form 1040NR, line 63. → 1040 / 1040A / 1040NR

Chapter 36

Education credits and other education tax benefits

ey.com/EYTaxGuide

Introduction

If you have eligible education expenses in 2011, you may be able to benefit from two education credits that can reduce your taxes. These are the American opportunity credit and the lifetime learning credit.

Here are some of the key details of the American opportunity credit:

1. The maximum amount of the credit is $2,500 per student. The credit can be claimed for qualified tuition and related expenses for the first four years of a student's post-secondary degree or certificate program.
2. The credit phases out if your modified adjusted gross income (AGI) is between $80,000 and $90,000 ($160,000 and $180,000 if you file a joint return).
3. Generally, up to 40% of the American opportunity credit is refundable (provided the taxpayer claiming the credit is not a child to whom the "kiddie tax" rules apply–discussed later). This means that you can receive up to a $1,000 refund even if the total amount of the credit exceeds your federal income tax liability. The term "qualified tuition and related expenses" includes expenditures for "course materials." These include books, supplies, and equipment needed for a course of study whether or not the materials are purchased from the educational institution as a condition of enrollment or attendance.

You might also be able to claim a lifetime learning credit of up to $2,000 on your tax return for educational expenditures incurred in any year of postsecondary education. However, you cannot claim both the lifetime learning credit and the American opportunity credit for the same student in the same year. For 2011, the amount of your lifetime learning credit is phased out if your AGI is between $51,000 and $61,000 ($102,000 and $122,000 if you file a joint return). The lifetime learning credit is nonrefundable. Although the lifetime learning credit can reduce your tax liability to zero, any credit excess of your tax liability is not refunded to you.

Amounts expended for education that are otherwise excludable from gross income or deductible as a business expense cannot be claimed as qualified tuition expenses for the American opportunity credit or the lifetime learning credit.

This chapter also discusses a variety of other education benefits that may be available to you–student loan deductions, Coverdell education savings accounts, deduction for qualified tuition expenses, and employer-provided educational assistance programs, among others.

Note

IRS Publication 17 (*Your Federal Income Tax*) has been updated by Ernst & Young LLP for 2011. Dates and dollar amounts shown are for 2011. Underlined type is used to indicate where IRS text has been updated. Places where text has been removed are indicated by the sentence: *Text intentionally omitted.*

ey.com/EYTaxGuide

Ernst & Young LLP will update the *Ernst & Young Tax Guide 2012* website with relevant taxpayer information as it becomes available. You can also sign up for email alerts to let you know when changes have been made.

What's New

American opportunity credit extended. The American opportunity credit is available for 2011.

Income limits for lifetime learning credit increased. For 2011, the amount of your lifetime learning credit is gradually reduced (phased out) if your modified adjusted gross income (MAGI) is between $51,000 and $61,000 ($102,000 and $122,000 if you file a joint return). You cannot claim a credit if your MAGI is $61,000 or more ($122,000 or more if you file a joint return). This is an increase from the 2010 limits of $50,000 and $60,000 ($100,000 and $120,000 if filing a joint return).

Text intentionally omitted.

TAXALERT

In December 2010, the President and Congress agreed to extend the so-called Bush tax cuts. Among the provisions extended is the availability of the American opportunity credit for 2011 and 2012. Unless Congress acts, the American opportunity credit will expire after 2012 and the Hope scholarship credit will return.

For 2011, there are two tax credits available to persons who pay expenses for higher (postsecondary) education. They are:

- The American opportunity credit, and
- The lifetime learning credit.

The chapter will present an overview of these education credits. To get the detailed information you will need to claim either of the credits, and for examples illustrating that information, see chapters 2 and 3 of Publication 970.

Can you claim more than one education credit this year? For each student, you can choose for any year only one of the credits. For example, if you choose to take the American opportunity credit for a child on your 2011 tax return, you cannot, for that same child, also claim the lifetime learning credit for 2011.

If you are eligible to claim the American opportunity credit and you are also eligible to claim the lifetime learning credit for the same student in the same year, you can choose to claim either credit, but not both.

If you pay qualified education expenses for more than one student in the same year, you can choose to take the American opportunity and the lifetime learning credits on a per-student, per-year basis. This means that, for example, you can claim the American opportunity credit for one student and the lifetime learning credit for another student in the same year.

TAXPLANNER

For 2011, it will be more beneficial for you to claim the American opportunity credit than the lifetime learning credit.

Differences between the American opportunity and lifetime learning credits. There are several differences between these two credits. These differences are summarized in Table 36-1, later.

Useful Items

You may want to see:

Publication

□ 970 Tax Benefits for Education

Form (and Instructions)

□ 8863 Education Credits (American Opportunity and Lifetime Learning Credits)

TAXPLANNER

The IRS launched a section on its website, *www.irs.gov*, highlighting various education incentives designed to help parents and students pay for college. The *Tax Benefits for Education: Information Center* section includes tips for taking advantage of long-standing education deductions, credits, and savings plans. In addition, there is a special section, *Tax Incentives for Higher Education*, with a summary of the education incentives and a link to frequently asked questions regarding the lifetime learning credit.

Who Can Claim an Education Credit

You may be able to claim an education credit if you, your spouse, or a dependent you claim on your tax return was a student enrolled at or attending an eligible educational institution. The credits are based on the amount of qualified education expenses paid for the student in 2011 for academic periods beginning in 2011 and in the first 3 months of 2012.

For example, if you paid $1,500 in December 2011 for qualified tuition for the spring 2012 semester beginning in January 2012, you may be able to use that $1,500 in figuring your 2011 education credit(s).

Tax Breaks and Deductions You Can Use Checklist

Education Tax Credits. There are two types of credits you can claim for post-high school expenses: the American opportunity credit (an expanded and renamed version of the Hope scholarship credit) and the lifetime learning credit. You can take an American opportunity credit of up to $2,500 per student for the first four years of college (a 100% credit for the first $2,000 in tuition and related expenses, and a 25% credit for the second $2,000). You can take a lifetime learning credit of up to $2,000 per family for postsecondary education (a 20% credit for up to $10,000 in tuition and related expenses). However, you cannot claim both the American opportunity credit and the lifetime learning credit in the same year on the same student. Each credit phases out depending on your adjusted gross income and your filing status. Up to 40% of the American opportunity credit may be refundable, which means you may be able to receive up to $1,000 even if the total credit you can claim exceeds your federal income tax liability. The lifetime learning credit is nonrefundable. See the discussion in this chapter for more information.

Qualified Tuition Programs (Section 529 Plans). A qualified tuition program lets you buy tuition credits for a child or make contributions to an account set up to meet a child's future higher education expenses. Qualified tuition programs can be established by state governments or by private education institutions. Contributions to these programs aren't deductible, but the earnings on the contributions accumulate tax-free until the college costs are paid from the funds. In addition, distributions from qualified tuition programs are tax-free to the extent the funds are used to pay qualified higher education expenses. Qualified expenses include tuition and fees, books, supplies and equipment. Beginning in 2011, however, expenses for computer technology and equipment, as well as Internet access, are no longer qualified expenses. Distributions of earnings that aren't used for qualified higher education expenses will be subject to income tax plus a 10% penalty tax.

Coverdell Education Savings Account (ESA). You can establish Coverdell ESAs and make contributions of up to $2,000 annually for each child under age 18. The right to make these contributions begins to phase out once your adjusted gross income (AGI) is over $190,000 on a joint return ($95,000 for singles). A child can make a contribution to his or her own account. As with Section 529 plans, the contributions aren't deductible but funds in the account aren't taxed, and distributions are tax-free if spent on qualified education expenses, which include pre-college expenses like private elementary school tuition.

Caution

You cannot use any amount paid in 2010 or 2012 to figure your 2011 education credit(s).

Caution

You can claim both the American opportunity credit and the lifetime learning credit on the same return—but not for the same student.

Academic period. An academic period includes a semester, trimester, quarter, or other period of study (such as a summer school session) as reasonably determined by an educational institution. In the case of an educational institution that uses credit hours or clock hours and does not have academic terms, each payment period can be treated as an academic period.

Eligible educational institution. An eligible educational institution is any college, university, vocational school, or other postsecondary educational institution eligible to participate in a student aid program administered by the U.S. Department of Education. It includes virtually all accredited public, nonprofit, and proprietary (privately owned profit-making) postsecondary institutions. The educational institution should be able to tell you if it is an eligible educational institution.

Certain educational institutions located outside the United States also participate in the U.S. Department of Education's Federal Student Aid (FSA) programs.

Who can claim a dependent's expenses. If a student is claimed as a dependent on another person's tax return, only the person who claims the student as a dependent can claim a credit for the student's qualified education expenses. If a student is not claimed as a dependent on another person's tax return, only the student can claim a credit.

TAXPLANNER

Who should claim the education credit. If you claim your child as a dependent, only you may claim the education credit for the child's qualified tuition and related expenses. If, however, you are eligible to claim your child as a dependent but choose not to do so, your child may claim the education credit for his or her qualified tuition and related expenses even if the tuition and expenses were paid by you, the parent. The American opportunity credit is not refundable to the child, however, if the kiddie tax rules apply to that child.

It is important to note, however, that if a parent who is eligible to claim a dependency exemption for a student does not do so, the student is not allowed to take a personal exemption for himself or herself on his or her own return. As a result, the exemption for the student may be lost. If you are subject to the income phaseout limitation of the education credits, you should review the overall tax effect of not claiming an exemption for your child and allowing your child to claim the education credits.

Generally, qualified education expenses paid on behalf of the student by someone other than the student (such as a relative) are treated as paid by the student. However, qualified education expenses paid (or treated as paid) by a student who is claimed as a dependent on your tax return are treated as paid by you. Therefore, you are treated as having paid expenses that were paid from your dependent student's earnings, gifts, inheritances, savings, etc.

Who cannot claim a credit. You cannot take an education credit if any of the following apply.

1. You are claimed as a dependent on another person's tax return, such as your parent's return.
2. Your filing status is married filing separately.
3. You (or your spouse) were a nonresident alien for any part of 2011 and did not elect to be treated as a resident alien for tax purposes.
4. Your MAGI is one of the following.
   a. American opportunity credit: $180,000 or more if married filing jointly, or $90,000 or more if single, head of household, or qualifying widow(er).
   b. Lifetime learning credit: $122,000 or more if married filing jointly, or $61,000 or more if single, head of household, or qualifying widow(er).

Figure 36-A, at the end of this chapter, may be helpful in determining if you can claim an education credit on your tax return.

Qualified Education Expenses

Generally, qualified education expenses are amounts paid in 2011 for tuition and fees required for the student's enrollment or attendance at an eligible educational institution. It does not matter whether the expenses were paid in cash, by check, by credit or debit card, or with borrowed funds.

Only certain expenses for course-related books, supplies, and equipment qualify.

- American opportunity credit: Qualified education expenses include amounts spent on books, supplies, and equipment needed for a course of study, whether or not the materials are purchased from the educational institution as a condition of enrollment or attendance.

Table 36-1. **Comparison of Education Credits**

Caution. You can claim both the American opportunity credit and the lifetime learning credit on the same return—but not for the same student.		
	American Opportunity Credit	**Lifetime Learning Credit**
Maximum credit	Up to $2,500 credit per **eligible student**	Up to $2,000 credit per **return**
Limit on modified adjusted gross income (MAGI)	$180,000 if married filling jointly; $90,000 if single, head of household, or qualifying widow(er)	$122,000 if married filling jointly; $61,000 if single, head of household, or qualifying widow(er)
Refundable or nonrefundable	40% of credit may be refundable	Credit limited to the amount of tax you must pay on your taxable income
Number of years of postsecondary education	Available **ONLY** for the first **4** years of postsecondary education	Available for all years of postsecondary education and for courses to acquire or improve job skills
Number of tax years credit available	Available **ONLY** for **4** tax years per eligible student	Available for an unlimited number of years
Type of degree required	Student must be pursuing an undergraduate degree or other recognized education credential	Student does not need to be pursuing a degree or other recognized education credential
Number of courses	Student must be enrolled at least half time for at least one academic period beginning during the tax year	Available for one or more courses
Felony drug conviction	No felony drug convictions on student's records	Felony drug convictions are permitted
Qualified expenses	Tuition and required enrollment fees. Course-related books, supplies, and equipment **do not** need to be purchased from the institution in order to qualify.	Tuition and required enrollment fees, including amounts required to be paid to the institution for course-related books, supplies, and equipment.
Payments for academic periods	Payments made in 2011 for academic periods beginning in 2011 and in the first 3 months of 2012	

- Lifetime learning credit: Qualified education expenses include **only** amounts for books, supplies, and equipment required to be paid to the institution as a condition of enrollment or attendance.

Qualified education expenses **do not** include amounts paid for:

- Room and board, insurance, medical expenses (including student health fees), transportation, or other similar personal, living, or family expenses.
- Any course or other education involving sports, games, or hobbies, or any non-credit course, unless such course or other education is part of the student's degree program or (for the lifetime learning credit only) helps the student acquire or improve job skills.
- Nonacademic fees, such as student activity fees, athletic fees, insurance expenses, or other expenses unrelated to the academic course of instruction.

Paid with borrowed funds. You can claim an education credit for qualified education expenses paid with the proceeds of a loan. Use the expenses to figure the credit for the year in which the expenses are paid, not the year in which the loan is repaid. Treat loan payments sent directly to the educational institution as paid on the date the institution credits the student's account.

Student withdraws from class(es). You can claim an education credit for qualified education expenses not refunded when a student withdraws.

No Double Benefit Allowed

You cannot do any of the following.

- Deduct higher education expenses on your income tax return (as, for example, a business expense) and also claim an education credit based on those same expenses.
- Claim more than 1 education credit based on the same qualified education expenses.
- Claim an education credit based on the same expenses used to figure the tax-free portion of a distribution from a Coverdell education savings account (ESA) or qualified tuition program (QTP).
- Claim an education credit based on qualified education expenses paid with educational assistance, such as a tax-free scholarship, grant, or employer-provided educational assistance. See *Adjustments to Qualified Education Expenses*, next.

Tip

There are a number of factors, such as your filing status, your MAGI, and whether you are subject to the alternative minimum tax, that will affect the amount of any education credit you are eligible to claim. When you figure your taxes, you may want to compare the different education credits in order to choose the method(s) that gives you the lowest tax liability. If you qualify, you may find that a combination of credit(s) and other education benefit(s) gives you the lowest tax. See Publication 970 for information on other benefits.

TAXALERT

One credit per customer. The American opportunity credit and lifetime learning credit are mutually exclusive. For each eligible student in each tax year, you must elect either one of the tax credits. The American opportunity credit and lifetime learning credit can be claimed in the same year that a distribution from a Coverdell education savings account or qualified tuition program is made, as long as the distribution is not used to cover the same expenses for which the education credits are claimed.

The American opportunity credit is phased out for single taxpayers with modified adjusted gross income (AGI) of $80,000 to $90,000 and for couples filing jointly with modified AGI between $160,000 and $180,000. The lifetime learning credit is phased out for single taxpayers with modified adjusted gross income (AGI) of $51,000 to $61,000 and, if married filing jointly, $102,000 to $122,000.

Adjustments to Qualified Education Expenses

If you pay qualified education expenses with certain tax-free funds, you cannot claim an education credit for those amounts. You must reduce the qualified education expenses by the amount of any tax-free educational assistance and refund(s) you received.

Tax-free educational assistance. This includes:

- Tax-free parts of scholarships and fellowships (see chapter 12 of this publication and chapter 1 of Publication 970),
- Pell grants (see chapter 1 of Publication 970),
- Employer-provided educational assistance (see chapter 11 of Publication 970),
- Veterans' educational assistance (see chapter 1 of Publication 970), and
- Any other nontaxable (tax-free) payments (other than gifts or inheritances) received as educational assistance.

Refunds. Qualified education expenses do not include expenses for which you, or someone else who paid qualified education expenses on behalf of a student, receive a refund. For more information, see *Refunds* in chapters 2 and 3 of Publication 970.

Amounts that do not reduce qualified education expenses. Do not reduce qualified education expenses by amounts paid with funds the student receives as:

- Payment for services, such as wages,
- A loan,
- A gift,
- An inheritance, or
- A withdrawal from the student's personal savings.

Do not reduce the qualified education expenses by any scholarship or fellowship reported as income on the student's tax return in the following situations.

- The use of the money is restricted to costs of attendance (such as room and board) other than qualified education expenses.
- The use of the money is not restricted and is used to pay education expenses that are not qualified (such as room and board).

For examples, see chapter 2 in Publication 970.

When Must the Credit Be Repaid (Recaptured)

If, after you file your 2011 tax return, you or someone else receives tax-free educational assistance for, or a refund of, an expense you used to figure an education credit on that return, you may have to repay all or part of the credit. You must refigure your education credit(s) for 2011 as if the assistance or refund was received in 2011. Subtract the amount of the refigured credit from the amount of the credit you claimed. The result is the amount you must repay. Add the repayment (recapture) to your tax liability for the year in which you receive the assistance or refund. See the instructions for your tax return for that year to find out how to report the recapture amount. Your original 2011 tax return does not change.

Figure 36-A. **Can You Claim an Education Credit for 2011?**

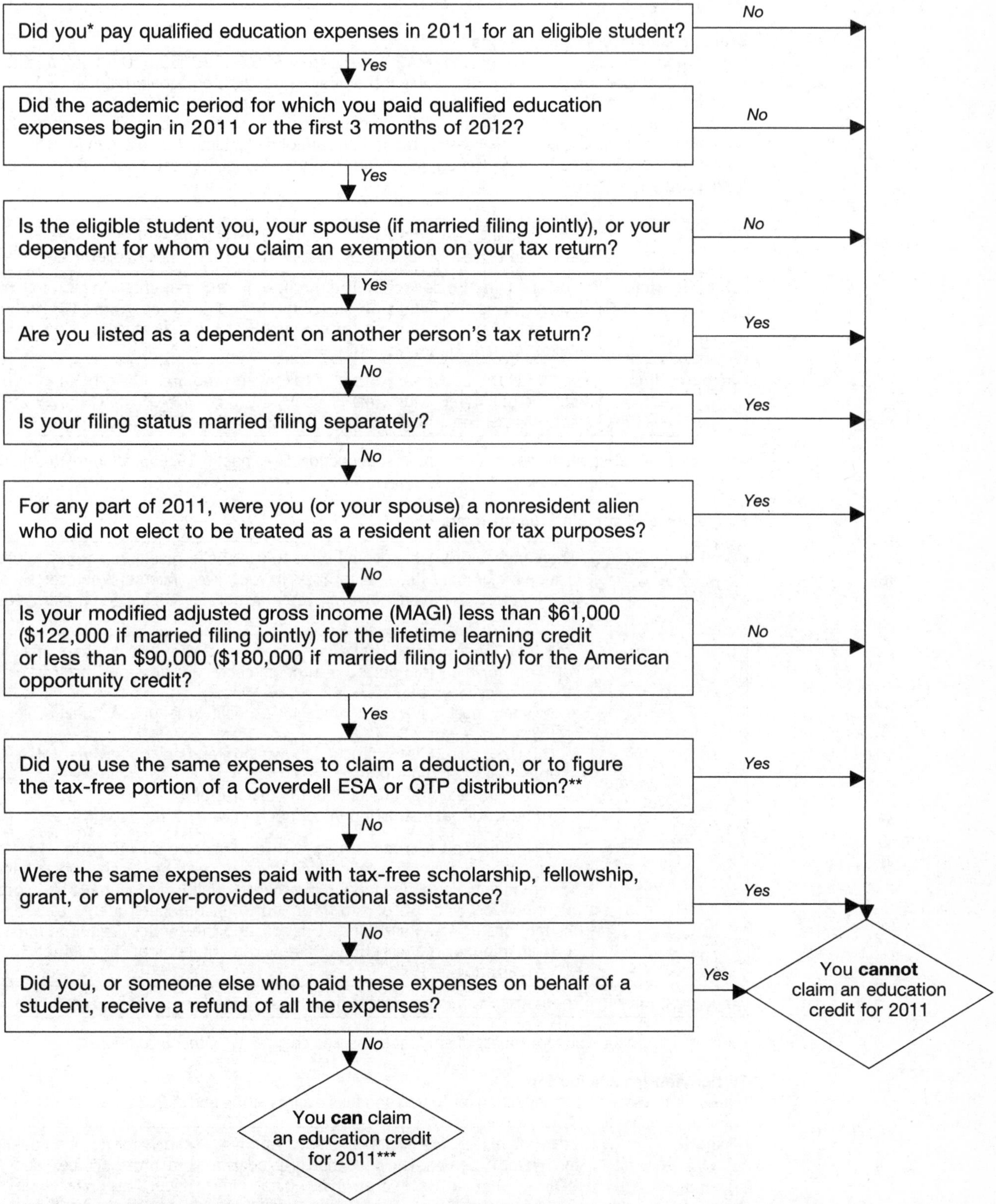
Did you* pay qualified education expenses in 2011 for an eligible student?
No
Yes
Did the academic period for which you paid qualified education expenses begin in 2011 or the first 3 months of 2012?
No
Yes
Is the eligible student you, your spouse (if married filing jointly), or your dependent for whom you claim an exemption on your tax return?
No
Yes
Are you listed as a dependent on another person's tax return?
Yes
No
Is your filing status married filing separately?
Yes
No
For any part of 2011, were you (or your spouse) a nonresident alien who did not elect to be treated as a resident alien for tax purposes?
Yes
No
Is your modified adjusted gross income (MAGI) less than $61,000 ($122,000 if married filing jointly) for the lifetime learning credit or less than $90,000 ($180,000 if married filing jointly) for the American opportunity credit?
No
Yes
Did you use the same expenses to claim a deduction, or to figure the tax-free portion of a Coverdell ESA or QTP distribution?**
Yes
No
Were the same expenses paid with tax-free scholarship, fellowship, grant, or employer-provided educational assistance?
Yes
No
Did you, or someone else who paid these expenses on behalf of a student, receive a refund of all the expenses?
Yes
You **cannot** claim an education credit for 2011
No
You **can** claim an education credit for 2011***

* Qualified education expenses paid by a dependent for whom you claim an exemption, or by a third party for that dependent, are considered paid by you.

** You cannot use the same expenses to claim more than 1 education credit.

*** Your education credits may be limited to your tax liability minus certain credits. See Form 8863 for more details.

Table 36-2. **Other Education Tax Benefits**

There are many education tax incentives in addition to the American opportunity credit and lifetime learning credit. Some of the more popular incentives are summarized below.

Student loan interest deductions

If your modified adjusted gross income (MAGI) is less than $75,000 ($150,000 if filing a joint return), student loan interest paid is deductible if the interest was paid on a loan that you took out to pay for qualified higher education expenses at an eligible education institution for yourself, your spouse, or your dependent. Qualified higher education expenses include the costs of tuition, fees, room and board, books, supplies, and equipment. You cannot deduct interest on a loan for which you are not legally obligated to make the payments nor can you deduct interest if you did not actually make payments.

Benefit	If you paid interest on a qualified education loan in 2011 you may be able to deduct up to $2,500 of the interest paid on your 2011 tax return.
Qualifications	You can claim the deduction if the following requirements are met: (1) Your filing status is any filing status except married filing separately, (2) No one else can claim an exemption for you on his or her tax return, (3) You paid interest on a qualified student loan.
Income Limits	For 2011, the phaseout range for taxpayers who are single, head of household, or qualifying widow(er) is $60,000 to $75,000. For taxpayers filing joint returns, the phaseout range is $120,000 to $150,000

For more information on the student loan interest deduction. See chapter 19, *Education-related adjustments.*

Forgiveness of certain student loans

Benefit	When any loan for which you are responsible is forgiven, you generally must include the amount that was forgiven in your gross income. When certain student loans are forgiven, however, you may not have to include the amount in income.
Qualifications	Your loan must provide that all or a portion of the debt will be canceled if you work for a certain period of time, in certain professions, and for a designated class of employers. The loan must have been made by a qualified lender. A qualified lender includes: • The U.S., a state (or political subdivision), and any governmental agency or instrumentality. • Certain tax-exempt public benefit corporations. • An educational institution in connection with certain programs. If you refinanced a student loan with a loan from an educational or tax-exempt organization, the refinanced loan may also be considered as having been made by a qualified lender. In order to qualify, it must have been made in connection with a program designed to encourage students to serve in occupations or areas with unmet needs, and the services required must be performed under the direction of a governmental unit or tax-exempt 501(c)(3) organization.
Income Limits	There are no specific income limits restricting the use of this provision.

For more information on forgiveness of student loans, see chapter 12, *Other income.*

Tuition and fees deduction

Unless Congress acts, the deduction for tuition and fees expires at the end of 2011.

Benefit	Certain taxpayers are eligible to deduct up to $4,000 paid for qualified tuition and related expenses. The deduction is an adjustment to gross income ("above-the-line") and is available even if you do not itemize deductions on Schedule A. The deduction for qualified tuition and fees are limited to those qualifying expenses paid during 2011 for 2011 enrollment periods, including any academic period that begins in 2011 or in the first three months of 2012.

Qualifications	Qualified tuition and related expenses are tuition and fees paid for you, your spouse, or a dependent for whom you claim an exemption. If your dependent pays qualified education expenses and you can claim an exemption for your dependent on your tax return, no one can take a tuition and fees deduction for those expenses. Neither you nor your dependent can deduct the expenses. This rule applies even if you do not claim an exemption for your dependent on your tax return. The expenses must be required for enrollment or attendance at an "eligible educational institution." A college, university, vocational school, or other post-secondary educational institution, which is eligible to participate in a student aid program administered by the Department of Education generally will be considered an eligible educational expense. Student activity fees and fees for course-related books, supplies, and equipment generally do not qualify unless they are paid to the education institution as a condition of enrollment or attendance. The cost of insurance, medical expenses, room and board, transportation, and similar personal expenses are not considered qualified tuition and related expenses even if paid to the institution as a condition of enrollment or attendance. The amount of qualified tuition and related expenses must be reduced by certain scholarships, educational assistance allowances, and other amounts paid for the benefit of such individual, and by the amount of such expenses taken into account for purposes of determining any exclusion from gross income of: (1) income from certain U.S. savings bonds used to pay higher education tuition and fees; and (2) income from a Coverdell education savings account. Additionally, such expenses must be reduced by the earnings portion (but not the return of principal) of distributions from a Section 529 qualified tuition program.
Income Limits	For 2011, you can deduct up to $4,000 if you are a qualifying taxpayer and your modified adjusted gross income is not more than $65,000, or $130,000 on a joint return. If your modified AGI is more than these amounts but not more than $160,000 ($80,000 for unmarrieds) you can deduct up to $2,000. These are absolute limits, not phaseouts. If your income is above those amounts, you cannot take any deduction. The deduction is also unavailable—regardless of your MAGI—if your filing status for 2011 is married filing separately or you can be claimed as a dependent on the tax return of another person. (You cannot take the deduction even if that other person does not actually claim you as a dependent.) In addition, the deduction is unavailable to a taxpayer for whom the American opportunity tax credit or lifetime learning credit would have provided a greater net reduction in tax liability, without regard to any disallowance or reduction in value of the credit as a result of the alternative minimum tax. Also, you cannot claim a deduction if you claimed an American opportunity or lifetime learning credit for the same student.

For more information on the tuition and fees deduction, see chapter 19, *Education-related adjustments*.

Tax-free scholarships and fellowships

In general, scholarships and fellowships received to assist an individual with payment of educational expenses are not considered taxable income. See the chart below for more details.

Benefit	A candidate for a degree at an education institution can exclude from income amounts received as a qualified scholarship or fellowship.
Qualifications	A candidate for a degree is defined as including a student who: 1. Attends a primary or secondary school or is pursuing a degree at a college or university, or 2. Attends a qualifying accredited educational organization that is authorized to provide a program: a. That is acceptable for full credit toward a bachelor's or higher degree, or b. That trains students for employment in a recognized occupation. A scholarship or fellowship grant is generally an amount paid for the benefit of an individual to aid such individual in the pursuit of study or research. A scholarship or fellowship grant does not include any amount provided by an individual to aid a relative, friend, or other individual if the grantor is motivated by family or philanthropic considerations.

	Amounts received that are used for qualified tuition and related expenses can be excluded from income. These expenses include tuition and fees required to enroll in, or to attend, an educational institution, and fees, books, supplies, and equipment required of all students in your course of instruction. Incidental expenses including room and board and travel expenses do not qualify. Although scholarships are usually taxable if they carry a future service requirement, qualified amounts received under the National Health Service Corps Scholarship Program or the Armed Forces Health Professions Scholarship and Financial Assistance Program will not be taxed.
Income Limits	There are no specific income limits restricting the use of this provision.

For more information on scholarships and fellowships, see chapter 12, *Other income*, and IRS Publication 520.

Withdrawals from IRAs before age 59½ to pay qualified higher educational expenses

Benefit	Generally, withdrawals from a traditional or Roth IRA before age 59½ are subject to an additional 10% tax on the part of distribution included in gross income. You will not be subject to the 10% additional tax, however, if for the year of withdrawal you have paid sufficient higher education expenses for yourself, your spouse, or for your or your spouse's children or grandchildren.
Qualifications	N/A
Income Limits	There are no specific income limits restricting the use of this provision.

Education savings bond program

Benefit	Interest earned on U.S. savings bonds is generally taxed either in the year the interest is earned or, more typically, in the year in which you cash in bonds. Under the education savings bond program, when you cash in qualified U.S. savings bonds, you may be able to exclude from your income all or a portion of the interest earned.
Qualifications	Only Series EE bonds issued after 1989 and Series I savings bonds qualify. In addition, the owner of the bond must be at least 24 years old before the bond's issue date, and cannot have a filing status of married filing separately. To be able to exclude interest from your taxable income, you must pay "qualified higher education expenses" for yourself, your spouse, or a dependent for whom you claim an exemption of your return. If the total that you receive when you cash in the bonds is not more than the available qualified expenses, part of the interest may be tax-free.
Income Limits	The interest exclusion is phased out for higher income taxpayers. The phaseout range for single taxpayers in 2011 is $71,100 to $86,100. For taxpayers filing joint returns, the phaseout range is $106,650 to $136,650.

For more information on the education savings bond programs, see chapter 7, *Interest income*.

Educational assistance as a working condition fringe benefit

Benefit	Certain educational expenses paid by your employer may be excludable from your income if the expenditures are considered a working condition fringe benefit.
Qualifications	Expenses qualify if the education you receive maintains or improves skills required in your employment or meets the express requirements of your employer or applicable law required as a condition of employment. Educational expenses that are incurred to meet minimum educational requirements or that qualify you for a new trade or business (such as a law or medical degree) do not qualify.

	Amounts paid by your employer will generally qualify as a working condition fringe benefit if the item would have been deductible as an employee business expense had you paid the expense. Treatment as a working condition fringe benefit is generally more beneficial than a deduction, however, since employee business expenses are deductible only if you itemize your deductions, and then only to the extent that they, in combination with other miscellaneous itemized deductions, exceed 2% of your adjusted gross income.
Income Limits	There are no specific income limits restricting the use of this provision.

For more information about working condition fringe benefits, see IRS Publication 15-B.

Employer-provided educational assistance programs
Your employer may assist you with educational payments, a portion of which may be excludable from your income (see chart below). Qualified payments include payments for tuition, fees, books, supplies, and equipment (not including meals and transportation). Courses in sports, games, or hobbies are not qualified expenses unless there is a reasonable relationship between the courses and the business of the employer or if the courses are required as part of a degree program.

Benefit	Up to $5,250 of employer-provided education assistance payments may be excluded from your income each calendar year when provided under an employer-sponsored educational assistance program. Qualifying payments are excludable from income whether or not the courses taken are job-related. This benefit covers educational assistance for undergraduate or graduate level courses.
Qualifications	Payments must be made under a qualifying written plan that does not discriminate in favor of highly compensated employees. Payments may be made for tuition, fees, books, supplies, and equipment. Payments made for meals, lodging, and transportation generally do not qualify.
Income Limits	There are no specific income limits restricting the use of this provision.

For more information on education as a working condition fringe benefit and on employer-provided educational assistance programs, see chapter 12, *Other income*, and chapter 29, *Tax benefits for work-related education*.

Coverdell education savings accounts

Benefit	There is no federal income tax on earnings in these accounts when distributions are used to pay qualifying educational expenses.
Qualifications	Qualified educational expenses include tuition, fees, books, supplies, and equipment, and costs of room and board. Qualified expenses include elementary and secondary school expenses. The purchase of computer equipment, Internet access, and related technology, if used by the student or the student's family, also qualifies. There is no federal income tax deduction for contributions to Coverdell accounts. Except in the case of a special needs beneficiary, you cannot contribute to a Coverdell account after the beneficiary reaches age 18. To the extent that distributions are not used for qualifying educational expenses, an income and penalty tax may apply to the distributed earnings.
Income Limits	The maximum contribution to a Coverdell account is $2,000 per year. The amount that a taxpayer is allowed to contribute to a Coverdell account is phased out for higher income taxpayers. In 2011 for joint returns, the phaseout range is $190,000 to $220,000. For other taxpayers, the phaseout range is $95,000 to $110,000.

TAXALERT
An individual who has received a military death gratuity or Servicemembers' Group Life Insurance (SGLI) payment may contribute all or a part of the amounts received to one or more Coverdell education savings accounts. The contribution is treated as a rollover, except that this type of rollover does not count when figuring the annual limit on the number of rollovers allowed.

Qualified tuition (Section 529) programs

A qualified tuition program allows you to prepay or contribute to an account that has been established to pay qualified higher education expenses. Unlike Coverdell education savings accounts, there are no income limits restricting the use of these accounts. Although contributions are not deductible for federal income tax purposes, many states permit you to deduct a portion or all of your contribution on your state income tax return.

Benefit	There is no federal income tax imposed when distributions from qualified tuition programs (popularly known as 529 plans) are used to pay qualifying higher education expenses.
Qualifications	There are two basic types of 529 plans. Under the prepaid educational service type plan, you purchase tuition credits today for use in the future. The other type of plan (often referred to as "college savings plan") permits you to contribute to a special higher education savings account for a designated beneficiary. In both types of plans, your initial investment is designed to grow over time and the value of that growth is not subject to federal income tax when distributions are made for qualifying higher education expenses. There is no federal income tax deduction for contributions to a 529 plan. Unlike distributions from Coverdell accounts, qualifying expenditures may only be made for higher education expenses. To the extent that distributions are not used for qualifying higher educational expenses, an income and penalty tax may apply. Higher educational expenses include tuition, required fees, books, and supplies. (Beginning in 2011, amounts paid for computer technology and equipment, as well as Internet access, are not qualified expenses.) For someone who is at least a half-time student, room and board also qualify as qualifying higher educational expenses.
Income Limits	529 plans are not subject to income limits and permit you to make contributions far in excess of the $2,000 annual contribution permitted for Coverdell accounts. The combination of benefits and flexibility offered by these plans make them the most widely used education tax incentive program. Be sure to discuss the investment options and limitations of the various programs with your financial advisor.

For more information on qualified tuition programs, Coverdell education savings accounts, and other education incentives, see Publication 970, *Tax Benefits for Education.*

Chapter 37

Other credits including the earned income credit

ey.com/EYTaxGuide

Note

IRS Publication 17 (*Your Federal Income Tax*) has been updated by Ernst & Young LLP for 2011. Dates and dollar amounts shown are for 2011. Underlined type is used to indicate where IRS text has been updated. Places where text has been removed are indicated by the sentence: *Text intentionally omitted*.

ey.com/EYTaxGuide

Ernst & Young LLP will update the *Ernst & Young Tax Guide 2012* website with relevant taxpayer information as it becomes available. You can also sign up for email alerts to let you know when changes have been made.

Introduction

This chapter discusses seventeen credits you may use to reduce your tax liability. Ten of these credits are nonrefundable; that is, although they may be used to bring your tax liability to zero, any credit in excess of your liability is not refunded to you. Seven of these credits are refundable. That means that any unused credit is refunded to you.

The ten nonrefundable credits discussed in the this chapter are:

1. Alternative motor vehicle credit
2. Alternative fuel vehicle refueling property credit
3. Credit to holders of tax credit bonds
4. Foreign tax credit
5. Mortgage interest credit
6. Nonrefundable credit for prior year minimum tax
7. Plug-in electric drive motor vehicle credit
8. Plug-in electric vehicle credit
9. Residential energy efficient property credit
10. Retirement savings contributions credit (saver's credit)

Depending on the credit, part or all of a nonrefundable credit that is not utilized in the current year generally may be carried back or carried forward and utilized in another year.

Tax Breaks and Deductions You Can Use Checklist

Tax Credits. Unlike tax deductions, which reduce your taxable income, tax credits reduce your tax liability dollar-for-dollar, which makes them especially valuable. There are two types of credits: nonrefundable and refundable. Nonrefundable credits are limited to the amount of your tax liability. Refundable credits can reduce your tax liability to zero and beyond—actually entitling you to a refund. The credits available to individuals (nonbusiness-related) are:

1. Social security and railroad retirement tax overpayments (discussed in this chapter)
2. Tax withheld on wages, pension annuities, and other deferred income (chapter 4)
3. Tax withheld on interest, dividends, and patronage dividends (chapter 4)
4. Credit for interest on certain home mortgages (discussed in this chapter)
5. Credit from a regulated investment company (chapter 39)
6. Withheld gambling winnings (chapter 4)
7. Child tax credit (chapter 35)
8. Elderly and disabled credit (chapter 34)
9. Earned income credit (discussed in this chapter)
10. Credit for health insurance costs of individuals receiving a trade wadjustment allowance or a benefit from the Pension Benefits Guaranty Corp. (PBGC) (discussed in this chapter)
11. First-time homebuyer credit for D.C.
12. Child and dependent care credit (chapter 33)

The eight refundable credits discussed in this chapter are:

1. The adoption credit
2. Credit for tax on undistributed capital gain
3. First-time homebuyer credit (recapture)
4. Health coverage tax credit
5. Refundable credit for prior year minimum tax
6. Credit for excess social security tax or railroad retirement tax withheld
7. Earned income credit

What's New

Text intentionally omitted.

Making work pay credit. This credit has expired. It is not available for 2011.

Adoption credit or exclusion. The maximum adoption credit or exclusion for employer-provided adoption benefits has increased to $13,360. In order to claim either the credit or exclusion, your MAGI must be less than $225,210. See *Adoption Credit* for more information.

First-time homebuyer credit. You generally cannot claim the credit for a home you bought after April 30, 2010. *Text intentionally omitted.* However, certain members of the Armed Forces and certain other taxpayers have additional time to buy a home and take the credit. See *First-Time Homebuyer Credit*.

Recapture of first-time homebuyer credit. If you claimed the first-time homebuyer credit for a home you bought in 2008, you generally began repaying it on your 2010 return. In addition, you generally must repay any credit you claimed for 2008, 2009, or 2010 if you sold your home in 2011 or the home stopped being your main home in 2011. See *First-Time Homebuyer Credit*.

Retirement savings contribution credit income limits increased. In order to claim this credit, your modified adjusted gross income (MAGI) must be less than $28,250 ($56,500 if married filing jointly; $42,375 if head of household).

Health coverage tax credit (HCTC). Beginning after February 12, 2011, the credit has decreased to 65% (from 80%) for amounts paid for qualified health insurance coverage for you, your spouse, and other qualifying family members.

Nonbusiness energy property credit. This credit has been extended for 1 year with a reduced rate of 10%. Amounts provided by subsidized federal, state, or local energy financing do not qualify for the credit. The energy-efficiency standards for qualified natural gas, propane, or oil furnaces, or hot water boilers have been increased. For 2011, the credit is limited as follows.

- A total combined credit limit of $500 for all tax years after 2005 (Form 5695, Part I).
- A combined credit limit of $200 for windows for all tax years after 2005.
- A maximum credit for residential energy property costs of $50 for any advanced main air circulating fan; $150 for any qualified natural gas, propane, or oil furnace, or hot water boiler; and $300 for any item of energy-efficient building property.

Earned income credit (EIC). You may be able to take the EIC in 2011 if:

- Three or more children lived with you and you earned less than $43,998 ($49,078 if married filing jointly),
- Two children lived with you and you earned less than $40,964 ($46,044 if married filing jointly),
- One child lived with you and you earned less than $36,052 ($41,132 if married filing jointly), or
- A child did not live with you and you earned less than $13,660 ($18,740 if married filing jointly).

Also, the maximum AGI you can have and still get the credit has increased. You may be able to take the credit if your AGI is less than the amount in the above list that applies to you. The maximum investment income you can have and get the credit has increased to $3,150.

Advance payment of the EIC is no longer available. The advance payment option to receive the refundable portion of the EIC on the taxpayer's paycheck expired at the end of 2010 and is no longer available beginning in 2011.

This chapter discusses the following nonrefundable credits.

- Alternative motor vehicle credit.
- Alternative fuel vehicle refueling property credit.
- Credit to holders of tax credit bonds.
- Foreign tax credit.
- Mortgage interest credit.
- Nonrefundable credit for prior year minimum tax.
- Plug-in electric drive motor vehicle credit.
- Plug-in electric vehicle credit.
- Residential energy credits.
- Retirement savings contributions credit.

This chapter also discusses the following refundable credits.

- Adoption credit.
- Credit for tax on undistributed capital gain.
- First-time homebuyer credit.
- Health coverage tax credit.
- *Text intentionally omitted.*
- Refundable credit for prior year minimum tax.
- Credit for excess social security tax or railroad retirement tax withheld.

Several other credits are discussed in other chapters in this publication.

- Child and dependent care credit (chapter 33).
- Credit for the elderly or the disabled (chapter 34).
- Child tax credit (chapter 35).
- Education credits (chapter 36).
- Earned income credit (chapter 37).

Nonrefundable credits. The first part of this chapter, *Nonrefundable Credits,* covers ten credits that you subtract from your tax. These credits may reduce your tax to zero. If these credits are more than your tax, the excess is not refunded to you.

Refundable credits. The second part of this chapter, *Refundable Credits,* covers seven credits that are treated as payments and are refundable to you. These credits are added to the federal income tax withheld and any estimated tax payments you made. If this total is more than your total tax, the excess will be refunded to you.

Useful Items

You may want to see:

Publication

- □ **502** Medical and Dental Expenses (Including the Health Coverage Tax Credit)
- □ **514** Foreign Tax Credit for Individuals
- □ **530** Tax Information for Homeowners
- □ **590** Individual Retirement Arrangements (IRAs)

Form (and Instructions)

- □ **1116** Foreign Tax Credit (Individual, Estate, or Trust)
- □ **2439** Notice to Shareholder of Undistributed Long-Term Capital Gains
- □ **5405** First-Time Homebuyer Credit and Repayment of the Credit
- □ **5695** Residential Energy Credits
- □ **8396** Mortgage Interest Credit
- □ **8801** Credit For Prior Year Minimum Tax—Individuals, Estates, and Trusts
- □ **8828** Recapture of Federal Mortgage Subsidy
- □ **8834** Qualified Plug-in Electric and Electric Vehicle Credit
- □ **8839** Qualified Adoption Expenses
- □ **8880** Credit for Qualified Retirement Savings Contributions
- □ **8885** Health Coverage Tax Credit
- □ **8910** Alternative Motor Vehicle Credit
- □ **8911** Alternative Fuel Vehicle Refueling Property Credit
- □ **8912** Credit to Holders of Tax Credit Bonds
- □ **8936** Qualified Plug-in Electric Drive Motor Vehicle Credit

13. Adoption expense credit (discussed in this chapter)
14. Saver's credit for elective deferrals and IRA contributions (discussed in this chapter)
15. American opportunity credit and lifetime learning credit for higher education expenses (chapter 36)
16. Nonbusiness energy property credit for energy-efficient improvements to a principal residence (discussed in this chapter)
17. Residential energy-efficient property credit for photovoltaic, solar hot water, and fuel cell property added to a residence (discussed in this chapter)
18. Credit for alternative motor vehicles (discussed in this chapter)
19. Plug-in conversion credit (discussed in this chapter)
20. Plug-in electric vehicle credit (discussed in this chapter)
21. Plug-in electric drive motor vehicle credit (discussed in this chapter)
22. Alternative fuel refueling property credit (discussed in this chapter)
23. Foreign tax credit (discussed in this chapter)
24. Credit for prior year minimum tax (nonrefundable and refundable credits) (discussed in this chapter)
25. First-time homebuyer credit

Nonrefundable Credits

The credits discussed in this part of the chapter can reduce your tax. However, if the total of these credits is more than your tax, the excess is not refunded to you.

Alternative Motor Vehicle Credit

You may be able to take a credit if you place an alternative motor vehicle in service in 2011.

Alternative motor vehicle. An alternative motor vehicle is a new vehicle that qualifies as a *(text intentionally omitted)* qualified fuel cell vehicle. A credit is also allowed for the cost of converting a vehicle to a qualified plug-in electric drive vehicle.
Text intentionally omitted.

Amount of credit. Generally, you can rely on the manufacturer's (or, in the case of a foreign manufacturer, its domestic distributor's) certification that a specific make, model, and model year vehicle qualifies for the credit and the amount of the credit for which it qualifies.

Ordinarily the amount of the credit is 100% of the manufacturer's (or domestic distributor's) certification of the maximum credit allowable. However, the credit for converting a vehicle to a qualified plug-in electric drive vehicle is the smaller of (a) $4,000, or (b) 10% of the cost of the conversion.

> ***TAXALERT***
> At the time this book was published, the credit for installing an electric drive conversion kit will only apply for conversions made before December 31, 2011.

Text intentionally omitted.

How to take the credit. To take the credit, you must complete Form 8910 and attach it to your Form 1040. Include the credit in your total for Form 1040, line 53. Check box c and enter "8910" on the line next to that box.

More information. For more information on the credit, see the instructions for Form 8910.

Alternative Fuel Vehicle Refueling Property Credit

You may be able to take a credit if you place qualified alternative fuel vehicle refueling property in service in 2011.

Qualified alternative fuel vehicle refueling property. Qualified alternative fuel vehicle refueling property is any property (other than a building or its structural components) used to store or dispense alternative fuel into the fuel tank of a motor vehicle propelled by the fuel, but only if the storage or dispensing is at the point where the fuel is delivered into the tank.

The following are alternative fuels.

- Any fuel at least 85% of the volume of which consists of one or more of the following: ethanol, natural gas, compressed natural gas, liquefied natural gas, liquefied petroleum gas, or hydrogen.
- Any mixture which consists of two or more of the following: biodiesel, diesel fuel, or kerosene, and at least 20% of the volume of which consists of biodiesel determined without regard to any kerosene.
- Electricity.

Amount of the credit. For personal use property, the credit is generally the smaller of 30% of the property's cost or $1,000. For business use property, the credit is generally the smaller of 30% of the property's cost or $30,000. The amounts are different for hydrogen refueling property.

How to take the credit. To take the credit, you must complete Form 8911 and attach it to your Form 1040. Include the credit in your total for Form 1040, line 53. Check box c and enter "8911" on the line next to that box.

More information. For more information on the credit, see the instructions for Form 8911.

> ***TAXALERT***
> The rate for the 2011 credit dropped from the 2010 limit. The credit rate decreased from 50% to 30% of the cost of qualified property placed in service in 2011. The cap in place under this law is $1,000 for qualified property installed at a personal residence.

Credit to Holders of Tax Credit Bonds

Tax credit bonds are bonds in which the holder receives a tax credit in lieu of some or all of the interest on the bond.

You may be able to take a credit if you are a holder of one of the following bonds.

- Clean renewable energy bonds (issued before 2010).
- New clean renewable energy bonds.
- Qualified energy conservation bonds.
- Midwestern tax credit bonds.
- Qualified forestry conservation bonds.
- Qualified school construction bonds.
- Qualified zone academy bonds.
- Build America bonds.

In some instances, an issuer may elect to receive a credit for interest paid on the bond. If the issuer makes this election, you cannot also claim a credit.

Interest income. The amount of any tax credit allowed (figured before applying tax liability limits) must be included as interest income on your tax return.

How to take the credit. Complete Form 8912 and attach it to your Form 1040. Include the credit in your total for Form 1040, line 53. Check box c, and enter "8912" on the line next to that box.

TAXALERT

For 2011, if you are a holder of a tax credit bond, you may receive Form 1097-BTC, which will provide the amount of the credit you may be entitled to take against your tax liability.

More information. For more information, see the instructions for Form 8912.

Foreign Tax Credit

You generally can choose to take income taxes you paid or accrued during the year to a foreign country or U.S. possession as a credit against your U.S. income tax. Or, you can deduct them as an itemized deduction (see chapter 23).

You cannot take a credit (or deduction) for foreign income taxes paid on income that you exclude from U.S. tax under any of the following.

1. Foreign earned income exclusion.
2. Foreign housing exclusion.
3. Income from Puerto Rico exempt from U.S. tax.
4. Possession exclusion.

Limit on the credit. Unless you can elect not to file Form 1116 (see *Exception,* later), your foreign tax credit cannot be more than your U.S. tax liability (Form 1040, line 44), multiplied by a fraction. The numerator of the fraction is your taxable income from sources outside the United States. The denominator is your total taxable income from U.S. and foreign sources. See Publication 514 for more information.

EXPLANATION

To take the foreign tax credit, the foreign taxes must have been imposed on you, and you must have paid or accrued the taxes during your tax year. Furthermore, if you work overseas and elect to claim the foreign earned income exclusion or the foreign housing exclusion, the amount of foreign taxes eligible for credit is reduced. The foreign earned income exclusion allows U.S. citizens or residents, who meet one of the tests for living abroad, to exclude up to $92,900 in 2011 of foreign earned income from their gross income. The foreign housing exclusion allows U.S. citizens or residents to exclude excess foreign housing costs from their gross income. See chapter 41, *U.S. citizens working abroad: Tax treatment of foreign earned income*, for a more complete discussion of these subjects.

The amount you may claim as a foreign tax credit is limited. You can figure your maximum credit by performing the following calculation:

$$\frac{\text{Taxable income from sources outside the U.S.}}{\text{Taxable income from all sources}} \times \text{U.S. income tax} = \text{Maximum credit}$$

Separate foreign tax credit limitations must be calculated for passive income and several other categories.

However, while you are limited in the amount of credit for foreign taxes you may claim in any one year, you are able to carry back or carry forward the unused credits. See chapter 41, *U.S. citizens working abroad: Tax treatment of foreign earned income*, for a further discussion of how to calculate your foreign tax credit.

TAXALERT

For tax years beginning on or after October 23, 2004, you may carry back the unused credits for 1 year and carry forward the unused credits for 10 years.

TAXPLANNER

It is usually better to claim a credit for foreign taxes than to deduct them as itemized deductions. Credits reduce your U.S. tax on a dollar-for-dollar basis, whereas a deduction just reduces the amount of income subject to tax. (For an example of this point, see chapter 23, *Taxes you may deduct.*) Another advantage of claiming the credit is that you can choose to take the foreign tax credit even if you do not itemize your deductions. You then are allowed the standard deduction in addition to the credit.

How to take the credit. Complete Form 1116 and attach it to your Form 1040. Enter the credit on Form 1040, line 47.

Exception. You do not have to complete Form 1116 to take the credit if all of the following apply.

- All of your foreign source gross income was passive income, which generally includes interest and dividends.
- All of your foreign source gross income and the foreign tax paid on it were reported to you on a qualified payee statement, which includes Form 1099-INT and Form 1099-DIV.
- The total of your creditable foreign taxes was not more than $300 ($600 if married filing jointly).
- You elect this procedure for the tax year.

For more details on these requirements, see the instructions for Form 1116.

TAXPLANNER

If you cannot utilize all of your $300 ($600 if married filing jointly) foreign tax credit to offset income tax in the current year, you must file Form 1116 to carry the unused amount forward to future tax years, even if you meet all the other exceptions listed earlier.

Mortgage Interest Credit

The mortgage interest credit is intended to help lower-income individuals own a home. If you qualify, you can take the credit each year for part of the home mortgage interest you pay.

Who qualifies. You may be eligible for the credit if you were issued a qualified mortgage credit certificate (MCC) from your state or local government. Generally, an MCC is issued only in connection with a new mortgage for the purchase of your main home.

Amount of credit. Figure your credit on Form 8396. If your mortgage loan amount is equal to (or smaller than) the certified indebtedness (loan) amount shown on your MCC, enter on Form 8396, line 1, all the interest you paid on your mortgage during the year.

If your mortgage loan amount is larger than the certified indebtedness amount shown on your MCC, you can figure the credit on only part of the interest you paid. To find the amount to enter on line 1, multiply the total interest you paid during the year on your mortgage by the following fraction.

$$\frac{\text{Certified indebtedness amount on your MCC}}{\text{Original amount of your mortgage}}$$

Limit based on credit rate. If the certificate credit rate is more than 20%, the credit you are allowed cannot be more than $2,000. If two or more persons (other than a married couple filing a joint return) hold an interest in the home to which the MCC relates, this $2,000 limit must be divided based on the interest held by each person. See Publication 530 for more information.

Carryforward. Your credit (after applying the limit based on the credit rate) is also subject to a limit based on your tax that is figured using Form 8396. If your allowable credit is reduced because of this tax liability limit, you can carry forward the unused portion of the credit to the next 3 years or until used, whichever comes first.

If you are subject to the $2,000 limit because your certificate credit rate is more than 20%, you cannot carry forward any amount more than $2,000 (or your share of the $2,000 if you must divide the credit).

How to take the credit. Figure your 2011 credit and any carryforward to 2012 on Form 8396, and attach it to your Form 1040. Be sure to include any credit carryforward from 2008, 2009, and 2010.

Include the credit in your total for Form 1040, line 53. Check box c on that line and enter "8396" in the space next to that box.

Reduced home mortgage interest deduction. If you itemize your deductions on Schedule A (Form 1040), you must reduce your home mortgage interest deduction by the amount of the mortgage interest credit shown on Form 8396, line 3. You must do this even if part of that amount is to be carried forward to 2012. For more information about the home mortgage interest deduction, see chapter 24.

Recapture of federal mortgage subsidy. If you received an MCC with your mortgage loan, you may have to recapture (pay back) all or part of the benefit you received from that program. The recapture may be required if you sell or dispose of your home at a gain during the first 9 years after the date you closed your mortgage loan. See chapter 15 for more information.

Nonrefundable Credit for Prior Year Minimum Tax

The tax laws give special treatment to some kinds of income and allow special deductions and credits for some kinds of expenses. If you benefit from these laws, you may have to pay at least a minimum amount of tax in addition to any other tax on these items. This is called the alternative minimum tax.

The special treatment of some items of income and expenses only allows you to postpone paying tax until a later year. If in prior years you paid alternative minimum tax because of these tax postponement items, you may be able to take a credit for prior year minimum tax against your current year's regular tax.

You may be able to take a credit against your regular tax if for 2010 you had:

- An alternative minimum tax liability and adjustments or preferences other than exclusion items,
- A minimum tax credit that you are carrying forward to 2011, or
- An unallowed qualified electric vehicle credit.

Refundable credit. If you had a minimum tax credit carryforward to 2009 (on your 2008 Form 8801, line 31), you may qualify for a refund of that credit amount. For more information, see *Refundable Credit for Prior Year Minimum Tax*, later.

How to take the credit. Figure your 2011 nonrefundable credit (if any), and any carryforward to 2012 on Form 8801, and attach it to your Form 1040. Include the credit in your total for Form 1040, line 53, and check box b. You can carry forward any unused credit for prior year minimum tax to later years until it is completely used.

More information. For more information about the credit, see the instructions for Form 8801.

TAXPLANNER

If you report varying income from year to year, you may find yourself in a regular tax position in one year and in an AMT position the next. By accelerating income into an AMT year and deferring expenses until a regular tax year, you may take advantage of the different tax rates between the regular tax and the AMT. The effect of such a strategy is reduced due to the AMT credit, which is designed to even out the effect of AMT over time. However, the AMT credit will be of no benefit for AMT arising from the exclusion of items such as certain itemized deductions, certain tax-exempt interest, depletion, and the exclusion for gains on the sale of certain small business stock. This should be considered if you undertake any plans to defer or accelerate income or expenses.

TAXPLANNER

Where possible, you should arrange income and deductions so that any AMT incurred will result in an AMT credit that is quickly usable.

Plug-in Electric Drive Motor Vehicle Credit

You may be able to take this credit if you placed in service for business or personal use a qualified plug-in electric drive motor vehicle in 2011.

Generally, you can rely on the manufacturer's (or, in the case of a foreign manufacturer, its domestic distributor's) certification that a vehicle qualifies for the credit.

Amount of credit. The amount of the credit varies depending on the battery capacity and ranges from $2,500 to $7,500 per vehicle.

Qualified vehicle. A qualified plug-in electric drive motor vehicle is a motor vehicle the original use of which starts with you and that:

1. Has at least four wheels,
2. Is acquired for your use or lease and not for resale,
3. Is made by a manufacturer,
4. Is manufactured primarily for use on public streets, roads, and highways,
5. Has a gross vehicle weight rating of less than 14,000 pounds,
6. Is a motor vehicle for purposes of the Clean Air Act, and
7. Is propelled to a significant extent by an electric motor that draws electricity from a battery that:
   a. Has a capacity of at least 4 kilowatt hours, and
   b. Is capable of being recharged from an external source of electricity.

How to take the credit. To take the credit, you must complete Form 8936 and attach it to your Form 1040. Include the credit in your total for Form 1040, line 53. Check box c and enter "8936" on the line next to that box.

TAXALERT

The base amount of the plug-in credit is $2,500. If the qualified vehicle draws propulsion from a battery with at least five kilowatt hours of capacity, the credit increases by $417 for each extra kilowatt hour of battery capacity. The limit on the additional credit available is capped at $5,000. Consequently, the maximum credit per vehicle is $7,500. Taxpayers may claim the full amount of the allowable credit up to the end of the first calendar quarter in which the manufacturer records its 200,000th sale of a plug-in electric drive vehicle. The credit is reduced in following calendar quarters. The credit is allowed against the AMT.

TAXPLANNER

IRS Notice 2009-89 (available online at *www.irs.gov*) provides guidance for you to know when you can rely on the vehicle manufacturer's certification in determining whether a credit is allowable with respect to a vehicle.

Plug-in Electric Vehicle Credit

You may be able to take this credit if you acquired a qualified plug-in electric vehicle in 2011. For this credit, the vehicle can have 2, 3, or 4 wheels. A vehicle with 4 wheels must be a low speed vehicle.

Generally, you can rely on the manufacturer's (or, in the case of a foreign manufacturer, its domestic distributor's) certification that a vehicle qualifies for the credit.

Amount of credit. The credit is 10% of the cost of the vehicle, limited to $2,500 per vehicle.

Qualified vehicle. A qualified plug-in electric vehicle is a motor vehicle the original use of which starts with you and that:

1. Is acquired for your use or lease and not for resale,
2. Is made by a manufacturer,

3. Is manufactured primarily for use on public streets, roads, and highways,
4. Has a gross vehicle weight rating of less than 3,000 pounds if it has 4 wheels and less than 14,000 pounds if it has 2 or 3 wheels,
5. Is a low speed vehicle if it has 4 wheels, and
6. Is propelled to a significant extent by an electric motor that draws electricity from a battery that:
   a. Has a capacity of at least 4 kilowatt hours (2.5 kilowatt hours in the case of a vehicle with 2 or 3 wheels), and
   b. Is capable of being recharged from an external source of electricity.

How to take the credit. To take the credit, you must complete Form 8834 and attach it to your Form 1040. Include the credit in your total for Form 1040, line 53. Check box c and enter "8834" on the line next to that box.

> **TAXPLANNER**
> IRS Notice 2009-89 (available online at *www.irs.gov*) provides guidance for you to know when you can rely on the vehicle manufacturer's certification in determining whether a credit is allowable with respect to a vehicle.

Residential Energy Credits

You may be able to take one or both of the following credits if you made energy saving improvements to your home located in the United States in 2011.

- Nonbusiness energy property credit.
- Residential energy efficient property credit.

If you are a member of a condominium management association for a condominium you own or a tenant-stockholder in a cooperative housing corporation, you are treated as having paid your proportionate share of any costs of the association or corporation for purposes of these credits.

Nonbusiness energy property credit. You may be able to take a credit of 10% of the costs paid or incurred in 2011 for any qualified energy efficiency improvements and any residential energy property. Amounts provided by subsidized federal, state, or local energy financing do not qualify for the credit.

For 2011, the credit is limited as follows.

- A total combined credit limit of $500 for all tax years after 2005 (Form 5695, Part I).
- A combined credit limit of $200 for windows for all tax years after 2005.
- A maximum credit for residential energy property costs of $50 for any advanced main air circulating fan; $150 for any qualified natural gas, propane, or oil furnace, or hot water boiler; and $300 for any item of energy-efficient building property.

Text intentionally omitted.

Qualified energy efficiency improvements are the following improvements that are new, can be expected to remain in use at least 5 years, and meet certain requirements for energy efficiency.

- Any insulation material or system that is specifically and primarily designed to reduce heat loss or gain of a home.
- Exterior windows (including skylights).
- Exterior doors.
- Any metal or asphalt roof that has appropriate pigmented coatings or cooling granules specifically and primarily designed to reduce heat gain of the home.

Residential energy property is any of the following.

- Certain heat pump water heaters; electric heat pumps; central air conditioners; natural gas, propane, or oil water heaters; and stoves that use biomass fuel.
- Qualified natural gas, propane, or oil furnaces; and qualified natural gas, propane, or oil hot water boilers.
- Certain advanced main air circulating fans used in natural gas, propane, or oil furnaces.

For 2011, the energy-efficiency standards for qualified natural gas, propane, or oil furnaces, or hot water boilers have been increased. For more information, see Form 5695, Part I.

TAXALERT

Tax legislation enacted in 2010 extended the availability this credit, albeit at the levels that were in effect before the enactment of the *American Recovery and Reinvestment Act of 2009* on February 17, 2009. Unless Congress acts, the current credit will expire after December 31, 2011.

TAXPLANNER

You must reduce your basis in your property by the amount of the credit claimed.

TAXALERT

The December 2010 tax law that extended the so-called Bush tax cuts also extended the ability to offset both your regular tax liability and alternative minimum tax (AMT) liability with the nonbusiness energy property credit and also the residential energy efficient property credit (discussed later). See *Alternative Minimum Tax* in chapter 31, *How to figure your tax*, for more information on the AMT.

Residential energy efficient property credit. You may be able to take a credit of 30% of your costs of qualified solar electric property, solar water heating property, fuel cell property, small wind energy property, and geothermal heat pump property. The credit amount for costs paid for qualified fuel cell property is limited to $500 for each one-half kilowatt of capacity of the property.

Basis reduction. You must reduce the basis of your home by the amount of any credit allowed.

How to take the credit. Complete Form 5695 and attach it to your Form 1040. Enter the credit on Form 1040, line 52.

More information. For more information on this credit, see the instructions for Form 5695.

TAXALERT

This credit applies to property placed in service after December 31, 2005, and before January 1, 2017. The credit is equal to the sum of 30% of expenditures for the following:

- qualified solar electric property,
- qualified solar water heating,
- small wind energy property,
- qualified fuel cell property,
- qualified small wind energy property, and
- qualified geothermal heat pump property.

In the case of any amounts paid for qualified fuel cell property, the maximum credit is $500 for each 0.5 kilowatt of capacity.

The credit is nonrefundable and reduces the basis in the depreciable property it relates to. The credit may also be used to offset AMT. If the credit is limited (due to an overall limit on the various nonrefundable personal credits that are allowed in a tax year), it may be carried forward to the next tax year.

Retirement Savings Contributions Credit (Saver's Credit)

You may be able to take this credit if you, or your spouse if filing jointly, made:

- Contributions (other than rollover contributions) to a traditional or Roth IRA,
- Elective deferrals to a 401(k) or 403(b) plan (including designated Roth contributions) or to a governmental 457, SEP, or SIMPLE plan,
- Voluntary employee contributions to a qualified retirement plan (including the federal Thrift Savings Plan), or
- Contributions to a 501(c)(18)(D) plan.

However, you cannot take the credit if either of the following applies.

1. The amount on Form 1040, line 38, or Form 1040A, line 22, is more than $28,250 ($42,375 if head of household; $56,500 if married filing jointly).
2. The person(s) who made the qualified contribution or elective deferral (a) was born after December 31, 1993, (b) is claimed as a dependent on someone else's 2011 tax return, or (c) was a student (defined next).

Student. You were a student if during any part of 5 calendar months of 2011 you:

- Were enrolled as a full-time student at a school, or
- Took a full-time, on-farm training course given by a school or a state, county, or local government agency.

School. A school includes a technical, trade, or mechanical school. It does not include an on-the-job training course, correspondence school, or school offering courses only through the Internet.

How to take the credit. Figure the credit on Form 8880. Enter the credit on your Form 1040, line 50, or your Form 1040A, line 32, and attach Form 8880 to your return.

TAXALERT

The credit for savers is allowed to the full extent of your regular tax and alternative minimum tax. See *Alternative Minimum Tax* in chapter 31, *How to figure your tax*, for more information on the AMT.

Refundable Credits

The credits discussed in this part of the chapter are treated as payments of tax. If the total of these credits, withheld federal income tax, and estimated tax payments is more than your total tax, the excess can be refunded to you.

Adoption Credit

You may be able to take a tax credit of up to $13,360 for qualified expenses paid to adopt an eligible child. The credit may be allowed for the adoption of a child with special needs even if you do not have any qualified expenses.

If your modified adjusted gross income (AGI) is more than $185,210, your credit is reduced. If your modified AGI is $225,210 or more, you cannot take the credit.

TAXALERT

The adoption credit is fully refundable; you can receive a refund for the full amount of the credit you claim, even when your credit exceeds your tax liability.

Qualified adoption expenses. Qualified adoption expenses are reasonable and necessary expenses directly related to, and whose principal purpose is for, the legal adoption of an eligible child. These expenses include:

- Adoption fees,
- Court costs,
- Attorney fees,
- Travel expenses (including amounts spent for meals and lodging) while away from home, and
- Re-adoption expenses to adopt a foreign child.

Nonqualified expenses. Qualified adoption expenses do not include expenses:

- That violate state or federal law,
- For carrying out any surrogate parenting arrangement,
- For the adoption of your spouse's child,
- For which you received funds under any federal, state, or local program,
- Allowed as a credit or deduction under any other federal income tax rule, or
- Paid or reimbursed by your employer or any other person or organization.

Eligible child. The term "eligible child" means any individual:

- Under 18 years old, or
- Physically or mentally incapable of caring for himself or herself.

TAXALERT

Qualified adoption expenses eligible for the credit include expenses paid or incurred in an unsuccessful effort to adopt an otherwise eligible child who is a citizen or resident of the United States. In the case of a child who is not a citizen or resident of the United States, the credit is available only for adoptions that become final.

Child with special needs. An eligible child is a child with special needs if all three of the following apply.

1. The child was a citizen or resident of the United States (including U.S. possessions) at the time the adoption process began.
2. A state (including the District of Columbia) has determined that the child cannot or should not be returned to his or her parents' home.
3. The state has determined that the child will not be adopted unless assistance is provided to the adoptive parents. Factors used by states to make this determination include:
   a. The child's ethnic background,
   b. The child's age,
   c. Whether the child is a member of a minority or sibling group, and
   d. Whether the child has a medical condition or a physical, mental, or emotional handicap.

TAXALERT

In the case of the adoption of a child with special needs, you may claim a credit of $13,360 when the adoption becomes finalized, regardless of whether you have actually paid qualified adoption expenses.

When to take the credit. Generally, until the adoption becomes final, you take the credit in the year after your qualified expenses were paid or incurred. If the adoption becomes final, you take the credit in the year your expenses were paid or incurred. See the instructions for Form 8839 for more specific information on when to take the credit.

Foreign child. If the child is not a U.S. citizen or resident at the time the adoption process began, you cannot take the credit unless the adoption becomes final. You treat all adoption expenses paid or incurred in years before the adoption becomes final as paid or incurred in the year it becomes final.

Substantiation requirements. For 2011, you must include a copy of one or more adoption-related documents with your return to claim the credit.

Adoption finalized in the United States. For a domestic or foreign adoption finalized in the United States, you must provide a copy of an adoption order or decree.

Domestic adoptions that are not final. For domestic adoptions that are not final, you must include an adoption taxpayer identification number, obtained for the child, on your tax return or provide a copy of one of the following documents.

1. A home study completed by an authorized placement agency.
2. A placement agreement with an authorized placement agency.
3. A document signed by a hospital official authorizing the release of a newborn child from the hospital to you for legal adoption.
4. A court document ordering or approving the placement of a child with you for legal adoption.
5. An original affidavit or notarized statement, signed under penalties of perjury, from an adoption attorney, government official, or other person, stating that he or she (a) placed or is placing a child with you for legal adoption or (b) is facilitating the adoption process for you in an official capacity.

Adoptions of special needs children. If you are adopting a special needs child, you also must attach a copy of the state determination of special needs to your tax return.

For more information, including what documents to include for adoptions finalized outside of the United States, see the instructions for Form 8839.

TAXALERT

You may claim a credit for qualified adoption expenses of up to $13,360 per adopted child. The credit is phased out for taxpayers with an adjusted gross income between $185,210 and $225,210. Taxpayers with adjusted gross income of $225,210 or more are not entitled to the credit. Qualified adoption expenses include reasonable and necessary adoption fees, court costs, attorney fees, and other expenses that are directly related to the adoption of a child by the taxpayer. The principal purpose of the expenses must be the adoption of an eligible child. An eligible child is an individual who has not attained the age of 18 or who is physically or mentally incapable of caring for himself or herself. The expenses cannot be in violation of federal or state law or for carrying out any surrogate parenting arrangement. You may not claim a credit for expenses incurred in adopting the child of your spouse. You may also not claim a credit for expenses reimbursed by a program of your employer; a federal, state, or local program; or other types of programs. You are eligible for a separate credit for each child whom you adopt. Thus, you may claim a credit of up to $26,720 if you adopt two children and meet all of the other requirements.

How to take the credit. To take the credit, you must complete Form 8839 and attach it and your adoption-related documents to your Form 1040. Include the credit in your total for Form 1040, line 71, and check box b on that line.

TAXALERT

Beginning in 2010, proof of adoption must be attached to the tax return for the year you claim an adoption credit. For adoptions finalized in the United States, you must attach an adoption order or adoption decree to your tax returns. For foreign adoptions, required documentation differs depending on whether or not the adoption took place in a country that is party to the Hague Convention on Protection of Children and Co-operation in Respect of Intercountry Adoption (Hague Convention). If the foreign adoption took place in a Hague Convention party country, you must attach a Hague Adoption Certificate, IH-3 visa, or a foreign adoption decree translated into English. For adoptions in all other countries, the adoptive parents may attach a foreign adoption decree translated into English or an IR-2 or IR-3 visa.

If the credit claimed is for the adoption of a special needs child, you must also furnish documentation provided by your state that shows determination of special needs.

Credit for Tax on Undistributed Capital Gain

You must include in your income any amounts that regulated investment companies (commonly called mutual funds) or real estate investment trusts (REITs) allocated to you as capital gain distributions, even if you did not actually receive them. If the mutual fund or REIT paid a tax on the capital gain, you are allowed a credit for the tax since it is considered paid by you. The mutual fund or REIT will send you Form 2439, Notice to Shareholder of Undistributed Long-Term Capital Gains, showing your share of the undistributed capital gains and the tax paid, if any. Take the credit for the tax paid by entering the amount on Form 1040, line 71, and checking box a. Attach Copy B of Form 2439 to your return. See *Capital Gain Distributions* in chapter 8 for more information on undistributed capital gains.

First-Time Homebuyer Credit

In general, you can claim this credit if:

- You bought your main home in the United States before May 1, 2011 (before July 1, 2011, if you entered into a written binding contract before May 1, 2011, to buy the home before July 1, 2011), and
- *Text intentionally omitted.*
- You (or your spouse, if married) were on qualified official extended duty outside of the United States for at least 90 days between January 1, 2009, and May 1, 2010, as a member of the uniformed services or Foreign Service, or an employee of the intelligence community, and
- You did not purchase the home from a person related to you (or your spouse if you were married)

No credit is allowed for a home bought after April 30, 2011 (after June 30, 2011, if you entered into a written binding contract before May 1, 2011, to buy the home before July 1, 2011).

TAXALERT

The deadline for eligible members of the military and certain other federal employees to qualify for the first-time homebuyer credit was April 30, 2011. Members of the uniformed services or Foreign Service and employees of the intelligence community who are on qualified official extended duty outside the United States had to enter into a binding contract by April 30 and close on the purchase by June 30, 2011, to get a refundable tax credit of up to $8,000 when eligible. Individuals who served on qualified official extended duty outside of the United States for at least 90 days after December 31, 2008, and before May 1, 2010, were eligible for this special provision.

Text intentionally omitted.

Main home. Your main home is the one you live in most of the time. It can be a house, houseboat, mobile home, cooperative apartment, or condominium.

Home constructed by you. If you constructed your main home, you are treated as having bought it on the date you first occupied it.

Who cannot claim the credit. You cannot claim the credit if any of the following apply.

1. You are a nonresident alien.
2. Your home is located outside the United States.
3. You sell the home, or it stops being your main home, before the end of 2011.
4. You acquired your home by gift or inheritance.
5. Your modified adjusted gross income (MAGI) is $145,000 or more ($245,000 or more if married filing jointly). See *Modified adjusted gross income (MAGI)*, later.
6. Your purchase price is more than $800,000.
7. You can be claimed as a dependent on someone else's return.
8. You (and your spouse, if married) were younger than 18 when you bought the home.
9. You acquired your home from a related person. A related person includes:
   a. Your spouse, ancestors (parents, grandparents, etc.), or lineal descendants (children, grandchildren, etc.).
   b. Your spouse's ancestors or lineal descendants.
   c. A corporation in which you directly or indirectly own more than 50% in value of the outstanding stock of the corporation.
   d. A partnership in which you directly or indirectly own more than 50% of the capital interest or profits interest.

For more information about related persons, see *Nondeductible Loss* in chapter 2 of Publication 544, *Sales and Other Dispositions of Assets*.

Amount of the credit. Generally, the credit is the smaller of:

- $8,000 ($4,000 if married filing separately), or
- 10% of the purchase price of the home.

Text intentionally omitted. You are allowed the full amount of the credit if your MAGI is $125,000 or less ($225,000 or less if married filing jointly). The credit is reduced if MAGI is more than $125,000 ($225,000 if married filing jointly). The credit is completely eliminated if MAGI is $145,000 ($245,000 if married filing jointly) or more.

Modified adjusted gross income (MAGI). Your MAGI is the amount from Form 1040, line 38, increased by the total of any:

- Exclusion of income from Puerto Rico, and
- Amount from Form 2555, line 45 and line 50; Form 2555-EZ, line 18; and Form 4563, line 15.

Repayment of credit. If you bought the home after 2008, you generally must repay the credit if you dispose of the home or the home stops being your main home within the 36-month period beginning on the purchase date. This includes situations where you sell the home, you convert it to business or rental property, the home is destroyed, condemned, or disposed of under threat of condemnation, or the lender forecloses on the mortgage. You repay the credit by including it as additional tax on the return for the year the home stops being your main home. If the home continues to be your main home for at least 36 months beginning on the purchase date, you do not have to repay any of the credit.

If you and your spouse claim the credit on a joint return, each spouse is treated as having been allowed half of the credit for purposes of repaying the credit.

Exceptions. The following are exceptions to the repayment rule.

- If you sell the home to someone who is not related to you, the repayment in the year of sale is limited to the amount of gain on the sale. (See item 9 earlier under *Who cannot claim the credit* for the definition of a related person.) When figuring the gain, reduce the adjusted basis of the home by the amount of the credit.
- If the home is destroyed, condemned, or disposed of under threat of condemnation, and you acquire a new main home within 2 years of the event, you do not have to repay the credit.
- If, as part of a divorce settlement, the home is transferred to a spouse or former spouse, the spouse who receives the home is responsible for repaying the credit if required.
- If you die, repayment of the credit is not required. If you file a joint return and then you die, your surviving spouse must repay his or her half of the credit if required.
- In some cases, there is an exception for members of the uniformed services or Foreign Service and for intelligence community employees.

Home bought in 2008. If you claimed the credit for a home you bought in 2008, you generally must begin repaying it on your 2010 return and continue the repayment for 14 more years. In addition, you generally must repay any credit you claimed for a home you bought in 2008 if you sold the home in 2011 or the home stopped being your main home in 2011. However, you do not have to repay the credit if one of the exceptions to the repayment rule applies.

EXPLANATION

The credit claimed on a home you bought in 2008 essentially operates much like an interest-free loan.

How to take the credit. To take the credit, complete Form 5405 and attach it to your Form 1040. Enter your credit on Form 1040, line 67.

How to repay the credit. If you are required to repay the credit, complete Parts III and IV of Form 5405. Attach the form to your Form 1040. Include the repayment on Form 1040, line 59b.

More information. For more information, including special rules for members of the Armed Forces, see Form 5405 and its instructions.

Health Coverage Tax Credit

TAXALERT

Under the American Recovery and Reinvestment Act (ARRA), the credit decreases from 80% to 65% for amounts paid for qualified health insurance coverage after February 2011.

You may be able to take this credit for any month in which all the following statements were true on the first day of the month.

- You were an eligible trade adjustment assistance (TAA) recipient, alternative TAA (ATAA) recipient, reemployment TAA (RTAA) recipient, or Pension Benefit Guaranty Corporation (PBGC) pension recipient (defined later).
- You were covered by a qualified health insurance plan for which you paid the entire premiums, or your portion of the premiums, directly to your health plan (including months for which you paid premiums to "U.S. Treasury–HCTC").
- You were not entitled to Medicare Part A or enrolled in Medicare Part B or C.
- You were not enrolled in Medicaid or the Children's Health Insurance Program (CHIP).
- You were not enrolled in the Federal Employees Health Benefits Program (FEHBP) or eligible to receive benefits under the U.S. military health system (TRICARE).
- You were not imprisoned under federal, state, or local authority.
- Your employer did not pay 50% or more of the cost of coverage.
- You did not receive a 65% COBRA premium reduction from your former employer or COBRA administrator.

But, you cannot take the credit if you can be claimed as a dependent on someone else's 2011 tax return. If you meet all of these conditions, you may be able to take a credit in 2011 of up to 80% for the months of January and February and 65% of the amount you paid for March through December for qualified health insurance coverage for you and any qualifying family members. You cannot take the credit for insurance premiums on coverage that was partially paid for with a National Emergency Grant. The amount you paid for qualified health insurance coverage must be reduced by any Archer MSA and health savings account distributions used to pay for the coverage.

You can take this credit on your tax return or have it paid on your behalf in advance to your insurance company. If the credit is paid on your behalf in advance, that amount will reduce the amount of the credit you can take on your tax return.

TAA recipient. You were an eligible TAA recipient on the first day of the month if, for any day in that month or the prior month, you:

- Received a trade readjustment allowance, or
- Would have been entitled to receive such an allowance except that you had not exhausted all rights to any unemployment insurance (except additional compensation that is funded by a state and is not reimbursed from any federal funds) to which you were entitled (or would be entitled if you applied).

Example. You received a trade adjustment allowance for January 2011. You were an eligible TAA recipient on the first day of January and February.

Alternative TAA recipient. You were an eligible alternative TAA recipient on the first day of the month if, for that month or the prior month, you received benefits under an alternative trade adjustment assistance program for older workers established by the Department of Labor.

Example. You received benefits under an alternative trade adjustment assistance program for older workers for October 2011. The program was established by the Department of Labor. You were an eligible alternative TAA recipient on the first day of October and November.

RTAA recipient. You were an eligible RTAA recipient on the first day of the month if, for that month or the prior month, you received benefits under a reemployment trade adjustment assistance program for older workers established by the Department of Labor.

Example. You received benefits under a reemployment trade adjustment assistance program for older workers for January 2011. The program was established by the Department of Labor. You were an eligible RTAA recipient on the first day of January and February.

PBGC pension recipient. You were an eligible PBGC pension recipient on the first day of the month, if both of the following apply.

1. You were age 55 or older on the first day of the month.
2. You received a benefit for that month that was paid by the PBGC under title IV of the Employee Retirement Income Security Act of 1974 (ERISA).

If you received a lump-sum payment from the PBGC after August 5, 2002, you meet item (2) above for any month that you would have received a PBGC benefit if you had not received the lump-sum payment.

TAXALERT

For January and February 2011, spouses and dependents (family members) are considered recipients and are eligible to receive the Health Coverage Tax Credit in the event that the TAA, ATAA, or RTAA recipient or PBGC payee dies or with whom they finalized a divorce. Qualified family members can receive the credit for up to 24 months from the event, ending in February 2011. Months after February 2011 cannot be claimed. For example, your spouse was a PBGC payee and died on August 20, 2010. You are eligible to receive the HCTC for August 2010 through February 2011.

How to take the credit. To take the credit, complete Form 8885 and attach it to your Form 1040. Include your credit in the total for Form 1040, line 71, and check box d.

You must attach invoices and proof of payment for any amounts you include on Form 8885, line 2. For details, see Publication 502 or Form 8885.

More information. For definitions and special rules, including those relating to qualified health insurance plans, qualifying family members, the effect of certain life events, and employer-sponsored health insurance plans, see Publication 502 and the instructions for Form 8885.
Text intentionally omitted.

Refundable Credit for Prior Year Minimum Tax

If you paid the alternative minimum tax for 2010 or you had a minimum tax credit carryforward to 2011, you may be able to take a credit for prior year minimum tax. For information about the nonrefundable credit for prior year minimum tax you may be able to take, see Nonrefundable Credit for Prior Year Minimum Tax, earlier. However, for 2011, you may qualify for a refundable credit for prior year minimum tax if you had a minimum tax credit carryforward to 2009 (on your 2008 Form 8801, line 28) and you have not used all of that carryforward, even if the total amount of your current year credit is more than your total tax liability. To figure the amount of any 2011 refundable credit, complete Part IV of Form 8801. Include any refundable credit on Form 1040, line 71, and check box c.

TAXALERT

Accelerated Recovery of Alternative Minimum Tax (AMT) Refundable Credit. A 2008 tax law accelerated the amount of refundable AMT credit you may recover for AMT you paid in past years to the extent that your AMT liability was attributable to the exercise of incentive stock options and other deferral adjustments. Under this law, 50% of long-term unused minimum tax credits may be refunded over each of 2 years, rather than 20% a year over 5 years. Additionally, the adjusted gross income phaseout is eliminated. As a result of these changes, you are able to recover the entire balance of long-term unused minimum tax credits over 2 years regardless of your adjusted gross income. Since this is a refundable credit, you can receive a refund even when the credit exceeds your total tax liability for the year.

TAXALERT

This refundable credit is available for unused minimum tax credits that are attributable to deferral adjustments. Deferral items—such as accelerated depreciation or the spread on incentive stock options (ISO)—are those that have the effect of reducing your regular taxable income relative to alternative minimum taxable income in early years, but subsequently the situation reverses over time. This provision may be particularly beneficial to option holders who recognized large ISO adjustments in a year they exercised ISOs. Such taxpayers may have generated taxable income for calculating AMT that far exceeded their average annual income and, as a consequence, faced substantial AMT bills that were a challenge to pay. Furthermore, these taxpayers are often unable to utilize any significant portion of available minimum tax credits in subsequent years.

For 2011, a portion of any unused minimum tax credit carryforward from 2007 or earlier years may be refunded. Your long-term unused minimum tax credit is the amount of your minimum tax credit carryforward from 2007 reduced by the amount of any minimum tax credits you claimed for 2008, 2009, and 2010.

Since this provision expires after 2012 for calendar year taxpayers, only those unused credits that arose before 2009 can be eligible for recovery as a refundable credit. Unused credits realized after 2008 can only be claimed under the preexisting rules for claiming minimum tax credits.

Example

Assume in 2011 you have a regular tax of $45,000, a tentative minimum tax of $40,000, no other credits allowable, and a minimum tax credit for the taxable year (before limitation) of $1.1 million, of which $1 million is a long-term unused minimum tax credit.

The AMT refundable credit amount for the taxable year is calculated as follows:

1. The lesser of $5,000 or long-term unused minimum credit	$5,000
2. 50% of long-term unused credit $1,000,000 × 50%	$500,000
The greater of these lines 1 and 2	$500,000
AMT refundable credit	$500,000

In this example, you are able to claim a $500,000 credit, which is $460,000 more than the total taxes due for the year. The remaining $600,000 minimum tax credit is carried forward to future tax years.

Credit for Excess Social Security Tax or Railroad Retirement Tax Withheld

TAXALERT

Since 1994, there has not been a cap on wages subject to the 1.45% Medicare tax. However, there is still a cap for social security taxes. In 2011, employees are subject to 4.2% social security tax on the first $106,800 of wages. If you worked for two or more employers during the year, you may have had excess social security or railroad retirement taxes withheld on your wages, for which you can claim a credit.

Caution

All wages are subject to Medicare tax withholding.

Tip

Use Form 843, Claim for Refund and Request for Abatement, to claim a refund of excess tier 2 RRTA tax. Be sure to attach a copy of all of your W-2 forms. See the worksheet in Publication 505, Tax Withholding and Estimated Tax, *to help you figure the excess amount.*

Most employers must withhold social security tax from your wages. If you work for a railroad employer, that employer must withhold tier 1 railroad retirement (RRTA) tax and tier 2 RRTA tax.

If you worked for two or more employers in 2011, you may have had too much social security or tier 1 RRTA tax withheld from your pay. You can claim the excess social security or tier 1 RRTA tax as a credit against your income tax. The following table shows the maximum amount of wages subject to tax and the maximum amount of tax that should have been withheld for 2011.

Type of tax	Maximum wages subject to tax	Maximum tax that should have been withheld
Social security or RRTA tier 1	$106,800	$4,485.60
RRTA tier 2	$79,200	$3,088.80

Employer's error. If any one employer withheld too much social security or tier 1 RRTA tax, you cannot take the excess as a credit against your income tax. The employer should adjust the tax for you. If the employer does not adjust the overcollection, you can file a claim for refund using Form 843.

Joint return. If you are filing a joint return, you cannot add the social security or tier 1 RRTA tax withheld from your spouse's wages to the amount withheld from your wages. Figure the withholding separately for you and your spouse to determine if either of you has excess withholding.

EXAMPLES

Example 1

Marie Gibson earned $108,000 during 2011. Her sole employer for the year inadvertently withheld $7,000 in social security and Medicare taxes from her salary. The amount that should have been withheld was $6,051.60 (4.2% × $106,800 plus 1.45% × $108,000). She may not claim the $948.40 overwithholding as a credit on her return. Instead, her employer should adjust her next check for this amount.

Example 2

Assume instead that Marie worked for two different employers during the year, and that her total withholding for social security and Medicare taxes was $7,000. She should now claim the $948.40 excess withholding as a credit.

How to figure the credit if you did not work for a railroad. If you did not work for a railroad during 2011, figure the credit as follows:

1. Add all social security tax withheld (but not more than $4,485.60 for each employer). Enter the total here	______
2. Enter any uncollected social security tax on tips or group-term life insurance included in the total on Form 1040, line 61	______
3. Add lines 1 and 2. If $4,485.60 or less, stop here. You cannot take the credit	______
4. Social security tax limit	4,485.60
5. Credit. Subtract line 4 from line 3. Enter the result here and on Form 1040, line 69 (or Form 1040A, line 44)	______

Example. You are married and file a joint return with your spouse who had no gross income in 2011. During 2011, you worked for the Brown Technology Company and earned $60,000 in wages. Social security tax of $2,520 was withheld. You also worked for another employer in 2011 and earned $55,000 in wages. $2,310 of social security tax was withheld from these wages. Because you worked for more than one employer and your total wages were more than $106,800, you can take a credit of $344.40 for the excess social security tax withheld.

1. Add all social security tax withheld (but not more than $4,485.60 for each employer). Enter the total here	$4,830.00
2. Enter any uncollected social security tax on tips or group-term life insurance included in the total on Form 1040, line 61	-0-
3. Add lines 1 and 2. If $4,485.60 or less, stop here. You cannot take the credit	4,830.00
4. Social security tax limit	4,485.60
5. Credit. Subtract line 4 from line 3. Enter the result here and on Form 1040, line 69 (or Form 1040A, line 44)	$344.40

How to figure the credit if you worked for a railroad. If you were a railroad employee at any time during 2011, figure the credit as follows:

1. Add all social security and tier 1 RRTA tax withheld (but not more than $4,485.60 for each employer). Enter the total here	
2. Enter any uncollected social security and tier 1 RRTA tax on tips or group-term life insurance included in the total on Form 1040, line 61	
3. Add lines 1 and 2. If $4,485.60 or less, stop here. You cannot take the credit	
4. Social security and tier 1 RRTA tax limit	4,485.60
5. Credit. Subtract line 4 from line 3. Enter the result here and on Form 1040, line 69 (or Form 1040A, line 44)	

How to take the credit. Enter the credit on Form 1040, line 69, or include it in the total for Form 1040A, line 44.

EXAMPLE

In 2011, Maurice Evans worked for a railroad for 7 months and had $1,573.00 in tier 1 railroad retirement tax, $601.75 in Medicare tax, and $1,826.00 in tier 2 railroad retirement tax withheld. He worked the remaining 5 months for a nonrailroad employer and had $3,705.00 in social security tax and $1,100.36 in Medicare tax withheld. He had no income from tips or group-term life insurance on either job. His credit is calculated as follows:

1. Total social security and tier 1 RRTA tax withheld (do not include more than $4,485.60 for each employer)	$5,278.00
2. Total social security and tier 1 RRTA tax on tips or group-term life insurance included on line 61, Form 1040	0
3. Total: Add lines 1 and 2	5,278.00
4. Limit	$4,485.60
5. Credit: Subtract line 4 from line 3	$792.40

Earned Income Credit (EIC)

What's New

Earned income amount is more. The maximum amount of income you can earn and still get the credit has increased. You may be able to take the credit if:

- You have three or more qualifying children and you earned less than $43,998 ($49,078 if married filing jointly),

- You have two qualifying children and you earned less than $40,964 ($46,044 if married filing jointly),
- You have one qualifying child and you earned less than $36,052 ($41,132 if married filing jointly), or
- You do not have a qualifying child and you earned less than $13,660 ($18,740 if married filing jointly).

Your adjusted gross income also must be less than the amount in the above list that applies to you. For details, see Rules 1 and 15.

What's New for 2012

You can no longer get advance payments of the credit in your pay during the year as you could in 2010 and earlier years. This is because the law changed. However, if you are eligible, you will still be able to claim the credit on your return, as explained in this chapter.

TAXALERT

A 2010 tax law eliminates the ability for taxpayers to elect to receive advance payments through their paychecks of their refundable portion of the EIC. Beginning in 2011, taxpayers eligible for the refundable portion of the EIC will need to wait to claim a refund on their tax return filed by April 15 of the following year.

TAXPLANNER

You can still effectively receive the nonrefundable portion of the EIC through the your paycheck, by adjusting withholding, to the extent you otherwise have positive tax liability.

Reminders

Increased EIC on certain joint returns. A married person filing a joint return may get more EIC than someone with the same income but a different filing status. As a result, the EIC table has different columns for married persons filing jointly than for everyone else. When you look up your EIC in the EIC Table, be sure to use the correct column for your filing status and the number of children you have.

Online help. You can use the EITC Assistant at www.irs.gov/eitc to find out if you are eligible for the credit. The EITC Assistant is available in English and Spanish.

EIC questioned by IRS. The IRS may ask you to provide documents to prove you are entitled to claim the EIC. We will tell you what documents to send us. These may include: birth certificates, school records, medical records, etc. We will also send you a letter with the name, address, and telephone number of the IRS employee assigned to your case. The process of establishing your eligibility will delay your refund.

The earned income credit (EIC) is a tax credit for certain people who work and have less than $49,078 of earned income. A tax credit usually means more money in your pocket. It reduces the amount of tax you owe. The EIC may also give you a refund.

How do you get the earned income credit? To claim the EIC, you must:

1. Qualify by meeting certain rules, and
2. File a tax return, even if you:
   a. Do not owe any tax,
   b. Did not earn enough money to file a return, or
   c. Did not have income taxes withheld from your pay.

When you complete your return, you can figure your EIC by using a worksheet in the instructions for Form 1040, Form 1040A, or Form 1040EZ. Or, if you prefer, you can let the IRS figure the credit for you.

TAXALERT

The EIC is a credit available to certain low-income taxpayers. For 2011, a taxpayer without any qualifying children (see later) may be eligible for a maximum credit of $464.

A taxpayer with one child may be eligible for a maximum credit of $3,094 for 2011, while a taxpayer with two qualifying children may be eligible for a maximum credit of $5,112, and a taxpayer with three or more qualifying children may be eligible for a maximum credit of $5,751.

TAXALERT

You are not eligible to claim the EIC if your investment income exceeds $3,150 in 2011. Investment income includes dividends, interest, tax-exempt interest, net capital gain, net passive income, and net rental and royalty income not derived in the ordinary course of a trade or business.

TAXALERT

Taxpayers claiming the EIC must include a taxpayer identification number for themselves, their spouses (if married), and any qualifying children on the return. For this purpose only, a taxpayer identification number is a social security number issued by the Social Security Administration, rather than one issued to an individual for the purpose of applying for federally funded benefits.

How will this section help you? This section will explain the following.

- The rules you must meet to qualify for the EIC.
- How to figure the EIC.

Useful Items

You may want to see:

Publication

- □ **596** Earned Income Credit (EIC)

Form (and Instructions)

- □ **Schedule EIC** Earned Income Credit (Qualifying Child Information)
- □ **8862** Information To Claim Earned Income Credit After Disallowance

TAXALERT

You must file a tax return to receive the earned income credit. If the tax you owe is less than the amount of the earned income credit, you will receive a refund from the government. Therefore, even if you are not required to file a tax return because your income is less than the income required to file, you still must do so in order to receive the credit.

Do You Qualify for the Credit?

To qualify to claim the EIC, you must first meet all of the rules explained in *Part A, Rules for Everyone*. Then you must meet the rules in *Part B, Rules If You Have a Qualifying Child*, or *Part C, Rules If You Do Not Have a Qualifying Child*. There is one final rule you must meet in *Part D, Figuring and Claiming the EIC*. You qualify for the credit if you meet all the rules in each part that applies to you.

- If you have a qualifying child, the rules in *Parts A, B,* and *D* apply to you.
- If you do not have a qualifying child, the rules in *Parts A, C,* and *D* apply to you.

Table 37-1, Earned Income Credit in a Nutshell. Use Table 37-1 as a guide to *Parts A, B, C,* and *D*. The table is a summary of all the rules in each part.

Do you have a qualifying child? You have a qualifying child only if you have a child who meets the four tests described in *Rule 8* and illustrated in Figure 37-1.

If Improper Claim Made in Prior Year

If your EIC for any year after 1996 was denied or reduced for any reason other than a math or clerical error, you must attach a completed Form 8862 to your next tax return to claim the EIC. You must also qualify to claim the EIC by meeting all the rules described in this chapter.

Table 37-1. **Earned Income Credit in a Nutshell**

First, you must meet all the rules in this column.		**Second, you must meet all the rules in *one* of these columns, whichever applies.**		**Third, you must meet the rule in this column.**
Part A. Rules for Everyone		**Part B. Rules If You Have a Qualifying Child**	**Part C. Rules If You Do Not Have a Qualifying Child**	**Part D. Figuring and Claiming the EIC**
1. Your adjusted gross income (AGI) must be less than: • $43,998 ($49,078 for married filing jointly) if you have three or more qualifying children, • $40,964 ($46,044 for married filing jointly) if you have two qualifying children, • $36,052 ($41,132 for married filing jointly) if you have one qualifying child, or • $13,660 ($18,740 for married filing jointly) if you do not have a qualifying child.	**2.** You must have a valid social security number. **3.** Your filing status cannot be "Married filing separately." **4.** You must be a U.S. citizen or resident alien all year. **5.** You cannot file Form 2555 or Form 2555-EZ (relating to foreign earned income). **6.** Your investment income must be $3,150 or less. **7.** You must have earned income.	**8.** Your child must meet the relationship, age, residency, and joint return tests. **9.** Your qualifying child cannot be used by more than one person to claim the EIC. **10.** You cannot be a qualifying child of another person.	**11.** You must be at least age 25 but under age 65. **12.** You cannot be the dependent of another person. **13.** You cannot be a qualifying child of another person. **14.** You must have lived in the United States more than half of the year.	**15.** Your earned income must be less than: • $43,998 ($49,078 for married filing jointly) if you have three or more qualifying children, • $40,964 ($46,044 for married filing jointly) if you have two qualifying children, • $36,052 ($41,132 for married filing jointly) if you have one qualifying child, or • $13,660 ($18,740 for married filing jointly) if you do not have a qualifying child.

However, if your EIC was denied or reduced as a result of a math or clerical error, do not attach Form 8862 to your next tax return. For example, if your arithmetic is incorrect, the IRS can correct it. If you do not provide a correct social security number, the IRS can deny the EIC. These kinds of errors are called math or clerical errors.

If your EIC for any year after 1996 was denied and it was determined that your error was due to reckless or intentional disregard of the EIC rules, then you cannot claim the EIC for the next 2 years. If your error was due to fraud, then you cannot claim the EIC for the next 10 years.

More information. See chapter 5 in Publication 596 for more detailed information about the disallowance period and Form 8862.

Part A. Rules for Everyone

This part of the chapter discusses Rules 1 through 7. You must meet all seven rules to qualify for the earned income credit. If you do not meet all seven rules, you cannot get the credit and you do not need to read the rest of the chapter.

If you meet all seven rules in this part, then read either Part B or Part C (whichever applies) for more rules you must meet.

Rule 1. Your AGI Must Be Less Than:

- $43,998 ($49,078 for married filing jointly) if you have three or more qualifying children,
- $40,964 ($46,044 for married filing jointly) if you have two qualifying children,
- $36,052 ($41,132 for married filing jointly) if you have one qualifying child, or
- $13,660 ($18,740 for married filing jointly) if you do not have a qualifying child.

Adjusted gross income (AGI). AGI is the amount on line 38 (Form 1040), line 22 (Form 1040A), or line 4 (Form 1040EZ). If your AGI is equal to or more than the applicable limit listed above, you cannot claim the EIC.

Example. Your AGI is $36,550, you are single, and you have one qualifying child. You cannot claim the EIC because your AGI is not less than $36,052. However, if your filing status was married filing jointly, you might be able to claim the EIC because your AGI is less than $41,132.

Community property. If you are married, but qualify to file as head of household under special rules for married taxpayers living apart (see Rule 3), and live in a state that has community property laws, your AGI includes that portion of both your and your spouse's wages that you are required to include in gross income. This is different from the community property rules that apply under <u>*Rule 7*</u>.

Rule 2. You Must Have a Valid Social Security Number (SSN)

To claim the EIC, you (and your spouse if filing a joint return) must have a valid SSN issued by the Social Security Administration (SSA). Any qualifying child listed on Schedule EIC also must have a valid SSN. (See <u>*Rule 8*</u> if you have a qualifying child.)

If your social security card (or your spouse's if filing a joint return) says "Not valid for employment" and your SSN was issued so that you (or your spouse) could get a federally funded benefit, you cannot get the EIC. An example of a federally funded benefit is Medicaid.

If you have a card with the legend "Not valid for employment" and your immigration status has changed so that you are now a U.S. citizen or permanent resident, ask the SSA for a new social security card without the legend.

U.S. citizen. If you were a U.S. citizen when you received your SSN, you have a valid SSN.

Valid for work only with INS or DHS authorization. If your social security card reads "Valid for work only with INS authorization," or "Valid for work only with DHS authorization," you have a valid SSN.

SSN missing or incorrect. If an SSN for you or your spouse is missing from your tax return or is incorrect, you may not get the EIC.

Other taxpayer identification number. You cannot get the EIC if, instead of an SSN, you (or your spouse if filing a joint return) have an individual taxpayer identification number (ITIN). ITINs are issued by the Internal Revenue Service to noncitizens who cannot get an SSN.

No SSN. If you do not have a valid SSN, put "No" next to line 64a (Form 1040), line 38a (Form 1040A), or line 8a (Form 1040EZ). You cannot claim the EIC.

Getting an SSN. If you (or your spouse if filing a joint return) do not have an SSN, you can apply for one by filing Form SS-5, Application for a Social Security Card, with the SSA. You can get Form SS-5 online at <u>*www.socialsecurity. gov*</u>, from your local SSA office, or by calling the SSA at 1-800-772-1213.

Filing deadline approaching and still no SSN. If the filing deadline is approaching and you still do not have an SSN, you have two choices.

1. Request an automatic 6-month extension of time to file your return. You can get this extension by filing Form 4868, Application for Automatic Extension of Time to File U.S. Individual Income Tax Return. For more information, see <u>chapter 1</u>.
2. File the return on time without claiming the EIC. After receiving the SSN, file an amended return (Form 1040X, Amended U.S. Individual Income Tax Return) claiming the EIC. Attach a filled-in Schedule EIC if you have a qualifying child.

Rule 3. Your Filing Status Cannot Be Married Filing Separately

If you are married, you usually must file a joint return to claim the EIC. Your filing status cannot be "Married filing separately."

Spouse did not live with you. If you are married and your spouse did not live in your home at any time during the last 6 months of the year, you may be able to file as head of household, instead of married filing separately. In that case, you may be able to claim the EIC. For detailed information about filing as head of household, see <u>chapter 2</u>.

Rule 4. You Must Be a U.S. Citizen or Resident Alien All Year

If you (or your spouse, if married) were a nonresident alien for any part of the year, you cannot claim the earned income credit unless your filing status is married filing jointly. You can use that filing status only if one spouse is a U.S. citizen or resident alien and you choose to treat the nonresident spouse as a U.S. resident. If you make this choice, you and your spouse are taxed on your worldwide income. If you (or your spouse, if married) were a nonresident alien for any part of the year and your filing status is not married filing jointly, enter "No" on the dotted line next to line 64a (Form 1040) or in the space to the left of line 38a (Form 1040A). If you need more information on making this choice, get Publication 519, *U.S. Tax Guide for Aliens*.

Rule 5. You Cannot File Form 2555 or Form 2555-EZ

You cannot claim the earned income credit if you file Form 2555, Foreign Earned Income, or Form 2555-EZ, Foreign Earned Income Exclusion. You file these forms to exclude income earned in foreign countries from your gross income, or to deduct or exclude a foreign housing amount. U.S. possessions are not foreign countries. See Publication 54, *Tax Guide for U.S. Citizens and Resident Aliens Abroad*, for more detailed information.

Rule 6. Your Investment Income Must Be $3,150 or Less

You cannot claim the earned income credit unless your investment income is $3,150 or less. If your investment income is more than $3,150, you cannot claim the credit. For most people, investment income is the total of the following amounts.

- Taxable interest (line 8a of Form 1040 or 1040A).
- Tax-exempt interest (line 8b of Form 1040 or 1040A).
- Dividend income (line 9a of Form 1040 or 1040A).
- Capital gain net income (line 13 of Form 1040, if more than zero, or line 10 of Form 1040A).

If you file Form 1040EZ, your investment income is the total of the amount of line 2 and the amount of any tax-exempt interest you wrote to the right of the words "Form 1040EZ" on line 2.

However, see *Rule 6* in chapter 1 of Publication 596 if:

- You are filing Schedule E (Form 1040), Form 4797, or Form 8814,
- You are reporting income from the rental of personal property on Form 1040, line 21, or
- You are a member of a qualified joint venture that is a passive activity reporting on Schedule C or C-EZ (Form 1040) rental real estate income not subject to self-employment tax.

Rule 7. You Must Have Earned Income

This credit is called the "earned income" credit because, to qualify, you must work and have earned income. If you are married and file a joint return, you meet this rule if at least one spouse works and has earned income. If you are an employee, earned income includes all the taxable income you get from your employer. If you are self-employed or a statutory employee, you will figure your earned income on EIC Worksheet B in the instructions for Form 1040.

Earned Income

Earned income includes all of the following types of income.

1. Wages, salaries, tips, and other taxable employee pay. Employee pay is earned income only if it is taxable. Nontaxable employee pay, such as certain dependent care benefits and adoption benefits, is not earned income. But there is an exception for nontaxable combat pay, which you can choose to include in earned income, as explained below.
2. Net earnings from self-employment.
3. Gross income received as a statutory employee.

Wages, salaries, and tips. Wages, salaries, and tips you receive for working are reported to you on Form W-2, in box 1. You should report these on line 1 (Form 1040EZ) or line 7 (Forms 1040A and 1040).

Nontaxable combat pay election. You can elect to include your nontaxable combat pay in earned income for the earned income credit. Electing to include nontaxable combat pay in earned income may increase or decrease your EIC. Figure the credit with and without your nontaxable combat pay before making the election. If you make the election, you must include in earned income all nontaxable combat pay you received. If you are filing a joint return and both you and your spouse received nontaxable combat pay, you can each make your own election. The amount of your nontaxable combat pay should be shown in box 12 of your Form W-2 with code "Q".

Self-employed persons and statutory employees. If you are self-employed or received income as a statutory employee, you must use the Form 1040 instructions to see if you qualify to get the EIC.

Approved Form 4361 or Form 4029

This section is for persons who have an approved:

- Form 4361, Application for Exemption From Self-Employment Tax for Use by Ministers, Members of Religious Orders and Christian Science Practitioners, or
- Form 4029, Application for Exemption From Social Security and Medicare Taxes and Waiver of Benefits.

Each approved form exempts certain income from social security taxes. Each form is discussed here in terms of what is or is not earned income for the EIC.

Form 4361. Even if you have an approved Form 4361, amounts you received for performing ministerial duties as an employee count as earned income. This includes wages, salaries, tips, and other taxable employee compensation. A nontaxable housing allowance or the nontaxable rental value of a home is not earned income. Also, amounts you received for performing ministerial duties, but not as an employee, do not count as earned income. Examples include fees for performing marriages and honoraria for delivering speeches.

Form 4029. Even if you have an approved Form 4029, all wages, salaries, tips, and other taxable employee compensation count as earned income. However, amounts you received as a self-employed individual do not count as earned income. Also, in figuring earned income, do not subtract losses on Schedule C, C-EZ, or F from wages on line 7 of Form 1040.

Disability Benefits

If you retired on disability, taxable benefits you receive under your employer's disability retirement plan are considered earned income until you reach minimum retirement age. Minimum retirement age generally is the earliest age at which you could have received a pension or annuity if you were not disabled. You must report your taxable disability payments on line 7 of either Form 1040 or Form 1040A until you reach minimum retirement age.

Beginning on the day after you reach minimum retirement age, payments you receive are taxable as a pension and are not considered earned income. Report taxable pension payments on Form 1040, lines 16a and 16b (or Form 1040A, lines 12a and 12b).

Disability insurance payments. Payments you received from a disability insurance policy that you paid the premiums for are not earned income. It does not matter whether you have reached minimum retirement age. If this policy is through your employer, the amount may be shown in box 12 of your Form W-2 with code "J."

Income That Is Not Earned Income

Examples of items that are not earned income include interest and dividends, pensions and annuities, social security and railroad retirement benefits (including disability benefits), alimony and child support, welfare benefits, workers' compensation benefits, unemployment compensation (insurance), nontaxable foster care payments, and veterans' benefits, including VA rehabilitation payments. Do not include any of these items in your earned income.

Earnings while an inmate. Amounts received for work performed while an inmate in a penal institution are not earned income when figuring the earned income credit. This includes amounts for work performed while in a work release program or while in a halfway house.

Workfare payments. Nontaxable workfare payments are not earned income for the EIC. These are cash payments certain people receive from a state or local agency that administers public assistance programs funded under the federal Temporary Assistance for Needy Families (TANF) program in return for certain work activities such as (1) work experience activities (including remodeling or repairing public housing) if sufficient private sector employment is not available, or (2) community service program activities.

Conservation Reserve Program (CRP) payments. If you were receiving social security retirement benefits or social security disability benefits at the time you received any CRP payments, your CRP payments are not earned income for the EIC.

Community property. If you are married, but qualify to file as head of household under special rules for married taxpayers living apart (see *Rule 3*), and live in a state that has community property laws, your earned income for the EIC does not include any amount earned by your spouse that is treated as belonging to you under those laws. That amount is not earned income for the EIC, even though you must include it in your gross income on your income tax return. Your earned income includes the entire amount you earned, even if part of it is treated as belonging to your spouse under your state's community property laws.

Nontaxable military pay. Nontaxable pay for members of the Armed Forces is not considered earned income for the EIC. Examples of nontaxable military pay are combat pay, the Basic Allowance for Housing (BAH), and the Basic Allowance for Subsistence (BAS). See Publication 3, *Armed Forces' Tax Guide*, for more information.

Tip

Combat pay. *You can elect to include your nontaxable combat pay in earned income for the EIC. See* Nontaxable combat pay election*, earlier.*

Part B. Rules If You Have a Qualifying Child

If you have met all of the rules in *Part A*, read *Part B* to see if you have a qualifying child.

Part B discusses *Rules 8* through *10*. You must meet all three of these rules, in addition to the rules in *Parts A* and *D*, to qualify for the earned income credit with a qualifying child.

Caution

If you do not meet Rule 8, *you do not have a qualifying child. Read* Part C *to find out if you can get the earned income credit without a qualifying child.*

You must file Form 1040 or Form 1040A to claim the EIC with a qualifying child. (You cannot file Form 1040EZ.) You also must complete Schedule EIC and attach it to your return. If you meet all the rules in *Part A* and this part, read *Part D* to find out what to do next.

Rule 8. Your Child Must Meet the Relationship, Age, Residency, and Joint Return Tests

Your child is a qualifying child if your child meets four tests. The four tests are:

1. Relationship,
2. Age,
3. Residency, and
4. Joint return.

The four tests are illustrated in Figure 37-1. The paragraphs that follow contain more information about each test.

Relationship Test

To be your qualifying child, a child must be your:

- Son, daughter, stepchild, foster child, or a descendant of any of them (for example, your grandchild), or
- Brother, sister, half brother, half sister, stepbrother, stepsister, or a descendant of any of them (for example, your niece or nephew).

The following definitions clarify the relationship test.

Adopted child. An adopted child is always treated as your own child. The term "adopted child" includes a child who was lawfully placed with you for legal adoption.

Foster child. For the EIC, a person is your foster child if the child is placed with you by an authorized placement agency or by judgement, decree, or other order of any court of competent jurisdiction. An authorized placement agency includes a state or local government agency. It also includes a tax-exempt organization licensed by a state. In addition, it includes an Indian tribal government or an organization authorized by an Indian tribal government to place Indian children.

Figure 37-1. **Tests for Qualifying Child**

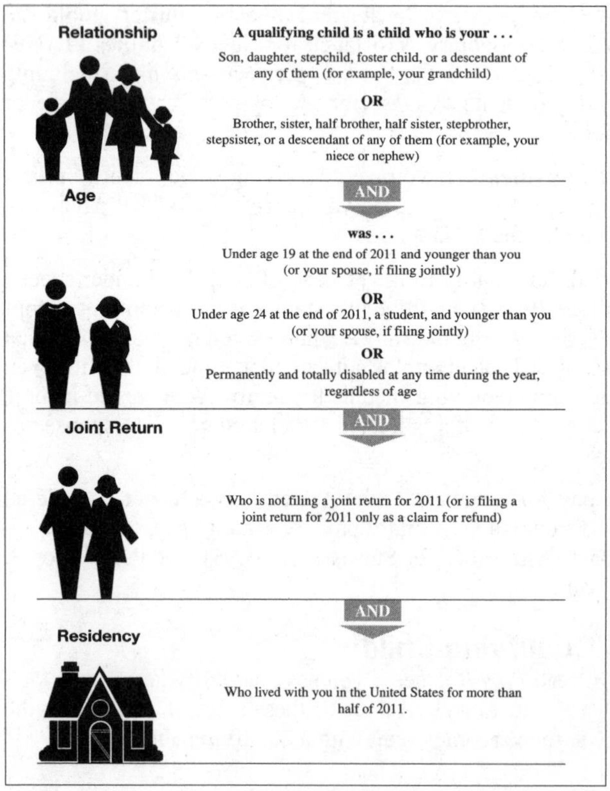

Example. Debbie, who is 12 years old, was placed in your care 2 years ago by an authorized agency responsible for placing children in foster homes. Debbie is your foster child.

Age Test

Your child must be:

1. Under age 19 at the end of 2011 and younger than you (or your spouse, if filing jointly),
2. Under age 24 at the end of 2011, a student, and younger than you (or your spouse, if filing jointly), or
3. Permanently and totally disabled at any time during 2011, regardless of age.

The following examples and definitions clarify the age test.

Example 1. Your son turned 19 on December 10. Unless he was permanently and totally disabled or a student, he is not a qualifying child because, at the end of the year, he was not under age 19.

Example 2. Your 23-year-old brother, who is a full-time student and unmarried, lives with you and your spouse. He is not disabled. Both you and your spouse are 21 years old and you file a joint return. Your brother is not your qualifying child because he is not younger than you or your spouse.

Example 3. The facts are the same as in *Example 2* except that your spouse is 25 years old. Because your brother is younger than your spouse, he is your qualifying child even though he is not younger than you.

Student defined. To qualify as a student, your child must be, during some part of each of any 5 calendar months during the calendar year:

1. A full-time student at a school that has a regular teaching staff, course of study, and regular student body at the school, or
2. A student taking a full-time, on-farm training course given by a school described in (1), or a state, county, or local government.

The 5 calendar months need not be consecutive.

A full-time student is a student who is enrolled for the number of hours or courses the school considers to be full-time attendance.

School defined. A school can be an elementary school, junior or senior high school, college, university, or technical, trade, or mechanical school. However, on-the-job training courses, correspondence schools, and schools offering courses only through the Internet do not count as schools for the EIC.

Vocational high school students. Students who work in co-op jobs in private industry as a part of a school's regular course of classroom and practical training are considered full-time students.

Permanently and totally disabled. Your child is permanently and totally disabled if both of the following apply.

1. He or she cannot engage in any substantial gainful activity because of a physical or mental condition.
2. A doctor determines the condition has lasted or can be expected to last continuously for at least a year or can lead to death.

Residency Test

Your child must have lived with you in the United States for more than half of 2011. The following definitions clarify the residency test.

United States. This means the 50 states and the District of Columbia. It does not include Puerto Rico or U.S. possessions such as Guam.

Homeless shelter. Your home can be any location where you regularly live. You do not need a traditional home. For example, if your child lived with you for more than half the year in one or more homeless shelters, your child meets the residency test.

Military personnel stationed outside the United States. U.S. military personnel stationed outside the United States on extended active duty are considered to live in the United States during that duty period for purposes of the EIC.

Extended active duty. Extended active duty means you are called or ordered to duty for an indefinite period or for a period of more than 90 days. Once you begin serving your extended active duty, you are still considered to have been on extended active duty even if you do not serve more than 90 days.

Birth or death of a child. A child who was born or died in 2011 is treated as having lived with you for all of 2011 if your home was the child's home the entire time he or she was alive in 2011.

Temporary absences. Count time that you or your child is away from home on a temporary absence due to a special circumstance as time the child lived with you. Examples of a special circumstance include illness, school attendance, business, vacation, military service, and detention in a juvenile facility.

Kidnapped child. A kidnapped child is treated as living with you for more than half of the year if the child lived with you for more than half the part of the year before the date of the kidnapping. The child must be presumed by law enforcement authorities to have been kidnapped by someone who is not a member of your family or your child's family. This treatment applies for all years until the child is returned. However, the last year this treatment can apply is the earlier of:

1. The year there is a determination that the child is dead, or
2. The year the child would have reached age 18.

If your qualifying child has been kidnapped and meets these requirements, enter "KC," instead of a number, on line 6 of Schedule EIC.

Joint Return Test

To meet this test, the child cannot file a joint return for the year.

Example. You supported your 18-year-old daughter, and she lived with you all year while her husband was in the Armed Forces. The couple files a joint return. Because your daughter filed a joint return, she is not your qualifying child.

Exception. An exception to the joint return test applies if your child and his or her spouse file a joint return only as a claim for refund.

Example 1. Your 18-year-old son and his 17-year-old wife had $800 of interest income and no earned income. Neither is required to file a tax return. Taxes were taken out of their interest income due to backup withholding, so they filed a joint return only to get a refund of the withheld taxes. The exception to the joint return test applies, so your son may be your qualifying child if all the other tests are met. *Text intentionally omitted.*

Married child. Even if your child does not file a joint return, if your child was married at the end of the year, he or she cannot be your qualifying child unless:

1. You can claim an exemption for the child, or
2. The reason you cannot claim an exemption for the child is that you let the child's other parent claim the exemption under the *Special rule for divorced or separated parents or parents who live apart,* described later.

Social security number. Your qualifying child must have a valid social security number (SSN) unless the child was born and died in 2011 and you attach to your return a copy of the child's birth certificate, death certificate, or hospital records showing a live birth. You cannot claim the EIC on the basis of a qualifying child if:

1. Your qualifying child's SSN is missing from your tax return or is incorrect,
2. Your qualifying child's social security card says "Not valid for employment" and was issued for use in getting a federally funded benefit, or
3. Instead of an SSN, your qualifying child has:
   a. An individual taxpayer identification number (ITIN), which is issued to a noncitizen who cannot get an SSN, or
   b. An adoption taxpayer identification number (ATIN), which is issued to adopting parents who cannot get an SSN for the child being adopted until the adoption is final.

If you have more than one qualifying child and only one has a valid SSN, you can claim the EIC only on the basis of that child. For more information about SSNs, see Rule 2.

Rule 9. Your Qualifying Child Cannot Be Used By More Than One Person To Claim the EIC

Sometimes a child meets the tests to be a qualifying child of more than one person. Although the child meets the tests to be a qualifying child of each of these persons, only one person can actually treat the child as a qualifying child. Only that person can use the child as a qualifying child to take all of the following tax benefits (provided the person is eligible for each benefit).

1. The exemption for the child.
2. The child tax credit.
3. Head of household filing status.

4. The credit for child and dependent care expenses.
5. The exclusion for dependent care benefits.
6. The EIC.

The other person cannot take any of these benefits based on this qualifying child. In other words, you and the other person cannot agree to divide these tax benefits between you. The other person cannot take any of these tax benefits unless he or she has a different qualifying child.

The tiebreaker rules explained next explain who, if anyone, can claim the EIC when more than one person has the same qualifying child. However, the tiebreaker rules do not apply if the other person is your spouse and you file a joint return.

Tiebreaker rules. To determine which person can treat the child as a qualifying child to claim the six tax benefits just listed, the following tiebreaker rules apply.

- If only one of the persons is the child's parent, the child is treated as the qualifying child of the parent.
- If the parents do not file a joint return together but both parents claim the child as a qualifying child, the IRS will treat the child as the qualifying child of the parent with whom the child lived for the longer period of time during the year. If the child lived with each parent for the same amount of time, the IRS will treat the child as the qualifying child of the parent who had the higher adjusted gross income (AGI) for the year.
- If no parent can claim the child as a qualifying child, the child is treated as the qualifying child of the person who had the highest AGI for the year.
- If a parent can claim the child as a qualifying child but no parent does so claim the child, the child is treated as the qualifying child of the person who had the highest AGI for the year, but only if that person's AGI is higher than the highest AGI of any of the child's parents who can claim the child. If the child's parents file a joint return with each other, this rule can be applied by treating the parents' total AGI as divided evenly between them. See Example 8.

Subject to these tiebreaker rules, you and the other person may be able to choose which of you claims the child as a qualifying child. See Examples 1 through 13.

If you cannot claim the EIC because your qualifying child is treated under the tiebreaker rules as the qualifying child of another person for 2011, you may be able to take the EIC using a different qualifying child, but you cannot take the EIC using the rules in Part C for people who do not have a qualifying child.

If the other person cannot claim the EIC. If you and someone else have the same qualifying child but the other person cannot claim the EIC because he or she is not eligible or his or her earned income or AGI is too high, you may be able to treat the child as a qualifying child. See Examples 6 and 7. But you cannot treat the child as a qualifying child to claim the EIC if the other person uses the child to claim any of the other six tax benefits listed earlier.

Examples. The following examples may help you in determining whether you can claim the EIC when you and someone else have the same qualifying child.

Example 1. You and your 2-year-old son Jimmy lived with your mother all year. You are 25 years old, unmarried, and your AGI is $9,000. Your only income was $9,000 from a part-time job. Your mother's only income was $20,000 from her job, and her AGI is $20,000. Jimmy's father did not live with you or Jimmy. The special rule explained later for divorced or separated parents or parents who live apart does not apply. Jimmy is a qualifying child of both you and your mother because he meets the relationship, age, residency, and joint return tests for both you and your mother. However, only one of you can treat him as a qualifying child to claim the EIC (and the other tax benefits listed earlier for which that person qualifies). He is not a qualifying child of anyone else, including his father. If you do not claim Jimmy as a qualifying child for the EIC or any of the other tax benefits listed earlier, your mother can treat him as a qualifying child to claim the EIC (and any other tax benefits listed earlier for which she qualifies).

Example 2. The facts are the same as in Example 1 except your AGI is $25,000. Because your mother's AGI is not higher than yours, she cannot claim Jimmy as a qualifying child. Only you can claim him.

Example 3. The facts are the same as in Example 1 except that you and your mother both claim Jimmy as a qualifying child. In this case, you as the child's parent will be the only one allowed to claim Jimmy as a qualifying child for the EIC and the other tax benefits listed earlier for which you qualify. The IRS will disallow your mother's claim to the EIC and any other tax benefits listed earlier unless she has another qualifying child.

Example 4. The facts are the same as in *Example 1* except that you also have two other young children who are qualifying children of both you and your mother. Only one of you can claim each child. However, if your mother's AGI is higher than yours, you can allow your mother to claim one or more of the children. For example, if you claim one child, your mother can claim the other two.

Example 5. The facts are the same as in *Example 1* except that you are only 18 years old. This means you are a qualifying child of your mother. Because of *Rule 10* discussed next, you cannot claim the EIC and cannot claim Jimmy as a qualifying child. Only your mother may be able to treat Jimmy as a qualifying child to claim the EIC. If your mother meets all the other requirements for claiming the EIC and you do not claim Jimmy as a qualifying child for any of the other tax benefits listed earlier, your mother can claim both you and Jimmy as qualifying children for the EIC.

Example 6. The facts are the same as in *Example 1* except that your mother earned $50,000 from her job. Because your mother's earned income is too high for her to claim the EIC, only you can claim the EIC using your son.

Example 7. The facts are the same as in *Example 1* except that you earned $50,000 from your job and your AGI is $50,500. Your earned income is too high for you to claim the EIC. But your mother cannot claim the EIC either, because her AGI is not higher than yours.

Example 8. The facts are the same as in *Example 1* except that you and Jimmy's father are married to each other, live with Jimmy and your mother, and have an AGI of $30,000 on a joint return. If you and your husband do not claim Jimmy as a qualifying child for the EIC or any of the other tax benefits listed earlier, your mother can claim him instead. Even though the AGI on your joint return, $30,000, is more than your mother's AGI of $20,000, for this purpose half of the joint AGI can be treated as yours and half as your husband's. In other words, each parent's AGI can be treated as $15,000.

Example 9. You, your husband, and your 10-year-old son Joey lived together until August 1, 2011, when your husband moved out of the household. In August and September, Joey lived with you. For the rest of the year, Joey lived with your husband, who is Joey's father. Joey is a qualifying child of both you and your husband because he lived with each of you for more than half the year and because he met the relationship, age, and joint return tests for both of you. At the end of the year, you and your husband still were not divorced, legally separated, or separated under a written separation agreement, so the special rule for divorced or separated parents or parents who live apart does not apply.

You and your husband will file separate returns. Your husband agrees to let you treat Joey as a qualifying child. This means, if your husband does not claim Joey as a qualifying child for any of the tax benefits listed earlier, you can claim him as a qualifying child for any tax benefit listed for which you qualify. However, your filing status is married filing separately, so you cannot claim the EIC or the credit for child and dependent care expenses. See *Rule 3*.

Example 10. The facts are the same as in *Example 9* except that you and your husband both claim Joey as a qualifying child. In this case, only your husband will be allowed to treat Joey as a qualifying child. This is because, during 2011, the boy lived with him longer than with you. You cannot claim the EIC (either with or without a qualifying child). However, your husband's filing status is married filing separately, so he cannot claim the EIC or the credit for child and dependent care expenses. See *Rule 3*.

Example 11. You, your 5-year-old son and your son's father lived together all year. You and your son's father are not married. Your son is a qualifying child of both you and his father because he meets the relationship, age, residency, and joint return tests for both you and his father. Your earned income and AGI are $12,000, and your son's father's earned income and AGI are $14,000. Neither of you had any other income. Your son's father agrees to let you treat the child as a qualifying child. This means, if your son's father does not claim your son as a qualifying child for the EIC or any of the other tax benefits listed earlier, you can claim him as a qualifying child for the EIC and any other tax benefits listed for which you qualify.

Example 12. The facts are the same as in *Example 11* except that you and your son's father both claim your son as a qualifying child. In this case, only your son's father will be allowed to treat your son as a qualifying child. This is because his AGI, $14,000, is more than your AGI, $12,000. You cannot claim the EIC (either with or without a qualifying child).

Example 13. You and your 7-year-old niece, your sister's child, lived with your mother all year. You are 25 years old, and your AGI is $9,300. Your only income was from a part-time job. Your mother's AGI is $15,000. Her only income was from her job. Your niece's parents file jointly, have an AGI of less than $9,000, and do not live with you or their child. Your niece is a qualifying child of both you and your mother because she meets the relationship, age, residency, and joint return tests for both you and your mother. However, only your mother can treat her as a qualifying child. This is because your mother's AGI, $15,000, is more than your AGI, $9,300.

Special rule for divorced or separated parents or parents who live apart. A child will be treated as the qualifying child of his or her noncustodial parent (for purposes of claiming an exemption and the child tax credit, but not for the EIC) if all of the following apply.

1. The parents:
   a. Are divorced or legally separated under a decree of divorce or separate maintenance,
   b. Are separated under a written separation agreement, or
   c. Lived apart at all times during the last 6 months of 2011, whether or not they are or were married.
2. The child received over half of his or her support for the year from the parents.
3. The child is in the custody of one or both parents for more than half of 2011.
4. Either of the following statements is true.
   a. The custodial parent signs Form 8332 or a substantially similar statement that he or she will not claim the child as a dependent for the year, and the noncustodial parent attaches the form or statement to his or her return. If the divorce decree or separation agreement went into effect after 1984 and before 2009, the noncustodial parent may be able to attach certain pages from the decree or agreement instead of Form 8332.
   b. A pre-1985 decree of divorce or separate maintenance or written separation agreement that applies to 2011 provides that the noncustodial parent can claim the child as a dependent, and the noncustodial parent provides at least $600 for support of the child during 2011.

For details, see chapter 3. Also see *Applying Rule 9 to divorced or separated parents or parents who live apart,* next.

Applying Rule 9 to divorced or separated parents or parents who live apart. If a child is treated as the qualifying child of the noncustodial parent under the special rule just described for children of divorced or separated parents or parents who live apart, only the noncustodial parent can claim an exemption and the child tax credit for the child. However, the custodial parent, if eligible, or another eligible taxpayer, can claim the child as a qualifying child for the EIC and other tax benefits listed earlier. If the child is the qualifying child of more than one person for these benefits, then the tiebreaker rules determine which person can treat the child as a qualifying child.

Example 1. You and your 5-year-old son lived all year with your mother, who paid the entire cost of keeping up the home. Your AGI is $10,000. Your mother's AGI is $25,000. Your son's father did not live with you or your son. Under the special rule for children of divorced or separated parents or parents who live apart, your son is treated as the qualifying child of his father, who can claim an exemption and the child tax credit for the child. However, your son's father cannot claim your son as a qualifying child for head of household filing status, the credit for child and dependent care expenses, the exclusion for dependent care benefits, or the EIC. You and your mother did not have any child care expenses or dependent care benefits. If you do not claim your son as a qualifying child, your mother can claim him as a qualifying child for the EIC and head of household filing status, if she qualifies for these tax benefits.

Example 2. The facts are the same as in *Example 1* except that your AGI is $25,000 and your mother's AGI is $21,000. Your mother cannot claim your son as a qualifying child for any purpose because her AGI is not higher than yours.

Example 3. The facts are the same as in *Example 1* except that you and your mother both claim your son as a qualifying child for the EIC. Your mother also claims him as a qualifying child for head of household filing status. You as the child's parent will be the only one allowed to claim your son as a qualifying child for the EIC. The IRS will disallow your mother's claim to the EIC and head of household filing status unless she has another qualifying child.

Rule 10. You Cannot Be a Qualifying Child of Another Person

You are a qualifying child of another person (your parent, guardian, foster parent, etc.) if all of the following statements are true.

1. You are that person's son, daughter, stepchild, grandchild, or foster child. Or, you are that person's brother, sister, half brother, half sister, stepbrother, or stepsister (or the child or grandchild of that person's brother, sister, half brother, half sister, stepbrother, or stepsister).

2. You were:
   a. Under age 19 at the end of the year and younger than that person (or that person's spouse, if the person files jointly),
   b. Under age 24 at the end of the year, a student, and younger than that person (or that person's spouse, if the person files jointly), or
   c. Permanently and totally disabled, regardless of age.
3. You lived with that person in the United States for more than half of the year.
4. You are not filing a joint return for the year (or are filing a joint return only as a claim for refund).

For more details about the tests to be a qualifying child, see *Rule 8*.

If you (or your spouse, if filing a joint return) are a qualifying child of another person, you cannot claim the EIC. This is true even if the person for whom you are a qualifying child does not claim the EIC or meet all of the rules to claim the EIC. Put "No" beside line 64a (Form 1040) or line 38a (Form 1040A).

Example. You and your daughter lived with your mother all year. You are 22 years old, unmarried, and attended a trade school full time. You had a part-time job and earned $5,700. You had no other income. Because you meet the relationship, age, residency, and joint return tests, you are a qualifying child of your mother. She can claim the EIC if she meets all the other requirements. Because you are your mother's qualifying child, you cannot claim the EIC. This is so even if your mother cannot or does not claim the EIC.

Caution

If you have a qualifying child, the rules in this part do not apply to you. You can claim the credit only if you meet all the rules in Parts A, B, *and* D. *See* Rule 8 *to find out if you have a qualifying child.*

Part C. Rules If You Do Not Have a Qualifying Child

Read this part if you:

1. Do not have a qualifying child, and
2. Have met all the rules in *Part A*.

Part C discusses *Rules 11 through 14*. You must meet all four of these rules, in addition to the rules in *Parts A* and *D*, to qualify for the earned income credit without a qualifying child.

Rule 11. You Must Be at Least Age 25 but Under Age 65

You must be at least age 25 but under age 65 at the end of 2011. If you are married filing a joint return, either you or your spouse must be at least age 25 but under age 65 at the end of 2011. It does not matter which spouse meets the age test, as long as one of the spouses does.

If neither you nor your spouse meets the age test, you cannot claim the EIC. Put "No" next to line 64a (Form 1040), line 38a (Form 1040A), or line 8a (Form 1040EZ).

Death of spouse. If you are filing a joint return with your spouse who died in 2011, you meet the age test if your spouse was at least age 25 but under age 65 at the time of death.

Example 1. You are age 28 and unmarried. You meet the age test.

Example 2. You are married and filing a joint return. You are age 23 and your spouse is age 27. You meet the age test because your spouse is at least age 25 but under age 65.

Example 3. You are married and filing a joint return with your spouse who died in August 2011. You are age 67. Your spouse would have been age 65 in November 2011. Because your spouse was under age 65 when she died, you meet the age test.

Rule 12. You Cannot Be the Dependent of Another Person

If you are **not** filing a joint return, you meet this rule if:

- You checked box 6a on Form 1040 or 1040A, or
- You did not check the "You" box on line 5 of Form 1040EZ, and you entered $9,500 on that line.

If you are filing a joint return, you meet this rule if:

- You checked both box 6a and box 6b on Form 1040 or 1040A, or
- You and your spouse did not check either the "You" box or the "Spouse" box on line 5 of Form 1040EZ, and you entered $19,000 on that line.

If you are not sure whether someone else can claim you (or your spouse if filing a joint return) as a dependent, read the rules for claiming a dependent in chapter 3.

If someone else can claim you (or your spouse if filing a joint return) as a dependent on his or her return, but does not, you still cannot claim the credit.

Example 1. In 2011, you were age 25, single, and living at home with your parents. You worked and were not a student. You earned $7,500. Your parents cannot claim you as a dependent. When you file your return, you claim an exemption for yourself by not checking the "You" box on line 5 of your Form 1040EZ and by entering $9,500 on that line. You meet this rule.

Example 2. The facts are the same as in *Example 1*, except that you earned $2,000. Your parents can claim you as a dependent but decide not to. You do not meet this rule. You cannot claim the credit because your parents could have claimed you as a dependent.

Rule 13. You Cannot Be a Qualifying Child of Another Person

You are a qualifying child of another person (your parent, guardian, foster parent, etc.) if all of the following statements are true.

1. You are that person's son, daughter, stepchild, grandchild, or foster child. Or, you are that person's brother, sister, half brother, half sister, stepbrother, or stepsister (or the child or grandchild of that person's brother, sister, half brother, half sister, stepbrother, or step-sister).
2. You were:
   a. Under age 19 at the end of the year and younger than that person (or that person's spouse, if the person files jointly),
   b. Under age 24 at the end of the year, a student (as defined in *Rule 8*), and younger than that person (or that person's spouse, if the person files jointly), or
   c. Permanently and totally disabled, regardless of age.
3. You lived with that person in the United States for more than half of the year.
4. You are not filing a joint return for the year (or are filing a joint return only as a claim for refund).

For more details about the tests to be a qualifying child, see *Rule 8*.

If you (or your spouse if filing a joint return) are a qualifying child of another person, you cannot claim the EIC. This is true even if the person for whom you are a qualifying child does not claim the EIC or meet all of the rules to claim the EIC. Put "No" next to line 64a (Form 1040), line 38a (Form 1040A), or line 8a (Form 1040EZ).

Example. You lived with your mother all year. You are age 26, unmarried, and permanently and totally disabled. Your only income was from a community center where you went three days a week to answer telephones. You earned $5,000 for the year and provided more than half of your own support. Because you meet the relationship, age, residency, and joint return tests, you are a qualifying child of your mother for the EIC. She can claim the EIC if she meets all the other requirements. Because you are a qualifying child of your mother, you cannot claim the EIC. This is so even if your mother cannot or does not claim the EIC.

Rule 14. You Must Have Lived in the United States More Than Half of the Year

Your home (and your spouse's, if filing a joint return) must have been in the United States for more than half the year.

If it was not, put "No" next to line 64a (Form 1040), line 38a (Form 1040A), or line 8a (Form 1040EZ).

United States. This means the 50 states and the District of Columbia. It does not include Puerto Rico or U.S. possessions such as Guam.

Homeless shelter. Your home can be any location where you regularly live. You do not need a traditional home. If you lived in one or more homeless shelters in the United States for more than half the year, you meet this rule.

Military personnel stationed outside the United States. U.S. military personnel stationed outside the United States on extended active duty (defined in *Rule 8*), are considered to live in the United States during that duty period for purposes of the EIC.

Part D. Figuring and Claiming the EIC

Read this part if you have met all the rules in *Parts A* and *B*, or all the rules in *Parts A* and *C*.

Part D discusses *Rule 15*. You must meet this rule, in addition to the rules in *Parts A* and *B*, or *Parts A* and *C*, to qualify for the earned income credit.

This part of the chapter also explains how to figure the amount of your credit. You have two choices.

1. Have the IRS figure the EIC for you. If you want to do this, see *IRS Will Figure the EIC for You*.
2. Figure the EIC yourself. If you want to do this, see *How To Figure the EIC Yourself*.

Rule 15. Your Earned Income Must Be Less Than:

- $43,998 ($49,078 for married filing jointly) if you have three or more qualifying children,
- $40,964 ($46,044 for married filing jointly) if you have two qualifying children,

- $36,052 ($41,132 for married filing jointly) if you have one qualifying child, or
- $13,660 ($18,740 for married filing jointly) if you do not have a qualifying child.

Earned income generally means wages, salaries, tips, other taxable employee pay, and net earnings from self-employment. Employee pay is earned income only if it is taxable. Nontaxable employee pay, such as certain dependent care benefits and adoption benefits, is not earned income. But there is an exception for nontaxable combat pay, which you can choose to include in earned income. Earned income is explained in detail in *Rule 7*.

Figuring earned income. If you are self-employed, a statutory employee, or a member of the clergy or a church employee who files Schedule SE (Form 1040), you will figure your earned income when you fill out Part 4 of EIC Worksheet B in the Form 1040 instructions.

Otherwise, figure your earned income by using the worksheet in Step 5 of the Form 1040 instructions for lines 64a and 64b or the Form 1040A instructions for lines 38a and 38b, or the worksheet in *Step 2* of the Form 1040EZ instructions for lines 8a and 8b.

When using one of those worksheets to figure your earned income, you will start with the amount on line 7 (Form 1040 or Form 1040A) or line 1 (Form 1040EZ). You will then reduce that amount by any amount included on that line and described in the following list.

- Scholarship or fellowship grants not reported on a Form W-2,
- Inmate's income, and
- Pension or annuity from deferred compensation plans.

Scholarship or fellowship grants not reported on a Form W-2. A scholarship or fellowship grant that was not reported to you on a Form W-2 is not considered earned income for the earned income credit.

Inmate's income. Amounts received for work performed while an inmate in a penal institution are not earned income for the earned income credit. This includes amounts received for work performed while in a work release program or while in a halfway house. If you received any amount for work done while an inmate in a penal institution and that amount is included in the total on line 7 (Form 1040 or Form 1040A) or line 1 (Form 1040EZ), put "PRI" and the amount on the dotted line next to line 7 (Form 1040), in the space to the left of the entry space for line 7 (Form 1040A), or in the space to the left of line 1 (Form 1040EZ).

Pension or annuity from deferred compensation plans. A pension or annuity from a nonqualified deferred compensation plan or a nongovernmental section 457 plan is not considered earned income for the earned income credit. If you received such an amount and it was included in the total on line 7 (Form 1040 or Form 1040A) or line 1 (Form 1040EZ), put "DFC" and the amount on the dotted line next to line 7 (Form 1040), in the space to the left of the entry space for line 7 (Form 1040A), or in the space to the left of line 1 (Form 1040EZ). This amount may be reported in box 11 of your Form W-2. If you received such an amount but box 11 is blank, contact your employer for the amount received as a pension or annuity.

Clergy. If you are a member of the clergy who files Schedule SE and the amount on line 2 of that schedule includes an amount that was also reported on line 7 (Form 1040), subtract that amount from the amount on line 7 (Form 1040) and enter the result in the first space of the worksheet in Step 5 of the Form 1040 instructions for lines 64a and 64b. Put "Clergy" on the dotted line next to line 64a (Form 1040).

Church employees. A church employee means an employee (other than a minister or member of a religious order) of a church or qualified church-controlled organization that is exempt from employer social security and Medicare taxes. If you received wages as a church employee and included any amount on both line 5a of Schedule SE and line 7 (Form 1040), subtract that amount from the amount on line 7 (Form 1040) and enter the result in the first space of the worksheet in Step 5 of the Form 1040 instructions for lines 64a and 64b.

Caution

Do not ask the IRS to figure your EIC unless you are eligible for it. Read the rules in Parts A, B, C, *and* D *to see if you qualify.*

IRS Will Figure the EIC for You

The IRS will figure your EIC for you if you follow the steps explained in this section.

Form 1040

If you file Form 1040 and want the IRS to figure your credit for you, follow these steps.

1. Put "EIC" on the dotted line next to line 64a. Then, if you have any of the types of income described earlier under *Inmate's income*, *Pension or annuity from deferred compensation plans*, or *Clergy*, follow the instructions given there.

2. If you received nontaxable combat pay and are electing to include it in your earned income for the EIC, enter the amount on line 64b. For details, see *Nontaxable combat pay election* in *Rule 7*.
3. Complete all other parts of your return that apply to you (including line 59a, 59b, and 60), but do not fill in lines 72, 73, 74a, and 76. If you do not have a qualifying child, stop here.
4. If you have a qualifying child, complete Schedule EIC according to its instructions. Be sure to enter the child's social security number on line 2 of that schedule. If you do not, your credit may be reduced or disallowed. Attach Schedule EIC to your return.

Tip

If you want the IRS to also figure the amount of your income tax, see chapter 31.

Form 1040A

If you file Form 1040A and want the IRS to figure your credit for you, follow these steps.

1. Put "EIC" to the left of the entry space for line 38a. Then, if you have any of the types of income described earlier under *Inmate's income* or *Pension or annuity from deferred compensation plans*, follow the instructions given there.
2. If you received nontaxable combat pay and are electing to include it in your earned income for the EIC, enter the amount on line 38b. For details, see *Nontaxable combat pay election* in *Rule 7*.
3. Complete all other parts of your return that apply to you, but do not fill in lines 41, 42, 43a, and 45. If you do not have a qualifying child, stop here.
4. If you have a qualifying child, complete Schedule EIC according to its instructions. Be sure to enter the child's social security number on line 2 of that schedule. If you do not, your credit may be reduced or disallowed. Attach Schedule EIC to your return.

Form 1040EZ

If you file Form 1040EZ and want the IRS to figure your credit for you, follow these steps.

1. Put "EIC" in the space to the left of line 8a. Then if you have any of the types of income described earlier under *Inmate's income* or *Pension or annuity from deferred compensation plans*, follow the instructions given there.
2. If you received nontaxable combat pay and are electing to include it in your earned income for the EIC, enter the amount on line 8b. For details, see *Nontaxable combat pay election* in *Rule 7*.
3. Complete all other parts of your return that apply to you, but do not fill in lines 9, 11a, or 12.

How To Figure the EIC Yourself

To figure the EIC yourself, use the EIC Worksheet in the instructions for the form you are using (Form 1040, Form 1040A, or Form 1040EZ).

Form 1040 and EIC Worksheet. If you file Form 1040 and want to figure the credit yourself, follow these steps.

1. Go to your form instruction booklet and turn to the instructions for lines 64a and 64b, and look for Worksheet A or Worksheet B.
2. Complete the EIC Worksheet that applies to your situation according to its instructions. Complete Worksheet B if you were self-employed at any time in 2011, a member of the clergy or a church employee who files Schedule SE, or a statutory employee filing Schedule C or C-EZ. Find the amount of your credit in the EIC Table in your instruction booklet.
3. Enter the amount of your earned income credit from Worksheet A or B on Form 1040, line 64a.
4. Keep the EIC Worksheet for your records. Do not attach it to your income tax return. If you do not have a qualifying child, stop here.
5. If you have a qualifying child, complete Schedule EIC according to its instructions. Be sure to enter the child's social security number on line 2 of that schedule. If you do not, your credit may be reduced or disallowed. Attach Schedule EIC to your return.

Form 1040A and EIC Worksheet. If you file Form 1040A and want to figure the credit yourself, follow these steps.

1. Go to your form instruction booklet and turn to the instructions for lines 38a and 38b, and look for the EIC Worksheet.
2. Complete the EIC Worksheet according to its instructions. Find the amount of your credit in the EIC Table in your form instruction booklet.
3. Enter the amount of your earned income credit from line 6 of the EIC Worksheet on Form 1040A, line 38a.

4. Keep the EIC Worksheet for your records. Do not attach it to your income tax return. If you do not have a qualifying child, stop here.
5. If you have a qualifying child, complete Schedule EIC according to its instructions. Be sure to enter the child's social security number on line 2 of that schedule. If you do not, your credit may be reduced or disallowed. Attach Schedule EIC to your return.

Form 1040EZ and EIC Worksheet. If you file Form 1040EZ and want to figure the credit yourself, follow these steps.

1. Go to your form instruction booklet and turn to the instructions for lines 8a and 8b and look for the EIC Worksheet.
2. Complete the EIC Worksheet according to its instructions. Find the amount of your credit in the EIC Table in your form instruction booklet.
3. Enter the amount of your earned income credit from line 6 of the EIC Worksheet on Form 1040EZ, line 8a.
4. Keep the EIC Worksheet for your records. Do not attach it to your income tax return.

Examples

The following two comprehensive examples (complete with filled-in forms) may be helpful.

1. John and Janet Smith, a married couple with one qualifying child and using Form 1040A.
2. Kelly Green, age 30, a student, with no qualifying child and using Form 1040EZ.

Example 1. John and Janet Smith (Form 1040A)

John and Janet Smith are married and will file a joint return. They have one child, Amy, who is 3 years old. Amy lived with John and Janet for all of 2011. John worked and earned $9,500. Janet worked part of the year and earned $1,500. Their earned income and AGI are $11,000. John and Janet qualify for the earned income credit and fill out the EIC Worksheet and Schedule EIC. The Smiths will attach Schedule EIC to Form 1040A when they send their completed return to the IRS.

They took the following steps to complete Schedule EIC and the EIC Worksheet.

Completing Schedule EIC

The Smiths complete Schedule EIC because they have a qualifying child. They enter "John and Janet Smith" and John's SSN (the SSN that appears first on their Form 1040A) on the line at the top of Schedule EIC. The Smiths then fill out *Qualifying Child Information* (lines 1–6).

Completing the EIC Worksheet

Next, the Smiths will complete the EIC Worksheet to figure their earned income credit.

Line 1. The Smiths enter $11,000 (their earned income).

Line 2. The Smiths go to the Earned Income Credit Table in the Form 1040A instructions. The Smiths find their income of $11,000 within the range of $11,000 to $11,050. They follow this line across to the column that describes their filing status and number of children and find $3,094. They enter $3,094 on line 2.

Line 3. The Smiths enter their AGI of $11,000.

Line 4. The Smiths check the "Yes" box because lines 1 and 3 are the same ($11,000). They skip line 5 and enter the amount from line 2 ($3,094) on line 6.

Line 6. The Smiths' EIC is $3,094.

SCHEDULE EIC
(Form 1040A or 1040)

Department of the Treasury
Internal Revenue Service (99)

Earned Income Credit

Qualifying Child Information

Complete and attach to Form 1040A or 1040 only if you have a qualifying child.

1040A
1040
EIC

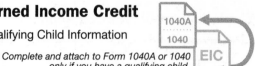

OMB No. 1545-0074

2011

Attachment Sequence No. **43**

Name(s) shown on return	Your social security number
John and Janet Smith	**222-22-2222**

Before you begin:

- See the instructions for Form 1040A, lines 38a and 38b, or Form 1040, lines 64a and 64b, to make sure that **(a)** you can take the EIC, and **(b)** you have a qualifying child.
- Be sure the child's name on line 1 and social security number (SSN) on line 2 agree with the child's social security card. Otherwise, at the time we process your return, we may reduce or disallow your EIC. If the name or SSN on the child's social security card is not correct, call the Social Security Administration at 1-800-772-1213.

CAUTION

- If you take the EIC even though you are not eligible, you may not be allowed to take the credit for up to 10 years. See page 2 of schedule for details.
- It will take us longer to process your return and issue your refund if you do not fill in all lines that apply for each qualifying child.

Qualifying Child Information	Child 1	Child 2	Child 3
1 Child's name If you have more than three qualifying children, you only have to list three to get the maximum credit.	First name Last name **Amy Smith**	First name Last name	First name Last name
2 Child's SSN The child must have an SSN as defined in the instructions for Form 1040A, lines 38a and 38b, or Form 1040, lines 64a and 64b, unless the child was born and died in 2011. If your child was born and died in 2011 and did not have an SSN, enter "Died" on this line and attach a copy of the child's birth certificate, death certificate, or hospital medical records.	**000-00-2222**		
3 Child's year of birth	Year 2 0 0 8 *If born after 1992 **and** the child was younger than you (or your spouse, if filing jointly), skip lines 4a and 4b; go to line 5.*	Year __ __ __ __ *If born after 1992 **and** the child was younger than you (or your spouse, if filing jointly), skip lines 4a and 4b; go to line 5.*	Year __ __ __ __ *If born after 1992 **and** the child was younger than you (or your spouse, if filing jointly), skip lines 4a and 4b; go to line 5.*
4 a Was the child under age 24 at the end of 2011, a student, and younger than you (or your spouse, if filing jointly)?	☐ **Yes.** *Go to line 5.* ☐ **No.** *Go to line 4b.*	☐ **Yes.** *Go to line 5.* ☐ **No.** *Go to line 4b.*	☐ **Yes.** *Go to line 5.* ☐ **No.** *Go to line 4b.*
b Was the child permanently and totally disabled during any part of 2011?	☐ **Yes.** *Go to line 5.* ☐ **No.** The child is not a qualifying child.	☐ **Yes.** *Go to line 5.* ☐ **No.** The child is not a qualifying child.	☐ **Yes.** *Go to line 5.* ☐ **No.** The child is not a qualifying child.
5 Child's relationship to you (for example, son, daughter, grandchild, niece, nephew, foster child, etc.)	**Daughter**		
6 Number of months child lived with you in the United States during 2011 • If the child lived with you for more than half of 2011 but less than 7 months, enter "7." • If the child was born or died in 2011 and your home was the child's home for the entire time he or she was alive during 2011, enter "12."	**12** months *Do not enter more than 12 months.*	____ months *Do not enter more than 12 months.*	____ months *Do not enter more than 12 months.*

For Paperwork Reduction Act Notice, see your tax return instructions. Cat. No. 13339M **Schedule EIC (Form 1040A or 1040) 2011**

Part 1

All Filers

1. Enter your earned income from Step 5. | 1 | 11,000 |

2. Look up the amount on line 1 in the EIC Table to find the credit. Be sure you use the correct column for your filing status and the number of children you have. Enter the credit here. | 2 | 3,094 |

   If line 2 is zero, STOP You cannot take the credit. Enter "No" to the left of the entry space for line 38a.

3. Enter the amount from Form 1040A, line 22. | 3 | 11,000 |

4. Are the amounts on lines 3 and 1 the same?

   ☒ **Yes.** Skip line 5; enter the amount from line 2 on line 6.

   ☐ **No.** Go to line 5.

Part 2

Filers Who Answered "No" on Line 4

5. If you have:
   - No qualifying children, is the amount on line 3 less than $7,600 ($12,700 if married filing jointly)?
   - 1 or more qualifying children, is the amount on line 3 less than $16,700 ($21,800 if married filing jointly)?

   ☐ **Yes.** Leave line 5 blank; enter the amount from line 2 on line 6.

   ☐ **No.** Look up the amount on line 3 in the EIC Table to find the credit. Be sure you use the correct column for your filing status and the number of children you have. Enter the credit here. | 5 | |

   Look at the amounts on lines 5 and 2. Then, enter the smaller amount on line 6.

Part 3

Your Earned Income Credit

6. This is your earned income credit. | 6 | 3,094 |

Enter this amount on Form 1040A, line 38a.

Reminder—

√ If you have a qualifying child, complete and attach Schedule EIC.

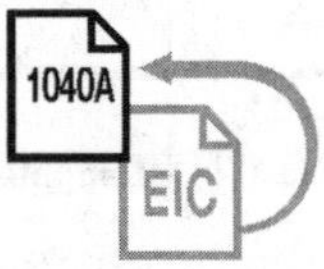

CAUTION *If your EIC for a year after 1996 was reduced or disallowed, see Form 8862, Who Must File, earlier to find out if you must file Form 8862 to take the credit for 2011.*

Example 2. Kelly Green (Form 1040EZ)

Kelly Green is age 30 and a full-time student. She lived with her parents in the United States for all of 2011. She had a part-time job and earned $6,240. She earned $20 interest on a savings account. She is not eligible to be claimed as a dependent on her parents' return. Although she lived with her parents, she is not their qualifying child because she does not meet the age test. She does not have any children.

Kelly qualifies for the earned income credit. Kelly will file Form 1040EZ and complete the EIC Worksheet.

Completing the EIC Worksheet

Kelly figures the amount of her earned income credit on the EIC Worksheet as follows.

Line 1. She enters $6,240 (her earned income).

Line 2. Kelly goes to the Earned Income Credit Table in the forms instruction booklet. She finds her earned income of $6,240 in the range of $6,200 to $6,250. Kelly follows this line across to the column that describes her filing status and finds $464. She enters $464 on line 2.

Line 3. Kelly enters $6,260 (her AGI).

Line 4. Kelly checks the "No" box because lines 1 and 3 are not the same.

Line 5. Kelly checks the "Yes" box because the amount on line 3 ($6,260) is less than $7,600. She leaves line 5 blank and enters the amount from line 2, $464, on line 6.

Line 6. She enters $464 here and on Form 1040EZ, line 8a. Kelly's earned income credit is $464.

Earned Income Credit (EIC) Worksheet—Lines 8a and 8b

1. Enter your earned income from Step 2 on page 14 . . . . **1.** 6,240
2. Look up the amount on line 1 above in the EIC Table on page 16 to find the credit. Be sure you use the correct column for your filing status (Single or Married filing jointly).
   Enter the credit here **2.** 464

   If line 2 is zero, STOP You cannot take the credit. Enter "No" in the space to the left of line 8a.
3. Enter the amount from Form 1040EZ, line 4 . . . . **3.** 6,260
4. Are the amounts on lines 3 and 1 the same?
   - ☐ **Yes.** Skip line 5; enter the amount from line 2 on line 6.
   - ☑ **No.** Go to line 5.
5. Is the amount on line 3 less than $7,600 ($12,700 if married filing jointly)?
   - ☑ **Yes.** Leave line 5 blank; enter the amount from line 2 on line 6.
   - ☐ **No.** Look up the amount on line 3 in the EIC Table on page 16 to find the credit. Be sure you use the correct column for your filing status (Single or Married filing jointly).
     Enter the credit here . . . . **5.** ______
     Look at the amounts on lines 5 and 2. Then, enter the **smaller** amount on line 6.
6. **Earned income credit.** Enter this amount on Form 1040EZ, **line 8a** **6.** 464

CAUTION *If your EIC for a year after 1996 was reduced or disallowed, see above to find out if you must file Form 8862 to take the credit for 2011.*

EIC Eligibility Checklist

Keep for Your Records

You may claim the EIC if you answer "Yes" to all the following questions.*

	Yes	No
1. Is your AGI less than: • $13,660 ($18,740 for married filing jointly) if you do not have a qualifying child, • $36,052 ($41,132 for married filing jointly) if you have one qualifying child, • $40,964 ($46,044 for married filing jointly) if you have two qualifying children, or • $43,998 ($49,078 for married filing jointly) if you have more than two qualifying children? (See *Rule 1*.)	☐	☐
2. Do you, your spouse, and your qualifying child each have a valid SSN? (See *Rule 2*.)	☐	☐
3. Is your filing status married filing jointly, head of household, qualifying widow(er), or single? (See *Rule 3*.) **Caution:** If you or your spouse is a nonresident alien, answer **"Yes"** only if your filing status is married filing jointly. (See *Rule 4*.)	☐	☐
4. Answer **"Yes"** if you are not filing Form 2555 or Form 2555-EZ. Otherwise, answer **"No."** (See *Rule 5*.)	☐	☐
5. Is your investment income $3,150 or less? (See *Rule 6*.)	☐	☐
6. Is your total earned income at least $1 but less than: • $13,660 ($18,740 for married filing jointly) if you do not have a qualifying child, • $36,052 ($41,132 for married filing jointly) if you have one qualifying child, • $40,964 ($46,044 for married filing jointly) if you have two qualifying children, or • $43,998 ($49,078 for married filing jointly) if you have more than two qualifying children? (See *Rules 7* and *15*.)	☐	☐
7. Answer **"Yes"** if you (and your spouse if filing a joint return) are not a qualifying child of another person. Otherwise, answer **"No."** (See *Rules 10* and *13*.)	☐	☐
STOP: If you have a qualifying child, answer questions 8 and 9 and skip 10 – 12. If you do not have a qualifying child, skip questions 8 and 9 and answer 10 – 12.*		
8. Does your child meet the age, residency, and relationship tests for a qualifying child? (See *Rule 8*.)	☐	☐
9. Is your child a qualifying child only for you? Answer **"Yes"** if your qualifying child also meets the tests to be a qualifying child of another person, but the other person is not claiming any child-related tax benefits using that child. Answer **"No"** if you do not know whether the other person is claiming any child-related tax benefits using that child.	☐	☐
10. Were you (or your spouse if filing a joint return) at least age 25 but under 65 at the end of 2011? (See *Rule 11*.)	☐	☐
11. Answer **"Yes"** if you (and your spouse if filing a joint return) cannot be claimed as a dependent on anyone else's return. Answer **"No"** if you (or your spouse if filing a joint return) can be claimed as a dependent on someone else's return. (See *Rule 12*.)	☐	☐
12. Was your main home (and your spouse's if filing a joint return) in the United States for more than half the year? (See *Rule 14*.)	☐	☐

* **PERSONS WITH A QUALIFYING CHILD:** If you answered **"Yes"** to questions 1 through 9, you can claim the EIC. Remember to fill out Schedule EIC and attach it to your Form 1040 or Form 1040A. You cannot use Form 1040EZ. If you answered **"Yes"** to questions 1 through 8 and **"No"** to question 9, see *Rule 9* to help you determine whether you can claim the EIC. If you answered **"Yes"** to questions 1 through 7 and **"No"** to question 8, answer questions 10 through 12 to see if you can claim the EIC without a qualifying child.

PERSONS WITHOUT A QUALIFYING CHILD: If you answered **"Yes"** to questions 1 through 7, and 10 through 12, you can claim the EIC.

If you answered "No" to any question that applies to you: You cannot claim the EIC.

Part 7

Special situations and tax planning

ey.com/EYTaxGuide

The first seven chapters in this part discuss some special situations. Chapter 38, *Self-employment income: How to file Schedule C,* is essential reading for anyone who is self-employed–freelancers, artists, and small business owners. Mutual fund investors will want to pay special attention to chapter 39, *Mutual funds.* It discusses what you need to know about the tax treatment of gains, losses, dividends, and distributions from a mutual fund. Chapter 40, *What to do if you employ domestic help,* will be of interest to taxpayers who employ domestic help, whether it is to care for their children or a disabled or elderly dependent. Chapter 41, *U.S. citizens working abroad: Tax treatment of foreign earned income,* discusses how U.S. citizens working abroad should handle their taxes. Among other matters, it explains how you can get a credit against your U.S. taxes for taxes you have paid to a foreign government. Chapter 42, *Foreign citizens living in the United States,* discusses the tax rules applicable to foreign citizens living in the United States. Chapter 43, *Decedents: Dealing with the death of a family member,* discusses a broad range of special issues that survivors face in handling the final tax matters of a deceased family member. Generous-spirited readers will want to peruse chapter 44, *Estate and gift tax planning.* It explains the tax intricacies of giving assets to others while you are alive and also discusses the estate tax and various strategies you can use.

Following these chapters on special situations, the next chapters offer a further helping hand. Chapter 45, *Everything you need to know about e-filing,* leads you through the electronic filing process. With luck, you won't need to refer to chapter 46, *If your return is examined,* but, in case your tax return is examined and you are subject to an audit, you will find it useful. Chapter 47, *Planning ahead for 2012 and beyond,* can help you save money on your taxes next year and beyond. It discusses tax developments in 2012 and after.

Chapter 48, *Tax rate schedules,* is the final chapter. It provides the 2011 tax rate schedules that you need to complete your tax return. The 2011 Tax Tables can be easily viewed and printed out at *www.irs.gov*. The tax tables must be used by taxpayers with taxable income of less than $100,000. Taxpayers with taxable income of $100,000 or more should use the tax rate schedules.

Chapter 38

Self-employment income: How to file Schedule C

ey.com/EYTaxGuide

Note

ey.com/EYTaxGuide
Ernst & Young LLP will update the *Ernst & Young Tax Guide 2012* website with relevant taxpayer information as it becomes available. You can also sign up for email alerts to let you know when changes have been made.

Introduction

More and more people work for themselves. Whether your business is your sole source of income, or it supplements other income, or it is new or existing, you will face a number of perplexing tax questions that ordinary wage earners do not face What income do you report? What expenses can you deduct? What forms do you need to file?

Unlike a partnership or a regular corporation, a sole proprietorship is not a separate entity. [A limited liability company (LLC) which has only one member is treated as a sole proprietorship for tax purposes.] In a sole proprietorship, you and your business are one and the same. You report net profit or loss for the year from a sole proprietorship on Form 1040, Schedule C (or Schedule C-EZ), and it becomes part of your adjusted gross income. In addition to owing income tax on such income, you, as the sole proprietor, usually will be liable for self-employment tax, and will also be required to make payments of estimated taxes. A net loss from the business generally can be deducted when you compute your adjusted gross income (see hobby loss rules, later in this chapter).

This chapter concentrates on how a sole proprietorship recognizes business profit and losses on Form 1040, Schedule C, and Schedule SE. Examples of completed forms are included at the end of this chapter.

Tax Breaks and Deductions You Can Use Checklist

Self-employment. Millions of Americans are self-employed. The good news is that self-employment can provide a number of tax advantages not available to employees. For example, expenses you incur as an entrepreneur are deductible in calculating your adjusted gross income (AGI), but an employee can only deduct such expenses as miscellaneous itemized deductions, if they itemize, subject to a 2% of AGI floor. Self-employed individuals can also establish their own retirement plans and deduct contributions to those plans. On the other hand, the self-employed have to pay a larger amount of social security and Medicare taxes than employees.

Useful Items

You may want to see:

Publication

- □ **15** Circular E, Employer's Tax Guide
- □ **15-A** Employer's Supplemental Tax Guide
- □ **225** Farmer's Tax Guide
- □ **334** Tax Guide for Small Business
- □ **463** Travel, Entertainment, Gift and Car Expenses
- □ **535** Business Expenses
- □ **541** Partnerships
- □ **587** Business Use of Your Home (Including Use by Day-Care Providers)

Who Must File Schedule C

If you are a sole proprietor, an independent contractor, a statutory employee, a statutory nonemployee, or a single member LLC, you may be required to report business income and expenses on Schedule C.

Sole proprietor. If you operate a business as a sole proprietor, you must file Schedule C to report your income and expenses from your business. If you operate more than one business, or if you and your spouse had separate businesses, you must prepare a separate Schedule C for each business.

TAXPLANNER

Husband-wife businesses. If spouses carry on a business together and share in the profits and losses, they may be partners whether or not they have a formal partnership agreement. If so, they should report income or loss from the business on Form 1065, U.S. Return of Partnership Income. They should not report the income on Schedule C (Form 1040) in the name of one spouse as a sole proprietor. However, a husband and wife can elect not to treat the joint venture as a partnership if they meet each of the following requirements:

1. The only members of the joint venture are the husband and wife
2. The husband and wife file a joint return
3. Both spouses materially participate in the business
4. Both spouses elect this treatment.

Note: The election not to treat the joint venture as a partnership is not revocable without IRS consent.

Independent contractor. A person whose work hours and procedures are not controlled by another and who is therefore deemed to be self-employed for tax purposes must also file a Schedule C.

Statutory employee. If you are a statutory employee, you should file Schedule C. If you file Schedule C, you can deduct certain business expenses when computing your adjusted gross income. A statutory employee's business expenses will not be subject to the reduction by 2% of his or her adjusted gross income that applies to "regular" employee business expenses reported as a part of Schedule A, Itemized Deductions. A statutory employee includes the following occupations:

1. Certain agent and commission drivers
2. Full-time life insurance sales representatives
3. Certain home workers performing work, according to specifications furnished by the person for whom the services are performed
4. Certain traveling or city salespeople who work full-time (except for sideline sales activities) for one firm or person, soliciting orders from customers

If you meet the definition of a statutory employee, your employer will indicate this classification by checking box 13, "Statutory employee," on your Form W-2. This indicates to the IRS that you have the right to report your income and expenses on Schedule C.

As a statutory employee, you are considered an employee for social security and Medicare purposes. However, if you and your employer agree, federal income tax withholding is optional, rather than mandatory.

A statutory employee reports his or her wages from box 1 of Form W-2 on line 1 of Schedule C. He or she then deducts allowable expenses on Part II of Schedule C to arrive at reportable income.

Statutory nonemployee. If you are a statutory nonemployee, you must file Schedule C to report your income and expenses.

Explanation

There are two categories of statutory nonemployees. The two categories are a direct seller of consumer products and a licensed real estate agent. They are treated as self-employed for federal income tax and employment tax purposes if:

1. Substantially all payments for their services as direct sellers or real estate agents are directly related to sales or other output, rather than to the number of hours worked; and
2. Their services are performed under a written contract providing that they will not be treated as employees for federal tax purposes.

Direct sellers. Direct sellers are persons:

1. Engaged in selling (or soliciting the sale of) consumer products in the home or at a place of business other than a permanent retail establishment; or
2. Engaged in selling (or soliciting the sale of) consumer products to any buyer on a buy-sell basis, a deposit-commission basis, or any similar basis prescribed by regulations for resale in the home or at a place of business other than a permanent retail establishment.

Direct selling also includes activities of individuals who attempt to increase direct sales activities of their direct sellers and who earn income based on the productivity of their direct sellers. Such activities include providing motivation and encouragement; imparting skills, knowledge, or experience; and recruiting.

Licensed real estate agents. This category includes real estate agents as well as individuals engaged in appraisal activities for real estate sales, if they earn income based on sales or other output.

TAXALERT

Unlike a statutory employee, a statutory nonemployee is not subject to social security and Medicare withholding. Therefore, he or she is required to pay self-employment tax on net earnings. Additionally, federal income tax withholding is not required; therefore, estimated taxes must be paid.

Single Member LLC (limited liability company). If you operate your business through a single member LLC (this is generally done for liability purposes), you should report your income and expenses with respect to the LLC activity on Schedule C.

What's Included on Schedule C

Schedule C is used to report income and related expenses applicable to the above activities. Income includes cash, property, and services received from all sources, unless specifically excluded under the tax code. Expenses include all ordinary and necessary expenses incurred in connection with the activity.

For sole proprietorships in the business of selling goods or inventory, the primary expense will be the cost of goods sold. The cost of goods sold represents the cost of materials, labor, and overhead included in the inventory sold during the year. Other expenses you may deduct on Schedule C include salaries and wages, interest on loans used in the activity, rent, depreciation, bad debts, travel, 50% of entertainment expenses, insurance, real estate taxes, state and local taxes, and an allocable portion of your tax return preparation fee.

TAXPLANNER

Schedule C-EZ. You may use Schedule C-EZ instead of Schedule C if you operated a business or practiced a profession as a sole proprietorship and you have met all of the requirements listed below:

- Had business expenses of $5,000 or less
- Used the cash method of accounting
- Did not have an inventory at any time during the year
- Did not have a net loss from your business
- Had only one business as a sole proprietor

and you:

- Had no employees during the year
- Are not required to file Form 4562, Depreciation and Amortization, for this business
- Do not deduct expenses for business use of your home
- Do not have prior year, disallowed passive activity losses from this business

Where to Report on Your Return

The net income or net loss calculated on Schedule C is reported on page 1 of Form 1040. The net income or net loss (subject to certain limitations) generated on your Schedule C will cause either an increase or a decrease to adjusted gross income (AGI).

TAXALERT

It is important to note that if you are filing Schedule C or Schedule C-EZ, you must use Form 1040, not Form 1040A or Form 1040-EZ.

Losses. If Schedule C expenses exceed Schedule C income, a loss will result. There is a possibility the amount of Schedule C loss that can be deducted on your current year's income tax return may be limited. The amount of the loss that can be deducted on your return depends on whether you materially participate in the operation of the business (defined below), and/or whether you have enough investment at risk to cover the loss.

TAXALERT

Reporting losses several years in a row on Schedule C may increase the risk that you will be subject to an IRS audit. The IRS monitors Schedule C filers to see if the "hobby loss" rules apply to their returns. Schedule C filers should make sure they understand the hobby loss rules (see below) when entering into ventures that will produce losses in the early years of operation. The ability to prove material participation will most likely result in no change to the amount of loss you claim on Schedule C, should you be audited.

Defining material participation. You are treated as a material participant only if you are involved in the operations of the activity on a regular, continuous, and substantial basis. If you are not a material participant in an activity, but your spouse is, you are treated as being a material participant, and the activity is not considered passive. A passive activity involves the conduct of any trade or business in which you do not materially participate.

For more information about passive activities and the at-risk limitation, see chapter 12, *Other income*, and IRS Publication 925, *Passive Activity and At-Risk Rules*.

What is a hobby loss? The IRS presumes that an activity which produces net income in 3 or more taxable years within a period of 5 consecutive years is engaged in for profit. Therefore, if an activity produces a loss for 3 or more years in a consecutive 5-year period, the IRS may infer that the activity is not engaged in for profit and disallow the loss.

Carrybacks and carryforwards. If you have incurred a Schedule C loss, it is possible that the loss may be large enough to offset all taxable income reported on your Form 1040. If this is the case, you may have generated a net operating loss (NOL).

TAXALERT

Net operating loss. If you have incurred a net operating loss (NOL) in 2011, you can carry back or carry forward the loss and utilize it to offset income in other years. Generally, an NOL can be carried back 2 years and forward 20 years.

Exceptions:

- A business owner with an NOL realized in a year beginning or ending in 2008 or 2009 may elect to carry back the NOL to as many as 5 previous tax years rather than 2 years. This applies to owners of businesses that operate as partnerships and S corporations, as well as sole proprietorships.
- NOLs incurred in 2001 and 2002 could also be carried back 5 years instead of 2 years.
- Earlier NOLs from pre-1998 tax years expire after 15 carryforward years.
- Victims of theft or casualty and sole proprietorships with less than $5 million in gross receipts that incurred losses attributable to presidentially declared disaster areas are subject to a 3-year carryback period.

You may elect not to carry back your NOL. If you make this election, you may use your NOL only during the 20-year carryforward period. To make this election, attach a statement to your tax return for the NOL year. This statement must show that you are electing to forgo the carryback period under Section 172(b)(3) of the Internal Revenue Code. If you do not make this election with your timely filed return in the NOL year, you are required to carry back the loss to prior years.

Example. In 2011, Robert Jones, the sole proprietor of a small business, has a net operating loss of $66,000. In past years, Jones reported the following amounts of taxable income: in 2009, $82,000, and in 2010, $10,000. The NOL can be carried back 2 years to 2009 and offset $66,000 of taxable income in that year. If Robert anticipates income in 2012, he may prefer to elect to carry forward his loss to 2012 by attaching an election under Section 172(b)(3) to his timely filed 2011 return .

TAXSAVER

If your income was subject to tax at a lower tax bracket during the carryback period and you expect future income to be subject to tax at a higher tax bracket, you may wish to elect to forgo the carryback of the NOL, and carry it forward instead. This may be especially relevant for net operating losses arising in 2012, if the so-called Bush tax cuts expire as scheduled at the end of 2012 and marginal income tax rates rise beginning in 2013.

Example. In 2012, Mark's business incurs an NOL of $20,000. It had been profitable in the 2 previous years, and the profits have been taxed at a 15% tax rate. He expects to generate large income in future years, which will be taxed at a 39.6% tax rate, assuming higher marginal tax rates take effect with the expiration of the Bush tax cuts. By electing to forgo the carryback of the NOL, he can save $4,920 in taxes [$20,000 × (39.6% – 15%)].

For more information on net operating losses, see Form 1045 and Publication 536, *Net Operating Losses.*

Self-Employment Income and Social Security Tax

Income reported on Schedule C is classified as self-employment income for sole proprietors, independent contractors, and statutory nonemployees. It is not classified as self-employment income for statutory employees, and is therefore not subject to self-employment tax.

Self-employment tax is calculated on Form 1040, Schedule SE.

TAXALERT

The December 2010 tax law that extended the so-called Bush tax cuts also reduced the social security tax rate applied in 2011 to net earnings from self-employment to 10.4% (down from 12.4%). Unless Congress acts, the social security rate is scheduled to return to 12.4% beginning in 2012.

For 2011, self-employment tax is composed of social security tax of 10.4% and Medicare tax of 2.9%. For 2011, the maximum amount of wages and/or self-employment income subject to the social security portion of the self-employment tax is $106,800. All net earnings are subject to the Medicare portion of self-employment tax. Therefore, if your salary income as an employee is $106,800 or above, you would have already paid all the social security tax you owe. Your self-employment income would, however, be subject to the Medicare tax of 2.9%. There is no limit on the amount of earnings subject to the Medicare portion of the self-employment tax. A comprehensive example at the end of this chapter shows how to calculate self-employment tax when you also have salary income.

You may be able to use the short Schedule SE if:

1. Your self-employment earnings and wages subject to social security were less than $106,800;
2. You did not receive tips reported to your employer;
3. You are not a minister or member of a religious order; and
4. You did not report any wages on Form 8919, Uncollected Social Security and Medicare Tax on Wages.

If your net self-employment income multiplied by 0.9235 is below $400, you are not subject to self-employment tax on your self-employment income.

TAXALERT

Estimated income taxes. You may be required to pay estimated tax on your self-employment income. This depends on how much income and self-employment tax you expect for the year and how much of your income will be subject to withholding tax. For more information, see chapter 4, *Tax withholding and estimated tax*.

TAXPLANNER

If you are self-employed but also a salaried employee, you may cover your estimated self-employment tax payments by having your employer increase the amount of income tax withheld from your pay.

TAXSAVER

If you have more than one trade or business, you must combine the net earnings from each business to determine your net self-employment income. A loss that you incur in one business will offset your income in another business.

When an individual's self-employment earnings multiplied by 0.9235 are less than $400, he or she is not required to file Form 1040, Schedule SE, or to pay self-employment tax.

Joint returns. Show the name of the spouse with self-employment income on Schedule SE. If both spouses have self-employment income, each must file a separate Schedule SE. If one spouse qualifies to use Short Schedule SE and the other has to use Long Schedule SE, both can use one Schedule SE. One spouse should complete the front (short form) and the other the back (long form).

Include the total profits or losses from all businesses on Form 1040, as appropriate. Enter the combined Schedule SE tax on Form 1040.

TAXSAVER

Self-employment tax deduction. You can deduct one-half of your self-employment tax in figuring your adjusted gross income. This is an income tax adjustment only. It does not affect either your net earnings from self-employment or your self-employment tax. To deduct the tax, enter on Form 1040, line 27, the amount shown on line 6 of Short Schedule SE or line 13 of Long Schedule SE and include Schedule SE with your 1040.

What Is Included in Net Self-Employment Earnings?

In most cases, net earnings include your net profit from a farm or nonfarm business, plus the following items:

- Rental income from a farm if, as landlord, you materially participated in the production or management of the production of farm products on this land.
- Cash or a payment in kind from the Department of Agriculture for participating in a land diversion program.
- Payments for the use of rooms or other space when you also provided substantial services. Examples are hotel rooms, boarding houses, tourist camps or homes, parking lots, warehouses, and storage garages.
- Income from the retail sale of newspapers and magazines if you were age 18 or older and kept the profits.
- Amounts received by current or former self-employed insurance agents that are:
  1. Paid after retirement but calculated as a percentage of commissions received from the paying company before retirement;
  2. Renewal commissions; or
  3. Deferred commissions paid after retirement for sales made before retirement.
- Fees as a state or local government employee if you were paid only on a fee basis and the job was not covered under a federal-state social security coverage agreement.
- Interest received in the course of any trade or business, such as interest on notes or accounts receivable.
- Fees and other payments received by you for services as a director of a corporation.
- Fees you received as a professional fiduciary.
- Gain or loss from Section 1256 contracts or related property by an options or commodities dealer in the normal course of dealing in or trading Section 1256 contracts.

Income and Losses Not Included in Net Earnings from Self-Employment

- Salaries, fees, and so on, subject to social security or Medicare tax that you received for performing services as an employee.
- Income you received as a retired partner under a written partnership plan that provides for lifelong periodic retirement payments if you had no other interest in the partnership and did not perform services for it during the year.
- Income from real estate rentals, if you did not receive the income in the course of a trade or business as a real estate dealer. This includes cash and crop shares received from a tenant or sharefarmer.
- Dividends on shares of stock and interest on bonds, notes, and so on, if you did not receive the income in the course of your trade or business as a dealer in stocks or securities.
- Gain or loss from:
  1. The sale or exchange of a capital asset;
  2. The sale, exchange, involuntary conversion, or other disposition of property unless the property is stock in trade or other property that would be considered inventory, or held primarily for sale to customers in the ordinary course of the business; or

3. Certain transactions in timber, coal, or domestic iron ore.
- Net operating losses from other years.

Statutory employee income. If you were a statutory employee, do not include the net profit or loss from that Schedule C (or the net profit from Schedule C-EZ) on Schedule SE. A statutory employee is defined above.

Self-Employment Tax Calculation
Self-employment tax can be calculated under one of the following methods: the regular method, the farm optional method, and the nonfarm optional method.

Regular Method. Under the regular method, your self-employment tax should be calculated as follows:

1. Figure your net self-employment income. The net profit from your business or profession is generally your net self-employment income.
2. After you figure your net self-employment income, determine how much is subject to self-employment tax. The amount subject to self-employment tax is called net earnings from self-employment. It is figured on Short Schedule SE, line 4, or Long Schedule SE, line 4a. It is generally 92.35% of net self-employment income.
3. Figure your self-employment tax as follows:
   - If, for 2011, your net earnings from self-employment plus any wages and tips are not more than $106,800 and you do not have to use Long Schedule SE, use Short Schedule SE. On line 5, multiply your net earnings by 13.3% (0.133). The result is the amount of your self-employment tax.
   - If you had no wages or tips in 2011, your net earnings from self-employment are more than $106,800, and you are not required to complete Long Schedule SE (see guidelines at the top of Short Schedule SE), use Short Schedule SE. On line 5, multiply the line 4 net earnings by 2.9% (0.029) Medicare tax and add the result to $11,107 (10.4% of $106,800). The total is the amount of your self-employment tax.
   - If you received wages or tips in 2011 and your net earnings from self-employment plus any wages and tips are more than $106,800, you must use Long Schedule SE. Subtract your total wages and tips from $106,800 to find the maximum amount of earnings subject to social security tax. If more than zero, multiply the amount by 10.4% (0.104). The result is the social security tax due. Next multiply your net earnings from self-employment by 2.9% (0.029). The result is the Medicare tax due. The total of the social security tax and the Medicare tax is your self-employment tax.

Optional Methods. Generally, you can use the optional methods when you have a loss or small amount of net income from self-employment and:

1. You want to receive credit for social security benefit coverage (in 2011, the maximum social security coverage under the optional methods is four credits, the equivalent of $4,480 of net earnings from self-employment);
2. You incurred child or dependent care expenses for which you could claim a credit (this method will increase your earned income, which could increase your credit); or
3. You are entitled to the earned income credit (this method will increase your earned income, which could increase your credit).

TAXALERT

The ability to use an optional method of calculating self-employment tax allows you to maintain the benefits of contributing to social security and eligibility for credits based on income even in a down year in your business. In a year where your self-employment earnings are lower, you can use the optional methods below to achieve the result of contributing the maximum amount to social security. Also, an optional method would permit you to take the earned income or child and dependent care credit (depending on eligibility). This benefit is allowed only five times during your lifetime. To be eligible for these methods, net earnings from self-employment must have been $400 or more in 2 out of the previous 3 years. The optional methods are as follows:

- If gross income from self-employment falls between $600 and $2,400, report 2/3 of gross or actual net earnings; or
- If gross income is greater than $2,399 and actual net earnings are $1,600 or less, report either $1,600 or actual net earnings.

For tax years after 2008, the maximum amount reportable using this method will be equal to the amount needed to get four work credits for a given year. For example, for tax year 2011, the maximum amount reportable using the optional method would be $1,120 × 4, or $4,480.

How to Determine Items of Income and Expenses

Start-Up and Pre-Operating Expenses

Start-up expenditures are the costs of getting started in business before you actually begin doing business. Start-up costs may include expenses for advertising, travel, utilities, repairs, or employees' wages. These are often the same kinds of costs that can be deducted when they occur after you open for business.

Pre-operating costs include what you pay for both investigating a prospective business and getting the business started. For example, they may include costs for the following items:

- A survey of potential markets
- An analysis of available facilities, labor, supplies, etc.
- Advertisements for the opening of the business
- Salaries and wages for employees who are being trained and their instructors
- Travel and other necessary costs for securing prospective distributors, suppliers, or customers
- Salaries and fees for executives and consultants or for other professional services.

Start-up costs do not include deductible interest, taxes, or research and experimental costs. Therefore, subject to other limitations, these items are currently deductible.

The deductibility of your start-up expenditures depends on whether you actually begin the active trade or business.

If you go into business, start-up expenses of a trade or business are not deductible unless you elect to deduct them.

TAXALERT

For tax year 2011, the deductible amount of start-up expenditures is the lesser of:

1. The amount of the start-up expenditures for the active trade or business; or
2. $5,000, reduced (but not below zero) by the amount by which the start-up expenditures exceed $50,000

Any remaining start-up expenditures are to be claimed as a deduction spread over a 15-year period.

All start-up expenditures related to a particular trade or business are considered in determining whether the cumulative cost of start-up expenditures exceeds $50,000.

TAXPLANNER

If you have start-up costs in 2011 for a new business exceeding the $5,000 limited amount, you should attach a statement to your tax return electing to amortize the portion exceeding $5,000 ratably over a period of 15 years. Complete and attach Form 4562, Depreciation and Amortization, for start-up expenses you are beginning to amortize in 2011.

Example. Tony's repair shop started business on June 2, 2011. Prior to starting business, Tony incurred various expenses totaling $11,000 to set up shop. Tony can deduct $5,000 of these expenses in 2011 and deduct the balance of $6,000 ratably over 15 years.

TAXALERT

Although the IRS has been instructed to do so, no guidance has been issued as to when a trade or a business begins. When it does so, the IRS is likely to take a conservative stance. In the meantime, there has been substantial litigation about this issue. The generally accepted rule seems to be that even though a taxpayer has made a firm decision to enter into a business, and over a considerable period of time has spent money in preparation for entering that business, he or she still has not engaged in carrying on any trade or business until such time as the business has begun to function as a going concern and has performed those activities for which it was organized.

Failure to go into business. If an attempt to go into business is not successful, your ability to deduct the expenses incurred trying to establish your business depends on the type of expenses incurred.

Investigatory expenses. The costs incurred before making a decision to acquire or to begin a specific business are classified as personal and therefore are not deductible. Investigatory expenses include costs incurred in the course of a general search for, or preliminary investigation of, a business prior to reaching a decision to acquire or enter any business. Examples include: expenses incurred for the analysis or survey of potential markets, products, labor supply, transportation facilities, and so on.

Start-up expenses. The costs incurred after making a decision to acquire or to establish a particular business, and prior to its actual operation, are classified as capital expenditures and may be deductible in the year in which the attempt to go into business fails, if prior to the end of the amortization period.

Business sold. If you completely dispose of a trade or a business before the end of the amortization period you have selected, any deferred start-up costs for the trade or business that have not yet been deducted may be deducted to the extent that they qualify as a loss from a trade or a business.

Tax Year

Every taxpayer must determine taxable income and file a tax return on the basis of an annual accounting period. The term "tax year" is the annual accounting period you use for keeping your records and for reporting your income and expenses. The accounting periods you can use are as follows:

1. A calendar year
2. A fiscal year

A tax year is adopted when you file your first income tax return. It cannot be longer than 12 months.

Calendar tax year. If you adopt the calendar year for your annual accounting period, you must maintain your books and records, and report your income and expenses for the period from January 1 through December 31 of each year.

Fiscal tax year. A regular fiscal tax year is 12 consecutive months, ending on the last day of any month except December.

If you adopt a fiscal tax year, you must maintain your books and records, and report your income and expenses using the same tax year.

TAXALERT

If you filed your first return using the calendar tax year and you later begin business as a sole proprietor, you must continue to use the calendar tax year, unless you get permission from the IRS to change. You must report your income from all sources, including your sole proprietorship, using the same tax year.

Accounting Methods

Accounting methods are described in chapter 1, *Filing information*. The discussion that follows relates mainly to self-employed entrepreneurs, sole proprietors, and others who file Schedule C. No single accounting method is required for all taxpayers. Generally, you may figure your taxable income under any one of the following accounting methods:

1. Cash method
2. Accrual method
3. Special methods of accounting for certain items of income and expenses
4. Combination (hybrid) method using elements of (1), (2), or (3)

Cash method. The cash method of accounting is used by most individuals and many small businesses with no inventories. However, if inventories are necessary in accounting for your income, you must use the accrual method for your sales and purchases of merchandise. If you are not required to maintain inventories, it is often more advantageous to use the cash method, because it allows more flexibility and control over your income.

Income. All items of income are generally included in gross income when actually or constructively received. Income is constructively received when an amount is credited to your account or made available to you without restriction. This does not mean you need to have possession of it. Your agent is also allowed to receive income for you (if you authorize them).

Expenses. Usually, you must deduct expenses in the tax year in which you actually pay them. However, you may be required to postpone the deduction for expenses you pay in advance. In addition, you may have to capitalize certain costs.

Accrual method. Under an accrual method of accounting, income generally is reported in the year in which it is earned, regardless of when the income is actually collected, and expenses generally are deducted in the year in which they are incurred, regardless of when the expenses are paid. The purpose of an accrual method of accounting is to match your income and your expenses. If inventories are necessary in your business, only the accrual method of accounting can be used for purchases and sales.

Income. All items of income are generally included in your gross income when you earn them, even though you may receive payment in another tax year. All events that fix your right to receive the income must have happened, and you must be able to determine the amount with reasonable accuracy.

Example. You are a calendar year taxpayer. You sold a radio on November 25, 2011. You billed the customer 3 days later but did not receive payment until February 2012. You must include the amount of the sale in your income for 2011 because you earned the income in 2011.

Income received in advance. Prepaid income is generally included in gross income in the year you receive it. Your method of accounting does not matter as long as the income is available to you. Prepaid income includes rents or interest received in advance and compensation for services to be performed later.

If, under an agreement, you receive advance payment for services to be performed by the end of the next tax year, you can defer the inclusion in income of the payments received until you earn them by performing the service. You **must** be an accrual method taxpayer to defer recognition of income on advance payments for services. You cannot defer the income beyond the year after the year you receive the payment.

Example 1. You are in the television repair business. In 2011, you received payment for 1-year contracts under which you agree to repair or replace certain parts that fail to function properly in television sets that were sold by an unrelated party. You include the payments in gross income as you earn them (which is by performing the contracted services).

If for any reason you do not perform part of the services by the end of the following tax year, 2012, you must include in gross income for 2012 the amount of the advance payments that are for services yet to be performed.

Example 2. You own a dance studio. On November 7, 2011, you received payment for a 1-year contract, beginning on that date and providing for 48 1-hour lessons. You gave 8 lessons in 2011. If you recognize income under the accrual method of including advance payments, you must include one-sixth (8/48) of the payment in income for 2011 and five-sixths (40/48) of the payment in 2012.

Expenses. You deduct expenses when you become liable for them, whether or not they are paid in the same year. Before you can deduct expenses, all of the events that set the amount of the liability must have happened, you must be able to determine the amount of the liability with reasonable accuracy, and economic performance (see below) must occur.

Economic performance rule. Even if all of the events that determine the amount of your expenses have occurred, you still cannot deduct business expenses until economic performance occurs. If your expense is for property or services provided to you, or for use of property by you, economic performance occurs as the property or services are provided or as the property is used. If your expense is for property or services that you provide to others, economic performance occurs as the property or services are provided, or as the property is used.

Special rules for related persons. An accrual basis taxpayer cannot deduct business expenses and interest owed to a related cash basis taxpayer until the amount is actually paid. For purposes of applying this rule, related persons include, but are not limited to:

1. Members of the immediate family, including only brothers and sisters, husband and wife, ancestors, and lineal descendants
2. An individual and a corporation, if more than 50% in value of the outstanding stock is owned, directly or indirectly, by or for such individual
3. An S corporation and any individual who owns any of the stock of such S corporation
4. A partnership and any person who owns any capital interest or profits interest of such partnership

Special methods. In addition to the cash or accrual methods, certain items of income or expenses are accounted for under special methods. They include:

- Depreciation
- Amortization and depletion
- Bad debts
- Installment sales

The method of accounting for depreciation and bad debts is discussed later in this chapter. Methods for deducting amortization and depletion are discussed in IRS Publication 535, *Business Expenses.* Methods for reporting installment sales are discussed in IRS Publication 537, *Installment Sales.*

Combination (hybrid) method. Any combination of cash, accrual, and special methods of accounting can be used if the combination clearly reflects income and is consistently used. As an example, if you maintain inventory, the accrual method of accounting for purchases and sales must be used; however, you may use the cash method for all other items of income and expenses.

Two or more businesses. If you operate more than one business, you generally may use a different accounting method for each separate and distinct business if the method you use for each clearly reflects your income. For example, if you operate a personal-service business and a manufacturing business, you may use the cash method for the personal-service business, but you must use the accrual method for the manufacturing business.

How to Complete Schedule C

Schedule C is divided into five parts:
Part I: Income
Part II: Expenses
Part III: Cost of Goods Sold
Part IV: Information on Your Vehicle
Part V: Other Expenses

In addition, Schedule C requires that you answer a number of general questions about the activity.

Completing the General Information Sections

Line A asks for the principal business or profession, including the product or service that provided your principal source of income.

Line B asks for the six-digit code that identifies your principal business or professional activity. The instructions to Schedule C contain a list of the principal business or professional activity codes that you should use.

Line C asks for your business name. If none, leave this line blank.

Line D asks for your employer identification number (EIN). An EIN is needed only if you had a Keogh plan, a SIMPLE, or a SEP (discussed later in this chapter and in chapter 17, *Individual retirement arrangements (IRAs)*), or if you were required to file an employment or excise tax return. If you do not have an EIN, do not enter your social security number. To apply for an EIN, you may either file Form SS-4 with the IRS where you file your individual tax return or apply online at *www.irs.gov*.

Line E requests your business address. If you conducted business out of your home, you do not have to complete this line.

Line F asks for your accounting method, as discussed earlier in this chapter and in chapter 1, *Filing information*.

Line G asks whether or not you "materially participated" in the business. If you did not, your losses from the business that you can deduct currently may be limited. See chapter 12, *Other income*.

Line H must be checked if this is the initial Schedule C filed for this particular business.

Line I must be checked if you are required to file any Form 1099s. You may have to file information returns for wages paid to employees, interest, rents, royalties, etc. You may also need to file Form 1099 if you sold $5,000 or more worth of goods to someone for resale.

In addition, Part III of the form asks two additional questions. Line 33 asks for the method used to value closing inventory, if your business maintains inventory. The inventory can be valued under any one of the following three methods: (1) cost, (2) lower of cost or market, or (3) any other method approved by the IRS. Methods of valuing inventory will be discussed later in this chapter.

Line 34 does not need to be answered if your business does not have inventory. If the business does maintain inventory and there was a change in determining quantities, costs, or valuations between opening and closing inventories, answer the question "yes" and attach an explanation for the change.

Income

Part I of Schedule C is used to report the gross income from the business. You should include on line 1a gross merchant card and third party network receipts and sales. All other gross receipts or sales should be included on line 1b. Do not combine receipts from two separate businesses on this line. Remember that you must file a separate Schedule C for each business. Statutory employees enter the amount from box 1 of Form W-2 on line 1c.

On line 2, report such items as sales returns, rebates, and allowances. For example, if an item you previously sold is returned for a cash refund, the cash refund should be reported here and not included as a reduction of the gross receipts or sales reported on line 1d.

Subtract line 2 from line 1d, and enter the difference on line 3. From this amount, deduct the cost of goods sold. After deducting the cost of goods sold, you arrive at the gross profit from the business.

Costs of Goods Sold

Part III of Schedule C is used to determine your cost of goods sold. If you make or buy goods to sell, you are entitled to deduct the cost of the goods sold on your tax return. One of the most important costs that must be determined is the cost of your inventory.

Inventories are required to be determined at the beginning and end of each tax year for manufacturers, wholesalers, retailers, and every other business that makes, buys, or sells goods to produce income. Inventories include goods held for sale in the normal course of business, work in process, and raw materials and supplies that will physically become a part of merchandise intended for sale.

Add to your beginning inventory the cost of inventory items purchased during the year, including all other items entering into the cost of obtaining or producing the inventory. From this total, subtract your inventory at the end of the year. The remainder represents the cost of goods sold during the tax period. It should not include selling expenses or any other expenses that are not directly related to obtaining or producing the goods sold.

Inventory methods. To determine the value of your inventory, you need a method for identifying the items in your inventory and a method for valuing these items. In general, there are three methods of identifying items in inventory: (1) specific identification; (2) first in, first out (FIFO); and (3) last in, first out (LIFO).

The specific identification method is used to identify the cost of each inventoried item by matching the item with its cost of acquisition in addition to other allocable costs, such as labor and transportation. This method is most often used by retailers of unique items.

If there is no specific identification of items with their costs, you must make an assumption to decide which items were sold and which remain in inventory. You make this identification by either the FIFO or the LIFO method.

The FIFO method assumes that the items purchased or produced first are the first items you sold, consumed, or otherwise disposed.

The LIFO method assumes that the items of inventory purchased or produced last are sold or removed from inventory first.

The FIFO method and the LIFO method produce different results in income, depending on the trend of price levels of the goods included in those inventories. In times of inflation, when prices are rising, LIFO will produce a larger cost of goods sold and a lower closing inventory. Under FIFO, the cost of goods sold will be lower and the closing inventory will be higher. However, in times of falling prices, LIFO will produce a smaller cost of goods sold and a higher closing inventory. Under FIFO, the reverse will be true.

Valuing inventory. Valuing the items in your inventory is a major factor in figuring your taxable income. The two common ways to value your inventory if you use the FIFO method are the specific-cost identification method and the lower-of-cost-or-market method.

Adopting LIFO method. To adopt the LIFO method, you are required to file Form 970, Application to Use LIFO Inventory Method, or a statement that has all the information required in Form 970. You must file the form (or the statement) with your timely filed tax return for the year in which you first use LIFO.

Once a method is selected you may not change to another method without the permission of the IRS. For a further discussion of inventory, see Publication 334, *Tax Guide for Small Business.*

Expenses

Part II of Schedule C is used to report expenses associated with your business. To be deductible, a business expense must be both ordinary and necessary. An ordinary expense is one that is common and accepted in your field of business, trade, or profession. A necessary expense is one that is helpful and appropriate for your trade, business, or profession. An expense does not have to be indispensable to be considered necessary. Examples of deductible business expenses include (1) reasonable allowance for salaries and other compensation, (2) traveling expenses while away from home, and (3) rentals or other payments for property used in a trade or a business.

You must keep business expenses separate from personal expenses. If you have any expense that is partly business and partly personal, a reasonable allocation should be made to separate the personal part from the business part.

Capital expenditures. A capital expenditure is defined as an expense that must be capitalized rather than deducted. These costs are considered a part of your investment in your business. There are, in general, three types of costs that must be capitalized: (1) costs of going into business, (2) costs to purchase business assets, and (3) cost of improvements.

Although you generally cannot directly deduct a capital expenditure, you may be able to take deductions for the amount you spend through a method of depreciation, amortization, or depletion.

A discussion of some of the more common expenses you will encounter in your business follows.

Bad debts. If someone owes you money that you cannot collect, you have a bad debt. You may be able to deduct the amount owed to you when you figure your business income in the year in which the debt becomes worthless. There are two kinds of bad debts: business bad debts and nonbusiness bad debts. A business bad debt generally is one that comes from your trade or business. All other bad debts are nonbusiness bad debts. For a discussion of nonbusiness bad debts and when a debt becomes worthless, see chapter 14, *Sale of property.*

Business bad debts usually occur because of credit sales to customers. They can also be loans to suppliers, employees, and others associated with your trade or business. These debts are usually shown on your books as either accounts receivable or notes receivable. If you are unable to collect any part of these accounts or notes receivable, the uncollectible part is a business bad debt.

You may take a bad debt deduction on your accounts and notes receivable only if you have basis in the debt; that is, you already included the amount you are owed in your current or earlier gross income (i.e., accounts receivable), or you actually loaned the money (i.e., notes receivable). Only individuals filing a Schedule C using either the accrual or hybrid (cash accrual) accounting method will be able to deduct bad debts relating to accounts receivable. Cash method taxpayers do not report income that is due them until they actually receive payment. Therefore, they cannot take a bad debt deduction on payments they cannot collect.

Example 1. Paul, who uses the accrual method on his Schedule C, reported income in 2010 of $1,000 related to an account receivable from a customer. In 2011, that account receivable became worthless. Because Paul is on the accrual method and has already included the $1,000 in income, he is permitted to recognize a bad debt deduction in 2011.

Example 2. Assume the same facts as in Example 1, except that Paul is on the cash method. Because Paul has not recognized the $1,000 income in 2010, he cannot take a bad debt deduction when the debt becomes worthless in 2011.

The net effect on Paul's income in either situation is the same.

	Accrual	**Cash**
Income recognized in 2010	$1,000	-0-
Less bad debt deduction in 2011	1,000	-0-
Net effect	-0-	-0-

Methods of treating bad debts. The method of accounting for bad debts is referred to as the "specific charge-off method," because it requires the specific identification of the debt that has become worthless. Using the specific charge-off method, you can deduct specific business bad debts that become either partly or totally worthless during the tax year.

Partially worthless debts. You may deduct specific bad debts that are partially uncollectible. To take the deduction, however, the amount must be written off on your books; that is, you must eliminate the worthless portion of the debt from your books as an asset. You do not have to write off and deduct your partially worthless debts annually. Instead, you may delay the write-off until a later year. Also, you may wait until more of the debt has become worthless or until you have collected all you can on the debt and it is totally worthless. You may not, however, deduct any part of the bad debt in a year after the year in which the debt becomes totally worthless. This rule affords you the opportunity to select the year in which to claim the partial bad debt deduction.

Totally worthless debts. A totally worthless debt is deducted only in the tax year in which it becomes totally worthless. The deduction for the debt must not include any amount deducted in an earlier tax year when the debt was only partially worthless. You are not required to make an actual write-off on your books to claim a bad debt deduction for a totally worthless debt. However, you may want to do so. If a debt you claim to be totally worthless is not written off on your books and the IRS later rules that the debt is only partially worthless, you will not be allowed a deduction until the amount is actually written off your books.

Recovery of bad debt. If you deducted a bad debt and in a later tax year recover (collect) all or part of it, you may have to include the amount you recover in your gross income. However, you may exclude from gross income the amount recovered, up to the amount of the deduction that did not reduce your tax in the year in which it was deducted.

Example. In 2010, Beatriz had a $25,000 bad debt loss relating to her Schedule C. She also had $25,000 of income from the activity. Beatriz had no taxable income for 2009.

In 2011, Beatriz recovered the entire $25,000 debt. To figure how much she should include in her 2011 income, see the following calculation.

	2010 with bad debt	**2010 without bad debt**
Income:		
Schedule C	$25,000	$25,000
Bad debt loss	(25,000)	-0-
Adjusted gross income	-0-	25,000
Less:		
Standard deductions	-0-	5,800
Personal exemption	-0-	3,700
Taxable income	-0-	15,500

The calculations show that Beatriz's 2010 taxable income was reduced by $15,500 by including the bad debt. Therefore, $15,500 is included in Beatriz's taxable income for 2011, the year in which she collected the $25,000 debt.

Automobile and truck expenses. If you use your automobile for business purposes, you may be able to deduct expenses associated with the business use of the automobile. You generally can use one of two methods to figure your expense: actual expenses or the standard mileage rate. Refer to chapter 27, *Car expenses and other employee business expenses*, for more information on expenses for business use of your automobile.

TAXALERT

You can report business vehicle information on Part IV of Schedule C rather than Form 4562 if you are claiming the standard mileage rate (51 cents per mile for miles driven January 1, 2011, through June 30, 2011; 55.5 cents per mile for miles driven after June 30, 2011), you lease your vehicle, or your vehicle is fully depreciated. However, if you wish to deduct actual automobile expenses, or if you must file Form 4562 for any other reason, you must continue to use Part V of Form 4562 to report the vehicle information.

Depreciating and Expensing Certain Assets

When you use property in your business, you are permitted to recover your investment in the property through tax deductions. You do this by "depreciating" the property—that is, deducting some of your cost on your income tax return each year. You depreciate "tangible" property, such as a car, a building, or machinery. You amortize "intangible" property, such as a copyright or a patent. Your depreciation deduction is generally based on the cost of the qualifying property. However, the total amount you can elect to deduct is subject to a dollar limit and a business income limit. These limits apply to each taxpayer, not to each business. Depreciation is reported on Part II or Part III of Form 4562, whereas amortization is reported on Part VI of Form 4562. You cannot depreciate land, property you rent from a third party, or inventory.

Property is depreciable if it meets the following requirements:

1. It must be used in business or held for the production of income.
2. It must have a determinable life, and that life must be longer than 1 year.
3. It must be something that wears out, decays, gets used up, becomes obsolete, or loses value from natural causes.

In general, if property does not meet all three of these conditions, it is not depreciable.

The amount of depreciation you can deduct depends on (1) how much the property costs, (2) when you began using it, (3) how long it will take to recover your cost, and (4) which one of the several depreciation methods you use.

You begin to claim depreciation on property when you place it in service in your trade or business or for the production of income. You continue to depreciate the property until you recover your basis (generally the cost) in it, dispose of it, or stop using it for business or investment purposes.

Form 4562, Depreciation and Amortization, is used to report your depreciation. Additional information can be found in Publication 946, *How to Depreciate Property.*

TAXALERT

Expensing certain assets (Section 179 deduction). You can elect to deduct all or part of the cost, up to specified limits, of certain qualifying property in the year in which the property is purchased, rather than capitalizing the cost and depreciating it over its life. This means that you can deduct all or part of the cost up front in one year rather than take depreciation deductions spread out over many years. You must decide for each item of qualifying property whether to deduct, subject to the yearly limit, or capitalize and depreciate its cost.

Qualifying property is property purchased for use in your trade or business and property that would have qualified for the investment tax credit.

Specified limits. Under the Small Business Jobs Act of 2010, the maximum Section 179 deduction available for qualifying property placed into service during taxable years beginning in 2011 (and 2010) is $500,000. This limit is reduced dollar for dollar once the cost of qualifying property placed in service during the year exceeds $2,000,000. Within those thresholds, this 2010 tax law also allows taxpayers to expense up to $250,000 of the cost of qualified leasehold improvement property, qualified restaurant property, and qualified retail improvement property placed into service during taxable years beginning in 2011.

In 2012, the maximum Section 179 deduction will be reduced to $125,000 with an investment ceiling of $500,000. After 2012, the maximum Section 179 deduction is scheduled to drop to $25,000, with an investment ceiling of $200,000. After 2011, qualified property no longer includes qualified leasehold improvement property, qualified restaurant property, or qualified retail improvement property.

Basis of qualifying property. The amount you elect to deduct is subtracted from the basis of the qualifying property. If you elect the Section 179 deduction, the amount of your allowable ACRS or MACRS deduction for this property will be reduced. If you and your spouse file separate returns in 2011, you can each deduct only $250,000, unless you and your spouse agree on a different split of the $500,000.

Other restrictions. The amount of the Section 179 deduction cannot be greater than the income derived from the active conduct by the taxpayer of any business during such taxable year (computed without regard to the property to be expensed). This rule prevents you from generating or adding to a net operating loss due to the Section 179 expense. Any Section 179 deductions disallowed under this income limitation are carried forward to the succeeding taxable year and added to the allowable amount for such year. Therefore, in the following year, you are eligible to receive the deduction ($125,000 in 2012) plus the carryover from the preceding year, limited to the amount of income. Also, the $500,000 amount is reduced dollar for dollar for property investments in excess of $2,000,000 in 2011.

Cost. The cost of property for the Section 179 deduction does not include any part of the basis of the property that is determined by reference to the basis of other property held at any time by the person acquiring this property. For example, if you buy a new truck to use in your business, your cost for purposes of the Section 179 deduction does not include the adjusted basis of the truck you trade in on the new vehicle.

Example. You buy a new piece of equipment, paying $2,500 cash and trading in your old equipment, which had an undepreciated cost to you of $4,000. Even though the new equipment has a tax basis to you of $6,500, you may claim the Section 179 deduction only on the $2,500 you paid out.

When to elect. You must make an election to take the Section 179 deduction, which can only be made in the first tax year in which the property is placed in service.

If you elect to deduct the cost of qualifying property, you must specify the items to which the election applies and the part of the cost of each you elect to deduct. If in 2010 you purchase and place in service two items of qualifying property costing $450,000 and $50,300, and you want to elect the $500,000 deduction, you must specify what part of the $450,000 property and the $50,300 property you want to deduct. You may arbitrarily allocate the maximum $500,000 between the two properties. Your remaining basis of $300 ($500,300 total cost of property placed in service, less $500,000 maximum Section 179 expense) may be depreciated.

Use Form 4562 to make the election and report the Section 179 deduction. The election is made by taking the deduction on Form 4562, filed with your original tax return. The election can be made on an amended tax return filed after the due date (including extensions), and can be revoked as long as the statute of limitations for the return is still open. Consult your tax advisor regarding the Section 179 rules.

TAXALERT

100% bonus depreciation. The December 2010 tax law that extended the so-called Bush tax cuts also provided that qualified property placed in service after September 8, 2010, and before January 1, 2012, is eligible for 100% first-year depreciation. (Tax laws enacted in 2009 and 2010 allowed an additional first-year depreciation deduction equal to 50% of the adjusted basis of qualified property placed in service after December 31, 2007, and before September 9, 2010.) For 2012, the bonus depreciation allowed for investments placed into service generally drops from 100% to 50% of the depreciable basis of qualified property.

Qualified property includes MACRS (Modified Accelerated Cost Recovery System) property with a recovery period of 20 years or less, computer software not covered under Section 179, and qualified leasehold improvement property.

The rules for claiming depreciation are complex. See Publication 946, *How to Depreciate Property,* for more information.

Computers. If you use a computer for both business and personal use, there are special rules that may limit the amount of depreciation that can be deducted.

The amount of depreciation you are allowed to deduct depends on what percentage of use was business and what percentage was personal. The allocation is made on the basis of the most appropriate unit of time. For example, determine the percentage of use in a trade or a business for a tax year by dividing the number of hours the computer is used for business purposes by the total number of hours the computer is used for any purpose for that tax year.

Luxury automobiles. See chapter 27, *Car expenses and other employee business expenses*, for a discussion of luxury cars and depreciation.

Amortization. Capitalized costs of certain intangible property acquired and held in connection with the conduct of a trade or business, or an activity engaged in for the production of income, may be amortized. The amount of the deduction is determined by amortizing the adjusted basis (generally the cost) of the intangible property ratably over a 15-year period. The amortization period begins with the month the intangible property is acquired.

These amortization rules apply to "Section 197 intangible" property. "Section 197 intangible" property is defined as any property that is included in any one or more of the following categories:

1. Goodwill and going concern value
2. Certain specified types of intangible property that generally relate to workforce, information base, know-how, customers, suppliers, or other similar items
3. Any license, permit, or other right granted by a governmental unit or agency, or instrumentality thereof
4. Any covenant not to compete (or other arrangement to the extent that the arrangement has substantially the same effect as a covenant not to compete) entered into in connection with the direct or indirect acquisition of an interest in a trade or business (or substantial portion thereof)
5. Any franchise, trademark, or trade name

Special rules apply if a taxpayer disposes of some, but not all, "Section 197 intangible" property that was acquired in a transaction. No loss is to be recognized by reason of such a disposition. Instead, the adjusted bases of the retained "Section 197 intangible" properties acquired in connection with such transaction are increased by the amount of any loss not recognized.

Leasing Business Assets

Many sole proprietors decide to lease a business asset, rather than purchase it. This is ideal if the asset is only needed for a limited period of time. For example, a tax practitioner may only need a computer for the months of February through April. Instead of incurring the large capital outlay required to purchase the asset, he or she can free up cash by leasing a computer.

Generally, the entire expense for leasing a business asset is deductible. This assumes the asset is used 100% of the time for business purposes. If, however, the asset is for both business and personal use, only the portion attributable to business use is allowed as a deduction. The most common business asset leased by a sole proprietor or a statutory employee is an automobile.

If you lease an automobile, you can deduct the portion of each lease payment related to the use of the automobile in your business or work. You cannot deduct any part of a lease payment that is for commuting to or from your regular job, or other personal use of the automobile. You must amortize any advance payments made on the lease over the entire lease period.

Autos leased after December 31, 1986, and used in a business, for a lease term of 30 days or more, may require an "inclusion amount" in income each year. If the fair market value of the automobile when the lease began exceeds the amounts depicted in the chart below, you must include in your gross income an inclusion amount each tax year during which you lease the automobile. For more about leasing, see chapter 27, *Car expenses and other employee business expenses*.

Year Lease Began	Base Value
2007	$15,500
2008	$18,500
2009	$18,500
2010	$16,700
2011	$18,500

Health Insurance

Self-employed individuals, including those filing Schedule C, may deduct the amount paid for health insurance premiums on behalf of themselves, their spouses, and—beginning March 30, 2010—their child who was under age 27 at the end of 2011, even if the child was not their dependent.

A child includes your son, daughter, stepchild, adopted child, or foster child. A foster child is any child placed with you by an authorized placement agency or by judgment, decree, or other order of any court of competent jurisdiction.

This deduction is only available if you had net profits from self-employment for the year and were not eligible to participate in a subsidized health plan maintained by you or your spouse's employer. The determination of whether a self-employed individual or his or her spouse may be eligible for employer-provided health benefits is made on a monthly basis.

Medicare premiums you voluntarily pay to obtain insurance that is similar to qualifying private health insurance can be used to figure the deduction. If you previously filed a return without using Medicare premiums to figure the deduction, you can file an amended return to refigure the deduction. For more information, see Form 1040X, Amended U.S. Individual Income Tax Return.

The allowable deduction is limited to the lesser of (1) 100% of the amount paid for health insurance premiums during 2011 for the self-employed individual, spouse, and children under age 27 as of the end of 2011, or (2) the net profit from the trade or business less the amount claimed for a Keogh plan, SIMPLE, or a SEP deduction on Form 1040, line 28.

The deduction is not claimed on Schedule C but is instead claimed on Form 1040, line 29, as an adjustment to income. Any medical insurance expenses in excess of the allowable deduction may be claimed as an itemized deduction on Schedule A (Form 1040), subject to the 7.5% (10% in the case of alternative minimum tax) of adjusted gross income floor for medical expenses.

TAXALERT

For tax years beginning during 2010 only, self-employed individuals were allowed to reduce the amount of their self-employment income subject to self-employment tax in 2010 by the amount of qualifying health insurance premiums paid. This deduction for purposes of calculating self-employment tax is no longer available for tax years after 2010.

Employees

Who are employees? Before you can know how to treat payments that you make for services rendered to you, you must first know the business relationship that exists between you and the person performing those services. The person performing the services may be: (1) an independent contractor, (2) a common-law employee, (3) a statutory employee, or (4) a statutory independent contractor.

The determination of a worker's classification can have significant tax consequences to an employer. When workers are not treated as employees, the employer can avoid employment tax and wage withholding responsibilities, as well as costs related to pension plans, health insurance, and other fringe benefits.

Independent contractors. People, such as lawyers, contractors, subcontractors, public stenographers, auctioneers, and so on, who follow an independent trade, business, or profession in which they offer their services to the general public, are generally not employees. However, whether such people are employees or independent contractors depends on the facts in each case. The general rule is that an individual is an independent contractor if you, the employer, have the right to control or direct only the result of the work and not the means and methods of accomplishing the result.

You do not have to withhold or pay taxes on payments made to independent contractors.

Common-law employees. Under common-law rules, every individual who performs services subject to the will and control of an employer, as to both what must be done and how it must be done, is an employee. It does not matter that the employer allows the employee discretion and freedom of action, so long as the employer has the legal right to control both the method and the result of the services.

Two usual characteristics of an employer-employee relationship are that the employer has the right to discharge the employee, and that the employer supplies the employee with tools and a place to work.

No distinction is made between classes of employees. Superintendents, managers, and other supervisory personnel are all employees. An officer of a corporation is generally an employee, but a director is not. An officer who performs no services or only minor services, and neither receives nor is entitled to receive any pay, is not considered an employee.

You generally must withhold and pay federal, social security, and Medicare taxes on wages you pay to common-law employees.

Statutory employees and statutory independent contractors are discussed at the beginning of this chapter.

Salaries, wages, and other forms of pay that you make to employees are generally deductible business expenses. However, a deduction for salaries and wages must be reduced by any work opportunity credit determined for the tax year. This will be discussed later in this chapter.

Tests for deductibility. To be deductible, employees' pay must meet all of the following four tests:

Test 1–Ordinary and necessary. You must be able to show that salaries, wages, and other payments for employees' services are ordinary and necessary expenses directly connected with your trade or business.

Test 2—Reasonable. What is reasonable pay is determined by the facts. Generally, it is the amount that would ordinarily be paid for these services by like enterprises under similar circumstances.

Test 3—For services performed. You must be able to prove that the payments were made for services actually performed.

Test 4—Paid or incurred. You must have actually made the payments or incurred the expense during the tax year.

If you use the cash method of accounting, the expense for salaries and wages can be deducted only in the year in which the salaries and wages were paid. If you use the accrual method of accounting, the expense for salaries and wages is deducted when your obligation to make the payments is established and economic performance occurs (generally, when an employee performs his or her services for you). In addition, the expense must be paid within 2½ months after the end of the tax year. However, the deduction of an accrual of salary to an owner may be limited. (See the previous discussion on the deduction of an accrual to a related party.)

Payroll taxes-general rules for withholding. As an employer, you must generally withhold income taxes, social security, and Medicare taxes from wages that you pay employees. In addition, the amounts withheld with respect to social security and Medicare taxes will have to be matched by you, the employer. Also, unemployment tax payments may be required.

For information about the payroll tax deposit rules, see Publication 15 as well as IRS Circular E, *Employer's Tax Guide*.

TAXSAVER

You may find it helpful to remember the following general rules for withholding:

1. **Independent contractors.** Do not withhold income tax or social security and Medicare taxes from amounts you paid to an independent contractor.
2. **Common-law employees.** You generally have to withhold income tax, social security tax, and Medicare tax from the wages paid to common-law employees. Employers pay federal unemployment tax and their share of social security and Medicare taxes on these wages.
3. **Statutory employees.** You are not required to withhold income tax from the wages of statutory employees. You must withhold and pay social security and Medicare taxes. Unless they are full-time life insurance sales agents or work at home, you must also pay federal unemployment tax on their wages.
4. **Statutory nonemployees.** You do not withhold or pay taxes on payments to statutory nonemployees.

Reporting payments to independent contractors and statutory nonemployees. If payments made to an independent contractor or a statutory nonemployee equal $600 or more during the year in the course of your trade or business, you must file with the IRS and provide the independent contractor a Form 1099-MISC, Miscellaneous Income.

Reporting payments to common-law employees. To report wages paid to a common-law employee, you must complete a Form W-2. The Form W-2 must show the total wages and other compensation paid, total wages subject to social security taxes, total wages subject to Medicare taxes, the amounts deducted for income, social security, and Medicare taxes, as well as any other information required on the statement. For information on preparing Form W-2, see the Instructions that come with Form W-2.

Reporting payments to statutory employees. To report wages paid to a statutory employee, complete a Form W-2. Report the same information that you reported for common-law employees. If the statutory employee has not elected to withhold income tax, this information does not have to be furnished. Also, the employer must check the box for "statutory employee" on Form W-2.

When hiring new employees, you are required to have the employee complete a Form W-4, Employee's Withholding Allowance Certificate, and a Form I-9, Employment Eligibility Verification Form. For more information on which payroll forms must be filed, see IRS Circular E, *Employer's Tax Guide*.

Office in the Home and Form 8829

It is not unusual for a person filing a Schedule C to use part of his or her home for business. If you use part of your home regularly and exclusively for business, you may be able to deduct certain operating and depreciation expenses on your home.

Requirements for claiming the deduction. You may deduct certain expenses for operating out of a part of your home only if that part of your home is used regularly and exclusively as:

1. Your principal place of business for any trade or business in which you engage (including administrative use, as further defined below), or
2. A place to meet or deal with your patients, clients, or customers in the normal course of your trade or business

TAXALERT

The Taxpayer Relief Act of 1997 provided that for tax years beginning after December 31, 1998, a home office qualifies as the principal place of business if:

1. The office is used to conduct administrative or management activities of a trade or business, and
2. There is no other fixed location of the trade or business where you conduct substantial administrative or management activities.

Example. John Smith is a salesperson. His only office is a room in his house used regularly and exclusively to set up appointments and write up orders and other reports for the companies whose products he sells. John's tax year is the calendar year.

John's business is selling products to customers at various locations within the metropolitan area where he lives. To make these sales, he regularly visits the customers to explain the available products and to take orders. John makes only a few sales from his home office. John spends an average of 30 hours a week visiting customers and 12 hours a week working at his home office.

The essence of John's business as a salesperson requires him to meet with customers primarily at the customer's place of business. The home office activities are less important to John's business than the sales activities he performs when visiting customers. Nevertheless, John is entitled to deduct his home office expenses. You may also deduct certain expenses for operating out of a separate structure that is not attached to your home, if you use it regularly and exclusively for your trade or business. (See chapter 29, *Miscellaneous deductions*, for more about deducting these expenses.)

TAXSAVER

Even if you do not qualify for a business use of the home deduction, you may be allowed to take a depreciation deduction or elect a Section 179 deduction for furniture and equipment you use in your home for business or work as an employee.

If you use part of your home for business and meet the requirements discussed earlier, you must divide the expenses of operating out of your home between personal and business use. Some expenses are divided on the basis of square footage. Some of these are further divided on a time-usage basis. If neither of these methods is appropriate, you can choose any other reasonable method to figure the business part of the expense.

What to deduct. Some expenses you pay to maintain your home are directly related to its business use; others are indirectly related; some are unrelated. You can deduct direct expenses and part of your indirect expenses, both subject to certain limitations. If you are a cash-basis taxpayer, you can deduct only the expenses you pay during the tax year.

TAXALERT

The deduction for expenses related to a storage unit in the taxpayer's home that is regularly used for inventory of the taxpayer's business of selling products in which the home is the sole fixed location of the business has been expanded to cover product samples as well as inventory.

Taxpayers are not required to use the space *exclusively* for the storage of inventory or product samples in order to be eligible for the deduction. The new rule adds "product samples" to clarify the current rule, so taxpayers need not attempt to distinguish between inventory and product samples.

Example. Joe Smith is in the business of selling cosmetics. Joe's residence is the only location of his business. He uses space in the study of his home to store cosmetic samples. Joe may deduct the expenses related to the portion of his residence used to store the product samples. It does not matter if Joe uses the study for additional purposes.

Direct expenses. Direct expenses benefit only the business part of your home. They include a separate phone line installed for the business, painting, or repairs made to the specific area or room used for business. You can deduct direct expenses in full.

Indirect expenses. Indirect expenses are for keeping up and running your entire home. They benefit both the business and personal parts of your home. Examples of indirect expenses include:

- Real estate taxes
- Deductible mortgage interest
- Casualty losses
- Rent
- Utilities and services
- Insurance
- Repairs
- Security systems
- Depreciation

You can deduct the business percentage of your indirect expenses.

Figuring the business percentage. To figure deductions for the business use of your home, find the business percentage. You can do this by dividing the area used for business by the total area of your home. You may measure the area in square feet. To figure the percentage of your home used for business, divide the number of square feet of space used for business by the total number of square feet of space in your home. If the rooms in your home are about the same size, figure the business percentage by dividing the number of rooms used for business by the number of rooms in the home. You can also use any other reasonable method to determine the business percentage.

Example 1. Your home measures 1,200 square feet. You use one room that measures 240 square feet for business.

Therefore, you use one-fifth (240 ÷ 1,200), or 20%, of the total area for business.

Example 2. If the rooms in your home are about the same size, and you use one room in a 5-room house for business, you use one-fifth, or 20%, of the total area for business.

Real estate taxes. If you own your home, you can deduct part of the real estate taxes on your home as a business expense. To figure the business part of your real estate taxes, multiply the real estate taxes paid by the percentage of your home used for business.

Deductible mortgage interest. If you pay deductible mortgage interest, you can generally deduct part of it as a business expense. To figure the business part of your deductible mortgage interest, multiply this interest by the percentage of your home used in business. You can include interest on a second mortgage in this computation.

Casualty losses. If you have a casualty loss on your home or other property you use in business, you can deduct the business part of the loss as a business expense. Treat a casualty loss as an unrelated expense, a direct expense, or an indirect expense depending on the property affected.

In a partial destruction, the deductible loss is the decrease in fair market value of the property or the adjusted basis of the property, whichever is less. You must reduce this amount by any insurance or other reimbursement received.

If your business property is completely destroyed (becomes totally worthless), your deductible loss is the adjusted basis of the property, minus any salvage value and any insurance or other reimbursement you receive or expect to receive. Figure the loss without taking into account any decrease in fair market value.

Rent. If you rent, rather than own, a home and meet the requirements for business use of the home, you can deduct part of the rent you pay. To figure your deduction, multiply your rent payments by the percentage of your home used for business.

Utilities and services. Expenses for utilities and services, such as electricity, gas, trash removal, and cleaning services, are primarily personal expenses. However, if you use part of your home for business, you can deduct the business part of these expenses.

Telephone. The basic local telephone service charge, including taxes, for the first telephone line into your home is a nondeductible personal expense. However, charges for business long-distance phone calls on that line, as well as the cost of a second line into your home used exclusively for business, are deductible business expenses for the business use of your home. Deduct these charges separately on the appropriate schedule. Do not include them in your home office deduction.

Insurance. You can deduct the cost of insurance that covers the business part of your home.

Repairs. The cost of repairs and supplies that relate to your business, including labor (other than your own labor), is a deductible expense. For example, a furnace repair benefits the entire home. If you use 10% of your home for business, you can deduct 10% of the cost of the furnace repair.

Repairs keep your home in good working order over its useful life. Examples of common repairs are patching walls and floors, painting, wallpapering, repairing roofs and gutters, and mending leaks.

Security system. If you install a security system that protects all the doors and windows in your home, you can deduct the business part of the expenses you incur to maintain and monitor the system. You can also take a depreciation deduction for the part of the cost of the security system relating to the business use of your home.

Depreciation. The cost of property that can be used for more than 1 year, such as a building, a permanent improvement, or furniture, is a capital expenditure.

Land is not depreciable property. You generally cannot recover the cost of land until you dispose of it.

Permanent improvements. A permanent improvement increases the value of property, adds to its life, or gives it a new or different use. Examples of improvements are replacement of electric wiring or plumbing, a new roof, an addition, paneling, remodeling, or major modifications.

Depreciating your home. If you use part of your home for business, depreciate that part as nonresidential real property under the Modified Accelerated Cost Recovery System (MACRS). Under MACRS, nonresidential real property is depreciated using the straight-line method over 39 years.

To figure depreciation on the business part of your home, you need to know:

1. The business-use percentage of your home
2. The first month in your tax year for which you can deduct business use of your home expenses
3. The adjusted basis and fair market value of your home at the time you qualify for a deduction

Adjusted basis of home. The adjusted basis of your home is generally its cost plus the cost of any permanent improvements that you made to it minus any casualty losses deducted in earlier tax years.

When you change part of your home from personal to business use, your basis for depreciation is the business-use percentage times the lesser of:

1. The adjusted basis of your home (excluding land) on the date of change; or
2. The fair market value of your home (excluding land) on the date of change.

Unrelated expenses benefit only the parts of your home that you do not use for business. These include repairs to personal areas of your home, lawn care, and landscaping. You cannot deduct unrelated expenses. For more information, also see chapter 29, *Miscellaneous deductions*.

Recordkeeping. You do not have to use a particular method of recordkeeping, but you must keep records that provide the information needed to figure your deductions for the business use of your home. Your records must show the following:

1. The part of your home you use for business
2. That you use this part of your home exclusively and regularly for business as either your principal place of business or as the place where you meet or work with clients or customers in the normal course of your business
3. The depreciation and expenses for the business part of your home

Generally, you must keep your records for at least 3 years from the date the return was filed or 2 years from the date the tax was paid, whichever is later. Keep records that support your basis in your home for as long as they are needed to figure the correct basis of your home.

Deduction limit. If your gross income from the business use of your home equals or exceeds your total business expenses (including depreciation), you can deduct all of your expenses for the business use of your home. But if your gross income from the business is less than your total business expenses, your deduction for certain expenses for business use of your home is limited. The total of your deductions for otherwise nondeductible expenses, such as utilities, insurance, and depreciation (with depreciation taken last) cannot be more than your gross income from the business use of your home minus the sum of:

1. The business percentage of the otherwise deductible mortgage interest, real estate taxes, and casualty and theft loss, and
2. The business expenses that are not attributable to the business use of your home (e.g., salaries or supplies).

If you are self-employed, do not include in (2) above your deduction for half of your self-employment tax.

You can carry forward to your next tax year deductions over the current year's limit. These deductions are subject to the gross income limit from the business use of your home for the next tax year. The amount carried forward will be allowable only up to your gross income in the next tax year from the business in which the deduction arose, whether or not you live in the home during the year.

Figuring deduction limit and carryover. If you file Schedule C (Form 1040), figure your deduction limit on Form 8829, Expenses for Business Use of Your Home. Enter the amount from line 35 of Form 8829 on Schedule C, line 30.

Deductible mortgage interest. After you have figured the business portion of the mortgage interest on Form 8829, subtract that amount from total mortgage interest. The remainder is deductible on Schedule A; do not deduct any of the business portion on Schedule A. If the amount of interest allowed on Schedule A for home mortgage is limited, because it exceeds the maximum allowed (see chapter 24, *Interest expense)*, the portion of the disallowed interest allocable to the business use of the home may be taken on Form 8829 (see instructions to line 16 of Form 8829 for further explanation).

Real estate taxes. If you file Schedule C, enter all your deductible real estate taxes on Form 8829. After you have figured the business portion of your taxes on Form 8829, subtract that amount from your total real estate taxes. The remainder is deductible on Schedule A; do not deduct any of the business part of real estate taxes on Schedule A.

Daycare facility. You can deduct expenses for using part of your home on a regular basis to provide daycare services if you meet the following requirements:

1. You must be in the trade or business of providing daycare for children, for persons age 65 or older, or for persons who are physically or mentally unable to care for themselves.
2. You must have applied for, been granted, or be exempt from having a license, certification, registration, or approval as a day care center or as a family or group daycare home under applicable state law. You do not meet this requirement if your application was rejected or your license or other authorization was revoked.

Meals. If you provide food for your day care business, do not include the expense as a cost of using your home for business. Claim it as a separate deduction on your Schedule C. You can deduct 100% of the cost of food consumed by your daycare recipients and 50% of the cost of food consumed by your employees as a business expense. You cannot deduct the cost of food consumed by you and your family.

Do not deduct the cost of meals for which you were reimbursed under the Child and Adult Care Food Program administered by the U.S. Department of Agriculture. The reimbursements are not included in your income to the extent you used them to provide food for the eligible recipients.

Retirement Plans

If you are self-employed, you can take an income tax deduction for certain contributions that you make for yourself to a retirement plan. You can also deduct a trustee's fees if contributions to the plan do not cover them.

TAXALERT

Under current law, small businesses, with 100 or fewer employees who collectively received a minimum of $5,000 in wages from the business in the preceding year, are eligible for a tax credit of 50% of the expenses to establish a new retirement plan. The maximum allowable credit is $500 for the first 3 years of the plan, beginning the year prior to the effective date of the plan. Deductible contributions plus the plan's earnings on them are tax-free until you receive distributions from the plan in later years. As a sole proprietor, you can deduct contributions made for your common-law employees, as well as contributions made for yourself. A common-law employee cannot take a deduction for your contributions. This law is set to expire for tax years beginning after December 31, 2012.

The common types of plans a self-employed person may establish are Keogh plans, Simplified Employee Pension (SEP) plans, and SIMPLE plans.

Keogh plans. A Keogh (HR 10) plan is a retirement plan that can be established by a sole proprietor. The plan must be for the exclusive benefit of employees or their beneficiaries. As an employer, you can usually deduct, subject to limits, contributions you make to a Keogh plan, including those made for your own retirement. You can contribute up to 20% of your self-employment income to a defined contribution Keogh plan (up to a maximum of $49,000 in 2011), which may be deductible as described below. Even more may be contributed to a defined benefit Keogh plan, depending on your age.

Where to deduct on Form 1040. Take the deduction for contributions for yourself on line 28 of Form 1040. Deduct the contributions for your common-law employees on Schedule C.

Because the deduction for your contribution to a Keogh plan for your benefit is reported on Form 1040, line 28, not on Schedule C, the contribution does not reduce your self-employment income subject to tax.

Reporting requirements. As the Keogh plan administrator or the employer, you may have to file an annual return or report form by the last day of the seventh month following the end of the plan year (July 31 for calendar year filers).

Simplified Employee Pension (SEP). A simplified employee pension (SEP) is a written plan that allows an employer to make contributions toward an employee's retirement, and his or her own, if the employer is self-employed, without becoming involved in a more complex Keogh retirement plan.

For further information about SEPs, see chapter 17, *Individual retirement arrangements (IRAs).*

SIMPLE retirement plan. Small businesses that normally employ 100 or fewer employees, who earned at least $5,000 in compensation in the preceding year, and do not maintain another qualified plan, may establish a Savings Incentive Match Plan for Employees (SIMPLE plan). A SIMPLE plan can be in the form of either an individual retirement arrangement (IRA) for each employee or part of a qualified cash or deferred arrangement (401(k) plan). Employees may make elective contributions of up to $11,500 for 2011 to a SIMPLE plan, and employers must make matching contributions. Employees are not taxed on account assets until distributions are made, and employers generally may deduct their contributions to the plan.

Individual retirement arrangements (IRAs). In addition to the retirement plans already discussed, a self-employed person may also make a contribution, which may or may not be deductible, to an individual retirement arrangement (IRA).

TAXALERT

The earnings on contributions generated by IRAs are generally not subject to tax. The distributions of deductible contributions and earnings from the plan, which are subject to certain limitations, may be taxable to you upon withdrawal.

For further information about IRAs, see chapter 17, *Individual retirement arrangements (IRAs).*

For more information about tax credits for small businesses related to retirement plans, see IRS Publication 560, available at *www.irs.gov*.

Travel and Entertainment

Business travel and meals and entertainment expenses are deductible, subject to certain limits, assuming that these amounts are both ordinary and necessary, as defined earlier in the chapter.

For a self-employed person, the meals and entertainment expenses to be deducted are subject to the 50% limit. Also note there are certain documentation requirements, as discussed in chapter 27, *Car expenses and other employee business expenses.* (Chapter 27 also contains a more complete discussion of the deductibility of both travel and meals and entertainment expenses.)

Other Schedule C Deductions

Various other expenses not previously mentioned are allowed as a deduction on Schedule C. Examples of these expenses are advertising, commissions and fees, insurance (other than health), interest, legal and professional services, office expenses, including supplies and other items used in the office, general rent, repairs and maintenance, taxes, utilities, and any other business expense that can be classified as ordinary and necessary.

Sales of Business Property Used in Your Business

How Different Assets Are Treated

A sole proprietorship may have many assets. When sold, these assets must be classified as either depreciable personal property used in the business, real property used in the business, or property held for sale to customers, such as inventory or stock in trade or capital assets.

The gain or loss on each asset is figured separately. The sale of inventory results in ordinary income or loss and is reported on Schedule C. The sale of a capital asset results in a capital gain or loss and is reported on Schedule D. The sale of depreciable personal property and real property used in the business results in Section 1231 gains or losses and is reported on Form 4797. (For further information about Section 1231 transactions, see chapter 16, *Reporting gains and losses.)*

Any gain realized on sales and certain other dispositions of depreciable personal property and, under certain circumstances, depreciable real property, is treated as ordinary income to the extent of depreciation deductions taken prior to the sale. The amount of depreciation recapture is the lesser of (1) the gain recognized or (2) depreciation taken on the property. For more information, see chapters 13, *Basis of property*, 14, *Sale of property*, and 16, *Reporting gains and losses*.

Section 1231 business gain or loss. Once you have determined the gain or loss on personal and real property not subject to depreciation recapture, you must combine all gains and losses from the sale and disposition of Section 1231 property for the tax year including Section 1231 gains and losses reported to you through partnerships and S corporations in which you have an interest. In general, if all of your Section 1231 transactions resulted in a net gain, the gain is treated as a long-term capital gain. If all of your Section 1231 transactions resulted in a net loss, the loss is treated as an ordinary loss. See chapter 16, *Reporting gains and losses*, for a further discussion of how to treat Section 1231 gains and losses.

Recapture of net ordinary losses. A net Section 1231 gain is treated as ordinary income to the extent that it does not exceed your nonrecaptured net Section 1231 losses taken in prior years. Nonrecaptured losses are net Section 1231 losses deducted for your 5 most recent tax years that have not yet been applied (recaptured) against any net Section 1231 gains in a tax year beginning after 1984. Losses are recaptured, beginning with the earliest year subject to recapture.

Sale of the Entire Business

Because a sole proprietorship is not a separate entity, a sale of the business will be treated as if each asset in the business had been sold separately. The gain or loss on such a sale is the total of the gains or losses as separately computed for each individual asset.

Both the buyer and the seller of a group of assets constituting a trade or a business must report to the IRS on Form 8594 various information about the acquisition of assets, including the following:

1. The name of the buyer and seller of the assets
2. The fair market value of the assets transferred
3. The allocation of the sales price to the assets transferred
4. Whether the buyer purchased a license, covenant not to compete or entered into a lease agreement, employment contract, management contract, or similar arrangement with the seller

Business Tax Credit

Tax credits are distinguished from deductions in that a deduction reduces taxable income and a credit reduces tax liability. Consequently, $1 in tax credit is more valuable than $1 in tax deduction.

Form 3800. The general business tax credit includes the following:

1. The investment credit (Form 3468)
2. The work opportunity credit (Form 5884)
3. The credit for increasing research activities (Form 6765)
4. The low-income housing credit (Form 8586)
5. The disabled access credit (Form 8826)
6. The credit for small employer pension plan start-up costs (Form 8881)

Form 3800 is filed to claim any of the general business credits listed on Part III, lines 1a through 4z. If your only source of credits listed on Form 3800 is from pass-through entities, you may not be required to complete the source credit form. Instead you may be able to report the credit directly on Form 3800. For more details, see the instructions for Form 3800.

Special Situations

Artists and Authors

The proper way for artists and authors to account for their expenses has been the topic of much debate in recent years. A special exception excludes authors and artists from the uniform capitalization rules for certain qualified creative expenses that they incur in their trade or business. As a result, these expenses can be currently deducted and not capitalized. A "qualified creative expense" is defined as any expense that is paid or incurred by an individual in the trade or business of being a writer or an artist and that would be allowable as a deduction for the taxable year.

Although you are allowed currently to deduct those expenses that are classified as qualified creative expenses, there are some expenses that need to be capitalized. Examples of such expenses include any expense related to printing, photographic plates, motion pictures, videotapes, and similar items.

There is an alternative way for an artist or an author to treat his or her qualified creative expenses. If the artist or author so chooses, he or she can capitalize all qualified creative costs. In the current year he or she is able to deduct 50% of the eligible costs and then deduct the remaining 50% ratably over the next 2 years. The reason one may choose this method over deducting all qualified creative expenses currently is that the meaning of a qualified creative cost is broader in this instance. It includes the costs of films, sound recordings, videotapes, and books. These expenses would otherwise be capitalized and amortized over their estimated useful lives.

How to Complete Schedule SE Line by Line, Briefly

Self-employed individuals filing Schedule C may be required to pay self-employment tax. Self-employment income and the related tax are discussed earlier in this chapter.

When completing Form 1040, Schedule SE, you must first determine whether you need to file the short Schedule SE form or the long Schedule SE form. You must use the long Schedule SE form if any of the following apply:

- You received wages or tips and the total of all of your wages (and tips) subject to social security, Medicare, or railroad retirement taxes plus your net earnings from self-employment are more than $106,800.
- You use either "optional method" to figure your net earnings from self-employment.
- You are a minister, a member of a religious order, or a Christian Science practitioner and you received IRS approval (by filing Form 4361) not to be taxed on your earnings from these sources, but you owe self-employment tax on other earnings.
- You had church employee income of $108.28 or more that was reported to you on Form W-2.
- You received tips subject to social security, Medicare, or railroad retirement taxes, but you did not report those tips to your employer.
- You reported wages on Form 8919, Uncollected Social Security and Medicare Tax on Wages.
- If none of these conditions exist, you are able to use the short Schedule SE form.

As a Schedule C filer, report Schedule C income on line 2 of Section A of the short Schedule SE form, or Section B of the long Schedule SE form (remember, do not include the income reported on Schedule C as a statutory employee).

Long Schedule SE Example

Peter Doyle is single. He is employed as a full-time Latin professor at a university. His wages from this job were $97,100. Dr. Doyle also gives lectures around the country on a freelance basis. His net profit from these lectures was $15,000, which he reported on Schedule C-EZ (Form 1040).

His net profit from lecturing and his wages total more than $106,800, so he must fill out Long Schedule SE.

1. On his Long Schedule SE, Doyle has no farm income, so he leaves line 1 blank.
2. Doyle enters the net profit from his Schedule C-EZ, $15,000.
3. Doyle has no farm income, so he enters the same amount on line 3, $15,000.

4a. Doyle multiplies the $15,000 by 92.35% (.9235) to get his net earnings and enters $13,853.

4b. Doyle did not elect an optional method, so he leaves this line blank.

5a-b. Doyle had no church employee income, so he leaves these lines blank.

6. Line 5b is blank, so Doyle enters the same amount he entered on line 4c, $13,853.

8a. Doyle enters his total wages, $97,100.

8b-c. These lines do not apply to him, so Doyle leaves them blank.

8d. Lines 8b and 8c are blank, so he enters the same amount he entered on line 8a, $97,100.

9. He subtracts line 8d ($97,100) from line 7 and enters the result, $9,700.
10. Doyle multiplies the smaller of line 6 ($13,853) or line 9 ($9,700) by 10.4% (.104) and enters the result, $1,009.
11. Doyle multiplies line 6 ($13,853) by 2.9% (.029) and enters the result, $402.
12. Doyle adds lines 10 and 11 and enters the total, $1,411, here and on line 56 of Form 1040 (not illustrated).
13. Doyle multiplies line 10 by 59.6% ($601) and line 11 by 50% ($201) and enters the result ($802) on Line 13 of this schedule, and Line 27 of Form 1040. This is the amount of SE tax he can deduct.

Comprehensive Schedule C/Self-Employment Example

John Paul Jones is a self-employed comic book salesman. He does business as JPJ Comics. The majority of his business consists of retail sales of comic books. John Paul works out of his home, located at 6409 79th Street, Queens, New York 11379, where he has been running the business since January 1, 1994. One-fourth of his home is used solely for the purpose of running his business. John Paul accounts for his purchases and sales on the accrual method. All other income and expense items are accounted for by use of the cash method. He is also a professor of civil law studies and has $54,000 of W-2 wages in 2011. John Paul Jones had the following income and expenses during 2011:

Gross receipts from sales of comic books–accrual basis	$35,000
Beginning inventory	2,200
Purchases	13,000
Ending inventory	2,700
Business subscriptions	350
Advertising	1,700
Legal fees	200
Supplies	1,200
Meals and entertainment	600
Travel	900
Telephone	300
Annual home insurance	900
Annual mortgage interest	6,000
Annual real estate taxes	4,000
Annual utilities	1,200
Basis of home purchased on 6/4/92	220,000
Amount attributable to land	40,000
Amount attributable to house	180,000

John Paul Jones has established a profit-sharing plan, providing for a maximum contribution of 25% of compensation. For 2011, he has made the maximum contribution before filing his tax return.

TAXORGANIZER

Records you should keep:

- Cancelled checks, receipts, and other documents for evidence of expenses paid
- Any 1099-Misc forms provided to you from the operation of the business
- A record of time spent using your home office for business

Name of person with **self-employment** income (as shown on Form 1040)	Social security number of person with **self-employment** income ▶	
Peter Doyle		001-12-2333

Section B—Long Schedule SE

Part I Self-Employment Tax

Note. If your only income subject to self-employment tax is **church employee income,** see instructions. Also see instructions for the definition of church employee income.

A	If you are a minister, member of a religious order, or Christian Science practitioner **and** you filed Form 4361, but you had $400 or more of **other** net earnings from self-employment, check here and continue with Part I . . . . ▶ ☐			
1a	Net farm profit or (loss) from Schedule F, line 34, and farm partnerships, Schedule K-1 (Form 1065), box 14, code A. **Note.** Skip lines 1a and 1b if you use the farm optional method (see instructions)		1a	
b	If you received social security retirement or disability benefits, enter the amount of Conservation Reserve Program payments included on Schedule F, line 4b, or listed on Schedule K-1 (Form 1065), box 20, code Y		1b	( )
2	Net profit or (loss) from Schedule C, line 31; Schedule K-1 (Form 1065), box 14, code A (other than farming); and Schedule K-1 (Form 1065-B), box 9, code J1. Ministers and members of religious orders, see instructions for types of income to report on this line. See instructions for other income to report. **Note.** Skip this line if you use the nonfarm optional method (see instructions) . . .		2	15,000
3	Combine lines 1a, 1b, and 2		3	15,000
4a	If line 3 is more than zero, multiply line 3 by 92.35% (.9235). Otherwise, enter amount from line 3 **Note.** If line 4a is less than $400 due to Conservation Reserve Program payments on line 1b, see instructions.		4a	13,853
b	If you elect one or both of the optional methods, enter the total of lines 15 and 17 here . .		4b	
c	Combine lines 4a and 4b. If less than $400, **stop**; you do not owe self-employment tax. **Exception.** If less than $400 and you had **church employee income,** enter -0- and continue ▶		4c	13,853
5a	Enter your **church employee income** from Form W-2. See instructions for definition of church employee income . . .	5a		
b	Multiply line 5a by 92.35% (.9235). If less than $100, enter -0-		5b	0
6	Add lines 4c and 5b		6	13,853
7	Maximum amount of combined wages and self-employment earnings subject to social security tax or the 4.2% portion of the 5.65% railroad retirement (tier 1) tax for 2011		7	106,800 00
8a	Total social security wages and tips (total of boxes 3 and 7 on Form(s) W-2) and railroad retirement (tier 1) compensation. If $106,800 or more, skip lines 8b through 10, and go to line 11	8a 97,100		
b	Unreported tips subject to social security tax (from Form 4137, line 10)	8b		
c	Wages subject to social security tax (from Form 8919, line 10)	8c		
d	Add lines 8a, 8b, and 8c		8d	97,100
9	Subtract line 8d from line 7. If zero or less, enter -0- here and on line 10 and go to line 11 . ▶		9	9,700
10	Multiply the **smaller** of line 6 or line 9 by 10.4% (.104)		10	1,009
11	Multiply line 6 by 2.9% (.029)		11	402
12	**Self-employment tax.** Add lines 10 and 11. Enter here and on **Form 1040, line 56,** or **Form 1040NR, line 54**		12	1,411
13	**Deduction for employer-equivalent portion of self-employment tax.** Add the two following amounts. • 59.6% (.596) of line 10. • One-half of line 11. Enter the result here and on **Form 1040, line 27,** or **Form 1040NR, line 27**	13 802		

Part II Optional Methods To Figure Net Earnings (see instructions)

Farm Optional Method. You may use this method **only** if **(a)** your gross farm income[1] was not more than $6,720, **or (b)** your net farm profits[2] were less than $4,851.

14	Maximum income for optional methods	14	4,480 00
15	Enter the **smaller** of: two-thirds (2/3) of gross farm income[1] (not less than zero) **or** $4,480. Also include this amount on line 4b above	15	

Nonfarm Optional Method. You may use this method **only** if **(a)** your net nonfarm profits[3] were less than $4,851 and also less than 72.189% of your gross nonfarm income,[4] **and (b)** you had net earnings from self-employment of at least $400 in 2 of the prior 3 years. **Caution.** You may use this method no more than five times.

16	Subtract line 15 from line 14	16	
17	Enter the **smaller** of: two-thirds (2/3) of gross nonfarm income[4] (not less than zero) **or** the amount on line 16. Also include this amount on line 4b above	17	

[1] From Sch. F, line 9, and Sch. K-1 (Form 1065), box 14, code B.

[2] From Sch. F, line 34, and Sch. K-1 (Form 1065), box 14, code A—minus the amount you would have entered on line 1b had you not used the optional method.

[3] From Sch. C, line 31; Sch. K-1 (Form 1065), box 14, code A; and Sch. K-1 (Form 1065-B), box 9, code J1.

[4] From Sch. C, line 7; Sch. K-1 (Form 1065), box 14, code C; and Sch. K-1 (Form 1065-B), box 9, code J2.

Schedule SE (Form 1040) 2011

SCHEDULE C
(Form 1040)

Department of the Treasury
Internal Revenue Service (99)

Profit or Loss From Business
(Sole Proprietorship)

▶ **For information on Schedule C and its instructions, go to** *www.irs.gov/schedulec*
▶ **Attach to Form 1040, 1040NR, or 1041; partnerships generally must file Form 1065.**

OMB No. 1545-0074

2011

Attachment
Sequence No. **09**

Name of proprietor	Social security number (SSN)
John Paul Jones	111-22-3344

A	Principal business or profession, including product or service (see instructions)	B Enter code from instructions
	Retail Sales of Comic Books	▶ 4 5 1 1 2 0

C	Business name. If no separate business name, leave blank.	D Employer ID number (EIN), (see instr.)
	JPJ Comics	1 3 2 9 9 9 9 0 9

E	Business address (including suite or room no.) ▶ 6409 79th Street
	City, town or post office, state, and ZIP code Queens, NY 11379

F Accounting method: (1) ☐ Cash (2) ☐ Accrual (3) ☐ Other (specify) ▶ Hybrid

G Did you "materially participate" in the operation of this business during 2011? If "No," see instructions for limit on losses . ☐ Yes ☐ No

H If you started or acquired this business during 2011, check here ▶ ☐

I Did you make any payments in 2011 that would require you to file Form(s) 1099? (see instructions) ☐ Yes ☐ No

J If "Yes," did you or will you file all required Forms 1099? ☐ Yes ☐ No

Part I Income

1a	Gross merchant card and third party network receipts and sales (see instructions)	**1a** 35,000	
b	Gross receipts or sales not entered on line 1a (see instructions)	**1b**	
c	Income reported to you on Form W-2 if the "Statutory Employee" box on that form was checked. **Caution.** See instr. before completing this line	**1c**	
d	**Total gross receipts.** Add lines 1a through 1c 	**1d**	35,000
2	Returns and allowances plus any other adjustments (see instructions)	**2**	
3	Subtract line 2 from line 1d 	**3**	35,000
4	Cost of goods sold (from line 42) . .	**4**	12,500
5	**Gross profit.** Subtract line 4 from line 3	**5**	22,500
6	Other income, including federal and state gasoline or fuel tax credit or refund (see instructions) . . .	**6**	
7	**Gross income.** Add lines 5 and 6 ▶	**7**	22,500

Part II Expenses Enter expenses for business use of your home only on line 30.

8	Advertising 	**8**	1,700	18	Office expense (see instructions)	**18**	
9	Car and truck expenses (see instructions) 	**9**		19	Pension and profit-sharing plans	**19**	
10	Commissions and fees .	**10**		20	Rent or lease (see instructions):		
11	Contract labor (see instructions)	**11**		a	Vehicles, machinery, and equipment	**20a**	
12	Depletion 	**12**		b	Other business property . .	**20b**	
13	Depreciation and section 179 expense deduction (not included in Part III) (see instructions) 	**13**		21	Repairs and maintenance . .	**21**	
				22	Supplies (not included in Part III) .	**22**	1,200
				23	Taxes and licenses . . .	**23**	
14	Employee benefit programs (other than on line 19) .	**14**		24	Travel, meals, and entertainment:		
				a	Travel 	**24a**	900
15	Insurance (other than health)	**15**		b	Deductible meals and entertainment (see instructions) .	**24b**	300
16	Interest:			25	Utilities 	**25**	300
a	Mortgage (paid to banks, etc.)	**16a**		26	Wages (less employment credits) .	**26**	
b	Other 	**16b**		27a	Other expenses (from line 48) .	**27a**	350
17	Legal and professional services	**17**	200	b	**Reserved for future use** . . .	**27b**	

28	**Total expenses** before expenses for business use of home. Add lines 8 through 27a ▶	**28**	4,950
29	Tentative profit or (loss). Subtract line 28 from line 7 	**29**	17,550
30	Expenses for business use of your home. Attach **Form 8829.** Do **not** report such expenses elsewhere . .	**30**	4,554
31	**Net profit or (loss).** Subtract line 30 from line 29.		
	• If a profit, enter on both **Form 1040, line 12** (or **Form 1040NR, line 13**) and on **Schedule SE, line 2.** If you entered an amount on line 1c, see instr. Estates and trusts, enter on **Form 1041, line 3.**	**31**	13,096
	• If a loss, you **must** go to line 32.		
32	If you have a loss, check the box that describes your investment in this activity (see instructions).		
	• If you checked 32a, enter the loss on both **Form 1040, line 12,** (or **Form 1040NR, line 13**) and on **Schedule SE, line 2.** If you entered an amount on line 1c, see the instructions for line 31. Estates and trusts, enter on **Form 1041, line 3.**	32a ☐ All investment is at risk. 32b ☐ Some investment is not at risk.	
	• If you checked 32b, you **must** attach **Form 6198.** Your loss may be limited.		

For Paperwork Reduction Act Notice, see your tax return instructions. Cat. No. 11334P Schedule C (Form 1040) 2011

Part III Cost of Goods Sold (see instructions)

33 Method(s) used to value closing inventory: a ☐ Cost b ☐ Lower of cost or market c ☐ Other (attach explanation)

34 Was there any change in determining quantities, costs, or valuations between opening and closing inventory? If "Yes," attach explanation ☐ Yes ☐ No

35	Inventory at beginning of year. If different from last year's closing inventory, attach explanation	35	2,200
36	Purchases less cost of items withdrawn for personal use	36	13,000
37	Cost of labor. Do not include any amounts paid to yourself	37	
38	Materials and supplies	38	
39	Other costs	39	
40	Add lines 35 through 39	40	15,200
41	Inventory at end of year	41	2,700
42	**Cost of goods sold.** Subtract line 41 from line 40. Enter the result here and on line 4	42	12,500

Part IV Information on Your Vehicle.

Complete this part **only** if you are claiming car or truck expenses on line 9 and are not required to file Form 4562 for this business. See the instructions for line 13 to find out if you must file Form 4562.

43 When did you place your vehicle in service for business purposes? (month, day, year) ▶ ____ / ____ / ____

44 Of the total number of miles you drove your vehicle during 2011, enter the number of miles you used your vehicle for:

a Business ________ b Commuting (see instructions) ________ c Other ________

45 Was your vehicle available for personal use during off-duty hours? ☐ Yes ☐ No

46 Do you (or your spouse) have another vehicle available for personal use? ☐ Yes ☐ No

47a Do you have evidence to support your deduction? ☐ Yes ☐ No

b If "Yes," is the evidence written? ☐ Yes ☐ No

Part V Other Expenses.

List below business expenses not included on lines 8–26 or line 30.

48 **Total other expenses.** Enter here and on line 27a	48

Schedule C (Form 1040) 2011

SCHEDULE SE (Form 1040)

Department of the Treasury
Internal Revenue Service (99)

Self-Employment Tax

▶ Attach to Form 1040 or Form 1040NR. ▶ See separate instructions.

OMB No. 1545-0074

2011

Attachment Sequence No. 17

Name of person with **self-employment** income (as shown on Form 1040)	Social security number of person with **self-employment** income ▶
John Paul Jones	111-22-3344

Before you begin: To determine if you must file Schedule SE, see the instructions.

May I Use Short Schedule SE or Must I Use Long Schedule SE?

Note. Use this flowchart **only if** you must file Schedule SE. If unsure, see *Who Must File Schedule SE* in the instructions.

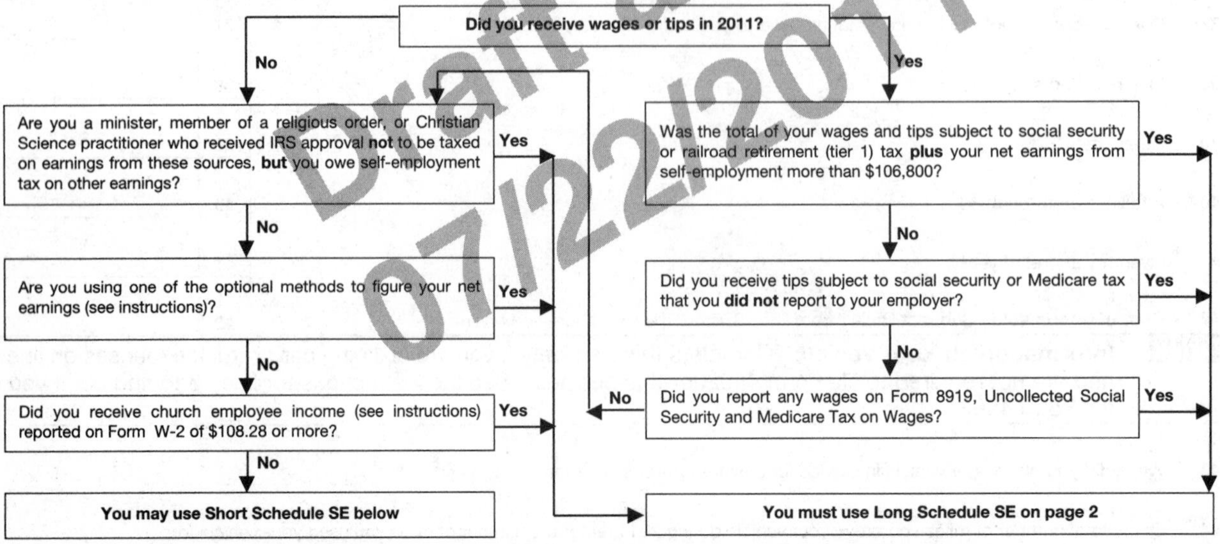

Section A—Short Schedule SE. Caution. Read above to see if you can use Short Schedule SE.

1a	Net farm profit or (loss) from Schedule F, line 34, and farm partnerships, Schedule K-1 (Form 1065), box 14, code A . . .	**1a**	
b	If you received social security retirement or disability benefits, enter the amount of Conservation Reserve Program payments included on Schedule F, line 4b, or listed on Schedule K-1 (Form 1065), box 20, code Y	**1b**	( )
2	Net profit or (loss) from Schedule C, line 31; Schedule K-1 (Form 1065), box 14, code A (other than farming); and Schedule K-1 (Form 1065-B), box 9, code J1. Ministers and members of religious orders, see instructions for types of income to report on this line. See instructions for other income to report . . .	**2**	
3	Combine lines 1a, 1b, and 2 . . .	**3**	
4	Multiply line 3 by 92.35% (.9235). If less than $400, you do not owe self-employment tax; **do not** file this schedule unless you have an amount on line 1b . . . ▶	**4**	
	Note. If line 4 is less than $400 due to Conservation Reserve Program payments on line 1b, see instructions.		
5	**Self-employment tax.** If the amount on line 4 is: • $106,800 or less, multiply line 4 by 13.3% (.133). Enter the result here and on **Form 1040, line 56,** or **Form 1040NR, line 54** • More than $106,800, multiply line 4 by 2.9% (.029). Then, add $11,107.20 to the result. Enter the total here and on **Form 1040, line 56,** or **Form 1040NR, line 54** . . .	**5**	
6	**Deduction for employer-equivalent portion of self-employment tax.** If the amount on line 5 is: • $14,204.40 or less, multiply line 5 by 57.51% (.5751) • More than $14,204.40, multiply line 5 by 50% (.50) and add $1,067 to the result. Enter the result here and on **Form 1040, line 27,** or **Form 1040NR, line 27** . . . **6**		

For Paperwork Reduction Act Notice, see your tax return instructions. Cat. No. 11358Z **Schedule SE (Form 1040) 2011**

Name of person with **self-employment** income (as shown on Form 1040)	Social security number of person with **self-employment** income ▶	
John Paul Jones		111-22-3344

Section B—Long Schedule SE

Part I Self-Employment Tax

Note. If your only income subject to self-employment tax is **church employee income,** see instructions. Also see instructions for the definition of church employee income.

A If you are a minister, member of a religious order, or Christian Science practitioner **and** you filed Form 4361, but you had $400 or more of **other** net earnings from self-employment, check here and continue with Part I . . . . ▶ ☐

Line	Description			Line	Amount
1a	Net farm profit or (loss) from Schedule F, line 34, and farm partnerships, Schedule K-1 (Form 1065), box 14, code A. **Note.** Skip lines 1a and 1b if you use the farm optional method (see instructions)			1a	
b	If you received social security retirement or disability benefits, enter the amount of Conservation Reserve Program payments included on Schedule F, line 4b, or listed on Schedule K-1 (Form 1065), box 20, code Y			1b	( )
2	Net profit or (loss) from Schedule C, line 31; Schedule K-1 (Form 1065), box 14, code A (other than farming); and Schedule K-1 (Form 1065-B), box 9, code J1. Ministers and members of religious orders, see instructions for types of income to report on this line. See instructions for other income to report. **Note.** Skip this line if you use the nonfarm optional method (see instructions) . . .			2	13,096
3	Combine lines 1a, 1b, and 2 . . .			3	13,096
4a	If line 3 is more than zero, multiply line 3 by 92.35% (.9235). Otherwise, enter amount from line 3 **Note.** If line 4a is less than $400 due to Conservation Reserve Program payments on line 1b, see instructions.			4a	12,094
b	If you elect one or both of the optional methods, enter the total of lines 15 and 17 here . .			4b	
c	Combine lines 4a and 4b. If less than $400, **stop**; you do not owe self-employment tax. **Exception.** If less than $400 and you had **church employee income,** enter -0- and continue ▶			4c	12,094
5a	Enter your **church employee income** from Form W-2. See instructions for definition of church employee income . . .	5a			
b	Multiply line 5a by 92.35% (.9235). If less than $100, enter -0- . . .			5b	
6	Add lines 4c and 5b . . .			6	12,094
7	Maximum amount of combined wages and self-employment earnings subject to social security tax or the 4.2% portion of the 5.65% railroad retirement (tier 1) tax for 2011 . . .			7	106,800 00
8a	Total social security wages and tips (total of boxes 3 and 7 on Form(s) W-2) and railroad retirement (tier 1) compensation. If $106,800 or more, skip lines 8b through 10, and go to line 11	8a	54,000		
b	Unreported tips subject to social security tax (from Form 4137, line 10)	8b			
c	Wages subject to social security tax (from Form 8919, line 10)	8c			
d	Add lines 8a, 8b, and 8c . . .			8d	54,000
9	Subtract line 8d from line 7. If zero or less, enter -0- here and on line 10 and go to line 11 . ▶			9	52,800
10	Multiply the **smaller** of line 6 or line 9 by 10.4% (.104) . . .			10	1,258
11	Multiply line 6 by 2.9% (.029) . . .			11	351
12	**Self-employment tax.** Add lines 10 and 11. Enter here and on **Form 1040, line 56,** or **Form 1040NR, line 54**			12	1,609
13	**Deduction for employer-equivalent portion of self-employment tax.** Add the two following amounts. • 59.6% (.596) of line 10. • One-half of line 11. Enter the result here and on **Form 1040, line 27,** or **Form 1040NR, line 27** . . .	13	925		

Part II Optional Methods To Figure Net Earnings (see instructions)

Farm Optional Method. You may use this method **only** if **(a)** your gross farm income[1] was not more than $6,720, **or (b)** your net farm profits[2] were less than $4,851.

Line	Description	Line	Amount
14	Maximum income for optional methods . . .	14	4,480 00
15	Enter the **smaller** of: two-thirds (2/3) of gross farm income[1] (not less than zero) **or** $4,480. Also include this amount on line 4b above . . .	15	

Nonfarm Optional Method. You may use this method **only** if **(a)** your net nonfarm profits[3] were less than $4,851 and also less than 72.189% of your gross nonfarm income,[4] **and (b)** you had net earnings from self-employment of at least $400 in 2 of the prior 3 years. **Caution.** You may use this method no more than five times.

Line	Description	Line	Amount
16	Subtract line 15 from line 14 . . .	16	
17	Enter the **smaller** of: two-thirds (2/3) of gross nonfarm income[4] (not less than zero) **or** the amount on line 16. Also include this amount on line 4b above . . .	17	

[1] From Sch. F, line 9, and Sch. K-1 (Form 1065), box 14, code B.

[2] From Sch. F, line 34, and Sch. K-1 (Form 1065), box 14, code A—minus the amount you would have entered on line 1b had you not used the optional method.

[3] From Sch. C, line 31; Sch. K-1 (Form 1065), box 14, code A; and Sch. K-1 (Form 1065-B), box 9, code J1.

[4] From Sch. C, line 7; Sch. K-1 (Form 1065), box 14, code C; and Sch. K-1 (Form 1065-B), box 9, code J2.

Schedule SE (Form 1040) 2011

Form **8829**

Department of the Treasury
Internal Revenue Service (99)

Expenses for Business Use of Your Home

► File only with Schedule C (Form 1040). Use a separate Form 8829 for each home you used for business during the year.

► See separate instructions.

OMB No. 1545-0074

2011

Attachment Sequence No. **176**

Name(s) of proprietor(s): **John Paul Jones**

Your social security number: **111-22-3344**

Part I Part of Your Home Used for Business

1	Area used regularly and exclusively for business, regularly for daycare, or for storage of inventory or product samples (see instructions)			1	200SF
2	Total area of home			2	800SF
3	Divide line 1 by line 2. Enter the result as a percentage			3	25 %
	For daycare facilities not used exclusively for business, go to line 4. All others go to line 7.				
4	Multiply days used for daycare during year by hours used per day	4	hr.		
5	Total hours available for use during the year (365 days x 24 hours) (see instructions)	5	8,760 hr.		
6	Divide line 4 by line 5. Enter the result as a decimal amount	6	.		
7	Business percentage. For daycare facilities not used exclusively for business, multiply line 6 by line 3 (enter the result as a percentage). All others, enter the amount from line 3 ►			7	25 %

Part II Figure Your Allowable Deduction

			(a) Direct expenses		(b) Indirect expenses		
8	Enter the amount from Schedule C, line 29, **plus** any gain derived from the business use of your home and shown on Schedule D or Form 4797, minus any loss from the trade or business not derived from the business use of your home and shown on Schedule D or Form 4797. See instructions					8	17,550
	See instructions for columns (a) and (b) before completing lines 9–21.						
9	Casualty losses (see instructions)	9					
10	Deductible mortgage interest (see instructions)	10			6,000		
11	Real estate taxes (see instructions)	11			4,000		
12	Add lines 9, 10, and 11	12			10,000		
13	Multiply line 12, column (b) by line 7			13	2,500		
14	Add line 12, column (a) and line 13					14	2,500
15	Subtract line 14 from line 8. If zero or less, enter -0-					15	15,050
16	Excess mortgage interest (see instructions)	16					
17	Insurance	17			900		
18	Rent	18					
19	Repairs and maintenance	19					
20	Utilities	20			1,200		
21	Other expenses (see instructions)	21					
22	Add lines 16 through 21	22			2,100		
23	Multiply line 22, column (b) by line 7			23	525		
24	Carryover of operating expenses from 2010 Form 8829, line 42			24			
25	Add line 22 column (a), line 23, and line 24					25	525
26	Allowable operating expenses. Enter the **smaller** of line 15 or line 25					26	525
27	Limit on excess casualty losses and depreciation. Subtract line 26 from line 15					27	14,525
28	Excess casualty losses (see instructions)			28			
29	Depreciation of your home from line 41 below			29	1,429		
30	Carryover of excess casualty losses and depreciation from 2010 Form 8829, line 43			30			
31	Add lines 28 through 30					31	1,429
32	Allowable excess casualty losses and depreciation. Enter the **smaller** of line 27 or line 31					32	1,429
33	Add lines 14, 26, and 32					33	4,454
34	Casualty loss portion, if any, from lines 14 and 32. Carry amount to **Form 4684** (see instructions)					34	
35	**Allowable expenses for business use of your home.** Subtract line 34 from line 33. Enter here and on Schedule C, line 30. If your home was used for more than one business, see instructions ►					35	4,454

Part III Depreciation of Your Home

36	Enter the **smaller** of your home's adjusted basis or its fair market value (see instructions)	36	220,000
37	Value of land included on line 36	37	40,000
38	Basis of building. Subtract line 37 from line 36	38	180,000
39	Business basis of building. Multiply line 38 by line 7	39	45,000
40	Depreciation percentage (see instructions)	40	3.175 %
41	Depreciation allowable (see instructions). Multiply line 39 by line 40. Enter here and on line 29 above	41	1,429

Part IV Carryover of Unallowed Expenses to 2012

42	Operating expenses. Subtract line 26 from line 25. If less than zero, enter -0-	42	
43	Excess casualty losses and depreciation. Subtract line 32 from line 31. If less than zero, enter -0-	43	

For Paperwork Reduction Act Notice, see your tax return instructions. Cat. No. 13232M Form **8829** (2011)

Chapter 39
Mutual funds

ey.com/EYTaxGuide

Note

ey.com/EYTaxGuide

Ernst & Young LLP will update the *Ernst & Young Tax Guide 2012* website with relevant taxpayer information as it becomes available. You can also sign up for email alerts to let you know when changes have been made.

Introduction

A mutual fund is an investment created by "pooling" money from many investors and investing the money in stocks, bonds, short-term money market instruments, or other securities. A mutual fund will have a fund manager that buys and sells stocks, bonds, and other securities according to the style dictated by the fund's investment objectives. Reviewing a mutual fund's investment objective is an important consideration for any investor as the thousands of different mutual funds have different features, risks, and rewards. Aggressive growth funds, for example, are characterized by high risk and high potential return. These funds typically seek long-term capital appreciation and do not produce significant interest income or dividends. The objectives of balanced funds, on the other hand, are to conserve an investor's initial principal, pay current income through dividends, and promote the long-term growth of both principal and income. While aggressive growth funds generally invest only in stocks, balanced funds typically invest in both bonds and stocks. There are many other kinds of mutual funds—growth and income funds, bond funds, sector funds, index funds, and the like—all with different investing objectives and different strategies to achieve them. A general rule to keep in mind: The higher the potential reward from your investment, the greater risk of loss.

This chapter explains how differing distributions you may receive from a mutual fund are taxed, as well as the different methods by which you may calculate your gain or loss when you sell your mutual fund shares. It also discusses some of the expenses you may incur when investing in mutual funds.

Tax Breaks and Deductions You Can Use Checklist

Avoiding Unexpected Taxable Income from a Mutual Fund. If you buy mutual fund shares right before a dividend distribution, you may be buying a tax liability. The share price you pay reflects this dividend right. For example, say that you buy 1,000 mutual fund shares for $20 a share shortly before the fund declares and pays a dividend of $4 per share. As a result of the dividend, the price per share will drop to $16. You will have to include the $4,000 ($4 per share × 1,000) dividend in your income even though there has been no increase in the overall value of your investment. If the investment had been delayed until after the dividend, the same $20,000 investment would have purchased 1,250 shares (at $16 per share) and this problem would have been avoided.

Tax-Managed and Index Funds. A "tax-managed" mutual fund is a type of mutual fund where the fund's managers are required to employ a series of strategies designed to keep the investors' tax-consequences to a minimum. Most large fund companies have tax-managed funds, and taxpayers often own these types of mutual funds in a taxable account (versus a tax-deferred account like a 401(k) or IRA). In addition to tax-managed funds, you might want to also consider stock index funds within a taxable account, which invest in the stocks making up a particular market index; for example, the Standard & Poor's index of 500 large companies. Since these funds stay invested only in the stocks making up the particular index, there

TAXPLANNER

Kinds of Mutual Funds

A mutual fund is a regulated investment company generally created by "pooling" funds of investors to allow them to take advantage of a diversity of investments and professional management. The advantages that investment companies can offer you are numerous, including:

- Professional investment management of assets at a relatively low cost
- Ownership in a diversified portfolio
- Potentially lower commissions, because the investment company buys and sells in large blocks
- Prospectuses and reports of various periodicals to assist people in readily accessing information needed to perform fund comparisons
- Other special services, such as dividend reinvestment plans, periodic withdrawal and investment plans, the ability to switch between funds by telephone or over the Internet, and in some cases, check writing privileges

Investment Objectives

Mutual funds are classified according to their investment objectives. Following is a summary of common types of funds categorized by their investment objective.

Aggressive growth funds. These funds are characterized by high risk and high potential return. They typically seek capital appreciation and do not produce significant interest income or dividends.

Growth funds. Growth funds aim to achieve an increase in the value of their investments over the long term (capital gains) rather than paying dividends.

Growth and income funds. Also called "equity-income" and "total return" funds, these funds aim to balance the objectives of long-term growth and current income.

Balanced funds. These funds have three objectives: to conserve investors' initial principal, to pay high current income through dividends and interest, and to promote long-term growth of both principal and income. Balanced funds invest in both bonds and stocks.

Bond funds. Bond mutual funds invest primarily in bonds. Some funds may concentrate on short-term bonds, others on intermediate-term bonds, and still others on long-term bonds.

Sector funds. Sector funds invest in one industry, such as biotechnology or retail, and therefore do not offer the diversity you generally receive from a diversified growth mutual fund, which might invest a portion of the fund assets in a variety of sectors.

Index funds. Index mutual funds re-create a particular market index (e.g., the S&P 500). The holdings and the return should mirror that of the index.

Target date retirement funds. A fund that invests in both stocks and bonds for specific long-term periods that you can match with your anticipated retirement date. Also referred to as lifecycle funds, they automatically rebalance their investment portfolios to a more conservative asset allocation as the participant approaches their retirement target date.

Money market funds. This is a type of mutual fund that is required by law to invest in low-risk securities. These funds have relatively low risk compared to other mutual funds and pay dividends that generally reflect short-term interest rates. Unlike a "money market deposit account" at a bank, money market funds are not federally insured.

Types of regulated investment companies

In addition to categorizing investment companies by their investment objectives, investment companies are classified by three types of capital structures:

- Closed-end funds
- Unit investment trusts
- Open-end funds

Closed-end funds. Closed-end investment companies have a set capital structure with a specified number of shares. For this reason, investors must generally purchase existing shares of closed-end funds from current stockholders. Investors who wish to liquidate their position in closed-end investment companies must sell their shares to other investors. Shares in closed-end funds are therefore traded on the open market just like the stock of publicly held corporations. As a result, closed-end funds have an additional risk that isn't present in open-end funds (discussed below)—their price does not necessarily equal their net asset value. Therefore, there is a risk that the fund's shares could sell for less than the value of the underlying investments. However, closed-end funds that are purchased at a discount from the value of the underlying investments can produce an opportunity for greater return.

Unit investment trusts. Unit investment trusts are a variation of closed-end funds. Unit investment trusts typically invest in a fixed portfolio of bonds that are held until maturity rather than managed and traded, as is the case with bond mutual funds. As an investor you purchase units that represent an ownership in the trust assets. Because the bonds are not actively traded, the annual fees charged for unit trusts may be lower than those charged by bond mutual funds. The unit trust collects the interest income and repayment of principal of the bonds held in the portfolio and distributes these funds to the unit holders. Unit investment trusts can provide you with a portfolio of bonds that have different maturity dates and an average holding period that meets your objectives. Cash flow is relatively predictable, because the intention is to hold the bonds until maturity.

Open-end funds. Commonly referred to as mutual funds, open-end funds differ from closed-end funds in that they do not have a fixed number of shares to issue. Instead, the number of shares outstanding varies as investors purchase and redeem them directly from the open-end investment company. An investor who wants a position in a particular mutual fund purchases the shares from the fund either through a brokerage firm or by contacting the fund company directly. Conversely, mutual fund shareholders who want to liquidate their position sell their shares back to the company. The value of a share in a mutual fund is determined by the net asset value (NAV). Funds compute NAV by dividing the value of the fund's total net assets by the number of shares outstanding.

Mutual Funds Fees

The costs associated with open-end fund shares resemble those for closed-end funds. Like closed-end funds, open-end funds bear the trading costs and investment management fees of the investment company. However, mutual fund investors may or may not be subject to a sales charge referred to as a "load."

Open-end mutual funds are classified by their type of load charge. These are:

- No-load funds
- 12b-1 funds
- Load funds

No-load funds. No-load funds don't impose a sales charge on their investors. Purchases and sales of shares in a no-load fund are made at the fund's NAV per share. Consequently, every dollar invested gets allocated to the fund for investment rather than having a portion permanently kept back to cover sales charges.

12b-1 funds. 12b-1 funds are a variation on no-load funds. While every dollar paid into the fund is committed to investment, the 12b-1 fund shareholders indirectly pay an annual fee to cover the fund's sales and marketing costs. This 12b-1 fee typically ranges from 0.1% to the maximum 1% of total fund net assets. *Note*: The 12b-1 fee is assessed every year (instead of only once); thus, the longer you hold your 12b-1 fund shares, the greater the sales charge you will bear.

Load funds. Load funds charge the shareholder a direct commission at the time of purchase and/or when the shares are redeemed and may also assess ongoing 12b-1 fees. "Front-end loads" are charged to the investor at the time of purchase and can be as high as 8.5% of the gross amount invested. On the other hand, some load funds charge their shareholders the load at the time their shares are redeemed. This cost will be either a "back-end load" or a "redemption fee." A back-end load is based on the lesser of the initial cost or final value of the shares redeemed and may disappear after a certain number of years. A redemption fee is similar to a back-end load, but is based on the value of the shares you choose to redeem rather than your initial investment. It typically applies if the investor sells within a very short period of time (usually 30 to 90 days). The purpose of such fees is to discourage shareholders from short-term trading of fund shares.

All fees, loads, and charges reduce your investment return. Therefore, you should consider not only a fund's return, but all of the expenses that affect this return.

Foreign Stock Mutual Funds

Many stock mutual funds invest in foreign stocks. They are divided into the following categories:

- *Global or world funds.* These funds invest anywhere in the world, including the United States.
- *International or foreign funds.* Such funds invest anywhere in the world except the United States.
- *Emerging markets funds.* These funds invest in financial markets of a single developing country or a group of developing countries. A developing country is categorized by the prospect of economic growth and potential vulnerability to economic and political instability. These funds are sought by investors for the prospect of higher returns but generally carry additional risk.
- *Regional funds.* These invest in specific geographic areas, such as Europe, Latin America, or the Pacific Rim.
- *Country funds.* Funds of this sort invest entirely in a specific country. For the most part, single country funds are closed-end mutual funds that typically trade on either the New York Stock Exchange or the American Stock Exchange.
- *International index funds.* These are mutual funds that parallel the concept of a domestic equity index fund. They are designed and operated so that their portfolios mirror the composition of the market index after which the funds are named.

are relatively few sales of stock from the portfolio and only a small amount of realized capital gain.

Foreign Bond Mutual Funds
In addition to foreign stock funds, numerous foreign bond funds are available for investment. Because economic conditions differ from country to country, interest rates vary as well. At any given time, you can usually find several countries with interest rates higher than those in the United States. There is a downside to consider, though. Overseas interest rates may be more attractive, but language barriers, differing regulations, and illiquid markets all increase the challenge of foreign investments. Fluctuating currency values, although a potential advantage, can work against you if the currency of your foreign investment loses value relative to the U.S. dollar.

Useful Items

You may want to see:

Publication

- □ **550** Investment Income and Expenses

TAXALERT

Effective April 1, 2011, the IRS eliminated the option for taxpayers to use the double category method in tracking their basis. Formally, the IRS allowed two options under the average cost method–single category and double category. Under the new regulations, taxpayers using the double category method as of April 1, 2011, must re-calculate the basis of identical mutual fund shares held in their account regardless of holding period.

TAXALERT

Beginning with the 2011 tax year, the IRS is requiring all brokers to report adjusted cost basis in addition to gross proceeds for covered securities and also to report whether the related gain or loss is long-term or short-term. Regulated investment company (RIC) and dividend reinvestment plan (DRP) shares are classified as covered securities if these types of investments are purchased or acquired on or after January 1, 2012. See chapter 16, *Reporting gains and losses*, for further information on covered securities and the three-year implementation period for the new regulations.

For RIC and DRP shares, brokers must report the adjusted cost basis in accordance with their default method unless a taxpayer notifies the financial institution in writing to use a different method.

EXPLANATION

Throughout this chapter, the term mutual fund is used in place of RIC when discussing the new basis reporting rules. However, a broker will determine if a mutual fund should be classified as a RIC and therefore be subject to the new basis reporting requirements in 2012. It will be important for taxpayers to understand if their mutual fund investments are considered RICs by their broker and therefore any purchases beginning on or after January 1, 2012, will be covered.

Caution

You may be treated as having received a distribution of capital gains even if the fund does not distribute them to you. See Undistributed capital gains *under* Capital Gain Distributions.

Tax Treatment of Distributions

A distribution you receive from a mutual fund may be an ordinary dividend, a qualified dividend, a capital gain distribution, an exempt-interest dividend, or a nondividend distribution. The fund will send you a Form 1099-DIV or similar statement telling you the kind of distribution you received. This section discusses the tax treatment of each kind of distribution, describes how to treat reinvested distributions, and explains how to report distributions on your return.

TAXPLANNER

How mutual funds are taxed. Which mutual fund or funds you choose will depend largely on your own investment objectives. One factor you should definitely consider is how your mutual fund investment will be taxed. Generally, a mutual fund is a conduit for tax purposes–that is, the fund does not ordinarily pay income taxes, but its shareholders do. Interest, dividends, gains, and losses are generally passed through to shareholders in a fund in the form of dividends and capital gains distributions. As a shareholder, you are liable for any taxes due on these distributions. Consequently, it can matter enormously how those gains and losses are taxed.

Dividends declared during the last quarter of one year but not paid until the next year. Often, a mutual fund will declare a dividend in October, November, or December of one year but not pay it until January of the following year. Nevertheless, you are treated as having received the dividend in the year in which it was declared.

Example. A fund declares a dividend in December 2011 payable to shareholders owning stock on that date. This is known as the record date. The dividend is not paid until January 2012. You are treated as having received the dividend on December 31, 2011.

TAXSAVER

Timing your purchase of a mutual fund. You should pay close attention to the timing of your purchase of a mutual fund. For example, if you invest in a fund near the end of the year and the fund shortly thereafter makes a year-end distribution, you will have to pay tax on the distribution even though from your point of view you are simply getting back the capital you just invested in the fund. In effect, all you've done is "bought" taxable income that the fund earned earlier in the year but had not yet paid out to shareholders. Typically, the fund's share price drops by the amount of the distribution. Your cost basis in the mutual fund, however, will be the pre-distribution price you paid for the shares.

There is one consolation. Your higher basis will reduce any capital gain on a later sale. Moreover, if you sell the fund at a loss, it will increase your capital loss. If you want to limit your current tax liability and lower your basis in the shares, you should delay your purchase of fund shares until after the record date for the distribution. Usually, a fund can tell you when distributions, if any, for the year are expected. Alternatively, you can consult investment publications, such as *Morningstar Mutual Funds*, which indicate distribution dates for the previous year.

Example. ABC Fund declares and distributes a $1 dividend on December 1, 2011. If you purchased 1,000 shares at $10 per share on November 29, 2011, you will have to report $1,000 of income for 2011. If instead you bought the shares on December 2, 2011, after the record date, you will pay $9 per share and have no taxable income to report in 2011. Of course, for the shares bought on November 28, your basis would be $10 per share instead of $9.

TAXSAVER

Year-end selling. If you are thinking of selling shares in a mutual fund, particularly near the end of the year when many funds pay dividends, you should consider redeeming your shares before any upcoming dividend is paid by the fund. If your shares are worth more than you paid and are held for more than one year, it might be to your advantage to sell the shares before a dividend is declared to take advantage of the 15% maximum long-term capital gains tax rate. If you wait until after the dividend is declared to sell, there is the possibility that some portion of the dividend may not be qualified dividend income and therefore be taxed at the higher ordinary income tax rates. Additionally, if your shares are worth more than you paid and if you have capital losses available in the current year, it might be to your advantage to sell the shares before a dividend is declared. The gain on the sale of the mutual fund shares, unlike the dividend income, can be offset by the capital losses. However, if your shares are worth less than what you paid for them, you can minimize your capital losses by selling the shares before the dividend is paid. Remember, the net asset value per share of the fund (that is, the amount you would receive on the redemption of your shares) decreases by the amount of the dividend.

Community property states. If you are married and receive a distribution that is community income, one-half of the distribution is generally considered to be received by each spouse. If you file separate returns, you must each report one-half of any taxable distribution. See Publication 555, *Community Property,* for more information on community income.

If the distribution is not considered community income under state law and you and your spouse file separate returns, each of you must report your separate taxable distributions.

Share certificate in two or more names. If two or more persons, such as you and your spouse, hold shares as joint tenants, tenants by the entirety, or tenants in common, distributions on those shares are considered received by each of you to the extent provided by local law.

Tax-exempt mutual fund. Distributions from a tax-exempt mutual fund (one that invests primarily in tax-exempt securities) may consist of ordinary dividends, capital gain distributions, undistributed capital gains, or return of capital like any other mutual fund. These distributions generally are treated the same as distributions from a regular mutual fund. Distributions designated as exempt-interest dividends are not taxable. (See *Exempt-Interest Dividends*, later.)

All other distributions generally follow the same rules as a regular mutual fund. Regardless of what type of mutual fund you have (whether regular or tax-exempt), when you dispose of your shares (sell, exchange, or redeem), you usually will have a taxable gain or a deductible loss to report.

For more information on figuring taxable gains and losses see *Sales, Exchanges and Redemptions*, later. Also see chapter 16, *Reporting Gains and Losses*, for further information.

Ordinary Dividends

Ordinary (taxable) dividends are the most common type of distribution from a mutual fund. They are paid out of earnings and profits and are ordinary income to you. This means they are not capital gains. Generally, dividends you receive on common or preferred stock are ordinary dividends unless the mutual fund tells you otherwise. Ordinary dividends will be reported in box 1 of the Form 1099-DIV or on a similar statement you receive from the mutual fund.

TAXALERT

Dividend distributions from a mutual fund, such as dividends earned from the fund's investment securities, are generally treated as a net capital gain for purposes of applying the capital gain tax rates for both the regular tax and the alternative minimum tax. In order to be eligible for the lower capital gain (versus ordinary) income tax rate, the mutual fund must hold the underlying stock for a specified time period. Each year, the mutual fund will be required to report to each shareholder the amount of dividends that qualify for the favorable capital gain and/or ordinary income tax treatment.

Qualified Dividends

Qualified dividends are the ordinary dividends subject to the same 0% or 15% maximum tax rate that applies to net capital gains. They will be shown in box 1b of Form 1099-DIV or on a similar statement you receive from the mutual fund.

Qualified dividends are subject to the 15% rate if your regular marginal tax rate is 25% or higher. If your regular marginal tax rate is lower than 25%, qualified dividends are subject to the 0% tax rate.

To qualify for the 0% or 15% maximum rate, all of the following requirements must be met:

1. The dividend must have been paid by a U.S. corporation or a qualified foreign corporation. See chapter 1 of Publication 550 for the definition of a qualified foreign corporation.
2. The dividend must not be of a type excluded by law from the definition of a qualified dividend. See chapter 1 of Publication 550 for a list of these types of dividends.
3. You must meet the holding period requirement (discussed next).

Holding period

You must have held the stock for more than 60 days during the 121-day period that begins 60 days before the ex-dividend date. The ex-dividend date is the first date following the declaration of a dividend on which the buyer of a stock is not entitled to receive the next dividend payment. When counting the number of days you held the stock, include the day you disposed of the stock, but not the day you acquired it. See chapter 1 of Publication 550 for more information about qualified dividends.

TAXALERT

Mutual funds that pass through dividend income to their shareholders must meet the holding period test for the dividend-paying stocks that they hold in order for the amounts they pay out to be reported as qualified dividends on Form 1099-DIV. In addition, investors must then meet the holding period test for the shares owned in the mutual fund in order for the qualified dividends reported to them to be taxed at the lower rates. If investors do not meet the holding period test, they cannot claim the lower tax rate on the qualified dividend income reported to them on Form 1099-DIV and must classify the qualified dividends as ordinary dividends.

Capital Gain Distributions

Capital gain distributions (also called capital gain dividends) are paid to you or credited to your account by mutual funds. They will be shown in box 2a of the Form 1099-DIV (or similar statement) you receive from the mutual fund.

Report capital gain distributions as long-term capital gains, regardless of how long you owned your shares in the mutual fund.

EXPLANATION

A capital gains distribution from a fund represents net long-term capital gains realized by the fund. While a fund may also realize net long-term losses from the sale of securities, it is not permitted to pass through these losses to shareholders. Instead, the fund must carry net capital losses forward to offset any future capital gains. Generally, all dividend and capital gains distributions from a fund are subject to federal and state income taxes. Dividends from municipal bond or municipal money market funds are the exception. These dividends are usually exempt from federal income tax and may also be exempt from state and local income taxes, depending on where you live and your state's tax law. See the above discussion on tax-exempt mutual funds. For more information on reporting capital gains and losses from the sale of mutual fund shares, see the discussion on gains and losses later in this chapter.

High-turnover funds. Before you invest in a mutual fund, you should consider the rate at which the fund turns over its assets. A fund with a high turnover rate will generate frequent gains and losses, increasing the chances that capital distributions will be short-term, rather than long-term. Short-term capital gain distributions are reported and taxed as ordinary income dividends and are subject to a higher tax rate.

Undistributed capital gains of mutual funds. Some mutual funds keep their long-term capital gains and pay tax on them. You must treat your share of these gains as distributions, even though you did not actually receive them. However, they are not included on Form 1099-DIV. Instead, they are reported to you in box 1a of Form 2439, Notice to Shareholder of Undistributed Long-Term Capital Gains.

Form 2439 will also show how much, if any, of the undistributed capital gains is:

- Unrecaptured section 1250 gain (box 1b),
- Gain from qualified small business stock (section 1202 gain, box 1c), or
- Collectibles (28%) gain (box 1d).

The tax paid on these gains by the mutual fund is shown in box 2 of Form 2439.

Basis adjustment. Increase your basis in your mutual fund by the difference between the gain you report and the credit you claim for the tax paid.

Exempt-Interest Dividends

Exempt-interest dividends you receive from a mutual fund or other regulated investment company are not included in your taxable income. Exempt-interest dividends should be shown in box 8 of Form 1099-INT.

EXPLANATION

A mutual fund may pay exempt-interest dividends to its shareholders if it meets certain requirements. These dividends are paid from tax-exempt interest earned by the fund. Since the exempt-interest dividends keep their tax-exempt character, do not include them in income. However, you may need to report them on your return. See *Information reporting requirement*, next.

Information reporting requirement. Although exempt-interest dividends are not taxable, you must show them on your tax return if you have to file a return. This is an information reporting requirement and does not change the exempt-interest dividends to taxable income.

Alternative minimum tax treatment. Exempt-interest dividends paid from specified private activity bonds may be subject to the alternative minimum tax. The exempt-interest dividends subject to the alternative minimum tax should be shown in box 9 of Form 1099-INT. See Form 6251 and its instructions for more information.

Nondividend Distributions

A nondividend distribution is a distribution that is not paid out of the earnings and profits of a mutual fund. You should receive a Form 1099-DIV or other statement showing you the nondividend distribution. On Form 1099-DIV, a nondividend distribution will be shown in box 3. If you do not receive such a statement, you report the distribution as an ordinary dividend.

Basis adjustment. A nondividend distribution reduces the basis of your mutual fund. It is not taxed until your basis in your shares is fully recovered. This nontaxable portion is also called a return of capital; it is a return of your investment in the company. If you buy mutual funds investments in different lots at different times, and you cannot definitely identify the shares subject to the nondividend distribution, reduce the basis of your earliest purchases first.

When the basis of your shares has been reduced to zero, report any additional nondividend distribution you receive as a capital gain. Whether you report it as a long-term or short-term capital gain depends on how long you have held the mutual fund.

EXAMPLE

In 1997, Jane Smith bought shares in ABC Mutual Fund for $10 a share. In 1998, she received a return of capital distribution of $2 a share, which reduces her basis in each share by $2 to an adjusted basis of $8. In 1999, Jane received a return of capital of $4 per share, reducing her basis in each share from $8 to $4. In 2011, the return of capital distribution from the mutual fund is $5 a share. Jane will report the $1 excess per share as a long-term capital gain on Form 8949 and Schedule D.

Reinvestment of Distributions. Most mutual funds permit shareholders to automatically reinvest distributions in more shares in the fund, instead of receiving cash. You must report the reinvested amounts the same way as you would report them if you received them in cash. This means that reinvested ordinary dividends and capital gain distributions generally must be reported as income. Reinvested exempt-interest dividends generally are not reported as income. Reinvested return of capital distributions are reported as explained under *Nondividend Distributions*, earlier. See *Keeping Track of Your Basis*, later, to determine the basis of the additional shares.

Money Market Funds. Report amounts you receive from money market funds as dividend income. Money market funds are a type of mutual fund and should not be confused with bank money market accounts that pay interest.

How To Report

Generally, you can use either Form 1040 or Form 1040A to report your dividend income. Report the total of your ordinary dividends on line 9a of Form 1040 or Form 1040A. Report qualified dividends on line 9b.

If you receive capital gain distributions, you may be able to use Form 1040A or you may have to use Form 1040. If you receive nondividend distributions required to be reported as capital gains, you must use Form 1040. You cannot use Form 1040EZ if you receive any dividend income.

Table 39-1, *Reporting Mutual Fund Distributions on Form 1040 or Form 1040A*, explains where on Form 1040 or Form 1040A or its related schedules to report distributions from mutual funds.

EXPLANATION

If your only capital gains are from mutual funds distributions, you should report them on line 13 of Form 1040 or line 10 of Form 1040A and not on Form 8949 or Schedule D. In addition, check the box on line 13 of Form 1040 that you are not required to file Form 8949 or Schedule D. Make sure you calculate the tax using the table in the instructions.

Foreign tax deduction or credit. Some mutual funds invest in foreign securities or other instruments. Your mutual fund may choose to allow you to claim a deduction or credit for the taxes it paid to a foreign country or U.S. possession. The fund will notify you if this applies to you. The notice will include your share of the foreign taxes paid to each country or possession and the part the dividend derived from sources in each country or possession.

EXPLANATION

In most cases, you must complete Form 1116 if you choose to claim the credit for income tax paid to a foreign country. You do not have to complete Form 1116 if your total foreign taxes paid are $300 or less for the year ($600 if married filing jointly). You can claim the credit for the full amount of the taxes paid as long as your foreign income is all passive (i.e., interest, dividends, etc.). Under certain circumstances, however, it may be to your benefit to treat the tax as an itemized deduction on Schedule A (Form 1040).

For a discussion of the foreign tax credit and whether you should claim the credit or a tax deduction, see chapter 23, *Taxes you may deduct*.

Table 39-1. **Reporting Mutual Fund Distributions on Form 1040 or 1040A**

		Then report the distribution on	
If you receive ...	**AND ...**	**Form 1040 ...**	**Form 1040A ...**
ordinary dividends (Form 1099-DIV, box 1a)	• your total ordinary dividends received are $1,500 or less, and • you did not received any ordinary dividends as a nominee	line 9a	line 9a
	• Your total ordinary dividends received are more than $1,500, or • You received ordinary dividends as a nominee	• line 9a, and • Schedule B, line 5	• line 9a, and • Schedule 1, line 5
qualified dividends (Form 1099-DIV, box 1b)		• line 9b, and • Qualified Dividends and Capital Gain Tax Worksheet, line 2, or Schedule D Tax Worksheet, line 2, whichever applies	• line 9b, and • Qualified Dividends and Capital Gain Tax Worksheet, line 2
capital gain distributions (Form 1099-DIV, box 2a)	you do not have to file Form 1040, Schedule D	• line 13, and • Qualified Dividends and Capital Gain Tax Worksheet, line 3	• line 10, and • Qualified Dividends and Capital Gain Tax Worksheet, line 3
	you have to file Form 1040, Schedule D (see Schedule D instructions for line 13)	Schedule D, line 13	you must use Form 1040; you cannot use Form 1040A
section 1250, 1202, or collectibles gain (Form 1099-DIV, box 2b, 2c, or 2d)		Schedule D (see the Schedule D instructions)	you must use Form 1040; you cannot use Form 1040A
nondividend distributions (Form 1099-DIV, box 3)		generally not reported*	Generally not reported*
exempt-interest dividends (Form 2439, boxes 1a-1d)		line 8b	line 8b
undistributed capital gains (Form 2439, boxes 1a-1d)		Schedule D (see the Schedule D instructions)	you must use Form 1040; you cannot use Form 1040A

*Report any amount in any excess of your basis in your mutual fund shares on Form 8949. Use Part II if you held the shares more than one year. Use Part I if you held your mutual fund shares 1 year or less.

Sales, Exchanges, and Redemptions

When you sell or exchange your mutual fund shares, or if they are redeemed (a redemption), you will generally have a taxable gain or a deductible loss. This also applies to shares of a tax-exempt mutual fund. Sales, exchanges, and redemptions are all treated as sales of capital assets. The amount of the gain or loss is the difference between your adjusted basis (defined later) in the shares and the amount you realize from the sale, exchange, or redemption.

In general, a sale is a transfer of shares for money only. An exchange is a transfer of shares in return for other shares. A redemption occurs when a fund reacquires its shares from you in exchange for money or other property.

TAXORGANIZER

When there is a sale, exchange, or redemption of your shares in a fund, keep the confirmation statement you receive. The statement shows the price you received for the shares and other information you need to report gain or loss on your return. Although brokers will be required to track adjusted basis for mutual fund shares acquired after December 31, 2011, it will be important to retain confirmation statements for all shares acquired prior to that date.

TAXSAVER

Exchanging funds in the same family. You will incur a taxable capital gain or loss when you exchange shares of one fund for shares in another, regardless of whether the new fund is in the same fund family. So, for example, if you exchange shares in ABC Growth Fund for shares in ABC Technology Fund, you will have to recognize a capital gain or loss. Any service fee charged for the exchange may be added to your basis of the shares you acquired.

You will not have to recognize a capital gain or loss, however, if the shares in one mutual fund are converted to the shares of another pursuant to a tax-free merger of the two funds, or if the redemption of your shares is treated as a dividend.

Information returns. Mutual funds and brokers must report to the Internal Revenue Service the proceeds from sales, exchanges, or redemptions. They must give each customer a written statement with that information by February 15 of the year following the calendar year the transaction occurred. Form 1099-B, *Proceeds From Broker and Barter Exchange Transactions*, or a substitute, may be used for this purpose. Report your sales shown on Form(s) 1099-B (or substitute) on Form 8949 and Schedule D (Form 1040) along with your other gains and losses. If the total sales reported on Form(s) 1099-B is more than the total you report on Form 8949 and Schedule D, attach a statement to your return explaining the difference.

Taxpayer identification number. You must give the broker your correct taxpayer identification number (TIN). Generally, an individual will use his or her social security number as the TIN. If you do not provide your TIN, your broker is required to withhold tax at a rate of 28% on the gross proceeds of a transaction, and you may be penalized.

Keeping Track of Your Basis

You should keep track of your basis in mutual fund shares because you need the basis to figure any gain or loss on the shares when you sell, exchange, or redeem them.

TAXSAVER

For mutual fund and DRP shares purchased or acquired after January 1, 2012, brokers will be required to keep track of adjusted cost basis and holding period information. For mutual fund and DRP shares purchased or acquired prior to January 1, 2012, it will be important to continue to keep track of your basis in order to accurately report any gain or loss upon sale.

Original basis. As explained in the following paragraphs, original basis depends on how you acquired your shares.

Adjusted basis. As described later under *Adjusted Basis*, your original basis is adjusted (increased or decreased) by certain events. You must keep accurate records of all events that affect basis so you can figure the proper amount of gain or loss.

Shares Acquired by Purchase

The original basis of mutual fund shares you bought is usually their cost or purchase price. The purchase price usually includes any commissions or load charges paid for the purchase.

EXAMPLE

Martin Brown bought 200 shares of XYZ Mutual Fund for $10 a share (total of $2,000). He paid a $100 commission to the broker for the purchase. His cost basis for each share is $10.50 ($2,100 ÷ 200).

TAXORGANIZER

Confirmation statements. When you buy shares in a fund, keep the confirmation statements you receive. The confirmation statement shows the price you paid for the shares and the purchase date. This information will help you figure your basis in the fund. As previously mentioned, the new basis reporting requirements for mutual fund and DRP shares become effective for purchases on or after January 1, 2012. It is important to retain confirmation statements for all holdings acquired prior to that date.

Commissions and load charges. The fees and charges you pay to acquire or redeem shares of a mutual fund are not deductible. You can usually add acquisition fees and charges to your cost of the shares and thereby increase your basis. A fee paid to redeem the shares is usually a reduction in the redemption price (sales price).

You cannot add your entire acquisition fee or load charge to the cost of mutual fund shares if *all* of the following conditions apply.

1. You get a reinvestment right because of the purchase of the shares or the payment of the fee or charge.
2. You dispose of the shares within 90 days of the purchase date.
3. You acquire new shares in the same mutual fund or another mutual fund, for which the fee or charge is reduced or waived because of the reinvestment right you got when you acquired the original shares.

The amount of the original fee or charge in excess of the reduction in (3) is added to the cost of the original shares. The rest of the original fee or charge is added to the cost basis of the new shares (unless all three conditions above apply to the purchase of the new shares).

Reinvestment right. This is the right to acquire mutual fund shares in the same or another mutual fund without paying a fee or load charge, or by paying a reduced fee or load charge.

Shares Acquired by Reinvestment

The original cost basis of mutual fund shares you acquire by reinvesting your distributions is the amount of the distributions used to purchase each full or fractional share. This rule applies even if the distribution is an exempt-interest dividend that you do not report as income.

TAXORGANIZER

Dividend reinvestment plan. If you participate in a dividend reinvestment plan, you should keep a record of the dividends and of the shares purchased with the reinvestment. The reinvested dividends are part of your cost basis for the shares. You will need these records to figure your cost basis when you sell all or some of your shares. See Identifying the Shares Sold, later in this chapter.

Shares Acquired by Gift or Inheritance

Mutual fund shares received as a gift. If you receive a gift of mutual fund shares, your basis is determined by the donor's basis (or fair market value of the shares if this is less than the donor's basis). Your holding period is considered to have started on the same day that the donor's holding period started.

TAXALERT

For gifted mutual fund and DRP shares, a broker is required to report all covered securities to another broker in a written statement with all necessary information required for the receiving broker to meet basis reporting requirements. Mutual fund and DRP shares become covered securities if purchased or acquired on or after January 1, 2012.

TAXALERT

Inherited mutual fund shares. If you inherited mutual fund shares prior to 2010 or inherit them after 2010, your basis in the shares is:

1. The fair market value at the date of the decedent's death (or the alternate valuation date), or
2. The decedent's adjusted basis where the decedent received the shares as a gift in the year prior to the decedent's death.

This is known as "stepped-up basis." You are considered to have held the shares for more than 1 year (even if you disposed of the shares within 1 year after the decedent's death). Report the sale of mutual fund shares inherited before or after 2010 on line 8 of Schedule D and write "Inherited" in column (b) instead of the date you acquired the shares.

On the other hand, mutual fund shares acquired from a decedent dying in 2010 do not have an automatic increase in basis. Your basis will depend on whether or not the executor of the decedent's estate elects to have the estate tax apply to the decedent's estate. If the estate tax applies, then the shares you inherit will qualify for the automatic step up in basis. If the executor chooses not to have the estate tax apply, then your basis in the inherited shares will generally be equal to the lesser of the fair market value of the property on the date of the decedent's death or the decedent's adjusted basis in the property. This is known as "carryover basis." If carryover basis applies, the executor may also elect to make additional adjustments that could increase the amount of basis in the shares you inherit. See *Property inherited from a decedent who died during 2010* in chapter 13, *Basis of property*.

TAXPLANNER

For inherited mutual fund and DRP shares after December 31, 2011, brokers must report adjusted basis equal to the fair market value of the shares on the date of death unless the financial institution receives different instructions from the estate representative.

Adjusted Basis

After you acquire mutual fund shares, you may need to make adjustments to your basis. The adjusted basis of your shares is your original basis (defined earlier), increased or reduced as described here.

Addition to basis. Increase the basis in your shares by the difference between the amount of undistributed capital gain you include in income and the tax considered paid by you on that income.

The mutual fund reports the amount of your undistributed capital gain in box 1a of Form 2439 and any tax paid by the mutual fund in box 2. You should keep Copy C of all Forms 2439 to show increases in the basis of your shares.

TAXORGANIZER

Confirmation statements. You should keep all confirmation statements for purchases of mutual fund shares as well as records of dividends that are automatically reinvested in your account. Your basis is increased by amounts reported to you by the fund on Form 2439 as undistributed capital gains you are required to report as income less the tax paid by the fund on the undistributed gains. Your basis is reduced by nontaxable dividends that are a return of your investment.

Reduction of basis. You must reduce your basis in your shares by any nondividend distributions that you receive from the fund. The mutual fund reports the amount of any nondividend distributions on Form 1099-DIV, box 3. You should keep the form to show the decrease in the basis of your shares.

Basis cannot go below zero. Your basis cannot be reduced below zero. If your basis is zero, you must report the nondividend distribution on your tax return as a capital gain. Report this capital gain on Schedule D (Form 1040). Whether it is a long-term or short-term capital gain depends on how long you held the shares.

No reduction of basis. You do not reduce your basis for distributions from the fund that are exempt-interest dividends.

Identifying the Shares Sold

To figure your gain or loss when you dispose of mutual fund shares, you need to determine which shares were sold and the basis of those shares. If your shares in a mutual fund were acquired all on the same day and for the same price, figuring their basis is not difficult. However, shares are generally acquired at various times, in various quantities, and at various prices. Therefore, figuring your basis can be more difficult. You can choose to use either a cost basis or an average basis to figure your gain or loss. See Table 39-2, *Choosing a Basis Method.*

Cost Basis

You can figure your gain or loss using a cost basis only if you did not previously use an average basis for sale, exchange, or redemption of other shares in the same mutual fund. To figure cost basis, you can choose one of the following methods.

- Specific share identification, or
- First-in first-out (FIFO)

TAXALERT

The IRS eliminated the average cost (double category) method for tracking basis effective April 1, 2011. If taxpayers formally used the double category method, they must re-compute their basis as of April 1, 2011, by averaging the basis of all identical shares in an account regardless of holding period. Taxpayers must use the single category method or another elected method prospectively.

TAXALERT

For mutual fund and DRP shares acquired on or after January 1, 2012, financial institutions will use their default method to determine adjusted basis unless the taxpayer selects another method. A taxpayer must notify their broker in writing if they wish to use another approved method.

Specific share identification. If you can adequately identify the shares you sold, you can use the adjusted basis of those particular shares to figure your gain or loss.

You will adequately identify your mutual fund shares, even if you bought the shares in different lots at various prices and times, if you:

1. Specify to your broker or other agent the particular shares to be sold or transferred at the time of the sale or transfer, and
2. Receive confirmation in writing from your broker or other agent within a reasonable time of your specification of the particular shares sold or transferred.

You continue to have the burden of proving your basis in the specified shares at the time of sale or transfer.

First-in first-out (FIFO). If the shares were acquired at different times or at different prices and you cannot identify which shares you sold, use the basis of the shares you acquired first as the basis of the shares sold. In other words, the oldest shares still available are considered sold first. You should keep a separate record of each purchase and any dispositions of the shares until all shares purchased at the same time have been disposed of completely. Table 39-3, *How to Figure Basis of Shares Sold*, illustrates the use of the FIFO method to figure the cost basis of shares sold, compared with the use of the single-category method to figure average basis.

Average Basis

You can figure your gain or loss using an average basis only if you acquired the shares at various times and prices, and you left the shares on deposit in an account handled by a custodian or agent who acquires or redeems those shares.

Table 39-2. **Choosing a Basis Method**

Basis Method	Advantages/Disadvantages
Specific identification	The most flexible way to determine your gains and losses. But there are important restrictions governing its use.
FIFO (first-in first-out)	The simplest approach. But it may mean a large gain if your shares have appreciated significantly and you are redeeming only part of your account.
Average cost (single category)	The middle ground, A more modest tax burden than the FIFO method but more tedious calculations if you sell shares frequently.

To figure average basis, you can use one of the following methods:

- Single-category method
- Double-category method

Once you elect to use an average basis, you must continue to use it for all accounts in the same fund. (You must also continue to use the same method). However, you may specify cost basis for shares in other funds, even those within the same family of funds.

TAXPLANNER

Beginning with shares acquired after December 31, 2011, a taxpayer may elect different cost reporting methods for the same mutual fund shares held in different accounts. For example, a taxpayer may elect to use specific identification in one account and the average method in another account although the underlying mutual fund shares are identical. In addition, a taxpayer may make one election with a financial institution to cover all eligible accounts and future accounts. The election statement must clearly identify each account to which the election applies.

TAXALERT

Taxpayers may use the average method for shares acquired after December 31, 2010, through a DRP provided that at least 10% of every dividend paid is invested in identical stock. A DRP may also average the basis of stock acquired by reinvesting distributions that are not considered dividends such as capital gain distributions, nontaxable returns of capital, and cash in lieu of dividends.

EXAMPLE

You own two accounts in the aggressive fund issued by Company XYZ. You also own 200 shares of the bond fund issued by Company XYZ. If you elect to use average basis for the first account of the aggressive fund, you must use average basis for the second account. However, you may use cost basis for the bond fund.

Tip

You may be able to find the average basis of your shares from information provided by the fund.

Single-category method. Under the single-category method, you find the average basis of all shares owned at the time of each disposition, regardless of how long you owned them. Include shares acquired with reinvested dividends or capital gain distributions.

Table 39-3 illustrates the use of the single-category method to figure the average basis of shares sold, compared with the use of the FIFO method to figure cost basis.

Even though you include all unsold shares of a fund in a single category to compute average basis, you may have both short-term and long-term gains or losses when you sell these shares. To determine your holding period, the shares disposed of are considered to be those acquired first.

EXAMPLE

John Smith bought the following shares in the GLM Mutual Fund: 100 shares in 2008 at $10 per share, 100 shares in 2009 at $12 a share, and 100 shares in 2011 at $26 a share. The 300 shares cost a total of $4,800. The average basis per share is $16 ($4,800 ÷ 300).

Remaining shares. The average basis of the shares you still hold after a sale of some of your shares is the same as the average basis of the shares sold. The next time you make a sale, your average basis will still be the same, unless you have acquired additional shares (or have made a subsequent adjustment to basis).

Double-category method. In the double-category method, all shares in an account at the time of each disposition are divided into two categories: short-term and long-term. Shares held one year or less are short-term. Shares held longer than one year are long-term.

The basis of each share in a category is the average basis for that category. This is the total remaining basis of all shares in that category at the time of disposition divided by the total shares in the category at that time. To use this method, you specify, to the custodian or agent handling your account, from which category the shares are to be sold or transferred. The custodian or agent must confirm in writing your specification. If you do not specify or receive confirmation, you must first charge the shares sold against the long-term category and then charge any remaining shares sold against the short-term category.

Table 39-3. **How to Figure Basis of Shares Sold**

This is an example showing two different ways to figure basis. It compares the cost basis using the FIFO method and the average basis using the single-category method.				
Date	**Action**	**Share Price**	**No. of Shares**	**Total Shares Owned**
02/04/10	Invest $4,000	$25	160	160
08/05/10	Invest $4,800	$20	240	400
12/15/10	Reinvest $300 dividend	$30	10	410
09/01/11	Sell $6,720	$32	210	200
COST BASIS (FIFO)	To figure the basis of the 210 shares sold on 09/01/11, use the share price of the first 210 shares you bought, namely, the 160 shares you purchased on 02/04/10 and 50 of those purchased on 08/05/10. $4,000 (cost of 160 shares on 02/04/10) + $1,000 (cost of 50 shares on 08/05/10) **Basis =** $5,000			
AVERAGE BASIS (single-category)	To figure the basis of the 210 shares sold on 09/01/11, use the average basis of all 410 shares owned on 09/01/11. $9,100 (cost of 410 shares) ÷ 410 (number of shares) $22.20 (average basis per share) $22.20 × 210 **Basis =** $4,662			

Changing categories. After you have held a mutual fund share for more than one year, you must transfer that share from the short-term category to the long-term category. The basis of a transferred share is its actual cost or other basis to you, unless some of the shares in the short-term category have been disposed of. In that case, the basis of a transferred share is the average basis of the undisposed shares at the time of the most recent disposition from this category.

Making the choice. You choose to use the average basis of mutual fund shares by clearly showing on your income tax return, for each year the choice applies, that you used an average basis in reporting gain or loss from the sale or transfer of the shares. You must specify whether you used the single-category method or the double-category method in determining average basis. This choice is effective until you get permission from the IRS to revoke it.

> ***TAXALERT***
> Although the double category method was eliminated as of April 1, 2011, a taxpayer may still use this method for sales prior to April 1, 2011.

Shares received as gift. If your account includes shares that you received by gift, and the fair market value of the shares at the time of the gift was less than the donor's basis, special rules apply. You cannot choose to use the average basis for the account unless you submit a statement with your initial choice. It must state that the basis used in figuring the average basis of the gift shares under either method will be the FMV at the time of the gift. This statement applies to gift shares you receive before and after making the choice, as long as the choice to use the average basis is in effect.

Gains and Losses

You figure gain or loss on the disposition of your shares by comparing the amount you realize with the adjusted basis of your shares. If the amount you realize is more than the adjusted basis of the

> **Records**
> *When there is a sale, exchange, or redemption of your shares in a fund, keep the confirmation statement you receive. The statement shows the price you received for the shares and other information you need to report gain or loss on your return.*

shares, you have a gain. If the amount you realize is less than the adjusted basis of the shares, you have a loss.

Amount you realize. The amount you realize from a disposition of your shares is the money and value of any property you receive for the shares disposed of, minus your expenses of sale (such as redemption fees, sales commissions, sales charges, or exit fees).

Adjusted basis. Adjusted basis is explained under *Keeping Track of Your Basis*, earlier.

Reporting information from Form 1099-B. Mutual funds and brokers report dispositions of mutual fund shares on Form 1099-B, or a substitute form containing substantially the same language. The form shows the amount of the sales price and indicates whether the amount reported is the gross amount or the net amount (gross amount minus commissions).

If your Form 1099-B or similar statement from the payer shows the gross sales price, do not subtract the expenses of sale from it when reporting your sales price in column (e) on Form 8949. Instead, report the gross amount in column (e) and increase your cost or other basis, column (f), by any expense of the sale. If your Form 1099-B shows that the gross sales price less commissions was reported to the IRS, enter the net amount in column (e) of Form 8949 and *do not* increase your basis in column (f) by the sales commission.

TAXALERT

In connection with the new basis reporting requirements, the IRS has introduced a new Form 8949 to report sales of investments reported on Form 1099-B. Sales details will no longer be directly reported on Schedule D but rather on Form 8949. You will have to use a different copy of Form 8949 for each of the following conditions:

1. Basis was reported on Form 1099-B
2. Basis was NOT reported on Form 1099-B
3. Sale not reported on Form 1099-B

The totals from each Form 8949 will then flow to Schedule D and onward to Form 1040. Since mutual fund and DRP shares are not considered covered securities until January 1, 2012, gains and losses associated with these investments will most likely be reported on Form 8949 and by checking box B "Form 1099, box 3, does not show basis."

EXAMPLES

Example 1. Linda Jones sold 200 shares of Fund B for $5,000. She paid a $150 commission to the broker for handling the sale. Her Form 1099-B shows that the net sales proceeds, $4,850 ($5,000 – $150), were reported to the IRS. Report this amount in column (e) of Form 8949.

Example 2. Joe Green sold 100 shares of Fund KLM for $5,000. He paid a $50 commission to the broker for handling the sale. He bought the shares for $2,500. Joe's broker reported the gross proceeds of $50,000 to the IRS on Form 1099-B, so he must increase his basis in column (f) of Form 8949 to $2,550.

Holding Period

When you dispose of your mutual fund shares, you must determine your holding period. Your holding period determines whether the gain or loss is a short-term capital gain or loss or a long-term capital gain or loss.

Short-term gain or loss. If you hold the shares for one year or less, your gain or loss will be a short-term gain or loss.

Long-term gain or loss. If you hold the shares for more than one year, your gain or loss will be a long-term gain or loss.

Determining period held. Determine your holding period by using the trade dates of your purchases and your sales. The trade date is the date on which you contract to buy or sell shares. Most mutual funds will show the trade dates on confirmation statements showing your purchases and sales.

To find out how long you have held your shares, begin counting on the day after the trade date on which you bought the shares. (Do not count the trade date itself.) The trade date on which you dispose of the shares is counted as part of your holding period.

EXAMPLE

Assume Lori Hill bought shares in XYZ Mutual Fund on January 11, 2010 (trade date). She starts counting on January 12, and the 12th of each following month is the beginning of a new month. Therefore, if she sells the shares on January 7, 2011 (trade date), her holding period would not be more than 1 year. However, if she sells them on January 13, 2011, her holding period would be more than 1 year (12 months plus 1 day).

Mutual fund shares received as a gift. If you receive a gift of mutual fund shares and your basis is determined by the donor's basis (or fair market value of the shares if this is less than the donor's basis), your holding period is considered to have started on the same day that the donor's holding period started.

Reinvested distributions. If your dividends and capital gain distributions are reinvested in new shares, the holding period of each new share begins the day after that share was purchased. Therefore, if you sell both the new shares and the original shares, you might have both short-term and long-term gains and losses.

Certain short-term losses. Special rules may apply if you have a short-term loss on the sale of shares on which you received an exempt-interest dividend or a capital gain distribution.

Exempt-interest dividends before short-term loss. If you received exempt-interest dividends on mutual fund shares that you held for 6 months or less and sold at a loss, you may claim only the part of the loss that is more than the exempt-interest dividends. On Form 8949, column (e), increase the sales price by the amount of exempt-interest dividends. Report the loss as a short-term capital loss.

EXAMPLE

On January 5, 2011, you bought a mutual fund share for $50. On February 2, 2011, the mutual fund paid a $3 dividend from tax-exempt interest, which is not taxable to you. On February 9, 2011, you sold the share for $45. If it were not for the tax-exempt dividend, your loss would be $5 ($50 - $45). However, you can deduct only $2, the part of the loss that is more than the exempt-interest dividend ($5 - $3). On Form 8949, column (e), increase the sales price from $45 to $48 (the $3 portion of the loss that is not deductible).

Capital gain distribution before short-term loss. Generally, if you received capital gain distributions (or had to report undistributed capital gains) on mutual fund shares that you held for 6 months or less and sold at a loss, report only the part of the loss that is more than the capital gain distribution (or undistributed capital gain) as a short-term capital loss. The rest of the loss is reported as a long-term capital loss.

EXAMPLE

On April 13, 2011, Ben Simms bought one share of ABC Mutual Fund for $25. On June 30, 2011, the mutual fund paid a capital gain distribution of $1 a share, which is taxed as a long-term capital gain. On July 19, 2011, he sold the share for $22.50. If it were not for the capital gain distribution, Ben would have had a $2.50 ($25 - $22.50) short-term loss. However, the part of the loss that is not more than the capital gain distribution ($1) must be reported as a long-term capital loss. The remaining $1.50 of the loss can be reported as a short-term capital loss.

Wash sales. If you sell mutual fund shares at a loss and within 30 days before or after the sale you buy, acquire in a taxable exchange, or enter into a contract or option to buy substantially identical property, you have a wash sale. You cannot deduct losses from wash sales. In determining whether the shares are substantially identical, you must consider all the facts and circumstances. Ordinarily, shares issued by one company are not considered to be substantially identical to shares issued by another company. For a further discussion of wash sales, see chapter 14, *Sale of property*.

How to Figure Gains and Losses on Form 8949 and Schedule D

Separate your short-term gains and losses from your long-term gains and losses on all the mutual fund shares and other capital assets you disposed of during the year. Then determine your net short-term gain or loss and your net long-term gain or loss.

EXPLANATION

Net capital loss. If you have a net capital loss, your allowable capital loss deduction is the smaller of:

1. $3,000 ($1,500 if you are married and filing a separate return)
2. Your net capital loss

Enter your allowable loss on line 13 of Form 1040.

Example 1. Margaret has capital gains and losses for the year as follows:

	Short-term	Long-term
Gains	$700	$400
Losses	($800)	($2,000)

Margaret's deductible capital loss is $1,700, which she figures as follows:

Short-term capital losses	($800)
Subtract short-term capital gains	$700
Net short-term capital loss	($100)
Long-term capital losses	($2,000)
Subtract long-term capital gains	$400
Net long-term capital loss	($1,600)
Deductible capital loss	($1,700)

Example 2. Art and Karen file a joint return. Their capital gains and losses for the year are as follows:

Net short-term capital gain	$450
Net long-term capital loss	($5,600)
Deductible capital loss	($3,000)

Their net capital loss is $5,150 ($5,600 - $450). Because their net capital loss exceeds $3,000, the amount they can deduct for the current year is limited to $3,000; however, the capital loss carryover is $2,150.

Capital loss carryovers. If your net capital losses are more than your allowable net capital loss deduction, you may carry over the excess to later years until it is completely used up. To determine your capital loss carryover, subtract from your capital loss the lesser of:

1. Your allowable capital loss deduction for the year, or
2. Your taxable income increased by your allowable capital loss deduction for the year and by your deduction for personal exemptions.

If your deductions exceed your gross income, you start the computation with a negative number.

When carried over, the loss will keep its original character as long-term or short-term. Therefore, a long-term capital loss carried over from a previous year will offset long-term gains of the current year before it offsets short-term gains of the current year.

In determining your capital loss carryover, apply your capital loss deduction to reduce your net short-term losses first. If after applying the short-term losses, the capital loss limit has not been reached, then apply the long-term losses until you reach the limit.

Use the Capital Loss Carryover Worksheet at the end of chapter 16, *Reporting Gains and Losses*, to figure your capital loss carryover.

Capital loss carryovers from separate returns are combined if you file a joint return for the current year. However, if you once filed jointly and are now filing separately, a capital loss carryover from the joint return can be deducted only on the separate return of the spouse who actually had the loss.

Investment Expenses

You can generally deduct the expenses of producing investment income. These include expenses for investment counseling and advice, legal and accounting fees, and investment newsletters. These expenses are deductible as miscellaneous itemized deductions to the extent that they exceed 2% of your adjusted gross income. See chapter 29 for further information.

Publicly offered mutual funds. Most mutual funds are publicly offered. Expenses of publicly offered mutual funds are not treated as miscellaneous itemized deductions. This is because these mutual funds report only the net amount of investment income after your share of the investment expenses has been deducted.

Nonpublicly offered mutual funds. If you own shares in a nonpublicly offered mutual fund during the year, you can deduct your share of the investment expenses on your Schedule A (Form 1040) as a miscellaneous itemized deduction to the extent your miscellaneous deduction exceeds 2% of your adjusted gross income. Your share of the expenses will be shown in box 5 of Form 1099-DIV. A nonpublicly offered mutual fund is one that:

1. Is not continuously offered pursuant to a public offering.
2. Is not regularly traded on an established securities market.
3. Is not held by at least 500 persons at all times during the tax year.

Contact your mutual fund if you are not sure whether it is nonpublicly offered.

TAXSAVER

If you own shares in a publicly offered mutual fund, you do not have to pay tax on your share of the fund's expenses. There should be no entry in box 5 of Form 1099-DIV. However, expenses of a nonpublicly offered fund may be subject to tax. You should consult your tax advisor for details.

TAXSAVER

Front-end fees. "Front-end," or purchase, fees (also known as "load charges") reduce your investment in a mutual fund, but they are still considered part of your cost basis for tax purposes.

Example

You invest $10,000 in a fund that charges a 1% load on portfolio transaction (purchase) fee. Your account statement reports a net balance of $9,900 ($10,000 minus the 1% fee). For tax purposes, however, your cost remains at $10,000.

Exception

Your basis in mutual fund shares does not include load charges (sales fees) paid after October 3, 1989, on the purchase of shares if you held the shares for 90 days or less and then reinvested the proceeds in a fund within the same fund family with a reduced load charge. Instead, the load charges become part of your basis in the shares of the new fund into which you put your investment.

TAXSAVER

Sales charges and redemption fees. Before you buy a mutual fund, you should examine the sales charges and redemption fees it charges, if any. No-load funds do not have a sales charge. Mutual fund listings in newspapers generally indicate whether there is a sales charge. No-load funds have the same purchase and redemption price for fund shares. Your broker or financial advisor should be able to tell you which funds charge commissions.

Explanation

Back-end fees. Fees may also be deducted from your fund when you redeem or sell shares. These are generally called redemption or "back-end" fees. (Certain back-end fees called "contingent deferred sales charges" or "contingent deferred sales loads" typically decline and eventually disappear over a set period of time.) If your mutual fund reports all proceeds net of redemption fees on your Form 1099-B, you do not need to adjust your tax cost. However, if your mutual fund reports gross proceeds before any redemption fees on Form 1099-B, you should increase your cost basis by the amount of the fee you paid when calculating your capital gain or loss.

Other fees. Custodial and account maintenance fees are deductible as investment expenses on Schedule A of your income tax return, subject to certain caveats. See *Investment Expenses*, earlier, and chapter 2, *Filing status*.

Expenses allocable to exempt-interest dividends. You cannot deduct expenses that are for the collection or production of exempt-interest dividends. Expenses must be allocated if they were partly for both taxable and tax-exempt income. One accepted method for allocating expenses is to divide them in the same proportion that your tax-exempt income from the mutual fund is to your total income from the fund.

Limit on Investment Interest Expense

The amount you can deduct as an investment interest expense may be limited. See chapter 24, *Interest Expense*.

TAXORGANIZER

Records you should keep:

- Confirmation statements. Keep a copy of all mutual fund confirmation statements reflecting all purchases and sales, as well as records of dividends that are automatically reinvested in your account.
- A copy of Form 1099-DIV, Dividends and Distributions, or a substitute form supplied by the mutual fund or brokerage firm containing substantially the same language. This form will tell you what you must report or take into account on your income tax return.
- A copy of Form 1099-B, Proceeds from Broker and Barter Exchange Transactions, or a substitute form supplied by the mutual fund or brokerage firm containing substantially the same language. This form will summarize the proceeds from sales, exchanges, or redemptions.
- Confirmation from mutual fund company on specific share identification method. This confirmation by the mutual fund company must confirm that you instructed them to sell particular mutual fund shares.
- A copy of Form 2439, Notice to Shareholders of Undistributed Long-Term Capital Gains, showing your share of undistributed capital gains and any tax paid by the mutual fund.

Chapter 40

What to do if you employ domestic help

ey.com/EYTaxGuide

Note

IRS Publication 17 (*Your Federal Income Tax*) has been updated by Ernst & Young LLP for 2011. Dates and dollar amounts shown are for 2011. Underlined type is used to indicate where IRS text has been updated. Places where text has been removed are indicated by the sentence: *Text intentionally omitted*.

ey.com/EYTaxGuide

Ernst & Young LLP will update the *Ernst & Young Tax Guide 2012* website with relevant taxpayer information as it becomes available. You can also sign up for email alerts to let you know when changes have been made.

Introduction

If you have a domestic helper who qualifies as your employee, you may have to pay social security and Medicare taxes, as well as federal and state unemployment taxes. You may also have to withhold federal income tax. In general, a person who works in or around your house qualifies as your employee if you control his or her working conditions—pay, work schedule, conduct, and appearance. This chapter spells out what federal tax rules govern domestic help and advises you on how to comply with them.

Both you and your employee are subject to social security and Medicare taxes if you pay your employee $1,700 or more during any calendar year. If you have paid any employee $1,000 or more in any calendar quarter during the current or preceding year, you are also subject to federal unemployment taxes on every employee during the current year.

Your employee may ask you to withhold federal income tax from compensation. If you decide to do so, you must withhold the proper amount from each paycheck. This withholding must be remitted to the IRS.

Use Schedule H (Form 1040) to compute federal taxes for your household employees and attach it to your personal income tax return.

If you pay your income taxes late, penalties and interest will be due by you on the taxes described in this chapter as well as on your personal income taxes.

This chapter only discusses the federal taxes applying to household employees. There may be additional taxes due depending on the state and city where the services are performed.

You may also be subject to federal and/or state rules regarding employees' pay and benefits. For example, state laws may dictate the maximum number of hours an employee may work, the amount to be paid for overtime, and/or the number of days of paid vacation and holidays the employee is entitled to.

Even if your domestic employee does not have legal authorization to work in the United States, you are still liable for the payroll taxes discussed in this chapter.

Tax Breaks and Deductions You Can Use Checklist

Paying Employment Taxes. In most cases, you are required to collect, and remit social security and Medicare taxes on wages paid to your domestic employee(s). Fortunately, the federal government allows you to make these payments along with your personal income tax payments—either through withholding or estimated taxes. You file Schedule H with your Form 1040 to report these amounts.

Are Your Employees Working Legally in the U.S.? Federal law requires you to verify that your new employees are eligible to work in the United States. You and your employee must complete USCIS (U.S. Citizenship and Immigration Services) Form I-9, Employment Eligibility Verification, and you should keep it for three years from hiring or one year from termination of employment, whichever is later. You can get Form I-9 at *www.uscis.gov*.

Federal Employer Identification Number. If you employ someone to work in your home, you should apply for a federal employer identification number (EIN) to use when you file required forms. You can file for an EIN online. Go to *www.irs.gov* and enter keywords "Apply for an EIN Online" in the upper right-hand corner. For more information, see *Employer Identification Number* in this chapter.

Table 40-1. **Household Employer's Checklist**

You may need to do the following things when you have a household employee.

When you hire a household employee:	• Find out if the person can legally work in the United States. • Find out if you need to pay state taxes.
When you pay your household employee:	• Withhold social security and Medicare taxes. • Withhold federal income tax. • Decide how you will make tax payments. • Keep records.
By January 31, 2012:	• Get an employer identification number (EIN). • Give your employee Copies B, C, and 2 of Form W-2, Wage and Tax Statement.
By February 29, 2012 (April, 2, 2012 if you file Form W-2 electronically):	• Send Copy A of Form W-2 to the Social Security Administration (SSA).
By April 17, 2012:	• File Schedule H (Form 1040), Household Employment Taxes, with your 2011 federal income tax return (Form 1040, 1040NR, 1040-SS, or Form 1041). If you do not have to file a return, file Schedule H by itself.

TAXPLANNER

The rules in this chapter relate to someone who works for you in the United States or who is a U.S. citizen or green card holder. If you are employing someone to work outside of the United States, you will need to investigate your responsibilities under the laws of that country.

Reminder

Social security and Medicare wage threshold is $1,700. The social security and Medicare wage threshold for household employees is $1,700 for 2011. This means that if you pay a household employee cash wages of less than $1,700 in 2011, you do not have to report and pay social security and Medicare taxes on that employee's 2011 wages. For more information, see *Social Security and Medicare Wages* in Publication 926, *Household Employer's Guide (For Wages Paid in 2011)*.

Employment Taxes for Household Employers

If you pay someone to come to your home and care for it, your dependent, or your spouse, you may be a household employer. If you are a household employer, you will need an employer identification number (EIN) and you may have to pay employment taxes. If the individuals who work in your home are self-employed, you are not liable for any of the taxes discussed in this section. Self-employed persons who are in business for themselves are not household employees. Usually, you are not a household employer if the person who cares for your dependent or spouse does so at his or her home or place of business.

EXCEPTION

Employees under the age of 18 at any time during the year are exempt from social security and Medicare taxes, regardless of how much they earn, provided household services is not their main job. If the employee is a student, providing household services is not considered to be his or her principal occupation.

TAXPLANNER

Paying the "nanny" tax. Employers are required to report the social security, Medicare, and federal unemployment taxes due on domestic workers' wages on the employers' Form 1040, Schedule H. The taxes can be paid through the employers' estimated tax payments. Alternatively, the employer could increase federal withholding on his or her own wages and pay these taxes on the domestic worker in that manner.

If you use a placement agency that exercises control over what work is done and how it will be done by a babysitter or companion who works in your home, that person is not your employee. This control could include providing rules of conduct and appearance and requiring regular reports. In this case, you do not have to pay employment taxes. But, if an agency merely gives you a list of sitters and you hire one from that list, the sitter may be your employee.

If you have a household employee you may be subject to:

1. Social security and Medicare taxes,
2. Federal unemployment tax, and
3. Federal income tax withholding.

Social security and Medicare taxes are generally withheld from the employee's pay and matched by the employer. Federal unemployment (FUTA) tax is paid by the employer only and provides for payments of unemployment compensation to workers who have lost their jobs. Federal income tax is withheld from the employee's total pay if the employee asks you to do so and you agree.

For more information on a household employer's tax responsibilities, see Publication 926 and Schedule H (Form 1040) and its instructions.

State employment tax. You may also have to pay state unemployment tax. Contact your state unemployment tax office for information. You should also find out whether you need to pay or collect other state employment taxes or carry workers' compensation and/or disability insurance. A list of state employment tax agencies, including addresses and phone numbers, is in Publication 926.

EXPLANATION

You may be able to claim a child and dependent care credit for the expenses you incur for domestic help.

Example

Janice Johnson is single and works to keep up a home for herself and her dependent father. Her adjusted gross income of $25,000 is entirely earned income. Her father was disabled and incapable of self-care for 6 months. To keep working, she paid a housekeeper $600 per month to care for her father, prepare lunch and dinner, and do housework. Her credit is as follows:

Total work-related expenses (6 × $600)	$3,600
Maximum allowable expenses	$3,000
Amount of credit (30% of $3,000)	$ 900

Explanation

Employee or independent contractor? Whether or not a person who provides services in and around your house is your employee depends on the facts and circumstances of the situation. In general, a person is your employee if you control his or her working conditions and compensation. A person does not have to work for you full-time to qualify as your employee.

Generally, workers are classified based on how they perform their work and their accountability for it. By definition, independent contractors are responsible for results, not how their tasks are accomplished. On the other hand, individuals who are instructed as to when, where, and how to complete their jobs would probably be considered employees. If you determine that your domestic helpers are employees, you must withhold and match social security and Medicare payments and may be subject to paying federal and state unemployment taxes as well.

To gain a better understanding of the distinction between an independent contractor and an employee, consider the person who mows your lawn. If the person works for an independent lawn service and is supervised by the lawn company that also provides its own equipment—all you provide is the grass—there's little question that the provider is an independent contractor. However, if a college student cuts your lawn using your mower, and you give specific instructions as to how and when to do the job, he or she will be considered your employee.

To enable you to determine whether a person is indeed an independent contractor, there are certain common indicators that can help. An independent contractor:

- Works for several homeowners
- Provides his or her own tools and supplies to perform the job
- Can bring in additional help if he or she deems necessary
- Determines how the results will be accomplished
- Is paid by the job, not by the hour
- Advertises his or her services
- May be fired at will
- Can set his or her own hours and leave when the job is completed

If you have reason to believe that a person is an independent contractor and not your employee, you should not withhold social security tax from his or her compensation. You may want to get a signed letter from this person indicating that he or she is an independent contractor and is responsible for his or her own employment taxes.

TAXPLANNER

Records you need. When you hire a household employee, make a record of that person's name and social security number exactly as it appears on his or her social security card. You will need this information when you remit social security, Medicare, federal unemployment, and withholding of federal income taxes.

An employee who does not have a social security number should apply for one using Form SS-5, Application for a Social Security Card. This form is available at all Social Security Administration offices, or on the Social Security Administration website at *www.socialsecurity.gov/online/ss-5.pdf*, as well as by calling 1-800-772-1213.

If your employee is not eligible to obtain a social security number, he or she may obtain an individual taxpayer identification number (ITIN) by filing Form W-7 with the IRS. The ITIN can be used on a tax return wherever a social security number should be used. You should note that the ITIN is for IRS records only. It does not change the employee's status with the USCIS or his or her entitlement to social security or other employment benefits.

Employer identification number (EIN). In order to pay federal taxes for your household employee, you will need an employer identification number (EIN). This is a nine-digit number issued by the IRS. It is not the same as your social security number. If you already have an EIN, use that number. If you do not have an EIN, you can apply for it online. Go to *www.irs.gov* and enter keywords "Apply for an EIN Online" in the upper right-hand corner. From this web page, you can access a web-based application that instantly processes requests and generates EINs in real time. You can also apply for an EIN by phone, fax, or mailing in Form SS-4, Application for Employer Identification Number. Form SS-4 is available at *www.irs.gov/pub/irs-pdf/fss4.pdf*. If you choose to submit Form SS-4 you will need to send it to the IRS office listed in Table 40-2 for your location. If you need further information regarding the IRS process for issuing an EIN number, call or fax the IRS office in your area or refer to Publication 926, *Household Employer's Tax Guide.*

Social Security and Medicare Taxes

If you pay a household employee cash wages of $1,700 or more during a calendar year, those wages are subject to social security and Medicare taxes. Payments in kind (meals, transportation, etc.) are not used to figure the $1,700 amount or to figure the taxes. The taxes are figured on all cash wage payments in the year, regardless of when they were earned.

What is taxable compensation? Table 40-3 may help to clarify what is reportable income to your employee. Remember that state and local income tax and unemployment or disability and other employment tax rules may be different.

Family members. Social security and Medicare taxes do not apply to household services performed by your spouse or by your child under 21. However, social security and Medicare taxes apply to wages you pay your parents for household services if:

1. You are a surviving spouse or a divorced individual who hasn't remarried or have a spouse living in the home who has a mental or physical condition which results in the spouse's being incapable of caring for a child or stepchild for at least four continuous weeks in the quarter in which the service is performed; and
2. Your child or stepchild is living in the home; and
3. Your child or stepchild is under age 18 or has a mental or physical condition which requires the personal care of an adult for at least four continuous weeks in the quarter in which the service is performed.

Table 40-2. **IRS Offices for EIN Application**

If your legal residence is located in:	Mail or Fax Form SS-4 to:
One of the 50 states or the District of Columbia	Internal Revenue Service Center Attn: EIN Operation Cincinnati, OH 45999 Fax-TIN: (859) 669-5760
If you have no legal residence, principal place of business, or principal office or agency in any state:	Internal Revenue Service Center Attn: EIN Operation Philadelphia, PA 19255-0525 Fax-TIN: (267) 941-1040

TAXALERT

If a person is an employee whom you pay a total of $1,700 or more per year, you have tax filing and payment responsibilities.

TAXPLANNER

Babysitters. If the babysitter watches your children in your house at the time you specify, IRS rulings conclude that the person is an employee. It's not enough to stop giving the sitter a ride home in an attempt to make him or her appear more independent. You would need to use sitters who watch children in their homes or other facilities during set business hours. Or you can rotate sitters to avoid paying anyone more than $1,700 per year. As previously noted, sitters under age 18 who are full-time students are exempt from social security and Medicare taxes.

Paying the tax. Both you and the employee pay a share of the social security and Medicare taxes on the employee's wages. For 2011, the tax rate for social security is 4.2% for the employee and 6.2% for you (a total of 10.4%). The tax rate for Medicare is 1.45% for both you and the employee (a total of 2.9%). The 10.4% social security tax applies only to the first $106,800 you paid each employee during calendar year 2011. The 2.9% Medicare tax applies to all wages.

TAXALERT

The December 2010 tax law that extended the so-called Bush tax cuts also cut the employee social security tax rate for 2011 to 4.2% from the usual 6.2% rate. The employer's social security tax rate remains at 6.2% for 2011. In addition, the social security wage base of $106,800 has not changed, meaning that the 10.4% social security tax applies only to the first $106,800 you pay each employee during calendar year 2011. Also, the Medicare tax rate of 1.45% for both the employer and the employee is unchanged from 2010.

You must pay the total of these taxes (your employee's and your share) yourself if you do not deduct the employee's share from his or her wages. Any of the employee's share you pay is added income to the employee. This income must be included in box 1, *Wages, tips, other compensation,* on Form W-2, Wage and Tax Statement, but do not count it as cash wages for social security and Medicare purposes. You must also include the employee social security and Medicare taxes you pay in boxes 4 and 6 of the employee's Form W-2, even though the taxes were not actually withheld.

TAXPLANNER

If you would rather pay your employee's share of social security and Medicare taxes without deducting it from wages, you may do so. Any portion you do pay, however, is added to the compensation to your employee, even though it does not constitute cash wages for social security and Medicare purposes. Although it may be easier if you pay your employee's share of social security and Medicare taxes, it does raise your cost. You should come to an agreement with your employee on this issue before he or she begins work.

Table 40-3. **What Is Taxable Compensation?**

	Federal Income Tax	Social Security and Medicare (FICA)	Federal Unemployment Tax (FUTA)
Salary paid by cash, check, or other means	Yes	Yes	Yes
Cash bonus (overtime, holiday, etc.)	Yes	Yes	Yes
Cash gifts (holiday, birthday, wedding, etc.)	Yes	Yes	Yes
Gifts of property (holiday, birthday, etc.)[1]	Yes	Yes	Yes
Vacation Pay	Yes	Yes	Yes
Sign-on bonus	Yes	Yes	Yes
Value of meals & lodging on your premises as part of job and for your convenience	No	No	No
Car provided to employee for commutation	Yes	Yes	Yes
Car provided to employee to do work for you only	No	No	No
Value of public transit passes provided (up to $230 for 2011)[2]	No	No	No
Value of parking provided (up to $230 per month for 2011)[2]	No	No	No
Insurance for employee's own car	Yes	Yes	Yes
Employee's medical insurance bills you pay	No	No	No
Uniforms you give to employee to wear on your premises	No	No	No
Cash uniform allowance	Yes	Yes	Yes
Value of vacation when nanny accompanies family to care for children	No	No	No
Employee's legal fees you pay	Yes	Yes	Yes
Employee's social security taxes you pay	Yes	No	Yes
Employee's income taxes you pay	Yes	Yes	Yes

[1] Taxable value is lesser of cost or fair market value. Certain gifts of nominal value may be excluded from income.

[2] Payment of occasional transportation expense, if infrequent, reasonable in amount, and not based on hours worked, may be excluded from an employee's taxable wage. See *De Minimis Transportation Benefits* in Publication 15-B for more details.

Example. Meredith Cabot pays her full-time housekeeper a $15,000 salary. She also pays both the employer's share of the social security and Medicare taxes (7.65% of $15,000, or $1,147.50) and the employee's share (5.65% of $15,000, or $847.50). For federal income tax purposes, the housekeeper's total compensation for the year is $15,847.50 ($15,000 plus $847.50), even though only $15,000 is subject to social security and Medicare taxes.

TAXPLANNER

If you and your employee agree that the employee will be responsible for his or her own share of the social security and Medicare taxes, you should also reach agreement on how it is to be paid. To minimize difficulties, you may want to start withholding immediately rather than wait until $1,700 has been earned each year. This avoids the problem of the employee having to pay you $96.05 (5.65% × $1,700) once the threshold has been met.

Federal Income Tax Withholding

If your household employee requests income tax withholding, and you agree, you must withhold an amount from each payment based on the information shown on Form W-4, Employee's Withholding Allowance Certificate, given to you by the employee. See chapter 5, *Wages, salaries, and other earnings,* for more information about Form W-4. Publication 15 (Circular E), *Employer's Tax Guide,* explains how to figure the amount to withhold.

TAXPLANNER

It is your decision whether or not to withhold income tax from your employee's compensation, even if withholding is requested by your employee. However, if you do withhold for an employee, everything that you pay your employee–whether cash or noncash–is income subject to withholding. Some of the more common forms of compensation for household employees are (1) salaries; (2) overtime and bonuses; (3) meals, unless provided in your home and for your convenience; and (4) lodging, unless provided in your home, for your convenience, and as a condition of employment. As a general rule, if you have live-in domestic help, any meals and lodging you provide are not considered compensation. A car that you provide solely for use in transporting family members and doing household errands would not be considered compensation. However, a car provided to a domestic employee for his or her personal use (including getting to and from your house) would be considered income to him or her. Other forms of compensation include cash reimbursement for the employee's personal expenses, such as car insurance and vacation expenses. However, up to $230 per month in public transit passes and up to $230 per month for qualified parking can be provided to an employee without any federal tax effect. State tax laws may be different.

Any income tax withholding you pay for an employee without deducting it from the employee's wages is added income to the employee and subject to income, social security, and Medicare taxes.

Form W-4 and Publications 15 (which explains employer responsibilities and requirements), 15-A (which supplements and explains the Publication 15 information in greater detail), and 15-B (which explains the employment tax treatment of fringe benefits) can be requested by calling 1-800-TAX-FORM (1-800-829-3676) or downloaded at www.irs.gov.

TAXALERT

Earned income credit advance payment. A 2010 tax law eliminated the ability for taxpayers to elect to receive advance payments through their paychecks of their refundable portion of the EIC. Beginning in 2011, if you are eligible for the refundable portion of the EIC, you will need to wait to claim a refund on your tax return filed by April 15 of the following year.

TAXPLANNER

You can still effectively receive the nonrefundable portion of the EIC through the your paycheck, by adjusting withholding, to the extent you otherwise have positive tax liability.

Notice about the earned income credit (EIC). Copy B of the 2011 Form W-2, Wage and Tax Statement, has a statement about the EIC on the back. If you give your employee that copy by January 31, 2012, you do not have to give the employee any other notice about the EIC.

If you do not give your employee Copy B of the Form W-2, your notice about the EIC can be any of the following items.

1. A substitute Form W-2 with the same EIC information on the back of the employee's copy that is on Copy B of the Form W-2.
2. Notice 797, Possible Federal Tax Refund Due to the Earned Income Credit (EIC).
3. Your own written statement with the same wording as in Notice 797.

If a substitute Form W-2 is given on time but does not have the required EIC information, you must notify the employee within one week of the date the substitute Form W-2 is given. If Form W-2 is required but is not given on time, you must give the employee Notice 797 or your written statement about the 2011 EIC by January 31, 2012. If Form W-2 is not required, you must notify the employee by February 7, 2012.

You must give your household employee a notice about the EIC if you agree to withhold federal income tax from the employee's wages and the income tax withholding tables show that no tax should be withheld. Even if not required, you are encouraged to give the employee a notice about the EIC if his or her 2011 wages are less than $36,052 ($41,132 if married filing jointly).

You must notify any employees not having federal income tax withheld that they may be eligible for an income tax refund because of the earned income credit.

For more information about employment taxes, see Publication 926, *Household Employer's Tax Guide.*

Federal Unemployment Tax (FUTA)
Federal unemployment tax (FUTA) is for your employee's unemployment insurance. If you paid cash wages of $1,000 or more to household employees in any calendar quarter this year or last year, you are liable for FUTA for any employees you have this year. However, the tax does not apply to wages paid to your spouse, your parents, or your children under 21 years old.

Rate. For the period of January 1, 2011, through June 30, 2011, the FUTA tax is 6.2% of your employee's FUTA wages. However, you may be able to take a credit of up to 5.4% against the FUTA tax, resulting in a net tax rate of 0.8%. After June 30, 2011, the FUTA tax decreased to 6.0% of your employee's FUTA wages. You may be able to take a credit of up to 5.4% against the FUTA tax, resulting in a net tax rate of 0.6%. Your credit for 2011 is limited unless you pay all the required contributions for 2011 to your state unemployment fund by April 17, 2012. (The due date is actually April 17, 2012, because April 15, 2012, falls on Sunday, and the following day, April 16, is the Emancipation Day holiday in the District of Columbia, which is observed as a legal holiday.) The credit you can take for any contributions for 2011 that you pay after April 17, 2012, is limited to 90% of the credit that would have been allowable if the contributions were paid by April 17, 2012.

The tax is imposed on you as the employer. Unlike social security, Medicare, and federal income tax, federal unemployment tax is solely an employer's responsibility. It is an additional cost to you of having domestic help. You must not collect or deduct it from the wages of your employees.

When you hire a household employee, you should contact your state employment tax office to get information on how to file the state return and to get a state reporting number. The state will help you to figure the amount of tax you will pay the state. See the instructions to Schedule H for how to claim the credit.

Example 1. George Darby paid his housekeeper $3,000 in cash during the first quarter of 2011. He must pay federal unemployment tax (FUTA) for any employees he has during any part of 2011. Since he was liable for FUTA in 2011, any cash wages he pays to his employees in 2012 will also be subject to FUTA.

Example 2. George Darby paid his housekeeper and sole employee $12,000 ($1,000 per month, paid monthly on the last day of each month) for all of 2011. Since FUTA is assessed only on the first $7,000 of cash compensation paid to each employee during the calendar year, George's FUTA liability (before any credit for state unemployment taxes) was $432.

Jan 1-Jun 30 wages × the applicable FUTA rate	$6,000 × 6.2% = $ 372
Jul 1-Jul 31 wages × the applicable FUTA rate	$1,000 × 6.0% = $ 60
Wages greater than $7,000 are not subject to FUTA	-0- = -0-
TOTAL FUTA TAX FOR 2011	
(before state unemployment credit)	$ 432

Reporting and Paying Taxes on Wages Paid to Household Employees

Unless you own a business as a sole proprietor, you should report these taxes on Schedule H attached to your 2011 Form 1040. These taxes are added to your income taxes. The total must be paid during the course of the year. See chapter 4, *Tax withholding and estimated tax*.

If you are a sole proprietor who has nonhousehold employees, you should be filing Form 940 (or 940-EZ) annually to report FUTA (unemployment taxes) and Form 941 quarterly (Form 944 annually for qualifying small businesses) to report and remit federal income tax and FICA (social security and Medicare) tax withholdings. The IRS gives sole proprietors the option of including withholdings and taxes paid for domestic employees with withholdings and taxes paid for nondomestic employees on Forms 940 and 941 or 944. Alternatively, sole proprietors can exclude domestic employees from Forms 940 and 941 or 944 and file Schedule H with their own income tax returns.

TAXALERT

The IRS notifies certain employers that they must file Form 944, Employer's ANNUAL Federal Tax Return, instead of Form 941, Employer's QUARTERLY Federal Tax Return. Form 944 is filed once a year, rather than quarterly as Form 941 is filed. Form 944 for calendar year 2011 will be due January 31, 2012. Employers that would otherwise be required to file Form 944 may opt out *for any reason,* if they want to file Form 941 quarterly instead of Form 944 annually. Complete details on the procedure for opting out of filing Form 944 are included in the Form 941 instructions, available at www.irs.gov. Employers who are required to file Form 944 have annual liability for social security, Medicare, and withheld income taxes of $1,000 or less. You cannot file Form 944 unless you have been notified by the IRS. However, if you believe you are eligible to file Form 944—and desire to do so in place of Form 941—you may opt in to filing Form 944 by contacting the IRS at 1-800-829-4933. If the IRS determines you are eligible to file Form 944, it will send you a written notice that your filing requirement has been changed. Note that you are ineligible to file Form 944 if you employ household employees only.

For more information about annual employment tax filing and deposit rules, see IRS Publication 15, Circular E, *Employer's Tax Guide,* available at www.irs.gov.

Whether or not you are a sole proprietor, once you withhold tax from an employee, you must remit the tax to the IRS. If you do not, you could be responsible for substantial fines and penalties.

Example. Paul and Irene Boyd employ Emily Whitney as a housekeeper and babysitter. Emily's weekly salary is $200, which is paid by Paul in cash each Friday. In addition, Irene pays Emily $50 for helping once a month on weekends when the Boyds entertain. Emily uses her own car to drive to and from the Boyd's home but is reimbursed weekly by Irene for gas to drive the children to school. Emily gives Irene a list of the actual miles driven and Irene pays her 51 cents per mile before July 1 and 55.5 cents per mile after July 1. Four times a year Paul pays $400 for Emily's medical insurance. Irene pays Emily's $300 vacation airfare in June and gives her a $500 bonus in December. Since Emily's annual compensation is expected to be over $1,700, the Boyds decide to deduct FICA from Emily's salary from the beginning of the year. Emily completes and provides to the Boyds a Form W-4. The Boyds agree to deduct income tax from Emily's compensation. Emily is a single person with no dependents. The Boyds will use the percentage method to calculate the federal withholding. See Publication 15, Circular E, *Employer's Tax Guide,* available at www.irs.gov, for instructions regarding the use of the percentage method and the 2011 Income Tax Withholding Tables. The state in which they reside has a flat income tax of 4% and total unemployment taxes of 9%—2% to be paid by Emily, and 7% to be paid by the Boyds on income up to $7,000.

Since Emily has provided documentation indicating how many miles were driven, for what purpose and when, and since the reimbursement is within the IRS guideline (the standard mileage rate is 51 cents per mile for business miles driven between January 1 and June 30, 2011, and 55.5 cents per mile for business miles driven between July 1 and December 31, 2011), Emily's reimbursement for gas is not taxable income to her. Also, since Emily does not have the option of receiving cash for the medical insurance premiums, the reimbursement for medical insurance is not taxable to her.

The worksheet in Table 40-4 summarizes the taxable compensation paid to Emily and the taxes required to be deducted from her pay. The Boyds would provide a Form W-2 to Emily showing taxable earnings of $11,800 and withholdings as indicated in Table 40-4. A copy would be sent to the Social Security Administration. They would report the federal income tax withholding and FICA and pay the required FUTA and their portion of social security and Medicare ($903) with their Form 1040, reflected on Schedule H. The state income tax and unemployment tax withholdings would be remitted as required by the state authorities. In addition, the Boyds would be liable for $490 of state unemployment tax, which would also be remitted as required, but not later than the due date for filing the Boyd's Form 1040. The employer is responsible for FUTA, which in this case would be $53 ($5,600 x 6.2%, plus $1,400 × 6.0%, less the 5.4% maximum credit).

The Boyds will have to either increase the withholding from their wages or increase their estimated tax payments by $2,654 in order to pay their household employee's taxes during the course of the year (total earnings of $11,800 × the total of employee and employer portions of social security [10.4%] and Medicare tax [2.9%] of 13.3%, plus $1,032 federal income tax, plus the net FUTA tax of $53).

TAXORGANIZER

Forms you will need. You will need the following federal tax forms if you employ household help:

- Schedule H
- Form W-2, Wage and Tax Statement
- Form W-3, Transmittal of Wage and Tax Statements
- Form W-4, Employees' Withholding Allowance Certificate

You will need to contact your state tax authorities for applicable state tax forms.

As an employer, you must keep records of any cash or noncash wages paid to your employee as well as any taxes withheld from those wages. Table 40-4 is designed to help you accumulate this information. You will need this information at year-end to prepare the employee's Form W-2, which must be given to the employee by January 31 of the following year. Even if you are preparing only one Form W-2, you also will need Form W-3, Transmittal of Wage and Tax Statements, to send copies to the Social Security Administration. The government copies must be sent by the last day of February of the following year.

Table 40-4. **Worksheet for Domestic Employee's Wages**

Employee's Name: Emily Whitney				**Employee's Social Security Number**			**123-45-6789**
	Cash Paid Directly to Employee	**Non-Cash Amount**	**Total Earnings for W-2 Purposes**	**Social Security and Medicare Tax Deducted**	**Federal Income Tax Deducted**	**State Income Tax Deducted**	**Other State Taxes Deducted**
January	$850		$850	$48	$71	$34	$17
February	$850		$850	$48	$71	$34	$17
March	$850		$850	$48	$71	$34	$17
April	$1,050		$1,050	$59	$86	$42	$21
May	$850		$850	$48	$71	$34	$17
June	$850	$300	$1,150	$65	$116	$46	$23
July	$1,050		$1,050	$59	$86	$42	$21
August	$850		$850	$48	$71	$34	$7
September	$1,050		$1,050	$59	$86	$42	
October	$850		$850	$48	$71	$34	
November	$850		$850	$48	$71	$34	
December	$1,550		$1,550	$88	$161	$62	
TOTAL	**$11,500**	**$300**	**$11,800**	**$667**	**$1,032**	**$472**	**$140**

TAXORGANIZER

Records you should keep:

- Employee's name and social security number exactly as it appears on the SSN card
- Employer identification number from the IRS
- Records of payments made to domestic help
- Copies of payroll tax forms (W-2, W-3, etc.) filed for domestic help

SCHEDULE H (Form 1040) Department of the Treasury Internal Revenue Service (99)	**Household Employment Taxes** (For Social Security, Medicare, Withheld Income, and Federal Unemployment (FUTA) Taxes) ▶ Attach to Form 1040, 1040NR, 1040-SS, or 1041. ▶ See separate instructions.	OMB No. 1545-1971 2011 Attachment Sequence No. 44

Name of employer	Social security number
Paul and Irene Boyd	Employer identification number 1 2 3 4 5 6 7 8 9

Draft as of 09/27/2011

A Did you pay **any one** household employee cash wages of $1,700 or more in 2011? (If any household employee was your spouse, your child under age 21, your parent, or anyone under age 18, see the line A instructions before you answer this question.)

- ☑ **Yes.** Skip lines B and C and go to line 1.
- ☐ **No.** Go to line B.

B Did you withhold federal income tax during 2011 for any household employee?

- ☐ **Yes.** Skip line C and go to line 5.
- ☐ **No.** Go to line C.

C Did you pay **total** cash wages of $1,000 or more in **any** calendar **quarter** of 2010 or 2011 to **all** household employees? (**Do not** count cash wages paid in 2010 or 2011 to your spouse, your child under age 21, or your parent.)

- ☐ **No. Stop.** Do not file this schedule.
- ☐ **Yes.** Skip lines 1-7 and go to line 8. (Calendar year taxpayers having no household employees in 2011 **do not** have to complete this form for 2011.)

Part I Social Security, Medicare, and Federal Income Taxes

1	Total cash wages subject to social security taxes	1	11,800		
2	Social security taxes. Multiply line 1 by 10.4% (.104)			2	1,227
3	Total cash wages subject to Medicare taxes	3	11,800		
4	Medicare taxes. Multiply line 3 by 2.9% (.029)			4	342
5	Federal income tax withheld, if any			5	1,032
6	**Total social security, Medicare, and federal income taxes.** Add lines 2, 4, and 5			6	2,601

7 Did you pay **total** cash wages of $1,000 or more in **any** calendar **quarter** of 2010 or 2011 to **all** household employees? (**Do not** count cash wages paid in 2010 or 2011 to your spouse, your child under age 21, or your parent.)

- ☐ **No. Stop.** Include the amount from line 6 above on Form 1040, line 59a. If you are not required to file Form 1040, see the line 7 instructions.
- ☑ **Yes.** Go to line 8.

For Privacy Act and Paperwork Reduction Act Notice, see the instructions. Cat. No. 12187K **Schedule H (Form 1040) 2011**

Part II Federal Unemployment (FUTA) Tax

			Yes	No
8	Did you pay unemployment contributions to only one state? (If you paid contributions to a credit reduction state, see instructions and check "No.")	8	✓	
9	Did you pay all state unemployment contributions for 2011 by April 17, 2012? Fiscal year filers see instructions	9	✓	
10	Were all wages that are taxable for FUTA tax also taxable for your state's unemployment tax?	10	✓	

Next: If you checked the **"Yes"** box on **all** the lines above, complete Section A.
If you checked the **"No"** box on **any** of the lines above, skip Section A and complete Section B.

Section A

11 Name of the state where you paid unemployment contributions ▶ Any state

12 Contributions paid to your state unemployment fund 12 490

13 Total cash wages subject to FUTA tax 13 7,000

14 **FUTA tax.** Multiply the portion of the wages on line 13 paid before July 1 by .008. Multiply the portion of the wages on line 13 paid after June 30 by .006. Enter the sum of those two amounts on line 14, skip Section B, and go to line 23 . . . . . . 14 53

Section B

15 Complete all columns below that apply (if you need more space, see instructions):

(a) Name of state	(b) Taxable wages (as defined in state act)	(c) State experience rate period From	(c) To	(d) State experience rate	(e) Multiply col. (b) by .054	(f) Multiply col. (b) by col. (d)	(g) Subtract col. (f) from col. (e). If zero or less, enter -0-.	(h) Contributions paid to state unemployment fund

16 Totals 16

17 Add columns (g) and (h) of line 16 17

18 Total cash wages subject to FUTA tax (see the line 13 instructions) 18

19 Multiply the portion of the wages on line 18 paid before July 1 by 6.2% (.062). Multiply the portion of the wages on line 18 paid after June 30 by 6.0% (.060). Enter the sum of those amounts on line 19 . . . 19

20 Multiply line 18 by 5.4% (.054) 20

21 Enter the **smaller** of line 17 or line 20 . . . . . .
(Employers in a credit reduction state must use the worksheet and check here) . . . . . ☐ 21

22 **FUTA tax.** Subtract line 21 from line 19. Enter the result here and go to line 23 22

Part III Total Household Employment Taxes

23 Enter the amount from line 6. If you checked the "Yes" box on line C of page 1, enter -0- . . . 23 2,601

24 Add line 14 (or line 22) and line 23 . . . . . . 24 2,654

25 Are you required to file Form 1040?

☑ **Yes. Stop.** Include the amount from line 24 above on Form 1040, line 59a. **Do not** complete Part IV below.

☐ **No.** You may have to complete Part IV. See instructions for details.

Part IV Address and Signature— Complete this part **only** if required. See the line 25 instructions.

Address (number and street) or P.O. box if mail is not delivered to street address | Apt., room, or suite no.

City, town or post office, state, and ZIP code

Under penalties of perjury, I declare that I have examined this schedule, including accompanying statements, and to the best of my knowledge and belief, it is true, correct, and complete. No part of any payment made to a state unemployment fund claimed as a credit was, or is to be, deducted from the payments to employees. Declaration of preparer (other than taxpayer) is based on all information of which preparer has any knowledge.

▶ Employer's signature ▶ Date

Paid Preparer Use Only	Print/Type preparer's name	Preparer's signature	Date	Check ☐ if self-employed	PTIN
	Firm's name ▶			Firm's EIN ▶	
	Firm's address ▶			Phone no.	

Schedule H (Form 1040) 2011

Chapter 41

U.S. citizens working abroad: Tax treatment of foreign earned income

ey.com/EYTaxGuide

Note

ey.com/EYTaxGuide
Ernst & Young LLP will update the *Ernst & Young Tax Guide 2012* website with relevant taxpayer information as it becomes available. You can also sign up for email alerts to let you know when changes have been made.

Introduction

U.S. citizens and *resident aliens* are taxed on their worldwide income regardless of where it is earned, paid, or received. But U.S. citizens living abroad get certain tax benefits that are not available back home. *Employees* and *self-employed* individuals living abroad may elect to exclude up to $92,900 of their foreign-earned income from taxation in 2011. Employees and self-employed individuals may also exclude or deduct part of their housing costs from *taxable income.* This chapter tells you about all the tax benefits you get from living abroad and what you have to do to qualify for them.

How to Qualify for the Foreign Earned Income Exclusion

You qualify for the foreign earned income exclusion if you are a U.S. citizen, you have a tax home in a foreign country, and you meet either the foreign residence test or the physical presence test, described below.

Generally, if you are a resident alien of the United States, you may qualify for the foreign earned income exclusion if you satisfy the physical presence test. This assumes that you have not permanently left the United States and that you plan to continue your resident alien status.

Tax home. Your tax home generally is the location of your principal place of employment, which may or may not coincide with the location of your family's residence. Among the factors that are important in determining whether or not your tax home is outside the United States are the anticipated duration of your overseas assignment and whether or not you will return to the same employment location in the United States. Under IRS guidelines, an anticipated short-term (1 year or less) assignment overseas, followed by a return to the same place of employment in the United States, would indicate that you do not have a tax home outside the United States.

If you meet either the foreign residence test or the physical presence test (discussed below) and have a tax home outside the United States, you are eligible for two exclusions—the foreign earned income exclusion and the foreign housing exclusion. Self-employed individuals are eligible for a housing deduction rather than the housing exclusion (see the discussion later in this chapter).

Foreign residence test. The foreign residence test requires that you be a "bona fide resident" of a foreign country (or more than one foreign country) for an uninterrupted period that includes an entire tax year. Whether or not you are a bona fide resident is a subjective question. The answer is determined by the facts and circumstances of your particular situation, including the purpose of your trip and the nature and length of your stay abroad, and your intent.

The following factors are considered by the IRS in determining your intent to be a "bona fide" resident in a specific place.

1. The type of quarters you occupy (hotel or rooming house, rented quarters, purchased quarters, or quarters furnished by your employer)
2. How long your family resided with you during the tax year
3. The length of the uninterrupted period of time during which you have been living outside the United States

4. The nature of any conditions or limitations concerning your employment agreement and the type and term of your visa to live/work in the foreign country
5. Whether you maintain a home in the United States and, if so, its rental status and the relationship of any tenants to you

If you make a statement to the authorities of a foreign country that you are not a resident of that country, and if you are not subject to tax by that country, you do not qualify as a bona fide resident of that country.

However, once you have met the foreign residence test for an entire tax year, your qualification is retroactive to the first day you established your bona fide residence. Occasional trips to the United States for business or vacation do not affect your qualification.

Example 1. You moved from the United States to a foreign country, arriving on September 15, 2011. You entered the country under a resident visa with your family for a 3-year assignment. You did not declare to the foreign authorities that you were not a resident of that country. You qualify as a bona fide resident of the foreign country if these facts remain the same through December 31, 2012. You may file your 2011 U.S. income tax return (or amend your original 2011 tax return) to claim the benefits of being a bona fide resident of a foreign country for the period September 15, 2011, through December 31, 2011.

Example 2. George has been a resident of the United Kingdom for 5 consecutive years. If he moves to France this year, he continues to be a bona fide resident of a foreign country. An uninterrupted period of bona fide residence may include residence in more than one foreign country in a given year.

Example 3. Amy moved to France with her family on June 15, 2010, for a job assignment of indefinite length. On December 3, 2011, she was transferred back to the United States. She did not satisfy the bona fide residence test in either year, since she did not maintain a bona fide residence in a foreign country for a period that includes a complete tax year. However, she may qualify for the foreign exclusions under the physical presence test (discussed below).

Physical presence test. This test simply requires that you be physically present in a foreign country (or countries) for 330 full days during any consecutive 12-month period. This is a purely objective test. There is no reference to your intentions or to any other factors that determine bona fide residence abroad.

Two important rules to keep in mind regarding this test are as follows:

1. A full day is a 24-hour period commencing at midnight. Thus, a day in which you travel *to or from the United States* is not a full day in a foreign country.
2. When you travel between *foreign countries*, the travel days will qualify as full days in a foreign country, provided that the time spent outside of either foreign country during the journey (i.e., time spent over international waters and/or time spent in the United States) is less than 24 hours.

TAXORGANIZER

Keep a calendar. Keep a record of your travel days in and out of the United States and retain it with your other important tax records. The calendar should be supported by airline tickets, stamped passports, or other evidence of arrival and departure dates.

The Foreign Earned Income Exclusion

If you qualify, you may elect to exclude a maximum of $92,900 in foreign earned income from your U.S. taxable income in 2011 . The amount of the exclusion is indexed annually for inflation.

The amount of earned income you may exclude depends on either (1) the number of days during the year in which you were a bona fide resident of a foreign country or (2) the number of days you were physically present in a foreign country during a 12-month period. These are known as your "qualifying days." If you are out of the U.S. for the entire year, you may exclude all of your earned income up to the $92,900 limit. However, if you are out of the U.S. for only part of the year, you generally must prorate the exclusion based on your number of qualifying days during the taxable year.

Example. You were a bona fide resident of a foreign country for 300 days during 2011. The maximum amount of income you may exclude from U.S. taxes is 300/365 × $92,900, or $76,356. Your exclusion is, of course, limited by the amount of foreign income you earn. If you earn less than the maximum allowed, you may exclude only that lower amount.

Only foreign earned income is eligible for the exclusion. Earned income is income you receive for the performance of personal services. It does *not* include dividends, interest, capital gains, rental property income, and other kinds of unearned income. For example, interest paid on a bank account in the United Kingdom to a U.S. expatriate on assignment in London is not eligible for the exclusion, since it is not foreign *earned* income.

Earned income may be received in cash or as benefits-in-kind and includes the following:

- Salaries, wages, bonuses, commissions, overseas incentive premiums, and so on.
- A housing allowance. This may take the form of a cash payment to you, a cash payment by your employer directly to a landlord, or housing provided by your employer. When a cash payment is made, you must report the full amount as income. When housing is provided, your employer should furnish you with an estimate of its fair market value, which is used for income-reporting purposes.
- An automobile allowance. A cash allowance for an automobile should be included in your income. When an automobile is provided by your employer, an amount representing the value of its personal use to you should be included in your income.
- A cost-of-living allowance.
- An education allowance (e.g., for the cost of schooling your children).
- Home leave. The value of home leave benefits provided to you and your family is included in your income. However, if you spend a significant portion of your home leave on business, you may be justified in characterizing your portion of the trip as a business trip and thereby exclude your travel expenses from income.
- Rest and relaxation airfare.
- A moving expense reimbursement or allowance, in certain cases.
- A tax reimbursement or allowance.

Source of earned income. The source of earned income depends on the place where the services are rendered. If the services are performed in the United States, the income is considered U.S. source income. On the other hand, if the services are performed in a foreign country, the income is foreign source. For the income to be excluded on your tax return, the earned income must be from sources within a foreign country (or countries) and relate to services rendered in the current year.

How to compute your foreign source income. To compute your foreign source income for purposes of the foreign earned income exclusion, you must determine your earned income from sources outside the United States.

Foreign source earned income includes all income received for personal services performed outside the United States. The place of payment is irrelevant: a payment made into a U.S. bank account by a U.S.-based employer for services performed outside the United States is foreign source income. If you perform services both inside and outside the United States during the tax year, you must determine what portion of your income is from U.S. sources and what portion is from foreign sources.

Example 1. You received $50,000 for services performed in 2011. You worked a total of 240 days during the year, 235 days in the United Kingdom on foreign assignment and 5 days in the United States for a technical meeting. The source of your earned income is as follows:

$$\frac{\text{5 days worked in the United States}}{\text{240 days worked worldwide}} \times \$50{,}000 = \$1{,}042$$

$$\frac{\text{235 days worked outside the United States}}{\text{240 days worked worldwide}} \times \$50{,}000 = \$48{,}958$$

Your U.S. source income is $1,042, and your foreign source income is $48,958.

There are several other considerations to keep in mind when you are figuring out the source of your income:

1. If there has been a significant change in your rate of compensation during the year, it may be appropriate to allocate your compensation separately for the days worked and income earned in the respective periods.
2. If a payment is received during the year for services performed in a prior year, it may be appropriate to compute the foreign source portion of that payment based on the days worked in the prior year. It is not possible to exclude this prior year foreign source income using the current year's foreign earned income exclusion, but it might be possible to exclude some or all of the income on your current year's tax return to the extent that last year's exclusion was not fully used up.
3. Do not take into account vacation or holiday travel to the U.S. as part of your workday calculation.

Example 2. In 2010, you were eligible for the full $91,500 foreign earned income exclusion but only had $81,500 of foreign source earned income that was excluded on your 2010 tax return. Therefore, you have $10,000 of unused exclusion from 2010. In 2011, your compensation includes $12,000 of foreign source income earned in 2010 (in this case, a bonus payment). You are able to exclude $10,000 of the $12,000 of income on your 2011 tax return. The $10,000 exclusion is in addition to any exclusion you might have for foreign compensation earned and received in 2011.

The Foreign Housing Exclusion

If you qualify as a U.S. citizen living abroad, you may elect to exclude from your U.S. taxable income the excess of eligible housing costs over a "base housing amount." Eligible housing costs that an individual may exclude are limited to 30% of the foreign earned income exclusion ($27,870 for 2011). However, the IRS issues guidance periodically establishing higher maximum housing costs for certain geographic locations–as high as $118,500 for Tokyo in 2011. This guidance can be found on the IRS website, *www.irs.gov*. The base housing amount is equal to 16% of the annual foreign earned income exclusion ($14,864 for 2011). The base housing amount is prorated by the ratio of the number of qualifying days to the total days in the year.

Example. You had $18,000 of qualified housing expenses in your 2011 qualifying period. Based on an allocation of your earned income, you determine that you had $98,000 of foreign source income. Furthermore, you had a qualifying period of 330 days in the tax year. The base housing amount is $14,864. Your housing exclusion is computed as follows:

1) Housing expenses	$18,000
2) Number of qualifying days	330
3) Total days in the tax year	365
4) Base housing amount	$14,864
5) 330/365 × $14,864	$13,439
6) Housing exclusion (line 1 – line 5)	$4,561

Assuming the same facts, you calculate your foreign earned income exclusion as follows:

1) Maximum foreign earned income exclusion	$92,900
2) Number of qualifying days	330
3) Total days in tax year	365
4) 330/365 × $92,900	$83,992
5) Total foreign source income	$98,000
6) Less: Housing exclusion	($4,561)
7) Total foreign source income available for exclusion	$93,439
8) Smaller of line 4 or 7	$83,992

Your foreign earned income exclusion is $83,992. In addition, your foreign housing exclusion is $4,561. Your total exclusion is $88,553.

Foreign housing deduction for self-employed individuals. If you are a self-employed individual and you do not have an employer to provide housing, you may deduct the cost of foreign housing, net of the base housing amount subject to the limitations discussed above, in computing your adjusted gross income. Your housing deduction is limited to the amount by which your foreign earned income exceeds your foreign earned income exclusion for that year.

If you are both an employee and a self-employed individual during the same tax year, see Publication 54, *Tax Guide for U.S. Citizens and Resident Aliens Abroad*.

TAXPLANNER

When to elect the foreign earned income exclusion and the foreign housing exclusion. You elect and calculate the foreign earned income exclusion and the foreign housing exclusion separately using Form 2555 or, in some cases, Form 2555-EZ. The elections can be made on a tax return that you file on time, on an amended tax return, or on a late-filed tax return that is filed within 1 year of the original due date. The IRS also allows the elections to be made later under certain circumstances. When you are deciding whether or not to use the exclusions, you should take into account a number of factors, including the level of taxation in the foreign country in which you are living, the type of foreign assignment you are on, and your employer's policies concerning individuals on foreign assignment.

When you elect the foreign income exclusion, you are required to reduce your otherwise deductible expenses that are associated with the excluded income. Similarly, foreign taxes available for the foreign tax credit must also be reduced (see *Foreign Tax Credit*, later).

If you are living in a foreign country with a high tax rate, you may be better off forgoing the exclusions and claiming a larger foreign tax credit. In this case, forgoing the exclusions might result in a higher current tax liability but may also create larger foreign tax credits that you might be able to use in other years to offset tax on foreign source income. In countries with moderate or low tax rates, it is usually to your advantage to claim the exclusions. In any event, you should calculate your taxes with and without the exclusions to see which is more beneficial to you.

Once you elect the exclusion(s), you may revoke either or both of them by attaching a statement to your return or your amended return stating that you do not wish to claim the exclusion(s). Once revoked, you may not claim the exclusions again for the next 5 years without obtaining IRS approval.

Employer-Provided Meals and Lodging

Meals and lodging provided in kind by, or on behalf of, an employer to an employee or to his or her spouse or dependents are excluded from taxable income if certain requirements are met:

1. The meals are provided on the business premises of, and for the convenience of, the employer.
2. Lodging is furnished on the premises of, and for the convenience of, the employer, and the employee is required to accept this lodging as a condition of employment.

The IRS has taken a narrow view of the lodging exclusion. As a result, most employer-provided lodging is not excludable from your income. However, the exclusion applies if the employee resides in a camp that is provided by the employer because the employee's work site is in a remote area where satisfactory housing is not available on the open market. The camp has to be located as near as is practicable to the work site and should be furnished with a common area or enclave that is not available to the general public and normally accommodates 10 or more employees.

TAXALERT

You do not have to be living abroad to take advantage of this exclusion for employer-provided meals and lodging. All taxpayers are entitled to exclude the value of meals and lodging from taxable income when they are provided on the employer's premises for the employer's convenience and when the lodging must be accepted as a condition of employment.

Foreign Tax Credit

You may elect to claim a credit for foreign income taxes paid or accrued during the tax year, or you may claim the taxes paid as an itemized deduction. Generally, claiming a credit is more beneficial, since it results in a dollar-for-dollar reduction in your tax bill. The foreign tax credit on your U.S. return is limited to the lesser of (1) the actual foreign income taxes paid or accrued during the year (including carrybacks or carryforwards) or (2) the amount of U.S. tax attributable to foreign source taxable income for the year. The foreign tax credit is elected and calculated on Form 1116 (see chapter 37, *Other credits including the earned income credit*).

As mentioned above, if you elect either the foreign earned income exclusion or the foreign housing exclusion, the amount of foreign taxes that is available for credit is reduced.

TAXORGANIZER

Keep a copy of your foreign tax return and receipts for taxes paid in order to support the foreign tax credit calculations. This may be needed if your return is audited by the IRS.

Example 1. You had $98,000 of foreign source income and $18,000 of qualified housing expenses in 2011. The total amount you may exclude from your income is $88,553. (See the *foreign housing exclusion example* above to learn how this number is calculated.) You paid $4,000 in foreign taxes for the year. You figure the amount that you may claim as a foreign tax credit as follows:

$$\frac{\$88{,}553}{\$98{,}000} \times \$4{,}000 = \$3{,}614$$

A maximum of $386 ($4,000 – $3,614) may be claimed as a foreign tax credit.

Example 2. You are an unmarried U.S. citizen currently residing in the United Kingdom. Your total gross income for the year is $120,000, all of which is compensation. You qualify for a foreign earned income exclusion of $92,900 and a housing exclusion of $5,000, for a total of $97,900. You spent 10% of your working days in the United States. You have $6,200 of itemized deductions, none of which directly relate to a particular class of income. The amount you may claim as a foreign tax credit is computed as follows:

Compensation from foreign sources (90% of $120,000)	$108,000
Deductions allocated to foreign source compensation:	
($6,200 × 90%)	($5,580)
Less: Foreign earned income and housing exclusions	($97,900)
Foreign source taxable income	$4,520
U.S. source compensation (10% of $120,000)	$12,000
Balance of itemized deductions ($6,200 minus $5,580)	($620)
Total taxable income before personal exemptions	$15,900

The foreign tax credit limitation is calculated by determining the ratio of foreign source taxable income to total taxable income (as shown above). The ratio in the above example would be

$$\frac{\$4{,}520}{\$15{,}900} = 0.2843$$

This ratio is then multiplied by the U.S. tax liability for the year to determine the maximum amount of foreign tax credit usable for the year. If we assume that the U.S. tax is $3,416, the maximum credit would be $971 (0.2843 × $3,416).

Carryback and carryforward of foreign tax credit. Example 1 (above) shows how to determine the amount of foreign taxes that may be used as a credit. Example 2 (above) shows how to determine the maximum amount of foreign tax credit that may be currently used as a credit against your U.S. taxes. If the amount of the foreign tax credit that is generated exceeds the amount that can be used currently, you may carry back the excess one year. The remainder, if any, may be carried forward for up to ten years. The excess credit must be carried back first, and used in the preceding year if possible, before it can be carried forward.

TAXPLANNER

Planning tips for individuals on international assignment. Here is a list of items you should consider in planning your tax affairs and preparing your tax return:

1. **Sale of your principal residence**. A taxpayer may claim an exclusion of up to $250,000 for single taxpayers ($500,000 for joint filers) once every 2 years if the taxpayer owned the residence and occupied it as a principal residence for at least 2 of the 5 years before the sale or exchange. New rules for 2009 and later years may limit the amount of gain which can be excluded if the property was used as a vacation or rental property or if the property was left vacant (see chapter 15, *Selling your home*).

There are no special rules for U.S. home sales by expatriates. If you have a significant gain built up in your home and you expect your assignment to last more than 3 years, you should give consideration to selling your home. Otherwise, if you decide to sell at a later date, you may fail the 2-year out of 5-year test and some or all of the exclusion may be lost (see chapter 15, *Selling your home*).

Keep in mind that if you purchase your primary residence in a foreign country, the amount of any gain will be affected by changes in the foreign exchange rate. In addition, principal payments on a foreign mortgage may result in a taxable exchange gain.

2. **Individual retirement arrangements (IRAs).** An expatriate who contributes to an IRA (see chapter 17, *Individual retirement arrangements [IRAs]*) must have earned income in excess of the total of his or her foreign earned income and foreign housing exclusions if he or she elects to use the exclusions.

   If you are covered by a company pension plan, your modified adjusted gross income must be below a certain level for your IRA contribution to be tax deductible. Similarly, your modified adjusted gross income must be below a certain level in order to make a contribution to a traditional IRA or a Roth IRA. Note that for purposes of computing modified adjusted gross income, the foreign earned income exclusion and the foreign housing exclusion amounts must be disregarded. For a more detailed discussion of IRAs, please refer to chapter 17, *Individual retirement arrangements (IRAs)*.
3. **Report of foreign bank and financial accounts.** You should become familiar with the filing requirements of Form TD F 90-22.1, which is a form that is used to provide information concerning foreign bank and financial accounts if in the aggregate their value exceeds $10,000. Significant penalties apply for noncompliance.

TAXORGANIZER

Records you should keep:

- A calendar of travel days to track workdays and non-workdays in the United States, the assignment country, and any other country. The calendar can be supported by airline tickets, stamped passports, or other evidence documenting arrival and departure dates.
- A list of housing expenses in the host country
- A copy of your foreign tax returns and receipts for foreign taxes paid or accrued during the tax year, depending on the method used for claiming the foreign tax credit

Chapter 42

Foreign citizens living in the United States

ey.com/EYTaxGuide

Note

ey.com/EYTaxGuide
Ernst & Young LLP will update the *Ernst & Young Tax Guide 2012* website with relevant taxpayer information as it becomes available. You can also sign up for email alerts to let you know when changes have been made.

Introduction

Whether a U.S. citizen or not, almost everybody living in the United States is subject to U.S. income tax laws. Foreign nationals working in the United States are either resident aliens or nonresident aliens. Resident aliens, like U.S. citizens, are subject to U.S. tax on their worldwide income. Nonresident aliens are subject to U.S. tax only on certain types of their U.S. source income.

Some foreign citizens living in the United States are not taxed at all—at least not by the U.S. government. A foreign citizen resident in the United States who works for a foreign government doing normal diplomatic work is exempt from the U.S. tax laws, provided that U.S. government employees working in that foreign country are exempt from its tax laws. Tax treaties between the United States and some foreign countries contain numerous other exceptions that alter the normal domestic U.S. tax laws.

This chapter tells you how to determine if you are a resident alien or a nonresident alien and how you should calculate your tax.

Determining Your Status

Whether you are a resident alien or a nonresident alien is of critical importance when you compute how much U.S. income tax you will pay. Your residency status will determine your filing status, the tax rate schedule applicable to your income, and the amount of your income that will be subject to U.S. income tax. Under rules that became effective in 1985, an alien must meet either one of the two following tests in order to be considered a resident of the United States for tax purposes:

1. **The green card test.** Have you been lawfully admitted to the United States for permanent residency? In other words, do you have a green card?
2. **The substantial presence test.** Have you been present in the United States for a substantial period of time? If you have been present in the United States for at least 31 days in the current year and if the total days you are present in the United States during the current year, plus one-third of the days present in the preceding calendar year, plus one-sixth of the days present in the second preceding calendar year, are equal to at least 183 days, you will meet the substantial presence test and be considered a resident alien in the current year.

If you are considered a U.S. resident under the substantial presence test (and you were not a U.S. resident in the prior year), your residency period generally begins on the first day you were present in the United States in the current year. However, if you have a brief visit (or visits) to the United States, and the total days you spend in the United States during the visit (or visits) amount to 10 days or less, you may, under certain circumstances, ignore those days for purposes of determining when your residency period begins.

Example. You move to the United States on June 1, 2011, and spend a sufficient number of days in this country in 2011 to meet the substantial presence test. Prior to your actual arrival on June 1, you spent 10 days in the United States from February 2 through February 11 to house hunt and to meet with your U.S. employer while you maintained your tax home in a foreign country. Your U.S. residency period begins on June 1. In the event you had stayed in the United States until February 12 (11 days), your U.S. residency period would have begun on February 2.

A similar rule applies in the year in which your U.S. residency terminates. Your residency period generally ends on the 31st of December. However, if you can show that you have closer connections to a foreign country for the remainder of the year, your U.S. residency generally ends on the last day you are present in the United States. Visits to the United States totaling 10 days or less following your departure may be disregarded in determining the last day of your U.S. residency.

TAXALERT

To take advantage of this closer connection rule and terminate your residency on the last day you are present in the United States, you may be required to attach a statement to your U.S. tax return for that year detailing the facts that support your closer connection to a foreign country.

Example. In 2011 you lived in the United States continuously from January 1 through October 31, when you moved to a foreign country and established a closer connection to it. Generally, you are considered to be a resident of the United States through October 31. If you return to the United States on business trips or on vacation during November and December and spend 10 days or less in total in the United States, your residency period terminates on October 31. If you spend more than 10 days in total in the United States in November and December, your U.S. residency period will be extended beyond October 31. The actual termination date will depend on the specific dates of your visits. You would also want to take into consideration any tax treaty benefits that might be available to you.

TAXORGANIZER

Arrival and departure dates. To substantiate your arrival and departure dates to and from the United States, copies of travel tickets (airline, boat, etc.), stamped passports, and other relevant documentation should be retained in your tax files.

TAXALERT

Resident alien status. Even if you meet the substantial presence test, you can avoid being considered a resident alien if you are present in the United States for less than 183 days in the current year and you can show closer ties to a tax home in a foreign country (or, in the case of a move, no more than two foreign countries) than to the United States for the entire year. Whether you have closer ties to the United States or to a foreign country depends on the facts and circumstances of your situation. Consult a tax advisor for details. You will be required to furnish a statement with detailed information to the IRS if you take this closer connection position.

Election to Be Treated as a Resident

The tax law contains a rule that allows an alien to elect to be treated as a resident of the United States for tax purposes (a "first year election"), even though he or she does not meet the green card or substantial presence test. The first year election allows an alien with significant U.S. presence toward the end of year 1 and who meets the substantial presence test in year 2 to elect to be treated as a U.S. resident alien in year 1. The alien can only make this first year election after he or she has met the substantial presence test in year 2. This may require filing an extension for the year 1 tax return. This election will be advantageous to some aliens, such as those who incur significant expenses when they first arrive in the United States (such as mortgage interest, deductible mortgage points, and real estate taxes related to a purchased home in the U.S.), which would be deductible for a resident but not for a nonresident. In addition, this election could also benefit married aliens who would otherwise be required to file using the married filing separate rates that apply to nonresidents. As U.S. residents under this election, they would be permitted to make a further election to be treated as residents for the entire year, thus permitting the filing of a joint return and the use of the more favorable joint return rates. An alien who meets the following criteria may make the election (see the following Example):

1. Doesn't meet the green card or substantial presence tests for the current year,
2. Was not a resident alien in the prior year,
3. Meets the substantial presence test in the following year,
4. Is present in the United States for at least 31 consecutive days in the current year, and
5. Spends at least 75% of the days between the first of the 31 consecutive days and year-end in the United States. (Note: Up to 5 non-U.S. days will be counted as U.S. days for the purposes of this test.)

An alien who makes the election to be treated as a resident may also make a similar election on his or her tax return on behalf of dependent children if the children are not required to file tax returns on their own, assuming, of course, that the children also meet the requirements of the election. The filing of the election will enable an alien to take dependent exemptions for the children.

Example. Assume that an alien is present in the United States for the following periods:

7/4-8/15	43 days
9/16-11/25	71 days
12/16-12/31	16 days

During the testing period of July 4 through December 31, the individual is in the United States 130 days out of 181 days total. Including the 5 additional non-U.S. days that can be counted as U.S. days, the individual is present in the United States on less than 75% of the days and cannot make the election for this period.

$$\frac{130+5}{181} = 74.6\%$$

However, since, during the testing period of September 16 through December 31, the individual was in the United States 87 days out of 107, which exceeds 75%, the individual could elect to be treated as a resident for the period of September 16 through December 31 (assuming that the other tests regarding the prior and subsequent years are also met).

TAXPLANNER

If you have a green card, you should be aware that you are considered a resident alien and that you are subject to tax on all of your worldwide income. If you have substantial U.S. or foreign investment income, you may want to transfer the income-producing assets to somebody else, for example, a spouse or other close relative who is still living abroad. Before making any transfers, however, you should consult with a tax advisor to consider possible gift tax and foreign tax implications.

TAXPLANNER

Substantial presence test. If you meet the substantial presence test described above, but you are present in the United States less than 183 days each year, you should examine your ties to another country. You might qualify for an exception to the substantial presence test if you can demonstrate that your ties to another country are stronger than your ties to the United States. You must file a statement with your tax return supporting your claim, or, if no return is required, a statement alone must be filed with the IRS.

If your ties are weak and you want to try to strengthen them, consider:

1. Maintaining a home in that country
2. Obtaining a driver's license issued by that country
3. Joining a religious, political, or cultural organization in that country
4. Maintaining or establishing a membership in a social organization in that country
5. Having a bank account in that country
6. Having personal property in that country such as cars, clothing, or jewelry
7. Continuing to vote in that country

If you spend a significant amount of time in the United States each year, you should carefully monitor the days to keep them below the 183-day threshold during the 3-year period considered under the substantial presence test.

TAXPLANNER

Do not assume that nonresident alien filing status necessarily results in greater savings than resident alien status. Resident alien status may result in a lower U.S. tax if you can use the lower joint return rates (for married resident aliens), if you are eligible for greater itemized deductions, and/or if you can benefit from the foreign tax credit.

Income tax treaties. Income tax treaties may have the effect of overriding the provisions of U.S. law. Consult a tax advisor for details.

Generally, tax treaties are consulted when an individual is a dual resident, that is, a resident of both the United States and a foreign country under each country's tax rules. When a treaty is used to claim that an individual is a nonresident of the United States, the individual must file Form 1040-NR and attach Form 8833, Treaty-Based Return Position Disclosure, to the return, presenting facts to support his or her claim of not being a U.S. resident.

An election to be treated as a nonresident of the United States under a treaty will apply for all purposes in computing the individual's income tax liability for the dual residency period.

TAXALERT

Filing Form 1040-NR may influence the determination by the U.S. Department of Homeland Security as to whether you continue to qualify as a U.S. resident for immigration purposes if you hold a green card. Consult with an immigration lawyer to evaluate the impact of this tax position on your immigration situation. In addition, you should consult with a tax advisor so that you understand all the implications of a treaty-based nonresident filing position.

Dual-status aliens. A dual-status alien is a person who is considered a resident alien and a nonresident alien during the same tax year.

You are most likely to have dual status in the year of your arrival in or departure from the United States. You could, for example, be a resident alien until your departure from the United States. Thereafter, you would be a nonresident alien.

For purposes of computing your tax liability, different rules apply to the time when you are a resident alien and the time when you are a nonresident alien. However, it is necessary to fill out only one tax return. You may make a special election that may decrease your taxes for some years in which you have dual status. This election is discussed in the following section.

TAXPLANNER

An alien's residency status may not be the same for all purposes. The definition discussed above applies for federal income tax laws. Different rules apply in determining residency for state income tax and for federal gift and estate tax purposes.

How Resident Aliens Are Taxed

Like U.S. citizens, resident aliens are subject to tax on the worldwide income they receive, regardless of its source. Resident aliens compute their taxable income and income tax liability the same way U.S. citizens do. They include the same items in income and are entitled to take the same deductions as U.S. citizens.

TAXALERT

Rules for Individuals Giving Up U.S. Citizenship or U.S. Residency

Recent legislation—The Heroes Earnings Assistance and Relief Tax Act of 2008—introduced significant changes to the tax rules for individuals giving up U.S. citizenship or U.S. residency. The new law applies to individuals who relinquish U.S. citizenship or terminate long-term residency on or after June 17, 2008. Individuals who relinquished their U.S. citizenship or terminated their U.S. residency prior to this date are subject to a different set of rules. However, the new law refers to some of the prior rules when determining who is subject to the new tax.

The prior rules applicable to individuals who expatriated between June 4, 2004, and June 16, 2008, are as follows:

- Objective standards are used to determine whether expatriated individuals are subject to U.S. tax on certain types of income. An expatriated individual is subject to U.S. tax on certain types of income unless the individual has an average annual U.S. federal income tax liability over the preceding five years of less than $139,000 for calendar year 2008, $145,000 for 2009 and 2010, or $147,000 for 2011, and a net worth of less than $2 million. Limited exceptions apply. In addition, the expatriated individual has to certify that he or she has complied with all U.S. federal tax obligations for the preceding five years, and prove this if required.
- A long-term resident is an individual who has held a green card for any part of 8 of the 15 tax years ending with the year of expatriation and has not relied on an international treaty in order to determine his or her country of residence.
- An expatriated individual continues to be treated as a U.S. citizen or long-term resident for U.S. tax purposes until he or she gives notice of an expatriating act or termination of his or her residency to the U.S. Secretary of State or the U.S. Secretary of Homeland Security, along with a statement containing information about his or her status. The statement provided has to comply with certain legal requirements.
- An expatriated individual subject to U.S. tax on certain types of income is subject to full U.S. federal taxation for any year in the 10 years following expatriation in which he or she is present in the United States for more than 30 days.
- Expatriated individuals are required to file annual returns for each year after expatriation that they are subject to U.S. tax on certain types of income, even if no U.S. federal tax is due.
- In addition, there may be U.S. gift and estate tax implications to the expatriated individual.

The new rules are applicable to U.S. citizens who give up their citizenship and to long-term residents who give up their green cards after June 16, 2008. Individuals who meet either the net worth or average income tax tests discussed above, or who have not complied with U.S. tax filing requirements for the prior five years, are referred to as "covered expatriates" and are subject to the new rules as follows:

Covered expatriates are subject to a special exit tax. The tax–known as the mark-to-market exit tax–is calculated as if the covered expatriate sold all of his worldwide property for fair market value on the day before he gave up his citizenship or surrendered his green card. A gain of up to $600,000 (indexed annually for inflation; in 2011, this amount is $636,000) is excluded from tax. Furthermore, you are allowed to increase your basis in your property to its fair market value at the time you became a U.S. resident for purposes of calculating your gain or loss on property.

Special tax rules apply to deferred compensation, specified tax deferred accounts, and interests in nongrantor trusts. Depending upon the situation, deferred compensation may either be taxed under the normal income tax rules (although subject to a 30% withholding tax), or the present value of the accrued benefit or the value of the property may be taxed on the day prior to expatriation. The balance in specified tax-deferred accounts (e.g., traditional IRAs, 529 plans, and health savings accounts) is taxed as if received on the day prior to expatriation. Note that Roth IRAs are not considered tax-deferred accounts and are subject to the general mark-to-market exit tax rules described above. Distributions of property from non-grantor trusts to covered expatriates are subject to withholding tax. Furthermore, any distribution of appreciated property subjects the nongrantor trust to tax on the appreciation. A covered expatriate is required to give IRS Form W-8CE to the payer of any of the items mentioned above. In addition, a covered expatriate must file IRS Form 8854 with the Internal Revenue Service.

Gifts and bequests from covered expatriates to U.S. citizens or residents are subject to tax at the highest gift tax rate (45% in 2008 and 2009, 35% for 2010 and 2011). Gifts below the annual exclusion amount ($12,000 for 2008; $13,000 for 2009, 2010, and 2011) and certain other gifts are excluded from this tax. The tax is paid by the recipient of the gift or bequest.

TAXPLANNER

New and additional rules apply for the purpose of determining whether a U.S. citizen or long-term resident has relinquished citizenship or residency for U.S. tax purposes.

If you are contemplating terminating residency or relinquishing U.S. citizenship, consult your tax advisor and immigration attorney. The rules are very complex, and special filings may be required.

Dual-Status Aliens

Dual-status aliens who are resident aliens for part of the tax year are taxed somewhat differently from U.S. citizens.

If you file a single return, you are taxed on your worldwide income for the part of the year in which you are a resident alien. For the part of the year in which you are a nonresident alien, only certain types of your U.S. source income are taxed.

Dual-status aliens who are married may not file a joint return or claim the standard deduction. Married taxpayers are taxed on their worldwide income for the part of the year in which they are resident aliens and only on certain types of their U.S. source income for the part of the year in which they are nonresidents. They are not, however, able to file a joint return and take advantage of the joint return rate schedule.

Exceptions. Dual-status aliens who are married have two other alternatives in the year in which they arrive in the United States:

1. **The Section 6013(h) election**. This election is available only in cases in which a U.S. citizen or resident alien is married to an individual who is a resident alien at the close of the tax year. An alien choosing this alternative is treated as a resident of the United States for the entire tax year. The most significant consequences of making this choice are:
   a. All income, whether from a U.S. or a foreign source, is subject to tax, including any income you had during the period in which you were not a resident of the United States. This income would have been exempt from U.S. taxes, or possibly taxed at a reduced rate, if you had not made the Section 6013(h) election.
   b. You may claim itemized deductions for the period in which you were not a resident of the United States, if such items would otherwise qualify for deduction. Some examples are foreign real property taxes, mortgage interest, and medical expenses.
   c. You may deduct, or elect to claim as a credit, foreign income taxes attributable to the period during which you were not a U.S. resident, which may substantially reduce or even eliminate U.S. income tax. Other benefits, however, like being able to file a joint return and thus be taxed at accordingly lower rates, are left intact. The result is that your net U.S. tax liability may be reduced.
2. **The Section 6013(g) election.** Under the Section 6013(g) election, a married couple may file a joint return as full-year residents of the United States if, at the end of the tax year, one spouse is a nonresident alien and the other is a citizen or resident of the United States.

   The effects of making this election are the same as choosing the Section 6013(h) election, with one very significant distinction. The Section 6013(g) election is valid for all subsequent years in which you and your spouse qualify, including the year in which the resident alien leaves the United States. Once made, the Section 6013(g) election can be revoked. However, if you revoke the election, you cannot make another such election in the future. On the other hand, the Section 6013(h) election cannot be made by the same two individuals in any future tax year.

Example. You and your spouse became U.S. residents on April 1, 2011. Prior to your arrival in the United States, you earned $5,000 in wages and your spouse earned $1,000 in wages. Both of you also had $500 in joint interest income for the first 3 months of the year. Once in the United States, you earned $75,000 from April through December. Your spouse did not work in the United States. You had an additional $700 in joint interest income. Your itemized deductions equal the standard deduction. Your tax liabilities are computed as follows:

Alternative 1: Dual-status return, married filing separately (for period while a U.S. resident)

Salary	$75,000
Interest	350
Itemized deductions	(5,800)
Exemptions	(3,700)
Taxable income	$65,850
Tax	$12,588

You would not be taxed on your non-U.S. source income.

Alternative 2: Full-year election, joint return

Salary	$81,000
Interest	1,200
Standard deduction	(11,600)
Exemptions	(7,400)
Taxable income	$63,200
Tax	$8,630

By electing to be treated as a resident alien for the entire tax year, you save $3,958 in federal income taxes. Note that your spouse could not be claimed as a dependent under Alternative 1, since your spouse had income during the U.S. residency period. Your spouse does not need to file a return under Alternative 1, since your spouse's income did not exceed the amount that requires you to file. (See chapter 1, *Filing information.*)

The $6,500 in income that you and your spouse had in your home country would probably be subject to tax there. If so, you would be eligible for the foreign tax credit if you filed under Alternative 2. The tax credit would further lower your taxes. See chapter 37, *Other credits including the earned income credit*, for a discussion of the foreign tax credit.

TAXPLANNER

In order to claim exemptions for a resident alien's spouse and/or children who are not eligible to obtain a social security number, an individual taxpayer identification number (an "ITIN") is required for each person. Obtaining such a tax ID number no longer necessitates going to the social security office with the family. Rather, these numbers are now obtained directly from the IRS when the tax return is filed. Alternatively, certain tax advisors are registered with the IRS to review your original documentation and obtain the ITIN for you.

How Nonresident Aliens Are Taxed

A nonresident alien is taxed as follows:

Compensation for services rendered in the United States or other income that is effectively connected with a U.S. trade or business is generally taxed at graduated rates, using the appropriate tax rate schedules. A nonresident alien may deduct certain expenses incurred in producing that income, such as business-related expenses and state and local income taxes. In addition, he or she may deduct casualty losses and qualifying charitable contributions. However, a nonresident alien may not claim the standard deduction.

TAXPLANNER

For taxable years beginning after 1986, income that is effectively connected with a U.S. trade or business at the time it is earned will be considered "effectively connected" at the time it is received, even if receipt occurs in a different tax year.

A nonresident alien is generally able to claim a personal exemption only for himself or herself. However, a nonresident alien who is a resident of Mexico or Canada, or a national of the United States (such as certain American Samoans or Northern Mariana Islanders), is also entitled to claim personal exemptions for

1. A spouse, if the spouse had no gross income for U.S. tax purposes and was not the dependent of another taxpayer
2. Other dependents, if they meet the same requirements as a U.S. citizen.

In addition, certain tax treaties allow for personal exemptions for a spouse and dependents in specific cases.

A married nonresident alien is taxed under the "married filing separately" Tax Rate Schedule, which is the highest Tax Rate Schedule applicable to individuals.

You may not claim head of household status if you are a nonresident alien. A nonresident alien who is single would use the "unmarried" Tax Rate Schedule.

Dividends, interest, royalties, pensions, annuities, and other types of U.S. source income that are not effectively connected with a U.S. trade or business are usually subject to a flat 30% tax rate unless a tax treaty allows for a lower rate of tax. No deductions or exemptions are allowed against this income. Interest earned on U.S. bank accounts, as well as certain other investments (known as "portfolio" debt instruments), is exempt from U.S. taxes.

Gains and losses from the sale of capital assets, other than real property situated in the U.S., may be taxed in either of two ways. If the gains and losses are not connected with a trade or business in the United States, any gain (after deducting losses) is taxed at a 30% rate if the nonresident alien is in the United States for 183 days or more during the tax year. If a gain is derived from the sale of capital assets effectively connected with a trade or a business in the United States, it is taxed in the same manner as it would be for a U.S. citizen. Capital gains from the sale of real property located in the United States are considered to be connected with a U.S. trade or business and are subject to special U.S. tax laws. (For a more detailed discussion of the tax treatment of gains and losses, see IRS Publication 519, *U.S. Tax Guide for Aliens.*)

Foreign students. Foreign students who enter the U.S. under an "F," "M," or "Q" visa (academic or language student) or a "J" visa (educational and cultural exchange visitor) are generally nonresidents for U.S. income tax purposes, as long as they substantially comply with the terms of their visa.

TAXPLANNER

Foreign nationals who become U.S. residents. Foreign nationals who become U.S. residents are taxed on their worldwide income from the day on which they become residents. You may, however, take several steps before you become a U.S. resident in order to limit your U.S. tax liability. Consider the following:

1. If you anticipate receiving a payment of compensation for past services, such as a bonus, arrange to receive this payment before becoming a resident of the United States. If this payment is received after you become a U.S. resident alien, it will be taxable in full by the United States, even though the related services were rendered prior to coming to the United States. Review tax treaty and foreign tax credit rules for possible relief if it is received after becoming a U.S. tax resident.
2. If you anticipate incurring expenses that will be deductible for U.S. income tax purposes, such as mortgage points, interest, or certain charitable contributions, consider deferring these payments until after you are a resident of the United States.
3. If you sell shares in a foreign corporation for a gain prior to your arrival in the United States, the entire gain is not subject to U.S. tax. However, if you sell shares at a profit after you become a U.S. resident, the entire gain is subject to U.S. tax, even if the entire appreciation of the shares occurred before you became a U.S. resident. You should consider selling shares and other investments in which you have a profit before you become a U.S. resident. By the same token, if you hold an investment that has a loss and the entire loss was generated before you became a U.S. resident, but you did not realize the loss until after you took up residency, you may deduct the loss on your U.S. tax return, subject to the normal rules (see chapter 16, *Reporting gains and losses,* for more information).
4. If you receive a lump-sum distribution from a government or private retirement plan after you have become a U.S. resident, the entire amount may be subject to U.S. tax. If at all possible, arrange to receive the payment before you become a U.S. resident, when it is not subject to U.S. tax. In addition, note that the American Jobs Creation Act of 2004 provides that distributions from foreign pension plans made on or after October 22, 2004, are taxable in the hands of a U.S. resident to the extent that the amount distributed has not been subject to U.S. or foreign tax previously. Again, review tax treaty and foreign tax credit rules for possible relief if it is received after becoming a U.S. tax resident.
5. If you sell your principal residence before becoming a U.S. resident, the proceeds are not normally subject to any U.S. tax. However, if you become a U.S. resident and elect to be taxed as a resident alien for the entire year to take advantage of lower joint filing rates (see *Exceptions,* earlier), you may end up paying tax on the sale of your principal residence, as well as tax on any exchange gain associated with the payoff of the mortgage. Be sure to consider this fact before you elect to be taxed as a resident alien for the entire year.

There is a $250,000 exclusion for single taxpayers ($500,000 for married taxpayers filing jointly) on the gain from the sale of a home if you have owned the home and lived in the home as your principal residence for 2 of the last 5 years. The use of the exclusion by foreign nationals who have ceased to be residents of the United States is permitted if the expatriation rules do not apply (see *Rules for Individuals Giving Up U.S. Citizenship or U.S. Residency*, earlier in this chapter). Given the fact that this area of law is complex, you should seek tax advice prior to disposing of your primary residence.

6. You may be able to take advantage of a "window between tax residencies," a situation in which certain income is never taxed. This requires analyzing the tax laws of your home country and the United States. A window may be created, for example, if you come from a country that does not tax income of its nonresident citizens.

Example. Humphrey Benson is a citizen of a country that does not tax its nonresident citizens, and he decides to move permanently to the United States. He owns securities that have appreciated by $10,000. On his move to the United States, Humphrey ceases being a resident of his home country and goes to a third country for 2 weeks. The tax rules in this third country are such that he is not subject to tax on sales of securities. While there, he sells all his securities. The result is that he does not have to pay any tax in his home country, in the United States, or in the third country.

TAXPLANNER

Minimizing your tax burden. The main point to remember is that the best time for you to minimize your U.S. tax burden is *before* you make an investment in the United States and *before* you become a U.S. resident.

Departing from the United States

Before you depart from the United States, you must obtain a certificate of compliance, indicating that you have satisfied your federal tax liability. This certificate, frequently referred to as a "sailing permit" or a "departure permit," is obtained by filing Form 1040-C or Form 2063. To get the permit, you must either pay all of the U.S. income tax due prior to departure or demonstrate that your departure from the United States will not impair the collection of the tax. The forms may be found on the IRS website (*www.irs.gov*). An exit permit is valid only for 30 days. If you postpone your departure, you probably have to apply for a new exit permit. See IRS Publication 519, *U.S. Tax Guide for Aliens*, for more details and for certain categories of individuals who are exempt from the "sailing permit" requirements.

TAXORGANIZER

Sailing permits. The IRS representative must see actual departure tickets in order to issue your "sailing permit." Make sure you bring these along to the IRS office. *A certificate of compliance is not a substitute for an annual income tax return.* A federal tax return still must be filed in accordance with regular filing procedures. Any payment in conjunction with the filing of Form 1040-C is treated as a payment on your annual tax return.

TAXPLANNER

Income from employment that is paid in a tax year after the individual's year of departure will be considered effectively connected with a U.S. business and taxed at the regular graduated rates. There could be significant U.S. tax savings if, for example, the individual was in the highest tax bracket in the year in which the income was earned, and if a portion of the income is foreign-source income. The receipt of the income in a subsequent year will cause it to be taxed at lower marginal tax rates. Care should be taken to understand any non-U.S. tax implications of deferring the receipt of income.

TAXPLANNER

Report of Foreign Bank and Financial Accounts. If you become a resident of the United States, you should become familiar with the filing requirements of Form TD F90-22.1, which is a form that is used to provide information concerning foreign bank and financial accounts if their aggregate value exceeds $10,000. Significant penalties apply for noncompliance.

TAXORGANIZER

Records you should keep:

- A calendar of travel days in and out of the United States as well as workdays in and out of the United States. Also retain copies of travel tickets, stamped passports, and other documentation to substantiate the dates. In some cases, you may need calendars for the current calendar year plus the two previous years.
- If you will be taxed as a resident of the United States and you have income/deductions from sources outside the United States, you will need to include those items on your U.S. return. Therefore, evidence of those items should be maintained. Note that the United States may tax certain items of income differently than other countries; you should consult a tax advisor to confirm proper U.S. tax treatment.
- A copy of your visa and permanent residence card (i.e., green card) if applicable
- A copy of your foreign tax returns and receipts for foreign taxes paid or accrued during the tax year, depending on the method used for the foreign tax credit
- A copy of your social security card or individual taxpayer identification number (ITIN) card(s) for yourself, your spouse, and your dependents

Chapter 43

Decedents: Dealing with the death of a family member

ey.com/EYTaxGuide

Note

ey.com/EYTaxGuide
Ernst & Young LLP will update the *Ernst & Young Tax Guide 2012* website with relevant taxpayer information as it becomes available. You can also sign up for email alerts to let you know when changes have been made.

Introduction

The death of an individual can cause special tax problems, many of which are likely to be unfamiliar and puzzling to his or her survivors. Among other things, the deceased's will, along with state inheritance laws, can create a bewildering array of questions about how income is to be allocated and which deductions may be claimed and by whom.

This chapter helps you sort out such questions. It is most helpful to a survivor who has to deal with a relatively uncomplicated situation and a small estate. When the assets are large and the situation is complex, professional assistance is recommended.

Reminders

Consistent treatment of estate items. Beneficiaries must generally treat estate items the same way on their individual income tax returns as they are treated on the estate's income tax return. For more information, see *How and When to Report under Distributions to Beneficiaries From an Estate* in Publication 559, *Survivors, Executors, and Administrators.*

This chapter discusses the tax responsibilities of the person who is in charge of the property (estate) of an individual who has died (decedent). It also covers the following topics:

- Filing the decedent's final return.
- Tax effects on survivors.

This chapter does not discuss the requirements for filing an income tax return of an estate (Form 1041). For information on Form 1041, see *Income Tax Return of an Estate–Form 1041* in Publication 559. This chapter also does not discuss the requirements for filing an estate tax return (Form 706). For information, see Form 706 and its instructions.

What's New

The December 2010 tax law that extended the so-called Bush tax cuts also:

1. Reinstated the estate tax for 2010,
2. Repealed the modified carryover of basis rules for property acquired from a decedent who died in 2010, and
3. Created a special election that allows the personal representative of an estate of a decedent who died during 2010 to elect out of the estate tax for 2010 and instead use modified carryover of basis rules to apply to property acquired from a decedent dying in 2010.

If the special election is not made, the rules for determining basis of property acquired from a decedent who died in 2010 are the same as the rules for property acquired from a decedent who died before or after 2010. See _Property inherited from a decedent who died during 2010_, for more information.

Explanation

Though this chapter mainly discusses the filing requirement of a final individual income tax return for a decedent, an explanation of the various potential filing requirements may be helpful. Generally, upon an individual's death, there are three types of taxes that should be addressed: estate tax, gift tax, and income tax.

The estate tax is reported on Form 706, *U.S. Estate Tax Return*. (If the personal representative of the estate of a decedent who died during 2010 elected not to have the estate tax apply in accordance with the special election enacted in late 2010, no estate tax applies and an estate tax return is not filed.) Form 706 is a return that is generally based on the value of the net assets of the decedent's "estate" at the date of death. The filing deadline for Form 706 is within nine months after the date of death, unless there is an extension of time to file. Form 706 is generally required to be filed if the gross estate (the value of the estate without subtracting debts and liabilities) is over the applicable estate tax exemption.

In addition to an estate tax return, the decedent's personal representative may be required to file a gift tax return (Form 709) on the decedent's behalf. This return would report any gifts made by the decedent in the year of death and indicate the amount, if any, of gift tax due.

There are two possible income tax returns that may need to be filed: Form 1040, *U.S. Individual Income Tax Return*, and Form 1041, *U.S. Income Tax Return for Estates and Trusts*. Form 1040 is generally used to report all the income that the decedent earned and received prior to death. Any income that was earned and received after the date of death is generally reported by the estate (or the trust, if the asset was held in trust) and is reported on Form 1041. This chapter focuses mainly on Form 1040 issues.

Useful Items

You may want to see:

Publication

- □ **3** Armed Forces Tax Guide
- □ **559** Survivors, Executors, and Administrators

Form (and Instructions)

- □ **56** Notice Concerning Fiduciary Relationship
- □ **1310** Statement of Person Claiming A Refund Due a Deceased Taxpayer
- □ **4810** Request for Prompt Assessment Under Internal Revenue Code Section 650 1(d)

Personal Representative

A personal representative of an estate is an executor, administrator, or anyone who is in charge of the decedent's property.

Executor. An executor (or executrix) is named in a decedent's will to administer the estate (property owned and debts owed by the decedent) and distribute property as the decedent has directed.

Administrator. An administrator (or administratrix) is appointed by the court if no will exists, if no executor was named in the will, or if the named executor cannot or will not serve.

Personal representative. In general, an executor and an administrator perform the same duties and have the same responsibilities. Because a personal representative for a decedent's estate can be an executor, administrator, or anyone in charge of the decedent's property, the term personal representative will be used throughout this chapter.

The surviving spouse may or may not be the personal representative, depending on the terms of the decedent's will or the court appointment.

Duties

The primary duties of a personal representative are to collect the decedent's assets, pay creditors, and distribute the remaining assets to the heirs or other beneficiaries.

The personal representative also must perform the following duties:

1. Notify the IRS (as discussed below) that he or she is acting as the personal representative.
2. File any income tax and estate tax return when due. (See Final Return for the Decedent, later.)
3. Pay any tax determined up to the date of discharge from duties.
4. Provide the payers of any interest and dividends the name(s) and identification number(s) of the new owner(s). (See Interest and Dividend Income [Forms 1099], later.)

For more information on the duties and responsibilities of the personal representative, see *Duties under Personal Representative* in Publication 559.

Notifying the IRS. If you are appointed to act in any fiduciary capacity for another, you must file a written notice with the IRS stating this. Form 56 can be used for this purpose. The instructions and other requirements are given on the back of the form.

Explanation

Form 56, Notice Concerning Fiduciary Relationship, is used to notify the IRS of the creation or termination of a fiduciary relationship. If notification is not given to the IRS, notices of taxes due will be sent to the last known address of the decedent. This is considered sufficient notice by the IRS. Therefore, Form 56 should be filed in a timely manner so that the personal representative is not considered personally liable for the taxes due, along with possible interest and penalties. Form 56 should be filed with the IRS Center where the decedent was required to file tax returns while alive.

Final Return for the Decedent

The same filing requirements that apply to individuals determine if a final income tax return must be filed for the decedent. Filing requirements are discussed in chapter 1, *Filing information*.

Filing to Get a Refund

A return should be filed to obtain a refund if tax was withheld from salaries, wages, pensions, or annuities, or if estimated tax was paid, even if a return is not required to be filed. See *Claiming a refund*, later. Also, the decedent may be entitled to other credits that result in a refund. See chapter 37, *Other credits including the earned income credit*, for additional information on refundable credits, and see chapter 35, *Child tax credit* for information on the child tax credit.

Determining income and deductions. The method of accounting regularly used by the decedent before death generally determines what income must be included and what deductions can be taken on the final return. Generally, individuals use one of two methods of accounting: cash or accrual.

Cash method. If the decedent used the cash method of accounting, include only the items of income actually or constructively received before death and deduct only the expenses the decedent paid before death. For an exception for certain medical expenses not paid before death, see Decedent in chapter 22, *Medical and dental expenses*.

Explanation

Examples of income actually or constructively received include such items as uncashed payroll and dividend checks, if they were received or were available to the decedent before death.

Example. If the decedent's payroll check for June 1 through June 15 is available on Wednesday, June 15, but she fails to pick it up and dies on Thursday, June 16, the income is included on the decedent's final individual income tax return. However, if the decedent would not have been paid until Friday, June 17–that date appears on the check and that is the first day it could have been picked up–the income is reported as part of the estate and not on the final Form 1040. In the latter case, the income is called *income in respect of a decedent (IRD)* and is discussed in the following section.

If the decedent was married and lived in a community property state–Arizona, California, Idaho, Louisiana, Nevada, New Mexico, Texas, Washington, or Wisconsin–half of the combined income and expenses of husband and wife up to the date of death may be attributable to the decedent. Wisconsin has a marital property law that is similar to community property law.

TAXSAVER

The person filing the decedent's final return may elect to include as income on that return all of the U.S. savings bond interest that had accumulated but had not been reported. If the decedent otherwise had low taxable income to report on his or her final return, this return could be the best one in which to recognize the interest income. To determine whether or not this is advantageous, you have to compare the tax rate of the decedent on the final individual income tax return with the tax rate of the recipient of the bonds. (For a further discussion of this point, see chapter 7, *Interest income*.)

Accrual method. If the decedent used the accrual method of accounting, report only those items of income that the decedent accrued, or earned, before death. Deduct those expenses the decedent was liable for before death, regardless of whether the expenses were paid.

Additional information. For more information on the cash and accrual methods, *see Accounting Methods* in chapter 1, *Filing information*.

Who must file the return? The personal representative (defined earlier) must file the final income tax return (Form 1040) of the decedent for the year of death and any returns not filed for preceding years. A surviving spouse, under certain circumstances, may have to file the returns for the decedent. See Joint return, later.

Example. Samantha Smith died on March 21, 2012, before filing her 2011 tax return. Her personal representative must file her 2011 return by April 17, 2012. (The due date is actually April 17, 2012, because April 15, 2012, falls on Sunday, and the following day, April 16, is the Emancipation Day holiday in the District of Columbia.) Her final tax return is due April 15, 2013.

Explanation

If the decedent had not yet filed a return for the previous year, the personal representative or surviving spouse should prepare and file the return, just as the decedent would have. The only differences are (1) the personal representative signs the return (see Signing the return, later) and (2) the estimated tax payments that are due after the decedent died are not required to be made. If a joint return is being filed, see the discussion of estimated tax payments under Joint return, later.

For the year of death, the decedent's final return covers income received and deductible items paid during the period from January 1 through the date of death (assuming that the decedent was a cash-basis taxpayer).

TAXSAVER

If the decedent was a member of the U.S. Armed Forces and dies while in active service in a combat zone or from wounds, disease, or other injury received in a combat zone, the decedent's income tax liability is forgiven for the tax year in which death occurred.

A decedent's income tax liability is also forgiven for any decedent who was either a military or civilian U.S. employee at death and dies from wounds or injury incurred while a U.S. employee in a terrorist or military action outside the United States.

For additional information, please seek advice from your tax advisor.

TAXSAVER

A surviving spouse may be able to reduce the tax on his or her income by filing a joint return with the decedent. Even if a taxpayer died on January 1 with no income earned by that date, the availability of joint tax rates to the surviving spouse could be beneficial. However, if the surviving spouse remarries before the end of the year, the decedent must file as married filing separately.

Filing the return. The word "DECEASED," the decedent's name, and the date of death should be written across the top of the tax return. In the name and address space, you should write the name and address of the decedent and, if a joint return, of the surviving spouse. If a joint return is not being filed, the decedent's name should be written in the name space and the personal representative's name and address should be written in the remaining space.

Example. John Stone died in early 2011. He was survived by his wife, Jane. The top of their final joint return on Form 1040, which includes the required information, is illustrated earlier in this chapter.

Signing the return. If a personal representative has been appointed, that person must sign the return. If it is a joint return, the surviving spouse must also sign it.

If no personal representative has been appointed, the surviving spouse (on a joint return) should sign the return and write in the signature area "Filing as surviving spouse." See Joint return, later.

If no personal representative has been appointed and if there is no surviving spouse, the person in charge of the decedent's property must file and sign the return as "personal representative."

TAXORGANIZER

After a person dies, it may be difficult for the family or personal representative to locate the information necessary to file the final tax return (e.g., charitable contribution receipts, interest payments, pay stubs, or Form 1099s). However, it is important to make a diligent search and to organize carefully the items located. See chart entitled "Important Tax-Related Actions to Take After a Death," on the next page.

DECEASED JOHN S. STONE FEBRUARY 28, 2011

Form **1040** Department of the Treasury—Internal Revenue Service (99)
U.S. Individual Income Tax Return **2011** IRS Use Only—Do not write or staple in this space.

For the year Jan. 1–Dec. 31, 2011, or other tax year beginning , 2011, ending , 20 OMB No. 1545-0074

Label (See instructions on page 14.) **Use the IRS label.** Otherwise, please print or type.

LABEL HERE

CAR-RT SORT**CR01
LP S29 30
JOHN S & JANE M STONE
1992 OAK ST 103
SHERIDAN WY 82801

IRS

Your social security number 765 00 4321
Spouse's social security number 123 00 4567
You **must** enter your SSN(s) above.

Presidential Election Campaign ▶ Check here if you, or your spouse if filing jointly, want $3 to go to this fund (see page 14) ▶ ☐ **You** ☐ **Spouse**
Checking a box below will not change your tax or refund.

Filing Status
Check only one box.

1 ☐ Single
2 ☐ Married filing jointly (even if only one had income)
3 ☐ Married filing separately. Enter spouse's SSN above and full name here. ▶
4 ☐ Head of household (with qualifying person). (See page 15.) If the qualifying person is a child but not your dependent, enter this child's name here. ▶
5 ☐ Qualifying widow(er) with dependent child (see page 16)

Third Party Designee
Do you want to allow another person to discuss this return with the IRS (see page 75)? ☐ **Yes.** Complete the following. ☑ **No**
Designee's name ▶ Phone no. ▶ ( ) Personal identification number (PIN) ▶

Sign Here
Joint return? See instructions. Keep a copy for your records.

Under penalties of perjury, I declare that I have examined this return and accompanying schedules and statements, and to the best of my knowledge and belief, they are true, correct, and complete. Declaration of preparer (other than taxpayer) is based on all information of which preparer has any knowledge.

Your signature	Date	Your occupation	Daytime phone number
Jane M. Stone	4/2/12	Engineer	( )
Spouse's signature. If a joint return, **both** must sign.	Date	Spouse's occupation	
Filing as surviving spouse			

Paid Preparer's Use Only
Preparer's signature ▶ Date Check if self-employed ☐ Preparer's SSN or PTIN
Firm's name (or yours if self-employed), address, and ZIP code ▶ EIN
Phone no. ( )

Form **1040** (2011)

Important Tax-Related Actions to Take After a Death	
Action	**Comments**
Obtain at least 10 death certificates from the local county clerk, mortuary, or funeral director.	The executor or personal representative (referred to as the "executor" in this chart) must file the death certificate with the estate tax return (Form 706) for the decedent. Also, death certificates will be needed to claim life insurance proceeds, change title to bank accounts, and transfer title to other assets. Death certificates usually will not be available until a week or two after the death.
Contact life insurance companies to claim the proceeds. The executor can usually find the telephone number on the life insurance policy.	Contact the insurance company as soon as possible. Insurance companies are sometimes slow to respond, and the decedent's family may need the insurance proceeds for support.
Notify the Social Security Administration of the death. Also notify banks and investment brokers.	The telephone number for the Social Security Administration is 1-800-772-1213.
Contact an estate planning or probate attorney to determine what court filings are necessary.	Select an attorney who has at least 5 years of significant experience handling probates and administrations of estates. See the attorney as soon as possible after the death. Referrals to attorneys can be obtained from friends or relatives, or often from a local Bar Association Referral Service.
Contact an accountant regarding all tax filings that will be necessary.	The personal representative or surviving spouse must file a final income tax return for the decedent (Form 1040). No further estimated taxes for the decedent must be paid after the death of the decedent.

	The "probate estate" (if a probate is necessary) becomes a new taxpayer and the personal representative must file a tax return (Form 1041). The estate may select a fiscal year which may result in beneficial tax deferral. If the decedent funded a "revocable living trust" during life that trust (which becomes irrevocable at death) also becomes a new taxpayer and may also be required to file a Form 1041. However, in certain cases, the probate estate and the trust may file consolidated income tax returns.
Obtain an Employee Identification Number (EIN) for the estate.	The estate will need an EIN to file tax returns and to open a bank account. In addition, an estate will be required to get a new EIN if the funds from the estate are used to establish a trust. The IRS provides an online application with an interactive, interview-style questionnaire that will guide you through the application process. There is no charge to obtain an EIN. The estate's attorney or accountant can also help with this process.
Open an estate checking account as soon as possible—deposit all checks due to the decedent and pay all debts and expenses owed (including funeral expenses and taxes) from this account.	It is critical that accurate records be kept. Do not commingle anyone else's income or expenses with the decedent's income and expenses, including income earned and expenses paid after date of death. The executor will need accurate information to report on the decedent's final income tax return, the estate's and/or trust's income tax return, and the estate tax return.
Search through the decedent's desk, office, safe deposit box, and files to locate information which is needed for the tax returns.	Specifically, look for the following: will, codicils to the will and trust agreements; addresses and social security numbers of beneficiaries; checking, savings money market, and CD statements; checkbook registers; brokerage statements; stock certificates; bonds; retirement plan and IRA benefit statements; life insurance and annuity policies; the last 3 years of state and federal income tax returns and all prior gift tax returns; property tax bill and deed for real estate; buy-sell or operating agreements for businesses; all outstanding bills (including last illness and funeral bills); and any undeposited checks.
Review the decedent's company retirement and benefit plans, as well as IRAs, with a tax advisor or attorney.	The beneficiary of these assets must make certain decisions regarding distributions from these plans and IRAs; the decisions made can have significant income tax consequences.

Example. Assume in the previous example that no personal representative has been appointed. The bottom of the final joint return, which shows that Jane is filing the return as the surviving spouse, is illustrated on the Form 1040 example.

Third party designee. You can check the "Yes" box in the Third Party Designee area of the return to authorize the IRS to discuss the return with a friend, family member, or any other person you choose. This allows the IRS to call the person you identified as the designee to answer any questions that may arise during the processing of the return. It also allows the designee to perform certain actions. See your income tax package for details.

Claiming a refund. Generally, a person who is filing a return for a decedent and claiming a refund must file Form 1310, Statement of Person Claiming Refund Due a Deceased Taxpayer, with the return. However, Form 1310 is not needed if the person claiming the refund is a surviving spouse filing a joint return with the decedent, or a court-appointed or certified personal representative filing an original return for the decedent. The personal representative must attach to the return a copy of the court certificate showing that he or she was appointed the personal representative.

If the personal representative is filing a claim for refund on Form 1040X, Amended U.S. Individual Income Tax Return, or Form 843, Claim for Refund and Request for Abatement, and the court certificate has already been filed with the IRS, attach Form 1310 and write "Certificate Previously Filed" at the bottom of the form.

Example. Mr. Green died before filing his tax return. You were appointed the personal representative for Mr. Green's estate and you file his Form 1040 for the prior year showing a refund due. You do not need Form 1310 to claim the refund if you attach a copy of the court certificate showing you were appointed the personal representative.

TAXPLANNER

To make sure that refunds are not delayed, attach Form 1310 to any return being filed for a decedent on which a refund is being claimed. This is true despite the fact that Form 1310 may not be required, as previously discussed.

Form 1310 can also be submitted to request that a refund check issued jointly to the decedent and surviving spouse be reissued to a surviving spouse.

When and Where to File

The final income tax return is due at the same time the decedent's return would have been due had death not occurred. The final return for a decedent who was a calendar year taxpayer is generally due April 15 following the year death occurred. However, when the due date falls on a Saturday, Sunday, or legal holiday, the return is filed timely if filed by the next business day. For 2012, the due date is actually April 17, 2012, because April 15, 2012, falls on Sunday, and the following day, April 16, is the Emancipation Day holiday in the District of Columbia.

TAXPLANNER

The personal representative or surviving spouse may request an extension of time to file the decedent's final income tax return by filing Form 4868, Application for Automatic Extension of Time To File U.S. Individual Income Tax Return. This will give an additional six months to file the return. Note that an extension of time to file does not mean an extension of time to pay tax. Hence, any tax liability owed must be paid in full by the due date of the return, excluding extensions. See *When Do I Have to File?* in chapter 1, *Filing information*.

You may obtain Form 4868 via the Internet by visiting the IRS website at *www.irs.gov*.

Generally, you must file the final income tax return of the decedent with the Internal Revenue Service Center for the place where you live. A tax return for a decedent can be electronically filed. A personal representative may also obtain an income tax filing extension on behalf of a decedent.

TAXPLANNER

A representative of a decedent's estate may be held personally liable by the IRS for later-discovered tax deficiencies if the representative has not retained enough of the estate's assets to pay those deficiencies. Therefore, many cautious representatives are slow to distribute the estate's assets to the heirs. Filing Form 4810, Request for Prompt Assessment Under Internal Revenue Code Section 6501(d), may shorten the period in which the IRS may hold the representative responsible for not paying enough tax, thereby potentially allowing the estate's assets to be distributed more promptly. However, the request may trigger an audit of those returns.

Joint return. Generally, the personal representative and the surviving spouse can file a joint return for the decedent and the surviving spouse. However, the surviving spouse alone can file the joint return if no personal representative was appointed before the due date for filing the joint return for the year of death. This also applies to the return for the preceding year if the decedent died after the close of the preceding tax year and before filing the return for that year. The income of the decedent that was includible on his or her return for the year up to the date of death (as explained under *Determining income and deductions*, earlier) and the income of the surviving spouse for the entire year must be included in the final joint return.

A joint return with the decedent cannot be filed for the year of death if the surviving spouse remarried before the end of the year of the decedent's death. The filing status of the decedent in this instance is married filing a separate return.

TAXPLANNER

If you are a surviving spouse and are filing a joint return with the decedent for 2011, you are not relieved of the obligation to make estimated tax payments for 2012 because of the death. See chapter 4, *Tax withholding and estimated tax*, for more information on estimated tax payments.

TAXSAVER

If the decedent was married, it is important to calculate whether the tax on a joint return would be less than the total tax on two separate returns.

Ordinarily, a joint return would result in the least overall tax for married couples, but only a complete computation will tell you for sure. Remember, the joint return will include all of the income and deductions of the survivor for the entire year, but those of the decedent are included only up to the date of death. If property was owned jointly with the surviving spouse, all of the income after death is required to be reported in the joint return, because it, along with the ownership of the property, passed to the surviving spouse. However, if the property was not owned jointly and passed to an executor at death, the subsequent income on that property would be reported on the income tax return for the estate for which the executor is responsible, and not on the joint return.

Personal representative may revoke joint return election. A court-appointed personal representative may revoke an election to file a joint return that was previously made by the surviving spouse alone. This is done by filing a separate return for the decedent within one year from the due date of the return (including any extensions). The joint return made by the surviving spouse will then be regarded as the separate return of that spouse by excluding the decedent's items and refiguring the tax liability.

Relief from joint liability. In some cases, one spouse may be relieved of joint liability for tax, interest, and penalties on a joint return for items of the other spouse that were incorrectly reported on the joint return. If the decedent qualified for this relief while alive, the personal representative can pursue an existing request, or file a request, for relief from joint liability. The amount of time to request equitable relief depends on whether you have a balance due or are seeking a credit or refund:

- Balance Due–You generally must file Form 8857 10 years from the date the tax liability was assessed. In certain cases, the 10-year period is suspended. The amount of time the suspension is in effect will be added to the time remaining in the 10-year period.
- Credit or Refund–You generally must file Form 8857 within 3 years after the date the original return was filed or within 2 years after the date the tax was paid, whichever is later. But you may have more time to file if you live in a federally declared disaster area or you are physically or mentally unable to manage your financial affairs. For more information, see Publication 556, *Examination of Returns, Appeal Rights, and Claims for Refund*.

For information on requesting this relief, see Publication 971, *Innocent Spouse Relief*, and see *Filing a Joint Return* in chapter 2, *Filing status*.

How to Report Certain Income

This section explains how to report certain types of income on the final return. The rules on income discussed in the other chapters of this publication also apply to a decedent's final return. See chapters 5 through 16, if they apply.

Interest and dividend income (Forms 1099). A Form 1099 should be received for the decedent reporting interest and dividends earned before death. These amounts must be included on the decedent's final return. A separate Form 1099 should show the interest and dividends earned after the date of the decedent's death and paid to the estate or other recipient that must include those amounts on its return. You can request corrected Forms 1099 if these forms do not properly reflect the right recipient or amounts.

For example, a Form 1099-INT reporting interest payable to the decedent may include income that should be reported on the final income tax return of the decedent, as well as income that the estate or other recipient should report, either as income earned after death or as income in respect of a decedent (discussed later). For income earned after death, you should ask the payer for a Form 1099 that properly identifies the recipient (by name and identification number) and the proper amount. If that is not possible, or if the form includes an amount that represents income in respect of a decedent, report the interest, as shown next under *How to report*.

See *U.S. savings bonds acquired from decedent* in Publication 559 for information on savings bond interest that may have to be reported *under income in respect of a decedent* on the final return.

How to report. If you are preparing the decedent's final return and you have received a Form 1099-INT, Interest Income, for the decedent that includes amounts belonging to the decedent and to another recipient (the decedent's estate or another beneficiary), report the total interest shown on Form 1099-INT on Schedule 1 (Form 1040A) or on Schedule B (Form 1040). Next, enter a subtotal of the interest shown on Forms 1099 and the interest reportable from other sources for which you did not receive Forms 1099. Then, show any interest (including any interest you receive as a nominee) belonging to another recipient separately and subtract it from the subtotal. Identify this adjustment as a "Nominee Distribution" or other appropriate designation.

Report dividend income for which you received a Form 1099-DIV on the appropriate schedule using the same procedure.

Note: If the decedent received amounts as a nominee, you must give the actual owner a Form 1099, unless the owner is the decedent's spouse. See *General Instructions for Forms 1099, 1098, 5498, and W-2G* for more information on filing Forms 1099.

TAXPLANNER

No matter how hard you try, you may have difficulty getting the payers of dividends and interest to reflect properly the amounts attributable to the decedent prior to death and the amounts that are paid to the decedent's successor in interest. It is therefore imperative that you follow the example below carefully in order to avoid bothersome inquiries from the IRS.

Example 1. Marty died on June 30, 2011. Marty owned 50 shares of ABC Corporation and 75 shares of XYZ Corporation, both of which paid a $1 per share quarterly dividend on February 1, May 1, August 1, and November 1. Upon Marty's death, all shares were transferred to his estate. XYZ Corporation has properly issued two Forms 1099-DIV. One Form 1099-DIV identifies Marty as the recipient of $150 (the dividends paid to Marty prior to death, from January 1, 2011, to June 30, 2011), and the other identifies Marty's estate as the recipient of $150 (the dividends paid to the estate, from July 1, 2011, to December 31, 2011). ABC Corporation, however, issued only one Form 1099-DIV, naming Marty as the recipient of the entire year's dividend ($200).

On Marty's final return, you must report total dividends as indicated on all Forms 1099-DIV issued in Marty's name ($150 from XYZ Corporation and $200 from ABC Corporation) on line 5, Part II of Form 1040, Schedule B. Several lines above line 6, write "Subtotal" and enter $350. Below this subtotal, write "Nominee Distribution" and enter $100 (the dividends paid by ABC Corporation to Marty's estate). Indicate the name and EIN of the nominee. Subtract the nominee distribution from the subtotal and report the net result of $250 on line 6. The same reporting procedure would apply to reporting interest. See the example below for an example of the language to put on Schedule B.

Example 2. John Johnson died on July 1, 2011. In January 2012, ABC Bank sent a Form 1099-INT to his executor reflecting interest paid during 2011 of $5,000. Because John was alive for only one-half of 2011, only one-half of the interest will be reported on his final Form 1040 for 2011. The other one-half of the interest will be reported on his estate's income tax return (Form 1041).

Schedule B of John's final Form 1040 should report the $2,500 of interest. Part I, line 1, should be completed as follows:

ABC Bank	$5,000
Less: Nominee distribution	($2,500)
(Estate of John Johnson: EIN: 00-0000000)	

Part 1, line 4, would show total interest income of $2,500.

The Form 1041 for the estate of John will report the other $2,500 of interest income.

TAXORGANIZER

You should keep a copy of the Forms 1099 that you receive as well as the tax worksheets showing pre- and post-death income for a minimum of three years.

Accelerated death benefits. Accelerated death benefits are amounts received under a life insurance contract before the death of the insured individual. These benefits also include amounts received on the sale or assignment of the contract to a provider of viatical settlements (life insurance payouts prior to death).

Generally, if the decedent received accelerated death benefits either on his or her life or on the life of another person, those benefits are not included in the decedent's income. This exclusion applies only if the insured was a terminally or chronically ill individual. For more information, see *Accelerated death benefits* under *Gifts, Insurance, and Inheritances* in Publication 559.

Business income. This section discusses some of the business income that may have to be included on the final return.

Partnership income. The death of a partner closes the partnership's tax year for that partner. Generally, it does not close the partnership's tax year for the remaining partners. The decedent's distributive share of partnership items must be figured as if the partnership's tax year ended on the date the partner died. To avoid an interim closing of the partnership books, the partners can agree to estimate the decedent's distributive share by prorating the amounts the partner would have included for the entire partnership tax year.

On the decedent's final return, include the decedent's distributive share of partnership items for the following periods:

1. The partnership's tax year that ended within or with the decedent's final tax year (the year ending on the date of death); and
2. The period, if any, from the end of the partnership's tax year in (1) to the decedent's date of death.

TAXALERT

A partnership's tax year closes with respect to a partner whose entire interest in the partnership is terminated by death. Therefore, the partnership income will have to be allocated between and reported by the decedent and the decedent's successor in interest. The final individual income tax return should include the decedent's share of partnership income and deductions for the partnership's tax year that ends within or with the decedent's last tax year (the year ending on the date of death). The final return must also include income for the period between the end of the partnership's last tax year and the date of death.

The income for the part of the partnership's tax year after the partner's death is reported by the estate or other person who has acquired the interest in the partnership.

Example. Jim, a partner in a law firm, died on December 1, 2011. The tax year for the partnership ends on June 30. Jim's partnership income of $100,000 for the fiscal year ending June 30, 2011, will be included on his 2011 individual income tax return. In addition, Jim's final income tax return for 2011 will also include his pro rata portion (154 days) of partnership income and deductions from July 1, 2011, to December 1, 2011, with the remainder to be reported to Jim's successor in interest.

TAXSAVER

Planning for partnership interests can save substantial amounts of income tax. For example, a partner should investigate the possibility of appointing his or her spouse as successor in interest to the partnership so that the income or loss for the year of death can flow onto the survivor's return and thus onto the joint return.

There is another way of ensuring the immediate transfer of the partnership interest to the spouse upon the partner's death so that the income or loss can be reported on the joint return. The spouses may own the partnership interest in joint tenancy. Be sure to check that the partnership will permit joint tenancy ownership. Also, if the executor has the assets and the legal authority to make an immediate distribution of the partnership interest to the spouse, all or a portion of the partnership income can be transferred to the final joint return. Prompt action may be necessary. Finally, consult with a tax advisor because there may be tax disadvantages to holding property in joint tenancy.

TAXPLANNER

If a decedent had an interest in a passive activity (e.g., a partnership or S corporation), the passive activity rules still apply on the decedent's final individual tax return. For example, the death of a partner does not trigger the deduction of any suspended passive activity losses associated with that partnership. (See chapter 12, *Other income*, for more information on passive activity losses.) Generally, the remaining suspended losses may not be transferred to the partner's successor in interest. However, these losses may have to be reduced depending on whether the interest received a step-up in basis. You should consult with your tax advisor for more information.

S corporation income. If the decedent was a shareholder in an S corporation, include on the final return the decedent's share of the S corporation's items of income, loss, deduction, and credit for the following periods:

1. The corporation's tax year that ended within or with the decedent's final tax year (the year ending on the date of death); and
2. The period, if any, from the end of the corporation's tax year in (1) to the decedent's date of death.

Example. Julia Jones was a 20% partner in XYZ Partnership and a 20% shareholder in ABC Corporation, an S corporation. The tax year for both the partnership and the corporation ends on December 31. Julia died on October 1, 2011. Had she lived Julia would have earned $100,000 of ordinary income in 2011 from the partnership and another $100,000 of ordinary income from the corporation.

Julia's final tax return for 2011 will include $75,068 (274 days) of income from ABC Corporation and $75,068 of income from XYZ Partnership. The remaining $24,932 of ABC Corporation income and the $24,932 from XYZ Partnership income will be included in the tax return of the successor in interest.

Self-employment income. Include self-employment income actually or constructively received or accrued, depending on the decedent's accounting method. For self-employment tax purposes only, the decedent's self-employment income will include the decedent's distributive share of a partnership's income or loss through the end of the month in which death occurred. For this purpose, the partnership income or loss is considered to be earned ratably over the partnership's tax year. For more information on how to compute self-employment income, chapter 38, *Self-employment income: How to file Schedule C.*

Coverdell Education Savings Account (ESA). Generally, the balance in a Coverdell ESA must be distributed within 30 days after the individual for whom the account was established reaches age 30 or dies, whichever is earlier. The treatment of the Coverdell ESA at the death of an individual under age 30 depends on who acquires the interest in the account. If the decedent's estate acquires the interest, the earnings on the account must be included on the final income tax return of the decedent. If a beneficiary acquires the interest, see the discussion under *Income in Respect of a Decedent*, later.

The age 30 limit does not apply if the individual for whom the account was established, or the beneficiary that acquires the account, is an individual with special needs. This includes an individual who because of a physical, mental, or emotional condition (including a learning disability) requires additional time to complete his or her education.

For more information on Coverdell ESAs, see Publication 970, *Tax Benefits for Education*.

Archer MSA. The treatment of an Archer MSA, a Medicare Advantage MSA, or a Health Savings Account (HSA) at the death of the account holder depends on who acquires the interest in the account. If the decedent's estate acquires the interest, the fair market value of the assets in the account on the date of death is included in income on the decedent's final return.

If a beneficiary acquires the interest, see the discussion under *Income in Respect of a Decedent*, later. For more information on Archer MSAs, see Publication 969, *Health Savings Accounts and Other Tax-Favored Health Plans*.

Exemptions, Deductions, and Credits

Generally, the rules for exemptions, deductions, and credits allowed to an individual also apply to the decedent's final income tax return. Show on the final return deductible items the decedent paid (or accrued, if the decedent reported deductions on an accrual method) before death.

Exemptions. You can claim the decedent's personal exemption on the final income tax return. If the decedent was another person's dependent (for example, a parent's), you cannot claim the personal exemption on the decedent's final return.

Standard deduction. If you do not itemize deductions on the final return, the full amount of the appropriate standard deduction is allowed regardless of the date of death. For information on the appropriate standard deduction, see chapter 21, *Standard deduction*.

Itemized deductions. If the total of the decedent's itemized deductions is more than the decedent's standard deduction, the federal income tax will generally be less if you claim itemized deductions on the final return. See chapters 22 through 29 for the types of expenses that are allowed as itemized deductions.

Medical expenses. Medical expenses paid before death by the decedent are deductible, subject to limits, on the final income tax return if deductions are itemized. This includes expenses for the decedent as well as for the decedent's spouse and dependents.

For information on certain medical expenses that were not paid before death, see *Decedent* in chapter 22, *Medical and dental expenses*.

TAXPLANNER

Funeral burial and probate expenses are not deductible on the decedent's or estate's income tax return. However, these may be deducted on the decedent's estate tax return.

TAXSAVER

The executor or executrix may elect to either claim certain medical and dental expenses as deductions on the estate tax return or as deductions on the decedent's final income tax return. The tax should be computed both ways to see which results in more tax savings.

If an election is made to include the medical and dental expenses on the decedent's income tax return rather than on the federal estate tax return, the executor or executrix must attach a statement to the income tax return stating that he or she has not claimed the amount as an estate tax deduction and that the estate waives the right to claim the amount as a deduction.

TAXSAVER

When death is expected in the near future, proper planning can save tax dollars. Deductible expenses, such as interest expense and accounting fees, that are due near the date of death may be paid before death, or after death. Choose the time offering the greater tax benefit. If you arrange to pay the expenses before death, they are deductible on the decedent's final Form 1040 if deductions are itemized. If you arrange to pay them after death, they are deductible on the estate's income tax return. Limitations as to deductibility may apply.

Unrecovered investment in pension. If the decedent was receiving a pension or annuity (with an annuity starting date after 1986) and died without a surviving annuitant, you can take a deduction on the decedent's final return for the amount of the decedent's investment in the pension or annuity contract that remained unrecovered at death. The deduction is a miscellaneous itemized deduction that is not subject to the 2% limit on adjusted gross income. See chapter 29, *Miscellaneous deductions*.

Deduction for losses. A decedent's net operating loss deduction from a prior year and any capital losses (including capital loss carryovers) can be deducted only on the decedent's final income tax return. A net operating loss on the decedent's final income tax return can be carried back to prior years (see Publication 536, *Net Operating Losses (NOLs) for Individuals, Estates, and Trusts*). You cannot deduct any unused net operating loss or capital loss on the estate's income tax return.

TAXSAVER

Net operating losses (or carryover losses) from business operations and capital losses (or carryover losses) of the decedent may not be carried over to the returns of executors or heirs. However, if a joint return is filed for the year of death, these losses may be used to offset the survivor's income for the entire year. In this case, it may be advantageous for the surviving spouse to incur capital gains and/or other income and to offset them with the capital losses and/or net operating losses that cannot be carried forward past the year of the spouse's death.

Example. Your spouse died on June 30, 2011, with $10,000 in **short-term capital losses** from his personal account. Because the maximum capital loss that can be deducted in a year is $3,000, only $3,000 of those losses will be allowed on your 2011 joint return, with no carryover of the remaining $7,000. However, if you could recognize an additional $7,000 in gains before the end of the year, you could use your deceased spouse's remaining $7,000 of losses to offset the gains by filing a joint return. If you waited until a later year to recognize those gains, they would be fully taxable, unless you had incurred other losses to offset them.

Credits. Any of the tax credits discussed in this publication also apply to the final return if the decedent was eligible for the credits at the time of death. These credits are discussed in chapters 33 through 37.

Tax withheld and estimated payments. There may have been income tax withheld from the decedent's pay, pensions, or annuities before death, and the decedent may have paid estimated income tax. To get credit for these tax payments, you must claim them on the decedent's final return. For more information, see Credit for Withholding and Estimated Tax in chapter 4, *Tax withholding and estimated tax*.

Explanation

Exemption allowances, the standard deduction, and itemized deductions are not prorated over that part of the year during which a now deceased taxpayer was alive. However, exemptions claimed for dependents could be a problem if the decedent did not live long enough during the year to provide the required amount of support. In most situations, potential problems will be alleviated if the surviving spouse files a joint return with the decedent. See chapter 3, *Personal exemptions and dependents*, for more information.

Tax Effect on Others

This section contains information about the effect of an individual's death on the income tax liability of the survivors (including the widow or widower and any beneficiaries) and the estate. A survivor should coordinate the filing of his or her own tax return with the personal representative handling the decedent's estate. The personal representative can coordinate filing status, exemptions, income, and deductions so that the decedent's final return and the income tax returns of the survivors and the estate are all filed correctly.

Explanation

Survivors. If you are a survivor, you may qualify for certain benefits when filing your own income tax return. This section addresses some issues that may apply to you.

Gifts and inheritances. Property received as a gift, bequest, or inheritance is not included in your income. However, if property you receive in this manner later produces income, such as interest, dividends, or rent, that income is taxable to you. If the gift, bequest, or inheritance you receive is the income from property, that income is taxable to you.

If you inherited the right to receive income in respect of a decedent, see *Income in Respect of a Decedent*, later.

TAXALERT

Property inherited from a decedent who died either before or after 2010. The cost basis of any asset distributed from the estate of a decedent who died either before or after 2010 (which he/she owned at death) via bequest or inheritance is "stepped up" to the fair market value at the date of the decedent's death or the alternate valuation date. See chapter 13, *Basis of property*, for more information.

Furthermore, the asset is deemed to be long-term capital gain property, so any capital appreciation on the asset above the fair market value on the date of the decedent's death will be taxed at the long-term capital gains tax rate.

Exception: If you or your spouse inherit property that you gave to the decedent within 1 year of death, your basis in the asset is what the decedent's adjusted basis in the asset was immediately before his or her death.

Property inherited from a decedent who died during 2010. The Tax Relief, Unemployment Insurance Reauthorization, and Job Creation Act of 2010 (the Act) that was passed in late 2010 complicated the matter of determining the basis in assets that you receive from a decedent who died in 2010. The new law provides executors of estates of 2010 decedents with a choice: to select either a stepped-up basis for the assets left by the decedent or to use a carryover basis for the assets—both of which are explained below.

Prior to the passage of the new law, the estate tax had been repealed for 2010, and new, complex rules applied for determining your basis in property inherited from a decedent who died during 2010. Property acquired from a decedent who died in 2010 would not get a "stepped-up" basis, meaning the new owner's basis in the property would not automatically be adjusted to the fair market value on the decedent's date of death. Instead, if you inherited property from a decedent who died in 2010, your basis would be equal to the lesser of the fair market value of the property on the decedent's date of death or the decedent's adjusted basis in the property. This is known as "carryover basis."

Exception: There is one key exception to this new carryover basis rule: A decedent's executor is allowed to increase (often referred to as "step up") the basis of assets transferred by a total of $1.3 million plus any unused capital losses, net operating losses, and certain "built-in" losses of the decedent. An additional $3 million basis increase is allowed for property transferred to a surviving spouse, which means that property transferred to a spouse will be allowed a basis increase of $4.3 million. However, certain types of assets are not eligible for this increase in basis. Nonresident aliens would only be allowed an increase in basis of $60,000 indexed for inflation after 2010.

The executor can choose to allocate the step up in basis on an asset-by-asset basis. For example, the basis increase can be allocated to a share of stock or a block of stock. However, in no case can the basis of an asset be adjusted above its fair market value. If the amount of basis increase is less than the fair market value of assets whose bases are eligible to be increased under these rules, the executor will determine which assets and to what extent each asset receives a basis increase. This could put the executor in an awkward spot: deciding which family members or other heirs get tax-free assets and which ones get assets with built-in capital gain.

The 2010 Act, however, retroactively reinstated the estate tax for estates of decedents who died during 2010. The 2010 Act also eliminated the "carryover basis" scheme for assets acquired from a decedent who died in 2010 and restored the stepped-up basis rules for assets acquired from a 2010 decedent. However, while the estate tax will apply for estates of decedents who died in 2010, the executor will be able to elect whether to apply the estate tax and use a stepped-up basis or use a "carryover" basis, whichever is more favorable. The "stepped-up" basis will be the default choice. The "carryover basis" will have to be elected. Generally, estates below $5 million would accept the default provision in order to get a step-up in basis without paying estate tax.

If you sold property in 2011 that you originally inherited from a decedent who died during 2010, you should contact the executor of the decedent's estate to confirm the basis in the property you received.

TAXALERT

Fees received by an executor or administrator for duties performed for an estate are includable in the gross income of the executor or administrator but are usually not subject to self-employment tax as long as you are not in the trade or business of being an executor or administrator.

However, a specific bequest to the executor is not treated as income. It is merely a gift to an heir who also happens to be serving as executor. Therefore, if you are the executor and an heir, you may consider declining to take a fee, in which case you will receive a larger portion of the estate that is not subject to income tax. Contact your tax advisor to assist you in determining which course of action is more beneficial.

Tip

If you have to include income in respect of a decedent in your gross income and an estate tax return was filed for the decedent, you may be able to claim a deduction for the estate tax paid on that income. For more information, see Publication 559.

Joint return by surviving spouse. A surviving spouse can file a joint return for the year of death and may qualify for special tax rates for the following two years. For more information, see *Qualifying Widow(er) With Dependent Child* in chapter 2, *Filing status*.

Explanation
After the two-year period following the date of death, a surviving spouse may still be able to qualify as a head of household and use the Tax Table and Tax Rate Schedules for head of household. While not as beneficial as joint return rates, they are better than those for single persons. See chapter 2, *Filing status*, for more details.

Decedent as your dependent. If the decedent qualified as your dependent for the part of the year before death, you can claim the exemption for the dependent on your tax return, regardless of when death occurred during the year.

If the decedent was your qualifying child, you may be able to claim the child tax credit. See chapter 35, *Child tax credit*.

Income in Respect of a Decedent
All income that the decedent would have received had death not occurred and that was not properly includible on the final income tax return, discussed earlier, is income in respect of a decedent.

How to Report. Income in respect of a decedent must be included in the income of one of the following.
- The decedent's estate, if the estate receives it.
- The beneficiary, if the right to income is passed directly to the beneficiary and the beneficiary receives it.
- Any person to whom the estate properly distributes the right to receive it.

Example 1. Frank Johnson owned and operated an apple orchard. He used the cash method of accounting. He sold and delivered 1,000 bushels of apples to a canning factory for $2,000, but did not receive payment before his death. The proceeds from the sale are income in respect of a decedent. When the estate was settled, payment had not been made and the estate transferred the right to the payment to his widow. When Frank's widow collects the $2,000, she must include that amount in her return. It is not to be reported on the final return of the decedent or on the return of the estate.

Example 2. Assume the same facts as in Example 1, except that Frank used an accrual method of accounting. The amount accrued from the sale of the apples would be included on his final return. Neither the estate nor the widow will realize income in respect of a decedent when the money is later paid.

Example 3. Cathy O'Neil was entitled to a large salary payment at the date of her death. The amount was to be paid in five annual installments. The estate, after collecting two installments, distributed the right to the remaining installments to you, the beneficiary. The payments are income in respect of a decedent. None of the payments were includible in Cathy's final return. The estate must include in its income the two installments it received, and you must include in your income each of the three installments as you receive them.

Transferring your right to income. If you transfer your right to income in respect of a decedent, you must include in your income the greater of:
- The amount you receive for the right, or
- The fair market value of the right at the time of the transfer.

Fair market value (FMV). FMV is the price at which the property would change hands between a buyer and a seller, neither having to buy or sell, and both having reasonable knowledge of all necessary facts.

Giving your right to income as a gift. If you give your right to receive income in respect of a decedent as a gift, you must include in your income the fair market value of the right at the time you make the gift.

Example. Tom has a right to receive a payment of $10,000 that represents income in respect of his deceased father (e.g., deferred compensation). He makes a gift of his right to receive the money. He would immediately have to recognize the $10,000 as income on his tax return.

Type of income. The character or type of income that you receive in respect of a decedent is the same as it would be to the decedent if he or she were alive. If the income would have been a capital gain to the decedent, it will be a capital gain to you.

Explanation
Installment obligations. If the decedent had sold property using the installment method and you have the right to collect the payments, use the same gross profit percentage the decedent would have used to figure the part of each payment that represents profit. Include in your income the same profit the decedent would have included had death not occurred. For more information on installment sales, see Publication 537, *Installment Sales*.

If you dispose of an installment obligation acquired from a decedent (other than by transfer to the obligor), the rules explained in Publication 537 for figuring gain or loss on the disposition apply to you.

Example. Andrew sold undeveloped real estate held as an investment in 2009 for $120,000, receiving a note payable in four annual installments of $30,000 each plus interest. Andrew's basis in the land was $40,000. Andrew died before the first installment was due, and the note was transferred to Helen, Andrew's heir. Helen collected the first installment of the note, $30,000, in 2010. When Helen was in need of additional cash in early 2011, she sold the note to a bank for its fair market value of $90,000. For 2010, Helen must recognize gain on the installment payment she received. Using the same gross profit percentage as the decedent's ($80,000/$120,000), she would recognize a $20,000 gain, computed as follows:

$$\$30{,}000 \times \$80{,}000 / \$120{,}000 = \$20{,}000$$

For 2011, Helen must recognize gain on the disposition of the installment obligation. The gain is the difference between her basis and the fair market value at the time of the disposition. Her basis in the obligation is the same as Andrew's ($40,000) less the payment of principal received by her in 2010 ($10,000). Hence, her gain is computed as follows:

$$\$90{,}000 - (\$40{,}000 - \$10{,}000) = \$60{,}000$$

Whether the gain recognized by Helen on her tax return is ordinary income or capital gain depends on what it would have been to Andrew had he lived to collect the payments.

Inherited IRAs. If a beneficiary receives a lump-sum distribution from a traditional IRA he or she inherited, all or some of it may be taxable. The distribution is taxable in the year received as income in respect of a decedent up to the decedent's taxable balance. This is the decedent's balance at the time of death, including unrealized appreciation and income accrued to date of death, minus any basis (nondeductible contributions). Amounts distributed that are more than the decedent's entire IRA balance (including taxable and nontaxable amounts) at the time of death are the income of the beneficiary.

If the beneficiary of a traditional IRA is the decedent's surviving spouse who properly rolls over the distribution into another traditional IRA, the distribution is not currently taxed. A surviving spouse can also roll over tax-free the taxable part of the distribution into a qualified plan, section 403(b) annuity, or section 457 plan.

Example. At the time of his death, Greg owned a traditional IRA. All of the contributions by Greg to the IRA had been deductible contributions. Greg's nephew, Mark, was the sole beneficiary of the IRA. The entire balance of the IRA, including income accruing before and after Greg's death, was distributed to Mark in a lump sum. Mark must include the total amount received in his income. The portion of the lump-sum distribution that equals the amount of the balance in the IRA at Greg's death, including the income earned before death, is income in respect of a decedent.

TAXALERT

Generally speaking, effective for distributions for calendar years beginning on or after January 1, 2003, a beneficiary may take distributions from an inherited IRA over his or her own life expectancy. For more information on inherited IRAs, see Publication 590, *Individual Retirement Arrangements (IRAs)*.

This rule also applies to Roth IRAs for post-death distributions. For more information on Roth IRAs, see Publication 590.

Roth IRAs. Qualified distributions from a Roth IRA are not subject to tax. A distribution made to a beneficiary or to the Roth IRA owner's estate on or after the date of death is a qualified distribution if it is made after the 5-year tax period beginning with the first tax year in which a contribution was made to any Roth IRA of the owner.

Part of any distribution to a beneficiary that is not a qualified distribution may be includible in the beneficiary's income. Generally, the part includible is the earnings in the Roth IRA. Earnings attributable to the period ending with the decedent's date of death are income in respect of a decedent. Additional earnings are the income of the beneficiary.

TAXALERT

The Department of Defense provides a payment of $100,000 to the survivors of a soldier killed in the line of duty. In addition, certain uniformed service members are automatically insured in the event of death under the Service Members Group Life Insurance (SGLI). The Heroes Earnings Assistance and Relief Tax Act of 2008 provides that a recipient of a military death gratuity or SGLI proceeds can contribute the amounts received to a Roth IRA, and treat these amounts as "qualified rollover contributions." If death results from injuries occurring on or after October 7, 2001, and before June 17, 2008, the rollover must be made no later than one year after June 17, 2008. For payments received on account of death from injuries occurring on or after June 17, 2008, the rollover must be made within one year of the date of payment.

Coverdell Education Savings Account (ESA). If the decedent's spouse or other family member is the designated beneficiary of the decedent's account, the Coverdell ESA becomes that person's Coverdell ESA. It is subject to the rules discussed in Publication 970.

Any other beneficiary (including a spouse or family member who is not the designated beneficiary) must include in income the earnings portion of the distribution. Any balance remaining at the close of the 30-day period is deemed to be distributed at that time. The amount included in income is reduced by any qualified education expenses of the decedent that are paid by the beneficiary within one year after the decedent's date of death.

Archer MSA. If the decedent's spouse is the designated beneficiary of the account, the account becomes that spouse's Archer MSA. It is subject to the rules discussed in Publication 969.

Any other beneficiary (including a spouse who is not the designated beneficiary) must include in income the fair market value of the assets in the account on the decedent's date of death. This amount must be reported for the beneficiary's tax year that includes the decedent's date of death. The amount included in income is reduced by any qualified medical expenses for the decedent that are paid by the beneficiary within one year after the decedent's date of death.

Other income. For examples of other income situations concerning decedents, see *Specific Types of Income in Respect of a Decedent* in Publication 559.

Deductions in Respect of a Decedent

Items such as business expenses, income-producing expenses, interest, and taxes for which the decedent was liable but that are not properly allowable as deductions on the decedent's final income tax return will be allowed as a deduction to one of the following when paid.

- The estate; or
- The person who acquired an interest in the decedent's property (subject to such obligations) because of the decedent's death, if the estate was not liable for the obligation.

Explanation

Deductions in respect of a decedent are items that would normally be deductible by the decedent except that he or she had not paid them before death. Typical examples are real estate taxes, state income taxes, and interest expense.

TAXSAVER

Expenses in respect of a decedent are deductible on both the estate's income tax return (Form 1041) and the estate tax return (Form 706). The estate tax and income tax are two different taxes with two entirely unrelated sets of rules. Taking a deduction on one return does not preclude taking the same deduction on the other return. When death is anticipated, planning the best possible use of double deductions may yield significant tax savings. A professional who specializes in this area should be consulted.

Example. When Oscar died in 2011, he owed accrued interest of $100. The marginal estate tax rate for Oscar's estate is 35%, and the estate's marginal income tax rate is 28%. The deduction on the estate tax return is worth $35 (35% of $100) and the deduction on the estate's income tax return is worth $28. Consequently, $63 of the $100 liability is recovered through tax savings.

On the other hand, less tax savings would be realized if Oscar had paid the $100 of interest before he died. He would have been able to take the interest deduction on his personal income tax return, paying $28 less in taxes, assuming he was in the 28% bracket. When he died, he would have been net out-of-pocket $72, his estate would be $72 less, and therefore his estate tax would be reduced by $25 (35% of $72). Thus, if he had paid the expense, his total tax savings would have been $53–$28 of income tax and $25 of estate tax–instead of the $63 tax saved because he had not paid the interest before he died, thus allowing the double deduction.

Estate Tax Deduction

Income that a decedent had a right to receive is included in the decedent's gross estate and is subject to estate tax. This income in respect of a decedent is also taxed when received by the recipient (estate or beneficiary). However, an income tax deduction is allowed to the recipient for the estate tax paid on the income.

The deduction for estate tax can be claimed only for the same tax year in which the income in respect of a decedent must be included in the recipient's income. (This also is true for income in respect of a prior decedent.)

You can claim the deduction only as a miscellaneous itemized deduction on Schedule A (Form 1040). This deduction is not subject to the 2% limit on miscellaneous itemized deductions as discussed in chapter 29, *Miscellaneous deductions*.

If the income in respect of a decedent is capital gain income, you must reduce the gain, but not below zero, by any deduction for estate tax paid on such gain. This applies in figuring the following:

- The maximum tax on net capital gain.
- The 50% exclusion for gain on small business stock.
- The limitation on net capital losses.

For more information, see *Estate Tax Deduction* in Publication 559.

TAXPLANNER

The deduction for federal estate tax attributable to income in respect of a decedent is complex. The good news is that the question does not arise if there is no federal estate tax on the decedent's estate. If the amount that each individual can leave estate-tax-free, $5 million in 2011, and the marital deduction is large enough to eliminate any federal estate tax liability, there cannot be an income tax deduction for federal estate tax.

If the estate incurs federal estate tax, the recipient of income in respect of a decedent may be entitled to an itemized deduction on his or her income tax return.

To determine the amount that can be deducted, you must first determine if the income and deductions in respect of the decedent result in net income. If so, you must then calculate the additional estate tax attributable to the net income in respect of a decedent.

To determine whether the items in respect of the decedent result in net income, you must deduct the total amount of deductions in respect of the decedent that appears on the estate tax return from the total amount of income in respect of a decedent that appears on that return. To calculate the additional estate tax, you must compare the actual estate tax with the estate tax that would have been paid if the net income in respect of a decedent had not been included. This amount is the deduction. The recipient's claim to the deduction is in the same proportion as his or her share in the total income in respect of a decedent.

Example. Assume that the estate tax return shows that the estate received salary income in respect of a decedent of $2,500 and had a deduction in respect of a decedent of $500 for unpaid real estate tax. The net of these two amounts is $2,000. Recomputation of the estate tax with $2,000 removed from the return shows that the estate tax caused by including these items is $740. If you, as one of two heirs of the estate, collect half of the $2,500 salary, you will be entitled to an income tax itemized deduction of half the $740, or $370.

TAXORGANIZER

Records you should keep:

- Power of appointment (or similar authorization to act as decedent's personal representative)
- Copies of decedent's wills, trust documents, and amendments to same
- Copies of decedent's death certificate
- Copies of all correspondence to and from attorneys, accountants, life insurers, and others related to administration of the estate
- Copies of all tax returns related to the decedent and copies of all source documents used to prepare these returns

Chapter 44

Estate and gift tax planning

ey.com/EYTaxGuide

Note

ey.com/EYTaxGuide
Ernst & Young LLP will update the *Ernst & Young Tax Guide 2012* website with relevant taxpayer information as it becomes available. You can also sign up for email alerts to let you know when changes have been made.

Introduction

Although it is not possible to take it with you, with careful thought and astute planning it is possible to provide your heirs, loved ones, and friends with a significant portion of your wealth. This chapter discusses the estate tax, the gift tax, and the generation-skipping transfer tax. The chapter also contains some estate planning ideas and techniques that may help you in making your plans for the future.

Frequent tax law changes continue to have a significant impact on estate planning. The tax law enacted in late 2010 contained significant changes with regard to estate, gift, and generation-skipping transfer taxes.

As a result of these changes, and because your goals and expectations constantly change as you go through life, you should periodically review your estate and gift tax plan. A review will help you (1) discover how your objectives may have changed; (2) assess whether your plan can still achieve your objectives; and (3) determine how legislative changes may affect existing plans and whether you can accomplish your goals more advantageously.

This chapter is intended as an introduction to estate and gift tax planning. You should seek professional advice, especially if your financial or family situation is complicated, if you own interests in closely held corporations or other illiquid assets, or if your spouse is not a U.S. citizen.

Getting Started

A periodic review of your personal financial plan makes sense. Filing an annual income tax return forces most taxpayers to look over their financial situation. Yet many–perhaps most–individuals allow years to go by without adequately considering changes in property titling, beneficiary designations, or key provisions in wills and trusts. To be on the safe side, you should periodically examine the following five basic tax and financial considerations:

1. Have there been any tax law changes, rulings, or other developments that might either adversely affect your present estate plan or offer an opportunity to pass more of your estate at a lower tax cost?
2. Does your estate have sufficient cash or other liquid assets to take care of debts, taxes, funeral expenses, and estate administration expenses?
3. Have there been any changes in your family's circumstances—births, adoptions, deaths, marriages, illness or disability, special schooling needs, and so on—that might call for revisions in your estate plan?
4. Should you initiate a plan to give some of your assets to your children, other family members, or charitable institutions? If you have already been making gifts, should you continue to do so? Which assets are now most appropriate for such a gift program?
5. Is the current form of ownership of your assets and the current designations of beneficiaries still appropriate, meaning that the assets will pass to the right people in the right fashion? Are they appropriate for saving taxes (both income and estate) and expenses?

Do You Need a Will?

A will is a legal document that specifies who receives what at your death and who will manage your estate. Even if you die without a will, you already have an estate plan of sorts. Generally, assets you own jointly with another person, such as a bank account, stock, personal residence, or business interest, or where you have designated a particular beneficiary, as under an insurance policy or IRA, will pass to the joint tenant or designated beneficiary. But assets you own in your name alone will be passed on in accordance with your state's laws if you die without a will.

If you die without a will—intestate is the legal term—state laws determine how your estate is divided up among your surviving spouse, children, and parents—and what happens when there is no surviving spouse. However, state law may not conform to your wishes. Often, the biggest problem is not the distribution of the property but rather the guardianship of minor children. If both parents die without a will that directs who will be guardian of a minor child, the court and the state social welfare department will make the decision. So, even if you do not have enough assets to have to pay federal estate tax, it's a good idea to draw up a will.

Estate Tax Fundamentals

Who Has to Pay Federal Estate Tax?

Until late in 2010, there was no estate tax for people who died (i.e., decedents) in 2010. However, the Tax Relief, Unemployment Insurance Reauthorization, and Job Creation Act of 2010 reinstated the estate tax but with some changes from prior law. The estate tax will apply for estates of decedents who died in 2010 and who die in 2011-2012. The estate exemption is $5 million and the top rate is 35%. The exemption is "portable" between spouses for 2011 and 2012, meaning the exemption amount of one spouse can pass on to the other at death. And, a spouse can still pass unlimited amounts to his or her surviving spouse without tax.

Unless Congress acts, after 2012, the estate tax laws will revert to 2001 levels—a 55% tax rate on estates worth more than $1 million.

The changes to the estate tax in 2010 mentioned above refer to the fact that while the estate tax will apply for estates of decedents who died in 2010, the executor is able to choose the method to calculate basis for inherited assets. The first method is to automatically apply the estate tax and a stepped-up basis on the assets held within the estate. A "stepped-up" basis means that the basis of the property is valued at its fair market price at the time of the decedent's death. The alternative method is to elect to apply the rules that had been in place in 2010 prior to the new law by adopting a carryover basis. A "carryover basis" means that the basis of the assets is the same as in the hands of the decedent before death. The automatic stepped-up basis rules will be the default method; the carryover basis must be specifically elected by the executor. Generally, estates below $5 million would use the default method in order to get a stepped-up basis while not paying estate tax. You should consult your tax advisor to determine which method will be more favorable.

Table 44-1. **Estate, Gift, and Generation-Skipping Transfer (GST) Tax Rates and Unified Credit**

Exemption Amount Calendar Year	Estate, Gift, and GST Tax Exemption	Highest Estate, Gift, and GST Tax Rates
2010	$5 million for estate, gift, and GST tax*	Estate and gift tax at 35%; GST at 0%
2011, 2012	$5 million for estate, gift, and GST tax	35%
2013	$1 million for estate, gift, and GST tax	55%

*Executor will be able to elect whether to apply the estate tax and use a stepped-up basis or the rules that had been in place for 2010, that is, no estate tax, but using a carryover basis.

TAXPLANNER

The significant estate tax exemption discussed above—exempting estates worth under $5 million from tax—certainly make estate tax planning easier for many Americans. But that should not lull you into thinking that planning is unnecessary. For starters, you may be worth more than you think. Despite the nationwide downturn in housing values, many middle-class families still own homes that are worth much more than what they cost. Moreover, even in this era of economic turmoil and heightened volatility in stock and bond prices, many investors still hold significant investment portfolios. And, in many cases, the proceeds of life insurance are also included in your taxable estate regardless of the beneficiary.

Even if your assets do not currently create a taxable estate, they might at the time of your death. Therefore, it is prudent to focus on strategies that help freeze the value of assets in your estate.

What Is Included in Your Estate

Assets subject to estate tax. Federal estate tax is a levy on the transfer of property at death. Your gross estate will include the value of all property to the extent of your interest in it at the time of death. Following are types of property included in your gross estate:

Tangible personal property, real estate, and other assets. This category includes property you own in your own name that is passed at death by your will or by state intestacy laws. Such property is commonly referred to as the probate estate. Examples include real estate, stocks, bonds, furniture, personal effects, jewelry, works of art, an interest in a partnership, an interest in a sole proprietorship, a bank account, and a promissory note or other evidence of indebtedness you hold.

Jointly owned property. In general, one-half of the value of property owned jointly by a husband and wife will be included in the estate of the first spouse to die. The unlimited marital deduction allows the transfer of the property from the deceased to the surviving spouse without being subject to federal estate tax. Upon the survivor's death, however, the entire property will be subject to tax (assuming it is still held at the time of death). However, if two people who are not married own property jointly, the entire value of the property is included in the gross estate of the first to die, unless the estate can prove that all or part of the payment for acquiring the property was actually furnished by the other joint owner. If you and another joint owner acquired property by gift or inheritance, only your fractional share of the property is included.

Jointly held property passes to the other owner automatically on death without regard to whether or not you have a will. In many states, Transfer on Death (TOD) or Totten Trust accounts allow securities and bank accounts to pass directly to a beneficiary even if the property is not held in joint name.

Life insurance. Your gross estate will include life insurance proceeds that are received (1) by or for the benefit of your estate or (2) by other beneficiaries if you own all or part of the policies at the time of your death. "Ownership" includes the power to change the beneficiary of the policy, the right to cancel the policy and receive the cash value, the right to borrow against the policy, and the right to assign the policy, among other things.

TAXSAVER

You can transfer ownership of a life insurance policy to your children or to a trust for your family's benefit and reap significant tax advantages. To be effective in keeping the proceeds out of your estate, the gift must be made more than three years before death. The three-year waiting period can be avoided for a newly purchased policy if proper steps are taken to have someone else (e.g., a trustee of an irrevocable life insurance trust) apply for the policy and own it from its inception. These types of irrevocable life insurance trusts can be structured so that your contributions each year to the trust can qualify for the annual gift tax exclusion (explained below). Setting up such a trust can be an effective way to get insurance proceeds to your heirs without incurring gift or estate tax.

Employee benefits. The value of payments from qualified pension plans, IRAs, and other qualified or nonqualified retirement plans payable to surviving beneficiaries or the estate of an employee (or the owner, in the case of a Keogh/HR 10 plan) generally is included in your gross estate.

Certain gifts and gift tax paid within three years of death. Gifts of property made during your lifetime are generally not included in your gross estate, but must be figured in the estate tax calculation if they exceed the $13,000 annual gift tax exclusion (discussed later). However, life insurance proceeds are included in your estate if the policies or ownership of the policies were given away within three years of your death. Also included is any gift tax you have paid within three years of your death. Lifetime gifts in which a decedent retains some interest (e.g., a life income interest) or control (e.g., voting rights in closely held stock given as a gift) will be included in the gross estate.

Allowable deductions and exclusions. Deductions are allowed for funeral and estate administration expenses, and debts–such such as unpaid mortgages–and other indebtedness on property included in the gross estate. Also allowed are special deductions such as the marital deduction and the charitable deduction. (See later sections for more details on the marital deduction.)

Funeral and administration expenses. Deductible funeral expenses include burial costs, costs for a burial lot, costs for future care of a grave site, and so on. Deductible administration costs include executor's commissions, attorney's fees, accounting fees, appraisal fees, and court costs.

Other deductible estate expenses. To be deductible, debts must be enforceable personal obligations of the decedent, such as mortgages or personal bank loans, auto loans, credit card balances, utility bills, and so on. The deductible amount also includes any interest accrued on such debt at the date of death. Transfers made under a marital property settlement because of a divorce may be treated as estate expenses. Taxes are also deductible debts if they are accrued and unpaid at date of death. Deductible taxes include accrued property taxes, gift taxes unpaid at death, and income taxes.

Valuing estate property. Property is included in an estate at its "fair market value," which is the price at which property would change hands between a willing buyer and a willing seller. Property that trades on an established market may be valued easily. For example, publicly traded stocks and bonds are valued based on the average of the high and low selling price on the date of death (or, if elected, the date six months after death). However, interests in closely held businesses or partnerships must generally be appraised, taking into account the business's assets, earning capacity, and other factors. An accountant can assist you in obtaining the appropriate appraisal of your business interests for estate or gift tax valuation purposes.

Your gross estate is valued as of the date of your death or six months later (also known as the alternative valuation date), whichever your personal representative elects. An election to value the estate six months after the date of death will generally apply to all assets in the estate, but is available only if the election results in a decrease in your gross estate and estate tax liability.

The amount remaining after subtracting any allowable deductions is your taxable estate. The federal estate tax is computed on this amount. Gifts made after 1976 are also factored in and can increase the marginal tax bracket of the estate.

If You Are the Beneficiary of an Estate

Property acquired from a decedent generally gets a new basis. Basis is generally the cost of an asset or the amount you will use to figure your tax when you sell the asset. In most cases, the new basis is the fair market value at date of death or alternative valuation date, whichever is used for estate tax purposes. If the new basis is greater than the old basis, this is known as your "stepped-up" basis.

TAXALERT

The basis of property acquired from a decedent who passed away in 2010 will depend on whether the executor of the estate elects to apply the estate tax and stepped-up basis rules or the rules formerly in place in 2010 (i.e., no estate tax but "carryover basis"). The stepped-up basis rules will be the default.

Consequently, if you inherit property from a decedent who died in 2010 and the estate's executor did not opt out of the estate tax, then you will get a stepped-up basis. However, if the estate did elect to not be subject to the estate tax, you will generally receive a "carryover basis" equal to the lesser of the fair market value of the property on the decedent's date of death or the decedent's adjusted basis in the property.

Example

Pedro had an estate valued at $4 million at the time of his death in 2010. Pedro's adjusted cost basis in his assets totaled $2.5 million. If the executor of Pedro's estate did not make an election when preparing his estate tax return, the stepped-up basis rules would apply, and the recipient of his assets would receive a basis equal to the fair market value on the date of Pedro's death or $4 million. If the executor elected to use the carryover basis rules, transferred assets would only receive a basis equal to $2.5 million.

Exception

There is one key exception to this carryover basis rule: The executor of a 2010 decedent can increase the basis of assets transferred by a total of $1.3 million plus any unused capital losses and net operating losses. An additional $3 million basis increase is allowed for property transferred to a surviving spouse, which means that property transferred to a spouse will be allowed a basis increase of $4.3 million. However, certain types of assets are not eligible for this increase in basis. Nonresident aliens would only be allowed an increase in basis of $60,000, indexed for inflation after 2011. This could put the executor in an awkward spot: deciding which family members or other heirs get tax-free assets and which ones get assets with built-in capital gain.

How Your Estate Is Taxed

Tax rates. The federal estate tax is progressive, ranging from a marginal rate of 18% to 35% in 2011. The 35% top rate will apply to estates larger than $5 million.

Credits and Exemptions

Your estate can claim certain credits and exemptions before figuring the amount of federal estate tax owed. These items include:

Estate tax exemption. Each individual is entitled to an estate tax exemption. For 2011 and 2012, the exemption is $5 million. In other words, no federal estate tax will be assessed on the first $5 million of an individual's combined taxable gifts and transfers at death. To the extent that the exemption has been used to offset gifts the decedent made during his or her lifetime, the exemption against the estate tax is reduced. While you should have your estate plan reviewed on a regular basis, it is especially important to be sure it is drafted to take advantage of the estate tax exemption available under the law in existence at the time of your death.

Example. Mary had an estate valued at $5 million at the time of her death in 2011. Two years before she died, she gave her son Bill a gift of $250,000 to help him buy a house. Instead of an estate tax exemption of $5 million, only $4.75 million of Mary's estate will qualify for the exemption.

The marital deduction. One of the most significant tax-saving provisions of the law is the marital deduction. As its name implies, it is a special deduction available only to married persons, where the spouse receiving the assets is a U.S. citizen. An estate is allowed an unlimited deduction for the value of property transferred to the spouse of the deceased. Thus, in effect, the marital deduction permits a couple to postpone paying any estate tax until the surviving spouse dies.

TAXSAVER

Most married individuals will want to take advantage of both the estate tax exemption and the unlimited marital deduction. This will reduce the federal estate tax to zero for the estate of the first spouse to die. The coordinated use of the exemption and the marital deduction is usually accomplished by placing property in a special type of trust, often called a bypass trust. These trusts, which are used to take full advantage of a spouse's estate tax exemption, typically provide income and discretionary distributions of principal to the deceased's surviving spouse. The amount that goes into these trusts is typically determined by a formula that puts the maximum possible amount into the trust without generating federal estate tax in the deceased spouse's estate. Assets in excess of the remaining exemption either pass to the surviving spouse outright or remain in a form of trust that will qualify for the estate tax marital deduction. The advantage of the bypass trust is that its assets will not be included in the surviving spouse's estate at his or her death, regardless of the amount in that trust at that time.

Portability. As of 2011, when a spouse passes away the surviving spouse can add to his or her own $5 million exemption, whatever amount of the exemption the deceased had not used during his or her lifetime. In order to take advantage of this option, an election must be made with a timely filed estate tax return for the deceased spouse, even though the estate of the deceased spouse many not be large enough to require the filing of an estate tax return.

After 2010, a surviving spouse will be able to use the deceased spouse's unused exemption for lifetime transfers as well as at the death of the surviving spouse. However, portability does not extend to the generation-skipping transfer (GST) tax exemption.

Prior to 2011 for estates in excess of the estate tax exemption equivalent, a typical estate plan would fund a bypass trust with the decedent's remaining unused amount of estate tax exemption equivalent. By funding the bypass trust at the death of the first spouse, the full, remaining amount of the estate tax exemption plus future appreciation would not be included and taxed in the estate of the surviving spouse. If an estate plan did not fund a bypass trust, all assets transferred directly to the surviving spouse upon the decedent's death would be includable in the surviving spouse's estate. Therefore, the full value of the exemption of the deceased could go unused and possibly be lost. Even though no estate tax would be due upon the death of the first spouse, a larger estate tax would be due upon the death of the surviving spouse.

Under the new portability rules, there would still be no tax due on the first-to-die, however the deceased's exemption would not be "wasted." Instead, any of the deceased's unused exemption carries over to the surviving spouse. While the portability rules provide relief in the ability to use a deceased's unused exemption, the funding of a bypass trust should continue to be considered in an estate plan. First, portability is not allowed for GST tax exemptions. Therefore, a surviving spouse would not be able to use the unused GST exemption of the first-to-die. Second, the funding of a bypass trust at the death of the first spouse removes the exemption equivalent amount and the associated future appreciation from the surviving spouse's estate. The traditional benefits of using a trust, such as creditor protection, should be considered as well as the possibility of the surviving spouse remarrying and the potential inability to use the first deceased spouse's unused exemption amount.

The following examples explain how an estate or gift tax exemption can be transferred from a deceased spouse to a surviving spouse.

Example 1. Assume that Husband 1 dies in 2011, having made taxable transfers of $3 million and having no taxable estate. An election is made on Husband 1's estate tax return to permit his Wife to use Husband 1's deceased spousal unused exclusion amount. As of Husband 1's death, the Wife has made no taxable gifts. Thereafter, Wife's applicable exclusion amount is $7 million (her $5 million basic exclusion amount plus $2 million deceased spousal unused exclusion amount from Husband 1), which she may use for lifetime gifts or for transfers at death.

Example 2. Assume the same facts as in Example 1, except that Wife subsequently marries Husband 2. Husband 2 also predeceases Wife, having made $4 million in taxable transfers and having no taxable estate. An election is made on Husband 2's estate tax return to permit Wife to use Husband 2's deceased spousal unused exclusion amount. Although the combined amount of unused exclusion of Husband 1 and Husband 2 is $3 million ($2 million for Husband 1 and $1 million for Husband 2), only Husband 2's $1 million unused exclusion is available for use by Wife, because the deceased spousal unused exclusion amount is limited to the lesser of the basic exclusion amount ($5 million) or the unused exclusion of the last deceased spouse of the surviving spouse (here, Husband 2's $1 million unused exclusion). Thereafter the Wife's applicable exclusion amount is $6 million (her $5 million basic exclusion amount plus $1 million deceased spousal unused exclusion amount from Husband 2), which she may use for lifetime gifts or for transfers at death.

Example 3. Assume the same facts as in Examples 1 and 2, except that Wife predeceases Husband 2. Following Husband 1's death, Wife's applicable exclusion amount is $7 million (her $5 million basic exclusion amount plus $2 million deceased spousal unused exclusion amount from Husband 1). Wife made no taxable transfers and has a taxable estate of $3 million. An election is made on Wife's estate tax return to permit Husband 2 to use Wife's deceased spousal unused exclusion amount, which is $4 million (Wife's $7 million applicable exclusion amount less her $3 million taxable estate). Under the provision, Husband 2's applicable exclusion amount is increased by $4 million (i.e., the amount of deceased spousal unused exclusion amount of Wife).

State death tax considerations. Most states impose some kind of inheritance or estate tax. In some states, the estate tax is simply the amount of the federal credit for state death taxes. However, since the federal state death tax credit had been eliminated for decedents dying in 2005 through 2009, there would be no state estate tax. To avoid this result, many states enacted estate taxes that are not tied to the federal credit. In addition, some states revised their tax laws to set their estate tax exemption at an amount that is less than the federal estate tax exemption. Furthermore, some states do not allow an unlimited marital deduction, as the federal government does. Consequently, in many states it is possible to have a taxable estate for state estate tax purposes but not for federal purposes. In these states, state death tax considerations may influence how your estate plan should be structured.

Foreign death tax credit. A credit is allowed against the federal estate tax for any death taxes actually paid to a foreign country, Puerto Rico, or the Virgin Islands on property that is also subject to the federal estate tax. The credit is limited to the U.S. tax attributable to the property taxed by the foreign country.

Credit for tax on prior transfers. Under certain circumstances a credit is allowed against the federal estate tax for part or all of any estate tax paid on property transferred to the present decedent.

TAXSAVER

Your will can be drafted so that your property is placed in a special type of trust that benefits a spouse who is not a U.S. citizen. The trust enables estate tax on the property to be postponed until the property is distributed out of the trust or the surviving spouse dies. This type of trust is called a Qualified Domestic Trust (QDOT). It permits property to qualify for the marital deduction if certain requirements—which provide that the property will eventually be subject to estate tax—are met.

EXAMPLE

Here is an example of a computation of the gross estate, the taxable estate, and the estate tax due for an unmarried individual who is assumed to die in 2011 as a resident of a state that has no estate tax. We assume that the estate tax laws for 2011, including the $5 million exemption, will be in place. The assets of the individual are listed in Step 1 below.

Step 1: Computing the gross estate

Cash	$1,400,000
Marketable securities	3,750,000
Residence	900,000
Personal property	350,000
Deferred compensation	300,000
Ordinary life insurance	1,000,000
Group-term insurance	300,000
Gross estate	$8,000,000

Step 2: Computing the taxable estate

The executor of the estate will subtract from the total value of the gross estate all those deductions allowable under the tax law, including the mortgage and any charitable bequest the individual made at his death.

Gross estate		$8,000,000
Deductions:		
Funeral expenses	(20,000)	
Estate administration expenses	(80,000)	
Debts	(900,000)	
Mortgages	(400,000)	
Marital deduction	-0-	
Charitable deductions	(1,000,000)	(2,400,000)
Total deductions		
Taxable estate		$5,600,000

Step 3: Computing the federal estate tax

To determine the amount of federal estate tax, calculate the tentative estate tax on the taxable estate, then reduce that amount by the estate tax exemption credit (the unified credit) to arrive at the net federal estate tax.

Gross estate	$8,000,000
Deductions	(2,400,000)
Taxable estate	5,600,000
Tentative estate tax	$1,940,800
Reduced by the unified credit	1,730,800
Federal estate tax	$210,000

The Fundamentals of the Gift Tax

You might think that the government would make it easy to give money away to non-charitable recipients. In some respects it does. You can give up to $13,000 annually ($26,000 if your spouse consents) in 2011 to as many individuals as you want without paying any gift tax. But, above that amount, gifts consume the lifetime gift tax exemption amount of $5 million and then can result in gift tax. The reason is that without such a tax, people could escape death taxes–assuming they were willing to give away a large portion of their property before death.

TAXALERT

Under the current tax law, the highest gift tax rate for 2011 is equal to the highest individual income tax rate, which is 35%.

Any gift you give above the annual amount that is exempt from tax is, in effect, included in your estate when you die. The value of the gift is not the value at the date of your death, but the value at the time you gave the gift. In addition, there are some special rules. A gift of a life insurance policy, for example, made within three years of your death will be included in your gross estate at its full face value. Any gift tax you pay on gifts made within three years of your death is also added to the value of your taxable estate. Nevertheless, giving gifts can substantially reduce your overall gift and estate taxes, as well as fulfill other desires. But gift-giving does require careful planning–and the commitment to make the gifts before it is too late.

Basis to the Recipient of a Gift

In general, the basis of appreciated property acquired by gift is the donor's basis for tax purposes. If a gift tax return was filed, the recipient–or donee–should examine it for information regarding the donor's basis, the holding period, and the amount of depreciation. The basis of gifts received after 1976 is increased by the amount of the federal gift tax attributable to the difference between the donor's basis and the gift's fair market value, if higher as of the date of gift.

How to Give Tax-Free Gifts

The gift tax annual exclusion. As noted above, in 2011 you may give up to $13,000 to as many individuals as you want without incurring any gift tax (the annual gift exclusion amount is indexed for inflation). And, if your spouse joins in making the gift (by signing a consent on a gift tax return), you may give $26,000 to each person annually without paying any tax. But this annual gift tax exclusion applies only to gifts of "present interests"–items that can be used, possessed, and enjoyed presently. Examples of a gift of a present interest include gifts of money, holiday presents, and so forth.

Gifts of "future interests" do not qualify for the annual exclusion. Gifts of future interests include remainder interests, reversions, or any other interest that will not give the recipient the right to possess, enjoy, or profit from the gift until some future date or time. There is an exception for gifts in trust to minors, which are subject to special rules that may allow an otherwise future interest to qualify for the annual exclusion.

Gifts to pay medical or educational expenses. In addition to the annual exclusion, an unlimited gift tax exclusion is available to pay someone's medical or educational expenses. The beneficiary does not have to be your dependent or even related to you, although payment of a grandchild's education expenses is perhaps the most common use of the exclusion. Also, contributions to a qualified tuition program (QTP) or a Section 529 plan will be eligible for the regular $13,000 exclusion. (See *Qualified Tuition Programs* under *Giving Gifts to Minors*, later.)

TAXSAVER

In order for a gift to be exempt from taxes, you must make the payment directly to the medical or educational institution providing the service. The beneficiary of the gift should not actually receive the payment. In addition, educational expenses include only tuition. Room and board, books, and other fees will not qualify for the unlimited exclusion, although they can, of course, qualify for the annual gift tax exclusion.

TAXSAVER

You can reduce your taxable estate substantially through a planned annual gifting program. All gifts within the exclusion limits are exempt from federal estate taxes. In addition, outright gifts that qualify for the annual exclusion are also protected from generation-skipping transfer taxes (see below). Obviously, you cannot hope to significantly reduce your estate tax by making gifts in a single year. But the estate tax savings can be substantial if you embark upon a carefully planned gift-giving program that extends for a number of years before your death.

TAXSAVER

A donor who makes contributions to a qualified tuition program (commonly known as a "Section 529 plan") in excess of the $13,000 annual exclusion amount may elect to recognize the contributions for gift tax purposes ratably over the five-year period starting with the year of the contributions. This means a donor can make a $65,000 tax-free contribution in one year—or $130,000 if the donor is married and the donor's spouse consents to gift-splitting. If the donor dies before the end of the five-year period, the portion of the contribution allocable to the period after the donor's date of death is included in the donor's gross estate.

TAXSAVER

Another major tax advantage of making a gift is that future appreciation in the gift's value and after-tax income earned on the property are not included in your estate. Example: Suppose you give stock worth $50,000 to your children now. If you die in 10 years and the stock is worth $130,000, the $80,000 of appreciation will not be included in your estate. Nor will you (or your estate) include any dividends paid on the stock after the gift.

Gift tax charitable contribution deduction. An unlimited gift tax deduction is available for gifts to qualified charitable organizations.

The gift tax marital deduction. The gift tax marital deduction allows you to transfer unlimited amounts of property during your lifetime to your spouse without gift tax.

Property can be transferred outright or in trust. Also, a gift of a lifetime income interest in property to your spouse can qualify for the marital deduction, if it is structured properly. You should consult with your tax advisor.

TAXSAVER

The gift tax marital deduction can help you lower the taxes on your estate. Consider that in order for one spouse to make full use of his or her estate tax exemption, it may be desirable to make gifts to that spouse so that he or she will have an estate at least equal to the estate tax exemption equivalent. Since the gift tax marital deduction allows you to make unlimited tax-free transfers to your spouse, you can build up your spouse's assets without worrying that your gifts will be taxable.

Some words of caution: The unlimited marital deduction is not allowed for gifts to a spouse who is not a U.S. citizen, although tax-free transfers of up to $136,000 (in 2011; this amount is adjusted annually for inflation) are permitted each year. (See the section on *Marital Deduction* under *Estate Tax Fundamentals*, earlier in this chapter.) Furthermore, the amount of the gift tax marital deduction for a particular state may differ from the federal amount. It is therefore vital to get professional advice before making any significant gifts.

Example: Giving gifts without paying gift tax. This example illustrates how you can set up a substantial gift program and avoid paying any gift tax. Note, however, that part of the $5 million gift tax exemption is being used.

During 2010, James made outright gifts of $200,000 to his wife, Helen, and $60,000 to each of his three children, for a total of $380,000.

James incurred no gift tax on Helen's gift because of the unlimited marital deduction. James and Helen were entitled to a total of $78,000 in annual exclusions (based on $26,000 for each child) because they elected to treat one-half of those gifts as made by Helen. That still leaves, however, a taxable gift of $102,000 to the three children. Since James and Helen have elected to treat the one-half of the gifts made by James as made by Helen, each parent has made $51,000 in gifts. By applying a portion of their respective gift tax exemptions, James and Helen can entirely eliminate paying gift tax. Assuming that this was their first gift using their exemptions, they will have reduced the remaining assets that will be considered tax-free for taxable gifts made in future years from $5 million to $4,949,000 each.

Giving Gifts to Minors

Before a parent or grandparent gives a gift to a minor child, certain legal and practical matters need to be considered. Because a child typically cannot manage his or her own affairs and because parents usually do not want to give young children unfettered control over gift property, some special arrangements need to be made. The tax law, too, poses some challenges since only gifts of a "present interest"—property for the beneficiary's immediate enjoyment—qualify for the annual gift tax exclusion, $13,000 in 2011. Furthermore, state laws frequently discourage outright gifts to minors. Many states commonly prohibit or discourage the registration of securities in the name of a minor and impose supervisory restrictions upon the sale of a minor's property. Consequently, gifts to minors can take different forms and have different tax consequences.

Outright gifts. The $13,000 annual gift tax exclusion is available for these gifts unless the property being given as a gift is a "future interest." Income from the property is taxed to the minor, and the property is included in the minor's estate if he or she should die. However, because of the "kiddie tax," which requires that a child's unearned income be taxed at the parent's rate until the child reaches age 18 (or age 24 if a student), your child may actually be taxed at your rates on any income he or she receives from the property.

Guardianship. A guardianship is an arrangement whereby property is under a guardian's legal control subject to formal (and possibly burdensome) accounting to a court. The gift, income, and estate tax consequences are the same as for outright gifts. Thus, such gifts also qualify for the $13,000 (in 2011) gift tax exclusion.

Custodial arrangements. To overcome the legal disability minors have in owning property outright, all 50 states, the District of Columbia, and the Virgin Islands have adopted the Uniform Gifts (or Transfers) to Minors Act. Under this act, a custodian may hold both cash and securities for a minor until he or she reaches adulthood. Securities may be registered in the name of any bank, trust company, or adult as custodian for the minor. Custodial gifts to minors are considered completed gifts for gift tax purposes, and such gifts are eligible for the annual gift tax exclusion. The income from the gift property during the custodial period is taxable to the minor (subject to kiddie tax provisions). However, if you use the income for your minor child's maintenance and support, it is taxable to you because you are the person legally obligated to support the minor.

TAXSAVER

Generally, you should not act as custodian of your own gifts to your minor child. If you do and die before your child becomes an adult, the value of the custodial account maintained for your child's benefit will be included in your estate. Instead, your spouse may be the custodian. If you and your spouse both make gifts to your minor child, in essence splitting your gifts to take advantage of the annual gift tax exclusion, you should consider making a third party the custodian for the child.

Present interest trust. Special rules enacted by Congress provide a method of making gifts to minors that qualify for the annual exclusion. Specifically, a gift to a qualifying trust established for an individual under the age of 21 will be considered a gift of a present interest and qualify for the annual gift tax exclusion. The trust instrument must provide that the gift property and its income:

- May be expended for the benefit of the beneficiary before reaching age 21, and
- To the extent not so expended, will pass to the beneficiary upon becoming age 21.

If the child dies before reaching age 21, the funds must be payable to the child's estate or as the child may designate under a general power of appointment. This rule applies to trusts for children under the age of 21, even if a state law has reduced the age of majority to age 19 or 18.

Crummey trust. This is a type of trust to which you can transfer property and have the gift qualify for the annual gift tax exclusion. The distinguishing characteristic of a Crummey trust (which takes its name from a court case) is that it gives the beneficiary the annual right to demand distributions from the trust equal to the lesser of the amount of the contributions to the trust during the year or some specified amount (e.g., $5,000 or 5% of the trust's value). The beneficiary (or legal guardian) must be notified of the power to withdraw from the trust, although the power is permitted to lapse or terminate after a short period of time, such as 30 days. If the beneficiary fails to make a demand during the window period, after being notified that a contribution was made, the right lapses for that year's contributions. To the extent the beneficiary (or legal guardian) has the right to demand distribution of the year's contribution, that contribution is considered a "present interest" and, therefore, qualifies for the annual gift tax exclusion.

A Crummey trust is very flexible. The trustee can be required to accumulate income until the child reaches a specified age above age 21. The trustee also can be restricted to using trust assets and income for specific purposes (e.g., college expenses). The trust is useful as a vehicle for permanently removing assets from the parents' gross estates.

Totten trust. An "In Trust For" or so-called Totten Trust is created when a donor deposits his or her own money into a bank account for the benefit of a minor and names himself or herself as trustee. Under the laws of certain states, this is an informal and revocable arrangement. Upon the donor-trustee's death, the funds avoid probate and pass directly to the minor. However, the trust is not considered a separate entity for tax purposes because the donor retains complete control over any property in the trust. Accordingly, the donor will be taxed on the income as if the trust were not in existence. Also, assets in the trust account will be included in the donor's estate.

Qualified tuition programs (Section 529 plans). Section 529 plans allow a donor to either buy tuition credits or contribute to a special higher-education savings account for a designated beneficiary. A donor can leverage the 2011 gift tax exclusion of $13,000 under a special gift tax rule that allows the donor to recognize any contribution to a qualified tuition program in excess of the annual exclusion amount as if it were made ratably over five years. This permits a donor to contribute up to $65,000 in one year—or $130,000 if gift-splitting with spouse—per beneficiary, free of gift tax.

Although the funds in a Section 529 account are treated as a completed gift, you can retain ownership and control over them. This unique provision allows you to decide when to distribute funds to the beneficiary. Subject to certain guidelines, you can even substitute a different beneficiary or revoke the account and take back the funds.

Earnings in the account are permitted to grow on a tax-deferred basis. In addition, under current law, no federal income tax is imposed on the earnings, provided that the funds are used to pay for qualifying higher education expenditures. Although contributions to Section 529 plans are not deductible for federal income tax purposes, a number of states offer a deduction against state income tax for contributions made to their programs.

Do You Need to File a Gift Tax Return?

Only individuals are required to file a gift tax return. If a trust, estate, partnership, or corporation makes a gift, the individual beneficiaries, partners, or stockholders are considered donors and may be liable for the gift tax. If a donor dies before filing a return, the donor's executor must file the gift tax return.

Although you may have made gifts during the year, you do not need to file a gift tax return so long as you meet all of the following requirements:

1. You made no gifts during the year to your spouse;
2. You gave no more than $13,000 in 2011 during the year to any one recipient; and
3. All of the gifts you made were of present interests.

Additionally, except in limited circumstances, you do not have to file a gift tax return solely to report gifts to your spouse (regardless of the amount of these gifts and regardless of whether the gifts are present or future interests).

You must file a gift tax return, however, if:

- Your spouse is not a U.S. citizen and the total gifts you made to your spouse during 2011 exceed $136,000;
- You make any gift of a terminable interest to your spouse that does not meet certain exceptions;
- You make a Qualified Terminable Interest Property election;
- You gave gifts to any donee, other than your spouse, which are not fully excluded under the $13,000 annual exclusion. Thus, you must file a gift tax return to report any gift of a future interest (regardless of amount) or to report gifts to any donee that total more than $13,000 for the year; or
- You elect to split gifts with your spouse (regardless of the amount of the gifts).

If you are required to file a gift tax return, use Form 709, United States Gift Tax Return.

When to File the Gift Tax Return

The gift tax return is an annual return. In general, you must file a gift tax return on or after January 1 but not later than April 15 (without extensions) of the year following the calendar year when the gifts were made. If the donor of the gifts died during the year in which the gifts were made, the executor must file the donor's gift tax return not later than the earlier of (1) the due date (with extensions) for filing the donor's estate tax return; or (2) April 15 of the year following the calendar year when the gifts were made. If no estate tax return is required to be filed, the due date for the gift tax return (without extensions) is April 15.

Extension of time to file. You can extend the time to file the gift tax return in either of two ways. First, you can request an extension by filing Form 8892 if you are not extending your Form 1040. Second, any extension of time to file your income tax return will also extend the time to file your gift tax return.

TAXPLANNER

Like the income tax return, an extension to file a gift tax return does not extend the time to pay the gift tax due. If you want an extension of time to pay the gift tax, you must make a separate request using Form 8892-V.

Gift Tax Return—Form 709

Form 709 is used to report transfers subject to the federal gift tax (as well as the generation-skipping transfer tax, not discussed here) and also to compute the tax, if any, due on those transfers. A married couple may not file a joint Form 709, even if the spouses elect gift-splitting. Instead, both the donor spouse and the consenting spouse must each file a separate gift tax return, unless either of two situations are met:

Situation 1. During the calendar year:

- Only one spouse made any gifts;
- The total value of these gifts to each third-party donee does not exceed $26,000; and
- All of the gifts were of present interests.

Situation 2. During the calendar year:

- Only one spouse (the donor spouse) made gifts of more than $13,000, but not more than $26,000 to any third-party donee;
- The only gifts made by the other spouse (the consenting spouse) were gifts of not more than $13,000 to third-party donees other than those to whom the donor spouse made gifts; and
- All of the gifts by both spouses were of present interests.

If either of these two situations is met, only the donor spouse must file a return and the consenting spouse signifies consent on that return.

TAXORGANIZER

Records you should keep:

- All gift tax returns filed by you and your spouse

The Generation-Skipping Transfer Tax

An additional tax may apply to gifts or bequests that skip a generation. For example, a gift of property directly from a grandparent to a grandchild (which effectively "skips" the intervening generation) would be subject to the generation-skipping transfer (GST) tax.

The reason for the tax is simple. It's designed to impose the equivalent of the gift or estate tax that would have been paid if the intervening generation had received the gift or bequest. So for a direct gift from a grandparent to a grandchild, the GST tax represents the amount of tax that would have been paid if the property had first been transferred to the child, who then died leaving the property to the grandchild.

The generation-skipping transfer tax is stiff. Under current law, the top tax rate on GST tax transfers in 2011 is 35%. It will be payable in addition to any estate or gift tax otherwise payable as a result of the transfer. Fortunately, most individuals will escape paying it. First, an outright gift under $13,000 from a grandparent to a grandchild ($26,000 if made with the consent of a spouse) that qualifies for the annual gift tax exclusion is exempt from this tax. Furthermore, each individual is entitled to an aggregate GST tax exemption for lifetime gifts and transfers at death.

TAXSAVER

A wealthy individual can maximize his or her opportunity to avoid the imposition of the GST tax on transfers to grandchildren and later generations by allocating the $5 million exemption for gifts during his or her lifetime.

If your living descendants are already well provided for, you may want to consider establishing a "dynasty trust." As its name implies, the trust can benefit future descendants by sheltering assets from estate, gift, and GST taxes for several generations.

How to Use Trusts

A trust is one of the most useful personal financial planning tools available. A trust is an arrangement under which one person or institution holds legal title to real or personal property for the benefit of another person or persons, usually under the terms of a written document setting forth the rights and responsibilities of all parties. Its primary virtue is that it can hold property for the benefit of other persons, now or in the future, and often avoid some taxes that otherwise would have to be paid.

Revocable trusts. A revocable trust (also known as a "living trust") is created during your lifetime, and you may amend or revoke it at any time. The trust instrument stipulates how the assets held by the trust are to be managed during your lifetime. This type of trust can also act very much like a will; the trust instrument can include instructions about how the assets in the trust should be distributed after your death.

What distinguishes a revocable trust from other kinds of trust arrangements is that you keep the power to reclaim the trust assets or contribute additional property to the trust at any time and for any reason. Thus, in effect, if you set up a revocable trust you really have not committed yourself to anything—at least until you die and the trust becomes irrevocable. For all practical purposes, you continue to own the trust property; the trust merely gets legal title. Since you keep complete control over the trust and its assets, the property held in it will be included in your gross estate for estate tax purposes. Also, all income and deductions attributable to the property in the trust will be included on your income tax return. On the other hand, you will not be liable for any gift tax when you contribute assets to the trust. This is the case even though the trust names the beneficiaries who will inherit the property upon your death. However, a gift will occur if you give up your power to revoke or amend the trust, or if income or principal is actually paid to someone else.

Essentially, there are no tax advantages gained by establishing a revocable trust. But there can be some real financial and administrative advantages, including:

Avoiding probate and ancillary administration. Revocable trust assets pass to the beneficiaries you name in the trust document and are not controlled by your will. This cuts out the costs and delays arising from the probate process, but first check the laws in your state. Many states have streamlined the probate process and reduced the associated costs. Also, unlike probate, with a revocable trust the identity and instructions for distributing estate property are not part of the public record. Further, if you own real property in a state other than your state of domicile, a revocable trust will avoid the ancillary probate administration in that state that would otherwise be required.

Avoiding legal guardianship. If you become incapacitated, the assets kept in your living trust would be managed by a trustee you named in the trust document. Otherwise, the determination of whether and to what extent you are disabled or incompetent and who is going to handle your affairs could be left to public, and potentially costly, guardianship proceedings. A durable power of attorney can also be an effective tool for prearranging the management of your affairs in the event you become incapacitated.

Irrevocable trusts. An irrevocable trust may not be changed or revoked after its creation. It is usually created to remove property and its future income and appreciation from the estate of the creator of the trust. A present interest trust and a Crummey trust, both of which are discussed above, are irrevocable trusts. You might also use an irrevocable trust if you want to make a gift to someone but want to prevent the assets from being spent too quickly. An irrevocable trust also can be used to protect assets you give from your beneficiary's creditors.

However, property placed in an irrevocable trust will not be removed from your estate if you retain certain interests or powers in the trust–such as an interest that entitles you to receive the income from the trust for the rest of your life or the power to determine which beneficiaries will receive distributions. In addition, any transfer to an irrevocable trust will be subject to gift tax to the extent you relinquish control over the property. If someone else will receive the current income from the trust, or if it is a present income trust, the $13,000 annual gift tax exclusion in 2011 can shield at least part of the property transferred to the trust from gift tax.

Besides saving you estate tax, irrevocable trusts created for your children can cut your income taxes. The amount of income tax savings depends on how much other income your children already receive and whether the "kiddie tax" applies to them. Also, there are very strict rules that limit the amount of control you or your spouse may keep over the trust in order for you not to include the trust's income on your tax return. The income from the trust will be taxed to you if the trust is used to pay for an item that you are legally obligated to provide as support for the beneficiary.

Relief from financial responsibility. If desired, an independent trustee can be used immediately to relieve you of the details of managing your property and investments, record-keeping chores, and the preparation and filing of income tax returns.

Living trusts have some drawbacks and are not suited for everyone:

- Expect to pay legal fees and other expenses, such as recording fees, to set up the trust and transfer property to it. You will also owe recurring trustee and administrative charges if you use a corporate trustee rather than managing the trust yourself.
- You will not necessarily save on other legal, accounting, and executor's fees paid to handle your estate. Whether your assets are held in a living trust or pass through probate, the same sort of work will generally be needed to value your assets, prepare federal and state tax returns, settle creditors' claims, and resolve disputes among beneficiaries.

TAXSAVER

Two reminders: (1) If you establish a living trust, be sure that any property covered by the trust is legally titled in the trust's name. This is a straightforward, but often overlooked, point. (2) After setting up a living trust, you must remember to conduct your personal business affairs through the trust. This is not difficult but can be a burden. Property held outside the trust at your death will be subject to probate–except for life insurance proceeds (payable to a beneficiary other than your estate) and property held jointly with right of survivorship, which by law would avoid probate.

How to Raise Cash to Pay Estate Taxes

In many instances, the estate of an owner of a closely held business–or for that matter, any estate–may not have sufficient cash to pay all the estate's obligations, including estate taxes. Without sufficient liquidity, the estate may be forced to sell a portion of the business to raise the necessary cash. But there are special rules for the estates of owners of closely held businesses. The techniques described below can help alleviate these problems.

Stock Redemptions to Pay Death Taxes

A special tax provision (Section 303 of the Internal Revenue Code) allows certain redemptions or partial redemptions of closely held stock to be treated as a sale or exchange, not as a dividend. Since the estate's basis in the decedent's stock will be the stock's fair market value at the date of death, only post-death appreciation will be taxed upon the redemption and only up to the maximum long-term capital gains tax rate (generally 15% for sales and exchanges).

TAXALERT

To qualify for what is called a Section 303 redemption, the value of all the stock of the corporation included in the decedent's gross estate must exceed 35% of the decedent's adjusted gross estate. The adjusted gross estate is the gross estate less the allowable deductions for funeral and administration expenses, debts, the family-owned business deduction, and certain losses (but before any charitable deduction or marital deduction). A qualifying redemption under Section 303 is limited in amount to the sum of the following items:

- Federal and state death taxes,
- Funeral expenses, and
- Estate administration expenses.

TAXALERT

The advantages of sale and exchange treatment under Section 303 may be somewhat diminished under the tax law, which taxes certain qualified dividends at the lower capital gains (vs. ordinary income) rate. As long as the redemption by the estate results in qualified dividend treatment, the estate would be taxed at 15% on post-death appreciation without meeting the Section 303 requirements.

TAXSAVER

An estate does not actually have to be illiquid in order to qualify for this special redemption. The estate may redeem stock up to the maximum amount referred to above, if the estate otherwise has sufficient liquid assets to take care of its expenses and taxes.

Installment Payment of Estate Tax

The estate taxes attributable to a decedent's closely held business can be paid over a 14-year period if certain conditions are met. This 14-year payout offers a very favorable interest rate plus a 5-year deferral on the first installment of estate taxes. The deferral provision only applies to an "interest in a closely held business." To qualify, the value of the closely held business must exceed 35% of the adjusted gross estate. The amount of estate tax that qualifies for a deferred payout is limited to the portion of the total tax that is attributable to the decedent's business interest. Thus, if the decedent's qualifying stock constitutes 62% of the adjusted gross estate, then 62% of the total estate tax liability may be deferred.

Even though none of the tax attributable to the closely held business interest is paid for five years, the interest on the tax for the first four years must be paid annually. Starting in the fifth year, the estate tax due plus interest may be paid in up to 10 yearly installments.

The interest rate charged on the deferred estate tax attributable to the first $1.36 million (in 2011) in value of the closely held business interest is 2%. An interest rate equal to 45% of the rate applicable to tax underpayments applies to the deferred estate tax in excess of that amount.

Concerns Regarding Community Property

Community property is most often property acquired by spouses while they are married and domiciled in a community property state. But not all property acquired during the marriage is community property. If one spouse individually receives a gift or inheritance, it is not community property but rather is "separate property" owned solely by the recipient. Property acquired or otherwise owned by each spouse prior to marriage is also considered separate property.

Community property and marital property are treated differently from non-community property when someone dies. In a non-community property state, the basis of the decedent's property is increased or decreased for tax purposes to fair market value as of the date generally of the decedent's death. However, when one spouse in a community property state dies, the basis of *both* spouses' interest in all community property is stepped up or down, that is, increased or decreased to the fair market value at date of death.

Estate Planning—Steps to Take Now

Here's a useful checklist of estate planning measures you should consider:

- Review with your spouse your current financial situation and your entire personal financial plan (including plans for your retirement as well as plans for the years after one of you has died).
- If any adult member of your family does not have a will, or if any wills have not been reviewed within the last three years, contact your attorney. This is especially important because of the frequency of tax law changes.
- Compile a list documenting where all your important financial and legal papers are located. Inform all appropriate persons of your list. If you have not already done so, be sure your spouse or whomever you designate as your personal representative knows your attorney, accountant, trust officer, broker, insurance advisor, and other appropriate individuals.
- Compile information on the cost and approximate purchase date of all your assets, including your residence.
- To reduce federal estate taxes, consider assigning ownership rights of your group term life insurance to children, a trust, or other appropriate recipient.
- Review whom you have designated as a beneficiary for your employee retirement or Keogh plan and other employee benefits.
- Review how your assets will be passed on to your beneficiaries.
- Make sure that you have provided for the legal guardianship and personal custody of your minor children.
- Review your will or any trust you have set up with your attorney. In particular, you and your spouse should check the provisions in your wills that pertain to what would happen to your estates if both of you died at the same time. Have you, for example, properly divided your assets to take maximum advantage of the marital deduction and the estate tax exemption?
- If you and your spouse do not have durable powers of attorney, health care proxies, or living wills, consider having them drawn up soon.

If the answer to any of the following questions is yes, you may need professional assistance to help you determine whether there are tax problems on the horizon. Remember: A "yes" answer is a warning flag, but not necessarily a signal that there is a problem.

Are you:

- Making significant cash gifts to members of your family that are likely to continue indefinitely?
- Planning to make gifts to grandchildren within the next few years? In your will?
- Anticipating a significant inheritance? Is your spouse?
- A non-U.S. citizen? Is your spouse?

Do you:

- Hold assets jointly with your spouse, other than your residence and a working banking account?
- Have a simple will that leaves all property you own at the date of your death outright to your spouse?
- Own any real property in a state other than the state of your residence?
- Have a child or other relative with a serious medical problem who may require special consideration in your will or trust instrument?
- Have substantially more or less property than your spouse?

Have you:

- Moved your residence to a different state since you last executed your will?
- Named your estate as the beneficiary of your life insurance or your retirement plan benefits?

Chapter 45

Everything you need to know about e-filing

ey.com/EYTaxGuide

Note

ey.com/EYTaxGuide
Ernst & Young LLP will update the *Ernst & Young Tax Guide 2012* website with relevant taxpayer information as it becomes available. You can also sign up for email alerts to let you know when changes have been made.

Introduction

E-filing has been a tremendous success. The IRS announced that more than one billion returns have been e-filed since 1986. The IRS also reports that for the 2011 filing season (for 2010 tax returns), over 100,000,000 returns were filed electronically, exceeding the record set in 2010 of over 93,000,000. This includes over 37,000,000 returns filed from home computers. Overall, about 75% of all individual returns were e-filed.

E-filing can offer a number of advantages. It's easy and efficient and, of course, eliminates filling out paper forms line by line. If you owe money, you can e-file and authorize an electronic funds withdrawal, pay by credit or debit card, or pay by enrolling in the Electronic Federal Tax Payment System (EFTPS). The electronic funds withdrawal and EFTPS payment options are offered for free; however, you should expect to pay a convenience fee if you pay your taxes by credit or debit cards. Generally, you receive electronic proof of submission within 48 hours of when the IRS has received your return. Your return can be quickly and automatically checked for errors and other missing information. The error rate for e-filed returns, according to the IRS, is less than 1%. If you are entitled to a refund, you can get it in half the time it takes for paper filers to get their refunds. Your chance of being audited does not differ whether you e-file or file a paper tax return. Finally, your bank account information, as well as your other tax return information, is safeguarded.

E-filing is increasingly becoming mandatory for many types of returns and in more states. This trend is expected to grow. A new IRS rule, being phased in over the next two years, requires many paid tax return preparers to electronically file federal income tax returns prepared and filed for individuals, trusts, and estates starting January 1, 2011. As a result, tax return preparers are required to start using IRS *e-file* beginning:

- January 1, 2011: for preparers who anticipate filing 100 or more Forms 1040, 1040A, 1040EZ, and 1041 during the year; or
- January 1, 2012: for preparers who anticipate filing 11 or more Forms 1040, 1040A, 1040EZ, and 1041 during the year.

While e-filing is available for all individual income tax returns, it might not be the right choice for you. This may be true if you prefer the familiarity of paper and pen or if you're simply not comfortable with computers and the Internet. If that is the case, although your paid tax preparer must follow the new federal e-file mandate, you still have an option to file your tax return on paper if you choose. Consult your tax preparer to discuss your options. If you choose to opt out of e-filing your federal return or if there is a particular reason why your tax preparer cannot e-file your return, Form 8948, Preparer Explanation for Not Filing Electronically, must be attached to your paper filed tax return by your tax preparer explaining why the return is not being e-filed.

Additionally, the following states allow resident taxpayers to file tax returns directly via their state website: California, Colorado, Connecticut, District of Columbia, Delaware, Hawaii, Illinois,

Indiana, Kansas, Louisiana, Massachusetts, Maryland, Maine, Montana, North Dakota, Nebraska, New Hampshire, New Jersey, New Mexico, Ohio, Pennsylvania, Tennessee, Utah, Virginia, and Wisconsin. You may consider using the online method of filing directly rather than using tax preparation software if you are familiar with the rules and requirements of filing your state tax return. There are additional states that offer e-file through the use of tax preparation software. Consult your tax preparer or your tax software provider for a listing of eligible states.

Like the IRS, many states are now mandating e-filing of state tax returns prepared by paid tax preparers; however, most offer opt-out provisions. Consult your tax preparer to discuss your state e-filing versus paper filing options.

This chapter discusses the three options available for e-filing and which one, if any, might be right for you.

Information You'll Need to E-File

Whether you decide to e-file or not, your first step is to get all your tax information together. That way you'll save time and won't have to stop in the middle of preparing your return to find a missing document. Here's what you'll need:

- Social security numbers for yourself, your spouse, and any dependents.
- Forms W-2, W-2G, and 1099-R from all employers or payors are required for yourself and your spouse. If you are filing electronic returns using a personal computer, you enter or transfer the data from the forms into the electronic filing software. This is similar to the attachment of Forms W-2, Forms W-2G, and Forms 1099-R to the face of paper tax returns. However, if you choose to use an "authorized IRS *e-file* Provider" (explained below), you must provide Forms W-2, Forms W-2G, and Forms 1099-R to the authorized IRS *e-file* provider before the provider sends the electronic return to the IRS. Providers are prohibited from submitting electronic returns to the IRS prior to receipt of all Forms W-2, Forms W-2G, and Forms 1099-R from the taxpayer. It is not required that you separately send these forms to the IRS.
- Forms 1099 for interest, dividends, retirement, or other income, or any Forms 1099 with income tax withholding.
- Schedules K-1 from pass-through entities including partnerships, S corporations, estates or trusts.
- Expense receipts for itemized deductions (Schedule A).
- Receipts and records for other income or expenses.
- Checking and/or savings account numbers and the routing number for your financial institution (for a fast refund, or to pay electronically).
- A copy of your prior year tax return.

Note: For a brief explanation of some of the details of e-filing, also see *Filing Information, Does My Return Have to Be on Paper?* in chapter 1, *Filing information*.

Signing Your Electronic Tax Return

You sign your electronic return by using a Self-Select PIN (see discussion later) for filing a completely paperless return. This allows you to confirm your identity with a five-digit PIN and your prior year's adjusted gross income (AGI). Or if you filed electronically last year, you can use the same PIN that you used to file last year's return. In most cases it is unnecessary to mail anything to the IRS when using e-file to transmit your return. In certain cases the IRS will require you to mail Form 8453, U.S. Individual Income Tax Transmittal for an IRS *e-file* Return, along with the supporting documents. See the *Supporting Documents* section for more information.

Self-Select PIN. The Self-Select PIN (Personal Identification Number) method allows you to electronically sign your e-filed return by selecting a five-digit PIN as your signature. The five-digit PIN can be any five numbers except all zeros. You can use your PIN whether you do your own taxes using a personal computer (described below) or have a tax professional prepare them for you.

You create your own PIN. You do not register the PIN with the IRS before filing or need to contact the IRS to get it. When you use one of the commercially available tax software packages on your personal computer that support the Self-Select PIN option, you will be guided through the process of entering your own PIN. If you use a tax professional, the preparer will help you. If filing a joint return, a PIN is needed for each taxpayer. The IRS has a new web-based application called "Electronic Filing PIN Help" that provides taxpayers with a PIN to be used when they cannot locate their prior year AGI or prior year PIN; refer to *www.irs.gov* for more information.

The following taxpayers are eligible to use the Self-Select PIN method:

- Taxpayers who are eligible to file Form 1040, Form 1040A, Form 1040EZ, and Form 1040-SS(PR) for Tax Year 2011.
- Taxpayers who did not file for Tax Year 2010, but have filed previously.
- Taxpayers who are age 16 or older on or before December 31, 2011, who have never filed a tax return.
- Taxpayers under age 16, filing as "primary" taxpayers, who have filed previously. A primary taxpayer is the taxpayer whose name appears on the first name line of the return.
- Taxpayers under age 16, filing as "secondary" taxpayers (spouse), who filed in the immediate prior year. A secondary taxpayer is the person whose name appears in the spouse line of the return.
- Military personnel residing overseas with an APO/FPO address.
- U.S. citizens and resident aliens residing in the American Possessions of the Virgin Islands, Puerto Rico, American Samoa, Guam and Northern Marianas, or with a foreign country address.
- Taxpayers filing a Form 4868, Automatic Extension of Time to File, or Form 2350, Extension for Certain U.S. Citizens Living Abroad.
- Those who are filing on behalf of deceased taxpayers.
- Taxpayers filing Form 8453, U.S. Individual Income Tax Transmittal for an IRS *e-file* Return, with required attachments.

The following taxpayers are not eligible to use the Self-Select PIN method:

- Primary taxpayers under age 16 who have never filed.
- Secondary taxpayers (spouse) under age 16 who did not file in the immediate prior year.

Supporting Documents

The IRS does require a select list of supporting documents to be mailed in hard copy. If you need to file any of the following forms or schedules, include a copy with Form 8453 (with the appropriate boxes checked) and send the package to the IRS after your e-filed return has been acknowledged and accepted by the IRS. Refer to Form 8453 for specific documents that must be attached in support of the following forms:

- Appendix A, Statement by Taxpayer Using the Procedures in Rev. Proc. 2009-20 to Determine a Theft Loss Deduction Related to a Fraudulent Investment Arrangement
- Form 1098-C, Contributions of Motor Vehicles, Boats, and Airplanes (or equivalent contemporaneous written acknowledgment)
- Form 2848, Power of Attorney (POA) and Declaration of Representative (or POA that states the agent is granted authority to sign the return)
- Form 3115, Application for Change in Accounting Method
- Form 3468, Investment Credit (if Historic Preservation Certificate is required)
- Form 4136, Credit for Federal Tax Paid on Fuels
- Form 5713, International Boycott Report
- Form 8283, Non-Cash Charitable Contributions (if Section A statement or qualified appraisal is required or if using Section B)
- Form 8332, Release of Claim to Exemption for Children of Divorced or Separated Parents
- Form 8858, Information Return of U.S. Persons With Respect to Foreign Disregarded Entities
- Form 8864, Biodiesel and Renewable Diesel Fuels Credit
- Form 8885, Health Coverage Tax Credit
- Form 8949, Sales and Other Dispositions of Capital Assets (or a statement with the same information), if you elect not to report your transactions electronically on Form 8949

Transmission and Acceptance Process

After you sign the return using a Self-Select PIN, the electronic record is transmitted to the IRS for processing. Once received at the IRS, the return is automatically checked by computers for errors and missing information. If it cannot be processed, it is sent back to the transmitter to clarify any necessary information. After correction, the transmitter retransmits the return to the IRS.

Within 48 hours of electronically sending your return to the IRS, the IRS sends an acknowledgment to the transmitter stating the return is accepted for processing. This is your proof of filing and assurance that the IRS has your return information. If you e-filed using your personal computer and have any of the items listed above under *Supporting Documents*, you need to mail the documents along with the completed Form 8453 to the IRS within three business days after receiving the acknowledgment. If a tax preparer e-filed your return, the preparer is responsible for sending Form 8453 to the IRS on your behalf within three business days after receiving the acknowledgment.

Errors/Rejections

Checks are built into return preparation software to catch errors in the process of preparing tax returns. Also, the IRS performs automatic checks when a return is initially e-filed and will "reject" the return if there are any errors or inconsistencies. If the IRS rejects an e-filed return you will receive electronic notification of the items causing the return to be rejected. You should promptly correct the issues and re-submit the return for e-file. It is critical that you monitor the e-file transmission until you receive the acknowledgment indicating the IRS has accepted your return in order to ensure your return is considered to be timely filed. Both your tax return preparation software and the IRS will provide assistance to resolve rejection notifications and facilitate acceptance of your e-filed return. However, in the rare event that you are unable to resolve the issues listed in the rejection notification, you will be required to submit the return in paper format. In order to timely file a paper return, you must file it by the later of the due date of the return (including extensions) or ten calendar days after the date the IRS rejects it. Again, there are many checks built into both the return preparation software and the IRS *e-file* process to locate errors before the final return is allowed to be transmitted, which makes IRS *e-file* returns virtually error-proof. The typical error rate for an e-filed return is less than 1%. IRS *e-file* greatly reduces the chance that you will later get a notice from the IRS.

Refunds

If you're due a refund, you can expect to receive it in approximately three weeks from the acknowledgment date—even faster if you choose the direct deposit method (possibly in as few as ten days if you both e-file and choose direct deposit of your refund). This is half the time as when filed on paper. The direct deposit method will enable you to direct your refund into up to three separate checking, savings, or other accounts (i.e., IRA, HSA, Archer MSA, Coverdell education savings account (ESA), or TreasuryDirect® online account) by providing the routing information for your financial institution and your bank account numbers. You can also request that your refund be used to buy up to $5,000 in paper U.S. Series I savings bonds. These requests are made using Form 8888, Allocation of Refund (Including Savings Bond Purchases).

Making Tax Payments

If you owe money, you can make payment in one of four convenient ways:

Option 1: By authorizing an electronic funds withdrawal from a checking or savings account. For electronic funds withdrawal, you include the routing information for your financial institution and your bank account number on the Form 1040 when you file electronically. You can designate the exact date (up to and including April 17, 2012) that you want the payment to be withdrawn (by the Department of Treasury financial agents) from either your checking or savings account at your bank,

Option 2: By credit card (American Express®, Discover®, MasterCard®, or VISA®) or debit card (Visa®, NYCE®, Pulse®, or Star® Debit Card), or

Option 3: By mailing a check or money order (made out to the United States Treasury) using Form 1040-V, Payment Voucher,

Option 4: By enrolling in the Electronic Federal Tax Payment System (EFTPS), which is a secure government website that allows users to make federal tax payments and schedule tax payments in advance conveniently 24/7 via the Internet. For more information on EFTPS go to the IRS website (*www.irs.gov*) and choose **"Make a payment"** under **"I Need To"** on the right-hand side of the website. Click on **"Electronic funds transfer"** under the heading **"How do I pay now?"** Note that you must enroll in the program before you utilize it. EFTPS allows individuals to schedule tax payments up to 365 days in advance of their due date and modifications to those payments can be made up to 2 business days in advance of the scheduled payment date.

One of the advantages of Options 1, 2, and 4 is that you receive an immediate acknowledgment when the IRS accepts your payment. A downside of using a credit or debit card is that the credit or debit card companies will charge a separate convenience fee for this service, in addition to any interest that might be charged on any outstanding credit card balance.

When to File and Pay Any Tax Due

If you use a tax professional, they can file your return electronically anytime during the filing season provided they have sufficient information from you to submit a complete and accurate return. However, sending the payment for a balance due by April 17, 2012, is still your responsibility. Your tax professional should advise you of the amount of any balance due by April 17, as well as provide you with Form 1040V, the voucher to transmit your payment to the IRS so that it is properly posted to your account, or discuss with you the alternative options to transmit your payment electronically as mentioned above. If you are not using a tax professional, you may file electronically as soon as you are ready and will receive a confirmation from the IRS within 48 hours of receipt of your return. All balance-due payments, regardless of method of payment, must be authorized or sent to the IRS by April 17, 2012, to avoid late payment penalties or interest charges. (The due date is actually April 17, 2012, because April 15, 2012, falls on Sunday, and the following day, April 16, is the Emancipation Day holiday in the District of Columbia, which is observed as a legal holiday.)

E-File for Your State Tax Returns

The option to e-file your state return (Federal/State e-file) is an extension of IRS *e-file* and is allowed in most states and the District of Columbia. However, not all Authorized IRS *e-file* providers offer this service. Your Authorized IRS *e-file* Provider can tell you if they participate in the Federal/State *e-file* program.

Extra Fees for E-Filing

The IRS does not charge a fee for electronic filing. However, some Authorized IRS *e-file* Providers (or Electronic Return Originators, "EROs") charge a fee for providing this service to their clients while others may offer it free of charge. This fee cannot be based on any figure from the tax return. Fees vary depending upon the tax professional you choose and the specific services you request.

With IRS *e-file* you can prepare your own return and pay a professional only to transmit it electronically, or you can pay to have your return both prepared and transmitted. Whichever you choose, shop around for a tax professional who offers the services you need at a cost acceptable to you.

Methods of E-Filing

There are three basic methods: using a tax professional, using your personal computer, and the IRS "Free File" option. We'll explain each of these methods in detail.

Tax Professional

Tax professionals who are accepted into the electronic filing program are called "Authorized IRS *e-file* Providers." In many cases, the tax professional is also the ERO who is authorized to file your return electronically with the IRS. If you've prepared your own return and are simply using a tax professional to transmit the return, the tax professional will need to convert the return into the appropriate format for e-filing.

Many tax professionals are mandated by the IRS to e-file eligible returns for their clients. To find a tax professional to file your return electronically, search online for the Authorized IRS *e-file* Provider nearest you or look in your local telephone directory under "Tax Return Preparation" for an Authorized IRS *e-file* Provider that meets your needs. Also, look for the "Authorized IRS *e-file* Provider" sign or decal in storefront windows.

Personal Computer

Instead of using the services of a tax professional, you can quickly and conveniently e-file your return using a personal computer. To do this you can:

- Purchase commercially available software,
- Download software from an Internet site and prepare your return offline, or
- Prepare and file your return online.

Note: The IRS cannot compete with private enterprise and does not offer free e-file software or direct filing. A number of companies, tested and approved by the IRS, do offer free use of their software and free filing, while others will charge nominal fees. Terms and conditions vary among companies and you are advised to review the information on each company's website and choose the product that is right for you.

Any way you choose, however, it's a simple process.

Who can file using a personal computer. Anyone can use this method of filing. Obviously, access to a personal computer is necessary. Software can be purchased, downloaded from the Internet, or accessed online.

Using this method, you prepare your tax return on a personal computer and transmit the information to the IRS. You can transmit up to five returns using tax preparation software, which enables you to prepare returns for family and friends with the same software and computer used for your return.

To actually e-file your return, the tax preparation software first converts your file to a format that meets IRS specifications and then transmits it to the IRS. The IRS checks the return and notifies the transmitter (who then informs you) whether the return has been accepted or rejected.

If your return is not accepted, the electronic return transmitter will provide you with customer support to correct your return and resubmit it.

Signing your return. You can sign the return using the Self-Select PIN, if you meet the eligibility requirements described earlier in this chapter. The IRS does not require you to mail your W-2 or any other form in hard copy, unless you are filing an item listed previously in the Supporting Documents section. Following the completion of your return, you should maintain copies of all items used in preparation and if applicable, copies of any documents sent to the IRS.

Extra fees for e-filing from a personal computer. The IRS does not charge a fee for e-file using a personal computer. However, an electronic return transmitter offering this service to taxpayers may charge a fee for transmission. Check out the IRS *e-file* Partners or Online Filing Software Companies listed at www.irs.gov to learn about free and low-cost e-file opportunities.

Payment methods and refunds. The same payment methods available using a tax professional are available with personal computer e-filing—check or money order, electronic funds withdrawal, credit or debit card, and EFTPS. Refunds should be in your savings or checking account within 2 weeks if you choose direct deposit, or in about 3 weeks if you choose a paper check. If you combine e-file with direct deposit, you could receive your refund in as few as 10 days.

If you have additional questions, you can also contact the IRS's toll-free customer service at 1-800-829-1040.

IRS Free File

This program began in 2003 and has been used to file more than 30 million returns to date.

Through a public-private partnership between the IRS and the tax software industry (i.e., Free File Alliance, LLC), you may access free, online tax preparation and electronic filing services through www.irs.gov. Eligible taxpayers may prepare and file their federal income tax returns using online software provided by the Free File Alliance companies—not the IRS.

The partnership agreement calls for the Free File Alliance to provide free tax preparation and filing to at least 70% of all taxpayers. Each participating software company has its own eligibility requirements.

The difference between Free File and the first two methods is that the entire filing process takes place online—there is no need to visit a tax professional or purchase or download software. You just input data while you're on the provider's website to complete your return.

Privacy and security concerns. Your tax information and data will be protected. To ensure your data's safety, the IRS requires participating companies to obtain both privacy and security seal certifications. These certification programs, administered by third-party providers, certify your tax return information is protected from unauthorized access during the tax preparation process. In addition:

- Tax return preparation is accomplished using proprietary software approved by the IRS; transmittal is through the established IRS *e-file* system.
- Alliance companies must comply with all federal rules and regulations on taxpayer privacy for paying and free customers. These rules prohibit use of tax return data for purposes not specifically authorized by the taxpayer.
- The IRS monitors the progress of each of the companies. If any problems develop, the companies are required to alert the IRS. If appropriate, the IRS will remove the company from the www.irs.gov website until the problem is resolved.

For more information, you should visit the company's privacy and security policy located on the company's website.

Step 1. How to Get Started: You start at the IRS website (www.irs.gov) and choose "e-file My Return for Free" under "I need to" on the right-hand side of the website. Click on "Option 2: Browse the list of Free File companies." The program can also be accessed through the IRS website at the following link: www.irs.gov/efile/article/0,,id=118986,00.html#moreinfo. You will go to a www.irs.gov Free File page where you may start your search for a Free File company.

Step 2. Determine Your Eligibility: You must first determine your eligibility for using a particular company. Each company has a simple description of its eligibility criteria for using its free service.

Step 3. Link to Free File Company Service: After choosing a company, click on the company's name, which sends you directly to the company's website (you will be notified you are leaving www.irs.gov and being sent to a commercial website). Follow the instructions on that company's website to begin the preparation of your tax return.

Alternatively, if you are having trouble choosing by scanning the list of Free File companies, you may want to use the interactive help tool. Choose "Option 2-Get Help finding a Free File company" to narrow down the possible companies offering free preparation and e-filing for you. Answer the questions and click "Submit."

If you are uncertain about your answers for the questions contained, you may want to view the complete list of companies and their services. The accuracy of the results is dependent on the accuracy of the information you provide in the tool.

Step 4. If You Do Not Qualify for the Selected Company's Free Offer: You may want to check other Free File company offers by accessing the www.irs.gov Free File page. If you are on the company's website, look for the link that takes you back to www.irs.gov and search for another Free File service. Go back and scan the listing of free company services as described in Step 3.

If you do **not** qualify for the company's free offer but continue with the preparation and e-filing process with this company, be aware you will be charged a fee for preparing and e-filing your federal tax return.

Example. If you select a company whose free services are provided to individuals with an adjusted gross income (AGI) of $26,000 or less and, based on your tax data, the company determines your AGI exceeds the $26,000 limit, you will be notified you may be subject to a fee. It is important you understand each of the company's eligibility criteria before selecting a company. You may find the fee by looking under "more details" next to the company's description on the Free File pages.

Step 5. Prepare and E-File Your Federal Income Tax Return: The company's software prepares and e-files your income tax returns using proprietary processes and systems right over the Internet. Electronically filed returns are transmitted by the company to the IRS using the established e-file system. An acknowledgment file, notifying you that the return has been either accepted or rejected, is sent via e-mail from the company.

Refunds and payments using Free File are handled the same way as they are for the other e-filing options.

Free File Fillable Forms. Beginning in 2009, the IRS started a program called "Free File Fillable Forms." This program opens up free online filing to everyone regardless of income level by providing the online equivalent of a paper return. All forms needed to prepare and electronically file your federal income tax return are available (state return forms are not available). The program can be accessed through the IRS website at the following link: *www.irs.gov/efile/article/0,,id=237156,00.html?Freefile=FFlink*.

Once you access the program, you may select the federal income Free File Fillable Forms and schedules you plan to submit, fill in the tax data, perform basic mathematical calculations, sign electronically, print for recordkeeping, and e-file your return. Most federal forms are available and can be used by 1040, 1040A, or 1040EZ filers. Please note, this program does not include questions or guidance that could assist you in preparation of your return. Free File Fillable Forms will be most helpful to those who are familiar with the tax law, know what forms they need to use, and do not need assistance to complete their returns. If you are not comfortable with this method, you may want to access the www.irs.gov Free File home page and check out the list of companies that offer free tax preparation assistance and e-filing services via the Free File program explained previously.

Chapter 46

If your return is examined

ey.com/EYTaxGuide

Note

ey.com/EYTaxGuide
Ernst & Young LLP will update the *Ernst & Young Tax Guide 2012* website with relevant taxpayer information as it becomes available. You can also sign up for email alerts to let you know when changes have been made.

Introduction

This chapter is probably not for you. Overall, the IRS examines only a small fraction of all tax returns that are filed. However, if you are contacted by the IRS about your tax return, this material may be very important to you. Just how important will depend on how carefully your return was prepared and the sources and amount of your income.

An IRS examination is nothing to be feared, if you have kept accurate records to support your deductions and all of your income has been reported. In most cases, IRS audits are rather routine. In fact, in about 25% of the cases, the IRS makes no changes or issues a refund. Whatever the result, you won't do yourself much good by making things difficult for the IRS. An IRS examiner has the legal power to force a taxpayer to produce books and records to complete the examination. The best strategy is almost invariably one of concluding the examination as quickly as possible by providing the facts needed and by meeting deadlines.

On the other hand, an IRS examination is nothing to take lightly. You should be prepared, and that preparation starts with keeping receipts and records, followed by careful preparation of your return. The IRS examiner must follow certain rules in conducting the examination. Since you'd be well advised to know what they are, this chapter tells you about them.

You will find a summary of your rights as a taxpayer at the beginning of this chapter. It may be especially helpful in cases that involve the delinquent payment of assessed taxes. This chapter tells you about your rights when your return is examined. You should know these rights, since they affect you and your pocketbook.

The first part of this section explains some of your most important rights as a taxpayer. The second part explains the examination, appeal, collection, and refund processes.

IRS Declaration of Taxpayer Rights

Protection of your rights. IRS employees will explain and protect your rights as a taxpayer throughout your contact with us.

Privacy and confidentiality. The IRS will not disclose to anyone the information you give us, except as authorized by law. You have the right to know why we are asking you for information, how we will use it, and what happens if you do not provide requested information.

Professional and courteous service. If you believe that an IRS employee has not treated you in a professional, fair, and courteous manner, you should tell that employee's supervisor. If the supervisor's response is not satisfactory, you should write to the IRS director for your area or the center where you file your return.

Representation. You may either represent yourself or, with proper written authorization, have someone else represent you in your place. Your representative must be a person allowed to practice before the IRS, such as an attorney, certified public accountant, or enrolled agent. If you are in an interview and ask to consult such a person, then we must stop and reschedule the interview in most cases.

You can have someone accompany you at an interview. You may make sound recordings of any meetings with our examination, appeal, or collection personnel, provided you tell us in writing 10 days before the meeting.

Payment of only the correct amount of tax. You are responsible for paying only the correct amount of tax due under the law—no more, no less. If you cannot pay all of your tax when it is due, you may be able to make monthly installment payments.

Help with unresolved tax problems. The Taxpayer Advocate Service can help you if you have tried unsuccessfully to resolve a problem with the IRS. Your local Taxpayer Advocate can offer you special help if you have a significant hardship as a result of a tax problem. For more information, call toll free 1-877-777-4778 (1-800-829-4059 for TTY/TDD) or write to the Taxpayer Advocate at the IRS office that last contacted you.

Appeals and judicial review. If you disagree with us about the amount of your tax liability or certain collection actions, you have the right to ask the Appeals Office to review your case. You may also ask a court to review your case.

Relief from certain penalties and interest. The IRS will waive penalties when allowed by law if you can show you acted reasonably and in good faith or relied on the incorrect advice of an IRS employee. We will waive interest that is the result of certain errors or delays caused by an IRS employee. While the IRS can waive or remove penalties based on reasonable cause, removal of most penalties is automatic if it is the first time you have incurred any penalties. You just have to ask the IRS to waive them. If you are not certain if you have had a penalty assessed on a prior return, you can contact the IRS and request an account transcript or ask the IRS assistor to check the account(s) for you and provide you with that information. There is no charge for this service. You can visit an IRS office where taxpayer assistance walk-in services are available or call the IRS on 1-800-829-1040 regarding individual tax returns and 1-800-829-4933 for business returns.

Examinations, Appeals, Collections, and Refunds

Examinations (Audits)

We accept most taxpayers' returns as filed. If we inquire about your return or select it for examination, it does not suggest that you are dishonest. The inquiry or examination may or may not result in more tax. We may close your case without change; or, you may receive a refund.

The process of selecting a return for examination usually begins in one of two ways. First, we use computer programs to identify returns that may have incorrect amounts. These programs may be based on information returns, such as Forms 1099 and W-2, on studies of past examinations, or on certain issues identified by compliance projects. Second, we use information from outside sources that indicates that a return may have incorrect amounts. These sources may include newspapers, public records, and individuals. If we determine that the information is accurate and reliable, we may use it to select a return for examination.

Publication 556, *Examination of Returns, Appeal Rights, and Claims for Refund,* explains the rules and procedures that we follow in examinations. The following sections give an overview of how we conduct examinations.

By mail. We handle many examinations and inquiries by mail. We will send you a letter with either a request for more information or a reason why we believe a change to your return may be needed. You can respond by mail or you can request a personal interview with an examiner. If you mail us the requested information or provide an explanation, we may or may not agree with you, and we will explain the reasons for any changes. Please do not hesitate to write to us about anything you do not understand.

By interview. If we notify you that we will conduct your examination through a personal interview, or you request such an interview, you have the right to ask that the examination take place at a reasonable time and place that is convenient for both you and the IRS. If our examiner proposes any changes to your return, he or she will explain the reasons for the changes. If you do not agree with these changes, you can meet with the examiner's supervisor.

Repeat examinations. If we examined your return for the same items in either of the 2 previous years and proposed no change to your tax liability, please contact us as soon as possible so we can see if we should discontinue the examination.

The Examination Process

The IRS examines returns for accuracy or correctness of income, exemptions, credits, deductions, and losses. Indeed, the IRS can examine any line item on the return.

Who Gets Audited?

The odds that your return will be examined by the IRS are, in fact, quite low. According to the most recent Treasury tables, the IRS examined only approximately 1% of all individual returns, down from about 5% in the mid-1960s. The odds shift substantially, depending on your income level and types of income.

TAXALERT

In 2007, the IRS received Congressional permission to study individual returns so that it can update the criteria it uses to select which tax returns it will audit. Less than 50,000 returns out of the 132 million individual returns filed will be sampled in the IRS study, known as the National Research Program (NRP). The results of the study will allow the IRS to update the statistical models it uses to assess the audit potential of various types of returns. The bottom line for individuals is that as a result of the study, your chances of being audited could increase.

TAXPLANNER

While IRS statistical models impact your chances of being audited, here is a list of some items or circumstances that also frequently draw the IRS's attention:

- Reported income does not agree with information on information returns, Forms 1099 and W-2 filed by the payor with the IRS.
- Married taxpayers filing separately. Many such taxpayers do not report items consistently between returns (e.g., itemized deductions, zero bracket or standard deduction amount elections).
- Returns with significant items that may trigger alternative minimum tax (e.g., significant miscellaneous itemized deductions and state, local, and property taxes).
- Taxpayers who may receive substantial cash payments in the normal course of business (e.g., doctors, lawyers, retail establishments, waiters, etc.).
- Deductions that seem unusually large compared to your income level.
- Total Schedule C (business income) gross receipts of $100,000 or more. According to one recent study, the IRS has concluded that individuals filing Schedule C are most likely not to report all business income or receipts.
- Large business expenses in relation to your income.
- A return submitted by an accountant or a tax preparer who is on an IRS list of problem preparers because they have repeatedly violated the law. The IRS has the power to conduct an examination of virtually all returns prepared by preparers who have been determined to be unscrupulous or have a proven history of filing returns with errors claiming large refunds.
- Complex investment or business transactions without clear explanations.
- Schedule F (farm) losses, particularly where the taxpayer has significant salary income.
- Earned income credit. Because there is the perception of potential abuse in this area, returns claiming the earned income credit are more closely scrutinized.
- Taxpayers' returns that fall in an area included in the IRS Market Segment Specialization Program (MSSP) such as automobile dealers, taxi services, air charters, attorneys, gas retailers, and others in a series of businesses or occupations that the IRS believes to need examination attention.

In addition, a local IRS district may undertake an Information Gathering Project (IGP) to more specifically focus on what they perceive as local compliance problems.

TAXALERT

The IRS is also realigning its audit resources to focus on key areas of noncompliance with the tax laws. This strategy represents a new direction for the agency's compliance effort. The new approach will focus on high-risk areas of noncompliance. The IRS effort will generally focus first on tax shelter or abusive scheme promoters and then on participants in these various schemes. The initiative will feature new and enhanced efforts in several priority areas, including:

- Offshore credit card users
- High-risk, high-income taxpayers
- Abusive schemes and promoter investigations
- High-income nonfilers
- Unreported income
- The National Research Program (NRP)

The strategy reflects a new way of doing business at the IRS. Several of these efforts–such as the National Research Program, described earlier in this chapter, and the credit card initiative–reflect innovative approaches to tackle long-standing tax problems.

Fairness If Your Return Is Examined

Only a small percentage of filed returns are actually examined by the IRS. But, even if your return is selected for examination, it does not suggest that you are dishonest. The inquiry or examination may or may not result in more tax. Your case may be closed without change or you may even receive a refund. The mission of the IRS is to determine the correct tax liability for returns examined, regardless of the outcome.

Courtesy and consideration. You are entitled to courteous and considerate treatment from IRS employees at all times. If you ever feel that you are not being treated with fairness, courtesy, and consideration by an IRS employee, you should ask to speak to the employee's supervisor. Publication 1, *Your Rights as a Taxpayer,* explains the many rights you have as a taxpayer. You can get free publications by calling 1-800-829-3676 or view them online at *www.irs.gov/pub/irs-pdf/p1.pdf.*

Your rights as a taxpayer. While the Taxpayer Bill of Rights does not break new legal ground, it does create a single document that informs you of your rights. It is useful to review it to be aware of the rights you have. A summary of the most important points follows.

Pay only the required tax. You have the right to plan your business and personal finances in such a way that you will pay the least tax that is due under the law. You are liable only for the correct amount of tax. The purpose of the IRS is to apply the law consistently and fairly to all taxpayers.

Privacy and confidentiality. You have the right to have your tax case kept confidential. Under the law, the IRS must protect the privacy of your tax information. However, if a lien or a lawsuit is filed, certain aspects of your tax case will become public record. People who prepare your return or represent you must also keep your information confidential.

You also have the right to know why the IRS is asking you for the information, exactly how the agency will use it, and what might happen if you do not give it. You also have the right to ask the question, "Why was my return selected for audit?" In most cases, however, the examiner will not know exactly why the return was selected, particularly if the return was selected as a result of an IRS computer-based statistical screening program that singles out certain items on your return.

Examination of Returns

An examination usually begins) when the IRS notifies you that your return has been selected. The IRS will tell you which records you will need. The initial contact can come in the form of a phone call followed by a confirmation letter or just a letter notifying you of the examination. If you gather your records and organize them before the examination, it can help speed the examination along with the least amount of effort.

How returns are selected. The IRS selects returns for examination by several methods.

1. **Discriminant Function System (DIF).** A computer program, developed under the National Research Program (NRP) called the Discriminant Function System (DIF) is used to select most returns for audit. Basically, DIF assigns a numerical value to certain items on your return. If the total of all the values equals or exceeds a minimum set by the IRS, the computer will single out the return for a possible audit. IRS agents or tax auditors will then check the return to see if it is worth the IRS's time to conduct an audit. This will depend on, among other things, staffing in your IRS district office. Even if your return is selected for an audit, it is likely that only specific items, such as charitable contributions or employee business expenses, would be examined, not your entire return.

It's a closely guarded secret what weight DIF assigns to which items. Some things this computer program is on the lookout for include:

- Large amounts of income not subject to withholding
- More deductions than seem to be reasonable for your income level
- Claims for an unusual number of dependency deductions as compared to withholding and other items on the return
- Discrepancies such as a change of address combined with deductions claimed for owning a residence when you have not reported that you sold your old residence

The DIF system is being used less as a selection source in recent years, especially in the case of Schedule C filers.

2. **Random selection.** Some returns are selected at random. The IRS uses the results of examining these returns to update and improve its selection process.
3. **Claims for credits and refunds.** The IRS also selects returns by examining claims for credit or refund and by matching information documents, such as Forms W-2 and the 1099 series, with returns.
4. **Information from outside sources.** Your return can be selected as a result of information received from other sources on potential noncompliance with the tax laws or inaccurate filing. This information can come from a number of sources, including the media, public records, or possibly informants. The information is evaluated for reliability and accuracy before it is used as the basis of an examination or investigation.
5. **The Market Segment Specialization Program (MSSP) and other special projects.** In 1991, the Internal Revenue Service began a project in the Los Angeles District Office focusing on developing highly trained revenue agents for a particular business market segment. Prior to this initiative, the IRS had not been training their revenue agents to be specialists within any certain business market segment. From that LA initiative, the IRS has expanded the program to cover more business market segments and has formally named the program the Market Segment Specialization Program (MSSP). The following is a list of these market segments:

Air charter
Alaska commercial fishing
Alaska placer gold mining
Architectural services
Art dealers
Attorneys
Auto body shops
Auto repair shops
Bail bondsmen
Bankruptcy
Beauty shops/barber shops
Bed & breakfast
Building maintenance services
Cable TV
Car washing and detailing
Casino gambling
Cattle
Check cashing establishments
Child care
Citrus industry
Commercial baking
Community banks
Construction/general building contractors
Construction industry
Cooperative housing corporations
Electronic components
Emergency care clinics
Employment tax–pizza drivers
Entertainment industry:
- Contracts–audit applications
- Foreign athletes and entertainers
- Motion pictures/television
- Music (Nashville)
- Theater–live performances

Escort service
Federal excise tax, coal mining
Financial institutions
Foreign tourism
Form 1042S withholding agents
Furniture manufacturing
Garment industry
Gas retailers
Golf courses
Grain and milo growers
Grocery stores
Health care
Insurance agencies
IRC Section 936 corporations
Jewelry dealers
Laundromat
Life insurance
Liquor stores
Low-income housing credit
Ministers
Mobile cart vendors
Mortuaries

Motor fuel tax
Nursing/rest homes
Offshore captive insurance co.
Oil and gas operators
Parking lots
Passive activity losses
Pawn shops
Petroleum contamination cleanup
Pizza parlors
Plastic surgeons
Port of Houston
Poultry
Printing
Real estate agents/brokers
Real estate developers
Recycling
Reforestation
Rehabilitation credit
Rent to own
Restaurants/bars/eating places
RTC project (forgiveness of debt)
Scrap metal
Seafood purchases
Selling door-to-door/telephone
Taxicabs
Timber sales
Time-sharing
Tobacco
Tour bus industry
Travel agency
Trucking industry
Used auto dealers
Wine industry

The scope of the MSSP will affect virtually every taxpayer who has a Schedule C attached to his or her return whose business operations come under one of the many business market segments. Once a business market segment is identified, the IRS issues detailed audit guidelines to their specialists as a guide to conduct an audit of the tax return. These guidelines will detail various issues and practices within a market segment that should be scrutinized by all revenue agents for potential adjustment. The IRS has issued formal audit guidelines to their examiners with respect to 27 market segments, including, but not limited to, gas retailers, attorneys, trucking, mortuaries, air charters, bed and breakfasts, taxicabs, the music industry, foreign athletes and entertainers, architectural services, bars and restaurants, mobile food vendors, resolution trust corporations, the wine industry, passive activity losses, and the rehabilitation credit.

In addition, the IRS initiates compliance projects on an area-by-area basis to identify areas of noncompliance which could also lead to your return being selected for examination. For example, one area examined all the drywall contractors in a major metro area and claims to have found widespread underreporting of gross receipts as well as nonfilers. Another area selected returns of individuals who had renegotiated loans and examined them to determine if they were subject to tax because an indebtedness had been forgiven.

Verification methods for proper payment. Besides the methods identified earlier that are used to select returns for examination and check the accuracy and proper reporting of tax, the IRS also uses several other methods and techniques to attempt to verify that the proper amount of tax is being paid by taxpayers:

1. **Document perfection.** Every return is checked for mathematical, tax calculation, and clerical errors in initial processing. If a mistake is discovered, a recalculation of the tax due and a notice of explanation are sent to the taxpayer. This procedure is not an audit—an important distinction.

   The IRS determines whether the return is in "processible form." The law lets the IRS avoid payment of interest on any refund until the return contains the taxpayer's name, address, identifying number, and required signature. Furthermore, the return must be on the permitted form and contain sufficient information to permit the mathematical verification of the tax liability shown on the return.

   The IRS has carried this to extremes by sending tax returns back to taxpayers for failing to check a box, not attaching all required forms, and not making alternative minimum tax computations when it is obvious no such action is due. While the IRS concentrates on refund returns with small errors that permit them to avoid large refunds, it has also sent balance-due returns back after depositing any checks attached. If the return is not perfected and returned before the due date, the IRS says the return is delinquent. The IRS has lost this issue in the Tax Court but persists in its position.
2. **Document-matching program.** The IRS matches the information supplied by your bank, your employer, and others on Forms W-2 and 1099 and other information documents with the information supplied on your return. If an item is omitted from your return or conflicts with what is reported to the IRS, the IRS computer will generate a notice that recalculates

your tax with corrections for the omitted income or overstated deduction. The Revenue Reconciliation Act of 1989 repealed the section of the tax law that gave the IRS the presumption of being correct in asserting a negligence penalty if you fail to report correctly relevant amounts reflected on information returns. The change applies to returns filed after December 31, 1989. It is probable that the IRS will continue to assert not only the negligence penalty but also the substantial understatement penalty. This procedure does not technically constitute a formal examination.

IRS service centers conduct other projects. Several service centers screened returns to determine if taxpayers who requested extensions of time to file were understating the tax that would be due. The IRS then treated extensions as invalid when the difference between the tax shown on the return and the extension exceeded certain tolerances.

3. **Economic reality audits.** Once an examination is started, the IRS instructs their examiners to examine the taxpayer, not just the return. This means that all information on the return and any additional internal information or documentation the IRS has access to is considered to assess an individual's financial status, particularly if the return includes a Schedule C or Schedule F business or farm operation. This often involves an examination of the taxpayer's lifestyle as an additional check on whether the taxpayer had unreported income. Areas of inquiry may include standard of living, accumulated wealth, economic history, business environment, and potential nontaxable income.

   Since the passage of the Internal Revenue Service Restructuring and Reform Act of 1998, economic reality audits have been severely restricted. These audit techniques were extremely intrusive and their use has been limited to situations where the IRS already has indications of unreported income. However, if the IRS does have indications of unreported income or if a taxpayer's income appears to be insufficient to support his or her lifestyle, the examiner is authorized to dig deeper into the apparent discrepancy or issue. In these cases, the examiners have been instructed to discuss their concerns with the taxpayer and give him or her an opportunity to explain and/or resolve any discrepancies. However, due to the potential serious nature of this type of issue, the well-informed taxpayer should consider contacting a tax advisor. Because of the delicate balance between what is and what is not a proper subject of inquiry of the IRS examiner, some care should be exercised.

   If your return reflects losses from Schedule C or F operations that reduce overall income to near or below zero, there is a good chance the auditor will consider an economic reality type of examination. If the auditor begins questioning personal living expense amounts, bank account and loan balances at the beginning and end of the year, you can probably assume that an economic reality audit is under way. If this is the case, the auditor will be working toward determining all sources of funds, both taxable and non-taxable (i.e., gifts, loans, etc.), as well as all personal and business expenses incurred during the year. The auditor will then compare the total amount spent during the year to the total sources of funds, and if the expenditures exceed the identified sources of funds, the auditor is within his or her authority to propose adding the difference to income as "unreported income." If that does happen, you would be advised to seek assistance from your tax preparer or other representative.

Arranging the examination. Many examinations are handled by mail. However, if the IRS notifies you that your examination is to be conducted through a personal interview, or if you request an interview, you have the right to ask that the examination take place at a reasonable time and place that are convenient for both you and the IRS. If the time or place the IRS suggests is not convenient, the examiner will try to work out something more suitable. However, the IRS will make the final determination on how, when, and where an examination takes place. The difference between the correspondence and office audit is as follows:

Correspondence audit. After a tax return is initially selected for examination, the IRS may first conduct a correspondence audit, requesting that documentation of a specific item on your tax return be submitted by mail. If it is more convenient, you may request that the audit be held at the IRS's local district office. However, by law, the IRS has the right to make the final decision on where and how an examination will be conducted, as long as it is not unreasonable in exercising its discretion. The Taxpayer Bill of Rights directed the IRS to publish regulations defining reasonable time and place. These regulations were published in temporary form, effective June 4, 1990.

Office audit. If the examination is conducted at an IRS office, its scope may be expanded to cover all questionable items. Although correspondence audits may be resolved more quickly than examinations conducted at an IRS office, there is no rule of thumb for which type of audit would be more beneficial to you. However, it is generally to your disadvantage to request that a correspondence audit be changed to an office audit or a field audit. Correspondence audits are limited in scope. If you request an interview audit at an IRS office or an audit at your place of business, you open up the opportunity for the examiner to question other items.

The easier you make the IRS's job, the less the amount of time required to conclude the audit and the greater the likelihood that you will avoid any arbitrary adjustments.

An examination verifies the accuracy of your tax liability on a specific item as reported on a tax return, claim, or other filing. An examination is generally limited to the study of those matters bearing directly on the tax question at hand. The IRS has the authority to examine information that may not appear to be directly related to your tax liability. For example, the IRS may study your living expenses to determine if your reported income can support your lifestyle or whether you may have unreported income.

Transfers to another district. Generally, your individual return is examined in the IRS district office nearest your home. However, not all offices have examination facilities. Your business return is examined where your books and records are maintained. If the place of examination is not convenient, you may ask to have the examination done in another office or transferred to a different district.

Representation. Throughout the examination, you may represent yourself, have someone else accompany you, or, with proper written authorization, have someone represent you in your absence. If you want to consult an attorney, an enrolled agent, a CPA, or any other person permitted to represent a taxpayer during an examination, the auditor has the latitude to schedule the audit appointment to allow sufficient time for you to contact your tax preparer or representative to assist you with the audit. If the examination has started and you become uncomfortable with the way the audit appears to be going, you still have time to consult with your tax preparer or representative, even if you have not had them involved in the process previously. The IRS can stop and reschedule the interview or appointment. The IRS will generally not suspend the interview if you are there because of an administrative summons.

If you use Form 8821, Tax Information Authorization, to name a representative for you, the representative is only authorized to receive information and cannot fully represent you by taking action on the information. If you use Form 2848, Power of Attorney, to name your representative, the representative is fully authorized to represent you and take any action necessary, including signing an agreement for a deficiency or overassessment of tax to conclude the case.

In recent years, some districts and some examiners have been very aggressive in demanding that the taxpayer, even though represented by a qualified practitioner with a power of attorney, appear personally to answer questions. This practice was admittedly to probe for unreported income and to establish if the taxpayer's lifestyle might suggest other problems in compliance with tax laws. The Taxpayer Bill of Rights now specifies that the IRS "may not require a taxpayer to accompany the representative in the absence of an administrative summons," and a properly qualified practitioner with a power of attorney is authorized to represent a client in any interview without the taxpayer's presence, except for criminal cases or matters involving the integrity of an IRS employee. Furthermore, the law specifies that "if a taxpayer clearly states at any time during an interview," except where an administrative summons has been enforced or accepted, "that the taxpayer wishes to consult with an attorney, certified public accountant, enrolled agent, enrolled actuary, or any other person permitted to represent the taxpayer," the IRS "shall suspend such interview, regardless of whether the taxpayer may have answered one or more questions."

TAXPLANNER

Do you need professional help? The answer is: It depends on the issues involved and your ability to represent yourself. If the amounts involved are small, it may not be worth it to pay for an advisor's time. If your return was prepared by a certified public accountant or a lawyer, you will want to inquire whether his or her fee included representing you at an audit. If it didn't and you want him or her to represent you, you should agree on a fee at the beginning of the process. You will certainly want an accountant or a lawyer to represent you if (1) the law involved in the audit is unclear or complicated, (2) highly technical supporting information may be required, (3) you think other issues may come up, or (4) you are too nervous or emotionally involved to handle the matter yourself.

Tape recording meetings with the IRS. You can generally make an audio recording of an interview with an IRS examination officer. Your request to record the interview should be made in writing. You must notify the IRS at least 10 days before the meeting and bring your own recording equipment. The IRS also can record an interview. If the IRS initiates the recording, it will notify you 10 days before the meeting, and you can get a copy of the recording at your expense.

Repeat examinations. The IRS tries to avoid repeat examinations of the same items, but sometimes this happens. If the IRS examines your tax return for the same items in either of the 2 previous years and proposed no change to your tax liability, you should contact the IRS as soon as possible so that the agency can see if it should discontinue the examination.

Generally, in connection with auditing your return for a particular year, the IRS may inspect your books only once. But there may be a second examination if you request it or if the IRS notifies you in writing that an additional audit is necessary. A further investigation could be considered necessary simply if the IRS suspects that additional tax is owed. You may refuse the IRS's request to make a second examination. In fact, if you do not object, you have, in effect, given your consent for the examination to take place. If you refuse to produce records, the IRS must issue a summons. If you still resist, the IRS will be forced to obtain court assistance to enforce the summons.

The ban on second examinations does not apply:

1. When the original audit, although prolonged and characterized by IRS staffing changes, is still going on.
2. When the examination is not considered an examination as such (e.g., when the IRS contacts you to verify the amount of dividends or interest on your return because that figure does not match what was otherwise reported).
3. When the second examination is for a different kind of tax (e.g., employment or excise tax, instead of income tax) than was dealt with in the first examination.
4. When a mere visual inspection of the return has taken place, not an examination of your books and records.
5. In cases involving the year of deduction of a net operating loss carryback (or similar type of carryback).
6. In cases in which there have been involuntary conversions and the taxpayer has not recomputed the tax liability after the replacement period has expired.

In summary, it is difficult for the IRS to justify a second examination of your books and records for the same year, but if there is a legitimate reason to do so, the IRS is usually within its rights. However, if your return has been examined and you have received a final closing letter indicating that no changes were made nor any additional tax or refund was due, the IRS is required to undertake a formal re-opening of the return for examination. Permission for such a formal re-opening is difficult for an examiner to obtain. In any case, it is important that you keep all correspondence from the IRS, especially if your return was examined.

Explanation of changes. If the IRS proposes any changes to your return, it will explain the reasons for the changes. It is important that you understand the reasons for any proposed change. You should not hesitate to ask about anything that is unclear to you.

Agreement with changes. If you agree with the proposed changes, you may sign an agreement form and pay any additional tax you may owe. You must pay interest on any additional tax. If you pay when you sign the agreement, the interest is generally figured from the due date of your return to the date you paid.

The IRS uses misleading language when it describes this consent form as an "agreement form." When you sign a Form 870 or Form 4549, you are simply permitting the IRS to make its assessment of tax without waiting 90 days, as required by law, and you are forfeiting your right to go to the Tax Court. You are not bound to follow the IRS position in subsequent years and may even file a claim for a refund for the years covered by the Form 870 after the tax has been paid.

If you do not pay the additional tax when you sign the agreement, you will receive a bill. The interest on the additional tax is generally figured from the due date of your return to the billing date. However, you will not be billed for more than 30 days' additional interest, even if the bill is delayed. Also, you will not have to pay any additional interest or penalties if you pay the amount due within 10 days of the billing date.

If you are due a refund, the IRS can refund your money more quickly if you sign the agreement form. You will be paid interest on the refund.

An IRS examiner's authority. An IRS examiner has virtually unlimited authority to determine the facts. Since most examination issues concern factual matters, the examiner has considerable discretion in accepting secondary evidence and in deciding what constitutes acceptable proof. On technical legal issues, though, he or she must adhere to established IRS policy. Therefore, even if certain court cases support your argument, the examiner must disallow it if the IRS has decided not to follow the precedents established by these cases.

In theory, IRS examiners are also not permitted to trade off items, letting you take one deduction in return for disallowing another. In practice, negotiations with the IRS are commonplace.

An important reminder. IRS examiners are under considerable pressure to close cases by reaching an agreement at the initial examination. An agent is given high marks for explaining the IRS position in a convincing manner. Contrary to popular belief, examiners are not rated by the amount of money they bring in or by the number of cases they close.

While all examination reports have a chance of being reviewed, except for cases that fall into a mandatory review category, the review is on a sample basis, so only a small percentage of cases are actually reviewed. The mandatory categories include cases involving refunds in excess of $2 million, tax shelters, NRP, and fraud. All unagreed cases are subject to a limited review on receipt of a protest asking for an Appeals hearing. This review is primarily focused on perfecting the IRS case based on your arguments in the protest. An examination of your return is not complete, however, until you receive a "closing" letter from the IRS. Even if the agent completes the examination and you agree and pay any tax due, the examination results will still be reviewed by the examiner's manager or further up the line by a "quality reviewer." These reviewers can still send the case back to the agent to correct any problem identified.

Appeals

If you do not agree with the examiner's proposed changes, you can appeal them to the Appeals Office of the IRS. Most differences can be settled without expensive and time-consuming court trials. Your appeal rights are explained in detail in both Publication 5, *Your Appeal Rights and How to Prepare a Protest If You Don't Agree*, and Publication 556, *Examination of Returns, Appeal Rights, and Claims for Refund.*

If you do not wish to use the Appeals Office or disagree with its findings, you may be able to take your case to the U.S. Tax Court, U.S. Court of Federal Claims, or the U.S. District Court where you live. If you take your case to court, the IRS will have the burden of proving certain facts if you kept adequate records to show your tax liability, cooperated with the IRS, and meet certain other conditions. If the court agrees with you on most issues in your case and finds that our position was largely unjustified, you may be able to recover some of your administrative and litigation costs. You will not be eligible to recover these costs unless you tried to resolve your case administratively, including going through the appeals system, and you gave us the information necessary to resolve the case.

EXPLANATION

Appealing the Examination Findings

If you and the IRS auditor reach an agreement on the issue under examination, the auditor will be on your side if his or her report is reviewed by his or her boss.

If you do not agree with the examiner's report, you can meet with the examiner's supervisor to discuss your case further. If you still do not agree after receiving the examiner's findings, you have the right to appeal them. The examiner will explain your appeal rights and give you a copy of Publication 5, *Your Appeal Rights and How to Prepare a Protest If You Don't Agree*. This free publication explains your appeal rights in detail and tells you exactly what to do if you want to appeal.

The IRS now offers fast-track mediation services to help taxpayers resolve many disputes. Most cases that are not docketed in any court qualify for fast-track mediation. Mediation can take place as early as the conference you requested with the examiner's supervisor. The process involves an Appeals Officer who has been trained in mediation.

If you disagree with the IRS. If you and the IRS examiner disagree over the proper interpretation of a point of law, either you or the examiner may request technical advice from the IRS national office. Technical advice will be given only if the issue is unusual or complex, or if there is a lack of uniformity within the IRS about its treatment. If you ask for technical advice and the examiner denies the request, you may appeal to the Territory Manager and Area Director for your area. If he or she also denies the request and you disagree with the denial, all data will be forwarded to the national office for review. Action on the disputed issue generally will be suspended until it is decided whether or not technical advice will be issued.

Technical disagreements may be resolved by taking them to the agent's supervisor. However, this course of action is not recommended unless you are absolutely certain you are correct. The supervisor could point out an alternative position that might be more favorable to the examining agent.

Appeals. There is a single level of administrative appeal within the IRS. You make your appeal about the findings of the examiner to the Appeals Office in your region. Appeals conferences are conducted as informally as possible.

If you want an appeals conference, address your request to your Area Director according to the instructions in the IRS letter to you. Your case will be forwarded to the Appeals Office, which will arrange for a conference at a convenient time and place. You or your representative should be prepared to discuss all disputed issues and to present your views at this meeting in order to save the time and expense of additional conferences. Most differences are resolved at this level.

If agreement is not reached at your appeals conference, you may, at any stage of the proceedings, take your case to court. See *Appeals to the courts*, later.

Written protests. Along with your request for a conference, you may be required to file a written protest with your District Director.

You do not have to file a written protest if:

1. The proposed increase or decrease in tax, or claimed refund, is not more than $25,000 for any of the tax periods involved.
2. Your examination was conducted by correspondence or in an IRS office by a tax auditor.

To request an appeal, follow the instructions in the letter to you by sending a letter requesting Appeals consideration, indicating the changes you don't agree with and the reasons why you don't agree.

If a written protest is required, you should send it within the period granted in the letter that you received with the examination report. Your protest should contain all of the following:

1. A statement that you want to appeal the findings of the examiner to the Appeals Office
2. Your name and address and a daytime phone number
3. The date and symbols from the letter, showing the adjustments and findings you are protesting
4. The tax periods or years involved
5. An itemized schedule of the adjustments with which you do not agree and why you do not agree
6. A statement of facts supporting your position in any issue with which you do not agree
7. A statement outlining the law or other authority on which you rely

You must sign the written protest, stating that it is true, under penalties of perjury as follows:

"Under the penalties of perjury, I declare that I have examined the facts stated in this protest and in any accompanying schedules and, to the best of my knowledge and belief, they are true, correct, and complete."

If your representative submits the protest for you, he or she may substitute a declaration stating the following:

1. That he or she prepared the protest and accompanying documents
2. Whether he or she knows personally that the statement of facts contained in the protest and accompanying documents is true and correct

Representation. You may represent yourself at your appeals conference, or you may be represented by an attorney, a certified public accountant, or a person enrolled to practice before the IRS.

If your representative attends a conference without you, he or she may receive or inspect confidential information only if a power of attorney or a tax information authorization has been filed. Form 2848, Power of Attorney and Declaration of Representative, or Form 8821, Tax Information Authorization, or any other properly written power of attorney or authorization may be used for this purpose.

You may also bring witnesses to support your position. You should consider consulting an attorney specializing in tax law before you do this.

Bargaining with the IRS. Whereas an IRS examiner must follow established IRS policy on statutory and procedural points, the appeals officer may bargain with you. He or she may consider whether litigation is worthwhile, given the strength of the views at odds with the IRS's position. If you make an unsuitable good faith settlement offer, the appeals officer may reject it but indicate a settlement he or she would recommend be accepted. In arriving at a figure, the appeals officer may calculate the chances of the IRS prevailing in court. Generally, however, the IRS will not settle a case just because it is a nuisance to continue to pursue it.

Appeals officers do not have final settlement authority in all cases and for all issues. Accordingly, it is good practice in negotiating a settlement to ask the appeals officer if any part of a settlement proposed is subject to a supervisory review.

If no agreement can be reached at the appeals conference, you have two options:

1. Pay the additional tax generated by the disputed issue and sue for the refund of this payment in your District Court or the U.S. Court of Federal Claims (formerly the U.S. Claims Court; see *Appeals to the courts*, later).
2. Wait for the arrival of your closing letter and select a course of action at that point. If you do not pay the disputed amount, you will receive from the IRS a notice of deficiency, which is also known as a 90-day letter. This notice authorizes you to file a petition in the U.S. Tax Court without first having to pay the tax. A Tax Court suit may not be filed before receipt of the 90-day letter.

TAXPLANNER

Partnerships and S corporations. Special procedures apply to certain partnerships and S corporations. The amount of any adjustment is determined at the partnership or S corporation level. The procedures are complex, regular statutory notices are not issued, and you should consult a professional if you want to contest a partnership or S corporation issue raised in the examination of your return.

Appeals to the Courts

Depending on whether you first pay the disputed tax, you can take your case to the U.S. Tax Court, the U.S. Court of Federal Claims, or your U.S. District Court. These courts are entirely independent of the IRS. However, a U.S. Tax Court case is generally reviewed by an Appeals Office before it is heard by the Tax Court. As always, you can represent yourself or have someone admitted to practice before the court represent you.

Tax Court. If your case involves a disagreement over whether you owe additional income tax, estate tax, gift tax, windfall profit tax on domestic crude oil, certain excise taxes of private foundations, public charities, qualified pension and other retirement plans, or real estate investment trusts, you may take it to the U.S. Tax Court. For you to appeal your case to the Tax Court, the IRS must first issue a formal letter, called a *notice of deficiency.* You have 90 days from the date this notice is mailed to you to file a petition with the Tax Court (150 days if it is addressed to you outside the United States). If you do not file your petition within the 90 or 150 days, you lose your opportunity to appeal to the Tax Court.

Generally, the Tax Court hears cases only if the tax has not been assessed and paid; however, you may pay the tax after the notice of deficiency has been issued and still petition the Tax Court for review. You must be sure that your petition to the Tax Court is filed on time. If it is not, the proposed liability will be automatically assessed against you. Once the tax is assessed, a notice of tax due (a bill) will be sent to you, and you may no longer take your case to the Tax Court. Once the assessment has been made, collection of the full amount due may proceed, even if you believe that the assessment was excessive. Publication 594, *What You Should Know About the IRS Collection Process*, explains IRS collection procedures.

If you filed your petition on time, the Tax Court will schedule your case for trial at a location that is convenient to you. You may represent yourself before the Tax Court, or you may be represented by anyone admitted to practice before the Tax Court.

If your case involves a dispute of not more than $50,000 for any 1 tax year, the Tax Court provides a simple alternative for resolving disputes. At your request, and with the approval of the Tax Court, your case may be handled under the small case procedures, whereby you can present your own case to the Tax Court for a binding decision. If your case is handled under this procedure, the decision of the Tax Court is final and cannot be appealed. You can get more information about the small case procedures and other Tax Court matters from the U.S. Tax Court, 400 Second Street, N.W., Washington, D.C. 20217.

TAXALERT

Representing yourself. Since many taxpayers represent themselves in small cases, the IRS has a very high win record. Filing your own petition may not be a good idea, especially if the amount is substantial to you. In any event, be careful in following the instructions *to the letter,* especially regarding the date for filing, the required fee, and the address of the Tax Court. The date of mailing a petition to the Tax Court is the filing date, but you should use certified mail and carefully retain the receipt with a legible postmark.

District Court and U.S. Court of Federal Claims. Generally, the District Court and the U.S. Court of Federal Claims hear tax cases only after you have paid the tax and have filed a claim for a credit or a refund. As explained later under *Claims for Refund*, you may file a claim for a credit or a refund with the IRS if, after you pay your tax, you believe that the tax is incorrect or too high. If your claim is rejected, you will receive a notice of disallowance of the claim, unless you signed a Form 2297, Waiver of Statutory Notification of Claim Disallowance. If the IRS has not acted on your claim within 6 months from the date on which you filed it, you may then file suit for refund. You must file suit for a credit or a refund no later than 2 years after the IRS disallows your claim or a Form 2297 is issued.

You may file your credit or refund suit in your U.S. District Court or in the U.S. Court of Federal Claims. However, the U.S. Court of Federal Claims does not have jurisdiction if your claim was filed after July 18, 1984, and is for credit or refund of a penalty that relates to promoting an abusive tax shelter or to aiding and abetting the understatement of tax liability on someone else's return.

For information about procedures for filing suit in either court, contact the Clerk of your U.S. District Court or the Clerk of the U.S. Court of Federal Claims. The addresses of the District Courts and the U.S. Court of Federal Claims are in Publication 556, *Examination of Returns, Appeal Rights, and Claims for Refund.*

Before you file suit. Here are some of the factors that you might want to consider before you decide to file your suit in Tax Court, District Court, or the U.S. Court of Federal Claims:

1. Which court has most recently arrived at favorable rulings on similar disputed issues.
2. The amount of tax involved. You may file a suit in Tax Court without paying the IRS the amount it claims you owe. If the tax has already been paid and you wish to file suit to obtain a refund, the U.S. District Court and the U.S. Court of Federal Claims are your only choices. However, to stop the accumulation of interest, you can at any time make a deposit in the nature of a cash bond of the tax that an examiner says you owe. *Note:* Such a remittance must be clearly labeled as a deposit. If you are successful in an appeal, you will draw no interest on the deposits returned. A deposit does not prevent you from going to the Tax Court. Once you file a suit in Tax Court, you may then pay the alleged tax deficiency and your suit will not be thrown out of court. If you do make the payment at this point in the process, you will not be liable for interest charges past the payment date. If you win, the government will then owe you interest from the date on which you made the payment. A deposit will be converted to a payment of the tax when you file a petition with the Tax Court. It is important to distinguish between payments of tax and deposits to stop the accumulation of interest.
3. Jury trials are available only in the District Courts. If your case rests on a question of equity, rather than on a finer point of tax law, a jury might be more responsive to your arguments. Remember, however, that both parties may appeal a District Court or a Tax Court decision.
4. A representative who is not an attorney may appear before the Tax Court if admitted to practice before that court.
5. Filing a suit before the Tax Court suspends the statute of limitation for assessment on the tax return that you are contesting. Consequently, if the IRS chooses, it could raise new issues and assert additional tax while your case is pending in court.
6. You're more likely to avoid embarrassing publicity before the Court of Federal Claims. The U.S. Court of Federal Claims is located in Washington, D.C. There is a U.S. District Court near your hometown. The Tax Court tries cases on a circuit-riding basis in most major cities.
7. You may file suit in Tax Court within 90 days (150 days if outside the United States) after the IRS issues a statutory notice of deficiency. You have more time to file before the U.S. District Court and the U.S. Court of Federal Claims.
8. In Tax Court, attorneys from the Office of Chief Counsel represent the IRS. In District Court and U.S. Court of Federal Claims, attorneys from the Tax Division of the Department of Justice will oppose your case.
9. Tax Court and District Court cases are appealed to the Circuit Court of Appeals and then to the Supreme Court. U.S. Court of Federal Claims decisions may be appealed to the Court of Appeals for the Federal Circuit and then to the Supreme Court.
10. Any court of the United States may now award attorney's fees and other costs for cases initiated after December 31, 1985, including certain costs incurred in an administrative appeal if the IRS's position was not substantially justified.

Recovering litigation expenses. If the court agrees with you on most of the issues in your case and finds the IRS's position to be largely unjustified, you may be able to recover some of your litigation expenses from the IRS. But to do this, you must have used up all the administrative remedies available to you within the IRS, including going through the appeals system. You may also be able to recover administrative expenses from the IRS. Free Publication 556, *Examination of Returns, Appeal Rights, and Claims for Refund*, explains your appeal rights.

The Taxpayer Bill of Rights corrects an inequity in prior law by permitting the courts to award costs, not only for litigating but also for administrative proceedings once a taxpayer's administrative appeal rights have been exhausted and a "notice of decision" by the IRS or a statutory notice of deficiency has been issued, whichever occurs earlier. The prior law had been interpreted to permit recovery only after the IRS's attorneys had taken a position before the courts. To recover, a taxpayer must substantially prevail through a determination in an administrative proceeding, after the point specified previously, or in a court of law and must establish that the position of the United States in the proceeding was not substantially justified. In collection matters, when neither notice is issued, only litigation costs are recoverable.

Reasonable administrative costs include the following:

- Fees or charges imposed by the IRS
- Reasonable expert witness fees
- Reasonable costs of studies and analyses
- Costs associated with engineering or test reports
- Reasonable fees (generally not in excess of $150 per hour) for a qualified representative of the taxpayer in connection with the administrative action

Collections

Publication 594, *What You Should Know About the IRS Collection Process,* explains your rights and responsibilities regarding payment of federal taxes. It describes:

- What to do when you owe taxes. It describes what to do if you get a tax bill and what to do if you think your bill is wrong. It also covers making installment payments, delaying collection action, and submitting an offer in compromise.
- IRS collection actions. It covers liens, releasing a lien, levies, releasing a levy, seizures and sales, and release of property.

Your collection appeal rights are explained in detail in Publication 1660, *Collection Appeal Rights.*

Innocent spouse relief. Generally, both you and your spouse are responsible, jointly and individually, for paying the full amount of any tax, interest, or penalties due on your joint return. However, if you qualify for innocent spouse relief, you may be relieved of all or part of the joint liability. To request relief, you must file Form 8857, Request for Innocent Spouse Relief, no later than 2 years after the date on which the IRS first attempted to collect the tax from you. The 2-year period for filing your claim may start if the IRS applies your tax refund from one year to the taxes that you and your spouse owe for another year. For more information on innocent spouse relief, see Publication 971, *Innocent Spouse Relief,* and Form 8857.

Potential Third Party Contacts

Generally, the IRS will deal directly with your or your duly authorized representative. However, the IRS can and will sometimes talk with other persons if it needs information that you have been unable to provide, or to verify information it has received. If the IRS intends to contact third parties for information on you, they are required to give notice to you that they intend to do so. The examiner may contact other persons, such as a neighbor, bank, employer, or employees to verify or gather information needed to complete the examination. The law prohibits the IRS from disclosing any more information than is necessary to obtain or verify the information it is seeking. The IRS's need to contact other persons may continue as long as there is activity in your case. If the IRS does contact other persons, you may have a right to request a list of those contacted.

Claims for Refunds

You may file a claim for refund if you think you paid too much tax. You must generally file the claim within 3 years from the date you filed your original return or 2 years from the date you paid the tax, whichever is later. The law generally provides for interest on your refund if it is not paid within 45 days of the date you filed your return or claim for refund. Publication 556, *Examination of Returns, Appeals Rights, and Claims for Refund,* has more information on refunds.

If you were due a refund but you did not file a return, you must file within 3 years from the date the return was originally due to get that refund.

EXPLANATION

If you believe that tax, penalty, or interest was unjustly charged, you have rights that can remedy the situation.

Claims for refund. Once you have paid your tax, you have the right to file a claim for a credit or refund if you believe the tax is too much. Be aware that informal claims that mention vague and general future possibilities to justify a refund will not be considered valid. The procedure for filing a claim is explained in chapter 1, *Filing information*.

If you do file a claim, you should keep all support or documentation used when the claim was prepared. In the event you are notified by the IRS that the claim will be examined, you will need to provide the documentation to support the claim upon request. The IRS will not allow time for you to gather the documentation requested. The IRS's position is that if you filed a claim, you had to have a basis for filing the claim and that should have been adequate support at that time and should not have to have time to gather the documentation. You will generally be given only one opportunity to provide the requested information and if you can't provide it within a reasonable amount of time, the claim will be disallowed and you will not receive the requested refund.

Some courts have held that an informal claim for a refund will, under certain circumstances, prevent the statutory period from expiring before you can accumulate and submit all your data. An informal claim should be in writing, should notify the IRS that a right to a refund is being asserted, and should tell as fully as possible the reasons why you feel the refund would be valid. A formal claim for the refund filed on official IRS forms should be made as soon as practical thereafter.

If you file with the wrong IRS center. If you file an amended return with the wrong IRS Service Center, it is under no obligation to forward that return to the correct Service Center. If you do not hear from the IRS within 6 months of filing Form 1040X, you should make a point of contacting it to determine the source of the delay.

Claims (Form 1040X) should always ask for a specific dollar amount or "for such greater amount as is legally refundable" to ensure that you receive a refund of interest and interest on such interest where appropriate.

Cancellation of penalties. You have the right to ask that certain penalties (but not interest, as discussed later) be canceled (abated) if you can show reasonable cause for the failure that led to the penalty (or can show that you exercised due diligence, if that is the standard for the penalty).

If you relied on wrong advice from IRS employees given to you by phone, the agency will cancel certain penalties that may result. But you have to show that your reliance on the advice was reasonable.

Reduction of interest. If the IRS's error caused a delay in your case, and this is grossly unfair, you may be entitled to a reduction of the interest that would otherwise be due. Only delays caused by procedural or mechanical acts that do not involve exercising judgment or discretion qualify. If you think the IRS caused such a delay, please discuss it with the examiner and file a claim.

TAXSAVER

If the IRS makes an error. If the IRS made an error, sent you a refund check, and then made you pay interest when you repaid it, you can strike back. According to the Tax Reform Act of 1986, the IRS may not charge you interest from the date of the erroneous refund to the date they demanded you repay it. The law has also given the IRS the discretion to refund or abate excessive interest that you may have paid on an underpayment of your tax if an IRS employee was dilatory or made an error in processing it. To qualify, you must not have caused the error in any way. The erroneous refund must have been less than $50,000. Use Form 843 to file your claim.

Past-Due Taxes

The Taxpayer Bill of Rights recognized that taxpayers occasionally may have problems paying taxes due on their returns because of unanticipated changes on examination or other unexpected difficulties. To ensure fair treatment, the Taxpayer Bill of Rights made some changes in how notices are issued, how much time is allowed for payment, how taxpayers can get help, and so on. The key provisions relating to past-due taxes are as follows:

1. The period from when the IRS provides written notice to a taxpayer to the first permissible date on which the IRS can levy on bank accounts, wages, and so on is increased from 10 days to 30 days. The IRS also cannot levy on property on any day on which the person appears before the IRS in response to a summons, unless the IRS determines the collection of the tax is in jeopardy. In addition, financial institutions are required to hold accounts garnished by the IRS for 21 days after receipt of the notice of levy.
2. The IRS established a formal system for the appeal of liens similar to that existing in the income tax deficiency area. The appeals procedures are printed on the notice of lien. See Publication 1660, *Collection Appeal Rights.*
3. The IRS now has the legal right to enter into installment agreements with taxpayers so that they can more easily pay delinquent taxes. The agreement will remain in effect unless the taxpayer has provided inaccurate information, does not pay an installment when it is due,

fails to respond to a reasonable request for updated financial information, or the collection of the balance is in jeopardy. In addition, the IRS may only modify or terminate an agreement if the taxpayer's financial condition has significantly changed. Notification of the reason for the action has to be given at least 30 days prior to any action.

4. The Taxpayer Advocate is authorized to issue a taxpayer assistance order (TAO) in any situation in which the taxpayer is suffering or about to suffer a significant hardship as a result of the manner in which the IRS laws are being administered. During the period in which the order is in effect, the statute of limitations is suspended and any further IRS action is halted. Only the Commissioner, Deputy Commissioner, or Taxpayer Advocate can modify or rescind the order. The Taxpayer Advocate administers the IRS Problem Resolution Program, which was created to resolve problems not remedied through normal operating channels.

One avenue for possible resolution of issues is to contact the Taxpayer Advocate Office (TAO). In 1996, the Taxpayer Bill of Rights established the Office of the Taxpayer Advocate and described its function as:

1. To assist taxpayers in resolving problems with the Internal Revenue Service;
2. To identify areas in which taxpayers have problems in dealings with the Internal Revenue Service;
3. To the extent possible, propose changes in the administrative practices of the IRS to mitigate those identified problems; and,
4. To identify potential legislative changes which may be appropriate to mitigate such problems.

Taxpayers who have tried, unsuccessfully, to resolve a pending issue with the IRS may be able to receive assistance from the TAO office. Generally, the TAO can help a taxpayer if, due to the administration of tax laws, the taxpayer:

a. Is experiencing economic harm or significant cost;
b. Has experienced a delay of more than 30 days to resolve a tax issue; or,
c. Has not received a response or resolution to the problem by the date promised by the IRS.

To receive assistance, the taxpayer must provide the following information:

a. Name, address, and social security number (or Employer Identification Number);
b. Telephone number and best time to call; and,
c. A description of the problem or hardship, detail on previous attempts to resolve the problem and the office(s) contacted if known.

The TAO will provide qualifying taxpayers with:

a. An assigned case advocate's contact number;
b. An impartial and independent review of the problem and updates on progress;
c. Advice on preventing future federal tax problems.

The TAO is not designed to assist taxpayers in avoiding valid tax liabilities or to interfere with the normal examination or collection process within the IRS. But, it can assist if the IRS is not following procedural guidelines or there is a significant financial hardship as a result of the IRS actions. The IRS has designed Form 911, Application for Taxpayer Assistance Order (TAO), for requesting TAO assistance in instances when there is significant financial hardship.

Chapter 47

Planning ahead for 2012 and beyond

ey.com/EYTaxGuide

Note

ey.com/EYTaxGuide
Ernst & Young LLP will update the *Ernst & Young Tax Guide 2012* website with relevant taxpayer information as it becomes available. You can also sign up for email alerts to let you know when changes have been made.

Introduction

At the eleventh hour in December 2010, Congress passed the Tax Relief, Unemployment Insurance Reauthorization and Job Creation Act (the Act) of 2010. This act extended the majority of the Bush tax cuts through 2012, and extended through 2011 other tax provisions set to expire at the end of 2009. The act also increased the exemption amounts for the calculation of alternative minimum tax (AMT) through 2011. And while an increasingly partisan debate over taxing and spending policies continues to rage through much of 2011–and is likely to continue through November 2012–it seems unlikely, as of the date this book was published in October 2011, that there will be major new tax legislation until after the next election. Even if significant tax law changes or even overall tax reform are somehow enacted before then, it is unlikely such changes will take effect until 2013 or beyond.

So tax planning through 2012 can be done with some relative degree of certainty. On the other hand, effective tax planning *after* 2012 remains a challenge given sharp differences about future tax policy and reform, the continued unwillingness of Democrats and Republicans to compromise, and still struggling U.S. and global economies.

Given the uncertain political and financial environment, it is even more important for taxpayers to start planning at the beginning of each tax year and regularly update their planning as new tax legislation is passed and their own personal circumstances change, in other words, well before their taxes are due. You should consult your tax advisor to determine how any new tax legislation passed in late 2011 and 2012 will affect your individual tax situation for 2012 and future years. In the meantime, here is a summary of some of the major items from recent tax legislation that may affect your tax returns in the future.

The information contained in this chapter is current through the date this book went to press in October 2011. Updated information about future tax law changes will be available on *ey.com/EYTaxGuide*. Purchase of this book includes free access throughout the 2011 tax return filing season.

Changes in Tax Rates, Deductions, and Credits

Individual Tax Rates Increase After 2012

The so-called Bush tax cuts that were enacted in 2001 and 2003 were extended for tax years through 2012. As a result, the marginal income tax rates for individual taxpayers on ordinary taxable income will remain at 10%, 25%, 28%, 33%, and 35% through 2012. Absent Congressional action, the scheduled rates in 2013 will increase to 15%, 28%, 31%, 36%, and 39.6%.

As of the date this book went to press in October 2011, Republicans have vowed to keep the Bush tax cuts in place after 2012. President Obama has proposed that higher tax rates apply to single individuals with income of more than $200,000, and married couples filing jointly with income of more than $250,000. The President has also called for the 10% and 25% brackets to be permanently restored, the 31% bracket to be eliminated, and the 28% rate bracket to be expanded so that low and middle income taxpayers will not see their taxes rise as a result of the increased tax rates. The President's proposals would essentially leave the 10%, 15%, 25%, and 28% tax rate brackets unchanged from their 2012 levels. These same rates would also apply to income taxes paid by trusts and estates.

Tax Rates for Qualified Dividends Increase After 2012

For 2011 and 2012, certain dividend income, referred to as "qualified dividend income," will continue to be taxed at a maximum rate of 15%. This lower rate on qualified dividend income (but not interest income) applies for both the regular tax and the alternative minimum tax. The tax rate on qualified dividends will remain at zero for taxpayers in the 10% and 15% tax brackets. With the scheduled expiration of the Bush tax cuts at the end of 2012, qualified dividends will be subject to tax at ordinary income tax rates, which are scheduled to be as high as 39.6%.

President Obama has called for the zero and 15% tax rates on qualified dividend income to be extended permanently for taxpayers with income in the 10% through 28% tax brackets, and a 20% tax rate to apply on qualified dividend income for taxpayers in the 36% and 39.6% tax brackets. Republicans have vowed to keep the low zero and 15% tax rates on qualified dividend income in place for all taxpayers, regardless of their level of income.

For a dividend to be eligible for the 15% reduced tax rate, you must own the underlying stock for more than 60 days during the 121-day period beginning 60 days before the "ex-dividend date," the day on which the stock starts trading without its next dividend. In the case of certain preferred stock, the holding period is increased to more than 90 days during the 181-day period beginning 90 days before the ex-dividend date. For more information, see chapter 8, *Dividends and other corporate distributions*.

Tax Rates on Capital Gains Increase After 2012

The top individual tax rate on long-term capital gains will remain at 15% through 2012, but is scheduled to increase to 20% in 2013. For 2011 and 2012, taxpayers in the 10% and 15% brackets will pay 0%. The 15% rate applies to assets held for more than one year under both the regular tax and the alternative minimum tax calculation. Similar to his proposals on qualified dividend tax rates, President Obama has called for the zero and 15% tax rates on long-term capital gains to be extended permanently for taxpayers with incomes in the 10% through 28% tax brackets, and a 20% tax rate to apply on qualified dividend income for taxpayers in the 36% and 39.6% tax brackets. Republicans have vowed to keep the current favorable capital gains tax rate in place after 2012 for all taxpayers, regardless of their level of income.

No Limit on Personal Exemption Through 2012

For 2011 and 2012, the personal exemption phaseout is fully repealed, allowing taxpayers at all income levels to deduct the full amount of their personal exemptions. (The personal exemption amount for 2011 is $3,700.) After 2012, however, the old phaseout rules are scheduled to return in full force. This means that, absent Congressional action, in 2013, taxpayers with adjusted gross income in excess of $171,100 ($256,700 for married filing jointly)—both numbers will be adjusted for inflation for 2013—will lose 2% of their personal exemption amount for each $2,500 (or portion thereof) of income over the threshold amount.

President Obama's tax proposals call for the personal exemption phaseout to be reinstated after 2012. However, the AGI levels at which the phaseout would begin would be increased. For 2013, the AGI floors would be adjusted for inflation starting at $200,000 ($250,000 for married taxpayers filing jointly), indexed for inflation from 2009. Republicans have vowed to repeal the personal exemption phaseout for all taxpayers, regardless of their level of income.

No Limit on Itemized Deductions Through 2012

For tax years 2011 and 2012, the itemized deduction phaseout remains fully repealed and higher income taxpayers are not required to reduce their total itemized deductions based on an adjusted gross income (AGI) limitation. After 2012, the old phaseout rule is scheduled to return in full force. Under the phaseout rule, allowable itemized deductions (other than medical expenses, casualty and theft losses, and investment interest) are reduced by an amount equal to 3% of a taxpayer's adjusted gross income in excess of $171,100 (as of 2011; but will be adjusted for inflation for 2013), not to exceed 80% of otherwise allowable itemized deductions.

The President's tax proposals call for the phaseout to be reinstated after 2012, but at a higher income level. The AGI floors would be indexed annually for inflation. For 2013, the AGI floors would be adjusted for inflation starting at $200,000 ($250,000 for married taxpayers filing jointly), indexed for inflation from 2009. The President has also proposed capping the tax value of itemized deductions to 28% for taxpayers in the 36% and 39.6% tax brackets. Republicans have vowed to permanently repeal the itemized deduction phaseout for all taxpayers, regardless of their level of income.

Alternative Minimum Tax Exemptions Decrease for 2012

The tax laws give preferential treatment to certain kinds of income and allow special deductions and credits for certain kinds of expenses. The alternative minimum tax (AMT) attempts to ensure that anyone who benefits from these tax advantages pays at least a minimum amount of tax. The AMT is a separately computed tax that eliminates many deductions and credits that are allowed in computing your regular tax liability.

The AMT is the government's mechanism through which taxpayers with a large amount of deductions still pay some income tax. The tentative minimum tax rates on ordinary income are 26% and 28%. The tax rates on qualified dividends and capital gains that apply for regular tax purposes in 2011 and 2012 also apply when calculating the AMT. If the Bush tax cuts are allowed to expire after 2012, qualified dividends will be subject to the same tax rates starting in 2013 that apply to other ordinary income, while the maximum rate on long-term capital gains for both regular tax and AMT will be 20%. If your taxable income for regular tax purposes, plus any adjustments and preference items you have, total more than the exemption amount, then you may have to pay the AMT.

In recent years, Congress has repeatedly enacted temporary measures that significantly raised the applicable exemption amounts above the levels that last applied in 2000. True to form, the Act passed in December 2010 raised the exemption amounts for 2010 and 2011. However, as of the date of publication of this book in October 2011, the last temporary increase will expire at the end of 2011. Without Congressional action, the AMT exemptions for 2012 and beyond will revert back to the levels that existed prior to 2001 as follows:

1. $45,000 (down from $74,450 in 2011) for married filing jointly/qualified widow or widower.
2. $33,750 (down from $48,450 in 2011) for single or head of household.
3. $22,500 (down from $37,225 in 2011) for married filing separately.

For updated information on this and any other tax law changes that occur after this book was published, see our website, ey.com/EYTaxGuide.

For an explanation of the AMT, see chapter 31, *How to figure your tax*.

AMT Refundable Credit

You are allowed a refundable credit for AMT you paid in past years to the extent that your AMT liability was attributable to the exercise of incentive stock options and other deferral adjustments. Eligible long-term unused minimum tax credits may be refunded over two years (50% per year). Since the credit is refundable, you can receive a refund even if the refund exceeds your total tax liability for the year. For 2012, a portion of any unused minimum tax credit carryforward from 2008 or earlier years may be refunded. Since this provision expires after 2012 for calendar year taxpayers, only those unused credits that arose before 2009 can be eligible for recovery as a refundable credit. Unused credits realized after 2008 can only be claimed under the pre-existing rules for claiming minimum tax credits. For more information on this credit, see *Refundable Credit for Prior Year Minimum Tax* in chapter 37, *Other credits including the earned income credit.*

Certain Credits Not Allowed to Offset AMT Beginning in 2012

The ability to offset both regular tax liability and AMT liability with specific nonrefundable personal credits–the credit for child and dependent care expenses, credit for the elderly or the disabled, Lifetime Learning Credit, nonbusiness energy property credit, and mortgage interest credit– has been extended through 2011. Unless Congress acts to extend this tax benefit, it will expire after 2011, and beginning in 2012, these credits will be allowed only to the extent that your regular income tax liability exceeds your tentative minimum tax, determined without regard to the minimum tax foreign tax credit. (The child credit, the saver credit, and the residential energy efficient property credit will continue to be allowed to the full extent of the individual's regular tax and AMT.) For updated information on this and any other tax law changes that occur after this book was published, see our website, ey.com/EYTaxGuide.

"Marriage Penalty" Slated to Return After 2012

Although married couples may elect to file separate returns, the tax rate schedules and other tax provisions are structured so that a married couple filing separate returns usually has a higher combined tax than when filing a joint return. Different rate schedules and tax provisions apply to single taxpayers. A "marriage penalty" is said to exist when the tax liability of a married couple filing jointly is greater than the sum of the tax liabilities that would apply if each taxpayer were single.

A 2003 tax law pegged the standard deduction amount for joint filers at twice the standard deduction amount for single filers. This 2003 law also provided relief for the marriage penalty that resulted due to the fact that the upper band on the 15% tax bracket was considerably lower for married filing jointly taxpayers than it was for unmarried taxpayers. Two unmarried individuals thus could have a greater amount of income taxed at the lower 15% tax rate than a married couple with similar income. This 2003 law extended the range of the 15% rate bracket for joint returns to twice the size of the corresponding rate bracket for single returns. The Act extended both of these provisions through 2012. Unless Congress acts, the so-called marriage penalty will return starting in 2013 and married taxpayers will once again find themselves paying more than two similarly situated unmarried individuals. For updated information on this and any other tax law changes that occur after this book was published, see our website, *ey.com/EYTaxGuide*.

Child Tax Credit Benefit Extended Through 2012

An individual may claim a child tax credit for each qualifying child under the age of 17. Through 2012, the maximum amount of the credit per child is $1,000. The credit is also refundable to the extent of 15% of the taxpayer's earned income in excess of $3,000. In addition, families with three or more qualifying children can determine the additional child tax credit using the "alternative formula" if this results in a larger credit than determined under the earned income formula. (Under the alternative formula, the additional child tax credit equals the amount by which the taxpayer's social security taxes exceed the taxpayer's earned income credit (EIC).) Through 2012, the credit is also allowable against both the regular tax and alternative minimum tax (AMT).

Unless Congress acts, after 2012, the maximum credit will be cut in half to $500. The ability to determine the refundable child credit based on earned income in excess of the threshold dollar amount will expire. As a result, families with fewer than three children will not be eligible for a refundable credit. While families with three or more children can still receive a refundable credit, the so-called alternative formula becomes the only manner for figuring the refundable portion. Also, the ability to offset the AMT expires.

The President supports extending the $1,000 credit and allowing the child tax credit against both regular income tax and AMT. The President also supports permanently extending the earned income formula for determining the refundable child credit, with an earned income threshold of $3,000. For updated information on this and any other tax law changes that occur after this book was published, see our website, *ey.com/EYTaxGuide*.

Earned Income Credit (EIC) Increase for Families with Three or More Children Expires After 2012

The American Recovery and Reinvestment Act of 2009 temporarily increased the earned income credit (EIC) for working families with three or more children for 2009 and 2010, and the Act extended these benefits through 2012. Unless Congress acts, this provision will expire after 2012, at which point workers with three or more children will receive the same EIC as similarly situated workers with two qualifying children. See chapter 37, *Other credits including the earned income credit*, for more information.

The President supports making the expansion of the EIC for workers with three or more children permanent. For updated information on this and any other tax law changes that occur after this book was published, see our website, *ey.com/EYTaxGuide*.

Adoption Tax Credit Extended Through 2012

Taxpayers who adopt children can receive a tax credit for qualified adoption expenses. A taxpayer may also exclude from income adoption expenses paid by an employer. The Bush tax cuts increased the credit and exclusion amount from $5,000 ($6,000 for a special needs child) to $10,000 (indexed for inflation from 2002). These benefits are phased out for taxpayers with AGI between $185,210 and $225,210. A 2010 tax law made the adoption credit fully refundable so that you can receive a refund for the full amount of the credit you claim even when your credit exceeds your tax liability. The Act extended the increased credit and exclusion amounts, as well as refundability, through 2012. See chapter 37, *Other credits including the earned income credit*, for more information.

American Opportunity Credit Extended Through 2012

The American Recovery and Reinvestment Act of 2009 expanded the existing Hope credit for tax years 2009 and 2010, making it available to a broader range of taxpayers, including many with higher incomes as well as those who owe no tax. This expanded version of the Hope credit was renamed the American opportunity credit. The Act extended the benefits of the American opportunity credit through 2012. For information on this expanded credit, see chapter 36, *Education credits and other education tax benefits*. The President has proposed making the expansion of this credit permanent. However, unless Congress acts, the American opportunity credit will expire and the smaller Hope credit will re-emerge after 2012. For updated information on this and any other tax law changes that occur after this book was published, see our website, *ey.com/EYTaxGuide*.

Additional Education Tax Benefits Extended Through 2012

The Act extended several tax benefits through 2012 related to education expenses. These benefits are:

1. Student loan interest deduction: Taxpayers who have paid interest on qualified education loans may claim an above-the-line deduction for the interest paid up to $2,500. The deduction is subject to phaseout depending on the income level of the taxpayer. See chapter 19, *Education-related adjustments*.
2. Coverdell account benefits: Coverdell Education Savings Accounts are tax-exempt savings accounts used to pay the higher education expenses of a designated beneficiary. Under the Bush tax cuts, the annual contribution amount was increased from $500 to $2,000, and the definition of education expenses was expanded to include elementary and secondary school expenses. The Act extends these benefits through 2012. See chapter 36, *Education credits and other education tax benefits.*
3. Exclusion for employer-provided educational assistance: The Act extended through 2012 the provision allowing an employee to exclude from gross income up to $5,250 of employer-provided education assistance. This provision applies to assistance received for both undergraduate and graduate education expenses. See chapter 36, *Education credits and other education tax benefits.*

Exclusion from Gross Income of Certain Discharged Mortgage Debt

Legislation passed in 2008 in response to the economic crisis extended through 2012 the temporary exclusion from gross income of income realized from the discharge of qualified principal residence indebtedness. Under this provision, up to $2 million ($1 million if married filing separately) of qualified principal residence indebtedness may be forgiven, and no income would have to be recognized related to the cancellation of debt. However, your basis in your principal residence would be reduced by the amount excluded from income.

Qualified principal residence indebtedness is defined as acquisition indebtedness with respect to your principal residence. Acquisition indebtedness generally means debt you incurred in the acquisition, construction, or substantial improvement of your principal residence that is secured by the residence. It also includes the refinancing of such debt to the extent the new loan balance is attributable to qualified principal residence indebtedness.

Section 179 Expense Deduction Decreased for 2012

Section 179 of the tax code allows you to deduct all or part of the cost—up to specified yearly limits—of certain qualifying property in the year in which the property is purchased and placed into service, rather than capitalizing the cost and depreciating it over its life. This means that you can deduct all or part of the cost up front in one year rather than take depreciation deductions spread out over many years. You must decide for each item of qualifying property whether to deduct, subject to the yearly limit, or capitalize and depreciate its cost. Qualifying property is property purchased for use in your trade or business and property that would have qualified for the investment tax credit. Under the Act, for taxable years beginning in 2012, the maximum deduction that can be claimed for the cost of equipment placed into service has been decreased to $125,000 (down from $500,000 in 2011). The allowable deduction is reduced dollar for dollar once the cost of qualifying property placed in service during the year exceeds $500,000 (down from $2,000,000 in 2011). In addition, you are no longer able to expense up to $250,000 of the cost of qualified leasehold improvement property, qualified restaurant property, and qualified retail improvement property.

After 2012, the maximum deduction decreases to $25,000 and the threshold for figuring the reduction in the credit allowed declines to $200,000.

Special Depreciation Allowance Decreased for 2012

Under the provisions of the 2010 Act, an accelerated write-off (referred to as bonus depreciation) of acquisitions of depreciable property is allowed for 2011 and 2012. The bonus depreciation for capital expenditures placed in service after September 8, 2010, and through December 31, 2011, is 100% of the cost of the property. For 2012, the bonus depreciation allowed for investments placed into service generally drops from 100% to 50% of the depreciable basis of qualified property.

Tax Benefits Expiring in 2012

The Tax Relief, Unemployment Insurance Reauthorization, and Job Creation Act (the Act) extended the following benefits through 2011. However, if legislation is not passed to further extend these benefits, they will no longer be available for 2012 and future years. These benefits include:

1. Deduction for state and local general sales taxes. See chapter 23 for the deduction available for 2011.
2. Above-the-line deduction for certain expenses of elementary and secondary school teachers. See chapter 19 for the deduction available for 2011.
3. Above-the-line deduction for qualified tuition and related expenses. See chapter 19 for the deduction available for 2011.
4. Contributions of capital gain real property made for conservation purposes. See chapter 25 for the deduction available for 2011.
5. Premiums for mortgage insurance deductible as qualified residence interest. See chapter 24 for the deduction available for 2011.
6. Tax-free distributions from individual retirement plans for charitable purposes. See chapter 17 for the deduction available for 2011.
7. Nonbusiness energy property credit. See chapter 37 for the deduction available for 2011.
8. District of Columbia first-time homebuyer credit.

For updated information on this and any other tax law changes that occur after this book was published, see our website, *ey.com/EYTaxGuide*.

Income Fully Recognized in Year of Conversion or Rollover to Roth IRA

After 2010, income from the conversion or rollover of a traditional, SEP, or SIMPLE IRA or a qualified employer retirement plan account to a Roth IRA must be fully reported as taxable income in the year the conversion or rollover is made. If the conversion is made in 2012, any taxable amounts will be included in income in 2012. For conversions and rollovers made in 2010, any taxable amounts were to be included in income in equal amounts in 2011 and 2012, unless you elected to include the entire amount in income in 2010. Accordingly, if no election was made to include the entire amount in income in 2010, then the remaining one half of the conversion will need to be reported as income in 2012. For more information, see *Can You Move Amounts into a Roth IRA?* in chapter 17, *Individual retirement arrangements (IRAs)*.

Inflation Adjustments for 2012

Each year a number of tax benefits and income limitations for tax benefits are indexed for inflation. Some of the items typically adjusted annually for inflation include:

1. Tax rate tables
2. Standard deduction
3. Personal exemption
4. Income limitations for the child tax credit, the education credits, interest on education loans and the adoption credit
5. Medical savings accounts
6. Contribution limits to qualified retirement plans and IRAs

As of the date this book was published, the contribution limits for 2012 had not yet been published. The limits applicable to 2012 will be posted on *ey.com/EYTaxGuide* after the IRS announces them.

Additional Taxes on Earned and Investment Income to Apply in 2013

Under the health care reform legislation enacted in 2010, starting in 2013, high-income taxpayers will be subject to two additional taxes:

- An additional Medicare tax of 0.9% on wages and other compensation over $200,000 for unmarried taxpayers, and $250,000 for married taxpayers filing jointly ($125,000 if married filing separately). For married couples filing jointly, the additional tax will be imposed on the combined wages of the employee and the employee's spouse. The imposition of this tax in 2013 means that if individual tax rates increase to 39.6% for high-income taxpayers, the marginal tax rate on their wages will increase to 40.5% for tax years beginning after December 31, 2012.

- An additional 3.8% tax on the lesser of net investment income (e.g., interest, dividends, capital gains, and certain types of business income, but excluding tax-exempt interest) or the amount modified adjusted gross income over a $200,000 threshold amount for unmarried taxpayers, and $250,000 for married taxpayers filing jointly ($125,000 if married filing separately). This additional tax will also be imposed on certain trusts and estates. The imposition of this tax in 2013 means that if the top individual tax rate rises to 39.6% for high-income taxpayers starting in 2013, the marginal tax rate on net investment income subject to the 3.8% tax would climb to 43.4% for tax years beginning after December 31, 2012; 23.8% on long-term capital gain income.

Temporary Changes to Gift, Estate, and Generation-Skipping Transfer (GST) Taxes Expire After 2012

The December 2010 Tax Act that extended the so-called Bush tax cuts also made significant changes to the gift, estate, and GST tax rules. For 2011 and 2012, the maximum tax rate on taxable transfers is 35% and the cumulative amount of otherwise taxable transfers that are exempted from gift, estate, and GST tax is $5 million. Unless Congress acts, beginning in 2013, the gift, estate, and GST tax laws are scheduled to revert to what they were before 2001 (top tax rate climbs to 55% and cumulative exemption amount drops to $1 million). For more information about the changes made to the gift, estate, and GST rules, see the *Changes in the Tax Law You Should Know About* section in the front of the book and chapter 44, *Estate and gift tax planning.*

A Summary for 2012 and Beyond

Although no increases to tax rates or significant changes to allowable deductions or credits are currently being considered for 2011 and 2012 by Congress and the President as of the date this book went to press, there is growing clamor on both sides of the aisle—with sharp differences of opinion as to what should be done—for fundamental tax reform that could impact all of these in 2013 and beyond. The upcoming Presidential and Congressional elections could fundamentally change the prospects to what is done and when. All of this uncertainty makes it even more important for you to monitor this debate, watch for new, perhaps sweeping, changes to the tax code, and analyze your tax situation in anticipation of any such tax changes.

Taxpayers in the lower income brackets may see their tax liability increase somewhat in 2013 and beyond, but higher income taxpayers could be presented with the biggest changes—both in their tax rates and their overall tax liability.

The uncertain environment certainly makes tax planning for the rest of 2012, and for 2013 and beyond, more difficult than usual. Here are a number of items to consider:

- High-income individuals may face an increase in the top income tax rate, a higher tax rate on qualified dividends, an increase in the capital gains rate, and a new Medicare tax on compensation and net investment income. The magnitude of the tax effect and where it will hit hardest will depend largely on the level and composition of your income, and on whether you are subject to the alternative minimum tax (AMT). Taxpayers who pay the AMT may find that the change in the effective rate on dividends and capital gains may have a more significant effect than the increase in the top marginal rates.
- To plan for rising tax rates, higher income individuals should review their portfolio allocations now. If the Bush tax cuts are allowed to expire, accelerating capital gains so they are taxed at the 15% rate in 2012, instead of a potential 20% rate in 2013, could be advantageous. Conversely, deferring the recognition of capital losses until 2013 to offset future gains that would be taxed at a higher rate may make sense. A $3,000 limitation on the use of capital losses applies if the taxpayer does not have any offsetting capital gains, so if losses are deferred, they will not provide a significant tax benefit unless there are gains to offset.
- Deferring itemized deductions, such as charitable contributions, to 2013 could offset a portion of the higher tax you may have to pay in 2013. However, taxpayers considering deferring itemized deductions should also consider the 3% phaseout on itemized deductions scheduled to be reinstated starting in 2013, and the potential exposure to the AMT, which may limit, or even eliminate, the tax benefit from claiming certain types of

itemized deductions. In addition, President Obama has proposed capping the tax value of itemized deductions at 28% for taxpayers in the 36% and 39.6% brackets. If the President's proposal is enacted, affected taxpayers should evaluate accelerating deductions into 2012.

- Other strategies might include a shift from taxable to tax-exempt investments, although taxpayers should analyze whether the benefit of the lower tax would outweigh potentially lower returns from the tax-exempt investment. Individuals might also explore adjusting their taxable and tax-deferred investment portfolios to take into account the likely increase in the tax rate on dividends.
- 2012 may be a good time for investors with traditional IRAs to consider the possibility of converting to a Roth IRA and making the election to pay the tax on the conversion in 2012, while tax rates are lower than they are likely to be in the future. In light of the scheduled reinstatement of the higher gift, estate, and generation-skipping transfer (GST) tax rates and lower exemption amount in 2013, you should revisit your estate plans.
- In light of the potential for significant legislative changes through 2013, and the alternative strategies available, taxpayers should work with their advisors to model out various scenarios before deciding on a course of action.

Chapter 48

2011 Tax rate schedules

ey.com/EYTaxGuide

Introduction

This chapter contains the 2011 final Tax Rate Schedules that taxpayers with taxable income of $100,000 or more must use. The 2011 Tax Tables must be used by taxpayers with taxable income of less than $100,000. Those Tax Tables can be found at *www.irs.Qov/pub/irs-pdf/i1040tt.pdf*.

Schedule X—If your filing status is **Single**

If your taxable income is: Over–	But not over–	The tax is:		of the amount over–
$0	$8,500	....	10%	**$0**
8,500	34,500	**$850.00**	**+ 15%**	**8,500**
34,500	83,600	**4,750.00**	**+ 25%**	**34,500**
83,600	174,400	**17,025.00**	**+ 28%**	**83,600**
174,400	379,150	**42,449.00**	**+ 33%**	**174,400**
379,150	....	**110,016.50**	**+ 35%**	**379,150**

Schedule Y-1—If your filing status is **Married filing jointly** or **Qualifying widow(er)**

If your taxable income is: Over–	But not over–	The tax is:		of the amount over–
$0	$17,000	....	10%	**$0**
17,000	69,000	**$1,700.00**	**+ 15%**	**17,000**
69,000	139,350	**9,500.00**	**+ 25%**	**69,000**
139,350	212,300	**27,087.50**	**+ 28%**	**139,350**
212,300	379,150	**47,513.50**	**+ 33%**	**212,300**
379,150	....	**102,574.00**	**+ 35%**	**379,150**

Schedule Y-2—If your filing status is **Married filing separately**

If your taxable income is: Over–	But not over–	The tax is:		of the amount over–
$0	$8,500	....	10%	**$0**
8,500	34,500	**$850.00**	**+ 15%**	**8,500**
34,500	69,675	**4,750.00**	**+ 25%**	**34,500**
69,675	106,150	**13,543.75**	**+ 28%**	**69,675**
106,150	189,575	**23,756.75**	**+ 33%**	**106,150**
189,575	....	**51,287.00**	**+ 35%**	**189,575**

Schedule Z—If your filing status is **Head of household**

If your taxable income is: Over–	But not over–	The tax is:		of the amount over–
$0	$12,150	....	10%	**$0**
12,150	46,250	**$1,215.00**	**+ 15%**	**12,150**
46,250	119,400	**6,330.00**	**+ 25%**	**46,250**
119,400	193,350	**24,617.50**	**+ 28%**	**119,400**
193,350	379,150	**45,323.50**	**+ 33%**	**193,350**
379,150	....	**106,637.50**	**+ 35%**	**379,150**

Note

ey.com/EYTaxGuide
Ernst & Young LLP will update the *Ernst & Young Tax Guide 2012* website with relevant taxpayer information as it becomes available. You can also sign up for email alerts to let you know when changes have been made.

Index

Symbols

A

B

C

D

E

F

G

H

I

N

Q

R

S

T

U

V

W

Z